The New York Times

ULTIMATE CROSSWORD OMNIBUS

Edited by
Will Shortz

ST. MARTIN'S GRIFFIN ☲ NEW YORK

INTRODUCTION

If I may be frank, this book contains more crossword puzzles than any sane person would ever consider trying at once. It's a ridiculously large number—1,001, more puzzles than most people do in years (or in a lifetime). These happen to be the first 1,001 daily crosswords that I edited for *The New York Times*, from 1993 to 1997, representing the cream of the crop of the thousands of puzzles submitted to me until then.

Let's say, hypothetically, that you can solve these in an average of 20 minutes each, including the tough ones. This would be a much better time than the typical solver . . . but then, if you're looking at this book, you're probably not a typical solver.

At 20 minutes each, assuming you work nonstop, 24 hours a day, never pausing for sleep, food, personal hygiene, job, or housework (housework? ha!), it will take you almost two weeks to finish this book.

At the end of this time you will be haggard, filthy, bleary-eyed, dangerously starved, and hated by all your friends and family (if, in fact, you have any friends and family left). But your brain will have grown to approximately twice its size (results may vary), and you will feel an immense sense of power and accomplishment. Clearly, the benefits are appealing.

Instead of the gonzo approach to doing this book, let's say you follow the more traditional course of eating, sleeping, bathing, and performing other basic activities as you solve. Maybe the puzzles will take you more than

20 minutes apiece on average. Whatever. Let's just agree right now that this book will last a looooong time.

Since the puzzles here span almost four years, they are not all of exactly the same style. For one thing, I think the puzzles got better through the years. As the contributors improved their skills, their work became fresher, sharper, and more colorful.

Also, in my capacity as editor, I think I got better at honing the difficulty of the clues. The easy puzzles at the start of the week got easier and the hard puzzles at the end of the week got harder, so that all skill levels would be catered to. In addition, I got more insistent about precise definitions, I included more references to classical culture, and I reduced the number of proper names and tests of specialized knowledge.

The *Times*'s crossword audience is so diverse, I've discovered, that it's difficult to find common ground on proper names. The things a twenty-year-old solver knows are quite different from what an eighty-year-old knows. So increasingly over the years I've tried to steer the puzzles toward the middle, emphasizing vocabulary familiar to everyone.

Since all but the last 150 puzzles in this book appear in random (not chronological) order, you won't be able to discern this gradual change in style. But take my word for it—it's there.

Now lock the door, unplug the phone, lay out a supply of pencils or pens, and turn the page. . . .

—Will Shortz

1 by Nancy B. Ross

ACROSS

1 "Charlie's Angels" actress
5 Jimmies
10 One who follows orders?
14 The cheaper spread
15 Campus clubs, for short
16 He jumps through hoops
17 New York cultural site
20 Squirrellike monkey
21 Weird
22 Molly Bloom's last word
23 Smidgens
25 Tempest locale
29 Ambience
30 Vote (for)
33 Woody's son
34 Not on all fours
35 Fido's foot
36 London cultural site
40 Juliette Low org.
41 Dearest ones
42 ___ of Samothrace
43 Poetic contraction
44 Bad day for Caesar
45 Moulin Rouge attraction
47 1947 Pulitzer composer
48 1987 Michael Jackson album
49 Swiss capital
52 Universal
57 Milan cultural site
60 Spur
61 More frigid
62 It sticks out of a scabbard
63 Emulate Icarus
64 Suspicious
65 Wordsworth works

DOWN

1 Rich soil
2 Tenor Luigi
3 Bucks, e.g.
4 Coed quarters
5 Press type
6 Jimmies
7 Bridge position
8 ___ degree
9 Compass pt.
10 Phoenix source
11 Yellowstone sighting
12 Singaraja's island
13 Vogue rival
18 Tom Smothers' plaything
19 Manufacturer's come-on
23 Quartet after a breakup?
24 Mischievous
25 "T" to ham operators
26 VCR function
27 Sacrifice site
28 Baked Hawaiian dish
29 City where van Gogh painted
30 Of the eye
31 Skier's garment
32 10-to-12 year-old
34 Gutter locale
37 Dickens waif
38 Lymph ___
39 Actress Reinking
45 Informer
46 Puts two and two together
47 ___ alia
48 Field worker
49 Heat quantities: Abbr.
50 Mr. Saarinen
51 Shankar piece
52 Ballet bend
53 Quick comeback?
54 One of a "Mikado" trio
55 "Winnie ___ Pu"
56 Musical that opened 10/7/82
58 Kind of painting
59 Sizzling serve

2 by Stanley Newman

ACROSS

1 Fight locale
6 Rhyme scheme
10 Fitzgerald specialty
14 Lonesome George
15 Third Vice President
16 Nope
17 Of one of the senses
18 Neck of the woods
19 Linger
20 Hot stuff
22 No contest, e.g.
23 NASA affirmative
24 Suitor
26 Man with a horn
30 Can't stand
32 Hideouts
33 Untrustworthy sort
34 Former nuclear agcy.
37 Being broadcast
38 The Rumba King
39 Colleague of Scotty and Spock
40 Road material
41 Showed the world
42 Keepers of the flame
43 Obsolete typewriter necessity
45 Memorable shepherd
46 Public fuss
47 "___ you!"
48 Congressional caucus
49 Hot stuff
56 Coin in the Trevi, once
57 Nobelist Wiesel
58 Herbert Hoover, by birth
59 Reckons
60 Hirschfeld's daughter
61 ___ garde
62 Letter closing
63 Lincoln in-law
64 Actress Evelyn

DOWN

1 Arab nobles
2 Lopsided win
3 Iberian river
4 "Hud" star
5 Attentive
6 By surprise
7 Ambience
8 ___ Rabbit
9 Pentagon pooh-bah
10 Inferior
11 Hot stuff
12 Isherwood collaborator
13 "Take ___ Train"
21 ___ to mention
25 Taipan frypan
26 Like crazy
27 Superboy's girlfriend
28 Hot stuff
29 Sportscaster Cross
30 Hot stuff
31 Bit of wampum
33 Beyond question
35 Sommer of the screen
36 Zodiacal border
38 Window type
39 Sample soup
41 Outlaw
42 Apple Computer co-founder
44 Slant differently
45 Spelldown
46 Bad news on Wall Street
47 Place
48 Give away
50 Miscellany
51 Barnum's soprano
52 Robert Indiana painting
53 On vacation
54 It's blowin' in the wind
55 Some carpenters

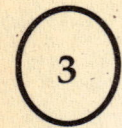

3 by Timothy S. Lewis

ACROSS

1 Lowly homes
5 One of the Simpsons
9 Abundantly supplied
13 Dairy section purchase
14 Overly sentimental
15 60's singer Sands
16 Knitting loop
17 Crude transportation?
18 House cat
19 House shader
20 Baseball's Canseco
21 "On Golden Pond" Oscar winner
22 With 34-Across and 48-Across, Wordsworth lines on Lucy
26 Fur type
27 Otto I's domain: Abbr.
28 Dig this
29 Sax, for one
30 "Take the ___"
33 Road hazard
34 See 22-Across
37 N.Y.C. subway
40 "___ Restaurant"
41 "Amo, ___, I love a lass . . ."
45 Sweep at sea
46 Japanese discipline
47 Pennsylvania folks
48 See 22-Across
53 Site of the Cambrian Mountains
54 Turkish bread
55 ___ Palmas, Canary Islands
56 Model Macpherson
57 Equatorial capital
59 Huff and puff
60 Dissembled
61 Shark's line
62 Source of sake
63 "The ___ doth protest . . ."
64 High point
65 German border river

DOWN

1 Desire
2 Wail
3 It can eat you out of house and home
4 La preceder
5 Verdi's "___ Miller"
6 Jersey and Guernsey
7 "___ walks in beauty . . ."
8 Burns's birthplace
9 Cut again
10 Rowena's inamorato
11 Grate expectations?
12 Six-carbon molecules
14 Farm sounds
20 Bump
21 Diva Mirella
23 Make over
24 Banquo, e.g.
25 Astronomical butter
30 "Anthony Adverse" author
31 Making bows
32 Transportation for Sinbad
35 Nuremberg defendants
36 Aforementioned
37 Dr. Johnson's biographer
38 First name in gospel
39 Warbled
42 Lost
43 Obliquely
44 Not one to trust
47 Sleuth's cry
49 Strapped
50 Home of the Trojans
51 KNO₃
52 Home of the Trojans
57 Sine ___ non
58 Home of the Trojans
59 Old hand

4 by Bryant White

ACROSS

1 Producer Ponti
6 Madras mister
9 Ruinous
14 Southeast Asia product
15 Perfect rating
16 Make ___ (get tagged, e.g., in baseball)
17 Month before Iyar
18 Soft-toned flutes
20 A STEIN'S LIQUEUR (anag.)
22 Shields for men-at-arms
23 Parodists
24 Left on the farm
26 Bishopric
27 Recipe meas.
28 Flora and fauna
30 Black tea
32 Coat
33 This puzzle's theme
35 Some Arabs
37 Poet's ponds
38 "Marriage Italian Style" star
39 Vigor, to Virgil
40 Spotted
43 "Lord of the Rings" creature
44 Earmark
47 Actor Robert
48 SIPS LAGER ON GIN (anag.)
52 Flight
53 The deep
54 Finnish coin
55 Scoreboard score
56 Thrash
57 Firework?
58 It makes molehills out of mountains
59 Record

DOWN

1 Tales of adventure
2 Each
3 Blue
4 Island feasts
5 Prefix with science
6 Short of cash, informally
7 Candy manufacturer Harry
8 Acquire
9 Actor Jamie
10 The Beatles' "___ Love Her"
11 Pavlova's slippers
12 Golden
13 Capt.'s subordinates
19 Common buttons
21 They may be batted
25 Type of paint
27 Botulin, e.g.
28 Czech statesman Eduard
29 Signs, in a way
30 Twining plant stem
31 Benbow or Farragut: Abbr.
32 Macho
33 1938 "invaders"
34 Deeply respectful
35 Violinist Bull
36 Chimera or Sphinx
40 Most cunning
41 Congenitally attached
42 Much-sought-after baseball card
44 Varnish ingredient
45 In pieces
46 Warrant officer
47 ___ Highway
49 El ___ (weather phenomenon)
50 Jack-o'-lantern feature
51 "___ it" ("Amen")
52 Belgian resort town

5 · by Sidney L. Robbins

ACROSS
1 "My Fair Lady" miss
6 ___ Air
9 Drop explosives on
13 Sal, in song
14 King topper
15 Kind of eclipse
16 Beethoven classic
19 Poker opener
20 Classic auto
21 Accountants' activities
22 Be under the weather
23 Electrical units
24 Horizontally
28 Leave the ground
29 Hint of scandal
30 "Gee whiz!"
31 Yearn (for)
35 Rarely
38 Jury member
39 Nobelist Wiesel
40 Adored
41 Mr. Musial
42 Evaluate
43 Adherents of Allah
47 Mine output
48 Gasoline rating
49 List ender
50 Native of old Peru
54 My sweetheart, in an old song
57 Core belief
58 Unknown John
59 Street urchin
60 Winged god
61 Neighbor of Syr.
62 Portents

DOWN
1 Austen heroine
2 City on the Rhône
3 "___ Rhythm"
4 Western novelist Grey
5 The whole shebang
6 Breakfast roll
7 Bounce back
8 Tennis call
9 German political groups
10 TV studio light
11 Lusterless finish
12 Copper-zinc alloy
15 Jeweler's eyeglass
17 Eye part
18 Chinese liquor
22 Spumante city
23 Bridal path?
24 Upon
25 Chaplin trademark
26 Houston school
27 Lollapalooza
28 Batman's partner
30 Swank affairs
31 Famous cookie man
32 Cabot ___ ("Murder, She Wrote" town)
33 Works the garden
34 Pass receivers
36 Tennis players
37 Otherwise
41 French legislature
42 St. Louis landmark
43 Grove of trees, in the Southwest
44 Yellow-orange
45 Dictation taker
46 Injures
47 Aquatic animal
49 Son in Genesis
50 Midwestern V.I.P.
51 Alaskan city
52 Originate, as a phrase
53 Miller and Sothern
55 Uganda's Amin
56 Self

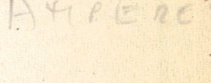

6 · by Randy Sowell

ACROSS
1 Keep ___ (persevere)
5 Sitcom diner
9 Most of Iberia
14 Dial sound
15 In ___ (mired)
16 Fake jewels
17 Goldwyn discovery Anna ___
18 Houston university
19 Get the lead out
20 Geology, e.g.
23 Gibson of tennis
24 Three, in Thüringen
25 Sheepcote comment
28 Baseball's Maglie
29 ___ rod (biblical item)
31 Airborne particulates
34 Where Lois and Clark work
38 Hook's henchman
40 River, in 9-Across
41 "American Gigolo" actor
42 Athlete's ambition
47 Pitch
48 Post-W.W. II Prime Minister
49 Golfer Woosnam
51 ___ Percé Indians
52 Imitated
55 High points
59 Shakespearean showplace
61 Cousteau concern
64 Pivot
65 Follow
66 Slick vehicle?
67 Seasons on the Somme
68 Gen. Robt. ___
69 Annual tournaments
70 Tweed Ring lampooner
71 Monster's loch

DOWN
1 On the briny
2 Utter
3 Like argon
4 Tithing portions
5 Sicilian port
6 Idle of "Monty Python"
7 Clear
8 Guide
9 Regular programming pre-emptor
10 Peel
11 Naked ___ jaybird
12 1986 hit "___ Only Love"
13 Born
21 Kind of waiter or water
22 Tide type
25 Noted Seine landscapist
26 End of ___
27 Late bloomer
30 Old barroom tune
31 City on the Nile
32 Slew
33 Airport booth leaser
35 Anger
36 Permit: Abbr.
37 "___ hoo!"
39 Pipe connection
43 From whom buyers buy
44 Cult film "___ Man"
45 Superlatively wealthy
46 The brave do it
50 Tidy up
53 Buddy of TV
54 Actress Burke
56 Out-of-date
57 Hears, as a case
58 Graf rival
59 Secluded valley
60 Calendar abbr.
61 Court
62 Start of a cheer
63 Pub brew

7   by David J. Kahn

ACROSS

1 Israel's Dayan
6 Baby's bed
10 Attire for Dracula
14 Varsity starters
15 Frost
16 Plow animals
17 Comedy sketch with 29- and 44-Across
20 Pizza ingredient
21 Roseanne, once
22 Do art on glass
25 Luv
29 50's TV comedienne
32 Suspend
34 Oklahoma city
35 Fleur-de-___
36 Choir voice
37 Election winners
38 Golden-voice Fitzgerald
39 "Agnus ___"
40 Yearly records
43 Kind of pad
44 50's TV comedian
47 Detail maps
48 Soot particle
49 ___ part (play on stage)
51 Envoy
56 Comedy sketch with 44-Across
61 "Do ___ others . . ."
62 DNA component
63 Bears' places
64 Continue
65 Happy
66 Sgt. Bilko

DOWN

1 Cartoonist Groening
2 Roman emperor of A.D. 69
3 Appear
4 Mirthful reaction
5 Did B-grade stage work
6 Onetime Fidel ally
7 Circus stars Siegfried & ___
8 Metric foot
9 Expand
10 "Lord Jim" writer
11 Fireman's equipment
12 Apiece
13 U.S.C.G. officer
18 ___ Dame
19 Hill nymph
23 Giving up, as territory
24 Church songbooks
26 "First, You Cry" author Betty
27 "___ Survive" (disco hit)
28 Test format, often
29 Shenanigans
30 Italian actor Tognazzi
31 Islam adherent
32 31-Down who's been to Mecca
33 ". . . ___ and hungry look"
38 "Xanadu" rock group
40 Letter after gee
41 Money put aside
42 ___ Ste. Marie
45 Allen's "Annie Hall" co-star
46 Addison associate Richard
50 Genesis brother
52 Growl
53 Tennis score
54 Actress Copley
55 Gaelic
56 Wine container
57 Yoko ___
58 W.W. II area
59 Literary olio
60 Crimson

8   by Cathy Millhauser

ACROSS

1 Elbowroom
6 Unchanged
10 Like the yang: Abbr.
14 Analogy mark
15 Caterer's item
16 Gung-ho about
17 Bowed
18 L. Frank Baum sequel to "The Blob"?
20 Indianapolis's ___ Dome
21 Frantic
22 Vermont ski resort
23 Where one learns to make bubbles?
27 Wagon alternative
28 Slug kin
29 Lets off the hook
31 "Harper's Bazaar" artist
32 Orbital point
35 Suffix akin to -ence
36 Item in Satan's grooming kit?
39 Half of sei
41 Karras of football
42 Aid for Santa
45 Orléans's department
47 "GoodFellas" actor
49 "Fatagaga" collagist
50 Catcher's lunch?
54 Sneaky peeker
56 Emulate a loon
57 Contend
58 Euphoria?
60 Revival shouts
62 Pulitzer-winning critic Richard
63 Lean
64 Nuclei
65 Audio industry giant
66 Lushes
67 Daniel follower

DOWN

1 Wolfs
2 Fat and grunting
3 Spanish Moors' palace
4 Runner Sebastian
5 Period of play in curling
6 Impassive
7 On ___ (having success)
8 Miata maker
9 Object on the back of a dollar bill
10 Basil, e.g.
11 Phillips Academy site
12 Hold stuff
13 Defrauds
19 Professional grp.
21 Typist's output: Abbr.
24 Autoharp, e.g.
25 Robt. ___
26 Egyptian canal
30 Chow chow brand
32 Whole
33 Grand ___ ("Evangeline" locale)
34 Clinton blows it
37 Overdue
38 Shouts for Juan Belmonte
39 Funnel site
40 Unwrap indelicately
43 Phil of "Top Banana"
44 Checkout line lengthener?
45 Ties
46 Notice
47 Dr. of rap
48 "Potemkin" mutiny port
51 Twin Peaks state
52 Fringes worn by Orthodox Jews
53 Ties
55 Music, Nashville-style.
59 Result of too much V.O.?
60 Berlin "alas"
61 Jersey "alas"

9   by Betty Jorgensen

ACROSS
1 Pack (in)
5 List ender
9 Huzzah for Horne
14 Canyonlands National Park site
15 Mathematical sets
16 Exxon Valdez, e.g.
17 Bayes who sang "Over There"
18 Give ___ up
19 "Thaïs," e.g.
20 Start of a quip
23 Nettled, with "off"
24 Rimrock locale
25 Base runner's feat
28 Word with season or secret
30 Seamstress's strip
34 Desists
36 Uppity one
38 Lady's man
39 More of the quip
42 Antietam general
43 Show bias
44 Aft
45 Lucille's love
47 "Born Free" lion
49 In a difficult position
50 One's entity
52 Adriatic seaport
54 End of the quip
61 "Abdulla Bulbul ___" (old song)
62 Brouhaha
63 Villa decoration
64 Stradivari's teacher
65 At any time
66 Trim, as a photograph
67 Like some myths
68 Florida county
69 Interpret

DOWN
1 Kind of sandwich
2 Superimposed
3 Japanese merchant ship
4 Pipe dream: Var.
5 Put on cloud nine
6 "Holy ___!"
7 Sampras, at times
8 Bone connector
9 These may be hit or cooked
10 Shop tool
11 Ex-British P.M. ___ Douglas-Home
12 40's-50's singer ___ Lynn
13 Ireland's ___ Islands
21 Pick
22 Foreign lady
25 Burn
26 Where Indians raise a flap?
27 Disburdens
29 Warm-up exams, for short
31 First name in cosmetics
32 Cuba ___
33 Graph depiction
35 Police badge
37 Eatery
40 Star-crossed
41 More regimented
46 Keys
48 Stood
51 A la King?
53 Worship
54 "Misery" co-star
55 Armory holdings
56 Regan's father
57 Popular salmon
58 Time's partner
59 Gymnast Korbut
60 Musical pipe

---

10   by Joe DiPietro

ACROSS
1 ___ de Mallorca
6 Unsteady
15 Studio light
16 Certain bunny
17 Brief job
18 Poe refrain
19 Author Sheldon
21 Emerson's "___ to Beauty"
22 Financial average
23 Prefix with -derm
24 Apes
27 Took the foot off the accelerator
29 Certain account
34 Newton, for one
35 Found fault with
37 Titian's "The ___ of Europa"
38 John Ciardi's "___ Man"
40 Electric swimmer
41 Ways
42 Wide-mouthed vessel
43 Part of an electric eye
45 Bank statement abbr.
46 Living
48 Tell
50 Takes off
52 Phone abbr.
53 Not to mention
56 Locks that can be picked?
57 Deserted animal
59 Kind of income
63 Strike ___ (model)
64 Like some Christians
65 Domingo, for one
66 Utmost
67 Anthony and Barbara

DOWN
1 Mine, for instance
2 It goes pfft!
3 Buried
4 "Gilligan's Island" boat
5 "De ___ Poetica"
6 Hideout
7 Ticket request
8 Cow of English origin
9 Unearthed, with "up"
10 Way out
11 Outer limit
12 Name in fashion
13 "Quo Vadis?" character
14 Developed
20 "Star Wars" sage
25 100 cents, abroad
26 Attaches
28 Baseball stat
30 ___-Magnon
31 Ship's communication device
32 Good time to take shots?
33 Coloradans, Utahans, etc.
36 Cow of ads
39 Kind of service
41 "Happy Days" dad, informally
43 Lineate
44 ___ buco (Italian dish)
47 Denoting some modern music
49 Cut (off)
51 Moving quickly and freely
53 Mirrored
54 St. Petersburg's river
55 Apothecary's measure
58 Word with prime or cut
60 "Moneyline" network
61 Las' followers
62 Routine

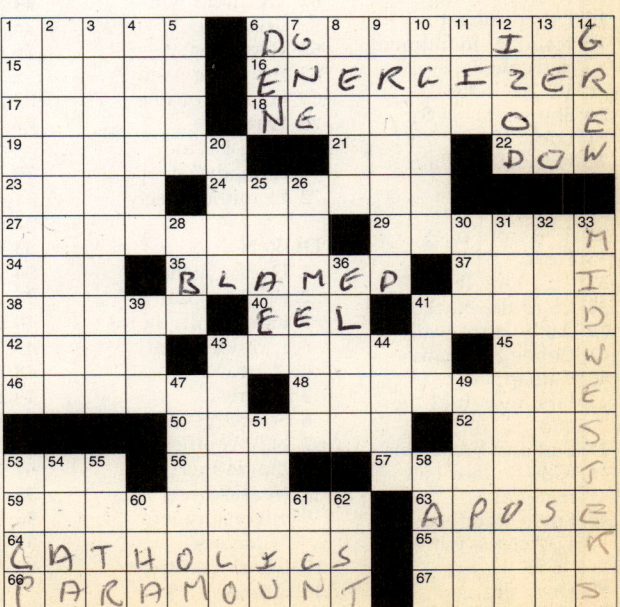

11 by Sidney L. Robbins

ACROSS

1 Thick slice
5 To the rear, nautically
10 First of all
14 June honoree
15 Fracas
16 Taunt
17 Pennsylvania and Park, e.g.: Abbr.
18 Elephant of children's lit
19 Burden
20 Ad puff
23 Not so much
24 One of Alcott's "Little Women"
25 "Jingle Bells" conveyance
28 Osmose
30 Pie ___ mode
33 Covering for a baby's bottom
34 Fire
35 Future blossom
36 Ad puff
40 Hawaiian garland
41 ___-Chalmers (farm machinery name)
42 "The jig ___!"
43 Printers' measures
44 Baby-faced
45 Most skilled
47 Wall Street operator, for short
48 "This one's ___!"
49 Ad puff
57 Pitch
58 "Pal Joey" writer John
59 15th or so
60 Poet Lazarus
61 Bay window
62 Alternatives to pastes
63 Socials
64 Jell-O shapers
65 Angel's topper

DOWN

1 Armed forces chow item
2 Popocatepetl emission
3 Uppermost point
4 Papal throne site
5 Surprise attack
6 A-frame supports
7 Priests' robes
8 Achievement
9 Polished mosaic floor
10 Ecstasy's opposite
11 Game show answer signal
12 Adjoin
13 Intertwine
21 Sister of 24-Across
22 Eastern V.I.P.
25 No longer fresh
26 Burdened
27 Hip swiveler of fame
28 Any song by 27-Down
29 Schmoes
30 Mistreat
31 Dillies
32 Modify to fit
34 Skirt accessory
37 Mother-of-pearl
38 Site for a poker game
39 ___ City (Denver's nickname)
45 Historical records
46 Yuppie's auto
47 Rand McNally book
48 Paddled
49 Sharpen
50 Actor Cronyn
51 ___ la Douce
52 "Comin' ___ the rye"
53 Ice pellets
54 Bright thought
55 Archer William
56 Bygone gas brand

12 by Rich Norris

ACROSS

1 Friendly
5 Pro ___ (perfunctory)
10 Vegas calculation
14 Lip balm ingredient
15 Ryan or Tatum
16 Urban unrest
17 National monument dedicated 10/28/1886
20 Show respect for
21 Dress
22 Fairy tale villain
25 Spies' org.
26 PC key
29 47-Across poet
35 Farce
37 "___ Like It Hot"
38 Clear the blackboard
39 Ambulance wail
41 Coffee alternative
42 Catnapper
43 First month of the año
44 Bed-and-breakfasts
46 Kids' indoor ball material
47 Poem inscribed on 17-Across, with "The"
50 Draft org.
51 Place for thieves
52 Send out
54 Lawrence of Arabia portrayer
58 Cry of delight
62 President who dedicated 17-Across
67 Take it easy
68 Adhesive resin
69 Huron, for one
70 Watcher
71 "The Divine Comedy" poet
72 Examine closely

DOWN

1 Do the dishes
2 Palo ___, Calif.
3 Horse with a gray-sprinkled coat
4 "Ditto"
5 Enemy
6 Songstress Yoko
7 N.B.A. official
8 ___ de mer (seasickness)
9 Silverstone of "Clueless"
10 Lunch box treat
11 Grime
12 Biblical verb
13 Eye inflammation
18 Prod
19 Burned brightly
23 Apt. divisions
24 Strong feeling
25 Make pure
26 German city north of Cologne
27 "Rise and ___!"
28 Seven-time A.L. batting champ Rod
30 Prayer responses
31 Elvis ___ Presley
32 Utterly destroys
33 Computer operators
34 Feudal workers
36 First planet: Abbr.
40 Piece of pasta
45 Total
48 Gave a longing look
49 Small, medium or large
53 Turnpike tabs
54 Give a longing look
55 Waiter's load
56 Seep out
57 Finished
59 W.W. II females' service gp.
60 Durante's "___ Dinka Doo"
61 Idyllic place
63 Tax return preparer, for short
64 Actor Chaney
65 Abbr. after a telephone number
66 Eustacia of "The Return of the Native"

13 by Frank Longo

ACROSS

1 European farm unit
8 Land whose name means "west island"
12 Gallery fare
14 Gland: Prefix
15 Common insecticide
16 Mideastern fiddles
18 Control
19 Lined up
20 Ethyl acetate, for one
21 Jet-setter's way of life
23 Parkway pulloffs
26 "Seascape" playwright
27 B-vitamin compounds
29 Plumlike fruit
32 What kitsch shows
33 Sonoma County firm
34 Transplants
40 Pen names adopted from others' real names
42 Oven-dry
43 Tactless
44 Sea quality
47 Like some South American cultures
48 Like a Nin novel
49 Amount after the decimal point
50 Go off
51 Early American patriot and journalist Benjamin
52 Jukebox supply

DOWN

1 Quite a stumble
2 Cut out
3 Safekeeping sites
4 Shoulder cape with hanging ends
5 Can't stomach
6 Inlets
7 Feminine name suffix
8 Sloth's order
9 Take another vote
10 Like rocky soil
11 Lack of objections, in a phrase
13 Cool
14 Onassis and others
17 ___'pea
22 Capital
24 TV knob
25 Slot machine feature
28 Nice notion
29 Caballed
30 Recent epoch
31 Rust-colored mineral deposits
32 "The Four Deuces" star
33 Completely infatuated
35 Merman of myth
36 Gym activity, with "up"
37 Secular
38 Subject of passing concern?
39 Barbers
41 Desires
45 Son of Hera
46 French novelist Pierre

14 by Sidney L. Robbins

ACROSS

1 Courtyards
6 ___ d'etat
10 Part of a gateway
14 Middays
15 Facilitate
16 Denver's home: Abbr.
17 Disoriented
20 Dancers Fred and Adele
21 ___-Japanese War
22 Actor Sparks
23 ___ end (very last part)
25 Prime-time hour
26 Soviet labor camp
30 Party to a defense pact
31 Spirited horse
32 Prophet who anointed Saul
34 Mimic
37 Disoriented
40 Jet to Heathrow
41 Vigorous
42 Actress Spelling
43 Operatic prince
44 Dead, as an engine
45 Had been
48 Guinness Book suffix
49 One of the Gershwins
51 Once more
53 Captain Picard series
58 Disoriented
61 State south of Ky.
62 Kind of smasher
63 Sharp as ___
64 Chair
65 They hold hymnals
66 Where Seoul is

DOWN

1 Paul who sang "Having My Baby"
2 Shipping units
3 Cheer (for)
4 Andean of old
5 Inquiring
6 Relinquished
7 Schmoes
8 G.I. entertainers
9 Each
10 Rights protection grp.
11 Chicken house
12 In the ball park
13 Board, as a trolley
18 "Able was I ___ . . ."
19 Historic county of Scotland
23 Botches
24 Native Alaskan
26 Wanders (about)
27 "Exodus" author
28 Endure
29 Roseanne's network
30 Love, in Lourdes
32 Urban woes
33 Monastery V.I.P.
34 Over
35 Where the Amazon originates
36 Make a change for the verse?
38 China and environs, with "the"
39 One ___ time
44 Noted site of Egyptian ruins
45 Floats gently
46 Be of one mind
47 Finnish bath
49 News paragraphs
50 "Far out"
52 "Money ___ everything!"
53 Pack
54 Dog in Oz
55 Bring up
56 Suffix with exist
57 America's first commercial radio station
59 Seance sound
60 Dined

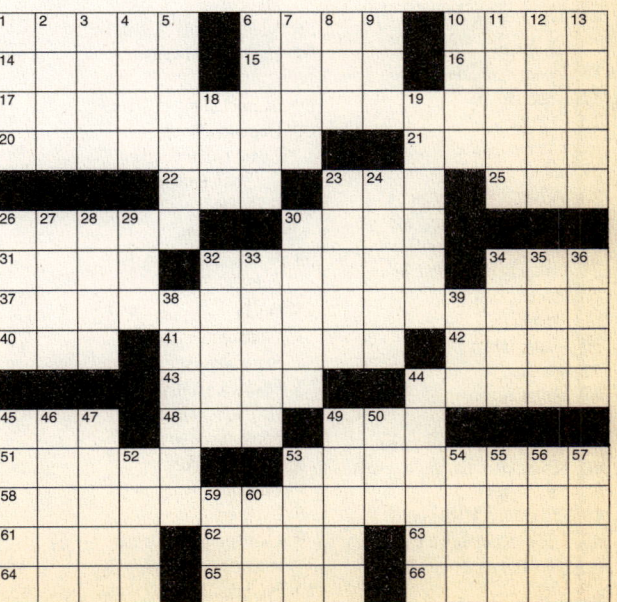

15 by James Neal

ACROSS

1 Food critic Sheraton
5 In the van
10 ___ law (rule of electricity)
14 Green acres?
15 Brendan Byrne, e.g.
16 Muumuu accessories
17 Tilt
18 Jabbered
19 Alternative word
20 Massachusetts musical ensemble
23 Othello's nemesis
24 Louvre annex architect
25 Soviet space station
27 Brussels ___
31 Fill driveway holes
33 In back
35 Somme summers
36 Parental substitutes, emotionally
40 Swamp
41 Hairsplitter
42 Wore away
45 Chapel next to St. Peter's
48 It's often seen ringside
49 Carpet down
51 Get ___ the ground floor
52 Harvestman
57 French novelist Pierre
58 Skiing mecca
59 Grammatical subject
61 Sponsorship
62 Shiny fur
63 Mrs. Dithers
64 Yiddish writer Sholem ___
65 Western "justice"
66 Genesis locale

DOWN

1 Actor Brooks
2 Eye malady
3 Bad luck
4 Kind of circuit
5 Vegas game
6 Retirement nest eggs
7 Flat payment
8 Person with a big nose?
9 "The Resurrection of Lazarus" painter
10 Backdrop for a TV scene
11 Spouse
12 Letters
13 Compass dir.
21 Salvation Army founder
22 Eskimo ___
26 Latin thing
28 Suffix with press or moist
29 Maryland athlete
30 They're sometimes cracked
32 Aptness
34 "___ Pagliaccio"
36 Andirons
37 Sweet-smelling
38 Fill-up filler
39 "___ Tomorrow" (Sammy Kaye hit)
40 Columnist Greenfield
43 Windup
44 Wright-Patterson base site
46 Worthless
47 Nail down
50 Greek Academy founder
53 Gossip
54 "___ be in England . . ."
55 Turndowns
56 "Sommersby" star
57 ___ & Perrins
60 Bert Bobbsey's twin

16 by David A. Rosen

ACROSS

1 Uniform material
6 Islamic pilgrimage
10 Late opponent of apartheid
14 "___ do" (turndown)
15 One of the back 40, perhaps
16 Pole, for instance
17 Listens to
18 "Candida" playwright
19 Rent
20 Where this was
23 Grow together again
24 Savonarola's offense
25 Utterly miserable
28 Be the victim of a sting?
30 Vulgarian
31 Meals
32 Semi's front
35 What this is
39 Laertes, to Polonius
40 Knocked in, as a putt
41 Farm feed
42 Admiral Rickover
43 "___ a Small Hotel!" (Rodgers and Hart hit)
45 Portuguese colony until 1975
48 Just conclusion?
49 What this is
55 One given to stretchers
56 More than a celebrity
57 Reddish-brown
58 Re
59 Schedule position
60 Brookhaven Laboratory site
61 ___ off (began)
62 Patroness of the Argonauts
63 Hacienda hands

DOWN

1 Granny, e.g.
2 Sundowner
3 Didn't just pass
4 Rapids shooters
5 Matched precisely
6 Lacks, briefly
7 Pine
8 Pull in
9 Cowboy's music maker
10 Suddenly
11 Wheelchair accessway
12 Bounders
13 "___ Little Movement" (Dorsey Brothers hit)
21 Go unused
22 Proust's "A la Recherche du Temps ___"
25 Essentials
26 Bklyn., e.g.
27 "Benny & ___" (1993 film)
28 MTV correspondent Tabitha
29 Anti-D.W.I. org.
31 Gaucho's weapon
32 Basil, e.g.
33 Part of an Adenauer epithet
34 Catfish Row soprano
36 Without confidence
37 Feminine
38 Animation toy
42 Flashy car
43 "___ Waterfowl" (Bryant poem)
44 Minor setback
45 Major key
46 Bedlam
47 Fuel holder
48 "Animal House" house
50 Fruitless
51 Hussein's queen
52 VIII, to Virgil
53 By and by
54 Minus

17   by Ed Pegg Jr.

ACROSS

1 "___ Without a Cause"
6 Musical scale letters
11 Joker
14 Smell
15 Of great scope
16 Electric ___
17 Proverb
18 Old-fashioned picture taker
20 Elevator name
22 Victory symbol
23 Norse Zeus
24 Candidate Landon
26 Was sore
28 Having divergent lines
29 Backside
31 DNA shapes
33 Letter getter
35 Seize
36 That lady
39 Make into a spiral
40 Book after Deuteronomy
42 Opposite of SSW
43 ___ Mahal
45 12, at dice
46 Leisurely study

48 Eric of "Monty Python"
49 October gems
52 ___ Rouge
54 Olive ___
55 Sushi go-with
56 National anthem contraction
57 Author Irwin
59 Intercom
62 Smoldering spark
65 Unfashionable
66 "___ a Rainy Night" (1981 hit)
67 On top of
68 Formerly named
69 One of life's certainties, in a saying
70 Deep-___ (discarded)

DOWN

1 Type of computer chip
2 Historical time
3 Ticket booth
4 Discharge
5 Keats poem
6 Recede
7 Beg shamelessly

8 Trapped
9 European freshwater fish
10 Medicine watchdog: Abbr.
11 Uncared-for, as a lawn
12 Eagle's nest
13 Liver or thyroid
19 Extinct birds
21 Rhodes ___
24 Jingle writers
25 Greg Evans cartoon
27 Use voodoo on
28 Crate up again
30 ___ Jo, of the '88 Olympics
32 Coaxes
34 Mosquito marks
36 Train for the ring
37 ___-burly
38 Artist's prop
41 ___-fi
44 Diner music maker
45 "Kapow!"
46 Entreaty
47 ___ Tuesday
49 Director Welles
50 Irritate
51 Not obtuse

53 Three-toed birds
56 Neighbor of Ark.
58 Both: Prefix
60 Acumen
61 Illiterates' signatures

63 The day before
64 Ruby

18   by Fred Piscop

ACROSS

1 Protection in a purse
5 Start, as a trip
11 Actor Max ___ Sydow
14 Lawyer Dershowitz
15 Dragon's prey
16 Author Levin
17 Ex-heavyweight champ
19 Galley slave's tool
20 "___ been had!"
21 Bad grades
22 "Is that so?"
24 Colonist
26 Rock's ___ Vanilli
27 Brit. ref. work
28 Triangular-sailed ships
30 Pencil name
33 Hotel lobby
34 "Ich ___ ein Berliner"
36 "Famous" cookie man
37 Little bits
38 Dumb ox
39 Fourposter
40 Linen shades
41 Leafy shelter
42 Small seals

44 Journalist Nellie
45 Get rid of, in slang
46 Deejay's need
50 Los Angeles player
52 Orbit period
53 Lumberjack's tool
54 Singer ___ Rose
55 Noble acts
58 ___ time (golfer's starting point)
59 Niagara Falls craft?
60 "Java" player Al
61 "___ day now . . ."
62 The "E" of H.R.E.
63 Chocolate-covered morsels

DOWN

1 Baseball's Roger
2 Extant
3 Middy opponent
4 Epilogue
5 Ran the show
6 Almighty
7 Lobster eaters' accessories
8 Hubbub
9 Second drafts
10 Pew attachment

11 A concertmaster holds it
12 Kind of vaccine
13 Not any
18 Ambitionless one
23 Pub drink
25 Stocking parts
26 Yucatán people
28 Name in computer software
29 7D, e.g.
30 Early Beatles describer
31 "Rag Mop" brothers
32 Legendary bluesman
33 Onward
35 Neither's mate
37 It sometimes comes in bars
38 Cassidy portrayer William
40 Uganda airport
41 Boombox sound
43 Jazz date
44 Long-eared pooch
46 Witch, at times
47 Fine cloth
48 Strive
49 Schick et al.
50 Disk contents

51 The yoke's on them
52 Cosmonaut Gagarin
56 Dada founder
57 ___ Na Na

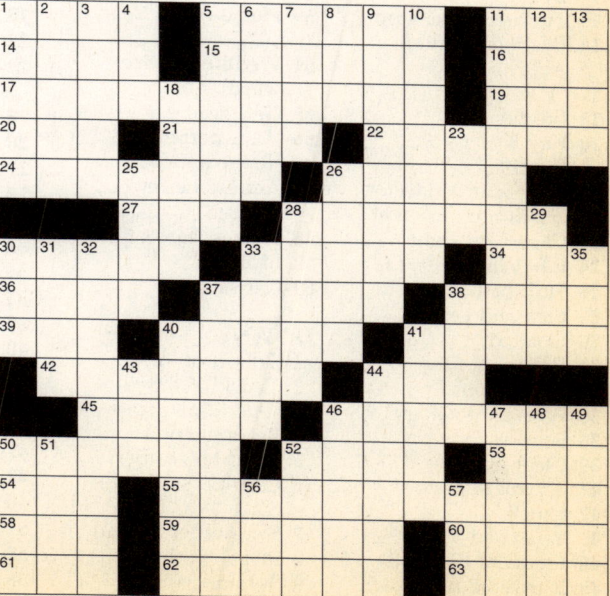

ACROSS

1 B followers
4 Philippine island
9 Writer LeShan
12 Penned
14 Thin pancake
15 Campaign donor, for short
16 Have airs, like Rover?
18 Dockers' org.
19 Gleaming
20 Shady
22 Washington's Mount St. ___
24 Director Fred et al.
25 Have it rough, like Asta?
30 "___ make myself clear?"
32 Hockey feint
33 Art school subj.
34 Author Ferber
36 Transplant
39 Goods: Abbr.
40 Sleeps in a sitting position
41 Spanish other
43 Tom Jones's "___ Not Unusual"
44 Get Marmaduke's reaction?
49 Rock's ___ Straits
50 Clothes
52 Patron of France
55 Remedial workshop
57 Inventor's cry
58 Visit the pound?
61 Dickens pen name
62 "Oklahoma!" aunt
63 Relaxing bath
64 Afore
65 Plow man
66 180° from NNW

DOWN

1 Teen love
2 Jitterbug
3 Prima ballerina
4 Acad. or univ.
5 "___ you for real?"
6 Doc
7 Moral fable: Var.
8 Sliding-door grooves
9 Of great size
10 Mustachioed artist
11 "___ may look on a king"
12 F.D.R. program
13 Group of nine
17 Proffer
21 Ali's faith
23 Benefit
26 Station
27 Native
28 Eschew food
29 Hot times in Saint-Tropez
30 Fender bender
31 Skunk's defense
35 Stage mutter
37 Will-___-wisp
38 Soldier's line of defense
42 Discombobulates
45 Imparted a slight taste to
46 Baltimore bird
47 Get cozy
48 "A Dog of Flanders" author et al.
51 Actress ___ Hasso
52 Kemo ___ (trusty scout)
53 Air Force missile
54 Flabbergast
56 Inits. for R. E. Lee
59 "___ the ramparts . . .'"
60 Uno + due

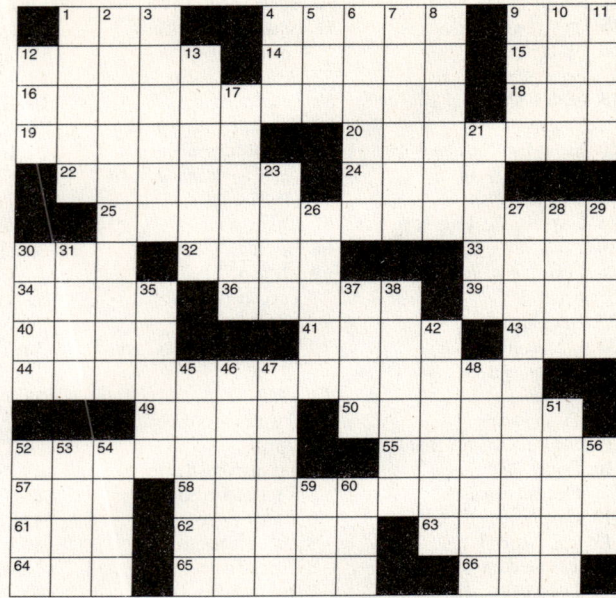

ACROSS

1 Twin
5 Market Square Arena team
11 Dog command
14 Eye
15 Turkish travel stop
16 Bygone coalition: Abbr.
17 "E.R." rival
19 Brother
20 Kay Kyser's "___ Reveille"
21 Hide-hair connector
22 ___ in the ointment
23 Cape Cod sight
24 E.B. White output
26 Stultified
28 Free and easy
30 Isolated
31 Religious rift
33 Anomalous
36 Works into shape
38 Scull
39 Clear-eyed
41 Chunk of history
42 Gulch
45 Wretched
46 Frequent dice rolls
48 It may be laid down
50 Confused
52 Pitch
53 60's coif
54 Mate for Bambi
57 Outback egg-layer
58 Western Indian
59 Horse of the Year, 1977
64 Wedding notice word
65 Get more gas
66 "___ perpetua" (Idaho's motto)
67 Actress Lesley ___ Warren
68 Shakespeare's Duke of Illyria
69 Canvasback

DOWN

1 Cohort of Wyatt
2 "Yuck" relative
3 "Aladdin" prince
4 Reprimanded
5 Farm newcomers
6 Catullus's "Odi et ___"
7 Songwriter Sammy
8 Switch ending
9 Subdue
10 Sault ___ Marie
11 Subject of an E.E. Cummings "portrait"
12 Civil War general, loser at Waynesboro
13 Becomes grizzled
18 Japanese aborigine
22 Film speed no.
23 Former New York Mets manager
25 Tasks for calculators
26 "Woe ___!"
27 Jordanian queen
28 Turmoil
29 Light and open
32 Mawkish material
34 Poet Walter ___ Mare
35 Lured
37 Goal preventer
40 Trite
43 Forest denizen
44 1982 James Earl Jones role
47 The big I
49 Actor Cronyn
50 Creatures
51 Many times
55 Dunces
56 Toiletries case
59 Kind of hotel, for short
60 X
61 Southeastern Conference sch.
62 Catchall abbr.
63 Stir-fry vessel

ACROSS

1 Woman's pronoun
5 "___ were the days!"
10 Discontinued Dodge
14 Apartment
15 Boots
16 Epitome of thinness
17 Worthless agreements?
19 Case for the military police
20 Primp
21 Flag
22 Emergency CB channel
23 Kind of seat
25 Flag
27 ___ pit (rock club area)
29 Twists
32 Oriental cookware
35 Private gesture
39 It's found dans le bain
40 Keeps
41 1958 Pulitzer-winning writer?
42 "The Catcher in the ___"
43 Grabbed a bite
44 Stew ingredient

45 Fence's opening, perhaps
46 Lob
48 Actress Allgood
50 Composure
54 Ebert's co-critic
58 Two shots, maybe
60 Kind of tide
62 Overfamiliar
63 Pizzeria appliance
64 Nonchalant view of fortune?
66 Carter's middle name
67 Protective layer
68 It often comes with points
69 Murder
70 "Young Mr. Lincoln" star
71 Seeing red

DOWN

1 Mini-mountains
2 ___ nous
3 Mature
4 Runs
5 Arnold or Dewey
6 Quatre doubled
7 Actor Davis
8 Like old schoolmasters

9 Problems for Sylvester the Cat
10 Florida product
11 Carol Burnett and Mary Tyler Moore, e.g.?
12 Very bright
13 Loafing
18 Aware of
24 Virginia Woolf piece
26 "___ your pardon!"
28 Shortwavers
30 Salad ___
31 Animal fat
32 "Eh?"
33 Curse
34 Fatalist's favorite song?
36 Warrant
37 Applications
38 "___ Theme" (1939 film song)
41 Lower jaw
45 Art crayons
47 Without secrets
49 Gain in status
51 ___ the boys
52 Certain soprano
53 Streep's "River Wild" co-star
55 Toy instrument

56 "King Olaf" composer
57 Sierra ___
58 Bucks' mates

59 Window shape, maybe
61 Golden, for one
65 "Give ___ break!"

ACROSS

1 Yields
10 Kind of stew
15 Political surprise
16 Time being
17 Bent backward
18 Spud
19 Spleen
20 Guns
21 Most high, in titles
22 They're dubbed
24 "Couplehood" author
26 Come by
27 Diary protectors
29 Ersatz
30 Louis Philippe, e.g.
31 60's Presidential in-law
34 Auden's "The ___ of Anxiety"
35 Black rights org. since 1912
36 Mourn
38 Spout
40 Two-piece piece
41 Pod starter
42 Shaping tool
43 Attention
44 Close

46 Shoot-'em-up
50 Naphthol, e.g.
51 Flaunt
54 Clean
55 Pencil name
57 Sweet-talk
59 One in a club: Abbr.
60 Dripping
61 Late-summer concern
63 Discrimination
64 Approved
65 City north of Cologne
66 Apparatus

DOWN

1 Loud
2 Isaac Albéniz composition
3 The electorate
4 Asian lead-in
5 Warehouse abbr.
6 Tender
7 Escape facilitator
8 Establishment in a new habitat
9 Mardi Gras V.I.P
10 Short musical work
11 More than laugh

12 Basic
13 Dramatic opening
14 Dissenter
21 Neptune, e.g.
23 Active
25 Journalist Alexander
28 Quiet
32 Of the north
33 Tobacco pipe
36 Grade school supplies
37 Infrequency
39 Fire
40 Intimate
45 Gap
47 Hot ___
48 Regulating device
49 Solution
52 Kind of column
53 Geocentric center
56 Garden access
58 Missing floor in Caesar's Palace?
61 "Tell ___" (1963 hit)
62 Recycled item

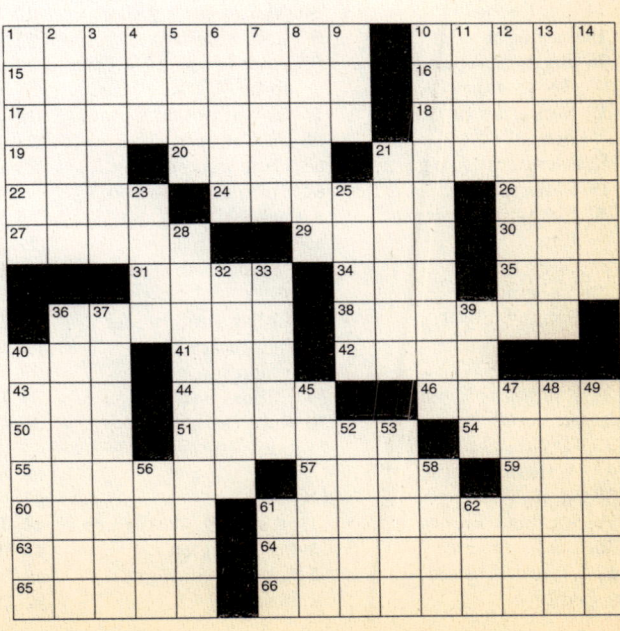

23   by Norma Steinberg

ACROSS
1 "Greetings ___ . . ."
5 "Stop, sailor!"
10 Gets older
14 Queue
15 Knight's weapon
16 Command at the Iditarod
17 QE2, e.g.
19 "Do ___ others . . ."
20 Patina
21 Microscope part
22 Tiff
23 Guard
25 Sound system
27 Piggies
29 Newsman Newman
32 "___ jail" (Monopoly directive)
35 Beast
39 Scooby ___
40 Volcano fallout
41 Ornamental work
42 Purpose
43 "Steady as ___ goes"
44 Eagerly wish
45 Mars's Greek counterpart
46 Is wearing
48 Measureless
50 Actress Anjelica
54 "___ 17"
58 "Shoo!"
60 Breakfast restaurant chain, informally
62 By oneself
63 Pea holders
64 Mississippi riverboat stop
66 Skin cream ingredient
67 Pickling solution
68 Slinky fabric
69 Mr. Gingrich
70 Christmas visitor
71 Understands

DOWN
1 Dental care item
2 Nouveau ___
3 ___ a million
4 Had the intention
5 Winner's take
6 Colorado ski town
7 Rice and Bancroft
8 Fragrance
9 Succinct
10 "We are not ___"
11 Content of some shells
12 "Cómo ___ usted?"
13 Whisky glass
18 Claudius's stepson
24 Calendar periods
26 Depend (on)
28 Cinch
30 Actress Skye
31 Signals assent
32 Knife wound
33 Dept. of Labor division
34 Lamont Cranston
36 Here, in Québec
37 TV's Griffin
38 Vicinities
41 Cures, as leather
45 Befuddled
47 Beginning
49 Polaris, e.g.
51 Mr. ___ (Poitier role)
52 Name on the Tara deed
53 Out
55 Name repeated in a 1963 hit song
56 Perspective
57 Nerds
58 Bridge
59 Composer Porter
61 French bridge
65 Cult. events funder

24   by Karen Hodge

ACROSS
1 Roasting rods
6 Sunscreen ingredient
10 Hacks around the city
14 ___ Dame
15 Hot spot
16 Brigham Young's destination
17 Barbarian of pulp fiction
18 Mennonites, e.g.
19 Make yawn
20 Elementary piano tune
22 Book before Nehemiah
23 Spanish artist
24 Ogler
26 Boy king
29 Rationalistic believer
31 Antiquated
35 Having zero rainfall
37 Actress Gardner
38 More ideal?
39 Southern France
40 L.B.J., for one
42 Volunteer State: Abbr.
43 Fine as can be
45 Uneven
46 Ax
47 Tree-lined walk
48 Have fun with
50 Matter for a judge
51 Lab weight
53 Course for an M.D.-to-be
55 Couch potato's place
58 Not be frank
63 Oral, maybe
64 Tommie of 60's–70's baseball
65 Singer Chris
66 "Sommersby" star, 1993
67 Collar straightener
68 Inamorata of Valentino
69 Billfold stuffers
70 Robin's home
71 Fuels (up)

DOWN
1 60's Black Power grp.
2 Pal of Piglet
3 Give ___ thought
4 Pitfalls
5 Had a feeling
6 100% sure
7 Opposite of sans
8 Canterbury dignitary
9 Impatient
10 Math extractions
11 Full, as an index
12 Attorney General under Bush
13 Mets' home
21 Versailles document
25 Ambulance rider, briefly
26 St. Pete's neighbor
27 Milton's "Regent of the Sun"
28 Kind of wave
30 Early Brit
32 Use a harpoon
33 Subsequently
34 Pershing's men
36 Chuck-a-luck and craps
38 Ruined
41 Next-door
44 That girl
48 Refugee
49 Slightly off course
52 With all one's might
54 "Bobby Shaftoe's gone ___"
55 Flower of 16-Across
56 The yoke's on them
57 What's for dinner?
59 Modernists
60 Destitution
61 Have the nerve
62 Rossignol gear

ACROSS

1 Hotel posting
6 Roast cut
10 Paper airplane part
14 W.W. II plane ___ Gay
15 Uzbekistan's ___ Sea
16 Treat the lawn
17 Not fulfilled
18 Like Marx Brothers humor
19 From the top
20 1996 event
23 "Tarzan" star Ron
24 Prominent donkey features
25 "___ the ramparts . . ."
26 Arabian demon
28 French nobleman
29 Halloween cry
32 Jelly holder
33 "Dallas" ranch
36 Theme song for 20-Across
39 Least comfortable
40 Record producer Brian
41 Derek and Jackson
42 Shtick
43 Did 100
45 Presidential nickname
46 Grandpa on "The Waltons"
48 Like grandpa
51 Site of 20-Across
55 Jai ___
56 Slippery
57 Baby conveyance
58 Lugosi of fright films
59 Neil Armstrong movement
60 Comedienne Cleghorne
61 Terminated
62 Posted
63 Tractor man

DOWN

1 Be economical with, as resources
2 Cancel
3 60's singer with the Shondells
4 K-6, schoolwise
5 Glossy fabric
6 Stubble remover
7 Eurasian mountain range
8 Multitude
9 Grand Voyager maker
10 Aptitude
11 "Mod Squad" member
12 "My Cup Runneth Over" singer
13 Cathedral seat
21 Competed in a marathon
22 ___ Melba (French dessert)
27 "My friend" of early TV
28 What two can coo
29 Giant waste of money
30 Black-and-white cookie
31 Rubber-stamps
32 O'Casey's "___ and the Paycock"
33 Editor's mark
34 Surprised cries
35 At no cost
36 Long sandwich
37 Kobe's bay
38 Congeniality
43 Go to, as a doctor
44 Investigated
45 Trojan War epic
46 Pioneer anatomist
47 Sphinx site
49 Feline crossbreed
50 Pop singer Taylor ___
51 Author Haley
52 Suspicious story
53 Head of France
54 Referee's guideline
55 "The ___ Daba Honeymoon"

ACROSS

1 Cry for "poor Yorick"
5 Brothers' keeper?
10 Chase flies
14 Fountain choice
15 Hotelier Helmsley
16 Not well
17 NAFTA fighter
19 Fed
20 Uneven
21 Related
23 Gets the better of
25 Paradise
26 Madrid Mrs.
27 Like an old record
31 Blond shade
34 One place to find Franklin
36 ___-Ball (arcade game)
37 Duffer's goal
38 Creator of the Morlocks
41 Important period
42 "___ first . . ."
44 Kind of chart
45 Hide-hair connector
46 It's all in the family
49 Decks
51 Limey
52 Goes off
56 Sign-reading site
60 Get used (to)
61 Frequent caller?
62 Noted 1973 resignee
64 Eye of ___ (witch's item)
65 The best and the brightest
66 Starts a lawn
67 Part of A.D.
68 Tamerlane sacked it in 1398
69 Shoe insert

DOWN

1 Throbbed
2 Greenstreet cohort in "The Maltese Falcon"
3 Removed
4 Disrespects
5 Gran Paradiso, e.g.
6 Summons, in a way
7 Crashing type?
8 ___ off (switch choice)
9 Rip to shreds
10 Official seals
11 "The American Language" author
12 Ex-Sen. Cranston
13 "Peer ___"
18 Kind of party
22 Lupino of film
24 Bite
27 Power source for Fulton
28 Scot, for one
29 Sub
30 Wine label info
31 ". . . hear ___ drop"
32 Ump's call
33 Black activist of the 60's
35 Has
39 Charles or George, e.g.
40 Inclined
43 SkyDome locale
47 "___ the season . . ."
48 Yearned
50 Most level-headed
52 Ruination
53 Kind of mill
54 Vocation
55 Taste, e.g.
56 Mandlikova of tennis
57 Hot spot
58 Heraldic charge
59 One of the Everly Brothers
63 Ring around the collar?

27 — by Trip Payne

ACROSS
1 Tater separator
6 Electric Company neighbor
15 It's carried through the air
16 Express wonderment
17 "I'm all ___"
18 Vulgarity
19 "Later"
21 Word in a store-hours sign
22 One overseas
23 Way up
24 In flawless shape
25 Lech's look
27 Harding and Wilson
28 40-card game
29 Popular Trekkie zine
31 Seat of Penobscot County
32 Tropical pastes
33 Zest for life
34 Moreno's real first name
37 Place for a grease well
40 Monologue ad-lib
41 "Topaz" author
42 Quick to the helm
44 Pizzeria desserts
45 Individually
47 Louse-to-be
48 Sega rival, for short
49 "Local Hero" director
51 Sexy person
53 Where millions of connections are made every year
54 "Women in Love" star
55 Gambler
56 Commercial challenge
57 750-year-old literary works

DOWN
1 Former shortstop Belliard
2 Twist endings, e.g.
3 Noble wear
4 Discharge
5 "Jabberwocky" creatures
6 Battle types
7 Using a recorder
8 Robed vocalists
9 Sets back
10 One chip, perhaps
11 Nutritionist's abbr.
12 Permanent
13 Gradually destroy
14 Quarters
20 Footnote phrase
24 Poem of lament
26 White water feature
28 Miss
30 Alternative to the new math
31 County of a TV western
33 Most epigrammatic
34 It keeps your hair drier
35 Seminole War leader
36 Breaks for the Mexican border?
37 Parts of humidifiers
38 Nautical line
39 U.N. member since 1993
41 Working through the night
43 Common solvents
45 Strive for
46 Whittle away
49 1995 Best Picture nominee
50 Migrating fish
52 It does a bang-up job

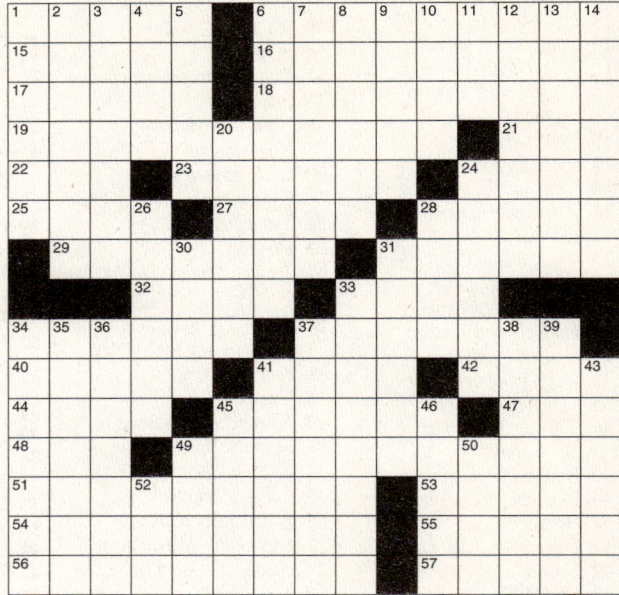

28 — by Rich Norris

ACROSS
1 Certain party
10 Floats
15 End of a routine
16 Mall forerunner
17 Embryological layers
18 Former Chiefs' coach Hank
19 Squeeze (out)
20 Businessmen, slangily
22 Send
23 Words of warning
26 Postponement
27 Unfavorably
28 John ___, California gold rush figure
30 Calendar periods: Abbr.
31 Manitoba native
32 Lipton alternative
34 Some artists
36 "Crimes and Misdemeanors" actor
37 Prefix with space
38 Mainstay
41 Is suspicious
44 Most eligible, once
45 AAA's opposite?
47 Late Mexican-American vocalist
49 Alicia of "Falcon Crest"
50 Poker choice
52 Some spreads
53 Guns
55 Al-Assad's land
57 Abbr. next to a telephone number
58 Fancy
60 Hog with erect ears
63 Madonna role
64 Talents
65 "Walk Away ___" (1966 hit)
66 Convention figures

DOWN
1 Zips
2 Get a break
3 Triple ___
4 "Green": Prefix
5 Scholar's goal
6 Motivation for Manolete
7 Bug
8 Rancor
9 Turnpike locales
10 Used to be
11 Govt. employees
12 Available
13 Kind of park
14 Salesman's load
21 Kind of analysis
24 Capital on the Rideau Canal
25 "I cannot ___ lie"
29 Satisfaction
31 Spiny cactus
33 1958 #1 song
35 Undesirable
38 Transient
39 Shake up
40 Do not delete
42 Not make an issue of
43 Villain, at times
46 Land on the Mediterranean
48 Size up
51 Epithet for Harry Callahan
54 Fill
56 Similar
59 Pearl Bailey's middle name
61 I stand: Lat.
62 Shack

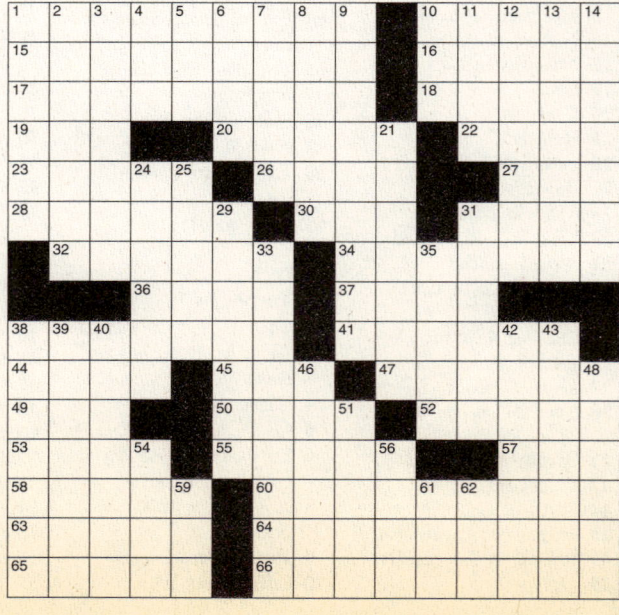

29 by Fred Piscop

ACROSS

1 Understood
4 Some tracks
9 ___ Rizzo ('69 Hoffman role)
14 Santa ___ winds
15 Actress Anouk
16 Significant person?
17 Kauai keepsake
18 Small person
20 Legit
22 Caroline Schlossberg, to Ted Kennedy
23 Type style: Abbr.
24 Big Mama
25 Church part
29 Rummy variety
32 The mark on the C in Čapek
33 Calendar period, to Kirk
37 Caustic substance
38 Traditional tune
40 Pub quaff
42 Logical newsman?
43 Long-lasting curls
45 Depicts
49 Health-food store staple
50 Jerry Herman composition
53 Dash
54 Michelangelo masterpiece
56 Journalist Greeley
58 Used booster cables
62 Tina's ex
63 Correspond, grammatically
64 Regarded favorably
65 Pince-___
66 Former Justice Byron
67 Air-show maneuvers
68 Palindrome center

DOWN

1 French
2 ___ time (singly)
3 Taipei's land
4 Honolulu locale
5 Fat fiddle
6 Fuse word
7 First name in hotels
8 Big rigs
9 Campus mil. grp.
10 Daughter of Zeus
11 Calendar abbr.
12 Theology sch.
13 Eye
19 ___-man (flunky)
21 Hooch container
24 Magna ___
26 Rights grp.
27 "Oy ___!"
28 ___ out (supplement)
30 Hoosegows
31 Footrace terminus
32 Stage actress Hayes
34 MS follower?
35 Love, Italian style
36 Newcastle-upon-___, England
38 Esne
39 Judge's exhortation
40 Prone
41 Name of 13 popes
44 Oscar the Grouch, for one
46 Julia Louis-Dreyfus on "Seinfeld"
47 Pool-ball gatherer
48 Common cause for blessing
50 Strawberry, once
51 "Any Time ___" (Beatles tune)
52 Auto-racer Andretti
55 Words of comprehension
56 "David Copperfield" character
57 Ten to one, e.g.
58 Gossip
59 "That's disgusting!"
60 High-tech med. diagnostic
61 Foreman stat

30 by Fred Piscop

ACROSS

1 "West Side Story" girl
6 200 milligrams
11 Low island
14 1968 song "All ___ the Watchtower"
15 River to the Missouri
16 Fuss
17 Seaver's nickname
19 Robert Morse Tony-winning role
20 House cleaner, in England
21 "Absolutely"
22 Legal profession
24 Queen Victoria's house
26 Freight charge
27 Half-wit
28 Better than a bargain
29 Polynesian carvings
33 "Hail, Caesar!"
34 Netman Nastase
37 Sheepish
38 Cup's edge
39 Battery part
40 Anti-prohibitionists
41 Disfigure
42 Get extra life from
43 Portaged
45 Patriotic uncle
47 Rocket's cargo
49 Crib-sheet contents
54 Earthy colors
55 Veneration
56 Hand-cream ingredient
57 "Harper Valley ___"
58 Decorative shrub
61 Sock in the jaw
62 Address grandly
63 Coeur d'___, Idaho
64 Flood relief?
65 Pave over
66 Coiffed like Leo

DOWN

1 "Concentration" objective
2 Hello or goodbye
3 Type type
4 Opening
5 Stone, for one
6 Kitchen gadgets
7 Garage-sale words
8 Spitfire fliers, for short
9 Work up
10 Electronics whiz
11 Western spoof of 1965
12 "What ___" ("I'm bored")
13 "___ Sixteen" (Ringo Starr hit)
18 Package-store wares
23 Skater Zayak
25 Place for posies
26 Call back
29 Wrecker
30 "___ had it!"
31 News locale of 12/17/03
32 Shoe part
33 Auto option, informally
35 Wallet contents, for short
36 Shoebox letters
38 Alan or Cheryl
39 Kind of buildup
41 Gauge
44 Inertia
45 Finn's pal
46 Once again
47 "Where's ___?" (1970 flick)
48 Part owner?
50 Half of a Western city name
51 Pulitzer-winning novelist Glasgow
52 TV exec Arledge
53 Basted
55 Cinema canine
59 ___ out (missed)
60 Descartes's conclusion

31 — by Ernie Furtado

ACROSS

1 Swiss city on the Rhine
6 "Jake's Thing" author
10 Nice shindigs
14 Allan-___ (Robin Hood cohort)
15 Carry on
16 "___ Fire" (Springsteen hit)
17 *Paris site*
18 "___ partridge in a . . ."
19 Kind of fountain
20 Runaway, of a sort
22 Runway, of a sort
24 Book-lined rooms
25 *London site*
27 Cartoonist Bushmiller
29 Twofold
32 Game award, for short
35 Make a pot
36 Skin layer
38 *Rome site*
40 *Amsterdam site*
41 Drop out
42 Seat for two or more
43 "You don't ___!"
44 ___-tiller
45 They beat deuces
47 *Florence site*
50 Not on land
54 Upset-minded teams
57 Positions
59 Big 10's ___ State
60 Letter encl.
62 *Moscow site*
63 Derby
64 Ended
65 Off
66 River to the North Sea
67 Corn bread
68 Having an irregular edge

DOWN

1 With ___ breath
2 One of the Astaires
3 Dresden dweller
4 Slip by
5 ___ majesty
6 Mr. Parseghian
7 Sea cow
8 Kipling story locale
9 Legendary Packers QB
10 Surgical knife
11 Love, Spanish-style
12 Italian town, site of a 1796 Napoleon victory
13 Fastener
21 N.F.L. standout Lott
23 Not a main route
26 Naldi of silents
28 1964 Four Seasons hit
30 "___ 'n' Andy"
31 Trevi Fountain coin
32 Classic sports cars
33 Turn sharply
34 Somewhat, in music
36 Loss
37 High overhead?
39 Money for Mason
40 "Cheers" role
42 Harold of politics
46 Pianist Gyorgy
48 Noted children's writer
49 An encouraging word
51 Defunct treaty org.
52 Group character
53 Unanimously
54 Nimble
55 Birds Eye product
56 ___ over
58 "___ kleine Nachtmusik"
61 Afore

32 — by A.J. Santora

ACROSS

1 1980 Olympics host
5 Writer ___ Louise Huxtable
8 Setting
13 Computer list
14 Outfielders' throws
16 Sleeping problem
17 One-legged ballet pose
19 "Swan Lake" wardrobe
20 Ballet spin
22 Fernando of "The French Connection"
23 ___ Grande, Ariz.
24 Café cup
26 Bull in Chihuahua
29 New Mexico artists' town
31 Spots on the face
34 Drinkers' heavens
37 1935 Astaire/Rogers musical
39 "Great Expectations" boy
40 Helpmate of sorts
42 Oil-rich ___ Dhabi
43 "In" site, in a phrase
45 Took hold again, as a plant
47 Riga resident
48 Old Syria
50 Latin life
51 "If ___ Hammer"
53 Where Cuzco is
56 Took it easy
58 Hopping step, in ballet
61 Plié spots
63 Anna Pavlova, e.g.
66 Accustom
67 Garfield pal
68 Desirous Greek god
69 ___ incognita (old map notation)
70 D.C. lawmaker
71 Writer Kantor

DOWN

1 Thurman of "Henry & June"
2 Eccl. talk
3 Lose it
4 Limiting line
5 Lhasa ___ (hairy terriers)
6 Pas ___ (dance for four)
7 The shivers
8 Contents
9 Computer's heart, for short
10 Ballet leaps
11 Opposite of alte
12 Smooth
15 Begin in earnest
18 Time of importance
21 Sampler
25 Weaken
26 "Fiddler" actor
27 Express a view
28 Ballet coach
30 Ad ___ per Aspera (Kansas's motto)
32 Local theaters
33 Old music magazine
35 Cote sound
36 Rub
38 Cortés's quest
41 Series of connected ballet movements
44 Biblical verb ending
46 Artists' lifeworks
49 Stallone role
52 Voyaging
54 Stephen Foster's "___ Bayne"
55 Female ruff
56 Theatrical bit
57 Murray of song
59 Softens
60 Aer Lingus land
62 Be wrong
64 "___ a chance!"
65 Oar wood

ACROSS

1 Overabundance
9 More expeditious
15 Superior
16 Secret
17 Corrupts
18 Granitelike rock
19 Poetic tribute
20 Actress Winwood
22 They're usually found in beds
26 Orsk's river
27 Isr. neighbor
28 Change the sticker
30 Newscaster Lindstrom
33 S-shaped molding
35 City with a view of Mt. Everest
37 Some stitches
39 Wedding column word
40 Ball
41 Factory feature
44 Lawyer Roy
45 Appetite
46 Sewing machine attachment
48 Warrant
49 Cut into kabobs
50 Prophet
52 Apollo 7 astronaut
55 Jazz org.
56 It follows San or Dan
57 Splitting
62 Some chalcedonies
63 Made tracks
64 Holiday Inn alternative
65 Longer

DOWN

1 Advanced deg.
2 Canard
3 Object of a hunt
4 Afghan
5 Soccer maneuver
6 Sequential
7 Paris's ___ La Fayette
8 It's behind the altar
9 Legendary leaf source
10 Heated, as glass
11 Balloon
12 Follow
13 Gaelic
14 Rural rtes.
21 Vassalry
22 Beatrix Potter character
23 Pea, e.g.
24 Moon of Uranus
25 More oblique, colloquially
29 Of a particular locale
30 Corn flour
31 Moves at a snail's pace
32 Proxies
34 Wapiti
36 Resin
38 Glittery, as a gown
42 Confidentially
43 Most enthusiastic
47 Sale incentive
49 Dancer-actress Rivera
51 "Rapper" of verse
52 Tale of derring-do, e.g.
53 Study feverishly
54 Yearn
56 Deface
58 Undisciplined
59 The Beatles' "___ I Love Her"
60 Thousand, to a yegg
61 Actor Byrnes

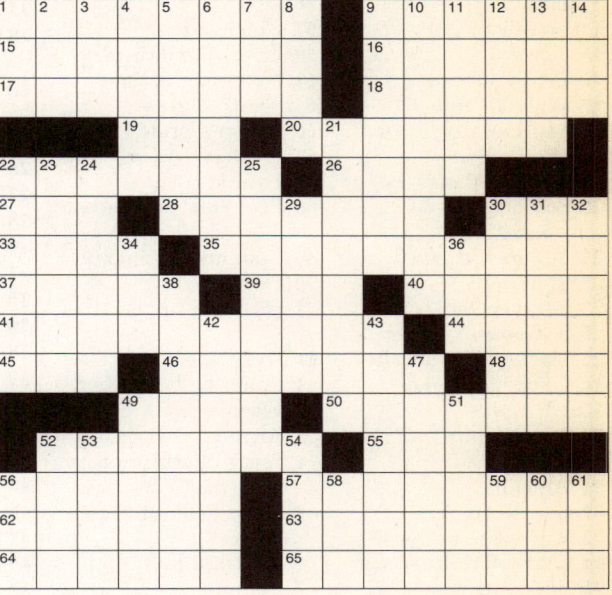

ACROSS

1 Boxer's weakness
9 Discharges
14 Type of canine
15 Einstein
17 Marinated dish
18 Matriarch, often
19 Reason for parental discretion
21 Big ___, Calif.
22 Bombard
25 Nigh
27 PC display
28 Teutonic one
29 Wither
31 Belligerent he-men
35 Commencement
36 CO$_2$ and methane, to a ecoscientist
41 Bushels
42 IV drip
43 Cleaned a windshield
47 Nova Scotia ___
48 Injury
49 Lead
50 Ostentatious
52 Morrow of "Northern Exposure"
53 Nap
55 Astronomer's Muse
59 Computer info
63 Toe trouble
64 Retired
65 Mota of the diamond
66 Medicine injectors

DOWN

1 Grasp
2 Drain opener ingredient
3 ___ Lingus
4 Tour of duty
5 1967 launch
6 Steinbeck family name
7 Grand Ole Opry's Mr. Guitar
8 Clinton staffers
9 One of a dozen, maybe
10 It surrounds St.-Pierre
11 Musical instrument: Suffix
12 Glitter
13 John of "Crossfire"
16 Vermont product
20 Seamen tell them
22 Wayward ice
23 Mythomaniac
24 "She Believes ___" (1979 hit)
26 Results of bull markets
27 Rock and roll genre
30 "La Dorotea" writer
32 Plagued (by)
33 Way back when
34 Chases flies
37 Playwright Clifford
38 MX housing
39 Plenty, previously
40 Hot
43 Groundskeeper's concern
44 Number needed
45 University of Illinois site
46 Off in la-la land
50 Glower
51 Custom
54 Prank ending
56 "A Spy in the House of Love" author
57 Item always charged
58 Whichever
60 Bar mem.
61 Boy in a Cash song
62 Part of a Road & Track test

35 · by Sidney L. Robbins

ACROSS
1 Out on ___ (vulnerable)
6 Jefferson's predecessor
11 Bleat
14 Novelist Puzo
15 Craze
16 Elbow's locale
17 With 37- and 64-Across, a seasonal observation
19 Here, in Paris
20 Secondhand transaction
21 Summer in Le Havre
22 Thin nail
23 Red vegetable
25 Scales, as a ladder
27 Sheltered, nautically
30 Cribbage marker
32 It's a plus
33 "Coriolanus" costume
34 Antenna
37 See 17-Across
43 Agreeable responses
44 Corncob or briar, e.g.
45 Shopping run

49 Health club
50 Strategize
51 ___ house (carnival attraction)
54 Star-Kist product
56 Dry
57 Greek letters
59 Easter floral display
63 Newsman Rather
64 See 17-Across
66 Pindar's pride
67 Mystery writers' award
68 Poet Stephen Vincent ___
69 Commit matrimony
70 Oceans
71 Heavenly spots

DOWN
1 From the U.S.: Abbr.
2 Wash
3 Angers
4 French Revolutionary statesman
5 Actor Peter of "Taxi Driver"
6 Electrical unit
7 Venture

8 Author Loos
9 "Back to the salt ___"
10 Droop
11 Scottish kids
12 Roofed-in gallery
13 In the center of
18 Cause of unwanted moisture
22 Egyptian god of music
24 Overflows (with)
26 Baby bovine
27 One ___ time
28 Actress Myrna
29 Sense of self
31 Lawn greenery
35 All thumbs
36 Battery's partner
38 Reply to a refusenik
39 Horrified
40 Zero
41 Tax figurer, for short
42 Urge
45 Figure at one's side
46 Macy's event
47 Destroyed
48 Terminus
52 Ooze

53 Mournful tune
55 Weeper of myth
58 Rice Krispies sound
60 "The Last Days of Pompeii" girl
61 On the level
62 Rigidifies
64 Koppel or Kennedy
65 Grads-to-be

36 · by Jon Delfin

ACROSS
1 Twaddle
4 Obvious fact
10 Swiss peaks
14 Where Tel Aviv is: Abbr.
15 Illustrator Beardsley
16 Skin opening
17 Any ship
18 Brooklyn pitching legend
20 Ancient storyteller
22 Bowling alley button
23 Mass. senatorial monogram
24 ___ out (just managed)
26 Horned zoo animals, briefly
28 "Forrest Gump" author
33 Picnic pest
34 Dormitory disturbance
35 Capital of Bolivia
39 Super server, in tennis
41 Song syllables
43 Bridge feat
44 Chocolate substitute

46 Be of use
48 Belief
49 Subject of a 1956 film "search"
52 Overly rushed
55 Nose-in-the-air type
56 Moray
57 Jai alai basket
61 Take over
64 Former Idaho Senator
67 Pub quaff
68 Fork part
69 Major blood vessels
70 Howard or Ely
71 Safecracker
72 Fire stirrers
73 Sot's ailment

DOWN
1 Italian flower town
2 Court star Arthur
3 Awards show V.I.P.
4 Machine rods
5 Capek play
6 Over, to Otto
7 "Dies ___"
8 Parts of mins.
9 "You saved me!"
10 Showery mo.

11 Actress Sophia
12 Teaser ad
13 Hunts for
19 Groups' tenets
21 Authorizes
25 Word of warning
27 Radio wise guy Don
28 W.W. II woman
29 Old-time Peruvian
30 Missile-warning grp.
31 Serious
32 Team track event
36 Coach's prop
37 Too hasty
38 TV prize
40 Gen. ___ E. Lee
42 Gets ready to fire
45 Building block
47 Expense account expenses
50 Polar cover
51 Milne's Baby ___
52 Packing a little weight
53 Creepy
54 Trolley sound
58 "Go away!"
59 Istanbul native
60 Commedia dell' ___
62 Cabal

63 Change for a twenty
65 Not pos.
66 Mercury or Saturn, e.g.

by James L. Beatty

ACROSS

1 Fight (with) down and dirty
7 Low in pitch
11 Merchandise: Abbr.
14 Enfeeble
15 Rights org. since 1920
16 Meadow
17 With 36- and 59-Across, words of Alexander Pope
19 Strike caller
20 Autumn occurrence
21 Exigency
22 Post-sunburn experience
23 Actor Cariou
24 Draft letters
26 Go by
28 To be, to Tacitus
30 Ballet step
32 Manacles
33 Skill
35 Hams it up
36 See 17-Across
38 Visitors from afar
40 Succinct
41 French pronoun
42 Part of a shepherd's flock
43 Seven ___
47 Changes the décor of
49 Sorority letter
51 Born
52 Class in which Keynes is taught
53 One Miss America measurement
56 Military group
58 "Caught you!"
59 See 17-Across
61 Obtain
62 Big name in little blocks
63 Have relevance
64 Superman's symbol
65 At the apex of
66 Worshiper

DOWN

1 Mix up, as a deck of cards
2 Ovid work
3 Fishing lures
4 Actor Mineo et al.
5 Organizers' aids
6 Blunder
7 Morally low
8 Yearn (for)
9 Baseball runner's tactic
10 Baltimore paper
11 These have sticky sticks
12 Land for a manor house
13 Dry, as a plant
18 Liable to cause injury
22 Springs from a pen
25 Boxes
27 7-Up flavorers
29 Level of authority
31 Part of many university names
34 Tennis player Richards
35 Plumed heron
36 What the dissolute sow
37 Most recent
38 Farmland, e.g.
39 Spongers
44 Make beloved
45 Charge with gas
46 Farm machine
48 Linen item
50 Trod the boards
54 "Othello" villain
55 Support
57 Singer Guthrie
59 Site of many keys: Abbr.
60 ___ pro nobis

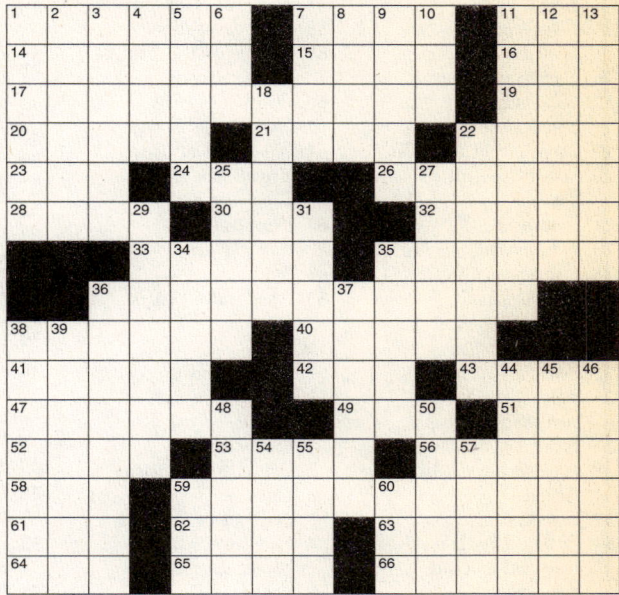

by Richard Silvestri

ACROSS

1 Sing "shooby-doo"
5 Below, to Byron
10 British colonial rule
13 Vogue rival
14 Shade of red
16 Stat for Christy Mathewson
17 Humdinger: Var.
19 Siege weapon
20 Amatory
21 Harden
22 At low ___ (declined)
23 Lampoon
26 Punch in the shop
28 House of lords
29 Armadas
32 Procter & Gamble brand
35 Help with the dishes
37 Challenge
38 Uris hero
39 Certain board members
42 White ___
43 Tibetan holy man
45 Hatcher of "Lois & Clark"
46 Minuscule
48 Finger movements
50 Maze notation
52 3-point Scrabble tile
53 Olympians
57 Oliver Stone film
59 Pompous person
62 Nook
63 Poetic pugilist
64 Excitement
67 Oxford tutor
68 Money in coin
69 Nevada city or county
70 Kind of basket
71 Instructional units
72 Big bucks, perhaps

DOWN

1 Graf rival
2 Bow of the silents
3 Appropriate
4 Brighton break
5 Supply in fresh meat
6 Photographer's abbr.
7 Brouhaha
8 Castilian kinsmen
9 Visibility problem
10 Cinematic encore
11 Descendant of Ishmael
12 Doorway sidepiece
15 Dating from birth
18 Copyright violator
24 "Outtasight!"
25 Neighbor of Sudan
27 Yoke
29 ___-de-lance (pit viper)
30 Innovative 1982 movie
31 Alluring
32 Baby whale
33 Spoken
34 Making like
36 Exact moment
40 Wino's woe
41 1947 Kim Hunter Broadway role
44 Cable award
47 Put up
49 "The Mermaid Tavern" poet
51 Pre-Socratic philosopher
54 Linen fabric
55 Conjure up
56 Toledo title
57 Shade of green
58 Wield the whip
60 Tries the wine
61 Galley marking
65 Kind of beer
66 Pitcher projection

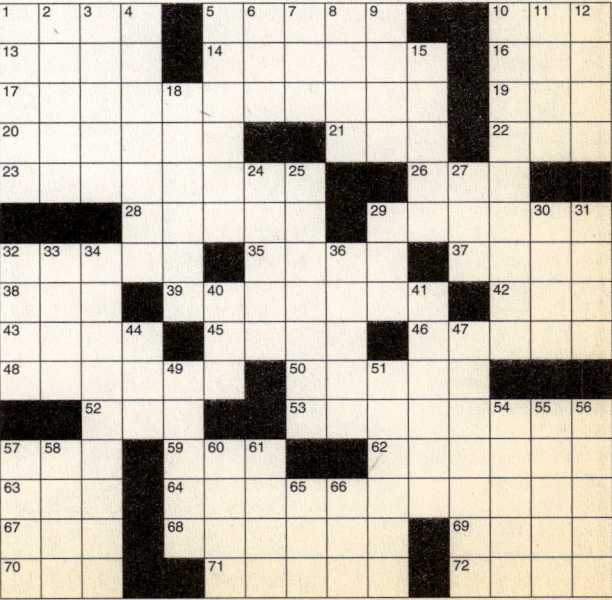

ACROSS

1 First course, maybe
5 Mans
11 Kind of site
14 About 30% of the earth
15 "Anybody ho-o-ome?"
16 Car m.p.g. raters
17 "Hee Haw" comedienne
19 Cave-dwelling fish
20 Second-brightest stars
21 Stormed
23 What Jesus spoke
26 High school class, informally
27 Broad ties
30 Architect Jones
33 Tough turkeys
36 Take ___ (accept congratulations)
37 Israeli desert
38 Health care lobby: Abbr.
39 Chicken ___
41 Otto I's realm: Abbr.
42 London cricket ground
44 Vega's constellation
45 W.W. II gun
46 Risible
47 Ancient Mexican
49 Farm field, maybe
51 Specious debater
55 Amber wines
59 Home of the biblical city Ephesus
60 Flightless bird
61 Noted Swiss item
64 No-good ending
65 Yupik speaker
66 Case for a vet
67 Presidential monogram
68 Salt
69 Associate: Suffix

DOWN

1 Afro-Brazilian dance
2 Willow switch
3 Range of the Rockies
4 Straw hats
5 Word for a storm
6 Choose
7 Epithet of Athena
8 Not increasing, as earnings
9 Loud
10 Comforting
11 Traditional homework time
12 Sporting sword
13 Coming out on top?
18 "A miss ___ good . . ."
22 Volcano's shape
24 Suffix with egotist
25 Shade of blue
28 Godzilla's target
29 Ice cream features
31 Actor Richard
32 Kind of mitt
33 Drying powder
34 Melville novel
35 The Winslows' family dog
39 Imputes
40 Org. whose symbol is a four-pointed compass
43 Reno cubes
45 Teaches
48 Big story
50 Expunge
52 Preferred term for 65-Across
53 Until now
54 Starchy food, informally
55 Repair
56 In the center of
57 "You Are My Destiny" singer
58 Slide sideways
62 Latin 101 word
63 Wheel part

ACROSS

1 Seven-time Wimbledon champ
11 Dam up
15 "Greetings!"
16 Off
17 "The Breakfast Club" actress
18 Emperor in a Mozart opera
19 Microscopic
20 Evening, in Avila
21 Beat by a tiny bit
22 Spot
24 Greenness
28 Kurosawa characters
31 Foe of 26-Down
32 Writer Waugh
33 Capt.'s heading
34 Mild oath
37 Dating term
39 Word in many cathedral names
41 Andean city
42 Rathskeller items
44 "Huh-uh"
46 Over
47 Fascinated by
48 Derisive ones
50 Court stat
53 Thoroughly enjoyed
54 "Macarena" singers Los ___ Rio
55 Bracing
57 Bar work
60 Term terminator
62 Run up to the Hill?
64 World's seventh-longest river
65 "Cimarron" co-star, 1931
66 Christian Science founder
67 It's on a roll

DOWN

1 "Heartbreak House" playwright
2 Conference lead-in
3 Part of Canada's Arctic Archipelago
4 The birds and the bees do it
5 Promote
6 Penelope, for one
7 Deli supply
8 Oliver of "Oliver!"
9 "As You Like It" forest
10 Whimsically strange
11 Remained idle
12 Piper PA-31P Navajo, e.g.
13 "Weird Al" Yankovic parody
14 Shortsighted person
23 Contemporary of Leoncavallo
25 Relief
26 Foe of 31-Across
27 Republic formerly called New Hebrides
28 Body cavities
29 Got down
30 Trumpeters, e.g.
35 Road to Rome
36 Lugs
38 Red army members?
40 "Hey Jude" chorus
43 Sir Toby Belch, e.g.
45 Quite the dish or hunk
49 Hairlines do it
50 Rochester's ward
51 Part of a sch. health class
52 Unit of cordwood
56 Kind of column
58 Tetracycline target
59 Herbicide target
61 New Jersey's Cape ___
62 Nickname in the family
63 Toys ___

ACROSS

1 Bart Simpson and others
12 Key letter
15 Hindrances
16 Common Market abbr.
17 Lengthy enumeration
18 ___ kwon do
19 Sister of King Arthur
20 "When I was ___ . . ."
21 Drama critic Richard et al.
23 Classified abbr.
24 Lack
25 Where the Rhône rises
28 ___ table (dessert buffet)
30 "Serpico" author
31 Sign up
32 Descartes's thought
33 Mat wins
34 "The Girl From Ipanema" composer
35 Precisely
36 Table-talk collections
37 Dazzles
38 Pantheon ruler
39 Affidavit takers
41 Smack
42 Taillike
43 Crown
44 Owning land
45 Stress, for one
47 Old cars
51 Flesh and blood
52 Aircraft maneuvers
55 Netherlands city
56 Dust Bowl feature
57 Moldavia, once: Abbr.
58 Craftsmen

DOWN

1 Uris's "___ 18"
2 Noted fashion model
3 Worked a jenny
4 ___ exeat (certificate phrase)
5 Byrnes of early TV
6 Ex-Senator Fong and others
7 Organic radicals
8 The Sail constellation
9 Phillips University site
10 Some linemen: Abbr.
11 Glossy fabric
12 Ran down
13 Peace of mind
14 Greenland feature
22 Hebrew tribe members
23 Musical notes
24 Think
25 Lysine and tryptophan
26 "Homecoming" star, 1948
27 Short-lived love affair
28 Feelings
29 Messenger of the gods, in the "Iliad"
31 Legendary Detroit Red Wing
33 Flattens informally
34 Lock up
38 Shoot
40 Salad item
41 One wearing a capote
43 Lightly moisten
45 Abecedary phrase
46 Make deceptively attractive
47 Kennedy Cabinet member
48 Put-in-Bay's locale
49 ___ about (legal phrase)
50 Personnel data abbr.
53 "___ thousand times . . ."
54 Geologic feature

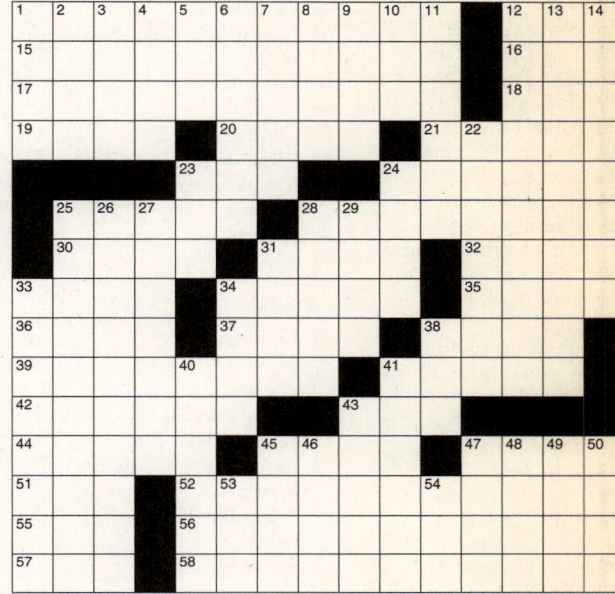

ACROSS

1 Monopoly property next to Community Chest
8 Fill the bill
15 Old-fashioned contraction
16 Scott novel or Sullivan opera
17 Most upbeat
18 Jurassic Park terrors
19 Money in the bank
20 Start of a laugh
22 Seeded
23 Elec. company, e.g.
24 Fictional salesman
26 Sassy
27 N.Y.S.E. regulator
28 In a way
30 Teachers' grp.
31 It's touched by the thumb
33 Noodge
35 Squander
37 Kiddingly
40 Succeeded, as a wish
44 Pasture plaint
45 Dangerous one
47 ___-Locka, Fla.
48 Little introduction
50 Olympic milieus
51 "The War of the Worlds" base
52 News subject
54 It rides the rails
55 City dept.
56 Christmas light?
58 Say yes
60 Certain cordial
61 Detective
62 Graffiti or litter
63 Actress Ann who played Maisie

DOWN

1 "Vienna Blood" composer
2 Fox trot, e.g.
3 "Who Framed Roger Rabbit?" rabbit
4 Sylvia Plath title
5 Face up to
6 Dash sizes
7 Charlotte Amalie's island
8 Shakespearean term of address
9 Actress Gardner
10 Night music
11 Being led
12 Obviously pregnant
13 Emulate Cassandra
14 Spouse's assent
21 Britannica alternative
24 Maine export
25 Obscurities
28 Earthquake
29 No-cal drink
32 Alphabet trio
34 Pick up
36 Collectors, informally
37 Dunk
38 Without understanding the consequences
39 Anonymous lady
41 Island where Virginia Dare was born
42 Like St. Paul, vis-a-vis St. Louis
43 Washington time
46 Christians' ___ Creed
49 "The Wreck of the Mary Deare" author Hammond ___
51 Drillmaster's command
53 Like some deli orders
55 Little row
57 Herr, here
59 Adept

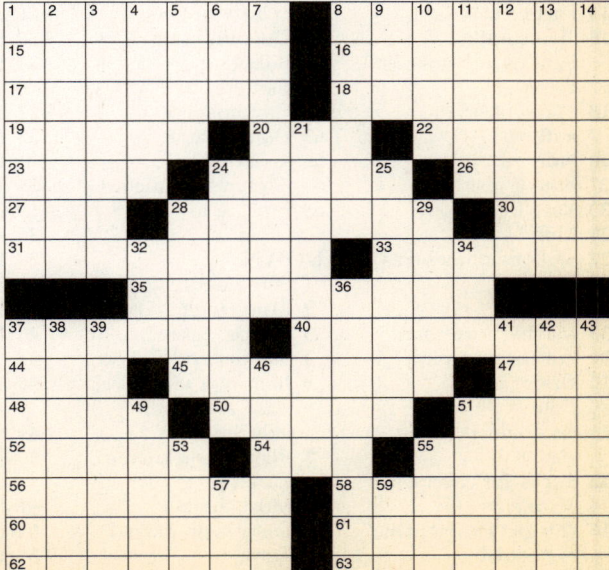

43 by Fred Piscop

ACROSS

1 Smelling things?
6 Howard and Brown
10 Hill-climber of rhyme
14 Well-nigh
15 Hand-cream additive
16 Writer Wiesel
17 "___ Davis Eyes"
18 1982 Beineix thriller
19 Flat amount?
20 Subject of this puzzle
22 Designer Gernreich
23 Opulence
24 ___ Islands
26 Hamilton of the Carter White House
30 "Topper" pooch
31 Tom Joad, e.g.
32 Bond
35 Fixed-up building
39 Accord signer of '78
41 G.I. address
42 Tool for bending cold metal
43 Laugher?
44 Bumper blemish
46 Noted name in lithography
47 TV palomino
49 Maintain
51 Promised Land
54 Bumpkin
56 Barbra's costar in '68
57 Noted performers on 20-Across's show
63 Falling-out
64 "___ Man" (Estevez flick)
65 Kind of cannon
66 Opposed
67 Geometry datum
68 Wipe out
69 It may generate interest
70 Clobber
71 Jinni

DOWN

1 Kemo ___
2 Sacked out
3 A good deal
4 1984 Nobelist
5 "___ by Starlight"
6 Base of a number system
7 "Thimble Theater" name
8 Smoked salmon
9 Rap session?
10 Performer on 20-Across's debut show
11 Alimentary canal part
12 Yorba ___
13 Admit
21 Bronchiole locale
25 Snobbery
26 Playwright Logan
27 Rubber-stamp
28 The Cyclone, e.g.
29 Performer on 20-Across's debut show
30 Light gas
33 Alan or Cheryl
34 News org. founded in 1958
36 Wealthy person
37 Ripening agent
38 Insurance writer A.M. ___
40 Georgia home
45 Mr. Kaplan
48 Draw in
50 Used wax, perhaps
51 ___ Sea (W.W. II site)
52 ___ acid
53 Gore/Perot debate topic
54 Beat the offense
55 Lusitania sinker
58 "You are ___"
59 Ran like mad
60 Rich soil
61 Former Sinclair competitor
62 Examined

44 by Jim Page

ACROSS

1 On which Irish linens are made
6 Chase flies
10 Krazy ___
13 Fort Knox deposit
14 Part of U.N.C.F.
16 "Foucault's Pendulum" novelist
17 Festive
18 "The Informer" author
20 Not fair
22 Bits of history
23 Ye ___ Shoppe
24 Mob
27 Stallone namesakes
28 Vex
29 Muddy
33 Mayberry resident
34 European capital
35 Draw ___ on
39 Date
41 Sisal and Bombay, e.g.
42 Bucks for captives
44 Scuffle
46 "Hagar the Horrible" cartoonist
47 Conform
48 Yokel
52 Look for flaws
54 60's hit "Let ___ Me"
55 Brewer of 50's pop
57 Presider in the 103d Congress
59 "Duffy of San Quentin" star
62 Bubbling
63 Remote
64 Circumspect
65 Donnybrook
66 To's opposite
67 Alphabet sequence
68 Put ___ to

DOWN

1 Some dance contests
2 Josie Hogan creator
3 "Sweet Rosie ___"
4 Samuel and Robert
5 Item in a pig's eye?
6 ___ Cat (Aspen vehicle)
7 Playboy nickname
8 Lace tip
9 Most somber
10 Larry who played Tony
11 ___ of the Apostles
12 G.I. Joe, e.g.
15 Character actor Dan
19 Lock up
21 Hardly a Prince Charming
25 Rainbow
26 Artist Georgia
30 Sire's mate
31 Stat for Alan Greenspan
32 All right
33 Mystery writer Lillian
35 Wall Street operator, for short
36 Kind of graph
37 Rock's Brian
38 Turning
40 Playwright Bogosian
43 Mark of the N.H.L.
45 "___ girl!"
48 13½-ton tourist attraction
49 "Murphy's War" star
50 1940 Rockne portrayer
51 Pulled (in)
53 Blacktops
55 Bygone despot
56 Kind of dollars
58 Spiritual leader
59 Not working
60 Wiliness
61 Big Apple sch.

45 by Trip Payne

ACROSS
1 Wrought-up
6 City near Phoenix
10 Melodramatic cry
14 Cottonwood, in Spanish
15 Burns one up
16 Perambulate
17 One past his prime
20 On the other hand
21 Essentials
22 Summer top
23 Skedaddle
24 Wish
25 Least significant
28 Bluesman Robert
29 Coffee-break brake
32 Independently
33 "You there!"
34 Relief pitcher's feat
35 Hot time
38 Makes like
39 Man with a lift
40 Échecs piece
41 N.Y.C. cultural site
42 Litigant
43 Most fit
44 Sir overseas
45 Biter
46 Plays the zither
49 Picked up on
50 ___ Vicente, Brazil
53 It won Hepburn an Oscar
56 One of the O'Neills
57 Iditarod terminus
58 World's largest cobalt exporter
59 Attributes
60 Gumption
61 Register

DOWN
1 Lots
2 Tissue addition
3 Santa drawer
4 Dennis the Menace, e.g.
5 Site of a May 1942 battle
6 Chop finely
7 Work units
8 Dry
9 Camels' destinations?
10 Marquis protagonist
11 Hel's father, in myth
12 Maintain
13 Faxed
18 "Yeah, sure!"
19 Brit's phrase
23 Wards (off)
24 Instructors, for short
25 Mary Stewart's "___, Will You Talk?"
26 Waive one's rites?
27 Physician-turned-wordsmith
28 The Mighty Clouds of Joy, e.g.
29 Farr of "M*A*S*H"
30 Hot spots
31 Nice topper
33 Daisylike bloom
34 Silvery fish
36 Elton John's first hit
37 Make citified
42 Penultimate round
43 From square one
44 Great shakes?
45 "The Maids" playwright
46 Quash
47 What you used to be
48 Flat rate
49 ___ Valley, Calif.
50 The joint
51 Prefix with space or stat
52 Mr. Hershiser
54 Postal Creed word
55 Children's author Agle

46 by A.J. Santora

ACROSS
1 1965 disturbance site
6 Reserved
14 Flog
15 Booker T. Washington, e.g.
16 Fallaci of "If the Sun Dies"
17 Overshadow
18 Half man, half goat of myth
20 Got together
21 Part of 46-Across: Abbr.
22 Rhapsodic
26 Itinerary word
27 Hag's cry
29 Zilch
30 J.F.K. portraitist
34 Spike
35 Eagerly expectant
36 Variety
37 J.F.K. biographer
40 Group shop
41 ___ Fail (ancient Irish stone)
42 British actress Bartok
43 Where runs are made
46 "Sweet 16" org.
48 Cow
49 Decking out
53 In the background
57 "G.W.T.W." role
58 Permit
59 Beijing belief
60 Followers
61 Driving hazard

DOWN
1 Guarded
2 Seed covering
3 Drudgery
4 Deli order
5 Bestrides
6 Cold-war forces
7 Conductor de Waart
8 Breadbasket
9 Less hospitable
10 Bar
11 Correlation ratio symbol in statistics
12 Nullifier
13 Trevi coin count
14 ___ Alamitos, Calif.
19 One way to get the blame
22 Sinister part?
23 Heads of ancient Rome
24 Designer Simpson
25 Escapade
26 Red-eyed birds
28 J.F.K. Library architect
30 Rodeo yell
31 Marquis Hirobumi ___
32 Average name
33 Trial
34 Delineate
38 Anodynes
39 Son of Cedric the Saxon
44 William ___ Gladstone
45 Grand
47 Overlays
49 Lime finishes
50 Opponent of Jimmy and Arthur
51 Vespiary
52 Campus facility
53 Actress Hagen
54 Ice cream ___
55 Traffic caution
56 Time abroad

47 by Stanley Newman

ACROSS

1 Adam and Eve locale
5 Pecan or poplar
9 Track official
14 Fully cooked
15 Do damage to
16 Become used (to)
17 Chew like a beaver
18 Radiate
19 Out of practice
20 Popular topping
22 Fire-gone conclusion
23 Film extras?
24 German-Polish border river
25 Industrial tub
26 Buttermilk's rider
28 Metal-in-the-rough
31 Comfortably inviting
34 Thick strings
35 Fix a squeak
36 Prayer ending
37 Mock-innocent query
38 Some med. insurance cos.
39 ___ good turn (help)
40 Suspicious
41 "All That Jazz" director Bob
42 Write hastily

43 "Gilligan's Island" homes
44 Hasty escape
45 Pager's sound
47 Put away (for)
51 Ahab's sighting
53 Popular topping
55 Corridors
56 Shirt brand name
57 "Do ___ others as . . ."
58 Kate's TV mate
59 Suffix with switch
60 No de Cologne?
61 Heston role
62 Called up
63 Matches a bet

DOWN

1 The F.B.I.'s J. ___ Hoover
2 "No man is an island" writer
3 Pass, as laws
4 Yale's home
5 Phillies park, familiarly
6 Film director Harold
7 Cleveland's lake

8 911 responders: Abbr.
9 Irrational speeches
10 Occupied, as a bathroom
11 Popular topping
12 Art Deco artist
13 Alejandro and Fernando
21 Say yes to
24 Ye ___ Book Shoppe
26 Jim Morrison's group, with "the"
27 Palmer's gallery
29 Ocho ___, Jamaica
30 Choice word
31 Muslim pilgrimage
32 Melville romance
33 Popular topping
34 Schmooze
37 Defeat, à la Ali
38 Base clearers
40 Gouda and Edam, e.g.
41 Top choice, so to speak
44 Pomeranian, for one
46 Miss ___ of "Dallas"
47 Dish's beloved, in rhyme

48 Gift recipient
49 Loosen the laces
50 Subatomic particles
51 Smack!
52 Angel's headgear
53 Berth place
54 Nehemiah preceder

48 by Albert J. Klaus

ACROSS

1 Scenic view
6 Hombres' homes
11 E.T.S. offering
14 Back way
15 "Yup"
16 Four-in-hand
17 John ___
19 Military inits.
20 Kind of diet
21 Tango requirement
22 Cob or drake, e.g.
23 Well-groomed
25 Red wine
27 ___ Mahal
30 Wineglass part
32 Right: Prefix
33 Sharif and Bradley
35 Mr. Fixit
39 Backgammon equipment
40 Attribute
41 River of northern France
42 Sure thing?
44 Mooring site
45 Exposed
46 Campus building
48 ___ Palmas, Spain
49 Guiding light

51 Logs some z's
53 Log some z's
54 Auditor, for short
57 Arabian coffees
61 Skill
62 John ___
64 Half of a 1955 merger
65 Serf
66 Garden bulb
67 At any time, poetically
68 British ___
69 Musial and Laurel

DOWN

1 Like fireplace logs
2 Advertising award
3 "___ right with the world"
4 Relative of the weasel
5 Huxley's "___ in Gaza"
6 Wrigley Field player
7 "Cat on ___ . . ."
8 Third place
9 Overlord
10 "Listen!"
11 John ___

12 Bride's path
13 Bit of dogma
18 Immediately, in the operating room
22 Diacritical mark
24 ___ firma
26 Garland
27 One of Taylor's exes
28 Friend of François
29 John ___
31 1971 hit "___ Bobby McGee"
34 Edit
36 Mountaineer's spike
37 Voyaging
38 Seines
40 Infantry lines
43 Spanish treasure
44 Customs duties
47 Incline
49 Drill grip
50 Halloweenlike
52 Advance person
55 Medicinal tablet
56 Medicinal plant
58 Hawaiian dance
59 "Z ___ zebra"
60 Weakens
62 Upsilon's successor
63 "___ De-Lovely"

49 by Manny Nosowsky

ACROSS

1 Quite ___(many)
5 Greenish-blue
9 City south of Gainesville
14 Phnom ___
15 Kiss
16 Sonoran snacks
17 Insomniac's bane
20 Shade maker
21 Unforced
22 State frankly
23 Meddlesome
25 IBM's and clones
28 Pyramids, e.g.
30 Weaned pig
32 Ogles
36 Complete failure
37 Lyric for an insomniac?
39 Author Fallaci
40 Attempt to impress, as in conversation
41 Set locks?
42 Wastes time
43 Jargon suffix
44 Trans-Siberian Railroad stop
45 Garb
50 Quickly, quickly
52 Magnetite, e.g.
54 What an insomniac would like to do, minimally
58 Alternative to Midway
59 Rake
60 Bump into
61 Grew in intensity
62 A-one
63 Whirlpool

DOWN

1 Church nooks
2 "Most happy" one
3 Ally's opposite
4 Sharpens
5 Willing follower?
6 Subject of a Mercutio monologue
7 Naval letters
8 Size up
9 Mayberry sot
10 Sly
11 Cry in Coblenz
12 He fled Sodom
13 Beast of burden
18 Diet sheet group
19 Vote against
24 Deadens
25 Puzzle
26 Chocolate source
27 Jazz dance
29 Pelion's sister peak
30 Second act?
31 Difficult
32 Calculus calculation
33 Radials
34 Burning
35 500 sheets
36 Fortune's partner
38 Hype
42 Drag on the balance of trade
44 Clumsy one
46 Lively: Fr.
47 Like a filet
48 Annoyed
49 Ill-tempered
50 Maybe it's all a plot?
51 Drop off
53 They may be seeded
54 "Don't have a ___, man!"
55 "So that's why!"
56 Common add-on
57 Aussie hopper, for short

50 by Nancy S. Ross

ACROSS

1 Art ___
5 Falcon-headed Egyptian god
10 One of those
14 "___ on both your houses!"
15 Shoulder warmer
16 Abominate
17 Spongy toy material
18 Beef cut
19 New Haven students
20 Setting of Verdi's "Simon Boccanegra"
22 #45
24 #94
27 Left ventricle's outlet
28 Campus V.I.P.
29 Sleeve
30 Like some stocks, for short
33 Lupino of the movies
35 Brando howl
39 What this puzzle's numbers refer to
43 Looney Tunes and ___ Melodies
44 Each
45 Halves of qts.
46 Spring mo.
47 Kind of fence
50 Series ender
53 #103
57 #100
59 Tiptoe
61 New World abbr.
62 Starring roles
65 Sprint
66 Globin lead-in
67 Craze
68 Thessaly peak
69 "S ___ sugar"
70 Ignition problem?
71 Advertising sign

DOWN

1 Swearer's euphemism
2 Fencing weapons
3 Horn-shaped part
4 #92
5 F.D.R. Veep
6 Horse-racing fan's hangout: Abbr.
7 Urban sunning sites
8 Radii neighbors
9 Oracle
10 1936 Clare Boothe Luce play
11 More healthy
12 Inclined
13 ___ coil (1891 invention)
21 Copycat
23 Keep one's ___ the ground
25 Elevator
26 Memorial Day weekend event
29 Hindu retreat
30 Electrical unit
31 ___ kwon do
32 St.-___-l'École, France
34 Hi-fi component
36 Sass
37 Authorize
38 Dolt
40 Plow attachment for maintaining uniform depth
41 Nearly catch, as the heels
42 Huascarán is its highest point
48 Collection org.
49 #104
50 City east of Boys Town
51 Silent types
52 Varnish resin
53 Gloomy, to poets
54 Meg and Nolan
55 Renter's contract
56 Catch, out West
58 Soprano Gluck
60 Tatar ruler
63 God, in 20-Across
64 Japanese honorific

51 by David J. Kahn

1 Drive
6 Four Tops leader ___ Stubbs
10 Breakfast cereal
14 City near Utah Lake
15 Leave
16 First name in country
17 Muslim group
18 "Anything ___"
19 Southwest California town
20 Curtain call that never ends?
23 Philip Sidney's "Astrophel and ___"
26 Teases maliciously
27 Object to a squelching remark?
32 Revival shouts
33 Whence the phoenix rose
34 Foxx of "Sanford and Son"
35 Admit
36 Sound frustrated
40 Lend ___
41 Actress Picon
42 Tenement?
45 Proust hero
47 Conceptualize

48 Pilot's joke to passengers?
53 Parts
54 Not straight
55 Answer to "Who did this?"
59 Island necklaces
60 Ground ___
61 Minolta rival
62 Old slave
63 Onetime Hagman co-star
64 Zuñi home

DOWN
1 Speed letters
2 Man-mouse link
3 1937 play "High ___"
4 Makes too great an advance
5 City founder of legend
6 Kind of blocks
7 Ex-Nebraska Senator James
8 Perspective
9 "___ wrap!"
10 Evening news anchor
11 Answer, legally
12 Toward the stern

13 Artless ones
21 Softness provider
22 80's mergers, for short
23 Pentagram
24 Break, in a way
25 Made (out)
28 Ancient: Prefix
29 Soc. Security Act, e.g.
30 Prickly item
31 Water droplets
35 "___ the Angels Sing" (1939 hit)
36 Motor coil
37 Actress Chase
38 Oversupply
39 Publicity
40 ___ regni (in the year of the reign)
41 "Truth or Dare" subject
42 Collect, as bucks
43 Disquiet
44 Repartee
45 Used
46 Merchandise
49 Disconcert
50 Escaped
51 Read attentively, with "over"

52 It follows once
56 Fight result
57 Criminal set
58 Chemical ending

52 by Cathy Millhauser

ACROSS
1 Expire
6 Dismissive interjections
10 It's often wiped
14 Lightsome
15 "That's what ___ for . . ." ("Stupid me!")
16 Rockies animal
17 Ditty about a retired city official?
20 Dwell (on)
21 Rat-___
22 Frau's iron
23 Spanish step
25 Thomas Gray's alma mater
27 Some horses?
33 Country rocker Steve
34 St. Bernards' beat
35 Caveman from Moo
36 Unpretentious carriage
37 Japanese electronics brand
39 Nonsense
40 On a date
41 Mil. option
42 Like some skirts

43 Howling leader of the Miracles?
47 Campus sports org.
48 ___ dire (court oath)
49 It's a good thing
52 Start of some restaurant names
54 Meaning
58 Do a veterinarian's task?
61 Napoleon biographer Ludwig
62 Cousin of the pintail
63 The king of Champagne?
64 Nasty remarks
65 Avion destination
66 Religious figure

DOWN
1 Builder's backing
2 Turkish bigwig
3 Berth place
4 Sans precision
5 Smoked or jellied dish
6 Hallux
7 Pearl Mosque site
8 With vehemence
9 Neatnik's horror

10 Bogart's role in "Casablanca"
11 Popular fast-food chain, informally
12 Wide-range reed
13 Frayed
18 Track event
19 Kit chat
24 Historic period
26 ___ Gigio (Ed Sullivan mouse)
27 Poet laureate ___ Tate
28 Calliope colleague
29 House dressing?
30 River of Tours
31 "-phile" meaning
32 Hotfooted it
33 Those, in Madrid
37 High-protein bean
38 Welder, e.g.
39 Car thief, maybe
41 Straight: Prefix
42 Moo goo ___ pan
44 Prepares to be knighted
45 Singer Phil or Don
46 Jerk
49 Laid up
50 Conductor's start?

51 Take a shot?
53 Mend
55 Mrs. Cooperfield
56 Designer von Furstenberg

57 ___ were
59 Car of a '64 song
60 "Alice" spinoff

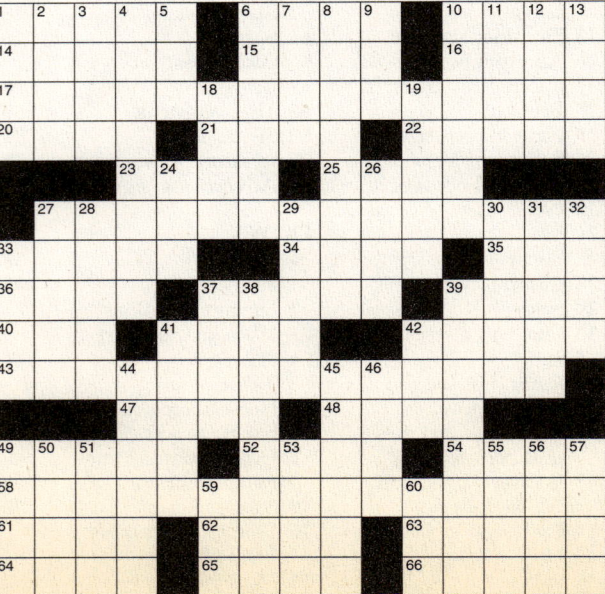

53 by Gregory E. Paul

ACROSS

1 Droops
5 Dutch engineering feat
9 Capital on the Seine
14 Prefix with port or pad
15 Spew
16 Separately
17 Historic periods
18 New Year's Eve figure
20 Machine for removing cloth waste
22 Chinese: Prefix
23 Forty winks
24 Made a ___ case of
26 Not windy
28 Of kings and queens
30 Cried like a Siamese
34 "Philadelphia" star Tom
37 Kemo ___ (the Lone Ranger)
39 Little hopper
40 Skin soother
41 Flower feature
42 Dance at a Jewish wedding
43 "Phooey!"
44 Angers
45 Abdomen
46 ___ d'Arc
48 Hardship
50 Play area
52 Most extended
56 Put 2 and 2 together
59 Gum or plum, e.g.
61 Brewer Coors
62 1938 movie with Ronald Reagan
65 CBer's end-of-message word
66 Newswoman Shriver
67 St. Patrick's land
68 ___ qua non
69 Proust hero
70 Femur-tibia go-between
71 Villa d'___

DOWN

1 Continental ___
2 Cliff dwelling
3 Thyroid, e.g.
4 1946 Rosalind Russell role
5 Bear part of, as expenses
6 "___ Yankee Doodle dandy"
7 Model sets
8 Moral precept
9 Conditional release
10 Prone
11 Parade spoiler
12 "___ la Douce"
13 Word repeated by a drill sergeant
19 Nail polish
21 Greek Cupid
25 Surgical beam
27 Nursery name
29 Slangy goodbye
31 Winter fabric
32 ___ of Suffolk
33 June 6, 1944
34 Pilgrimage to Mecca
35 Wings: Lat.
36 Nick's "Thin Man" wife
38 Pesto herb
41 Coyote State's capital
45 007
47 Lane of "The Birdcage"
49 Trimmed beard
51 Actress Bo
53 Ed Sullivan guest of 9/9/56
54 Worn-out
55 Babe Ruth's number
56 Some military defenses: Abbr.
57 Sketch
58 "Cannery Row" character
60 "___ go bragh!"
63 Can material
64 Exist

54 by Dorothy E. Donaldson

ACROSS

1 "Waterloo" pop band
5 First of a familiar trio
9 Border on
13 Action word
14 On the up and up
16 ___ of one's existence
17 Prefix with -logue
18 Acid/alcohol reaction product
19 Bygone Fords
20 Long-distance communications?
22 Cars discontinued in 1960
24 Shoelace problem
25 Environmental study: Abbr.
26 Fairylike
28 Director Peckinpah
31 Expressions of approval
34 ___ Juana (name in old Mexico)
35 Embark on a voyage
38 Top dog, for short
39 Owns
40 Second of a familiar trio
41 "Cool!"
42 Bankbook entry: Abbr.
43 Contacted by shortwave
44 Pilot's announcement, for short
45 Places for needles
47 "___ the season . . ."
48 Creme cookies
50 Armchair athlete's channel
52 Abbr. on a love letter
53 Ship's platform
56 The least possible
59 "Oh, sure"
60 Fog
62 Missile storage site
63 Grasslands
64 Idolize
65 Outside: Prefix
66 Actor Talbot
67 Moved rapidly
68 Worn out

DOWN

1 Budget rival
2 George Eliot's Adam
3 Food in a bowl
4 Improved: Fr.
5 Winter driving hazard
6 Robert Stack TV role
7 Ten-percenter; Abbr.
8 Like Hamelin's piper
9 In flower
10 Place name on a 3-Down box
11 Nullify
12 Hardy girl
15 Genealogist's handiwork
21 Force into service
23 Reduce
26 Principles of good conduct
27 Tropical vine
28 German town
29 Computer code
30 Powerful sharks
32 Marvy
33 Ice cream drinks
36 Historical period
37 ___ de France
46 African fly
49 Elevates
51 "Super" star
52 Fathered
53 Leave no part empty
54 Follow instructions
55 Footballer's protection
56 Sir Thomas
57 Voice below soprano
58 Booty
61 Third of a familiar trio

ACROSS

1 Polaroid
5 Against: Abbr.
8 Original
14 Points on a math test?
15 Three times, in prescriptions
16 Rings
17 Drink for Captain Midnight
19 Kind of car
20 Hairline feature
22 Do a teamster's job
23 Nice time of year
24 Friend abroad
25 Prefix with skeleton
26 Rotating engine piece
28 Secure for a cause
30 Agonize (over)
31 Nobleman, informally
33 Bender, of a sort
35 Detectives
37 Chipped stones of archaeological interest
41 Soviet cooperative
43 Idolize

44 "Dark Lady" singer
47 Game of which black lady is a variation
49 Familiar appellation for a cowpuncher
50 Take it easy
51 Knife, in old dialect
52 Utterance of mockery
54 Last leader of Communist Albania
55 Aluminous mineral
59 Abutting
61 Sweetie pies
62 It superseded the lute
63 Flock member
64 Candlemaker's supply
65 Coca-Cola introduction of 1961
66 The elder: Abbr.
67 Comic Austen work

DOWN

1 Dense
2 ___ Sad (Yugoslavia's second-largest city)
3 Collegedom
4 Mark Twain was one

5 Colonial pamphleteer James
6 Man of letters?
7 One in an incubator
8 River steamer
9 Transfer ___
10 Up on things
11 Horror film figure
12 Refer
13 Find concealment
18 Stereo part
21 Party divider on the Hill
26 Tractor, slangily
27 J.F.K. info
29 Long Island area
32 Composer of "Il Tigrane"
34 Ancient mariner, surely
36 Evil lead-in
38 Steel ingredient
39 Eur. inits. until 1806
40 Kind of kitten
42 "I am justly kill'd with mine own treachery" speaker
44 Sounds of San Francisco

45 Hide
46 Panacea, maybe
48 Celebrity
53 1946 Literature Nobelist
56 Jan Smuts, for one
57 Suppose
58 This, to Juan
60 Use a shuttle

ACROSS

1 Rushes (along)
5 Amassed
10 They cover Highland heads
14 Neglect
15 Mes numero uno
16 "In a cowslip's bell ___": "The Tempest"
17 One nourished by daydreams?
19 Rotten to the ___
20 One of "Them!" things
21 Author O'Brien
22 Ready for framing
24 Genealogical chart
25 New Rochelle college
26 One who counts calories?
32 Perspiration perforations
33 Alternative to a watering can
34 Khan married to Rita Hayworth
35 Detective Charlie
36 Dress style
38 Classic art subject
39 Elephant's weight, maybe

40 Israeli Abba
41 "For ___ sake!"
42 One with a high-iron diet?
46 Hollywood giants?
47 Jemima, for one
48 Farm trough
51 ___ .45
52 Dallas school, for short
55 Strip of wood
56 One fond of dining on tongue?
59 Florence's river
60 Destroy
61 Motion supporters
62 High schooler's test, briefly
63 Went out with
64 Key letter

DOWN

1 "J'accuse" author
2 Springsteen's "___ Fire"
3 English P.M. called "The Great Commoner"
4 Alphabet trio
5 Carolina river
6 More ridiculous

7 "I ___ Song Go Out of My Heart"
8 Before, to a poet
9 Member of Alice's tea party
10 Popular breath mint
11 Loads
12 Slough
13 Burpee's bit
18 Some Bosnians
23 ___ Morrow Lindbergh
24 Feds
25 Clothes presser
26 Not at all
27 Heavens: Prefix
28 Tableware
29 ___ cuisine
30 Presbyter
31 Deli loaves
32 Election numbers: Abbr.
36 Sucked up
37 Statutes
38 Its eye is needed in a "Macbeth" recipe
40 Slight advantage
41 Sophia's Carlo
43 Boiling mad
44 "Tao Te Ching" author
45 Quieted

48 Part of an envelope
49 Auricles
50 Lab burner
51 Layer
52 Hebrides island

53 Make the acquaintance of
54 Twinkling bear
57 Man-mouse link
58 Taxi

ACROSS

1 Beckoned
5 Arroyo
9 Edith Evans, e.g.
13 Travel writer Thollander
14 Arrangement containers
15 Enthralled
16 Start of a quip
19 "___ was saying . . ."
20 "Women Who Run With the Wolves" author
21 Appearance
22 Stipple
23 Rent out
24 Quip, part 2
33 Punts, e.g.
34 Out of place
35 "Bleak House" girl
36 Moons
37 TV adjusters
38 Court score
39 1959 Kingston Trio hit
40 ___ nous
41 In reserve
42 Quip, part 3
45 Stable particle

46 Super Bowl QB Dawson
47 "Kenilworth" novelist
50 "Luck and Pluck" writer
53 As well
56 End of the quip
59 A Guthrie
60 Marshal
61 Other
62 Jim Morrison, e.g.
63 Nanny, perhaps
64 Home bodies?

DOWN

1 Kind of star
2 Comments to a doctor
3 Half of sechs
4 High ways?
5 Bulb measure
6 Court V.I.P. Arthur
7 Tunisian rulers, once
8 Theory
9 Lennon's last home, with "The"
10 Exchange premium
11 One of Chaucer's travelers

12 Hash-house order
14 Horizon, maybe
17 Persian cries
18 Bright-eyed and bushy-tailed
22 Silent-spring causers
23 More than snips
24 Frightful force
25 It comes from the heart
26 Capital on the Bou Regreg river
27 Reach in total
28 Vast, in the past
29 Name on a pencil
30 Point of greatest despair
31 Order
32 Decreases
37 Puzzle
38 Betimes
40 Woman with a lyre
41 "Siegfried," e.g.
43 Lusting after
44 Thomas Gray piece
47 A herring
48 Mackerellike fish
49 Ibsen's home
50 Farming prefix
51 Turkish money

52 Backbiter?
53 Prefix with port or play
54 Drying oven
55 Hugo works
57 Piano tune
58 Up on

ACROSS

1 Manatee
7 Desert bloomer
12 Sheepherder's bane
14 Slices of life
17 Broadway tribute to wine?
19 O.T. book before Jer.
20 Imprint, as in the memory
21 Dr. Scholl's purchase
22 Hong Kong, e.g.
23 Relax
25 Up to the task
26 Cheerleaders' number
28 "El ___" ('67 Wayne film)
31 Headed up
32 Kind of crazy
34 Under-the-sink item
36 A "dear" French wine?
39 Insurance payment
41 Toning salons
44 Ill-wisher
45 Add a design to
48 Flintstones' pet
50 Goes (for)

52 Architectural overhang
54 Foyer spread
55 Sale locale
58 Multipurpose protein source
59 Lasorda or LaRussa: Abbr.
60 Artsy wine center?
63 Flower good for winter bouquets
64 Involves
65 Mailroom gizmo
66 Literary heptad

DOWN

1 Add NaCl to
2 Maroons
3 Culpable
4 Ernesto Guevara, familiarly
5 Bay window
6 All for naught
7 Health org.
8 Dry Mongolian expanse
9 Sherman Hemsley TV series
10 Vice follower
11 Dignify

13 Brand of craft knife
15 Person with many bills
16 Pegasus, e.g.
18 Symbol of poverty
24 Barely tinged
27 Rickey ingredient
29 "___ Rosenkavalier"
30 Propels, in a way
33 Colosseum setting
35 TV's "___ Blue"
37 Pick-up-sticks game
38 Part of a sentence: Abbr.
39 Roy Lichtenstein works
40 Item good for another go-round?
42 Skywriting?
43 Be cozy
44 Noted world traveler and namesakes
46 A Franklin invention
47 Penning up the pigs
49 Fairy tale meanie
51 Before Anita or Clara
53 Conference site of '45
56 Carriage
57 Nietzsche's "___ Homo"

61 Not him!
62 Retriever, informally

59 by Bette Sue Cohen

ACROSS

1 Bend
5 Exchange
9 Polite form of address
13 Actor Calhoun
14 Make ___ for (argue in support of)
15 Ray of Hollywood
16 This puzzle's mystery subject
19 "The Joy Luck Club" author
20 Fuzzy
21 Rule
22 Yield
23 Dubbed one
24 1951 movie with 16-Across
31 Stumble
32 River to the Caspian
33 Veterans Day mo.
35 Daly of "Gypsy"
36 Competition for Geraldo
38 Trig function
39 Wynken, Blynken and ___
40 They're sometimes wild
41 Earth mover
42 1957 movie with 16-Across
47 Thumbnail sketch
48 16-Across's "Cat on ___ Tin Roof"
49 Étagère piece
52 County north of San Francisco
54 Neighbor of Ind.
57 1946 movie with 16-Across
60 "___ known then what . . ."
61 Cancel
62 "A" code word
63 Greek portico
64 Use épées
65 Half a fortnight

DOWN

1 Stew
2 "Damn Yankees" seductress
3 Green land
4 ___ Affair
5 Play's start
6 He coined the term "horsepower"
7 Pallid
8 Caress
9 MGM's Louis B. and others
10 "___ know is what . . ."
11 Sick as ___
12 Dawn
14 Put up with
17 Novelist Waugh
18 Disney mermaid
22 Horn, for one
23 Iranian chief, once
24 Letter abbr.
25 Richard of "Bustin' Loose"
26 Newswoman Ellerbee
27 Tend to
28 Refrain syllable
29 Confederacy's opponent
30 Three trios
34 Exceedingly
36 Eight: Prefix
37 Through
38 Latched
40 Law professor Hill
43 Airline to Spain
44 Outpouring of gossip
45 Bit of fall weather
46 Miss O'Neill
49 Publisher Adolph
50 Sloop
51 Defense means
52 Diner's guide
53 First-class
54 Man or Ely, e.g.
55 16-Across's "___ With Father"
56 Plumber's concern
58 Travel (about)
59 16-Across's "The Last Time I ___ Paris"

60 by Janet R. Bender

ACROSS

1 Not fully shut
5 Penalty
9 Ragu competitor
14 Richness
15 Irish Rose lover
16 Prepared potatoes, in a way
17 POUND
20 Denials
21 Computer insert
22 Discharges
23 Earring site
24 "Ain't She Sweet?" composer
25 Guarantee
28 Scottish Highlander
32 RAND
34 Knock the socks off
35 Away from the wind
36 Sorority character
37 Muslim officers
38 Calif. neighbor
39 SCHILLING
43 Love-lies-bleeding, for one
45 Parsons' places
46 Inventor Rubik
47 "The Sweetest Taboo" singer
48 Timmy's dog
51 Pulitzer winner Quindlen
52 Take to court
55 YEN
58 Really hurt
59 Iron or foot preceder
60 Singer Pinza
61 Servings of ale
62 Profits, informally
63 Antiprohibitionists

DOWN

1 Wyoming's Simpson
2 O'Casey play "___ and the Paycock"
3 Turning point
4 "Losing My Religion" rock group
5 Bullet size
6 More than flabby
7 Swim's alternative
8 Gumshoe
9 Offspring
10 Stairway parts
11 Old French coins
12 Goldfinger portrayer Frobe
13 Lyric poems
18 Think the world of
19 Permitted
23 Time co-founder
24 To whom a caliph prays
25 Turkish city
26 Western capital
27 1983 Indy winner Tom
28 Work behind the plate
29 Biblical gift bearer
30 Cognizant
31 Hornets' homes
33 Fistfight
37 Bad marks?
39 Rinds
40 English novelist Hammond ___
41 Flow forth
42 Detection device
44 Take offense at
47 Move stealthily
48 Speech impediment
49 Prefix with skid
50 Throw for a loop
51 Jean Auel heroine
52 Capacity
53 Military group
54 Selves
56 Newt
57 Unused

61 by D. J. Listort

ACROSS

1 Barbecue rods
6 Newfoundland catch
9 Trouble
14 "Ready ___ ..."
15 Rap sheet abbr.
16 Kind of acid
17 Headed for the hills
19 Oregon's capital
20 With 34-Across, one example of 51-Across
22 Cash ending
23 Selma Lagerlöf hero
24 "___ bite"
25 As a whole
27 Western Indian
28 Path of virtuous conduct
31 [So written]
32 Responsibility
33 Media co. founded in 1919
34 See 20-Across
39 Corrida cheer
40 Geraint's beloved
41 Seine sight
42 Sir or ma'am preceder
43 ___ in xylophone
44 Item seldom seen in pockets
48 Boob
49 Rows
50 4:00 function
51 Difficult articulations
55 Salk's conquest
56 She-monsters: Var.
57 Troublesome gas
58 Egg producer
59 Steamed
60 Utopias
61 Assn.
62 Fodder figures

DOWN

1 Bombing run
2 Adapted for grasping
3 Blends
4 Crags
5 Ale servings
6 Beef
7 Approvals: Var.
8 June honorees
9 Completely untrue
10 Modern messages
11 Kimono fabric
12 Chemical suffixes
13 The piper's son
18 Bygone alliance
21 Ask for a loan
26 Not wait
27 A, in Arles
28 Three-sided
29 Swift, in music
30 Bucket material
32 Expensive ref. work
34 Kind of sauce
35 Honeycomb cells
36 More than a boo-boo
37 Part of H.R.H.
38 Family member
44 Crows' noise
45 ___ and Thummim (sacred Judaic articles)
46 Montaigne works
47 Lads' partners
48 Salad ingredient
49 Thomas Tryon chiller, with "The"
51 Tailless amphibian
52 Obsolete for "obsolete"
53 Canyon phenomenon
54 Actress Hatcher
55 View or record lead-in

62 by Lois Sidway

ACROSS

1 "No problemo!"
5 Like a contortionist
10 Way to go
14 Threesome
15 Crazy as ___
16 Poet Lazarus
17 Grp. joining a lawsuit
18 1969 Hitchcock film
19 A Barrymore
20 "Stop!"
23 Judge's issuance
24 ___ juice (milk)
25 The Last Frontier
28 Kind of zoo
32 Mr. McCarthy, familiarly
33 Erratum
36 Actor Homolka of "I Remember Mama"
37 C.D. collection?
38 "Look!"
40 Give-go link
41 Miller salesman
43 Ohio city
44 Wally's little bro
45 Take a gander at
47 Just about
49 Ricardo's river
50 20-Across, to Popeye
52 "Listen!"
58 One of Esau's in-laws
59 Prepared to propose
60 Hauls
62 Killer whale
63 Related on the mother's side
64 Bryce Canyon site
65 Bust's opposite
66 Shy guy of the 4077th
67 1983 Maltby/Shire musical

DOWN

1 Flight plan info: Abbr.
2 Principal
3 Storage tower
4 Coin flipper's declaration
5 It's almost past the deadline
6 Gershwin's "The Man ___"
7 Lush
8 Frozen dew
9 Pepsin, for one
10 Cinnamon candies
11 Katz of "Eerie, Indiana"
12 "Right on!"
13 Terrytoons' Deputy ___
21 Sobriquet for Dwight Gooden
22 From head ___
25 Springy
26 Artist Neiman
27 "What's in ___?"
28 Haiku, e.g.
29 Not as cordial
30 Kind of day
31 Extra benefit
34 Cheerleader's cheer
35 ___ Beta Kappa
38 Mobile home dweller?
39 Pursued
42 "Amadeus" star, 1984
44 Rubber duck pond
46 Sightseer
48 90 degrees from nord
50 "You're ___ duck!"
51 Italian physicist
52 Liquidy lump
53 Mr. Saarinen
54 Fast food offering
55 Tolstoy's Karenina
56 Minimal bit
57 Clear the decks?
61 Shrinking

63 by Chuck Deodene

ACROSS
1 Bad accident
8 Nettles
13 Scattering of a population
14 Kind of lines
15 Man-made
16 Turkeys
17 Ben-Gay, e.g.
18 Place to put bags
19 Activist
20 Kind of party
23 Soaking wet
25 Trumpet's sound
26 Lip
27 Lie in a sheltered spot
29 Galway Bay's ___ Islands
30 "___ Boot" (1981 film)
31 Extended rule?
34 Round: Abbr.
37 Jog
38 Rummage
42 Sugar suffix
43 Charged, in a way
45 1,000 liters
46 Events at Newport
49 Participating in 46-Across
50 Hateful
51 Cause turmoil in
53 Lugged
54 Dickens novel
56 Expunge
57 Tasty mollusks
58 De-ices, in a way
59 Tablet

DOWN
1 Glee club members
2 Bond's end
3 Foe of Laver and Newcombe
4 Exhausted
5 Jacuzzi
6 Swiss canton
7 ___ 10 conference
8 Résumé list
9 Acquired relative
10 Ferocious cat
11 Department stores
12 ___ analyst
13 Vacuum tube feature
15 Red Sea borderer
18 Sun helmets
21 Cash alternative
22 Role
24 Soothing words
28 Box score figure
32 "___ Barbara" (Gallegos novel)
33 Witt on ice
34 Prairie wolves
35 First name in dance
36 Conservatory offering
39 On again
40 Breakfast fare
41 Prelims
44 Lemonlike fruit
47 "The Lockhorns" cartoonist Bill
48 Edge
52 Pull up
54 "Star Wars" rogue
55 ___ system (blood typing)

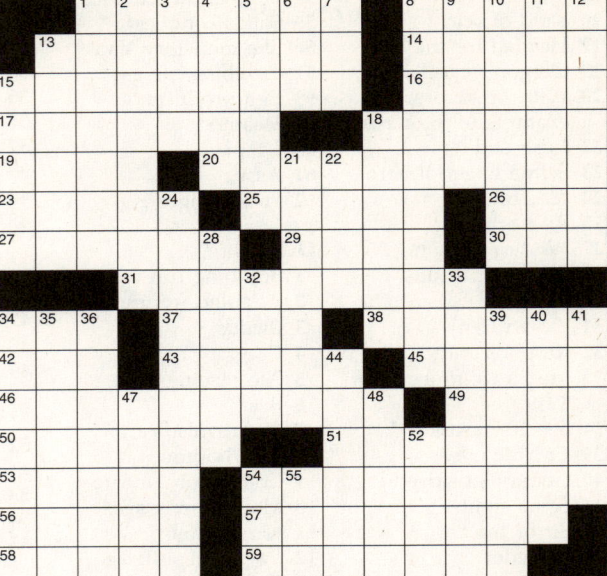

64 by Chuck Deodene

ACROSS
1 Vessel for Pasteur
6 Accord
10 Goofball
14 ___ Picchu (site of Incan ruins)
15 Tijuana eight
16 Race track
17 Illustrator's goof
18 Neeson of film
19 Coburg canine
20 Financial connivances
23 It gives you a charge: Abbr.
24 Hat tipper's word
25 Eggs ___ suisse
28 Odyssey
30 Red Cross procedure
34 Getting close
36 Think tank nugget
38 Burdened
39 1966 Naguib Mahfouz novella
42 Perfect copy
43 Lamb sandwich, in Greek cookery
44 Loam
45 "Black Beauty" author
47 Top-flight
49 Clinic heads, for short
50 Reaction to a pinch
52 Await
54 1994 Tobias Wolff memoir
60 Dreyfus ally, 1898
61 Second of a Latin trio
62 Fifth element
64 Name of two Danish kings
65 Pulitzer winner James
66 Feudal lord
67 #1 Presley hit
68 Minus
69 Rock's Van Halen

DOWN
1 Some radios
2 Beacon
3 ___-deucey
4 Brokerage unit
5 "On the Road" newsman
6 Narc's assistant
7 It reddens litmus paper
8 Crevasse
9 Tabby's courter
10 Coffeehouse denizens
11 Egg cell
12 First name in westerns
13 Auto pioneer
21 Type of badge
22 Roaring Camp writer
25 Radar system acronym
26 Chowder server
27 Pointer
29 Runner Kip Keino's homeland
31 Accepted statement
32 Icy
33 Jamesian scholar Leon et al.
35 Colliery access
37 Degenerates
40 Beau, slangily
41 Perfects
46 Relating to young insects
48 Empower
51 Satchel of baseball
53 Servant of the future?
54 ___ Lacoste
55 Ambivalent plea, for short
56 Blueprint
57 Words inspired by Erato
58 Equine on the tube
59 Hindu ascetic
63 Name part

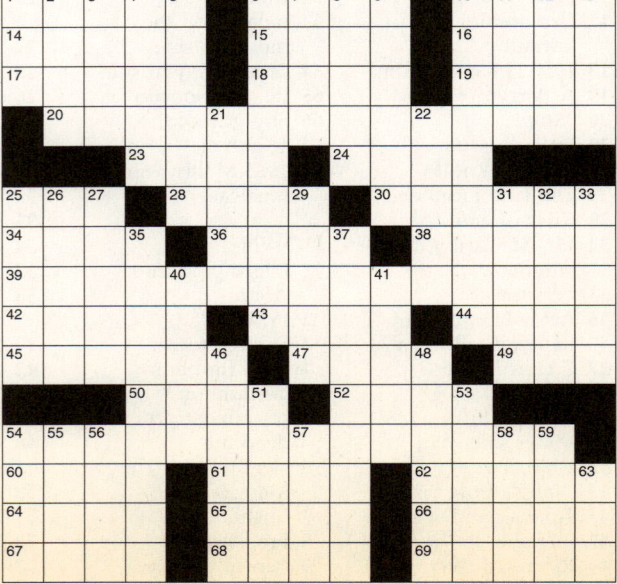

65 by Thomas W. Schier

ACROSS

1 Actress Theda of the silents
5 Fall flower
10 Girl- or boy-watch
14 Greek war god
15 Laminated rock
16 "QB VII" author
17 Attacks from hiding
19 Mr. Republican of the old G.O.P.
20 Giant star in Scorpius
21 Gnaw at corrosively
23 ___ Carlo
25 Desire
26 Colorado ski resort
29 Lumberjack's tool
31 Architectural arch
34 Bit of dental work
36 Yo-yo, e.g.
38 Condescending type
39 Suffix with doctor or elector
40 Holy sites
43 Hirt and Gore
44 Bowwow
46 D.C. V.I.P.
47 Fresca competitor
49 Broad necktie

51 Take steps
53 Actor Quinn
54 The "E" in Q.E.D.
56 Dancer Twyla
58 Sherry-like wine
61 Shock
65 En route on the QE2
66 Throat part
68 "The Chinese Parrott" detective
69 River embankment
70 To be, in Brest
71 Not his
72 Build ___ egg (save)
73 Heads, in slang

DOWN

1 Rum cake
2 Give ___ for one's money
3 Conclude one's case
4 Humiliated
5 Pale, as a face
6 California mount
7 Tic-___-toe
8 Actress Sommer
9 Spotted again
10 Picnics or barbecues
11 Money for a scholar
12 London elevator

13 "___ perpetua" (Idaho's motto)
18 Inequities
22 Chinese principle
24 Like the dodo
26 Addis ___
27 Spanish misses: Abbr.
28 A hole in the head?
30 Untold centuries
32 Upper ___ (Burkina Faso, once)
33 Buddy of "The Beverly Hillbillies"
35 Querying sounds
37 "You bet!"
41 New Deal prog.
42 Militaristic city of ancient Greece
45 Seoul mates?
48 Unwrap roughly
50 Mai ___ (drink)
52 River by Westminster Palace
55 Song syllables
57 It's a plus
58 Airspeed unit
59 Tennis's Arthur
60 Yemen port
62 ___ no good

63 Strike-monitoring agcy.
64 Barely passing marks
67 Blvd.

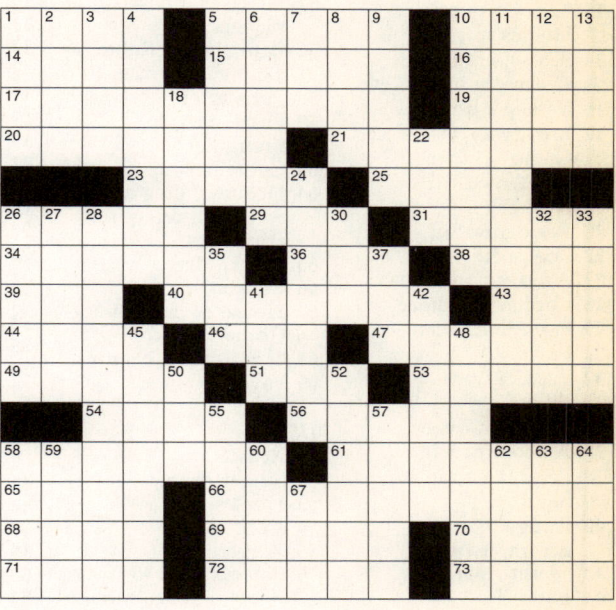

66 by Patrick Jordan

ACROSS

1 Grant's successor
6 Play, as a ukulele
11 Mil. command centers
14 Henry Ford's only son
15 Half of Hispaniola
16 Not at home
17 "The Winds of War" actress
19 British "relief station"
20 Zip, to Zapata
21 ___ the good (beneficial)
23 Nags
27 Digressed
29 Stimulate, as curiosity
30 Oration
31 Register receptacles
32 Ball-and-socket, for one
33 Conversational fillers
36 "SOS!"
37 Casts off the skin
38 Have memorized
39 TV Tarzan Ron

40 "Land ___!"
41 Led Zeppelin's "Whole ___ Love"
42 Jigsaw components
44 Corset material, once
45 More hair-raising
47 Hits the road
48 Goods for sale
49 Russian river
50 Aardvark's treat
51 "Sweet" girl of Irish song
58 Pasture plaint
59 Senseless
60 Eminent
61 Wayfarer's stop
62 Pencil wood, usually
63 Companions

DOWN

1 Cool, in the 50's
2 Hue and cry
3 Fashionable initials
4 Sinuous swimmer
5 Reynard's quality
6 Houses for hoses and hoes
7 Scarlett's home
8 Fix the outcome

9 Shoshonean
10 Mosque adjunct
11 "The Piano" player
12 Stock market stat
13 Endured
18 Unclothed
22 Fond du ___, Wis.
23 Scrub in the tub
24 Disney mermaid
25 "Here You Come Again" crooner
26 Eat greedily
27 Roasting rods
28 Addition column
30 Feet bottoms
32 One getting lost in the shuffle?
34 Sacred song
35 Graceful paddlers
37 Riot queller
38 Soft drink nut
40 Like fault-line activity
41 Northern European region
43 Wrath
44 Grin broadly
45 Hindu teacher
46 Church law
47 Salon apparatus

49 Forearm bone
52 It's "for the money"
53 Terhune dog
54 Mauna ___
55 Baseball's Mel

56 Prenuptial indicator
57 Begleys Sr. and Jr.

67   by Richard Hughes

ACROSS

1 Thrash
4 It gives a lift at the circus
9 Surrounded by
13 "___ Carousel" (1967 Hollies hit)
14 Sea separating Greece from Turkey
16 Yemen's capital
17 Broadway's "The ___ Game"
18 Fired, as a U.P.S. worker?
20 Residents: Suffix
22 Poe poem
23 Fired, as a salesclerk?
25 Capital of Bulgaria
29 Fairy tale villain
30 Furrow
32 T.L.C. givers
33 Bikini, e.g.
36 "M'aidez," e.g.
37 Algebra or trig
38 Fired, as a ranch hand?
42 Bridge accomplishment
43 Mouth, slangily
44 Enticed

45 Syr. neighbor
46 Morse role on Broadway
47 Med. school course
49 Authority
51 Fired, as a baseball player?
56 Batman and Robin, e.g.
58 Pot starter
59 Fired, as a firefighter?
63 Container metal
64 Jacques "alive and well and living in Paris"
65 One under
66 Molson, e.g.
67 House of ___-Coburg-Gotha
68 H.S. juniors' exams
69 Favorite

DOWN

1 Reasoning
2 Singer Bryant
3 Horses' hair
4 KLM rival
5 Waver
6 Pay no heed to
7 River of forgetfulness

8 Convenience for Blockbuster customers
9 ___ quarter (eschew assistance)
10 Month in Paris
11 Bed and breakfast
12 The U.N.'s Hammarskjöld
15 Noted paperback publisher
19 "___ la guerre"
21 Temple greeting: Var.
24 Eskimo home: Var.
26 Business misbehavior
27 Opening bars
28 Pale-faced
31 Dos Passos trilogy
33 Architectural recess
34 Oklahoma city
35 Eared seal
36 Bread, for stew
37 Sicilian height
39 Norse war god
40 What a strict captain runs
41 Deli side dish
46 Burg
47 Naval force
48 1944 Sartre drama
50 Carved stone slab
52 Tillers

53 From the barrel
54 Helpful
55 Belief
57 Where N.Y.C. horseplayers go

59 Literary monogram
60 Author Levin
61 Bother
62 Some M.I.T. grads

68   by A.D. Cover

ACROSS

1 Mah-jongg pieces
6 Van adjunct
10 Catered
13 Locale of Prince Albert and Prince George
14 Golden ___ (century plant)
15 Crew member
16 Start of an old song lyric
18 U.S. 101, e.g.: Abbr.
19 Visitor to Venus
20 Nothing
21 "___ better to have loved . . ."
22 Cat Nation
23 Kind of arch
25 Tie up
26 Moon vehicles, for short
27 Ren and Stimpy et al.
28 Minotaur's home
29 Dorothée, e.g.: Abbr.
30 Type set
31 Prayer
32 Lively dances
34 Sales lure

37 Snack of nuts, raisins, etc.
38 Part of H.M.S.
41 In reserve
42 Fabled racer
43 Small bag
44 Stuffing herb
45 Peace
46 Tended, with "for"
47 Period of decline
48 Pasty
49 Annul
51 Recipe title part
52 End of the lyric
54 Half a score
55 Christmas
56 Not take part in
57 Byrnes of "77 Sunset Strip"
58 "First Knight" star
59 Lilac, e.g.

DOWN

1 Upholstery fabric
2 How some partners work
3 Word on a door
4 Ideal sites
5 Hotel convenience
6 Cheerleader's cheer

7 Dress styles
8 Multiplex offering
9 Rind
10 Decade of this puzzle's theme song
11 Erode
12 Zwinger Museum site
13 Alternatives to Marlboros
17 Electric wire feature
24 Middle of the lyric
25 Jewish ritual
27 Ready
28 Cut, as a picture
30 Kismet
31 Meanie
32 Stand up to
33 Routine
34 Optimistic
35 Aided
36 Player of this puzzle's theme song
38 O'Neill's "Beyond the ___"
39 Manages
40 Cinnamon candy
42 Yearn
43 Gourmet's sense
45 Birchbark

46 Work in panels
48 Fly
50 & 53 A beverage brand since 1777

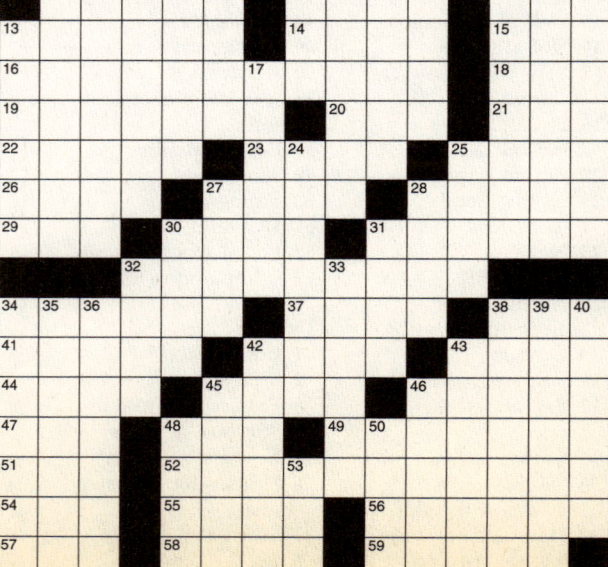

ACROSS

1 Proof of pedigree
7 One left holding the bag?
14 Kind of service
15 Through
16 Cobblers' forms
17 Pirates
18 J.F.K.'s service
19 Kennel club rejects
21 Annoyed with
22 Zippo
24 Gathering storm
26 Part of a pedigree
27 Used a prie-dieu
29 Giverny artist
31 Actor Ruman of "Ninotchka"
32 Concert hall
34 "___ My Heart"
35 Old bag
36 Bankruptcy listing
39 It's hard to get out of
42 Traffic cop?
43 Make tracks
46 N.T. book
47 Three-time Masters winner
49 Cloaks

51 Crockpot concoction
53 Rosencrantz and Guildenstern
55 Connecticut community
56 Shinto Temple gateway
58 Powerful ray
60 Hydromassage facility
61 Follower
63 Sanjo banjo
65 Not as clear
66 Dodgers
67 Locks
68 Puts another way

DOWN

1 Compatriot
2 Changed a bill
3 Life
4 Netherlands town
5 Incurred
6 Gambler's strategy
7 Nursery item
8 Schooner's contents, maybe
9 Knock
10 Old Norse collections

11 Inclined to sulk
12 Forcible seizure of a ship, in maritime law
13 Reserve
14 Moxie
20 Ricky's nightclub
23 Songwriter Wilder
25 Erector's set
28 Players take them
30 Olympics symbol
33 "___ my big mouth!"
37 They wish
38 Land
39 Computer command
40 Adequate
41 1979 film with a Best Actress nomination
44 Peregrination
45 Hardens, or softens!
48 Not as bright
50 Astin and Lennon
52 Thin strands
54 Forestall, with "off"
57 Medical suffix
59 You love, to Livy
62 Miss Peggy
64 Mrs. William McKinley

ACROSS

1 Not fiction
5 Prefix with legal or chute
9 Fire starter
14 Hand lotion ingredient
15 At any time
16 Macho dude
17 Author Fleming and others
18 Extinct bird not known for its intelligence
19 Sky-blue
20 Louisa May Alcott classic
23 Envision
24 Deli loaves
25 Participants in a debate
27 World's fastest sport, with 2-Down
29 Footfall
32 Sounds of satisfaction
33 Thomas ___ Edison
35 "Woe is me!"
37 Walkway
41 Nightgown wearer of children's rhyme
44 Four-door
45 It has a keystone
46 Lass

47 "Now ___ seen everything!"
49 Store, as a ship's cargo
51 Aye's opposite
52 Woven cloth or fabric
56 Not able to hear
58 "___ Believer" (Monkees hit)
59 Don Ho standard
64 Sprite
66 Destroy
67 ___ one's time
68 Its a piece of cake
69 Atlanta arena, with "the"
70 "What's ___ for me?"
71 Affirmatives
72 Endure
73 Kett of the comics

DOWN

1 Flunk
2 See 27-Across
3 Artificial
4 Irritable and impatient
5 Place for a statue or a hero
6 Affirm
7 Give a makeover

8 Fragrance
9 Major Chinese seaport
10 Candy that comes in a dispenser
11 Tickle the funny bone
12 Harder to find
13 Strike zone's lower boundary
21 "___ Miserables"
22 Memorable time
26 Taking advantage of
27 Shark tale
28 Sheltered from the wind
30 First name in scat
31 Couples
34 Watch for
36 Religious splinter group
38 Miser
39 Trevi Fountain coin
40 Slippery
42 People asked to parties
43 Murder mystery
48 Yale grad
50 World Wide ___
52 A bit blotto
53 Writer Zola
54 The line y = 0, in math

55 Register, as a student
57 60's protest leader Hoffman
60 City in Arizona
61 Storage containers
62 Do magazine work
63 ___ high standard
65 Skating surface

ACROSS

1 "Shane" star
5 Late actor Phoenix
10 "Dark Lady" singer, 1975
14 "___ in a manger . . ."
15 Author Zola
16 "___ from New York . . ."
17 Haircuts?
19 Kathleen Battle offering
20 "___ we having fun yet?"
21 Glowing
22 Kuwaiti structure
24 Opening word
26 Broadway show based on a comic strip
27 Dubuque native
29 Imperturbable
33 Become frayed
36 Former spouses
38 Conceited smile
39 Hawkeye portrayer
40 Recording auditions
42 Garfield's canine pal
43 Pilots let them down
45 Cushy
46 Catches some Z's
47 ___ fugit
49 Gullible
51 Sufficient
53 Knucklehead
57 Horoscope heading
60 Police blotter abbr.
61 Prospector's find
62 World rotator?
63 Fake embroidery?
66 Augury
67 "This way in" sign
68 ___ carotene
69 Emcee Parks
70 Nursery packets
71 Flowery verses

DOWN

1 Actor Lorenzo
2 Conscious
3 Odense residents
4 Recolor
5 Critiqued
6 ". . . ___ a man with seven wives"
7 ___ ordinaire
8 "Candle in the Wind" singer ___ John
9 Copal and others
10 Vandalized art work?
11 Put on staff
12 Heinous
13 Kind of estate
18 Movie Tarzan ___ Lincoln
23 Whoppers
25 Smog?
26 Showy flower
28 Lumber camp implements
30 Verdi heroine
31 Stumble
32 Makes do, with "out"
33 Float
34 Madame's pronoun
35 Eden resident
37 Divan
41 Scoundrels
44 Its usefulness goes to waste
48 Cumin and cardamom
50 Test tube
52 Actor Greene
54 Courted
55 Livid
56 Ann Richards's bailiwick
57 Poor fellow
58 "Be our guest!"
59 Concluded
60 Thunderstruck
64 Part of a year in Provence
65 Cable add-on

ACROSS

1 Trounce
8 "My gal" of song
11 Castleberry of "Alice"
14 Have coming
15 Soldier's fare
17 Traveled militarily
18 Catch-22 situation
19 Black and white, e.g.
21 U.S.N. rank
22 Ireland
23 Cosmo and People, e.g.
26 I, to Claudius
27 "___ Lisa"
31 Shower mo.
32 Scruggs of bluegrass
34 Epithet for a tyrant
36 Not a warm welcome
39 Flower child
40 A big blow
41 De Maupassant's "___ Vie"
42 Some of Wordsworth's words
43 Legendary Hollywood monogram
44 Ed of "Daniel Boone"
45 Roller coaster cry
47 "Society's Child" singer Janis ___
49 Sang-froid
56 In progress
57 Vegetarian's no-no
59 Alley of "Look Who's Talking"
60 Rodeo ropes
61 Ship's heading
62 Always, poetically
63 Majority's choice

DOWN

1 S. & L. offerings
2 Lover's ___
3 Christiania, today
4 Scarlett and others
5 Bear Piccolo
6 Civil rights leader Medgar
7 Change the decor
8 Punic War general
9 Knight's attire
10 Slip-up
11 Fight sight
12 Mislay
13 Washington bills
16 Mai ___
20 Like Captain Ahab
23 Like a he-man
24 Sap sucker
25 Bellyache
26 Be off the mark
27 Denver summer time: Abbr.
28 Disgrace
29 Nary a person
30 Saint whose feast day is January 21
32 Biblical judge
33 Word of support
34 Bugs' voice
35 Hairy ancestor
37 Obsolescent disks
38 Engine part
43 Like slim pickings
44 Lacking iron, maybe
45 Essayist E.B.
46 Three-time skating gold medalist
47 Model
48 Novelist Malraux
49 Furnace fuel
50 Getting ___ years
51 Bogeyman
52 Pop music's ___ Lobos
53 Gardner of mysteries
54 Backside
55 Overindulge
58 Chairman's heart?

73 by Bob Sefick

ACROSS

1 Clicker that might be used on a trawler?
9 London elevator
13 Tibetan V.I.P.
14 Plume source
16 Starter at an Italian restaurant
17 Quick on one's toes
18 Shoshonean
19 Health resort
20 Department store employee
21 Behan's "___ Boy"
23 George Sand, e.g.
24 Gene Kelly's "___ Girls"
25 Loving touches
26 German coal region
28 Propelled a punt
29 Amtrak listing: Abbr.
30 One of the Astors
31 Is interested
32 Caddies carry them
33 Bank account amt.
34 Vatican City dwellers
35 Jetty
36 It causes a reaction
38 Great noise

39 Sparta was its capital
40 Have the chair
44 Resounding, as a canyon
45 TV knob abbr.
46 Statehouse V.I.P.
47 Left the chair
48 Cheese at an Italian restaurant
51 "Put up your ___!"
52 Relinquishes
53 Élan
54 Solemn hymn

DOWN

1 Piece of a poem
2 Change, as hems
3 Capuchin monkey
4 Racetrack informant
5 Confirmation slaps
6 Twangy
7 Ambulance attendant: Abbr.
8 Philosopher's universal
9 Scholarly
10 Eliza's 'enry
11 Chicken dish
12 Distance gauge

13 Paint unskillfully
15 Brewer and Wright
20 Parisian papas
22 Kill, as a dragon
23 Turns white
25 Meltdown areas
26 City south of Palo Alto
27 Salad ingredient
28 ___ New Guinea
30 Throw off the scent
31 Some lose sleep over it
32 Baking pans
34 Most runtlike
35 Polish dumpling
37 Yankee great Skowron et al.
38 Herds
40 Call up
41 Jim Croce's "___ Name"
42 Gift getter
43 Holiday nights
48 Cushion
49 Baseball hitter's stat
50 Household god, in Roman myth

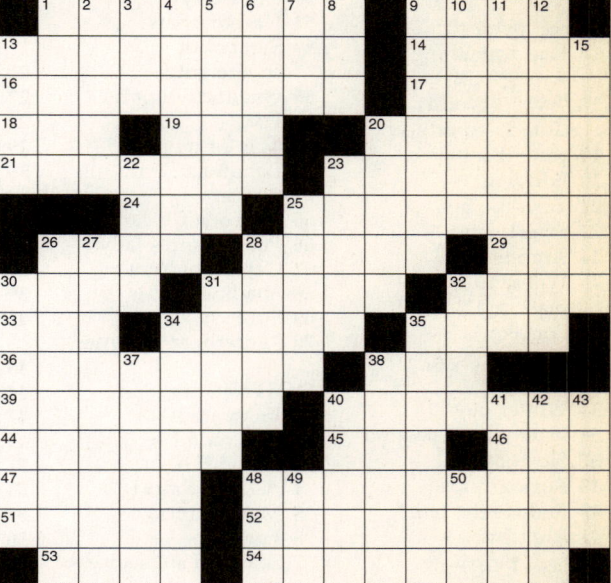

74 by Trip Payne

ACROSS

1 Tick off
5 Jerry Herman musical
9 Scarf
14 Tennis's Ivanisevic, often
15 "Fatal Attraction" villain
16 Bust finds
17 Diner's card
18 1953 Leslie Caron role
19 Long time
20 #1 song for Robert Palmer
23 At that point
24 Bookbinding leather
25 At regular intervals
28 Innocent one
29 Entirety
32 Communion table
33 TV's "Batman," e.g.
34 Oil of ___
35 Learning method that "works for me"
38 "Indecent Proposal" director Adrian
39 Jokesters

40 One quadrillionth: Prefix
41 Vane dir.
42 Ill will
43 #, & or %
44 Either star of "Tea and Sympathy"
45 To you, to Yves
46 Empty-calorie lover
52 Craze
53 Novel featuring Doctor Long Ghost
54 Bear in the sky
55 Keats or Wordsworth
56 Mash preceder
57 Sardine containers
58 Wash
59 Light submachine gun
60 Noted Renaissance name

DOWN

1 Doll's cry
2 Like some tea
3 Ward (off)
4 Yuletide snack
5 Ice cream treat
6 Xenophobe's fear
7 Pinochle combo

8 Turnoffs
9 It fell in 1979
10 Attach, as a feed bag
11 King Harald's father
12 Folk tales
13 Slalom shape
21 Beloved
22 Energy
25 Humorist Mort et al.
26 Artful dodges
27 Pay the penalty
28 "Tootsie" Oscar winner
29 Out on ___
30 Milk: Prefix
31 Popular disinfectant
33 Checking places
34 "Hold on . . ."
36 Happy, for one
37 1934 song "The Very Thought ___"
42 Goddess of Hades
43 One of the Virgin Islands
44 Filled turnover
45 Give ___ of one's own medicine
46 Nonsense song of 1918
47 Hand or foot

48 Exclude
49 Mr. Kristofferson
50 Does not exist
51 Life of Riley
52 Crowd around

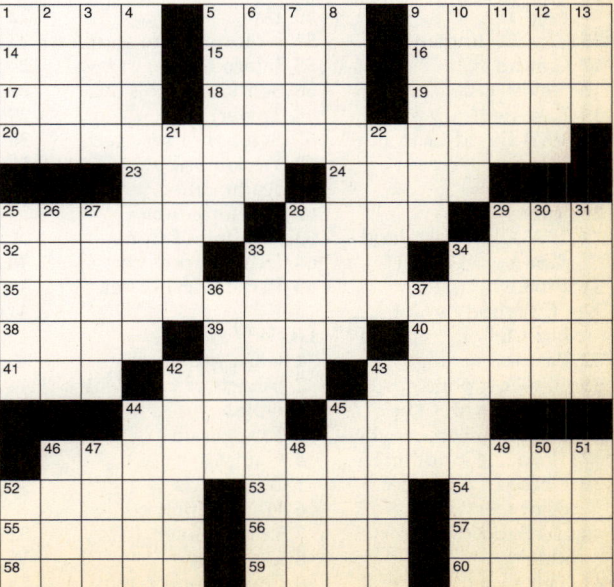

ACROSS

1 Butcher's hook
5 Exam for H.S. jrs.
9 Make nuts
14 ___ breve (2/2 time)
15 Aunt Millie's competitor
16 Had something wrong
17 "When Worlds Collide" producer
19 Knight spot?
20 Eddying
21 Take the bus
23 Sweet spud
24 Argo ending
26 Where to get plastered?
28 Forsake
31 "Cosby Show" co-star
34 Winter bug
35 Hate with a passion
37 Host Jay
38 Rock groups
40 Reduce the fare?
41 Runs into
42 "___ partridge . . ."
43 Levy
45 Peppermint Twister Joey
46 Yellowstone attraction
48 A month of ___
50 Unearthly
52 Harbor boats
53 Symbol of sovereignty
55 Quantico initials
57 Fix
61 Man of morals
63 Longtime Pirate pitcher
65 Lost one's balance?
66 Peter Gunn's lady
67 Capital of Yemen
68 Shadings
69 Split
70 "Enterprise" journey

DOWN

1 Infatuated
2 Pub round
3 Go with it
4 A Little Rascal
5 Musical intro
6 Enervate
7 Seaweed substance
8 Haarlem bloomer
9 Tourist's tote
10 Inlet
11 "Brat pack" actress
12 Epsilon follower
13 Holland export
18 Some pianos
22 Move like a dragonfly
25 Indian icon
27 South Seas site
28 Out in the cold
29 "Barnaby Jones" star
30 Tide types
32 Starts the pot
33 Pill allotment
34 Old Glory
36 Substantial
39 Let up
41 Civil-rights leader Evers
43 Flower of one's eye?
44 Extinguished
47 Hits the ceiling
49 Shortstop's stat
51 Barbecue leftover
53 Malt drier
54 Bank take-back
56 Spy writing
58 Bender
59 Feminine suffix
60 Neighbor of Sask.
62 "A Chorus Line" finale
64 Hopper

ACROSS

1 Poke
5 Alternative to whole
9 Nutty
13 CNN screen word
14 One size smaller than English
15 "To ___ human"
17 Candid
18 News piece
19 Base neutralizers
20 1970 David Lean film
23 Planet
25 Like soave
26 Runs
27 1970 Clint Eastwood film
31 Broadway's "Ev'rybody's Got ___ But Me"
32 Pastoral settings
33 60's–70's police drama, with "The"
36 Future queen, maybe
37 "You ___ kidding!"
39 Horse of a certain color
40 ___ Saud (Saudi king)
41 Tire
42 Latin land
43 "Where the elite meet to eat," in old radio
46 Lover
49 O'Hara's Joey
50 Date
51 Notorious fire starter
55 Intermediate, in law
56 San Francisco's ___ Tower
57 Symbol of servitude
60 Wicker willow
61 Author Rice
62 Author Ambler
63 Meeting of Cong.
64 Extreme poverty
65 Paradoxical Greek

DOWN

1 Gaza grp.
2 Stretch of turbulent water
3 Exaggerated
4 Gainsay
5 Book parts
6 Hardly high art
7 In the cooler
8 Doll's cry
9 Snoopy and family
10 Fallen features
11 Platitudinous
12 Joined forces (with)
16 Former states: Abbr.
21 "___ sow, so shall . . ."
22 W.W. II craft
23 Giraffe's cousin
24 Clinic program
28 Alphabet trio
29 Gray work
30 Stimpy's TV pal
33 Gave up: Var.
34 Vermont city
35 Vacuous
37 Actress Woodard
38 U.K. defenders
39 Prepare to drag
41 Indy 500 pit workers
42 Magnesium silicate
43 Hive loafers
44 Kim Philby activity
45 Likes and dislikes
46 Bullets
47 Prepare, as a turkey
48 Davis of "Evening Shade"
52 Rent-___
53 Author Jaffe
54 Court call
58 Brethren
59 Environmentally minded

ACROSS

1 Ideologies
5 ___ Jean aka Marilyn
10 On the briny
14 Harvest
15 Love affair
16 Command to a dog
17 Taj Mahal site
18 New Zealand native
19 ___ Krishna
20 Military officer in charge of food and clothing
23 Suffix with novel
24 Sign before Virgo
25 "Gosh!"
28 Not proper
32 Not together
34 Eva's half sister?
37 Cheap
40 A single time
42 Excludes
43 Ten: Prefix
44 Coat in a way
47 N.F.L. linemen
48 Cocteau's "The Blood of ___"
49 Troop encampment
51 Moon craft, for short
52 Shipment from Texas
55 Pay ___ mind
58 Frugal, disrespectfully
64 Italian car
66 Blackmore's "Lorna ___"
67 Writer James
68 ___ Boleyn
69 Toughen
70 Jersey five
71 April hath 30
72 Fall bloomer
73 Where the coin goes

DOWN

1 Baghdad's land
2 Musical transition
3 Corday's victim, 7/13/1793
4 Winner of the Peloponnesian War
5 Moniker
6 Actor Sharif
7 Space
8 Michelangelo work
9 Come up
10 Tennis great Arthur
11 Astronomer
12 Catch one's ___
13 Yes, to Rob Roy
21 Subject, to Puccini
22 Miniature hopper
26 Straight up
27 Lab burners
29 Whom fans adore
30 Ignoramus
31 Photographer's request
33 Peas' home
34 Of districts
35 Criticize, with "at"
36 Play second fiddle to, in a way
38 Coup d'___
39 "The Thin Man" dog
41 ___ out a living
45 007's alma mater
46 Grand story
50 Allen and Frome
53 "Gunga Din" setting
54 Capital of Rhone
56 Dr. Watson portrayer ___ Bruce
57 ___ a customer
59 Hot times in Bordeaux
60 Show petulance
61 Concerning
62 ___-do-well
63 Daring deed
64 Mini-craze
65 Put ___ good word for

ACROSS

1 Solon, e.g.
5 Galvanometers measure them
9 Turkish bigwig
14 Quark's place
15 Sir's opposite
16 At full speed, as a ship
17 Burglarize
18 Forearm bone
19 Concerto movement
20 "What's more . . ."
21 Dannay-Lee sleuth
23 Knock down a notch
25 Package ___
26 Eskimo region
29 Notice
33 Bing Crosby #1 hit
35 Officer-to-be
37 Scot's yes
38 "I've Got ___ in Kalamazoo"
39 BMW's 535i, e.g.
40 Gunslinger's command
41 Medic
42 South Pacific kingdom
43 Years and years
44 Not mono
46 Nail polish
48 A Guthrie
50 Video-store section
53 Legendary deejay
58 "Rock and Roll, Hoochie ___"
59 16th-century violin
60 Verdi villain
61 Valued fur
62 Beam fastener
63 Till bills
64 Poet Sexton
65 Gawk
66 Hatching site
67 "Omigod!"

DOWN

1 Dieter's meal
2 Do penance
3 Old Saturday Review humorist
4 Paramedic: Abbr.
5 Rabbit's foot, e.g.
6 Sears locale
7 Glass square
8 Brainy
9 Inlaid floor
10 Love affairs
11 Of sound mind
12 Trapper's ware
13 Before long
21 Emulate Dürer
22 Alpine song
24 Kind of hygiene
27 PC pic
28 Beg
30 "Nightingale" singer
31 "Sleepless in Seattle" co-star
32 Evergreens
33 Hires rival
34 "___ Plenty o' Nuttin!"
36 College V.I.P.
39 Dough
40 Have an opinion
42 Home wrecker
43 In a frenzy
45 Roof support
47 Greet brazenly
49 Bermuda for one
51 Golfer Caponi
52 Hooked up, as oxen
53 Part of V.F.W.
54 Neglect
55 Igneous flow
56 Mrs. Jetson
57 Years and years
61 Fannnie ___ (investment)

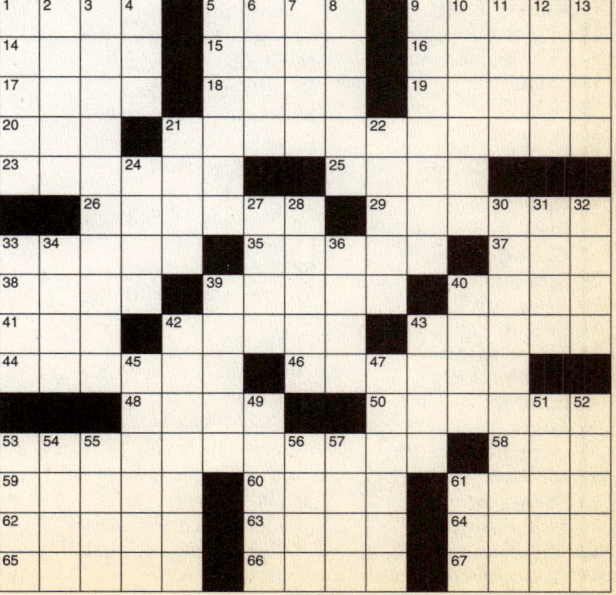

ACROSS
1 "___ off!" ("Congrats!")
5 Payola, e.g.
10 Sandler formerly of "S.N.L."
14 Object of an Army hunt
15 Wedding route
16 Deli sandwich
17 Dig, so to speak
18 "___ your life!"
19 Siberia's site
20 W.W. II fighter pilot
23 Nosh
24 Theater sections
25 Head out on the ranch?
27 Monopoly purchase
30 Nova ___
33 Hertz rival
36 Aplenty, in the past
38 "But ___ me, give me liberty . . ."
39 Children's card game
40 Changeable in shape
42 Last number before "Liftoff!"
43 Run off to the preacher

45 Take a ___ at
46 Fires
47 Signify
49 Photographer Adams
51 Cobbler's stock
53 Pindar's Muse
56 Foofaraw
58 1960 chart topper
62 G.O.P. insider Matalin
64 Skepticism
65 "My Way" lyricist
66 Old socialite Maxwell
67 "Sesame Street" Muppet
68 Champagne name
69 Appear
70 Intelligence
71 Mrs. Shakespeare

DOWN
1 50%
2 "Where there's ___ . . ."
3 1964 Olympics city
4 Vehicles with bells
5 Mafioso
6 Battle with the police
7 Italian wine center
8 Whips

9 Principles
10 "Caught you!"
11 Erwin Rommel's nickname, with "the"
12 La Scala song
13 Castle defense
21 Recent: Prefix
22 Preserve again
26 Dawn goddess
28 NASA chimp
29 Led Zeppelin's "Whole ___ Love"
31 Actress Skye
32 Trojan War god
33 Filled with wonder
34 Lowland
35 Locomotive
37 Withdraw, as from a dependency
40 One of the Benchleys
41 Kind of ballot
44 "The Purloined Letter" writer
46 Joe Namath's alma mater
48 Dodges
50 Unit of work
52 Dorm sound
54 Mortise insertion

55 Like some old buckets
56 City north of Des Moines
57 Cowgirl Evans
59 Senator Sam
60 Nile bird
61 Fixed fee
63 Sweet potato

ACROSS
1 Bad golf shot
5 Stuff
9 "Apollo 13" costar
14 Epithet for Athena
15 Ready for picking
16 Kind of artery
17 Site at the end of "Romeo and Juliet"
18 Satanic
19 Cabal
20 Aviary?
23 Search (out)
24 Marker
25 Rustic parents
28 Buck Rogers player Gerard
29 Monopolist's amount
30 Covenant
31 Bowling alley button
34 Junior Dumas
35 Sgt. Snorkel's bulldog
36 Bird call competition?
39 Modern music maker
40 Some Antilles, e.g.
41 Mother-of-pearl
42 First name in fashion
43 Antiquity, old-style

44 "Wanna ___?"
45 Bird's beak
46 Start of many Québec place names
47 Bodies of law
50 Why the crow wouldn't sing?
54 Girl of a Beatles title
56 Sharer's word
57 Attacks weeds
58 Made goo-goo eyes at
59 Bring to ruin
60 "___ Her on Monday" (1942 song)
61 Domineering
62 Mrs. Dick Tracy
63 Low state, with "the"

DOWN
1 Serious business loss
2 Cold
3 "Cherchez la ___"
4 Russian royal treasure
5 Embroidery yarn
6 Construction fastener
7 ". . . blackbirds baked in ___"

8 "Coca-Cola Cowboy" singer
9 Small, exquisite ornament
10 Reunion attender
11 Of the movies
12 Kind of bran
13 U.S.O. user
21 Shopworn
22 "The Planets" composer
26 Cast member
27 "What 'litho-' means
29 Pointed
30 Picnic bite
31 Novarro of "Ben Hur"
32 Molière's "L'___ des femmes"
33 Nile birds
34 Got plumper
37 Michelangelo marble
38 Concerning
44 Low singers
46 Darkened
47 Part of Miss Muffet's diet
48 Model Campbell
49 Caring

51 Connections
52 Start of summer
53 Sonic boom creators
54 Task
55 Italian dramatist ___ Betti

81   by A.J. Santora

ACROSS

1 Cabin attendants, slangily
6 Popular cuisine
10 One-named model
14 Flemish painter Michiel van ___
15 Layers
16 "Juke Box Baby" singer, 1956
17 Make ___ buck
18 Height of fashion
19 British pol portrayed in "Mission to Moscow"
20 Figure in a Super Bowl promo
23 Eastern New Year
24 Update, maybe
25 Sensational
27 Gentlemanly reply
30 Kind of wool
31 Privileged one
34 Amount to pay
35 Commercial broadcaster since 1941
39 Pro
40 Spanish scarfs
41 Valued violins

44 Post-disaster danger
48 Track official
49 Horned deity
51 Take-home
52 Hoop extravaganza
56 "The Jolly Trio" painter
57 Tibetan sighting
58 Accommodate oneself to
59 To ___ (exactly)
60 Architect Saarinen
61 Overact
62 Disarray
63 Pitcher Belinda
62 ___-ski

DOWN

1 Insubstantial
2 Problem for fillings
3 Glorifies
4 Madison's home: Abbr.
5 Fifth person
6 Infamous island name
7 Took evidence from
8 White
9 "You showed me"
10 Frosted

11 Musical direction
12 Cheese choice
13 United Nations vote
21 Wipers
22 The lot
26 Small amount
28 O.T. book
29 Rock's Adam ___
30 Third on a roll call
32 Party person
33 Doctrine since the 1850's
35 Delegates do this
36 Prickly shrubs
37 Jack of "Barney Miller"
38 Final closure
39 Lard
42 Picks on
43 Politico-military grp. in the news
45 Captivate
46 Couch potato's aid
47 Cubic measures
49 Speedy
50 Word in Kansas' motto
53 Soapmaker's supplies
54 Mother of Hera and Zeus

55 1994 Oscar-winning role
56 Grandstander

82   by Martin Ashwood-Smith

ACROSS

1 Belvedere, for one
6 Relief work?
15 Part of the stratosphere
16 Hope/Crosby film of 1947
17 Yuppie's salary, perhaps
19 Olympian: Abbr.
20 Herculean
21 Besides
22 Taper?
24 ". . . ___ saw Elba"
26 Emulate the birds and the bees
27 Fight (for)
28 Good buddy
29 Lee side?
31 Practically still
37 Alpinist
38 Sales
39 ___ Enterprise
40 Fire exit?
41 Suffix with fruit names
42 Like some political support
45 Gala affair

46 Martians and Venusians
47 ___-Magnon
48 Peeved, after "in"
50 NAFTA signatory
52 Like 501 to 502?
58 Raked over the coals
59 Tickle pink
60 Ones going along
61 Test-tube glass

DOWN

1 Business orgs.
2 Hospital addition
3 Pete Wilson, e.g.
4 Have ___ miss
5 Flat rate?
6 Suffix with boot
7 Folks
8 Faith developed in Iran
9 Redolence
10 Gambler's game
11 Message in a bottle?
12 Steamed
13 Children in an escuela
14 Theatrical title character who's never seen

18 Chicago team
22 Sunshade
23 Which: Fr.
25 Do another hitch
26 Biblical mother from Bethlehem
27 Improvise
28 Commends
29 Academic subject whose name means "pebble"
30 Slug, old-style
32 In one piece
33 Row
34 Wolf pack member
35 Posts
36 European language
42 Big name in opera
43 They put on a whale of a show
44 Government paperwork
45 She played Jezebel, 1938
46 At cock's crow
48 "___ example . . ."
49 "Hey you!"
51 Put one's foot down
53 Award for a lord?: Abbr.

54 Both Begleys
55 Mr. Potato Head accessory
56 Angers season
57 Wild West moniker

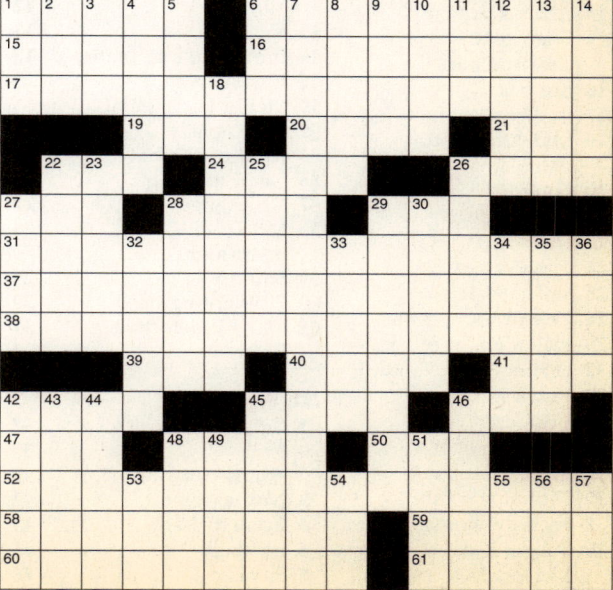

83   by Bob Sefick

ACROSS

1 Gallows
5 "___ So Lonely" (1954 hit)
9 Speck
13 Commendably
14 NASA firing
16 Take it from the top
17 "___ a Male War Bride" (Grant flick)
18 Studio sign
19 Footfall
20 Something to stand for
23 Environmentalists
24 Kind of order
25 Wheels of Fortune, for short?
26 "Take ___!"
29 Some Russians
32 Smithy
33 Work stations
34 Amtrak employee
39 Andy of the early 60's "Bob Newhart Show"
40 Baker's supply
41 Oppressor
43 60's dance

44 Decide to leave, with "out"
47 Smooths
49 Washington persona non grata
51 Unprepared
54 Suffix with poll
55 Kind of servitude
56 ___ country (natural rural area)
57 Old record label
58 Ice cream order
59 On the captain's good side?
60 Org. for Pelé, once
61 Judge's order
62 Reduced

DOWN

1 Stab
2 "Wanted" poster information
3 Delights
4 Oliver Wendell Holmes's "___ Venner"
5 Golfer's approach from the fairway
6 Actress Rowlands

7 Enumeration shortener
8 F-A-C, e.g., in music
9 One with plans
10 Air
11 Baseball's Blue Moon
12 Casual hairdo
15 "Like it ___ . . ."
21 Exactly
22 Artisan
27 N.R.C. predecessor
28 Donahue and others
30 One of old Hollywood's Big Five
31 Defunct pol. entity
32 Winter resort assignment
34 Dollop
35 Martinique, e.g.
36 To whom Dan Rather reports
37 Comedian Lehr
38 By the flock
42 Fill-ins
44 King Henry II portrayer of film
45 Crabapple Annies
46 Discards
48 Erupts
50 Author Erich

51 ___ Kett of old comics
52 "Get ___!"
53 Avis opener
54 ___ Sebastián, Spain

84   by Gregory E. Paul

ACROSS

1 Bushy coif
5 Belle or Bart
10 "Dancing Queen" pop group
14 It goes with runners
15 Army Corps of Engineers construction
16 Burrow
17 In direct competition
19 Mid 12th-century date
20 Long fish
21 Rich Little, e.g.
22 Drew out
24 Three-sided sword
25 Savage
26 One of the Greats
29 Half step, in music
32 Partner of ways
33 Shack
34 Corn crib
35 Early Andean
36 More rational
37 Diplomat's skill
38 Fr. holy woman
39 Burger King, to McDonald's

40 Where the loot gets left
41 Autumn drink
43 Crave, with "for"
44 "You Must Remember This" author
45 Kennel cry
46 Browning automatics
48 Effrontery
49 Menlo Park initials
52 Shut noisily
53 Kind of combat
56 Gambling, e.g.
57 ___ orange
58 Mitch Miller's instrument
59 Squint
60 Firefighting need
61 Old TV detective Peter

DOWN

1 Connors defeater, 1975
2 Hightail it
3 Not imagined
4 Roulette bet
5 Inclined
6 Snicker

7 Say it's so
8 New Deal proj.
9 Jesus Christ, with "the"
10 Virtually
11 One after the other
12 Ill temper
13 Saharan
18 Uses a camcorder
23 Resort near Copper Mountain
24 Soprano Berger
25 Angle on a gem
26 Plain People
27 Slowly, in music
28 In-person, as an interview
29 Sub detector
30 Recess
31 Computer command
33 Wealthy ones.
36 Two-headed lady exhibit, e.g.
37 Part of L.S.T.
39 Liturgy
40 Film producer Ponti
42 More tranquil
43 Horse restraint
45 Sheriff's star, e.g.
46 Invitation letters

47 Tennis's Nastase
48 Pesky insect
49 No-no: Var.
50 Erelong
51 First place

54 Simile center
55 Not a sharer

by Joy L. Wouk

ACROSS

1 Crocus bulb
5 "Son of the Sun"
9 Set-to
14 Pastiche
15 Score in pinochle
16 "A house is not ___"
17 Restaurant request
18 Vessel for Jill
19 "Anticipation" singer
20 Song by 11-Down
23 Vinegary
24 Scottish hillside
25 Westernmost Aleutian
27 A clef
32 Unsettle?
35 Scruff
38 "Aeneid" locale
39 Musical or song by 11-Down
42 Nobelist Wiesel
43 Rows before P
44 Gorky's "The ___ Depths"
45 Had a hunch
47 Carol
49 Daffy Duck talk
52 Bedtime annoyances
56 Song by 11-Down
61 Mercutio's friend
62 Cigar's end
63 Prefix with China
64 An acid
65 Alert
66 Ending with gang or mob
67 Guided a raft
68 Kane's Rosebud
69 Libel, e.g.

DOWN

1 Pause sign
2 Relating to $C_{18}H_{34}O_2$
3 Dyeing instruction
4 Some handlebars
5 Collision
6 Circa
7 Mountaineer
8 Psychiatrist Alfred
9 Tennessee Senator Jim
10 I.O.U.
11 Late, great composer
12 Mine: Fr.
13 "State of Grace" star
21 Thurber's Walter
22 Informal goodbye
26 Word on a coin
28 Student of animal behavior
29 Make coffee
30 Knowledge
31 Spectator
32 Farm mothers
33 Base
34 "The doctor ___"
36 Barley beard
37 Exploited worker
40 It may be golden
41 Actress Verdugo
46 Friend of Harvey the rabbit
48 Belgian port
50 Mergansers' kin
51 Perfumery bit
53 Showed allegiance, in a way
54 Downy bird
55 Stable sound
56 Envelop
57 Our genus
58 Biographer Ludwig
59 Hawaiian honker
60 To be, to Henri

---

by Robert Katz

ACROSS

1 Eye site
7 Freshens up baby
14 Canceled
15 P.O.W.'s
16 Partied hearty
17 Fossillike
18 "Liftoff" preceder
19 Early Beatle Sutcliffe
21 Phone button
22 Bottom line
25 Suffix with depend or descend
27 4.0, e.g.
30 "Hey! Jealous Lover" singer
33 Goofs
34 Italian epic poet
36 Showy moths
37 Take in
38 Nursery-rhyme queen's fare
41 Thespian's quest
42 Work unit
43 Shangri-las
44 Timetable divisions
45 Earth and moon, e.g.
47 Letter from Greece
48 Message from the Titanic
49 Satchel binder
53 Willing
57 "___ Lazy River"
59 "___ minute"
60 Twain and others
63 Cloys with adoration
66 Twilight time
67 Voucher
68 Supplies with new hands
69 Iroquoian people

DOWN

1 Computer salesman of renown
2 Maine college town
3 Musical direction
4 Question
5 Plumber's joint
6 Tote board stat
7 Apply lightly
8 ___ facto
9 Not under
10 Bundle
11 1977 Streisand hit
12 Abbr. in a military name
13 Compass dir.
15 Nursery-rhyme king's den
20 Gunpowder, e.g.
23 Black numbers
24 '63 film "David and ___"
26 Marched
28 Wishes
29 Image in Egyptian art
31 Intersections
32 Tribe of Israel
33 Repeated Jim Varney film role
34 Lifts of a sort
35 Charged at the bench
39 Some Dada works
40 Ovid products
41 Vim
46 Empath's skill
50 ___ Janeiro
51 Lark
52 Ziti or fusilli
54 Poet Bradstreet
55 ___ Hari
56 German biographer Ludwig
58 Fundamentals
60 Each
61 Oscar-winning Joanne Woodward role
62 Masthead listings, for short
64 Poet's word
65 Boxer's title: Abbr.

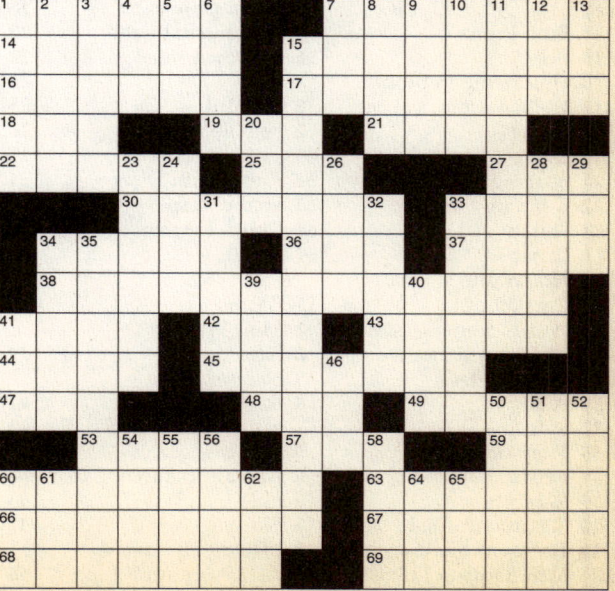

87   by Daniel R. Stark

ACROSS

1 Kind of fair
7 10th-century English king
12 Walden Pond habitué
13 One found in the stacks
15 Bandit's cry
16 Fine-wooled sheep
18 Beehives, for instance
19 From 8 to 11
21 Venison
22 Alda of "M*A*S*H"
23 "Cheaper by the ___"
24 Baseballer Maglie
25 View
26 Antique autos
27 Vain
29 Temporary hair tinter
30 Romance with the past
33 Rubberneck
36 Linked
39 Catamount
40 Thumbs through
41 ___ out (relax)
43 Not very competent
45 Furry companions
46 Allocate

47 Leggy one
49 Passengers
50 Birders' society
51 Duds
53 ___ piece
54 Volunteers
55 Super buys
56 Expunge

DOWN

1 Mademoiselle's hat
2 Short poems
3 Fire of the mind
4 Actor Parker
5 Letter after sigma
6 Most limber
7 King's fur
8 Consider
9 Rose up, in dialect
10 Newspaper part
11 Inhabitant
12 Dropping sounds
14 Lovers
17 Sixth ___
20 Searched thoroughly
22 Old radio favorite "Easy ___"
25 ___ gin

28 Delight beyond measure
29 Splits
31 Dawdled
32 Teeth holders
33 Bright star in Virgo
34 Mechanic's job
35 Revised
37 Hillary's conquest
38 Political thaw
40 Shells out
42 Hero's exploits
44 Shinbone
46 Actress Van Doren
48 Lifeguard's beat
49 Satisfy
52 One, in Aberdeen

88   by George Quincy

ACROSS

1 ___ at Work
4 Diesel-engine submarine
9 Hindu title of address
12 The "A" in U.A.R.
14 Bull: Prefix
15 Pole
16 First name in humor
17 13-Down musical form
19 Kigali's land
21 Soak again
22 Company V.I.P.'s
24 Stately 13-Down dance
26 Americano
28 Carried out
29 Words from Caesar
30 13-Down dance in triple meter
34 Acid
37 Suit to ___
38 They often have twists
39 Receipts
40 Neighbor of Leb.
41 13-Down medium for Jean Baptiste Lully

42 Reactor factor
43 Amigo
44 Baby wrigglers
46 13-Down dance, in France
52 English royal house
53 Flood protection
54 Ornamental band
56 13-Down musical form
58 Faithful
62 Female deer
63 ___-Bismol
64 Prefix with Disney
65 Snaky shape
66 Deuce toppers
67 Big ___

DOWN

1 Miss West
2 Slip
3 60's service site
4 Sundance Kid's girlfriend ___ Place
5 Manger locales
6 Literary pen name of old
7 Noisy
8 Woody Herman's "___ Autumn"

9 Give rise to
10 Judged
11 Hot under the collar
13 Highly embellished style
15 Slammin' Sammy
18 Circle
20 Sch. of the Northwest
22 Tart-tongued
23 Stage direction
25 "___ Fideles"
26 First side to vote
27 Old Chevrolet
31 "___ say!"
32 Lon ___
33 Western Indian
34 Not now
35 Baby bird?
36 Whom Reps. run against
39 Moderately quick 13-Down dance
41 Made hay?
43 Prayers
45 Drain cleaner ingredient
46 Clearing
47 Former Houston hockey team
48 Climbing plants

49 Marathoner
50 Hang
51 Deplete
55 Writer Anita
57 Inclined

59 Stroke
60 Yorkshire river
61 Long, long ago

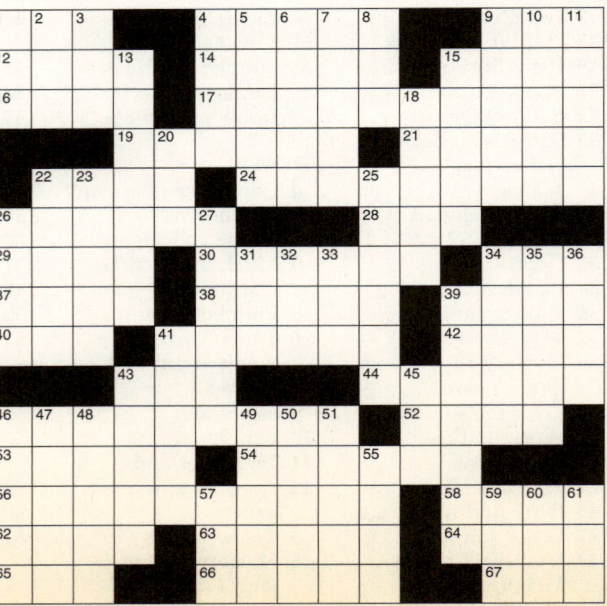

89   by Bryant White

ACROSS

1 Venezuelan lake or seaport
10 Lightheaded ones?
14 Pastime for two
16 Andean tuber
17 Tender
18 Middling mark
19 Giant Brave
21 Drinking spree
23 "Excuse me . . ."
24 Complacent
25 Fishermen
27 Caps
33 Some H.S. students
34 Up-and-comers, perhaps
35 Detectives' discoveries: Abbr.
38 Delusion
40 Wear
43 This, señor
44 Reclined
45 Vishnu incarnation
49 Sisters of Charity founder
50 Chronological division
51 Noblewoman
53 River to Solway Firth
54 The Southern Crown
59 Old means of punishment
60 Trees with dark, fragrant wood

DOWN

1 Year in Louis VII's reign
2 Rubber center
3 Gambrel, for one
4 Overhead
5 Intaglio's counterpart
6 Male: Prefix
7 Give ___ whirl
8 Science fiction writer Bova
9 Azog or Bolg of Middle-earth
10 Green-plumed tropical bird
11 Warnings, once
12 Place of one's own
13 Scorn, with "at"
14 Crows
15 Screen ___ (old TV company)
20 U.S. scientific satellite of the 60's
22 Dentures
23 Singer Jarreau and others
26 European language
28 Budge
29 More robust
30 Hoarder's goal
31 Conservative start
32 Cause of a blowup
35 Relate incorrectly
36 Formation of bone
37 Disciplines, in a way
38 Capture
39 Lilliputian
40 Smart one
41 Old European card game
42 Pageant prop
46 "This is ___!" (crimebuster's cry)
47 Volcano opening
48 Goose genus
49 Icy pinnacle
52 R. & B. singer James
55 Where lts. are educated
56 When doubled, a Gauguin book
57 Massachusetts cape
58 Three-toed sloths

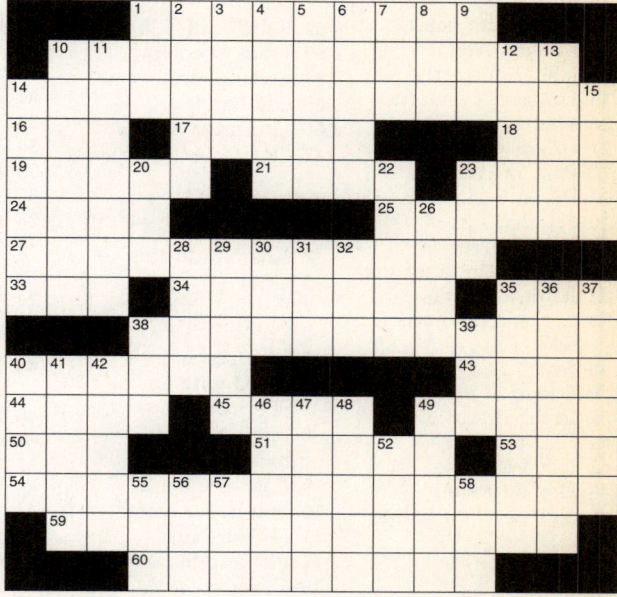

90   by Sidney L. Robbins

ACROSS

1 This might be a lot
5 Paradigm
10 Sprite
13 Word after long or dog
14 Fragrance
15 Compete
16 Sydney of "The Maltese Falcon"
18 Lady of Eden
19 Added too many pounds
20 Displayed contempt
22 Snick's partner
23 Burglarize
26 Bummer
27 Lost Ark seekers?
30 Snatch
33 Where to hang one's hat
36 "Carmen" or "Aida"
37 Moline manufacturer
38 Alluring woman
40 Despondent
41 Upright
42 Goodnight lass
43 Steps over a fence
45 Hush-hush govt. org.
46 Gardener's item
47 ___ Palace
49 Cape Canaveral org.
51 Hardly bold
52 Sandy's barks
56 Interviewer Barbara
59 Restaurant
61 Levin who wrote "Deathtrap"
62 "Of Thee I Sing" role
65 Kind of horn
66 It's enough to bring a tear to the eye
67 Swiftness
68 Owned
69 Neck parts
70 Steps on the evolutionary ladder

DOWN

1 Baseball's Hank
2 Minotaur's home
3 Short jacket
4 Poet Millay
5 Welcome giver?
6 Bruin Bobby
7 Accomplishes
8 Corrects
9 Afterward
10 Landscaping item
11 As we speak
12 Oats, e.g.
13 Urges, with "on"
17 Undress
21 Anxious
24 Texas city
25 Scolds
28 Top-notch
29 Red vegetable
31 Firecracker paths
32 Obsolescent VCR format
33 Letters before omegas
34 Cork's site
35 It was colonized circa A.D. 986
37 Fawn or doe
39 "This foolishness must ___ once!"
44 Kind of cake
47 Canopus's constellation
48 Minor despot
50 Affix, as a button
53 Della of pop
54 Stews
55 "Auld Lang ___"
56 Accompanying
57 Coloratura's piece
58 Cut
60 Turkish honcho
63 Shoe part
64 Printers' measures

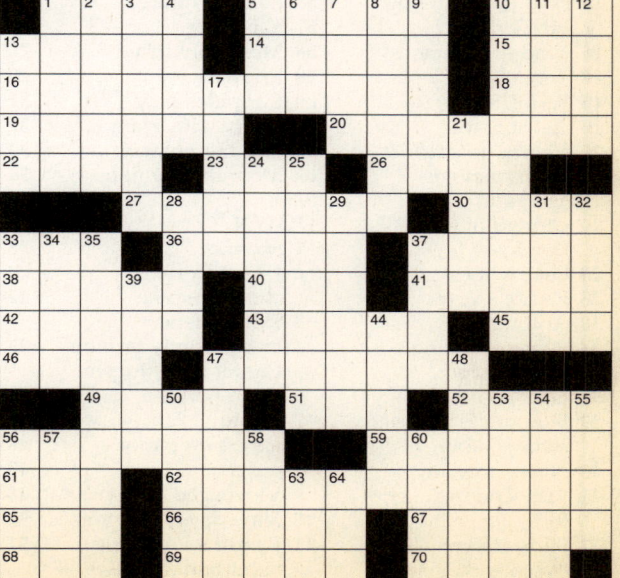

91 by Bernice Gordon

ACROSS
1 Skewered dish: Var.
6 Knifes
11 Bus. name ending
14 Bout site
15 Lose one's head
16 Prefix with natal
17 Kareem Abdul-Jabbar, formerly
19 Designer Claiborne
20 Mauna ___
21 Ungracefully thin
22 Post, of etiquette
24 Divorce demand
26 Hamlet, e.g.
27 French greeting
28 Wonderland creature
32 Rabin's people
35 "___ the ramparts we watched . . ."
36 Bryn ___, Pa.
39 Friend of Fran
40 In the distance
41 "___ Believer"
42 Fiancée
44 Domed rooms
46 Dumas's "La Tulipe ___"
50 Hence
51 Make damp

53 Nobelist Marie
55 Jail door sound
57 Clio honorees
58 Rock's ___ Rose
59 Old-time dancing song
62 Ranch call
63 Trace of color
64 Ecclesiastical wear
65 Old hand
66 Linksman Sam
67 Quarterback tackles

DOWN
1 Soprano Maria
2 Anatomical ring
3 Grieve
4 Put ___ show
5 Votes
6 Like porcupines
7 Word with gas or Sherman
8 English prince's nickname
9 Celebrity book
10 Fun house sounds
11 Rather than
12 Playwright Simon
13 Cover for a teapot

18 Preserve, as vegetables
23 L-P connection
25 "The Ghost and Mrs. ___"
26 Toweled off
28 Excises, as text
29 Actress Lena
30 Sargasso, e.g.
31 Flub
33 Sonata section
34 Neighbor of Sask.
36 Russian space station
37 Amas preceder
38 Final defeat
40 Hubbubs
42 Consumes
43 Posers
45 Spoon-bender Geller
47 Type of type
48 Lay to at another marina
49 Follows
51 Coupled
52 Warbler Yoko
53 Woody home
54 Wife, in old Rome
55 Motion picture
56 Org. overseeing courses for women?

60 Blood, so to speak
61 Singer Sumac

92 by Roger H. Courtney

ACROSS
1 Decorating ribbon
6 Not quite dry
10 André, Françoise, etc.
14 Loosened up, in a way
15 Poet translated by FitzGerald
16 Kind of testimony
17 Tongue-lash
18 K.G.B. worry
19 ___ of tears
20 Charming patriot?
23 Anthropologist Margaret
24 Dimwit of 80's–90's movies
25 Bear witness
28 Radio, TV, etc.
30 Anthracite
31 Home run king
32 Cross shape
35 Legislators' perks?
39 Summer Schenectady setting: Abbr.
40 Noses around
41 "___ Coming" (1969 hit)
42 Slims down
43 "Woe is me!"

45 ___ Equity (stage group)
48 Othello, e.g.
49 Gold?
55 Italian artist Guido
56 Still-life figure
57 Sheeplike
58 Monopoly token
59 Privy to
60 Euripides play
61 Prefix with gram
62 Sale tag notation
63 Mountain nymph

DOWN
1 Sacrifice
2 Like a German chocolate cake
3 Skin softener
4 In disorderly fashion
5 Cantor and Murphy
6 Round on top
7 Cupid
8 Ice-cream parlor order
9 Victimized
10 Nine days' devotion
11 Pontiff's vestment
12 Suburban expanses

13 Winter driving hazard
21 Louisville Slugger
22 Fetch
25 Flu symptom
26 "The Wind in the Willows" character
27 Like some nerves
28 Sprays rioters, e.g.
29 Cupid
31 Throw ___ (explode)
32 Prefix with gram
33 Atlas section
34 Lenin's land: Abbr.
36 Church topper
37 Aeschylus trilogy
38 Children's outdoor game
42 Fats of "Blueberry Hill"
43 Sluggee's exclamation
44 Santa's exclamation
45 Skylit courts
46 Dear, in Dijon
47 Purport
48 Dawns
50 Plant bristles
51 Pope called "The Great"

52 Lake Nasser site
53 Draft status
54 Rip

93 by Julie Hess

ACROSS

1 Pocket bread
5 Pulitzer-winning Ferber novel
10 At a distance
14 Land of the Peacock Throne
15 Novelist Louise de la Ramée
16 Wrist-elbow connector
17 Daughter of Powhatan
19 "Auld Lang ___"
20 Spellbind
21 Barbecue sites
23 Montana native
24 Become established
25 ___ torte
28 Throttle
31 Mr. 'iggins
32 "Land ___!"
34 Gulf war missile
35 Muslim general
36 Wire measure
37 Fix
38 "___, With a Z"
40 Turns over
42 Emblem of England
43 Midwest crop
45 Helped sail a boat
47 Falcon-headed deity
48 Pupil's place
49 Not concerned with ethics
51 Quiescent
55 Master Simpson
56 Wampanoag chief who led a 1675–76 war
58 Instead
59 Professeur's place
60 "___, vidi, vici"
61 Title
62 Seashore features
63 Top dog

DOWN

1 Prop for Santa
2 Shade of gray
3 Savoir-faire
4 Bedlam or worse
5 Oklahomans
6 Little bit
7 Dentist's request
8 Mrs. McKinley
9 Cigarettes, in British slang
10 Classic British cars
11 Seneca chief during the American Revolution
12 Part of A.D.
13 Charlotte and others
18 Fabled racer
22 ___ standstill
24 Engraved marker
25 Elite Navy group
26 Prefix with -plasty
27 Oglala chief at Little Big Horn
28 Cargo planks
29 Rainer of "The Good Earth"
30 Nosed (out)
33 Service closers
39 Stopped at Cape Canaveral
40 Applied oakum to
41 Abrasions
42 Fidgety
44 Notable time
46 Opulent
48 Fireplace
49 Still sleeping
50 Like a stag
51 Aware of
52 Holly
53 One climbing the walls
54 "Iliad," e.g.
57 Hospital dept.

94 by Harvey Estes

ACROSS

1 On the loose
8 Jefferson's '61 counterpart
15 Unselfish folks
16 Raises a fuss
17 Took a sample
18 Shopaholic's aid
19 First name in clowns
20 Dwarf, with "over"
21 "Equatorially" ample
22 Port. is part of it
23 Shore of America
27 Sermon starter
29 Musical finale
30 Film set around 73 B.C.
35 Malcolm-___ Warner
36 Bush whacker
37 Period in human history
39 Despise
40 The Man of a Thousand Faces
42 Zero-wheeled vehicle
43 Smith or Jones
44 Squirts
46 Pull some strings
47 Black Sea cottage
52 Baseball card essentials
54 Collapsed
55 Square meal?
58 One way to settle a fight
59 For
60 Vulnerable to being shot
61 Nebraska natives
62 Quotable Yankee

DOWN

1 TV dog
2 Pound
3 "Mule Train" singer
4 Fields
5 Like some days
6 Part of a control tower screen
7 Direction in France
8 Trouper
9 Swat
10 Really mattered
11 Uncle Sam's stuff
12 Mischief
13 Constellation near Telescopium
14 "No ___"
20 Attire for walking on tiptoe
22 Make A's, e.g.
24 Start of a quote ending "it tolls for thee"
25 Dull saw, maybe
26 "R-O-C-K" singer, 1956
28 After-grace directive
30 Tennis shot
31 Poet Neruda of "Il Postino"
32 Ibuprofen targets
33 ___ man (early human)
34 Resiliency
35 Tractor handle
38 Big initials in records
41 Poet's output
45 Broke in, as a hole in a hull
46 Brouhahas
48 "The Tell-Tale Heart" teller's heart?
49 Hold tight
50 Swinging connection
51 Hell's follower
53 Face saver?
54 "Candid Camera" host
55 20-year sleeper
56 Santa ___
57 Old G.I.'s group
58 Knock, in 90's slang

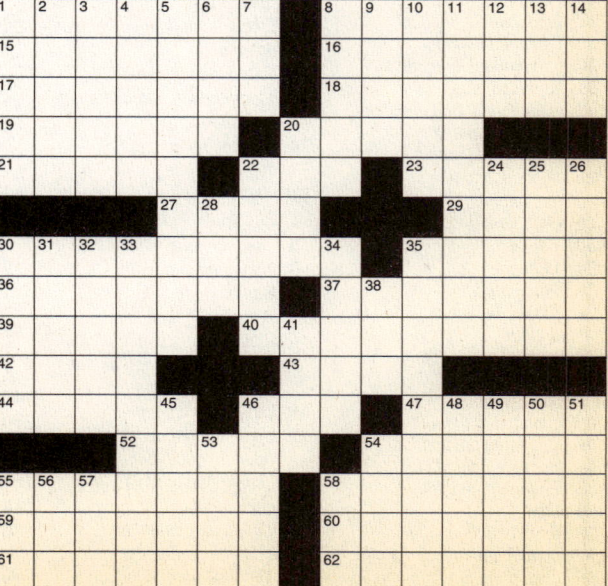

95   by Martin Ashwood-Smith

ACROSS

1 "Dennis the Menace" girl
9 Word on a door
13 Taskmaster
14 Bring about
17 Goodbye abroad
18 Photographer's chemical
19 Former Mideast inits.
20 Sidekick
22 Italian number
23 Econ. figure
24 Nail site
25 Goddess whose name means "chosen one"
26 Kind of pack
27 Decrease?
29 "Gigi" star
30 Adapt, in a way
33 Pulsar studier
34 Every which way
35 ___ d'Aosta (region of Italy)
36 Stygian
37 Up-to-the-minute
38 Kindergarten learning
39 ___ juris (legal term)
40 Pink lady ingredient
41 Jungle climber
42 24-Across's opposite
43 Seasoning for pommes frites
44 Took a stab at?
46 List ender
51 Another list ender
52 Put two and two together
53 Bereft
54 Play to the balcony

DOWN

1 Calendar divs.
2 Actress Gardner
3 Alfonso, e.g.
4 Foundation timbers
5 Child's play
6 Bring up
7 Alway
8 Semis
9 Excite
10 U.S. coin word
11 Much-debated defense prog.
12 Late September or early October event
15 Caustic
16 Actress Parker and others
21 Respectful one
23 "___ Diary" (1943 movie)
25 Onetime P.O.W. site, slangily
26 Lament
27 "If ___ a nickel . . ."
28 Dregs
29 Oblique line
30 Working, as a car
31 Lacquered metalware
32 Pseudo
39 City on the Meuse
40 Ninnies
42 One may be apparent
43 Deface
45 Day-___
47 Mark aimed at in curling
48 Alfonso's queen
49 Rosy
50 Drink suffix

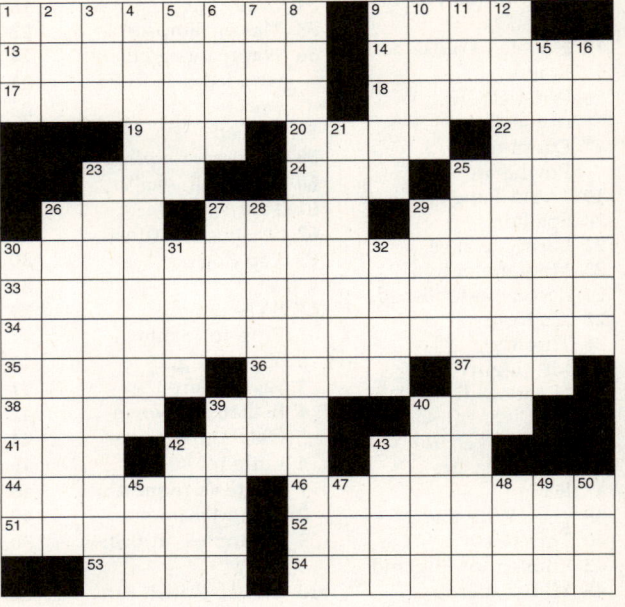

96   by Jeremiah Farrell [NOTE: This puzzle was originally published on Election Day, 1996.]

ACROSS

1 "___ your name" (Mamas and Papas lyric)
6 Fell behind slightly
15 Euripides tragedy
16 Free
17 Forecast
19 Be bedridden
20 Journalist Stewart
21 Rosetta ___
22 60's espionage series
24 ___ Perignon
25 Quilting party
26 "Drying out" program
28 Umpire's call
30 Tease
34 Tease
36 Standard
38 "The Tell-Tale Heart" writer
39 & 43 Lead story in tomorrow's newspaper(!)
45 Gold: Prefix
46 ___ Lee cakes
48 Bobble the ball
49 Spanish aunts
51 Obi
53 Bravery
57 Small island
59 Daddies
61 Theda of 1917's "Cleopatra"
62 Employee motivator
65 Otherworldly
67 Treasure hunter's aid
68 Title for 39-Across next year
71 Exclusion from social events
72 Fab Four name
73 They may get tied up in knots
74 Begin, as a maze

DOWN

1 Disable
2 Cherry-colored
3 Newspaperman Ochs
4 Easel part
5 Actress Turner
6 Ropes, as dogies
7 Place to put your feet up
8 Underskirt
9 First of three-in-a-row
10 Lower in public estimation
11 Onetime bowling alley employee
12 Threesome
13 English prince's school
14 60's TV talk-show host Joe
18 Superannuated
23 Sewing shop purchase
25 TV's Uncle Miltie
27 Short writings
29 Opponent
31 Likely
32 Actress Caldwell
33 End of the English alphabet
35 Trumpet
37 Ex-host Griffin
39 Black Halloween animal
40 French 101 word
41 Provider of support, for short
42 Much-debated political inits.
44 Sourpuss
47 Malign
50 "La Nausée" novelist
52 Sheiks' cliques
54 Bemoan
55 Popsicle color
56 Bird of prey
58 10 on a scale of 1 to 10
60 Family girl
62 Famous ___
63 Something to make on one's birthday
64 Regarding
65 Quite a story
66 Dublin's land
69 ___ Victor
70 Hullabaloo

ACROSS

1 Clogs
8 Like some ears
15 It's found according to schedule
16 Requiring adherence
17 Overruns
18 Reason for a reserve
19 1964 Ronny and the Daytonas hit
20 Bowling alley equipment
22 Truss
23 Sportscaster Albert
25 Not lead
26 Natl. Courtesy Month
27 "As You Like It" locale
29 Theater letters
30 Prize money
31 Fancy dance movement
33 Spoke out for
35 Basically
37 Choppy
40 Create
44 Put aside
45 Samoa's official plant
47 Potbelly
48 Differently
49 Stews
51 When tourists take tours of Tours
52 Opposite of fail
53 Skier's aid
55 Sanskrit term of respect
56 Flamenco immortal Carlos
58 Office supply item
60 Houdini, e.g.
61 Mean
62 Judges, old-style
63 Passed

DOWN

1 Blots
2 Announcement for a king
3 Dress shoes
4 Cambrian lead-in
5 Some teen talk
6 Out-and-out
7 Emulate Dennis the Menace
8 Wreath adornment
9 Like helium, e.g.
10 Pond denizens
11 Loot
12 Holes in the ground
13 Overshadow
14 Took out
21 Buys out
24 Buggy, e.g.
26 Tropical tree with yellow berries
28 '30s Vice Presidential middle name
30 Part of a magician's incantation
32 Vote for
34 Kind of test
36 Top movie of 1977
37 Irate
38 Like some powder
39 Lack
41 Jumpin' joint
42 Pigged out
43 Lived
46 Without delay
49 Entrance
50 Fishing kit item
53 Drink like a fish
54 View from the Ionian Sea
57 Place for a pompom
59 Letter abbr.

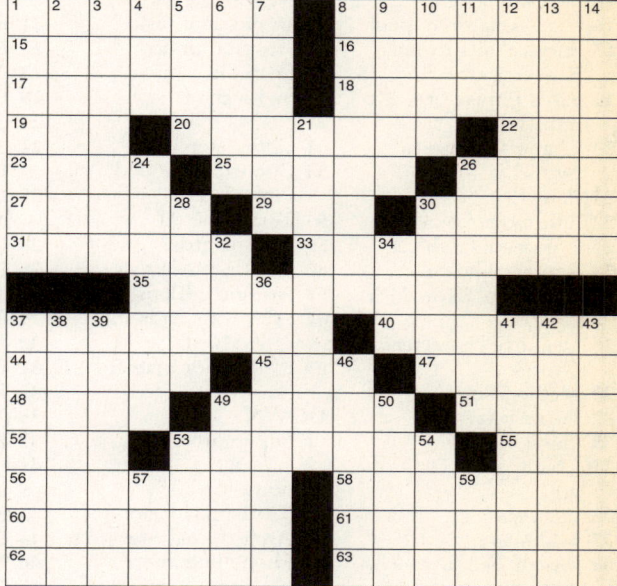

ACROSS

1 Catch-22
5 Nimble
9 Paul of "American Graffiti"
14 Where pirates moor
15 Queen of scat
16 Khomeini, for one
17 Ugandan tyrant
18 Carpenters' work?
19 Frankie or Cleo
20 "Citizen Kane" spoiler
23 First-class service
24 Diamonds, to hoods
25 Scattered
29 Oversized
31 ___ and Span (cleaner brand)
35 Poi ingredients
36 Bring in
37 Roxy Music co-founder Brian
38 "Planet of the Apes" spoiler
42 Cartoon dog
43 Provides machine maintenance
44 Venusian, for one
45 Lobster pot
47 In high spirits
48 Bells and whistles
49 Kind of shore
51 Afflict
52 "The Crying Game" spoiler
61 Salad bar implement
62 Unpleasant person
63 Roast beef request
64 Hello in Hilo
65 Concept of Descartes
66 Deck hands
67 Snappish
68 Copper
69 Vehemence

DOWN

1 Lasting impression?
2 Pitcher Hideo
3 Budget alternative
4 Kind of pool
5 Figure out
6 Give the slip
7 Whipped along
8 "Toodle-oo!"
9 Violet shade
10 Gets the lead out
11 Knights' garb
12 Actress Jeffreys
13 Bound
21 Opera villain, often
22 Autographs
25 Kick off
26 Times or Post
27 Omni or Forum
28 Donnybrook
29 In the worst way
30 Spring flower
32 Hidden rocks, to a ship
33 Microchip giant
34 Lawyer Roy and family
36 Hollywood's Kazan
39 "I read you"
40 Baseball's Wynn
41 Champion of 10/30/1974
46 Pickle
48 Choice cut
50 School assignment
51 #1 Green Mountain Boy
52 G.D.P., for one
53 Swimming
54 Hazzard County deputy
55 "War and Peace," e.g.
56 One who takes messages
57 Military parade passageway
58 Dam
59 Rug figure
60 Former House Speaker Gingrich

99   by Stephanie Spadaccini

ACROSS

1 27, to 3
5 Virgule
10 St. Nick accessory
14 The top
15 "Remember the ___!"
16 "Ars Amatoria" poet
17 Surgical site in the Beaver State?
19 Kid's phrase of request
20 Chang's Siamese twin
21 Itch
22 Full moon color
24 Commedia dell'___
25 Rapper who co-starred in "New Jack City"
26 Le Carre character George
29 Methodology
32 Estate papers
33 Gunk
34 Champagne Tony of golf
36 ___ vera
37 Middays
38 Money to tide one over

39 It's west of N.C.
40 Just
41 "What ___ I do?"
42 Nielsen stats
44 Comic Charles Nelson ___
45 Unpleasant task
46 Hospital unit
47 Declarer
50 Swiss river
51 "___ is me!"
54 Glitzy sign
55 Doc from the Old Line State?
58 Cartoonist Al
59 Chorus girls?
60 The first: Abbr.
61 Fashion's Klensch
62 1956 Four Lads hit "___ Much!"
63 It's just for openers

DOWN

1 Supergarb
2 "___ the housetop . . ." (Christmas lyric)
3 Arctic Ocean sighting
4 Phone line abbr.
5 ___-pants (wise guy)

6 Jessica of "Frances"
7 Right-hand person
8 ___-cone
9 Decorated officers
10 Driver's license in the Gem State?
11 Russian "John"
12 Engine knock
13 Actress McClurg
18 Fishing gear
23 ___ room
24 Sound system in the Keystone State?
25 Humor not for dummies
26 Quite a hit
27 Distance runner
28 Actress Massey
29 Chlorinated waters
30 1988 Olympics site
31 Inconsequential
33 Pagoda sounds
35 "Handy" man
37 Rural
41 Goddess of agriculture
43 Suffix with elephant
44 Least cooked
46 "Yippee!"
47 Suffix with utter

48 ___ piccata
49 Kin of "Uh-oh!"
50 Envelope abbr.
51 Alert
52 Leave off

53 Periphery
56 "Strange Magic" rock band
57 1988 Dennis Quaid remake

100   by Rand H. Burns

ACROSS

1 Some of the Dead Sea Scrolls
7 Guitarist Hendrix
11 Bygone cause
14 Way to Brooklyn or Broadway in song
15 Breakdowns
17 Pithy depiction
19 Garnets
20 Mystery author Lathen et al.
21 Drive away
22 Brilliant conclusion
23 Fitness guru
25 Heed
26 Create a fragrant aura
28 The end to some
29 Baseball Hall-of-Famer Combs
31 Crystal mineral
33 Miniplay
35 Bad mouths
36 Faithless
40 Kiss to 47-Down
42 Massed forces
43 Full up
46 Spirit
48 Throw off

49 Neighbor of Scorpius
50 Catch on
52 Chuck
53 Tomb articles
55 1955 Preakness and Belmont winner
57 Study
58 Apt medium for 17-Across
61 From now on
62 Remove blubber from
63 ___ judicata
64 Plant-growth retardant
65 Turned out

DOWN

1 Soprano Munsel et al.
2 Reading room
3 Girl in a Beatles song
4 Tubers
5 Thorax protector
6 Private
7 "The Travels of ___ McPheeters"
8 Nonborder regions
9 Tricky shot on baize
10 Order

11 Job's forerunner
12 Take on more fuel
13 Not at sea
16 Sandburg's "___, the Dead Speak to Us"
18 Floor
23 Round coffeecake
24 Queen, to Juan Carlos
27 Quench
30 Churchill's successor in 1945
32 Craft with delta wings
34 Bowie the commish
37 Months of dawn-to-dusk fasting
38 Miss ___
39 Far out
41 Courtesan of ancient Attica
42 Disease, in combos
43 "She-Bop" singer, 1984
44 Check in
45 Flings of a sort
47 One who avoids "sissies"?
51 Matriculate

52 Little Iodine's creator
54 Dover or Hormuz: Abbr.
56 Defunct sports grp.

59 She was Glory In "Mad Dog and Glory"
60 Bus. mogul

101 by A.J. Santora

ACROSS

1 Word with blood or touch
5 Pouch
8 Dollop
11 Fantasized
13 For
14 Bovarism
15 TV host
17 Abbr. on a grocery list
18 TV host
20 With rapid tempo
21 Golf course supply
22 Letters of invitation?
25 Network: Abbr.
26 One of the Chaplins
28 & 29 An anatomical part
31 Produce
32 TV host
36 Insubstantial
38 Women's wear daily
39 Cicero speaking site, with "the"
40 Mine-car load
42 Ending for pay
45 TV's Sharkey et al.
46 W.W. II enlistee
49 Threefold
51 TV host
54 ___ tree
56 TV host
57 Kind of Buddhism
58 Stooge name
59 Doo-wop's ___ and the Dreamers
60 Passbook abbr.
61 Junior
62 Crow's-nest site

DOWN

1 Christmas events, sometimes
2 Goads a hillbilly
3 ___ way (yield a return)
4 Staff
5 Dick's Veep
6 Like hung streamers
7 Roy of Senate hearings
8 Bust site
9 Give it ___
10 From A ___
11 Grocery section
12 ___ T
15 Honored players, for short
16 "Bugs"
19 Beastly
23 James Herriot, e.g.
24 Before beginning
27 Marino of Miami
28 Man-mouse link
30 Needle
31 Navigator's work area
32 More than snooty
33 Vivify
34 Substance's partner
35 Cortez quest
36 Man in the mil.
37 Alley ___
41 Sappho's poet friend
42 Kind of wonder
43 Lash of the West
44 Wings
46 Rodeo yell
47 Asylum seeker
48 Fifth-century date
50 Russian Johns
52 45 and 78, e.g.
53 Cranky
54 Banned gun
55 Write

102 by Harvey Estes

ACROSS

1 Insertion mark
6 Rock layers
12 Kojak portrayer
14 It frequently finds itself in hot water
16 Cracker Jack prize
17 Peter Finch movie "Raid on ___"
18 Saw
19 Chicken ___ king
21 Standing near home, maybe
22 Communion or baptism
23 SALT concern
25 China: Prefix
26 Path for Confucians
27 Language from which "sarong" comes
29 Article in Der Spiegel
30 Hollered
32 Kon-Tiki wood
34 Cool, as coffee
35 Computer unit
36 Idiot box
38 Cash reserves
42 Loan org.
43 Beatty's co-star in "Bonnie and Clyde"
45 Paul's singing partner
46 Watermelon waste
48 To ___ mildly
49 Actor John
50 Word with jack or label
52 "I ___ You Babe"
53 Prize money
54 Sugar type
56 Gym exercises
58 Enters helter-skelter
59 Works a deal on
60 Least done
61 Founded

DOWN

1 Of the heart
2 Amelia Earhart, e.g.
3 Roundup site
4 Actress Sommer
5 ___ kwon do
6 X-rated
7 Countdown beginning
8 Pro follower
9 Aids and ___
10 House cats
11 Balkan country
12 Fits' companion
13 Quarterback Ken
15 Divulge
20 Put ammo in
23 Hot-dog
24 Tended tots
27 Became hitched
28 Cooper's ___ Bumppo
31 Superman symbol
33 Grant opponent
35 Enchant like Samantha
36 Where things vanish
37 Absolutely bland
38 Group with HQ in Brussels
39 Debate stifler
40 Understood
41 Underline
42 Dowdy person
44 Guitarist Ted
47 Spoiler
49 Em and Bee
51 Schnozzola
53 Tilting-tower town
55 Mom's girl
57 Spokes' intersection

103 by Nancy Joline

ACROSS
1 Tops of wine bottles
6 Wreak havoc upon
12 Gorge
13 Undergoes again, as an experience
14 Fund-raiser
15 Requiring immediate action
16 Postprandial drinks
18 Dessert pastry
19 ___ hurrah
20 Actor Jannings
22 Chest rattle
23 Brightened
25 Burghoff role on "M*A*S*H"
27 Columbia, vis-à-vis the ocean
28 Entraps
30 Nullifies
32 Hash house sign
34 Info
35 Reduces
38 Glass ingredient
42 Tex-___ (hot cuisine)
43 DeMille films
45 Exorcist's adversary
46 Elderly
48 Angry to-do
49 Cable TV's C-___
50 Scuttlebutt
52 Take to court
55 Burst inward
57 Aficionado
58 It stretches across a tennis court
59 Bellyached
60 They may be liquid
61 Tried to catch a conger

DOWN
1 Variety of rummy
2 William Tell and others
3 Prevalent
4 Make a sweater
5 Hunting dog
6 Tyrannosaurus ___
7 Parted company with a horse
8 Good physical health
9 Nothing special
10 Calms
11 Hold in high regard
12 Stay
13 Sojourned
14 Strike alternatives
17 Muscat is its capital
21 Former capital of Nigeria
24 "___-porridge hot . . ."
26 Word before fire or transit
29 Hitchcock's "The Thirty-Nine ___"
31 Hubble, e.g.
33 Cut, as roses
35 Peanuts, e.g.
36 Frees from liability
37 Disfigure
39 Ascribed
40 Like nuts at a chocolatier's
41 French year
42 Boater's haven
44 Plodding person
47 Fellini's "La ___ Vita"
51 Cheer (for)
53 Devoid of moisture
54 The dark force
56 O.R. personnel

104 by Wayne Robert Williams

ACROSS
1 Forlorn
4 Poker actions
10 Is appropriate
14 Actress MacGraw
15 State boldly
16 British title
17 Cover
18 Animated myope
20 Type of lily
22 Neighbor of Switz.
23 Oriental tea
24 Plant with cup-shaped flowers
26 Skirt opening
27 Communists
28 Clamorous advertising
32 Part of a book
34 Down the ___
35 Word of rejection
36 Escape vehicles
37 Misprint
38 Mr. Kadiddlehopper
39 In the past
40 False temptress
41 Targets of 40-Across
42 "Ta-ta"
44 Fictional plantation
45 Gypsies
46 Cold dessert
49 One of the Borgias
52 Rimsky-Korsakov's "Le Coq ___"
53 Rival of Brown
54 Aussie hopper
57 Actor Cariou
58 First name in mysteries
59 Flair
60 Any person
61 Son of Seth
62 Small piano
63 The "o" in Cheerios

DOWN
1 Latin beat
2 1979 sci-fi hit
3 Musical instrument from Down Under
4 Collide head-on
5 Vietnamese and Nepalese, e.g.
6 Point of contention
7 Match parts
8 Afore
9 Tot toter
10 Allegiance
11 Venetian troublemaker
12 1982 Disney film
13 Work long and hard
19 Works long and hard
21 Portents
25 Pindar piece
26 Wooden shoe
28 Beast of burden
29 Uproar
30 S-shaped curve
31 Resistance units
32 Tiff
33 Okefenokee resident
34 Small combos
37 Strunk and White's "The ___ of Style"
38 Transport
40 Botanist's concern
41 West of Hollywood
43 Big quackers
44 Seat of power
46 Philosopher Kierkegaard
47 Russian writer Bonner
48 Religious principle
49 Ontario tribe
50 Merit
51 Town near Caen
52 Dream pictures artist
55 Hiatus
56 Legendary Giant

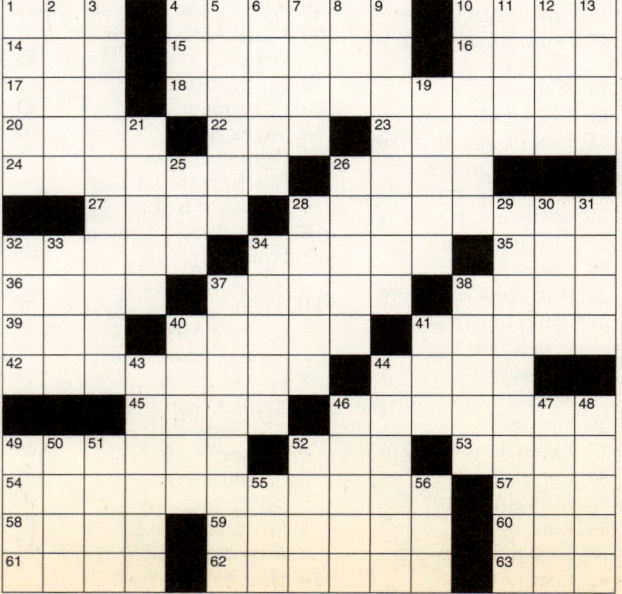

105 by Christopher Page

ACROSS

1 Prank
5 Brazilian dance
10 Trade
14 Needing irrigation
15 Actor Delon
16 "Oliver Twist has asked for ___!"
17 Marco Polo had it
19 Disconnect
20 Nautical sheet
21 Suffix
22 "Thar ___ blows!"
23 Crooked copy
25 Area for anchor cables
29 Vagrant
31 Somme's capital
33 Dubious
34 Tues. preceder
37 Dryer residue
38 Discombobulated
40 Soccer legend
41 Gave nourishment
42 Carrot, on occasion
43 Loewe collaborator
45 Of indeterminate gender
48 Liberate
49 Comes
51 Jar top
53 Like an old mattress
54 Maine's symbol
59 Rapier
60 Young genius
62 Legal writ, for short
63 Willow
64 Discontinued Dodge
65 Perceives
66 Actor George of "Cheers"
67 Board membership

DOWN

1 Scare film of '75
2 Smell ___(detect wrongdoing)
3 ___ colada
4 Christian Scientist Mary Baker ___
5 Actress Bernhardt
6 On the same side, in war
7 Manhandle
8 Twice: Lat.
9 Aardvark morsel
10 Blur
11 Awe
12 Love
13 Big bloomer
18 German industrial city
21 Too stylish, perhaps
23 Colonial flute
24 Butcher's byproducts
25 ___ nelson
26 French friend
27 Oscar Wilde lady
28 Ready-go connector
30 Gone up
32 Tartar ___
35 Mr. Cassini
36 Imperious emperor
39 Very: Fr.
40 Early start
42 Latin literary lion
44 Respected tribesman
46 Lab measurers
47 Skipped over
49 Baldwin and Guinness
50 Calcutta coin
52 Like some gases
54 Nabokov novel
55 Some ring decisions
56 Frost
57 Central Sicilian city
58 Blue-pencil
60 "Hubba-hubba!"
61 "___ as directed"

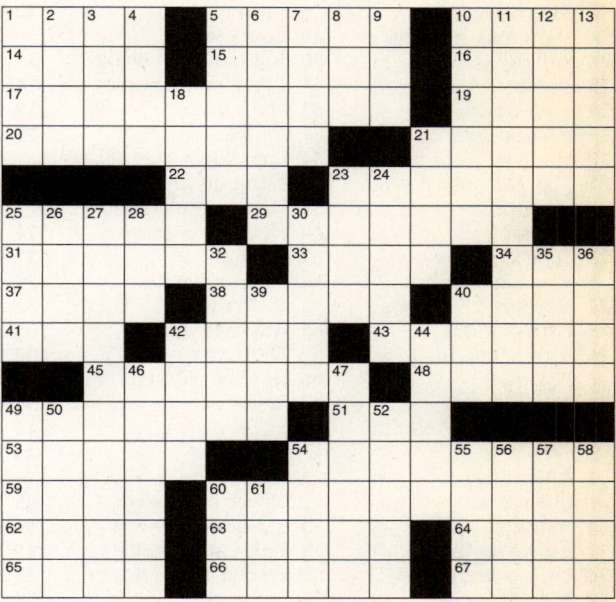

106 by Bryant White

ACROSS

1 Some microwaves
7 Bully
10 Good luck charm of the Middle Ages
14 Comeback
15 Chemistry pioneer Andrew
16 Science series since 1974
17 Wrong idea
20 Nimbi
21 Sorceress of Aeaea
22 Butterfly's sash
25 Capital of Cuba
26 Knitted shoes
28 Wires by wireless
30 Bee, in a way
31 Coalesce
32 Ticked off
33 Lakes in the distance
39 Gnaws
40 File
42 Show fear
46 Sandpiper
47 Of the skull
48 Phonograph inventor's monogram
49 Jeanne d'Arc, e.g.: Abbr.
50 Pines
51 Three-time British Open winner
53 Eyeball bender
59 Now's companion
60 Pince-___
61 Hard, dry, one-seeded fruit
62 London park
63 Baker's abbr.
64 Was impolite

DOWN

1 Sandy's remark
2 1958 song "Make ___ Miracle"
3 Azores' loc.
4 Quick bite
5 Hawaii's is 808
6 Rural steps
7 Tarot suit
8 Celebrated Bruin blueliner
9 Minute
10 Type of inspection
11 Pears, in Paris
12 Long-legged shore bird
13 Alleys have them
18 Shemp and Curly's brother
19 Part of the U.K.
22 Regalia item
23 Unadorned
24 ___ fixe
26 Enemy of Rocky and Bullwinkle
27 Rara avis
29 Officeholders
30 Positivism founder Auguste
32 Play for time
34 Singer McEntire
35 Flume
36 Shooter
37 Grigs
38 Please
41 Compass dir.
42 Mounted antlers, to some
43 Blew one's stack
44 Battering ram or catapult
45 Hodgepodge: Abbr.
46 Cowboy's home
47 Calico, e.g.
48 Chess champion of 1960
51 Effervescence
52 Part of the Dept. of Labor
54 Plus
55 Singer Sayer
56 Front end?
57 Together
58 Writer Buntline

107   by Michael S. Maurer

ACROSS

1 Laissez ___
6 Element of disguise
11 Alternative to 65-Across
13 Alternative to 31-Across
15 Rapidly
16 Irritate
17 G.I. carrier
18 Musical interval
20 Mauna ___
21 "___ conclusion . . ." (wrapping-up phrase)
23 "The G-String Murders" author
24 Approach
25 Cartridge fill
26 Alternative to 22-Down
28 Worthless
30 Come before, as the eyes
31 Alternative to 13-Across
33 Feminine ending
34 Sports period
36 Drop a line?
38 Assault
40 Alternative to 24-Down
42 Sashes
46 Eliot's miser
48 Alternative to 64-Across
49 Court seat
50 Something to shake
51 Toy manufacturer
53 Phillips 66 competitor
54 Eng. king
55 Clip out
59 Houston interstate
60 Nixon predecessor
62 Opening
64 Alternative to 48-Across
65 Alternative to 11-Across
66 Kind of clippers
67 Relies

DOWN

1 Gross
2 Never surpassed
3 ___ de France
4 Rules, informally
5 French 101 verb
6 Hit gently
7 Fix permanently
8 Model of honesty
9 Most repulsive
10 Rot
11 ___ needles
12 From Stalingrad, e.g.: Abbr.
13 Motion picture
14 Lachrymose
19 Home additions
22 Alternative to 26-Across
24 Alternative to 40-Across
26 ___-C.I.O.
27 Help for a pedestrian
29 Defendants, at law
32 Skelton character
35 Fruit beverage
37 Debussy's "La ___"
38 Elizabethan knight
39 Rings of color
41 Rubs out
43 Fortress
44 Entomophobic's fear
45 Biscuits
46 Molten matter
47 Withdraw as a judge
52 Schindler document
55 Noted presentation?
56 Loudly lament
57 Vaccine type
58 Vex
61 Stashed
63 Ala. neighbor

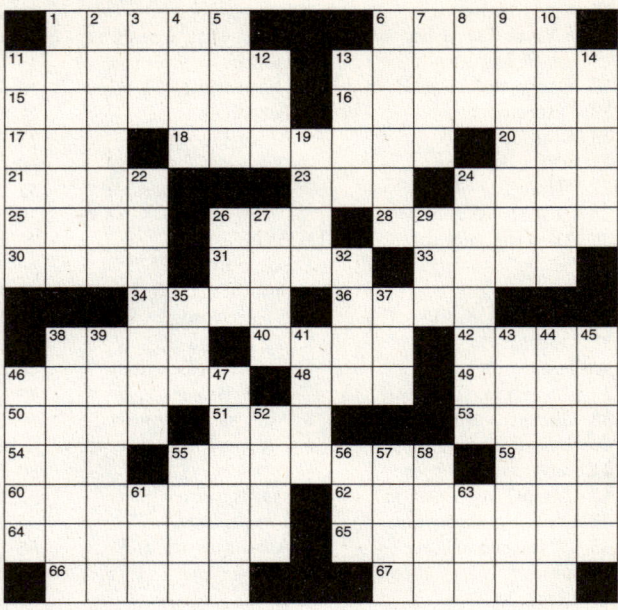

108   by Fred Piscop

ACROSS

1 Insolent talk
5 Talk, talk, talk
8 Trousers
13 On the main
14 "Famous" cookie name
16 Actress Aimée
17 Cannonball Adderley tune
20 Public madness
21 Coal bed
22 Pacific island
23 Give the nod
25 Compass doodles
27 Some boxing wins, for short
29 2 and 3, to 6
34 Mil. addresses
38 Women's links org.
40 "I see"
41 Beach Boys tune
44 Overpowering fear
45 Fed lines to, as an actor
46 Canton cookware
47 Soup cracker
49 Pat gently
51 Kind of list
53 Big toy company
58 Cole ___
62 Dinner freebie
64 1972 Derek and the Dominos hit
65 Teresa Brewer tune
68 Yoke
69 In ___ (completely)
70 Old-fashioned learning
71 Kind of test
72 Just minted
73 Snake eyes

DOWN

1 Delta preceder
2 "___ directed"
3 Seedless plants
4 Prima ___
5 Sweet potato
6 ___ Brothers ("Rag Mop" quartet)
7 Seoul's land
8 Actress Dawber
9 Once again
10 Nick and ___ Charles
11 Legendary friar
12 ___ terrier
15 Like Capone
18 American
19 Community athletic events sponsor: Abbr.
24 Squealed
26 Gulf War missile
28 Dazed and confused
30 January "warming"
31 "This can't be!"
32 Wrinkle
33 Ladies
34 Tacks on
35 Prefix with graph
36 Like Nash's lama
37 Jazz performance
39 Wildebeest
42 Blue-pencil
43 Wax-coated cheese
48 Average guy?
50 Unguent
52 TV announcer Johnny
54 Bull: Prefix
55 Heavyweight Mike
56 Top-class
57 Skates have them
58 Porn
59 Kind of moth
60 Seller's stipulation
61 Skater Katarina
63 Lo-cal
66 Middling mark
67 "Holy ___!"

by Jonathan Schmalzbach

ACROSS
1 "The Cryptogram" playwright
6 Like most workhorses
10 "___ you know!"
14 Calculating snake?
15 Hockey great Gordie
16 Shoreline recess
17 Versatile one
20 "___ my brother's keeper?"
21 Announcer's call on a pitch
22 Slot cars, e.g.
23 "A ___ 'clock scholar"
24 Comic Jacques
25 Pappy Boyington, for one
30 Food writer Rombauer et al.
31 Up ___ good
32 Topper
34 Paper quantity
35 Guitar ridges
37 ___ Marie Presley
38 Japanese honorific
39 Bellicose Olympian
40 Dumb mistake
41 Hobo
45 Geologic time divisions
46 Lie next to
47 Parasitic grub
50 Some nest eggs: Abbr.
51 Slugger's stat
54 1951 Oscar film for Bogart
57 Intl. business accord
58 Perfume
59 Deprive of courage
60 Being, to Brutus
61 Grow dim
62 Bridge positions

DOWN
1 Goya's "Naked ___"
2 First of all
3 Start of the 17th century
4 Comic strip shriek
5 Bricklayers' tools
6 Peter Pan's loss
7 Golfer's object
8 Athena's symbol
9 Gets off a Pullman
10 Locust
11 Prospector's bonanza
12 Out's partner
13 "Guarding ___" (1994 movie)
18 Discover
19 Price-earnings ___
23 Trolley
24 Harness race
25 Inflict
26 Muscat native
27 Bikini blast
28 Sèvres or Wedgwood
29 Relieved
30 4/15 inits.
33 Driveway cover
35 Best seats in the house
36 Arbitrators, for short
37 Pirate's recompense
39 Make ___ (err)
40 Curt
42 Nullify
43 Capital of Zimbabwe
44 Israel's Abba
47 Homeowner's payment: Abbr.
48 Cries of discovery
49 Secures
50 Screen symbol
51 X-ray measurements
52 ___ Generation (Kerouac et al.)
53 Hostelries
55 Wash. neighbor
56 Spenserian heroine

by Gregory E. Paul

ACROSS
1 Mideast ship
6 Garden smoother
10 Peepers
14 Siesta sound
15 Dining sites
16 Stubborn one
17 Future oak
18 Of old poetry
19 Author Harte
20 Talk, talk, talk
21 1985 Streep/Redford film
24 Overlook
26 Pass on
27 Ring figure
30 Pledge
34 Island in New York Harbor
35 Fruit container
38 Annual deposit: Abbr.
39 North Carolina college
40 Tinge
41 Trim
42 Fifty-four, to Flavius
43 Leaf aperture
44 Carbonated drinks
45 Have underlying anger
47 "La Desserte" artist
49 Caught on the ranch
52 Hawaiian tuber
53 William Bendix 50's sitcom, with "The"
57 Home loan grp.
60 Stratford's river
61 "Just this ___ . . ."
62 Deere product
64 Sighting from the crow's-nest
65 Singer Coolidge
66 Hip
67 First name on "60 Minutes"
68 College official
69 Social misfits

DOWN
1 National anthem start
2 Old Peruvian
3 "Casino Royale" song, with "The"
4 Go off course
5 Some Impressionist paintings
6 Supreme comedy
7 Combination conjunction
8 Scalpel
9 Step up
10 First stage
11 Soviet leader Andropov
12 T.V.A. output: Abbr.
13 ___ good example
22 Opponent of Kit Carson
23 Grooviest one
25 "Don't Fence ___"
27 Bobbins
28 Mayberry druggist
29 Chamber sound
31 Herman Wouk novel, with "The"
32 Divas' songs
33 Backslide
36 Butt
37 West of Hollywood
40 Ira Levin's "The ___ Wives"
41 Evian evening
43 "Buzz off!"
44 ___ convention, in bridge
46 Chic
48 Noshed
50 Cartoonist Bushmiller
51 Mandates
53 Carol syllables
54 Wall Street's Boesky
55 Adoring, with "of"
56 Mrs. Sprat's no-no
58 Grazing group
59 Greek Mars
63 Have bills

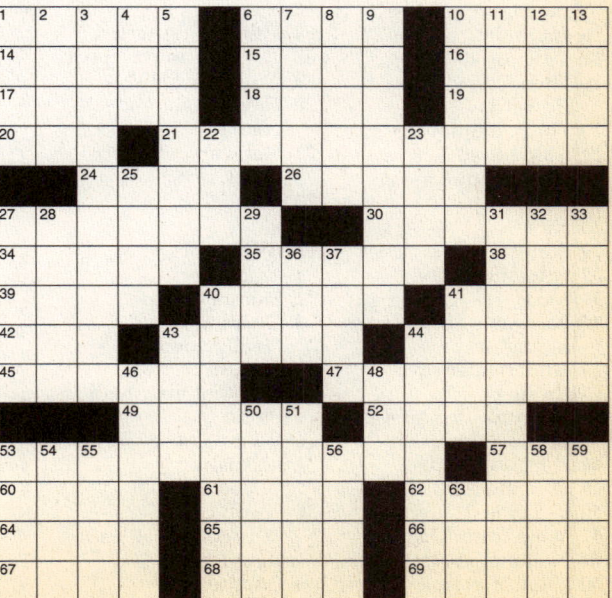

111 by Jonathan Schmalzbach

ACROSS

1 Union flouters
6 It's mined in South Australia
10 Legendary Memphis recording company
14 City near Leipzig
15 Gossiper Barrett
16 Wyoming town named for a frontiersman
17 "___ With a View"
18 Scored 100 on
19 Bailiff's cry
20 Pickup line
23 Famous twin
24 Slacker at the track
25 Name on old Asian maps
28 Pickup line
33 ___ Tuck
35 Association: Abbr.
36 Vast amount
37 "___ people go"
38 Babe in the woods
39 Sorry ones
41 Somewhat: Suffix
42 Impediment
43 This may have fallout
44 Pickup line
49 Coup ___
50 Welcome item
51 Govt. pension agcy.
54 Blanket pickup line rejection
58 Jai
61 Spoken
62 Take ___ (plop down)
63 Bath powder
64 Incense
65 Bridge, in Bologna
66 Rams' mates
67 Predicament
68 Show of derision

DOWN

1 Ghost
2 "Gigi" star
3 Song from "Call Me Mister," 1946
4 Ink smudge
5 Religious school
6 Jungle swingers
7 Somewhat, in music
8 Freshly
9 It's spotted in a garden
10 Turns inside out, so to speak
11 Mattel item
12 "Fables in Slang" author
13 ___ Affair
21 "Krazy" one
22 "___ House" (1983 hit)
26 Play staging
27 Maturation catalysts
29 Ingredient in a Western 47-Down
30 The Beatles' "Baby ___ a Rich Man"
31 Spinner in space
32 Harper's Weekly cartoonist
33 Cannes cop
34 Fix the lawn
38 Train unit
39 Hovels
40 Western Indian
42 Race track supporters
45 Legal subject
46 "Bali ___"
47 See 29-Down
48 Marvy
52 Roll right along
53 China ___
55 Misstep
56 Angelic headgear
57 "The race ___!"
58 Broke bread
59 Fortas's forte
60 Half pints, maybe

112 by Michael S. Maurer

ACROSS

1 Kind of blocker
5 Twinge
9 Big dos
14 Philosopher Hoffer
15 Award for "Curse of the Starving Class"
16 Intimidate
17 Title for 40-Across
19 "Ben Casey" star Edwards
20 Hosp. employee
21 Title for 40-Across
23 Horse command
26 Part of i.p.s.
28 Kiln
29 Sunny
32 Salutation abbr.
36 Incite
37 Saroyan's "My Name Is ___"
39 Underwater cave dweller
40 Multitalented subject of this puzzle
44 Dangerous curve
45 Emerald ___
46 ___ time
47 View from Klamath National Forest
50 Kind of permit
52 Hang
54 N.Y.C. sports venue
55 Certain training
56 Title for 40-Across
60 Third word of "America"
62 Name in puppetry
63 Title for 40-Across
68 "La vita nuova" poet
69 Gulf War V.I.P.
70 Have ___ in one's bonnet
71 Stack up
72 Quick drive
73 Borough

DOWN

1 "___ sport . . ."
2 Stub one's toe
3 Opening in "Hollywood Squares"
4 Workout aftermath
5 Blotto
6 White House nickname
7 "Good work!"
8 "I can't ___ satisfaction" (1965 song lyric)
9 Counsel
10 Keels over
11 Archaeological inscription
12 Whenever
13 Suffix with mob
18 Old Chevy
22 Symbol of magnetic field strength
23 Deceits
24 Tangle
25 Wife, in Madrid
27 Understands
30 Farm layer
31 Like St. Nick's "little mouth," in "The Night Before Christmas"
33 Recipient
34 Happens again
35 Maximally cunning
38 Take away, at law
41 Gay
42 Unspoiled
43 Traveler's stop
48 Cheerleading maneuvers
49 Conical homes
51 Backward
53 Administers medicine
56 Scotch's partner
57 Symbol of happiness
58 Skeleton part
59 Forces on horses: Abbr.
61 R.B.I., e.g.
64 Junior's junior
65 Native Nigerian
66 Put in stitches
67 List complement

113   by Michael W. Perry

ACROSS

1 Handle
9 Coach
15 "Taltos" writer
16 Page identifier
17 Screens
18 Dressy attire
19 Baseball figure
20 Egg cream additive
22 Harvey Kurtzman was its first editor
23 Nostalgic time
25 "Today" forecaster
26 Issuer of a famous report
27 Rifle strap
29 Heavenly body?
30 Some ancient mosaic designs
31 Financier's business
33 "Devices and Desires" author
35 Preserves
37 Hillary's aides
39 Power source
42 Carapace
43 "Caroline in the City" character
45 Freshen

47 Performas and PowerBooks
48 Cut up
50 Lahore's river
51 Like the mot juste
52 Cult director Abel
54 Minute
55 Scanner
57 "Married . . . With Children" co-star
59 Deep dish
60 Fiddled (with)
61 100 and 400, to a photographer
62 Gym locker items

DOWN

1 Chicago political family
2 Hot
3 London's location
4 No longer in the U.S.N.
5 Barbra's 1976 co-star
6 More subtle
7 Spotted wildcat
8 Family skeletons, e.g.
9 Following
10 Gloomy

11 ___ pop.
12 Run down
13 Puts under
14 Undergoes nivation
21 Black Michael's castle, in book and film
24 Japan and others
26 Treadwheel operator
28 Twist
30 Where the lord dwells
32 Nurse
34 "Lord ___"
36 Depths
37 Develop
38 Sizable amount of land
40 Site of a 1990 film "Bird"
41 Party animal
42 Savvy
44 Start of a segue
46 Exercises
48 Actors Bruce and Laura
49 Queen's mate
52 Network transmission

53 Singer who appeared in "The Longest Day"
56 Aberdeen's river
58 Cousin of "Yikes!"

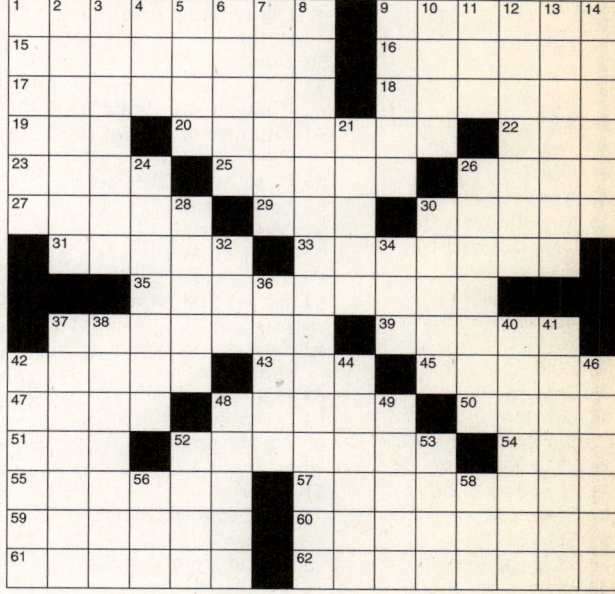

114   by Fran and Lou Sabin

ACROSS

1 Brighton pub
6 Retreat
10 Pull an all-nighter
14 Mitchell family name
15 One, to Wilhelm
16 Proctor & Gamble soap
17 Like an inner tube, geometrically
18 Catch
19 Kind of rock
20 Lo-o-o-ong efforts from a QB?
23 It must be followed
24 Hot times on the Riviera
25 It runs up trees
28 Computer adjunct
30 Jack of clubs, in cards
33 Geographical datum
35 Early baby word
36 One who's practical and tidy, they say
38 Switches receivers?
42 Tin can's target
43 60's singer Little ___
44 Memorable New York Met Tommie

45 Prospector's need
46 Pompous pronoun
50 Minerva, symbolically
51 Coin catalogue rating
52 Swamp thing
54 Navy's anti-Army strategy?
60 Betting sum
61 Suffix with switch
62 More foxy
63 Teen Beat cover subject
64 Ivy League power
65 Floor worker
66 Address with ZIP code 10001: Abbr.
67 Elder or alder
68 Pimlico garb

DOWN

1 Sen. Trent
2 Cry of excitement
3 N.F.L. co-founder Joe
4 Constellation near Perseus
5 Prepare to tie shoes
6 Envoy's assignment
7 Open to breezes
8 Peeved

9 Payback
10 Teacher's charge
11 Word with arms or foot
12 Hertz rival
13 Daft
21 Gloomy tune
22 Do one's duty
25 Became alert
26 Island NE of Maracaibo
27 He was called "El Lider"
29 Bumps
30 Polite Italian word
31 Discredited Veep
32 Fashion figure
34 Alicia of "Falcon Crest"
37 Tax-deferred plan, for short
39 Uncomplaining
40 Burnt, or practically so
41 Man's man
47 Broken, as promises
48 Parent
49 Luaus
51 Bad move
53 CCCXXVI doubled

54 Good wine quality
55 Screwball
56 ___ of the above
57 Hunter's take
58 Onion's kin
59 Misreckons
60 Hem holder

115 by David J. Kahn

ACROSS

1 Construction lifts
7 "If ___ a nickle . . ."
11 Pointed criticism
14 You can say that again!
15 Section flanked by aisles
16 Hubbub
17 Appoint
18 Spring zoo attraction
20 Tick off
21 Dearie
22 Ambles (along)
23 Magellan, e.g.
27 Crescent-shaped figure
28 Olive ___
29 Beach time in Buenos Aires
32 Retired
33 Struggle
34 O'Brien of "The Barefoot Contessa"
36 TV news time
37 Namesakes of a literary fox
39 Suffix with saw
40 Plain homes
42 Eight pts.
43 Not occurring naturally
44 ___ voce
45 Adaptable truck, for short
46 Stonewort, e.g.
47 Confederate soldier, at times?
50 Pundit
53 Where to hear "All Things Considered"
54 Number of articles in the Constitution
55 New York City opera benefactor?
57 Melon originally from Turkey
60 Tide rival
61 Noted first name in jazz
62 Like Alban Berg's music
63 Get spliced
64 ___-poly
65 Metric units

DOWN

1 Med. care provider
2 Sweep
3 World's fair pavilion
4 Famished
5 Tot's transport
6 Start of many Western place names
7 Theme of this puzzle
8 1492 Columbus discovery
9 Dow Jones fig.
10 Pool areas
11 Item in a trunk
12 Together, musically
13 Feints in boxing
19 "Air Music" composer
21 Contribute, as to an account
23 Criticize in no uncertain terms
24 Red corundums
25 Continues
26 Razzed
30 Louis XIV, to himself?
31 Wound up
35 Cheerless
37 Attorney's request
38 Critic
41 Old words from which modern words are derived
43 Half of the Odd Couple
48 Sound of passage
49 Not perfectly round
50 Fish-eating duck
51 Ginger Rogers tune "___ in the Money"
52 Not much
56 Day-___
57 Be-bopper
58 "Phooey!"
59 Capp and Capone

116 by Bryant White

ACROSS

1 Foretell
5 Recipe ingredient
14 Greedy, in Grenoble
16 Backward: Fr.
17 Carpenter's aid
18 Exiles
19 Oil containers
20 Child's measures: Abbr.
21 Do
22 Poet ___ Wheeler Wilcox
23 Dress necklines
24 Gridiron positions: Abbr.
25 Scold
26 District in Arabia
28 Rock musician ___ Vicious
30 Name in detective fiction
34 "Naked Gun" hero
35 ___ of troubles (beset on all sides)
36 Short race
41 Use cross hairs
42 1980's TV police comedy
43 Hold up
44 Postgraduate science deg.
46 Comic Gilliam and namesakes
48 "The Godfather" figure
49 "Mazel ___!"
50 Venetian blind component
51 Tropical ray
52 Fig marigolds
55 Deposit in a tomb
56 Wicked one
57 Color television inventor
58 Bowler merchants
59 Damsel

DOWN

1 Nonsense
2 Surmounted, as with gold
3 Stool pigeon
4 Swelling
5 Part of Santa's team
6 What Bush Sr. served
7 Like crocodile tears
8 Trains informally
9 Parts of joules
10 Songstress Zadora
11 Firecracker
12 Uplift
13 Half and whole, e.g.
15 Discontinued trains
23 Article of food
26 Philatelist's need
27 Climb a pole
28 Sea dog's ropes
29 "___ boy!"
31 Utah town
32 Looks
33 Skeleton's head
36 Free-swimming worms with developed sense organs
37 Some parents
39 Say again
40 Instrument panels
41 Quickly, to a grammarian
44 Line of poetry
45 Hot beverage
46 Haphazardly
47 "La Plume de Ma ___"
48 Waterway
50 Put down
51 Kid's marble
53 Early starter
54 Promgoers: Abbr

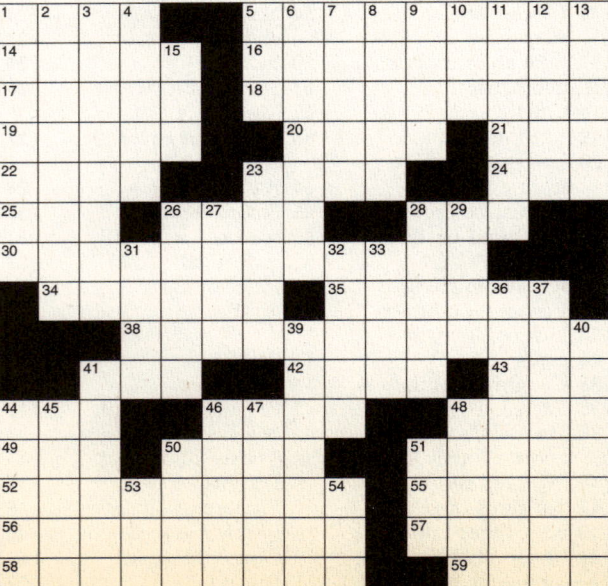

117 ACROSS

1 Paint layer
5 Best of old films
9 Plays at Pebble Beach
14 Greengrocer's pods
15 Controversial 70's sitcom
16 Lit
17 Menu appetizer
20 Titter
21 Bambi and kin
22 Hints at the pool table?
23 ___ fixe
25 Ta-ta in Turin
27 Hollywood's Barbara or Conrad
30 Menu entree
35 Lew Wallace's "Ben ___"
36 Word before mother or lively
37 1975 Clavell best seller
38 Slack-jawed
40 Hoover, e.g.
42 Clean, as a computer disk
43 Beaverlike fur
45 Collars
47 Herbal soother
48 Menu side order
50 Carrel
51 G-men
52 Mr. Carnegie
54 Mystery dog
57 Hacker, e.g.
59 Revises
63 Menu dessert
66 Lady's alternative?
67 Kind of log
68 Hammer part
69 1941 Bogart role
70 Sediment
71 Ocean flyer

DOWN

1 Egyptian church member
2 "The Grapes of Wrath" worker
3 Foot part
4 Provide lodging for
5 Vane dir.
6 Walked unevenly
7 Scruff
8 Each
9 Dentist's anesthetic
10 Risqué
11 Stead
12 Parole
13 Televisions
18 Calculator display: Abbr.
19 Crossword diagrams
24 Newt
26 Pines
27 Hallucinogenic drink
28 Bode
29 Seething
31 Toothpaste once advertised by Grace Kelly
32 Type size for fine print
33 Ponders
34 Underhanded fellow
36 View from the Quai d'Orsay
39 Introduced
41 Barbara with two sisters
44 "Straight up" singer Paula
46 Youth grp. founded in 1910
49 Classic Montaigne work of 1580
50 Dock
53 The M-G-M lion
54 Book after John
55 Lollipop was a "good" one
56 Roman get-up
58 Needle case
60 Sunny vacation spot
61 Ruler until 1917
62 Basted
64 Vein find
65 Ran into

118 ACROSS

1 Spit the kabobs
7 ___ Noël ((holiday figure)
11 Nosy Parker
12 Accommodating
14 At her small condo, actress Glenn was ___
17 "The ___ Progress"
18 1903 Nobelist
19 "Go, team!"
20 Time for les vacances
21 Mount
22 Foreign-exchange cost
23 Novelist Buntline
24 French friend's pronoun
25 Failing
27 Hot spots
29 Levels
30 In her corset, actress Beatrice was ___
34 Operetta composer
35 Kind of cake
36 Cowcatcher
38 Before time
39 Friday, e.g.: Abbr.
42 "___ may look on a king": Heywood
43 Hold forth
46 Broadway's "High ___"
47 Cal. pages
48 Kind of bar
49 V sign
51 The holiday gathering at actress Betty's was ___
54 Bolt down
55 Click beetles
56 Retreats
57 Watch mechanism

DOWN

1 Natural
2 Chaffed
3 Axis end
4 Army addresses
5 Guitarist ___ Paul
6 Making a stand?
7 Scotland yards?
8 Republic since 1948
9 Unloyal sort
10 Make it keep going, and going, and . . .
11 Lorelei
12 Unvarnished
13 Finished second
15 Canadian prov.
16 Brake equipment
21 Recital works
22 Put on ___
24 Miss America prop
26 Clean
27 Deadly reptile
28 Skittish
30 Dugongs
31 Drubbed
32 Did not move decisively
33 Wash
34 Source of fine fleece
37 Gin hounds
39 Bee's target
40 Tyke's four-wheeler
41 Lock
44 Ethnic group
45 "___ du lieber!"
48 Knock for a loop
49 Rel. of college boards
50 Cigar's end
52 Italian ___
53 Réunion, e.g.

ACROSS

1 Juice obstruction
12 Calligraphy
14 Adds picturesque details (to)
16 Canaanite people
17 Lower part of the pistil
18 Dive
19 Belittle, in slang
22 Indy winner Luyendyk
23 Sidelong look
24 Encroaches
26 TV luminary and namesakes
28 Swinging star
32 Some bank offerings
33 Blood derivatives
34 Soil combiner
38 Rent-___
39 Middle grade
40 Inguinal parts
42 Morrison and Tennille
44 Vixen's mate
45 Had a big mouth
49 Mouth waterer
50 Unsanctioned class communicators

DOWN

1 Kind of ring
2 Giraudoux play
3 Storm from the Pacific
4 "Oklahoma!" aunt
5 Classic cars
6 Wall St. initials
7 Actress Hagen
8 ___ Aviv
9 With a bow, musically
10 John, at the Vatican
11 Swells
12 Wild
13 Bloody to the max
14 Fall behind
15 Baker's offerings
19 Epidemiologist's concern
20 "That is to say . . ."
21 Yards
25 Passbook abbr.
26 Archeological find
27 Kind of layer
28 Phrase after "Cheese it!"
29 Dracula, e.g.
30 Texas town
31 Dear one
33 Boaters
34 Good for growing
35 Approach
36 Puerto ___ (Caribbean natives)
37 Erect
40 Golfer Norman and others
41 S.A.T. takers
43 Skirt feature
44 ___ ed.
46 First lady
47 Fish lightly
48 La-la lead-in

ACROSS

1 Day in Hollywood
6 Like a V.P.
10 Hula hoops, mood rings, etc.
14 Live
15 Talk drunkenly
16 Revise
17 Like Macaulay Culkin, in a 1990 movie
19 Mr. Mostel
20 Diner signs
21 The Boston ___
23 Sense of self
24 ___ Moines
26 One of the Greats
28 Loathed
33 Zilch
34 Egyptian deity
35 Jeanne d'Arc and others: Abbr.
37 Asp
41 Straddler's spot
44 Ordinary talk
45 Roman "fiddler"
46 Composer Thomas
47 Western Indian
49 Hair curls
51 Cheerleader's prop
54 Kind of nut or brain
55 Live
56 Verne captain
59 Cut in a hurry
63 Poses
65 Intersection concern
68 Mound
69 Tickled-pink feeling
70 Declaim
71 Confederate
72 Paradise
73 Big books

DOWN

1 N.J. neighbor
2 Plow pullers
3 Abundant
4 Ratio words
5 Bleachers
6 Mary Kay of cosmetics
7 Hog filler?
8 Certain wrestler
9 Boring tool
10 Turk topper
11 Run like ___
12 Somber tune
13 Remained firm
18 Trypanosome carrier
22 Divide the pie
25 ___ fire (ignite)
27 Certain wallpaper design
28 Dewy
29 Eastern V.I.P.
30 Fuss
31 Finishes
32 Postpone
36 Not a one-panel cartoon
38 Yawn inducer
39 Go into hysterics
40 Soft drinks
42 Pretend
43 "I'm telling the truth!"
48 Appear
50 Awkward bloke
51 Bygone title
52 Bay window
53 Kind of detector
57 Fine, temperaturewise
58 Convex/concave molding
60 Dated hairdo
61 Did laps in the pool
62 Abhor
64 Mata Hari, e.g.
66 Hatcher
67 Favorable vote

121

ACROSS

1 "60 Minutes" producer Hewitt
4 Press on
9 Invitation replies
14 Bachelor's last words
15 "___ circumstances beyond . . ."
16 Before-dinner tidbit
17 Really calm
20 Cube inventor Rubik
21 1987 film flop
22 Mach topper
23 Govt. permit
25 Sargasso, e.g.
27 Really tidy
36 Breakfast fish
37 Santa ___, Calif.
38 Card with a message
39 Baseball tags
41 Summon
43 "Star Trek" crewman
44 Bridgestone products
46 Auguries
48 Yore
49 Really fit
52 Calendar abbr.
53 Dancer Charisse
54 Pixie
57 One who leads the way
61 Something to think about
65 Really gone
68 Spoken language
69 Big-city newspaper heading
70 Fury
71 Floozies
72 Ordinary lines
73 Census datum

DOWN

1 Rearview mirror decoration
2 Redolence
3 When shadows shorten
4 Actress Lupino
5 Soirée entertainment
6 They're often split
7 Put art on glass
8 Palooka
9 Tag line?
10 Slippery ___
11 Household rivals
12 Nights, in classifieds
13 Spanish muralist
18 1970 Kinks hit
19 1987 Wimbledon winner
24 Back of the bus.?
26 Gray and others
27 Priesthood, metaphorically, with "the"
28 DeVito's "Taxi" role
29 Hollywood walk-on
30 "Stompin' at the ___"
31 Perfume
32 Rouses
33 More faithful
34 Lounges
35 Piano practice
40 Ending for him or her
42 Lawmakers
45 Baby rivers
47 Lacking
50 Notorious Alger
51 Asgard chief
54 Rework, as a story
55 Swan's partner, in myth
56 Equitable
58 With with boot or summer
59 Silesian river
60 ___-Rooter
62 Orator's perch
63 Dublin's land
64 "Roots" writer Haley
66 E, in Morse code
67 Agile deer

122

ACROSS

1 Smashing pumpkins' sounds
7 Silent signals
15 Muse of astronomy
16 Ecuadorean volcano
17 Lyrical poem
18 Saskatchewan city
19 At any time
20 Betel palms
22 Stood
23 Web
24 Unexpected victory
29 Breathing
31 Ecdysiast
32 Public relations matter
35 Devotees: Suffix
37 Royal residence of old Ireland
38 Loser to 4-Down in 1992 and 25-Down in 1994
41 Fireplace fuel
42 ___ Xiaoping
43 Cash in hand, e.g.
44 Burdens
46 Tragedy
48 Or, in a musical score
49 Crimebuster
50 Actress Rogers
54 Erotic
56 Stick with a stick
57 Wavering
61 Zimbabwe's capital
63 Thinner than thin
64 Spouts speeches
65 Russian for "comrade"
66 Most prudent

DOWN

1 More likely
2 Brigham Young University site
3 Country ways
4 1992 Wimbledon winner
5 Deuce
6 Sandwich meat
7 Last words at Wimbledon
8 "___ Arden"
9 Greek portico
10 Kleenex, e.g.
11 Function
12 English rule in India
13 Alfonso's queen
14 Spotted
21 Come back to life
25 1993 and 1994 Wimbledon winner
26 Some Eastern Europeans
27 Gooseflesh-making
28 Pamphlet
30 Sportscaster Berman
31 "___ Love You"
32 White house
33 Indian time periods
34 Hundred-eyed creature of myth
36 Persistence of memory
39 Age proof
40 Spade or Malone
45 Spring time
47 Regardless
49 Of RNA
51 Really miffed
52 "O tempora! O ___!"
53 That is to say
55 Checker, maybe
57 Boater or bowler
58 Brian, formerly of Roxy Music
59 From Stalingrad, e.g.: Abbr.
60 Writer Levin
62 Hebrew name meaning "lion"

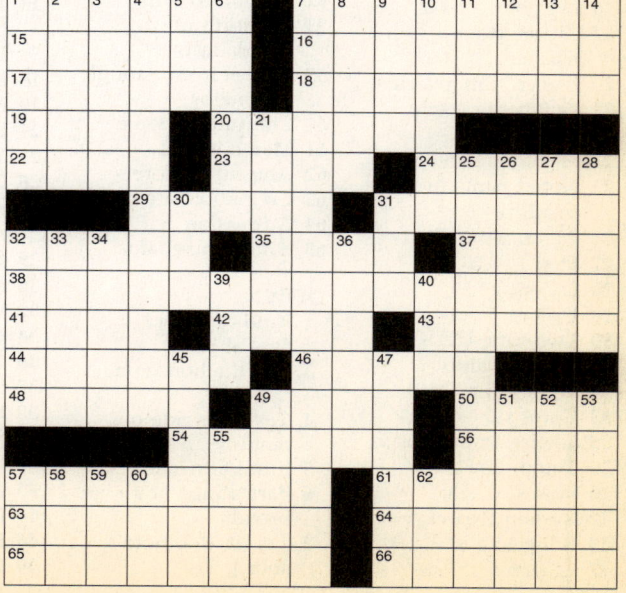

123   by Rich Norris

ACROSS

1 Architectural spaces
5 Skill
8 Computer language
14 Result of a bite, maybe
15 Compete
16 Profane
17 Line
19 Not as fresh
20 Ready
22 First name in sopranos
23 See 18-Down
24 Covet
25 Corrodes, with "away"
26 Devilkin
28 Shipwreck site
29 Helper: Abbr.
30 Southfork locale
34 Act like a baby
36 Light song
38 Shopping aid
42 Pushers' chasers
44 Clad like Claudius
45 Raised
48 Football Hall-of-Famer Graham

50 This yr.'s grads
51 Vocalist Horne
52 Carol
53 Bar abbr.
55 Oriental servant
56 Gardener's forte
60 Pax
62 Delegated, as powers
63 Equalizer
64 Alfonso's queen
65 Ending with insist or persist
66 Infrequently
67 Maritime
68 Title

DOWN

1 Lively, to Liszt
2 "Blame ___ Rio" (1984 film)
3 Fait ___
4 Oscar-nominated western of 1953
5 Hertz rival
6 Mob member
7 Cut for a mortise
8 Show timidity
9 Worker ___
10 "Hurry up!"

11 Butterfly genus
12 All-points bulletins
13 Orpheus, musically
18 With 23-Across, popular cuisine
21 Three-time Wimbledon champ
26 Rhoda's TV mom
27 Vitiate
31 Help out
32 ___ loss
33 Achieve by force
35 Siouan Indian
37 Thespian
39 Old-fashioned petticoat
40 ___ Lingus
41 Merchandise: Abbr.
43 Works the waterfront
45 Plays at high volume
46 Distance
47 Cloisonné requirement
49 Liquid fat
53 It's two before iota
54 Trace
57 University sports org.
58 Defense mechanism?

59 Ran
61 Recent beginning

124   by Matt Gaffney

ACROSS

1 Uncleaned
6 Street pavement sign
9 Biscayne Bay site
14 Poe poem "For ___"
15 Whole bunch
16 Li'l one
17 Choice from a masher
20 French film award
21 University motto word
22 "I can't believe it!"
23 Noted name in retailing
25 Advertising pitch
27 Step
28 O.J. judge
29 Up
30 Two-time U.S. Open tennis champ
31 Froot Loops bird
33 Corot subject
35 Choice from Elvis
39 Tough one
40 Powwow site
42 Certain Peruvian
45 Bring to a boil
47 ___-haw

48 Model from Mogadishu
49 Hum soothingly
50 Trader's shout
51 "___ sure!" (Valley girl comment)
52 Is afflicted with
53 It's north of Bangladesh
55 Choice from a tough negotiator
60 Computer people
61 Memo letters
62 Ancient explorers
63 Cremation sites
64 Admission ___
65 Southern Senator

DOWN

1 Kind of school
2 One abroad
3 Left the house on tiptoe
4 Cavaliers ride on them
5 Rural affirmatives
6 Bart, Ringo and Brenda
7 ___ cit. (footnote abbr.)

8 Bon mot
9 Pop singer Richard
10 Big Blue
11 20 Questions category
12 Hazard
13 Three empresses of the Eastern Roman Empire
18 Barrio residents
19 Not safe
23 Dog command
24 Yours, in Paris
26 Choice from a cross-examiner
27 Annoyance
29 Blabbered
30 Show contempt
32 Washington channel
34 Concentrated
36 Loses effectiveness
37 Some collectibles
38 Director's unit
41 Sushi choice
42 Hoist
43 Agreeable remark
44 Chit
46 Last line of defense
49 Fiddle's partner

50 Enjoy
52 Defendant of 1949
54 Belted one out
56 Before
57 Catcher's spot

58 Belief
59 Pro ___

125 by Raymond Hamel

ACROSS

1 Subdue
10 Electric flux symbols
14 New York City's ___ Park
15 Baseball's 1980 Player of the Year
16 Like some bratwursts
17 Keats narrative poem
18 Made bubbly
19 Kind of power
21 Radioactive
22 Long opening?
23 Geometric sign-off
24 Muskeg
25 Part of H.R.H.
26 Unattired
27 Gerry Adams's org.
28 Pub decoration
31 Alcoholic beverages
32 Actor Pendleton
33 Blubbered
34 Blubbering
35 Cracker topping
36 Notable time
37 Squander
38 Feeling no pain
39 Outback runner
40 ___ law (1827 discovery)
41 Golf target
42 Pop quartet ___ Tuesday
43 Potential pike
44 Cambridge campus
45 "Exodus" hero
48 Item of court attire
50 Native
52 Decorative garment fastener
53 Weave together
55 Agile swimmer
56 Zend-Avesta name
57 Youth
58 "The Sound of Music" song

DOWN

1 Daughter-in-law of Naomi
2 Winged insectivore
3 Turn outward
4 Midianite leader of the Old Testament
5 Collagen, e.g.
6 Wickerwork branches
7 "A Woman of No Importance" writer
8 City southeast of Amsterdam
9 Noted march site
10 Ask
11 Tournament game
12 Travel a regular circuit, as a judge
13 Was in a rut
15 Skater's equipment
20 Victoria's Secret purchase
25 Chart topper
26 ___-foot oil
28 Place to get good strokes
29 Discontinue
30 Doorman's ornament
31 Spellbind
34 Truckee River outlet
35 "Great Expectations" boy
37 Serf
38 Beat in a duel
41 Ether in eucalyptus oil
44 Downing Street distance
45 Valued violin
46 Fixes potatoes, maybe
47 Cupcake toppers
49 Solar disk
51 Different
54 Agree, visibly

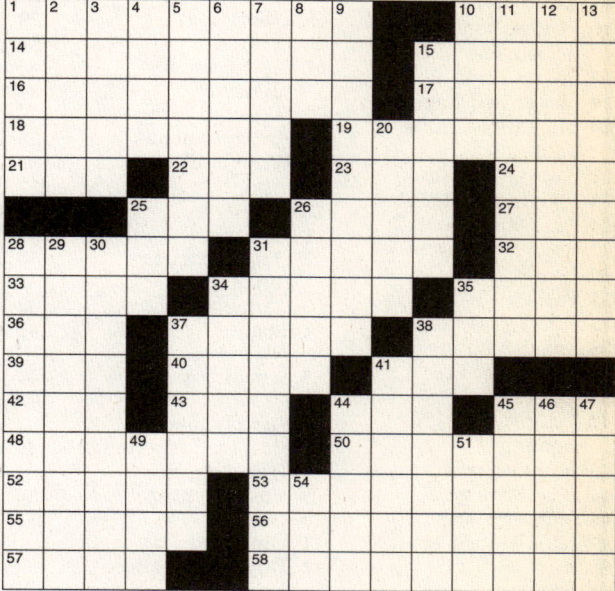

126 by Stanley B. Whitten

ACROSS

1 Dock
5 Sandwich stores
10 Extend over
14 Not at work
15 Texas shrine
16 Big Apple university
17 1944 Crosby/Fitzgerald film
19 Simians
20 Election selections
21 Most bright
23 Iowa college town
25 "___ the ramparts . . ."
26 Toy store ___ Schwarz
29 Treated badly
33 Scottish headwear
36 Chef's protector
38 Wallet items
39 French novelist André
40 1995 Cage/Shue film
43 Yemen's capital
44 Trot or canter, e.g.
45 The end
46 Heart readout, for short
47 Tourney
49 ___ judicata
50 Car m.p.g. raters
52 Mid-sixth-century date
54 Like an Acura or Toyota
59 Response
63 God of war
64 1978 Fonda/Voight film
66 Hive denizens
67 Lift
68 "Ars Amatoria" poet
69 50% off event
70 Four Holy Roman Emperors
71 Mr. T's family name

DOWN

1 Sty residents
2 Matinee hero
3 Lamb's pen name
4 Oscar de la ___
5 One "in distress"
6 Tarzan portrayer
7 Statutes
8 Mosque priest
9 Type of bean
10 Outpouring
11 One who looks powerful but isn't
12 Part of a dead man's hand
13 Home built in the spring
18 May-June sign
22 Reel's companion
24 Motto
26 Incorrect
27 Vertically, in nautical talk
28 Drink garnish
30 Dark
31 In a chair
32 Double curve
34 Proverb
35 Flat-topped hills
37 Eggs
39 Treasure
41 Vietnam's ___ Dinh Diem
42 November activity
47 Juice container
48 Leans
51 Old hat
53 "___ an arrow . . ."
54 Certain punches
55 Vicinity
56 Reverberate
57 Chimney dirt
58 Give off
60 Made by hand, as a rug
61 Kuwaiti leader
62 Change the decorations
65 Prefix with bar or butane

ACROSS

1 Islamic leader
5 Madrid museum
10 "___ reminds me . . ."
14 Chess finale
15 Eagle's claw
16 Half nelson or full nelson, e.g.
17 Set up camp
19 Singer Redding
20 Biographee ___ B. Toklas
21 Grew suddenly
23 Like terra-cotta tiles
26 "___ Miss Brooks"
27 Boy
30 Uno + due
31 Parties
33 R-rated, as humor
35 Spanish airline
38 Composer Erik
39 Curse
42 Peninsula in 1967 fighting
43 Impolite criticisms
44 Like Scrooge
46 Stubborn one
47 Hula-Hoops, once
50 Jiffy
51 Rooster's partner
53 Chinese Water Torture Cell inventor
56 Beginning
59 Venom, for one
60 ___ d'oeuvres
62 Lose on purpose
65 Whetstone
66 Eat into
67 ___-Tass news agency
68 "Bonanza" role
69 Ancient letters
70 Wriggly fish

DOWN

1 Collision
2 Handy postal container
3 Garments
4 Goal of a Muslim pilgrimage
5 School org.
6 Fink (on)
7 Pub potables
8 Hawaiian entertainer
9 Traveling, as a musical group
10 Ten C-notes
11 Ministove
12 Three-time Frazier foe
13 Six-pointers, for short
18 Skirt's bottom
22 Melancholy
24 "What's the big ___?"
25 Toes' woes
28 Landed
29 H.S.T.'s successor
32 Loudonville, N.Y., college
34 Contemptuous comments
35 Where Tabriz is
36 Dilapidation
37 Gorillalike
39 1976 bestseller "The ___ Report"
40 Mythical beasts
41 ___ facto
42 Draft org.
45 Prefix with day or year
47 Obsess (on)
48 Twenty Questions category
49 Greasy spoons
52 India's first P.M.
54 Actress Hagen
55 In song, one that needs to "git along"
57 "A thousand and one ___"
58 Jeff Bridges film of 1982
60 1968 election monogram
61 Tic-tac-toe win
63 "___ to a Nightingale"
64 Jazzman Montgomery

ACROSS

1 The Crimson Tide
5 Trucker's concern
9 Benchwarmer
14 Bulldogs
15 Tra trailer
16 Bel ___ cheese
17 Stadium walkway
18 Awestruck
19 Key
20 "My joy" and "my delight," in an old song
23 Ill-humored
24 ___ effect (electrical phenomenon)
28 Sloppy digs
29 "It's freezing!"
31 Basketball's Thurmond
32 Star
35 Summer tops
37 Abu Dhabi's federation: Abbr.
38 Microscope slide subjects
40 "___ real!"
41 Haunted house hazards
43 Looks from Groucho
45 Radius's partner
46 Oz. and lb.
47 Accepted greedily, with "up"
48 Rob or Laura of "The Dick Van Dyke Show"
50 Ultimatum words
53 Symbol of dependency
57 What people in a line may be doing
60 Kind of value
61 Clanton gang foe
62 Par ___
63 ___-Tass news agency
64 ___-Ball (arcade game)
65 Woman of letters
66 Conservative
67 Henri's head

DOWN

1 It may go with the floe
2 Auto accessory
3 Dupe
4 Malign
5 Like some eyes
6 Score in this puzzle's theme
7 Cream ingredient
8 Frenzy
9 Did moles' work
10 Famed couturier
11 Fam. member
12 Take habitually
13 "You ___!"
21 O.K.
22 Vice follower
25 NCO's nickname
26 Web-footed mammal
27 Fits together
29 Rathskeller offerings
30 Confederates
32 Class clown
33 Hall-of-Famer Combs
34 Wasn't upright
35 Binge
36 ___-skelter
39 Tractor attachment
42 Nonpareil
44 Most slippery
47 Main road
49 Old toothpaste brand
50 Boxer De La Hoya
51 Moccasin, e.g.
52 Heron
54 "Wanna make something ___?"
55 Brussels-based org.
56 Germany's Graf von ___
57 Cleveland hoopster, for short
58 Lab eggs
59 "House of Incest" novelist

129 by A.D. Cover

ACROSS

1 Cola container
8 Stuck together
15 Ancient capital of Israel
16 Need to have it all
17 Rock group with the hit "Shake It Up"
18 Key
19 TV news director Roger
20 Cower
22 Nos. in a travel guide
23 Cads
24 Caviar
27 Pose
28 Living daylights
29 Obliged
31 "Great weeds do grow ___": "Richard III"
32 Stone roller
33 TV series whose title is this puzzle's theme
36 Rain protectors, in London
37 French cheeses
38 Military assignments
39 King and others
40 The Financial Times abbr.
43 Close (in)
44 Situation
45 Beget
46 Place of disgrace
48 And, to Caesar
49 Electric cell component
52 Lock up
54 Purify
55 Knock out of position
56 Windlass
57 Navigated

DOWN

1 MTV favorites
2 Where Papeete is
3 Breakfast choice
4 Dueling distance
5 Tomorrow, to Tacitus
6 Intake intake
7 Early development
8 Herbal tea: Var.
9 Potters' chambers
10 Depend
11 Art Deco designer
12 Title city in a Fred Astaire hit
13 Coin of Old France
14 Françoise Sagan's "___ bleus à l'âme"
21 Takes after
23 Makes well
24 Bombed area in W.W. II
25 Load
26 Hands of Time, for short
28 Shadows
29 Computer capacity
30 Unfolds, in poetry
31 Eastern prince
32 Chapel name
33 Bering Sea sighting
34 Homecoming visitor
35 Spiders
36 Thin soup
39 Smarts
40 Kind of cabinet
41 Cut short
42 Transferred, as property
44 "El Capitan" composer
45 Operagoer's wear
46 Tenets
47 Suggest
48 Church area
49 New Deal prog.
50 Cookbook phrase
51 Bankbook abbr.
53 NASA recruiting site

130 by Frank Longo

ACROSS

1 Raises
7 Coal-mining waste
11 Interruption
14 Cores
15 Grand Prix, for instance
17 One of the lanthanides
18 Accumulates
19 What's NEW?
21 Hugs, symbolically
22 Spanish dramatist ___ de Vega
23 What's KNEW?
30 Fragrant resin
31 Member of the flock
32 Spill the beans
36 What's GNU?
40 Opposite of bless
41 River to the Mississippi
42 Provincial pronoun
43 What's NU?
46 Athens's home
49 Suffix with libel
50 What's NOUS?
56 "A Raisin in the Sun" writer Hansberry
57 Quiver contents
60 Support
61 Where to get fast service?
62 Derek and Diddley
63 Honky-___
64 Ancient Qumran inhabitant

DOWN

1 Abbr. at the bottom of a letter
2 Curse the day
3 Brown shade
4 Illegal block
5 German
6 Violent Saharan wind
7 Pane's place
8 Pear-shaped instrument
9 Fermi's fascination
10 How horror scenes are often depicted
11 Refuel
12 Intense
13 "___ Le Moko" (1937 Duvivier drama)
16 Slots site
20 Water tester
23 Intellect
24 ___ Romeo
25 Skin: Suffix
26 "___ love!"
27 Gettysburg victor
28 Have the rights to
29 No longer active: Abbr.
32 Stain
33 Ill-mannered one
34 Basilica section
35 Cold one
37 Opposite of dep.
38 Obit word
39 Trash bins, graffiti, etc.
43 Track speedster
44 Chinese diplomat Wellington ___
45 Crescent-shaped
46 Down East college town
47 Zebra groups
48 Pertaining to
50 Bungle
51 Seat of Hawaii County
52 Nabokov novel
53 Stench
54 Tomb items
55 Not a lick
58 Carry the day
59 Wind dir.

131 by Martin Ashwood-Smith

ACROSS

1 Historic introduction?
4 Clamorous
9 Gothic architectural feature
14 Grp. overseeing early reactors
15 Slowly
16 Auriculate
17 Start of an Erma Bombeck quip
19 "___ Honey Are You?" (Fats Waller hit)
20 Dey TV series
21 Kind of wheels
23 He's a real doll
24 Rapper?
26 Terrorize
28 Quip, part 2
32 Dieter's no-no
35 ___ operas (Gilbert and Sullivan works)
36 ___ Jima
37 Quip, part 3
40 First mate?
41 Rib-ticklers
44 Set straight
47 Quip, part 4
50 Actress Donohoe
51 Sticking point?
55 Ax
57 Crack or jack follower
58 Twilled fabric
59 Stomach ___
61 End of the quip
65 The merry widow in "The Merry Widow"
66 "Aha!"
67 London Zoo feature?
68 'Mid
69 Trades
70 GQ staff, e.g.

DOWN

1 Barn items
2 Summation
3 Dangerous bacteria
4 Female member of the bar?
5 Churchill's "so few": Abbr.
6 Famous Bruin
7 Gone by
8 The Desert Fox
9 Baubles
10 Word to a doctor
11 Covered costs
12 ___-majesté
13 Paradise lost
18 Corday's victim, 1793
22 "___ luck?"
25 Astronauts' ade
26 Arrestee's rights, familiarly
27 Half a dance
29 Debussy subject
30 Gad about
31 Got a load of
32 Suva is its capital
33 Takes one's breath away
34 Longtime NBC Symphony conductor
38 Flight formation
39 Long spar
42 The piper's son
43 Rebukes sharply
45 Four o'clock services
46 Lawn tool
48 ___-Cat
49 Luggage necessities
52 Nibble
53 Encouraged, with "on"
54 Saxophonist's supply
55 Ones going through a stage?
56 Have ___ (flip out)
60 Fort ___, N.J.
62 Fiddle stick
63 LAX info
64 Kind of treatment

132 by Ed Pegg, Jr.

ACROSS

1 Kind of wrench
7 Venomous, as a snake
13 Do well
14 Not real
16 Reducer
17 Eavesdropped
19 With 49-Across, underlying theme of 24-Down
1 Prefix with stasis
"___ only"
Appropriate, in a way
hool subj.
of fame
-cured cheeses
keptic
hested
e worst
nces
ns
Inc.
-Down

40 Undermine
41 Vituperates
43 Gift ___
47 Site of temptation
49 See 19-Across
52 Nice work if you can get it
54 James Russell Lowell, for one
55 Freshens, in a way
56 Bow out
57 Illegal race track workers
58 Secret fraternity

DOWN

1 Put on
2 "Goody"
3 Desire
4 Wind-up toys?
5 Incessantly
6 Arctic ___
7 Very much
8 Climb
9 Wallop
10 Some investors' income: Abbr.
11 Pipe part
12 Truthful qualities
15 Actress Laurie of "Roseanne"
18 Parts of meeting rooms
20 Hairy-chested
24 Theme of this puzzle, with "The"
26 The believer
27 Spanish stew
29 Object of March celebrations
30 Made more precipitous
31 "Double Indemnity" novelist
32 Phlebotomy target
33 Defensive ditches
34 Land of peace and simplicity
35 Heaven
37 Relevance
39 Bothersome bedmate
42 Critical
43 Fieri facias and others
44 Statistical bit
45 It's put away for winter
46 Mourning sites
48 Student of Seneca
50 Give a wave?
51 Essay's basis
53 Kind of gun

ACROSS

1 Rolling stone's deficiency
5 Anchor position
10 Complain
14 Aleutian island
15 ___ Loa
16 Literally "high wood"
17 Obstinate
20 Royal spouses
21 Be on the brink
22 Professional bean counters
23 Designer Christian
24 Hardy's pal
27 Describe
28 Org. founded in 1948
31 Bandleader Shaw
32 Imparted
33 Sondheim's "___ the Woods"
34 Elusive
37 Branch Davidians, e.g.
38 Speaker's platform
39 Worker's wish
40 Off ___ tangent
41 Curb, with "in"
42 Daredevil acts
43 Actor Sean
44 Lady in an apron
45 "Yessir," e.g.
48 Moon of Jupiter
52 In the altogether
54 Final notice
55 Teach one-on-one
56 Lion's den
57 Like 52-Across
58 Atlanta university
59 Thompson of "Howards End"

DOWN

1 Opposite of fem.
2 Mr. Preminger
3 Daze
4 Like the 2 in B$_2$
5 Not knowing right from wrong
6 Small pies
7 Hosiery snags
8 Actress Claire
9 Diversions
10 Future star
11 Border on
12 Actor's part
13 Look with squinty eyes
18 Sheepish lass
19 A long time
23 Prima donnas
24 Rope a dogie
25 Senator Specter
26 City east of Syracuse
27 Store up
28 ___ a million
29 Alamogordo event, 7/16/45
30 Shoe bottoms
32 Rye or corn
33 Silent, or almost so
35 Toothless
36 With pretentiousness
41 Tear
42 $200,000, for Clinton, once
43 Pro golfer Calvin
44 TV's "___ Dad"
45 Presently
46 "Elephant Boy" star, 1937
47 Have brake problems
48 Roman statesman and censor
49 Thailand, once
50 Adjust the sails
51 Polish border river
53 Add

---

134 | by Cathy Millhauser

ACROSS

1 Slates
6 Provinces
11 Part of a footnote abbr.
14 Way of speaking
15 Slacken
16 Paul's "Exodus" role
17 Kind of scout
18 River to the Missouri
19 Charles S. Dutton sitcom
20 Performed a Herculean feat #1
23 Fray
25 Preliminary figure: Abbr.
26 "A Letter for ___" (1945 movie)
27 Manipulate
28 Crony
30 Uncle Sam poster words
31 Performed a Herculean feat #2
36 Île-de-France river
37 Tart apples, informally
38 Performed a Herculean feat #3
44 ___ Bornes (classic card game)
45 "Hey, you!"
46 Bravo, e.g.
47 Heraldic band
48 Treaty org. since 1948
50 Painter Hooper
53 Performed a Herculean feat #4
56 List ender
57 Bad, bad Brown of song
58 Appoggiaturas
61 Hilo souvenir
62 Honeymoon follower
63 Pauperized
64 Fast wings, for short
65 Save up
66 Attach an ell

DOWN

1 Become prone
2 TV's Mrs. Morgenstern
3 Aimed
4 Rental sign
5 Suggest, with "of"
6 Baseball's Moises
7 Change "potatoe" to "potato," e.g.
8 Our 50, to Francois
9 Zero
10 Admiral sunk with the Scharnhorst
11 Truck: lorry:: trailer: ___
12 Type of board
13 Summons
21 Unseat
22 ". . . consider her ways, and ___": Proverbs
23 Baby bloomer?
24 "Do ___ say!"
29 Made fun of, in a way
30 Yen
32 Column bases, in architecture
33 Nature outing
34 Mischief-makers
35 More substantial
38 1979 World Series champs
39 Backdoor
40 Results
41 Precision-made
42 Tell the world
43 Staff
44 Mushrooms
48 Concert site
49 Skylit courts
51 Former Cabinet Secretary Shalala
52 Wined and dined, perhaps
54 Wagner heroine
55 Regards
59 Tokyo, once
60 Dict. listing

135   by Bob Lubbers

ACROSS

1 Monopoly purchase
6 ___ of office
10 Singing Beatle
14 Maytag rival
15 German numeral
16 Shade of red
17 Kind of dressing
18 Boccaccio work, with "The"
20 Actress Swenson
21 GLASGOW: ___
22 E. B. White piece
24 Put on ___
25 Toulouse tams
27 Art ___ (master keyboardist)
29 Get up
30 1987 Wimbledon winner
31 Actor Jannings
35 ___ Tin Tin
36 From Novi Sad
39 "___ No Hooks"
40 Boat's backbone
42 Geissler tube illuminant
43 Winding paths
45 Fall flower

47 Long-legged shorebird
48 Actress June
50 Memorable shrine
51 MONACO: ___
54 Satan's doing
57 LEM driver
58 Ballerina Shearer
59 Spanish province or capital
60 Andrews Sisters, e.g.
61 Shenanigan
62 Quiet street
63 Drains of stamina
64 Ninnies

DOWN

1 Mata ___
2 Arabian sultanate
3 TANGIER: ___
4 Sheathes
5 ___-di-dah
6 Strange to say
7 Kind of rug
8 Gumshoes
9 Son of the West Wind
10 Before kickoff
11 Goldfinger's first name

12 Convoy chaser
13 Boston suburb
19 Waiter's handout
21 Tums target
23 Fr. holy women
25 Sergeant's voice
26 Canal opened in 1825
27 Olden drum
28 "It's ___ to tell a lie"
30 Manitoba Indian
32 MOSCOW: ___
33 "Oh, that's what you mean!"
34 Paris's Gare de ___
37 Contest responders
38 St. Petersburg's river
41 Shotz Brewery worker of 70's TV
44 Gershwin's "___ to Watch Over Me"
46 Utah's state flower
47 Tankard tipple
48 Hebrew prophet
49 Writer Chekhov
50 Detroit output
51 Shopping center
52 ___ Delano (F.D.R.'s mother)
53 Witticism
55 Spring flower

56 Teddy material
58 People or GQ

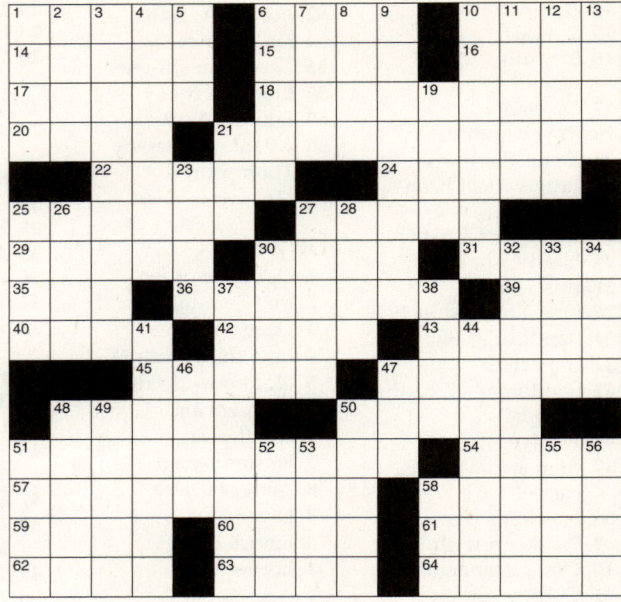

136   by Harvey Estes

ACROSS

1 Jam maker
8 Mounds of arms
14 Facsimile
15 Tour follower
16 Occupy
17 Treadmill
18 They may try you
19 RR depot
21 Borders
22 Look up and down
23 "No bid"
25 Curve between musical notes
26 "Agnus ___"
27 Crustacean catcher
29 Before
30 Scopes Trial defender
32 Fit into the schedule
34 Coal container
35 Razor-billed bird
36 Reindeer relative
40 Like this answer
43 Constellation next to Scorpius
44 Membership fee for 39-Down?
46 Shipping letters
48 "___ Was a Rollin' Stone" (1972 hit)

50 Picker-uppers
51 Stories
52 Uses a knife
54 Sullivan Award grp.
55 Sommelier's offerings
56 "Four Quartets" poet
58 Temporary
60 Sprays, perhaps
61 Ruin, as plans
62 Naguib's successor
63 Originally

DOWN

1 Shooter supporter
2 Took back
3 Highest orbital points
4 Get wider
5 Whopper juniors
6 Henri's here
7 Dupe
8 Bathing suit top
9 Bit
10 Takes to the street edge
11 Uniform attachment
12 Visualize
13 Is incensed
15 Comprehends
20 Drink opener

23 Resolve, as differences
24 Consoles
27 Kid corrals
28 City on the Loire
31 Baseball stat
33 Ring result
36 Where nautical rope is wound
37 Uzbek lake
38 Duelers' equipment
39 W.W. II craft
40 Masters tournament location
41 Freeloader
42 Cracker toppers
45 Certain code carrier
47 Ruthless ruler
49 Book containing legends
51 Florentine painter
53 Spot
55 "Star Trek" Klingon
57 Finish'd
59 Youngster

137 by Daniel R. Stark

ACROSS

1 Coming down lightly
8 Sparkle
15 Feeler
16 "Tinker, Tailor, Soldier, Spy" author
17 Cavalry mount
18 Ready for romance
19 Time with monsieur
20 Baker's meas.
22 Silent screen's Nita ___
23 Cliff dweller
24 Paris's darling
26 Coasted
27 Oddity
28 Usurper in "The Castle of Otranto"
30 Summer in Haiti
31 Modern Abyssinia
33 Was a stockbroker
35 Just fine, thank you
37 Midnight rider
40 Air
44 Ex of Ol' Blue Eyes
45 Concert conclusions
47 Lip
48 Cheesy sandwich
50 Rani's garments
51 Bobtail mouse
52 Body-building goal
54 Thesis beginning
55 More pure
56 Easy
58 Hoop
60 Credit
61 Down to a ___ (exact)
62 Outstanding
63 Film and TV trio

DOWN

1 Jungle slasher
2 Come into
3 Not fickle
4 Neighbor of Vénus
5 "Splendor in the Grass" screenwriter
6 Capt.'s heading
7 Fragrant blossom
8 Pottery worker
9 Apollo 11's Eagle, e.g.
10 "User friendly" feature
11 ___ Bulba (Gogol's Cossack warrior)
12 Sang merrily
13 Learned
14 Had an address
21 Kind of nerve
24 Comes about
25 Bugs
28 Silverheels's partner
29 Evaporates
32 Hard water?
34 Hovercraft, for short
36 Haunting quality?
37 Dry ravines
38 Conquest of 5/29/53
39 Window adornment
41 Pressing work
42 Calm
43 Materializes
46 Furniture mover
49 Follow the majorettes
51 Olive-green songbird
53 Actor ___ Patrick Harris
55 Cold in Tijuana
57 Where Shaq attacks: Abbr.
59 Get busy

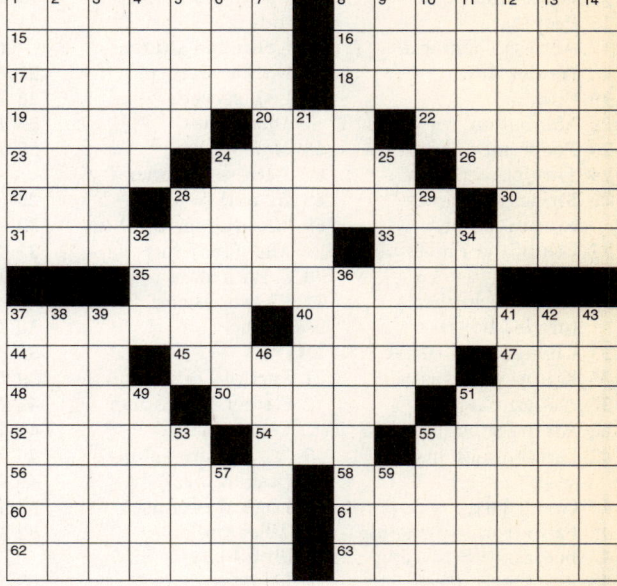

138 by Sidney L. Robbins

ACROSS

1 ___ Park, N.Y.
5 Cider season
9 Layer of paint
13 Kind of collar
14 Together, musically
15 1982 Stallone action role
16 Florsheim product
17 With 62-Across, words of caution
19 Sen. Kennedy
20 Mr. Lugosi
21 Athletes' negotiators
22 Spartacus, e.g.
24 Wing: Prefix
26 Intelligent sea creature
28 Early American statesman ___ King
33 Vituperate
35 How some packages are sent
37 Small rail bird
38 Ones who don't enunciate
40 Lashes down
42 City near Monaco
43 Restaurant bill
45 Tropical eels
46 Scouts do good ones
48 Diet
50 Australian marsupial
52 Muse of poetry
55 Catered event
59 Lawyers' degrees
61 Auto part
62 See 17-Across
64 "___ boy!"
65 Sea eagles
66 Actor James ___ Jones
67 "Portnoy's Complaint" author
68 6-3, 4-6, 6-1, e.g.
69 "___ bien!" (French accolade)
70 Carpet layer's calculation

DOWN

1 Pauses
2 Singer Waters
3 With 30-Down, what 17- and 62-Across are
4 A quarter of four
5 Lose color
6 Newspaper publisher Ochs
7 Asylum resident
8 Permit
9 Neanderthals' home
10 Harbinger
11 Adjoin
12 Take these out for a spin
15 Harshness
18 Civil War vets' org.
20 ___ of the ball
23 Canceled
25 Biblical son
27 Sprightly
29 Underworld money lender
30 See 3-Down
31 Chemistry Nobelist Harold
32 Lip
33 Sunder
34 Writer Wiesel
36 Moore of "Indecent Proposal"
39 F.D.R.'s mother ___ Delano
41 Arrives
44 Protective glass cover
47 On the ___ (declining)
49 In abundance
51 ___ pro nobis
53 Sip
54 D-Day beach
55 Thumbs-up votes
56 Golfer's shout
57 Allen of "Candid Camera"
58 War deity
60 Oil quantities: Abbr.
63 Still and all
64 Mr. Gershwin

139   by Gregory E. Paul

ACROSS

1 Handed out
6 Ditto
10 ___ Raton, Fla.
14 Goldbrick
15 Wallet fillers
16 Peepers
17 Actress Diamond
18 Fender flaw
19 Pronto
20 Manhattan, for one
23 Poetic monogram
24 Tiny powerhouse
25 Modeling agency executive Ford
27 Foe of the Philistines
30 RV
32 "Rumble in the Jungle" boxer
33 Changed the décor
35 Krupp works city
38 Assign places to
40 Alpine song
42 Ophthalmologist's case
43 Greek Pax
45 Palindromic principle
47 Before, to Browning
48 Plumber's need

50 Enjoyed a wad of tobacco
52 Flatter, with "up"
54 Impulse
55 Miscalculate
56 Crème gauloise, today
62 Columbia student
64 Rockies resort
65 Fish served amandine
66 Narrow way
67 Actress Sommer
68 By and by
69 "___ Rather Be With Me" (1967 hit)
70 Satyr's stare
71 Please no end

DOWN

1 Part of D.J.
2 Cather biographer Leon
3 "___ vostra salute" (Italian toast)
4 Logical premises
5 Tiller puller
6 Sinful city
7 De novo

8 Fix
9 Prize
10 "___ sport . . ."
11 Christmas Eve dish
12 Halt
13 Quaking ___
21 "___ I'm home!" (sitcom opener)
22 Mature
26 Not so much
27 Draped dress
28 Former orchard spray
29 Trattoria treat
30 Autumn drink
31 Yemen port
34 Love excessively, with "on"
36 Rochester's beloved
37 Must have
39 Group of toads
41 Nobelist Walesa et al.
44 Hgt.
46 Meadow bloom
49 Nonsense
51 Ethically neutral
52 Poe poem, with "The"
53 Dickens's ___ Heep

54 "Ben-Hur" director William
57 Racer Yarborough
58 Quarterback's bark
59 Scintilla

60 Kind of pudding
61 To be, to Satie
63 Actor Beatty

140   by Gregory E. Paul

ACROSS

1 "How sad!"
5 Sources of milk
10 Unhealthy air
14 When hot cross buns are eaten
15 Buick model
16 One of the Jackson 5
17 Simone Signoret role
19 Italian wine city
20 Genesis mountain
21 Western hat
23 Vagabond
26 Big birds
27 Lady at a ball
30 Attention
32 Bartletts
35 "Dies ___"
36 Welcome
38 Northern Ireland's ___ Paisley
39 California fort
40 Ship's medical facility
41 Car in a 1964 song
42 Stocking stuffer
43 Barton and others
44 Othello, e.g.
45 "Ragged Dick" author

47 Plunked oneself down
48 "Death Be Not Proud" poet
49 Not written
51 Dakota Indian
53 Aïda's love
56 Portuguese West Africa, today
60 Relative of the heron
61 Robin Hood's love
64 Word after take or high
65 "Golden" song
66 Bulldogs
67 Panic
68 Hornets' homes
69 Muse's instrument

DOWN

1 Michigan college
2 Limerick man
3 "___ partridge in . . ."
4 Surprise
5 Miss Garbo
6 Above, to Key
7 Gone by
8 Moscow news name
9 Roofing tile

10 Public square decoration
11 1991 Broadway smash
12 Palindromic name
13 Enter
18 Stable mate
22 Gas gauge level
24 Places that draw crowds
25 Hoarder
27 Life of a region
28 Swashbuckler Flynn
29 "Bareback" rider
31 Money back
33 Boca ___, Fla.
34 Saw wood
36 Be ill
37 Audio systems, for short
40 "Beat it!"
44 Not purebred
46 Pencil part
48 Senhora
50 Tart flavor
52 Subdues
53 Repeated musical phrase
54 Lover of an Irish Rose

55 Store news
57 Unctuous
58 Hideout
59 "As I Lay Dying" character

62 Wallet items
63 Dah's partner

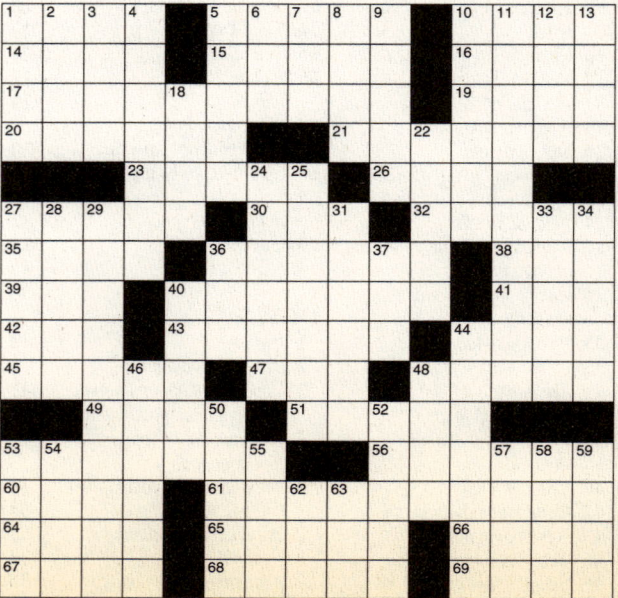

141   by Cathy Millhauser

ACROSS

1 13 popes
5 Trimming target
9 One of Donald's exes
14 Hamburg's river
15 Antiquity
16 Works by Jack and Robert Frost
17 Rotarian Muslim?
20 Spain's patron saint
21 Kimono accessory
22 Dilettantish
23 Montréal, Tahiti, etc.
26 Where to earn a B.A.
28 Rotarian, proverbially?
33 Metric measure
34 Brit. record label
35 Caesar's peepers
37 Rotarian's charge-account feature?
42 Debussy contemporary
43 Tic-tac-toe row
44 Metro or Storm, e.g.
45 Rotarian's favorite song of 1969?
50 Pulitzer-winning critic Richard
51 "The Good Earth" woman
52 Merit
55 Hunky-dory
57 Throwaway
61 Rotarian's favorite movie of 1977?
65 Breaks
66 Land of the Blarney stone
67 Spreadsheet material
68 Quarters
69 Prie-___ (prayer desk)
70 Site of ancient Olympia

DOWN

1 Off-color
2 K-12, educationally speaking
3 Cousin of a Tony
4 Brazilian musician Mendes
5 Post-it-note abbr.
6 Cambodia's ___ Nol
7 Jason's craft
8 Unwelcome hotel guest
9 Like some verbs: Abbr.
10 Orally
11 Arab leader
12 Stick-y position?
13 Pallid
18 Hang out
19 One of a Kind
24 Hgt.
25 Venture County's ___ Valley
27 Like ___ not
28 Departments
29 Intensify
30 Curtain fabric
31 "Get it?" motion
32 Architect Saarinen Sr.
33 Kennel cry
36 Judge Lance
38 Spatially adjusted
39 Impart
40 Kind of dancer
41 Monk's attire
46 Problematic for presbyopes
47 Wrinkle-free
48 Door fastener
49 Make secret
52 Singer James
53 Captain of literature
54 Adventurer-hero ___ Williams
56 Soprano Te Kanawa
58 Iranian coin
59 No voter
60 Home-sch. liaisons
62 Milk, in a way
63 Nietzsche's never
64 Cousin of the eland

142   by Sidney L. Robbins

ACROSS

1 Blockheads
6 Late tennis V.I.P.
10 Dirty literature
14 Evangelist ___ Semple McPherson
15 Wander
16 El ___, Tex.
17 With 36- and 56-Across, an announcer's plea
19 "Leaving on ___ Plane"
20 Rooster's mates
21 Melee
22 Stingless bee
23 Female deer
24 Woman in charge of a prison
25 Keep
29 What a dinner partner might pick up
31 European autos
32 Came up
33 Louis XVI, e.g.
36 See 17-Across
39 Observe
40 Eggs on
41 Reach in total
42 Left-hand pages
44 Sinew
45 In the center of
47 Fish eggs
48 Count with an orchestra
49 Profit
51 Kind of processing
55 Cecil B. DeMille work
56 See 17-Across
58 "Thanks ___!"
59 Comic Johnson
60 Flee to wed
61 Department store department
62 Army chow
63 Irritates

DOWN

1 Bills and coins
2 Lower-calorie beer
3 Mideast sultanate
4 Old Tunisian rulers
5 Stitch
6 Shaw of "Star Dust"
7 Big Apple area
8 ___ monde (high society)
9 German spa
10 Ancient Greek city
11 Like many advertised appliances
12 "___ hooks"
13 "On a scale of one ___"
18 Golf club
22 Oasis sight
23 Spend
24 Netting
25 Tiers
26 Fencer's sword
27 Much-used advertising medium
28 Sum total
29 Endeavors
30 Doesn't share
32 Jason's ship
34 Numerical prefix
35 Sacred image: Var.
37 Formerly, once
38 Burger roll
43 Decrees
44 Chinese secret society
45 90 degrees from fore-and-aft
46 Shade tree
47 Religious observances
49 Clinton's Veep
50 Picnic pests
51 Limp watch painter
52 Army deserter
53 Stock ticker output
54 Nays' opposites
56 Hoover, e.g.
57 "___ the ramparts we . . ."

143 by David J. Kahn

ACROSS

1 Buckwheat was a little one
7 Third Hebrew month
13 Rubbing compound ingredient
15 Clash
16 It often comes down to this
17 A bogey, to par
18 Electrical unit
19 Herald's locale
21 Camping equipment
22 Plainly
26 ___ Brothers
27 Matriarch buried at Hebron
28 Strain
29 Stock page listing
32 "A Room With a View" view
33 Colorado native
34 Football lines
39 Chemical suffix
40 ___ Bear ("Uncle Remus" character)
41 Trickster
42 Glen Canyon ___
43 Suffix with switch
44 Shocks
48 1968 Rock Hudson film
53 ___ expense
54 Kilmer poem ending
55 South Africa's ___ Paul Kruger
56 Kind of leader
59 "Black Magic Woman" rock group
61 Auction reaction
62 Arranged
63 1986 World Series losers
64 Actress Bullock

DOWN

1 Decorate again
2 Minerva's Greek counterpart
3 Chess expert Lyman
4 Cornfield sound
5 Inner personality, to Jung
6 Ending with folk
7 "___-Tiki"
8 Seine scene
9 Deadly sin
10 Revel
11 Lacking teeth
12 Geometric points
14 Deep throat
15 Phrase inventors
20 Awkward
23 Idle
24 Baseball's Bichette
25 Spindle part
30 "Lost Horizon" setting
31 Home planet
34 Divorce participant, sometimes
35 Not working
36 Mad
37 Skintight outfit
38 "For what profit has a man, ___ . . .": Matthew
45 On base
46 Domestic worker
47 Best Western rival
49 Whisky drinks
50 Approximately
51 Approximates
52 "The Prisoner of ___"
57 80's merger inits.
58 ___-en-Provence
60 Gymnast's goal

144 by Sidney L. Robbins

ACROSS

1 Free-for-all
6 Welshman or Scot
10 Paint unskillfully
14 Critical, as a shortage
15 Seaweed product
16 Florence's river
17 Eastern ascetic
20 Kennedy matriarch
21 Lover's sounds
22 Downy duck
23 It's "big" in London
24 Venomous vipers
25 Insincere sentimentality
29 Cries one's eyes out
31 Of bees
32 French capital, in song
33 Man of tomorrow
36 Daytime serial since 1956
39 One born in early August
40 Carved gem
41 Speck
42 Whalers and such
43 Drinking spree
44 "Scram!"
47 Remote
48 Lumberjack
49 Employer
51 Money-losing proposition
55 Space-efficient floor connector
58 Mailed
59 Leave out
60 Harbor
61 Ransom, the car maker
62 Part of V.F.W.
63 Mountain nymph

DOWN

1 Bryn ___ College
2 Canyon feature
3 "The Bridge of San ___ Rey"
4 To be, in Picardy
5 Conger
6 Church law
7 Frozen waffle brand
8 Youngsters
9 Uno, due, ___
10 St. ___ (famous Welsh cathedral)
11 Take for ___
12 Racer Al
13 Family of Danish physicists
18 Hot-weather desserts
19 Outstanding, as a day
23 Fine dinnerware
24 Quite impressed
25 False god
26 Church nook
27 Yugoslav hero
28 "So there!"
29 Uncovers
30 Singer Guthrie
32 Grand display
33 Slender nail
34 Fairy tale starter
35 River to the North Sea
37 Linger
38 Coffee server
42 Race openers
43 Italian port on the Adriatic
44 Deep-voiced singer
45 Oust
46 "___ is a terrible thing to waste"
47 Achievements
49 West Point inits.
50 Agitate
51 Capone feature
52 Grotto
53 Out of port
54 Darn
56 Near the ground
57 Sigma's predecessor

145 by Bob Klahn

ACROSS

1 Minds
8 Conks
12 Deserted
13 Baby boobook
15 Improve a text
16 Bother terribly
18 Evensong
19 On the line
20 Squire
21 "East of Eden" protagonist
22 Grp. making barrels of money?
23 Ancient Roman tunic
24 Frequent restaurant order, with "the"
25 Persian pooh-bah
26 California dessert wine
29 Junior's junior
30 Detective's cliché
34 Bradley Intl. letters
35 Dr. Seuss classic
36 Barker of Hollywood
38 Balanced
39 Commander of the Enterprise
43 Plant, in combos
44 Literary monogram
45 "Le Diable boiteux" novelist
46 City north of Seattle
48 Elbows
49 Venus follower
50 One providing the big picture?
51 Foment anew
52 Medes and Minoans
53 Hide but not hair
54 Part of Jordan's border

DOWN

1 Least likely to bite
2 "Oedipe" composer
3 Temperate, e.g.
4 Urbanite's vacation spot
5 Institute
6 Rug rats
7 Opening number
8 Modern collectible
9 Has something outstanding
10 "___ Republic"
11 Sistine Chapel figures
12 Nîmes dreams
14 Point (at)
17 Electronics expert
19 "Bear of little brain" creator
21 Italian turnover
24 Ignore, as faults
27 Nowhere, now
28 Above, in a sense
30 Scratched
31 Entertains at home
32 Guinness data
33 A lot of the New Testament
37 Exposed
40 Baseball's Mr. Tiger
41 Waste matter
42 Breaks
45 Spanish writer García ___
47 Patron saint of goldsmiths
48 Kind of wedding
50 Nuts or crackers

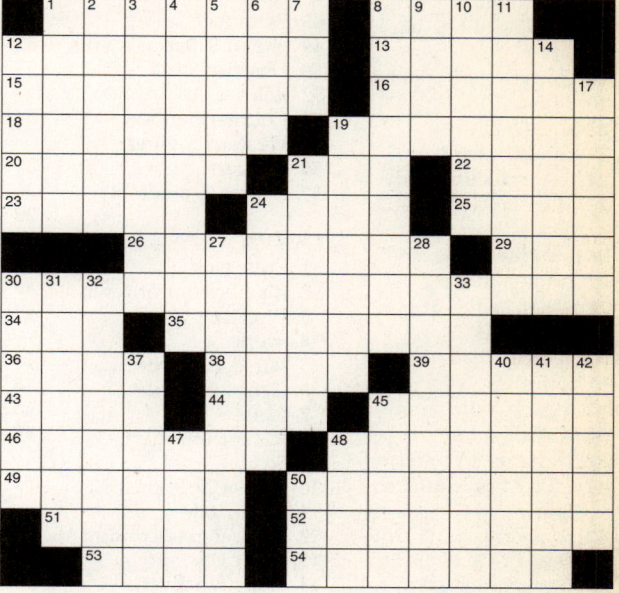

146 by Gregory E. Paul

ACROSS

1 Poverty
5 Mutual of ___
10 Track tipster
14 Neighborhood
15 Artist Bonheur and others
16 Like Solomon
17 Watch face
18 Whitney's partner in airplanes
19 Pizazz
20 1970's New York Knick's nickname
23 Western alliance: Abbr.
24 Sidestep
28 Grotto
32 20- and 51-Across, e.g.
35 States firmly
36 To ___ (precisely)
37 "___ the season to be jolly"
38 Hank Ketcham comic strip
42 Purpose
43 Harrow's rival
44 Dog: Fr.
45 When American elections are held
48 Rio ___ (border river)
49 Take care of, as duties
50 Nearly worthless coin
51 1960–66 N.B.A. scoring leader, informally
59 Jellystone Park bear
62 "I don't give ___!"
63 Scent
64 G.I. addresses
65 Jazz singer Vaughan
66 Burn soother
67 Didn't part with
68 Pickpocketed
69 Physics unit

DOWN

1 Walk in the baby pool
2 La Scala solo
3 Not distant
4 Six-foot or more
5 Annie, e.g., in the comics
6 Folkways
7 "Rush!"
8 Abhor
9 30's movie dog
10 Midnight
11 Source of Rockefeller money
12 Red, white and blue initials
13 Hamilton's bill
21 Trunks
22 Seminary subj.
25 Reach
26 Cleared, as a winter windshield
27 Ancient Palestinian
28 West Pointers
29 Boulevard
30 Buyer
31 Suffix with east or west
32 One of the Three Musketeers
33 MTV's target viewer
34 Haw's partner
36 Bar member: Abbr.
39 Poseidon's realm
40 Pale colors
41 Shelter grp.
46 Double curve, as in yarn
47 "How ___ love thee? Let me . . ."
48 "Faust" dramatist
50 Sand bar
52 Sweetheart
53 "Anything but ___!"
54 Bullfight bull
55 "The Wind in the Willows" character
56 Without thought
57 Diving bird
58 Chestnut or walnut
59 Talk, talk, talk
60 Unlock, in poetry
61 Republicans, collectively

147 by Manny Nosowsky

ACROSS

1 Holds back
8 Watery
15 Do tests on
16 Africa's ___ Faso
17 Port sight
18 They're not as big as jars
19 Gilmore of basketball
20 Grave
22 ___-di-dah
23 Cynic's retort
24 Reproductive body
25 She played Gilda in "Gilda"
26 Peeples of "Fame"
27 It may be dirty
28 Chief Justice after Marshall
29 "Ditto"
31 Dries up
32 Refuse help
34 Kvetch a lot
37 Daytime TV offering
41 Like Miss Muffet's fare
42 Saavedra ___ (1936 Peace Nobelist)
43 In vitro items
44 Pouch holders, for short
45 "V" villain
46 No stay-at-home
47 Certain photo order: Abbr.
48 Palm leaf
49 Site of Tiberius's villa
50 Obscure stuff
52 Release
54 Countermanded
55 Western ravines
56 Daggers
57 Overseas assembly

DOWN

1 Preserves
2 It's way out of town
3 Wrestling duo
4 Scope
5 Jamaica's Ocho ___
6 Genes material
7 Isolate
8 Recant officially
9 So
10 Give a little push
11 Ticker tale?
12 Vital engine conduit
13 Left over
14 Steps fancily
21 "Huh?"
24 V.I.P. from Araby
25 Wrecks
27 Theatrical
28 Points at the dinner table
30 "Heavens to Betsy!"
31 "___ of the Year"
33 One losing power, perhaps
34 Puts on for a certain audience
35 Hut style
36 Surgical specialty
38 Notoriously malodorous birds
39 Manage
40 Least confident
42 Big name in insurance
45 French traffic order
46 British pens
48 Big bash
49 Shoe impression, maybe
51 Former world chess champion from Russia
53 "Smoking or ___?"

148 by Frank A. Longo

ACROSS

1 Luminesced
10 Course
15 Fatalness
16 J. P. Donleavy novel
17 Kudos
18 Like many teacups
19 Ultimate
20 Tropical fruit tree
21 Split
22 Most newspapers
24 Plot
25 Sea eagles
26 Search party members
27 Backsliding
30 1981 Beatty-Keaton epic
31 Mountaineers
33 Canine cries
37 Hires too many employees
42 Spayed
44 Lofty nest: Var.
45 Snubbed
46 Bygone empress
48 City on the Bay of Bengal
49 Nectar flavor
50 Male cat
51 Nom de guerre
52 Chew
54 Shade
55 Linked in a series
56 Fired up
57 Vulgarity

DOWN

1 Throw dirt on
2 2.471 acres
3 Restless
4 Conductance unit
5 Feelings of discomfort
6 Cheer
7 Disneyland attractions
8 Parisian summers
9 Functional prefix
10 Absterges
11 Student
12 TV show's spot
13 Having protective wrapping
14 Dispirits
21 Brainteasers
23 Manannan's father, in myth
24 Stand in (for)
26 Aheap
28 Makes baskets
29 Made a copy on a floppy
32 Candle-wax compounds
33 Vivify
34 King's privileges
35 Financial support
36 Safekeeping
38 Burgh on the Firth of Clyde
39 Aircraft carrier escort
40 Sets that have limits
41 Ocean floors
43 Pencil topper
46 Seed coat
47 Overindulges
49 Famous name in TV talk
52 Year in King John's reign
53 Hoosegow

ACROSS

1 P's ___ (this puzzle's theme)
6 ___ happened
10 Ewes, e.g.
14 "Whippersnapper" of films
15 Asian princess
16 Have too little
17 Landing site
18 Poet's inspiration
19 Wingate of W.W. II
20 Clinch
21 Jimmy Carter's birthday: Abbr.
22 Incense
23 Scuttled
25 Second-row occupant
27 Warm-up
28 Slips
29 Compass point
30 "Enough ___!"
32 Arrange, as the hair
34 Nuzzled
35 Bird groups
39 Conical candy
42 Circus prop
44 Asian honorific
47 Dig out
49 Kind of doctor
50 Lampoon
52 Part of 25-Down
53 Stadium section
54 15th-century date
55 Obsolescent
56 Problem for a masseur
57 Word before pittance
58 Heating setting
61 Good source of starch
62 Start of a Cockney toast
63 Bewilders
64 Letter opening?
65 Time out for music
66 Sport with traps

DOWN

1 Roker and others
2 "Unforgettable" singer
3 Racks for washed dishes
4 Glance
5 Decidedly not marshy
6 Sandhurst arsenal
7 Sci-fi transport
8 As a proxy
9 Connect with
10 Come down in a hurry
11 ___ nails
12 Grants, perhaps
13 "A Sentimental Journey" writer
23 Cross
24 Alice's chronicler
25 Letters of triumph
26 Finnish bath
31 "See you"
33 Runt
36 Make a substitution?
37 Mary's "South Pacific" costar
38 Post
40 Weight Watchers member, maybe
41 Square-dealing
42 Like a #1 housekeeper
43 Address abbr.
44 Perfumes
45 Brat
46 They're bicoastal
48 Inner circles
51 Pursuit
55 Tout's topic
59 Jay follower?
60 N.Y.C. zone

ACROSS

1 Tot's talk, perhaps
5 Encourages
9 First-grade instruction
13 Stinks
15 "Thanks ___!"
16 Swing around
17 Like factory workers
19 U, for one
20 Elsie's bull
21 "Mommie ___" (Christina Crawford book)
23 "What's ___ for me?"
25 Take a potshot
26 Teller of white lies
29 Stage whisper
30 Give the eye
31 Quick bites
33 Advances
36 Baseball's Gehrig
37 Trunk
39 Runner Sebastian
40 Remains
43 Person of action
44 King's address
45 Illegal inducement
47 Mexican dishes
49 Speakeasy offering
50 Saxophonist Getz
51 Candid
53 Waiter's jotting
56 Actress Archer
57 Kind of jury
61 Bucks and does
62 Otherwise
63 Singer ___ Neville
64 Lawyer: Abbr.
65 Tackle-box item
66 City inside the Servian Wall

DOWN

1 Tennis shot
2 Run in neutral
3 Body's partner
4 Logician's start
5 Sidekick
6 Sum total
7 Wart giver, in old wives' tales
8 Emphasis
9 On a horse
10 Edit
11 No blessing, this!
12 Shipped
14 Fragrance
18 Marco Polo area
22 Dye color
appropriate to this puzzle
24 Vacuum tube
26 Go belly up
27 Borodin's prince
28 Texas' state flower
29 Balance-sheet pluses
32 Golf club V.I.P.
34 Illustrator Gustave
35 Comprehends
38 Patrick Henry, e.g.
41 Bodega
42 Clothing specification
44 Boating hazard
46 Saharan tribesman
48 Newswoman Shriver
49 Intelligence-testing name
51 Actress Thompson
52 Glamour rival
54 River of Spain
55 Leeway
58 "It's no ___!"
59 Slippery one
60 Opposite SSW

151 by Ernie Furtado

ACROSS

1 Dogpatch's creator
5 Palindromic term of address
9 Talked, old-style
14 Nose tweaker
15 Willa Cather's "One of ___"
16 With sickly pallor
17 Dream
18 Till's bills
19 Rags-to-riches writer
20 Start of an old motto
22 List ender
23 Shooter ammo
24 Part 2 of motto
26 Take-___ (accompaniers)
29 ___ of one's own medicine
30 Part 3 of motto
31 Bulldog
32 Twosome
36 Martinique, e.g.
37 Environmentally minded, for short
39 Hook shape
41 "Don't Bring Me Down" rock group
42 Miami's county
44 Blanche in "The Golden Girls"
46 Part 4 of motto
48 Particle
50 Conquering hero
51 Part 5 of motto
54 Aerialist's safeguard
55 Theater people
56 End of motto
61 Sightseeing sight
62 Golfer Isao ___
63 Singleton
64 Ball
65 A night in Paris
66 Exterior: Prefix
67 Blackthorn shrubs
68 1949 erupter
69 Creep through the cracks

DOWN

1 Search thoroughly
2 Together, musically
3 On hold
4 Make believe
5 Heath
6 Godmother, often
7 Rings of color
8 Orig. texts
9 Mower's trails
10 Mouth parts
11 White, informally
12 Last name in fashion
13 Nest for 21-Down: Var.
21 See 13-Down
22 "Me" types
25 Thumb-twiddling
26 Fatty ___
27 Refrain part
28 1985 Danielle Steel best seller
33 Regretfulness
34 Choir voice
35 Koh-i-___ (famed diamond)
38 Pinch reaction
40 Cut of meat
43 Nitty-gritty
45 Just managed
47 Streets
49 Medea's ill-fated uncle
51 Miss Muffet edible
52 Business as ___
53 Zoo heavyweight
57 Related
58 Comic Rudner
59 Spot
60 "Avast!"
62 Actress Sue ___ Langdon

152 by Harvey Estes

ACROSS

1 It goes from stem to stern
5 Ten Commandments word
10 Companion of Ollie
14 Dancer Pavlova
15 Champing at the bit
16 A billion years
17 Con game
18 Vacant
19 Soap unit
20 Stoves that don't work?
23 "Diamonds ___ a girl's ..."
24 "Gidget" star
25 Perform perfectly
28 Hägar the Horrible's honey
30 It was banned in 1973
33 Beatniks beat it
34 Interjections
36 ___in apple
38 Iamb and dactyl
39 Filming actors?
43 Pasture sounds
44 Carl of baseball, informally
45 Tic-toe bridge
46 Lady ___, founder of the Girl Guides
48 Trouble in France
50 Frame
54 Itch initiator
56 Partake of
58 Calendar abbr.
59 Arson?
63 West of Gotham City
65 "I'm ___ duck"
66 ___ hemp (fiber plant)
67 "I Spy" star
68 List of candidates
69 It may come with points
70 Grown-up grigs
71 Biblical king with 10 wives
72 Muffs

DOWN

1 North African fortress
2 Concert cry
3 Filling surrounder
4 "Mrs. Battle's Opinions on Whist" writer
5 Île de la Cité site
6 The ___ Man (tarot card)
7 Actor John
8 First name in supper club entertainment
9 Drift
10 Not at a distance
11 Logician
12 Flight approval
13 22° 30'
21 Baking potato
22 Lump
26 "Rock of ___"
27 Young 'un
29 Thrilled response
31 Tony of "Who's the Boss?"
32 License
35 Pen
37 Trans-Atlantic flier
39 Emerson, the ___ of Concord
40 Game originally called "fives"
41 Descartes conclusion
42 Fashion
43 Sot's spot
47 Big ___, Calif.
49 Not staccato
51 A sew-and-sew?
52 Hubbub
53 Is foppish
55 Grind
57 Kind of attraction
60 Run in place
61 About
62 No ___ (register button)
63 Plane downer
64 Like threatening bills

153 by Randall J. Hartman

ACROSS

1 ___ throat (winter ailment)
6 Duelists' steps
11 "20/20" network
14 Actress Dunne
15 Spartan magistrate
16 Interminable ride
19 Heavy reading
20 Mine yield
21 Parade stopper
22 Zenith
23 Each
24 Paragraph start
27 A.P. competitor
29 Where ships run aground
31 ___ Paulo
32 Grand site?
35 Speaker's stand
37 German article
38 "Sting like a bee" champion
39 Gum ball
41 Sony rival
42 Bit of butter
43 Castaway's call
44 Mighty mite
46 Portuguese money
48 Suffix with correspond
49 Client
51 Unit of radio frequency: Abbr.
52 Zone
55 "Savvy?"
57 Poet Pound
60 ___ Diamond
61 Diamonds, in slang
62 Applaud
63 Children's game
67 Kind of closet
68 Taco sauce
69 Understand
70 Amherst, school, for short
71 More crafty

DOWN

1 Sis or bro
2 Scout unit
3 Parent, e.g.
4 Went in
5 Letterman's Stupid ___ Tricks
6 Nut for a nutcracker
7 Plant louse
8 Intricate problems
9 Long time
10 Matamoros Mrs.
11 Nick and Nora's pooch
12 Coalition
13 Mao's domain
17 Lachrymose
18 Aperture
25 Spring nymph
26 Lone Ranger's pal
28 Hawkeye State
30 Canal site
32 Gardner's stories
33 Single
34 "It's ___ way"
36 It's between Alta. and Man.
40 John ___ Passos
45 The M of "M.E."
47 One means of payment
50 With bounteousness
53 Shades
54 Unfolds
56 Gaggle members
58 Steak order
59 Church niche
63 Actor Gulager
64 Not her
65 Road curve
66 Mercury or Saturn

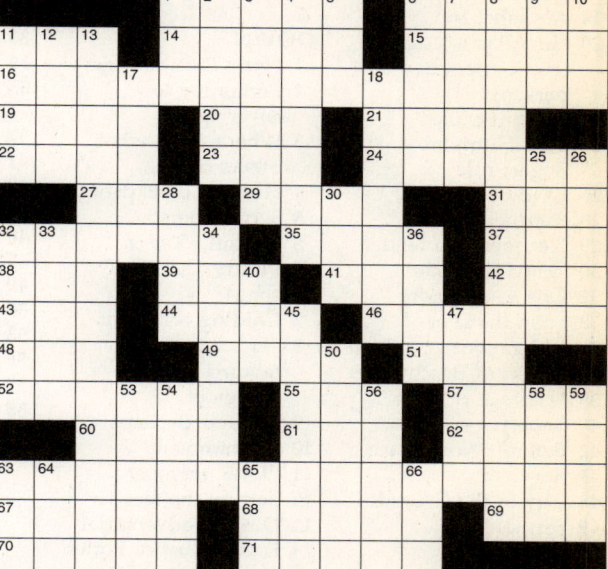

154 by A.J. Santora

ACROSS

1 Hubbub
4 Tray filler
7 "No, sirree!"
12 1972 Olympics star
16 In harmony
17 OPEC member
18 Man in red
19 "The Ferrari in the Bedroom" author
21 Start off
24 Doll's name
25 Appeal
26 Crossing word
27 Proven sound
30 Whiff
31 Dream team
36 "Heaven Must Have Sent You" singer
40 Unrigid
41 Barker
43 Track down
46 Upscale singer?
47 "Is it a boy ___ girl?"
48 "Now I know why!"
51 Did with a passion?
53 West Coast Senator
57 Obscure
58 Charity
62 Jimmy Dorsey hit "Maria ___"
63 Original Woodstock rocker
64 Synthetic fabric
65 From ___ Z
66 TV actor Jack

DOWN

1 Bon follower
2 Baseball's Quisenberry
3 California fort
4 Grant portrayer
5 Canine command
6 Belonging to Li'l Abner
7 Lid fastener
8 Bonneville Flats site
9 Genuine
10 Not genuine
11 Chaired
13 Lollipop cop
14 "___ sad sight to see the year dying": FitzGerald
15 Newswoman Paula
20 Involve
21 Night shift worker
22 Ancient Dead Sea kingdom
23 Pro ___ (like some legal work)
28 Atlantic flier
29 Atl. flier
31 Operating without ___
32 One-dimensional
33 Set the pace
34 Bath bath
35 Book of the Apocrypha: Abbr.
37 Scottie Pippen's org.
38 Rephrase
39 Wander
42 Wander
43 Hurled, as grenades
44 By swallowing
45 List
46 Language of ancient Rhodes
49 Pilgrimage
50 Peek ending
51 On the money
52 Kind of ism.
54 Curse
55 Sea east of the Caspian
56 Fit to serve
59 Accepts
60 Prefix with realism
61 Sign of popularity

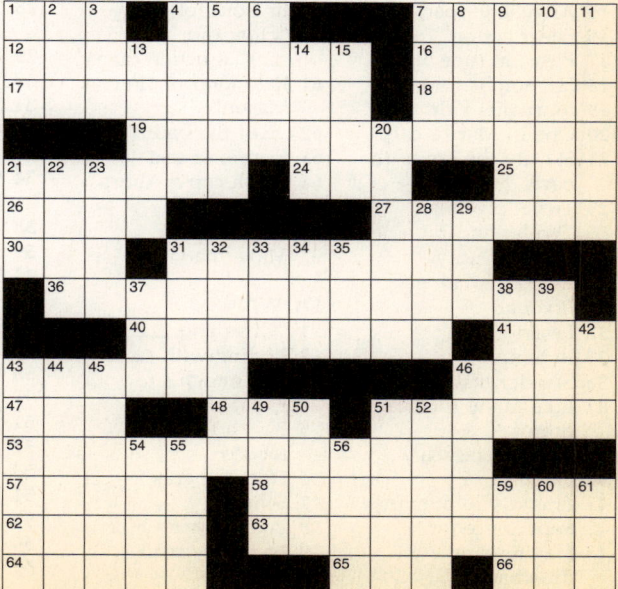

155 by A.J. Santora

ACROSS

1 Evening hours
10 They come in shells
15 Like new
16 Religious art figure
17 Differ amicably
19 Alphabet trio
20 Guardian ad ___ (court-appointed person)
21 Kind of camp
22 1941 Humphrey Bogart role
26 Lead ore
28 Kindness
29 Not merely a lender
30 "Lord Jim" star
32 One in a hundred
33 Food thickener
36 Obligations
38 Works of Bacchylides
39 "Have ___!"
40 Squash
42 Bellini's Norma, e.g.
45 Survivor
48 City in the Crusades
49 Sermonist
51 Isr. neighbor
52 Bristles
54 Copycat
55 Nation's width
60 Psyched
61 Impetrated
62 Put up
63 Stone-broke

DOWN

1 Hyde Park strollers
2 Pertaining to a sovereign
3 Where to do what others do
4 Howard of slapstick
5 Second person
6 "I Taut I Taw a Puddy ___" (1950 song)
7 Chiding comment
8 "Let ___ in a tavern . . .": The Archpoet
9 Shorten, perhaps
10 Unanimously
11 O.A.S. member
12 Soft on the feet
13 Directly adversarial
14 Former Justice Potter et al.
18 Bell-shaped flower
23 Sound sleepers?
24 Crater
25 Smidgen
27 Concise
29 Hindrances
31 D-Day ship: Abbr.
33 One taxed
34 ___ blimp
35 Strength of electric current
37 Graf ___
41 Schnozz continuation
43 Catalogue
44 Dundee turndowns
46 Forbearing, in a way
47 Flap-door shelters
49 Care
50 Interprets
53 "Take ___ Train"
56 Dick
57 Embitterment
58 Clear
59 One at a hoedown

156 by Sidney L. Robbins

ACROSS

1 Chef's serving
5 ___ a plea (works a deal with the D.A.)
9 "Skiddoo!"
14 Margarine
15 Angelic topper
16 Sheer cotton
17 Pleasant tune
18 ___ bomb
19 Journalist Pyle
20 One in Mary's care
21 Hardly the life of the party
23 Ticket profiteer
25 "Yo-ho-ho, and a bottle of ___"
26 Octogenarian, e.g.
28 Bivouac
32 Pester
35 Ill temper
36 Slender instrument
37 Like many modern dorms
38 Church council
40 Queue
41 Friendly to humans
42 Sept. preceder
43 Having no drawbacks
44 Like work horses
45 Some Belgians
48 Medical charge
49 F. Murray ___
53 Refreshment for 007?
58 Lasso
59 In front (of)
60 "How much am ___?" (auction query)
61 Raymond of "Perry Mason"
62 ___of the ball
63 Excise, as text
64 Not a copy: Abbr.
65 Business job
66 Midterm, e.g.
67 Make mad

DOWN

1 "Guys and ___"
2 Ending with sacro-
3 60's march site
4 Excitable
5 Had a wad of tobacco
6 Horse operas
7 Scheme
8 Pedro's hat
9 Be plenty mad
10 Toe woe
11 Skating oval
12 "I cannot tell ___"
13 Track competition
22 Enticed
24 Ask persistently
27 Trace
28 Virginia Civil War battle site
29 His Rose was Irish
30 "___ Lisa"
31 Sunburn result
32 Book after John
33 Ark skipper
34 Captain for many a league
38 More secure
39 Noel season
43 Syr. neighbor
46 Kind of folder
47 Footnote notation
48 Loses brightness
50 Beautiful woman of paradise
51 Showery month
52 Join
53 Uses a powder puff
54 Mother of Zeus
55 Scream
56 Kind of bonding
57 Wild goat

ACROSS

1 Reindeer herder
5 Wilson's predecessor
9 Public spat
14 Brainstorm
15 Take on
16 Midwest Indians
17 Tilt
18 Dash
19 Wine sediment
20 Without warning
23 Opposite of black-tie
24 Hobby room
25 Talon
29 Green hazard
31 Daily dread
33 Mind-reading
36 Government agt.
38 Frost-covered
39 Kit and caboodle
43 Goddesses of the seasons
44 Chinese dollar
45 Where swine dine
46 Asmara is its capital
49 Computer unit
51 ___-majesté
52 Bikini top
54 Lathered

58 The Queen of Country
61 Diving bird
64 Craftiness
65 Unexpected trouble
66 Titan's tripod
67 Military sch.
68 "___ deal!"
69 City on the Aire
70 Howard and Maynard
71 Refusals

DOWN

1 Perfume scent
2 ___ Rogers St. Johns
3 Rings
4 Succeed in the end
5 Texas shrine
6 Feels bad
7 Consumer affairs topic
8 Somewhat sore
9 Team
10 Farm storage site
11 Meadow mom
12 Henpeck
13 Double curve
21 More distant

22 Gene ID
26 Fernando or Lorenzo
27 Without ___ to one's name
28 Like pie slices
30 Buddy
32 1776 battle site
33 Singer Merman
34 Prop (up)
35 Persian sprites
37 Napoleonic general
40 It can rock you to sleep
41 Hero
42 Rubes
47 Recede
48 Caribbean native
50 Dines at home
53 Liturgical scarf
55 Colorful horse
56 Rub clean
57 "The Ballet Class" painter
59 Congers
60 Family
61 Hair preparation
62 "Norma ___"
63 WNW's opposite

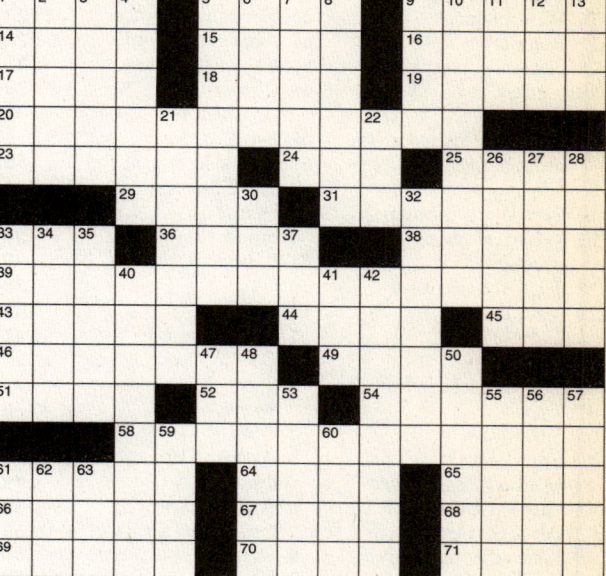

ACROSS

1 Gave a face lift to
6 Barter
10 Amazes
14 Swiftly
15 Rock's Turner
16 Coo's partner
17 Swell, formally?
19 First name in jazz
20 Existence
21 Kind of radio show
23 Imperfect
25 X
26 Professional suffix
27 Actress Brennan
28 1991 movie "___ & Louise"
30 Up, in baseball
31 "The Red"
32 Madame Bovary
35 Difficult journey
36 Looked suspicious
37 At a distance
38 Withered
39 Sneaker brand
40 In unison
41 Tire patterns
43 18-and-over crowd
44 Turf

46 It might need refining
47 Go too far, with "it"
48 Pants line
50 Pancake relative
51 Phoned
52 Olympics vehicle, formally?
57 Boy or girl preceder
58 Creative start
59 Film actress Anders
60 Look with effort
61 Sonneteer
62 W.W. I battle site

DOWN

1 Dominion, in old India
2 Govt. watchdog grp.
3 Block
4 Conversation starter, maybe
5 Early Mormon land
6 Military defense
7 Museum add-on
8 What's more
9 Worker's due
10 Famed fratricide victim

11 Place to put money, formally?
12 Island in New York Bay
13 Perspective
18 ___ Bien Phu, Vietnam
22 Be unwell
23 Bishop topper
24 Way of cooking, formally?
25 It may be fine when company comes
27 Chow
28 Ways of London
29 Makes the grade
31 Piano exercise
33 ___-man defense
34 Consort of Aphrodite
36 Finger food
40 With skill
42 Dawn goddess
43 Have one's say
44 Junk
45 Emulate Pliny the Younger
47 Mountain nymph
49 Food thickening agent
50 One with a handle

53 Harem room
54 Roman household god
55 Opposite WSW
56 Govt. lawyers

159 by Patrick Jordan

ACROSS

1 Puts a limit on
5 Duroc domiciles
10 Vaudeville segments
14 Atlas section
15 Busch Gardens locale
16 Wife of Jacob
17 Reinstate
18 Screened messages?
19 Culp/Cosby TV series
20 Breakfast order at the Storybook Cafe?
23 Clear
24 Star Wars initials
25 Where to get a draught
28 T.L.C. dispensers
29 Mrs. David Copperfield
33 Park activity
35 The Confessor king
37 Tops
38 Side order at the Storybook Cafe?
43 Military command
44 Addled by age
45 Pentecost events
48 Where to nosh on a knish
49 Hill builder
52 "I am," to Descartes
53 Battering beam
55 Hebrew prophet
57 Dessert order at the Storybook Cafe?
62 Garden entrance
64 Andean animal
65 Barrel diameter
66 Center of a revolution
67 Kind of down
68 Greek love god
69 The Shakers, e.g.
70 Public embarrassment
71 Fender flaw

DOWN

1 Wyoming city
2 To the rear
3 Some Renaissance works
4 Gorges
5 Arthur Murray lesson
6 Author Janowitz
7 One-named model
8 DeMille specialties
9 Leafy courses
10 "I cannot tell ___"
11 Sump
12 Open, as a keg
13 Deficient
21 ___-Wip (dessert topping)
22 Medic's bag
26 Armbone
27 Huffed and puffed
30 Have deed to
31 Start of an Alger story?
32 In a trajectory
34 Level, in Leeds
35 Stretches, with "out"
36 "It's a deal!"
38 Switch settings
39 Stead
40 Striking in effect
41 "___ Darlin'" (jazz standard)
42 Root or Yale
46 Prefix with corn or corder
47 Luxurious furs
49 Like sailors on leave
50 Impulse carrier
51 Most docile
54 Kind of acid
56 Spherical
58 "___ we forget . . ."
59 Invited
60 Prayer closing
61 Swiss river
62 Shell product
63 It may swing in the jungle

160 by John R. Conrad

ACROSS

1 Roman sun god
4 Neighbor of Montenegro
10 Disparaging comments
14 Start of a quip
16 Green concern: Abbr.
17 Unite
18 Freedom fighter, for short?
19 Pilot's instrument
20 Disney Store item
21 Gridiron opener
22 Quip, part 2
26 R.N.'s service
29 Alphabet trio
30 ___ Tin Tin
31 Narrow inlet
32 Mathematician Turing
34 Gaping grin
37 Quip, Part 3
40 Hyperactive ones
41 Remedy
42 TV host Peeples
43 Québec's ___ d'Orléans
44 Sudden flight
45 "How sad"
46 End of the quip
51 Trail
52 Psychic Geller
53 Part of the eye
57 ___ Beach, Fla.
58 Not worth ___
62 Word in a spiritual
63 Author of the quip
64 Lip
65 Do a longshoreman's job
66 Alpine road feature

DOWN

1 Alone
2 "Goodness gracious!"
3 Shakespeare's "very foolish fond old man"
4 Hidden mike
5 "___ pro nobis" (Latin motto)
6 Academic period: Abbr.
7 Kweisi Mfume's org.
8 Pentium chip maker
9 "Die Fledermaus" maid
10 Dante's beloved
11 Figurehead?
12 "The Planets" composer
13 Illegal political money
15 Arafat's org.
22 Less available
23 Cools one's heels
24 Grist
25 Roman galley
26 Neat
27 Actress Bonet
28 Dangerous dinosaurs
33 Big Apple inits.
34 Farmerish
35 Les États-___
36 Neb. neighbor
38 Airplane wing flaps
39 Part of an orange
46 Some salmon
47 Swelling
48 Ring heavyweights
49 "___ my case!"
50 Kind of pie
53 Prefix with valence
54 Repulsive
55 Loose parts
56 Eons
59 ___ kwon do
60 Journalist Kupcinet
61 Have bills

161 · by Nancy Joline

ACROSS

1 Out of place
11 Tiny bit
15 Better
16 Like Nash's lama
17 "Mansfield Park" author
18 Tabula ___
19 Occasional
20 Holiday abroad
21 1972 Billy Wilder film
23 Orchestra section
26 Contemptible and not to be trusted
28 Collector's items
30 Train part
31 Maintain
32 Easter preceder
33 Ivan's da
34 Check
36 Storyteller
39 Walken's gift in "The Dead Zone"
42 Gosh, British-style
44 "___ House"
48 Soccer great Diego
51 Setting
52 Conditional
54 Desmond of "Sunset Boulevard"
55 Thin layer
56 Mathematics writer ___ Stewart
58 Chap, affectionately
59 Inter ___
60 Synthetic fabric
64 Kind of egg
65 Toon bird
66 Shoe width
67 Lifeguards wear them

DOWN

1 Mediterranean holiday spot
2 1984 Oscar winner
3 Banks, e.g.
4 Porter
5 Airline to Karachi
6 Wipeout
7 1987 skating champ Brian
8 Paisley, e.g.
9 Suffix with Capri
10 Like some committees
11 U.S.O.'s concern
12 Stupid joke
13 Having a will
14 Renowned New York eatery
22 Energy
24 Burns out
25 Kind
27 Combine
29 Museum of natural history exhibits
35 Kind of recording
37 Not now
38 Law used to fight organized crime, acronymically
39 Board the Concorde: Var.
40 Food industry giant
41 Oath
43 Perth Amboy's river
45 Emil's "Blue Angel" co-star, 1930
46 Brand of brandy
47 They're followed
49 Fly
50 Racket
53 Sports page numbers
57 Dealer's nemesis
61 Bud's comedy sidekick
62 Big ___
63 French article

162 · by Michael W. Perry

ACROSS

1 Bankrolls
5 Gumbo vegetable
9 Military group
14 Take on
15 "Gallipoli" director
16 Mozart offering
17 Start of a quote by 39-Across
20 Old schoolhouse item
21 Nostradamus, e.g.
22 Where the worm turns
23 Geisha's garment
25 Droop
27 Function
28 Record producer Brian
29 ___-ran
32 Noble's partner
34 Tear asunder
36 Tombstone lawman
38 Comedian Foxx
39 See 17-Across
42 Open a bit
44 Rock music's Ford
45 Trans World Dome team
49 Like a harvest moon
51 Popular race
53 The pause that refreshes?
54 Fish cookout
55 Sweet potato
57 Radio antenna
59 Folder's locale
61 Gilbert of "Roseanne"
64 John Lennon hit
65 End of the quote
68 Where the buffalo roam
69 Town in Nevada
70 Otherwise
71 Single-masted vessel
72 Audition for a part
73 Textile worker

DOWN

1 Narrow margin of victory
2 Carrier
3 "Get real!"
4 Former defense collective
5 Bird of prey
6 Ivories and others
7 Get carried away?
8 One born on April 1
9 Debate side
10 Chooses
11 Echo
12 Exalted
13 "Lone Star" director John
18 Singer Horne
19 Colorless
24 Designer Cassini
26 Actress with a "Tootsie" role
30 Spinnaker or jib
31 Satellite's path
33 Bring up
35 Actress Cannon
37 Gov. Wilson
40 Bacchanalian event
41 Money in Johannesburg
42 Advent
43 He's on "Tonight" tonight
46 Irregularity
47 Lethargic feeling
48 Not a saver
49 Auction bids
50 Daybreak direction
52 New Zealander
56 "Politically Incorrect" host Bill
58 Sat (for)
60 Proof word
62 Provoke
63 "Lonely Boy" singer
66 Slangy affirmative
67 The Eternal

163 by Richard Hughes

ACROSS
1 Lived it up
10 Wedge-shaped inserts
15 Too keen
16 Site of two of the Ancient Wonders
17 Ace
18 Slag
19 Put ___ ease
20 Tore
21 Third rock from the sun
22 Toward the end
24 Rap's Dr. ___
25 Marching band instruments
29 Detects
31 Italian count?
35 Actress Balin
36 Commando's outing
37 He was Amin guy
38 Crate component
39 CNN parent co.
40 Partner
42 Spoiled rotten
44 Hungry
45 It's equal to 100 ergs per gram
46 Deeply personal
50 Ford's folly?
52 First name in coaching
53 "___ Andy Warho!" (1996 movie)
58 Buddha's birthplace
59 Discordant
61 Herd
62 Mesmerized
63 Sandburg's "farewell-summer flower"
64 Called into question

DOWN
1 Jolly sound
2 Calling company?
3 Strike out
4 Field
5 "___ ever so humble . . ."
6 Airline to Chile
7 Site of the Temple of Hephaestus
8 Foreign assembly
9 Ontario's ___ Canal
10 Certain home improvers
11 Ring dance
12 Excessive
13 Was unkind to
14 Casements
22 Shaq's alma mater
23 Really big shoe
25 Hudson's Bay Company, e.g.
26 Poorly situated
27 Impose
28 Roush of the Reds
30 Risotto alternative
32 It may block the Rhein
33 Fall sports stats
34 "Wild Orchid" locale, 1990
38 Fall from grace
40 Author Rand
41 Director's cry
42 Rhoda's sister
43 Rudder attachment
47 Frenzied
48 Northeast college town
49 Prince of Darkness
51 Sun shade
53 About
54 L.I.R.R. stops
55 Stalk
56 Years ago
57 Prepared to drive, with "up"
60 Multinational business inits.

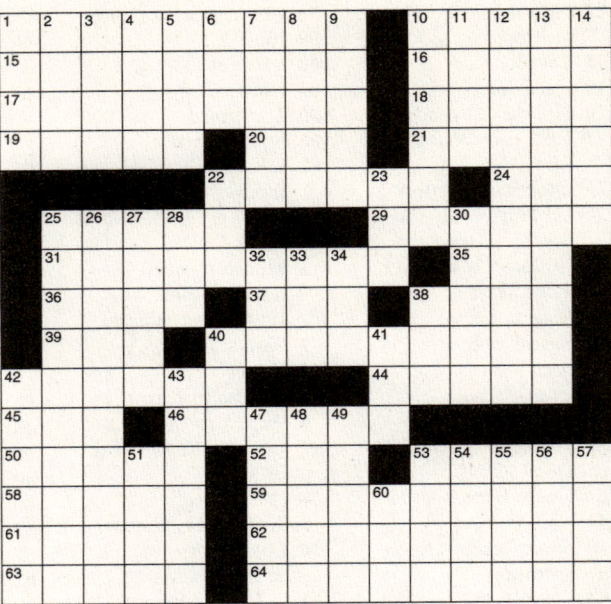

164 by Manny Nosowsky

ACROSS
1 Build-up
7 Literally, soft technique
14 Cheyenne ally of old
15 Extremely important
16 Inflammation of the respiratory tract
17 In a silly fashion
18 Boomer
19 Garcia Marquez's "___ Writes to the Colonel"
21 James and Clark
22 Business start
24 Young boxer, e.g.
26 Goes downhill
27 Classic name in mail order
29 He can hardly give a hoot
31 Compass dir.
32 Rush
34 Actions
36 Pictorial
38 Secondary listing
41 "Ready ___"
44 Agcy. that monitors smoking hazards
45 Dr. Zhivago and others
47 Vaccine name
49 To be, to Henri
51 12-point types
53 Old columnist Maxwell
54 Kind of gun
56 Unabridged editions
58 Something to believe in
59 Old profs
61 Curt
63 Pensioner
64 First and Second places?
65 Prizes
66 Fixes

DOWN
1 Old homesteads
2 Dive
3 ___Locka, Fla.
4 Counsel, perhaps
5 Chuck
6 Comment from Santa
7 Glyptologist
8 ___ tree,
9 Athletic sort
10 30's Interior, Secretary
11 Paris art treasure, with "The"
12 Soup go with
13 Book set entirely on the date 6/16/04
14 Pretend to be
20 Land of Enchantment
23 Mideasterner
25 R.&B. singer Bryson
28 Poker faced
30 Red foes
33 Become eventually
35 Arm parts
37 Facts
38 Start of a chewing out
39 Computers' working hours
40 Browning, originally
42 Biased
43 Cold comfort?
46 Deer with three-pointed antlers
48 Finger points, when said twice
50 Odd
52 Put into play
55 Desperate
57 Petitioned
60 Pro ___
62 ___-Cat (winter vehicle)

165　by Nancy Joline

ACROSS

1 Name from 50's TV
9 Baseball's Doubleday
14 Romberg product
15 Filmdom's Lawrence
16 Infant's game
17 Infant's shoe
18 Showed fear
19 Stupidity
20 Sting
24 Mal de ___
26 Words of enlightenment
27 Mars sighting
29 Bestow
32 Blow the cover of?
34 Puts back
38 ___ Juana
39 Urban noise maker
41 Take this out for a spin
42 University founded in 1253
44 Locust
46 Exhortation
48 Pitcher Ryan
49 "___ of you . . ."
52 Ear-related
54 "The ___ From Brazil"

55 Defective stop sign?
58 "I ___ You Babe"
60 Yogi's cartoon sidekick
61 Blubbered
66 Like spring flowers
67 Battery type
68 Physicist Freeman
69 Innkeeper

DOWN

1 Person with a collar?
2 One rung on the evolutionary ladder
3 Spike, for one
4 Biblical vessel
5 Coach Bryant
6 Up
7 High
8 Vietnamese money unit
9 Accelerator item
10 Sticks
11 Dostoyevsky's "___ From Underground"
12 Beethoven dedicatee
13 Singer Della
15 ___-Wan Kenobi
19 Star in Cygnus
20 Rabbits' tails

21 "Pagliacci" husband
22 Menachem's peace partner
23 Deface
25 Agony
28 Item of love?
30 Bk. of Revelation
31 Poison
33 Pioneering video game
35 Writer Calvino
36 TV show since 1/14/52
37 Wings have them
40 Wambaugh's "The ___ Field"
43 Bogey
45 Male swan
47 1980 Richard Gere portrayal
49 Hooked in a way
50 Definitely not a brain surgeon
51 Chemical compounds
53 Kind of tour
56 Continue
57 South Africa's ___ Paul
59 "___ does it!"
61 Phooey's cousin

62 Novelist Rölvaag
63 Medium for Matisse
64 Ending with acetyl or butyl
65 ___ Spiegel

166　by Fred Piscop

ACROSS

1 ___ Islands (Pacific group)
9 Pink end
15 Type of music
16 Generic
17 Whenever
18 VCR user's need
19 Props (up)
20 Faith
22 N.B.A.'s Archibald
23 Kind of crazy
24 Tennis score
25 Perplexed
26 Arch site
27 Complaint
28 Chemical salt
31 Postal abbr.
32 Monte ___
35 Marshaled
37 Apollo component
38 Having rectangular cells, as a ceiling
42 Hue and cry
44 Wyoming's Simpson
45 Lose it
49 Early stock speculator Russell
50 Common side order
51 "See you"

52 In ___ (doubled up)
54 Serve
56 Moolah
57 Heartfelt
59 Park, e.g.
60 Kind of exam
61 A day ago, dialectally
62 Stopped

DOWN

1 Name in aviation
2 Hello and goodbye
3 VCR user's need
4 Gets stuffed
5 Word repeated before "show"
6 The Beatles' "Yes ___"
7 Info on a French passport
8 Big name in small construction
9 On the ocean: Fr.
10 Word with block or test
11 Temper
12 Lori of "Petticoat Junction"

13 Make thin
14 Yielded
21 Singer Coolidge
23 Dipsomaniac
26 Throat problem?
27 Bushed
29 "Up and ___!"
30 Govt. investigator
32 Graduates' celebration time
33 Correspondent
34 Conjures up
36 Auden verses
39 Big blow
40 Hugged
41 Eddie Murphy flick
43 Something remembered
46 Floating
47 Forthwith
48 Respired, dog-style
50 Clydesdale outfitter
53 Rock music's Mötley ___
54 Some live by them
55 Culture starter
58 Small note

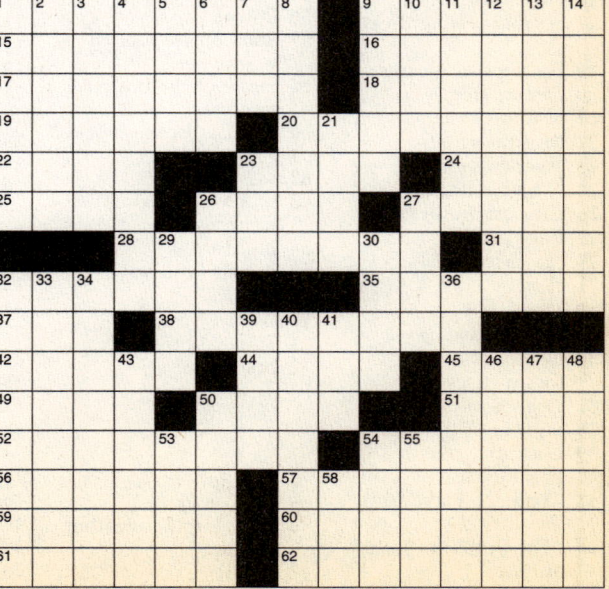

ACROSS

1 Book of the Apocrypha
7 Apse setting
15 Catchall phrase
16 Esthete
17 Uncompromising
18 Swain song
19 Doctrinal holding
20 French assembly
21 Teachers' grp.
22 They have namesakes: Abbr.
23 Grammy-winning country group
25 Results of conks
26 Farm building
30 Guarding mobilely
34 Its fruit is monkey bread
36 It's played at the 7-Down
38 Rose's home
39 Without concern for the future
40 Baron in "Der Rosenkavalier"
41 Wistful one
42 Epcot neighbor
44 Computer add-on?

47 G. & S. princess
50 Embarrass
51 Strauss's "Ariadne auf ___"
53 Transportation Secretary Pena
55 Theater's Willy, Linda, Happy and Biff
56 St. Louis arch designer
57 Charlotte ___, Virgin Islands
58 Printed, as a quote
59 Way with words?

DOWN

1 One-liners
2 Complete
3 Fills in a hole
4 Tennis hothead
5 XXX activity
6 Derby
7 36-Across's site
8 Circus locales
9 Sportscaster Hank
10 "___ song go . . ."
11 Mr. Chaney
12 A Karamazov
13 Part with

14 Purlieu
20 Southernmost U.S. point
24 Michaels of "Saturday Night Live"
26 ___ speak (as it were)
27 Footnote abbr.
28 Literally, superior one
29 Be loyal to
30 Knowing
31 Pusher's nemesis
32 Chief god of Memphis
33 Afflicts
34 Howled
35 Copernican concern
37 Lustrous velvet
41 Kind of mining
42 Umpire for the duel in "Hamlet"
43 Zoo critter
44 Rate highly
45 Artist Delaunay
46 Car of the 20's
47 Conditional words
48 College leader
49 Month after Shevat
52 "___ for All Seasons"

54 Prior to
55 Scale notes

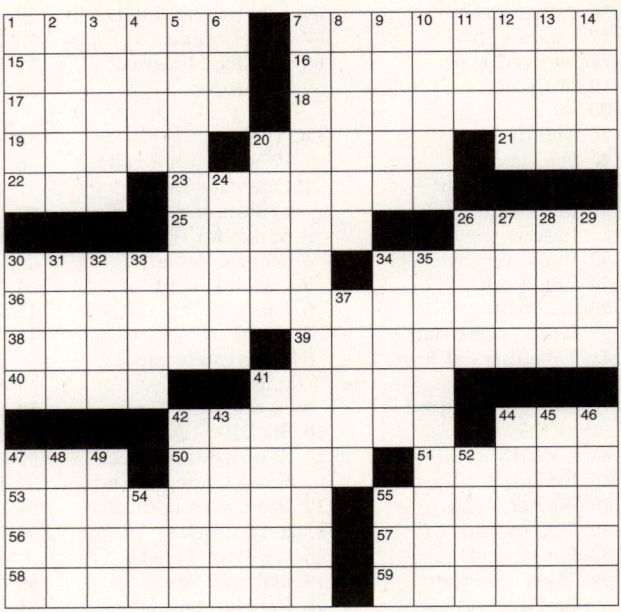

ACROSS

1 Say "I do" again
6 March starter
9 Diplomatic skills
14 Dwelling place
15 U.N. member
16 Honolulu hello
17 Scrabble, anagrams, etc.
19 Bottoms of graphs
20 Disney dog
21 Madam's mates
22 Mosque chiefs
23 Ave. crossers
24 "I've been ___!"
25 City on the Brazos
27 Ear cleaner
29 ___ race (finished first)
30 Lived
33 Oaxaca waters
35 Dictionaries and thesauruses
37 Organic soil
38 Subject of this puzzle
39 Lockup
40 Preambles
42 "You ___ Have to Be So Nice"
43 "The Sultan of Sulu" author

44 Crooner Williams
45 Jokester's props
46 Nightclub bits
47 Tricia Nixon ___
48 New Deal org.
51 Move furtively
54 Barely open
56 Bewail
57 Start of the French workweek
58 Some of them are famous
60 Not ___ in the world
61 Prayer part
62 ___ nous
63 Ex-baseball commish Ueberroth
64 Light time
65 Lucy's landlady

DOWN

1 Singer Lou
2 Enemy vessel
3 T H I S
   H E R E
   I R O N
   S E N T
4 Whirlpool
5 B.A. or Ph.D.
6 Like August weather, perhaps
7 Client

8 Computer access codes
9 City vehicle
10 Battle depicted in "The Last Command"
11 Hip joint
12 Not us
13 Freshness
18 Quickly: Abbr.
24 Towel word
26 Connectors
28 Housebroken
29 Circumlocutory
30 Poet laureate, 1843–50
31 Similar
32 Mil. officer
33 ___ Romeo
34 Well-mannered
35 Incoherent speech
36 Off Broadway award
38 Is obstinate
41 More erratic
42 Humanitarian Dorothea
45 Where a cruise calls
46 Previn or Kostelanetz
47 Disk jockey Kasem
49 San Diego pro
50 Photographer Adams

51 Masher's comeuppance
52 Politico Clare Boothe ___
53 ___ the finish

55 Al Hirt hit
56 ___ Blanc
59 Itsy-bitsy

169 by Chet Currier

ACROSS

1 Mulligan, for one
5 Red Bordeaux
10 Script starter
14 "Rule, Britannia" composer
15 Throes and woes
16 Worn-out
17 Foie gras fan
19 Actress Skye
20 Author Tan
21 Undocumented person
22 Dialect
23 Failed attempt
24 Prefix with act or state
26 Country singer Cowboy ___
29 Backus was his voice in 60's TV
31 ___ Guevara
34 Kicked off
36 Svelte in those days
38 Works by sculptor Hans
39 Ejects
41 S.F. train system
42 Adhesive, for one
44 "Idylls of the King" maiden
46 Diffident
47 Add more cushioning
49 Trial companion
50 Recumbent, in a way
52 Change for a five
54 Rumor
56 Severity
58 Agenda items
61 Bumbler's blurt
62 Barely discernible aroma
64 Apartment building head, slangily
65 Honeybunch
66 "Scram!"
67 Attention-getters
68 Mine excavation
69 Mountain cat

DOWN

1 Casa room
2 Tonsorial procedure
3 Begrudge
4 Minute
5 Shopping havens
6 "I" problem
7 Peace symbol
8 1958 Elvis hit
9 St. ___-l'École, France
10 Tangential remark
11 Church seat
12 Up ___ good
13 Inventory unit
18 Employee's delight
22 Lay ___ thick
23 Parson's home
25 Racket
26 Checkroom articles
27 Competitor of Phil
28 Lively new pet
30 Disoriented
32 "Tell ___" (1965 Zombies hit)
33 Computer command
35 Senior fellow
37 Ski lifts
40 Potent punch
43 Harness race
45 Casts desirous eyes
48 Pinch a pooch
51 Climbs
53 ___ Dame
54 Poppycock
55 Sensualist
57 "Othello" villain
58 Moist
59 ___ even keel
60 Charon's crossing
62 60's draft org.
63 Silent ___ (20's moniker)

170 by Nancy S. Ross

ACROSS

1 Naïve ones
6 Crosswise to a ship's middle
11 ___ Malaprop (Sheridan character)
14 Massey of "Love Happy"
15 Yankee Yogi
16 Hour on a grandfather clock
17 Twiggy broom
18 End-all's companion
19 One-liner
20 "Unfinished"
23 "Glitter and Be ___" ("Candide" song)
24 Coop denizen
25 State of France
26 Relieved sound
29 "Foucault's Pendulum" author
31 "Ich bin ___ Berliner"
33 Lennon's lady
34 Crack the case
36 More pleasant
40 "Classical"
43 Reddish dye
44 ". . . and ___ grow on"
45 Ingested
46 Approves
48 ___ Lanka
49 Home of Iowa State
50 Severe disappointment
53 Overhead rails
55 Hokum
57 "Kaddish"
63 Great many
64 Coordination loss: Var.
65 Pavarotti, for one
66 Prefix with sex or cycle
67 Beau ___
68 Mother's-side relative
69 Aerialist's safeguard
70 Clockmaker Thomas et al.
71 M.P.A.A.-approved

DOWN

1 Lobster eaters' needs
2 British P.M. Douglas-Home
3 Hokum
4 Ample
5 Dance in Rio
6 A.M. or P.M., e.g.
7 "Pastoral"
8 Remove chalk
9 Francis of "What's My Line"
10 Neighbor of Senegal
11 Strength
12 Cowboy's rope
13 Tourist attraction
21 Ken Follett's "___ the Needle"
22 Bottled spirits
26 Undergrad
27 Apropos of
28 Thug
30 Sister of Euterpe
32 Dope
34 Good, long bath
35 Always
37 Study for finals
38 Villa-building family
39 Hwy. numbers
41 Understood
42 Swizzles
47 Certain sofa
49 Parthenon goddess
50 Kid's shooter
51 Sierra ___
52 Trip that's out of this world?
54 Slightest
56 Aquatic mammal
58 Loses rigidity
59 Actress Carrie et al.
60 ___ the kill
61 Learning method
62 1857's ___ Scott Decision

171 — by Jeremy Thomas Paine

ACROSS

1 Fantastik competitor
7 Minimum
12 60's space project
13 Polyester sheets
15 Show horse
16 Trident carrier
18 Jewel
19 "___ Rhythm"
21 Riyadh residents
22 Blitzed
24 TV's "Tales from the ___"
25 Weaselly animal
28 Boston airport
30 Doe follower, in song
31 Botticelli subject
32 Lawyers' org.
35 Budget item
36 Fits (inside)
37 Kind of history
38 Compass heading
39 Aligns, temporally
40 Bring forth
41 Disney dog
42 Father of the Titans
43 50's White House name
46 Tap type

48 Item in this puzzle's theme
50 Results
51 Warning to Bo-Peep
54 Buckle up
56 Offering a neologism
58 Meaning
59 A Mouseketeer
60 Ground
61 Nullify

DOWN

1 Parisian head
2 Utah city
3 Street drug
4 Florida city
5 Eugene's place
6 "The Prisoner of Chillon" poet
7 K-O string
8 Potato buds
9 Guanaco relatives
10 General Motors product
11 Hubert's wife, in the comics
12 Food additive
14 Trim a tress
17 Superlative suffix

20 Means of spotting this puzzle's theme?
22 Editor's notation
23 Some pieces of advice
25 Damages
26 Summer beverages
27 Artist Magritte
29 Astronaut Grissom
31 Relieves
32 Elvis's middle name
33 Capital on the Caspian
34 XXX drinks
36 Big Apple sch.
37 Ellipsoid
39 Train car
40 Causing to disappear
41 Mexican festival feature
42 Ruined
43 Brit. legislators
44 Prefix with meter
45 1918 battle site
47 Like some pre-Columbian art
49 Hue
51 Ship post
52 Part of A.M.
53 Point in life

55 Advanced degree?
57 Teachers' grp.

172 — by Gerald R. Ferguson

ACROSS

1 Over-the-shoulder item
6 Beliefs
12 Conciliatory
14 Euphoria
16 Sour note
17 Comeback
18 Cousin of slander
19 More than encourages
21 "___ Stoops to Conquer"
22 Hospital inits.
23 Journalism, for one
25 Sought reparations from
26 Mill locale
28 Animals in Pharaoh's dream, in Genesis
29 Dear, in Dijon
30 Kind of suspicion
32 Brought up
33 Bean-sprout bean
34 Kind of loser
35 Mystery awards
38 Feature of Sinatra and Newman
42 Drive out
43 Codger

44 "Two Years Before the Mast" writer
45 Insurance agent's calculation
46 "Swann's Way" novelist
48 16th-century date
49 Pretend
50 Water pipes
51 Oklahoma tribe
53 Carpenters' devices
55 Singer Kitt et al,
57 Danger for a low-flying plane
58 Hemingway's "Islands in the ___"
59 Children's author Le Cain et al.
60 It might be past

DOWN

1 ___ Valley
2 Roman officer
3 Peace Nobelist Cassin
4 Horse's hock
5 Chart shape
6 Cylindrical and tapered
7 Typewriter type

8 Cats catch them
9 W.W. II front: Abbr.
10 Sneezer's needs
11 Gloater's phrase
13 Packing, as fruit
15 Not optional
16 Desk items
20 Kaboom!
24 Trappers' wares
25 Used a buffer
27 Linen fabric
29 Supervision
31 Russell of Hollywood
32 Shellackings
34 Tops, of a sort
35 Roving
36 Kin of "So what?"
37 More breezy
38 Largess
39 Some road bikes
40 Chess finale
41 Instruments for Clarence Clemens
43 Baked desserts
46 Word of mouth
47 1971 batting champ Joe
50 "Take ___ your leader"

52 Light submachine gun
54 Celtic Neptune
56 Blue-chip symbol

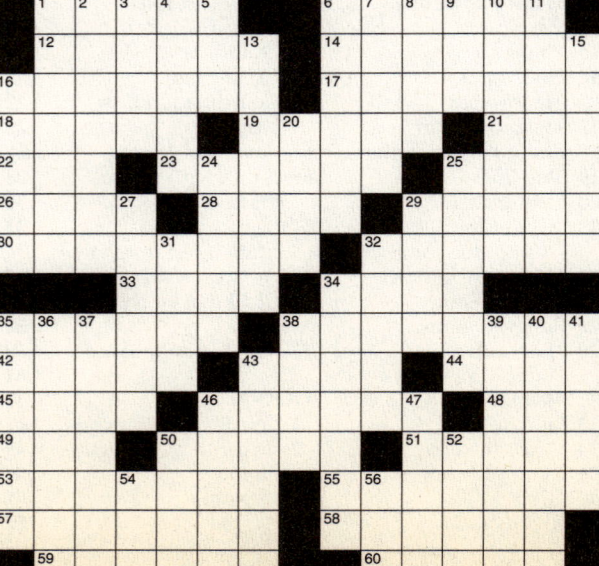

ACROSS
1 "Idylls of the King" setting
8 Sticks
14 Its chief port is Ciudad Bolívar
15 Roadside hazard
16 Labor Day event
18 Mt. Hood site
19 Pilot's heading
20 Kind of shot
22 Wellness provider: Abbr.
23 Suffix with tip
25 Newshawk
27 Sea
29 "A Bridge Too Far" co-star
30 Incongruousness
31 Eroded
32 Pest control brand
36 Filmdom's Wertmuller
37 Certain farmhand
38 Old book's content
39 English author ___ Phillpotts
40 Under observation
41 Fashion capital
42 Hook
44 Rushlight
45 Emend, in a way
48 Quarter
49 First name of a Fighting Irish legend
50 Subordinates
52 Benefits org.
55 Old Rolling Stones record label
57 1948 Triple Crown winner
59 Windup
60 Petition
61 (The) Stage
62 Chalk deposit sites

DOWN
1 Temporary accommodations
2 Assister of the Trojans
3 Significant event
4 Chemical ending
5 Millionaire producer
6 Muted colors
7 Beep
8 Bet middler?
9 Polygraph inventor John
10 "___ been thinking . . ."
11 "S'long"
12 Fairy-tale character
13 Cervantes title
17 More than sleepy
21 Verged toward
24 Enjoyment of a position
26 Cancel, in a way
27 Stratagem
28 Nonproductive
31 Entries
33 Highly aloof
34 Unwritten
35 Gray-brown goose
37 Dress ornamentations
41 Sicilian wine
43 Three-time Tour de France champion
44 "No, No, Nora" singer
45 Jephunneh's son
46 Town on the Penobscot
47 Stuffed carnival prize, maybe
51 Department of northern France
53 It's après après-midi
54 Farm dwellers
56 Profession of 36-Across: Abbr.
58 Third word of "America"

ACROSS
1 Sanction
10 Elements found once each in 1-, 15-, 57- and 62-Across, and 30-Down
15 Pulmonary problem
16 Tots' cries
17 To the point
18 Heated and then some
19 ___ squares (statistical method)
20 Untouched by time
22 Summer D.C. clock setting
23 Consumer Reports feature
26 Brazil's biggest city
29 Wraparound dresses Var.
33 Fort Peck site
35 Kind of cup
36 Together
38 Set of dishes
40 Words before "diamond" and "pearl" in an Irving Berlin song
41 It's directly south of the White House lawn
43 Old store counter
45 Commuter country
48 Catches
50 Response: Abbr.
51 River port in Kentucky
54 Political societies
56 Run into a hitch?
57 Harem woman
61 Helicopter part
62 Works by Plato
63 Generation Y
64 Dressmakers' materials

DOWN
1 Trick-or-treaters' treats
2 Old biscuit brand
3 Tumorous growths
4 Shacks
5 Pass over
6 80's White House name
7 Like Bruckner's Symphony No. 7
8 California wine, familiarly
9 Worry greatly
10 "The Sound of Music" farewell
11 Probably not a night owl
12 Zoological name suffix
13 Haggis ingredient
14 Applications
21 Literary monogram
23 "___ have promises to keep": Frost
24 Gladden
25 Trinity member
27 Seize with alacrity
28 TV employees
30 "Macbeth" stage direction
31 Die Zeit article
32 Grasp
34 Misbehave
36 Turkish leader
37 Cry
39 City, to Cato
42 Sender of monthly checks: Abbr.
44 L.A.'s Union, e.g.
46 Provided: Var.
47 Evaluate
49 Little ___ (state nickname)
51 Sassy
52 Drug-yielding plant
53 Spoil, with "on"
54 Literary genre: Abbr.
55 "Let ___ then, you and I": Eliot
58 24 hours, to Diego
59 Alpine river
60 Legal deg.

175 by Janet R. Bender

ACROSS
1 Sixth sense
4 Suit part
8 Fr. holy women
12 Donjon
14 River of Hesse
15 Author Gardner et al.
17 Suffix with cigar or major
18 Hawaiian goose
19 Della or Pee Wee
20 English writer who applied Darwinian principles to philosophy
23 Mill output
24 Football lineman
25 Coll. senior's test
27 Bridge support
30 Synagogue-goer
33 "Speed" star
35 Ott or Gibson
36 It helps build character
37 Broadway conductor Lehman ___
38 Bewitch
39 Defeats
40 Borscht ingredient
41 Select number
42 Olympian Jackie Joyner-___
43 Poetic contraction
44 Bedroom furniture piece
46 Be at fault
47 Certain intersection
48 "Thou shalt not covet" Commandment
50 ABC sitcom star
56 Playboys' looks
57 "___ Only Just Begun"
58 Actress Sommer
60 Intuit
61 "___ Tu" (1974 hit)
62 Govt. agents
63 Suffix with pun
64 Monthly due
65 Match part

DOWN
1 Just make, with "out"
2 Thomas of timepieces
3 "Where Have All the Flowers Gone" songwriter
4 Surfaces
5 First woman swimmer of the English Channel
6 Mailed
7 Uno y dos
8 Placid
9 Polling news
10 Util. power
11 Zaire's Mobutu ___ Seko
13 Saucy
16 Sun. speech
21 Kind of palm
22 Claiborne of Rhode Island
25 Diving bird
26 Newswoman Poussaint
28 Small ducks
29 1982 Matt Dillon movie
30 Southern senator
31 Reply to a knock
32 Bremen's river
34 Certain doc
36 Neighbor of Lux.
38 TV's "___ Haw"
39 "Games People Play" author Eric
41 ___ Basset of the comics
42 Most acute
44 More compact
45 Director Spielberg
47 Concise
49 Weight allowance
50 Chicago transports
51 Wine sediment
52 Spring time
53 Juice server
54 "Primal Fear" star
55 ___-Ball (arcade game)
59 Tolkien creature

176 by Elizabeth C. Gorski

ACROSS
1 Movie souvenir
5 E. coli watchdog: Abbr.
8 Neil Simon's "___ Suite"
13 Moon goddess
14 Unaccompanied
15 Arthur Miller's salesman
16 Genesis son
17 Opposed to, in dialect
18 Do penance
19 Noted Ballet Russe dancer
22 The "A" in Thomas A. Edison
23 ___-Cat (winter vehicle)
24 "Network" satirist
31 Birds at sea
32 Was in debt
33 Kind of soup
34 Duds
35 Algebraic grouping
37 Halcyon
38 Prefix with lateral
39 Swiss river
40 Marx and Malden
41 "Pulcinella" composer
45 Biblical verb suffix
46 ___-Day vitamins
47 Eighth in a Taylor series
54 J.F.K. terminal architect
55 Pay to play, with "up"
56 Mrs. Chaplin
57 Three-time P.G.A. tournament champ
58 Pastry chef, at times
59 Resort near Mt. Jackson
60 Swarm
61 Law, to Lucius
62 "Laugh-In" name

DOWN
1 Eastern European
2 Bottom brass
3 French articles
4 Chopin compositions
5 After-dinner sipping
6 Sixth-century date
7 And, e.g.: Abbr.
8 Mapped out
9 Many
10 Run ___ (go off course)
11 Off the wall
12 Chemical suffix
14 "Get it?"
20 Local legislators: Abbr.
21 "The best ___ to come"
24 Pitchfork part
25 Surgical procedure, for short
26 Hebrew prophet
27 Wonder
28 Explosion's cause
29 Shade of green
30 Candied items
31 Holder for needles and things
35 Frazzled comic strip heroine
36 Puckster Bobby
37 Womanizer
39 Spanning
40 Baby bouncer
42 Go over again
43 Maelstrom
44 Lay to rest
47 Alphabetic run
48 Copycat
49 Bomb
50 "___ bitten, twice shy"
51 Fly high
52 Sweater, usually
53 Word on a lock
54 Language suffix

177 by Jim Page

ACROSS
1 50's portrait?
8 Excoriates
13 Like some dental checkups
15 Become intense
16 Hither and yon
17 Punctual
18 "The French Connection" co-star
19 Place to doodle
21 Certain NCO
24 Proceeds slyly
25 Spanish religious center
27 Hit the dirt
28 "___ Drives Me Crazy" (1989 hit)
31 It may be blocked
32 "Don't rub ___!"
33 Site for a seat of honor
34 Manhattan district
36 Trims
38 Ex-sportscaster Hodges
39 Coulombs per second
41 Quizmaster
42 Verb suffix
43 Biblical invocation to God
44 Long ___
45 Flight
47 Santa ___
48 1984 Coppola film, with "The"
52 Milne character
55 Acropolis figure
56 It's receptive to new ideas
59 Song stanzas
60 Alumnus at an alumni party, e.g.
61 Actress Sally Ann
62 Demagogues

DOWN
1 German preposition
2 Beget
3 "Forrest Gump" Oscar nominee
4 Messenger ___
5 ___ Rutledge (Abe Lincoln's betrothed)
6 Meshuga
7 Takes a powder?
8 Got rid of while they were hot?
9 Homebuilder's supplies
10 Expectant
11 Colorado River city
12 Shot, in a way
14 Orpheus, for one
15 White House connection
20 Wings it
22 Reasons for retakes
23 Mason's job
25 Jeff Bagwell, e.g.
26 Bug
28 Overly sentimental
29 "Car 54, Where Are You?" creator
30 Classics trio
32 Like much of Wordsworth's poetry
33 Energetic one
35 Changing places
37 ___ vu
40 Kind of game
43 Makes up (for)
45 Canyon, for one
46 Custodian
48 Kind of cow
49 "High Noon" actor Kruger
50 Relax
51 Phase constant, in physics
53 Critical spelling feature of "Caribbean"
54 Works of Anacreon
57 Susan Sarandon in "Dead Man Walking"
58 80's TV celeb

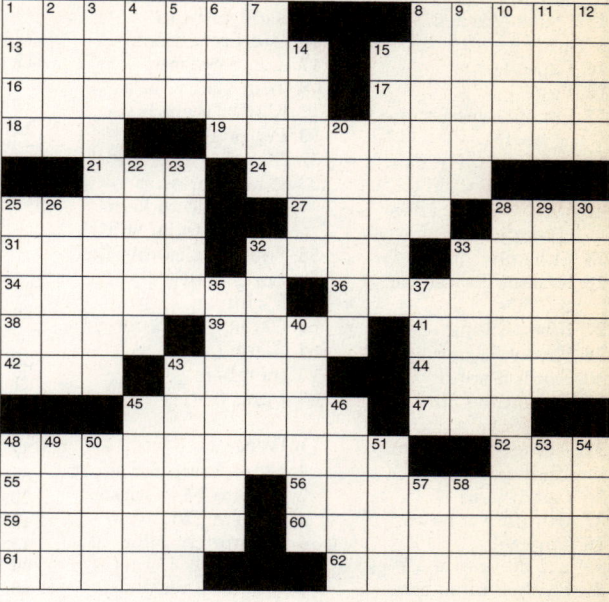

178 by Gerald R. Ferguson

ACROSS
1 Pickle container
4 Motionless
9 Fashion
14 Matriarch of all matriarchs
15 Actor Romero
16 Boiling
17 Weighed in
20 Light lunches
21 To any extent
22 List-ending abbr.
23 Moo juice container
25 Grp. overseeing toxic cleanups
28 Perfect rating
29 Most prudent
31 Become raveled
32 Painful spots
33 Carroll adventuress
34 Caused disharmony
38 Napping spots
39 Magazine exhortation
40 Break in relations
41 Out of business
43 Compaq products
46 ___ Miss
47 Engulfs in amusement
48 Cream ingredient
49 Tear to shreds
51 Part of MOMA
53 Blabbed
57 ___ pedis (athlete's foot)
58 Take to the stump
59 Certain shirt
60 Anxiety
61 Wanderer
62 Japanese honorific

DOWN
1 High-fliers
2 Fly
3 Change tactics
4 Like an eclair
5 Composer Rorem and others
6 Superlative ending
7 Short cheer
8 Firestone features
9 Clergyman
10 Kind of surgery
11 Indoor court
12 Indian with a bear dance
13 Some M.I.T. grads
18 Chum
19 Leave be
23 Wielded
24 Partner of search
26 Warsaw ___
27 Word of assent
29 Canton cookware
30 Land west of Eng.
31 Current
32 Sing "shooby-doo"
33 Out for the night
34 Aggravate
35 Part of a church service
36 Piano-playing Dame
37 Ariz.-to-Kan. dir.
38 Sign of stage success
41 Professor Plum's game
42 Pomeranian, for one
43 Stitched folds
44 Window of an eye
45 Breath mint brand
47 Sloppy-landing sound
48 Suffix with stock
50 France's ___ de Glenans
51 Queens team
52 Follow the code
53 ___ Puf fabric softener
54 Wrestler's goal
55 Have a go at
56 Gen. Arnold of W.W. II fame

179 by Stephanie Spadaccini

ACROSS
1 Stage between egg and pupa
6 "Durn it!"
10 Head of hair, slangily
13 "Silas Marner" author
14 Exploiters
16 Eggs
17 Teensy-weensy piece of beef?
19 Seat in St. Paul's
20 ___ Rosa, Calif.
21 1984 World Series champs
23 The sun
26 Johnnie Ray hit of the 50's
27 Biblical king
28 Sleazy
30 Sandlot sport
33 Cottonlike fiber
34 Without
35 Actress ___ Dawn Chong
36 Got 100 on
37 Dot on a monitor
38 Tiny bit
39 ___-de-France
40 Radius, ulna, etc.

41 U.C.L.A. player
42 Big North Carolina industry
44 "Dirty Rotten Scoundrels" actress ___ Headly
45 Kind of bean
46 Old French coin
47 ___ es Salaam
48 Tom Canty, in a Mark Twain book
50 Pedestals, e.g.
52 Mornings, for short
53 What stand-up comics do to keep their material shiny?
58 Soupy Sales missile
59 Long bout
60 Vicinities
61 Catalogue contents
62 Some P.T.A. members
63 Long (for)

DOWN
1 Moon craft, for short
2 Actress MacGraw
3 ___ Tin Tin
4 "Comment allez-___?"
5 Embassy worker

6 Name for a cowpoke
7 Movie pooch
8 Society page word
9 Like a proper rescuee
10 Ride an engine-powered bike?
11 Finished
12 Furry feet
15 Poodle and dirndl, e.g.
18 Professor 'iggins
22 Sailor
23 Sea route
24 Delphic shrine
25 "My gold dress isn't back from the cleaners yet" and others?
27 Sharpens
29 Caesar of "Caesar's Hour"
30 At ___ and sevens
31 Chicana
32 Horseshoes shot
34 Sal of "Giant"
37 Instant picture
38 Anger
40 They're big in gyms
41 Colorful, crested bird
43 Strike lightly
44 "No kidding!"
46 MS. enclosures

48 Madonna's "___ Don't Preach"
49 In the center of
50 Dallas's nickname
51 Achy
54 Meadow
55 Mauna ___
56 It may be pulled in charades
57 ID digits

180 by Robert H. Wolfe

ACROSS
1 Kind of race or queen
5 ___ point
10 Malign
14 Morning wind personified
15 Rocket stage
16 Actress Sedgwick
17 End of "America the Beautiful," in brief
20 Circus workers
21 All-purpose song lyrics
22 Society page word
23 Put on board
24 1987 #1 hit by Heart
26 Playmate
29 Learned
33 Success story
38 To be, in Paree
39 Beatitudes phrase, in brief
43 Cotton pod
44 They're alphabetized in phone directories
45 Books that suffer where and tear?
49 Queensland neighbor: Abbr.

50 Customs
52 Broadway's Harold
56 1981 Blake Edwards comedy
58 Plaster backing
60 Thermoplastics
62 Event of 12/16/1773, in brief
65 Deputy
66 Actress Verdugo
67 Debt satisfier
68 Winning margin, maybe
69 Haggadah reading occasion
70 Peeved

DOWN
1 Unhinged
2 Part of R.E.A.
3 Bouquet
4 Staked
5 Congratulates in a way
6 Kind of mania
7 Inventer Nikola
8 Take a drag on
9 Shakespeare's Robin Starveling
10 Schuss
11 Boston suburb

12 Push for
13 Iditarod, e.g.
18 Brunch fare
19 Part of Mork's sign-off
25 Swelling
27 ___ alque vale
28 Ruled
30 Particular
31 Math diagram
32 Comic screams
33 Palindromic pop group
34 Coagulate
35 "The Divine Comedy" locale
36 Arabic word meaning "submission"
37 B.&O., and others
40 Large wine cask
41 Nolte's "48 ___"
42 Bundle up
46 Tutti's opposite, in music
47 Does away with
48 Finalize
51 Like some horses
53 Feared exams
54 Linguist Pei
55 Register

56 Saxophonist Getz
57 Columbus's home
58 Some of them are twins
60 Wisher's sight
61 New Year's word
63 Busy one
64 Ship's heading

ACROSS

1 Colorful salad ingredient
10 Plant pest
15 Throw some light on
16 El ___ (Spanish painter)
17 Acting ambassador
19 Mooring rope
20 The sky, maybe
21 Perry's creator
22 Pop's Carly or Paul
25 It's a drag
27 Country rtes.
28 It has its ups and downs
30 Turner of Hollywood
31 "Duke Bluebeard's Castle" composer
32 Super-soaked
33 Literature as art
36 Urger's words
37 Aloha State
38 Ooze
39 Bombast
40 70's sitcom "___ Sharkey"
43 Watered-down ideas
44 Subsequently
45 Teri of "Tootsie"

46 "___ Andronicus"
48 Samantha's "Bewitched" husband
50 Facetious advice in a mystery
54 Indoor design
55 Carouse
56 Birthplace of 16-Across
57 By and large

DOWN

1 "... for ___ for poorer"
2 Founder of est
3 Talks Dixie-style
4 Diagram a sentence
5 Competitive advantage
6 Boat's departure site
7 Rocket's departure site
8 It's after zeta
9 Foul caller
10 One more time
11 Schoolmarmish
12 Birthright
13 Bar accessory
14 ___ Passos

18 Go with the ___
22 Layup alternative
23 Quarantine
24 Be militaristic
26 Manner
28 It can sting
29 Before, in palindromes
30 Actress ___ Singer
31 Radar screen image
32 Rouse to action
33 Brief break
34 It's worth looking into
35 Clavell's "___-Pan"
36 Recipe abbr.
39 Mess-hall meal
40 Clint Eastwood's city
41 Kind of scream
42 Obstinate
44 Pelf
45 Miss Garbo
47 Jog
48 Hamlet, for one
49 Nowhere near
50 Fed. medical detectives
51 Sunny-side-up item
52 Lawyer Baird
53 Cambodia's ___ Nol

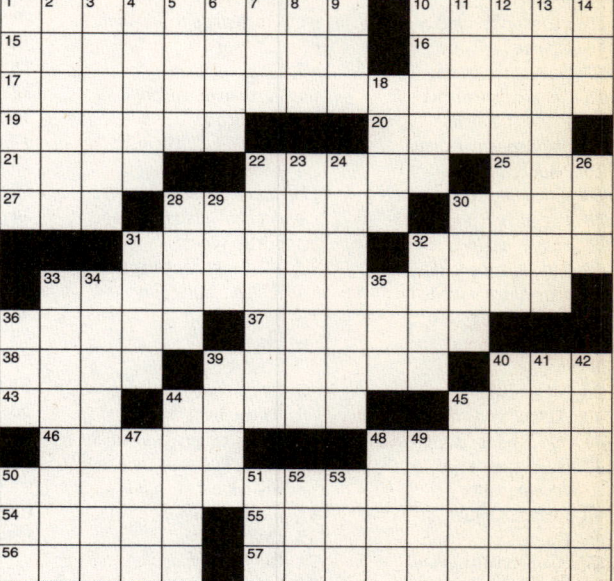

ACROSS

1 Give tit for tat
5 Pillow covers
10 Bunco
14 It debuted in Cairo, Dec. 24, 1871
15 Video screen dot
16 So long
17 What's my line: #1
20 Guard
21 They make colorful displays
22 Transcending
23 Have trouble on the ice
24 Gas, in Greenwich
27 Wine casks
28 Cleopatra biter
31 The A in "CAT scan"
32 Cartoonist Peter
33 Utah ski center
34 What's my line: #2
37 Nautical direction
38 Danza of "Who's the Boss?"
39 Refine, as 53-Down
40 Old Ford model
41 Dickey fastener
42 Thinks out loud
43 Level

44 Amatory writing
45 Brutality
48 Ghostly
52 What's my line: #3
54 First name in fashion
55 Prefix with figure or form
56 G.P.A., in slang
57 "Not my ___"
58 Intelligence
59 Mr. Culbertson and others

DOWN

1 Easy marks
2 Telegraph
3 Mideast gulf
4 Rural-themed opera
5 Crystalline gemstone
6 Stowaway
7 Leaf angle
8 One of Alcott's Little Women
9 Boy Scout tie
10 Reserved
11 Musical with the song "Memory"
12 ___ smasher
13 Viking touchdown site

18 Villa d'Este locale
19 Speaker at Cooperstown
23 Cheerful
24 Of the Vatican
25 Glorify
26 "Dead"
27 Vogue
28 Green-card applicant
29 Hackneyed
30 Cords, e.g.
32 Love, in Le Havre
33 Signature event
35 Goes for
36 Phase
41 Acapulco assent
42 Danish city
43 Bit of color
44 Certain tournaments
45 Difficult position
46 Confederate
47 Philosophical
48 Comics publisher Lee
49 Actor Julia
50 "Go ___!"
51 Cleaning agents
53 Ferriferous rock

183 by Rich Norris

ACROSS
1 Fitzgerald's forte
5 Inter ___
9 W.W. I battle site
14 Science fiction's ___ Award
15 Persuade cagily
16 Prime
17 Bon Ami rival
18 Dog command
19 Robert Louis Stevenson home
20 NO RUNS
23 Conservatory site?
24 Prepare to shoot
25 Have a few
28 Takes away (from)
33 Very, to Vivaldi
34 Muscovite, e.g.
35 Ring around the collar
36 NO HITS
40 Actor Wallach
41 1962 Met ___ Chacon
42 Backspace, on a computer
43 Lorenz Hart, for one
46 Razzed
47 Music hall tune
48 Linkletter subjects
49 NO ERRORS
57 Reddish equines
58 Baker
59 Vitamin D source
60 ". . . the better ___ you with"
61 Memphis's locale
62 ___ vera
63 Flag features
64 Without much thought
65 TV's "___ Blue"

DOWN
1 Ayatollah preceder
2 King work
3 Mideast potentates
4 E.P.A. concern
5 Mount up
6 Slack
7 Sonnet part
8 Kerrigan feat
9 "You bet!"
10 Sci-fi energy source
11 The Apostle of the Franks
12 Coll. course
13 Buck
21 Be pushy
22 Corrode
25 Drive
26 Tart-tongued writer ___ Ivins
27 Washington's ___ House
28 One, for one
29 Cavern phenomenon
30 Exonerate
31 Coquette
32 Fathered
34 Thickness units
37 Be lordly
38 Beginnings
39 Pledge, probably
44 One whose work is decreasing?
45 Reasons why
46 Bus
48 Sound at sundown
49 Some are liberal
50 Geezer
51 ___ Grande, Ariz.
52 Grammy winner Braxton
53 More than willing
54 Too glib
55 Sit (down)
56 Managed, with "out"

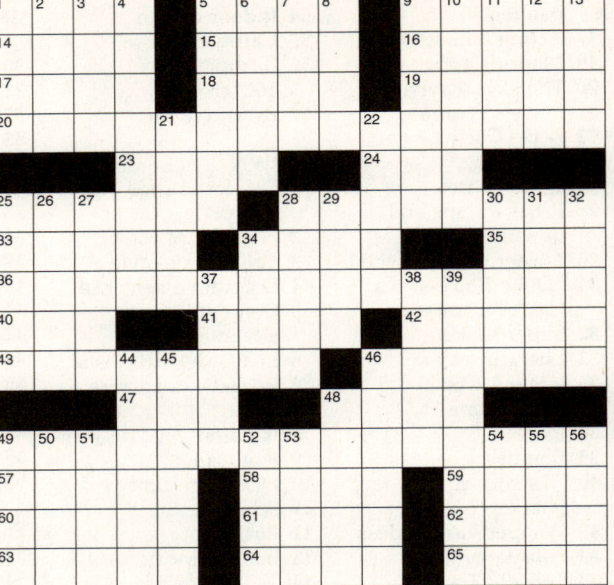

184 by Stanley Newman

ACROSS
1 He reached his peak in 1806
5 Wahine's welcome
10 Steep
14 "___ close to schedule"
15 Screened over
16 "___ Ever Need Is You"
17 Overpriced insects?
20 "Naughty, naughty!"
21 Three minutes in the ring
22 Kosher
23 O.R.'s locale
24 Party cheese
26 ___ oneself (go)
29 Aussie's hello
30 Mortgage agcy.
33 Skylit courts
34 Hoodlum
35 Oscar role in "The Killing Fields"
36 Where to buy Maid Marian mums?
39 Goes out with
40 Filthy lucre
41 "I Love Trouble" star
42 Pre-Columbian
43 Like falling off a log
44 Climbed up
45 40's White House name
46 Fraud
47 March honoree, for short
50 Express alternative
52 Kicker
55 Scans departure screens?
58 Science magazine
59 "Cookery is become ___": Burton
60 Film
61 Look
62 Looks at
63 Tabloid topics

DOWN
1 Spender, for one
2 "New Sensation" rock group
3 Crackpot
4 Go wrong
5 Tuneful
6 Abate
7 "The Plague" setting
8 Relinquished, as a football
9 Farm critter
10 Western capital
11 First name in fashion
12 Jai ___
13 Star-___ tuna
18 Rather rival
19 Castigate
23 Components of locks
25 Part of Boone's signature
26 He sings low
27 Mrs. Mertz
28 Cornered
29 Devout
30 Something extra
31 Expeditiousness
32 Chipped in
34 Agrees
35 Tournament type
37 Shade of gray
38 Available for duty
43 Grub
44 Treats treacherously
45 Hindu ascetic
46 Alarm
47 Hog food
48 Considerable volume
49 Corn product
51 Kind of tradition
52 End-of-week exclamation
53 "This can't be!"
54 Vous ___ (you are): Fr.
56 Toy merchant Schwarz
57 Emer. locale

185 by Cathy Millhauser

ACROSS
1 Singer Vikki
5 Dadaist Hans
8 Rabbitlike animals
13 Stage award
14 Didst exist
16 Mutual of ___
17 Spool decoratin' Granny Smiths?
20 Deck officer
21 Bulgar, e.g.
22 Cloned computers
23 Weekday abbr.
25 Southwest New York city
27 Bird sittin' atop a stogie?
33 Nantucket I.'s in it
34 Joke
35 Richards of tennis
37 Cork, e.g.
40 Scraped the bottom of
42 "Dynasty" actress Garber
43 ___ Canals
44 Keats's "The ___ of St. Agnes"
45 Result of currants marryin'?

50 "West Side Story" song
51 "Love Story" composer Francis
52 Greenish-blue
55 Pods for stews
57 Map dot, maybe
61 Actor havin' missed his seat?
64 Payment for dozens?
65 Dweeb
66 Purviance of Chaplin films
67 Hoard
68 Córdoba couple
69 Ooze

DOWN
1 Our Gang's Fat Joe
2 "Peek-___"
3 Some are spare
4 Blunt turndown
5 Barley beard
6 KO callers
7 Extend
8 Balloon sound
9 Encroached
10 TV journalist Marvin
11 "Psst" alternative

12 Smart talk
15 Refrain syllables
18 Cross inscription
19 With: Fr.
24 Pulitzer dramatist of 1953
26 Yorkshire river
27 Former life
28 Put into words
29 Biota part
30 One of a pair at Henley
31 Provoke
32 Actor Christopher
36 P.M. before Macmillan
38 Humans and monkeys
39 City on the Arno
40 Play-___ (kids' art medium)
41 Churn
43 Wolfed (down)
46 Nutritional necessity
47 Canon rival
48 Nonclerical
49 Set on the table
52 Puts on
53 Surrender

54 Plebe's place: Abbr.
56 ___-American
58 Load cargo
59 Strauss's "___ Nacht in Venedig"

60 Golfing snag
62 Ending with oaf
63 PBS no-no

186 by Gregory E. Paul

ACROSS
1 Office note
5 Buss
10 Fiddler, for one
14 Gung-ho
15 It's grasping
16 Catcher's base
17 Margaret Rutherford film portrayal
19 Skin cream ingredient
20 Peculiar
21 Goddess of discord
22 Apprehend
24 Part of R.O.T.C.
26 1963 Pulitzer biographer Leon
27 Gettysburg general
28 1984 Tom Selleck film
32 Author ___ Chandler Harris
35 Tartan wearer
37 Succinctly worded
38 Worrier's woe, they say
40 Weed digger
41 Vista
42 Tiny: Prefix
43 Poet Sexton
45 Canine command

46 Utah banned it in 1882
48 Doctors' org.
50 Wisecrack
51 Lobbed explosive
55 Polemist
58 Humanities
59 Checkers side
60 Auto racer Yarborough
61 Mickey Spillane film portrayal
64 Quiz choice
65 "The Tempest" sprite
66 "Earth in the Balance" author
67 Detected
68 Mary Poppins, e.g.
69 Hoarse horse?

DOWN
1 Thatcher's successor
2 Dodge
3 In one's ___ eye
4 Pindar product
5 Goes on a crash diet
6 One of the Osmonds
7 Heidi's home
8 Newspaper feature: Abbr.
9 Prepares dough

10 Warner Oland film portrayal
11 Part to play
12 Andy's pal on old radio
13 Sugar source
18 Only
23 Takes five
25 Ralph Bellamy film portrayal
26 Chowed down
28 Bonkers
29 Nest site
30 Anglo-Saxon worker
31 Lively dance
32 Start, as a dead battery
33 Mishmash
34 Book after Proverbs: Abbr.
36 ___ at the bit
39 Scalawag
44 Temporal
47 Eddie Rickenbacker, e.g.
49 Arizona city
51 Environmentally minded
52 Knight's suit
53 Plow man
54 King Edmund's successor

55 "Hamlet" has five of them
56 Pink, as steak
57 Borden product
58 Analogous

62 Kin of a Keogh plan: Abbr.
63 Selznick studio

187   by Gregory E. Paul

ACROSS

1 Like Zeno
6 ___ onto (seize)
10 Completely fill
14 Kemo Sabe's companion
15 Country's McEntire
16 Popeye's greeting
17 Stream animal
18 Subj. for Milton Friedman
19 Burrow
20 Shade of blond
21 Quickly
24 Prefix meaning 25-Down
26 "... but is it ___?"
27 Romeo's belle
29 Armada ships
34 "___ You Glad You're You?"
35 State again
36 "___ on your life!"
37 Joe DiMaggio's number
38 Melodramatic
39 Normandy campaign town
40 Lawyer's charge
41 Popular department store
42 Cartoonist Wilson
43 Midseason honorees
45 University of Oregon's site
46 Dancer Charisse
47 Circus employee
48 Official
53 "Well done!"
56 Peel, as an apple
57 Butterine
58 A.J. Foyt, e.g.
60 ___ Clayton Powell
61 Pillow candy
62 "The Old ___ Bucket"
63 Weak, as an excuse
64 Hash house sign
65 Antiquated

DOWN

1 Greek portico
2 Day-care users
3 Honest
4 Follower: Suffix
5 Small crown
6 Miss Garbo
7 Poland's Walesa
8 Orchestral instrument
9 Myanmar city
10 "Cheers!": Ital.
11 Melville hero
12 Slave away
13 "Jane ___"
22 Butterfly catcher's need
23 Air France airport
25 Full complement of planets
27 Tel Aviv-___
28 An archangel
29 What a shift shifts
30 Nile snakes
31 In big trouble
32 "The Man Without a Country" man
33 Pebble
35 Leonine sound
38 Floating airport
39 "Riders of the Purple ___"
41 Eye affliction
42 Small candy
44 Stratagem
45 A muff covers it
47 Honeybunch
48 Milky gem
49 Zilch, to Zapata
50 Streetcar
51 Lamb's alias
52 "Red" coin
54 Dregs
55 Sea eagle
59 Auto club letters

188   by Norman S. Wizer

ACROSS

1 "What ___ is new?"
5 The Bible's Kingdom of ___
10 Probability
14 Strange: Prefix
15 Reckon
16 Needle
17 Start of a Wayne Gretzky quote
20 Sun. delivery
21 Limit 10 ___ (checkout sign)
22 Fisherman in the Sargasso
23 Railroad bridge
25 Existential writer
26 Part 2 of the quote
29 Sharp irritation
32 Stationery order
33 Table leaving
36 Opposite of flunked
37 Word before box or proof
39 Like a buck or boar
40 British ending
41 Covered walkway
42 Arched ceiling
43 Part 3 of the quote
46 Affidavit taker
49 Undertones
53 Parroting
54 Palm leaf
56 Enthusiast, slangily
57 End of the quote
60 Loads from lodes
61 Bewildered
62 Ill temper
63 Blowout
64 Run-down
65 "___ lively!"

DOWN

1 Be real
2 Type of hosen
3 A little night music?
4 Long time
5 Jar
6 Maintenance
7 Cir. bisector
8 Soldiers of a sort
9 TV's "___ Haw"
10 Them
11 Resided
12 More ominous
13 Cubic meter
18 Fief fee
19 "___ to please"
24 Card game
25 Card game
27 ___ Heep
28 Corp. head
29 Peace in Bolivia
30 Diamonds
31 Geometry abbr.
33 Physics particle
34 "___ be seeing you"
35 Term of endearment
37 ___-bitty
38 Wall Street figure, with "the"
39 Impair
41 Kind of protector
42 Luisa Miller's creator
43 Kick out
44 Acted amateurishly
45 Where models model
46 Daddy Warbucks, e.g.
47 Output of 42-Down
48 Mah-jongg pieces
50 Not turned on
51 Moscow moola
52 Sheer
54 Wine and dine
55 Skyrocket
58 Duct
59 Dieter's worries: Abbr.

189   by Matt Gaffney

ACROSS

1. Moreover
8. Former Senate V.I.P.
15. Behead, maybe
16. Camden Yards birds
17. Problem solved with drops
18. Stores on the Plaza del Sol
19. More diminutive comic?
21. L.A. campus
22. Author
23. Pool activity
26. Mess up
27. Halloween garb
32. Self-proclaimed psychic Geller
33. Indian attire
35. Porter nom de plume
36. Quicker writer?
39. 1751 Fielding novel
40. [uh-oh!]
41. "The Island of the Day Before" novelist
42. Noted consumer advocate
43. With 38-Down, a Chinese dish
44. The "A" in M.A.

45. Actress Barbara ___ Geddes
46. Beach shade
48. Taller actress?
55. Pol's media event
56. Former French colony
58. Roll-on alternative
59. Staggering
60. Seaside factory
61. Singular

DOWN

1. Sacramento newspaper
2. Final
3. Antitoxins
4. Son of Daedalus
5. Tear channels
6. Puritan work ___
7. Visualized
8. Bug
9. "Platoon" movie studio
10. Oktoberfest order
11. No-no
12. Like many a shoppe
13. Shakespearean king
14. Twisty curve
20. With elasticity

23. Bush Cabinet member Manuel
24. Fragrance
25. Had a yen
26. Pitchers want it low
27. Send
28. Playboy mansion boss
29. Stage direction
30. Build
31. Neophytes
33. Recipe word
34. Detective's cry
35. Hooter
37. Hearty brew
38. See 43-Across
43. With all one's heart
44. Bassett of "Waiting to Exhale"
45. Main street of Toronto
46. Flat sign
47. Tee off
48. Stadium seating 55,601
49. Brass piece
50. British prep school
51. Get upset
52. Friend of Sven

53. Moran of "Happy Days"
54. Proposer's offering
55. ___-Man

57. Subject of an ID check

190   by Jim Page

ACROSS

1. Isolated
9. Low-fat
13. Erin minority
14. Johnny Carson's magician
16. Earmark
17. Provoke
18. Inventor's monogram
19. Elvis Presley's label
21. Worn-out model
24. Eisenhower and others
25. Opal finish
26. Epinephrine combats it
27. U.S. Amb. to the U.N., 1961–65
28. Dominoes
30. Former defense grp.
32. Like a pitcher's bag
34. Child's needs
36. Sharpened
38. Swim contests
41. Ship's opposite
42. Bridge strength?
44. Hurts
46. Asian holiday
47. Strong ___ ox

48. Quite a bargain
49. Bosses at bonus time
52. Sch. in Troy, N.Y.
53. Sebastian's bride in "Twelfth Night"
54. Real brain
58. Dallas family
59. Hockey taboo
60. Bed check?
61. Kicks back, in a way

DOWN

1. Weightlifter's lift
2. Sub-launched missile
3. Legally off base
4. Grande opening?
5. Meteor's path
6. Opposite of noche
7. Adriatic peninsula
8. Cab driving, e.g.?
9. Punjabi garb
10. McDonald's founder Ray
11. Useless
12. Made with bricks
14. Cleveland five
15. Goddess of agriculture

20. "The Eagle and the Arrow" writer
22. Riddle
23. It's left behind
28. Dermatologists' cases
29. Six-footer
31. Dead, as a bulb
33. "Cheers" bar owner
35. Leave off
36. Hayes's Veep
37. Activate illegally
39. "___ lies a tale"
40. Maritime tree
41. Sharpen
43. Store on the farm
45. Missile launchers
47. Nabokov heroine and namesakes
50. Popular theater name
51. "Hud" director Martin
55. Its slogan was once "Parade of Stars"
56. Back burner?
57. Prefix with light

191   by Stanley B. Whitten

ACROSS

1 Football executive Hunt
6 Proofreader's direction
10 Opposite of "absent"
14 Run off together
15 Olympic sport discontinued after 1936
16 Poles' connector
17 Spills (over)
18 Garden site
19 Equips
20 1957 Cooper/ Hepburn film title, literally
23 Fleet runner
25 Circular homes
26 Some art
27 Biographical data
30 Fuel that's burned
31 Makes livable, as a house
35 Escape
36 1980's invasion site
38 Gnaw at
39 Settles elsewhere
41 Batting backstop
42 Bowling alleys
43 Hold protectively
45 Ditch
48 Aquatic bird
49 1951 Grable/Carey film title, literally
53 Pub round
54 Way to go
55 Former swimsuit cover model
58 Building regulations
59 "Caro nome," e.g.
60 Zhou ___
61 Jailer's need
62 1994 Jodie Foster film
63 Musical bars?

DOWN

1 Article in France-Soir
2 Exclusively
3 1941 Ameche/Grable film title, literally
4 Select
5 Vacation destination
6 Incantation
7 Kind of list
8 Mountain sign abbr.
9 ___ of voice
10 Bring under control
11 Leaves
12 Amendment subject
13 Largest section of a dictionary, usually
21 TV's "Emerald Point ___"
22 Where George Orwell was born
23 PowerBook maker
24 Fantasize
27 Beach terrain
28 Times to remember
29 Intention
31 Entertain grandly
32 1979 Heard/Hurt film title, literally
33 Boy Scout rank
34 "Skittle Player Outside an Inn" painter
36 Place for peaks
37 Competed
40 Specs
41 Purplish-red
43 Former mile record holder
44 Scoundrel
45 Pancake arrangement
46 Daphnis's lover, in Greek romance
47 Slender
48 Take first, second or third, in the Olympics
50 Mediterranean port
51 Exhausted, with "out"
52 Letters
56 Gangster's gun
57 Family member

192   by Randall J. Hartman

ACROSS

1 Boxer's pokes
5 Hammond book
10 "Dragnet" star
14 Norway's capital
15 Mutt
16 Film director Kazan
17 "Let's get outta here!"
20 Catch, as a criminal
21 Spots in the Seine, for instance
22 Grad student exams
23 Moray
24 Dull blow
26 Kentucky Derby
33 Goes it alone
34 Merits
35 ___ kwon do (martial art)
36 The triple in a triple play
37 "L'Étranger" novelist
38 Groucho or Zeppo
39 Neighbor of Syr.
40 Perry Mason stories
41 Stout
42 Outlaw's order, in a western
45 Mortgage
46 Gobbled up
47 Hearing-related
50 Kiln for drying hops
52 Winter bug
55 Show patriotic respect
59 London's Hyde, e.g.
60 ___ brûlée (French custard)
61 Banister
62 "One-hoss" vehicle
63 Made dove sounds
64 Memorial Day race, informally

DOWN

1 First name of four Presidents
2 On the briny
3 Tell all
4 Yard square
5 Moon-landing program
6 Hightailed it
7 Plenty
8 Alas, in Augsburg
9 "___ Cried" (1962 hit)
10 Nut
11 Scat queen Fitzgerald
12 Invoice
13 Paul McCartney's instrument
18 Feudal estates
19 A doctor keeps them
23 Son of Seth
24 Rocket engine force
25 Roosters' mates
26 Wake up
27 The "U" of UHF
28 Why's answer
29 Circus performer
30 Bare
31 Ahead of schedule
32 Alluring
33 "Bon ___" (good evening, abroad)
37 Eatery
38 Calliope, e.g.
40 Kid
41 Singer Midler
43 Making hitting sounds, as an engine
44 Chopped up
47 Horned vipers
48 Home of Brigham Young
49 ___ avis
50 Sandwich cookie
51 "Look ___ (I'm in Love)"
52 Custard tart
53 Set down
54 "The ___ American"
56 ABC and CBS regulator
57 Spanish gold
58 Thur.'s follower

193 by Daniel R. Stark

ACROSS

1 Numinous
9 Try out
15 Independence
16 Donny or Marie Osmond
17 Monk's garment
18 Extends
19 Charade
20 Running slow
22 "Tag"
23 Shake
25 More slippery
27 ___ Bernardino
28 On the main
29 Vanilla, e.g.
30 City founded as Naniwa
32 Kings' group, for short
34 Like loaf bread
36 Lowering
40 Rainbows
41 Witch hazel is one.
43 Previous word
44 First name in cosmetics
45 Parts of joules
47 Siva's consort, in Hinduism

51 Blonde shade
52 Clip
54 French family members
55 Rebuffs
57 Busy
59 Carnival site
60 One with a foil
62 It's hard to hit
64 "___ Bath Book" ("Sesame Street" volume)
65 Managed
66 Brain stumper
67 Meat tenderizer

DOWN

1 Ancient fortress on the Dead Sea
2 Joshua trees
3 Bronze, e.g.
4 Exceed
5 Arctic dweller
6 Weak, as a scent
7 Charlotte ___, V.I.
8 Melodious
9 Big polling news
10 Worried, with "at"
11 "Buddenbrooks" author

12 Dish at a royal feast
13 Member of Congress
14 Baja California city
21 Good gymnastics scores
24 Girl in a Robert Burns poem
26 Pirate
29 One side in the Civil War
31 Drop out
33 Realtor's concerns
35 Galoots
36 Poisonous shrub
37 Famous surrender site
38 Ultimately
39 Rude look
42 Window variety
46 Unaged Italian brandy
48 Slips on a slip?
49 Like Salome
50 Wagner soprano
53 Richard III's need
54 Kind of dish
56 Gradually fell
58 Gallery
61 Sea shocker
63 Sure competitor

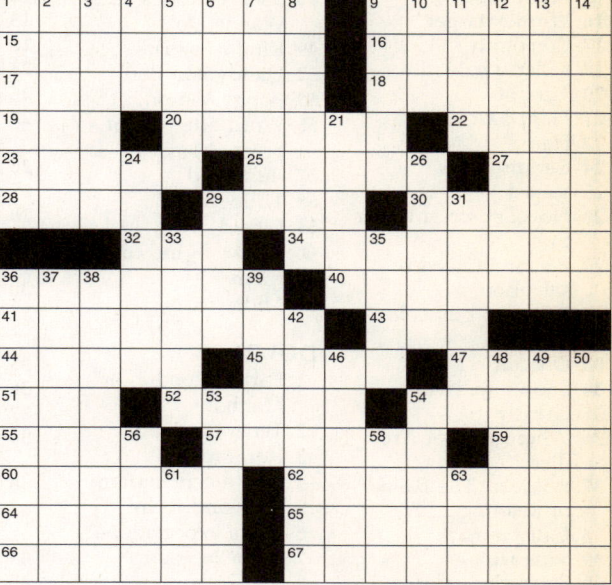

194 by Dean Niles

ACROSS

1 Charlie Chan portrayer Warner
6 Letters after a proof
9 1908 Peace Nobelist Fredrik
14 Auger or drill
15 ___ Today
16 A McCoy, to a Hatfield
17 747 and DC-10
19 "___ which will live in infamy": F.D.R.
20 Greek earth goddess
21 British submachine gun
22 Temporary stay
26 Literally, face to face
29 Accents in "résumé"
30 Precooking solution
31 18-wheelers
32 Founder of a French dynasty
33 Meadow
34 Ninnies
35 Seeker of the Golden Fleece
36 Take ___ at (criticize)
37 Singer Kamoze
38 Spanish gent

39 "Zorba the Greek" setting
40 Genius
42 Attired for a frat party
43 Convertibles
44 Additional helpings
45 Moonshine containers
46 Phnom ___
47 Old adders
49 Nickname for DiMaggio
54 Italian bowling game
55 Record speed: Abbr.
56 Role for Valentino
57 Some sharks
58 Caribbean, e.g.
59 Circumvent

DOWN

1 Goal: Abbr.
2 Singer Rawls or Reed
3 Pitcher's pride
4 Lincoln's state: Abbr.
5 Small parachutes
6 Wicked "Snow White" figure
7 "¿Como ___ usted?"
8 Prosecutors, for short

9 Skedaddles
10 Like the Incas
11 "Les Miserables" protagonist
12 C.P.R. administrat
13 Deli bread
18 See 30-Down
21 Theda Bara, e.g.
22 With more attitude
23 Pacific islands, collectively
24 Single calisthenic
25 Big name in elevators
26 Gaseous mist
27 Conceptualized
28 Where oysters sleep?
30 With 18-Down, home canning items
32 ___ Major (southern constellation)
35 Army vehicles
36 35-Across's vessel
38 Cheap cigars
39 Apache chief
41 Plaster finish
42 Camp sight
44 Alabama city
46 Pontiff
47 Defense syst.
48 Feathered stole

49 Some namesakes, for short
50 Gretzky's grp.
51 Game, in France
52 Ending with human or planet
53 Supplement, with "out"

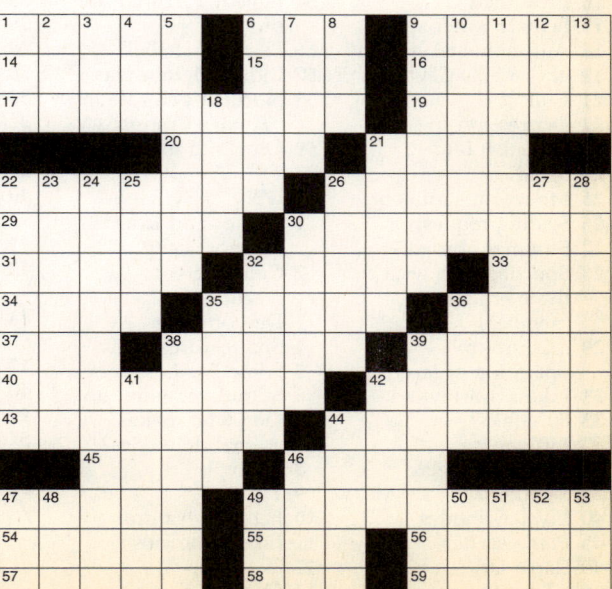

195 by Gregory E. Paul

ACROSS

1 Farm structure
5 Kon-Tiki wood
10 Boutique
14 Rev. Roberts
15 From the East
16 Windex target
17 Conjointly
19 Killer whale film
20 Till bill
21 Plant part
22 Ham
24 Certain pints
25 Vessel
26 Novelist-screenwriter Eric
29 Person in need of salvation
32 Places to buy cold cuts
33 Dugout
34 Showtime rival
35 Greatly
36 Where Joan of Arc died
37 Wilde's "The Ballad of Reading ___"
38 Catty remark?
39 Vine fruit
40 Snorkeler's sight
41 "O Pioneers!" setting
43 Talkative
44 Joins the team?
45 Stable newborn
46 Insignia
48 Sheryl Crow's "___ Wanna Do"
49 Kind of story
52 Handyman Bob
53 Bobby Vinton hit
56 Word after pig or before horse
57 Burdened
58 Tittle
59 Ribald
60 Works in the cutting room
61 Midterm, e.g.

DOWN

1 Part of London or Manhattan
2 Teheran's land
3 Rural route
4 Like a centenarian
5 Back-and-forth
6 Grate expectations?
7 Actor Neeson
8 ___ Diego
9 "Father Knows Best" family name
10 Lampoons
11 Sidney Sheldon TV series
12 Some time ago
13 Fruit cocktail fruit
18 Tropical getaways
23 Pal, Down Under
24 Dismounted
25 "We'll go to ___, and eat bologna . . ."
26 Rhett's last words
27 Free-for-all
28 Detailed account
29 Singer Nyro or Branigan
30 German sub
31 Candy on a stick, informally
33 Parts of wine bottles
36 Look like
37 Soccer score
39 Enter a Pillsbury contest
40 Mountain range
42 Hero of early French ballads
43 Punctuation marks
45 Armada
46 Like Satan
47 Bog
48 German auto
49 Gin flavor
50 Scoreboard stat
51 Cop's milieu
54 Youth
55 Bridle part

196 by Rich Norris

ACROSS

1 Shadowy
7 Throe
12 Informant
14 Brownish grays
16 Presumed
17 Female water spirit
18 Agronomists' studies
19 N.C.A.A.'s Cavaliers
21 Collect
22 Depression
23 Greenish blue
24 Scold
25 Mountain sign abbr.
26 Seating request
27 Summer abroad
28 Sporting org. with three million members
29 ___ jure (by operation of law)
31 Like Errol Flynn
33 80 winks?
37 Little, e.g.
38 Musical syllable
39 Ventured
40 Elysian abodes
43 Plane starter
45 Rap's Dr. ___
46 Allow the use of
47 Burden
48 Antipasto ingredient
50 Oldest city in Ohio
52 Friendly
53 Bring out
54 Benedict Arnold, for one
56 Fix, as a chair
57 Inducted, in a way
58 Norman Fell role in "Three's Company"
59 On cloud nine

DOWN

1 Snakes and lizards, taxonomically
2 Causes great resentment
3 Deli offerings
4 Spa features
5 Some Ivy Leaguers
6 Stimulate, with "up"
7 One who makes special deliveries?
8 Twinge
9 Try out
10 Echidna features
11 Like some jobs
12 Skewered
13 Theatrical event
15 Black Panthers leader
20 Poem that ends "I am the captain of my soul"
22 Egregious
25 River to Donegal Bay
26 Cinematic pooch
28 Tiny portions
30 Legal lead-in
32 Golfer's concern
34 Relinquish
35 Saturated
38 Made resolute
40 Gyrocompass inventor Sperry
41 Merchant
42 First name among tenors
44 Modern physics particle
47 Mink relative
48 Ending
49 Frothy
51 Der Spiegel article
52 Shade of blue
55 Chemical ending

by Eric Albert

ACROSS

1 Shrimp ___
9 Hemingway and others
14 "No Time for Sergeants" playwright
15 1969 Super Bowl M.V.P.
16 Given similar parts
17 Kind of punch
18 "The Twittering Machine" artist
19 Drink of the gods
20 Youngest
24 "Java" man
25 Buckeye
26 From Trondheim
28 Element #5
29 Rum cake
30 Make it up, musically
33 Kitchen gizmo
35 Cover up
38 Gridiron stat: Abbr.
39 River past Bern
41 Dance line
42 Repeat sign
44 Pitcher Jim
45 "Black Beauty" author
48 Bridge, often
50 Become breathless?
51 Juveniles
52 "Peanuts" girl
53 Prattle
58 Glue brand
59 Watercolor?
60 Poor
61 Proceed toward the target

DOWN

1 With, in Wiesbaden
2 Ending with honor
3 Kind of sheet
4 ___ de la Cité
5 Collar holder
6 1990 Levinson film
7 Staircase piece
8 It catches some waves
9 Comic strip units
10 "Cocoon" Oscar winner
11 Page of music
12 Fighting
13 Height-challenged
15 Jewish, for example
20 Capitol group
21 "You've Really Got ___ On Me"
22 Begets
23 Jessica Rabbit, for one
27 The duck in "Peter and the Wolf"
29 Healthful breakfast food
30 Intriguing group
31 Rival of Sparta
32 Has in mind
34 Baby baldies
36 "Taxi Driver" director
37 Sudden ouster
40 Like a swindler
42 Zipped
43 First name in mysteries
44 Chaos
45 Low card in skat
46 Napoleon, twice
47 Disingenuous cry
49 Common rental
54 LXVII x III
55 Solo in space
56 Service mail drop: Abbr.
57 Common base

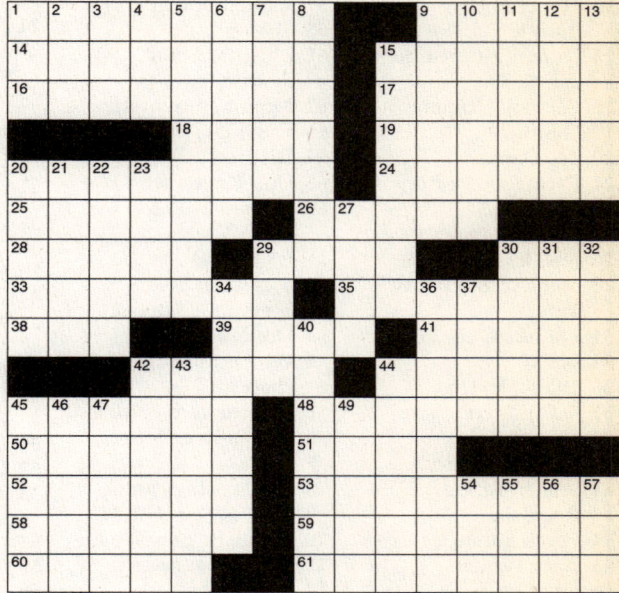

---

by Janet R. Bender

ACROSS

1 Wrongs
5 Stockyard group
9 Sail supports
14 Govt. agents
15 War of 1812 battle site
16 Member of a crowd scene
17 Give stars to
18 Basketball's Chamberlain
19 1993 Formula One winner Prost
20 Old "House Party" host
23 Knocks down
24 Reserved
25 1975 Stephanie Mills musical, with "The"
28 Hot time in Paris
29 Take turns
33 Kind of package
34 More albinolike
35 Phobic
37 P.G.A.'s 1992 leading money winner
39 Rickey Henderson stat
41 Hunter of myth
42 Well ventilated
43 Least exciting
45 Rotary disk
48 Sign of summer
49 Mathematician's letters
50 Throw
52 N.F.L. receiver for 18 seasons
57 Booby
59 Not in use
60 Crips or Bloods
61 Uris' "___ Pass"
62 Baylor mascot
63 Skirt
64 Check writer
65 Slumped
66 Actress Charlotte et al.

DOWN

1 Attack by plane
2 Turkish hostelry
3 Stinging plant
4 Fish-line attachment
5 Axed
6 Dancer Bruhn
7 Small brook
8 Loathe
9 Substantial
10 Wheel shaft
11 Noted film trilogy
12 Angle starter
13 ___ José
21 Hebrew for "contender with God"
22 Eponymous poet of Greek drama
26 Temper
27 British alphabet ender
30 Elderly one
31 Gumshoe
32 "___ With a View"
33 Columnist Herb
34 Supplicate
36 Thread of life spinner, in myth
37 Savageness
38 Late actress Mary
39 NaCl, to a pharmacist
40 Truss
44 Deviates from the script
45 Party to Nafta
46 Exact retribution
47 Enters a freeway
49 Persian Gulf land
51 Trevanian's "The ___ Sanction"
53 Green target
54 Madison Avenue product
55 Ardor
56 Boor
57 Cutup
58 Noche's opposite

199 by Lois Sidway

ACROSS

1 Whip end
5 Mystery writer's award
10 Sassy young 'un
14 " ___ silly question . . ."
15 Painter Andrea del ___
16 Portnoy's creator
17 "Hmm?"
20 ___ Dame
21 Packwood, for one
22 Curse
25 Purse fastener
26 Jeweler's weight
28 Some of the Brady bunch
31 Eat like a chicken
34 Blend
36 Utah's Hatch
37 D.D.E.'s command
38 "Hmm . . ."
40 Volga tributary
41 Writer Terkel
43 Requisite
44 Porch adjunct
45 Arab capital
46 Ignoramus
48 South African statesman Jan
51 Gospel singer Jackson
55 Many TV shows
57 Cathedral displays
58 "Hmm!"
61 Mitch Miller's instrument
62 Mountain nymph
63 Electricity carrier
64 District
65 Don Knotts won five
66 Actress Young

DOWN

1 Suburban greenery
2 Seeing ___ (since)
3 Do figure eights
4 Where to hang your chapeau
5 Biblical verb ending
6 "Zip-a-Dee-Doo-___"
7 Alum
8 Relics collect here
9 The "R'" in H.R.H.
10 Pugilistic muscleman
11 Famous debater
12 Rat chaser?
13 Talese's "Honor ___ Father"
18 Word repeated after "Que"
19 Speaker
23 In a line
24 Eagle's nail
27 Like Neptune's trident
29 Adidas rival
30 Break sharply
31 Annoyance
32 Famous last words
33 Camp V.I.P.
35 Concert hall
38 Debate subjects
39 Irish novelist O'Brien
42 Like a golf ball
44 Manatees
47 Word sung twice before "cheree"
49 Lake near Carson City
50 Drang's partner
52 DeVito's "Taxi" role
53 Venous opening
54 Gray
55 Ms. McEntire
56 Cherry leftover
58 "Far out!"
59 Spring time
60 Lots of ft.

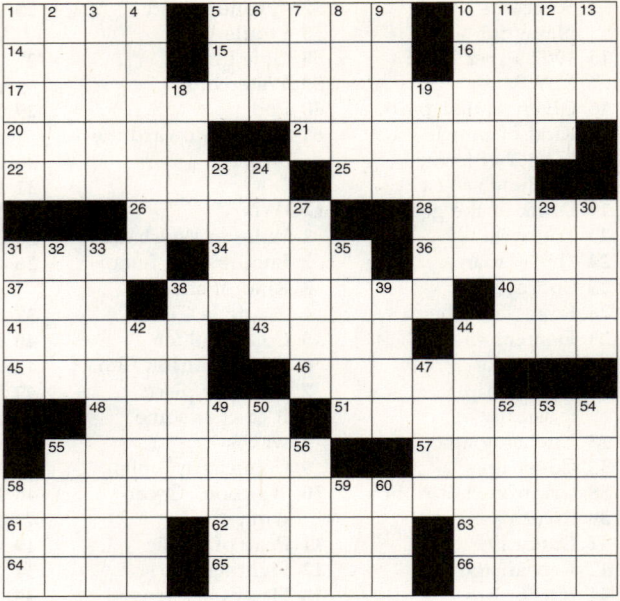

200 by Gregory E. Paul

ACROSS

1 First name in Solidarity
5 Festive
9 Philatelist's item
14 Jai ___
15 Mideast gulf
16 Eunomia, Dike and Irene
17 Partner of pieces
18 Schindler's request
19 Kind of orange
20 Feminine suffix
21 1928 A.L. batting champ
23 Correspondence
25 "It's a sin to tell ___"
26 Alias of Romain de Tirtoff
27 Substitutes
31 Tupelo's favorite son
33 Impersonators
34 Nosh
35 Fizzles out
36 "___ Jacques"
37 Carol syllables
38 Ex-governor Richards
39 Kind of table, informally
40 She played Lady L in "Lady L"
41 Singer Jim and others
43 Novi Sad native
44 "Diary of ___ Housewife"
45 Parched
48 CNN newsman
52 Thou, today
53 Poet's almost
54 Frown
55 Bulkhead
56 Terrify
57 Folk follower
58 Hazzard County officer, on TV
59 Risk
60 Butterine
61 1169 erupter

DOWN

1 Stick-on
2 Molière girl
3 "Peace Train" singer
4 Towel word
5 Aplenty
6 Felipe's farewell
7 Minus
8 U.C.-Irvine's nickname
9 Easy winners
10 Type of salad
11 Uzbekistan's ___ Sea
12 Crèche figures
13 Hammer part
21 "Smoke ___ in Your Eyes"
22 Tinted windows prevent it
24 Cleveland's Speaker
27 Scharnhorst commander et al.
28 Crimson Tide coach
29 Buckley's "God and Man at ___"
30 Cartoonist Drake
31 Cheese town
32 Part of a fishing trio
33 Sticky-tongued critter
36 Newspaper edition
37 Actress Loughlin
39 Tambourine
40 Comic Lew
42 Expedition in Kenya
43 Mono's successor
45 Sky-blue
46 Athenian statesman
47 Oral Roberts University site
48 Big stinger
49 Formerly
50 Limerick man
51 Wrench, e.g.
55 Tiny

201   by Rich Norris

ACROSS

1 Chief
5 Opposite of fem.
9 Carries on
14 "That's a laugh"
15 Capital on the 60th parallel
16 Newbery-winning author Scott
17 Tied
18 Object of devotion
19 Playwright Maxim
20 Three-time Wimbledon champ
23 Kind of image
24 Swordsman
27 "Jane ___"
28 What a vacuum vacuums
30 Car radio feature
31 Goal
33 Brouhaha
35 Scurrier
36 "Ruthless People" actor
40 Account exec
41 Prof. ___ (ex-academic)
42 Swindle
43 Things to be hedged
45 German river
47 D'Urbervilles lass
50 Triathlon competitor
52 Cultural
54 Longtime role for Shelley Long
57 June honorees
59 Golf stroke
60 Popular cookie
61 Norman's motel
62 Soprano Te Kanawa
63 City south of Salt Lake City
64 Cubic meter
65 British weapon
66 Actress Carol

DOWN

1 "Beg pardon"
2 Desolate
3 Sundae garnish
4 Parked, at O'Hare
5 Rippled fabric
6 Mount
7 Type of machine
8 Mozart compositions
9 Miscreant
10 Cherishes
11 Plumb
12 Lodge member
13 Stone for Stallone
21 Pay back
22 Showing a preference
25 Smooth, in a way
26 Cable network
29 Grenoble is its capital
32 Humiliate
34 Beat
36 Boo
37 Current
38 Some rubes
39 Kind of exam
40 Diamond stat
44 Ebbets Field hero Duke
46 Terminate a termination
48 "High ___" (1941 film)
49 Filter
51 Minnesota Fats stroke
53 Hakeem Olajuwon score
55 I.O.U.
56 Several
57 Literary monogram
58 Squeal (on)

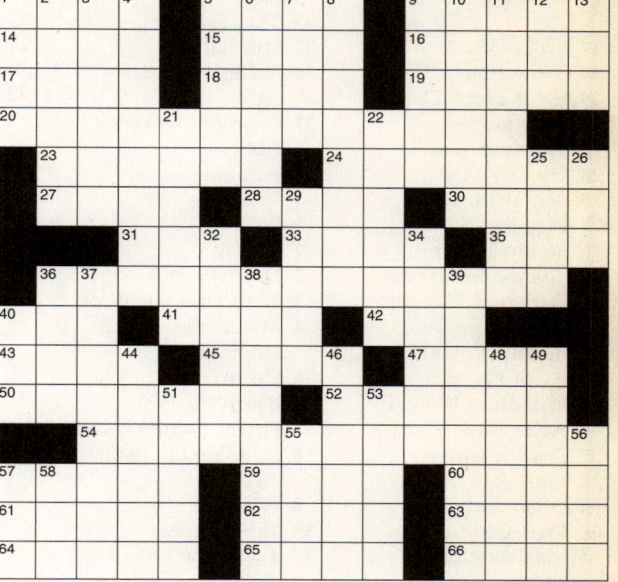

202   by Jim Page

ACROSS

1 Meeting: Abbr.
5 Byron's "best of prophets"
12 Freight carrier
14 1979 hit by the Police
15 Convert a message
16 Renunciation of faith
18 Poirot's "Mon ___!"
19 "No Time for Sergeants" playwright
21 Mr. Ziegfeld
22 Place of drudgery
24 ___ Valley, Calif.
26 Alloy
27 Account receivable
28 Actress Samantha
31 "Mr. ___ Builds His Dream House" (1948 film)
36 Old World deer
37 She played 50-Down's partner
38 "I read you"
39 Mugfuls
41 "Allah ___!" (Teheran cry)
42 Dig in
43 Hangs five
45 "Pique Dame," e.g.
48 Arthur Miller play, with "The"
52 ___ Tin Tin
53 Palette pigment
55 Pipe hole
56 Move
59 Words to the wise
61 Crackpot
62 Vassals
63 Son of a ___ (nautical epithet)
64 "Cabaret" star

DOWN

1 Actress Braga
2 Hyundai model
3 Tonto's equestrian role?
4 Long-faced
5 Robert E. Lee's reins?
6 Rain dancer, maybe
7 Nebraska Senator James
8 ___ de deux
9 Army crawler
10 Super blooper
11 Induction motor pioneer
12 Hospital count
13 Turned back on
17 Relative of "Ouch!"
20 Permit
23 French sea
24 Turf
25 Lone Ranger's "Giddyap"?
27 Current administration
28 Flub
29 Gunk
30 Graphic start
32 Give confidence to
33 San Francisco's ___ Hill
34 Transcript figure, for short
35 Mideast land: Abbr.
37 "___ real!"
40 Ewe said it
41 Annual playoff grp.
44 Arcadian
45 Three-time Hart Trophy winner
46 Old Milwaukee competitor
47 Result
49 Earth tone
50 Title character in an 80's police drama
51 Barely makes, with "out"
53 Cartoon canine
54 Muse of history
57 Bambi's aunt
58 Second O of O-O-O
60 "Savvy?"

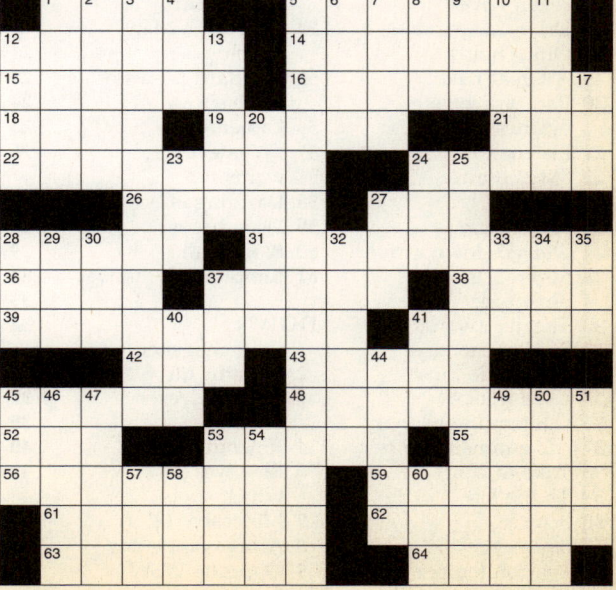

203 by Randolph Ross

ACROSS
1 1990 U.S. Open tennis winner
9 Start of dirty pool?
13 Wipe out
15 Guitarist Eddie Van ___
17 Broker
18 Show ring
19 River to the Danube
20 Infrequency
22 Times abroad
24 Destroy
25 Set (against)
26 Piggery
28 Football filler
29 Spanish wine bag
30 Darlene's TV mom
33 "The wages of ___ death": Romans
34 Award won by Woodrow Wilson
36 Actress Woodard
37 Brunch entree
38 Markers
39 Dijon donkey
40 Prussian pronoun
41 Magazine revenue source

42 Venturing, after "on"
44 Adoption agcy.
47 Interior work
50 Sgt. Friday's employer
52 Laud
53 Catalyst
55 Stiff hairs
56 Refreshment stand order
57 Chamber workers: Abbr.
58 Straightened up

DOWN
1 Big rig
2 Dawn
3 Without a talent for
4 Mail-order employees
5 Up to
6 Beach treats
7 Finger pointer
8 Rudolph Giuliani, e.g.
9 Winner
10 Take home
11 Take time for a decision

12 Attune
14 Sofa flanker
16 Connors contemporary
21 Tommy Dorsey chart topper "___ Love"
23 Archaeological find
27 Mouth off
29 Origin
30 Desk organizers
31 Cloud
32 Just born
33 Architect's info
34 Aquatic nymphs
35 Samuel's predecessor
39 Oklahoma city
42 Commedia dell' ___
43 ___ nous
45 Start of a Tennessee Williams title
46 A pig in ___
48 Wang Lung's wife, in fiction
49 Prefix with cycle
51 Stowe novel
54 Dachshund doc

204 by Sidney L. Robbins

ACROSS
1 Senegal's capital
6 Hobbler's support
10 Male deer
14 Pal, in Panama
15 "... I met ___ with seven wives"
16 Drive-___ window
17 Office hours
19 A Great Lake
20 Part of a jewelry business
21 Listens to
22 "My country, ___ of thee..."
23 Kiowa homes
24 Floated down a river
28 St. Francis's birthplace
30 Theater awards
31 Spot to sanctify
32 It's a little louse
35 Used a loom
36 Contemptuous look
37 ___ gunman theory
38 Take to court
39 To the left
40 Scorch
41 Say yes
43 Peevish temper

44 Damaged, as a fender
46 Mil. address
47 Chief god of the early Hindus
48 Old navigational instrument
54 "The Thin Man" pooch
55 Standard pieces of lumber
56 Lamented
57 "Whatever ___ wants..."
58 Dazzling effect
59 Deep urges
60 Blood ball
61 Jump out of the way

DOWN
1 Copenhagener
2 Dictator Idi
3 Double-decker checker
4 Ripening agent
5 Revolves
6 Lunch spots
7 Mideast V.I.P.
8 Army competitor
9 Opposite WSW

10 Soaks, as tea bags
11 Multipurpose
12 Take for ___ (deceive)
13 Twenty questions attempt
18 "The Art of Love" poet
21 Will figure
23 Nicholas, e.g.
24 Noisy fights
25 ___ Ben Adhem
26 Woolworth's, way back when
27 Links peg
28 All ears
29 Let stand
31 Quot. attribution
33 "Picnic" writer
34 Generation Y member
36 Raced
37 Diamond ___
39 On the briny
40 Lampooned
42 Precious violins
43 Nimble
44 Anne Frank work
45 Follow
46 Facing the pitcher

48 Army no-show
49 Virtuoso performance?
50 Plumb crazy
51 "___ Lang Syne"

52 Boast
53 Villa d'___
55 R.N.'s touch

205 — by Mark Elliot Skolsky

ACROSS
1 Five-time Socialist candidate
5 Florida city
10 Man, e.g.
14 Perry's creator
15 Tomato, technically
16 LSD
17 Olympic endeavor
20 Nicholas and Alexander
21 As well
22 Please, overseas
23 Enola Gay payload
25 Actress Carrere
27 Eagle on a par 3
28 TV's Dr. Frasier ___
29 Lane's partner
30 490 B.C. battle site
33 Garbage boat
34 Brawling
37 Surgical device
40 Kind of indicator
44 Longtime fraternal order
45 Lyndon's 1964 opponent
47 Palindromic songstress
48 Age at which to get a chariot license?
49 Analyze grammatically
50 High up
52 Protect, as in a museum
54 Sports center
55 Premiere of 12/15/39
59 Ran in the wash
60 Jurist Salmon P. ___
61 Analogy words
62 Father
63 Northwestern capital
64 1929 hit "___ Funny That Way"

DOWN
1 B.A. or Ph.D.
2 Blue literature
3 Scorch
4 French assembly
5 Liquidates
6 ___ Magnon
7 Gold: Prefix
8 Electronics giant ___ Industries
9 In
10 Shakespearean villain
11 Moped
12 Light and rhythmic, as a song
13 Actor Kookie Byrnes
18 Coll. sr.'s test
19 Decline
22 "Batman" sound
23 Elvis ___ Presley
24 Sausages, in England
26 Chowed down
28 T'ai ___ ch'uan
29 The Green Hornet's sidekick
31 Long time
32 Craggy hill
33 Farm container
35 Farm unit
36 Trifle
37 Law, to Livy
38 Air cells
39 Noted American behaviorist
41 Fickle
42 Spanish prince
43 Army bed
45 ABC's
46 Queen of Soul
49 Feline foot.
50 "___ you kidding?"
51 Clark's fellow explorer
53 Yield
54 "Excuse me . . ."
55 Literary monogram
56 Fictional supercomputer
57 Lao-___
58 Hairstyles

206 — by Gayle Dean

ACROSS
1 Prefix with -genarian
5 Mercury model
10 Braid
14 No longer new
15 Bay window
16 Unhinged
17 Put out
18 Esteemed fish escort?
20 Capital on the Barada River
22 Declares
23 Map features: Abbr.
24 Italy's Gulf of ___
26 Let the baby fish beware?
30 You can believe it
31 Ready follower
32 Filet, maybe
36 Energy
37 Horticulturist's box
41 Lend a hand
42 Otherwise
44 Japanese novelist ___ Kobo
45 Wan
47 Musical TV fish game?
51 Eared flask
54 Opole's river
55 Kind of nerve
56 Slandered
60 Fish's courting place?
63 Catch some Z's
64 Ohio or New York county
65 Martinique volcano
66 Commits a faux pas
67 Dupes
68 Eggs on
69 Security breach

DOWN
1 Had to give it to?
2 Robin Cook bestseller
3 In good condition
4 Thunder Bay locale
5 Kin of rugby
6 Stir up
7 Some auction action
8 Constellation with the star Regulus
9 Toymaker's assistant
10 Shorebirds
11 Not the social type
12 Squirrel's prize
13 Certain sculpture
19 Nimbus
21 Characteristic mark
24 Rain slightly
25 Tommy Dorsey's "Oh, Look ___ Now"
26 Garment for Batman
27 Figure skating jump
28 Bigwigs
29 "Absinthe Drinker" artist
33 Site of the Koolau Range
34 Debt security
35 Novelist Ferber
38 Glittery fabric
39 Spy Rudolf
40 Graded
43 Tempts
46 Pastry whose name means "whirlpool"
48 Principal
49 One with a sting operation?
50 Sayings
51 Contends (with)
52 "Ernani," e.g.
53 Möbius piece
56 Grouter's target
57 Reactor part
58 Poet Pound
59 Office station
61 Whirlpool
62 Modern information source, with "the"

ACROSS

1 Poland's Walesa
5 Prop for a Valkyrie
10 Break in relations
14 Post-weeding blues
15 Couric of "Today"
16 Nabisco snack
17 Song question of 1966
20 Neither's partner
21 Native Oklahoman
22 Duel personalities
23 Loch of song
26 Doberman doc
27 Bray
29 Spacewalking inits.
31 School zone caution
35 The sun, in Sonora
36 Sharp-witted columnist Molly
38 ___ nutshell
39 Moviegoer's question
42 ___ Grande
43 Casino employee, maybe
44 Make one's case
45 E-mailed
47 Bernardo's bear
48 Most important figures

49 Devil's disciple?
51 Sequel
53 Noted Seminole chief
57 Formerly named
58 Radio operator
61 Partygoer's question
64 Venetian resort
65 "___ Navidad!"
66 Get through the cracks
67 Tore (off)
68 Scorecard
69 Bismarck's state: Abbr.

DOWN

1 Spot for tennis
2 Repeat exactly
3 Fort Sumter locale
4 Riled (up)
5 Ride up the mountain
6 "Cry, the Beloved Country" author
7 Pilot's info, for short
8 Doesn't feel right
9 Apropos
10 Labor savers

11 Heavy metal
12 More than an argument
13 Little ones
18 Mogadishu residents
19 One in the hand?
24 "Oops!"
25 Flesh out
27 Certain beneficiaries
28 Beast of Borden
30 Lab glass
32 Probability
33 Lakers star
34 Fairies' props
36 Cow-headed goddess
37 Pearly Gates figure
40 Pocket at the mall
41 ___ Mountains
46 Car steering element
48 Informal, as conversation
50 1994 Men's Downhill gold medalist Tommy
52 Smithy's need
53 Nocturnal preyers
54 Windjammer
55 Yield

56 Between ports
59 San Francisco's founder Juan Bautista de ___
60 Undemanding

62 Building wing
63 Hither and ___

ACROSS

1 School subj.
4 Burst
9 Overfill
13 Puddin'
14 Triangular toast topping
16 Kind of tomato
17 Car trunk item
19 As well
20 Rock's ___ Vanilli
21 Serious words are said in this
23 Ft. Bragg constabulary
25 What a waste!
26 Finds oneself with a pink slip
30 "Rich Harbor" and others
31 S.F., for one
32 Some dashes
33 Honorarium
34 Creep
37 "Howards End" author
41 Lummox
42 Evil, to Yvette
43 Mission closing
44 State in NE India

47 Wilderness Road traveler
50 Invitation to dance
52 Eggy prefix
53 Vamooses
54 Tickle
58 Like some hands
59 Remote area
63 Poetic contraction
64 Living room piece
65 Tennis call
66 Race track figures
67 Having beams of light
68 Wonderment

DOWN

1 1954 #1 hit by the Crew-Cuts
2 Thus, to Luciano
3 Like some airports: Abbr.
4 Theater lines
5 Rep.'s or Dem.'s money source
6 Charlottesville campus, for short
7 Razz
8 Kind of show
9 Fabric add-ons

10 Aver
11 Shoving match
12 Plays the ham
15 Interpret
18 Some are slippery
22 TV weatherman
24 Bundle
25 Slips
26 Roam
27 Prefix with center
28 Crag
29 3-Down lang.
33 Original Shakespeare edition
35 Bank giveaways
36 Furniture materials
37 It shoots the breeze
38 Thou-shalt-not
39 Directional suffix
40 Deli request
42 Murray of the silents
44 White mouse, for example
45 Like Muscat raisins
46 Lost freshness
47 Tizzy
48 Got around
49 Wheels on Oscar night
51 Vamooses

55 Kareem's alma mater
56 Depict unfairly
57 Marchese d' ___ (Italian nobleman)
60 J.F.K. info

61 Take
62 Born

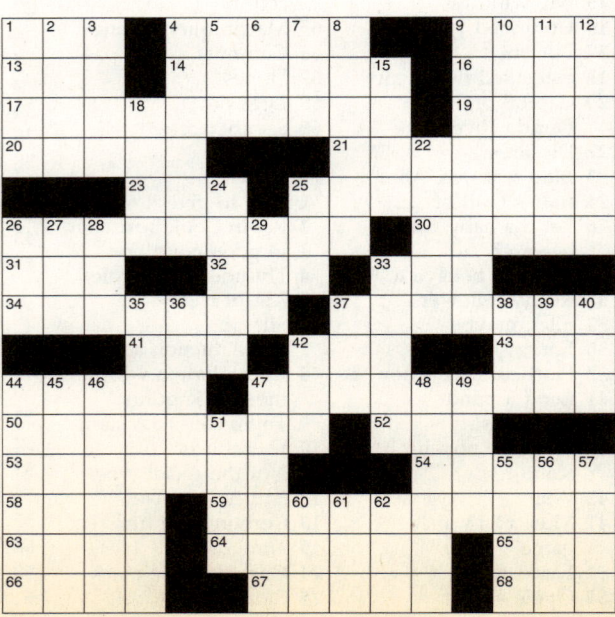

209 by Rich Norris

ACROSS

1 Dig, perhaps
10 Quibbles
15 Stay calm, slangily
16 Forestall
17 Actually
18 Track competitor
19 Alliance formed in 1860–61: Abbr.
20 Advance cautiously
21 Rock salt
22 Dance
23 Meet
24 Parks, in a way
25 Emcee's responsibility
27 Role for Lorre
28 Pulls
29 Creates
31 Affectation
32 He refused a 1970 Oscar
35 High school subj.
36 Ate
37 Geiger of Geiger counter fame
38 Comp
40 Hearty cheer
41 Opening
42 Civil War guerrilla
46 Fell heavily
48 "Any fool knows that!"
49 Hart Trophy winner, 1970–72
50 Teacher's goal
51 "Black Beauty" star Freeman
52 ___ Vicente, Brazil
53 Cherish
54 Dead in the water
56 Top of a form to be filled out
57 Follows, timewise
58 Injured indelicately
59 School requirement, sometimes

DOWN

1 Overly stylish
2 "Merry Mount" composer
3 Delighted
4 Kind of limit
5 Formulates a strategy
6 Recital performer
7 Loading apparatus
8 Bone: Prefix
9 Christie contemporary
10 Mustang competitor
11 1954 A.L. batting champ
12 Gospel
13 Facade
14 Spoke with an accent?
21 Some ring occupants
24 Gluttonous meal
26 "Phooey!"
27 Rouen Cathedral depicter
30 Early Judean king
31 Patchy
32 Plant exchanges
33 Removed from circulation
34 Kind of competition
36 Old liners
38 Bolt
39 Some dyers
41 Holiday meal, informally
43 Get the worst of
44 Wiped out
45 ___ Pointe, Mich.
47 Reduce to mush
48 Search, in a way
51 Secure
54 Shipment notation: Abbr.
55 France/Switzerland's ___ Léman

210 by Chet Currier

ACROSS

1 Conspiracy
6 Thundering
11 Quipster
14 Diminish
15 Stir up, in a way
16 Billy Joel's "___ to Extremes"
17 Limited group?
19 Oriental absolute
20 Kind of steel
21 Astronaut in 1996 news
23 Undercover operative
24 "Frasier" character
25 Communion dishes
28 Like TV's Jaime Sommers
30 Nile bird
31 Academy student
32 Prearrange
35 Suede feature
36 Straw hats
38 Part of a name on a menu
39 Surprising "gift"
40 This comes in as March goes out
41 Quite some distance off
42 Gofer's assignment
44 Joan of Arc, e.g.
46 Salon treatment
48 Figures
49 Gentle as ___
50 Unexpected
55 Malaysian export
56 Vein
58 "The Island of the Day Before" author
59 Broadcast
60 Bristles
61 Consult
62 Unkempt
63 Discernment

DOWN

1 Stadium souvenirs
2 Blind as ___
3 Theda the vamp
4 Now and then
5 Inaugural Rock and Roll Hall of Fame inductee
6 Jibe
7 Flagwoman?
8 Circus cries
9 Elvis's "A Fool Such ___"
10 Moves in the garden
11 Sorcery
12 "Not ___!"
13 Former Philly mayor Wilson
18 Right-angle joints
22 News inits.
24 Activist
25 Loblolly, e.g.
26 Down with: Fr.
27 Harrison sobriquet
28 Like some breath
29 Time to beware
31 "The Postman Always Rings Twice" author
33 "Now ___ me down . . ."
34 Actress who played Tootsie's tootsie
36 One whom Pilate pardoned
37 Kind of history
41 Uzbek lake
43 Hoops target
44 Sportscaster Albert
45 Bear witness
46 Clotho and Lachesis
47 Author Walker
48 To whom "my heart belongs"
50 Resentful
51 Pigeon-___
52 Political suffixes
53 Spiffy
54 Jubilation
57 Golfer's concern

211   by Brendan Emmett Quigley

ACROSS

1 Made fun of
6 Comic Martin
11 Object of invective often
14 Concert venue
15 Site of Western Michigan University
17 1959 Philip Roth book
19 Part of the Holy Trinity
20 First name on Capitol Hill
21 Cold war side, with "the"
22 Seats with cushions
23 1932 and 1981 "Tarzan" films, e.g.
26 Inevitably
29 Dove rival
30 Coin no longer minted
31 Gen. Powell
32 Charge
35 Hemingway novel of 1929
39 Abbr. for 20-Across, in two ways
40 Watergate co-conspirator
41 Nonsense word repeated in a 1961 hit
42 Chemistry measurements
43 1902 Physics Nobelist Pieter
45 Loudly laments
48 Add color to
49 Seat
50 The "pneumo" in pneumonia
51 Untapped
54 1958 Mario Lanza song
59 Popular motor home
60 Writer Shute
61 Article in France Soir
62 Give
63 Ennoble

DOWN

1 Certain sports cars, informally
2 Suffix with buck
3 Drudge
4 Get rid of
5 Actor Coleman
6 Biases
7 Mediator's skill
8 "Hold On Tight" rock band
9 Kilmer of "The Saint"
10 Aussie bird
11 Language spoken in Tashkent
12 Cursor mover
13 Puts up, as a computer message
16 Home products company
18 Evergreens
22 Jack of 50's–60's TV
23 Come-from-behind attempt
24 Send out
25 Jorge's hand
26 Winglike
27 Never-ending sentence?
28 Scarf
29 Causes of some absences
31 Turns over
32 Gift tag word
33 Austen heroine
34 Cable staple
36 "The Time Machine" race
37 Something left behind
38 Help
42 Cheech of Cheech and Chong
43 Vitamin additive
44 Head of a train
45 More than a scuffle
46 Chill-inducing
47 Alerts
48 "Presumed Innocent" author
50 Lincoln Log competitor
51 Astronomer's sighting
52 Disney's "___ and the Detectives"
53 Cartoonist Kelly
55 Churchill symbol
56 Surveyor's dir.
57 Pop
58 Latin ruler

212   by Charles E. Gersch

ACROSS

1 Leaves in a huff
10 Calender abbr.
13 Warning for the inattentive
15 Actress Maryam
16 Some fast-food offerings
17 "___ do you good!"
18 Prefix with benzene
19 ___ de veau (sweetbread)
20 Outcome
22 Rain check
24 Designation
27 Frigidaire rival
28 Matriculate
30 ". . . ___ to breathe free" (Statue of Liberty Inscription)
32 Ropes
34 Herders' sticks
35 Commercially, O.K.
37 Pair
41 ". . . ___ a good night!"
43 Armenia's capital: Var.
44 Shows glee
47 About
48 Noted "Porgy and Bess" soprano
49 Sound
51 Actor David of "Rhoda"
52 Hoodwink
54 Rock's ___ Rose
56 Actor Gulager
57 Kon ___
58 More fast-food offerings
62 Dripping wet
63 Keep going
64 Albanian coin
65 Inexpensive telegram, once.

DOWN

1 Woollies
2 Country since 1964
3 1881 fight site
4 Pre-show show: Abbr.
5 ___ Woods (California tourist site)
6 Bowler's problem
7 "The Plough and the Stars" playwright
8 It goes in one era and out the other
9 Ala. neighbor
10 Prophet who reprimanded David
11 Rectangular
12 Pioneer physicist Alessandro
14 Baton Rouge coll.
15 Letting go
21 Curious one
23 Crisp
25 Polit. label
26 Business hub
29 Hard hat
31 Poet laureate Nicholas
33 Part of a blind
36 Office workstations maybe
38 Winter wear
39 Legendary Spanish matador
40 Cheerleader in a way
42 Actress Thompson
44 Popular vacation trip
45 Name in Western lore
46 Rather fashionable
48 Labellum
50 Remove
53 Answer to "How did you know?"
55 Hydro or electro follower
59 Organized
60 ". . . man ___ mouse?"
61 Project

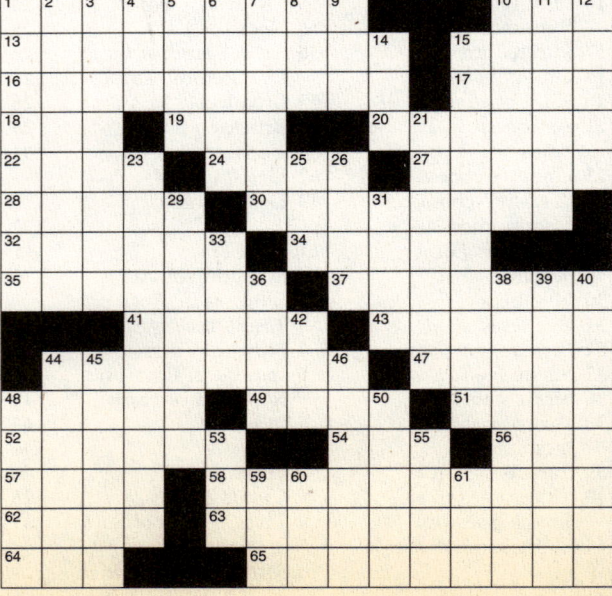

ACROSS

1 Snake with a nasty bite
4 Snide
9 Doggone pest?
13 Rung
15 Sap sucker
16 Galley propellers
17 Tight closure
18 Bulls and Bears, e.g.
19 Abdul-Jabbar's alma mater
20 Slippery
21 "Cubist" Rubik
22 Nixon's infamous '72 org.
23 Aftershock
25 Poisonous Asian snake
27 Some General Motors cars
29 Flower named for a Swedish botanist
33 Freighters' delays
37 Sea bird
38 Friendship
39 Disencumber
40 Oncoming
41 Well-off
42 "And *then* . . ." stories
44 "Light" ammunition?
46 ". . . bombs bursting ___"
47 ___ a million
49 Nag
53 Easily split rock
56 Eye
58 Unsavory bar
59 It can be a stretch
60 Witch's home
61 First name in cookies
62 Astronaut Shepard
63 Radio hostess Hansen
64 Harness fitting
65 Award for "Kiss of the Spider Woman"
66 Hen, perhaps
67 Just in

DOWN

1 Figure in black?
2 Guide
3 Painter Charles Willson ___
4 Party provider
5 Mimic
6 November 25, some years
7 Indonesian island
8 Football gains: Abbr.
9 Date for 6-Down
10 Doily material
11 First name in detective fiction
12 Immediately
14 Site of the first 6-Down
22 O.S.S. successor
24 Grand Ole ___
26 Plugs, of a sort
28 Hog fat
30 Lecherous look
31 "Dies ___"
32 No ifs, ___ . . .
33 Bull's-eye hitter
34 Abu Dhabi V.I.P.
35 Isinglass
36 Churchill successor
40 End in ___ (draw)
42 "We ___ not amused"
43 Officer in charge of the king's table linen
45 Wind dir.
48 Ancient land on the Aegean
50 "___ of Athens"
51 Bring out
52 Fix stitching
53 Louver
54 Hawaiian port
55 "That's one small step for ___ . . ."
57 Solitary
60 Building wing

ACROSS

1 Shakes up
5 Moonshine-to-be
9 Architectural afterthought
14 Like crazy
15 Until
16 Hang (over)
17 Patrick's "Ghost" co-star
18 Knock out
19 Like interstates
20 Practical joker's buy
23 Kind of fin
24 Sapporo sash
25 Fake jewelry
27 Marked a ballot
29 Charming
33 Publicize
34 Banana oil, e.g.
36 Major affiliation
37 Practical joker's buy
41 Centers of activity
42 Bucks
43 Impress mightily
44 Once around the sun
45 Will-o'-the-wisp site
46 Special interest grps.
48 Pithecologist's study
50 Lhasa ___ (terrier type)
51 Practical joker's buy
58 See 6-Down
59 Brazen
60 Bring on board
61 Sound
62 Kaput
63 Similar
64 Smile upon
65 Cleaning solutions
66 Work at a bar

DOWN

1 Figurine material
2 ___ Raymond, originator of "Flash Gordon"
3 Easy victory
4 Clown's props
5 Least lucid
6 With 58-Across, certain victims
7 Stagger
8 "Dukes of Hazzard" boss
9 Robin Williams forte
10 Involve with, unwillingly
11 Seaman-novelist who served on the Pilgrim
12 Abbr. on a phone
13 Nancy Drew's boyfriend
21 "Shane" or "Stagecoach"
22 How some pkgs. come
25 Nettle
26 Resort island off Venezuela
27 TV tube material
28 Consequently
30 Artist Grant Wood, e.g.
31 Steamship staffs
32 Rochester's beloved
33 Wan
35 What the hands may show
38 Sharon and Shamir
39 Charleston ladies
40 "Will Rogers Follies" prop
45 Turkish topper
47 "Big deal!"
49 Change at Chihuahua
50 Jibe
51 Music category
52 Junction point
53 Whom a wannabe wants to be
54 The Midshipmen
55 Water barrier
56 Green land
57 Split apart
58 Wisk rival

215   by Mel Taub

ACROSS
1 Ezio Pinza, e.g.
6 Leak
10 Mention publicly
14 Mythological figure
15 It's found on the end of a string
16 Hogarth depiction
17 Texas A & M student
18 Untimely arrival
20 National anthem?
22 907 kilograms
23 Sip
27 Houston, for one
28 "To ___" (with 44-Across, tune to which U.S. anthem was set)
31 Belli's bailiwick
34 Gold Cup Day site
36 "Holy cow!"
37 Cross to bear
39 Not by a long shot
40 Lay by
41 Straight prefix
42 Yemeni's neighbor
43 Took the van
44 See 28-Across
46 Pourboire
49 Direct
50 Obsolescent occupation
53 National anthem?
58 Whoop it up
61 Nick of "Cape Fear"
62 Impersonator
63 Hold overseas
64 Grenoble's river
65 Shadows
66 More than cheerfulness
67 Relinquished

DOWN
1 Whilom airline inits.
2 About 1% of the atmosphere
3 Transition
4 Louis and Paul, e.g.
5 Folk singer from Birmingham
6 Most populous N.Y.C. boro
7 Former Irish Prime Minister Cosgrave
8 Alaskan wildlife refuge site
9 Killer ___
10 Gains
11 Beat it
12 Maui strings
13 Neighbor of Pol.
19 U.S. Pres., militarily
21 Peter I, II or III
24 Splendid
25 Italian white wine
26 Ran its course
28 Israelite stoned for stealing at Jericho
29 Twelve
30 Moving jerkily
31 Bulgarian king, 1918–43
32 As to
33 Pleated trimming
35 A number of
38 Four-time Super Bowl champs
45 Ancient Syria
47 Peaceful
48 Hirsute
50 Distinctive manner
51 In bundles
52 Among: Fr.
54 Burglar
55 Rigorous test
56 Cleaving tool
57 Actual performance
58 Touched
59 Mail abbr.
60 Tapster's unit

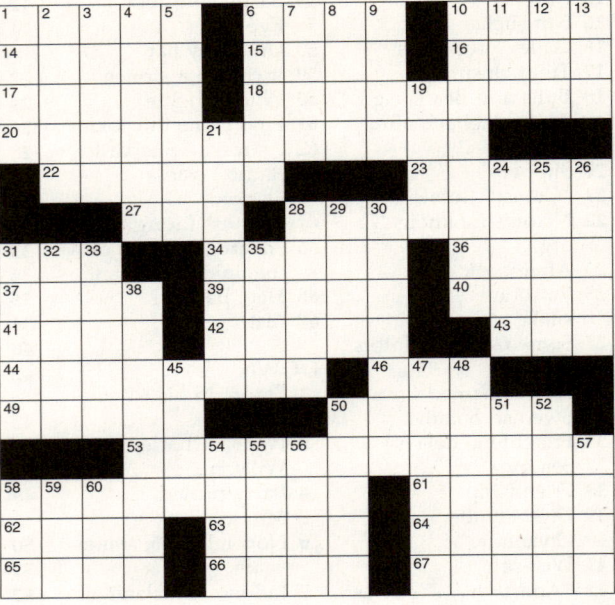

216   by Wayne Robert Williams

ACROSS
1 Comic Martha
5 Bamboozle
9 Stoppers
14 Height: Abbr.
15 Face-to-face exam
16 Beau at the balcony
17 Town near Caen
18 Chockablock
20 Headlong
22 Resident's suffix
23 Racetracks
24 Dormitory din
28 New York's Twin ___
30 Offspring, genealogically: Abbr.
31 Celtic Neptune
32 Centers
33 Walk-on
34 Chancellorsville victor
35 Western Indian
36 Enmity
38 Sugar suffix
39 Singer Tillis
40 Word after many or honey
41 Conflict in Greek drama
42 French dance
43 A.L. or N.L. honorees
44 "Phèdre" dramatist
46 Flummoxes
48 Spring fragrance
49 Picture blowup:Abbr.
50 Head count
53 Game of digs and spikes
57 Parts of pelvises
58 Greek poet saved by a dolphin
59 Fit
60 Oodles
61 Mississippi Senator ___ Lott
62 Branch headquarters?
63 "Auld Lang ___"

DOWN
1 Answer: Abbr.
2 Der ___ (Adenauer moniker)
3 Cowardly one
4 Changes with the times
5 Carpentry pins
6 Europe/Asia separator
7 Dark shadow
8 Building wing
9 1984 Goldie Hawn movie
10 Look threatening
11 Actress Thurman
12 Solidify
13 Our sun
19 Xmas tree trimming
21 Spoil
24 Interstate trucks
25 Without rhyme or reason
26 "Schindler's List" star Liam
27 Novelist Graham
28 Hitches, as a ride
29 Surpass at the dinner table
30 Natural alarm clocks
33 Hoofbeats
36 About to occur
37 Pulchritudinous
41 Gum arabic trees
44 Garden brook
45 Completely
47 Juicy fruit
48 Takes it easy
50 Contemporary dramatist David
51 King of the beasts
52 Deceased
53 Large tub
54 Hockey's Bobby
55 Golf-ball position
56 Prohibit

ACROSS

1 Suspect's "out"
6 Start of an invention
10 ___ to riches
14 Chance
15 Potter's furnace
16 Taj Mahal site
17 "Slow down!"
19 Freshwater duck
20 Swapped
21 Villain's laugh
22 Peruvian native
23 Illiterates' signatures
25 Hammed it up
27 Army need
31 Got up again
34 Roebuck's partner
36 Aquarium fish
37 Charged atom
40 "Slow down!"
43 Antlered animal
44 Assessed
45 To incorrectly write
   an infinitive
46 Provide with feathers
48 Actress Harper
49 "Ridi, Pagliaccio"
   singer
53 Koch and others
55 Dublin's land

56 Defective missile
59 Hardened
64 X-ray vision blocker
65 "Slow down!"
67 Not punctual
68 Tire parts
69 Kind of ray
70 Glacial ridges
71 "No more!"
72 Wheat bundle

DOWN

1 Aid and ___
2 Tragic king
3 "___ boy!"
4 Hopalong Cassidy
   portrayer
5 The Dow, e.g.
6 50's voters "liked"
   him
7 TV signal receiver
8 Lamb pseudonym
9 Flower development
10 Proportion
11 Insurance worker
12 Princess of Monaco
13 Waldorf ___
18 German border river
24 Unruffled
26 Cat calls

27 Late tennis V.I.P.
28 Banquet
29 Lone Ranger attire
30 Table crumb
32 Cleared leaves
33 Jittery
35 Feudal workers
37 Capri, e.g.
38 Elevator pioneer
39 Earns as profit
41 Nose offenders
42 Likely
47 Cut-and-paste
49 String quartet
   member
50 Regions
51 Lariat
52 Beneath
54 Hosiery risks
57 Army outfit
58 Sample record
60 Mormons' home
61 Relative of hoarfrost
62 Poet Lazarus
63 Fall on ___ ears
66 Cobra

ACROSS

1 Altar robes
5 "Wake Me Up Before
   You Go-Go" group
9 Basic ball game
14 Kitty cry
15 New York college
16 Council Bluffs
   neighbor
17 Silly author?
20 Like church music
21 "Dies ___"
22 "Help!"
23 Traditional Easter
   fare
25 Xenia's state
27 Not for the faint of
   heart
30 Senior's nest egg, for
   short
32 Ruined
35 Black cuckoo
36 Tennis score
38 Shell food?
40 French direction with
   ESP?
44 Ziti or linguine
45 Mrs. David
   Copperfield
46 Wind dir.

47 Pillages
49 Christmas quaff
50 Play the lead
51 Zola heroine
53 Unthinking
55 Write (down)
58 Peru's capital
60 Kind of bread
64 Person with a polite
   message?
67 Actor Toomey
68 The ___ Reader
   (eclectic magazine)
69 Actress Raines
70 Genuflected
71 "Phooey!"
72 Kaiser or Parker
   House

DOWN

1 Latin 101 verb
2 Actress Olin
3 Bygone airline
4 Helical
5 Quixote's opponent
6 ___ polloi
7 Years, to Tiberius
8 Computer shortcut
9 Acquire by accident
10 Rocker's equipment

11 ___ Ski Valley, N.M.
12 Ending for "ah"
13 Occurs, poetically
18 Q.E. 2 setting
19 Pearl Harbor site
24 Bette Midler's "A
   View From a ___"
26 Singer Anita
27 John Irving title
   character
28 Barry Lyndon
   portrayer, 1975
29 Detergent brand
31 Word on a French
   postcard
33 Pessimist's phrase
34 Part of DKNY
37 Boo-boo
39 Ending with seam or
   team
41 English school
42 Instigator
43 Unpredictable events
48 Use scissors
50 Evidence of a fistfight
52 It makes le monde
   go round
54 Was impassive
55 Yank
56 Foreshadowing

57 Buster Brown's dog
59 Nick and Nora's dog
61 Go it alone
62 "___ be a cold day in
   hell . . ."
63 Actress Patricia
65 Diamond ___
66 Explosive stuff

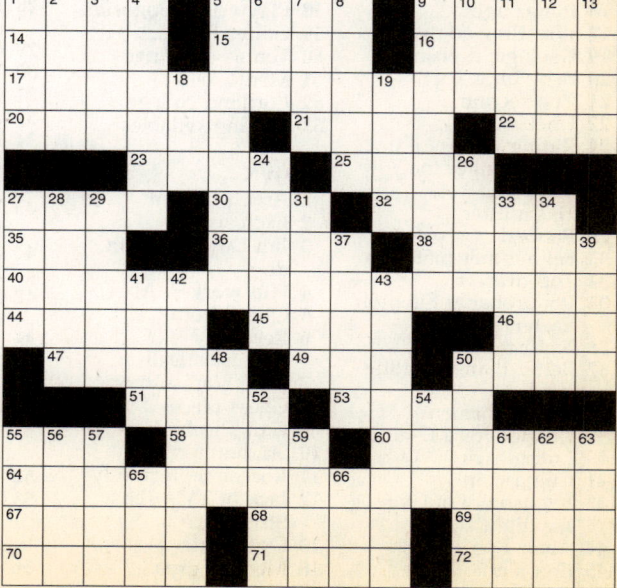

219 by Ed Early

ACROSS

1 Starting four
5 Nicholas or Peter
9 Not fat
13 Side-splitting comedy
14 Benoit ___ of the N.H.L.
16 London's ___ Park
17 Emaciated
20 Under the weather
21 Make sure of, as a victory
22 Holly trees
23 Did business (with)
25 More nuts
28 Waste
30 Require
31 Two cups, basically
34 Fugue master
35 Outmoded
36 Asset
37 With nothing in reserve
41 Eye part
42 Spanish chess piece
43 River to the Ubangi
44 Shelley tribute
45 Noodle
46 Rapunzel feature
48 Some tableware
50 Kind of gum
52 First U.S. spacewalk mission
55 Koch and others
57 9 or 66, e.g.: Abbr.
58 More than ready for battle
62 Manipulator
63 Ohio college
64 French Sudan, today
65 Minus
66 Bell ___
67 Timetable, for short

DOWN

1 Police announcement: "This is ___!"
2 Like pelicans and hospital patients
3 Shoulder part
4 Skid row woe
5 Stylish
6 Like most city land
7 ___ Khan
8 Baseball score
9 Stable worker
10 ___ eyed (sharp-sighted)
11 French notion
12 Imbroglio
15 Deleted from galley proofs
18 Hardly fine art
19 Extorted from
24 Covers with rich soil
26 Pain allayer
27 Hat material
29 Show generosity to
31 Very fast talk
32 Gully
33 Eruption fallout
36 Frigid spots
37 Mr. Ziegfeld
38 Bloodshot
39 Adroit
40 Least
45 Deep knee ___
47 Come to terms
48 Harbor structures
49 Kind of center
51 Concealed again
52 Ancient France
53 European language
54 Sras. across the Pyrenees
56 G.O.P. opponents
59 Slippery stuff
60 Song syllable
61 Printer's measures

220 by Lois Sidway

ACROSS

1 Bullwinkle, e.g.
6 Unit of sugar
10 One with a handle
14 Algebraic exponent
15 Carpet cutter's calculation
16 Lunar light
17 Wrestling coups?
19 Geologic divisions
20 Baby blue, e.g.
21 Zoo section
22 Unctuous
24 Riding whip
25 Lone Ranger foe Black ___
26 Has a litter
29 Pooped
33 Set another match to
34 Top-drawer
35 It's probably filled on Easter
36 Not care ___
37 Better-than-middling grade
38 ___ at (torment)
39 Change for a C-note
40 Lummoxes
41 China man
42 It's usually out for the night
44 Actor Lon
45 Brooklet
46 Jam-pack
47 Work
50 Hooey
51 It starts in Apr.
54 Oscar-winning Pasteur portrayer
55 Many a drug pusher?
58 Playwright Bogosian
59 Golfer Isao ___
60 Tennis exchange
61 Memo
62 Portland college
63 Singing syllables

DOWN

1 Attic problem
2 Exclusively
3 Jim Davis cartoon dog
4 Hill worker: Abbr.
5 Quote from
6 Receive enthusiastically
7 "The Haj" author
8 Chess pieces
9 Gail Sheehy book
10 Student's crib?
11 Roseanne, formerly
12 Jack of TV's "Easy Street"
13 Optimistic
18 Medical grps.
23 Lawrence Tero, professionally
24 Dog groomer's specialty?
25 Worker's reward
26 Tom Joad felt it
27 "___ go again . . ."
28 Relative of the dik-dik
29 Gave (out)
30 Yakety-yakked
31 Get around
32 1948 also-ran
34 Fencing movement
37 Frisco transporter
41 Movers' partners
43 Word with head or line
44 Bean
46 Intelligible
47 Sign of things to come
48 ___ Disney
49 Hawkeye's MASH, for one
50 Make brownies
51 Farmer's place, in song
52 Part of S.A.S.E.
53 "___ Little Tenderness" (old hit song)
56 Lobster coral
57 "The Way"

221   by Manny Nosowsky

ACROSS

1 Fowl entrées
7 Minolta rival
12 Fingernail crescent
13 Hard rock
15 Filmdom's "My Sister ___"
16 Duck hunter's scope
17 Permanently abroad, maybe
18 Load
19 Alphabetic run
20 ___ Tiki
21 Games people play
23 Computer function
24 When écoles let out
26 Firefighting equipment
27 Odd
28 Furniture wood source
30 Fred Flintstone's workplace
31 "Joyeux ___"
32 Actor Ke Huy ___
33 Meal maker?
36 Bee workers
40 Match
41 Thigh muscle, informally

42 Without ___ (riskily)
43 "Sister Act" extras
44 Old and charming
46 Article in "Die Welt"
47 Tease
48 One of a fivesome, for short
49 Cologne's Church of St. ___
51 Milk purchase
53 Chokers
54 "The Cannonball Run" actor
55 Computer programmers
56 Infection cause
57 Hardly dense

DOWN

1 Comparatively smooth
2 Don of fiction
3 Like most stationery
4 "The Mammoth Hunters" author
5 Censor
6 Gidget in "Gidget"
7 "Peanuts" character
8 Jug ___

9 Start of "The Yankee Doodle Boy" chorus
10 Overcome
11 More sore
13 Easy 2-pointers
14 1939 movie lawman
16 Dead duck
22 "The Fusco Brothers" dog, in the funnies
23 Amounts
25 Christmas temps
27 Kind of analysis: Abbr.
29 Take it easy
30 Busybodies
32 Le Havre lading place
33 Tarkington opus
34 Zebras, e.g.
35 Population boom area
36 Dress designer Mary
37 Ultimate consumer
38 Sots, at times
39 Road in the Ruhr
41 Stationery amount
44 Suppress
45 Go as a group
48 Wilde comment
50 Fountain potable

52 In the capacity of

222   by Fran and Lou Sabin

ACROSS

1 Knife wound
5 Stair part
9 Clear the blackboard
14 Like linoleum floors
15 West Virginia export
16 Banister post
17 Cake decorator
18 Facility
19 Kind of preview
20 Oscar
23 On, as a lamp
24 Panhandle
25 Inlaid design
29 "___ whillikers!"
31 Feasts upon
35 Sailor's "Stop!"
36 Alan of "The Four Seasons"
37 Fraternity letter
38 Oscar
42 Singer/poet Yoko
43 Other: Sp.
44 "That's the truth!"
45 Paper quantity
47 Serenade the moon
48 Sweet and hard drinks
49 Runner Sebastian
51 "Full," at a theater

52 Oscar
61 Love affair
62 Many a Disney character
63 Caesar's worst day
64 ___ face (grimace)
65 Poker payment
66 Jump
67 British guns
68 Pay mind to
69 "That was no ___, that . . ."

DOWN

1 Gulp down
2 South-of-the-border sandwich
3 Ice show jump
4 Polar explorer Richard
5 Eye-pleasing, as a view
6 "To your health!" is one
7 Asia, with "the"
8 Courtroom bargain
9 Follow
10 Go back on one's word
11 Mad as ___ hen

12 Plane reservation
13 Actress Sommer
21 Haves
22 Letter-shaped girder
25 College concentration
26 Sheeplike
27 Mead's "Coming of Age in ___"
28 Cigar tip
29 Denzel Washington's 1989 Oscar film
30 Author Ferber
32 Computer firm
33 Not your or our
34 Locations
36 "The Thin Man" dog
39 Annual prize
40 Teamsters, e.g.
41 Place for peas
46 Poet Rod
48 Strained to see
50 Gumbo vegetables
51 Whomped à la Samson
52 Plays extemporaneously
53 Amo, amas, ___
54 Pepsi rival
55 Mormon stronghold
56 Out of sight

57 Streamlet
58 Concert halls
59 X-ray vision blocker
60 Catch sight of

223 by Fred Piscop

ACROSS

1 Give a Bronx cheer to
5 Camel features
10 Dog's annoyance
14 Region
15 W.W. II plane ___ Gay
16 Melon throwaway
17 Party munchies, e.g.
19 Within: Prefix
20 Comic book heroes
21 "Return to ___"
23 Smart, as students
26 Waterfall
27 Submarine detection systems
28 Big name in copiers
29 "___ luck!"
30 Army vehicle
31 Brothers
35 "I'd hate to break up ___"
36 Ram, astrologically
37 Rolling in money
38 Like most postage stamps: Abbr.
39 Female sweetheart
40 Spotted horse
41 Politico North
43 Teeter-totter
44 Fix indelibly
47 Equilibria
48 Evolution theorist Charles
49 Leopold and ___ (1920's murder case)
50 Bright thought
51 How a surprise might catch you
57 Stadium level
58 Utah's ___ Mountains
59 De ___ (opulent): Fr.
60 Hourglass fill
61 Japanese camera
62 Nerve cell part

DOWN

1 Brit. W.W. II fliers
2 Mr. Onassis
3 Buddhist sect
4 Zig's opposite
5 Greek messenger of the gods
6 Starved
7 Apollo 11's goal
8 Arafat's org.
9 Inept soldiers
10 Burger side order
11 Figure skater Fratianne
12 Open-___ (unrestricted)
13 Revere
18 Newsboy's cry
22 "___ Beso" (1962 song)
23 Christmas bird
24 The "I" in ICBM
25 VCR button
26 Movie theaters
27 Personal affront
28 Hoist
30 Choo-choo
32 Get the suds out
33 Play the role of
34 Third place at the race track
36 Jokingly
40 Singer Bryson
42 My ___, Vietnam
43 Edberg of tennis
44 Prepares for publication
45 Gymnast Comaneci
46 Golf hole's locale
47 ___ voce
49 Thin
52 52, to Flavius
53 Rock-___ (jukebox brand)
54 Oft-rented outfit
55 Outside: Prefix
56 Cub Scout group

224 by Brendan Emmett Quigley

ACROSS

1 Epsilon follower
5 Maze choices
10 Diner side dish
14 Tributes in verse
15 Not far off
16 March blower
17 Scouting units
18 Prairie dog?
20 Its job is taxing
21 Calligrapher
22 Hilo hello
24 Angel, perhaps
28 Made of clay
31 High school for Hercule
32 Great valor
36 Kind of trick
37 Dog identification?
41 "My man!"
42 Stanley ___ (early auto)
43 Pertaining to element 56
46 Regan's poisoner
50 The Ox-Bow Incident; e.g.
54 Freedom within a relationship
55 Queen's subject
58 Animation unit
59 Play with a dog?
62 Coors drink advertised as "zomething different"
63 Enroll in
64 "Nixon" director
65 ___ instant (at once)
66 Hitch
67 Steve Forbes is surrounded by them
68 Remain undecided

DOWN

1 High signs?
2 Channel swimmer Gertrude
3 Certain muscle
4 Donkey's uncle
5 Reduce, as expenses
6 Like ___ out of hell
7 Scout's rider
8 More colossal
9 Noted shock jock
10 Turbulent
11 1964 Murray Schisgal play
12 1860's White House name
13 Tolstoy topic
19 Convincing
21 Less convincing
23 Sarcastic laugh
25 Comeback
26 Straight
27 Hanoi New Year
29 Gets under one's skin
30 Bargaining basis
33 Mineral suffix
34 Rug variety
35 Office communiqué
37 Fracture detector
38 Eve's counterpart
39 Smarts
40 Ready for surgery
41 Petroleum meas.
44 Chinese book of divination
45 Blender setting
47 "Phèdre" playwright
48 Delivery person of old
49 University founder Stanford
51 Occupied
52 Fits snugly
53 Greek fast food
56 Response to "Come va?"
57 Former partners
59 Breakfast drinks
60 Years and years
61 24 horas
62 Spice

225

ACROSS
1 Filthy lucre
5 House holds
11 Grunts
14 "I kissed thee ___ kill'd thee:" Othello
15 Personae non ___
16 Snippets of information
17 Tennis referee's cry
18 Investing, in a way
19 Temporary computer storage
20 Extremely rare
22 Year in St. Gregory I's papacy
23 It has a cupule
24 Corn-coction
25 Brings in
26 Angle's partner
27 Unification Church member
29 Claim
32 Christie adaptation
38 Impetuous
39 Eat exclusively
40 Ebenezer's partner
45 They go bananas over bananas
46 Bluejackets

50 Former Spanish president Manuel ___
51 Common conjunction
52 St. Lawrence sight
54 Literary monogram
55 Oscar winner, 1974 and 1980
56 Brest milk
57 Box score notation
58 Taken out
59 River to Donegal Bay
60 "Independence Day" attackers
61 Weigh
62 They may have it

DOWN
1 King who sent Jason for the Golden Fleece
2 Work with a famous Funeral March
3 Pop singer Annie
4 Beaumarchais's barber
5 Soil: Prefix
6 Band
7 Banned
8 Suffix with add or part

9 Birch society members?
10 Deseret bloom
11 Billie Holiday trademark
12 Idleness
13 Geishas' instruments
21 The Crossed Harpoons, in "Moby-Dick"
25 Words of denial
28 Fort near Monterey
29 H.S. subject
30 Make out
31 Title for Gilbert or Sullivan
32 Title for Gilbert and Sullivan
33 Lay eggs, as a field cricket
34 Young hares
35 Provokes
36 Race car driver ___ Fabi
37 Ballroom couples
40 Carrier to Kyoto
41 Flower whose name means "dry"
42 One who sings
43 1939 Giraudoux play

44 Clubs
47 O'Neill and others
48 Arrowrock Dam's river
49 Begets

52 Glimmering
53 Lays down the lawn

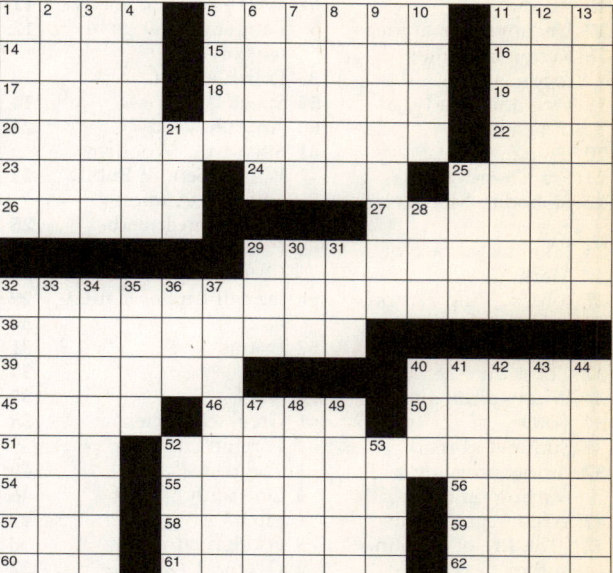

---

226 by David J. Kahn

ACROSS
1 Wee bit
4 Sticking point
8 Ethanol, to dimethyl ether
14 Longtime Frazier foe
15 Flunky
16 Actor William of "Knots Landing"
17 Sunday reading
19 Wilderness home
20 Explosives and such
21 "The Raggedy Man" poet
23 Frostiness
24 Latitude
25 ___ Verde National Park
26 "Bird on ___" (Gibson film)
28 Together, musically
29 Upbeat, in music
31 The yoke's on them
32 Patrick Ewing, for one
34 Quechua, e.g.
36 Musical that premiered 3/29/1951
39 "The Faerie Queene" character

40 Thatched
43 A.L. player
46 Smack
48 Coty of France
49 Places for hats?
51 Fraternity letters
52 Lot
53 Kind of card
54 Golden Horde member
56 Mint
57 Beer, sometimes
59 Pacific divider
61 Popular Hershey bar
62 Repute
63 B.&O. stop
64 Furtive
65 TV Guide span
66 Guitarist Nugent

DOWN
1 Southeast Florida city
2 Pie preference
3 Gymnast's finale
4 Airport queue
5 Bravo, e.g.
6 Any one of the Magi
7 Song from 36-Across
8 Nothing doing?
9 "Bye!"

10 Fertilization sites
11 60's–70's TV sleuth
12 Uncut
13 End a shutdown
18 With 27-Down, song from 36-Across
22 Psychiatrist/author R. D. ___
25 Sell
27 See 18-Down
30 States of alarm
33 Suffix with slogan
35 Actress Sue ___ Langdon
37 Not suitable
38 VISTA worker, perhaps
41 Understanding
42 Pool area
43 Footprints
44 ___ reason
45 Con
47 Pep talk, sometimes
50 Chateaubriand
55 Pretentious
56 Weight lifting maneuver
58 Reggae variation
60 Part of Italy

227 by Dean Niles

ACROSS
1 Some clauses
11 Pond dross
15 College in 1995 headlines
16 Account
17 Unconventional ideas
18 Kennedy Center focus
19 Fine and dandy, in old slang
20 On ___ with
21 French crowd?
22 Slobodan Milosevic, e.g.
24 Like the surface of Mars
27 John's "Pulp Fiction" co-star
28 Stockpiled
32 Chest muscle
33 What spirits may do
34 Total
36 Summer abroad
37 Axioms serving as starting points
41 What I may mean
42 "The Joy of Cooking" author
43 Mail abbr.
44 Simile center
45 Wound
48 Date for Dizzy
49 Spanish novelist who won a 1989 Nobel
51 1980's police comedy
53 Language that gave us "kayak"
55 Polish export
59 Speck
60 Ampule's kin
61 Site of the Woodrow Wilson Sch. of Public and Intl. Affairs
64 Basic French verb
65 Preserved oral history, e.g.
66 Jazz drummer Catlett et al.
67 Exams

DOWN
1 Greek character?
2 Foreign currency
3 The rest
4 One with perfect pitch?
5 Foreign currency
6 Over
7 "There!"
8 Osmics is the study of these
9 Sergeant Preston's horse
10 Rocky, really
11 Antares, for one
12 "If I Loved You" musical
13 Eventual
14 E-mail
21 Computer experts, e.g.
23 They may be made in clubs
25 French city on the Moselle
26 Deliver
29 Take away
30 Horn in (on)
31 Standard
35 Canadian pol. party
37 Excuses
38 Q45, e.g.
39 60's militant
40 ___-dieu
46 High, in a way
47 Midday event
50 They have low pH's
52 Harness features
54 Mer sights
56 "Get ___!" (boss's order)
57 1988 film "Rent-___"
58 "___ joy keep you": Sandburg
61 Show of support
62 Herb of grace
63 Keep time

228 by Manny Nosowsky

ACROSS
1 Longtime New Yorker cartoonist
10 Doctors' professional magazine
14 Kind of booth
15 Business department
16 Fan
17 Typical subjects in a psych study
18 Grilling spots
19 Beach item
20 Unhappy crowd sound
21 Spanish quarters
22 Number five iron
26 Taken in a sedan
27 Llama herder, once
28 Lots
32 Kaiser kin
33 In a blah manner
34 Gambler's game
35 Means of support?
37 Bee's landing platform
38 Rockwell and Clark
39 Buying a quart of milk, e.g.
40 Star attractions?
43 Zetterling of "All Those Tomorrows"
44 Excise
45 Short hole, perhaps
50 In readiness
51 Go to bed
52 Fur pieces
53 Exactly
54 Last column in addition
55 In need of exorcism

DOWN
1 Tut-tut
2 This: Sp.
3 Lawsuit basis
4 "___ Coming" (1969 pop hit)
5 Makes lots, as money
6 "Don't be such ___!"
7 Mob scenes
8 Entre ___
9 Thunder Bay prov.
10 Candy store purchase
11 Court defense
12 ___ Park
13 Fools
15 Literary Laurence
19 Have a ball
21 Bubbles
22 Neighbor of 9-Down
23 San Francisco founder
24 Have a look-see
25 "School" lessons?
26 Chicago five
28 Call it ___
29 VHS alternative
30 Words before instant or uproar
31 Blabbed
33 He went through Hell
36 Giants coach Dan
37 Please, to Shakespeare
39 Kipling's "When ___ Last Picture is Painted"
40 Advertising film
41 Prominent Red Square name
42 Chemical compound
43 Dillon and Biondi
45 Spanish conifer
46 They peck at their food
47 Greek letters
48 The life of Riley
49 Gave the once-over
51 Short trip

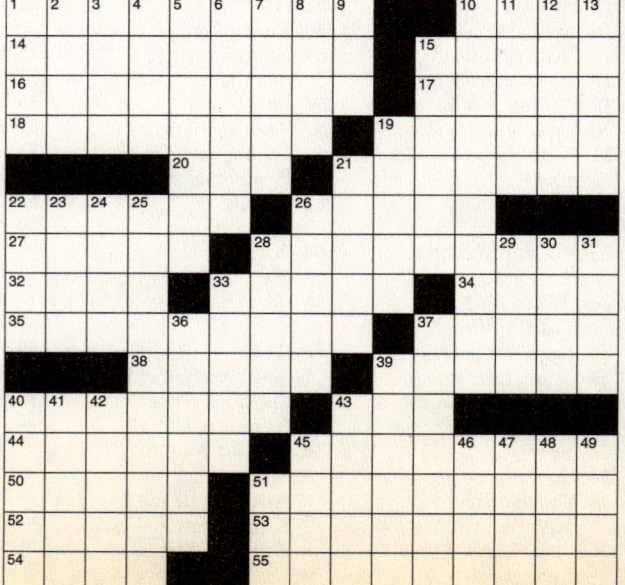

ACROSS

1 Dog star
5 Gull's cousin
9 Eyeball bender
14 Ground grain
15 Mini revelation
16 Red-eyed bird
17 Haitian despot
20 Cordwood measure
21 Israeli dance
22 Out's opposite
23 Vidal's Breckinridge
25 Actor Young of TV's 67-Across
27 Is grief-stricken
30 Book subtitled "His Songs and His Sayings"
35 Supped
36 Relative of a Bap. or Presb.
37 Balkan capital
38 Gabor sister
40 Thimbleful
42 Dryden work
43 Help get situated
45 Plugs of a sort
47 Saturn's wife
48 1956 Rosalind Russell role
50 "For ___ us a child is born"
51 Headlight?
52 Survey chart
54 Seaweed product
57 ___ fixe
59 Reached the total of
63 Popular psychologist
66 Paul Anka hit
67 See 25-Across
68 Deep blue
69 Throat malady
70 Achy
71 James Mason sci-fi role of 1954

DOWN

1 Rock band equipment
2 Usher
3 Mend, in a way
4 Alternatives to The Club
5 Round stopper
6 Delights
7 Change the décor
8 Kind of network
9 Roman breakfast?
10 Light beers
11 "Jewel Song," e.g.
12 Mariner's peril
13 Raced
18 She played Grace Van Owen on "L.A. Law"
19 Passepartout, to Phileas Fogg
24 Strongly scented plant
26 Stellar Ram
27 Fiji neighbor
28 City in northern Japan
29 Set in motion
31 Dinnerware
32 Building contractor
33 Not suitable
34 Final authority
36 Madness
39 Oust
41 Nurse, maybe
44 Directed toward a goal
46 Hair fixative
49 Office connections?
50 Donny Osmond, e.g.
53 Record-holding N.F.L. receiver ___ Monk
54 Postfixes
55 Sandpaper surface
56 Opened a crack
58 Catalonian river
60 Hawaiian hen
61 In shape
62 Kon-Tiki Museum site
64 Shrill bark
65 Lyric poem

ACROSS

1 Twelve ___ ("G.W.T.W." home)
5 Cousin of the cobra
8 Pelt
12 Insomnia causes
14 Sausage, e.g.
16 Having no deferments
17 "___ akbar" (Arab cry)
18 The Sphinx and the Parthenon?
20 Available
22 Speech problem
23 Until
24 Author Murdoch
26 Took the most credit
28 Socks and Millie?
32 Popular Dutch export
33 Zero-shaped
34 Mr. Hulot's portrayer
36 Gossip-column snippet
38 Poe story setting
39 Piers 19 and 20?
41 Tony-winner Caldwell
43 Ending for tip or team
45 The Untouchables
46 Russian sea
47 Goneril's father
49 Two-spot and six-spot?
51 Helter ___
54 Problem for Superman
55 Unsafe, in a way
56 1982 Stein / Pimpton biography
58 Subject of Freudian study
61 20 cents?
64 Obloquy
66 Blueprint
67 Bald head
68 Cry from the sick ward
69 Barks
70 Town on Long Island Sound
71 Unclothe

DOWN

1 Seraglio room
2 Singer Guthrie
3 Potter's need
4 Kind of sense
5 Concert hall equipment
6 Bewhiskered animal
7 City of Light
8 ___ polloi
9 Light entertainments
10 Farm-gear pioneer
11 Sugar-coated
13 Nattily clad
15 Kind of test
19 Floral spike
21 Attraction at St. Peter's
25 Show alarm
27 Squeal
28 Top 40 music
29 Budget rival
30 Jalopy
31 Notary public's need
35 Exemplar
37 Lows
39 Jabbered
40 "No right ___"
42 Turgenev's "On the ___"
44 Conger
46 Made sense
48 Gave a room a face lift
50 Hall-of-Fame Brave
51 Excessively sentimental
52 ___ Lumpur
53 Inflexibility
57 Prize since 1948
59 River through Leeds
60 Chew (on)
62 Years in 7-Down
63 Date
65 Country singer McDaniel

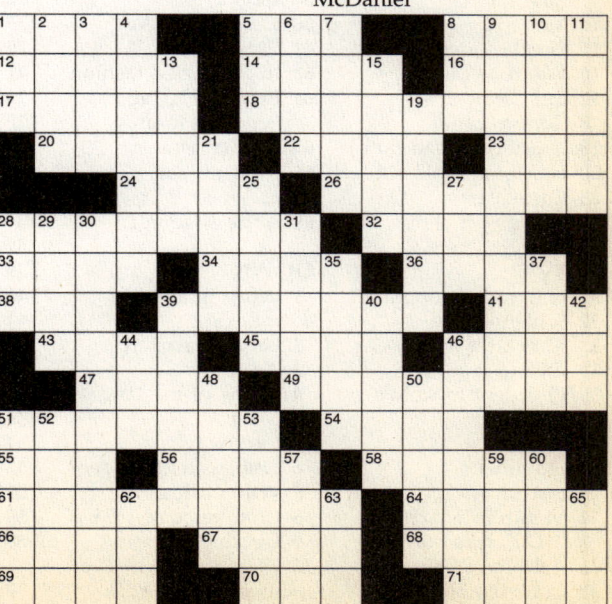

231   by Harvey Estes

ACROSS
1 "Star Wars" group
7 ___ card (wallet item)
13 "Walk on the Wild Side" singer
15 Puget Sound city
17 Feeler
18 "L'École des Femmes" writer
19 Retard
20 "Make ___ double!"
22 Introvert
23 Sticky strip
24 Static
26 Thurmond of hoops
27 ___ flash
28 Hang on the line
30 Medicine amounts: Abbr.
31 Some shooters
33 Singer Kitt
35 Subject of the book "Perjury"
36 Open-weave fabric
37 Examine again
40 We're all in this together
44 Addison's "___ to Creation"
45 Leathernecks
47 ___ anemone
48 High time?
50 Tar from the Thames
51 Italian bread
52 ___ Park, Colo.
54 Masc. alternative
55 Niamey's country
56 Lucky, like sesame seeds?
58 Shiite leader
60 Loose
61 Double negative follower
62 Not worn out
63 Ran the show

DOWN
1 Adjustable
2 Four-time Super Bowl QB
3 Housed in
4 "The Forsyte Saga" lady
5 Overhead expense
6 Poet's adverb
7 On ___ (when wanted)
8 Ab ___ (from the start)
9 Dudley Do-Right's love
10 M-G-M or TriStar rival
11 Show historically
12 Seventh-inning activity
14 Newspapers
16 Mother of Calcutta
21 Advice
24 Glassware
25 Grant's opponent, 1872
28 Jeffersonian belief
29 1979 Richard Gere film
32 Any miss
34 Artist Lichtenstein
36 Center, for one
37 Beaus
38 Six-time Emmy-winning actor
39 With a will
40 Quiet, expressive one
41 Pioneer pilots
42 Golden
43 Long in the past
46 Rummaged in an arsenal?
49 Vassals
51 Digs
53 Alphabetize
55 Second starter
57 Majors in acting
59 Chew the fat

232   by Fred Piscop

ACROSS
1 Land for development
6 Small nail
10 ___ Observer (1992 mission)
14 Move like a chopper
15 Greek liqueur
16 Wanted G.I.
17 ___ Gay
18 Comics canine
19 ___ fide (in bad faith)
20 Heirloom tool?
23 Carte start
24 Run an art show
25 Red giant, e.g.
28 TV's "___ Academic"
31 N.L. cap monogram
32 Schlemiel
33 Knock for a loop
35 Casino request
39 President Lincoln's tools?
42 Hightail it
43 Hummer's instrument
44 Month in which D.D.E. was born
45 Astronaut Grissom
47 Cornell's Big ___
48 Disturb, with "up"
49 Peloponnesian War participant
52 Antipollution grp.
54 Secret military tool?
59 100 kurus
60 ___ du Lac, Wis.
61 Puts out
63 In a frenzied fashion
64 Former Hawaii Senator Hiram
65 Annual visitor
66 Kind of loaf
67 ___-eyed
68 Actress Georgia

DOWN
1 Word ignored in indexing
2 Gossipy Barrett
3 Admit
4 Home of the 1962 Mets
5 Park way
6 Flub, as a grounder
7 Wife of Boaz
8 Conqueree of 1521
9 Goofball
10 Class to which all of us belong
11 Look for
12 Esther of "Good Times"
13 Dispatch
21 Attaches
22 Joint: Prefix
25 Drenches
26 1 on the Mohs' scale
27 Way off
29 Transported
30 Until now
33 Our longest bones
34 Level
36 Commandment starter
37 Certain raingear
38 C.P.R. specialists
40 1945 blast site
41 Augured
46 Doesn't tip
48 Lunatic
49 Goo
50 Word of mouth
51 Play for ___
53 Bel ___ cheese
54 Decked out
55 ___ time (right away)
56 1988 Dick Francis thriller, with "The"
57 Throw barbs at
58 Kitchen addition?
62 Pitcher Maglie

ACROSS

1 "Even Cowgirls Get the Blues" star
11 "Star Wars" sage
15 Modern-day 20-Across
16 Common first floor apt. no.
17 Riding around town, maybe
18 Former Pistons coach Chuck
19 Cartouches
20 Radio message
21 "Lord of the Rings" tree people
22 "Mmmmmm!"
25 Back biters
26 1993 Peace Prize winner
30 Word part: Abbr.
32 Hank Aaron stat
33 Assign too high a rating to
35 Best in a race
37 Jeans maker Strauss
38 Smart
40 Mata ___
41 Smart Alex?
43 Singer from Ottawa
45 Hammer's location
46 Kind of order
48 Walked on
49 First name in mysteries
51 Queen of the Misty Isles, in the comics
53 Drumsticks, basically
54 Spot in the mer
55 Leonardo's ladies
60 Latin lover's word?
61 Tabula rasa
64 Colorado resort
65 Photo retoucher
66 Last of the Stuarts
67 Get penalized, in some games

DOWN

1 Golden rule word
2 Nuclear missile
3 Celebes ox
4 Apple targeter
5 Hip hugger?
6 One, to Antoine
7 Fernando, por ejemplo
8 Humidified
9 Miffs
10 Darkroom items, for short
11 Novelty song
12 Out grocery shopping, maybe
13 Comic TV actress
14 Brindled cat
23 Yukon neighbor
24 Film director Gus Van ___
25 Winter woe
26 Kilauea flow
27 John Doe
28 Start of many resolutions
29 Small amount
31 Modern breakfast
34 Laotian money
36 Senator Cochran
39 Basketball's Archibald
42 Freudian study
44 Fills with cargo
47 Roman proconsul in a biblical dispute
50 Weaver's fiber
52 Unwelcome looks
54 Suffix with myth or monarch
56 To boot
57 When doubled, a fish
58 Heliolater's deity
59 Spanish painter
62 Presidential nickname
63 Inits. of 1933

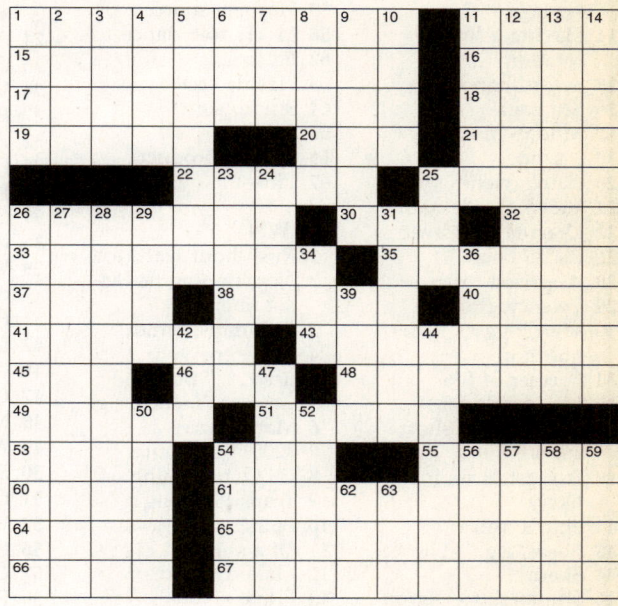

ACROSS

1 Writer Tom or Thomas
6 Help in crime
10 One ___ (form of baseball)
14 Of the lower intestine
15 Ready for picking
16 Canceled, as a launch
17 Neato
19 One more time
20 Glimpses
21 ___-do-well
23 Referee's count
24 Household power: Abbr.
26 Phoenix neighbor
28 ___-been
31 Cuticle shaper
36 Patriot Allen
38 "Crazy" bird
39 Hydroxyl compound
40 Eins + zwei
41 Court center, usually
42 Hawaii's state bird
43 Loses all power
44 Did better than a B
45 Welsh dog
46 Curry favor with
49 ___ Diego
50 Golfer Ballesteros
51 List ender
53 ___-jongg
55 "Masque of Alfred" composer
58 Eats away, as soil
62 ". . . ___ saw Elba"
64 Kid's bike part
66 Polaris, e.g.
67 Scent
68 Crowded
69 Fictional Mr.
70 Exhibit boredom
71 Mr. Kefauver

DOWN

1 Towel (off)
2 Corrida cheers
3 Jump
4 Prima ___ evidence
5 Level of command
6 Couples' transportation?
7 Good: Fr.
8 Fencer's blade
9 Urban housing
10 End ___ high note
11 Receptacles
12 "A Death in the Family" writer James
13 Burg
18 River through Flanders
22 Legal matter
25 Printed cloth
27 Shorthand taker
28 Gossipy Hopper
29 In position, as a sail
30 ___ Bay, Brooklyn
32 Unusual
33 Sweet treat
34 Afro-Cuban drum
35 Anne of fashion
37 Usher's route
41 Fledgling entrepreneur
45 Message in mime
47 ___ Marie Saint
48 Anna who played Nana
52 Comes in last
53 Netting
54 Pretentious
56 It means nothing to Julio
57 Plenty, old-style
59 Fender bender memento
60 Ill at ___
61 Fr. holy women
63 Dander
65 Prince Valiant's son

235 by David J. Kahn

ACROSS

1 La ___, Calif.
6 George Michael's old musical group
10 Shuts up, as a hostage
14 Having a line of rotation
15 Sword handle
16 Sea eagle
17 Mild, white cheese
19 ___ tide
20 Cain's victim
21 Video arcade name
22 Dracula portrayer
26 Radio knob
28 Apprised (of)
29 Twenty: Prefix
30 Miss Piggy's question
31 Partner of life
35 List concluder
36 More than a short story
40 August birth, most likely
41 Ship's trail
43 Niece, e.g.: Abbr.
44 Sham
46 Shipment to Detroit
48 Disburses
49 Three-time N.L. M.V.P.
53 "Let's Make ___"
54 Critic Greene
55 Hashish source
56 Lively folk dance
62 Fit to ___
63 Needle case
64 Studio sign
65 Sole
66 Steno's product
67 Link

DOWN

1 Rush-hour feature
2 Nonwinning tic-tac-toe line
3 Columnist Smith
4 "Give me your tired . . ." poet
5 George Wallace, e.g.
6 Marine snail
7 "2001" computer
8 C.I.O. beginning
9 Transit of song
10 Polite
11 Of a surface
12 Make twisted
13 Photo color
18 French president Coty
21 Cabinet dept.
22 Shepherd's charge
23 Thin plate, anatomically
24 Army problem
25 Catch, slangily
26 Vista
27 Eight: Prefix
32 Actress Massey
33 Darn
34 Lads
37 City near Utah Lake
38 Agnew, once
39 Wisconsin city, childhood home of Harry Houdini
42 Loose nut?
45 Greek
47 Chess champ Mikhail
48 Mr. Connery
49 Auto racing's Bobby
50 Schiller's "___ Joy"
51 Gulf of Aden land
52 Writer Marsh
56 Pro ___
57 Consumed
58 Pirate drink
59 West Coast airport, briefly
60 N.Y.C. school
61 ___ gratia artis

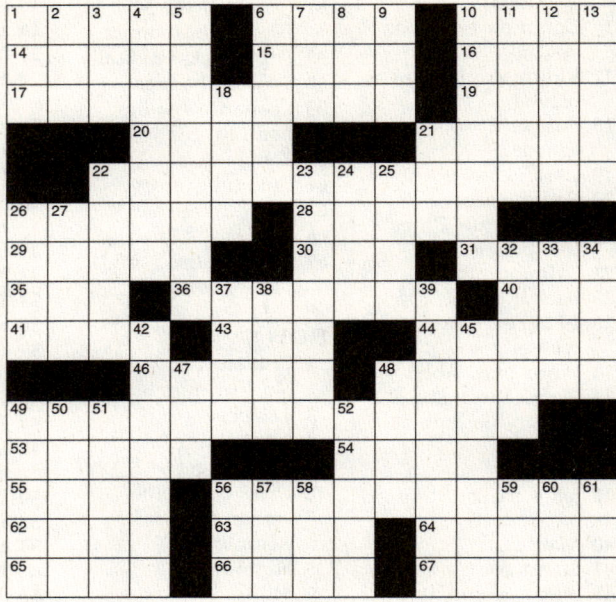

236 by Gregory E. Paul

ACROSS

1 Lullaby
5 "Betty ___" (1930 hit)
9 Tin Pan Alley grp.
14 "It's a Sin to Tell ___"
15 Proficient
16 Billow
17 Camera's eye
18 Italia's capital
19 Look of scorn
20 William Randolph Hearst's home
22 Like neon
23 "Who has an answer?"
24 No sweat
26 Pleased
29 "Hey, ___!"
33 Wood shaper
37 Rock's ZZ Top, e.g.
39 "Othello" villain
40 It's west of Wales
41 Out of place
42 Feet
43 Nonesuch
44 Start for a hero
45 Wiesbaden's state
46 Thwart
48 Majesty lead-in
50 Savings plans, for short
52 Silent's successor
57 Disciple of Socrates
60 Michael Jackson's home
63 Salesman Willy
64 One who's adored
65 "Snug as ___ . . ."
66 Words of wisdom
67 Medicine tablet
68 Polyhymnia, e.g.
69 KNO$_3$
70 Kett of the comics
71 Ballantine and others

DOWN

1 Party dip
2 City SSE of Buffalo
3 Fool
4 Plaster painting surface
5 Mount ___, Israel
6 Bassoon relative
7 Adm. Zumwalt
8 Patriot Silas
9 Saintly city
10 Washington Irving's home
11 Algonquian Indian
12 Ending with teen or golden
13 Saucy
21 Pulitzer playwright
25 Biblical prophet
27 Prefix with sphere
28 Prospect for oil
30 Southwestern art colony
31 Hatchery items
32 Blush shade
33 Composer Janácek
34 Grammarian's eyebrow raiser
35 Deuce topper
36 Andrew Jackson's home, with "The"
38 Man, e.g.
41 Vicinity
45 Consider, as a case
47 Laundry worker
49 "A Streetcar Named Desire" name
51 Long-billed bird
53 Incan transport
54 Afghan capital
55 Occupied
56 Fringes
57 Keogh, for one
58 Felician College site
59 Latin 101 verb
61 Rework, as copy
62 Bit of a shock

237 by Fran and Lou Sabin

ACROSS
1 Blasé
6 Horse show command
10 Panasonic products
14 Pianist Claudio
15 Diamond Head site
16 Cooper's cleaving tool
17 Geese may be found in it
19 Mrs. Chaplin
20 Cleo's biter
21 Word with floor or peace
22 Arctic whale: Var.
24 Ampule
25 Griffin of "Jeopardy!"
26 Quick breads
29 Persuade to accept
33 Radio station supplies
34 Reasons against
35 Group enterprise
36 Set up
37 Kind of deg.
38 Botanical opening
39 Make 1-Down, e.g.
40 "Later"
41 Cartridge content

42 Deck hands
44 One way to put things
45 Pond sight
46 City desk shout
47 Temple
50 Matador's foe
51 Burns film role
54 Moises, for one
55 Abecedary phrase
58 Night sightings
59 Russian soldier
60 Lawn tool
61 Summer camp site
62 ___ libre
63 Henhouse

DOWN
1 Joe
2 Barks
3 Downslide
4 Musical gift
5 Least kept up
6 All-Bran rival
7 Drizzle
8 "What's this?"
9 Secret passages, maybe
10 Churchill sign
11 Eschew humility

12 First name in gossip
13 Harbor ___
18 " 'Tis a pity"
23 Couples-only craft
24 Middy
25 Heaven-sent help
26 Basketball infraction
27 Seven-time A.L. batting champ
28 "Le Coq d'Or," e.g.
29 Sugar pie
30 1963 Ray Charles song
31 Volumes
32 It's eye-catching
34 Cautious
38 Visit briefly
40 Shalom Tower site
43 Two hearts, e.g.
44 Of two minds
46 Creates
47 Newsman Harvey
48 A, in code-speak
49 Makeup, informally
50 Romanov leader
51 Full of energy
52 Barcelona boosters
53 Tapered seam
56 Forum farewell

57 "Deed ___" (Jazz Age tune)

238 by Frank A. Longo

ACROSS
1 Dairy treats
16 Cotopaxi and Hekla, e.g.
17 Novel featuring Jake Barnes
18 Makes an archaeological error
19 List shortener
23 Hard hitter
27 Pout
28 Org. in which Jordan is a member
31 Get hip
32 Screen siren
33 Rabbit whose ears stick out at right angles to the head
35 Year in Benedict IV's papacy
36 Over
37 ___ pactum (simple contract)
38 Shreds
39 Capek classic
40 Knock down a peg
41 River to the Mediterranean
42 Like a good egg
44 Half a cartoon duo

45 "The Brady Bunch" regular
46 Assaults
47 Unaccompanied part song
48 Flower's distinguishing feature
54 IV drips, often
61 Cozy cover
62 Colorado, with "the"

DOWN
1 Tiger
2 Methylene group, chemically
3 Taxonomic suffix
4 U.S.S.R.'s successor
5 Egg
6 Director Riefenstahl
7 Gardner and others
8 Let the cat out of the bag
9 Old socialite Maxwell
10 Lerwick ladies
11 Ellie May Lester feature, in "Tobacco Road"
12 Drink flavorings
13 Sends to the canvas

14 Shoe-store letters
15 Conscription org.
19 Prohibition
20 Perfectly
21 Dawns
22 Intuitive step
24 Acoustic unit
25 Eucalyptus
26 Installment
28 Occidental
29 "Father Goose" author
30 Passion
34 Renaissance instrument
38 "Wozzeck" composer
40 Absence of war
43 Characterize
49 Q-queen connector
50 Places
51 Terra ___ (powdery substance)
52 Wing shape
53 Airport approximations, familiarly
54 Brief moment?
55 Leicester libation
56 Writer Deighton
57 Passbook abbr.

58 Volga feeder
59 Bottom line?
60 Catherine, e.g.: Abbr.

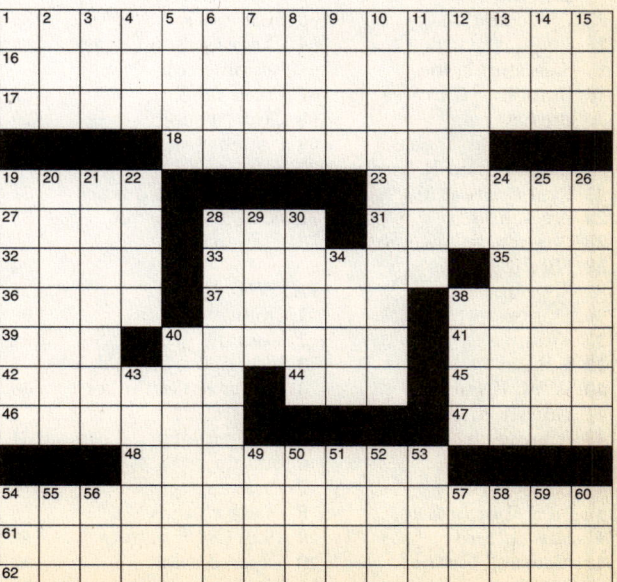

239 by Chuck Deodene

ACROSS

1 "Backdraft" gear
6 Approximates
15 Wind: Prefix
16 Credit card cost
17 G.I.'s bills
18 Prospectors' helpers
19 Formal footwear
20 Place for a hole, often
21 Square dance partners
22 When repeated, a 1968 pop hit
23 Certain trousers
25 Knot
26 Acting Gardner
27 Have ___-see
29 Pollster's finding
31 State of emergency
33 Attacker
34 Cold war headquarters
35 Fetter
39 Cartoon brawl exclamation
40 Locker room discussion
41 Pari ___ (at an equal rate)
44 Tender looks
45 Catchall abbr.
46 Smelter input
47 Scottish clan leader
49 Skiing mecca
50 Kind of fall
52 CPR administrator
53 Tonto's Scout, for one
54 Schedule
57 Geometer's concern
58 Like brewers' hops
59 Escape the understanding of
60 University Park campus
61 Counted tree rings, e.g.

DOWN

1 #
2 Head-to-toe look
3 Outdoor air
4 70's radical ___ Harris
5 Saturates
6 Song from the 'hood
7 Getting crocked
8 Pop
9 Microwaved
10 Stop up
11 Turnstile cheater
12 Recently
13 "___ Stronger Every Day" (1973 hit)
14 Owned (up)
23 Succotash ingredient
24 Stepping spots
27 To the max
28 70's singer Garrett
30 Bring in
32 Israeli writer ___ Oz
33 Public regard
35 English garden feature
36 Looking freshly groomed
37 Leeway
38 Fenced-in
40 Series of troubles
41 Soda can feature
42 Reach
43 Galleon crew
44 Africa's smallest country
48 Compassion
49 Cy Young winner, 1988
51 Volunteer's home: Abbr.
53 Made, as a case
55 Scores at R.F.K.
56 City near Arnhem

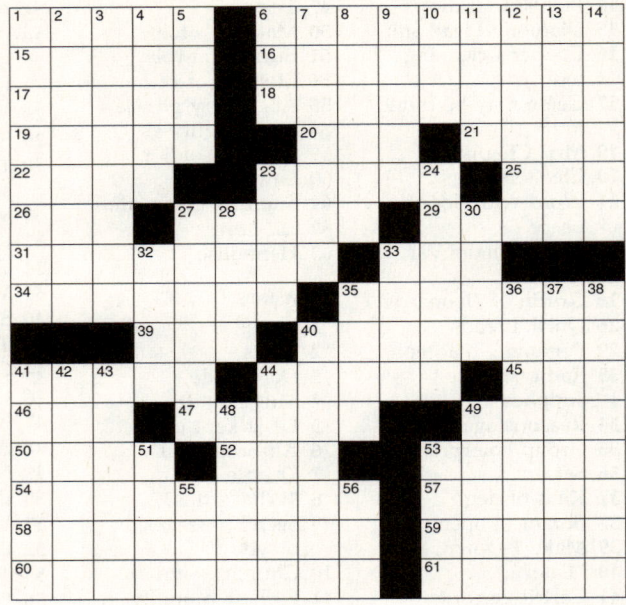

240 by Gregory E. Paul

ACROSS

1 Shut noisily
5 Trouser parts
9 Iridium, e.g.
14 Sound of contentment
15 Cleveland's lake
16 Playing marble
17 Sale stipulation
18 Bumbling Carol Burnett role
20 Prefix with meter
22 Cumberland R. locale
23 Real estate unit
24 Sty sound
26 Pharmacist's weight
28 Nitwit
32 Sign up
36 Opposer
37 Trounce
39 Edition
40 W.W. II gun
41 Downy duck
43 It grows from the neck
44 Bedevil
46 Neighbor of Belg.
47 Lab culture
48 National Guard building
50 Three Rivers Stadium team
52 Lack
54 1169 erupter
55 Clean air gp.
58 Stallion's mate
60 Fish hawk
64 Greer Garson Oscar-winning role
67 Fixed fee
68 Church song
69 I came: Lat.
70 Soup pods
71 Parenthetical remark
72 A.C./D.C. power
73 Classmate

DOWN

1 Quarrel
2 Verdant
3 Indy 500's Luyendyk
4 Simon & Garfunkel hit
5 Picnic quaff
6 Bungle
7 Essence
8 Made clothes
9 1955 Oscar actress
10 Kind of salad
11 Head's opposite
12 ___ time (never)
13 "___ we forget"
19 Regarding
21 Russian space station
25 Popular Japanese beer
27 "Allegory on the banks of the Nile" speaker
28 Linguine, e.g.
29 Reply to a knock
30 TV soldiers of fortune, with "The"
31 Matisse subjects
33 Lake of the Ozarks' river
34 Kind of eclipse
35 Lechers' looks
38 Singer Midler
42 Empty talk
45 Loner
49 Give birth, as a sheep
51 U.S.N.A. grad
53 Beverly Hills' Rodeo ___
55 Madame Bovary
56 Partner of cons
57 Italian wine center
59 Daredevil Knievel
61 Autumn tool
62 French 101 verb
63 Vintage
65 Club ___
66 Okla.-to-Ky. direction

241 by Frances Hansen

ACROSS

1 Billy Budd's affirmatives
5 Cio-Cio-San's marriage broker
9 Land in the Rub al Khali
13 Almost red
14 One may be found near a cloverleaf
15 Mental barrier
16 Start of a tribute to the Metropolitan Opera's James Levine
19 Like soap operas
20 Sgt. Bilko
21 E.T. carriers
22 Ship of myth
24 More of the tribute
31 Hawaiian "gathering place"
32 Points of difficulty
33 Met guest artist DeLuise
34 Ship ropes
35 Detroit Dark Red and others
37 Flag
38 Additionally
39 Kind of dance
40 Regretful one
41 More of the tribute
46 Maximum degree
47 Letters from Greece
48 Expect
51 Expiate
55 End of the tribute
58 "Der fliegende Holländer" tenor
59 ___ Park
60 Singer's concern
61 Department store department
62 Walton opera, with "The"
63 Coast

DOWN

1 "Vissi d'___" (Puccini aria)
2 Squawk
3 ". . . ___saw Elba"
4 Like Salome's dance
5 Card game similar to authors
6 Of the ear
7 Pastor, informally
8 Cheer for Escamillo
9 Weber opera
10 Loud complaint
11 Rural prefix
12 Stock page heading
14 Me's partner, in a 1936 song
17 Modern protein source
18 Safecrackers
22 Month of l'été
23 Cookout fare
24 Minute amounts
25 Refuse
26 Vamp Bara
27 16th-century council site
28 Abhorrence
29 Composer of "Miss Julie"
30 Manicurist's board
35 Object of Canaanite worship
36 Once
37 Cuts geometrically
39 "Mefistofele" composer
42 Speculates
43 Utmost extent of one's strength
44 Western tribe
45 Peerce and Smuts
48 "Pardon . . ."
49 Had being
50 Related
51 Boy preceder
52 Silly billy
53 Author Sarah ___ Jewett
54 Sax or oboe
56 Spiders parlor
57 Compass point

242 by Patrick Jordan

ACROSS

1 Some sports cars, for short
5 Foundation
10 Yield
14 Grimm villain
15 Novelist Jong
16 Jump at the Ice Capades
17 British heavy metal group
19 Canned meat brand
20 Disney's Dwarfs, e.g.
21 Printings
23 Support for Tiger Woods?
24 Pop singer Peeples
26 Prepares leather
27 Do a few odd jobs
32 ___ Ababa
35 Cape Cod resort town
36 Acuff of the Country Music Hall of Fame
37 Androcles' friend
38 Headgear for Hardy
39 Celebration
40 Worshiper's seat
41 Bruce Wayne's home, for one
42 Valentine's Day gift
43 Inexpert motorist
46 Klondike strike
47 Org. that advises the N.S.C.
48 Computer key abbr.
51 One who works for a spell?
55 Sauteed shrimp dish
57 Not this
58 Huck Finn portrayer, 1993
60 Bring to ruin
61 As a companion
62 To be, in Tours
63 Afrikaner
64 London length
65 Fortuneteller

DOWN

1 Ceiling supporter
2 Conform (with)
3 Search blindly
4 E-mailed
5 "Hit the bricks!"
6 Jackie's second
7 Pro or con
8 Chilled the Chablis
9 Hygienic
10 Dealer's employer
11 Film box datum
12 Cain of "Lois & Clark"
13 Stately shaders
18 Luncheonette lists
22 Tropical root
25 Look after, with "to"
27 Wrestler's goal
28 Diamond flaw?
29 Decorative heading
30 Bit of marginalia
31 Changes color, in a way
32 European chain
33 The Almighty, in Alsace
34 Reduce in rank
38 Class distraction
39 On behalf of
41 Having a Y chromosome
42 Boxer's stat
44 Alter deceptively
45 Countenance
48 Overplay onstage
49 Fern fruit
50 Autumn beverage
51 Hit, as the toe
52 "You gotta be kidding!"
53 Model Macpherson
54 Very funny fellow
56 Makes one's jaw drop
59 Dad's namesake: Abbr.

243   by Norman S. Wizer

ACROSS

1 Serve with a summons
5 "Casino" co-star, 1995
10 Castaway's transportation
14 Copper containers
15 Hybrid citrus fruit
16 Perry's creator
17 Egyptian actress?
19 Jar
20 Ar's follower
21 Novelist Jean
22 Come to
24 Last frame, sometimes
26 Chorus syllables
28 Winter resort rentals
30 Like some drugs
33 It may be hooked
36 Philippic
38 Navigator's dir.
39 Garfield's predecessor
41 Setting for a place setting
42 Room to ___
44 "Gotcha!"
45 Guesses
48 ___ out (manages)
49 Pleasing to the ear
51 Bridge
53 Waste gases, e.g.
55 Storm
59 Fivesome
61 Twelve Oaks neighbor
63 Trifle
64 House of Leo?
65 Egyptian heavyweight?
68 1995 N.C.A.A. basketball champs
69 Overact
70 Personal prefix
71 "___ My Girl" (1967 hit)
72 Fabulous
73 Get dewy-eyed

DOWN

1 Hale-Bopp, e.g.
2 People with "O' " names
3 Flirt
4 Paranormal ability
5 Strong praise
6 Where 2-Down live
7 Baby-size
8 Murmur
9 Went all the way, as a smoker
10 Used car deal, e.g.
11 Egyptian second banana?
12 Kind of pipe
13 Ky.-Ala. divider
18 Amount of hair
23 Evanesces
25 Salinger dedicatee
27 Playing marbles
29 "My love is like a red, red rose," e.g.
31 Apropos of
32 Medium grades
33 "Eh?"
34 Island near Kauai
35 Egyptian actor?
37 Commanded
40 Bulgaria's capital
43 Pocket protector items
46 Splash sites
47 Thinner
50 They're cast in a cast of thousands
52 "Immediately!"
54 Sitting place
56 Offhand remark
57 Ancient land on the Aegean
58 Egypt's Temple of ___
59 In addition
60 Individually
62 You have to be upfront about this
66 Big bird
67 Top 10 song, say

244   by Derderian Brown

ACROSS

1 Battle of 1836
6 Snoozes
10 Read, as bar codes
14 Actress Linda
15 Song for one
16 Tropical food plant
17 "Great!"
18 Shaker contents
19 ___-European
20 Rarely
23 Zero
24 They use lassos
25 Product with Ammonia-D
29 Ineptly
31 Counterpart of Mars
32 Jai ___
33 Kind of cow, dog or horse
36 Hercule Poirot's pride
41 Feminizing suffix
42 The last word?
43 Seamstress Betsy
44 Cons
45 TV secretary
47 New York's ___ Island
50 Wide's partner
51 Surrenders
58 Double-reed woodwind
59 "The Wind in the Willows" character
60 Something to fall back on?
61 Stir up
62 Toledo's lake
63 Heavy reading
64 Lump
65 Auction off
66 Baker's need

DOWN

1 In addition
2 White House area
3 With: Fr.
4 Roger Bannister's distance
5 Connected to the information superhighway
6 Twang type
7 Show horse
8 Tablet
9 Sinatra's "___ Night"
10 Part of a 90's TV duo
11 Transport for Hiawatha
12 Zeal
13 Middays
21 Overrule
22 Windblown
25 Cloth texture
26 Showy flower
27 Snares
28 Summer hrs.
29 Owls' hangouts
30 Pub draught
33 ___ gin fizz
34 Otherwise
35 Like some profs.
37 Intertwines
38 Flows forth
39 Small wonder
40 Blunder
44 Addison contemporary Richard
45 Plopped (down)
46 Peace maker
47 Like some enemies
48 No-no
49 Eschew
50 Cuba's Castro
52 Had on
53 "___, Caesar!"
54 Ice chunk
55 South American capital
56 "Honest" one and namesakes
57 Essence

245 by Fred Piscop

ACROSS
1 Six-Day War commander
7 Music makers
10 Paul Fusco TV role
13 Oregon city
14 First name in tennis
15 My ___
16 Chico, really
18 Common vow
19 Snorkel, for one: Abbr.
20 Rocky Road servings
21 Chair person?
23 Gauge
25 Chan portrayer
26 Flummox
29 Like some polynomials
31 Bud's home
32 St. John's player
36 Reps.
39 Blow it
40 Bubby of the N.F.L.
42 L.L. Cool J's genre
43 Affix a brand to
45 San ___, Tex.
46 Wanted-poster abbr.
47 Untrue
49 Norton's workplace
51 Spokes
53 Linguine toppings
57 Blue, in a way
58 What's more
59 Kettle and others
62 Dear one?
63 Head of surveys
67 Sleep disturber, possibly
68 De Valera's land
69 10-Across and others
70 Lie on the beach
71 Driller's deg.
72 Floating

DOWN
1 Poivre's mate
2 Lemon and orange, e.g.
3 Het up
4 Airport pickup
5 ___ string
6 Squares
7 Yearbook signer
8 S or E: Abbr.
9 "All My Pretty Ones" poet
10 "Goodbye, Columbus" star
11 Burdened
12 Arctic finger: Var.
14 Pucks
17 It impresses
22 Saturn's end?
24 Novi Sad native
26 Steinfuls
27 Film producer ___ Schary
28 Simon LeBon's band
30 Like Nash's lama
33 Bullpen stats
34 Outmoded items
35 "No ___" (menu phrase)
37 Fish haul
38 Practice with a palooka
41 Charlie Hustle
44 Ruffle
48 Of nobility
50 Sparkle
51 Barely talks
52 Word for a person on the go?
54 What George couldn't tell
55 Letters before a state name, perhaps
56 Cagney role
60 Gazetteer data
61 ___ Fein
64 Sci-fi suffix
65 Carte start
66 Wings of a sort

246 by Ernie Furtado

ACROSS
1 Play opening
5 Ran
9 Shawl or afghan
14 Forsaken
15 Yellow brick, e.g.
16 Moonshine
17 Unencumbered
19 Composed
20 Follower of 21-Across?
21 Follower of 20-Across?
22 Small: Suffix
23 Ripped
24 Dems. opposition
27 Proverbial distancer
32 Sleepy Hollow schoolmaster
34 Ampersand
35 Firpo of the ring
36 Folk tales
37 Ship's officers
39 ___ time (never)
40 Upshots
41 Morning hrs.
42 Waffle topping
43 Kind of disease, facetiously
47 Hook shape
48 Alphabet quartet
49 Unmixed, as a drink
51 Character actor George
54 Starts
58 In the thick of
59 Be afraid to offend
60 Hope of Hollywood
61 Manhattan campus
62 Gamblers' game
63 Boorish
64 Some combos
65 Sharp put-down

DOWN
1 ___ Romeo (automobile)
2 Hip
3 De ___ (too much)
4 Words before "red" or "running"
5 Literary sister
6 Give some slack
7 Maneuver slowly
8 White House monogram
9 Block
10 Fun and games
11 Kind of beer
12 Eight, in combinations
13 A question of time
18 Singer Lenya
21 Merchandise
23 Manner of speaking
24 Staff leader
25 University of Maine site
26 TV announcer Don
28 1980 DeLuise movie
29 Bizarre
30 "Peanuts" character
31 Stock plans providing worker ownership: Abbr.
33 Young'uns
37 Horace and Thomas
38 BB's
42 Disreputable
44 Some are spitting
45 World cultural agcy.
46 Flirts
50 Stylish Brits
51 Baby powder
52 Poet Khayyám
53 ___ fide
54 Where humuhu-munuku-nukuapuaa might be served
55 Filly or colt
56 Roman marketplaces
57 Quit
59 Abbr. in a mail-order ad

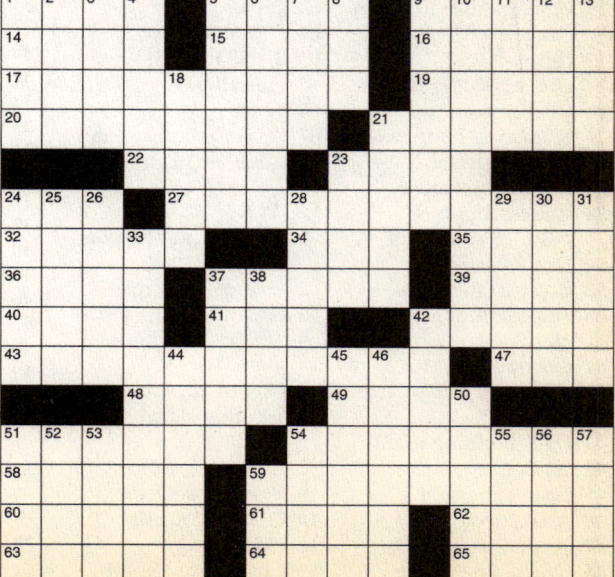

247 by Roger H. Courtney

ACROSS

1 Cremona violinmaker
6 Henri's squeeze
10 Tennis units
14 Quarrel
15 Stadium protests
16 Wynken, Blynken and Nod, e.g.
17 Criticize a prizefight?
19 Small brook
20 Transgression
21 Blackmailed
22 Cold stick
24 Le Sage's "Gil ___"
25 One way to run
26 Instruments for Rostropovich
29 Economic hostility
33 Poet T. S.
34 Trumpeter Al
35 ___ morgana (mirage)
36 Highway caution
37 Skater Sonja
38 Late king of Norway
39 "I ___ Got Nobody" (20's hit)
40 Mare's feed
41 Jacques, in song
42 Rings loudly
44 Bell's signal
45 Itineraries: Abbr.
46 Handed-down stories
47 Expensive
50 Bit
51 Word with date or process
54 Imitator Little
55 Boxing commission?
58 Medicinal plant
59 Killer whale
60 "Happy Birthday" medium
61 Cravings
62 Shade of blue
63 Cup of thé

DOWN

1 Clumsy boats
2 Actor Paul
3 Ever and ___
4 Idiosyncrasy
5 Imagination tester
6 French clergymen
7 "___ Indigo"
8 Chit
9 Guesswork
10 How hard Riddick Bowe can hit?
11 Rock star Clapton
12 Cash drawer
13 Fileted fish
18 "What a pity!"
23 Delivery letters
24 Items used in "light" boxing?
25 "Mrs. ___ Goes to Paris"
26 Actor Romero
27 "Dallas" matriarch Miss ___
28 Detroit footballers
29 Hues
30 Charles's princedom
31 Old name in game arcades
32 "Nevermore" quoter
34 Call at a coin flip
37 Winnie-the-Pooh receptacle
41 Awhile
43 Shoshonean
44 Humorist Lazlo
46 Not an express
47 Devoutly wish
48 Annoy
49 Religious image
50 Peruvian Indian
51 Speaker's spot
52 Coffee dispensers
53 Fisher's "Postcards From the ___"
56 Suffix with fail
57 Wood sorrel

248 by Peter Gordon

ACROSS

1 Bedwear, informally
4 Essen exclamation
7 Move back
13 Sports org.
14 ___ tai
15 Ethanol and dimethyl ether, e.g.
17 Germinating
19 One of 38-Across
20 Unchanged
21 Sounds of happiness
23 Hose material
24 One of 38-Across
28 Actress Lupino
29 Distinctive quality
30 Drink cat-style
33 River to the Seine
36 Telecommunications giant
37 Uncommon
38 Theme of this puzzle
42 Missing
43 Dam-building org.
44 Gather
45 Gaze at
46 Afrikaner
47 To and ___
48 One of 38-Across
53 Lumberjacks' competition
56 Vote for
57 It is in Spain
58 Concern of 38-Across
61 Beg
63 Fame
64 Nipper's co.
65 Black and tan ingredient
66 Texas city
67 Driver's license info
68 Cobb and Hardin

DOWN

1 Pari ___ (at an equal rate): Lat.
2 One of 38-Across
3 Finland, to the Finns
4 "What ___, chopped liver?"
5 One of 38-Across
6 Weather data
7 Semi
8 Language suffix
9 Pupil's protector
10 Oscars' cousins
11 Good buy
12 Cubemaker Rubik
16 Antonym's antonym: Abbr.
18 Add color to again
22 Shower's counterpart
25 River in Germany
26 Saturn or Mercury; e.g.
27 Not kosher
30 Pelée output
31 Lover of Aphrodite
32 Bics, e.g.
33 Homeowner's pymt.
34 Sailor's cry
35 Actress Russo
37 More distant
39 Sioux Indian
40 Iris's place
41 Wraparound dress
46 Litters
47 One of 38-Across
48 Type
49 Rathskeller servings
50 "Have ___" (interviewer's request)
51 One of 38-Across
52 N.B.A.'s Thurmond and Archibald
53 Scale notes
54 Eight: Prefix
55 Fill, as bases
59 Yr. parts
60 Singer Sumac
62 Strain

ACROSS

1 Opposing sides
5 Mr. Kadiddlehopper
9 ___ belli (cause of war)
14 Part of a foot
15 Prince, in a way
16 Ultraviolet ray absorber
17 Actress Kedrova
18 Drawn carriages
19 Magna cum ___
20 1991 Sally Field film
22 Fred Dryer police drama
23 Inputs
24 Abound
26 "48 ___"
27 Uses rollers
29 Yiddish crook
31 Quantity of groceries
34 Declaration of Independence signer John
38 Hautboy
40 Thole insert
41 Alice's Restaurant patron
42 City on Great Slave Lake
47 London's ___ Gardens
48 Transplant patient
49 Theatrical lament
51 One way to fish
53 Annexes
55 Baseball bird
59 Estuary features
61 Quadrennial event
63 Verbalize
64 Vatican City site
65 Wedding finery
66 Terra ___
67 Dr. Seuss's "If ___ the Zoo"
68 Writer Wiesel
69 Pooh-pooh, with "at"
70 Automobile pioneer
71 Papas

DOWN

1 Quiz response
2 Film company
3 Acclamation
4 Fashions
5 Corpus ___
6 Floral wear
7 V-___
8 Wife, with "the"
9 Newspaper features
10 Call from a minaret
11 "Dallas" ranch
12 Secondary to
13 Prognosticators
21 Took a straw
22 Get an earful
25 Female adviser
28 Supplied with fuel
30 Auto-testing grp.
31 ___ George
32 Honest man
33 Some tableware
35 Solo of "Star Wars"
36 "Hurrah!"
37 Equality grp.
39 "Xanadu" band, for short
43 Rampaging
44 Unites
45 Mr. Ziegfeld
46 Carter's middle name
50 Crabbed
51 Harrow blades
52 Composer Bruckner
54 Vowed
56 City in Florida's horse country
57 Of sound mind
58 Swords
60 Major ending
62 Gulf War ally
64 Poke fun at

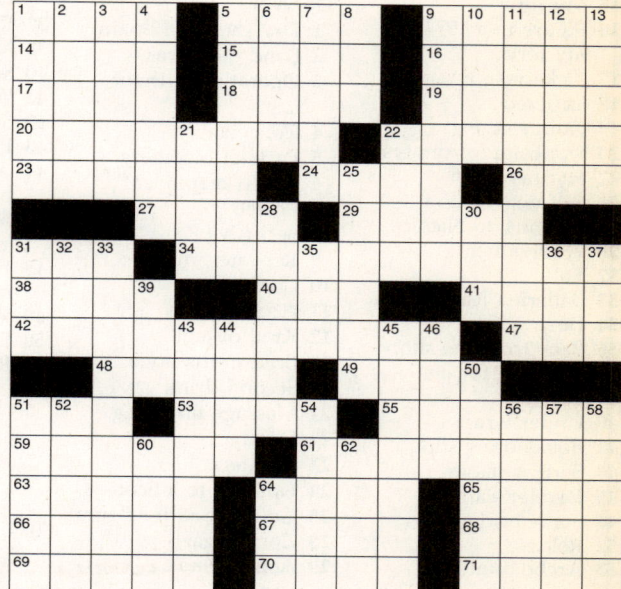

ACROSS

1 Literally, "gem of buildings"
9 Florentine : spinach :: lyonnaise : ___
15 Make match
16 Yoplait competitor
17 Can't sell anymore, by necessity
18 Chrétien's capital
19 ___ tai
20 Pestles' companions
22 Vet
23 Multivitamin ingredient
25 Conspicuous signs
26 Picard predecessor
27 Innsbruck's province
29 Phoebus, with "the"
30 Reagan Cabinet member
31 Singer Sheena
33 In use, as an apartment building
35 They're busy in Apr.
37 Dry: Prefix
38 Clinched
42 Postprandial chore
46 Reamed
47 One of the services: Abbr.
49 "Butterfield 8" author
50 Cousins of the cassowary
51 Head
53 Since
54 "Encore!"
55 Wasn't passive
57 Noshed
58 Access
60 Danish cheeses
62 Baseball's Martinez et al.
63 Good way to serve curry
64 30's leading lady Farrell
65 Something Alaska lacks

DOWN

1 Member of the order Isoptera
2 Glass houses?
3 Sons
4 Kind of jacket
5 Former student
6 Harass, in a way
7 Ponta Delgada is its capital
8 Unincluded
9 Fetors
10 Turner and others
11 Passbook abbr.
12 Like Oprah, perennially
13 Just as good
14 Noshed
21 Wing
24 Scoring records
26 Lake Michigan city
28 Proceeded easily
30 Novelist Puzo
32 Catch
34 Mr. Flanders of "The Simpsons"
36 Coffee-aisle item
38 Arctic sight
39 Hardly worth mentioning
40 Con artist's words
41 Wide, calf-length trousers
43 Attacks
44 "Kama-Sutra," e.g.
45 90's catch phrase
48 Prague's river
51 ___ ghost (hallucinates)
52 Flatten
55 Split
56 Truth alternative
59 Author-vet Kovic
61 Monopoly acquisitions: Abbr.

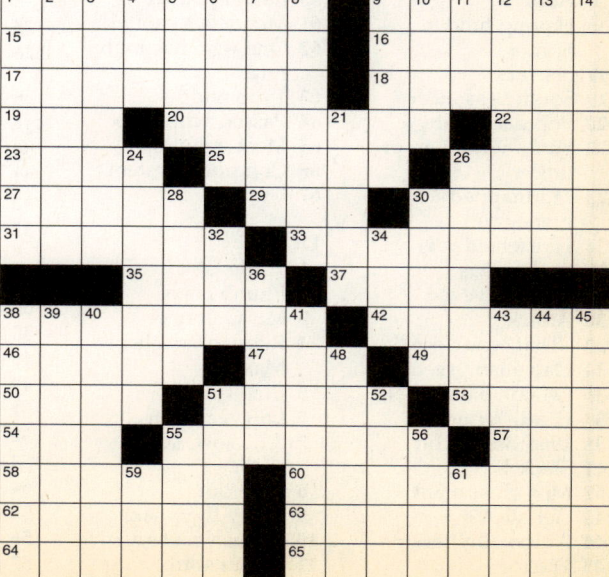

251   by Gerald R. Ferguson

ACROSS
1 Blended desserts
8 Nursery item
12 Trailblazed
14 "Crazy" singer
15 Murmur
16 Figure in a 1971 mystery
17 Lickety-split
18 Suffered
19 Guinness, e.g.
20 Opposite of runners
22 Hydras
26 Self-deprivation
27 Notions, to Nicole
28 Woolgather
32 Toll
33 Ballerina Jeanmaire
34 Destroy
36 Back from the shop
38 Mekong, for one
39 Bounce
40 Under wraps
41 Bookstore visitor
44 Song syllables
45 Jeweler's aid
46 Some bridge bids
52 Release
53 Arctic hunting grounds

54 Blissful locales
55 Some Cadillacs
56 Miffed
57 Suddenly hits

DOWN
1 Dry sherry of Spain
2 Land measures
3 Operating without ___
4 Conceivably
5 Parts of bloomers
6 Like a maple leaf
7 Posted
8 Seclusive
9 Repeater, maybe
10 Construe
11 Abacus parts
12 Kind of tent
13 Bred-in-the-bone
14 Second drink
21 Message taker, e.g.
22 Dandy
23 Theaters
24 Faithful, to a Scot
25 Good wood for floors
28 Corn sugar
29 Actress Sue ___ Langdon

30 1771 ballad," ___, Robin Gray"
31 Minim
33 Angry reaction
35 Pulitzer-winning writer Robertson
37 Red flares
38 Make out
40 Screen Jean
41 Willie Dixon genre
42 Sonata finale
43 Peripheral
44 ___ charmed life (be lucky)
47 South African grassland
48 First king of Phliasia, in myth
49 Venetian beach
50 Pianist Fleisher
51 Radiator sound

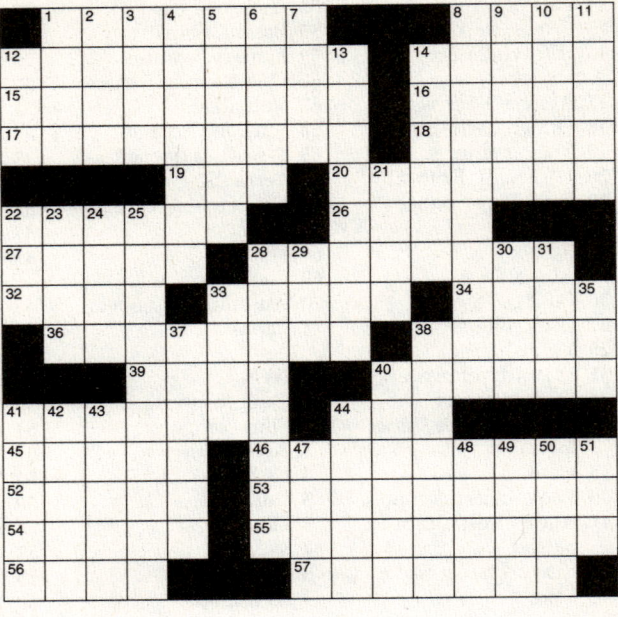

252   by Ben Wheelock

ACROSS
1 Smelter waste
5 Cry to Bo-Peep
8 Grammatical case
14 Game with mallets
15 Football positions: Abbr.
16 Having hidden humor
17 Sourness
19 South Seas attire
20 Popular lullaby
22 Suffix with item or union
23 "Kidnapped" monogram
24 Household sets
27 Backwoods affirmative
30 Attack
33 "That was close!"
34 Hawaiian greeting
36 Oil company of old
37 Hindu princess
38 1966 Beatles hit
41 Stack
42 Medicinal plant
43 Get all A's
44 Author Blyton
45 Fracases

47 They're either A.M. or P.M.
48 Bear's home
49 Russ. or Ukr., once
50 U.S. soldiers
52 Wrestling move
58 Italian painter
61 Mandela's capital
62 One who has more fun?
63 Type widths
64 Passed with ease
65 Most cunning
66 Computer system
67 Girl

DOWN
1 Trade jabs (with)
2 Plumb crazy
3 Mr. Guinness
4 Russian novelist Maxim
5 Corrupts
6 Lawyer: Abbr.
7 "___ sow, so shall . . ."
8 Rule out
9 Many Egyptians
10 English conservative
11 Italian suffix

12 Bordeaux or champagne
13 Hosp. instrument
18 Mideast market
21 BBQ dish
24 Old-fashioned roofing
25 Woodworker's facade
26 Fudge ice cream features
27 Talked noisily
28 Actress May
29 Ribbed fabric
31 Arctic hunters
32 Scarf
33 ___ fixe (menu notation)
35 Follow, as advice
39 Baby basket
40 Don't say yes
46 Female monster
49 Lots
51 Sandbank
52 Trig function
53 Rushed
54 "Yes ___?"
55 Killer whale
56 Fibs
57 Family members

58 Atlanta-based cable channel
59 Not well
60 Item in Santa's bag

253 by Norma Steinberg

ACROSS

1 Zilch
5 Stored, as papers
10 60's–70's hairdo
14 Secondhand
15 ___ fell swoop
16 Beat soundly
17 Film for which Daniel Day-Lewis won an Oscar
19 Ascended
20 Congresswoman Abzug
21 A single time
22 Like printers' fingers
23 Elevator alternative
25 Short
27 Trawler's equipment
29 Panache
32 Apex
35 Olympics ceremony music
39 Goal
40 ___ Guevara
41 "Off-limits"
42 Sleep phenomenon: Abbr.
43 Spicy
44 Append
45 ___ St. Vincent Millay

46 Actor Tom of "The Seven Year Itch"
48 New Yorker writer E.J. ___
50 Go on and on
54 Comstock Lode site
58 "Desire Under the ___"
60 Fox's shrill cry
62 Tree exudation
63 Stock exchange position
64 "Night Gallery" host
66 Follow
67 Ryan or Tatum
68 Keats's works
69 Rooney of "60 Minutes"
70 "Phooey!"
71 Saucy

DOWN

1 Desensitizes
2 To date
3 Perry's secretary
4 Sweet girl of song
5 Suit
6 Data
7 "On Golden Pond" birds

8 Tennyson's "___ Arden"
9 Impede, as an attack
10 Unanchored
11 Place for a lawn
12 J.F.K.'s Secretary of State
13 Follow orders
18 $1.50 for the first 1/5 mile, e.g.
24 Onset
26 "Woe ___!"
28 Tantrum
30 Mortgage
31 Poet Lazarus
32 Symptom for a dentist
33 Grub
34 Municipal employee in a Beatles song
36 New Deal proj.
37 Chop none too carefully
38 Patriot Allen
41 Tree in Miami
45 Wrap
47 "As the final point . . ."
49 German mister
51 Justice White
52 Sierra ___
53 Kind of statesman

55 All kidding ___
56 Informal eatery
57 High anxiety
58 "Cómo ___ usted?"
59 Like Jack Sprat's diet

61 11th grader's exam: Abbr.
65 Raised railways

254 by Randall J. Hartman

ACROSS

1 Second-string player
6 Sharp breath
10 Baby skin problem
14 Billy Joel's instrument
15 Simba's cry
16 Light beige
17 Teacher's duty (the basis for five anagrams in this puzzle)
19 Gorge
20 "The Catcher in the ___"
21 Appearance determinant
22 Parts of ecosystems
24 Five-time Wimbledon champ
25 Expensive coat
26 Fountain treat
29 Orderly lion's lair?
33 ___-garde
35 Functions
36 4:00 function
37 Actor Chaney
38 Placate
41 Blow it
42 So, in Latin

43 Sharp
44 Kind of boom
46 Beachgoer's goal?
50 Western Indians
51 Macaulay Culkin's home status
52 Electrical unit
54 Verdigris
56 Scintilla
57 16th-century date
60 Ceremony
61 Actor Beatty fasts?
64 First garden
65 Arboretum item
66 Fad
67 Wired
68 Bus rider's prize
69 Where to get down from?

DOWN

1 Practice boxing
2 Metro
3 Fare
4 Article in "Le Figaro"
5 Beatnik's drum
6 Football great Red
7 Top-flight
8 Pouch

9 Introduces
10 Denouement
11 Tepee with poles?
12 Madrid miss: Abbr.
13 Shades
18 "The 'Burbs" costar
23 Humiliates
24 60's slogan "___ the bomb"
25 Greek meeting place
26 Hot sauce
27 Egg-shaped
28 Sock hop notice?
30 007, e.g.
31 Weird
32 Undercover police
34 Hire
39 Some titles
40 Tennis's Sampras
45 Not safe
47 Grisham nailbiter, with "The"
48 Marsh bird
49 ___ chance
53 Kind of corporal
54 D.C. V.I.P.
55 Adjutant
56 Brainchild
57 Fermented drink
58 Almost knock out

59 Roman road
62 Byron's before
63 Chemistry prefix

255　by Fred Piscop

ACROSS

1 Opposite of guerra
4 Oscar contender
9 Noted diarist
14 "___ pig's eye!"
15 "Maria ___" (1941 hit)
16 Toiled in the galley
17 Nurse
18 Composer Ned
19 Tallow sources
20 "I was ___"
23 Turkey, e.g.
24 Rubber tree yields
27 Bed support
28 "Hedda Gabler" dramatist
31 Hobgoblin
32 Marvel comics hero
34 Toothsome
36 "I am ___"
39 It may have a well
41 Before, in Brest
42 Kind of nut
43 Rustic
45 Sexual desire
49 Centers of commerce
52 Off the mark
54 "I'll be ___"
57 Dallied (with)

59 Ore carriers
60 Relations
61 Castle of the ballroom
62 Media whiz Roger
63 Dos halved
64 Trunk
65 Actress Davis
66 Set, as an exchange rate

DOWN

1 Galileo and others
2 Kind of magnetism
3 "Viva ___!"
4 Word on mail from Mexico
5 Cutting up
6 Trillion: Prefix
7 Lulu
8 Not get to the point
9 Assume as fact
10 ___ Cologne
11 Come before
12 To this point
13 Radical 60's org.
21 Kind of nut
22 Was published
25 C.P.R. expert
26 Le Carré figure

29 Where to get shots
30 Weasel
33 "___ the ramparts..."
34 Site for Hamilton
35 Rearward
36 W-2 receiver
37 City map abbr.
38 Late additions to a jury
39 That ship
40 Pro ___
43 Negative, in Chinese philosophy
44 Poster material
46 Amass
47 Using CompuServe
48 Dictation taker
50 Auguries
51 Fun for cowboys
53 Baseball's Tony La ___
55 Native New Yorker
56 Locksmith Linus
57 Bit of retribution
58 Rio de ___

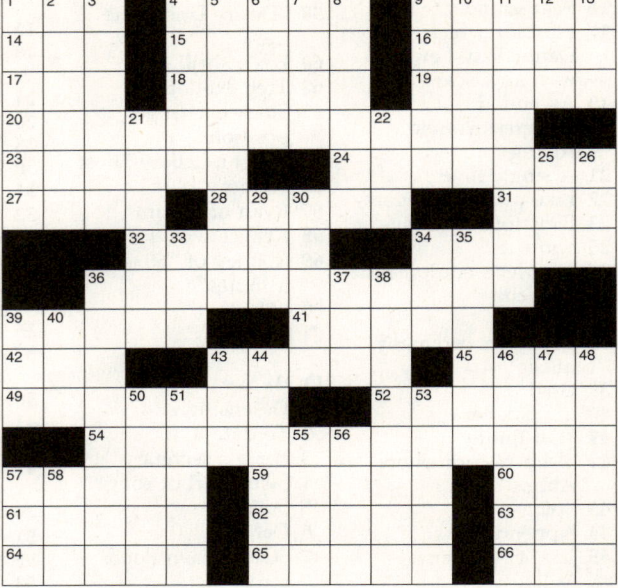

256　by Gerald R. Ferguson

ACROSS

1 Shoulder of a road
5 Magician's word
9 Succotash ingredients
14 Sneaking suspicion
15 Wheels of fortune?
16 ___ Gay
17 Dove rival
18 Forefather of the Edomites
19 Jane Smiley's "A Thousand ___"
20 Place for picky people?
23 Audio systems, for short
24 Blended ___
25 Noted Arctic explorer
28 London terminus
32 Nut favored in Chinese cooking
34 50's political inits.
35 Gaelic "Oh my!"
36 Friend of Charlie Brown
40 Ariz.-to-Kan. dir.
41 Suffix with resident
42 Algonquian chief
43 One in a million

46 Make a temporary stitch
47 Writer Silverstein
48 Monte Rosa, e.g.
49 Diet setback, maybe
57 A feather in one's cap
58 Delft, e.g.
59 "The Talmadge Girls" author
60 Goes up against
61 African despot
62 Find fault
63 Sworn body
64 Blathers
65 Up for grabs

DOWN

1 Two hearts and others
2 Touch up, in a way
3 Backside
4 Language blooper
5 Commoners
6 Department north of Paris
7 First name in Persian poetry
8 Hercule Poirot's home on Farraway Street

9 Go for
10 One way to pay
11 Cartoonist Walker
12 Novelist Waugh
13 Pane holder
21 "McQ" star
22 Bakers' supplies
25 First-anniversary gift
26 Turgenev lady
27 Swelling, in England
28 Loudly commends
29 Authors Henry and Philip
30 Mendelssohn's ___ in E flat major
31 Lamenter's question
33 Gibberish
37 Send (for)
38 Poet Neruda
39 Mexican cruise port
44 Scarves worn to the races
45 Exchange for "my kingdom"
48 Church cries
49 Bloke
50 King of the road
51 Burden

52 Janowitz who wrote "Slaves of New York"
53 QB Kramer
54 Bar stuff
55 Needing liniment
56 Armchair athlete's channel

ACROSS

1 City west of Guantánamo
9 Phenomenon of paramnesia
15 Fragrant, poisonous shrub
16 Passes over
17 Squarely
18 Pistil-packing
19 Kind of grass
20 Inferior
22 What a tabaquero makes
23 What's cooking
24 Subject of a Cézanne series
26 Jazz pianist Ahmad
29 United States's second-smallest state capital
31 Magic 8 Ball
33 Curtain fabric: Var.
37 Do like Dürer
38 Swahili and related tongues
40 "Shoot!"
41 Chicken dish
43 Pincered insect
45 Yellow-flowered herb

47 Not clean, as a garment
48 Escorts
51 Fine fiber
53 "___ Pretty" ("West Side Story" song)
54 Roger's co-star on "77 Sunset Strip"
56 Buddy
59 Title character in a Peter Hoeg bestseller
61 Go-getter
63 Talk radio need
64 Theoretical
65 Within the legal area of play
66 Milton topic

DOWN

1 Fair
2 Michigan town or its college
3 Pinlike
4 Tic-toe tie
5 Aid to John Hancock
6 Enhancement
7 Get prepared
8 Planetarium sights
9 Awesome, in teen slang
10 Former Buick model

11 Seattle-born '60s rock star
12 Saw
13 Of the soft palate
14 Gold diggers, in a way
21 1975 Pulitzer-winning critic
23 "The Prince" writer
25 Speak in court
26 Young kangaroo
27 Greek city known to the ancients as Ambracia
28 Hollywood mogul Sennett
30 Like some columns
32 Black
34 It breaks every day
35 Name part: Abbr.
36 Rich, as food
39 Hit the deck, so to speak
42 Sang merrily
44 Walk in the shade
46 Kilimanjaro is there
48 Kid's name
49 "The Rights ___"
50 Simon and others
52 Burton of "Star Trek"
55 Brouhaha

56 Maurice Chevalier's theme song
57 Diminutive Greek names
58 Gospel singer Winans
60 "___ we having fun yet?"
62 Combine

ACROSS

1 Catch
5 Long Island airfield
10 Bureau projection
14 Nightmarish boss
15 Rhône feeder
16 Actress Skye
17 Class-action suit?
20 Act gung-ho
21 Dahl and Francis
22 They may have brand identification
23 Globe part
24 Kind of call
27 Magnetism
32 "Roots," e.g.
36 Emulate Odysseus
38 Exxon Valdez, for one
39 Playsuit?
42 Company that produced the game Pong
43 Sans purpose
44 Caricaturist Thomas
45 Send back
47 Think of it!
49 Owl's hangout
51 Overcharges
56 Follow suit

60 Knight's superior
62 Trump suit?
64 Actress Baclanova of old films
65 Soft palate
66 Opponent
67 Norman of sitcom fame
68 Lift up
69 Singer Russell of 70's music

DOWN

1 Alumni ___
2 Instrument
3 Fit to be tied
4 Madre's milk
5 Wife of Osiris
6 Fit to be tried
7 Record
8 Pizarro's conquest
9 Bradley University site
10 Relative of a falcon
11 You name it
12 "The joke's ___!"
13 Some parties
18 Smart
19 Lillehammer event
23 Disney hit of '92

25 Treasure of the Sierra Madre
26 Loughlin of "Full House"
28 Club member since 1917
29 It's near the crazy bone
30 Bench's benchmates
31 Formerly, once
32 Traumatize
33 Adenauer moniker Der ___
34 "Where America's Day Begins"
35 "East of Eden" woman
37 Salsa specification
40 Storied sailor
41 Alway
46 It's a case
48 Israeli port
50 Party
52 Neighborhood
53 Fatuous
54 Basil-based sauce
55 Stout vessel
56 Elvis, for one
57 Source of a leak
58 Actress Swenson

59 Rimsky-Korsakov's Saltan, e.g.
60 Like some champagne
61 Zenith
63 Commercial suffix with Motor

259 by Jeff Herrington

ACROSS
1 Slugger's stats
5 Theme of this puzzle
10 Capital of Italia
14 Burn soother
15 Filibuster, in a way
16 Hawaiian music makers
17 Editor's definition of this puzzle's theme
20 Prevent legally
21 Popular beverage brand
22 Shea nine
25 More crafty
26 Allowable
30 Beckon
33 University of Maine site
34 ___-do-well
35 Dickens protagonist
38 Mapmaker's definition of this puzzle's theme
42 Compass heading
43 Pseudonymous short-story writer
44 Backing for an exhibit
45 Peaceful
47 Sentient
48 Insurance giant
51 Negative in Nuremberg
53 Competed in the Hambletonian
56 Ribeye, e.g.
60 Physician's definition of this puzzle's theme
64 Bank claim
65 Battery part
66 Second in command, once
67 Driver's license prerequisite
68 The ___ Prayer
69 Interested look

DOWN
1 Genre for Notorious B.I.G.
2 Depressed
3 Charged particles
4 Split-off group
5 Stylish auto
6 Man-mouse link
7 Back muscle, familiarly
8 Redding of 60's soul
9 "Open 24 hours" sign, maybe
10 Muss up
11 Animal with zebra-striped legs
12 Actress Oberon
13 Questioner
18 Indian drum
19 Political cartoonist Thomas
23 Kid's make-believe telephone
24 Elude the doorman
26 Canter
27 Ayatollah's land
28 Dunce cap, essentially
29 ___ pinch
31 Where St. Mark's Cathedral is
32 Investment vehicle, for short
35 Famous tower locale
36 Roman road
37 See 49-Down
39 Enzyme suffix
40 Shanty
41 Bird's cry
45 Purpose
46 "Phooey!"
48 Not perfectly upright
49 With 37-Down, famous W.W. II correspondent
50 Big handbags
52 Wight and Man
54 List shortener
55 Singer Martin, to friends
57 Therefore
58 In awe
59 Basketball's Malone
61 Neither's companion
62 Do basic arithmetic
63 Society column word

260 by Rand H. Burns

ACROSS
1 Babushkas
7 Juliet's cousin
13 MOMA artist
14 Sports car event
15 Wheeler dealer type
18 Finstersaarhorn, for one
19 Material used in making insulation
20 Kind of testing
21 Hoofbeat
23 Disaccustoms
24 Year in Etheired the Unready's reign
25 Sub
26 Battle song
27 Draw toward evening
28 Thing
30 Willful liars
32 Clean, with force
34 Like possums and squirrels
37 Chico's partner
41 Aquatic birds
42 Chief Justice in the 1920's
44 Zsa Zsa Gabor's real given name
45 Little pieces of France
46 Groove holding a gem in place
47 He played Ponch on "CHiPs"
48 Grassland
49 Expunged
51 Winner at Chancellorsville
52 Prey of 15-Across
55 Colanders
56 Stage direction
57 "Communist Manifesto" co-author
58 Part of Egypt's boundary

DOWN
1 Bulging
2 Mustang's shelter
3 Noted name in abstract sculpture
4 Letters from Greece
5 City on the Maumee River
6 Assassin
7 Ship timber peg
8 Fabrications
9 Slate-colored, in Scotland
10 Heavyweight poet
11 Explosive made of picric acid
12 More wee
15 Secrete
16 Daniel Boone for one
17 Soakers
22 Contaminates
24 Mediterranean language
27 Guitarist Phil
29 Gobs
31 No shrinking violet, she
33 Alone
34 Inclined
35 Unhand
36 Watergate, for starters
38 Film star's autobiography, 1990
39 Shorter version of 26-Across
40 Some sportswear
43 Chain
46 Cut obliquely
49 Went headlong
50 1856 Stowe novel
53 Brain wave readout, "for short"
54 Astronaut Grissom

261 by Arthur W. Palmer

ACROSS
1 Not piquant
5 Israelite at the conquest of Canaan
10 Fortune's partner
14 Rustic
15 More than fubsy
16 Part of an été
17 About 17 million square miles
18 Get even, in a way
19 Germany's Oscar
20 Start of an adage
23 Infamous Ugandan
24 "Third Man" director
25 Subservient
28 Mash
30 Computer code
34 Son of Hera
35 Type of window
37 Mason's aid
38 Cornishman
39 Web-footed animal
40 Use a whetstone
41 Four-time Japanese P.M.
42 Mugs
43 Tag words
44 Tithing
46 ABC, for short

47 Making a stand?
48 1905 Secretary of State
50 Shoshone
51 End of the adage
59 Word with fire or no
60 Paris official
61 Pop singer Burdon
62 Some charts
63 Essence
64 Late-night star
65 Fly ash
66 Some homes
67 Crackpot

DOWN
1 Prankster
2 Rummy
3 Anne Nichols stage hero
4 Exciting to the max
5 Welsh dog
6 Incite
7 Wife of Jacob
8 Steep slope
9 Actress Davis
10 Oslo and others
11 Taurus or Aries, e.g.
12 Paw

13 Western Electric founder ___ Barton
21 Preternatural
22 Binge
25 Wordless
26 Alpine feature
27 Item in a patch
28 Make powerful
29 Big-band name
31 X'd
32 Type of column
33 Words of explanation
35 "i" piece?
36 Oral stumbles
40 Wood hyacinth
42 Type of gun
45 Like best friends
47 Theta preceder
49 Isle ___
50 Patrons
51 Indiana Jones perils
52 Actor Scott
53 Stick in the fridge?
54 Tiny imperfections
55 "Darn it all!"
56 Nabisco product
57 El ___
58 Coll. course

262 by A.J. Santora

ACROSS
1 Does over
10 Dogie catcher
15 Clear
16 Molière's "L'___ des femmes"
17 Fame
18 Engraver's tool
19 Fr. holy woman
20 Legendary name in sitcoms
21 Replay technique
22 S.A.T. org.
23 Former aviation agcy.
26 Z ___ zebra
27 Grate
30 1942 Jimmy Dorsey hit
32 Load-bearing steel
34 "Another year ___ ..."
35 Hebrew letter after shin
36 Farm male
37 Ending for cash
39 Flying Cloud, in old automobiling
40 Give ___ rest
41 "How ___ doing?"

42 Café additive
44 Dispatch
46 She played Alice in "Alice"
48 Early weather satellite
49 Choreographer White of "The Music Man"
50 Dauphin
51 Two-piece part
53 Ayn and Sally
55 Steadfast
57 ___ Lingus (Irish carrier)
60 One of 27 works by Chopin
61 The privileged
63 '60 Wimbledon champ ___ Fraser
64 Welcomed to the fold
65 Canadian physician Sir William
66 Justice chief

DOWN
1 Fam. tree listings
2 Kind of poll
3 Iditarod terminus
4 Solitary
5 Grassland

6 Aggressive one, they say
7 Car owners need them
8 Kosher
9 Prepared
10 Johnny ___ (soldiers)
11 Eyepiece
12 Hollowness ratios
13 Does away with
14 Splitsville?
22 Clean air agcy.
24 Hurricane of 1992
25 1958 Pulitzer winner for fiction
27 Oscar, Tony, Grammy and Emmy winner
28 Loathes
29 Like recommended dental visits
30 Bullfighter
31 Magazine for which publisher Ralph Ginzburg went to jail
33 See-through silicate
38 Is off base
43 Four-time Super Bowl QB
45 Kind of brain

47 Fiddle ___ (nonsense)
51 Big Sky Country city
52 Send payment
54 Diviner
56 Botch

57 Chip in
58 Eve's place
59 Try again
61 Alphabet trio
62 Galley blade

263   by Mark Diehl

ACROSS

1 Jubilate or Miserere
6 "Paradise Lost," for one
10 Wee bit
13 Standard
14 Pane holder
15 Kind of pen
16 Cause of a good belly laugh?
18 Peter Gunn's girlfriend ___ Hart
19 Mona Lisa attribute
20 Optimism
22 Flowers for floats
24 Souvenir shop items
25 Sacrifices
29 Mideast capital
30 W.W. I battle site
31 Attacked vigorously
33 Multipurpose truck
36 "Ricochet" co-star
37 Flash
38 Lordly one
39 Start of a hole
40 70's singer Freda
41 De ___ (actual)
42 Appear
44 Annual Labor Day event
46 Combined, in a way
49 "Tuna-Fishing" artist
50 Idée fixe, for example
52 Mussolini's air marshal Balbo
55 Mount north of Catania
56 Hindquarters?
59 Cunning
60 Tale opener
61 Western airline
62 T, to Morse
63 Going-away party?
64 Iron Mike

DOWN

1 Zing
2 Termini: Abbr.
3 Like a beehive
4 Embrocation
5 News syndicate founder Samuel
6 Night school subject: Abbr.
7 Modest hand
8 Ain't right?
9 Knights' group
10 Where Howard Stern rides horses?
11 The elite
12 Wish the best for
15 Nigeria neighbor
17 Takes up
21 "If ___ a Hammer"
23 Hardly polite
25 Drop
26 Die feature
27 What there's no such thing as at NASA?
28 Put on a coat
32 Struck a low blow
34 Barker of filmdom
35 Dark, poetically
37 "Wheel" or "Pyramid"
38 In a pleased way
40 Famed traveler
41 Homburg
43 Chicago-based TV show
45 Of the flock
46 All-time P.G.A. tour leader
47 Exotic fish
48 Book subtitled "Her True Story"
51 Use a straw
53 Plain of Jars locale
54 Cuatro y cuatro
57 Society page word
58 Colo. neighbor

264   by Sidney L. Robbins

ACROSS

1 Hypothetical eccentricities in time
6 Competition
10 Jail unit
14 "___ man with seven wives"
15 Miss Cinders of old comics
16 Singer Guthrie
17 Brightly sunburned
19 Leaning
20 60's space chimp
21 Heroic legends
22 Teen woe
23 Beelzebub
24 Aware of
25 French painter Jean
29 Hesitation sounds
30 ___-di-dah
31 Sports sites
33 Mr. Whitney
35 Slippery one
38 Calms medically
40 Car gear
42 Mount St. Helens spew
43 "How dry ___"
44 Cylindrical
45 Self
47 Pass receiver
50 "M*A*S*H" character
51 Flake material
52 Boors
54 Cordial
55 They get smashed
56 Clumsy ships
60 One of five
61 Oscar winner for "Sayonara"
63 Lease
64 ___ Stanley Gardner
65 Boundary
66 Advantage
67 Philosopher A.J. ___
68 Versifiers

DOWN

1 Use Western Union
2 Prayer's closing
3 Effect a makeover
4 School orgs.
5 Airline to Stockholm
6 Cash back
7 Sour brew
8 Under-the-sink item
9 Sups
10 Poolside hut
11 Greenland settler
12 Grassy plain
13 Mislay
18 Botanist Gray
23 Depot
24 Hardy and North
25 Pedro's house
26 Silver holders
27 It misleads
28 Broadway's "Three Men ___ Horse"
32 Ocean
34 Permit
36 This, in Barcelona
37 Amorous gaze
39 Place of refinement
41 Baseball stat
46 Reproductive cell
48 Kind of soup
49 Not so clever
51 Exposed
53 Houston sch.
54 Had been
55 Length × width, for a rectangle
56 Prefix with sphere
57 Judicial cover?
58 Mend, as bones
59 Speedy planes
62 Spigot

265 by Jon Delfin

ACROSS

1 Hair lines
6 Neeson of "Darkman"
10 Toe woe
14 Influence
15 Chills and fever
16 Margarine
17 Renowned cabaret crooner
19 Wee
20 Addison's literary partner
21 Marsh bird
23 Geese formation
24 Onetime Mideast inits.
26 Vacillates
28 Staircase adjunct
33 Water ___ ("Wind in the Willows" character)
34 Sandler of "Saturday Night Live"
35 Designer von Furstenberg
37 Gay city
41 Harry Kemelman sleuth
44 Flock of geese
45 Singer Horne
46 Blackhearted
47 Murphy, for one
49 Portray as satanic
51 Electrical units
55 123-45-6789, e.g.: Abbr.
56 "L'état c'est ___": Louis XIV
57 A little night music
59 More spooky
64 Bide ___ (stay a bit): Scot.
66 Vegas impressionist
68 Epsilon follower
69 1994 film "___ Lies"
70 Magicians' props
71 Part of Q.E.D.
72 Actress Lamarr
73 "___ in the Dark"

DOWN

1 Cancer-causing compounds
2 "Thanks ___!"
3 After-shower wear
4 Toothpaste holder
5 Phonograph needle
6 ___-di-dah
7 Lab assistant
8 Astral glows
9 Field of achievement
10 Folding 47-Across
11 Baseballer Tony
12 Extend a subscription
13 Poet Alfred
18 Like passengers during takeoff
22 Bounds
25 Fit for a king
27 Male flower part
28 Captain's insignia
29 Aleutian island
30 Local theater, to Variety
31 Drink
32 Wandered
36 Dressed to the ___
38 Sitarist Shankar
39 The Queen: Abbr.
40 Model Macpherson
42 Not moving
43 Distressed one?
48 Lack
50 New York lake
51 Stun
52 Lawn equipment
53 Michelangelo work
54 Steeple
58 Mideast missile
60 A.A.A. offerings
61 Longing
62 Nevada town
63 There's none for the weary
65 Dine
67 "Yoo-hoo!"

266 by Wayne Robert Williams

ACROSS

1 Patagonian plains
7 Background setting for 7-Down
15 Jay's home
16 Burn soother
17 Abate
18 Least
19 Surgery spots: Abbr.
20 Buyer's bottom line
22 Animal doc
23 Friend to Fido, for short
25 Contented comments
26 Take lunch
27 Stead
28 Supermarket tabloid subject
29 Stripped
31 Oodles
32 Diarist Anaïs
33 In imitation of
34 Best Picture of 1954
40 White House nickname
41 Haw's partner
42 Rapier
43 Traveled like Hiawatha
46 Time remembered
47 Stimulus
48 Ireland's ___ Islands
49 Hosp. diagnostic
50 Kind of warning
51 Cold war flier
52 Angels' home
55 Our sun
56 Deli offering
58 End
60 Still in bed
61 Overjoys
62 Make wedding plans
63 Fast-lane malady

DOWN

1 City near San Francisco
2 Antipathy
3 Squandered
4 ___ de deux
5 Sphere
6 Since, in Scotland
7 1941 Lillian Hellman play
8 Lower-priced spreads
9 Agile deer
10 Fast time
11 Twice CCLIII
12 Destructive beetle
13 Lupin of mysteries
14 Told (on)
21 Cheap rum
24 Banquette item
26 Honey
28 Single
29 Italian cheese city
30 Sprite
35 Supplement, with "out"
36 Haunted
37 Facing
38 Psychological problems
39 Unconditional
43 College setting
44 Dukas opera "___ et Barbe-Bleue"
45 Annoys
49 "Glengarry Glen Ross" dramatist
50 Got a noseful
52 Needing rain
53 Discovery grp.
54 March time
57 Song syllable
59 Disfigure

267 ACROSS

1 Salon concern
5 Case for the consumer affairs bureau
9 One-two link for Welk
13 Motor
14 River to the Ligurian Sea
15 Show displeasure
16 Gradually passed
18 "Two Women" Oscar winner
19 Tie-up
20 Insolence
21 Mogadishu resident
22 Take an overly young bride
25 Drugstore cowboys, often
28 Shampoo ingredient
29 It follows St. or Mrs.
30 Lower the price of
35 Actor Morales
36 Fence stairs
38 Gallic girlfriend
39 Discard
41 Switch
42 Half of Mork's greeting
43 Get mad
44 Have some Halloween fun
49 Turns away
50 Berliner's article
51 Soft splashing sound
54 "I ___ my way"
55 Ingratiate oneself with
58 One of the seven principles of Kwanzaa
59 Concerning
60 Years and years
61 Little chap of the comics
62 Life stories, in short
63 Dwindle

DOWN

1 Trip for a 21-Across
2 General look
3 Particular
4 Brawl
5 Mahouts' masters
6 Stole
7 Literary olio
8 Like some 60's fashion
9 Bakery treat?
10 "WarGames" locale
11 Live
12 Sharpshooter Oakley
15 Dann of TV's "Law & Order"
17 Then, in Thiers
21 Go over big
22 Museum piece
23 Overact
24 Mideast carrier
25 Fuel price setter, for short
26 Knife mark
27 Pearl City party
31 Braves
32 Gen. Bradley
33 Astray
34 Straits
36 Skyrockets
37 Casserole staple
40 Complex
41 Minute
43 Vacation souvenirs
44 Reprobate in slang
45 Sheeplike
46 Obscure
47 Popular corn chip
48 Peter, in Puebla
51 Nancy Lopez's org.
52 Egyptian sun god
53 Put forward
55 Chest protector
56 Prefix with cameral
57 A.F.L.-C.I.O. constituent

268 ACROSS

1 Artists' headwear
7 "So?"
15 1994 World Cup finalist
16 Fort Shafter site
17 Indiana squad
18 Bad
19 Bar fruit
20 President pro ___
21 Not naturally colored
22 Dough
23 Cable staple
25 Stops broadcasting
27 Reduced to shreds
32 A new beginning
33 Actress Mimieux
34 Uxmal residents
39 A sib
41 Wow
42 1988 Michener epic
44 Moron's comment
46 Himalayan area
47 Bobsled team member
53 Eagles do it
55 Uncivilized one
56 Greenish-yellow pear
60 Big-selling card game
61 Famous landing site
62 Sen. John McCain, e.g.
64 Exemplar of cruelty
65 Like some differences
66 Opposite of "Attention!"
67 After-dinner order
68 General reply

DOWN

1 Rifle stands
2 And others
3 Stepping on it
4 Football team
5 Ones who are getting weary
6 Hairstylist Vidal
7 Vehicle in the news, 1995
8 Sharpens
9 Bad way to run
10 Cape ___ (Buzzards Bay locale)
11 "Put ___ on it!"
12 Shade of red
13 Model Macpherson
14 Wooed
24 Old Chevy model
26 Second of 12: Abbr.
28 Rock group from Athens, Georgia
29 Sorority letter
30 1989 Bruce Chatwin novel
31 It precedes cue
34 Parents
35 N.F.L. kicker ___ Haji-Sheikh
36 Chatter
37 Cross-examine
38 Tommy Moe transportation
40 "___ Town"
43 Comes (to)
45 Expresses one's view
48 Japanese for "empty hand"
49 Dodges
50 Shriver and others
51 Chang rival
52 Certain fisherman
54 Writer Nin
56 Pyramid part
57 Miner matters
58 Easy mark
59 Old-time dictator
63 Countdown penultimate

269 by Charles Gersch

ACROSS

1 Chou ___
6 Winner's prize, maybe
10 Winner's prize, maybe
13 Entertainer born 1/20/1896
16 Concert finale
17 Partner of 13-Across
18 Game-winning cry
19 Warwick's river
20 Raise
22 Estate division
24 First name in frontiersmen
26 Blast furnace input
27 1847 sea adventure
28 Smooth
29 Hewlett-Packard products
30 Where Forrest Gump served
31 Book before Amos
32 Family member, informally
35 1975 film co-starring 13-Across
38 Outdated
39 Fancy feather sources
40 Common caustic, chemically
41 Not hither
42 Ninnies
43 Start of a children's rhyme
44 Force in Bosnia
46 Extent of damage
47 "Yanks" star
48 Soviet premier Kosygin
50 Pinguid
52 Vaudeville singer's prop
53 1980 film starring 13-Across
58 Electromotive force pioneer
59 Word for 13-Across
60 First degrees
61 Receives
62 Canvases

DOWN

1 Kind of cream
2 Relative of King Saul
3 Mauna ___
4 Five-time Derby winner
5 "Uncle!"
6 ___-de-sac
7 Longtime "What's My Line" name
8 Bell sound
9 Olden slave
10 13-Across, for a famous example
11 Yoke
12 Ones in sashes
14 Help-wanted abbr.
15 Exchanges
21 Dict. content
22 Gian Carlo Menotti hero
23 13- and 17-Across, and others
25 Plant once considered a medical panacea
27 Latch ___
28 Poet's spring
29 Chief exec
31 Explorer Cabrillo
32 Zoo beasts
33 "___ and Only"
34 Grayish
36 Shimmied
37 Opposite of burst
42 Très chic
43 Pal of Pooh
44 Big wheel
45 Pacific greeting
46 Snicker
47 Say "I told you so!"
49 Assns.
51 Arab name part
54 Game finales, for short
55 Relations
56 "Ten thousand saw ___ a glance": Wordsworth
57 Election victors

270 by Sidney L. Robbins

ACROSS

1 Tale with a point
6 Dutch portraitist Frans
10 Slightly wet
14 Wing it, speechwise
15 Rock's Clapton or Carmen
16 Theater award
17 Diver's inspiration?
19 Facilitate
20 Extremities
21 "The Zoo Story" playwright
22 Escalator segment
23 "___ De-Lovely"
24 Restaurant patrons
26 Hijacker's destination, once
30 Mock
32 Hebrew "A"
33 Bride's route
34 Arab name part
37 1995 Whitney Houston movie
40 Zero
41 ___ bourguignon
42 Debate (with)
43 Bees' homes
44 Bounced back
45 Make calm
48 Squeal (on)
49 "You said it!"
50 Lads and dads, e.g.
53 Three-player card game
57 Gale
58 In suspense
60 Otherwise
61 "Yikes!"
62 Central artery
63 Like Easter eggs
64 Surveyor's measures
65 Quartet member

DOWN

1 Lose brightness
2 Yemeni port
3 Blackmailed
4 Revlon targets
5 Flow back
6 Dressy shoes
7 Yemeni, e.g.
8 Miller beer brand
9 Timetable
10 "___ scratch" (old cleanser slogan)
11 Lessen
12 Super-skinflint
13 Chicks' sounds
18 ___-tat-tat
23 Repress
25 Not precise
26 Actress Goldie
27 Jai ___
28 Bit of wedding garb
29 Prone
30 Shakespeare's "___ Andronicus"
31 From
33 "Let Us Now Praise Famous Men" writer
34 Othello's ensign
35 Like robins' eggs
36 Penury
38 Election time
39 Royal initials
43 Personally gave
44 Bridge seat
45 Was a cutup?
46 Etiquette arbiter Post
47 Thick
48 Is a bookhound
51 Jason's ship
52 Conduct
53 Blackthorn fruit
54 Composer Jerome
55 Concerning
56 Romanov V.I.P.
59 Derby, e.g.

271 by Gregory E. Paul

ACROSS
1 Part of D.J.
5 Florida's ___ Bay
10 Trucker with a radio
14 Worshiped one
15 Kitchen bulb
16 Guthrie the younger
17 State flower of Texas
19 Bakery offering
20 Having a notched edge
21 Elbowroom
23 Misfortunes
24 Dwarfs' group
25 Civic leader
28 Left in the lurch
31 Lend ___ (listen)
32 Wild plums
33 Comedian Philips
34 Coffee grinder
35 It may be rounded on a diamond
36 B.M.O.C.'s house, maybe
37 Hoopster Manute
38 Kind of note
39 Dwayne Hickman role, in 60's TV
40 Mountain demarcation
42 Actress Streep et al.
43 Durum, for one
44 Huff and puff
45 First name in fugues
47 Necessary nutrients
51 Fiery gem
52 Vietnam vet
54 Location
55 Jousting weapon
56 Command to Fido
57 Pianist Myra
58 Terminator
59 Dried up

DOWN
1 Rights
2 Run in neutral
3 Tart
4 Of the cloth
5 Flute sound
6 Queen ___ lace
7 Look after
8 Master of the macabre
9 Like an elk
10 Take a corner too fast
11 Famed Hollywood eatery, with "the"
12 Actress Raines
13 ___-poly
18 Farm machine
22 Stowe girl and others
24 Mall unit
25 Door parts
26 Charged atom
27 Buddhist sect
28 Cut through
29 Cyberspace messages
30 Loves excessively, with "on"
32 Old-fashioned contraction
35 Y.M.C.A. logo
36 Castle
38 Narrow valley
39 Star in Cygnus
41 Subjects of study at Woods Hole
42 Cut of one's jib
44 "Now for the ___ de résistance"
45 Kid
46 Andy Taylor's son
47 Fix
48 Jokester Johnson
49 Limerick man
50 Eye sore
53 Jogged

272 by Randall J. Hartman

ACROSS
1 Pequod skipper
5 Mizzen and jigger, e.g.
10 Engine disks
14 Lascivious look
15 Abbr. on a record label
16 Skin cream ingredient
17 Song a.k.a. "Somewhere, My Love"
19 Noon, in Nantes
20 Potbelly, e.g.
21 Society page word
22 Black, in poetry
23 1982 Meryl Streep film
27 Gangsta ___
29 Gymnast's goal
30 Word before rod or staff, in Psalms
31 Brother of Jacob
33 Gallery display
35 Prom couples
40 Popular mail order company
44 Look of contempt
45 Bit of paronomasia
46 Floor square
47 Patty Hearst's kidnap gp.
50 Foot in the forest
52 Nile viper
53 Saul Bellow's Pulitzer-winning novel
59 Out of port
60 Hubbub
61 Cowardly Lion portrayer and family
64 Thanksgiving dishes
65 "Anything that can go wrong will"
68 Freudian topics
69 "Green ___"
70 Singer Tennille
71 Lucy's partner
72 "Now you ___, now . . ."
73 Pique

DOWN
1 "___ Well That Ends Well"
2 Miami five
3 Lockheed Martin field
4 Acclaim for Pavarotti
5 Pin location
6 Volcanic fallout
7 Vista
8 Most docile
9 Cry at an awards ceremony
10 Minor role
11 Excuse
12 Oregon Indian
13 English Channel feeder
18 Be Kind to Editors and Writers Month: Abbr.
24 "___ me out"
25 Crucifix letters
26 Jekyll's counterpart
27 Races, as a motor
28 Z ___ zebra
32 Salt Lake City athlete
34 Spigot
36 Dramatize, with "out"
37 Iron man event
38 Wriggly fish
39 Escalator part
41 Approximately
42 Has dinner
43 Hidden catch
48 Alpaca cousins
49 Bring forward as evidence
51 Scheming
53 Did fieldwork?
54 Grammarian's concern
55 Office notes
56 Deep voices
57 Baseball manager Joe
58 Prison protests
62 Punjabi princess
63 Hot Lips Houlihan player
66 Canton-born architect
67 Former White House inits.

273 by Jeremy Thomas Paine

ACROSS
1 Yarn
7 "Jupiter" composer
13 Insect
15 Blotched, as the skin
16 Fancy
17 Wail
18 Ratlike rodent
19 California's ___ Range
21 Rock endings
23 "___ alike!"
24 A.B.A. member
25 It's said for openers
27 ___ gratia
28 Quarry
29 Kitchen worker
31 Cookware
32 Prone to excess
34 Chills
35 Medical tracer, at times
36 "Uncle Remus" epithet
37 Degree for one who's studied calculus
38 Botanist Gregor
42 Friendly question
43 Conjuring
45 Kind of pad
46 One receiving measured blows?
49 Prizes for MTV artists
50 New Jersey river
51 1975 Doctorow novel
53 Holiday beverages
54 Swindler
55 Appetite
56 Collectible cars

DOWN
1 Salad bar offering
2 Barely connected
3 Elevates
4 Employee
5 Prefix with -zoic
6 Chaney, Jr. and Sr.
7 Nyasaland, now
8 Eye: Prefix
9 Buthelezi, for one
10 One way to order
11 Flightless birds
12 Agreement
14 One of the '30s Gas House Gang
15 Grumbled
20 Message on a bottle?
22 "L.A. Law" actor
26 Compass dir.
28 Sovereigns
30 Bits
31 Philatelic purchases
32 Ocean hazards
33 Goaltending concern
34 When alphabetic writing became widespread
36 Was tuned up
37 Wreck
39 Patent subject
40 Cloisonné material
41 Ne'er-do-wells
43 Word with car or court
44 "At Random" autobiographer
47 Sub-subcompact
48 Bronchial sound
52 Dropout's goal, for short

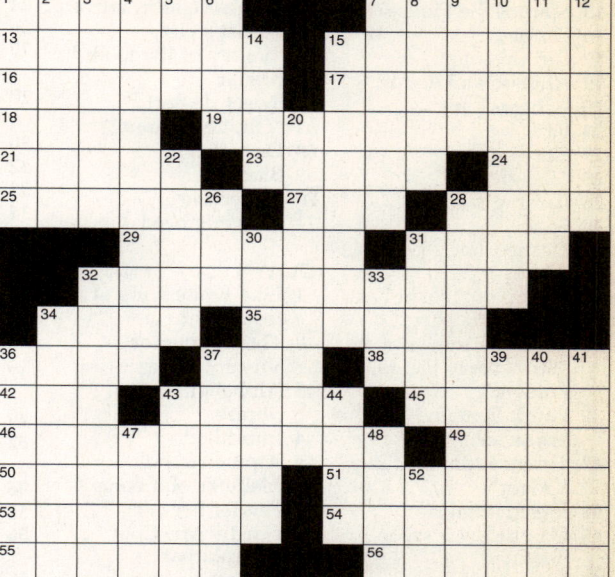

274 by Jim Page

ACROSS
1 Glower
6 Yuri's love
10 Crooked
13 "Hill Street Blues" star
14 Athletic supporter?
17 With lance in hand
18 W.W. II fighter planes
19 Indiana city or college
21 Sent into orbit
22 Pen name
25 Soak flax
26 Composer of "The Christmas Song"
29 Opener, of sorts
33 Farm females
34 ___ culpa
35 Constitutional
36 Seam
37 Holes over which timber is cut
39 1969 Super Bowl
40 Olympus support
42 Post-op destination
43 Barker of filmdom
44 Undertake
45 "Best of luck!"
47 Court matter
48 Petty criticism
49 It's used for trim
52 "The Wizard of Oz" prop
56 Direction at sea
59 Game, to Guglielmo
60 Paint additives
61 Gumbo dishes
62 Temple University athlete
63 Reduced-fare program?
64 Drill targets

DOWN
1 Pretended
2 "Bye!"
3 Old song "Abdul Abulbul ___"
4 Survivors
5 Corrida cynosure
6 Contents of some sleeves
7 Dada figure
8 Make muddy
9 Group once directed by Lee Strasberg
10 "As you ___"
11 Thatcher's need
12 Jr. et al.
15 Feigns
16 Singer of the "High Noon" theme
20 Glenn Close stage role
23 Diving duck
24 Porpoises
26 Host of note
27 Juice holders
28 "The Chronicles of Narnia" author
30 Bruit (about)
31 Power ___
32 It's a long story
37 Unnamed person
38 Object of devotion
41 Ran smoothly
43 Simian
46 Tap
49 Animal stomach
50 Catapult
51 "Dear mother Ida, harken ___ die" (Tennyson refrain)
53 Like some beliefs
54 It may look on a king
55 Bite
56 Vietnam's Le Duc ___
57 Past-due amount?
58 Presidential inits.

ACROSS

1 Cockeyed
6 Stirs in ingredients
10 Emily of "Our Town"
14 Trig. function
15 Man of the House?
16 Oil of ___
17 Gin inventor
19 After-school drink
20 "Cheers" star
21 Fib
23 Cravings
25 "___ giorno!"
26 Bathing facility
29 Spot
31 Flashed one's pearly whites
35 Unagi, at a sushi bar
36 Lymphatic part
38 "Penny Lane," not "Strawberry Fields Forever"
39 Frank Fontaine TV character
43 Thomas Mann's "___ Kröger"
44 Presidential run
45 One below a second lieut.
46 Pursues
48 Government worry
50 Aves.
51 Sir Peter ___, painter of British royalty
53 Kind of toad
55 Leftover
59 Emphatic affirmative
63 Violist's clef
64 "Valley of the Dolls" co-star
66 Sweet dessert
67 "Oh, very funny!"
68 Line of type
69 Blackens
70 Yesteryear
71 Brewer's need

DOWN

1 Like white wine at a restaurant
2 Theme song of Vincent Lopez
3 Alphabet book phrase
4 Info-filled
5 Alpine sounds
6 Member of a colony
7 Fender bender
8 Hardly Mr. Cool
9 Victrola part
10 Not masculine
11 Mideast carrier
12 Neighbor of Java
13 Data unit
18 Diamond segment
22 Arthur Miller character
24 Full-bodied ale
26 Split-off groups
27 Candidate of 1992 and '96
28 George's talk show co-host
30 Put on a border
32 Property securities
33 Order
34 Floor models
37 Once-popular feather source
40 Gobs and gobs
41 On the team?
42 Life, in the early days
47 Like many a winter road
49 Itty-bitty
52 Popular Internet company
54 Compact name
55 Emergency vehicle
56 Miss Cinders of old comics
57 Play the lead
58 1964 Tony winner for "Foxy"
60 "Two Mules for Sister ___"
61 Reply to "Can this be true?"
62 Taken away by force, old-style
65 Caviar

ACROSS

1 Puget Sound city
7 Escorts of a sort
14 Left out
15 Away doing research, e.g.
16 Went by car
17 Raises the hem
19 Sassy
20 "Not guilty by reason of insanity," e.g.
21 Sticky place?
22 Wraps up
23 T, for one
24 Odium
25 Willis's "___ Hard"
26 Make up (for)
27 Word after flip or tip
28 Warmhearted
30 Ward off
32 Lover who lived by the Hellespont
33 Swing music
35 Crawls, in a way
38 Alecto, Megaera and Tisiphone
40 Actress Dawber
41 Added muscle with "up"
42 Answers for Nanette?
45 Tennyson's "Geraint and ___"
47 Gators' kin
48 Madras dress
49 Voting nay
50 Sign of a saint
51 Aired again
52 Not setting the agenda
54 Kind of room or legend
55 Soft shell clam
56 Repay, in a way
57 Not in so many words?
58 F.T.C. subject

DOWN

1 Bedeviled
2 Reuners
3 Charleston college, with "The"
4 Aromas
5 Athletic event
6 Connect
7 A little gander?
8 Exist naturally
9 Show impolite satisfaction
10 "___ the ramparts . . ."
11 Door closer
12 Was gluttonous
13 Barbara Boxer, for one
18 Won all the races
20 Record player
23 Paint can direction
26 Welcomes
29 A little resistance?
30 Cupidinous
31 Churchill's sign
33 Snowbird
34 Wraths
35 Asparagus unit
36 Most sick-looking
37 Be a copycat
38 Tom's behavior?
39 Entangling
41 Go places
43 Holland's royal family
44 Literature Nobelist, 1978
46 Food cubing gizmo
47 Ding-dong
48 Split up
51 Use a cleaver
53 Words of gratitude
54 Flight from justice

277 by Joel Davajan

ACROSS
1 College digs
5 Haggadah-reading time
10 Coarse hominy
14 Piedmont city
15 Cuisine type
16 The Magi, e.g.
17 Railbird's passion
20 Certain wind
21 Check
22 Opposite of "yippee!"
23 Buyer caveat
24 Bottoms
27 Darlings
28 Railroad abbr.
31 Old toy company
32 Trim
33 It's not a dime a dozen
34 Bettor's bible
37 Grocery buy
38 Sword of sport
39 Archaic "prior"
40 Political abbr.
41 Cutting reminder
42 Didn't quite rain
43 Broadcasts
44 Baptism, e.g.
45 Corner piece?
48 Some legal documents
52 Across-the-board bet
54 Mont. neighbor
55 Mercantilism
56 Mrs. Chaplin
57 Curaçao ingredient
58 Downy duck
59 Snoopy

DOWN
1 Desert dessert
2 Agcy. founded in 1970
3 Hwys.
4 Results of some errors
5 Summer wear
6 Some House of Lords members
7 Word before free or calls
8 Ike's command, for short
9 Double-check the seat belts
10 Muddles
11 "Judith" composer
12 Cold-war fighters
13 Starting gate
18 Like some gates
19 A Kringle
23 Penthouse home?
24 Pheasant broods
25 Words to live by
26 Stoop
27 Race-track runner
28 Snob
29 Notre planète
30 1947 Horse of the Year
32 "___ Got a Brand New Bag"
33 Track hiatus time
35 Have fun
36 Like trotters, e.g.
41 Dust collector?
42 Actor Martin
43 Dismay
44 "The Cloister and the Hearth" author
45 Switch
46 Roofing item
47 Chip in
48 Interpret
49 "Git!"
50 Geologists' times
51 Waffle
53 Dernier ___

278 by Lois Sidway

ACROSS
1 Agcy. vigilant about vittles
4 Make or break, e.g.
8 Two-fisted
13 Abbr. for an old soldier
14 Energy choice
15 Playwright Fugard
16 Gifted
17 Didja ever see a ___?
19 "I don't think so"
20 Mine, to Marcel
21 Parenthetical comments
22 Staff
24 Many a hip-hop poet
26 Didja ever see a ___?
29 Imprint
33 Jai ___
34 Team in an annual all-star game
37 Color
38 Didja ever see a ___?
41 Didja ever see a ___?
43 Bowl over
44 Thick slice
46 Newsy bit
47 Plight
49 Didja ever see a ___?
53 Some like it hot
56 Poet Teasdale
57 They get squirreled away
60 Lenin's police org.
63 Go vroom, vroom
64 Didja ever see a ___?
66 Sundial number
67 Antipasto goody
68 Plow man
69 Presidential monogram
70 Devonshire dad
71 Hairdresser, sometimes
72 Grin's stopping point

DOWN
1 Garçon's pourboire
2 Split
3 Where touts tout
4 "Va-va-va-___!"
5 Barcelona bull
6 Project glowingly
7 Buddy
8 Bit of poolroom finesse
9 Garb
10 Nigerian border lake
11 Grind, in a way
12 Ford contemporary
14 ___ Na Na
18 Breach
23 Constitutional
25 Child's ammo
27 Wails from baby
28 Bass ___
30 Hitch
31 Word on a diploma
32 Drill sergeant's call
35 Black & Decker competitor
36 Famous marshal
38 Certain missile
39 Be in the red
40 Sunscreen ingredient
42 Super Bowl III champs
45 Hogwash
48 Tried hard
50 Simon of fiction
51 French fries brand
52 Cincinnati university
54 Tick off
55 Controversial food additive
57 On
58 Some kind of a nut
59 Last writes?: Abbr.
61 Rumble of contentment
62 French article
65 Tack on

279   by Manny Nosowsky

ACROSS

1 Challenge authority
5 Acronym since 1960
10 Off one's trolley
14 Napoleon, twice
15 Shake makers
17 Guys may be attached to them
18 Appendectomy, for one
19 Mimic
21 Covers with a blanket
22 Subject of a Thomas Gray ode
23 Panama, e.g.
25 Physicist's ___ jar
29 Hearing aid?
30 Divine ___
32 Compelled
33 Superficial pretenses
35 ___-Day vitamins
36 Words on romance by Virgil
40 Similar
41 Schoolwork
42 Hold, as one's attention
44 Musical "repeat" sign
45 Calendar mo.
48 More expensive
50 "Get the point?"
51 Marginal mark
52 Give it ___
54 Bad weather for a sailor
56 Dessert for the mistaken?
60 Loose
61 Kind of booth
62 Gods' blood
63 Moist
64 Watch over
65 Energetic

DOWN

1 Convene after a break
2 Combo bet at Belmont
3 King's neighbor
4 First name in rock
5 Majesty preceder
6 Bernardo's bear
7 Acts on the basis of 36-Across
8 Churchill successor
9 Sing door-to-door
10 Famous standard maker
11 Mr. Onassis
12 Referee's decision
13 Nine-digit ID: Abbr.
16 Shot the breeze
20 Zoo critters
24 Ten-percenters
26 Honorific of Spain
27 Stuntman Knievel
28 "Hud" Oscar winner
30 Kind of room
31 Walk wearily
33 With worthiness of respect
34 Nets
36 Kitchen staple, once
37 Steinbeck emigrant
38 Brando's "___ Zapata!"
39 Pierce Arrow competitor
43 Nikola the inventor
45 At ___ door
46 "thirty-something" character
47 Stick in the salad?
49 Mitchell hero
51 Not a whiz kid
53 Andy Griffith's TV son
55 "Jeopardy!" is one
56 Shrouded
57 Purpose
58 Trim
59 Finale

280   by Randolph Ross

ACROSS

1 COPPER CHARGES
8 MERCURY WATER SOURCES
15 Furniture piece
16 Glee
17 Competitor
18 "O, where is ___?": Shakespeare
19 Hemingway novel setting
20 Bygone auto
21 Quarantine
22 Ship officers
24 Of oneself: Lat.
25 GOLDEN GALE
28 POTASSIUM PORTIONS
33 TIN SOURCE
34 HYDROGEN GAS
35 Auction offering
36 Mauritanian, e.g.
37 Like Oscar Wilde
38 Flintstone pet
39 Zip
40 Imagine that!
41 CARBON COOKER
42 SILVER DEBRIS
45 NEON PORTAL
46 O.T. book
47 Recreational drives
49 Grants
53 Take measures
54 Boz boy
57 Lets, in tennis
58 Bug River locale
60 Current instrument
61 Some new-car drivers
62 HELIUM DRINKS
63 ALUMINUM FISHING GEAR

DOWN

1 Mediocre marks
2 The ___ Reader (alternative press magazine)
3 Pro ___
4 Cabinet dept.
5 Scented blossom
6 He went to camp in a 1987 movie
7 ___ Hall
8 Port opening
9 Back-of-the-book section
10 Rad
11 Latin list extender
12 Actress Kedrova
13 Senator from Mississippi
14 Backwater
22 Bedroom community, for short
23 Kerrigan and company
25 Yoga position
26 Take apart
27 Strive mightily, with "out"
29 U.S. poet laureate ___ Dove
30 Former Twin batting champ
31 Largish singing group
32 Attack in a way
34 Bury
37 Recalled
38 Follows hostilely
41 Indispensable
43 ___ one's head
44 Slightly tapered
45 Monticello site
48 Comic Poundstone
49 Esau's wife
50 Approach
51 Search
52 Lith. and Lat., once
54 Deck
55 Memo words
56 Dining hall
59 Tempe sch.

281   by Wayne Robert Williams

ACROSS

1 Assists
6 Group that votes alike
10 Tennis score
14 "So long, Simone"
15 Verdi opera
16 Local theater
17 Systematic, as instructions
19 Looks at
20 Faux ___
21 Stymie
23 Wampum
27 6/6/44
29 Old-fashioned curse word
30 Baseball's Espinoza
31 Writer Murdoch
32 Tiny bit
33 Tiniest sound
34 Blacktop basketball contest
37 Painful points
39 "Am ___ blame?"
40 1983 film "El ___"
43 Everything being taken into account
46 DCCLII doubled
47 60 secs.
49 Hebrew dry measure
50 Conceive
52 Unaffiliated politically: Abbr.
53 Nimble
54 Bryce ___ National Park
55 One of the Fates
57 Suffix with beat or peace
58 Move about
59 How a pendulum swings
66 Hot chamber
67 Lamb's pen name
68 Bathroom hanger
69 Hardly Mr. Cool
70 Bambi, e.g.
71 Ring-shaped island

DOWN

1 Is down with
2 N.Y.C. summer hrs.
3 Prevaricate
4 Energy
5 Poor, as a performance
6 Contralto's counterpart
7 On, as a lamp
8 Lyric poem
9 Abraham Lincoln, in a Whitman poem
10 Once more
11 Continually
12 Spain's peninsula
13 Fitted one within another
18 Rube
22 Green tea
23 Rand McNally products
24 Margarine
25 Repeatedly
26 Place for a pin
27 Food-related
28 Oversalivate
35 San Francisco player, for short
36 Roman name
38 Walk through puddles
41 Former Yugoslav chief
42 Tied
44 Laid on, as taxes
45 Permitted by law
47 One-millionth of a meter
48 Smitten
51 Sioux Indian
56 Look after
57 Close
60 ___-de-France
61 Conk out
62 Drunkard
63 ___ Jima
64 Second smallest state: Abbr.
65 Right angle

282   by Ernie Furtado

ACROSS

1 Person with a beat
4 Mafia kingpin
8 Keeps one's fingers crossed
13 Voiced
15 Prime draft status
16 Maine college town
17 Deal with quickly
20 Isolate, in a way
21 I.O.U.
22 Phila. clock setting
23 N.F.L. linemen: Abbr.
24 Prince Valiant's firstborn
26 ___ Moines
28 Save steps
35 Point one's finger at
37 Panorama
38 Too
39 Prefix with type
40 Actress Thompson et al.
41 Traveling type
42 Mideast chief
43 "Gypsys, Tramps & Thieves" singer
44 Politico Jackson
45 Is easily riled
48 China's Chou En-___
49 Yang's partner
50 Ancient text "___ Te Ching"
53 They give you a shot in the arm
56 Pre-1917 honcho
59 Guitar feature
61 Be cheated
64 Speechify
65 "Pretty Woman" star
66 "Alas"
67 Morocco's capital
68 Medical suffix
69 Elephant's weight, maybe

DOWN

1 Promising rookie
2 Long-armed ape, informally
3 Islamabad denizens
4 Hold fast
5 Enero to diciembre
6 Fringe benefit, for short: Var.
7 ___ of office
8 Owl
9 Hockey's Bobby
10 Jab
11 Country Slaughter
12 Squeezable
14 "___ Misérables"
18 Allay, as thirst
19 Word before peak or walk
25 Indian rug
27 Wells Fargo vehicles
29 Unconcerned with right and wrong
30 East ___ (Manhattan resident)
31 Substantial, as a meal
32 Seal
33 Exploits
34 Ripped
35 Insipid
36 Peru's capital
40 Unstable person, slangily
44 Coup d'état group
46 Perfumed bag
47 Angles
51 Prefix with meter
52 Versifier Nash
53 Mr. Sikorsky
54 Actress Miles
55 Knife
57 Golden Fleece ship
58 Atlas lines: Abbr.
60 Genetic stuff
62 Amtrak term.
63 Dernier ___

283 by Trip Payne

ACROSS

1 "___ Breaky Heart"
5 Mavens
10 Apple of discord contender
14 Oxford, for one
15 Dickens's Heep
16 "___ calling"
17 Early TV western
20 State a new way
21 Near-homer
22 Hankers after
23 "Doggone it!"
25 Cessation
27 "Xanadu" band
28 Rose protector
29 Memory unit
30 Goes to sea
33 Former Attorney General Edwin
34 Flees after release
37 Substantive
40 Arm of the sea?
44 Queen and workers
45 In the future
47 ___ Tin Tin
48 Giant Mel
49 Tennis Hall-of-Famer Chris
50 "___, the final frontier . . ."
52 Doctored
54 Newsman Arledge
55 Beginning
59 African snakes
60 Extremely cold
61 Luxuriant
62 ___ noire
63 Idyllic spots
64 Captain Hook's right hand, so to speak

DOWN

1 Cigarette tip
2 Bach work
3 Wish otherwise
4 Matzoh's lack
5 Underwater hazard marker
6 Vase
7 ___ Newtons
8 Ingredient
9 Former Israeli defense minister
10 Fastening device
11 Hex sign
12 Mice, squirrels, etc.
13 At least one
18 ___ Vegas
19 Take a load off
22 Director Craven
23 Armada member
24 Gunfighter's wear
26 Scottish river
28 Mai ___
29 Mr. Lugosi
31 Jet-set jets
32 Word with light or write
33 Cal Tech rival
35 Pooped
36 Charades "little word"
37 Long March participant
38 Bubble over
39 Endeavor
41 A real head case?
42 Permit
43 Pilot's heading
45 Exact satisfaction for
46 Was noncommittal
49 Crimson rival
50 Soak (up)
51 Betting systems
53 Cathedral part
54 Country mail systems, for short
55 Poke
56 Flamenco cry
57 Five-spot
58 Charades "little word"

284 by Christopher Hurt

ACROSS

1 The year 1006
4 Hardware items
10 Kenya's Daniel ___ Moi
14 Crib
15 Bird with a fanlike crest
16 Israeli P.M. Golda
17 Cartoon dog sound
18 Measure of current
19 Unit of real estate
20 1939 Robert Donat film
23 Cores
24 Vote for
25 Elec. day
26 Chimney channel
27 Carp
30 Imagined
32 Guitarist Paul
33 "The Most Happy ___"
35 Brown seaweeds
36 1984 Diane Keaton film
38 Flaubert story
41 Egg producer
42 Acid
45 Cops' cry at the door
47 Before
48 In ___ parentis
49 Kitten's sound
50 Siesta
52 50's White House name
54 1990 Newman-Woodward film
58 Emilia's husband
59 1904 Physiology Nobelist
60 Bother
62 Stair part
63 Comfortable
64 Kind of dye
65 Roll-call response
66 Smell and taste, e.g.
67 Soak up

DOWN

1 Wharton degree
2 Slash
3 Clearly viewable
4 Window cover
5 Harvesting machines
6 Viscous
7 Dueling blade
8 Like bad apples
9 Be furious
10 Nanking nanny
11 Solo musicale
12 Service station feature
13 Gets the VCR ready
21 Bullfight hurrah
22 Starter of a sort
23 Super Bowl org.
28 Too
29 Mitt
31 Electric ___
33 German philologist Wilhelm
34 "It's ___ cry . . ."
36 K2, e.g.: Abbr.
37 Country music giant of the 40's and 50's
38 Michael Chiklis TV series, with "The"
39 Be at the controls
40 Holist, perhaps
42 Open galleries
43 Playful musical passage
44 Period
46 Gauchos roam these
48 Slangy hat
51 Babble
53 Henry VIII sextet
55 Informal refusal
56 Bergman collaborator Nykvist
57 "Gil ___"
61 Film policeman

285 by Alex K. Justin

ACROSS

1 Not a dupl.
5 Part of Indochina
9 D or F, but rarely E
14 Photog's purchase
15 Narrow margin
16 Valuable timepiece
17 Display anger
20 Herolike
21 Noted acting family
22 Occupational suffix
23 Merrie ___ England
24 Eating places
26 Some footballers
27 At this point, in France
30 An astronaut gets into it
31 Temporal prefix
32 Beginning at
33 Display wrath
36 Thematic poetry
37 Water-skier's aid
38 Get lost
39 At the same time
40 Frightener
41 Hypochondriac's complaints
42 "Auld Lang ___"
43 Cinematographer's tool, for short
44 Seafood order
47 Disaffect
52 Display rage
54 Pandora's release
55 Don River's outlet
56 Cross initials
57 Theater capacity
58 Boxer's garb
59 Not restricted by sex

DOWN

1 "Carmina Burana" composer
2 Speaking ___
3 Russian writer Ehrenburg
4 Makes much of
5 Some cons
6 Army members
7 Big name in newspaper publishing
8 Cyndi Lauper's "___ Bop"
9 Steinways
10 Singer Blakley
11 "M*A*S*H" actor
12 Farmer's place, in rhyme
13 Divorcées
18 Argosies
19 "Picnic" star
23 In the lead
24 Dessert item
25 Monastery superior
26 Kind of fire
27 Grenoble's department
28 Fizzy drinks
29 Doubtful
30 Passé word in marriage vows
31 Words of wisdom
32 Short-breathed
34 Like many O. Henry stories
35 Walled side of a ditch
40 Kind of surgery
41 On duty
42 Refine
44 The Beatles' "___ Leaving Home"
45 It may be batty
46 Athletic shoe company
47 Auto designer Ferrari
48 Tuft-hunter
49 Boy abroad
50 Blood and guts
51 "Idylls of the King" lady
53 Dinghy thingie

286 by Alfio Micci

ACROSS

1 Woodman's memento
6 Once, once
10 Incognizant
14 Auto repair cost
15 Bull tosser?
16 Play the wolf
17 Place for garçons, e.g.
18 Actress Sommer
19 Arctic
20 Question from 34-Across
23 Sponge
24 Ones welcomed to the fold?
25 Drudges
28 Let ___ (reveal)
29 Place for a stone
31 "___ flowing with milk and honey"
34 See 20-Across
36 Egg holder
37 Insults
38 Mr. T's last name
39 See 50-Across
41 Pains, as the heart
42 Oddball
43 E-4 to E-9 rankings
45 Minneapolis suburb
46 Conceal profits illegally
47 Hikes
50 Answer from 39-Across
53 Part of a frat party chant
56 Suffix with flex
57 1960 Wimbledon champ ___ Fraser
58 Settled
59 You name it
60 Made do
61 Means of inheritance
62 Adventurous tale
63 French preposition

DOWN

1 A great many
2 Prefix with meter
3 Wolf pack member of WW II
4 Shed
5 Act
6 Comment from Holmes
7 Peeves
8 "Tobermory" writer
9 Intrude
10 Third degrees
11 It may be massaged
12 Dryden's "___ for Love"
13 Certain investigator
21 1940s Pacific battle site, informally
22 Fashion suffix
26 Best Actor of 1958
27 "Pretty stupid, huh?" speaker
28 Cow
29 Levee
30 Large, to Lafarge
31 Author Seton
32 Sierra ___
33 "___ is my witness..."
35 Eight-time Norris Trophy winner
37 Ignoring, as an order
40 Bilbao bath
41 Wine and dine
44 Paris business abbr.
46 Philippine natives
47 None too bright
48 Ferryman
49 Ingrid Bergman, e.g.
51 Orchestra part
52 Ultrabright
53 Name, slangily
54 Cousin of "Rah!"
55 Certain game ending

 **287** by Stephanie Spadaccini

ACROSS

1 Practice with Rocky
5 Fresh kid
9 Hop-jump intervener
13 Grow dim
14 Architect Saarinen
15 Salon job
16 Very thin noodles
19 80's–90's White House dog
20 Quickly pans (in)
21 Slippery stuff
22 Mornings, for short
24 Bread, for stew
25 Engine additive: Abbr.
28 Main battle line, with "the"
30 Playboy founder
32 Deface
35 Loathsome one
37 Go on and on
38 Marinated salad items
41 Mario's "handsome"
42 One-named soccer star
43 "Untouchable" Eliot
44 "No kidding!"
46 Celery unit
48 TV spots
49 ___ Alamos, N.M.
51 Gardner of film
52 Critic ___ Louise Huxtable
55 Perfect Sleeper maker
57 Mingo player on "Daniel Boone"
59 Afternoon tea accompaniment
62 Medicinal plant
63 "___ be a cold day in . . ."
64 ___ homo (biblical phrase)
65 Tidings
66 Feel sorry for
67 "___ I say . . ."

DOWN

1 Guru
2 Sudden terror
3 Corner shape
4 Film spool
5 Huge creature
6 "The Crying Game" star Stephen
7 N.M. neighbor
8 Bullring bulls
9 Headlong rush
10 Smooch
11 Bank acct. addition
12 School org.
17 Tale teller
18 Milne character
23 Nose (around)
25 Zzzz
26 Camp shelters
27 What the Gazette goes to
28 Extra
29 Grabs
31 Ol' Blue Eyes
32 Israeli native
33 Belief system
34 Mythical strongman
36 River's end
39 Bryn Mawr and others
40 Celestial
45 The olden days
47 Alan or Cheryl
50 Get undressed
52 Friend, in Florence
53 Bing Crosby's record label
54 Hearth residue
55 Problem solved by cable
56 Italian wine region
58 Impressed
59 Summer breeze source
60 Paris's ___ de la Cité
61 Supermodel Carol

 **288** by Pauline V. Wilson

ACROSS

1 Blue-ribbon position
6 Tiny aquatic plant
10 Radar screen dot
14 Thespian
15 "Crazy" bird
16 Moreno of "West Side Story"
17 School essay
18 Pepper's partner
19 "Oh, woe!"
20 Start of a comment by critic George Jean Nathan
23 Like hen's teeth
26 "I surrender!"
27 Part 2 of the comment
32 Washington Mayor Marion
33 Sharpens
34 Puppy's bite
37 Opera singer Pinza
38 Virile
39 Zola courtesan
40 Kind of whisky
41 Ill-fated ship Andrea ___
42 Olympian's prize
43 Part 3 of the comment
45 Atlantic fish
48 Fish-eating hawk
49 End of the comment
54 Helps
55 Natural balm
56 Prefix with -pedic
60 Prefix with logical
61 Not the front or back
62 Arctic, for one
63 Sign gas
64 "___ Dreams" (1994 documentary film)
65 Nairobi's land

DOWN

1 More than hefty
2 "___ bin ein Berliner"
3 Expy., e.g.
4 Hat for a siesta
5 Excessively sweet
6 As well
7 Goof off
8 Game on a green
9 Not pro
10 Intellectually gifted
11 State flower of New Hampshire
12 "Darn ___!"
13 Old hat
21 Joey ___ & the Starliters (60's group)
22 Chicago team
23 Cavalry sword
24 Nutso
25 Eagle's nest
28 Swiss ___ (vegetable)
29 Gin's partner
30 China's Zhou ___
31 Actress Susan
34 Ralph who wrote "Unsafe at Any Speed"
35 Silly
36 Very friendly
38 Dairy farm sound
39 Chief Joseph's tribe
41 Dumbbell
42 Identified wrongly
43 Special boy
44 Overly
45 Beau
46 Rebuke
47 Bucking bronco event
50 "Candy / Is dandy . . ." humorist
51 Mishmash
52 Kind of list
53 Mondale or Quayle, e.g.
57 Countdown start
58 Cow chow
59 Go ___ diet

289 by Fred Piscop

ACROSS

1 Genoan musical debutant, 1793
9 Parts of estates
15 Kind of exercise
16 Theater floodlight
17 Pool necessity
18 Samuel Richardson novel
19 Band-___
20 Designer's workplace
22 Kind of gas: Abbr.
23 Samuel Adams, e.g.
25 Soul singer Lattisaw
26 Spot for a mountain goat
27 Words from a Shakespearean question
29 Undivided
30 Idaho river
31 Red Sox great, for short
33 Ad slogan words before "you're a part of me"
35 Quite dry
39 Woodworking tools
40 Like "The Forsyte Saga," e.g.
42 Spleen
43 They're a formality
44 Kind of reflex
46 Throat medicine
50 ___-ear (tropical abalone)
51 ___-arms
53 Brochette
54 Skater Midori
55 Certain hospital patient
57 Sri Lankan export
58 ___ Alley
60 Aids in gnawing
62 Some seamstresses
63 Share a policy
64 Get snug
65 Rapprochements

DOWN

1 Skier Street
2 More pale
3 Propitious
4 From ___ Z
5 "A Doll's House" heroine
6 Some tree carvings: Abbr.
7 51 minutes past the hour
8 Onetime Danish province
9 Listless
10 Wing-shaped
11 Math game
12 Somewhat spoiled
13 Key stimulus, in animal behavior
14 Astonishes
21 Bakery gizmos
24 Shaped custards
26 Fuzz
28 Pacific tubers
30 Imperial, e.g.
32 Veer off in a new direction
34 Fluidity symbol, in mechanics
35 Add financial difficulties to
36 Caribbean leader elected in 1990
37 Billboard listings
38 Neighbor of Chad
41 First name in TV comedy
45 Get closer to
47 Decide to quit
48 Composer Boulez
49 Equilibria
51 Cleric's home
52 Unspoken
55 31-Across's first name
56 Theater
59 Darling
61 Nine-digit ID

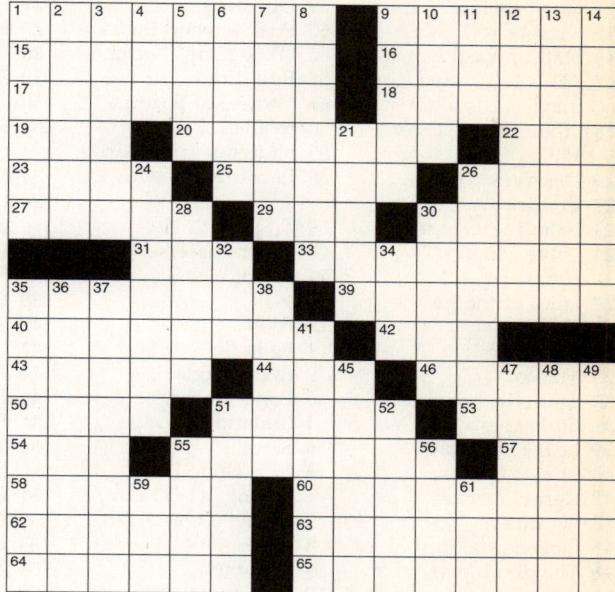

290 by Fred Piscop

ACROSS

1 Desert plants
6 Swap
11 Stomach muscles, for short
14 Extraterrestrial
15 King or queen
16 Do some soft-shoe
17 Big name in video rentals
19 Kimono accessory
20 Musical partner of Crosby and Stills
21 Madison Avenue worker
23 Big monkeys
27 French artist Henri
29 Adjusts to fit
30 Extreme cruelty
31 Religious factions
32 Top floor
33 Rainbow shape
36 Lodge members
37 Air raid alert
38 Words of comprehension
39 Tiny bit, as of cream
40 Asia's ___ Peninsula
41 Bus station posting: Abbr.
42 Mickey of "National Velvet"
44 Word said to a photographer
45 Split with a hatchet
47 Scorched
48 Contract with a car dealer
49 Limerick, e.g.
50 Bic filler
51 Yegg
58 "We're number ___!"
59 Eskimo boat
60 Lariat's end
61 Neighbor of Isr.
62 Little finger
63 Soaked

DOWN

1 Quick way around town
2 The whole shooting match
3 A.F.L.'s partner
4 Gumshoe
5 Tied up
6 Supporting beam
7 "High priority!"
8 Supermodel Carol
9 Ruby or Sandra
10 Unpredictable
11 Cyclotron
12 Rum cakes
13 Vertebra locale
18 Prohibits
22 Malign, in slang
23 Established
24 Writer ___ Rogers St. Johns
25 Exhausting task
26 Chooses
27 Chum, to a Brit
28 Tennis score
30 Homeless animal
32 Felt crummy
34 Pee Wee of Ebbets Field
35 Yielded
37 Having one's marbles
38 Cake finisher
40 Advances
41 Tribal healers
43 Western treaty grp.
44 Sonny's ex
45 Advertising awards
46 Comedian Bruce
47 Overly self-confident
49 Mountain
52 "___ Blue?" (1929 #1 hit)
53 Five smackeroos
54 Dove sound
55 Keystone character
56 Sixth sense, for short
57 Juan Carlos, e.g.

291 · by Rich Norris

ACROSS

1 They're not to be believed
6 Malice
11 Foot with a claw
14 Good-looker
15 Kind of roll
16 Stat for Yastrzemski
17 "This is ___ two can play!"
18 "Blue Eyes" singer, 1982
20 Deserves
22 Comics cry
23 Balm ingredient
24 "Blue Moon" composer
27 Janet of the Justice Department
28 Be a pain
29 Madcap
32 Scarlett's home
35 Biblical gift
39 Leave slack-jawed
40 Story of Jesus
42 Kernel carrier
43 Set down
45 Queens stadium
46 The good guys, in a chase film
47 VCR button
49 Shooter filler
51 "The Blue Knight" author
58 60's TV boy
59 Operated
60 Push beyond limits
62 "Blue Chips" actor
65 Bull: Prefix
66 "Wheel of Fortune" request
67 Shoreline irregularity
68 Encouraged, with "on"
69 Trap, with "in"
70 Oater chasers
71 Scouts' work

DOWN

1 Swindle
2 Even bigger
3 Pong maker
4 Imitation
5 Stew
6 "___ Done Him Wrong" (1933 film)
7 Propelled, as a raft
8 Bury
9 Assumed
10 Directional suffix
11 Manual laborer
12 Hate
13 Pouilly-Fuisse and others
19 Notched
21 Seasonal visitor
25 Bellows
26 Edith Evans, for one
29 Erase, as a PC file
30 Leatherworker's tool
31 King Features competitor
33 Stadium sound
34 Crosswind direction, at sea
36 Classic car
37 Salt-N-Pepa's music
38 Divs. of days
40 Tiniest complaint
41 Gentle ones
44 Alabama native
46 Pluck
48 Prefix with logical
50 Thickly entangled, as hair
51 Old Testament book
52 Imagine
53 Attack dog command
54 Maze parts
55 Pot amounts
56 Meter reader's reading
57 Took on
61 Appears to agree
63 Bite
64 Sorbonne summer

292 · by Manny Nosowsky

ACROSS

1 Centennial year of old
4 Part of a Hawthorne signature
8 Food critic Greene
12 Rachel's older sister
13 Together in music
14 Kind of belt
15 Phrase after "This is my final offer"
18 Inspired (very much so!)
19 ___ prof.
20 Remote
21 Bob Hoskins in "Hook"
22 Speed
25 Columbus sch.
27 Pearl Harbor ship of 1941
30 Does wrong
32 Treat too well
36 Begins campaigning
39 Eliminate
40 Ferris wheel cry
41 Coxae
42 Limit
44 Tidal bore
46 "Hard Road to Glory" writer
49 Like sashimi
51 Brute
54 Have a hobby
59 Be slightly nuts
60 New Mexico county
61 Bone: Prefix
62 Bowl over
63 Cheerful
64 Peel (off)
65 Lao

DOWN

1 Half of a comedy team
2 Solidifies
3 Overacts
4 A football conf.
5 "I now bid you a welcome ___": Artemus Ward
6 Relapse, with "a"
7 Andrew Wyeth's "The ___ Pictures"
8 Passes on
9 Crosswise to a ship
10 Establishment
11 Underworld river
12 Corp. name suffix
14 Lieutenant's insignia
16 "I can't believe ___ . . ."
17 Rain in Spain collector
23 Intersected
24 Ship in poetry
26 Object of 60's protest: Abbr.
27 Multipurpose truck
28 Bluejacket
29 Indication of another name
31 Actor John of "Missing"
33 Caen confirmation
34 Puck
35 They're groovy
37 Where the buoys are
38 Med. record
43 They get paid
45 Mideast weight
46 More than disdain
47 Former alliance
48 Allergic reaction
50 Tie
52 Is revolting
53 Come after
55 Principal principle
56 Physician's start
57 Water bearer?
58 Mil. officer

293 by Sidney L. Robbins

ACROSS

1 Gore's "___ in the Balance"
6 One who's "agin" it
10 Train unit
13 "___ Without Windows" ('64 song)
14 Supermarket meat label
15 Territory
16 Major Bowes updated?
18 Fat
19 Home on the range
20 Kind of signal
21 Part of SEATO
22 Mail HQ
23 Breakfast order
25 Lift up
29 Woodworker's choice
32 Belgian airline
34 Bests
38 Hemingway opus
41 Dub again
42 Took ten
43 Ingenious
45 Shows remorse
46 Up
50 Marinaro and others
52 Slough
53 Reckon
56 Bosom companions
60 "Remember the neediest," e.g.
61 Olympia Dukakis film
63 Fast time
64 Capri, for one
65 Misrepresent
66 Pupil's place
67 African lake
68 Volvo worker

DOWN

1 Bridge seat
2 Comic Johnson
3 Imitation morocco
4 Civil wrong
5 ___ Pinafore
6 Cottonwoods
7 Grammy-winning pianist
8 Yacht heading
9 Person of will
10 1929 event
11 High nest
12 "M*A*S*H" character
15 "Too bad"
17 Parapsychology study
22 Authentic
24 Singing sisters
25 D.C. zone
26 Comic Bert
27 Have ___ in one's bonnet
28 Probe
30 Flat sign?
31 Vienna is its cap.
33 In opposition to one another
35 River to the Seine
36 Town near Padua
37 Osmose
39 Melmackian of TV
40 60's org.
44 Craved
46 With room to spare
47 "Little Orphant Annie" poet
48 Goodnight girl
49 Pants part
51 ___ Plaines
54 Deluxe
55 Southeast Kansas town
56 Witch's ___
57 Golden, e.g.
58 Tart
59 ___ Ball (arcade game)
62 Kitchen meas.

294 by David J. Kahn

ACROSS

1 Colo. acad.
5 Start fishing
9 "Dancing Queen" pop group
13 Mata ___
14 Tear to shreds
16 Tactic
17 Singer Antoine from New Orleans
19 Intense anger
20 Carty of baseball
21 ___ and kin
23 "The Company"
24 Mister twister
28 San Francisco area
29 Antitoxins
30 Laughed, in a way
32 Transfer, as a legal proceeding
36 "Tie a Yellow Ribbon" tree
37 Native land
39 Inform (on)
40 Fantasized
44 Durante's "Mrs."
48 Cosmonaut Gagarin
50 1956 Oscar-winning actress
51 Birthday-suit activity
55 One of L.B.J.'s dogs
56 Munich's river
57 Max or Buddy
59 Till compartment
61 Film hit of 1934
65 Dermatologist's diagnosis
66 Underwater acronym
67 Tevye portrayer on stage
68 Feminist Millett
69 Mikulski and Murkowski: Abbr.
70 Once more

DOWN

1 TV initials
2 Region of heavy W.W. II fighting
3 Heart of the grocery?
4 Champion named 9/1/72
5 ___ Magnon
6 Goal
7 Acerbic
8 Acropolis attire
9 Bank loan abbr.
10 Longtime Supreme Court name
11 Humphrey, to Bacall
12 TV's "___ in the Life"
15 Commotion
18 Act like the Apostle Thomas
22 "___ goes!"
25 ___ Harbour, Fla.
26 Playoff breathers
27 Machine part
28 "___ she blows!"
30 Food fish
31 A dwarf
33 Syracuse players
34 Floral container
35 Biblical suffix
38 Moist
41 Novelist Rand
42 City bond, for short
43 Secret lovefests
45 Appearance at a sit-down?
46 Suspect's "out"
47 Top-rated TV show of the 60's
49 Baking potatoes
51 Kind of therapy
52 Moi's country
53 "___ my case"
54 "Goodnight" girl
58 Steak order
60 Marie, e.g.: Abbr.
62 Aruba product
63 Nolte's "48 ___"
64 Right away

295 by Jonathan Schmalzbach

ACROSS
1 Mercury or Mars
4 Good old boy
9 Double-crosser
14 1979 film "Norma ___"
15 W.W. I battle site
16 Pomme de ___ (French potato)
17 Modern bank "employee": Abbr.
18 "___ in Venice"
19 Feeling regret
20 Night photographer's work, with "a"?
23 Common connectors
24 Bother
25 Wears well
27 Kind of budget
32 Dustin, in "Midnight Cowboy"
33 Actress Ward of "Sisters"
34 Exist
35 Like an inept photographer's subject?
39 Christina's dad
40 Snoop Doggy Dogg songs
41 Plays
42 Indy and Daytona
45 Classified
46 Sleep stage: Abbr.
47 Family member
48 Photojournalists' choices?
54 "___ Paradiso" (1966 film)
56 Catalyst
57 Mining area
58 "___ of robins in her hair"
59 San ___, Calif.
60 Chemical suffix
61 Mill, to a cent
62 Embellish
63 ___ Guinea

DOWN
1 Fat, in France
2 Vow
3 Floor model
4 Owing to
5 Defeats
6 Imps
7 One of the March sisters
8 Netman Arthur
9 Road, in Roma
10 Reflex messenger
11 Composer Satie
12 Prince Valiant's son
13 Fraternity party staple
21 "Jerusalem Delivered" poet
22 ___ Lama
25 Author Esquivel
26 Greek
27 Computer sounds
28 Swiss range
29 Trigger
30 Fumbled
31 Grades below the curve
32 Surf sound
33 Open carriage
36 Chaplin persona
37 Shadow-y surname?
38 ___-frutti
43 One of the Gallos
44 Affluence
45 Spoiler
47 Vinegar: Prefix
48 British gun
49 Lady of Spain
50 "Holy moly!"
51 Unrestricted
52 Supreme Court complement
53 Brood
54 Topper
55 Single

296 by Ernie Furtado

ACROSS
1 Luggage
5 Sneaking suspicion
9 Waist material
13 Broadway aunt
15 "The Old Curiosity Shop" heroine
16 Words of enlightenment
17 Everybody's opposite
18 Brickbat
19 Bear head, once
20 Sgt. Friday's comment at the office equipment store?
23 Check-cashing needs
24 Insubstantial
25 Biblical initials
26 Lend a hand
27 Tour grp.
28 "Mighty ___ a Rose"
31 Big salmon order for a security firm?
36 Unvarnished
38 "Don't tell me!"
39 Goes it alone
41 ___-European
42 ___ the iceberg
44 Part of the cost of floor covering?
46 ___ Canals
47 Comic Philips
49 High dudgeon
50 "___ tell"
52 Clock part
54 Emulate
57 Musical instrument that throws Troy Aikman for a loss?
60 "___ never fly"
61 Nobel chemist Harold
62 Championship
63 Clock part
64 Clears (of)
65 Have the helm
66 Grand Ole ___
67 Crime battler of 60's TV
68 Once, once

DOWN
1 Movie pooch
2 Not sotto voce
3 Shine
4 Wired
5 Actress Stevens
6 More than ennoble
7 Exile site
8 Writer de Tocqueville
9 Eastern lute
10 Bushwhacker
11 Where ends meet
12 That ship
14 Kind of price
21 Squirrels away
22 Alphabet quartet
26 Peek ending
27 Wife, to Caesar
29 Verdi's slave girl
30 Landon's running mate, 1936
31 Pointillist's marks
32 Wheeling's river
33 Out of style
34 Bats
35 Suffix with pay
37 Lo-cal
40 Star in Virgo
43 Misgiving
45 Pitches, in a way
48 1989 Nancy Reagan book
51 Comeback
52 Bandleader Waring et al.
53 Gaping hole
54 Sunflower, in furniture decoration
55 Loses color
56 Wield
57 Ear spear
58 Albany-to-Buffalo route
59 Tom of golf
60 Words before a kiss?

297 by Manny Nosowsky

ACROSS

1 Pandora's release
6 "The Man Who Came to Dinner" playwright
10 Pointed criticisms
14 Alice's cat in "Alice in Wonderland"
15 Blue Bonnet product
16 Scope
17 "See if ___!"
18 Flip
19 Appearance
20 San Francisco site
23 Bridge support
24 "Red Roses for a Blue Lady" singer
25 That, in Tijuana
26 Euripides tragedy
30 Milieu for Edith Piaf
34 Search for
35 Corporate name in chemicals
36 Welland Canal terminus
37 Evening event
41 Performed badly
44 Have some faith
45 Prince Valiant's firstborn
46 Lasting introduction
47 Where Athens is
52 San Francisco site
56 Flash
57 Gaelic Ireland
58 Future star
59 Israeli airline
60 Editor's notation
61 Hersey locale
62 Kind of swoop
63 Miss Trueheart
64 Ernie and others

DOWN

1 Word from on high
2 Wakefield V.I.P.
3 Absurd
4 Greases up
5 Protection
6 Grilling site
7 Oceans
8 Lives
9 Proportional
10 Crowded
11 ___ da capo
12 It may have a head but not a tail
13 Sent to the bottom
21 Ultimatum word
22 Patella's place
27 One who sees red?
28 Devastation
29 Suit to ___
30 Hair raiser, perhaps
31 Shampoo ingredient
32 Sci. course
33 Best Picture of 1977
38 Golfer Ballesteros
39 Hillary's conquest
40 Home wrecker
41 Refrigerator decorators
42 Furies
43 Rainier cover?
48 Aunt of song
49 ___ Abdel Nasser
50 Peace goddess
51 60's hairdos
52 Where esnes slaved
53 Unoccupied
54 Imprimatur
55 War god

298 by Rich Norris

ACROSS

1 Unembellished
9 Breakfast cereal pioneer
15 This could have been fixed
16 Farmhand
17 Rude
18 Bring about
19 Words with hole or two
20 Very unpopular
22 Actor Chaney
23 Bad-mouth
24 Scavenger hunt participant
26 Market
27 Son of Adam
29 Debutante, for one
30 #1 song for the Association, 1967
31 Part of Cousteau's world
33 Candy
35 Beat it
36 Beat it
37 Kind of radio program
40 Brunei's island
43 Intimate center
44 Representation
46 Cobras
48 Over
49 Golf club feature
51 Kind of brain
52 Road map abbr.
53 Output
54 With
56 Go-___
58 Health club employee
60 Force out
61 Departures
62 Brews
63 Tie

DOWN

1 Cuttlefish kin
2 Bluefins
3 Comeback
4 Radio-controlled aerial bomb
5 British ___
6 Alphabet trio
7 Impetuous one
8 Pinches
9 Colonial newsman
10 Proceed
11 Steno's need
12 Sumptuous
13 Supports, in a way
14 Up-to-date
21 Actress Harper
25 Tropical resin
26 Congress site of 1814–15
28 Consecrate
30 Have on
32 Calamine lotion, e.g.
34 Treat unfairly
37 Circumstances
38 Irate
39 Lake Victoria outlet
40 Chains
41 Champion
42 The briny
43 Makes an unannounced entrance, with "in"
45 Settled
47 Most prudent
49 Removes, in a way
50 Uncomplicated
53 Kennel sound
55 Engage
57 Menlo Park monogram
59 Mrs., in Madrid

299   by Gregory E. Paul

ACROSS

1 Mineral powder
5 Country singer Buck
10 ___ Clayton Powell
14 Sills solo
15 Hypothesize
16 "___ la Douce"
17 Musical based on "The Taming of the Shrew"
19 Garden starter
20 Book after Nehemiah
21 "Oh, to be in ___": Browning
23 Infuriated
26 City near Provo
27 Mrs. Mertz
30 Parapsychology skill
32 "Wuthering Heights" man
35 ___ Rabbit
36 Wish for
38 Give ___ whirl
39 Cartoonist Keane
40 Musical based on "The Once and Future King"
41 Diamond stat
42 Wriggler
43 Without secrets
44 Keogh, for one
45 Waggish
47 Initials on a record label
48 "Play ___ for Me"
49 Bucks and does
51 Slip-up
53 Double-___ (rat)
56 Worry-free place
60 Scream
61 Musical based on "7½ Cents," with "The"
64 Sandwich shop
65 Poetry Muse
66 Suffix with cell or gland
67 Cowboy Rogers's real last name
68 Politician ___ Alexander
69 Adm. Zumwalt

DOWN

1 Seize
2 Onassis and others
3 Roster
4 One who works the till
5 "Fidelio," e.g.
6 Chinese cooker
7 That: Sp.
8 Day's opposite, in commercials
9 Court reporter
10 Having walkways
11 Musical based on the Supremes
12 Prayer ending
13 Hwy. safety org.
18 Blackbird
22 Welcome
24 One that swarms
25 Central nature
27 Receded
28 City on the Mosel
29 Musical based on "The Matchmaker"
31 Parthenon feature
33 Up, in baseball
34 Save for a ___ day
36 Dangle bait on the water
37 Artist Lichtenstein
40 Nat and Natalie
44 Indian dugout
46 Singer Uggams
48 Manny of the Dodgers
50 Drive back
52 Scuttlebutt
53 Dancer Charisse et al.
54 Lively dance
55 ___ avis
57 Gloomy shadow
58 Muslim leader
59 Flying: Prefix
62 Toast topper
63 One ___ time

300   by Jonathan Schmalzbach

ACROSS

1 Leave, slangily
6 New York's ___ University
10 Component part
14 Hardly eager
15 Muslim title
16 "Heartburn" writer Ephron
17 Carroll adventuress
18 Number of Beethoven symphonies
19 Winter Palace resident, once
20 "Guys and Dolls" guy
23 Do one's darndest
24 Actor Stephen
25 Elite military group
27 World Series of Poker winner
31 Dictatorial
34 Site of deposit withdrawals
35 African antelope
36 "That hurts!"
37 Deere products
39 Stamping tools
40 Neighbor of Leb.
41 Astronaut Bean
42 "___ Porridge Hot"
43 Radio drama "of mother love and sacrifice"
47 Lover
48 Feel unwell
49 Fore's partner
52 Jack Boyle detective
56 "Get going!"
58 Always
59 Transparent cloth
60 Artists' purchases
61 ___ avis
62 Columnist Goodman
63 Cotton bundle
64 One-armed bandit's gullet
65 Gobs

DOWN

1 Italics have it
2 Kind of bear or cap
3 Ordinary churchfolk
4 Yen
5 "Be all that you can be" group
6 Theban poet
7 She might get a billet-doux
8 Shoptalk
9 May birthstones
10 Loosens
11 Yearning for the past
12 Clinton aide Magaziner
13 Roofing substance
21 Teachers' org.
22 Siouan Indian
26 King Solomon's excavations
27 Bat wood
28 Actress Massey
29 Weather system
30 Meditate
31 Forest: Fr.
32 Evicts
33 Weirdo
37 Kind of punch
38 Terhune dog
39 Composer Josquin ___ Prés
41 Actress MacGraw et al.
42 Tasting sensibilities
44 Founder of Taoism
45 Experimental animal
46 Like Capp's Abner
49 "A View to ___"
50 ___ mignon
51 Adolescents
53 Track-shaped
54 Nephew of Caligula
55 R.C., e.g.
56 Kind of sister
57 Spook-y org.

301 by Randy Sowell

ACROSS

1 Invader of old Rome
5 Caper
10 W.W. II assault craft
14 After-shoveling feeling
15 Flora and fauna of a region
16 "It's ___!" (sportscaster's cry)
17 F-4, e.g.
19 Prego competitor
20 Slip up
21 Nabisco cookie
22 Undercut
24 Leaves
26 Got up
27 Unit of mass transit
28 Ran
31 Church recesses
34 Washington Mayor Marion
35 Deli loaf
36 ___ of Sanitation
37 Is overfond
38 Look for
39 "___ was going to St. Ives"
40 Vetoes
41 Fine jacket material

42 Further
44 "Sprechen ___ Deutsch?"
45 Mystery writer Michael
46 Flammable cleaner
50 "i" completer
52 London gallery
53 Kind of engineer: Abbr.
54 Hence
55 Author anonymously
58 Spray cleaner target
59 Spine-tingling
60 "The Good Earth" wife
61 da-DAH
62 Pilotless plane
63 Closed sac

DOWN

1 Opened wide
2 Earth tone
3 Choreographer Twyla
4 Layer
5 Cape Canaveral cancellations
6 1629 treaty city
7 Axis villain

8 Ending with Israel
9 Party aides
10 50's singer Julius
11 Maple or elm
12 Buster Brown's dog
13 Macho man
18 Doughnut, mathematically
23 Calhoun of "The Texan"
25 Aid's partner
26 After, in Arles
28 Western
29 Looked at
30 Astronaut Slayton
31 Genesis 2:7 subject
32 Mexican moolah
33 False beard attacher
34 Warehouse clutter
37 Forked off
38 Egyptian port
40 Zero
41 Tendon
43 Bury
44 Parlor piece
46 Tidal ___
47 With no warmth
48 Actress Talbot et al.
49 Track meet component

50 Name in old TV comedy
51 Ocean menace
52 Matador's foe
56 Part of H.R.H.

57 Mythical bird

302 by Matt Gaffney

ACROSS

1 Horace volume
5 "Cabaret" name
9 Door fasteners
14 Volcanic flow
15 Give ___ for one's money
16 West African capital
17 Film director Reitman
18 Washington medical center
20 Traitor to Norway
22 Best
23 Nitpicker
25 Source of a biblical jawbone
26 Involuntary muscle spasm
29 Unspecified number
30 Bleachers cry
31 Vermont-born President
33 Penalty
34 Traitor to Christ
38 Hearty laughs
39 Shakespeare hero
40 Aussie bird
41 Alphabet sequence
43 Bomb of a bomb

44 Dupin creator
47 Do technical film work
49 City known for rubber products
51 Traitor to the United States
56 Disasters
57 Enterprise competitor
58 "Maria ___" (1941 song)
59 O.K. Corral fighter
60 Say no to
61 Actor Merlin
62 Pops' mates
63 Place of temptation

DOWN

1 Singer Newton-John
2 Wales's St. ___ Cathedral
3 Gets around
4 Decaf brand
5 White House area
6 Invader of 1990
7 African language
8 Con
9 Motorcycle maker
10 Bitter

11 Hypothetical chain of events
12 Expecting
13 Pathetic
19 Cable staple
21 Extreme
24 More and merrier preceder
27 Not his or hers
28 You may get a peep out of this
29 Like a pendulum's path
31 Paid spots
32 ___ Today
33 Cone bearer
34 Basketball showdown
35 Kahoolawe instruments
36 Tempe sch.
37 Traffic tracker
38 Oui or si
41 He cometh
42 "Star Wars" knight
44 Showed
45 Sea rock
46 Finishes with
48 Ridiculous
50 Scamp
52 Agenda part

53 "Bye"
54 Time for a President or a convict
55 Mean snakes
56 Corp. honcho

303   by Mary E. Brindamour

ACROSS

1 Bygone leader
5 Kind of acid
10 Business sch. candidate's exam
14 1983 Michener novel
15 Easter Rebellion site, 1916
16 Fad
17 "___ right!"
18 1992 Pulitzer author Mark
19 Giordano opera "___ Chénier"
20 Spendthrifts
22 The S in "DOS"
24 Astronaut William of Apollo 8
25 Field goal pct., e.g.
26 Messy place
29 China's 1972 gift to the U.S.
32 "What was ___ think?"
33 Frost
34 African antelopes
36 Certain Slav
38 Davis or Midler
39 Umbrella parts
40 Mr. Hammer
41 They're typed with the left pinkie
42 Dye holder
43 Desert worry
45 Church aides
48 Heyerdahl's "Kon-___"
49 In stock
50 Places to sip mint juleps
53 Grammatical case
57 Bedouin
58 Part of a reservation, maybe
60 Ancient theaters
61 Send back
62 "Casino Royale" actress
63 Frau's partner
64 Kennel noises
65 Wind instruments
66 Peruvian, perhaps

DOWN

1 Gush
2 Georgetown athlete
3 Brews
4 Gymnastic feats
5 Best clothes
6 Pitcher Hershiser et al.
7 Undrunk portion
8 Improperly
9 Place for suckers
10 Showoff
11 Superette, e.g.
12 Writer James
13 Kind of spirit
21 No longer in the U.S.N.
23 Big mouth
25 Swings at
26 Tower location
27 Roman roads
28 Chowhound: Var.
29 Tribal object
30 Surviving
31 Ship grounder
33 Clothing merchant Bendel
35 Fast planes
37 Some outdoor musical combos
38 Left Bank sights
44 Pedro's aunt
45 Proviso word
46 ___ Na Na
47 Kind of combat
49 More than portly
50 Fluctuate
51 ". . . ___ saw Elba"
52 Highway exit
53 Zenith
54 ___ fixe
55 Miles of "Psycho"
56 Garner, as rewards
59 70's–80's pol. cause

304   by Manny Nosowsky

ACROSS

1 Haiti's François Duvalier, familiarly
8 Sistine Chapel figures
15 Cry of panic
16 Suffered humiliation
17 Astor Cup, e.g.
18 The beginning
19 Old as Methuselah, in a way
20 Floppy takers
22 Bee quest?
23 De Valera's country
24 Con
26 Convince
27 Three-striper, e.g.: Abbr.
28 Par amount
30 "Comprende?"
31 Citrus hybrids
33 Mugged
35 Kind of agreement
37 Important
40 Gets what's coming
44 City, informally
45 ___ Lee, who lived in a kingdom by the sea
47 Belli's bailiwick
48 Social affairs
50 Takes shape
51 It meant well to Caesar
52 Set in motion
54 Inn serving
55 Sidewalk hazard
56 Do-it-yourselfer
58 Alternative to a station wagon
60 Memorable 1969 hurricane
61 Whatnot
62 Prayer, often
63 Times-Mirror paper

DOWN

1 Omen
2 Historic plane of Adm. Byrd
3 Blast furnace product
4 Bagmate for a steelie
5 Spoil, with "on"
6 German compass point
7 Lovers' guide
8 Assents
9 Juin through septembre
10 Bring in the rye
11 Lots of land
12 March, perhaps
13 Dragon's home, in a song
14 Ballooned
21 Occasion to say "Whew!"
24 Site of the George Washington Br. tollbooths
25 Sewers have them
28 Nose parts
29 Nose
32 Mud
34 Versified salute
36 Pirates of Penzance, before they were pirates
37 Bush country
38 Serf's opposite
39 Warriors vs. Bulls, e.g.
41 Split
42 Trumpet blare
43 Bob ___, TV's Fibber McGee
46 More on target
49 "Gymnopédies" composer
51 Liner cans
53 "Little" Dickens girl
55 Be an eager beaver
57 Suffix with glob
59 Suffix with meteor

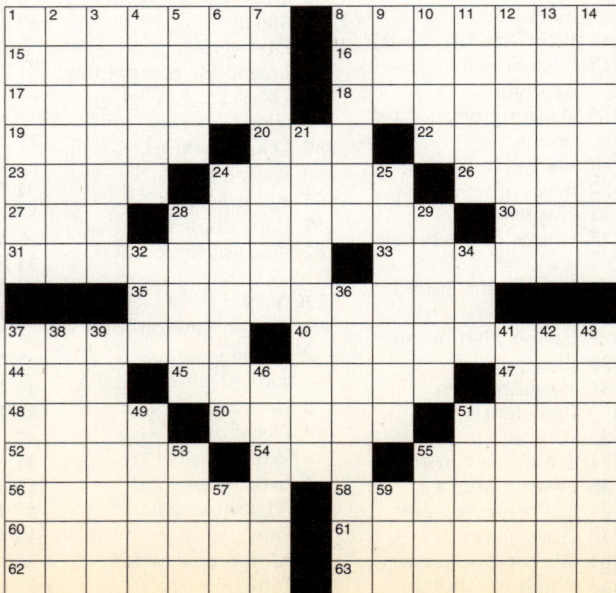

305 by Manny Nosowsky

ACROSS

1 Park, in a way
7 Breakfast order
14 Grammy winner Franklin
15 It gets its kicks
16 Lays low
17 Oil
18 Dick on TV
19 Apple thrower of myth
20 Film director Roach
21 "Be present," in a song
22 Velvet finish
23 1993 news site
24 Gide's "La symphonie ___"
26 Estonia's second-largest city
27 Shiloh priest
28 Has change
29 Assessing
35 Dazed
36 Ballyhoo
37 Steppes settler
38 Follow as an unexpected result
44 "South Pacific" role
45 Words of inquiry

46 Fan
47 Medit. land
48 Skip
49 50's tennis star Gibson
50 More impertinent
52 Venetian assembly
53 Like a Christmas tree
54 Metropolitan Opera V.I.P. James
55 Poked along
56 Puts up

DOWN

1 Tank top?
2 Navy group
3 Robs, to Robert Burns
4 Give one's word
5 "In the ___" (Presley hit)
6 Hunter's object
7 Actress North
8 Add to the stewpot
9 Common duck genus
10 Scale amts.
11 Casanova
12 "The Zoo Story" or "Riders to the Sea"
13 "Othello" topic

15 Big Three supplier
23 Flaw
25 Thrilla in Manila fighter
26 Whip but good
28 Word for an archdeacon
29 Champs
30 Friend of Henry Miller
31 First name in Olympic skating
32 "___ first you . . ."
33 Part of Scand.
34 Red carpet treader
38 Protective layer
39 It will curl your hair
40 Like some church candles
41 Kind of cuisine
42 Doesn't have to
43 Takes the lead
45 Boxer Griffith
48 European auto
51 "___ Love You"

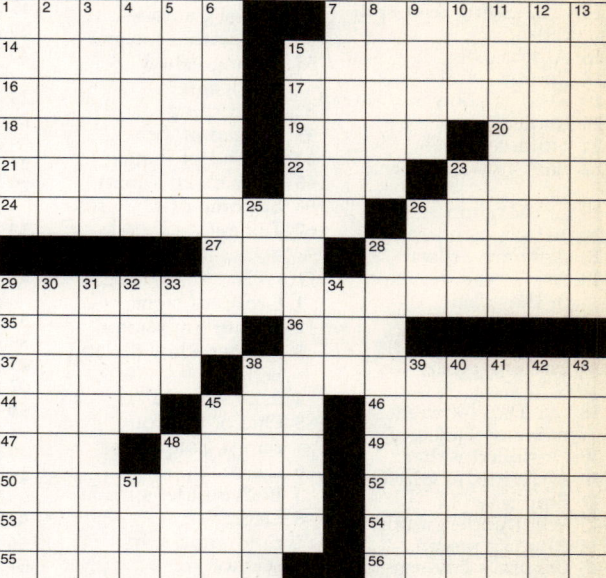

306 by Nancy S. Ross

ACROSS

1 Garden dweller
5 Cassius and company, in "Julius Caesar"
10 Achievement
14 Prefix with byte or buck
15 Run with a hon?
16 Site of the MGM Grand
17 December 25 activity
20 Severe
21 These may get a welcome sight
22 Pick apart
24 Hereabout
25 ___-relief
28 Creeks
30 Drafted
34 "What's the ___?"
35 Court org.
37 Wee bit
38 Convivial holiday affair
42 Pub needs
43 Positions
44 Part of TNT
45 Like Clifford Odets's "Waiting for Lefty"

48 "Whip It" rock group
49 Smoke signal message, maybe
50 Kind of bond
52 Baltic port
54 Used a caret-and-stick approach?
58 Pinpoint
62 Sign-off a la Clement Moore
64 Nefariousness
65 Opposite of viejo
66 Campus V.I.P.
67 ___ fide (bad faith)
68 Bit of parsley
69 Bristle

DOWN

1 Sheriff Tupper of "Murder, She Wrote"
2 Agric. or H.H.S., e.g.
3 Ripener
4 Frenzied
5 Political moderate
6 School subj.
7 Hits, in slang
8 Stage extension
9 Looked lasciviously
10 Unlimited choice
11 Counting-out word

12 Add to the pot
13 Play horseshoes
18 Mythical flier
19 Scorch
23 Oasis trees
25 British swaggerer
26 Pale
27 Maestro Koussevitzky
29 Sedate
31 Habits
32 In ___ (not yet born)
33 Golden apple bestower
36 Daisylike bloom
39 Patron of Columbus
40 Marine, informally
41 Equiangular geometrical shape
46 Sagan of "Cosmos"
47 Certain missiles
51 Mounter's assist
53 These can be citric
54 Gossip tidbit
55 Suddenly bright star
56 Spinnaker, e.g.
57 Active one
59 1957 Pulitzer winner
60 "___ does it!"
61 Sicilian sight

63 Egg: Prefix

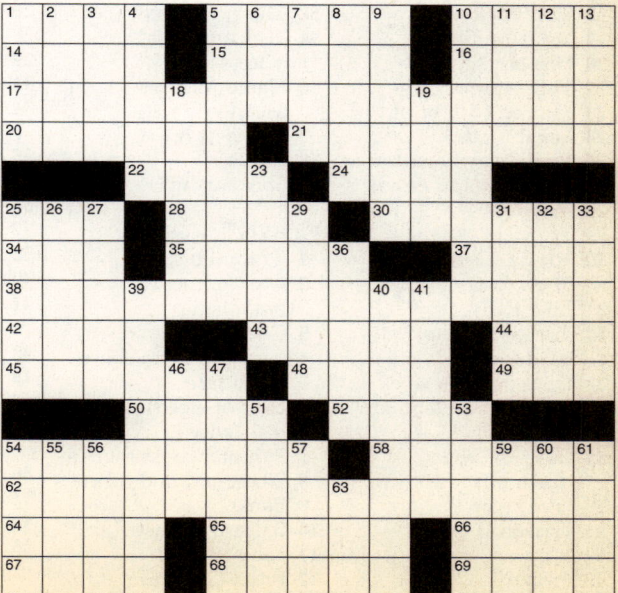

 by Mark Elliot Skolsky

ACROSS

1 Delete, in a way
4 Low blow?
8 Glacial ridge
13 Run of the ranch?
14 Riyadh resident
15 "___ crying over spilt milk"
16 Alpine aster
18 Pound
19 Kind of show
20 Radical
21 Fluid container
22 Baryshnikov's former co.
25 ___-Magnon
26 Attach, as a patch
28 Antwerp artisan
30 Saw in the direction of the grain
31 Jackie's second
32 Game plan
34 Pitching credit
35 Saki story
38 ___ Thai (official name of Thailand)
39 Unskilled writer
40 67-Across employee
41 Stupidity
43 Went underground
44 Rhoda's mom
45 Eskimo's environs
49 Corrida cheer
50 ___ deferens
51 Pilot's heading
52 God whose symbol was two horses' heads
53 Three on a match?
55 Model Campbell
57 Rod with a racquet
58 Distinguished politicians
62 Concerning
63 A head of Time
64 A head of France
65 They make a mint
66 Epitome of 41-Across
67 Tax agcy.

DOWN

1 Group of signs
2 Instant impression
3 Former Rhode Island Senator
4 ___ kwon do
5 One of the Four Forest Cantons
6 ___-relief
7 Bodybuilder's pride
8 Degree of randomness, in science
9 It's near Piccadilly
10 "Seven Samurai" director
11 Arcane
12 Yankee's foe
13 1988 Peter Allen musical
17 Doc's best friend
20 Brigs, e.g.
23 Where the U.S.S. Cyclops disappeared
24 Shocks
25 "Rambo" actor Richard and kin
27 Flirtatious signal
29 Prufrock creator's inits.
33 Bill
35 Canyon feature
36 Mike Hammer's creator
37 Restyled
39 33d Pres.
41 Distracts
42 Public to-do
46 Fraternal twin, in chemistry
47 Bill Haley's backup
48 Round-Manhattan cruise company
54 Outlet
56 Wine region
57 Varnish ingredient
58 ___-pitch softball
59 Formal wear, informally
60 Crackerjack
61 Part of a royal flush

 by Manny Nosowsky

ACROSS

1 Travelogue technique
10 Steady ___ goes
15 Owing
16 Ink dispenser
17 Sheet metal producer
18 Court activity
19 Pants preference
20 Has an egg
22 This señora
23 Minced oath of old
24 Legal matter
25 Radio wave emitter
27 Extra costs in movie making
29 Trips
30 Hit ___ (aggravate a 57-Across)
31 Like Esau
32 French Belgian border river
33 Do reporter's work for a certain tabloid?
35 Course average
38 Rusty on the diamond
39 Free again
41 Hassan II's land
44 X's
45 Properly
46 Set
47 Cartoonist Peter
48 Certain measurement: Abbr.
49 Popular dog name
51 Collimate
52 Museum piece
54 "Falcon Crest" actress
56 Ngaio Marsh's "___ a Murderer"
57 Where it hurts
58 Excuse
59 Sponsorship

DOWN

1 Unthinking
2 Development of an organism
3 Goes over again
4 It can be extra sharp
5 Sushi fare
6 Unit of electrical resistance
7 Summer dress fabrics
8 Fitzgerald and others
9 Bank
10 Balaam's beast
11 Kind of clean
12 From Genève
13 Suggest
14 Awards since 1947
21 Stockpile, with "away"
24 Shows the court how the crime was done
26 Let out line
28 Complain
29 Basque "game"
31 Center piece
34 ___ warranto (legal proceeding)
35 Grace Kelly's middle name
36 Repaying
37 Strike a chord
38 More like mush
40 Pacific Coast critter
41 Sierra ___ (Mexican mountains)
42 Acclimatize
43 Bridge of 1590
44 Split, so to speak
46 Columbus's birthplace
50 It's a lock
51 Pick of the litter?
53 1951 Johnnie Ray hit
55 Meteorological prefix

309   by Norman S. Wizer

ACROSS
1 Man has seven
5 Small groove
10 Trims the tree
14 Barbarian
15 Cut ___ swath
16 "___ Her on Monday" (1942 hit)
17 Mercury or Saturn
18 Treacherous person
19 Computer memory
20 LOCK . . .
23 Praise loudly
24 Giant's third word
25 Fling
28 Cherub
33 Coos' partner
34 Maintain
35 Word associated with light bulbs
36 STOCK . . .
40 That, in Sonora
41 Part of HOMES
42 Reagan Attorney General
43 Coffeecake topping
46 Mug
47 Turner or Cole
48 Kiddie talk?
49 BARREL . . .

57 Pealed
58 Double-check the check
59 "March Madness" org.
60 Energy source
61 N.R.A. symbol
62 Venetian strip
63 Flattop, of sorts
64 Hitler's architect
65 Gossips are all this

DOWN
1 "It's ___!" (wow!)
2 Foot problem
3 Luncheon follower
4 Work discussion
5 British taste
6 'Tween
7 Torn and tide, e.g.
8 The same, to Caesar
9 Gaseous
10 A nut for cooking
11 Novel set on Tahiti
12 President Fujimori's land
13 Blue-pencil notation
21 Fort on the Oregon Trail
22 Craggy hill

25 French clerics
26 & 27 Ground level
28 Use
29 Pool, in poetry
30 Movie shots
31 Items on hand
32 Western
34 Plot measure
37 Makes as good as new
38 Plain People
39 Knee jerk, e.g.
44 Mystery
45 Mideast inits.
46 It usually has a garten in back
48 Dipper
49 Pull an all-nighter
50 Odium
51 Years in Toledo
52 Gather
53 Knight's glove
54 Member of 59-Across
55 German river
56 Grub

310   by Joe Clonick

ACROSS
1 Started wrongly?
9 Mouse
15 Number after 1?
16 Ravel's "___ for a Dead Princess"
17 Is in the running
18 Unimak Island inhabitants
19 Home folks
20 Adriatic seaport
22 Endangered whale
23 African tyrant and namesakes
25 Like a wolf's howl
26 Furnish
27 Legal landmarks
29 Digital clock's light emitter
30 La Plata locale: Abbr.
31 Gary Cooper-ish?
33 Like "The Persistence of Memory"
37 6-0, courtesy of Steffi
38 Immortal Pirate
40 French sea
41 It's bound to show the way
42 Site north of Frederick, Md.

47 Emblem on an English shield
48 Fabulous finish?
49 Stories
50 Health org.
51 Film makers' equipment
53 Certain degrees: Abbr.
54 Crumples
56 Aeronautical inclination
58 Army command
59 Casts an absentee ballot
60 Designer Norman Bel ___
61 TV address, in short

DOWN
1 Cut the mustard
2 Cheap jewelry material
3 Anyone's game?
4 Angkor ___
5 Noted rapper
6 Host of a short-lived talk show
7 Swirls
8 Utah's early name

9 Outpouring
10 Hearty accompaniment?
11 "___ Gotta Be Me"
12 Upset
13 Double ___
14 Junk-mail addressee
21 A rug
24 1984 Jeff Bridges role
26 Not loose
28 Manitoba Indians
29 Went under
32 Puts a wrap on
33 No-goodnik
34 Superlative
35 Fed the Colt again
36 Maj.'s superior
39 Frostbite preventers
43 École employee
44 Scroll-shaped ornament
45 Decrees
46 Have an aversion to
48 Acts hangdog
51 Early actress Elèanora
52 God of destruction
55 Downcast
57 Name in voyeurism

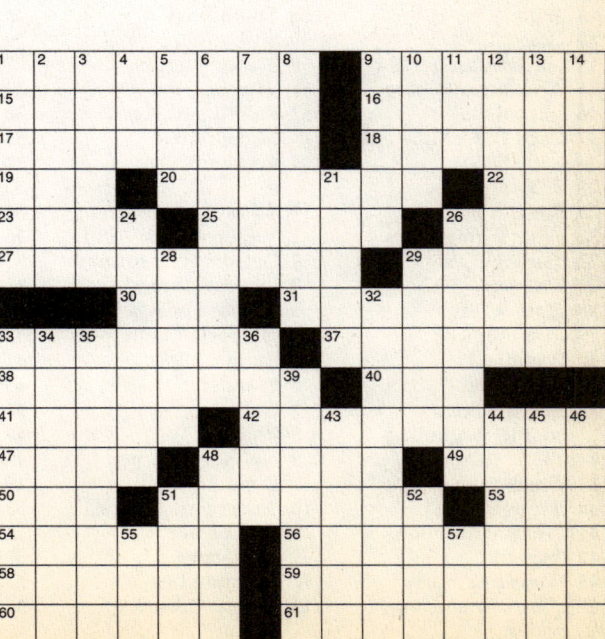

311 by Sidney L. Robbins

ACROSS

1 Mosque tops
6 Long Ranger attire
10 Strike caller
13 Dynamic
14 "I cannot tell __"
15 Mimic
16 Chinese principles
18 Lavish party
19 Tosspot
20 Worships
21 Freshly
22 Life, for one
23 Enlarge
24 Soup dipper
28 Six-stanza poem
31 Lily
32 Does, for example
33 Knot of hair
36 Procrastinator
40 Relative of the buttercup
42 Moral no-no
43 Tentmaker of fame
45 Kind of camera focus
46 Modified
49 Mount
50 Sighed (for)
52 Playboy pic
54 Took a taxi
55 Sound choice?
57 Busy person around Apr. 15
60 Smidgen that's smashed
61 Occasionally
63 Greek letters
64 Kurdish home
65 Throw out
66 N.Y. winter time
67 Trapper's trophy
68 Fires

DOWN

1 TV's "__ of Our Lives"
2 Hodgepodge
3 Money maker
4 "Uncle Tom's Cabin" girl
5 Spot for 100
6 Giuliani and others
7 Equipped with a theft protector
8 Trig function
9 Barrels
10 No longer bedridden
11 Fracas
12 Shrimp
15 Once more
17 Successor to H.S.T.
23 Telegram
24 Lassies' partners
25 Jai __
26 Homeless
27 Conducted
29 Melville novel setting
30 Countdown start
34 "Render therefore __ Caesar . . ."
35 It's a gas
37 Trucker's amount
38 Holy Roman, e.g.: Abbr.
39 Squealer
41 Alluring West
44 License extension
47 Considers
48 "The Story of Civilization" author
49 Hollow stones
50 Jabber
51 Specks
53 Bear's abode
55 Quick cut
56 Ripped
57 In high style
58 Captain Ahab of film
59 Busy ones
62 Initials of 1933

312 by Sidney L. Robbins

ACROSS

1 Extreme point in an orbit
6 "Hogan's Heroes" extra
10 Cole __
14 Hayes's predecessor
15 Arabian sultanate
16 __ colada
17 Cecil B. DeMille epic with "The"
20 Prohibition oasis?
21 Pilgrim John
22 What a ring lacks
23 "Finally!"
24 On ship
28 Plate scrapings
29 In a moment
30 Peculiar
32 Fast plane
35 English-French conflict beginning 1337
39 Greek vowel
40 Bay window
41 Prefix with pilot
42 "Scram!"
43 Went in a hurry
45 South American plains
48 Shock
50 __ acid
51 Jerk
56 What 17-Across had
58 Tooth pain
59 St. Louis 11
60 Skater's figure
61 "The __ the limit"
62 Relative of the heckelphone
63 Teacher's charge

DOWN

1 10-percenters: Abbr.
2 Get ready, informally
3 Of sound mind
4 Native Peruvian
5 "Dracula" author Bram
6 Wanderer
7 Gather
8 Wacky
9 Neither Rep. nor Dem.
10 Takes part in a bee
11 One of the McCartneys
12 Opening bets
13 Jimmy Dorsey's "__ It You?"
18 Repair
19 Make a difference
23 Sills song
24 Late tennis V.I.P.
25 Title
26 Mrs. Chaplin
27 Also
28 Pitcher Hershiser
30 Revise copy
31 Potato feature
32 Done laps
33 Surfeit
34 Trampled
36 Florid
37 Times to write about
38 __ Paulo, Brazil
42 Treats with malice
43 Bantu people
44 "Just a moment . . ."
45 Drug-yielding plants
46 "Alas and __"
47 Netted
48 Sad sack
49 The ones over there
51 Knife
52 Drop in a letter box
53 Actress Swenson
54 Old English letters
55 Beach-storming vessels: Abbr.
57 To and __

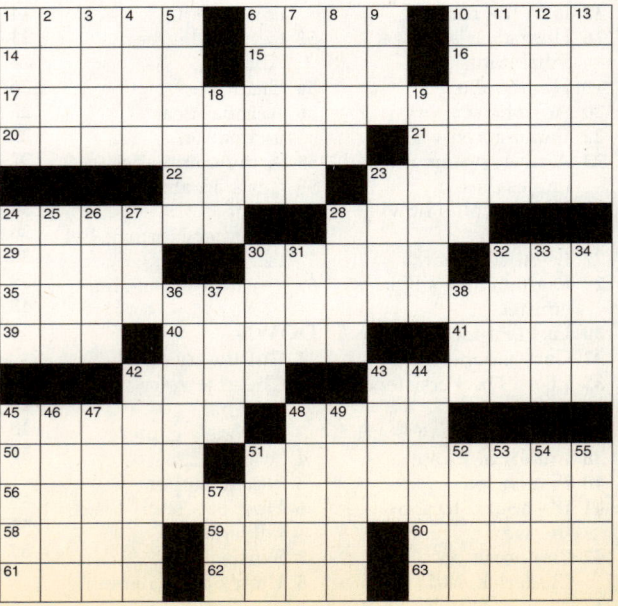

313 by Bernice Gordon

ACROSS
1 Man with a whale of a tale?
6 Texas city
10 Invoice stamp
14 Tickle one's fancy
15 Shah's land
16 Columnist Bombeck
17 Doctor
18 Pay no ___
19 Actor Richard ___
20 Cheap liquor
22 Unmixed
23 Go on
24 Emotional period
26 Airplane engine
30 Kind of booth or opposition
32 Basso Pinza
33 Ishmael's son-in-law
35 Obvious onlooker
39 Most bounteous
41 Make good as new
43 Fairy tale villain
44 Toward sunrise
46 Award given by The Village Voice
47 TV's "The ___ and the Restless"
49 Marzipan base
51 Children, in Scotland
54 Pro ___
56 Cartoonist Peter
57 Fair
63 Pharmacist's sale
64 Fizzled out
65 Oil, in Orléans
66 Quayle's successor
67 "___ dust shalt thou return"
68 Rub out
69 Water pitcher
70 Like Franklin's Richard
71 Did a cobbler's job

DOWN
1 Tight spots
2 Sign to heed
3 Manet's "Olympia," e.g.
4 30% of the world
5 Badger, as a speaker
6 Non-macho men
7 Piece for Pavarotti
8 Isn't able to
9 Next up
10 Voyeur
11 Monster with 100 eyes
12 Pottery from Japan
13 They may be great
21 "Rawhide" role for Eastwood
25 Antique autos
26 Plundered, old-style
27 Mediterranean's Côte d'___
28 "Venus de ___"
29 Flag for Captain Kidd
31 Not theirs
34 W.W. II gun
36 The gray wolf
37 Actress Moran
38 Marsh plant
40 North Carolina school
42 States, in St. Lô
45 Accept
48 Gone
50 Carpenter's machines
51 Sheriff's star
52 Symbol of straightness
53 Get used (to)
55 Dual conjunction
58 Italian wine
59 Prefix with centric
60 Poison holder
61 Other
62 Want

314 by Harvey Estes

ACROSS
1 Noted Lyceum instructor
10 Policy postscript
15 Mexican dance musicians
16 Dickens's ___ Heep
17 Say "WHAT!?"
18 Itsy-___
19 Funnyman Caesar
20 Center of interest
21 Organizational need
22 Yarn measure
23 Opening in the ice
24 Splotches
26 Sweaters?
27 Frightful, in slang
28 Evel Knievel, e.g.
32 Sea birds
33 Pub missiles
34 Garr of "Tootsie"
35 Alexander's home
37 Be an ecdysiast
38 Charges (at)
39 Collar victims
40 Cause to jump
43 Bartlett, for one
44 Synagogue scrolls
45 Wilderness home
46 Tender spot?
49 Give the slip to
50 Sewing machine's inventor
52 Bowling Hall-of-Famer Dick
53 Like Poe's "Letter"
54 Twinklers
55 They're not there

DOWN
1 Book after Joel
2 Sitarist Shankar
3 Plenty mad
4 Army address
5 Uncle Remus story, with "The"
6 Sinatra film "___ Eleven"
7 Word in an Oscar acceptance speech
8 Shellac
9 "C'___ la vie!"
10 Carmine
11 Hunting dog
12 The same
13 Canvas prop
14 Ditty
21 Fathers
22 Wheeler-dealer
23 Cardiologist's concern
24 Femme fatale Theda
25 ___ Hayes of TV's "Mod Squad"
26 Helen's abductor
27 Dress's bottom
28 Infernal writer?
29 Novelist Brittain
30 Showy flower
31 Edge
33 Guys' partners
36 Bumstead's boss
37 Affixes quickly
39 Having two X chromosomes
40 Does a slow burn
41 For rent
42 Caribbean isle
43 Figure skating event
45 Putter, for one
46 Paleontologist's discovery
47 "Just ___ bit"
48 1981 Beatty film
50 Ecol. org.
51 Top 40 song

315   by Chuck Deodene

ACROSS
1 Spicy dip
6 Mogul emperor
11 Compete in a Nordic combined
14 Allegheny River city
15 Ball girl?
16 School of whales
17 Drifters hit of 1963
19 "___ was saying . . ."
20 Raincoats
21 Liqueur named for an island
23 Three: Prefix
24 Motionless
25 Dick Van Dyke, in "Mary Poppins"
31 "Purgatory" dramatist
32 Slipped a Mickey
33 Diamond stat
36 With deftness
37 Impostors
38 Sightsee
39 Stock option
40 Erskine Caldwell's "Miss Mama ___"
41 Buffalo skater
42 Wiretapper, e.g.

45 Old World undergrowth
47 Composer Rorem
48 Capitol Hill sight
51 Nine-sider
55 Type of dye
56 Vulgar one
58 Vim
59 Key in
60 Renown
61 Sullivan and others
62 Change the grass
63 Spanish coins of yore

DOWN
1 Broth
2 Canine bowlful
3 Panetta of the White House
4 Holiness
5 Stirring songs
6 Lincoln and others
7 Splash or plunk lead-in
8 Alliance
9 Baseball's Felipe
10 Like bean-dip beans
11 Voyager 2, e.g.
12 N.F.L. QB Bernie
13 Blockhead

18 Cornet
22 Chemical suffix
25 Philippine isle
26 Women's summer wear
27 Wax-coated cheeses
28 Harnessed
29 Nazi architect Albert
30 Horror film director Craven
31 Mouth, slangily
34 Duelist of 1804
35 Pique
37 "For shame!"
38 Fast-paced entertainment
40 Superhero, often
41 Faerie Queene's creator
43 Tempe sch.
44 ___ about (legal time frame)
45 Concord, e.g.
46 Exuded
49 Frank Herbert saga
50 Bar mems.
51 Dweeb
52 Reptilian "monster"
53 Form of silica
54 Meshes

57 Auto racer ___ Fabi

316   by Rich Norris

ACROSS
1 Insult
8 Lives
15 Interstate overseer
16 Manifest
17 Cloth
18 Town east of Paramus, N.J.
19 I.C.C. issuance: Abbr.
20 Brand of glue
22 Close
23 Competent
25 Luke's "Star Wars" mentor
26 Put one past
27 Take over
29 Rent
33 Cesar of 60's-70's baseball
34 Dish sometimes made with leftovers
35 Auto accessory
37 Most chic
41 Hauled
45 Social
46 Hazardous locale
49 Emotional outburst
50 Cell chemistry: Abbr.
51 Riches
53 Appears

54 Career suffixes
56 1962 Tommy Roe hit
58 Last letters?
59 European kingdom until 1918
61 Kerchief
63 He or I may represent one
64 Fancy homes
65 Crystalline amino acids
66 Mideast money

DOWN
1 Draws
2 Plunder
3 Purple flower
4 Malarkey
5 Aunt Bee's charge
6 Nice one
7 Rapid repeat, in music
8 Go back over
9 Certain celebration times
10 Wrong
11 TV's Mrs. Morgenstern et al.
12 Best
13 Braid

14 Professionally barbered
21 Kind of cheese
24 Greek governor
28 Deal with
30 Addition
31 Paper units
32 Athens's district
36 Former N.H.L. great
38 Loathe
39 Guard
40 Infringe (on)
42 They may be worn with tails
43 Foil relative
44 "Coppélia" composer
46 Clans
47 Shoe part
48 Infer
52 Photographer's concern
55 Prefix with circle
56 Trigonometric ratio
57 Predeal requirement
60 Stag goers
62 Wild West terr.

317 by Robert Katz

ACROSS

1 Shut loudly
5 Summary
10 El ___, Tex.
14 Arrived
15 To love, in Torino
16 Notorious czar
17 "Thanks ___!"
18 "Melancholia" engraver
19 Shake up
20 Oxymoronic proverb
23 Čapek play
24 In ___ of (as a substitute for)
25 Like a low-watt bulb
28 Give off
31 Loath (to)
35 Literary olios
37 Old radio's "Easy ___"
39 News briefs
40 Parsimonious proverb
43 Huge, old-style
44 At hand
45 Suffix with super or major
46 Iroquoian language
48 "Cut it out!"
50 Loser to D.D.E.
51 Members of a wriggly field?
53 G.M. employees' union
55 Cautious proverb
63 Newsman Sevareid
64 Met offering
65 Bank offering
66 "The King and I" lady
67 Be in a bee
68 Beginner
69 Mover and shaker
70 Keys in
71 Skips over, as TV ads

DOWN

1 Swindle
2 ___ land (Los Angeles)
3 How not to run
4 European's "yard"
5 Control tower figure
6 Ostrich cousins
7 Grocery transporter
8 Whirling
9 Olden Iran
10 Ballet twirl
11 Confess
12 Go yachting
13 Nothing but
21 Shade
22 "Rosemary's Baby" writer Ira
25 1925 Nobel Peace Prize recipient
26 Nutty
27 Wall builder
29 Windows picture
30 What chapeaux cover
32 ___-car (Hertz, e.g.)
33 Struck down, in the Bible
34 Colorado's ___ Park
36 Vehicle with a bell
38 Hit, as a fly
41 Show's host
42 Wake-up calls
47 This doesn't count, in a saying
49 Furry foot
52 Mawkish
54 Viennese dance
55 President
56 River under the Ponte Vecchio
57 Trig function
58 Preserve
59 ___ Stanley Gardner
60 Kind of bean
61 Football field protector
62 Grandson of Adam

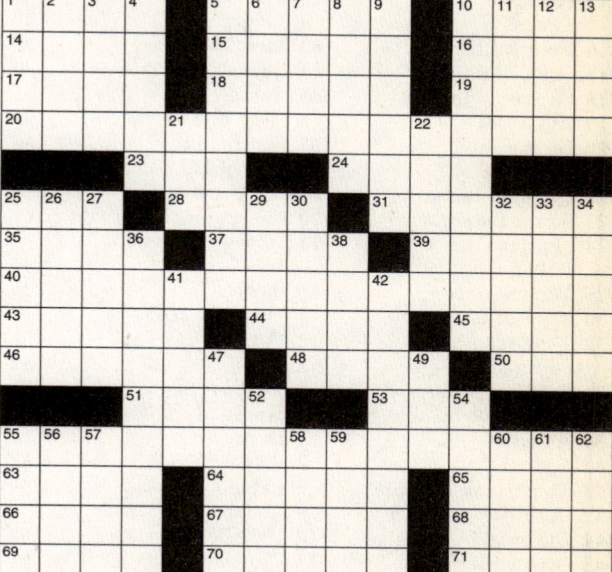

318 by John Scott Marrone

ACROSS

1 Pro ___
5 Both: Prefix
9 Slacken
14 Meanie
15 "Hee Haw" humor
16 Modern Persian
17 Landmark 20th-century ballet
20 The "S" in WASP
21 Openings
22 Foot: Lat.
23 Pax ___
26 Install
27 1966 Lovin' Spoonful hit
32 Italian wine region
33 Former rival of Jay and Dave
34 Rectory
36 Little sucker?
40 More like the Blob
46 Neophyte: Var.
47 1935 Vernon Duke song
51 Elevator man
52 One of the Nixons
53 Low-class newspaper
54 Brotherhood, for short
55 1970s music
60 1968 Hepburn/O'Toole film
64 Battling great Hank
65 Andrews or Carvey
66 Missing
67 Result
68 Author Haley
69 Patronizes the Four Seasons, e.g.

DOWN

1 Spoils
2 Turkish leader
3 "Jurassic Park" menace
4 Space prefix
5 It precedes "of God" or "of war"
6 A Stooge
7 Work shoes
8 Ravel's "Pavane pour une ___ défunte"
9 Kissers
10 Blunder
11 Chiang Kai-shek's capital
12 Messy
13 Symbol of messiness
18 About
19 Hall-of-Fame pitcher Warren
24 ". . . man ___ mouse?"
25 Russian "peace"
26 "Star Trek" engineer
27 Uncle ___
28 What 27-Down represents
29 Alp, e.g.: Abbr.
30 Wife, informally
31 Frozen Wasser
35 Shade tree
37 Brazilian getaway
38 Flightboard abbr.
39 In which dim sum may be cooked
41 Preface
42 Kind of rights, for a suspect
43 Beginning
44 S.A.S.E., e.g.
45 Defendants, at law
47 Main lines
48 Beehive State resident
49 Detroit nine
50 Desert streambed
54 Numismatist's classification
56 "Bus Stop" playwright
57 Portico
58 Copper
59 Mine rocks
61 Bud's comedy companion
62 Opposite SSW
63 Medium for Mme. Tussaud

ACROSS

1 Canvas
5 Moll Flanders, e.g.
10 Defeat
14 Like some medicines
15 Esther of "Good Times"
16 Colorful fish
17 Singer Minnelli
18 Heavenly hunter
19 Kill a bill
20 Dinner table centerpiece
22 Cliffside home
23 Somme summer
24 "Easter Parade" star, 1948
26 Yemen, once
30 Kind of town
32 They may be cultured
34 D.D.E.'s command
35 Fighter jet maneuver
39 As well
40 Loafed
42 Think tank output
43 Countless number
44 Classical beginning
45 Singer John et al.
47 Cancel

50 ___ Day
51 Drifted
54 Flag Day grp.
56 Bay window
57 1969 Creedence Clearwater Revival song
63 Moldiness
64 Purifies, as water
65 Gamete
66 Help at a heist
67 Figure out
68 Part of D.J.
69 ___ a one
70 Everything, to Ernst
71 "Cómo ___ usted?"

DOWN

1 Turnpike fee
2 "Un bel dì," e.g.
3 Tease
4 VCR button
5 Speckled ___
6 Derby entries
7 Pelvis parts
8 Extend
9 Marsh
10 1967 Beatles song
11 Donizetti work
12 Used, as a chair

13 Did a blacksmith's job
21 Sea World attraction
22 Biblical verb
25 Battery terminal
26 Baden and Bath, e.g.
27 High water's partner
28 Life of Riley
29 Baked dessert
31 Slave
33 Lightly burn
36 Dump problem
37 Pre-Easter period
38 Eye protector
41 Clint Eastwood film, with "The"
46 Ribald
48 Building annex
49 Develop
51 Dweller on the Tiber
52 Caribbean island
53 Scrooge, e.g.
55 Electric circuit safeguards
58 Small brook
59 Pop music's Depeche ___
60 Hertz rival
61 Oxidize
62 Gym site

64 "Be prepared" grp.

ACROSS

1 Hertz rival
5 Rug fiber
10 "Walk Like ___" (1963 hit)
14 Lincoln or Madison
15 Gay refrain
16 Olympic vehicle
17 Tied
18 Single-celled organism
19 Item in a carpenter's kit
20 FRIENDS
23 Plays (around with)
24 Co., in Cannes
25 Collect $200, in Monopoly
28 Elizabeth's sister
33 Foil's kin
34 Mother of Perseus
35 Devoured
36 ROMANS
40 Scrap for Fido
41 Hunter's lure
42 Director Jordan
43 Brief stay
45 Ukrainian port
47 Zoo attraction
48 Desert Storm target

49 COUNTRYMEN
57 Hideout
58 Dog walker's need
59 51-Down highlight
60 Reverse, as damage
61 World-weary feeling
62 Easter flower
63 Noggin
64 Removed from print
65 Resorts, of sorts

DOWN

1 Completed effortlessly
2 Cheer for Zapata
3 Particular
4 Summaries
5 Fortified French resort
6 They're kept in the keep
7 Kind of trap
8 Gain ___ on
9 Brightly speckled crustacean
10 Tennis champ Gibson
11 Pasteur portrayer Paul
12 Water, in Oaxaca
13 Takes home

21 Derby also-ran
22 Ty Cobb, e.g.
25 Legendary cowboy ___ Bill
26 To one side
27 Take care of
28 House of lords
29 Hardy boy
30 Is worthy of
31 Small needle cases
32 Unit of induction
34 Carp's kin
37 Take in, on or up
38 Divulged
39 Peerless people?
44 Supporter of the arts
45 Hothouse flower
46 Patriotic org.
48 Mint or print
49 Bungle
50 Tony winner Nathan
51 Verdi opera
52 Hawaii's state bird
53 Frontiersman Boone, informally
54 Stagehand
55 ___ monster
56 States

ACROSS

1 A way the wind blows
8 Skyscraper, e.g.
15 Columbus discovery of 1493
16 Successful detective
17 Tea of fabled powers
18 Quintessence
19 Mt. Rushmore site
20 Unschooled, as an artist
22 Britain's ___ Douglas-Home
23 One who works on a horse
25 It starts in Apr.
26 Colorful food fish
29 "God Save the Queen," e.g.
31 Shake
33 Had one's up and downs
37 Home of Carthage College
39 1984 World Series winners
40 Threadbare excuse
42 Yellowstone range
43 It's all the same
45 Loaded
46 Expression of comfort
49 Animals related to shrews
51 ___ Bator
53 Former East German secret police
54 Rumors
58 Ancient Roman coins
60 Composer Dvořák
62 As a preferred alternative
63 Heroine of Irish legend
64 Shipping channel
65 Movable cupboard

DOWN

1 Jet effects
2 Children's author Blyton
3 Lab item
4 Rival of Fab
5 Personnel datum
6 Like Brie
7 Noted Portuguese navigator
8 Chicago Loop feature
9 Inside info provider
10 French place
11 ___ morgana (illusion)
12 "___ you so!"
13 Shows up
14 Put up
21 They can put you up
23 Wrote anonymously
24 Lab personnel
26 Russia's ___ Region
27 Hang fire
28 "It's ___ Unusual Day"
30 Cuban patriot
31 Ring decision
32 ___ ridgeback (hunting dog)
34 Canine comment
35 German article
36 Withdrawal syndrome
38 Caribbean leader elected in 1990
41 City on the Colorado River
44 Dead Sea fortress
46 Quattros
47 Coeur d'___, Idaho
48 Medieval guild
50 Certain San Franciscan
52 Abbr. in many org. names
54 Ring combatant
55 The Beatles' "___ Love Her"
56 Transportation to N.Y.C.
57 Spot for a scrape
59 New Deal prog.
61 Director Burton

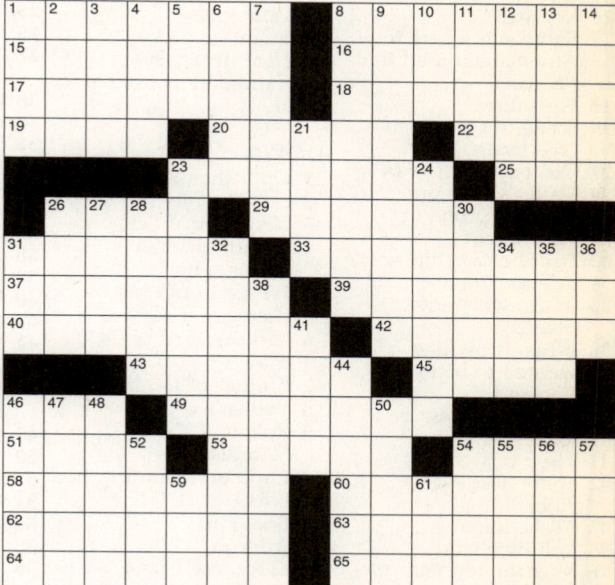

ACROSS

1 Sandwich shop
5 Fitzgerald and others
10 "We're looking for ___ good men"
14 North Carolina college
15 Gettysburg victor
16 Pepsi, for one
17 41339
20 Sweet liqueur
21 Gallic girlfriends
22 Ascot
23 ___-Coburg-Gotha (British royal house)
25 62060
33 Affixed with heat, as a patch
34 ___ number on (mess up)
35 Campground letters
36 20's gangster Bugs ___
37 Each of the numbers in this puzzle's theme
38 Being a copycat
40 They: Fr.
41 ___ Tse-tung
42 Tone deafness
43 49236
47 "Horrors!"
48 Hawaiian wreath
49 Companionless
52 They're handy by phones
57 97352
60 I in "The King and I"
61 Heathen
62 Glow
63 Cheer (for)
64 Lodge member
65 Reading light

DOWN

1 "It was ___ vu all over again"
2 Enthusiasm
3 Graph points
4 Signs, as a contract
5 Sentiment
6 Of the pre-Easter season
7 TV's Ricki
8 Summer refresher
9 Thurmond, e.g.: Abbr.
10 Shrewdness
11 Points of convergence
12 Actress Sommer
13 Streets and avenues
18 Places atop
19 Metered vehicle
23 Ladled-out food
24 Pie ___ mode
25 Copycat
26 On ___ (proceeding successfully)
27 Back: Prefix
28 Pig ___ poke
29 Dialect
30 Approving
31 Ancient Aegean land
32 Late astronomer Carl
37 Like the Marx Brothers
38 More pale
39 Taro dish
41 "Hi ___!" (fan's message)
42 Common solvent
44 Like many diet products
45 Quaker pronoun
46 Actress Massey et al.
49 Slightly open
50 Late-night host
51 ___ consequence (insignificant)
52 Canceled
53 Bells' sound
54 Water, to Joaquin
55 College student's home
56 Rice Krispies sound
58 Engine speed, for short
59 ___ Paulo, Brazil

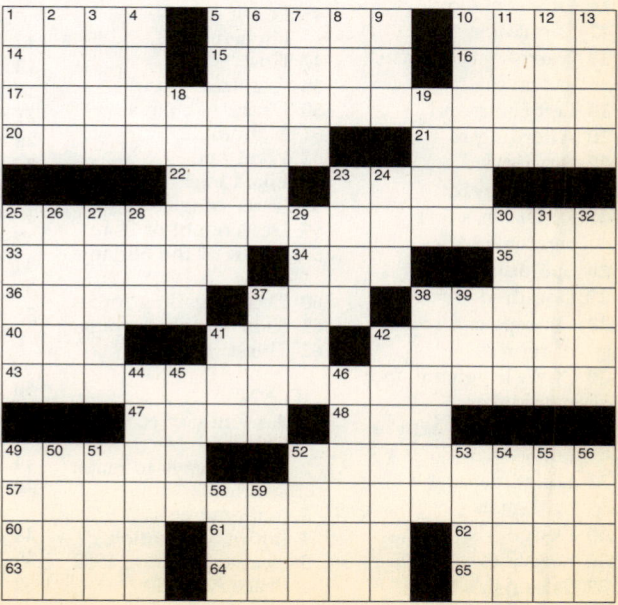

323   by Jonathan Schmalzbach

ACROSS

1 The beans in refried beans
9 Snail ___ (endangered fish)
15 City south of Tijuana
16 Register
17 Battle site where the Athenians routed the Persians
18 Ford flops
19 Scene of Operation Overlord
21 Old paper currency
24 Gaffer's assistant
29 Friends' pronoun
30 Pound part
33 Druidic worship sites
34 Science shop
35 In ___ (properly placed)
36 When Browning wanted to be in England
37 Montana massacre locale
41 Tired of it all
42 Some nest eggs: Abbr.
43 "Take me as ___"
45 Hill dwellers
46 Michael and Peter
48 Sunday seats
49 Site of many flicks
51 Poet Teasdale et al.
52 1781 surrender site
56 Violinist Menuhin
60 1862 Maryland battle site
64 Obliterates
65 Infant
66 Heat up again
67 Candidate Harold et al.

DOWN

1 Opposite of masc.
2 Genetic inits.
3 Neighbor of Leb.
4 Dream girl in a Foster song
5 Where to put the cherry of a sundae
6 "The Wizard of Oz" actor
7 Brother of Jacob
8 Yemen's capital
9 Role in TV's "Hunter"
10 Capp and Gump
11 B.&O. et al.
12 Boot part
13 Add-on
14 "Treasure Island" monogram

20 Peacock network
21 Letters on a Cardinal's cap
22 Where Attila was defeated, 451
23 Religious experience
25 "___ the mornin'!"
26 Obstacle
27 1945 island dogfight site
28 Couturier initials
30 Heating fuel
31 Southwestern Indian
32 Ancient kingdom on the Nile
35 Criterion: Abbr.
36 Cries of delight
38 Exam
39 Like "to be": Abbr.
40 Heating fuel
41 Flock sound
44 What eds. edit
46 Oriental philosophy
47 Hafez al-Assad's land: Abbr.
48 Juries
50 Actress Winona
51 Kind of cheese
53 Okla. neighbor
54 Carpenter's fastener
55 Other: Sp.
56 "Get ___ Ya-Ya's Out!" (Stones album)

57 Poet's "before"
58 Turn left
59 "Land of the free": Abbr.
61 Knot

62 Raggedy doll
63 Brit. sports cars

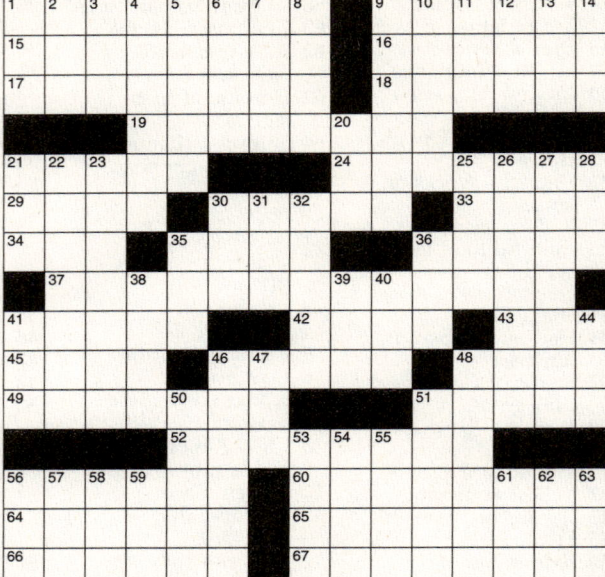

324   by Rand H. Burns

ACROSS

1 French composer Francis
8 Silent "ugh"
15 Kind of eclipse
16 Of a son's love
17 Stipulation
18 Narrow at the base, as leaves
19 Left command
20 Affording rest
22 Broadside
23 Potent leader
25 Letters in a 60's cigarette ad
26 Sub outlet
27 Dog tired
29 Off-repeated sound of reproof
30 W.W. II general and namesakes
31 Euphemistic oath of old
33 Longtime Israeli statesman
35 Dodge
36 Seneca foe
37 Salesman's line
39 1969 Luchino Visconti film, with "The"
42 Dessert introduced in 1897
43 Apply
45 Leave just the kitchen sink?
47 Host
48 "___ Irish Rose"
50 Dance to chants
51 Mauna ___
52 Went ape
54 Liked loads
55 Jesus' tongue
57 Descendant of Esau
59 Coach of the Nittany Lions
60 Countervailing force
61 Kids' support group
62 Thirst

DOWN

1 Ancient city of Cyprus
2 Access ways to major arteries
3 Not anyone's
4 Informal affection
5 ___ Ducommun, 1902 Peace Nobelist

6 Stuffy, in a way
7 Show decisiveness
8 Show dementedness
9 Counter
10 16 magazine profilee
11 Year in Ethelred the Unready's reign
12 Mexican packsaddle
13 Index
14 Fragrant resins
21 Outback denizen
24 Sans animation
26 Offbeat ordinal
28 Same: Prefix
30 Crops
32 Bisected fly
34 70's and 80's cause
37 Via the mouth
38 Capital of the Kazakh Soviet Republic
40 Professorial
41 Waters down
42 Capital of Veracruz
44 Nurse a brewski
46 Communication devices
48 Dress with a flare
49 Event of 4/16/03
52 The going price?

53 Item in a roundup
56 Rendezvoused
58 Hold down, in a way

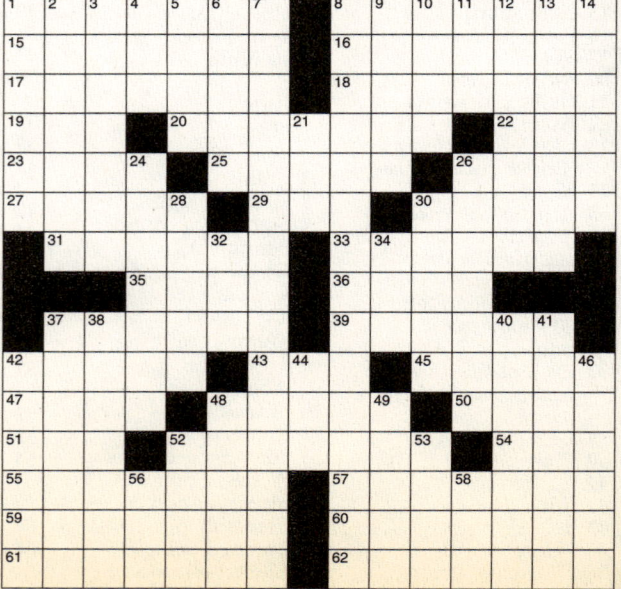

325 by Fred Piscop

ACROSS

1 Like Caspar Milquetoast
6 Yodeling locale
10 Quantities: Abbr.
14 City south of Gainesville
15 Chip's partner
16 Attack of the flu
17 Hook's flag
19 Florence's river
20 Like some shopping
21 Just say no?
23 Grp. founded in 1960
25 Present, for one
26 Antiknock number
30 ___ and hounds
33 Calhoun of "The Texan"
34 Swiss mathematician
35 Son-gun link
38 Dr. Seuss classic
42 Da or ja
43 Onetime pupa
44 Austen's Woodhouse
45 Duchamp subject
46 Gym class, for short
48 "Siddhartha" author
52 Stat starter
54 Craftsperson
57 Short vocal solo
62 "Jurassic Park" beast, for short
63 Ocean denizen
65 It's nothing
66 Split ___
67 Ottoman: Prefix
68 South-of-the-border shouts
69 Catch some Z's
70 Torpedoes

DOWN

1 Axis leader
2 Macintosh screen symbol
3 Type of bonding?
4 Miseries
5 Wright brothers' home
6 See 18-Down
7 Jet follower
8 No contest, e.g.
9 Belgrade resident
10 Cut down
11 Notorious Bugs
12 City near the ruins of Carthage
13 "JFK" director
18 With 6-Down, Ali maneuver
22 "Private Parts" author
24 Locomotive, perhaps
26 Overindulgence
27 Roy Innis's org.
28 Very, in Versailles
29 Parliament vote
31 What's more
32 Davidson's "The Crying Game" costar
34 "Holy cow!"
35 Resistance figures
36 Celebrity
37 Make ___ dash for
39 Dress to the ___
40 Cassowary kin
41 Susan of "L.A. Law"
46 Saucy
47 Block and tackle et al.
48 Little Iodine creator
49 "My Wicked, Wicked Ways" author Flynn
50 Eydie's partner
51 Boxcars
53 Medieval guild
55 Like some cheeses
56 El ___ (ocean current)
58 Lateral lead-in
59 Go sour
60 ___ off (anger)
61 Commotions
64 Cooper's tool

326 by Jonathan Schmalzbach

ACROSS

1 Scroogian comments
5 Grandson of Adam
9 Biblical possessive
12 Sheltered, at sea
13 Spot for Spartacus
14 Carnival ride cry
15 "Ho, ho, ho" fellow
18 Seems
19 Hockey's Bobby, et al.
20 Blue Eagle initials
21 Feasted
23 "My salad days when I was ___": Shakespeare
30 Favorite dog name
31 Closes in on
32 The East
33 Word in a price
35 Volcano spew
36 Deli cry
37 Cause for liniment
38 Not-so-prized fur
40 River inlet
41 Bucky Dent slew it at Fenway Park in 1978
45 Zorba portrayer
46 Tennis call
47 Sulk angrily
48 Many Dickens stories, originally
52 Civil War currency
56 Merit
57 Nintendo hero
58 One of the Simpsons
59 Sot's problems
60 Jot
61 Prepares the dinner table

DOWN

1 Mexican peninsula
2 Crooked
3 Maids
4 Moon goddess
5 Misreckons
6 Born
7 Indivisible
8 ___ Marcos, TX
9 Arid region of India
10 Chick watchers
11 Thus far
13 Take with ___ of salt
14 Utility employee
16 It comes in balls
17 Bad news at a talent show
21 "Bull ___" (Costner film)
22 Psyche parts
23 Word in a monarch's name
24 Extent
25 National treasuries
26 Tidy up
27 Teen heartthrob Priestley
28 Undeliverable letter, in post-office talk
29 13th-century invader
34 Monastery head
38 D.C. legislator
39 El Greco's "View of ___"
42 Nothing: Fr.
43 Pianist Peter
44 Part of rock's C.S.N. & Y.
47 Brotherhood
48 Comic bit
49 "I cannot tell ___"
50 Ultimate
51 Madrid Mmes.
52 Dropout's degree: Abbr.
53 Status letters, perhaps
54 "Say ___"
55 Dernier ___

327 by Harvey Estes

ACROSS

1 Espresso
7 Pocketbook material, maybe
14 Opens
16 Make too many eggs?
17 More than dull
18 Juicy morsels
19 Cabbies
20 Valuable deposits
22 Gymnast's need
23 Ticks off
24 Tea type
25 Deft
26 Zip
27 Point count bidding pioneer
28 Amaze
29 Flips out
31 Undiluted
33 Cycle starter
34 Crowd noise
35 Squirrels' sustenance
38 Game fad of the 50's
42 Shade of white
43 Pull strings
45 Preschooler
46 Standard
47 Religious devotion
48 "Star Trek" Klingon
49 Sphere opening
50 "Hans Brinker" author
51 "Madonna With Saints" artist
52 Comic Dick
54 Parasite
56 Activist actor
57 Clothing, informally
58 Lineups
59 Idi Amin, e.g.

DOWN

1 Boston cardinal Richard
2 Least great Great Lake
3 Spot for Howdy Dowdy
4 Y's
5 Crimson rivals
6 Expansion wing
7 They're up for discussion
8 Just like ewe?
9 Bolsheviks
10 Ball
11 Invitation to ride
12 Piece of junk mail
13 Kind of bar
15 Stern
21 ___ out (just manage)
24 Visit unexpectedly
25 Islands welcome
27 Game-show host Moore
28 Blunt
30 Gale of "Oh! Susanna"
32 Cartoon crime-fighter
35 It surrounds a pit
36 Popular cigars
37 Eight-footers
38 Most adorable
39 Makeshift
40 One cursed by Farragut
41 Initially
42 "Well, ___!"
44 Stocking stuffer
47 Logroller, in a way
48 Cellar contents
50 Unit of force
51 Wives' tales
53 Clock-resetting abbr.
55 Degree of distinction

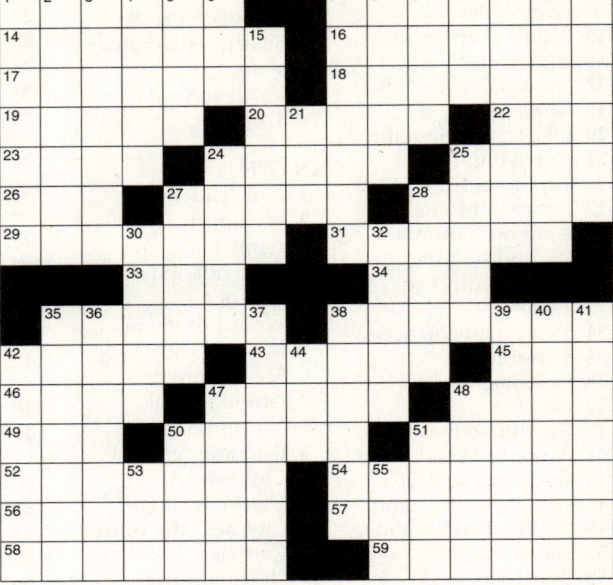

328 by Daniel R. Stark

ACROSS

1 Kind of sleeve
7 In the cards
15 Symphony written for Napoleon
16 Furniture polish ingredient
17 Spreads the news
18 With no exceptions
19 Poet's contraction
20 One who's squeezed in
22 Mauna ___
23 Rough it
25 Seating areas
26 Say truly
27 Up a ___
29 Kittenish response
30 Fiery dance
31 Team originally called the Colt .45s
33 Guard
35 Not clerical
37 Split
38 Founder of Detroit
42 Smith of sorts
46 Prince Valiant's wife
47 Fanatic
49 Succinct
50 Scream and shout
51 Traveling aids
53 Business letter encl.
54 Actor Vigoda
55 Quiescent
57 Poison ___
58 Nymph changed into a bear
60 Like Don Juan
62 Added up
63 Drill
64 Stonecutter
65 Less muscle-bound

DOWN

1 Daphne du Maurier novel
2 In ___ (behind)
3 Bon vivant
4 Year in Claudius's reign
5 Romans preceder
6 Countryish, in a way
7 Made a toast
8 Critic
9 A shaman uses them
10 Dull fellow
11 Jane Fonda farce "___ Wednesday"
12 Library item
13 Family tree
14 ___ of Aquitaine
21 Computer capacity, for short
24 Plant growth medium
26 Cloaks
28 Zoo critter
30 Adoxy
32 Part of R.S.V.P.
34 Small number
36 Kitchen container
38 Cat with tufted ears
39 Creek Indian land
40 Unfold
41 Charge
43 Wall hanging
44 Gist
45 Join again
48 Mai ___
51 Goddess of the hearth
52 Herbal alcoholic drink
55 Part that's thrown away
56 Catch hold of
59 Him, in Marseilles
61 Inspector Van ___ Valk (literary detective)

329 · by Gregory E. Paul

ACROSS

1. "Julius Caesar" role
5. Shall not, old-style
10. Actress Drescher of "The Nanny"
14. The third man
15. Red, white or blue
16. San ___ (Riviera resort)
17. Uncle Ben's dish
18. Rod Stewart's ex
19. "What's ___ for me?"
20. James Cook ship
22. Hardy heroine
23. FedEx rival
24. Words after "Oh yeah?"
26. Smiles smugly
30. Doe's mate
32. "Tippy" boat
33. Henry Hudson ship
38. Tough-guy actor Ray
39. Corday's victim
40. Gen. Robt. ___
41. William Bradford ship
43. Sports facility
44. Charged particles
45. Shorebird
46. Indiana college
50. Coach Parseghian
51. A Great Lake
52. Sir Francis Drake ship
59. Breakfast order
60. Neeson and O'Flaherty
61. German-Polish border river
62. Avec's opposite
63. Stan's friend, in old films
64. Tableland
65. First word of Massachusetts's motto
66. Lawman Earp
67. "___ as 1, 2, 3"

DOWN

1. Mystery writer John Dickson ___
2. He had an Irish Rose
3. Private eyes, in slang
4. Butterine
5. Diving ducks
6. Romance novelist Victoria et al.
7. Jai ___
8. Taboo
9. Conduct, as business
10. Sen. Hollings
11. Extend, as a subscription
12. Some Mennonites
13. Untrue
21. One of the Gospels
25. Swelled head
26. Ripoff
27. ___ fides (bad faith): Lat.
28. ___ 500
29. Heliport site, often
30. Fillies' fathers
31. Moscow ruler
33. Sunup
34. ___ Beach, Fla.
35. Hgt.
36. Artist Magritte
37. Vintage
39. Clair de lune
42. Tell a whopper
43. A. A. Milne's first name
45. Coffee-maker switch
46. V-formation fliers
47. Sidewalk grinder's instrument
48. "Stop" and "Merge," e.g.
49. Novelist Hermann
50. Fess up
53. Unctuous
54. Carol syllables
55. "Fourth base"
56. Notion
57. An Untouchable
58. Cart

330 · by Bob Klahn

ACROSS

1. Practical jokes
5. School founded by Henry VI
9. Sharp-smelling
14. For men ___ (stag)
15. "Kon-Tiki" craft
16. Haunted house noises
17. They're easily bruised
18. The ___ of the party
19. Leaning slightly, as a ship
20. Passenger restraints
22. Sudden shock
23. Change, as a hem
24. Paramount workplace
25. Path of Discovery
27. Island near Australia
29. White weasel
30. Followed tenaciously
32. Rainbows
33. Last mile in a car warranty, often
38. University founder Cornell
39. Shops
40. Be that as it may
42. Painstaking
47. TV host Gibbons
48. Cleopatra's biter
49. Artoo-___
50. Gottfried, in "Lohengrin"
51. Tour outline
53. Tour of duty
54. Nil, in Seville
55. Chorister
56. Eyelashes
57. Spanish crowd?
58. Haymarket Square event
59. Football's Papa Bear
60. "___ Grand Night for Singing"
61. Comic Carvey

DOWN

1. Attacks
2. Actress Lansbury
3. Is a bad winner
4. Word with solar or nervous
5. ___ Stanley Gardner
6. Firefly component?
7. Leading early in the race
8. Military experiment, perhaps
9. Key of Beethoven's Seventh
10. Play-by-play announcer's partner
11. Front-row racing fan
12. 1992 thriller "Basic ___"
13. Aug. clock setting
21. Diamond Jim
26. Musician/sportscaster John
28. "___ fast, buster!"
29. Car bomb?
31. "Medea" playwright
33. "I ___ Fine" (Beatles hit)
34. Russian newspaper
35. Voluntary capacity
36. Dar es Salaam's land
37. Stage comment
41. Christmas bell ringers
43. Actor Depardieu
44. It may be last on the list
45. Boxer Ken
46. Corolla, e.g.
48. "___ a stinker?": Bugs Bunny
52. Cape Canaveral acronym
53. Univ., e.g.

 by Jay Livingston

ACROSS

1 6-Down finales
6 Corn waste
9 Conductor Riccardo
13 Ancient Greek marketplace
14 ___ polloi
15 Physically squelch
16 1. e4; e5 2. Nf3; Nc6 3. Bg5
19 Detective's assignment
20 Sugar suffix
21 Actor Estevez
22 Cousin of "Mayday!"
23 Cut in thirds
24 Neighbor of a knight
28 Name of 12 popes
29 "So long"
30 Stocking material
31 Debussy's had quite an afternoon
35 1. e4; c5
38 Frozen dew
39 Steelmaker's need
40 Property taxes in London
41 Lotto variant
42 Sherwood, e.g.
43 Doctorow best seller

47 Lose energy
48 Filmdom's May
49 Here, in Hyères
50 ___ even keel
54 1. e4; e5 2. Nf3; Nc6 3. Nc3; Nf6
57 Playwright William et al.
58 "___ is the winter . . ."
59 Wiser's companion
60 Kickoff props
61 Gun lobby inits.
62 Relative of 41-Across

DOWN

1 ___ Antony
2 Juárez water
3 Hellman's were in the attic
4 Gardner of mysteries
5 ___ Paulo
6 This puzzle's theme
7 Seep
8 Life story
9 Some skirts
10 Practical
11 Pick-me-up
12 Gold bar
15 Interstate haulers

17 One of the decks
18 Old-fashioned wig
22 Musical genre
23 Mark for mañana
24 Big party
25 Prefix meaning peculiar
26 Film director Vittorio De ___
27 One next in line
28 Suspiciously left, 50's style
30 France's ___-et-Loire department
31 Dread
32 First chips
33 Exploits
34 Place for eggs
36 Onetime refrigerant suppliers
37 Tadpole, eventually
41 Twists in a line
42 ___ accompli
43 Change the equipment
44 Solo
45 Pressure measurer
46 Michelins, e.g.
47 Unstressed vowel
49 Frankenstein's helper

50 Give the eye
51 Nothing, to a Nuyorican
52 The last word
53 Famed fiddler
55 Hotel
56 Weep

---

by Judith Perry

ACROSS

1 L.A.-to-Seattle dir.
4 Afrikaner
8 Explorer's aids
12 Honolulu's island
14 Lofty home
15 Pavarotti selection
16 Gyrate
17 Magnificent Julia?
19 Recalcitrant Lucille?
21 Duck's gait
22 Master of unsavory film roles
23 Geometric shapes
24 Johns of "Mary Poppins"
26 Out-of-sorts Clara?
30 Renaissance fiddle
31 Cowl
32 French miss, for short
33 Black cuckoo
34 Self-absorbed person
37 "___ hail!"
38 "___ Breckinridge"
40 Miner's quest
41 Spanish soldier-hero
43 Blue Jeremy?
45 Volleyball shots
46 X-ray units

47 Scale
48 Vacillate
51 Happy Eliot?
54 Coy Joey?
56 Sea bird
57 Yugoslav hero
58 Isn't upright
59 Attracted
60 TV problem
61 Like the White Rabbit
62 Longing

DOWN

1 Snack
2 California wine region
3 Spinning Larry?
4 Uncle Miltie
5 Kind of surgery
6 German article
7 Sunburned James?
8 Muslim messianic belief
9 Nonfertile
10 Disagreeable person
11 "Smooth Operator" singer
13 Ruined
14 Culture mediums

18 What lots have lots of
20 Fanny of vaudeville
23 ___-Rivières, Que.
24 Lab weights
25 Austrian singer
26 Pigeon coops
27 Mournful Chuck?
28 Dragon puppet
29 Fuses
31 Satanic feature
35 Angelic George?
36 Not too hot
39 Fliers' performance
42 Delineated
44 Postwar Austrian chancellor
45 Rebuffs
47 Splitting image
48 Coll. entrance exams
49 Leprechaun's turf
50 Outer: Prefix
51 Steps leading down to the Ganges
52 Snick and ___
53 Stitched
55 Vast expanse

333   by Fran and Lou Sabin

ACROSS

1 Food maven Greene
5 Kind of mouth
10 Field food
14 Cuba or Puerto Rico
15 Live to ___ old age
16 Scrabble piece
17 King of Corn
19 Eftsoon
20 Straight
21 Wandered
23 Having new faith
25 Easy pace
26 ___ Bryant Ford
28 Beautifully imaginative
31 ___ Calais
34 Singer Stookey
36 Wishing site
37 Former auto inits.
38 Supermarket gizmo
41 It's sometimes crushed
42 Wisdom
44 Certain G.M. car
45 ___ in the bucket
47 Victimize
49 Alabama march town
51 Proceeds
53 Harvestman
56 Waders
59 Some computers
61 Money-changer's cut
62 Purse item
64 Powell or Scott: Abbr.
65 "Dallas" miss
66 Basso Pinza
67 Don't strike!
68 Scare off
69 Ophelia or Laertes, e.g.

DOWN

1 "The Whales of August" actress
2 According to
3 Type type
4 Superior bottom
5 Ballplayer's goal, with "the"
6 Aztec treasure
7 Salon job
8 "Lulu," e.g.
9 Have another bite
10 Essentials
11 It's found at the end of a lane
12 Natural balm
13 Tape
18 Diminishes
22 Nigerian native
24 Asian kingdom
27 Territory
29 Fictional ensign
30 Jockey's need
31 Feeler
32 Love, to Livy
33 Twisty-leafed tree
35 Big name in auto racing
39 Looked the other way
40 New Jersey's ___ Mountains
43 Metal fastener
46 Spotted
48 Plastic ___ Band
50 Calaveras competitor
52 Out of fashion
54 Higgins's prodigy
55 Ancient fly catcher
56 "Macbeth" trio
57 "___ Ideas" (1950 hit)
58 Bank deposit
60 Camera device
63 Golfer's position

---

334   by Matt Gaffney

ACROSS

1 Some
5 Briefing site
15 Famous 25-Down
16 1992 resort opening
17 Pearl Buck heroine
18 Calming words
19 Even
21 Spy novelist Deighton
22 Ancient greetings
23 Are
24 Hardly respectful
26 U2 producer Brian
27 ___ passim (common footnote)
28 Frequented spot
30 Kind of nerve
32 Did some editing
33 Tevye's wife in "Fiddler on the Roof"
34 Immune system members
36 Aloha State Senator
38 Police drama climax
39 Lock
40 Well-preserved leader
41 Lurk
42 Ex-employer of Aldrich Ames
45 Ledger abbr.
46 Pale
48 ___ friends
50 Angling need
52 Suffers from
53 Like many starlets
54 Utopian
57 Subject, usually
58 Noted curfew breaker
59 Alcott's Jo, for one
60 Fat city
61 So very

DOWN

1 Makes amends
2 1985 Neil Simon play setting
3 Type type
4 Mutes, with "down"
5 Dampens
6 "Whazzat?"
7 Whence the Kennedys
8 How some things are laid
9 Perfect spots
10 Success
11 Part of the Dept. of Labor
12 Without balance
13 Courtyard entertainment
14 Dump, e.g.
20 South Atlantic island
24 Pleads
25 Nationality beginning 1929
29 Exclusively
31 Brock and Ferrigno
32 First name in 50's TV
34 Often-vilified group
35 Rec. centers
36 Press
37 Powerful advertising word
38 Oscar-winning Jodie Foster role
39 Planking support
41 Enterprise weapon
42 English complexion
43 Like good pianos
44 42-Across workers
47 Tee, e.g.
49 ___ work
51 Kenny Rogers #1 song
53 Ella Fitzgerald forte
55 Late Secretary Aspin
56 ___ de Noirmoutier, France

335   by Norma Steinberg

ACROSS
1 Event for Cinderella
5 Father
9 Father
12 Jai ___
13 Washington's successor
15 Composer Bartók
16 Second man to set foot on the moon
18 Soothsayer's aid
19 With 60-Across, author of "The Joy Luck Club"
20 Whitish
21 Beethoven's Third
23 Marathon
24 Consider
25 Covet
28 Ad for the lovelorn
32 "___ think so!"
33 Currency in Capri, once
34 Kind of model
35 Chinese dynasty
36 Belief
37 Quick lunch
38 And others: Abbr.
39 Ruin's partner
40 Pondered
41 Like a nag
43 Also-rans
44 Eyebrow position
45 Maritime stop
46 Color à la the Grateful Dead
49 Filmdom's Vittorio De ___
50 Ebenezer's exclamation
53 Not busy
54 TV, movies, comics, etc.
57 Shakespearean king
58 Fires
59 Parched
60 See 19-Across
61 Observe Yom Kippur, in a way
62 Like Superman's vision

DOWN
1 Ali ___ of children's fiction
2 Reuniongoer, for short
3 Slothful
4 Actress Taylor
5 Regal home
6 Confuse
7 Shave
8 "___ my brother's keeper?"
9 Moore of "Ghost"
10 Actor Baldwin
11 "Two Years Before the Mast" author
14 Look down on
15 Like a volatile economy
17 In pieces
22 ___ ipsa loquitur
23 Cabal's head
24 Hollywood's Bo
25 March of ___
26 Novelist Wharton
27 Submarine system
28 "Collar"
29 Cacophony
30 Transform
31 City on the Aire
33 Dogwalker's line
36 Arm muscle
40 Virtuous
42 Kind of humor
43 Migratory insect
45 Guitar player's implements
46 Pinball no-no
47 Brainstorm
48 Panache
49 Org. that shelters strays
50 Duelist of 1804
51 Song from Plácido
52 Actress Lamarr
55 Bumpkin
56 Price add-on

336   by Andrew Goldstein

ACROSS
1 Confused
5 Lake in Africa
9 Detest
14 Carpet cutter's calculation
15 Prefix with dynamic
16 Solo
17 "The Gift of the ___"
18 Soft cheese
19 Distinctive glows
20 Where a student may solve a problem
23 "What I Am" singer Brickell
24 Actor Lukas of "Witness"
25 "Fat" Cosby character
27 Using the VCR
30 Marconi's field
32 Hearty brew
33 Enter, as a car
35 Frontiersman in a coonskin cap
39 Party line?
41 Fore's counterpart
42 Rubber hub
43 Domingo's voice
44 Skirt feature
46 Ike's W.W. II domain
47 Slack
49 Feels nostalgia for
51 Honesty
54 Shortly
55 God of war
56 Obsequious student
62 Defeats decisively
64 First name in fashion
65 "Big Mouth" Martha
66 The Pentateuch
67 Tallies
68 Balanced
69 Atlanta university
70 Track contest
71 Pause in the music

DOWN
1 Lion's trusting companion
2 Kind of hygiene
3 Electronic game giant
4 Chinese discipline
5 Sauerkraut, essentially
6 Grinders
7 Song for Madame Butterfly
8 Not an idler
9 Bond rating
10 Place for a student's essay
11 Crowd
12 Walking ___ (elated)
13 Put back to zero
21 Jumpy one
22 Pops
26 Wine poured to honor a deity
27 Diplomat's specialty
28 Healing plant
29 Teller's partner in magic
30 Biathlon equipment
31 Kitty starter
34 A little night music
36 Mineral rocks
37 Memorandum
38 Slaughter on the ballfield
40 Reward for a student
45 Surrounded by
48 Sphere
50 Nighttime noisemaker
51 A la ___
52 "___ with a View"
53 Prefix with surgeon or transmitter
54 Stockholm native
57 Wander
58 Ye ___ Shoppe
59 Stat for a goalie
60 Peepers
61 1996 Tony-winning musical
63 Timid

337 by Manny Nosowsky

ACROSS

1 Salmon variety
8 Stick in a case
15 Not in the store yet
16 Puts down
17 Some discomfort
18 Available, as money
19 Up
20 ___-square (odds calculation)
22 Solution strength, in Surrey
23 Wear well
24 Child supporter?
26 Pulitzer-winning writer on Vietnam ___ Sheehan
27 Kind of agent
28 Vibrate, as with heat waves
30 Tiny angular measurement
31 Snow lander
33 60's activist
35 Winter warmer
37 City on the Puyallup River
40 Julian the ___
44 Buff
45 32 laps in many pools
47 Country in N.A.
48 Constellation animal
50 Coeur d'___, Idaho
51 Bust maker
52 Best Actor of 1981
54 "...far ___ can see"
55 Compatriot of Golda
56 Made available
58 Expands
60 Like the West of yore
61 Just developing
62 Heart
63 Ball bearings, e.g.

DOWN

1 Some equatorial denizens
2 For fun
3 Easter Island statues, e.g.
4 Big cheese processor
5 Rewrite
6 "You bet!"
7 Building
8 Be fidgety
9 Barbarian
10 90°
11 Dizzy
12 1993 Hutton/Boyle thriller
13 Husband of Catherine de Medici
14 Actress Parsons of "Bonnie and Clyde"
21 Order to a chauffeur
24 Woodstock group, 1969
25 Area at each end of a basketball court
28 Replay technique
29 Step before spin-dry
32 Military-political grp. since 1964
34 "Hey, there!"
36 Court papers
37 Chocolate treat
38 Outdoor light shows
39 Rather beat?
41 Acquisitive one
42 "Lad, a Dog" author
43 Leaves out
46 Run out
49 H, e.g., in the literary world
51 Kind of word
53 Major fueling station for the Suez Canal
55 Strainer
57 L.A. campus
59 Twaddle

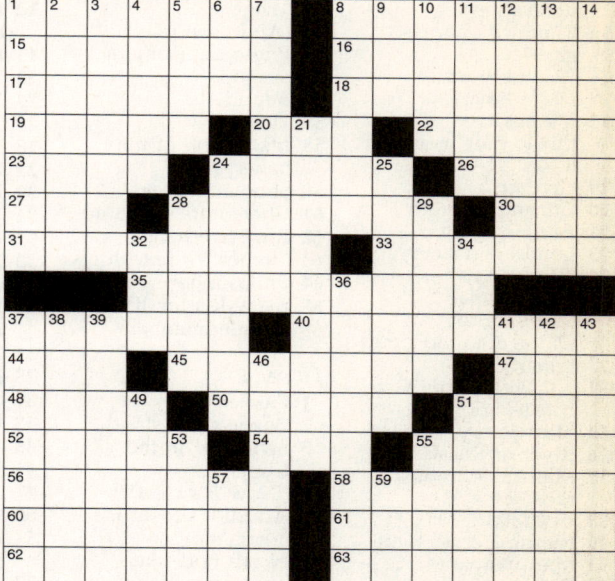

338 by Elizabeth C. Gorski

ACROSS

1 Anesthetize, in a way
4 Some chain clothing stores
8 Video game hub
14 Play the part
15 Zone
16 Stops the tape temporarily
17 "Little" extraterrestrials
19 Passé
20 Had a bug
21 Inspirationalist Norman Vincent ___
23 Before, in verse
24 Home on the Black Sea
26 Smart-alecky
28 Pop duo with the album "Swamp Ophelia"
34 Reply to a masher
38 Satellite ___
39 Bunk
40 Actress Anderson
41 Newton or Stern
43 Actress Thurman and others
44 Small choir
46 Outfielder's cry
47 Oct. precursor
48 Drinks with gin, Cointreau and lemon juice
51 Greeting at sea
52 Undignified landing
56 Hardly Mr. Right
59 Facilitates
62 Unpaid factory worker
64 "All ___!"
66 Some Gainsborough forgeries
68 Ice cream parlor order
69 Two-wheeler
70 Sometime theater funder: Abbr.
71 Be at
72 French holy women: Abbr.
73 Blow it

DOWN

1 Crazy (over)
2 Pungent
3 Inscribed column
4 Leader called Mahatma
5 Tattoo place
6 Coop sound
7 Psychologically all there
8 Noted Harlem hot spot, with "The"
9 Durham's twin city
10 Bossy's chew
11 Connors opponent
12 ___ John
13 Isabella d'___ (Titian subject)
18 Continental trading org.
22 Khyber Pass traveler
25 1941 Glenn Miller chart topper "You ___"
27 Reverent
29 Lets down
30 "Let me repeat..."
31 Where the Vatican is
32 Giant hop
33 Method: Abbr.
34 Leisurely
35 Ness, for one
36 One doing a con job?
37 Michelangelo masterpiece
42 So-so grades
45 Iran's capital
49 Stinking rich
50 Shopping binges
53 Defensive tennis shot
54 Have ___ to pick
55 One who's not playing seriously
56 Home for la familia
57 Go up against
58 Word of warning
60 Drops off
61 Cut
63 Pre-1917 ruler
65 Fruit juice
67 Hawaiian music maker

339 · by Fred Piscop

ACROSS
1 Indian title of respect
6 Love handles, essentially
10 Gad about
14 "Fur ___" (Beethoven dedication)
15 Clarence Thomas's garb
16 Second word of many limericks
17 It's not as threatening as it looks
19 Give up
20 Current strength
21 Antiaircraft fire
23 London lavatory
24 "Rocky ___"
25 ___ A Sketch (drawing toy)
26 Old age, in old times
27 Italian cheese
31 ___ Major (southern constellation)
35 Mat victory
36 River of Russia
37 Man ___ (famous race horse)
38 Jive talkin'
40 Running shoe name
41 Marquand's Mr. ___
42 Rotter
43 Does some lawn work
44 Disappear through camouflage
46 Mineral springs
48 Tended to the weeds
49 "High ___" (Anderson play)
50 Photo ___ (camera sessions)
53 Repudiate
56 Horrid
58 It's put off at the bakery
59 Shooter's target
61 Change for a C-note
62 Roof overhang
63 Homes for hatchlings
64 Philosopher
65 Exceeded the limit
66 Gaggle members

DOWN
1 Flower part
2 Bowie's last stand
3 Swimmer in the Congo
4 "Now it's clear!"
5 Additions to an ice cream sundae
6 North Pole-like
7 Theater section
8 Burrows of the theater
9 Chewing out
10 Geologist
11 ___-Day (vitamin brand)
12 Australian hard-rock band
13 Like a milquetoast
18 Party game pin-on
22 New Deal prog.
25 "___ go bragh"
28 Math subject
29 Money brought in
30 Pub quaffs
31 Toothed item
32 Roll call misser
33 Hoops great Archibald
34 Lou Gehrig nickname, with "the"
35 Seat cover
38 Arts' partner
39 Touch down
43 Bringing in
45 ___ Jones
46 Hung around
47 Splendor
50 Corpulent plus
51 Draws, as a line on a graph
52 Good judgment
53 Pencil-and-paper game
54 Brainstorm
55 Carol
56 Garroway of early TV
57 "The African Queen" scriptwriter
60 Drink like Fido

340 · by Bryant White

ACROSS
1 Highlands tongue
5 Name of two former Supreme Court Justices
10 London's Old ___ theater
13 Maximum bet
15 Image: Prefix
16 Constellation near Pavo
17 Digital music maker, in old Rome?
19 War site, informally
20 Grand
21 Give ___ whirl
22 Suffix with depart
25 Germany's Tirpitz, for one: Abbr.
26 Irritant
29 Maison window
31 First duke of Normandy
32 100 centimes
34 Coral reef predators
35 Actress Ullmann, in old Rome?
37 Discard
40 Soft silk fabric used for linings
44 Actress Gillette
45 More bryophytic
46 Sailor, in British slang
49 Clinch
50 French marshal Michel
51 Election-night abbr.
52 7-Up alternative
54 Ingested
55 007's boss, in old Rome?
60 Cologne's loc.
61 Imaginative tales
62 Boris Godunov's daughter
63 Football Hall-of-Famer Healey et al.
64 Used an abacus
65 Ceraceous

DOWN
1 Tolkien's Legolas, e.g.
2 1947 Hope-Crosby destination
3 Dallas inst.
4 Healer at Valhalla
5 Soother
6 Elec. abbr.
7 Capone rival
8 Anoint, old-style
9 Staff
10 Kind of bean
11 With a temper
12 Mustangs race them
14 Overwrought
18 Hang glider's aid
22 "X-Files" phenomenon
23 Stimpy's buddy
24 67.5°
27 They're saved in trunks
28 Actress Liz
30 Exhausted
33 Pitcher Young et al.
34 Rare-book binding
36 Hungry
37 Storm
38 Approved
39 Nervousness
41 "Delta of Venus" author
42 Shoe width
43 Hold in judgment
47 Land ___
48 Political analyst's topic
53 Cigar tip
55 Wood sorrel
56 Put in stitches
57 Bibliographic suffix
58 Prohibit
59 1878 Kentucky Derby winner ___ Star

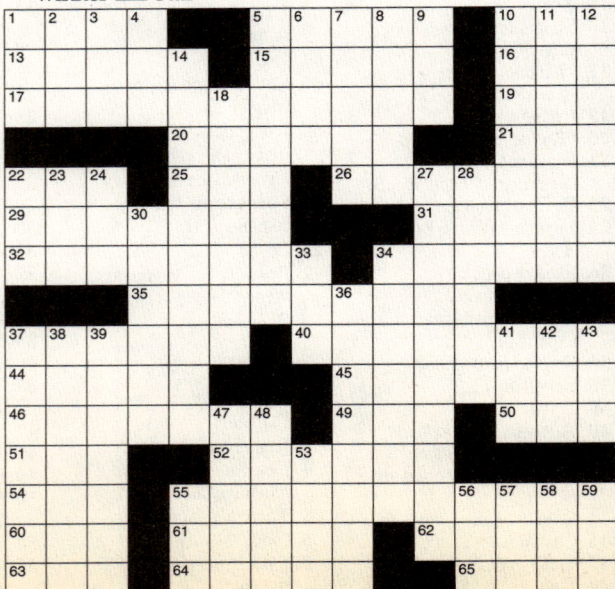

341 by Sidney L. Robbins

ACROSS

1 Women's mag
5 One-liners
9 Soccer legend
13 Egg-shaped
14 TV oldie "Green ___"
16 Vientiane's land
17 Building code requirement
19 Prod
20 Pilgrim John
21 Most pleasant
23 Madam's mate
25 July 4, 1776, e.g.
26 Opposite of vert.
29 W. Hemisphere org.
32 Mr. Arnaz
34 The lowdown on dancing?
36 Kind of car or sandwich
38 Use a crayon
41 Ratted (on)
42 Armbone
43 By oneself
44 Writer Hunter
45 Hauls
46 Stimulate, as curiosity
47 Measure out
48 Provence city
50 Stalin ruled it
52 "The Bridge of San Luis ___"
53 Stephen of "The Crying Game"
54 Late tennis V.I.P.
57 Dawn goddess
59 Lustrous fabric
61 "Faust," for one
65 Shocked sound
67 Summer treat
70 Matures
71 Go 1-1 in a doubleheader
72 Letterman's "Top Ten," e.g.
73 Model's position
74 "Auld Lang ___"
75 Not so much

DOWN

1 Divan
2 "Hear no ___ . . ."
3 Cooking fat
4 Hightails it
5 Oil alternative
6 U.N.C. and U.Va. grp.
7 In a lofty style
8 Artist's brown
9 +
10 Bulldozer
11 Captain's record
12 Language suffix
15 Church offshoot
18 Arthurian lady
22 Slippery one
24 Sum up
27 Not quite spherical
28 Los Angeles motorist King
29 Of the eyes
30 Magnetism
31 Shades
33 By oneself: Prefix
35 News entry
37 Home port
39 Burden
40 Hall-of-Famer Pee Wee
49 Was in session
51 Motel vacancy
55 Does needlework
56 Mounds
58 "How do you ___ relief?"
60 Church nook
62 Writer Wiesel
63 Flagmaker Betsy
64 Picnic pests
65 Cumberland, e.g.
66 In the past
68 One for Wilhelm
69 Numbered rd.

342 by Richard Silvestri

ACROSS

1 Honeydew kin
7 Fatherless fellow
11 Crow's feat?
14 Slurred over a syllable
15 Ring happening
16 Part of a flick?
17 College study
19 NNW antithesis
20 Gerund maker
21 It's sold in bars
22 Wrangle
23 Screech, for one
25 Bit for Fermi
26 Stories connector
27 Bring in the crops
29 In an evil way
31 Stealthily
33 Flying Peter
34 Carry
35 Type of tiger
38 Religious sch.
39 Reflected on
41 Abandoned
45 Penny or Lois
46 See eye to eye
47 Hertz alternative
48 Lose (to)
49 Way out
50 Slow down from a run
51 Start of the St. Ives riddle
53 Fleur-de-___
54 Trinidad and Tobago's capital
58 Exaggerator's suffix
59 Philharmonic instrument
60 Monopoly card
61 Hog haven
62 Obscene
63 Perfumed, in a way

DOWN

1 Animation frame
2 "Thrilla in Manila" victor
3 Ssspeak like thisss
4 Arabian Sea gulf
5 Glacier Bay sight
6 Orthodontist's org.
7 Seafood order
8 Scale opening
9 Jam ingredient
10 Short range?
11 One of the Magi
12 Lambaste
13 Light rowboat
18 Skin softener
22 Baseball's Old Professor
23 El Dorado treasure
24 Travel
25 "___ Goes By"
26 Kiosk
28 Piece of eight
30 Loses one's balance?
32 Annapolis freshman
35 Fish like a mackerel
36 Spirited steeds
37 Letterman rival
39 Swiveled
40 Drops in the morning
41 Soup scoops
42 Self-centered sort
43 Snowman of song
44 Cultivating tool
50 Option for Hamlet
51 "Off the Court" author
52 Stretch over
54 D.C. figure
55 TV watchdog
56 Rocks in a glass
57 Actor Beatty

ACROSS

1 Send a Dear John letter
5 Antarctica's ___ Coast
10 Stain on Santa
14 Medicinal herb
15 "Golden" song
16 Transportation Secretary Federico
17 Prefix with bucks or bytes
18 Ad: Part 1
20 Ad: Part 2
22 And others
23 Lennon's lady
24 Clinches
25 Ad: Part 3
28 Ad: Part 4
33 Beats
34 Judge
35 Dogpatch diminutive
36 Cabbies' credentials: Abbr.
37 Jabbed
38 Radio knob
39 And so forth, for short
40 Singular person
41 Gladiator's place
42 Medium in which this puzzle's ad appeared
45 Furnishes for a time
46 Twilights, poetically
47 Richmond was its cap.
48 Queen Victoria's husband
51 Ad: Part 5
55 Sponsor of the ad
57 Snead and Spade
59 15 miles of song
60 Floor pieces
61 Wasatch Range state
62 Prepared to drive
63 Unclogs
64 Glazier's section

DOWN

1 Predicament
2 "___ a song go..."
3 CBS's eye, e.g.
4 Genteel snack spots
5 Topper's first name
6 Wings
7 Peculiar: Prefix
8 Clear
9 Downcast
10 Quite an impression
11 Trompe l'___
12 "Dedicated to the ___ Love"
13 Noted Chaplin follower
19 Shoshoneans
21 Responsibility
24 Buries
25 Shiftless one
26 ___ Bandito of commercials
27 New Mexico's state flower
28 Offenses
29 "The Old ___ Bucket"
30 Martian or Venusian
31 Article of food
32 Actress Raines and others
37 Indicates
38 Concocts
41 In addition
43 Adjudged
44 "Buona ___" (Italian greeting)
47 Judit Polgar's game
48 Help a crook
49 Bait
50 Spreadable cheese
51 Tempest
52 Browning locale
53 "Do I dare to ___ peach?": Eliot
54 Muscat's land
56 Fashionable
58 That girl

ACROSS

1 Horoscope
6 Pachacuti was one
10 Safety specifications
14 Personal care workers
15 Dickensian orphan
16 Stormy greeting?
17 Fat City dwelling?
20 Loudness unit
21 Jots
22 Actor Davis
23 Gatsby portrayer, with 36-Across
25 Just those of Juan things?
27 Outwit, in Fat City?
33 Was a busybody
34 Gibbons
35 Common Market money
36 See 23-Across
37 Warp
39 Parts of matches
40 Unstop, poetically
41 Germany's ___ Mountains
42 Munchkins
43 Fat City office attire?
47 Bearing
48 Inspector
49 Sphere, e.g.
52 Paraphernalia
54 Final words
58 Be insincere, in Fat City?
61 Crow's-nest cry
62 "Little Sheba" playwright
63 Yellow-fever mosquito
64 "Ladders" in hose
65 Turned gray
66 Take by force

DOWN

1 1983 Tony musical
2 "Farmer in the Dell" syllables
3 Arabian Peninsula port
4 Prepared leftovers
5 General on Chinese menus
6 Bonkers
7 Requisite
8 Zoom-lens shots
9 Actor-director Kjellin
10 Ballroom glide
11 Boating couple
12 Actress Conn of "Benson"
13 Besides
18 Bountiful's state
19 Despoils
24 Old Ford
26 Printer's mark
27 Plot mathematically
28 Place to get down from
29 Fabric akin to felt
30 Chaucer pilgrim
31 Eightsome
32 Ado
33 Novelist's concern
37 Race's end
38 Using extortion
39 Barely mention
41 Johanna Spyri classic
42 Canton finish
44 Dickinson and Brontë
45 Halted
46 Rochester's beloved
49 Practice à la Marciano
50 Kauai neighbor
51 Where the Rhone meets the Saône
53 Sidle
55 Remain
56 Finishes the cake
57 Examine
59 ___ mater (brain membrane)
60 Like sashimi

345 by Fred Piscop

ACROSS
1 Dolphin family member
4 Terra ___
9 Mrs. Gorbachev
14 Comment from 33-Across
15 Oscar, e.g.
16 Mayflower Compact signer
17 ___ major (legal doctrine)
18 "Faust" character
19 New York's Little ___
20 Start of a lapel-button warning message
23 Cut down
24 Mexican snack
28 Hoo-ha
29 American rival
32 Words after see, hear or speak
33 Barnyard belle
34 Simplifies, with "down"
36 Rocket stage
37 Part 2 of the message
39 Capable of making mistakes
42 Football's Papa Bear, George ___
43 Wrecker
46 Come out
48 "Mayberry ___"
49 Singer Amos
50 Matt Dillon, e.g.
52 Snouted beast
53 End of the message (we warned you!)
57 Spice-rack item
60 Gettysburg victor
61 Jazz musician
62 Run off
63 Tidal ___
64 G.P. grp.
65 It's unfathomable
66 Chose, with "for"
67 Back talk

DOWN
1 Make unnecessary
2 ___ Coalition
3 Washington's ___ Range
4 Military group
5 One who charges
6 Rikki-tikki-___
7 Math subject
8 Wing it
9 Four Monopoly properties
10 Inseparable friend
11 G. & S. princess
12 French seasoning
13 ___ which way
21 Siouan Indian
22 Dog holder
25 "___ had it!"
26 ___ lizzie
27 Schnozz extension
29 Coal measure
30 Genie's grant
31 Hitching post?
34 Cask openings
35 Kind of portrait
37 Esculent roots
38 Groovy, these days
39 Border
40 Actress Thurman
41 Debussy's "La ___"
43 Kind of anesthetic
44 Paper art
45 Eavesdrop, in a way
47 Wear away
49 Smear
51 Bar dance?
52 The way things go
54 ___ tide
55 Skiing memento, perhaps
56 Garfield's pal
57 Maude portrayer
58 Priest's garment
59 Kind of sauce

346 by Raymond Hamel

ACROSS
1 Toasty
5 Pack in
9 Almanac tidbit
13 "Heat of the Moment" rock group
14 Used high beams, perhaps
15 Stern
16 Item in a giblets package
17 Engine sparkers
18 Aimless
19 Run off
22 Came to the rescue
23 The Breadbasket of America
24 Pseudopodal organisms
27 Bronze place
29 Bobby's follower?
30 Stepped-up pace
31 Sty chow
35 Pray for a miracle
38 Ascorbic acid, for one
39 Kachina doll makers
40 Hands up the ball
41 In other words
43 Cicero's birthplace
44 Mercury, e.g.
47 Northern abodes: Var.
49 Statue outside Three Rivers Stadium
54 Initials on old meeting halls
55 Industrialist Schindler
56 Resort near Copper Mountain
57 "Whip It" band
58 Choice
59 Sundance Kid's girl
60 Giver of regards
61 Lavish affection
62 Time for a whistle

DOWN
1 Shortage
2 Offshore
3 Basketball's ___ Barry
4 Waste no time in traveling to
5 Ravel's "Daphnis et ___"
6 Vacation purchase
7 Céleste being
8 U.S. Army gear
9 John Glenn capsule
10 Yellow-fever mosquito
11 Arum lily
12 Headlock?
14 Bone china
20 Bit of regalia
21 Cynical laugh syllable
24 "As Long ___ Needs Me" ("Oliver!" song)
25 Gaze dreamily
26 Fair
28 Hägar's daughter, in the comics
30 Kit Carson Home site
32 Enemy of Thor
33 Dentist's command
34 Eight reals, once
36 Isolated, in a way
37 Recite in a monotone
42 Essen article
43 With ears pricked
44 Hubris
45 Sarge's superior
46 In excess of
48 French dessert
50 Where the Storting sits
51 Its HQ is in Brussels
52 Mozart opera "La Clemenza di ___"
53 Panache

ACROSS

1 Ties one's shoes
6 Wise one
10 Haberdasher's wares
14 Full-price payer, at an amusement park
15 Female egg
16 Jai ___
17 Casals's instrument
18 Handful of hay
19 1994 Jodie Foster movie
20 Arranged unfairly
23 Caboodle's partner
24 Hearty draught
25 Demanded proof
34 Mountain nymph
35 "___ From Muskogee" (1970 hit)
36 The sun
37 Bundle up
38 Cloak-and-dagger types
40 Positive
41 ___ Alamos
42 Crimson rivals
43 Suit material
44 Upped the stakes
48 Actress Sue ___ Langdon

49 ___ de Cologne
50 Remained expressionless
58 Singer Brickell
59 Where Anna taught
60 Parade component
62 Type of group
63 ___ of Man
64 Stage in a butterfly's development
65 ___ 500
66 Require
67 All over

DOWN

1 Varnish ingredient
2 Summer refreshers
3 Unorthodox sect
4 Fitzgerald of scat
5 Supplied
6 Site of a 1976 South African uprising
7 Gung-ho
8 Sudden wind
9 Stress
10 "Messiah" composer
11 Sheltered
12 Bath product
13 Imported material
21 Tease

22 North Sea tributary
25 Monks' hoods
26 Traffic directional
27 Alternative to purchase
28 In the ___ of luxury
29 Hubbub
30 ___ out (supplement)
31 Seize without authority
32 Relinquish
33 Armada
38 Ignores the alarm
39 Wrestling finale
40 Understand
42 Sicilian spouter
43 Mix up kings and queens?
45 Diner
46 Considered
47 Paver's need
50 French military cap
51 Shangri-La
52 ___ Piper
53 River to the Seine
54 Hardy cabbage
55 Broadway's ___ Jay Lerner
56 Electricity carrier
57 Roof overhang

61 Little bit

ACROSS

1 Oscars org.
6 Novelist Waugh
10 Shade of blue
14 New York restaurateur
15 Student pilot's goal
16 Fine powder
17 Dairy product
18 Wedding cake feature
19 Kind of lens
20 Maine's junior Senator
23 Lobs
24 Dark brew
25 Toast topping
28 St. Louis team
31 In recent days
33 Umpire's call
37 Revolutionary War patriot
39 Making a hole-in-one
41 Dove's sound
42 More rational
43 "Airplane!" and "Airplane II" actor
46 Cysts
47 Anheuser-Busch, e.g.
48 Waggin' part

50 Long-running NBC show, for short
51 ___ de cologne
53 Missive
58 "Don't It Make My Brown Eyes Blue" singer
61 Tresses
64 Lose power
65 Actress Barkin
66 Moises of baseball
67 Hideous
68 Family member
69 Celtic language
70 Answer to "Shall we?"
71 Pub game

DOWN

1 Neckwear item
2 Actress Thomas
3 Victimizes, with "on"
4 Name of two Presidents
5 Silly smile
6 Sleuths' canine
7 TV's "___ and Clark"
8 Actress Verdugo
9 Flower part
10 Wood-dressing tool

11 Status ___
12 Road show grp.
13 Banking device
21 "No man ___ island"
22 Withdraws gradually
25 Former diplomat Kirkpatrick
26 Beat poet Ginsberg
27 Mike of 50-Across
29 Supersonic number
30 Summer ermine
32 Melt
33 Nasty remarks
34 Oak starter
35 Damage a reputation
36 Was aware of
38 Georgetown athlete
40 Actress Garson
44 Waiter's burden
45 Window part
49 Story of Robin Hood, e.g.
52 Custom
54 Actress Shire
55 Polk's predecessor
56 Choose
57 Descartes and others
58 Essential point
59 Lean
60 Playboy Khan et al.

61 Sandwich meat
62 ___ carte
63 Item in an electric discharge

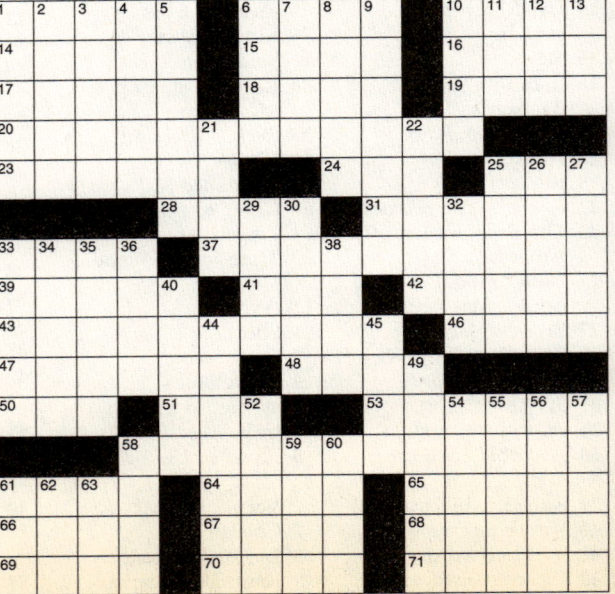

ACROSS

1 Reply to an insult
5 Fleece
10 On vacation
14 Prefix with scope
15 Robert of "G.E. College Bowl"
16 Toasty
17 Stratford's river
18 Jargon
19 Philosopher Hoffer
20 Franklin aphorism
23 Gilbert & Sullivan princess
24 Grab
25 Cagney's portrayer on 80's TV
27 Leading
30 Pirate's punishment
33 Ski lift
36 Old Capri currency
38 Hardly Mr. Cool
39 Looking peaked
40 Marzipan ingredients
42 Command to Rover
43 Intestine part
45 Practice pugilism
46 Extorted from
47 Is hip
49 Actor Martin
51 "Peter and the Wolf" bird
53 Protracted battles
57 Conclude, with "up"
59 Reply to a boaster
62 Miss Marple discovery
64 Motionless
65 Swenson of "Benson"
66 City south of Lillehammer
67 Comedienne Fields
68 Change course
69 Hoof it
70 Late bloomer
71 French 101 verb

DOWN

1 Shoe covers
2 "Rosemary's Baby" author
3 Redolence
4 Stickum
5 Beach memento
6 Abuse
7 Thus
8 Beside
9 Update, as a story
10 Overwhelm
11 Shermanism
12 Waterless
13 Community org.
21 First person in Bavaria
22 Dublin-born dramatist
26 Dallas-to-Austin dir.
28 Prepares to fire
29 Eye soothers
31 Canal opened in 1825
32 Hightailed it
33 Quirks
34 Gale
35 Night watchman's cry
37 Premed course: Abbr.
40 Fear and trepidation
41 Oscar winner Marie, 1931
44 "Put ___ Happy Face"
46 Apiary unit
48 Soft drink brand
50 Singer Damone
52 Some choristers
54 Old World animal with a ringed tail
55 Gung-ho
56 Frame score
57 Flatboat
58 "Lohengrin" miss
60 Eartha of song
61 Tennis's Nastase
63 Stir-fry fryer

ACROSS

1 What hopes may do
5 Word with code or colony
10 Copied
14 Tours to be?
15 ___ Gay
16 Get along
17 Have ___ (the poor)
18 First two of a short-story writer and poet
20 London area
21 Grounded ship's helper
22 ___-Magnon
23 Jewish month
24 First two of a novelist
29 Put the ball in play
31 Opposite of WSW
32 Liz Taylor's third
33 Surrendered
35 Recede
38 Physique, briefly
39 Lacking spontaneity
41 Display stands
43 Arab name part
44 Forty winks
46 Conductor Kurt
47 Drench
49 Serving of 61-Across
51 NBC newsman Lauer et al.
54 First two of an essayist
58 Twist around an axis
59 Abu Dhabi's land: Abbr.
60 Swiss river
61 It's both grown and eaten in rows
62 First two of an essayist and poet
66 Ambience
67 Resting on
68 Three English rivers
69 Artist Mondrian
70 Seabirds
71 Descartes and Auberjonois
72 Ferrara family name

DOWN

1 Intuits
2 "My Favorite Year" star
3 First two of a mystery writer
4 Motion's start
5 P.G.A.'s Calvin
6 Lived through
7 Bean
8 Resembling
9 Tough-wooded conifer
10 Still not sunk
11 Crony
12 70's-80's pol. cause
13 Lion's home
19 Send weapons to
25 So-so mark
26 First two of a novelist
27 Biblical no-no
28 Tacks on
30 Paradise
34 Spanish queen until 1931
36 Breakfast's partner
37 Ointment
39 Hankering
40 "O" to ham operators, once
42 Winslow Homer's "The Gulf Stream," e.g.
45 Garden sphere
46 Daughter of Minos
48 Noted Essen family
50 King Arthur's destination
52 Gunner's station
53 Capitol body
55 "Uh-huh"
56 Double-walled flask
57 Smelting waste
62 Dodge pickup
63 Had a bite
64 Volume setting
65 Roman greeting

351 by A.J. Santora

ACROSS

1 Peepers
5 Jumble
9 Waft
14 Milne's ___ Corner
15 Mr. Guinness
16 Beguiled
17 Being, to Brutus
18 ___ trough (rain runoff site)
19 Charged, in a way
20 A Yankee skipper
23 Marmalade tree
24 Pie style
28 1927 Yankee batting array
30 Cesar who played the Joker
33 Propellers, of a sort
34 Bach's Partita ___ minor
35 Have ___ good authority
36 One way to swing
37 Wise guy
38 Kvetch
39 Only
41 Sparkly minerals
43 Legendary Yankee nickname, with "the"
46 Summer garb
47 Team once called the Colt .45s
50 Yankee V.I.P.
53 Addams Family name
56 Hick
57 To be, in Paris
58 Sprang up
59 Panhandler's home?: Abbr.
60 Traipse
61 Take in
62 Shortage
63 Zoomed

DOWN

1 Gas shortage manipulators
2 Ponselle and Parks
3 ___ nova
4 Wool gatherers
5 Toscanini, e.g.
6 In hog heaven
7 Golfer Ballesteros
8 Game plan
9 Very attentive
10 Empires
11 Unmatched
12 Broadway's "Five Guys Named ___"
13 30's-50's actress Harding
21 "In ___ face!"
22 Site for a stream
25 Window style
26 Taker
27 Pitchers
29 Either Zimbalist
30 Altar exchange
31 City WNW of Sapporo
32 ___ David
36 Pantaloons presser
37 Belittlers
39 Classic sports cars
40 Theater award
41 Formed a wrong opinion of
42 Penny fee
44 Tax
45 Talk idly
48 Leading
49 Accommodate
51 Blow to kingdom come
52 Melodeon part
53 [yuck!]
54 Bruin of yore
55 Elsie utterance

---

352 by Matt Gaffney

ACROSS

1 Wheedles
8 Complete and orderly system
14 Kind of board
15 Army threats?
16 Not shaded
17 Heavy
18 Been angered
19 Loud
20 Pottery
21 Homecoming?
22 Labor Dept. section
25 Glum
26 "___ Boy" ("Tommy" song)
30 Noted Washington address
35 City on the Clark Fork River
36 "Interview with the Vampire" actor
37 Laser element
38 Ladies of the house
39 Chemistry Nobelist Onsager
40 Lucrative
41 Actor Jannings
44 Facing
48 37-Across, e.g.
52 ___-Romagna (region of Italy)
53 Atlanta corporate giant
54 Turn in
55 Peg
56 Existing
57 Stops

DOWN

1 Retina part
2 Amount to be raised?
3 Sherlock Holmes's chronicler
4 "Orfeo," e.g.
5 Vanquished
6 Dodge
7 Dict. listing
8 Plan jointly, as a prank
9 Great quantity
10 Military award
11 ___ operandi
12 Sports event
13 Produce strains
14 Wrong beginning
19 The Creator, in Hinduism
22 Ottoman dynasty founder
23 "Goosebumps" creator R.L. ___
24 Must
25 Guesstimates
26 Brains
27 Coronet
28 Sub standard?
29 Jawbone of ___
31 Phanerozoic, for instance
32 Reply in a French salon
33 Malt shop orders
34 Hamburger's connection
40 Hamburger accompaniment
41 Shorelines do it
42 Fends off, in a way, as a mugger
43 From Isfahan
44 She plays Lois on "Lois & Clark"
45 Augur
46 All-inclusive
47 Half pints, maybe
49 ___ alone (fly solo)
50 Swedish actor Kjellin et al.
51 For example
53 Eleventh-century hero

353 by Joe DiPietro

ACROSS

1 Publicizes
8 Start the ball rolling
15 Alert
16 Type of moth
17 Welcome guest
18 Boat akin to a canoe
19 Indication of contempt
20 "Take Me Home" singer
22 Altar in the sky
23 Kind of party
24 Lancaster, e.g.
26 Capital of Belarus
28 Promotional piece
29 Seattle attraction
30 Prefix with meter or sphere
33 ___ City, Ariz.
34 Ethnic ball
35 Victuals
36 Getty rival
38 Houston athlete of yore
39 Arousing
41 ___ choy (Chinese cabbage)
42 Workers
43 Deficit
44 Endowed (with)
46 "Raspberry ___" (Prince song)
47 Squalid
48 See 29-Down
51 True successor to the prophet, in Shiism
52 Swards
53 It's seen on Peru's coat-of-arms
55 It's a wrap
58 Less than neat
60 Make a pig of oneself
61 Nutty
62 Lose heart
63 Bric-a-brac

DOWN

1 Meat skewer
2 Trattoria offering
3 Shade of black
4 Lou's ex-wife on "Mary Tyler Moore"
5 Stellar
6 Directly
7 Rainbow coalition?
8 Unpopular person
9 Big name in Ajman
10 Calendar abbr.
11 ___ gratias
12 Back-to-school purchase
13 "Address" starter
14 Wacky exhibition
21 Was palsy-walsy
25 John of filmdom
26 Extinct cousin of the kiwi
27 All there
28 Type of pasta
29 With 48-Across, deli item
30 Made sour
31 Like a haiku
32 Bygone jewelry
37 Common side
40 Bankbook abbr.
45 Nicole Hollander comic strip
47 Put bottoms on
48 ___ stock (carried)
49 Relating to NH_2
50 "Olympia" painter
52 An auction bidder might give a high one
54 Time to give up?
56 Dandy
57 Spanish playing card
59 Devil follower

354 by Elizabeth C. Gorski

ACROSS

1 ___ blocker
5 Cabbie
9 Desert flora
14 Latin 101 word
15 Cousin of a Tony
16 Autumn color
17 Singer McEntire
18 Give the slip to
19 Squirrel away
20 Alien art form, some say
23 Magnum and others, for short
24 Give it ___ (try)
25 "Now, about . . ."
26 Getaways
28 Hilton Head Island, for one
30 Prohibitionists would like to prohibit it
33 Caught but good
36 Danish money
37 Agreement
40 Interrupt, as a dancer
42 Parroted
43 Fitzgerald and others
45 Bee and snake products
47 Boo-boos
49 Turkey moistener
53 Cartoon skunk ___ Le Pew
54 TV ad
56 "Norma ___"
57 SASE, e.g.
59 Fruit pastry
62 Ravel work, with "La"
64 Legal scholar Guinier
65 Villa d'___
66 "Give peace ___ time, O Lord": Morning Prayer
67 Prime time hour
68 Mets stadium
69 Gently gallops
70 Pub round
71 Like a Granny Smith apple

DOWN

1 Where train commuters drink
2 Come to the fore
3 No-nos
4 Pronto!
5 Kind of medicine
6 Call off a takeoff
7 50's western "The ___ Kid"
8 Ship's central beam
9 Russian horseman
10 Take steps
11 Auto disassembly site
12 Actress Hatcher
13 Gets one's goat
21 Singer Irene
22 Building wing
27 Quagmire
29 Recorded
30 Point after deuce
31 Single
32 Conducted
34 Disposable diaper brand
35 Bordeaux summer
37 Foot: Lat.
38 The works
39 Carriage horse sound
41 People who don't count
44 Evening meals
46 ___ Hari
48 Each
50 Country singer Yearwood
51 Resurrection Mass day
52 Warm up again
54 Escargot
55 Tubular pasta
57 Stephen King topic
58 Prefix with second
60 Arm bone
61 Hornets' home
63 Take to court

355 by Brendan Emmett Quigley

ACROSS
1 Like topiary
7 "The never failing vice of fools": Pope
12 Went into hiding
14 Brawl activity
16 Not in yet
17 Stirs
18 1993 musical with the Best Original Score
19 Product once pitched by Grace Kelly
21 Pandowdy, e.g.
22 Parseghian et al.
23 Multitude
24 Thomas Moore ballad locale
25 Artist Gerard ___ Borch
26 Eminent Washington family
27 Shakespearean female roles
28 "Shiloh" novelist Shelby
29 Strong
30 Standup comic with a sitcom
33 "G.W.T.W." extras

34 Whoop it up
35 In the back
36 Bristol-Myers Squibb brand
37 Eden and others, for short
40 Following
41 Surged
42 Stay fresh
43 911 responder
44 3-D graph lines
45 Dame's introduction
46 Raphael's "___ Madonna"
48 Victory site of March 1945
50 Japanese mats
51 Veto
52 Navajo home
53 City dweller's pocketful

DOWN
1 Barraged
2 Caricaturist Daumier
3 Baseball's Sandy
4 Salon orders
5 Go round and round
6 Anticipated
7 Ring up

8 1990 World Cup site, locally
9 "___ had it!"
10 Alacrity
11 100%
13 Before
14 Lots
15 Let up
20 Condition ahead of time, as film
23 Goes by foot, with "it"
24 Palatable
26 Summer intern, maybe
27 Tony winner Swoosie
28 E
29 Idiot
30 Old Testament book
31 Makes a choice
32 Enters, as a controversy
33 Most inferior
36 Quashes
37 Dress size
38 Sea creatures of myth
39 Catches, in a way
41 Arrived breathlessly
42 13th Precinct lieutenant

44 Coors product since 1992
45 Canceled
47 Moniker
49 Showery

356 by Randolph Ross

ACROSS
1 Sauce ingredient
12 Old spy novel grp.
15 Eden event
16 Trendy
17 Grew back
18 Verdi aria "___ tu"
19 Count, in a manner of speaking
20 S.A.T. takers
21 Police findings, for short
22 Lift giver
25 Arthur Miller's "All My ___"
27 Dear ones?
28 Golf-cartlike vehicles
30 Damask rose product
33 Pen brand
34 Main
36 Exchange for something precious
38 Deli order
41 Some woolens
42 Day's march
43 Indian name meaning "ruler"
44 Smart guy
47 H.S. requirements
48 In order

49 A few bucks
51 Pilot's heading
52 Philosopher ___ Yutang
53 Overseas pen pal?
55 Track components
58 Philippine native
59 Soap opera of 1954–74, with "The"
64 Its ZIP codes start 89-: Abbr.
65 Lucid
66 Describing some wines
67 Kind of sandwich

DOWN
1 Peak
2 Bank deposit
3 Onetime enemy plane
4 Song composer Milton
5 Off Broadway's "Tony n' ___ Wedding"
6 ___ customer
7 Raise a family
8 Like
9 Jets

10 Rank
11 QB targets
12 Track event
13 Piece of college jewelry
14 Ham companion
22 Summer resort south of Narragansett Pier
23 Scout out
24 Virginia creeper
26 Operated, in a way
27 Lily and rose, e.g.
29 Seasonal workers
31 Yes
32 Third man in a ring
35 Just out
37 It's stubbed
39 Narc's org.
40 Passbook info: Abbr.
45 Singer Peter
46 Carradine and others
50 VCR button
53 "The Apostle" novelist
54 Dramatic beginning
55 Specialist in 60-Down
57 Reward for merit
60 Modern music
61 Harem quarters
62 Ad ___

63 Year in Henry VII's reign

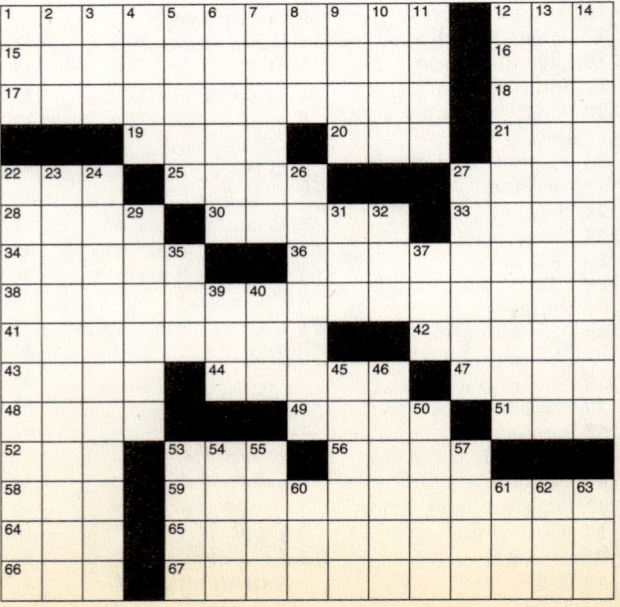

357 by Alex K. Justin

ACROSS

1 David Bowie's model wife
5 Famed Dublin theater
10 Terrier of fiction
14 Canceled
15 Pen
16 Paul of "CBS This Morning"
17 Burgeon
18 "Read my lips" declaration
20 Never
22 Actress Graff of "Mr. Belvedere"
23 It's forbidden
24 It may be blind
26 Veteran sailor
29 Polite refusal
33 Montreal street sign
34 Indian craft
35 Suffix with diet or planet
36 Bush Attorney General William
37 Become misty
38 Computer symbol
39 "How was ___ know?"
40 Buy a round
41 Cultural: Prefix
42 1987 Costner thriller
44 Carried on
45 PC operator
46 Country ballroom?
47 Alamogordo's county
50 "Jack Sprat could ___"
54 Straight from the shoulder
57 Bear up?
58 Kuwaiti ruler
59 Get ___ of one's own medicine
60 Go smoothly
61 Actress Thompson
62 Kind of situation
63 Noted Ferrara family

DOWN

1 Swenson of "Benson"
2 Satirist Sahl
3 Attic contest
4 "I'm not surprised!"
5 Storefront sight
6 Headache easer, for short
7 Twining stem
8 Riviera season
9 Material for archers' bows
10 Rhododendron
11 ___-Coburg (former duchy)
12 "___ He Kissed Me" (1963 hit)
13 Addie's husband in "As I Lay Dying"
19 Church gift
21 Drinking binge
24 Dunking item
25 Over
26 Polio fighter
27 Lyrist of myth
28 "This way" sign
29 Complain relentlessly to
30 Strauss's "Eine ___ in Venedig"
31 Jockey Julie
32 Religious council
34 ___ d'Alene, Idaho
37 Splitting tool
38 "I can't go on!"
40 Spinks defeater, 1988
41 Deserve
43 Roman Eos
44 Mediterranean vessel
46 Ezio Pinza and others
47 Singles
48 Tony Musante TV series
49 Novelist Bagnold
50 Sufficient, once
51 Lippo Lippi et al.
52 Didion's "Play It ___ Lays"
53 Chaucer piece
55 Antonio or Juan
56 Conductor de Waart

---

358 by Bob Lubbers

ACROSS

1 Kind of file
7 Dupe
11 Vacation spot
14 Razz
15 Speed
16 Total cost
17 Dear ones
18 Come before
20 Psychiatrist?
22 Mirror image?
23 Pain of a sort
24 Express
25 Cookout fare
28 Bus starter
30 Actor Jannings
34 Canter
35 Re-election runners
36 "___ to Psyche"
37 In a managerial position to
38 Self-diagnosis?
40 Fancy
41 It's bleu on maps
42 "Steve Allen Show" veteran
43 Detach, in a way
44 Hyde Park sight
46 "The Last Time I Saw Paris" composer
48 Oxygenators
49 Sci-fi objects
51 Shopper's helper
53 Where one is in the stadium?
56 Personal revelation?
59 Stove stuffing
61 Land, as a fish
63 Back
64 To be, abroad
65 Kind of kick
66 Of course
67 U.S. Army medals
68 Camera-shy critter?

DOWN

1 Forbes competition
2 Nostalgic soft drink name
3 Boy Scout's act
4 One who makes personal plugs?
5 "___ Restaurant'"
6 Condor condos
7 Tangle (with)
8 Ax
9 Demonstrator's doctrine
10 "With Reagan; The Inside Story" author
11 Dateless
12 Orbit
13 Help
19 Urgent
21 Native Nebraskan
24 Sigmund's daughter
25 Tiptoe's opposite
26 Fly like a flying saucer
27 Works
29 Party
31 Display
32 Standard
33 Is attracted
38 Section in a psychological test
39 This puzzle's punning theme
40 Self-defense testifier?
45 Make a proposal
47 Sergeant major: Abbr.
48 "Brighton Rock" novelist
50 Say "I do" again
52 Splatter safeguard
53 Questionable
54 Cassino cash
55 Romance symbol
56 Time in "Julius Caesar"
57 Boola-boola cheerers
58 "___ Pagliaccio"
60 Killer of the deep
62 Formerly

359 by Jonathan Schmalzbach

ACROSS

1 "... more than one way to skin ___"
5 Supply a party
10 Beast of burden
13 Fads
15 Speak publicly
16 Caltech rival
17 Cereal "fruit"
19 "___ of these days, Alice . . ."
20 Outdoor
21 Spiritual punishment
23 Meadow
24 Jockey Cordero
25 Civil War flash point
32 Nom de crook
33 Upset
34 Small dog, for short
37 Split
38 Grew ashen
40 Coffee, informally
41 Hat-room fixture
42 Salon offering
43 More painful
44 U.S. commodore in Japan, 1853-54
47 Letter-shaped metal bar
50 Señor Guevara
51 Lovebirds' destination, maybe
54 Paul of "Casablanca"
59 ___ Altos, Calif.
60 County of Northern Ireland
62 Had a little lamb?
63 First name in cosmetics
64 Novelist Françoise
65 Roll of bills
66 Looks (to be)
67 Unattached

DOWN

1 With the bow, in music
2 Bellyache
3 Malarial symptom
4 Part of T.V.A.: Abbr.
5 Hooded snakes
6 Exist
7 Diamond cover
8 To be, to Satie
9 "___ the Fox" (classic fable)
10 In the midst of
11 From the time of
12 Girder material
14 ___ of justice
18 Yesterday: Fr.
22 "___ luck?"
25 David's instrument
26 Downwind, nautically
27 Wedding sine qua non
28 Add to, unnecessarily
29 Smut
30 Prior to, in poems
31 Crimson
34 Henry VIII's VIth
35 "Reply completed," to a ham operator
36 Queen of Scots
38 Word before bull or stop
39 Grasshopper's rebuker
40 Baseball's DiMaggio
42 Mexican snacks
43 Isn't miserly
44 Cosmo, e.g.
45 Reverberations
46 At what time?
47 Wedding acquisition
48 Flora and fauna
49 Let up
52 Type of wine
53 Kitty starter
55 Kind of estate
56 Therefore
57 Major rug exporter
58 Unit of force
61 Rep. foe

360 by Christopher Hurt

ACROSS

1 Greatly impressed
5 Chairman ___
8 Poet Mandelstam
12 Charming
15 Viper
16 Moore of "A Few Good Men"
17 Sagan's "___ Brain"
18 40-Across's beloved 11
20 Shifty shoe?
22 African nation since 1993
23 Danger
25 Reps.
26 Close, as friends
29 Musician's job
31 Composer of "Socrate"
34 National park in Maine
36 Shem's father
38 Getting on
39 Indian writer Santha Rama ___
40 Theme of this puzzle
42 End up ahead
43 Frank Baum's initial initial
44 Angel's headgear
45 California's motto
47 Hebrew master
49 Dutch airline
51 Spinners, e.g.
52 Brain tests, for short
54 Essentials
56 Common speech
59 Bureau
63 Locale of 40-Across
65 Mourn
66 Prolific "author"
67 ___ pro nobis
68 Plains Indians
69 Items in a code
70 ___ Luthor
71 Boss Tweed lampooner

DOWN

1 Liturgical robes
2 Eroded
3 Bacchanalian cry
4 Crab, e.g.
5 Small rug
6 Late tennis great
7 It may be seria or buffa
8 Single-named folk singer
9 40-Across landmark
10 Hungary's Nagy
11 Galileo's home
13 40-Across's eastern border
14 Belgian river
19 Feature of 40-Across, according to Sandburg
21 Get-up
24 1860 nominee in 40-Across
26 Less cluttered
27 Florida city
28 1976 Nobel Prize winner from 40-Across
30 Indian district
32 "___ Ike" (50's slogan)
33 Millay and Ferber
35 Cry of discovery
37 Ripen
41 Kind
46 Type of roulette
48 Sets sail
50 Avg.
53 Pub perch
55 Therefore
56 Perfume holder
57 Humerus neighbor
58 Mary Robinson's land
60 Nintendo rival
61 Impending times
62 "Give it a ___"
64 Wailing instrument

361 by Judith Perry

ACROSS

1 Lupino et al.
5 Rock band equipment
9 Swabs
13 "Cheers" habitué
14 French landscape painter
16 Toward shelter
17 Talk show host's holiday songs?
19 Holler
20 Interstice in a leaf
21 Goes first
23 Hog heaven?
24 County bordering London
25 Window frame
27 Actor's first course?
31 Wine cask
32 Swing around
33 Spitting ___
34 Education for the deaf
36 Carrot cousin
38 Street show
39 Bit of medicine
40 Car in a 1964 hit song

41 Artist's soup ingredients?
44 H.S. jr.'s exam
45 Tempestuous
46 Legal matter
47 Smart alec
50 Jesse James, e.g.
53 Buffalo's lake
54 Playwright's rubbish?
56 Drum sound
57 Moonshiner's need
58 Look ___ (explore)
59 Grandson of Adam
60 Old record company
61 Auspices: Var.

DOWN

1 "To Live and Die ___"
2 Active one
3 English composer's trap?
4 Unwrinkled
5 Clearasil target
6 Bossy's call
7 Musical intro
8 Sherry classification
9 Actress-director's vegetables?

10 Source of trans-fatty acids
11 Ill-gotten wealth
12 ___-serve (gas sign)
15 Russian kings
18 Foxy
22 Wish for
24 Poor part of town
25 Baby bird?
26 Ear-related
27 Capp and Capone
28 Filmmaker's argot?
29 Heebie-jeebies
30 Station
32 Mexican's nap
35 General's catch of the day?
36 Slow
37 Balaam's mount
39 Black mark
42 Lomond and Ness
43 Mistakes
44 "Dick Van Dyke Show" family name
46 Dull routine
47 "___ all in this together"
48 Press clothes
49 Cylindrical building
50 Norse capital

51 Italian wine center
52 "___ on first?"
55 R.N.'s skill

362 by Wayne Robert Williams

ACROSS

1 TV interruptions
4 Support crew
9 Tough
14 Little 'un
15 Instrument played sitting down
16 A Kennedy
17 Singular 1960 musical?
19 Vacation destination
20 Toward shelter
21 Grub
22 Dispositions
23 Game of love
25 Those not listed
26 Singular celebrity?
30 Tight spot
33 Longfellow character
36 Way to go
37 Task for Holmes
38 Get on
39 Misreckon
40 Balked
41 Salinger dedicatee
42 Overrule
43 Deck or dock workers
44 Whippoorwill's bill

45 Singular club performer?
47 Knowledgeable about
49 Not quite
53 Walloping winds
55 Wagon train direction
58 Mr. Rubik
59 Muezzin's God
60 Singular cheer?
62 Grave marker
63 Pisces follower
64 Alibi guy
65 Church plate
66 Aquarium fish
67 Composer Rorem

DOWN

1 Ready to swing
2 "Charlie's Angels" co-star
3 "Skittle Players" painter
4 ___-fi
5 Actress Wright of "Mrs. Miniver"
6 Soprano Frances
7 Move like a butterfly
8 Opposing sides
9 Hypnotism pioneer

10 Partner of Porthos
11 Singular Christmas toy?
12 Stampeding group
13 Ring cheers
18 DDT ingredient
24 Gershwin's "___ It a Pity?"
25 Five-and-a-half yards
27 Love of money
28 It helps circulation
29 Münchhausen, e.g.
31 Played for a sucker
32 Cots and cradles
33 "So be it"
34 Mislay
35 Singular slug?
37 Smoothie
40 Cartoonist Silverstein
42 "Das Lied ___ der Erde"
45 "Land o' ___!"
46 "Death Comes for the Archbishop" author
48 Rembrandt, the painter
50 Senator Hatch
51 Hisser
52 Played (with)

53 Last breath
54 Neighbor of B.C.
55 "Huh?"
56 The old sod
57 Roasting device

61 Olympics chant

363 by Chuck Deodene

ACROSS

1 Nightcap accompaniment
8 In the sky
14 Zenith
15 Enervation
16 Living off another's largess
18 "Loverboy" singer Billy
19 Yarn spinner
20 Brace for trouble
21 Wild card, often
23 Actor Neeson
26 Elusive
27 Triumph
28 Lunar valley
29 Statuary art
31 Make safe
32 Experimental electrical materials
36 Hag
37 Center
38 Montgomery of film
39 Paddle
40 "Hawaii Five-O" actor Fong
43 Smooch
44 Burst
47 Fly alone
48 Ear malady
50 Loser to Dempsey, 9/14/23
51 One who can make brown eyes blue?
55 Resting
56 Locomotive's load
57 Arctic coats
58 TV news story

DOWN

1 Cosmetics applicator
2 Thoroughfare
3 Holy war
4 Mideastern gulf
5 Red-starred aircraft
6 Swiss river
7 Mishap
8 "___ Baby" (Crickets hit)
9 Global: Abbr.
10 Bums
11 Texas metropolis
12 Roman trio
13 Campaigned
14 Early synthesizers
17 Carpet cleaner, briefly
21 Platters
22 Inner, in combinations
24 Daminozide, familiarly
25 Quaint residential street
27 Sausage
28 Crop up again
29 Kind of tomato
30 Lorne Michaels's program, for short
31 Coin of old
32 Wallop
33 Wrinkly-skinned fruit
34 Detainee
35 Postern, e.g.
40 Seoul man
41 Herb of horns
42 Anchors
44 Eyesores or eye sores
45 Photo
46 Rehab candidates
47 From then on
49 "___ Heartache" (1978 hit)
50 Patina
51 Cleft
52 Letter from Plato
53 Scot's refusal
54 Musical engagement

364 by Manny Nosowsky

ACROSS

1 747, e.g.
9 Hotel posting
14 Basketball game
15 Follower of Santa
16 Pant waist inserts
17 "I, Robot" author
18 It can have pluses or minuses
19 Granada grizzlies
20 Twinkle-toed
21 Baking ___
23 One past due
24 More costly
25 Ultimate buyers
27 Perfect
29 Converge (on)
31 Feel sick
32 Tart
34 Early Biblical commentary
40 Aurora's counterpart
42 Mal de mer
43 Fabric design
49 Southwestern sights
50 "Strange Interlude" playwright
51 Actress Gardner
53 Boss: Abbr.
54 Courage
55 Govt. disaster agency
57 Inn drink
58 Excessive contraction of the pupil
59 Boys Town figure
61 Draws out
62 ___ glycol (antifreeze)
63 Stucco backing
64 Had a setback

DOWN

1 Liar in old car ads
2 Release, redundantly
3 Follows a stream's path
4 Cattle genus
5 Knowing about
6 Horizontal beam
7 Rerun of a telecast
8 Inlaid piece
9 More optimistic
10 Kind of cracker
11 Sound quality
12 Where professeurs profess
13 People of some account
15 Troubadour's instrument
22 Aligned, with "in"
26 "Sprechen ___ Deutsch?"
28 Lip
30 Like a lot of worry
33 As well
35 Flood control
36 Is contrite
37 Pacifies
38 Alaskan transport
39 Hurried up
41 Office employee
43 Beat
44 One of the Five Nations
45 Exhale
46 Art museum rejects?
47 Friends
48 Having a model's body
52 Menotti character
56 Author Seton
60 Monte Rosa, e.g.

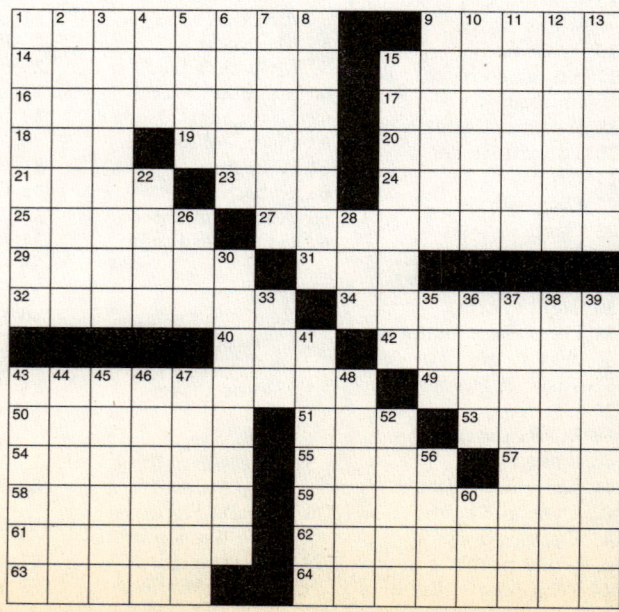

ACROSS

1 32-card game
5 Place
10 Actress Moore
14 Not pro
15 Creepy
16 Andy's partner
17 Place of Viking insurgence?
20 Banish
21 Raises
22 February 14 name
25 Opposite WNW
26 90's music genre
29 "Lucky Jim" author Kingsley
31 Not quite a homer
36 Org. for Johnnie Cochran
37 London paper, with "The"
39 Roger Rabbit, e.g.
40 Site of Celtic uprising?
44 Italian wine center
45 Liaison
46 Uno + due
47 County Cork roofing
50 "Beowulf," e.g.
51 Neighbor of Leb.
52 Jamaican liquor
54 Oahu goose
56 Japanese paper figures
61 Saturate
65 Location of Yankee massacre?
68 Portent
69 Approaches
70 Kitty feed
71 Olympic sword
72 ___ gum (paint ingredient)
73 Comforting reply to "When?"

DOWN

1 Not out
2 Fort ___ (U.S. gold depository)
3 Yours, in Paris
4 Duke, e.g.
5 Caribbean, e.g.
6 Part of ITT: Abbr.
7 First name in mysteries
8 Path to the altar
9 Loathe
10 Baby's utterance
11 Radiate
12 Grimace
13 Doctrines
18 Tongue-lash
19 State
23 Leave out
24 "The Lion King" lion
26 Capital of Morocco
27 Make embarrassed
28 Linguine, e.g.
30 Clothing splitting points
32 Los Angeles judge
33 Sulks
34 Sussex semi
35 Door sign
38 ___-Kettering Institute
41 Model airplane package
42 Racing sled
43 Skulls
48 Hermit ___
49 Compassionate
53 Odometer reading
55 Thompson and Samms
56 Hautbois
57 Steps bypass
58 Fortune-teller's start
59 Hereditary factor
60 Blinds crosspiece
62 Cher's ex
63 "Do ___ others . . ."
64 Biblical garden
66 Dr. ___ of 26-Across
67 Neighbor of Leb.

ACROSS

1 F.D.R.'s predecessor
4 Florida city
9 Make into law
14 The Greatest
15 Lexicon: Abbr.
16 Literary style
17 Tombstone letters
18 Slated for court
20 Tile work
22 See 25-Down
23 Painter Paul
24 Opposite of modern
26 Spots for Christmas decorations
28 Mobil rival
30 Plunder
32 French law
33 Senator / astronaut Garn
34 1982 Jeff Bridges cyberfilm
36 Prefix with -hedron
40 Breakfasted
41 Kettledrums
43 "Ben-___"
44 Hoffman role ___ Rizzo
46 Opera set in Egypt
47 Lane coworker
48 "Holy smokes!"
50 Small bite
51 Work units
52 Early Allen flick
56 Loverboy
58 "Get ___!" ("Start working!")
59 ___ Na Na
61 60's-70's TV western
64 1976 James Taylor album
67 Roller skate accessory
68 Seduced
69 "Do I dare to eat a peach?" poet
70 Baseball stat
71 Iditarod racers
72 "True Confessions" novelist
73 Quite a load

DOWN

1 Injure
2 Advertising award
3 It helps you shake a leg
4 Egg-shaped
5 Vivaldi's "The Four Seasons," e.g.
6 Pretense
7 Bert of "The Wizard of Oz"
8 At right angles to the keel
9 Freudian focus
10 Absence at "dress-down days"
11 Leg support
12 Angler's basket
13 Heads, in Le Havre
19 Poker command
21 Skin softener
25 With 22-Across, title role for Sally Field
27 Reply to the Little Red Hen
28 Slightly open
29 Pro ___
31 Arrive casually
35 Low point
37 Rod Laver's nickname
38 Crosspiece
39 These may be fine
41 Roger Rabbit, e.g.
42 Creamy pastry
45 Enveloped
47 Peachy-___
49 Kind of waist
52 Seethes
53 Make void
54 Saltpeter, in Salisbury
55 With oxfords
57 Photo finish
60 Org. that defends freedoms
62 Architect Saarinen
63 Actor O'Neal
65 Mag. workers
66 Relations

367 by Jonathan Schmalzbach

ACROSS
1 Convent attire
6 ___ mater
10 Over, in Bonn
14 Big name in microwaves
15 Anon
16 It borders the chancel
17 Wasserstein's 1989 Pulitzer drama winner, with "The"
20 ___ spumante
21 Boon
22 Volunteer
23 Stare stupidly
25 Small: Suffix
26 Three-part Galsworthy opus
32 Scholars' money
33 Sideways look
34 ___-la-la
35 Eden-to-Nod direction
36 Dancer Charisse
37 Recipe direction
38 Blast maker
39 Together, musically
41 "Ain't That ___"
43 1984 film based on a Fuller play

46 Says further
47 Russian despot
48 Sugar or flour, e.g.
51 Ewe's call
52 "Bye-bye"
56 14th-century literary classic, with "The"
59 Choir voice
60 French river or department
61 William Morris employee
62 Radar point
63 Small fry
64 Jai alai basket

DOWN
1 "Very funny!"
2 The ___ Brothers (40's–50's group)
3 Night crawlers, e.g.
4 Penniless
5 Mai ___ (cocktail)
6 More pallid
7 Surprised cry
8 ___ juice (milk)
9 Actress Bening
10 Vanya and Remus, e.g.
11 Island near Java

12 Holiday cusps
13 Relaxation
18 Mafia V.I.P.'s
19 Bury
24 Early P.M.
25 Observed
26 Part of TWA
27 Must
28 More cunning
29 Perfume ingredient
30 Not clean
31 Bern's river
32 "I Still ___ Thrill" (1930 hit)
36 Pool needs
37 Deficit
39 Nonplus
40 French philosopher Denis
41 Test, as ore
42 RR stop
44 Computer for a commuter
45 Long looks
48 Strikebreaker
49 Seven-foot, e.g.
50 Voting no
51 Statuary item
53 Tavern potables
54 Bivouac shelter

55 Hammett Schnauzer
57 Publicity info
58 Tic-___-toe

368 by Mark Elliot Skolsky

ACROSS
1 Inside the foul line
5 Like Ionesco's soprano
9 Romantic actor Charles
14 It parallels the radius
15 Perlman of "Pearl"
16 A month in Madrid
17 Robin
19 Actress Shire
20 Wall Street order
21 Brain test results, for short
23 Some linemen: Abbr.
24 Hopes
28 School failure
30 Alphabetic run
31 Kind of summit
33 All over
34 Pinkish color
36 Custard tart
38 Longtime Israeli foreign minister
41 Rock concert equipment
42 See 32-Down
43 Start of a Latin boast
44 ___ Alto, Calif.
45 Mobil rival

46 E-mail predecessor
47 Oklahoma city
49 1995 earthquake site
51 Potash
52 Conniver
55 Having deep pockets
57 Miler Sebastian
58 French tire
60 Shot over the head
61 D-Day beach
63 Legal-tender bill
68 Situation for Pauline?
69 Ice cream thickener
70 Industrial show
71 First name in cosmetics
72 Mother of Apollo
73 ___ ex machina

DOWN
1 Raccoon, e.g.
2 Bitter
3 Not the party type: Abbr.
4 Browning's Ben Ezra, e.g.
5 Supreme Court Justice Stephen
6 "Gotcha!"
7 ___-majesté

8 Saw
9 Trusts
10 ___ roll
11 Chicken, so to speak
12 "A Masked Ball" aria
13 Friars Club event
18 Part of R.F.D.
22 Super-duper
24 Royalties org.
25 Pore in a leaf
26 Service award
27 "60 Minutes" newsman
29 Irk
32 With 42-Across, a famous pirate
35 Together
37 Woolf's "___ of One's Own"
39 Words before and after "for"
40 Forbade
42 When doubled, a German city
46 Mortise's mate
48 Stick
50 Ravel composition
52 Sub's eye, for short
53 Shows up
54 Buick model

56 Fell off
59 Feel the ___
62 Make haste
64 Dinner table exhortation

65 Fire
66 Computer's heart, for short
67 Dempsey stat

369 by Glenton Petgrave

ACROSS

1 Dash
8 Landscaper's tools
14 Acquisition
15 Site of the world's first subway
16 Kind of carriage
17 Artificial channel
18 Winner of seven Emmys
19 Photographer Adams
21 Start of many poem titles
22 Country or its largest lake
23 Bullfinch topic
24 Kind of radio or wave
26 Angel's prayer
27 Milk protein
29 "Plan 9 From Outer Space" alien
30 Pave the way for
32 Time on the throne
34 Drummer's activity
36 Milk-yielding plants
40 In two
42 By and large
43 Word in some French restaurant names
46 Grow more intense
48 Kind of mother
49 Forced to go
51 Sound like an ass
52 Baryshnikov's birthplace
53 Brink
54 Winner of 18 majors
56 Sports show finale, perhaps
57 Gorge
59 Smith and wright
61 Disquiet
62 Win over
63 Outstanding
64 Understanding

DOWN

1 Cheer
2 Like some care
3 Felt (for)
4 Mjolnir's wielder
5 Blacken
6 Bacon pieces
7 Take part in again
8 Besides that
9 Runyon characters
10 Veldt grazer
11 Tina Brown, for one
12 Highly ornate
13 Casual footwear
14 Uses court bouillon, in cooking
20 Started
23 Frenzied follower
25 Painter Rousseau
27 Movie excerpt
28 Niger's capital
31 Horse marking
33 Sculptor ___ Lorenzo Bernini
35 Helldiver
37 Sign or symptom
38 Chic
39 Neurotransmitter's route
41 John O'Hara's "From the ___"
43 Innocent
44 Where Ponce de León died
45 News hour
47 Regular
50 Not very swift
52 Amber, e.g.
55 Shift course
56 Gauche introduction?
58 Publisher Ballantine
60 Amatol ingredient

370 by Fred Piscop

ACROSS

1 Scores for the Maple Leafs
6 Heavyweight champ dethroned by Braddock
10 In this way
14 Hold, as the attention
15 Any of three English rivers
16 Wax's opposite
17 In solitary
18 Dressed
19 As before, in footnotes
20 Batman and Robin, e.g.
22 Evening, informally
23 G.I. dinner
24 Kitty ___
26 Where to find Chile powder?
29 Vinegar: Prefix
31 Statement of belief
32 Obliquely
36 Diamond Head locale
37 Kind of mill
38 Within: Prefix
39 It's about thyme!
41 Impels
42 Expunge
43 Miniature map
44 50's–60's pitcher Don
47 Einstein's birthplace
48 Declare
49 Tinkers-Evers-Chance forte
56 New Zealander
57 Cartoonist Peter
58 Tylenol competitor
59 Mideast carrier
60 ___ Hari
61 Wouk work
62 Beach, basically
63 Kind of car
64 Handle a baton

DOWN

1 Mortarboard wearer
2 Overly smooth
3 View from Stratford
4 Horne who sang "Deed I Do"
5 Restrained, as a flow
6 Game with wooden balls
7 "___ Lang Syne"
8 Jacob's twin
9 Aromatic
10 Prominent Manhattan sight, once
11 Equestrian's garb
12 Bring together
13 Jewish feast
21 Apr. payee
25 Communications corp.
26 Give ___ (care)
27 Royal Crown Cola brand
28 Condition in kids' card games
29 ___ B. Toklas
30 Amontillado holder
31 Subjects for Barron's: Abbr.
32 Sp. ladies
33 "Picnic" writer
34 Manuscript mark
35 Dawn goddess
37 Sporty Pontiacs
40 Palindromic preposition
41 Not intentional
43 "Well, ___ be!"
44 Aral and Caspian Seas, really
45 Spanish tourist center
46 "Laugh-In" co-host
47 W.W. II predator
50 Kind of thermometer
51 Biblical preposition
52 Farm need
53 ___ Strauss jeans
54 Swear
55 "Gimme a C . . . !" is one

371 by Brendan Emmett Quigley

ACROSS

1 Screamer's necessity
6 Manhandle
9 "Peer Gynt" dramatist
14 "Otello," e.g.
15 ___ mode
16 It makes quite a bang
17 Sound of old floorboards
18 When Guy Fawkes Day is celebrated: Abbr.
19 It may be static
20 Cult Canadian comedy troupe, with "The"
23 Operates
24 Tara family
25 Flood stage
28 ___ Xing (sign)
29 "The Gold Bug" author
30 Need air conditioning
32 60's war capital
34 Boy or girl lead-in
35 1869 Twain novel, with "The"
41 Season of peace
42 Move stealthily
43 Provided for, as a widow
47 N.Y.C. clock setting
48 Liq. measures
51 Gives the green light
52 Of service
54 Untouched
55 1934 Lillian Hellman play, with "The"
58 Genius
60 Hood's gun
61 Item on a pole
62 Plane seating choice
63 Charlottesville sch.
64 And ___ grow on
65 Gibson, e.g.
66 Gibson, e.g.
67 Victim of a 1955 coup

DOWN

1 Poky
2 Revolt
3 Had to have
4 Not Astroturf
5 H.H. Munro, pseudonymically
6 Roman temple
7 56-Down salutation
8 Isn't decisive
9 If
10 Unwelcome mail
11 Heel style
12 Sea bird
13 Yule serving
21 Peter of Herman's Hermits
22 Hem's partner
26 Home video format
27 Carpenter's nail
29 Campaign money source
31 Harmless prank
32 Reason for darning
33 "___ De-Lovely"
35 Prefix with Chinese
36 Cranny's partner
37 10:00 program
38 Bony
39 "Homage to Clio" poet
40 Diner sandwich
44 Spoiler
45 Immigrant's study, for short
46 Cotton-pickin'
48 Citer
49 Loyally following
50 Address of St. Patrick's Cathedral?
53 Plucky
54 Drop a dime, so to speak
56 See 7-Down
57 Call it a day
58 Farm call
59 Rock's Ocasek

372 by Charles E. Gersch

ACROSS

1 "Fiddler" star
6 Dido
14 Prosper
15 Fliers collectively
16 Site in the "Aeneid"
17 Polite intro
18 Johnny and the Moondogs, more familiarly
20 Locks
21 Union, e.g.: Abbr.
22 Stays in line
24 Old trains
26 Get an ___ effort
27 Alphabet trio
30 Some Wall Street firms
35 Army bigwig
36 About 2 million in the U.S.
37 W.W. II craft
38 "Elle et Lui" author
39 Whirlwinds
40 Spotted horse
42 The Mormons, initially
44 Curtain accessory
48 Breathe deeply
52 Slothful
54 New York island
55 Halloween hanging
56 Adjective for a trifle
57 Issue, as a verdict
58 Put together

DOWN

1 Another name for God
2 Church areas
3 Artist Mondrian
4 Amphitheater
5 Smooth, in phonetics
6 Telesthesia
7 University officials
8 Support
9 Staff
10 Favorable factors
11 Bristles
12 Lady of the knight
13 Regards
14 It's good to keep these on kids
19 "To the best of my information . . ."
23 Hobgoblin
25 Glide, in Glasgow
26 Art Deco artist
27 Texas-New Mexico range
28 "The Ten Commandments" extras
29 Informal women's attire
30 Warehouse container
31 Stationary item: Abbr.
32 Cowpoke's charge
33 2 ___ (double-teamed)
34 Mercedes models
40 Blanched
41 Vinegary prefix
43 Posted
44 Mrs. Addams affectionately
45 Start of a Durante title
46 Sagan's "The Dragons of ___"
47 Gusty
49 West Point inits
50 Part of a pipe
51 Normal start
53 Nashville based cable service

ACROSS

1 Noodlehead
5 Dagger handles
10 Silver-tongued
14 Eminently draftable
15 He has "99 beautiful names"
16 San ___, Italy
17 "Murder in the Cathedral" setting
19 Faux pas follower
20 Auto part
21 Abe's "The Woman in the ___"
22 Bohea, e.g.
25 Caddies carry them
27 In fairness
28 Boulevard
30 Genteel
32 Aquarium fish
33 Humble toiler
34 Pick
37 Training-room complaint
38 Robbery
39 National Enquirer rival
40 66, e.g.: Abbr.
41 Like "Hee Haw" humor

42 Italian Renaissance poet
43 Two-time A.L. M.V.P.
45 Lecture
46 Reserve supply
48 Promise word
50 Beat one's gums
51 Brook
52 Writer Angelou
54 Eaglelike, perhaps
55 Perambulates
61 Plains Indian
62 Regarding
63 Xenia's home
64 First-rate
65 Violet relative
66 Arctic native

DOWN

1 Baseball's Gooden
2 ___ roll
3 Actor Cariou
4 "So long"
5 Yamaha rival
6 Noted absurdist
7 Kind of shot
8 Tobacco figure
9 Like a wallflower
10 Ptarmigan

11 Assassin's victim, 8/20/40
12 Spur
13 Imperious
18 Lagniappe
21 Con
22 Golden Horde member
23 Upright
24 Miss Marple film "Murder ___"
26 Upholstery concern
27 Stun
29 Up to
31 Cheerful
33 Persian sprite
35 Fettuccelle, e.g.
36 Scout group
38 ___ de combat
39 "They called her frivolous ___"
41 Tobacco wad
42 Singer Tucker
44 Deteriorates
45 Nice and warm
46 Work shoe
47 "Symposium" man
49 Sibyl subjects
53 Baseless?
55 Kind of dance

56 Cultural collection
57 Writer Auletta
58 "Great idea!"
59 Sass
60 Keystone fellow

ACROSS

1 "The Nazarene" writer
5 "Elephant Boy" boy
9 ___ night
12 Cheer noisily
14 "Am ___ Love?"
15 1990 Best Supporting Actress
17 Juárez river
18 Newswoman Compton
19 Twiggy willows
21 Singer James
23 Nurse a drink
25 Conductor Dorati
26 Poverty
27 "Waterlilies" artist
29 ___ Z
30 Partying with Eddie Cantor?
34 René or Renée
35 Toymaker
36 Noisy bird
43 Scale notes
44 Lambaste
45 Composition
48 Road from Dawson Creek
51 Kind of hill or lion

52 Feast
53 Canned-tomato style
55 Truckers' watchdog
57 Any ship
58 Nothing to shout about
62 "Xanadu" rock group
63 Noisy festivity
64 Manuel's intro
65 One of a trio in Scandinavian myth
66 Pursue

DOWN

1 ". . . ___ Christmas"
2 ___ up (film genre)
3 Bill's partner
4 "May I?" step
5 Hires
6 Act of contrition
7 Biblical month
8 Hairstyle that needs hairpins
9 Coordinate
10 Listen in on
11 Unappreciative one
13 Airline to Karachi
15 Songbird
16 Scouting org.
20 Kind of gin

22 Town in a W.W. II novel
24 Notre Dame bench
27 Copycat
28 Heat unit
31 Keystone officer
32 Rock ___ (jukebox brand)
33 Land ___ (night locale)
36 Package
37 Hair products maker Curtis and others
38 Warring Seminole chief
39 Brady bill opposer
40 Father
41 Become popular
42 Occurrence
46 Loose a bra
47 Filter
49 ___ Parker, 1904 candidate for President
50 Mint
54 How the answer to this goes
56 Ceiling
59 Greek letter
60 Typewriting abbr.

61 Start of a bray

ACROSS

1 Rear
6 Edible rodent
10 Address abbr.
13 Historic earldom
14 Jambalaya locale
15 Perrier, par exemple
16 Smog?
18 More than aloofness
19 Yves's eve
20 Write off
22 Belly laugh
25 Like Desmond Tutu
28 Synge's "___ Island"
29 Fred Harman's comics cowboy
32 Of ecological stages
34 Athlete's foot
35 Hack
36 Ownership
37 U.N. arm
38 Firms (up)
40 Bambi's aunt
41 Rings
43 Mountain capital
44 Freedom
46 Head overseas
47 Showed indecision
50 Sound of a live wire
51 Belle and others
53 Appear ahead
55 Comics interjection
56 How a young lady succeeds?
62 Sign
63 Goodbye
64 ___ Fountain
65 Dance step
66 Almost up
67 Indians whose name means "lovers of sexual pleasure"

DOWN

1 Actor Stephen
2 "Do ___ say!"
3 Medit. nation
4 At some times of the year
5 Fair
6 Something to be up to
7 One vote
8 Tell secretly
9 Overlords
10 Inaugural balls?
11 Confront
12 "Parigi, o cara," in "La Traviata"
14 Old dance site
17 Airline to Karachi
21 Bit of light
22 Low-priced lodging
23 ___ million
24 Results of deer hunting?
26 Cross-examiner
27 Jay and family
30 Uses force
31 Has a second meeting with
33 Ed Sullivan Theater host
34 Cañon feature
39 Hornswoggle
42 Diamond call
45 Comparative suffix
48 Tennyson's "doves in immemorial ___"
49 ___ good turn
51 She at sea
52 One of the Sinatras
54 Aware of
57 MNO, on a phone
58 Tippler
59 Storm producer
60 Time before
61 Family member

ACROSS

1 Mischief-maker
7 Pokes
13 Snub
14 Cartoon tot
15 Shocks
17 Guinea pigs
18 Numbers on a letter
19 Go-aheads
20 Bluejackets
22 Comedian Olsen
23 With a whole new appearance
27 Big Bill of the court
31 Kind of music notation
32 Sunburn soother
33 Music Appreciation, for one
35 Lead-in for flops or hertz
36 Certain crimes
38 Domain for Athena
40 Cleaned, in a way
42 Ending with pay or plug
43 Preparing, with "up"
46 Famously cold Maine town
49 "Step on the gas!"
52 Fruity beverage
53 Electron tube
54 "The Gathering" star
55 Plants used in ropemaking
56 Slip
57 Tantrums

DOWN

1 ___ Brothers (old film slapstick team)
2 Cultural opening
3 Fractures
4 Tête-à-tête
5 Fancy cabinet
6 S.A.T. taker's need
7 Shropshire mothers
8 Landlords
9 Tropical kernels
10 Attentive
11 Biblical verb
12 Mouth off
14 Attitudes
16 Hauler
21 All together
24 Pleading the Fifth
25 Edible rootstock
26 Ancient Khuzistan
27 Filing aids
28 Pelvic bones
29 Type of statistical distribution
30 Most pernicious
34 Texas ___
37 Swaziland's capital
39 Crackbrained
41 Sherman was his Veep
44 St. Olaf's subjects
45 More than a murmur
46 F or G, e.g.
47 Opera set in Memphis
48 Baltic Sea feeder
50 "Monty Python" regular
51 1979 Nastassja Kinski role

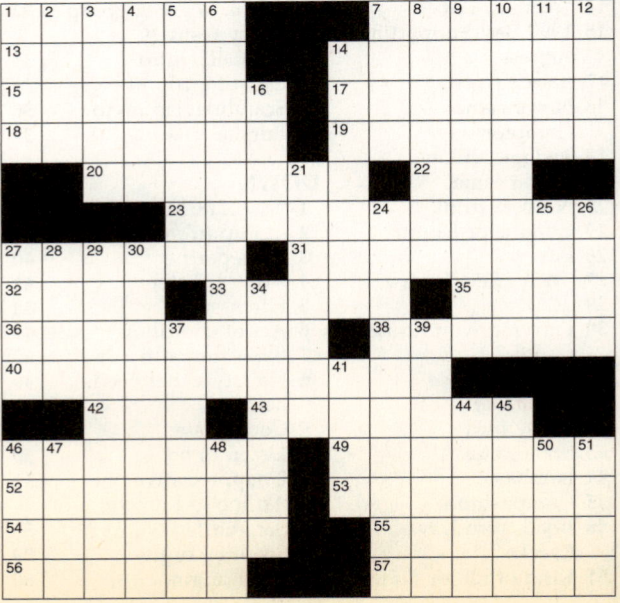

377 by Jonathan Schmalzbach

ACROSS
1 Boats like Noah's
5 Dove, for one
10 Swiss mountain
13 "Star Wars" princess
14 Terre ___, Ind.
15 Bread with seeds
16 Huey Long roman à clef
19 Judith Krantz novel
20 It's frozen in Frankfurt
21 "For ___ a jolly . . ."
22 Secretary, e.g.: Abbr.
23 Canyon effect
25 Shoe bottom
29 Made as good as new
37 Marry
38 Eugene O'Neill work
42 Dye container
43 Most foulmouthed
44 Q-tip, e.g.
46 Bulletin board sticker
50 "Syncratic" prefix
54 Mauna ___
57 Letter before sigma
58 Streisand film, after "The"
61 Tale of a Piggy's plight
63 Lumberjack's tool
64 Loved ones
65 "Is so!" rebuttal
66 The ___ Affair
67 Gardner and others
68 Perches

DOWN
1 Visigoth leader
2 Hot dog topper
3 Potter's oven
4 Paige, informally
5 1988 Tim Rice musical
6 Squirrels' hangouts
7 Single-named novelist
8 Lab burners
9 Kathie Lee's co-host
10 Host
11 Soap ingredient
12 Stylus
17 With 39-Down, a cornball variety show
18 Speedy jets
19 Prominent part of "Peter Piper picked a peck . . ."
24 Refinery shipment
26 Possess
27 "Malcolm X" director
28 Magazine chiefs, for short
30 River to the North Sea
31 Health club
32 ___ Aviv
33 Scrap of food
34 Louis XIV, e.g.
35 Prior, to Prior
36 LP spinners
38 Boob tubes
39 See 17-Down
40 It's two after epsilon
41 Giant giant
45 Basketball's Larry
47 Passionate
48 Pieces of bedroom furniture
49 Feats of Clay: Abbr.
51 Radio part
52 Use logic
53 In base 8
54 Loamy soil
55 Incorrect
56 Brother of Prometheus
58 Clinton, slangily
59 Honor: Ger.
60 Four on a sundial
61 Loose
62 Petroleum company, informally

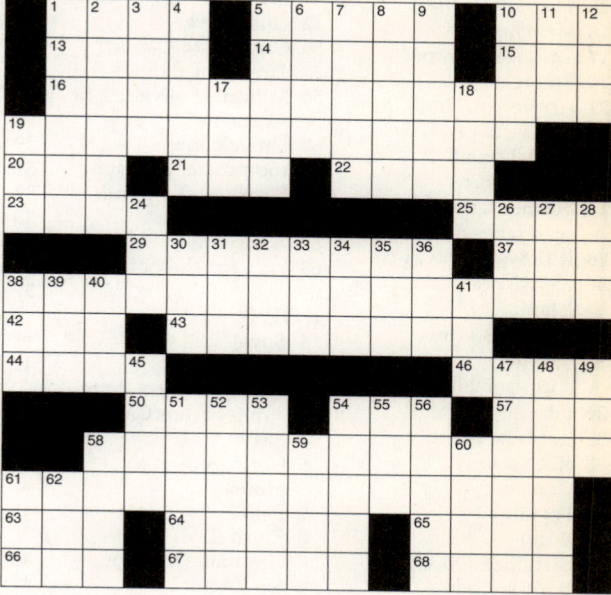

378 by Sidney L. Robbins

ACROSS
1 Israeli port
6 "Of ___ I Sing"
10 Flattened circle
14 Fall flower
15 Is under the weather
16 Accumulation
17 It's lined with bars
19 Palindromic pop quartet
20 Irritate
21 Snoozing
23 "Just a ___"
26 Failures
27 Leadership group
32 Rigorous exams
34 Bay window
35 1985 film "___ Williams"
36 Mexican coin
40 Carte blanche
43 Fly alone
44 Identical
45 Identically
46 Rancher's cattle
47 Lawn pests
48 Ravel work
52 Lair
54 Polar covering
55 Makes watertight
61 When doubled, a Samoan port
62 1959 Doris Day film
66 Airline to Jerusalem
67 ___ Lackawanna Railway
68 Hawaiian island
69 Cowgirl Evans
70 Actor Alan
71 Won't

DOWN
1 Door holder
2 Late tennis V.I.P.
3 Followers: Suffix
4 Yard sections
5 Comic Johnson
6 Shape of St. Anthony's cross
7 That guy's
8 Yale Bulldog
9 Bake in sauce
10 October stones
11 Feelings, in slang
12 Playwright Edward
13 Bounds
18 "The A-Team" star
22 Stranded sailor's call
24 Central arteries
25 Indulged in reveries
27 Corny throwaways
28 Folkie Guthrie
29 Watch's face
30 Nevada city
31 Moose
33 Electrical unit
36 Game with sticks
37 Sinful
38 "For heaven's ___!"
39 Bullring cries
41 Impediment, at law
42 Computer capacity, for short
46 Mrs. in Madrid
48 Two-legged
49 Florida city
50 Over 21, liquorwise
51 Pierre's school
53 Sgt. or cpl.
56 Shoemaker's tools
57 Beehive State
58 Actress Turner
59 Part of K.K.K.
60 Comical playlet
63 Mr. Gershwin
64 Cover
65 Conducted

379 by Richard Hughes

ACROSS
1 Guinness or Baldwin
5 Parisian coin
10 Resorts
14 Papal tribunal
15 Y's half brothers
16 Mr. Gingrich
17 Caesar's résumé?
20 Enters
21 Arrive feet first
22 Aunt ___ of "Oklahoma!"
24 Storm sirens
25 Former Clinton press secretary
28 It flows in the Ebro
30 New York's ___ Island
31 Geraint's wife
32 Passport endorsement
36 Fit
37 Century plant
38 Rock's Billy ___
39 Consider
40 Forum site
41 Bitter
42 Standard Oil logo
43 Barn sounds
44 Onetime phone company sobriquet
48 Russian ballet company
50 Moon-landing missions
52 Guard, e.g.
56 Cassius, to Caesar?
58 Turner of movies
59 Milton's "olive ___ of Academe"
60 Unwelcome roommate, perhaps
61 Barely makes, with "out"
62 Assistants
63 "___ for the poor"

DOWN
1 Bows
2 Boor
3 To be, to Bernadette
4 Advice from Caesar?
5 Easy
6 Get together, as grads
7 Pain
8 Entre ___
9 Graduation honors for Caesar?
10 Nasty
11 Pumpkin eater of rhyme
12 Expect
13 British guns
18 Man and Capri, e.g.
19 Handyman Bob
23 Went bananas
25 ___ ringer
26 North Sea feeder
27 Vogue rival
29 Award
31 Some are super
32 Caesar's opposite?
33 Think about it
34 Type
35 Priestly garb
37 Start of Caesar's comment at a museum?
41 "___ came a spider . . ."
42 Cockney greeting
43 Pickling solutions
44 Important Vermont tree
45 Approximately vertical, at sea
46 Carried
47 "___ Dream"
("Lohengrin" soliloquy)
49 "___ a Parade"
51 Asian dress
53 Shoppers' haven
54 Jot
55 Catches
57 Nonverbal affirmation

380 by Jonathan Schmalzbach

ACROSS
1 Parts of addresses
5 Like some religions
10 "Hurry!"
14 Pip
15 Thrill to pieces
16 Hip
17 Seagoing departure from a Scandinavian capital?
20 A Stooge
21 "As You Like It" forest
22 50's rocker Bill
23 One "T" of TNT
24 Item used in strokes
25 Anouk Aimée film in a Mideast capital?
33 Destinations
34 Mosquito genus
35 Pourboire
37 Dictum
38 Friend of the Red Cross
39 Overfeed
40 Picnic interloper
41 Ur's locale
42 Vieux ___ (New Orleans locale)
43 Aggressive personality trait in the Far East?
46 ___ King Cole
47 Function
48 ___ Heep
51 Latin "that is"
54 Trilogy that includes "1919"
57 South American football player?
60 Longish dress
61 Like Fellini's vita
62 Dash of panache
63 Barbados export
64 Sleipnir, for Odin
65 Computer unit

DOWN
1 Type of lens
2 ___ many words
3 One-name sports star
4 Box-office sign
5 Vaudevillian's bellwether
6 "When I was ___ . . ."
7 Scandal suffix
8 Memo abbr.
9 Paleo's opposite
10 Some things work like this
11 Ground
12 Bang-up
13 QB's call
18 Farm homes
19 Pandemonium
23 It's hard to believe
24 Debtor
25 Pearl Mosque site
26 Jockey's ride
27 W.W. II's most-bombed island
28 Ruth's mother-in-law
29 Cygnus shiner
30 Revere
31 Arcade name
32 Demolitionist's supply
36 Look closely
38 "Ma mère, je la vois," in "Carmen"
39 Cut costs
41 Algerian cavalryman
42 ___ wide net
44 Even, scorewise
45 Quieted
48 West Point inits.
49 Amtrak travel
50 ___-European
51 "___ Plenty o' Nuttin"
52 Big name in the pineapple biz
53 Behold, to Brutus
54 Hideous
55 Bucket in a Buick
56 Composer Thomas
58 Classified items
59 One of Stonewall's soldiers

381 by Cathy Millhauser

ACROSS
1 Kickapoos, e.g.
6 "Tuna-Fishing" painter
10 Silent one
14 Emulated the Blob
15 "My People" author
16 Dash
17 Like well-behaved clerics?
20 Singular
21 Mirror backing
22 It can bring a tear to your eye
23 The Great Commoner
24 Spelling on TV
25 Like mosquitoes at a camp?
32 Pernod ingredient
33 Hoopster Archibald
34 "Who, Horatius?"
35 Baker or Battle, e.g.
36 Producers of bangs?
38 Swindle, slangily
39 Put away the dishes
40 Exec's dispatch
41 Pickle
42 Like tie-dyed clothes?
46 Hem
47 Fritzi, to Nancy
48 Sally
51 Mercyhurst College site
52 Indian sovereignty
55 Like Cinderella before the Prince?
58 Blue dye
59 Kind of thermometer
60 Ticket imperative
61 20's heavyweight Tunney
62 Street band
63 Goes the distance

DOWN
1 Fast food option
2 Crucifix
3 Shirt label
4 High-riser, e.g.
5 High-rise, e.g.
6 Danny of "Taxi"
7 Old actor Walter
8 ___ Cruces
9 Mass sections
10 Deserved praise
11 O'Grady of "Eight Is Enough"
12 Ham bits
13 Screen
18 Reply to the Little Red Hen
19 Seine feeder
23 City on the Arno
24 Pre-1917 ruler
25 One of Polly Adler's ilk
26 Grammy-winning Baker
27 Hepatologist's specialty
28 Washington's ___ Station
29 Horse play?
30 "M*A*S*H" extra
31 Rake parts
36 Spinose mammal
37 Feminine friend
38 Junk
40 Ambulance driver
41 Dakar's land
43 Pot
44 Giving a darn
45 Trash
48 Decorative drapery
49 Caen's river
50 Harness part
51 Garden spot
52 ___ horn (shofar)
53 Keep ___ (persevere)
54 Jacuzzi set
56 60's singer Little ___
57 Vitamin bottle abbr.

382 by A.J. Santora

ACROSS
1 Queen Bilqis's land
6 Went for
9 Demean
14 Gold
15 Chemical prefix
16 Actress Thompson et al.
17 What tots did in the malt shop?
20 Auto item with rubber flanges
21 Best-furnished
24 ___ Cat (winter vehicle)
25 Application datum
26 Word to a doctor
27 Training system originated in Sweden
29 Sill cover
32 Walk-ons
35 Braced for a roller coaster ride
38 Comes down somewhat hard?
39 Lout
42 Overpamper
44 Prefix with 25-Across
45 Part of a "fully loaded" car
46 Powerful D.C. lobby
48 Good tidings
52 Not the independent sort
55 Shook hands?
59 Month in Managua
60 Tony-winning actress Salonga
61 North of Virginia
62 Deceived
63 Opposite of lack
64 Paintbrush material

DOWN
1 Decline
2 Wallace's "Ben-___"
3 Oxydol competitor
4 St. Louis's ___ Stadium
5 Copious
6 "___ I" (1970 gold record)
7 Car-racing org.
8 Southey's "Roderick, the Last of the ___"
9 Dixon line
10 M.T.A.: Boston:: ___: San Francisco
11 Fresh as ___
12 Went ballistic
13 20's auto
18 Danger for a U-Boot
19 Judo instructor
21 Cape Canaveral site
22 Row
23 Bygone leader
28 Part of the Labor Dept.
30 Foreign money
31 "Prelude to a Kiss" composer
32 TV producer Fred
33 Symbol of industry
34 Hood and others: Abbr.
36 Texas city on the Mexican border
37 Hood
40 Identical
41 Shortening kin
42 Water-soluble gas
43 Ready to go
45 Gradually increasing in speed, in mus.
47 Saxon predecessor
48 Water choice
49 Bigwig
50 Cooperstown's Cap ___
51 Just
53 Sleuth Wolfe
54 Increased
56 Afflicted
57 Madre's hermano
58 Poultry buy

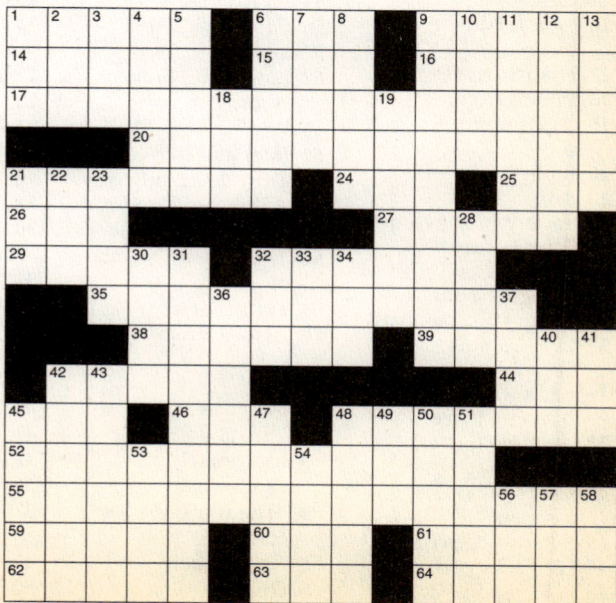

383 by Martin Schneider

ACROSS

1 ___ Doc Duvalier
5 J. ___ Hoover
10 ___ au lait
14 ___ Corporation (ammunition maker)
15 Jules ___
16 ___-friendly
17 "Of ___ and Men"
18 "___ the news today . . ." (Beatles lyric)
19 "Take ___ Train"
20 ___ basket
22 "The ___ Show on Earth"
24 "It's ___!" ("See you then!")
26 Camus's "The ___ of Sisyphus"
27 ___ so on
29 Nick at ___
31 ___ living
34 TV's "___ & Clark"
36 Hippocratic ___
38 On the ___
40 Title for this puzzle
43 "Van Gogh in ___"
44 "Que ___ . . ."
45 ___ River, N.J.
46 ___ the storm
48 Jay ___
50 Jacqueline Kennedy, ___ Bouvier
51 "___ Fiction"
53 British ___
55 "The ___ Heart"
59 Mount St. ___
62 ___ Canal
63 ___ finish
65 Get ___ the ground floor
66 "Rock of ___"
67 ___ nous
68 ___ spumante
69 ". . . gathers no ___"
70 ___ the course (perseveres)
71 "Have a ___"

DOWN

1 "___ and Circumstance"
2 Et ___
3 ___ Circus
4 Put ___ to
5 ___ notice
6 "___ Rosenkavalier"
7 Cyclist ___ LeMond
8 ___ and a leg
9 Take the ___ (fly at night)
10 ___ competition
11 Arthur ___
12 Legal ___
13 Quod ___ demonstrandum
21 ___ Fleming
23 "Not ___" ("Think nothing of it")
25 ___-Unis
27 ___ Romeo
28 Bête ___
30 ___ Merman
32 ___ panty hose
33 Billy Joel's "Don't ___ Why"
35 "___ in Seattle"
37 "Ready or not, ___ come!"
39 In ___ (actually)
41 The word ___
42 Rock's Siouxsie and the ___
47 Go down in ___
49 Grand ___ Opry
52 Manufacturing ___
54 ___ Howe
55 ___ player
56 "Cogito ___ sum"
57 "True ___"
58 ___ Kett of the comics
60 ___ bene
61 In a ___ (agitated)
64 The old college ___

384 by Stephanie Spadaccini

ACROSS

1 Yak
4 Ending with Dixie
8 Mountaineer's goal
12 Sharer's pronoun
14 Casanova
16 Item filed by a secretary?
17 Hydrox rival
18 Whatsoever
19 "___ hungry I could . . ."
20 Blue
23 Anger
24 Society page word
25 Sounds surprised
27 Long-___ owl
29 Designer Lauren
33 Suffix with bombard
34 Late Cabinet Secretary Aspin
36 Exclamation from Beaver Cleaver
37 ___ time (never)
38 Green
42 Captain Hook's assistant
43 S.F.-to-Vegas dir.
44 Neither's partner
45 G.I.'s address
46 Fight off
48 Winona Horowitz's professional name
52 Word with time or memory
54 Sturdy tree
56 First lady
57 Yellow
62 Linguistics branch: Abbr.
63 Whiff
64 Interlaken's river
65 Turn down officially
66 "___ is an island . . ."
67 Owllike
68 The Mideast's Gulf of ___
69 Transmitted
70 Actor Herbert

DOWN

1 Sweet treat
2 The dawn
3 Milwaukee profession
4 "The Bridge" poet Hart
5 No-goodnik
6 Oriental nurse
7 Phone or photo preceder
8 Jung's feminine component
9 Place for tents
10 Squander
11 "Hold On Tight" rock group
13 Family boy
15 Aged
21 Encyclopedia volume
22 "Yuck!"
26 Sold-out sign
28 Gen. Robt.
30 Go along (with)
31 Hawaiian accessory
32 Hammer end
35 Graf ___
37 "___ in the Dark"
38 Influenced, with "on"
39 Beginner
40 Sixth sense
41 Bellini opera
42 Mule of song
46 Kind of room
47 ___ Brothers (investment firm)
49 Bit of info
50 Very
51 Turn in for money, as bonds
53 Señor Bolivar
55 Inclined
58 Neb. neighbor
59 Cupid
60 Alaska gold rush town
61 In its natural state
62 Señora Perón

385 by Randolph Ross

ACROSS
1 Comparison maker
10 Rain check?
14 Monazite, e.g.
15 Plantation worker
16 Woolworth's, e.g.
17 High as ___
18 Suggestions
19 Free to attack
20 Turn black, then blue?
21 Date
22 Hanukkah dish
23 Sight at Dulles
24 Foldable furniture
26 Fusses
30 Most rundown
31 Cry of success
33 Gothic typeface: Var.
36 Spectacle
39 Like some motions
40 Feed bag morsel
42 Tart
43 Second of three X's
45 Magna ___
47 Spokes
48 Small chapels
50 Order
51 Jubilation
52 Lucky numero
53 Propagandist
54 Besmirches
55 Fall events

DOWN
1 Spirits
2 Least artful
3 ___ the teeth
4 Chary
5 Durango direction
6 Catarina's cat
7 Von Bulow portrayer, 1990
8 1990 remake of "The Texas Rangers"
9 "Men of honest report," in Acts
10 Sample
11 Somewhat
12 Second shots
13 Practice exam
15 Like Sinatra songs
25 Driver's needs
27 Precincts
28 Dental problem
29 Bandar ___ Begawan (Brunei's capital)
32 Structured like sodium chloride
33 Most meager
34 Pastoral land of ancient Greece
35 Comparatively poor
37 Prisoner taken 1/3/90
38 Gone
41 Samples
44 Dutch painter ___ Fabritius
45 Heating elements
46 Put the ___ (intimidate)
49 Repressed, with "on"

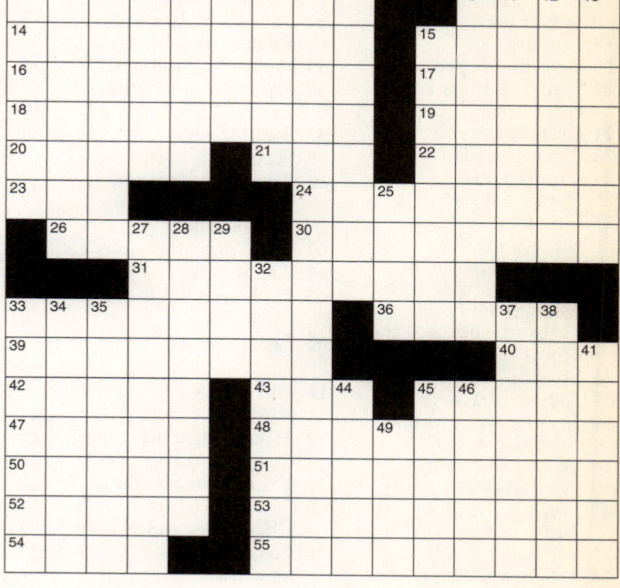

386 by Stephanie Spadaccini

ACROSS
1 Garb for Superman
5 Ice cream dessert
10 Work detail, for short
14 Singer Guthrie
15 Ness of "The Untouchables"
16 ___ Strauss (jeans maker)
17 What a ghost may give you
19 Coup d'___
20 Boundary
21 Meat cuts
22 Stockholmer
23 Wise one
24 Pay no attention
26 Georgia city where Little Richard was born
29 Western hero
31 Keeps away from
33 "Whose Life ___ Anyway?" (1981 movie)
34 Suffix with cash
37 Factory on a stream
38 Department at an auto shop
40 Fairy tale starter
41 Tally (up)
42 Bundled cotton
43 "Well said!"
45 Honkers
48 A Musketeer
49 Pass ___ (make the grade)
50 Poll amts.
52 Bar for a bird
53 California lake resort
55 Notwithstanding, briefly
58 Actress Chase
59 With feet pointing in
61 Above, in Berlin
62 Not moving
63 Singer Fitzgerald
64 Articulates
65 Go along (with)
66 Enemy's opposite

DOWN
1 Hamster's home
2 "East of Eden" brother
3 Slog (through)
4 Dawn goddess
5 Obscure
6 Hardy and North
7 Bearing
8 Most domineering
9 Numerical ending
10 Quite a few, after "a"
11 "Network" co-star
12 Dodge, as a question
13 Commend
18 African antelope
22 Perturbed state
23 Loam
25 Grain for grinding
26 Baby doll's cry
27 Enthusiastic
28 One way to quit
30 Personnel person
32 Outpouring
35 Reverberate
36 "Cheers" actor Roger
39 Emulating Paul Revere
40 Inning parts
42 This and that
44 Granola-like
46 Katharine Hepburn has four
47 Globe
49 Opera star Nellie
51 "Veddy" British actor Robert
52 Papal name
54 Finish for teen or golden
55 Auto commuter's bane
56 "War is ___"
57 Singer Anita
59 Actress Zadora
60 Wonderland drink

387 by Bob Klahn

ACROSS
1 Stereotypical swing voter
11 Luck, to some
15 Delusions
16 Dirk of yore
17 They don't play the net in tennis
18 Lowers
19 Amour-propre
20 It may have a big head
21 Brandy letters
23 Curry or Rice
24 Composed
26 Piano pieces?
27 Doc bloc
28 Gather on the surface, chemically
30 Things for one to do
32 Mangel-wurzels
35 Long of "Boyz N the Hood"
36 Stirring
37 Relief, of a sort
38 Immigrant's course, briefly
39 Driver's warning
40 "GoodFellas" group
42 Lemieux milieu: Abbr.
43 Scrooge
44 Towhead

45 How many manuscripts are submitted
47 Propel a shell
48 Fictional clue-sniffer
50 Nels of "Little House on the Prairie"
54 Sounds of Brahma, Vishnu and Siva
55 Peace, in Russia
56 Husband and wife, e.g.
57 Sect leader?
58 Sorority letter
60 Rock band named after the villain in "Barbarella"
63 Bank holding
64 Affranchise
65 Professor 'iggins, to Eliza
66 Press release?

DOWN
1 Agrees
2 Model railroad track measure
3 TV newsman David
4 "Get it?"
5 Christmas and Easter
6 Fox Mulder's obsession

7 Philatelist's purchase
8 Got fed up
9 Interviewer's surprises
10 Affectionate, in slang
11 It was dropped in the 60's
12 "A Girl Like I" autobiographer
13 Hester Prynne portrayer, 1995
14 Slave's response
22 Mountain on the Gulf of Salonika
25 Doesn't do takeout
26 Deity whose name means "black"
29 Bridge opening
31 Some are out of it in January
32 Buffalo
33 Where Rommel was routed
34 "Where Angels Fear to Tread" novelist
41 Leading man?
43 Sweet, in a way
46 Sudden seizure?
49 Top of a platter
51 Musical heirloom
52 Magniloquize
53 Number in NASA-speak

56 Twain's celebrated jumping frog
59 Some
61 Hammer sound
62 News letters

388 by Brett Blaylock

ACROSS
1 Logical thinker
6 Does laps
11 Scott Baio's "Happy Days" role
12 Least trusting
15 Reviewed with "up"
16 Agitated
17 Star seen late at night
19 "___ bien!" (all right!). Sp.
20 Tom Mix film
21 Kind of notation
24 Biblical measure
25 Helmet guardpiece
26 Sign
27 Nora portrayer in film
29 Makes rings in the hair
31 Joseph of ___ (follower of Jesus)
34 Snowmen?
36 Bit of snowman attire
40 Southwest Conf. team
41 Gift giver
43 Zeno's home

44 Where there's a lotta shakin' goin' on
46 Utter
47 Sandwich material
48 "Rhetoric" author
50 Wagner hero
53 Set off
54 Portuguese lady
55 Prepared for a wallop
56 Waif
57 Inflame

DOWN
1 "Eye" opener
2 1958 Literature Nobelist
3 Landscapist's color
4 "If I Could Turn Back Time" singer
5 Cruise companion
6 Playground equipment
7 Opposite of ruddy
8 Brit. adversary
9 Churl
10 Cast off
11 Smooth
13 Protests

14 Follow in another's footsteps?
15 Flowerage
18 Variety of gypsum
22 Price word
23 Muddy Waters's genre
28 Commence
30 Secretariat. e.g.
32 "___ Old Cowhand"
33 Chet Huntley, by birth
34 Furniture style
35 Appropriate
37 "Take ___" (order to a steno)
38 Swayed
39 Got along
40 Back-to-sch. times
42 Awn
45 Soft woolen fabric
46 Comedian Arnold
49 Sheppard and Turpin's gun
51 Gobbler
52 Mr. Onassis

ACROSS

1 Like Ike
5 Like most colleges today
9 One 39-Across
13 "I cannot tell ___"
14 Heraldic band
15 Sandbags, maybe
16 Holds up
17 Café additive
18 Chemically nonreactive
19 Chiffonier
21 One 39-Across
23 One 39-Across
25 Verboten: Var.
26 Cantankerous
32 Rep.'s rival
35 "___ be a cold day in Hell . . ."
38 Ancient region of Asia Minor
39 Each of eight in this puzzle
43 Like measles
44 Elliptical
45 Compass dir.
46 Home to Denali National Park
48 Teases
51 One 39-Across
56 One 39-Across
60 Stay informed
62 Island group near Fiji
63 Periodical of haute couture
65 Small dog breed, for short
66 One 39-Across
67 Plaintiff
68 Get ready
69 Fusses
70 Orly birds?
71 Lighten up

DOWN

1 Fishhook part
2 One way to read
3 Sign of autumn's beginning
4 Go AWOL
5 One 39-Across
6 ___ pro nobis
7 Statesman Root
8 Coup ___
9 Transportation Secretary Federico
10 Penultimate fairy tale word
11 Wonk, maybe
12 Pocket
15 Actress Ullmann
20 One-time link
22 Symbol for density
24 Expenditure
27 Singer Ocasek of the Cars
28 Classic drama of Japan
29 Seth's son
30 Ocho ___, Jamaica
31 One 39-Across
32 1982 movie thriller
33 Iniquitous
34 Pianist Hess
36 Broadway comedy of 1964
37 Live's partner
40 ___ Palmas (Canary Islands seaport)
41 Benevolent guy
42 Macs
47 King Kong, e.g.
49 Quilt-making gathering
50 Treeless plain
52 Like the Boston-accented pronunciation of many words
53 Card catalogue abbr.
54 Where the fat lady sings
55 Zaps
56 Ask to produce proof of age
57 Melville novel
58 Participates in a regatta, perhaps
59 One of the Bobbsey twins
61 ___ Le Pew
62 Loan-granting Fed. agcy.
64 Fill a flat?

ACROSS

1 *Break down grammatically*
6 *Items in a still life*
11 Braincase
13 "___ Fables"
15 Considers bond values again
16 Reduce to ashes
18 Fred's sister
19 ___ Speedwagon
20 Not give ___
21 Mediocre
22 Argued
24 Loudonville, N.Y., campus
25 Classical name in medicine
27 Sprinted
28 "___ Believer" (Monkees hit)
31 Barn topper
32 Football squad
36 Court ruling
37 Hint to solving the eight italicized clues
39 ___ Jima
40 Ignite
42 Plane or dynamic preceder
43 Actress Ryan
44 Deteriorate
45 Curses
47 Sprockets linker
50 Reps. counterparts
51 Riding whip
55 Natural gait
56 Emily, to Charlotte
57 Madrid attraction
58 Kind of lot
60 Zebralike
62 March laboriously
63 Paired nuclides
64 *Catch suddenly*
65 *Harvests*

DOWN

1 *Trims*
2 Kind of recording
3 Passage ceremony
4 Cash's "A Boy Named ___"
5 Printers' widths
6 Set the standard for
7 Architect Saarinen
8 Chemical suffix
9 Lettuce variety
10 *Bowling score*
11 Tomorrow: Lat.
12 Try again
14 Laurel or Musial
17 Wetlands watchdog
19 Deserters
22 Venus, for one
23 River to the Laptev Sea
24 Game fish
26 50's singer Frankie
27 Supplies with better weapons
28 Kind
29 ___ tai (cocktail)
30 Cereal bristle
33 Robust energy
34 Pronoun in a côte?
35 Norfolk ale
38 20 quires
41 Evaporated
46 Act niggardly
47 Actor Gulager
48 Emcee
49 *Copycats*
50 More extreme
52 *Mustard plants*
53 Baltic Sea feeder
54 Pea places
56 Long account
57 Swift sailing boat
59 B-F connection
60 Salutation for Edmund Hillary
61 Half a fly

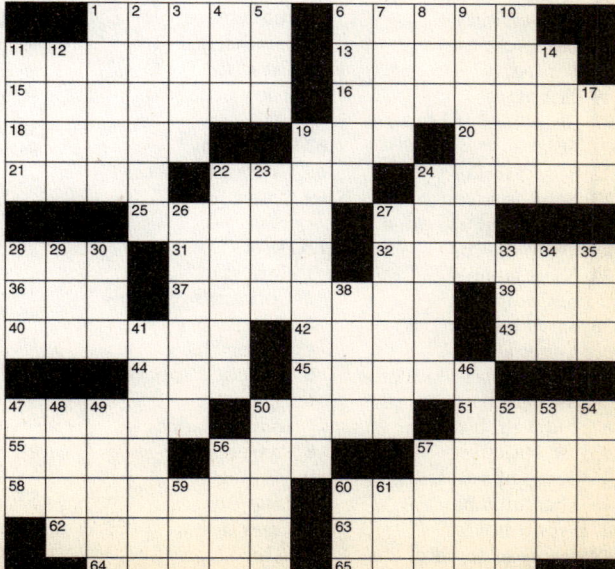

391 by Thomas W. Schier

ACROSS

1 Jerk
6 Netman Kriek
11 Peek
12 Even (with)
14 Bristles
15 Symbol of somberness, in poetry
17 Passbook amt.
18 Not a winner
20 Tell (on)
21 Fishes by dangling the bait on the water
23 Meadowlands hockey player
24 Lasso
25 "___ or lose it!"
27 June honoree
28 Farm worker
29 Xerxes ruled here
31 Directional sign
33 Bank burglars
35 Packaging material
36 Informational sign
39 Topped
42 Take ___ at
43 Düsseldorf dessert
45 White House resignee of 1988
46 Team finisher
47 Stenos' output
49 Dully colored
50 Author Kesey
51 Indiana town near South Bend
53 French city where Henry IV was born
54 Diane and Ruth
56 Portray, as historical events
58 Outbuilding
59 More ___
60 "Following the Equator" author
61 Bridge seats

DOWN

1 Cautionary sign
2 Not in France
3 Theater org.
4 Burn
5 Interfered (with)
6 Spur-of-the-moments trips
7 Magic's Shaquille
8 "Bird on a Wire" actress
9 Meet
10 Cautionary sign
11 Bribe, informally
13 "Grim" one
14 Make sense
16 Forever, to Keats
19 Race track
22 "Yes, sir," in Seville
24 Switched according to plan
26 Packed closely
28 Pluck a uke
30 Muslim honorific
32 ___ Schwarz
34 Thinks over
36 Difficult matters
37 Bony
38 Prom night transport
40 Stern and Newton
41 Coming out
44 Juliet's was "sweet"
47 Cuban patriot José
48 Metric measure
51 Yakutsk's river
52 Sigmoid swimmers
55 Go off course
57 End up with

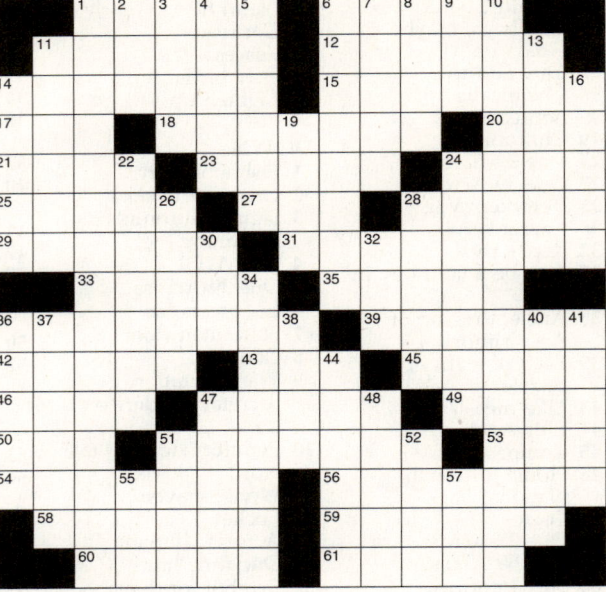

392 by Robert H. Wolfe

ACROSS

1 Funeral stand
5 Lick
8 A little night music
12 Like matzoh
16 Della's creator
17 18th-century monarch, too familiarly?
19 Tributary
20 Residents of Meshed
21 Still
22 Miss Merkel
23 Baby food
26 Items that are piled
29 Overwhelms
34 Shah Jahan's building site
36 Salve base
38 Ennoble
39 Lake Ontario outlet, too familiarly?
42 Indian follower
43 TV's Ricky
44 Tangent's cousin
45 Shenanigans
47 Frond holder
49 It makes towels plushy
50 Indy 500 advertiser
52 Actress Thompson
54 Available, as retail goods
59 Bill collector
63 Architectural refinement, too familiarly?
65 Press for
66 Took orders, in a way
67 By and by
68 Bygone platters
69 Those for

DOWN

1 Bare skin
2 Concerning, at law
3 Robt. ___
4 Singer Helen
5 Athletic supporter?
6 Against
7 Indian leader
8 Actress Garr
9 Vicinage
10 Map out
11 Goes down
13 "Do, ___, a female . . ."
14 Kind of reality
15 Academic heads
18 Beaver, for one
23 Turkish bigwig
24 In addition
25 Art sale item
27 Wrap name
28 Chafed places
30 W.W. II foe
31 Know-it-all
32 Full assemblies
33 Pharyngeal invader
35 "The King ___"
37 Aforetime
40 University of Arizona site
41 Surrenderer
46 Last item?
48 Verdun's river
51 Jail-related
53 Overeager
54 Greenish-blue
55 Crank
56 Utah's state flower
57 Adult-to-be
58 Small cut
60 Letters from Wall Street
61 Parmenides's birthplace
62 Stop lights
64 Como's "___ Impossible"

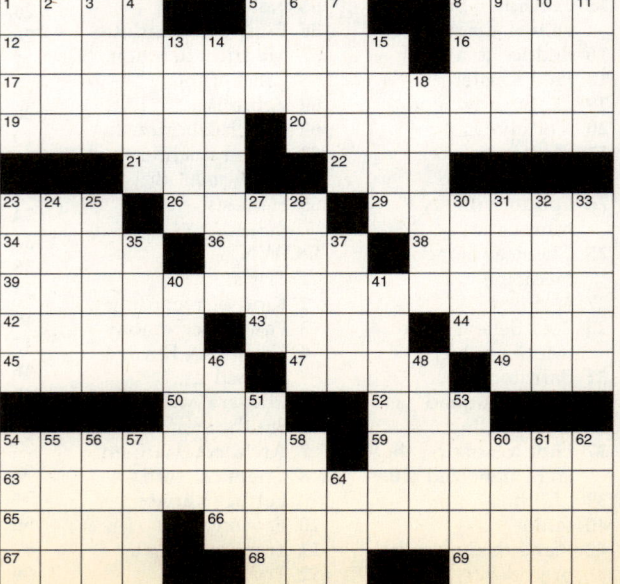

393 by Alfio Micci

ACROSS

1 Mugger subduer
5 Bathday cake?
9 Like a bairn
12 Press
13 Zoroastrian
14 Miss
16 M
19 Aficionado
20 Word of woe
21 Calorie counter
22 Less cordial
24 Palindromic org.
25 Actress Mary
26 O
30 Circumvent
31 ___ mutantur (all things change)
32 Group meal
33 Green ___
35 Neighbor of Ariz.
39 Dazzling effect
41 Arrange for orchestra
42 E
47 Downed
48 See red?
49 A.k.a.
50 Hard: Prefix
52 Date-setting phrase
53 Cask
56 Y
59 Eliel's son
60 Jam
61 "Judith" composer
62 Neighbor of Isr.
63 Yemen's capital
64 Pooped

DOWN

1 Upset
2 "Un bel di," for one
3 Wall moldings
4 Printer's dashes
5 Game hunter's trip
6 Table scraps
7 Timber wood
8 Former airline
9 Fizz flavor
10 Virgil's birthplace
11 Backward
13 Propelled a punt
15 Tatter
17 Sully
18 Dolphins' home
23 Constrict
24 Climber's goal
26 Notable uncle
27 First lady
28 Paraguayan compass point
29 Region of Spain, with "La"
33 Elaborate affairs
34 Overhang
36 Dew
37 Misdo
38 Crossed out
40 Brazilian dance band
41 Unbending
42 Thrash
43 Emulates Dürer
44 Sniggler's spot
45 1955 Belmont Stakes winner
46 One-master
51 ___ effort
52 "___ o'clock scholar"
54 Armbone
55 Da's opposite
57 Estuary
58 Alternative to a hook

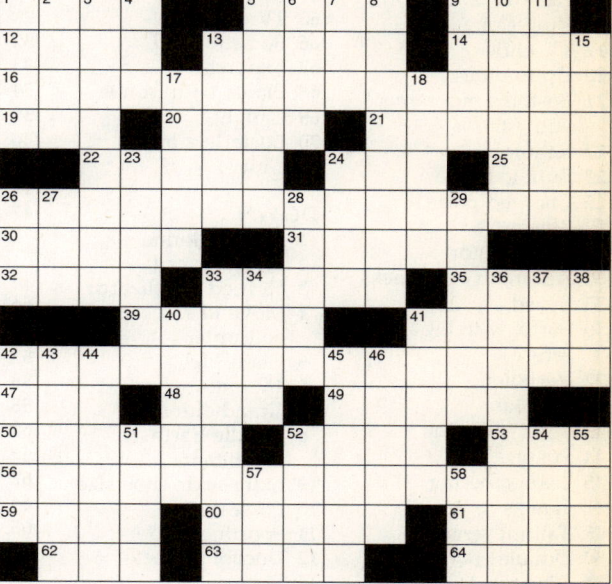

394 by Chuck Deodene

ACROSS

1 Lie poolside
5 Love of Lucy
9 Author ___ Gallant
14 Anderson of TV sitcoms
15 Nerve impulse conduit
16 Shelley's "Adonais," e.g.
17 Faulkner's "Requiem for ___"
18 About: Abbr.
19 Being male or female
20 Rolling Stones album of 1968
23 Word with coin or time
24 Handily subdues
25 Newly arrived
28 Pros' foes
29 Handel opera
30 Leaf
31 Big sandwich name
34 Niven film of 1937
38 British verb ending
39 Limerick, e.g.
40 Zeno of ___ (Greek logician)
41 Like a fair lass
42 Promoter of rooster fights
44 Tipsy
45 Blacken
46 Hemingway memoir
51 Cremona product
52 Pulitzer-winning writer Sheehan
53 Compatriot
54 Neighbor of Nigeria
55 Where water turned to wine
56 Rend
57 On, as medication
58 Skirt
59 Canadian baseballer

DOWN

1 Spill the beans
2 Top-of-the-line
3 Comfy
4 Caribbean capital
5 Clothing tag name
6 Live and breathe
7 Soak up
8 Personified
9 Smokehouse flavoring
10 Seal hunters
11 Nettles
12 "___ it!" ("Eureka!")
13 Baseball exec Thrift
21 Star of "The Greatest"
22 Chalk up
25 Skywalker, e.g.
26 Terrorists' tools
27 Kind of curve
28 Affected
30 Hoedown
31 Exploit
32 Fitting phrase ending
33 All-powerful one
35 Not fixed
36 1966 hit "Walk Away ___"
37 Stage anew
41 A B vitamin
42 Pincers
43 Big galoot
44 Sultan Qabus bin Said, e.g.
45 Adhere
46 City on the Skunk River
47 Bit of wampum
48 "A Clockwork Orange" droogie
49 Strike
50 Neophyte
51 ___ Bakr (first caliph of Mecca)

395   by Randall J. Hartman

ACROSS

1 The two together
5 "Woman ___ Year"
10 Egg layer
13 Distant
15 Nevada lake resort
16 King Kong, e.g.
17 TV oldie
20 Up-to-date
21 Boston's nickname, with "the"
22 Require
23 Buffalo locale
25 Charged particle
27 Blue
30 Prevaricator
31 Alternatives to tricks
35 Dined
36 Suffix with beat or refuse
37 Verboten
38 TV oldie
43 "I do" location
44 Possess
45 4:00 gathering
46 Gawks
48 Tail movements
50 Double curve
51 Dictator Amin
52 Hitchcock's "The 39 ___"
54 It might be a convertible
57 Flood's opposite
59 Comfort
63 TV oldie
66 Be bedbound
67 Expunge
68 Plants with fronds
69 Caught
70 Lusterless finish
71 Glut

DOWN

1 Healing lotion
2 Bread spread
3 Horned ___ (lizard)
4 Move like a helicopter
5 Giant Mel
6 TV oldie
7 Grand amount
8 Middle Earth inhabitant
9 Extra-wide shoe size
10 Possess
11 Sporting blade
12 Uncool fellow
14 Savage
18 Diamond division
19 Temper, as glass
24 Earth goddess: Var.
26 Morsels
27 Drawn-out tales
28 Inclined
29 T.W.A. rival
32 Lessen
33 Musical sounds
34 Ice cream drinks
39 Cowboy's rope
40 Angered
41 Police ___ team
42 Swallow
47 ___ Club (conservationists' group)
49 Lampoon
53 Blackthorn shrubs
54 Beau for a doe
55 Buckeye State
56 Pool table cover
58 Finish ahead of
60 Taj Mahal site
61 Not worth a red ___
62 Latin being
64 Skirt edge
65 Discern

396   by Richard Thomas

ACROSS

1 Mrs. F. Scott Fitzgerald
6 Three-legged ___
10 Laud loudly
14 Bubbling, as hot water
15 Panache
16 Elderly
17 British runner
20 Gigantic
21 The Wizard of Menlo Park
22 ". . . ___ any drop to drink": Coleridge
23 Blowout
24 Northern Canadian body of water
31 Urbane
32 Polo shirt brand
33 Prattle
34 Smog
35 Track athlete
37 Jack of "Dragnet"
38 Lowest bill
39 Zola tale
40 Trivial Pursuit's ___ Edition
41 Entrepreneur's funds
45 "And Then There Were ___"
46 Charged particle
47 Photog's flash
50 Overconfidence
55 Victor Hugo novel, with "The"
57 Show biz star
58 Resort near Venice
59 Taken ___ (surprised)
60 Putrefies
61 Sophomore, e.g.
62 Cheese nibbler

DOWN

1 40's boxer Tony
2 Noted Israeli diplomat
3 Western wolf
4 Designer Christian
5 Wellesley grads
6 Happens again
7 "What a shame!"
8 Dismiss, in slang
9 Attempt
10 Tire type
11 "It's ___!"("Groovy!")
12 Presidential no
13 Nirvana
18 Plant anchor
19 Waited around
23 Steady look
24 Organic fertilizer
25 Home wrecker
26 Genesis lady
27 Spring bloom
28 Gemini rocket stage
29 Afghan capital
30 Recedes
31 Third place at Belmont
35 Courteous
36 "Bus Stop" playwright
37 Anti-Prohibition
39 Weeper of myth
40 Summery fabric
42 Gentle hills
43 Set one's sights on
44 Be sullen
47 Commotion
48 Commotion
49 Haymarket Square happening
50 Fountain drink
51 Biblical summit Mt.
52 Jacob's twin
53 Jiffies
54 Japanese tipple
56 "Sprechen ___ Deutsch?"

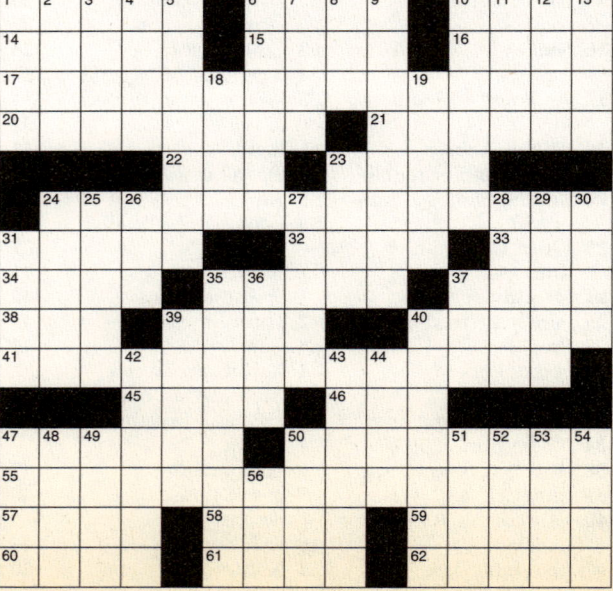

397 by Deborah Trombley

ACROSS
1 Twitch
6 Dispenser candy
9 Mumblety peg item
14 When repeated, an Evergreen State city
15 Dweller on the Mekong River
16 Countryish
17 Book filled with legends
18 W.W II tour sponsor
19 Leave ___ on (influence)
20 Pirate's exclamation
23 Sweetie
24 Country dance
25 Maiden name preceder
26 Sweet potatoes
27 Digs tunnels
31 March 17 celeb
34 "___ Rheingold"
35 One of Frank's exes
36 Pirate's situation
41 Two ___ time
42 1948 pact: Abbr.
43 Filmdom's Dr. Kildare
44 Robbers
47 Fairway warning
49 Opposite of a ques.
50 Lascivious
51 The Beatles' ___ Pepper
54 Pirate's destination
59 Upper crust
60 Horse's morsel
61 Threat for a Wild West outlaw
62 "So long, amigo"
63 Arthur Godfrey played one
64 Drawbridges cross them
65 Barely noticeable
66 U.A.R. member
67 Cherbourg shes

DOWN
1 Swagger
2 Prefix with logical or genic
3 Tuckered out
4 Bulgarian, e.g.
5 Pricey Italian car
6 Feathers
7 Writing pad support
8 Kind of suit
9 "Seinfeld" neighbor
10 Show song
11 Dies ___
12 Co-star of 55-Down
13 Lodge members
21 Dreamy acronym
22 Lavatory sign
26 Prattle
27 Scrooge exclamation
28 Gen. Bradley
29 Beef bourguignon ingredient
30 Fifth Avenue name
31 Hit the deck?
32 "Bye!"
33 Strategize
34 Sot's woe
37 "___ fast!"
38 High-test, e.g.
39 "So sorry"
40 Liquid in drums
45 Scopes trial locale, 1925
46 Kiddingly
47 Rankle
48 One who gives a hoot
50 Not watertight
51 Drinker's toast
52 Beau ___
53 Lock
54 Heedless
55 He was Pierce on "M*A*S*H"
56 Hour on a grandfather clock
57 We, oui?
58 Hip

398 by Glenton Petgrave

ACROSS
1 Charitable one
8 Aloof
14 Fish whose male hatches the eggs
15 Tree-held shelter
16 Heaven
17 Hard to move
18 In the know
19 Work of Homer
21 Ill temper
22 Sugar source
23 Chief
24 Intellectuals
26 "Am ___ believe . . . ?"
27 Confession maker
29 Arguable
30 Horses' sounds
32 Sourball
34 Breakfast cereal
36 1948 Literature Nobelist
40 Old hand
42 Crayola color
43 C.I.S. predecessor
46 Furtive one
48 Take captive
49 Domain
51 Winter need
52 Price
53 Hair-styling stuff
54 Oil, pharmaceutically
56 Scoundrel
57 Large lizard
59 Protective fence
61 Down below
62 Prominent
63 Hall of Fame members
64 Put on a pedestal

DOWN
1 Nonpotable
2 Irrational distrust
3 Alternative to Midway
4 Bump
5 ___ Lanka
6 Legendary Gaelic hero
7 Not steady on the feet
8 Jar
9 Gives special nursing care to
10 Airline watchdog grp.
11 Blue shade
12 Car option
13 Fair and square
14 Typist's concern
20 Sluggish
23 Duped
25 Roomy
27 Supplied with footwear
28 Reddish-brown winter apple
31 Contort
33 Israel's Golda
35 Fast
37 Produce new technology
38 Partial
39 Was a snitch
41 Veteran actor
43 Insistence
44 "If I Had a Hammer" singer
45 Bow to
47 "Hot" dish
50 Water lilies painter
52 Labor organizer Chavez
55 Swedish author Gustafsson
56 Belly flop, e.g.
58 "There you are!"
60 Soviet Physics Nobelist ___ Landau

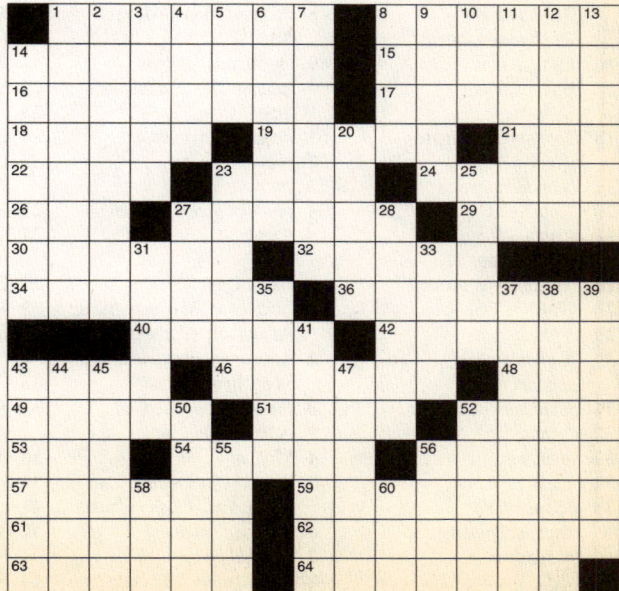

399 by Norman S. Wizer

ACROSS
1 Ivory tower figure
5 Cancel
10 Inferiors to cpls.
14 Girl's name ending
15 Missing Jimmy
16 God with a bow
17 Wall Street action
20 Know by sixth sense
21 These can close Mexican stores
22 Spain's Ibiza, e.g.
23 Indian title
24 Wall Street action
31 Little bits
32 Address nos.
33 Toronto's prov.
35 Sea east of the Caspian
36 Hunter's trail
38 Collateral
39 "Bei ___ Bist Du Schön" (1938 hit)
40 Diaphanous
41 Kind of cavity
42 Wall Street action
46 Sailor's assent
47 Primo
48 Net
52 Throaty
55 Wall Street action
58 Soft cheese
59 Dairymaid's seat
60 De ___ (too much)
61 Grub
62 Uptight
63 This does it!

DOWN
1 3, on a phone
2 Ornamental case
3 Envelope abbr.
4 Maritime
5 1962 #1 hit for Tommy Roe
6 Share top billing
7 New Deal lending org.
8 Alien craft
9 Rail
10 Source of an old rug
11 College party site
12 Caesar's partner in 50's TV
13 Trans-Atlantic fliers
18 Hard, crisp breads
19 Canada's Northwest ___: Abbr.
24 King's home, on Broadway
25 Doughnut-shaped
26 Japanese port
27 Rodeo horse
28 "Am ___ believe . . ."
29 Auctioneer's warning
30 Provide
34 Durbeyfield girl
36 Most gossamery
37 Neat article
38 Iron ore
40 Have a ___ (essay)
41 Foreign assembly
43 Kenmore products
44 Race in "Gulliver's Travels"
45 Major of the comics
48 River to the North Sea
49 Asta's mistress
50 Angry state
51 Art Deco artist
53 Marsh bird
54 Baseball's Slaughter
56 ___ ami
57 Peeper

400 by Mel Rosen

ACROSS
1 "I see," facetiously
5 Descendant of Fatima, to Shiites
9 Dash locale
12 Alfred the butler cares for it
14 Send elsewhere
16 Jazzed up
17 Place for an exchange
18 Crossword topics, often
19 Word of grace
20 Clean-cut
21 Plugs away (at)
23 Stuff in envelopes
26 Legation resident
28 Kind of column
29 Workplaces
30 Wordsworth's "We ___ Seven"
31 Lambaste slangily
32 Crud
33 Vino region
34 Sci-fi figures
35 People in compromising positions?
36 Kid?
37 War of 1812 locale
39 Humors, with "to"
40 Oblique
41 Oz visitor
42 Part of España
43 Malthus, for one
48 Powerful political duo
49 Destined to fail
50 Hägar the Horrible's dog
51 Peptic activity
52 New Left gp.
53 Wow
54 He became Earl of Avon

DOWN
1 End of a Muhammad Ali catch phrase
2 Renaissance artist Memling
3 Town liberated in July 1944
4 Minus
5 Region between Cape Roca and Cape Creus
6 1/60 fluid dram
7 "Black Stallion" boy
8 Top three finishers
9 Piatigorsky's instruments
10 Remembrance of things past
11 Second-time claimant
13 Too
14 Mishnah authorities
15 Reading and others: Abbr.
22 Symbol of life
23 "___ tov!"
24 Incitements
25 Like some minimum-wage workers
26 Scrap
27 They hold their horses
29 Bonuses
32 Swinger's shout
33 One way to decrease the work force
35 Dislike
36 Academese, for example
38 Experienced ones
39 Pass on
41 South Pacific nation
42 They're made by FB's and HB's
44 Radiator part
45 Footnote note
46 Dark purple fruit
47 Neighbor of Ark.

401 by A.J. Santora

ACROSS

1 Cut and filed
10 Lay up
15 Poker-faced
16 Hardly wimpy
17 Orbital rendezvous point
19 Like 17-Across, once: Abbr.
20 Sister of Erato
21 Crime boss
22 Site of a Hercules task
24 Underling
27 Vernaculars
31 ___ Plummer (Dickens character)
32 Defensive weapons, for short
35 River rising in the Cantabrian Mountains
36 "The Last Command" locale
37 Pop singer Tori
38 Things
40 Vingt-___ (casino game)
41 ___ Prospekt (old thoroughfare)
43 Head start
44 Cult film "___ Man"
45 Found riches
46 Gambler's secret
48 Copies
50 Stomached
53 Nail down
54 Mystery woman
58 Author Wallace
60 Time-off time
64 Hot time in Santiago
65 Some antibodies
66 Writer ___ Orne Jewett
67 Unmanly quality

DOWN

1 Flowers, for short
2 Hydroxide particle
3 Steadfastness
4 Architect Pei and others
5 Traffic reporter's transport
6 "Who's Afraid of Virginia Woolf?" Tony winner
7 Costa follower
8 Stuntman Knievel
9 Big name in '50s comedy
10 M.D. group
11 Ring covering
12 Embitter
13 Typical western
14 Half of a musical duo
18 Bit
23 Huge
25 Novelist ___ de Queiroz
26 Frank Capra's birthplace
28 Ensemble instruments
29 Hubert's wife, in the funnies
30 "Maria" and "Marie"
32 Place of drudgery
33 World Book rival
34 One-foot line of verse
39 Two-handed hoops
42 Revived: Prefix
47 List abbreviator
49 Antonio, e.g.
51 "Maria" or "Marie"
52 Ecclesiastical officials
55 Silences
56 "For ___ know . . ."
57 Accordingly
59 "Swiss Family Robinson" writer
61 L.A. lawyer Reiner
62 Cry of wonderment
63 B and B

402 by Matt Gaffney

ACROSS

1 Walker, in sign language
4 Thanksgiving dish
7 Engagement
13 Baritone in Rabaud's "Marouf"
14 First or second, e.g.
15 Habituates
16 With 63-Across, theme of this puzzle
18 See 6-Down
19 Xaviera Hollander book
21 Neighbor of Uganda
22 Boston suburb
23 6/6/1944
26 Gung-ho
31 Result of a firing
34 Corporate hotshot
36 Patriot of 1776
37 Common game show consolation prize
42 Meanie
43 Out of town
44 "Fantasy Island" prop
45 SE Mexican state
49 Words of Caesar
51 Senseless state
53 "All I gotta do ___ naturally" (Beatles lyric)
57 "The Jeffersons" co-star
62 It's often picked up in bars
63 See 16-Across
64 The Continent
65 Sonnies
66 City on Guanabara Bay
67 Made up (for)
68 Windy City sights
69 Door word

DOWN

1 Results of some handshakes
2 Peace Nobelist Root
3 Fell precipitately
4 Cry harshly
5 ". . . and make it snappy!"
6 With 18-Across, a two-time Oscar winner
7 Bucknell footballers
8 Lover in Dryden's "All for Love"
9 Izmir resident
10 Cherry or apple
11 Lecherous look
12 Psychic's claim
14 Not so spicy
17 Harry James's "___ the Craziest Dream"
20 Triangle part: Abbr.
24 Borden weapon
25 Cry of victory
27 Half a dance
28 Flag down a cab
29 Colleague of Claudia and Naomi
30 Lucy's husband
31 Tons
32 Nintendo rival
33 Mint or sage
35 1860's insignia
38 Shade of green
39 Have bills
40 Turner of note
41 Daily since 1851, briefly
46 Minor accident result
47 Searched thoroughly
48 Medical suffix
50 Soyuz launcher
52 Fish
54 Waker-upper
55 Whoopi, in "The Color Purple"
56 Holyfield beat him, 11/9/1996
57 Close
58 Submarine
59 Venerable English institution
60 Become better
61 Machiavellian concerns
62 Leaves at 4:00?

403   by Fred Piscop

ACROSS
1 Meal at boot camp
5 Sell tickets illegally
10 Sam the ___ of 60's pop
14 "Beetle Bailey" dog
15 It's a no-no
16 Car with a meter
17 Lose one's nerve
19 Israeli guns
20 Tennis great Rosewall
21 Bohemian
22 "Gunsmoke" star James
24 Vulgar one
26 Tyke
27 70's–80's Yankee pitching ace
34 Imus's medium
37 Goods
38 "Blue" bird
39 Abba of Israel
40 Opera headliners
41 Stupor
42 ___ easter
43 Sheets, pillowcases, etc.
44 Put on the payroll
45 Old instrument of punishment
48 "Who ___ you?"
49 Sounded, as a bell
53 Prestige
56 Villa d'___
58 Actress Gardner
59 Major league brothers' name
60 Quaint dance
63 "___ the Mood for Love"
64 Actress Samantha
65 Microwave, slangily
66 Grandmother, affectionately
67 Immunizations
68 ___ off (plenty mad)

DOWN
1 Treats cynically
2 Lucy's best friend
3 Children's author R. L. ___
4 League: Abbr.
5 Audiophile's setup
6 Quitter's word
7 "It's ___!" (proud parents' phrase)
8 Singer Rawls
9 Shepherd's pie ingredients
10 Publicity seekers' acts
11 Smog
12 X or Y, on a graph
13 Ole ___
18 Nonmusician's musical instrument
23 Flagmaker Betsy
25 Opposed to, in the backwoods
28 Playground equipment
29 Overhangs
30 Research money
31 Not quite shut
32 Stare, as at a crystal ball
33 Checked out
34 Pull apart
35 "___ Ben Adhem"
36 Jeanne ___ (French saint)
40 Eating alcoves
41 Pickle flavoring
43 Old Italian money
44 Nonsense
46 Hawaiian medicine man
47 Frolicking animals
50 Lash ___ of old westerns
51 Call forth
52 Went out with
53 Old Testament murderer
54 ___ mater
55 Nickel or copper, but not tin
56 Therefore
57 Three-player card game
61 "Yecch!"
62 Blaster's need

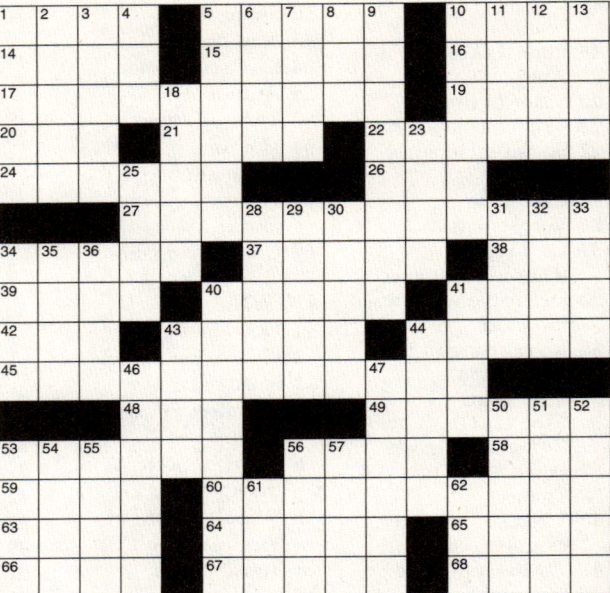

404   by Bryant White

ACROSS
1 Handel's "___, Galatea e Polifemò"
4 Pale purple
9 Stone: Lat.
14 Center square in a game
15 Architect Jones
16 Stand
17 Italian crowd?
18 Miss at the movies
20 Route near Bear Creek Pass
22 Trial
23 Lost enthusiasm
25 Limo figure, maybe
27 Papers for eds.
28 Shelter for troops
32 Actor Byrnes
33 Rivals
34 Thunder
35 This puzzle's theme
38 Service
39 "The Camp Meeting" composer
40 1949 Edmond O'Brien movie
43 Magnitude
47 Name part meaning "father"
49 Sweep
50 Archer's need
51 Physics topic
54 Fairy bluebird genus
55 Bakery purchases
60 Gaseous prefix
61 With all one's might
62 Black Bears' home
63 Alphabet trio
64 Slow
65 Massenet opera
66 Compass dir.

DOWN
1 State Department employee
2 Shipping unit
3 Freezing
4 Drew
5 Daughter of Cadmus
6 Historical Chinese name
7 Auden's "The ___ of Anxiety"
8 Reserved
9 Covert
10 Start of a children's rhyme
11 Soldiers of yore
12 Flashes
13 Hoaxes: Sl.
19 Hussein's queen
21 ET on TV
24 Flip one's lid?
25 Long-bladed hatchet
26 South Pacific Island
29 Actress Davidovich
30 Hubbub
31 Orange blossom ingredient
35 Hosp. ward
36 Educ. group
37 "It ___ Fair" (Sammy Kaye hit)
38 Arthur Curry's superhero identity
40 Some corners
41 Concord
42 Ancient goddess of fertility
44 Thunder
45 Hiver, e.g.
46 Sale item abbr.
47 Petrify
48 "Superfudge" author
52 Kabob thingamabob
53 Month: Prefix
56 Yankee Clipper's brother
57 Keogh plan relative
58 "___ Dieu!"
59 "Music for Airports" composer

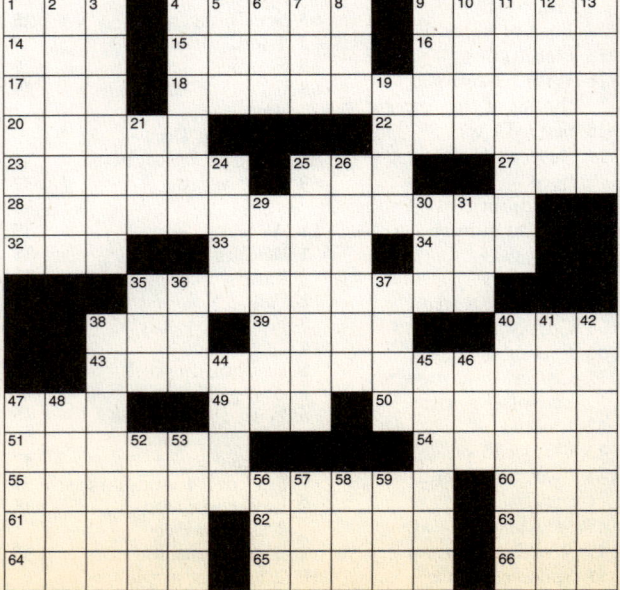

405 by Bill Click

ACROSS

1 1975 Wimbledon champ
5 ___ nova
10 High-ranking NCO
14 Oscar winner for "Moonstruck"
15 Sit up for
16 Ron Howard TV role
17 Irving Berlin song
20 Woolgatherer?
21 Winter forecast
22 Sioux Indians
23 "Gimme a G . . . ," e.g.
25 Org.
26 Word in Amtrak's slogan
28 N.H.L. legend Gordie
30 Wide's partner
33 "La Bohème" role
34 Louisiana inlet
35 One in France
36 Andrews Sisters hit
40 Speaker's pauses
41 Writer Cecil of "The Straight Dope"
42 ___ me tangere
43 Q followers
44 Strength, in Variety talk
45 Favor
47 Confused thoughts
49 Secretaries may file these
50 Alpha's opposite
52 Unified
54 Profit by
57 Andrew Lloyd Webber song, with "The"
60 Astound
61 Chisholm, e.g.
62 Tense
63 1/20/03 honoree
64 First-year law school class
65 "Rule, Britannia" composer

DOWN

1 Highest point
2 "Pygmalion" author
3 Beatles recording
4 Goof
5 Tried to save a sinking ship?
6 Steinbrenner to the Yankees
7 Wise
8 Search (through)
9 From ___ Z
10 Loses feathers
11 "Mary Poppins" tune, with "A"
12 Take's partner
13 Golfers' gadgets
18 River in Belgium
19 Revolted
24 "Aquarius" musical
25 Gone, but not forgotten?
26 Dinosaur DNA preserver
27 Coffin stands
28 Injures
29 Court cry
31 "Twisted" body part
32 Broadcast anew
34 Boast
37 "The Human Comedy" author
38 "Zip ___ Doo-Dah"
39 Like Nash's "lama"
45 Juries
46 Nothing: Fr.
48 Ripening
49 Like a pitcher's perfect game
50 Siberian city
51 Conductor Riccardo
52 60's hair style
53 Asterisk
55 Avoid
56 Cigar ending
58 Giant Mel
59 "Make ___ double"

406 by Manny Nosowsky

ACROSS

1 Suit
6 Bit of smoke
10 ___ scratch
14 Town near Bangor
15 "The ___!" (hmmph!)
16 Good enough to eat
17 One ___
19 Gray's subj.
20 Disprove
21 Go all-out
23 Washington story, maybe
25 Remembrance of things past
26 Easier to count
29 Turn-of-century Secretary of State
31 Fleece
33 Hurrays
34 U.C.L.A. rival
35 Knocked, in a way
37 She raised Cain
38 One side in an 1862 battle
40 1951 Johnnie Ray hit
41 Disk spinner
43 Exception word?
44 Deliberate
45 Vending machine part
46 Stewed
47 Firedamps
48 Name in robotry
50 "Once ___ a midnight . . ."
52 Dinner alfresco
55 Fancy-coiffed bird
59 Nobelist ___ von Behring
60 Two ___ (dilemma)
62 The L of L-dopa
63 Scads
64 ___ up (relented)
65 From the top
66 Popular source of quotes, for short
67 Sans élan

DOWN

1 Beethoven's birthplace
2 Spooky waterway?
3 80-day traveler
4 Gulps
5 Rock
6 Dorothy Parker, e.g.
7 G. & S. princess and others
8 Door stopper?
9 Army chaplain
10 Box label
11 Three ___
12 Type of glass
13 Dish (out)
18 Main
22 Worrier's risk, so they say
24 Turkish for "ruler"
26 Oscar-winning film director Zinnemann
27 Runoff site
28 Four ___
30 Convenient story
32 In itself
34 Not 100% open
35 Make a memo of
36 Aids in disguises
38 Photo choice
39 Balletic put-on
42 Mr. Average
44 Sports legend of 1920
46 With trumpets ablare
47 Spurred on
49 Symbol of vastness
51 Reward for yrs. of study
52 Gymnastics coach Karolyi
53 "I agree!"
54 Inflatable items
56 Bouquet
57 Heavily damaged city of W.W. II
58 Swirl
61 Somme summer

407 by Robert Zimmerman

ACROSS

1 Gregory Hines specialty
4 Take for granted
10 Colorless
14 Actress Gardner
15 Stay-at-home
16 Roof overhang
17 House member: Abbr.
18 Interior decorator's hiree
20 Wields the gavel
22 Swear (to)
23 Pinker inside
24 Opponent
25 Greek geometer
27 Premolar
31 Pallid
32 Secrete
33 Poi ingredient
34 Fed. power agcy.
35 Diffidence
38 Sword's superior, in saying
39 Craving
41 Ends' partner
42 More than fat
44 Stereo components
46 32-card card game
47 Effect a makeover
48 Napoleon's cavalry commander
49 Slow, in music
52 Bring an issue home
55 Pet rock, maybe
57 Hair application
58 Formerly
59 Mother
60 The 90's, e.g.
61 Goes out with regularly
62 Archeological finds
63 Director Howard

DOWN

1 Canvas cover
2 Declare positively
3 Houseman TV series, with "The"
4 Two are often prescribed
5 Under the elms
6 "Great!"
7 Salt Lake City team
8 Russian for "peace"
9 Makes more valuable
10 Person who's feeling down in the mouth?
11 Fad
12 Lexington and Madison: Abbr.
13 Lahr or Parks
19 One of the Aleutians
21 Shopper's lure
24 Adjutants
25 Noblemen
26 Exhaust
27 Ties
28 Toothless threat
29 "___ my case"
30 Gift recipient
32 Kind of power
36 Barn dances
37 Legendary hemlock drinker
40 Sidewinder lock-ons
43 False god
45 Actor Dullea
46 A form of 46-Across
48 Tycoon
49 Primates
50 Madonna's "Truth or ___"
51 Church area
52 Lo-cal
53 Mr. Mostel
54 Flair
56 Chow down

408 by Arthur S. Verdesca

ACROSS

1 Yin's partner
5 Toy gun ammo
9 Rift
14 ___ patriae (patriotism)
15 Together, in music
16 "It ___ Be You"
17 Parisian entree
18 Vatican City monetary unit
19 Down Under soldier
20 1954 Hitchcock hit
23 Bonny one
24 Singer Acuff
25 Beautify
28 Barley bristle
30 Buddy
34 Spanish wave
35 Passage
37 Cain's nephew
38 Behave
42 Clam supper
43 Sacred song
44 Onetime medicinal herb
45 German donkey
46 Élan
47 Charitable foundations, e.g.
49 Chinese ideal
51 Part of a wagon train
52 Merit award
59 Use
60 Candy brand
61 Paint unskillfully
62 Mesa ___ National Park
63 Felipe, Jesus or Matty
64 Former Mormon chief ___ Taft Benson
65 Shipping amount
66 Desires
67 ___ Bien Phu (1954 battle site)

DOWN

1 Croquet locale
2 French call for help
3 ___ cloud in the sky
4 Edsel feature
5 Soft leather
6 Farewell
7 Result of tummy rubbing?
8 Ore layer
9 Maria Rosario Pilar Martinez
10 Jacks-of-all-trades
11 Wood trimmer
12 Weekly World News rival
13 Beaded shoe, for short
21 Chinese-Portuguese enclave
22 Coffee server
25 Ice cream mold
26 Biblical prophet
27 Thanks, in Thüringen
28 Journalist Joseph
29 Grieved
31 "My Dinner With ___"
32 Brimless hat
33 Test car maneuvers
36 18-wheeler
39 Iron pumper's pride
40 Diligent
41 Lagoon former
46 Actress Caldwell
48 Lacked
50 Locale in van Gogh paintings
51 Breakfast fruit
52 At any time
53 Betting game
54 Kind of vision
55 Fiddlers' king
56 "Schindler's List" extra
57 Fix
58 Israeli diplomat
59 Dow Jones fig.

409 by Stanley B. Whitten

ACROSS

1 Beaver projects
5 Service item
10 Conceal
14 Of grand proportions
15 Flushed, as the cheeks
16 North Sea feeder
17 Relax
20 Maximal
21 Covered with scales
22 Hellenic H
23 Evocative of an earlier time, as fashion
24 Treadless
27 Excursion
29 Paul Anka's "___ a Lady"
33 Mil. address
34 Ride the waves
35 Raise
37 Rossini opera, with "The"
40 Card game for two
41 Tax deferral plans
42 Command to Dobbin
43 Actress Olin
44 Where some chichi ski
45 Difficult
46 Part of Iberia
49 "Ode ___ Nightingale"
51 Medicinal amount
53 1975 Beatty-Hawn film
57 Small pooch
59 Toward shelter
60 Counting everything
61 Denoting certain textbook publishers
62 Fastens
63 Spruce
64 Society gatherings

DOWN

1 Proofreader's mark
2 Summit
3 Catcher's glove
4 Tallied
5 Early
6 Misplace
7 Bat wood
8 Come-on
9 Undemocratic law
10 Seaplane attachment
11 "Time ___ the essence"
12 Moist
13 Coastal flier
18 After taxes
19 Čapek drama
23 Bully
24 Noisy confusion
25 Quickly
26 Navigational system
28 Spanish gold
30 Hägar's better half, in the comics
31 Swiss mathematician
32 1994 movie thriller
34 Bullheaded
35 In a hale manner
36 Hosp. devices
38 Number two woods
39 ___ Lanka
44 Type of sausage
45 Gertrude's son
47 Busy election-year org.
48 Once more
50 Pull, at sea
51 Sandwich shop
52 Farm team
53 NaCl
54 Soccer great
55 Worker-welfare watchdog: Abbr.
56 Medical suffix
57 Glove compartment item
58 Sombrero, e.g.

410 by David J. Kahn

ACROSS

1 Cake topper
6 Synagogue
10 Newborn equine
14 Movie rental
15 Come in second
16 Florence's river
17 Wine fermenter
18 Be an accessory to the crime
19 Tortoiselike
20 Telegraph language, formally
23 Yalta participant
26 Somersaulting dive
27 Apt anagram of 20-Across
31 Tease
32 Nat Turner was one
33 RBI's et al.
37 Old French coins
39 Sultan's subjects
41 Kind of team
42 Futures market commodity
44 All in ___ work
46 "You ___ There" (50's TV show)
47 Telegraph company
50 20 Questions category
53 Capri's Blue ___
54 Apt anagram of 47-Across
58 Malevolent
59 Have ___ (blow one's top)
60 Actress Aimée
64 Holler
65 "The Dram-Shop" author
66 Shiner
67 Pipe bends
68 W.W. I battle area
69 Patrick or J.R.

DOWN

1 Wall clinger
2 Fr. company
3 Miss Lupino
4 Crunch maker
5 Gloomy books
6 Wrestling maneuver
7 Vagrant
8 ___-friendly
9 Releases
10 Generalissimo Franco et al.
11 Sweater fabric
12 Terminal
13 Humble
21 ___ Gay
22 Roadside sign
23 Scold
24 Emulate Mr. Chips
25 Debate
28 French revolutionary
29 Get away from
30 Preclude
34 Be in store for
35 Fortune teller
36 Secretary, at times
38 Oregon workplaces
40 "Riders to the Sea" dramatist
43 Sign of pathos
45 For Americans, it's always last
48 Tawdry
49 "I'm busy!"
50 Keep ___ on
51 Bellow specialty
52 "___ Survive" (Gloria Gaynor hit)
55 Martian craft, maybe
56 "Cleopatra" locale
57 Celebrity
61 Yes, to Yves
62 Annapolis org.
63 College party staple

411 by Harvey Estes

ACROSS

1 Latin dance
7 Trees in "The Little Prince"
14 Perform perfectly
15 "Billy Budd" writer
16 Spectators' seating
17 Move, as with difficulty
18 Runs roughshod over
20 "Act your ___!"
23 Rowers grip it
24 157 ½°
25 Begin a fall
27 Brother's title
30 East Asian prefix
34 Marking with ridges
37 Hand-me-down
40 Head of the House, once
41 Dessert duo
44 Stretch the truth or stretch out
45 A Guthrie
46 Dictator from Gori
47 Yakutsk river
49 Branch
51 Angler's luck
52 Untrustworthy sort
55 Grp. of swingers
58 Train part
59 Haunt
65 Choral piece
66 Water temperature tester, maybe
70 Division division
71 Messengers from afar
72 This may get 40 lashes
73 Marquis ___

DOWN

1 S & L offerings
2 Roasting
3 ___ glance
4 Takes for a ride
5 Couldn't get out of it
6 On the ocean
7 Suds, so to speak
8 Low-voiced ladies
9 Round figures
10 Confirmation class gifts
11 Skin smoother
12 Fast runner on slow film
13 Hardens
15 Theater threesome
19 Sandy's line
20 Freely
21 Allen of comedy
22 Doreen of "Private Benjamin"
26 Photo
28 Unconfirmed info
29 Nutty-fruitcake center
31 *Like this*
32 Leonid predecessor
33 First game
35 Depression fighter: Abbr.
36 Luther's lang.
38 Nuts to editors
39 Mantis killer
42 Chef's phrase
43 Truck front
48 Vinegary
50 Pitched ball stat
53 Bouquet
54 More critical
56 Turn
57 With a flared bottom
59 Tequila additive
60 Domain
61 Does like "it"
62 Ship of 1492
63 "I've ___ a Secret"
64 Spurs
67 Indian export
68 Familiar
69 Jargon suffix

412 by Matt Gaffney

ACROSS

1 1993 Bulls feat
10 Red letters
14 Place to work out
15 With 41-Across, relax
16 Economist's figure
17 In the red
18 Cleveland's lake
19 Receiver-turned-sportscaster
21 TDs are worth six
22 Memo letters
23 Erasmus's birthplace
25 Obsolescence, in a way
28 Org.
31 Jeff Lynne's old rock band
32 Bits
33 In need of a chill pill
36 Like some traffic
38 Emotional tone
39 Alley ___
41 See 15-Across
42 Take, or authorize to give
46 Gotland's locale
47 CCXXI x V
50 Kingston music
52 Make permanent
53 One engaged in match play?
54 When the balcony scene occurs in "Romeo and Juliet"
56 Brunch dish
58 Skier Phil
59 Clear
60 Relative of Manx
61 Disco era

DOWN

1 "Stop, ___!"
2 Carl Anderson comic strip
3 Diameters halved
4 "Night" author Wiesel
5 And so on
6 Ancient lighthouse site
7 Kind of tax
8 John or Andrew
9 Volunteers' neighbors
10 Detroit group, for short
11 Diet dangerously
12 Commissioned
13 With 35-Down, the American Dream
15 Lincoln in-laws
20 53-Across's crime
23 Step
24 Conductor Kostelanetz
26 Literally, let it stand
27 Pathetic
28 Each
29 Photo lab rinses
30 Libya's Gulf of ___
33 Actress Thurman
34 "___ it" ("Get going!")
35 See 13-Down
37 Extent
40 Prospecting tool
43 Football Hall-of-Famer Matson
44 "Foundation's Edge" author
45 "Receiving poorly," in C.B. talk
47 Infamous massacre site
48 Land of Minos
49 Politician's acquisitions
50 Unvaried
51 Former Chrysler offering
53 Suave rival
55 Wrath
57 Boyz II ___

ACROSS
1 Beginning
5 Served perfectly, in tennis
9 "Can't take ___"
14 Supermarket section
15 Sub ___ (secretly)
16 Apply thoroughly, as lotion
17 Monopoly corner square
18 Sudden rush of air
19 Lasses
20 "JFK" co-star
23 Race driver Yarborough
24 "It must be him ___ shall die"
25 "Spoon River Anthology" poet
33 Service club members
34 Put on, as clothes
35 Burn soother
36 Summer clock setting: Abbr.
37 Most arduous
41 Burger cover
42 Audio feedback problem

44 Architect I. M.
45 Orchestra members
47 "The Cowboys" actor, 1972
51 Farming: Abbr.
52 Communist Karl
53 "Great Balls of Fire" singer
59 Couric of "Today"
60 Blunders
61 "The Wizard ___"
63 Cowgirl Dale
64 Daft
65 "What's to become ___?" (words of despair)
66 Soirees
67 Flower stalk
68 Used Miss Clairol

DOWN
1 Modifying word: Abbr.
2 Stool or stoop
3 Hodgepodge
4 Where a movie reel is stored
5 Historic county of Scotland
6 Grand ___ Dam
7 Existence: Lat.

8 Biblical fruit
9 Knight's clothes
10 Spanish girl of old song
11 Award of "Prelude to a Kiss"
12 Tykes
13 Nav. rank
21 Swamp
22 Blondell and Baez
25 Tribal V.I.P.
26 70's dance place
27 Ancient Teutons
28 Aviator Rickenbacker
29 A Stooge
30 Middle of a sleeve
31 Where Jeanne d'Arc died
32 Taste or feel
38 Mimicry
39 Electrical unit
40 Yankee manager Joe
43 Sweet potato
46 Material for engraver's blocks
48 Evil woman
49 Come from the shadows
50 Fir tree
53 Coffee, slangily

54 And others: Abbr.
55 Table supports
56 Part of Q.E.D.
57 Uncertain
58 Between all and none

59 Beer container
62 Last letter, in London

ACROSS
1 Boner
6 Horse's gait
10 Jacob's first wife
14 Pooped
15 Dublin's home
16 Res ___ loquitur
17 Follow strict rules of politeness
20 Bunny movements
21 Victory sign
22 Made an incursion
23 Screwball
24 Underground reservoir
25 Fir
29 Hay storage site
30 Signature on a bad check, maybe
31 18-wheeler
32 Swank
36 Not miss an opportunity
39 Electrical units
40 Historical periods
41 Award for "Braveheart"
42 Old TV host Jack
43 Does tailoring on

44 41-Across bestower, with "the"
48 Foxlike
49 They're needed for organ transplants
50 More than admiration
51 Actress Moreno
55 No longer be able to escape the facts
58 "This ___ outrage!"
59 Arthurian lady
60 To whom Muslims pray
61 W.W. II newsman Ernie
62 Set system
63 Landlord's paper

DOWN
1 Knife wound
2 Quartet member
3 Envelope part
4 50's car features
5 Pass receiver
6 Belief
7 Houston university
8 Silver container
9 "Wow!"

10 "___ one to a customer"
11 Lyric poem
12 Ed of "Lou Grant"
13 "Surprise Symphony" composer
18 Egg
19 N.F.L. conference
23 Cape Canaveral org.
24 Arrives
25 ___ California
26 Graduate, for short
27 Like a wet noodle
28 Schmos
29 "The Merry Widow" composer Franz
31 Err
32 Kind of tense
33 Fairy tale start
34 Capone feature
35 Word on a towel
37 Jimmy Hoffa follower
38 Sacred
42 Lima's land
43 Trebek of "Jeopardy!"
44 Leaky, as a faucet
45 Basketball great Bob

46 Historical record
47 "Lorna ___"
48 Stockholm native
50 Throw ___ (rant)
51 Straight line

52 Mallorca, e.g.
53 Socials
54 Late tennis V.I.P.
56 Warbler Yoko
57 Pres. Coolidge, informally

415 by Gerald R. Ferguson

ACROSS

1 Supports
6 Zoophilist's org.
10 The Crimson Tide, for short
14 Almost too coincidental
15 "Wellaway!"
16 Kind of empire
17 "Gigi" song, 1958
20 Members of the flock
21 Where King Zog I ruled
22 Western Indian
23 Dagger of yore
24 Willie Mays was one
28 Checked
30 1970 Medicine Nobelist Julius
32 Rubout
35 Increases
36 Phrase accompanying a finger-snap
40 Ticket office notice
41 Plead with
42 Set of kettledrums
45 Monty ___
49 Bad-mouth
50 Baron in "Der Rosenkavalier"
52 Cheer for Joselito
53 One of the ABC islands
56 Neptune and Uranus, e.g.
57 "You know what . . ."
61 Bandy words
62 Odd happenstance
63 Staggering
64 Venomous varmints
65 Deere competitor
66 Pithy

DOWN

1 Modern capital founded by the Phoenicians
2 Infuse with oxygen
3 Some liqueurs
4 Spy Philby et al.
5 Call the bet of
6 Jet-black
7 West Point freshman
8 Dear, to Dino
9 "B ___ bug"
10 Cry over
11 Hail from the past
12 Wire measure
13 ___ fours

18 It has 844 million native speakers
19 Buster Brown's dog
23 Architect José Luis ___
25 Kind of lily
26 "Negatory!"
27 N.F.L. scores
29 Sympathy's partner
30 Seed covering
31 Disciple of Socrates
33 Conductor's beginning
34 Diamond figure
36 Tidy
37 Site of scores of baseball players?
38 Prohibitionists
39 Bidder's failure
40 Aves.
43 Sulky pullers
44 In ___ (stagnant)
46 Dancer, slangily
47 Some are golden
48 Sit comfortably
50 Palette pigment
51 Africa's most populous city
54 Plant holder
55 ___ cost (free)

56 60's singer Lesley
57 Civil War letters
58 Goddess of plenty
59 War room fixture
60 Krazy ___

416 by Rich Norris

ACROSS

1 Fisherman's hook
5 Sting
10 Invites
14 Snack item since 1912
15 Transport for the brave?
16 Big dipper
17 See 12-Down
18 Incriminate
19 Coniferous
20 Mediocre, to a cabby?
23 Animation unit
24 Dine
25 Like a good-looking cabby?
32 Culled
34 Trounced, with "down"
35 Wonder
36 Kiln
37 Fills
38 Orange waste
39 Monopoly properties: Abbr.
40 Pitch
41 "The Great Forest" painter
42 The inevitable, to a cabby?
45 Preacher of baseball
46 Alternative to a Compaq
47 Question to a smitten cabby?
55 Goat-man, in myth
56 Bright lights
57 Carroll's "slithy" thing
58 Word with drawing or drive
59 The Sleeping Prophet
60 Jejune
61 Word often after "Ye"
62 Bitter ___
63 Olympics award

DOWN

1 The Masters game
2 Field
3 Heartquake
4 Rain, e.g.
5 Torah
6 "Yes, ___!"
7 Detractor
8 Cross
9 Lean

10 Ancient Rome's ___ Way
11 "Samson et Dalila" composer
12 With 17-Across, Shakespeare tragedy
13 Underhanded
21 Part of MTV
22 Star
25 Bandy about
26 At full speed
27 Famous
28 Resided
29 "___ So Fine" (1963 hit)
30 Has liabilities
31 Weaken, romantically
32 Tendon
33 Famous loser
37 Recuperative spot
38 Damage, so to speak
40 Took off
41 Final
43 Nonstudent living in a college community: Var.
44 Tickles
47 Call
48 Early Andean
49 Arrangement

50 It may walk the dog
51 Not enough, to Susann
52 Manolete opponent
53 Harmful
54 Funny Foxx
55 "Alice" spinoff

417 by Joe DiPietro

ACROSS

1 Cores
5 Traffic stopper
15 Shade of blue
16 Whence the phrase "I am Alpha and Omega"
17 German communications center in W.W. II
18 It has many diamond figures
19 Some shirts
21 Actor Jack
22 "WKRP" character
23 Hidden, as a pig
26 Small drawing?
28 Andy Kaufman TV co-star
31 Site of the Fletcher School of Law and Diplomacy
35 Proxy: Abbr.
36 Susan of "Goldengirl"
37 Dismantle
38 Be hopping mad
40 Kind of cartridge
42 Writer Janowitz
43 Actress Anderson et al.
45 Staff directives
47 Calendar abbr.
48 Fluid accumulation
49 1980 N.F.L. Player of the Year
51 Jim Bakker ministry, for short
53 Words of Jesus
54 Was up (for)
57 Tip, in a way
60 Testator
61 Site of a state university
65 Cape ___ (westernmost point in continental Europe)
66 Book-of-the-Month Club's owner
67 Pitch indicator
68 They sometimes get honked
69 Legion

DOWN

1 Welcoming
2 Mischievous
3 Noted name in book publishing
4 Title name in a 1965 #1 hit
5 Pepper, et al.
6 VCR option: Abbr.
7 State with conviction
8 Word before "#1"
9 Small blisters
10 ___ foot
11 "Am ___ blame?"
12 Phone
13 Veep from Tennessee
14 Cricket wickets
20 Lab reagent
24 "Metaphysics of Morals" writer
25 Bury
27 Short shot
29 Certain regulator
30 Lack of energy
32 One way to serve shrimp
33 Watches
34 Saucers and such
39 Favor one side
41 Surf's sound
44 Rested
46 Hit a ___
50 Discrediting act
52 Miller character
54 H.S. or coll. program
55 Seed appendage
56 1995 N.L. Rookie of the Year
58 Game in which all the spades are laid out
59 Swimming gear
62 Mint
63 Word on French gravestones
64 Hosp. units

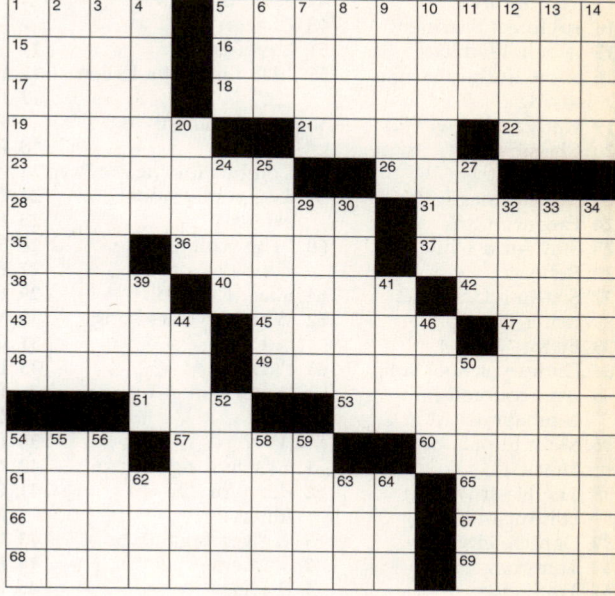

418 by D.J. DeChristopher

ACROSS

1 Promise
5 Lowers, as the lights
9 Biblical queen's home
14 Peculiar: Prefix
15 Olympics event since 1900
16 Ached (for)
17 Emulated the sirens
18 "Alas!"
19 End of a Pindar poem
20 Mythological sculptor who really loved his work
22 Church niches
23 "Shake ___!"
24 Round, full do
26 Court matter
29 Scott of antebellum legal fame
31 Crooked
35 Gladiator's place
37 Require
39 Vintage designation
40 "Nana" author
41 Nasal passage
42 38-Down, for example
43 German river
44 Disable
45 With glee
46 Deliver, in a way
48 Middle: Prefix
50 Slalom curve
51 Mineral suffixes
53 Emulates Xanthippe
55 Defeat
58 Athenian princess who was turned into a nightingale
63 Ouzo flavoring
64 Mother of Helen of Troy
65 Gen. Bradley
66 Arboreal animal
67 Ticked off
68 Fork prong
69 Snake, to Medusa?
70 Prepare 49-Down
71 Generations

DOWN

1 Thin strand
2 Singer Anita
3 Cabal
4 Inflexible teaching
5 Narc's collar
6 Daughter of Agamemnon and Clytemnestra
7 Office note
8 "... like you've ___ ghost!"
9 Weapons for the Myrmidons
10 Queen of the Amazons
11 Son of Seth
12 Eliot hero
13 Lime coolers
21 "Everyone Says I Love You" actor
25 Hula hoops and such
26 Chin smoother
27 Wear away
28 Graf rival
30 Casual cotton
32 Eagle's home
33 Things to be filed
34 Classical-sounding cities in New York and Michigan
36 Youth who fell in love with his reflection
38 Another name for the Furies
41 Bob Hoskins's role in "Hook"
45 Kind of dancer
47 Pronounces
49 Some lunches
52 Divvy up
54 Slew
55 Creator of Mickey and Goofy
56 Lollapalooza
57 Frost
59 Leander's lover
60 Nabob of the Near East
61 One of Artie's exes
62 Greek war god

419 by Susan Smith

ACROSS

1 Convince with smooth talk
5 Wallop but good
9 Like some pans
13 ___ lot (few)
14 Architect Saarinen
15 Is beholden to
16 Show authority, in a saying
19 Native of Novi Sad
20 Classic party activity
21 Rumpus
23 Sacred image: Var.
24 Fare-well link
25 Stay for a while
28 Reflects
32 Six-time U.S. Open tennis champ
33 Bistro
34 Divinity school subj.
35 Unaccounted-for combatants: Abbr.
36 Main impact of an attack
38 The Destroyer, in Hinduism
39 Danube city
40 Tom-tom
41 Traffic jam
42 Word with fruit or play
44 Famous park name, once
46 Baby sounds
47 Salve ingredient
48 Charm
51 Caverns
55 1948 film "The Fallen ___"
56 Be substantial, as a meal
58 Combustible heap
59 Two-dimensional extent
60 "The wolf ___ the door"
61 Slave to detail
62 Where oysters hang out
63 Parker and Waterman

DOWN

1 60's civil rights grp.
2 Beery of 20's–40's films
3 ___ vez (again): Sp.
4 Soldiers
5 Precise
6 Fix, as a paper clip
7 "Trinity" novelist
8 Slough
9 More intrusive
10 John Irving's "A Prayer for ___ Meany"
11 Square, updated
12 Is loyal to
17 People of eastern Siberia
18 It's not automatic
22 "Present"
24 Govt. agent
25 Heist words
26 St. Teresa of ___
27 Paper measures
29 Bay window
30 Variety show
31 Comedy type
33 Diploma word
36 Halloween transport
37 Box score column
38 Itinerary diversion
40 New Look designer
41 Certain investment, for short
43 Fishmonger's tool
44 Hauled
45 Island greetings
48 Crankcase item
49 Romantic interlude
50 Hurting
51 Skirt panel
52 French river
53 Israeli diplomat
54 Atl. speedsters
57 Check

420 by Bob Klahn

ACROSS

1 "Hide in Plain Sight" star
10 Drumbeat
14 Briefly
15 Yammer
16 "My ___" (1972 hit)
17 Preminger classic
18 Never ever
19 Submit
20 It clinks in drinks
21 Pretends not to see
22 Trump Castle, for one
26 Whitman bloomer
27 Behind, in a way
28 A number 1
32 Way to go
33 Hardly laid-back
34 Horse play?
35 Startling revelation
37 Pebble Beach contest
38 1967 Uris novel
39 Junior rocker
40 Blitzes with a blizzard
43 ___ kwon do
44 Nicholson film "Drive, ___"
45 Bent
50 Wax Websterian
51 Browne of "Black Like Me"
52 Moves cautiously
53 Irish Sea spot
54 Henna handler
55 Lombardi lecture

DOWN

1 Novelty hit of 1919
2 Working hard
3 "The Magic Mountain" author
4 Breakfast brand
5 Scheduling
6 Like Eugene Field's cat
7 Lively, in Lyon
8 Teen trauma
9 Battery term
10 "Pocketful of Miracles" director
11 Eulogizes
12 Places in the heart
13 "I ___ what I said"
15 Two-dimensional
19 Imagist poet Doolittle
21 Squeegee
22 Rise to the occasion
23 On the road
24 Planned setting
25 Steaming?
26 "If I Had a Hammer" singer
28 "Oh! Calcutta!" co-writer
29 Couples club
30 Upwardly mobile Israeli group?
31 Multiday building project?
33 Lukewarm
36 Nosegays
37 Make beforehand, as rice
39 Scrub
40 Like some horses
41 Square
42 Orange or Indian
43 Radio pioneer
45 Swanky
46 Avoirdupois
47 Michigan college town
48 1963 Best Actress
49 Six-mile-plus run
51 Ocasek of the Cars

421 by Stanley Newman

ACROSS
1 Yahoo
5 Pigeon drop, e.g.
9 Fill one's tank
14 Peace Nobelist Myrdal
15 Rival of Martina
16 Busy airport
17 Freud's home
18 Ticked off
19 Client of 16-Across
20 Princess Margaret's ex
23 Queue after Q
24 Fishing gear
25 Ended a bout early
27 Fishing gear
30 Barbering job
32 Really went for
36 Bakery enticement
38 Tide type
40 Nephew of Caligula
41 1991 Emmy-winning comic
44 Med. sch. subj.
45 Author Dinesen
46 Davis of "Do the Right Thing"
47 Tout's offering
49 Nudnik
51 Highway hazard
52 Uncommon sense
53 Music score abbr.
55 Experimentation station
58 1961 Inauguration speaker
64 Jordanian port
66 Word on a $1 bill
67 Hoedown prop
68 Blender setting
69 Blockhead
70 "If ___ You" (1929 hit)
71 Game-show group
72 Tom Smothers amusement
73 Courage

DOWN
1 Cry like a baby
2 Mixed bag
3 Walkie-talkie word
4 Leave time
5 Fight souvenir
6 Eastern region
7 One more time
8 Anti-D.W.I. group
9 Composer of Hitchcock's theme
10 Sounds of satisfaction
11 German coal region
12 "Trinity" author
13 Saucy
21 Attack
22 Giraffe kin
26 Taboos
27 Elephant rider, perhaps
28 Maine college town
29 Best Actor of '39
31 ___ Work (rock group)
33 Teammate of Robinson and Hodges
34 "To ___ human"
35 B₁₂ quantities
37 Photo finish
39 Betraying clumsiness
42 "Fantasia" ballerina
43 "___ I can help it!"
48 Sharon's land
50 Completely
54 Boris Badenov's boss
55 Reindeer herder
56 Water color
57 Stable home
59 Miss Marple discovery
60 Suffix for stink
61 Waikiki locale
62 Chair part
63 Koppel and Kennedy
65 Old-fashioned do

422 by Manny Nosowsky

ACROSS
1 Alias of Margaretha Zelle
9 Finish of the 50's
15 Sweet potatoes
16 Trucked
17 Au natural
19 Hoosier humorist
20 With whom Jacob contracted to marry Rachel
21 Cardinal sin
22 One of a vaudeville seven
24 Lip
26 Eight on the Mohs' scale
29 Civil War buff's favorite actress?
34 New news
35 At such a time that
36 At the summit of
37 Summer cooler
38 Two-striper
43 Bar drink, at times
45 Connector of song
46 Sirens
47 Just a bit
48 Golfer Alcott
49 Gulf in 1991 news
53 You can be slapped with these
55 Genes material
58 Just what we need
62 Revisionist?
63 Coffee shop freebies
64 They build up spirits
65 Added as an afterthought

DOWN
1 "The Best Little Whorehouse in Texas" lady
2 Mil. school
3 Receipts
4 Live
5 Kept out of sight
6 Take apart
7 Tabula ___
8 Largest of the Galápagos islands
9 They make a difference
10 What "that" ain't
11 Hick
12 Giant chemicals company
13 First name in TV talk
14 Nelson of 30's musicals
18 Tires
22 Fountain order
23 Master Melvin
25 Roman I
26 Mountebank
27 Author Sinclair
28 Dig for squares?
30 Kind of bead
31 Win by ___
32 Raider's chief
33 Peter and others
39 Sash
40 Top workers?
41 Lark
42 Most economical in business
43 Word in many tournament names
44 Proceed smoothly
49 Be loyal to
50 Whipped up
51 Solo
52 Meadowlands team
54 This señora
55 Fizzled
56 Poppaea's husband
57 Org.
59 Contrary indication
60 Bother
61 A crowd in Torino?

423 by Randy Sowell

ACROSS
1 Instance
5 Kind of metabolism
10 Loading site
14 ". . . ___ forgive our debtors"
15 Get the lead out?
16 "The Cherry Orchard" miss
17 18th-century poet (whose name shares a feature with 36- and 56-Across)
20 Sweetheart
21 February 14 figure
22 Major-league transaction
23 It may be proper
24 Opera composer Nikolai
26 Highlight
29 Relieved
32 Narrative Byron poem
33 Room to ___
34 Support
36 17th-century dramatist
40 United
41 Navratilova rival
42 Boston athlete
43 Natural habitat
45 "Martha" et al.
47 Isolated
48 TV sheriff Tupper
49 Plus
52 Onetime labor chief
53 Good name for a cook?
56 20th-century writer
60 Old song "___ She Sweet?"
61 Get ___ on
62 Churchill prop
63 Hwys.
64 "John Brown's Body" poet
65 Linemen

DOWN
1 Daisy Mae's drawer
2 "Days of Grace" author
3 "M*A*S*H" actress
4 That's a moray
5 Rough posting for a foreign correspondent
6 Illegal firing
7 Processes lumber
8 Quiet color
9 Dracula actor Christopher
10 Traverse a beat
11 "To Live and Die ___"
12 Looked at
13 Comic Martha
18 Ancient land of Spain
19 Leader of '45
23 Around
24 Eye-cue tests?
25 Ocean flier
26 Ken-L-Ration competitor
27 Queeg's command
28 Fish basket
29 Wear
30 "Oklahoma!" aunt
31 Singer Reese
33 Vista
35 Realizes
37 Not hands-on
38 Tied
39 Low-fat desserts
44 Picks
45 Spanish ___
46 Charles's game
48 Mightier than
49 Partly open
50 "___ was you!" (mystery denouement)
51 Nostalgic song ending
52 Middle name in Memphis
53 Mr. Musial
54 Take care of
55 Spends
57 Rainy day rarity
58 Soul, in Soissons
59 Virtuoso

424 by Raymond Hamel

ACROSS
1 Grinder
11 Magistrate in Dryden's "Absalom and Achitophel"
15 Sultry star of "A Man and a Woman"
16 Western wolf
17 Copying, with "after"
18 Shake, in a way
19 911 abbr.
20 Splinter group
21 Brown baggers?
22 Old Portuguese coins
24 Pet nickname
27 Dockworkers' grp.
28 Postman's challenge
30 1981 Rolling Stones hit
32 Short-bodied dog
34 Franck detective ___ Clovis Désiré Pel
35 It won't go along for the ride
38 Make balance
39 Reflecting reality as a single unit
41 Prefix with metrics
42 Shelf coverings
44 1961 fad, with "the"
48 Messenger ___
49 Lauder et al.
51 Unescorted
52 Brand advertised as "two mints in one"
54 Proceedings
56 Ruckus
57 Sharpen, as a knife
58 Would-be journeyman
61 Actor Mischa
62 Sponge
63 Passé hairstyle
64 Not the reigning champs

DOWN
1 Print media
2 Canine's coat
3 Richie's TV buddy
4 Shot or well follower
5 Squeezes (out)
6 Stood up, in dialect
7 Walks primly
8 Look like
9 Dawson of football
10 Part of a journey
11 1973 hit "___ Know"
12 Most thuggish
13 Sheer
14 Gets overexcited
21 Half a coin motto
23 Type of tank
25 Like some reviews
26 Kirkuk denizen
29 Scraps
31 Cat cries
33 Los ___, Calif.
35 Enlisted
36 Swollen
37 Chef's protector
39 Passage of poetry or music
40 Depreciate
43 Like some identities
45 Silver ___ (cloud seed)
46 Kitchen gadget
47 Cosmetic preparations
50 Stone marker
53 Mr. T's real name
55 Pretty soon
58 Half the N.F.L.: Abbr.
59 Turn ___ (start making money)
60 Tiny bit

425 by Sidney L. Robbins

ACROSS

1 Church seat
4 Advantage
8 One way to enlarge a family
13 Essayist Wiesel
15 Projecting rock
16 "Casablanca" star, informally
17 Org.
18 Halloween imps
20 Retained
21 Jupiter's mother
22 Keanu of "Speed"
23 Map lines: Abbr.
25 Super joke
26 Listened
28 Cluckers
29 River of W.W. I
30 Vampire's tooth
31 Oxford, e.g.
35 Halloween visitors
38 Graf ___
39 Wedding shower?
40 French topper
41 Alternative to charge
42 Luges
43 Freshen, in a way
46 Mimic
47 Place side by side

48 Evergreen
49 First of all
53 Halloween tale
55 Stare open-mouthed
56 Equestrian
57 City south of Moscow
58 Gaelic
59 Gland: Prefix
60 Small whirlpool
61 Court divider

DOWN

1 High spot
2 Otherwise
3 Tuft
4 Repeated
5 Throat-soothing candies
6 Chatters
7 Sunny-side-up item
8 Top nun
9 Measures (out)
10 Architectural arch
11 Moper
12 Hardy girl
14 Captivate
19 Juice source
24 Long journey
25 Style

26 Complain
27 Great Lake
28 Concoct
29 McKinley and others: Abbr.
30 Wiry rug fabric
31 Cheapest accommodations
32 Roundup group
33 Raw metals
34 N.Y. winter time
36 Declaims
37 Competent
41 Cuba's Fidel
42 With nimbleness
43 Garden insect
44 Lyric poem
45 1953 American League M.V.P. Al
46 Broadcast
47 Taj Mahal site
48 Tennessee Ernie ___
50 Mend
51 Church recess
52 Encounter
54 Stocking's end

426 by Sidney L. Robbins

ACROSS

1 Movie-spinoff TV series
5 "Arms and the Man" playwright
9 Little Goody Two-___
14 Director Preminger
15 Video
16 Blood vessel
17 With 37-Across and 59-Across, a familiar finale
19 With 58-Across, where to read 17-Across, etc.
20 Whooped
21 Combines
22 Appear
23 Sailor
24 Kind of ball
28 Naughty child's Christmas gift
32 Baden-Baden, e.g.
35 English scarf
36 Israeli native
37 See 17-Across
40 Boxing site
41 "___ say more?"
42 Morse code message
43 Marsh growth

44 Much more expensive
45 Had been
46 Impressed deeply
50 Did a con job on
54 Mollified
58 See 19-Across
59 See 17-Across
60 Askew
61 French statesman Coty
62 Ripped
63 Rain gear
64 Bohemian
65 Raced

DOWN

1 Hole maker
2 One of the Three Musketeers
3 Inscribed pillar
4 According to ___
5 Agitate
6 "___ a nice day!"
7 Copied
8 Tie the knot
9 More secure
10 Kind of frost
11 Not secondhand: Abbr.

12 To be, in Paris
13 Pronounces
18 Logician's propositions
21 Hopping ___
23 Utmost extent
25 Fire residue
26 Play parts
27 Where Inchon is
28 Toy gun "ammo"
29 Sashes
30 Mr. Guthrie
31 Emulates hens
32 Twinkler
33 Skin opening
34 Author James
36 Meadowsweet
38 Pass receiver
39 Summer drink
44 "Dear old ___"
45 Bridge seats
47 Gentle breezes
48 Legally prevent
49 Moline, Ill., company
50 Penetrate
51 Pact since 1949
52 Mishmash
53 Whipping reminder
54 Insist
55 Confined, with "up"

56 Birds of ___
57 ___ Scott Decision, 1857
59 Pitcher's stat

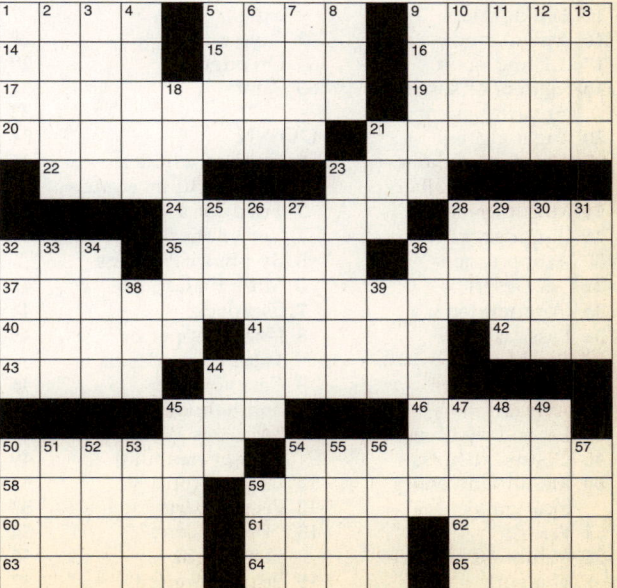

ACROSS

1 Good Queen ___
5 Paradisiacal spots
10 Interfraternity pres., e.g.
14 Latin 101 verb
15 On the up and up
16 ___ Major
17 Whopper maker
18 Delight
19 It gives skiers a lift
20 Clifton Webb film role
23 Carbon dater's calculation
24 Auto club letters
25 Amended
27 Suburbanite, perhaps
32 Seine feeder
33 Timetable abbr.
34 Delaware's capital
36 Cabinet post
39 Gulf war missile
41 Linda Blair in "The Exorcist"
43 Local theater
44 L'eggs rival
46 Wisconsin college
48 Mauna ___

49 "The More ___ You" (1945 song)
51 Toddler's transport
53 Côte d'Azur
56 One of the Three Stooges
57 Resident: Suffix
58 1971 Nitty Gritty Dirt Band song
64 Deuce or trey
66 Where vows are exchanged
67 Marshal Wyatt
68 Too
69 Aquarium fish
70 High gymnastic score
71 Da's opposite
72 Hopped out of bed
73 Stowe novel

DOWN

1 Wound soother
2 Abu Dhabi prince
3 Swedish auto
4 Gulf or jet follower
5 Grain ___
6 Proofreader's mark
7 "Holy moly!"
8 KNO$_3$
9 Sound system

10 On the other hand
11 Tom Selleck sports film
12 Kind of orange
13 Was concerned
21 Praise
22 Good's opponent
26 "This ___ outrage!"
27 The "C" in J.C. Penney
28 "Jaws" boat
29 Muscular moniker
30 In perpetuity
31 Kathie Lee's co-host
35 Engrossed
37 Relative of the English horn
38 "Step to the ___"
40 Lucy's son
42 Oscar-winning Sally Field role
45 Look like
47 Shootout time
50 Book boo-boos
52 Map feature
53 Puerto ___
54 Land of Milan
55 More fit
59 Football Hall-of-Famer Graham

60 They preserve preserves
61 Hideout
62 Sea eagle
63 Made haste

65 Complete an "i"

ACROSS

1 Thomas ___ Edison
5 Bartók et al.
10 Engine noise
14 "Witness" director Peter
15 Eye dazzlers
16 Apian abode
17 ___ and anon
18 Matters of some embarrassment
20 Tagalong
22 Tiny hydrophones
23 Room in an albergo
24 Most deplorable
26 Ill-gotten gains
30 At top speed
31 ___ Desert
35 Confounded
36 Pass, as time
38 Food bar
40 Blast measure
42 Aberration
43 Legendary bluesman
46 Doesn't dismiss
50 Miami University location
51 Wield
52 Mountain climbers, of a sort

56 1981 Gold Glove winner
59 Inner person
60 Turned off
61 Sow chow
62 Site of Napoleonic exile
63 Give a hand
64 On edge
65 Slant

DOWN

1 Inspires wonder
2 Manufacturer Strauss
3 Tried for a title
4 Very noticeable
5 By physical means
6 More than great
7 Escapade
8 Jazz's Pepper or Tatum
9 Case for an ophthalmologist
10 "A ___ Is Waiting" (Cassavetes film)
11 Depend (on)
12 Peeper parts
13 "The Balcony" playwright
19 Bearing freight

21 "The Boys of Summer" author Roger
24 Give the once-over
25 Unfit for farming
26 Latest thing
27 Mosque priest
28 Metallic fabric
29 Overturn
32 They're slow going
33 Reb Robt. ___
34 Sweetie
36 Kind of gun
37 Whale herds
39 Authorizes
41 ___ Island ("Jaws" locale)
42 Go belly up
44 Hayseeds
45 Violent wind carrying snow
46 Made over
47 Radiate
48 Electrical unit
49 Soviet co-op
52 Revue segment
53 Townspeople
54 Ointment container
55 Deli side order
57 Youth org.

58 Grain bristle

429 by Rich Norris

ACROSS
1 Kind of wool
6 San ___, Calif.
10 Ones making a scene
14 Let up, as a storm
15 Once follower
16 Lumberjack
17 Pamphlet writer's expertise?
20 Communicate silently
21 Decorate fancily
22 Incline
26 Mars or Venus
27 Tangle
28 Vault feature
29 Troublemaker
31 Ave. crossers
32 Gardener's need
33 Supermarket phenomenon
34 Studio technician's expertise?
41 Needing irrigation
42 Like a Jekyll-Hyde personality
44 Chest muscle
47 Barn toppers
49 They must be pitched
50 German pronoun
51 Barley bristle
52 Sought transportation, in a way
54 Arty
56 Not fully shut
57 Town planner's expertise?
63 Listen up
64 Ancient Rome conqueror
65 Fix, as a copier
66 C.I.S. predecessor
67 English
68 Dennis the Menace et al.

DOWN
1 Head for the hills
2 Atty.'s group
3 Guy
4 Air conditioner meas.
5 Yuletide, e.g.
6 Served on a panel, maybe
7 Dentist's request
8 Red or White team
9 "Now ___ . . ." (town line message)
10 Hot rod part
11 Postulates
12 Begins, as a task
13 Affair arrangements
18 Back talk
19 Logo
22 "Yuck!"
23 Cons' counterpart
24 Fair to middlin'
25 Stead
26 "Ars Amatoria" author
30 Give the slip
35 Kind of blanket
36 Random decision makers
37 Islamic spirit
38 Cheese in a ball
39 Sans senses
40 The red kind is especially sticky
43 Kind of trip
44 Machu ___, Peru
45 Sonar blips
46 Tower ringers
48 City on the Bay of Fundy
49 Get comfy
53 Hem's companion
55 U.S.N. rank
56 One opposed
58 "Keystone" character
59 Chemical conclusion
60 Some CD players
61 Piece
62 Printers' measures

430 by Manny Nosowsky

ACROSS
1 Prom staple
8 Faction makers
15 Stuck
16 Head of a pyramid scheme?
17 Fixing, maybe
18 Sandwich lettuce
19 Hero's award
21 Not touched
22 Sports happening since 1911
23 Stunning
27 Word root
31 Throw a curve
34 Salty letters
35 Absolutely, to Ahab
37 Maxim violated by a stool pigeon
40 Water pipe
41 Gung-ho feeling
42 Use a postscript
43 Feminizing suffix
44 Popular tourist area, with "the"
46 Certain bond, for short
48 Track figures
52 Movies
59 Duke of Normandy who was called "the Devil"
60 Wire-haired dog
61 Mesabi Range wealth
62 Food originally made by Brazilian Indians
63 Cutting tool with pulleys
64 Gelded

DOWN
1 Checks
2 Battle field?
3 It's a gas
4 High
5 Calif. neighbor
6 It may be dominant
7 Brain tests, for short
8 Arose
9 Set of keys?
10 Overdone
11 Of wrath, in a hymn
12 Port ___
13 Former U.S. poet laureate ___ Van Duyn
14 Illustrator Silverstein
20 Model T
24 Siamese employee, once
25 "A Chorus Line" character
26 Rocks
27 Poivre's partner
28 Dramatic intro
29 Noted with interest
30 Doctor
31 Tennis name of fame
32 Card at a party
33 Become solid
35 Petri dish contents
36 Yellow in white?
38 Just make, with "out"
39 Surfer's surface
44 For all to see
45 Combat pilot's flight
46 Some Spanish paintings
47 Extremely
49 Betty Ford process
50 Clear, in a way
51 Senior golf great
52 Former Big Apple newspaper, with "The"
53 Joyful dance
54 Bard's black
55 E-mail menu choice
56 Alphabet quartet
57 Search through
58 Long-running Fox show

431 by Sidney L. Robbins

ACROSS
1 Songs by Queen Latifah
5 Prefix with sphere
9 Cavalry sword
14 Dictator Idi
15 Hold (up)
16 Money holder
17 Classic bouquet tosser
19 Furious
20 Houston pro
21 Wooed with music
23 Kind of collision
25 Commercials
26 Highlander's skirt
29 ___ quo
34 Possesses
38 Skin opening
40 Chris of tennis
41 With 66-Across, an observation by Lowell
44 "___ Eat Cake"
45 Hard labor
46 Thick slice
47 Russian plain
49 Items hard to eat with a knife
51 German city on the Danube
53 Tics
58 Most stable
64 Pitch black
65 Winner's winning
66 See 41-Across
68 Older brother of Moses
69 Taj Mahal site
70 Curved molding
71 Pooped
72 Revolutionary Trotsky
73 Stalin's realm

DOWN
1 Former title in India
2 Entertain
3 One of Columbus's ships
4 Dummy Mortimer
5 Mar. follower
6 Speaker of baseball fame
7 Means
8 "Tosca" or "Thaïs," e.g.
9 Bachelorette of a certain age
10 Surrounding glow
11 Finishing nail
12 Town near Padua
13 Saxophone, e.g.
18 Enter criminal charges against
22 Actors Harris and Begley
24 Cheese ___ (popular snack food)
27 Missing
28 Boy Scout group
30 Fifth and Mad., e.g.
31 Dabbling duck
32 ___ Major
33 Injure with a pitchfork
34 Wise birds
35 Hone
36 Basketball great Thurmond
37 Bit of a climb
39 Toledo's lake
42 Sassy
43 "'Tis a pity!"
48 Israelite judge
50 Twirled
52 Veteran's pride
54 Region in the Loire Valley
55 Wallops
56 Excavates
57 Ranch head?
58 Ems and Baden-Baden
59 Snare
60 The auld sod
61 Radio-controlled aerial bomb
62 One sought for advice
63 Novice
67 Author Fleming

432 by Gregory E. Paul

ACROSS
1 This may have a hard or soft shell
5 Lionel Hampton's instrument
10 This may have a hard or soft shell
14 Mary Kay competitor
15 W.W. II's ___ Gay
16 Stockings
17 Video
18 White-plumed bird
19 Screen terrier
20 Uncommon sense
21 Cold war barrier
23 Caviar source
25 Poppycock
26 John ___ (the Lone Ranger)
27 Psychotherapy
32 Western resort lake
34 Hundred-dollar bill
35 Nationality suffix
36 Iowa State's locale
37 One slightly overweight
38 Merriment
39 ___ culpa
40 Hall's singing partner
41 Participated in a Christmas club
42 Publicly supports
44 French 101 verb
45 Paycheck amount
46 Indistinct, as speech
49 Oz denizen
54 Mustangs of the Southwest Conf.
55 Draft status
56 Pass on
57 Elemental unit
58 Pastry chef's aide
59 Squirrel's snack
60 Pro ___
61 Cooking fat
62 Singer Lenya
63 Ocho minus cinco

DOWN
1 "Soap" family
2 Nautical command
3 Venomous viper
4 Word on a penny
5 Changed direction
6 Fort Knox unit
7 ___ again
8 T.V.A. output
9 Waterlog
10 Loquacious
11 Spingarn Medal winner Parks
12 ___ spumante
13 Noodle
21 Rival of Bjorn
22 Romeo, e.g.
24 Classic cars
27 Peruvian peaks
28 Holiday drinks
29 Combat award
30 Response heard in 27-Across
31 Storage spot
32 Docile
33 Congregation's assent
34 Baby-faced
37 Idyllic
38 Actress Teri
40 Nabisco snack
41 Render speechless
43 Leader's exhortation
44 Comedienne Boosler
46 Bright
47 Play to the balcony
48 Camille's creator
49 Labor
50 Machu Picchu dweller
51 Not e'en once
52 See 57-Down
53 Coin opening
57 With 52-Down, 20's–30's design

by Mike Shenk

ACROSS

1 MG, e.g.
10 Pen name
15 "Here Is Your War" author
16 Frequent
17 In the doghouse
18 Essence
19 Clark's "Mogambo" co-star
20 Nebbish
22 Ensign's underling: Abbr.
23 "The Old Curiosity Shop" heroine
25 Items in a count
26 Bit of business
27 Misappropriate
29 Alternative to spring
30 Author on mythology Geoffrey ___
31 See 32-Down
33 Jurassic Park threat
35 Krypton, for one
38 Some pigs
39 Series start
40 "A ___ the Life" (Lennon-McCartney song)
41 Young oyster
42 Construction piece
44 Critic's awards
48 Wren's wings
49 One of the Churchills
51 Draft rating
52 Sound intensity unit
53 Swallow
55 Contract
56 "Once ___ Mattress"
58 Unhurried
60 School visitor?
61 "If Morning Ever Comes" author
62 Deal with
63 Mourners of August 9, 1995

DOWN

1 Carried chairs
2 Yard border
3 Reduced
4 Fix, in a way
5 Stretch
6 Canaries' owner
7 Iowa State team
8 Czar Nicholas II's heir
9 Biblical shortcut
10 Sport
11 Word in a Cagney impersonation
12 Ishmael and others
13 Album item
14 Batters with controlled swings
21 Trout catcher
24 Hidden fingerprints
26 Draw on
28 Seating request
32 With 31-Across, Best Supporting Actress of 1992
34 Stick through the middle
35 Gatherings in a Herrick poem
36 Traditionally American
37 1989 Jody Watley hit
38 1980s musical with mbaqanga music
40 Pop singer Love
43 Lay
45 Len's "Sweeney Todd" co-star
46 Rocked
47 Dionysus's entourage
50 Watered down
53 Card game with a bank
54 Judges' successor
57 Surfing site
59 ___, N.Y. (Barbara Bush's birthplace)

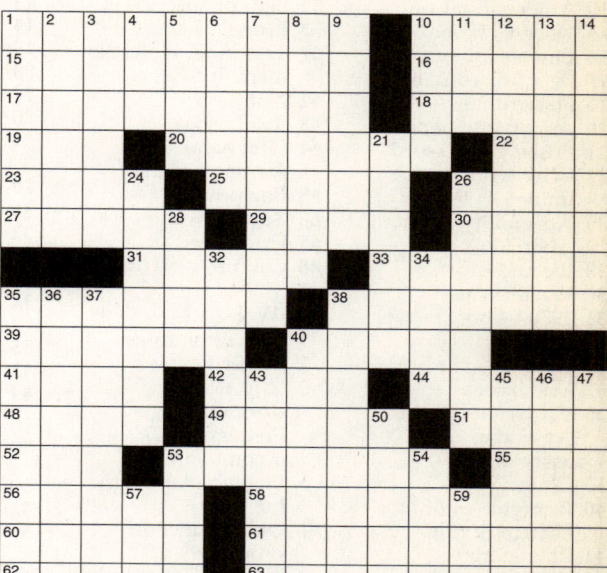

---

by Frances Hansen

ACROSS

1 Composer ___ Carlo Menotti
5 So-and-sos
9 "Goodbye, Mr. Chips" star, 1939
14 Liking
15 Semicircular room
16 Balearic resort isle
17 Flop
18 ___ to the throne
19 Locker art
20 Basic
23 Fish of which the male carries the fertilized eggs
24 Cocktail ingredient
25 ___ toot
26 Germ
30 Gentleman's evening clothes
35 Topper
36 Car bar
37 Agreeable word
38 Enthralled
39 Writer Hecht
40 Maugham satire
44 Ignorant (of)
46 Revivalist, informally
47 Brian of rock
48 Person with hives
53 1953 play, or consolation for a meatless meal?
56 Kind of board
57 Where Ron Howard was born: Abbr.
58 Betty of cartoons
59 Printing mark
60 Laugh ___
61 Like some tennis games
62 Walter Trampler's instrument
63 Elizabeth II's only daughter
64 Made do

DOWN

1 The Bee Gees
2 Harden
3 Confused
4 "Forget it!"
5 Extremely arid
6 Broaches, in a way
7 Backing vocal?
8 Author Ivo Andric, for one
9 Hinged pair of pictures
10 ___ dictum
11 Emergency CB channel
12 France's Cote d'___
13 Designate
21 Spanish lady's title
22 "Trinity" author
26 Failure
27 "Eugene Onegin" sister
28 Junior high subj.
29 Touchiness
30 Elephant Boy of 30's film
31 Team members
32 Arm part
33 Director W. S. Van ___
34 Charge
38 Darling
40 Popular game from Uruguay
41 Schoenberg's "Moses und ___"
42 Pep up
43 One of the tides
45 Toad Hall vandal
48 Show politeness at the door
49 Traffic cone
50 "___ a trip on a train . . ." (Benny Goodman lyric)
51 Leave, with "off"
52 Pounded the Underwood
53 Cuisine choice
54 A Saarinen
55 ___ Maar (Picasso subject)
56 Year in Septimius Severus's reign

435   by Gilbert H. Ludwig

ACROSS

1 Draft org.
4 "Immediately!"
7 The back of the choir?
13 American falcon
15 Queen's home
16 Emotes
17 Beans or corn, e.g.
18 Harvestman
20 Astronaut Shepard
21 Postal creed word
22 "Thy word is ___ unto . . .": Psalms
25 Air quality tester: Abbr.
28 Joe and others?
30 Writer Wiesel
31 1970 George Segal movie
36 Kind
37 Undergoes
38 ___ Group (Latin American association)
39 Chum
40 It might result in a change of title
41 Env. extra
42 1964 Cary Grant comedy-romance

45 Daughter of Laban
47 Glasgow refusal
48 ___ de Cologne
49 Combustible woodpiles
51 Sign of success?
53 Prong
57 1966 A. E. Hotchner memoir
61 Not basic
63 Really soak
64 First name in women's tennis
65 Poe poem
66 Young swan
67 Crew need
68 Cal. units

DOWN

1 Like some forces
2 Singer Payne
3 "My Roomy" storywriter
4 Frequent H_2O accompanier
5 English playwright Joe
6 Didn't function properly
7 Ancient Semitic idol
8 Sleep disturber

9 TV's "Living ___"
10 Town near the Golden Gate Bridge
11 Laundry room brand
12 Word part: Abbr.
13 Musical tail
14 Low island
19 Old name for the flu
23 Draws out, as humor
24 Orange ___
26 B'way showing
27 Hyphenate with American
29 Two-for-one?
31 Young lion
32 Dancer Carol of "The Pajama Game"
33 Landscaper's job
34 White, granular powder
35 Chlorophyta bit
43 Start of a toast
44 Lost interest in, in a way
46 Occasional parking requirement
50 Enliven
52 City on the Missouri
54 Johnny Cash's "___ the Line"
55 Big-time competition: Abbr.

56 Scrutinizes
58 Not enough room to swing ___
59 Ancient route
60 Heart
61 Cable network
62 Shy, but maybe not?

436   by Rich Norris

ACROSS

1 Self-supporting
10 According to
15 Turnpike sites
16 40's jazz-style singer Ella Mae
17 Cut off
18 Prime
19 Greek letters
20 Pulitzer-winning critic Richard
21 Naval acronym
22 Profits
23 Look
25 Albergo offering
26 "___ Lover" (1959 hit)
29 Herd orphan
31 Toe preceder
32 Focus
34 Hindu divinity
35 Had
36 Checks
40 Like a nursing infant
42 Cask
43 Choir members
45 Accelerate
46 Purge
47 Blackmore heroine

49 "The Merry Widow" star, 1952
53 Support payers
56 Tend the plants
57 Sacred serpent
58 Wounds
60 Elf of Persian folklore
61 Pop singer Stansfield
62 Fend (off)
63 Down-to-earth
65 Trevanian's "The ___ Sanction"
66 Following
67 Cinematographer's concern
68 Some leather garments

DOWN

1 Patron
2 One in a flat
3 Possessions
4 Times spent on la plage
5 Ancient Roman spirit
6 Like a rainbow
7 In demand
8 Mashpee's peninsula
9 Ovarian product

10 Old-time actor Leon
11 Recitals, often
12 Type of medical care
13 Raise
14 Went over
24 Snake, for one
27 Response to a revelation
28 "The Last Judgment," e.g.
30 Studio prop
33 Word after "look out"
36 Highlights
37 Starry-eyed
38 Minor
39 Down to one's last nickel
41 Fed. agency estab. in 1933
44 Future resident, perhaps
48 Make bubbly
50 Curaçao quaff
51 Delegate
52 Staggers, with "out"
54 A natural
56 Asperity
59 Arid
61 Shenanigan

64 High school subj.

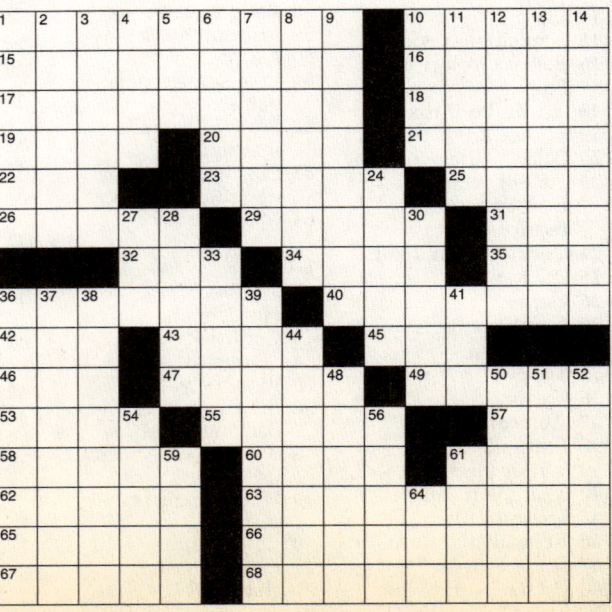

437 by Thomas W. Schier

ACROSS
1 Canyon sound
5 Cross-legged exercises
9 August forecast
14 Bumbler
15 50–50
16 Mohawk Valley city
17 Kitchen fat
18 Shea Stadium nine
19 Pressed one's luck
20 Big-eared animal
21 Vacation locale
23 In ___ (ready for release)
25 Sign of summer
26 Cordage
29 It will be printed tomorrow
34 Gerald Ford's birthplace
36 Banned apple spray
38 By way of
39 Vacation locale
42 Declare
43 Speaker Gingrich
44 Solemn procedures
45 "___ forget"
47 1959 Fiestas song
49 Comic Charlotte
51 Outcome
54 Vacation locale
60 Have a tab
61 Like gold
62 On-the-cob treat
63 Ilsa of "Casablanca"
64 Wrist movement
65 Tale starter
66 Pre-owned
67 Army vehicles (You're welcome)
68 Blue-green
69 Jolly, to the British

DOWN
1 Brilliance
2 Sharply disagree
3 Monmouth Park events
4 ___ man out
5 Sana native
6 "Back to you"
7 Fetches
8 Photographer Adams
9 Rock of Hollywood
10 Jazz locale
11 Muralist Joan
12 Cake decorator
13 Janet Reno's home county
21 Lacquer
22 Pine
24 Associate
27 Put the finger on
28 Is brilliant
30 Painter's mishaps
31 Russian parliament building
32 Sea swooper
33 "Broom Hilda" creator Myers
34 Whitish gem
35 Military command?
37 "Wheels"
40 Late-late show hour
41 Vacation events
46 Violent downfalls
48 Tornado part
50 Orlando attraction
52 Shareholder
53 Sleepwear item
54 ___-Hartley Act
55 Hip-shaking in Kauai
56 Actress Moran
57 Rube
58 TV knob
59 Whale of a movie
63 Broadway hit of 1964–65

438 by Stephanie Spadaccini

ACROSS
1 Casper or Balthazar, e.g.
6 Rope material
10 Chorale part
14 Florida city
15 Jai ___
16 La Scala presentation
17 NO UNTIDY CLOTHES
20 Walking on air
21 Macadam ingredient
22 ___ Cruces, N.M.
23 Prepared
24 Harem
26 Subordinate Claus
29 Apocalypse
31 Gene material
32 Seldom seen
34 "QB VII" author
36 Lump of jelly, e.g.
39 GOVERN, CLEVER LAD
43 "You said it!"
44 Writer Shere
45 Approve
46 W.W. II grp.
48 Agrippina's son
50 German pronoun
51 Answer to "What's keeping you?"
55 Mount near ancient Troy
57 Item in a lock
58 "I" affliction
59 1990 Bette Midler film
62 BLATHER SENT ON YE
66 Neighborhood
67 Le Mans, e.g.
68 Conductor Georg
69 Back-to-school time: Abbr.
70 Bouquet
71 Friend of Henry and June

DOWN
1 Word on the Oise
2 Long (for)
3 Food critic Greene
4 Arm bones
5 Fried lightly
6 Actor Charles of "Hill Street Blues"
7 Overhead trains
8 Not shiny
9 A captain of the Enterprise
10 Dance, in France
11 On ___ (doing well)
12 1979 treaty peninsula
13 Authority
18 Alternate road
19 Los Angeles suburb
24 Obviously pleased
25 Big name in viniculture
26 Physics unit
27 Zhivago's love
28 "It Came ___ Outer Space"
30 Mezz. alternative
33 "It's true," in Torino
35 French resort town
37 Forest florae
38 ___ B'rith
40 Fingernail polish
41 Realism
42 Salon selection
47 Rossini character
49 Potemkin mutiny site
51 Jots
52 Skiing's Phil or Steve
53 Tiptoe
54 Air Force arm: Abbr.
56 Illinois city
59 Cassandra
60 Falana or Montez
61 Opposing
63 Dracula, sometimes
64 Sgt., e.g.
65 Frozen Wasser

439   by Harvey Estes

ACROSS

1 Annie, for one
7 Sandwich often on toast
10 "___ 'em!"
13 Took refuge
15 ___ rights (police suspect's entitlement)
17 Bomber type
18 Noted Richard III portrayer
19 Congressional funding?
21 Memory unit
22 R.E. Lee's land
23 Three-time World Cup medalist
27 Many a time
29 It borders Tenn.
33 Declaration
36 Taj Mahal, e.g.
39 Most-wanted poster letters
40 Vatican Museum holdings?
43 ___ out a living
44 First name in game shows
45 "Brace yourself!"
46 He played Fred on "Sanford and Son"
48 Trading-bloc inits.
50 Particles
51 Make ___ story (lie)
54 Famous sewer
57 Vacation slides?
64 Tank gas
65 Forked over
67 Nineveh's nation
68 "Great Expectations" miss
69 Ben in the film "Ben"
70 O.K.
71 Well-___ (rich)

DOWN

1 Cries
2 Campus mil. grp.
3 ___-bargain
4 Jalopy
5 Make up on the spot
6 Harebrained
7 Coll. V.I.P.
8 Shade of purple
9 Stumbles
10 Irritated state
11 Bit of brainwork
12 Baseball's Yastrzemski
14 Pic
16 Birdy?
20 Table scraps
23 On ___ (theoretically)
24 Call forth
25 Ran at an easy pace
26 Lamb producer
28 Stroller passenger
30 Freighter filler
31 Ohio city
32 Pours
34 Provide weapons
35 Caustic
37 55 letters?
38 Fancy neckwear
41 Start to dominate
42 One at the beginning
47 Hardly svelte
49 Two-door vehicle
52 Admiral in the Arctic
53 Nickname in the Senior P.G.A.
55 Tennis kill
56 Bash, biblically
57 Boom or box
58 Nocturnal bear
59 "Make the ___ of it"
60 Votes for
61 "Zip-___-Doo-Dah"
62 Undulate
63 Christmastime
66 Itsy bit

440   by Jonathan Schmalzbach

ACROSS

1 Symbol of suburbia
5 Author Grey et al.
10 Joyful cries
14 Hand cream additive
15 Sommelier's stock
16 Crow's-nest spot
17 Storage spot in a Brooklyn home
19 Word with sound or dog
20 Jargon suffix
21 Hurry
22 Petrol amount
23 What a Brooklyn guy blames today's problems on
27 It's stuck on Brooklyn theater floors
30 Place that Lot fled
31 Eager
32 What Brooklyn students hate to take
36 Half of Mork's sign-off
37 Serra's title
39 Ages
41 What a Brooklynite catches at J.F.K.
43 Creeper
44 Too-too
46 Where a Brooklynite tipples
47 Body that busted a Brooklyn gangster
52 Anchor position
53 Three, to Gina
54 Job's lot
57 Role for Oland
58 Laundry chore in Brooklyn
62 Annoyed interjection
63 Liver, e.g.
64 Conception
65 Clumsy craft
66 Author Zora ___ Hurston
67 Shore flier

DOWN

1 Forced (to)
2 Pub brews
3 Hoop's locale, perhaps
4 Pastoral spot
5 Austrian-born writer Stefan
6 Anouk et al.
7 Wind dir.
8 Bard's twilight
9 Jet set's jet
10 Sphere of operation
11 Cole Porter's "Katie Went to ___"
12 Type of turf
13 Dutch artist Jan
18 Noah's eldest
22 Hamstrung
23 Unearthed
24 Sleepy ones
25 Fulda feeder
26 Repetition
27 Comic Aykroyd
28 "Heavens!"
29 Missing
33 Little Foys number
34 Newspaper nickname
35 Mens ___ in corpore sano
37 ___ Springs
38 One against
40 Sunday speech: Abbr.
42 Unit of sugar or coal
45 Star-shaped
46 Bunnies' mummies
47 Russian villa
48 Old anesthetic
49 China flaw
50 Sty sounds
51 "Forsyte Saga" heroine
54 Broad
55 Singular person
56 Actor Eddie
58 Slip into
59 Before, to Burns
60 Links grp.
61 Dog command

441 by Fran and Lou Sabin

ACROSS
1 One of the March sisters
5 Musical composition
10 Michener's "Hawaii," e.g.
14 Heckelphone
15 Win by ___
16 Verse pattern
17 TURKEY?
20 "___ Pay" (Faulkner's first novel)
21 Carpenter's supply
22 Shed
23 Break-even amount
24 Catalina, e.g.
27 Ornamental garden
31 Mediterranean port
32 View from I-90
33 Sharers' word
34 PLYMOUTH ROCK?
39 Supplement, with "out"
40 Med. course
41 Auricular
42 Assad's capital
44 Smooth-talking
46 Like many cakes
47 Weed killer
48 It's a wrap!
50 Tops in poker?
54 MAYFLOWER?
56 Pour
57 Comforts
58 When twice repeated, a 1970 war movie
59 Just for guys
60 Like modern bombs
61 Clairvoyant

DOWN
1 Haircuts
2 Spanish river
3 Cat's-paw
4 Impetuous
5 Least prepared
6 Windy City touchdown site
7 Some votes
8 "What's the ___?"
9 Handel's "Messiah," e.g.
10 Friendly cannonade
11 Get in touch with?
12 Needlefish
13 "The Woman in the Dunes" author
18 Fashionable name
19 Going along (with)
23 Grouse
24 Snagged dogies
25 Alexander of "The Cosby Show"
26 "The Crucible" setting
27 Baby brothers, typically
28 Atlas line
29 Arrest, in slang
30 Upright
35 Classic Sterling North book
36 Infuriates
37 Whittier heroine
38 Out-of-towners
43 TV broadcast
44 Timberland
45 Regan's father
47 Lumberjack
48 Tiff
49 "Se vuol ballare," e.g.
50 Soprano Ponselle
51 Sole possessor?
52 Joyce's land
53 Rigging supporter
54 Start of M-G-M's motto
55 Thanksgiving fare

442 by Fran and Lou Sabin

ACROSS
1 Karate blow
5 O'Neill specialty
10 Suffer consequences
13 Coleridge poem
14 Tyr, Balder, etc.
15 Magic incantation
16 Start of a quip
19 Amigo
20 Arp art
21 Boxer Griffith
22 Hard to corner
23 Arrogates
25 Strauss opera
28 Phylum subdivision
29 Botanist's angle
30 "Dangerous Liaisons" star
31 One who stoops to conquer
34 Part 2 of the quip
38 Isle of ___, England
39 "Werewolf of London" star, 1935
40 Erect
41 Tickle
42 Restraint
44 Curricula vitae
47 Startling success
48 Pass over
49 Factory
50 Emblem of sovereignty
53 End of the quip
57 Sunday wrap
58 Delete
59 Nonmainstream group
60 Spare item
61 Clemson player
62 What the genouillère protects

DOWN
1 Biker's aid
2 Round dance
3 Amphitheater
4 Darling
5 1992 Irons-Binoche film
6 Start of a marksman's orders
7 One of the Oceanides
8 Wire measure
9 Path of a pass
10 Feast of Lots
11 Hock
12 Approvals
15 Tale-spinning uncle
17 Port on the Ijsselmeer
18 Time sharer, e.g.
22 Big band drummer Cozy ___
23 Viva voce
24 Bratty talk
25 Reasoning
26 Oksana Baiul leap
27 Romany historian
28 Computer knockoff
30 Without couth
31 Strip
32 Time can do it
33 Gothic governess
35 Loser at El Alamein
36 Model binder
37 Do LSD
41 "City Without Walls" poet
42 Thunderclap
43 Basketball coach Adolph
44 Plot again
45 Varnish ingredient
46 Silent screen slinker
47 Portrait on a $10,000 bill
49 Unpartnered
50 Social reformer Robert
51 Camptown activity
52 "PC World" rival
54 Nevertheless
55 Title for Nehru
56 "Just ___"

ACROSS

1 Extremely unpleasant
6 One going downhill
10 Sand
14 Cosmetician Lauder
15 Peel
16 ___ Rooter
17 With 36-Across, shirker's comment
20 Manipulates a needle
21 60 minutes past 12
22 Thrusts back
23 ___ Glory
24 Glad rags
25 Changed into
29 English statesman William
30 Oak-to-be
31 ___ California
32 Land amount
36 See 17-Across
39 Lays turf
40 Biddies
41 Siouan Indian
42 Poses
43 Made beer
44 Inclines
47 Serling of "The Twilight Zone"
48 Actor Omar
49 Artfully shy
50 Gem
54 Evasion and pursuit
57 Came to earth
58 Leave out
59 British Museum's ___ marbles
60 The "B" in N.B.
61 Dig this!
62 Yorkshire city

DOWN

1 Front-page matter
2 Tennis V.I.P. Arthur
3 Goulash
4 Counting system
5 Still and all
6 Disburse
7 Spike, as the punch
8 Time for the history books
9 Of waste
10 Pick of the vineyard
11 Oarsman
12 Country in a grand tour
13 Santa's bagful
18 Bagel's middle
19 Mailed
23 Hotel chain name
24 South Pacific islanders
25 Faces the pitcher
26 Reverberate
27 Campus lass, in old lingo
28 Weaponry
29 Dupes
31 Borscht ingredients
32 Cathedral area
33 Eagle feature
34 Latest "in" fashion
35 Observed critically
37 Leader's office
38 The Almighty
42 Twirl
43 Word before and after "will be"
44 Laminated rock
45 Former language of 12-Down
46 Give a keynote address
47 Course
48 Sign of healing
49 Mint
50 Leer at
51 Senate runner
52 In the center of
53 Camera part
55 2,001, to Ovid
56 Slippery fish

ACROSS

1 Fence openings
6 ___ California
10 Airline to Tel Aviv
14 Open-eyed
15 Israeli statesman Abba
16 Casual dissent
17 Really small
19 "Concord Sonata" composer
20 Some walk-ups
21 Discharge
22 ___ de la Cité
23 Frost-covered
24 Iterated
28 On and off
32 Greetings at sea
33 Slick goo
34 Homophone for 50-Down
35 Poses (for)
36 String quartet member
37 Novelist ___ S. Connell Jr.
38 Em chasers
39 Housekeeper of 60's TV
40 El Greco's birthplace
41 Big city horizons
43 Troupe member
44 London gallery
45 Ryan's "Love Story" co-star
46 Prostrate
48 Like vending machines
54 Campus mil. org.
55 Really big to-do
56 ___ quam videri (North Carolina motto)
57 Gymnast Korbut
58 De-file a disk?
59 Remunerates
60 About midmonth
61 Wives of knights

DOWN

1 Intl. commerce org.
2 Nautical direction
3 Tiger Beat reader
4 Sea eagle
5 Holds up
6 Designer Geoffrey
7 Help a crook
8 Comedienne Hooks et al.
9 Whichever
10 Elgar's "___ Variations"
11 Really affectionate
12 Copies
13 For fear that
18 Fuse
21 Irish republic
23 "Arrivederci, ___"
24 Facilitates
25 Armorial flaw
26 Really fine
27 Cries of dismay
28 Blackthorns
29 Alternative to a caplet
30 Fit to be tied
31 Furniture worker
33 "One ___ fits all"
36 Windmill blade
37 Historical period
39 Sexologist Shere
40 Ascended
42 Jousters' equipment
43 Scheme
45 A two-dimensional world?
46 Kind of school
47 Civil rights figure Parks
48 "___ Lang Syne"
49 Egg on
50 New Age-ish glow
51 Cable car
52 Word in an ultimatum
53 Henna and others
55 ___ polloi

445 by Ernie Furtado

ACROSS

1 Long time
5 Son of Venus
9 Exhaust a person
14 "Cheers" stoolie?
15 Western wine valley
16 Prefix with centrism
17 Some exercises
18 Fed
19 South Sea isle
20 Dangerous drink
23 Classic auto
24 Numeral prefix
25 Atlanta-based cable channel
26 Fast fliers
27 Unaided
31 ". . . baked in ___"
33 Ticket info
34 Ask urgently
37 ___ pink
40 Wanted-poster letters
41 Usually
43 Alley ___
44 Senior member
46 Kind of sax
47 Court
48 Letter encl.
50 Missions
52 Accusation from Caesar
54 Big band ___
57 Ballad ending
58 Broadcast
59 Single engagement
64 Calliope power
66 Café additive
67 Novello of old films
68 "Maria ___" (40's hit)
69 Book after II Chronicles
70 Utah's state flower
71 Pretend
72 Dates
73 De ___ (too much)

DOWN

1 Whoever
2 Make a boo-boo
3 Hence
4 Intelligence
5 Workers' homes
6 Rosalind Russell Broadway role
7 Certain abstract paintings
8 Babbled
9 Out of juice
10 Polo Grounds great
11 Burg
12 Cove
13 Court pleas, briefly
21 Coring tools
22 One-time link
26 Kind of tax
27 Slender nail
28 John's mate
29 It's marked with an arrow
30 Guinness record, maybe
32 Cardin and Curie
35 "Right you ___!"
36 High point at the shore
38 Punk
39 Homeric poetry
42 Swit and Young
45 Water in a fontaine
49 Donne's dusk
51 Painter
52 Painter's prop
53 Sir or Dame, e.g.
55 Heats up
56 Staring
59 Kind of band
60 Take on
61 Swear up and down
62 Canceled
63 Word after ear or tear
65 Year in the Yucatán

446 by Harvey Estes

ACROSS

1 "Gone With the Wind" locale
8 Cousin of a terrarium
14 Area of early exploration
16 Senator Daniel
17 Maj. Strasser in "Casablanca"
18 Hung around
19 Cigar tip
20 Ages
22 Mustachioed artist
23 Backward
24 Coal porter
26 Ambrose Bierce, notably
27 Communicate through channels
29 Some trial evidence
30 Realty sign
31 Ed of Mingo fame
32 "Wanna ___?"
33 Employs pupils
35 Radii parallels
37 "Yeah, right"
38 Ky.-to-Okla. direction
39 Passed beautifully
40 Alternative to Le Bourget
42 Polluter-busting org.
43 Arm on a saucer
45 Ball's beau
47 "On the Beach" author
48 Sgt., e.g.
51 Objects of a 1950's scare
52 Wheat center
53 Eve's counterpart
54 Harden
56 Springs (from)
59 Depleted
60 Suckle
61 Skyscrapers
62 Most condensation-covered

DOWN

1 Lenten forehead smudges
2 You put them in your food
3 Churchgoers
4 Oxy-5 target
5 Common conjunction
6 Mai ___
7 Get higher
8 Sound like thisss
9 Neighbor of Minn.
10 Sycophant
11 Presently, to a shopaholic?
12 Part of a makeup kit
13 Set aside for some purpose
15 Completely, to a pitcher?
21 Scent
24 Country singer McDaniel
25 Bring about
26 Record replacers
27 "___ your old man!"
28 Vacation spot
30 Scoundrel, to Betsy Ross?
33 Initiate, as a warrant
34 After-dinner order
36 Certain car deal
37 Artful
39 Carpenter's tool
41 Charlotte of "Diff'rent Strokes"
44 Showed busyness
46 Words to the audience
48 ___ Dame
49 Salad green
50 Start
52 Works a deal on
53 Kahului's locale
55 Animal enclosure
57 Noshed
58 90 degrees from 38-Across

447   by David J. Kahn

ACROSS

1 Booty
5 Met singer
10 Untanned
14 As written, in music
15 "Encore!"
16 During
17 Sacramento's ___ Arena
18 60's actress Demick
19 ___ qua non
20 Metro cars
21 Wire: Abbr.
22 Toward the end
24 Exhortation from Horace's "Odes"
27 Get dark
29 The first H in 4-H
30 Straighten
31 French seasonings
32 A.F.L.-___
35 Pavarotti, to fans
39 Brain scan, for short
40 Bankrupt
41 Paris decree
42 TV's "The ___ Show"
43 Julianne or Marianne
44 Survives another night
48 Warhol's genre

50 ___ Paulo
51 Reebok rival
54 Newspaper item
55 "The Champ" star, 1931
57 Where Jackie Robinson lettered
58 Tenant problem, perhaps
59 "Darn ___!"
60 Extra
61 Hammer head
62 Armor plate
63 Erotic

DOWN

1 Cinder
2 Had on
3 Challenging in public
4 Zero on the scoreboard
5 "The Substance of Fire" playwright
6 Conclude negotiations
7 What pirates used to do
8 Subject of a sermon
9 Tethered
10 Trattoria offering

11 ___ Island ("Jaws" resort)
12 Come-on
13 Pulitzer-winning critic Richard
23 Tack (on)
25 ___ way (never)
26 Fabled beauty
27 Daytime talk show host
28 "I cannot tell ___"
31 Knievel feat
32 Narrative
33 Bakery worker
34 Bone: Prefix
36 Nipped in the winter
37 "___ Camera"
38 Adults
42 Neighbor of Switz.
44 Enlivener
45 Chewed up
46 Peerage members
47 "The Doings of Raffles Haw" writer
48 Splendor
49 Prize for "Prelude to a Kiss"
52 Ku ___ Klan
53 Effortless
56 Sorority letter

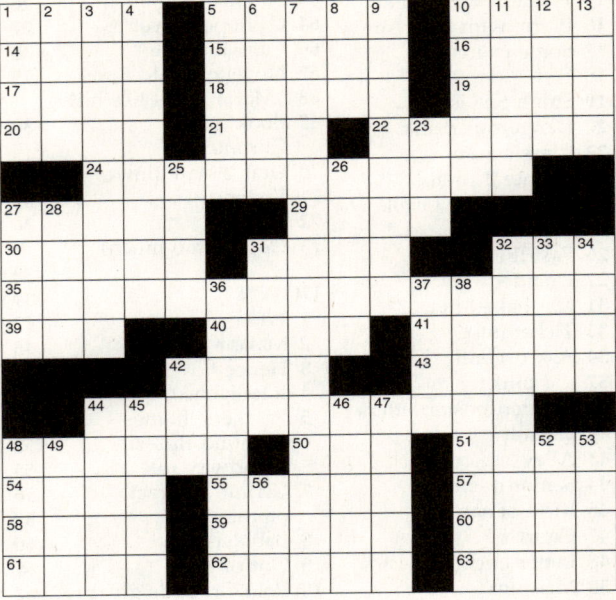

448   by Frank Longo

ACROSS

1 Lilliputian
6 "Delirious" co-star, 1991
15 Where the Gai Lan International Airport is
16 Drop-in?
17 Attachment
18 Owing money
19 Kind of china
21 Popular stuffed carnival prize
22 "Very well"
23 Londoner's sour brew
27 Pilgrimage
28 More icy, informally
30 Dander
31 Pa. hub
34 Star of a one-woman Broadway hit, 1980–82
35 Itinerary word
36 Exceeded
38 Drives insane
40 Onion bits?
41 One of a Chekhov trio
43 Gershwin hero

44 Subject of a 1973 ban
45 It's in the "I" column in bingo
47 Crocus or freesia
49 Primp
50 Jacuzzi site
53 Beats
55 Entertainment center
57 Where one draws the line?
61 Site of ancient Ephesus
62 Sources of plumes
63 Butchers' offerings
64 Scalpers
65 Age and weight, e.g.

DOWN

1 Questionable
2 Member of the familia
3 Mount Aconcagua's locale
4 Creator of Lorelei Lee
5 Vic Tayback's sitcom co-star
6 Asthma sufferer's relief
7 "Whew!"

8 "D.C. Cab" actor
9 Word to a doctor
10 Part of an Army chant
11 Enlightened Buddhist
12 Mancini masterpiece
13 Crumbling
14 "Blind tiger"
20 Ransom ___ Olds
24 Major mail ctr.
25 Inflatable camping item
26 "General Hospital" regular Sofer
28 ___-mo
29 Censors
31 Jeane Dixon, for one
32 Bring up, as an orphaned animal
33 Nature guides?
37 Land of poetry
39 Family head?
42 Teachers' advocate, for short
46 Letters on a shoe box
48 Raison ___
50 Braga of "Kiss of the Spider Woman"
51 Word with dew or view

52 Squirrel away
54 Windmill blade
56 Kind of canal
58 Year in Fabian's papacy

59 Everyday article
60 Burns's "___ the Water to Charlie"

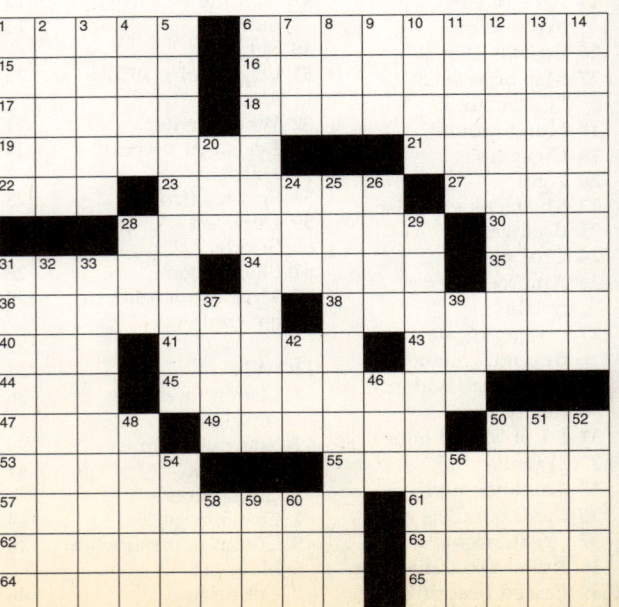

449 by Frank A. Longo

ACROSS

1 Office accessory
9 Emergency room supply
15 Certain rifle
16 Vital passages
17 409, e.g.
18 Track meet officials
19 Boons
20 Sheathe
21 United competitor
23 Ending with win or hand
24 Tangled hair mass
28 Catty comments
30 Eraser mate alternative
32 So far
34 Piece of hard candy
37 Insecticides
39 By the rules
40 Literal
42 Cut deeply
43 From Okla. City to Birmingham
44 Extra
46 In ___ (actually)
47 Adherents
50 Sneaked
52 Having a handle
54 Yank
59 Hang out
60 Crown, as a sovereign
61 History
62 Tissue paper sounds
63 Never forgive oneself
64 Sizes up

DOWN

1 Complete bore
2 Finnish skiing gold medalist Maentyranta
3 Put the pedal to the metal
4 Large green parrots
5 Spiked
6 Reparations
7 Butt in
8 Fast musical passages
9 Head
10 Section of the body
11 Noted name in steel
12 Health spa offerings
13 Large Mediterranean port
14 Cape fox
22 Lost leatherneck
24 Rung
25 Aces
26 Speaking to
27 Habiliments
29 Unique
31 Playwright Fitch
33 Member of the familia
35 Alternative to Magnavox
36 Cold north wind
38 Thimblefuls
41 ___ cane
45 They spread quickly
48 Khan's subject
49 Commemorative stone
51 100 öre
52 Wing-shaped
53 Once, long ago
55 Finalizes the deal
56 Jazzman Tjader et al.
57 To ___ (just right)
58 Early 60's TV hero

450 by C.F. Murray

ACROSS

1 Wood-turning tool
6 Welcome smell
11 Undergrad degrees
14 Disney mermaid
15 Site of golfing's Ryder Open
16 Genetic trait carrier
17 Make an error
19 Consume
20 Part to play
21 Teacher in a turban
23 Conciliate
27 Gotten back, as land in battle
29 Villain
30 Capital of Tasmania
31 Welles of "Citizen Kane"
32 Golden Horde member
33 Premium cable channel
36 Diana of the Supremes
37 Munchhausen's title
38 Lima, e.g.
39 Suffix with superintend
40 Rubbernecker
41 Fanny ___ of the Ziegfeld Follies
42 Area of Manhattan
44 Lighthouse light
45 Artist's studio
47 Make manhattans and such
48 Ear parts
49 Is up
50 Zoo bird
51 Be outrageous
58 ___ room
59 Deceive
60 Charge
61 "For shame!"
62 Mystery writer's award
63 Nairobi's land

DOWN

1 Terhune's "___: a Dog"
2 Opposite of "Dep." on a flight board
3 Tijuana uncle
4 With it, 40's-style
5 It loops the Loop
6 Dancer Astaire
7 Caftan
8 "... man ___ mouse?"
9 ___ de mer
10 Selected athlete
11 Get a party going
12 "What's in ___?"
13 Luxurious sheet material
18 Hydrant hookup
22 Card game for two
23 Dean Martin song subject
24 Juan of Argentina
25 Not take responsibility
26 1961 space chimp
27 Copter part
28 Israeli statesman Abba
30 Quarters in a sultan's palace
32 Grow narrower
34 Breakfast sizzler
35 Upturned, as a box
37 Cotton bundle
38 Baby sitter's nightmare
40 Chewy part of meat
41 Bananas
43 Hearty drink
44 Alternative to a shower
45 With ears pricked
46 Weighty books
47 Ulan ___, Mongolia
49 ___ carotene
52 Help
53 Beer barrel
54 Feed lines to
55 Massachusetts cape
56 Braggart knight of the Round Table
57 H, to Greeks

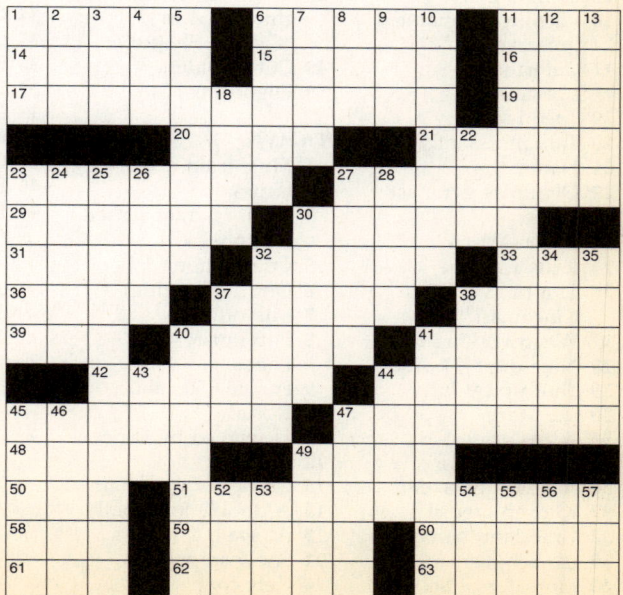

451 by Elizabeth C. Gorski

ACROSS
1 Utters
5 Military plane acronym
10 Desertlike
14 Wyoming neighbor
15 Striped critter
16 Hurting
17 State of financial independence
19 CAT ___
20 Singer Lopez
21 Kett of old comics
22 Little guitars
23 Singer Cara
25 Guard
27 It's a stitch!
29 Mint and sage
32 Stadium sounds
35 Basketball hoop site, often
39 Acorn, in 2020?
40 "Surfin' ___" (Beach Boys hit)
41 Gandhi's title
42 Ryan's "Love Story" co-star
43 Russian space station
44 Puzzle
45 4:1, e.g.
46 Mubarak's predecessor
48 Recipe direction
50 Some Broadway shows
54 Overhead shot
57 Last name in spydom
59 "There ought to be ___!"
61 Suggest itself (to)
63 Thrift shop stipulation
64 "The Birdcage" co-star
66 Possess
67 Whitney Houston's "All the Man That ___"
68 Verve
69 Parrots
70 Chooses actors
71 E-mail command

DOWN
1 Winter bird food
2 Video arcade name
3 Arafat of the P.L.O.
4 Wallflower's characteristic
5 Much-publicized drug
6 Existed
7 Helps in dirty deeds
8 El Greco's birthplace
9 Underworld figure
10 Guarantee
11 Ice cream parlor order
12 "Dies ___"
13 TV rooms
18 ___ qua non
24 1991 Tony winner Daisy
26 "Take ___ Train"
28 When repeated, a fish
30 Like a worn tire
31 T-bar sights
32 Jamaican exports
33 Pacific Rim region
34 Computer part
36 Joplin piece
37 24-hr. conveniences
38 Certain exams, for short
41 Prefix with physical
45 The Scriptures
47 Gets up
49 "___ Fire" (Springsteen hit)
51 Wired, so to speak
52 "The George & ___ Show" (former talk show)
53 Fills up
55 Union rate
56 Chinese province
57 Joker's gibe
58 Rush job notation
60 Stimulate
62 Rip apart
65 Want ___

452 by Randolph Ross

ACROSS
1 Siegfried Line of 1930's Germany
9 Lashes
14 Cherub
15 Gym activity
16 Like an uninhabited preserve
17 Colorful fish
18 ___ time
19 Teen idol
20 Talk incessantly
21 Name
22 Olympics gymnast's goals
23 Clear sky
24 Jesus was one
26 Tim of "WKRP in Cincinnati"
27 Woodworking tools
28 Nine-digit ID: Abbr.
29 Shut up by force
30 ___ Maria
33 Turns gray
35 Pith helmet
36 At one's wits' end
37 Kitchen utensil
38 Graceland name
39 ___ Lingus
40 Liberator of Scotland
41 Counts
43 Bind up
44 Detached
45 Yeast enzymes
47 To-dos
48 1969 rock concert site chronicled in "Gimme Shelter"
49 Cube holders
50 Flight finishes

DOWN
1 Mule train drivers
2 Issues
3 What Hamlet sensed
4 Doctored
5 Commotion
6 On ___ (binging)
7 Mil. officers
8 Pop music's ___ Lobos
9 Fortune 500 abbr.
10 Upset
11 Is swayed by logic
12 Nuts
13 Causes of gray hair
15 A double informally
19 At sea
21 Show stopper
24 Gets cozy
25 Far out
27 ___ Bay (New England site)
29 "Mrs." in dialect
31 Banker's point
32 Smog checks
34 Carrying on
35 Culpable
36 He reigned in Spain
37 Cold medicine
38 Imperative
40 Geom. figures
42 Clowns' shoe widths
45 Fictional dog
46 Pub drink

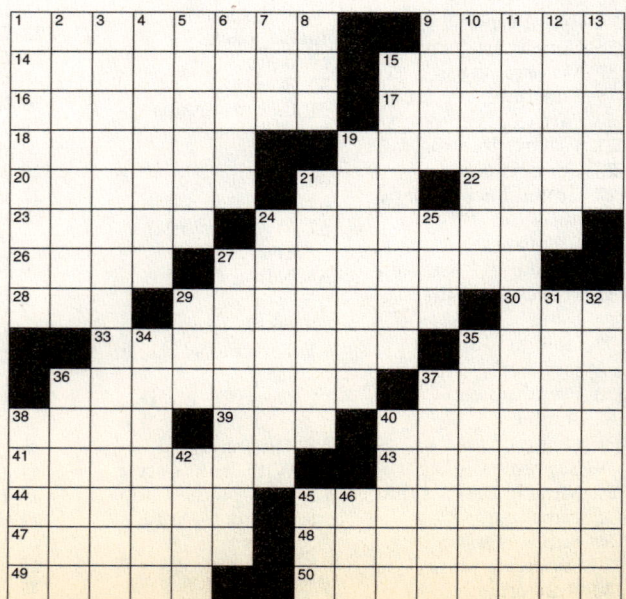

453   by Merl H. Reagle

ACROSS
1 Smooth wood
5 Treat like a pariah
9 Pin place
14 Mixed bag
15 "Self" starter
16 "Die Fledermaus" maid
17 Stay tuned, Part 1
20 Writer Danielle
21 She shares the wealth
22 Cut (off)
24 ___ gallop
25 Stay tuned, Part 2
34 "O.K., Ahab"
35 Actress Verdugo
36 Borden bovine
37 "Cool"
39 Gounod opera
41 Marion's finish
42 Island crooner
44 Slangy $100 bill
46 Sniggler's wiggler
47 Stay tuned, Part 3
50 Ankh's cross
51 Midwest Indian
52 Disparages
58 Ogden Nash's feet
62 Stay tuned, Part 4
64 Signal to slow
65 Unguarded, in football
66 Radiate
67 Full of vim and vinegar
68 Word to a refusenik
69 Thanksgiving side dishes

DOWN
1 Lays down the lawn
2 Much
3 Not quite Bo Derek
4 "No kidding!"
5 ___ Tomé and Principe
6 Hollywood 10 condemner: Abbr.
7 60's spy plane
8 Biblical 950-year-old
9 Gulf of Mexico pirate
10 Cute
11 A.k.a. Edson Arantes do Nascimento
12 Large lodge
13 Minus
18 Boston daily
19 Informal agreement
23 Ill-gotten gains
25 Fish in a John Cleese comedy
26 "___ newt . . ."
27 Listed
28 Boxer's asset
29 Operating
30 Reactions to aerialists
31 Fall bloomer
32 Given as a source
33 Falls (over)
38 London daily
40 Ballerina's strong points
43 Speaking skill
45 "Roughing It" writer
48 Hippo's wear in "Fantasia"
49 Dramatist Sean
52 Arts degs.
53 "Cope Book" Aunt
54 Arcing shots
55 Author Hubbard
56 Wordsmith Willard
57 The Graf ___
59 N.Y. institution on 53d Street
60 Fedora feature
61 Trans-Atlantic speedsters
63 Prov. on Niagara Falls

454   by Harvey Estes

ACROSS
1 Encircles
6 Word in old wedding vows
10 Door securer
14 "I ___ Him" (1963 hit by the Angels)
15 Tot's first word
16 Maintain
17 Photographer Bullaty
18 "Come ___!"
19 More than gratify
20 Blood supply
22 Fast planes from New York
24 Rebuke to Junior
26 Low-voiced ladies
27 Sunday book
29 Article in Le Monde
30 Catty remark
31 Primitive means of investigation
34 Former title in Tripoli
37 Howls
38 Guitar sound
39 Scruff
40 Flurry
41 Boxer's spot
42 Mixed drink made with an egg
43 Clear, with "of"
44 Open
46 Wise guys
49 Polling subjects
51 Dr. Johnny Fever and Venus Flytrap
53 Blocked
57 Uzbekistan's ___ Sea
58 Paradise evictee
60 Scrimshaw medium
61 "Who's the Boss?" mother
62 Vogue
63 Onetime colonial power
64 Memorial Day weekend event
65 Appraised
66 First name in cosmetics

DOWN
1 Shocked response
2 Pedestal figure
3 Barrett of gossip
4 Erving's cars
5 Tar
6 Prefix with meter
7 Players pick it
8 Uplift
9 W.W. II Army magazine
10 Big bother
11 Stop, at sea
12 Altercation
13 Basketball stratagem
21 Made fit
23 Ratted
25 Revealed, as an identity
27 Govern
28 Vacillate
29 In a state of mental collapse
30 C.E.O.'s degree
32 Neb. neighbor
33 All thumbs
34 MOMA work
35 "Iliad," e.g.
36 Uh-huh
39 Top gridiron players
41 One method of sealing
43 Instant ___
45 Cook slowly
46 Hindu honcho
47 Goodyear's home
48 Thou
49 9/2/45
50 Tree cultivated for hedges
52 "How ___ you!"
54 Onetime means of defense
55 Buffalo's county
56 Measure of force
59 ___ school

455   by Wayne Robert Williams

ACROSS

1 Interlaced
6 Canadian tree
11 Unit of chewing tobacco
14 Idiotic
15 Relieve
16 One of Frank's exes
17 Motion picture award
19 ___ Kippur
20 ___ ex machina
21 Red Square figure
23 Spacecraft sections
27 Tentative forays
29 Gone from the program
30 Shoulders-to-hips areas
31 "___ Irish Rose"
32 Paper purchases
33 Once existed
36 Guitarist Lofgren
37 See 30-Down
38 ___ fide
39 Farm enclosure
40 Crude characters
41 Gershwin hero
42 Jai alai ball
44 "Ode to ___ Joe"

45 Votes
47 Hamlet, at times
48 Shrine to remember
49 Spotted
50 Reunion-goers
51 Nature personified
58 First lady
59 "Middlemarch" author
60 Inventor Howe
61 Matched grouping
62 Tears
63 Show shock, e.g.

DOWN

1 Store-bought hair
2 Musician Yoko
3 Actor Kilmer
4 Football lineman
5 Tries to rile
6 John Fowles novel, with "The"
7 "___ Well That Ends Well"
8 Hebron grp.
9 Big, friendly dog, for short
10 Huxley's "___ in Gaza"
11 Teen film hit of 1992
12 To have, to Héloïse
13 Curses
18 Require
22 "Xanadu" musical grp.
23 Signifies
24 Pluto's path
25 Perry's paper
26 Functions
27 Bubble masses
28 Columnist Bombeck
30 With 37-Across, the ground
32 Wild times
34 1973 Rolling Stones hit
35 Word with nay or sooth
37 Bit of poetry
38 Manila machete
40 Early feminist
41 Avant-gardist
43 Slippery ___
44 Rabbit's title
45 Hardens, as clay
46 Breathing
47 Borscht ingredients
49 Bullet-riddled
52 Cheer
53 Malleable metal

54 Pale or Newcastle brown
55 Narrow inlet
56 Middle X or O
57 Presidential initials

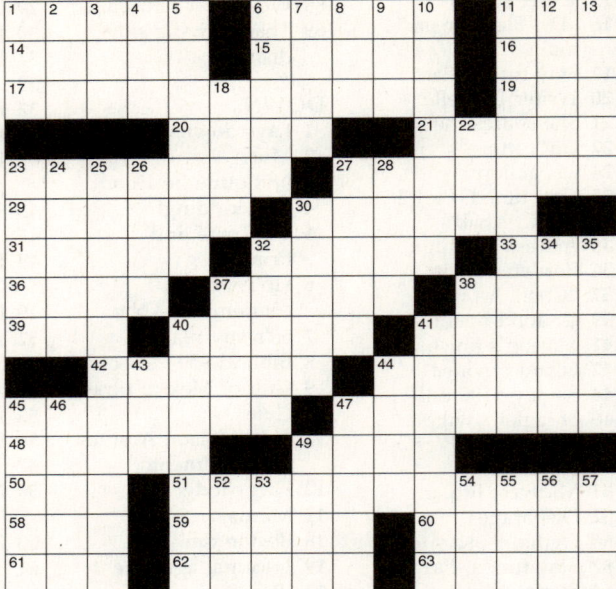

456   by Jonathan Schmalzbach

ACROSS

1 Son of Abraham
6 RR stops
10 Ill-considered
14 Hajj destination
15 Justice Black
16 ". . . and to ___ good night"
17 Whittles down
18 The sun, to the skin
19 Hera's husband
20 Noted baseball announcer
22 Give the boot to
23 Actor Ray
24 Lustily robust
26 Cervantes's ___ Panza
30 Improvise
32 Mountain of central Russia
33 Defense acronym
35 Actress Christine
39 Fixed shoes
41 Emancipates
43 Borgnine's "From Here to Eternity" role
44 Pronounced
46 Abstract artist Paul

47 Clear, as a tape
49 Loco
51 Quarterback, often
54 Misplace
56 Compassion
57 All worked up
62 Concept
63 Tastes
64 "___ of Athens"
66 First name in casino ownership
67 Option word
68 Gentry
69 Educator Sullivan
70 Noticed
71 Acted grandmotherly

DOWN

1 Mischief-maker
2 Cook quickly
3 Caldwell's "God's Little ___"
4 Scored on a serve
5 Algiers quarter
6 Archeologist's fragment
7 Harbor helper
8 Author James
9 Horse color
10 Clinton's home team

11 Certain Alaskan
12 Kind of fund
13 Cursory
21 By oneself
25 Is sickly
26 Malibu sight
27 Neighborhood
28 Cartoonist Thomas
29 Near miss
31 Celebrated Freud case
34 Hubbubs
36 Dance performed in a grass skirt
37 High schooler
38 Sinking-in phrase
40 Knowledge
42 "Aeneid" queen
45 Setback
48 Gets up
50 Cleared
51 Jazz trumpeter Louis
52 "The Age of Anxiety" poet
53 Shock jock Howard
55 Novelist Tillie
58 Cairo's river
59 Hawaiian seaport
60 Spew forth
61 Dull routine

65 Pulp penman Buntline

457   by Eileen Lexau

ACROSS
1 "Amo, ___, I love a lass"
5 Rowing crew
10 Nickname for Barbara
14 Whip
15 Something to plight
16 Tennis score
17 Dickens classic
19 Neighborhood
20 Not fresh, as water
21 Cry in "Arsenic and Old Lace"
23 Goes out, in a card game
24 Millet subject
25 Ships' cranes
28 Pipe type
29 Pisces's follower
30 Use the Osterizer
31 Hauler's truck
34 Shaw classic
37 Gal of song
38 "___ my case!"
39 ___ Mongolia
40 Is the worrywart
41 Olympics ceremony song
42 Peruvian pack animals
45 O.T. book
46 Scale's reading
47 He-man's display
51 Sham
52 Vincent Price classic
54 Applications
55 Eroded
56 Revenue
57 For fear that
58 Clown's prop, at times
59 British gun

DOWN
1 Priests' robes
2 Ice cream treat
3 Cruising
4 More like far-fetched dog stories?
5 Allen and Frome
6 Jeremy of stage and screen
7 Pain in the joints
8 Altitudes: Abbr.
9 Jail, slangily
10 Market
11 Decorate
12 Hardly a show of self-restraint
13 Villain's look
18 Opposite of a purl
22 Boss of bosses
24 Adjective for Alexander
25 Dits' counterparts, in Morse code
26 Neighborhood
27 Pharmacist's container
28 "God ___" (sneeze response)
30 Makes java
31 The Bambino
32 Words of understanding
33 Seed
35 Whispers
36 Wins the strongman contest
40 Most wise
41 Immigrant's giveaway
42 Dire
43 Rent
44 Toll roads
45 Artist's stand
47 Conductor Riccardo
48 Take a swipe at
49 Earn
50 Clumsy ones?
53 ___ bran

458   by Stanley B. Whitten

ACROSS
1 Event for Cinderella
5 Rewind function
10 Grow tiresome
14 Lily plant
15 Claw
16 Gobi Desert site
17 Cape Canaveral sights
19 Outbuilding
20 Noon
21 Hallowed
23 Women's fashion magazine
25 Innuendo
26 Nautical pulley
30 Hard, glossy finish
34 Mil. training site
35 Strip of equipment
37 Southern Filipino
38 Practical joker's items
42 Actress Albright
43 Triangular item
44 Co., in Caen
45 Absorb
48 Very hot day
50 Punishes in an old way
52 Folk dance
53 Earthly
56 Single shot, perhaps
60 One of the Beach Boys
61 1959 Day-Hudson film
63 Double curve
64 Bid one ___ (depart)
65 Ashtabula abuts it
66 Prohibits
67 Ferment
68 1860's Southerners

DOWN
1 Salve
2 Kyrgyzstan's ___ Mountains
3 Noisy
4 Bank, sometimes
5 Citrus colorant
6 Séance sound
7 "Welladay"
8 Fizzy drinks
9 Preserve fodder
10 Deli offering
11 Connors rival
12 More than misled
13 Young man
18 Summon for service
22 Sister
24 Bearing corn
26 Chickens and ducks
27 Cause for a blessing
28 Sicily, to Sicilians
29 Cuts into cubes
31 Sponge
32 Banks of Chicago
33 Misfit
36 Deep ravine
39 Squirrels' hangouts
40 Protruded
41 Farm implement
46 Egypt, formerly: Abbr.
47 Settle up beforehand
49 Film V.I.P.
51 Derogatory
53 Palatine garb
54 Level
55 Lamb's name
57 Rhine feeder
58 Having too-easy answers
59 ___ out (supplements)
60 Smash setup
62 Kelly's "___ Girls"

459 by Wayne Robert Williams

ACROSS

1 Revolutionaries
5 Improvises on the piano
10 Patrick White novel
14 Lateral beginning
15 Shakespearean sprite
16 Suffix with refer or prefer
17 Former capital of the Philippines
19 Panetta of the White House
20 News bit
21 Split hairs differently
23 Black bird
24 Saddam Hussein, e.g.
28 Nitrogen
30 Apollo's Eagle, for one
31 Bean paste
32 Elemental state
33 "Yes, that's clear"
35 Inventor's initials
36 Responsibilities
37 Rock variety
40 Steeply inclined
43 "___ alors!"
44 Runner Budd
48 "If you would . . ."
49 Pub potables
51 One in the middle of a fight
52 Swiss city on the Rhine, in old spelling
53 Drink impolitely
54 Slug
55 Wayside shelter
57 "And the Lord set a mark upon ___"
59 The gamut
60 Person with the answers
65 Molecular biology topic
66 Fully anesthetized
67 Poi base
68 Chances
69 Greek contests
70 Furthermore

DOWN

1 Necessary: Abbr.
2 Horses
3 Eventually, with "in"
4 Dimensions
5 Small-business vehicle
6 Semicircle
7 Pair of 501's
8 Culture dish
9 Leonard ___, alias Roy Rogers
10 "Surrender of Breda" artist
11 Oppressive
12 Terrier
13 One in a hundred: Abbr.
18 Delete
22 Whitewash
23 The Lion of God
25 Take turns
26 From a distance
27 Bird of the Aztecs
29 Mag. staffers
32 Hang around
34 Squares up
38 Big sports news
39 Bantu language
40 Police call letters
41 Wrote a scathing review of
42 Answer
45 Like satellites
46 Horseshoe points
47 Sternward
50 Watchdog watchdog: Abbr.
53 Suspended
56 Sea shade
58 Cinema pooch
59 In the past
61 Altar assent
62 Branch of Buddhism
63 ___ Calabash
64 Milne's Baby ___

460 by Martin Ashwood-Smith

ACROSS

1 It turns into a different story
16 Mother tongues
17 Collegiate goals
18 Enter as a group, with "in"
19 Commercial quotation
20 Actress Swenson
21 Bi-halved
22 Shades
24 Deucy preceder
25 Takes without authorization
27 Ballet step
30 Capone's nemesis
31 "N ___?" (Agatha Christie novel)
32 Forces open
34 Humankind
36 Acquires in large amounts
37 Court V.I.P.'s, for short
38 X rating?
39 Elisabeth, e.g.: Abbr.
40 Real people
44 Dosimeters measure them
46 "The Gypsy" painter
47 Heater
48 ___ many words
49 One who gives special service?
51 San ___, Calif.
52 Uppity
56 Lifeless
57 Forensic psychiatrists, at times

DOWN

1 Grab
2 "Author! Author!" actor
3 Inclined, in a way
4 Carpool
5 Hail from the past
6 Apollo part
7 Driving hazards?
8 South-of-the-border orders
9 Everyday connections
10 "___ Ideas" (1950 hit)
11 Throw
12 Ancient district in Asia Minor
13 Bureaus
14 Folk singer and family
15 Lamb products
22 Son of Maia
23 Nth
26 Nut
27 Doozie
28 Photo-developing powder
29 Vilifies
32 Tenor Peerce
33 Research facility: Abbr.
34 It's seen in bars
35 German pronoun
36 Take back lost territory
38 Certain tube
40 English author Asquith
41 Ancient squares
42 Film "star" since 1943
43 Girds
45 Balloon probe
46 Swiss miss
49 Like some eds.
50 Tobacco wad
51 Rock's Bon Jovi and others
53 Canal site
54 Title of respect: Abbr.
55 Initials on maps of old Eur.

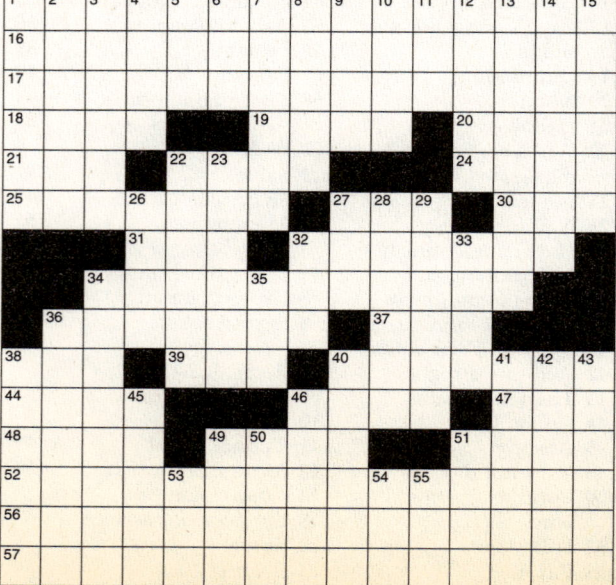

461 by Sidney L. Robbins

ACROSS
1 Macaroni or cannelloni
6 Socialist Eugene
10 Rainbows
14 Illinois city
15 "___ a man with seven . . ."
16 Dove or Dial
17 Locale for King Arthur
19 Japanese wrestling
20 Artist Magritte
21 Playing marbles
23 Prefix with natal
24 Curses
26 "I beg your ___"
28 Kind of cry
31 Most August births
32 Tater
33 Author Umberto
34 Nineveh was its cap.
36 Young fellows
39 Learned
41 Consumed
44 Emcee Jay
45 Trunk item
47 Word with sports or squad
48 Ballroom dance motions
51 Get the wrinkles out
52 Cathedral city
53 Shoe part
55 Pizza part
57 Op.___ (footnote abbr.)
58 Beach robe
60 "Listen!"
64 Summers on the Riviera
66 Kind of tournament
68 Russia's ___ Mountains
69 Puppeteer Tony
70 "All kidding ___ . . ."
71 Molassesslike
72 Gen. Robt. ___
73 Cacklers

DOWN
1 Catherine ___ (Henry VIII's sixth)
2 Skin soother
3 Stupefy
4 Sounded
5 Also
6 Doctors' determinations
7 Diplomat's post
8 Boxer's trophy
9 Soaks, as teabags
10 Silly one
11 Waltz or reel
12 Engraved gem
13 Act lovey-dovey
18 Most domesticated
22 Silly one
25 Jai ___
27 Reign
28 Grope
29 Good-sized plot
30 Cut of beef
35 Adjust
37 Kind of exhaust
38 Limber
40 "Go ahead!"
42 In the vicinity
43 Sawbucks
46 Film
49 Muscle-builder's pride
50 Not plentiful
53 Become frozen
54 Explosive
56 "___ were the days, my friend"
59 Young horse
61 His Rose was Irish
62 Clears (of)
63 Pants part
65 Wily
67 Old piano tune

462 by Randall J. Hartman

ACROSS
1 Nosegay
5 Stared at
10 Mex. miss
14 Pro ___
15 Stopped in one's tracks
16 Beatles' "Magical Mystery ___"
17 Prince William's school
18 British strand
19 Hick
20 Type of sonnet
23 J.F.K. jet
24 Avant-garde rocker Lou
25 Bill addition
28 Part of B.A.
29 "Frasier" setting
31 Top-notch
34 Conger
35 Luftwaffe foe: Abbr.
36 Hiking danger
41 Kimono sash
42 Corporal punishment, with "the"
43 Cowboy at roundup
44 Troughs
47 Stockholm sedan
49 Brace (oneself)
50 Horse feed
51 Boston baseball legend Williams
54 Crap shoot
58 Heartthrob actor Pitt
60 Set free
61 Love, in Oviedo
62 Film director Clair
63 Outboard motor's locale
64 Part
65 Chooses
66 Sharpens
67 Spock's voyage

DOWN
1 Fourth Estate
2 "Gosh darn!" and worse
3 Summer ermine
4 American
5 Compensate
6 Complains
7 Like oak leaves
8 Pound of poetry
9 Bambi, e.g.
10 Mariner's passage
11 Here to there to here
12 Not the sleekest ship
13 "Odds ___ . . ."
21 Swashbuckler Flynn
22 One for the history books
26 Gladden
27 Direct elsewhere
28 Qty.
29 Coral ___
30 Cousin of the moose
31 They're full of dates
32 Morocco's capital
33 Traveling salesman
34 Curtains, with "the"
37 Blow it
38 Sea plea
39 De-chalk
40 Bing's buddy in old films
45 Hollow rocks
46 Building wing
47 Juvenal's genre
48 Acropolis locale
50 Frequently
51 Indonesian island
52 Paris's ___ des Beaux-Arts
53 Bo of "10" fame
55 Opulent
56 Cognizant of
57 Pub throw
58 Pal
59 Newt Gingrich, e.g.: Abbr.

463 by Rich Norris

ACROSS

1 Some pens
5 Join, as hands
10 Ship of 1492
14 Zion National Park locale
15 Prefix with -gon
16 Part of Q.E.D.
17 "Never!"
19 Bother
20 Newt
21 "Never!"
23 Share (in)
26 Rap sheet word
27 Double curve
28 Mrs. Bunker and others
32 PC accessory
33 Opposite of ahead
36 Dirndl or sari
38 "Never!"
42 Gird (oneself)
43 Soothe
45 Civil War soldier
48 Popular cruise destination
50 "Norma ___"
51 Arabian Peninsula leader

53 It may be found in a table
56 "Never!"
60 At once
61 Affaires d'___
62 "Never!"
66 Winger co-star, 1982
67 "Rosemary's Baby" author
68 Shade trees
69 Shangri-la
70 Fashion
71 Stave

DOWN

1 Coiled hairdo
2 Judge in 1995 news
3 Tries to please
4 Treat unfairly, in slang
5 E.M.T. skill
6 Paged
7 Novelist Seton
8 Leave in after all
9 Rouen recreation spot
10 Katmandu's land
11 Peaceful
12 Org. for Cale Yarborough

13 Swear (to)
18 School org.
22 Bother
23 Stew item
24 Professional grp.
25 Hound hotel
29 Objects of worship
30 One-man Broadway hit of 1990
31 Like some tea
34 Saucer's contents, for short
35 Kind of club
37 Attack dog command
39 Assenting vote
40 Leave-taking
41 Spirit
44 Ran into
45 Go back (on)
46 Didn't act subtly
47 Word of caution
49 Ground
52 In the stomach
54 High school subj.
55 Malone of the N.B.A.
57 Send a Dear John letter
58 Standout
59 PC command
63 Ill. neighbor

64 Singer Sumac
65 Superlative suffix

464 by Randolph Ross

ACROSS

1 Cartoon deputy
5 Dot in the sea
10 "Oh! My ___" (Eddie Fisher tune)
14 Skating maneuver
15 Tide rival
16 List-extending abbr.
17 = ___
20 Highly regarded
21 Bring into harmony
22 Show one's appreciation
23 Like some type: Abbr.
24 Beatles music co.
27 Foodstuffs
31 Hosiery shade
32 Cropped up
33 Discoverer's cry
34 = ___
38 Bad temper
39 First name in cosmetics
40 "Born Free" lioness
41 Stomach calmer: Var.
43 Summer 1996 movie thriller
45 Snowman's comment?

46 "The Black Stallion" boy
47 "West Side Story" Oscar winner
50 Not go out
54 = ___
56 Concert receipts
57 Bottled water brand
58 Summoned
59 Asteroid discovered in 1898
60 Raison ___
61 Libelous remark

DOWN

1 Hamlet, for one
2 W.W. II powers
3 Left
4 Group working in harmony?
5 Jewel thief, in slang
6 Blind followers
7 Advance
8 Electric ___
9 Scholarly paper
10 Mortar's partner
11 Aleutian island
12 Used one
13 Lotion additive
18 Prefix with port

19 Pollen holder
23 Start of many bumper sticker slogans
24 Press
25 Part of a squirrel stash
26 Dressing place
27 Thin as ___
28 Christmases
29 Guess Who hit "___ Eyes"
30 Oceanographer's aid
32 Up and about
35 Memorized
36 In a holding account
37 Kind of pet
42 Wild goats
43 Comedienne Boosler
44 Alejandro and Fernando
46 Rose oil
47 F.H.A. loan
48 Horse racing's Man ___
49 Rooter starter
50 Tantrum
51 Race site
52 Software choices
53 M.I.T. grad: Abbr.

55 "The mother of all living"

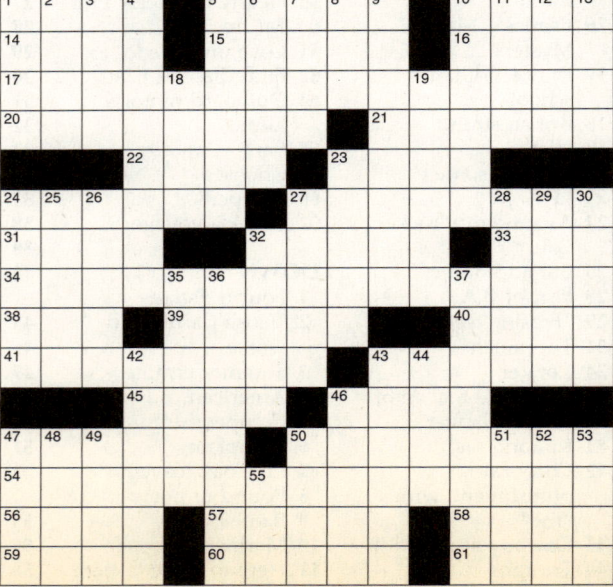

465 by Rich Norris

ACROSS

1 Chop phenomenon
9 South American prairie
14 Deli order
15 1983 N.B.A. champs
16 Satellites
17 Folds paper, as for packing
18 Eight-time Norris Trophy winner
19 Candy
21 Curtain-parting time
22 Show petulance
24 Actor Erwin
25 Binds
26 Is nervous
29 Ship built from trees on Pelion
31 Cable inits.
32 Track feature
34 Suffix with expert
35 Marquis de Sade novel
38 Caught, in a way
40 Galoot
41 Salad ingredient
43 Green target
44 Café cooler
45 Overthrow
49 "You ___ both!"
51 ___ Hay (Israeli memorial)
53 Mare's-nest
54 G.O.P. elephant's creator
55 Actress Lee
58 Rockies zone: Abbr.
59 Beethoven's "___ Variations"
61 Swamp
63 Blurred
64 Took dead aim
65 These, in Toledo
66 Lined up

DOWN

1 Expresses jubilance
2 Anguish
3 Stain
4 French pronoun
5 Tolkien tree giants
6 Deckhands
7 English romance writer Ruby
8 They're tender in una tienda
9 More, in music
10 Kind of symmetry
11 1936 John Barrymore role
12 Cover
13 Opposite of frustrated
15 Geometric figs.
20 Chocolate treat
23 Miss Manners subject
25 Seeks advice from
27 Quite a hit
28 The merry widow in "The Merry Widow"
30 Edna Ferber work
33 Arab, e.g.
35 Kind of beetle
36 Like an angry mob
37 Posts
39 Certain high schooler, for short
42 List
46 Perfumed ointment
47 Like some inventory, for accounting purposes
48 Offer
50 Peak of ancient Troy
52 Tablecloths, e.g.
55 Light line
56 Kind of cheese
57 Clove hitch, e.g.
60 Light wts.
62 ___ volente

466 by David J. Kahn

ACROSS

1 Airplane exit
5 Boat with a V-shaped transom
9 China-Russia boundary river
13 Finito
14 "... partridge in ___ tree"
16 15th-century maritime name
17 Tuscany ta-ta
18 Choice for a sand trap shot
19 "Even ___ speak . . ."
20 Start of a Will Rogers quip
23 Kind of parking
24 Miss America, to some
25 More of the quip
30 Sorrows
33 Algerian port
34 Sentimental stuff
35 Tax plan staples
36 Mallard-sized goose
37 San ___, Italy
38 Horse color
39 Craving
40 Considered, with "on"
41 More of the quip
45 Unencumbered
46 Writer Jong et al.
50 End of the quip
54 Jeer
55 Kind of seal
56 View from Sandusky
57 Pond swimmer
58 Tee off
59 Insect nests
60 Muffs
61 Film maker Joel or Ethan
62 Something to do

DOWN

1 "Fidelio" jailer
2 Birdlike
3 Board
4 Is a breadwinner
5 Occurred to, with "on"
6 Noted cartel
7 Go back to square one on
8 ___ Sant'Gria (wine brand)
9 Wreath for the head
10 Doesn't estimate correctly
11 Like some guests
12 Actress ___ Dawn Chong
15 Counting (on)
21 Malady suffix
22 Charlie Weaver's Mt. ___
26 Like some baseball games
27 Early Warhol film
28 A votre ___
29 Tough guy
30 Opera set near the Nile
31 Like Grape-Nuts vis-a-vis other cereals
32 Mustache style
36 Intermingled
37 Basic skill
40 Swamplike
42 Skis with high-speed turns
43 "Bali ___"
44 Make vapid
47 Senate house in ancient Rome
48 Litmus reddeners
49 Valentino role
51 Police decoy, sometimes
52 The Police in rock music, e.g.
53 Golfer Ballesteros
54 Mobilnet corp.

467 by Martin Ashwood-Smith

ACROSS
1 Whisk
6 Comforting words of empathy
11 Sound at the door
14 Barbera's partner in cartoons
15 Rover
16 Pueblo pronoun
17 Knock for ___
18 February birthstones
20 Decorates, in a way
22 Cork's place
23 Temple of Apollo site
24 "The Jungle Book" setting
25 Loser's place?
28 Bolts over
30 Pulver, e.g., in "Mister Roberts": Abbr.
31 Range rovers
33 Terminal activity
35 Ne plus ultra
36 Tip
37 Made a great point
39 Pitcher's place
41 Edit
42 Portmanteau

43 1976 Peck-Remick thriller
45 ___-Anne-de-Beaupre, Quebec
46 ___ Rogers St. Johns
48 Roundabout routes
50 Jaunt
51 Reacting to, as a bad joke
55 Some Cadillacs
57 Kind of fairy
58 Highway warning
59 In ___ (untidy)
60 Sharp ridge
61 Great amount
62 Best Picture of 1955
63 Copy at the office

DOWN
1 Tobacco wad
2 Syllables meaning "I forgot the words"
3 Hydroxyl compound
4 "You can't teach ___..."
5 Siesta takers
6 Shipshape
7 Boomerang
8 Foreign office?
9 "Darn!"

10 Old English letter
11 Quarters
12 Harsh
13 Impersonate
19 Long
21 It may come in cases
24 Man, e.g.: Abbr.
25 ___ Na Na
26 Slight sin
27 Decisive conflict
29 Fun, so to speak
32 Like one side of the aisle: Abbr.
34 Cartesian conclusion
36 Seat, slangily
38 Presidential monogram
40 Grp. throwing an open house
41 Loathing levies
42 Minimum
44 "___ Heldenleben" (Strauss opus)
47 Sign of summer
49 Overnight sensation?
51 Navigator Vasco da ___
52 Attendee
53 One-quintillionth: Prefix

54 TV's "___-Files"
56 Farm butter

468 by Bob Klahn

ACROSS
1 Millie, for one
8 Sites of many bars
15 Cookout sauce
16 Land "by the sea"
17 Printing
18 Couldn't resist
19 "Stage Door" actress
20 Literary monogram
22 Nancy Milford literary biography
23 Fictional newswoman
24 "The Dance of Life" author, 1923
26 Cartoonist Gross
27 "Music City Tonight" network
28 Julius, familiarly
30 Miss named?
31 Modern housing
33 Get at
35 Veranda refreshment
37 Impious
40 Spread
44 Curling target
45 Kahill Gibran's birthplace
47 First offender?
48 He wrote "To be loved, be lovable"

50 Toughness
51 Smudge
52 Actress Rosie
54 Literary monogram
55 "Atlantic City" director
56 Emphatic words
58 Jurgen Prochnow nail-biter of 1981
60 Free
61 Table centerpiece
62 Affectionate one, maybe
63 Less radioactive

DOWN
1 Hugger-muggery
2 Roles in "The Godfather"
3 Steadfast
4 Basketball's Thurmond et al.
5 "The doctor ___"
6 "Travels in Hyperreality" author
7 Like some friends
8 Cure
9 Pepin, e.g.
10 Lady in Meyerbeer's "L'Africaine"

11 "Days of Our Lives" town
12 Conservative
13 Christmas refuse
14 Drugs, perhaps
21 Work clothing
24 The Furies
25 "Merry Wives of Windsor" windbag
28 Bar companion
29 Main
32 Blue Cross offering
34 Y class
36 Expendable
37 Visionary
38 "I'll ___ the Same" ('32 tons)
39 She gets what's coming
41 One aspect of earthquake study
42 Old Nick
43 Struck out
46 Capra's "The ___ Tea of General Yen"
49 Stopping point
51 Native Israeli
53 George Burns buddy Harry Von ___

55 Very short time, for short
57 Map abbr.
59 Do Little work

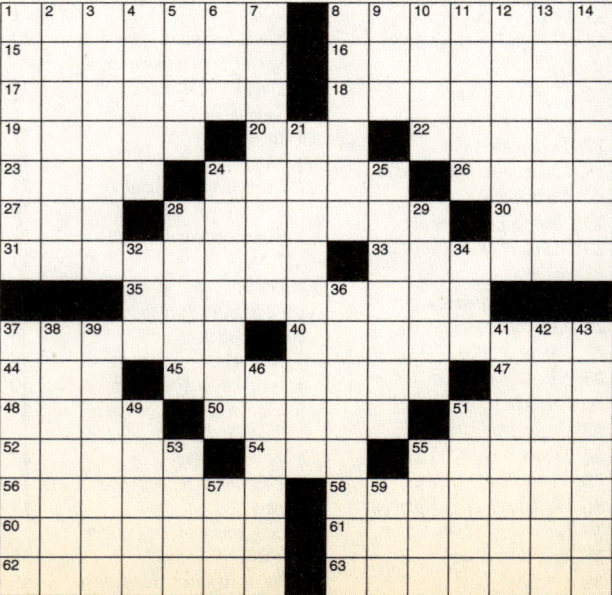

469   by Richard Silvestri

ACROSS

1 Iron-pumper's pride
5 Washerful
9 Make pigtails
14 Columbia athlete
15 Oppositionist
16 Diploma word
17 Rattles
19 Comatose
20 Came upon the maharajah?
22 F or G, for example, but not H
23 "___ Cane" (1963 movie)
24 Lead ore
27 Forming opinions
31 Hugo or Tony
32 Neighbor of Chad
34 Easter preceder
35 Gives no stars
36 Got a new address
37 Sneaky guy?
38 Scratch (out)
39 High numbers?
40 Oscar-winning film of 1955
41 Dislike to the max
43 Puts in the scrapbook
44 An Astaire
46 Destiny
47 Intrepid Eric?
54 Form-related
55 Double-crossers
56 Muscat resident
57 Point at the table
58 Mountain sign abbr.
59 Star's small role
60 Slaughter in Cooperstown
61 Decline

DOWN

1 Deep purple
2 German article
3 Overhead
4 Gym shoes
5 One of the Jacksons
6 One's partner
7 First-stringers
8 Ousts
9 Stupid error
10 Hit-or-miss
11 Autobahn auto
12 Creative input
13 "Jurassic Park" actress
18 The way things are going
21 "You're All ___ to Get By"
24 Goggled
25 Up and about
26 Strike locations
28 Still
29 Night, in Napoli
30 Lady Jane and Zane
32 Long short story
33 "___ Got My Eyes on You"
36 Silas Marner, e.g.
37 Hobbies
39 Beethoven opera
40 Aucklander, maybe
42 16th-century dance
43 China, perhaps
45 Word maven Newman
47 Coll. hotshot
48 It's on the Tevere
49 "Paradise Lost" character
50 Stereo precursor
51 Dudley Do-Right's love
52 ". . . ___ saw Elba"
53 Invitation letters

470   by Harvey Estes

ACROSS

1 Taj Mahal, e.g.
5 Leader from Talah Minufiya
10 Braces
14 Spy in a 1962 exchange
15 Wide open
16 "Listen up," old style
17 Chuck-a-luck equipment
18 Defunct award
19 Villa Maria College site
20 Start of a quip
23 Copied
24 Davis's home: Abbr.
25 Carmichael's "___ Buttermilk Sky"
26 Chaps
28 Scrap for Rover
31 Overlord
33 Subject of equitation
35 "Deep Space Nine" character
36 QB's want them
37 Quip, part 2
43 Union initials
44 Modern site of ancient Tyre
45 Minute ___
46 Lower
49 Mount
51 Onetime soldier
52 Twaddle
53 Tram load
55 Advance stealthily
57 Quip, part 3
62 Mavens
63 Attorney chaser
64 Garden dweller
66 May, for one
67 David Copperfield's mother
68 Sheltered spot
69 Inspected
70 First name in comedy
71 Coaster

DOWN

1 Jot
2 Final copy: Abbr.
3 Repairer
4 Censor, in a way
5 Vegetarian football game?
6 Family data
7 Dungeonlike
8 By the item
9 Rides herd on
10 Pronoun in a wedding vow
11 MOMA work
12 Field-guide listing
13 Make fun of mercilessly
21 "Is it soup ___?"
22 Carnival day
26 Marcus Loew founded it
27 Debussy's "Le Jet d'___"
29 Writing on an urn
30 Irrelevant facts, slangily
32 Locale in a Beatles song
34 Go soft
36 Disposable
38 On the other hand
39 Fish-line material
40 Flying cross, e.g.
41 More than aloofness
42 Partygoer
46 Ballet movement with the toe
47 Manhattan type
48 "Becket" co-star, 1964
49 Word in a detergent ad
50 Chic
54 Unwelcome tenant?
56 Decodes
58 Gone, with "up"
59 Fraternity
60 Bring home
61 Moolah
65 Kind of school

471 · by Bryant White

ACROSS
1 Hellenic mathematician
6 Hornet or Celtic, e.g.
11 Hot pepper
13 Having ice cream on top
16 Half of a murderous Broadway title
17 Headed off again
18 Higgins Clark, the novelist
19 Holstein part
21 "Half-off" event
22 Hidalgo time period
23 Hail, e.g.
25 "Henry & June" author
26 Harden
28 Hitler's one
29 Home-loan cost amt.
31 Hite who writes
33 Hades
34 Habits of a sort
37 Hair dye
38 Herman's Hermits' leader
39 Higher ___ (orbital point)
40 Highlands youth
43 Hueless
44 Hold in view
45 Honshu wraparound
46 Hundred bani
47 "Have a nice ___!"
49 Hiding places for aces
52 Hoop grp.
55 Heroine of an Austen novel
57 Husband of Patty Duke, once
58 Human #1
59 Hobos, in a way
61 Het-up states
63 Hard-news bit, TV-style
64 High in rank
65 Hours from now
66 Holy council

DOWN
1 H
2 Hard to pin down
3 Heredity unit
4 How to enter a scene properly
5 Harassed amiably
6 Heels over, as a ship
7 Highly vigilant
8 Helium, e.g.
9 Huge birds
10 H, once
11 Hospitalized condition
12 Humorous King
14 Hero's place
15 "Harper Valley P.T.A." star
20 Half of MCIV
23 Hits the spot, so to speak
24 Heralds
27 Hall-of-Famer Banks
30 Hangman's need
31 Hirohito's temple
32 Hardly square
35 Houston-to-Chicago dir.
36 Hatch, e.g.: Abbr.
40 "Hoop-Dee-Doo" lyricist
41 Help
42 Halves
47 Hard of hearing
48 Howitzer need
50 Hulking
51 Hatfield, to a McCoy
53 Hollywood's Barbara
54 He loves: Lat.
56 High, in place names
58 Hokkaido native
60 Have a bite
62 Historical Chinese leader ___ Piao

472 · by Sidney L. Robbins

ACROSS
1 Brazilian dance
6 Teen woe
10 Loot
14 "The Tempest" sprite
15 Avoid
16 Sherwood Anderson's "Winesburg, ___"
17 Letter turner
19 Home for some crocodiles
20 Crimson foes
21 Ones who brood
22 Sees socially
23 Artist Magritte
24 Measured (out)
25 Sir Isaac
29 Teeter
31 Singer Merman
32 Beauty's companion
33 Oklahoma city
36 Comedian Jerry
38 Neck artery
40 Tit for ___
41 Destroy for fun
43 Tip over
44 Storied Plaza girl
46 Alarms
47 Square, e.g.
48 Help in mischief
50 Makes a mess
51 Off base, maybe
52 Use a letter opener
56 Papal name
57 "Perils of Pauline" star
59 Otherwise
60 First name in mysteries
61 Movado rival
62 Not natural
63 Olympian's quest
64 You'll get a rise out of this

DOWN
1 Pack rat's motto
2 Asia's ___ Sea
3 60's fashion
4 Writer Hecht and others
5 Pie ___ mode
6 Wan
7 One-fifth of humankind
8 Goofy
9 Opposite WSW
10 "Moonlight," e.g.
11 Arkansas location
12 Felt below par
13 "Here ___!"
18 Invitation info
22 Ruin
23 Stylish desks
24 Tableland
25 Egg container
26 Ms. Kett of old comics
27 Executive branch
28 Part of ITT: Abbr.
30 Per
32 Women's support group?
34 Eat well
35 Puts two and two together
37 Admiral Perry victory site
39 W.W. II agcy.
42 Beach protector
45 Like an unpaid policy
46 Wall Street order
47 In a foxy way
49 Yawning?
50 Raced
51 Space prefix
52 Tree locale
53 Valentino co-star ___ Lee
54 Residents: Suffix
55 Not pictures
57 "___ o' My Heart"
58 Kind of humor

473   by Wayne Robert Williams

ACROSS
1 Ingenuity
5 Vocational identifiers
9 Singers Collins and Ochs
14 Roman emperor
15 Netman Arthur
16 Actress Taylor
17 1954 Gérard Philipe film
20 Guitar ridges
21 Pilot starter
22 Research room
23 Ogled
25 Had a lack
28 Worldwide lending org.
30 Yielding readily to pressure
32 Train freight holder
35 Clothes line
37 Malay boat
39 An Allman brother
40 1978 Ugo Tognazzi film
43 Coeur d'___, Idaho
44 Bruins' school
45 Luce magazine
46 Irving Berlin's "All by ___"
48 Thundering group
50 Adversary
51 N.H.L. city
53 Change the décor
55 Lummox
57 Brothers, e.g.
59 Deck out
62 1974 Richard Kiley film
66 "The Hustler" author Walter
67 Cad
68 Pocket bread
69 Fuse, as ore
70 Catch sight of
71 Miss America prop

DOWN
1 "The Call of the Wild" animal
2 Roman way
3 1957 Joanne Woodward film, with "The"
4 Black, as a chimney
5 Crone
6 On the briny
7 1987 Kevin Costner film
8 Siena seven
9 Start for fab or face
10 Biddy
11 1942 John Wayne film
12 "Star Wars" princess
13 Croat's neighbor
18 Functions
19 Leopold's partner in crime
24 Idiot
26 Idiot
27 Be jubilant
28 Mideast belief
29 ___-mouthed (insincere)
31 Lady of the haus
33 Wind: Prefix
34 Visit again
36 Artist Edouard
38 Car bar
41 Yiddish cash
42 "M*A*S*H" co-star Jamie
47 Eat not
49 "___ Diary . . ."
52 Willow twig
54 Faucet problems
55 Mel and family
56 "Excuse me . . ."
58 Ooze
60 Exploits
61 Slangy okay
63 ___ Abner
64 Adherent's suffix
65 Thickness

474   by Harvey Estes

ACROSS
1 Beat, as wings
5 Biblical symbol of patience
8 Spain's Bay of ___
14 Civil rights figure Parks
15 Unlatch, poetically
16 Skewer
17 "___ Breaky Heart"
18 Still, to Steele
19 Short stops
20 Intense interrogation
23 International traveler's need
24 Norse chief
25 Artery clogger
28 Pirate's sword
30 Lived
33 Lover of Narcissus
35 Albee's "The ___ Story"
36 Romeo's rendezvous
38 Journalists, collectively
42 Ionian island
43 ___ with (tease)
44 To be, in Paris
45 Clod buster
46 Picked up the dinner tab
50 Gyroscope's cousin
51 Counterfeit coin
52 Stairway component
54 Refusing to testify
60 Minor task
61 Old World deer
62 ___ vision (Superman skill)
63 Prattle
64 30's home run king
65 See 30-Down
66 Fast
67 Like: Suffix
68 Guitar's ancestor

DOWN
1 Sigma Chi, e.g.
2 ___ Ness
3 Ace-serving Arthur
4 Programs for purchase
5 Mendacious salesman of old car ads
6 O, on a telephone
7 River curve
8 They stand on their own two feet
9 Ezra Pound and Amy Lowell, e.g.
10 Reject with disdain
11 Four six-packs
12 Away from the weather
13 Oui or ja
21 Here: Lat.
22 ___ good turn
25 Go get
26 Sneeze sound
27 When repeated, a comforting phrase
29 1970 hit "Whole ___ Love"
30 With 65-Across, Dodge City lawman
31 Houston player
32 Brew in a teapot
34 Not working
37 Rd. or hwy.
39 Summarized
40 Flamboyant successes
41 Upper canines
47 Become depleted of water
48 Omelet need
49 Rock's ___ Leppard
51 Slide on ice
53 Computer dot
54 Catch animals
55 "Verrrrry interesting" Johnson
56 "Star Trek" counselor
57 Haus wife
58 Small pastry
59 Preposterous publicity
60 Nav. rank

475 by Richard Hughes

ACROSS

1 First name in talk radio
5 Garbed
9 Angry with
14 Story starter
15 Kibitzer's bit
16 Practice piece
17 Old Glory
20 One grieving
21 Soften
22 "Cloudy and warm," e.g.
24 High boot
28 Sticking point?
29 Roman goddess of abundance
32 Dimethyl sulfate, e.g.
33 Mom's mom
35 Taj Mahal site
36 Old Glory
39 Stitched
40 Defraud
41 Mountain crest
42 There are 100 in a cen.
43 ___-Cat
44 Mushroom features
45 Got a big head
48 Like some lawns
51 Vitamins' partners
56 Old Glory
58 Nabisco's ___ Wafers
59 "Rule, Britannia" composer
60 Indolent
61 Preferred group
62 Colored
63 Polio vaccine discoverer

DOWN

1 See 24-Down
2 "Do ___ others . . ."
3 Dueling memento
4 Mister, in Munich
5 Eat none too daintily
6 Queen Elizabeth, e.g.
7 Wrestling's "Giant"
8 The shakes
9 Least
10 Slanted
11 Trick
12 Gulf near Yemen
13 ___ match (cricket event)
18 Like Lucky Strikes, per old ads
19 Accident aftermath
23 Whip sound
24 With 1-Down, Old Glory V.I.P.
25 Wedding party member
26 Frets
27 Union, N.J. college
29 Wolf, in a way
30 Jabber
31 Savants
33 Get ready
34 ___ de la Plata
35 60's hair style
37 Verdi opera
38 Caught some Z's
43 "Who cares!"
44 Caught some rays
45 Chickens and turkeys
46 Abrasive powder
47 Sam's love on "Cheers"
48 Jug in old Rome
49 Astronaut Armstrong
50 16th-century date
52 Willie Mays stats
53 "California Suite" star
54 Soothe
55 Look for
57 Just a bit

476 by Rich Norris

ACROSS

1 Plant pest
6 Family member, for short
10 Surgery souvenir
14 Break
15 Gumbo ingredient
16 "___ want for Christmas . . ."
17 Craving of a kind
19 Apprehends
20 Stimulate affection for
21 Unsympathetic Simon
23 Harsh cry
25 Child of Loki, in Norse myth
26 Author Follett
27 Tempting
33 Tolstoy's Karenina
34 N.Y. commuter's transport
35 Big name in hotels
38 Checks
40 Fasten
41 Shade
42 Like sharp cheddar
43 New Orleans and Boston, e.g.: Abbr.
45 ___ fours
46 Not serious
49 ___ wolf
51 Limit
52 Affectionate sound
53 Tithes
55 Took in
60 Opie's dad, on 60's TV
61 Insincere talk
65 Ontario native
66 Notion
67 Conceal
68 Much-discussed 1997 movie
69 Hamlet
70 Bar, legally

DOWN

1 Church area
2 Cat's-paw
3 Tinged
4 Cousin of "uh-huh"
5 Clip
6 Muck
7 Onetime Hollywood letters
8 Knack
9 "Das Lied von der Erde" composer
10 Warbled
11 Subject of "Long Live the King"
12 "The Zoo Story" playwright
13 Ascended
18 Fish, in a way
22 Peace Prize recipient Root
24 Sits by the window, e.g.
25 Dissident
27 Agora
28 Draft classification
29 Accidental
30 Ballroom dance
31 Second-rate material
32 Attendant of Apollo
36 Quiz answer
37 Chore
39 Out of ___ (not together)
44 Night noise
47 Illuminated, as old streets
48 Force
49 Arrange neatly
50 Artist Toulouse-Lautrec
54 Parts of topsails
56 Rock video awards
57 Ancient Briton
58 Canyon sound
59 Abstruse
62 Promising words
63 Kind of bench
64 Jose or Juan preceder

477 by Manny Nosowsky

ACROSS
1 Good work, as by an auto mechanic?
10 Plague
14 Relative of a water ski
15 Indian soldier of old
16 Transfers
17 Dashed off
18 Navigation hazard
19 Ancient Brit.
20 Holdup man?
21 Tip off
23 Electrically transmitted picture
25 ___ Shah, Persian ruler who seized the Kohinoor diamond
26 Kink
27 Pulitzer author Herbert
28 Düsseldorf dessert
30 Drive-___
32 Québec's ___ Montréal
33 1954 Maxwell Anderson play, with "The"
37 Some summer cabins
39 My and thy
40 Already, in Allier
42 Clipped conjunction
43 Not much
45 Bills
47 1915 Gallipoli fighter
51 By the ___ (what's more)
53 Some canines
54 Actress Lords of "A Time to Die"
55 Some Arab kings
57 "Vissi d'___" (Puccini aria)
58 Outward, in anatomy
59 Carried away
61 View from Basel
62 Therapy
63 Part of CBS: Abbr.
64 Phone book info

DOWN
1 Masked savior
2 Constellation south of Cygnus
3 Took care of
4 Train signal frameworks
5 Shipping co.
6 Raindrop's fall
7 New York's ___ Center
8 Copper
9 Onetime Judy Garland co-star
10 W.W. I's Big ___
11 Augustine's "The City of God," e.g.
12 Less than rarely
13 Blemishes
15 Kind of meet
22 True companion
24 Gulf Coast bird
29 Mind
31 Doff one's derby
33 Ones with "I" problems?
34 Czarism, e.g.
35 ___ personae
36 Capital city once called Batavia
38 Needle holders
41 Lover of Héloïse
44 Pour, as port
46 Shot from cover
48 Flunking scores
49 Bring into harmony
50 Caissons
52 Procter & Gamble brand
56 Destiny
60 Commercial truck, for short

478 by Robert Zimmerman

ACROSS
1 Bed support
5 Race prelim
9 Austere
14 Story
15 Cooking pot
16 Golfer Palmer, to his pals
17 Author unknown, for short
18 Money for a poor box
19 Actress Jessica or Hope
20 Basketball tactic
22 "Let's Make ___"
23 Goes angling
24 Identical
26 Action word
29 Longtime convicts
33 Like some vegetables
37 Parched
39 On the main
40 "Figaro" song
41 Rocket stage
42 Type style: Abbr.
43 Actress Anderson
44 Not one red ___
45 Hang loosely
46 Of the stars
48 Dog in Oz
50 Faithful
52 Where les enfants learn
57 Measure of petrol
60 Morning meal
63 French spa
64 Forbids
65 Speechless
66 Henry or Jane of film
67 View from Buffalo
68 "Pretty Maids All in ___"
69 Classic Kilmer poem
70 Fathers
71 Gets some quick Z's

DOWN
1 Flagpole
2 Hawaiian veranda
3 At ___ for words
4 Decimal portion
5 Raspy-sounding
6 Mademoiselle
7 ___ mater
8 Chores
9 Sandwich meat
10 Product exhibition
11 William III's successor
12 Latvia's capital
13 Boat's bottom
21 Flock
25 Actor Alan
27 Storm
28 Presidential aide Scowcroft
30 "¿Cómo ___ usted?"
31 Harvest
32 Shopper's thrill
33 Song syllables
34 Greek love god
35 "That ___ hay!"
36 Market principle
38 "___ the valley of Death . . ."
41 Rights org.
45 Pier
47 Sports venues
49 Razzes
51 Waned
53 Paine's "The Rights ___"
54 1944 Tierney title role
55 Impede legally
56 Mulligans
57 Remaining
58 Actor Novello
59 Prong
61 ___ avis
62 Novelist Bagnold

479 by Janet R. Bender

ACROSS
1 Gymnast's move
5 Part of a regiment
10 Air pollution
14 Letter after theta
15 Singer Gorme
16 "Les Misérables" author
17 Scotch and Drambuie drinks
19 Not in use
20 Actress Skye
21 Fire starter
23 Bartenders' measures
27 Not him
28 N.F.L. gains
29 Signs up
30 Poland's capital
32 Three-time P.G.A. winner Sam
33 Labyrinth
34 Bulb unit
37 Pants part
38 Cleared leaves
39 Ending with origin
40 Gaelic
41 Daredevil Knievel
42 Vassal
43 Petty officers

45 Act traitorous to
46 C.I.A. forerunner
48 Rather of CBS
49 Euphoniums and tubas
50 Occur
52 Attorney's income
53 Lotion ingredient
54 1971 Clint Eastwood action film
60 What fans do
61 Make happy
62 Part of a sound stage
63 British princess
64 Keep (from doing)
65 Latest news

DOWN
1 Cone bearer
2 "Skip to My ___"
3 "___ My Party"
4 Frisk, with "down"
5 Choir members
6 "___ Daughter"
7 "Garfield" dog
8 Kuwaiti export
9 Annoyed
10 Much-kicked body part

11 Bluesman who sang "I've Got My Mojo Working"
12 Girl-watched
13 Active ones
18 Sign at merging traffic
22 Tax org.
23 Sen. Helms
24 Word before city or most
25 Not even a half-star restaurant
26 Pointed beard
27 Eye color
30 Arouse
31 Expects
33 Acknowledged expert
35 Forum robes
36 Low cards
38 Sent back to a lower court
42 Fido's restraint
44 Lyric poem
45 Supreme Court Justice appointed in 1994
46 Maureen of "Miracle on 34th Street"
47 Beauty shop

49 Singer Midler
51 Hall-of-Famer Maravich
52 Where boys will be boys

55 Paris's ___ de la Cité
56 Concert prop
57 ___ de la Plata
58 30's–40's film studio
59 "Uh-huh"

480 by Brendan Emmett Quigley

ACROSS
1 What Pandora released
6 Fuel from a marsh
10 Like some seas
14 City SE of Dayton
15 Flesh-eating giant
16 Roman historian
17 California's worry
19 Ireland
20 It may help you go on
21 "___ Lang Syne"
22 Its capital is Belgrade
24 Stick-to-it-iveness
25 Atheist Madalyn Murray ___
26 Best
29 Betty Boop feature
32 Poland Springs rival
33 Comes out of a coma
34 Comprehend
35 Actress Teri
36 "___ so!"
37 Detective Charlie
38 Summer drink
39 Complain
40 Handle
41 Plenty mad
43 Noxious gas

44 "Give it ___!"
45 Kind of list
46 Optic nerve toucher
48 Drive away
49 Call to a lamb
52 Far from land
53 Budget-busting 1955 movie
56 Soil fertilizer
57 Tiny bit
58 Noted modeling agency
59 Mug
60 Certain exercises
61 Exorcism battler

DOWN
1 Barron's reader
2 Côte de ___ (French entrée)
3 Concerning
4 Word with English or kiddie
5 Desertlike
6 Turkey tot?
7 "Yikes!"
8 Biblical vessel
9 Concert souvenir
10 Priest

11 Retouches, in a way
12 Chapter 57
13 Mimicking bird
18 Hang up one's spurs
23 Consumes
24 Paraphernalia
25 Think out loud
26 Ballerina painter
27 Skirt
28 Freak show attractions
29 "Every Breath You Take" singer
30 Area
31 ___ hand (help)
33 Good Samaritan and then some
36 "Over here!"
37 "Adios"
39 Reporters' question
40 Bereaved, in a way
42 Court TV broadcasts
43 Othello, e.g.
45 70's courtroom series
46 Thruway entrance
47 Genesis twin
48 What does attract
49 Sanka rival
50 Kind of sax

51 Mideast's Gulf of ___
54 ___ Z
55 Ring cheer

481 by Rich Norris

ACROSS

1 One not to criticize
10 Excitement
15 Musical tempo
16 Sprightly
17 Went up like a monkey
18 Foggy
19 Fusspots
20 Dynamic start
21 Proclamation
22 Kind of white
23 Key of Beethoven's Symphony No. 7: Abbr.
24 ___ precedent
25 Lock
27 Raskolnikov portrayer in 1935
31 Training unit
32 Soaked
34 Contentious promise
36 River to the Severn
38 ___-Aryan (language group)
39 Stunned
43 Collaborate (with)
47 Argument closer
48 Refrain from enforcing, as a sentence
50 Malign, with "at"
51 Cancel
53 Remaining
55 Some deg. holders
56 Common contraction
58 City named for a Civil War general
59 "___ true?"
60 "The Flying Dutchman" painter
61 Instructional
63 "I'd Be Surprisingly Good for You" musical
64 One giving sermons
65 "77 Sunset Strip" restaurant
66 Vaudeville fare

DOWN

1 Powder pads
2 How to play "Waltzing Matilda"
3 Rung
4 1980 Super Bowl losers
5 Go down
6 Fancy
7 Life, e.g.
8 Make more than happy
9 Words of collective consent
10 Wash out
11 "My word!"
12 Former Muslim officials
13 In
14 Government bonds?
23 Letter ender
26 Neb. neighbor
28 Francis I, e.g.
29 Shrimp
30 Like a tribal leader, perhaps
33 Bar ___
35 Advance
37 O.T. book
39 Balanced
40 Subject for Shakespeare
41 Gave as a bonus
42 Committed a football violation
44 Not compact, maybe
45 In jail?
46 Won't quit
49 Security of a kind
52 "You're ___ talk!"
54 Primary
57 Musical syllables
58 San ___
59 Pack ___
62 Richard's "Goodbye Columbus" co-star

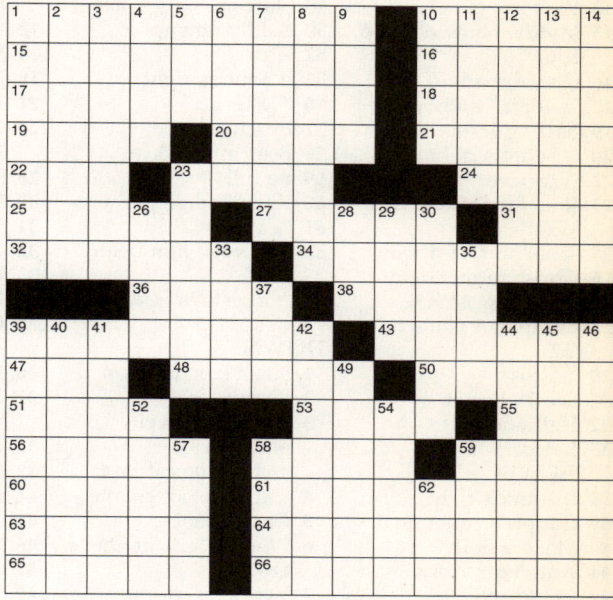

482 by Lois Sidway

ACROSS

1 Old actress Anna May
5 Kiwi soldier
10 It follows the Gospels
14 On ___ with
15 Goddess of fate
16 Miss Loughlin of "Full House"
17 "I'm off to bed," said Tom ___
19 Live wire
20 Obliterate
21 Disillusioned by
23 Takes in
26 Desert of dinosaur finds
27 Vicuña relative
29 Wear away
32 Fella
35 Ornery sort
37 Packed straw
38 Nest egg, for short
39 "I get a company car," said Tom ___
41 Dillydally
42 Peace Corps kin
44 Chunks in a Greek salad
45 Unit of force
46 It sounds like B flat
48 He's hard to find
50 "___ Dinka Doo"
51 Berate
54 Sheltered, in a way
58 Chair-back part
60 Impulse
61 "I sat in some poison ivy," said Tom ___
64 Cubbyhole
65 "Lunch Poems" poet
66 Macintosh sign
67 A final blow
68 ___ situation
69 Endangered goose

DOWN

1 Forks and spoons
2 "Lakmé," e.g.
3 Horoscope-related
4 You can chew on this awhile
5 Jack Horner's last words
6 Parisian vote
7 Sidesteps
8 Mr. Guthrie
9 An Iroquois
10 Search for the unknown?
11 "I'll have a curaçao," said Tom ___
12 The Bee Gees, e.g.
13 Speak with one's hands
18 Film short
22 Actor Benson
24 Tear
25 Blue fellow
28 Cockeyed
30 1934 baseball M.V.P.
31 Advantage
32 Met #1?
33 "The Haj" author
34 "Gotta run," said Tom ___
36 Lute's kin
39 Skiwear
40 Carol syllables
43 Fruit created circa 1904
45 Aquarium star
47 ___ Weems
49 Harrow blade
52 Author Walker
53 Avian preening aid
54 Twain hero
55 'Hood
56 Mimic
57 Gunslinger's command
59 One of the Dalys
62 Jackie's second
63 Famous Amy

483 by Mark Diehl

ACROSS

1 Section under the mezz.
5 Scuttlebutt
9 Send by parachute
13 Yarborough, et al.
15 Middle name of "The King"
16 One abroad
17 "Utopia" author
19 Earring locale
20 It sounds right
22 Aggrieve
23 Role for Shirley in '63
24 Transport, in a way
25 Christian monogram
26 They dog AWOL's
27 Campaign name of '52
29 ___ loss
31 See 26-Down
32 Half and half
33 Jonson's "Sweet Swan of ___!"
34 It sounds right
39 Couple's pronoun
40 Make a doily
41 Antonym: Abbr.
42 Contorted

43 ___ favor (please)
44 Baden-Powell offshoot org.
45 CNN parent company
48 Start of many a tale
50 Boldly attempt
52 Air
53 It sounds right
56 "Take ___"
57 Exactly
58 Bear in the sky
59 Be full
60 Kewpie doll, perhaps
61 Leave in
62 Bo Derek film before "10"
63 "Greystoke" extras

DOWN

1 Sushi bar selection
2 Peppy
3 New Mexico city noted for archaeological finds
4 Cut off from escape
5 Circus people
6 Woolf's "___ of One's Own"
7 Verdun's region

8 Socialized with
9 Street in old TV
10 Wayne-Martin western of 1959
11 Remote control feature
12 Milord
14 Kerouac's Paradise
18 Don
21 Treat a sprain
26 Cocktail, with 31-Across
28 Shale oil product
30 Whatever
31 Troy Aikman stats
32 Calendar abbr.
33 Roadie equipment
34 Bowl over
35 Economic association since 1957
36 Newborn attendant
37 Person who makes beds?
38 Clean air org.
43 Grade school ammo
44 Rodeo mount
45 ___ greens
46 Proceed easily
47 Accept a proposal
49 Sole attachment

51 Montezuma II, for one
52 Marketplace
53 Currency for 35-Down
54 Emerald City visitor
55 Forbidden City occupant: Abbr.

484 by John Greenman

ACROSS

1 Fitzgerald's forte
5 Shortening
9 "___ little piggy . . ."
13 Impetuous
14 Sunburn remedy
15 Rule the ___
16 Agitate
17 Have on
18 Simone's school
19 Epithet for a TV set
22 Jeanne or Thérèse: Abbr.
23 Believer in God
24 Podunk
30 Eucharistic plate
31 Lascivious looks
32 Set-to
35 On ___ with (equal to)
36 High in pitch
37 Mongol monk
38 Bandman Brown
39 Baseball's Doubleday
41 Bank patron
42 Fixation
44 "Queenie" author Michael
46 Get a move on

47 Gambler's tormentor
53 Beau ___
54 Flub
55 Eye layer
57 Take back to the car pound
58 Axlike tool
59 60's vocalist Vikki
60 German river
61 "Let's Make a Deal" choice
62 Make a cable stitch

DOWN

1 Last year's jrs.
2 Marcus Porcius
3 M ___ Mary
4 Farm machine
5 Maker of cases
6 Not aweather
7 Abbey or Tobacco, e.g.
8 Suffix for 41-Down
9 Alarm bell
10 Catcalls
11 Wee atoll
12 Ending for hip or hoop

15 Extends a subscription
20 School founded in 1440
21 Fragrance
24 October birthstone
25 Place for a necklace clasp
26 Hellenic H's
27 Obliqueness
28 Moray pursuer
29 Aquarium fish
32 Sitarist Shankar
33 Bodement
34 Voting district
37 Politician with a limited future
39 Hurricane of 1992
40 Smile broadly
41 Word before deep or dive
42 Demosthenes, e.g.
43 Impatient one
44 Bumped impolitely
45 Spanish direction
47 Grimm villain
48 "Yipes!"
49 Old fogy
50 Dolt
51 Netman Lendl

52 Garr of "Tootsie"
56 Trump's "The ___ of the Deal"

485 by Christopher Page

ACROSS

1 Literary Bret
6 From Cardiff
11 Fairy queen
14 Low-cholesterol spreads
15 Winged
16 Señora Perón
17 Rogue
19 Morning dampness
20 Not an expert
21 ___ greens
23 Protein source
24 Chicle product
26 Lemon zest source
27 ___ monkey
30 1945 meeting site
33 Fruit juice blend
36 ___ cit. (footnote abbr.)
38 Canal to the Baltic
39 Hubbub
40 Rowdy one
43 Granada gold
44 Pocket item?
46 Opus ___ (work of God)
47 Off-campus nonstudent
49 Circus walker
51 Mexican state bordering Arizona
53 Zhivago's love
55 Diarist Anaïs
56 Cousin of the emu
60 Brownie ingredients
63 Peanuts
65 "___ ever catch you . . ."
66 Stew
68 Avant-garde prefix
69 Sri Lankan native
70 Since: Sp.
71 Possess
72 Prepared to testify
73 $C_4H_8O_2$, e.g.

DOWN

1 Wedding dances
2 Hertz rival
3 Satisfy a debt
4 "Just for openers . . ."
5 Suffix with opal
6 Carroll's carpenter's companion
7 Addition
8 Secular
9 Small porch
10 Regatta site
11 Cab symbol
12 State categorically
13 Floozy
18 Bored
22 Washington news source, maybe
25 Vertical dividing bar in windows
28 Cry of glee
29 ___-disant (self-styled)
31 Actress Garr
32 Burn soother
33 Snoozes
34 Abridge, perhaps
35 Do for debs
37 Benin's largest city
41 Bandleader Brown
42 Neither's counterpart
45 Author Paton
48 Coloratura's sounds
50 They're sometimes blind
52 Be finicky
54 Attorney ___
57 Thieves' work
58 Wear away
59 "Mary Tyler Moore Show" co-star
60 Souse
61 "___ Good Men"
62 Oriental combat
64 Ye ___ Shoppe
67 Russian for "peace"

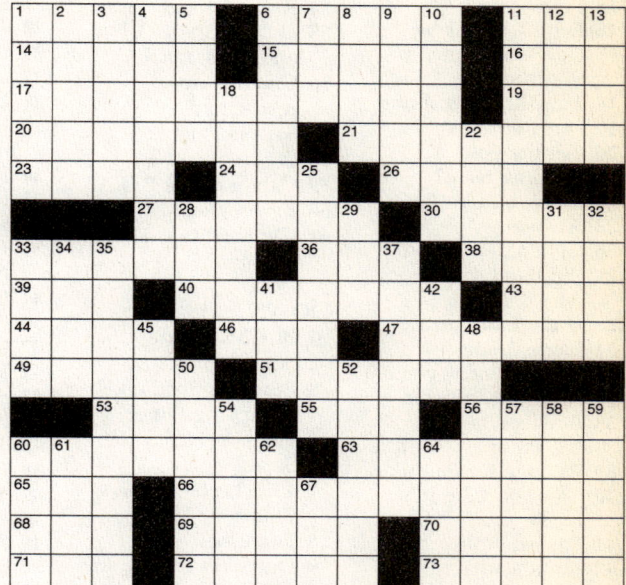

486 by Joan Scott

ACROSS

1 Access way
5 Golden oldie?
10 Sala site
14 H_2O
15 D-day beach
16 Rack's partner
17 Start of a breakfast order
20 Human culture phase
21 Laurel tree nymph
22 Draw
23 Meadow flowers
24 London or Manchester, e.g.
28 Lamebrain
29 Wedding necessity
30 Farm vehicle
31 Goddess pictured with an open papyrus
35 Continuation of 17-Across
38 In addition
39 First name in mysteries
40 Dome-top openings
41 Perón et al.
42 Tropical winds
43 Wall Street's ___ Burnham Lambert
46 Hosp. machine
47 Salts
48 Former British coins
52 End of 17-Across
55 Two before X
56 Sister of 31-Across
57 Old dog in a Stephen Foster song
58 Actor Jannings
59 Ignited a snuffed wick
60 Exclusive

DOWN

1 Indian rule
2 Here, en español
3 "The Ghost and Mrs. ___"
4 Spanish guitarist ___ De Lucia
5 Angora yield
6 Appearance
7 Baronet's wife
8 "I knew it!"
9 Youngsters' diamonds
10 ___ suzette
11 Zero
12 Inks
13 Handle: Fr.
18 Put in a vault
19 Paint poorly
23 Transported
24 Turkish V.I.P.
25 Russia's ___ Mountains
26 Word with ring or coin
27 Belly laugh
28 Scolds, with "out"
30 Lobster roe
31 Imogene of "Your Show of Shows"
32 Extol
33 Michigan's ___ Royale
34 Inventor Elisha
36 T-man
37 Former Ford
41 Corporate chief
42 Warp-knit fabric
43 Levi Strauss stock
44 Arms of a sort
45 Instant correspondence
46 Civvies
47 Banker's byword
48 Caged puck
49 Newts
50 Bygone hair style
51 Gummed flap
53 Prefix with date or dawn
54 Hurricane's center

487 by Raymond Hamel

ACROSS

1 Elephant boy of film
5 Hero-worshipers
9 Stringed instruments
14 Shell
15 Polo ground?
16 Echo was one
17 Garfield's bane, in the comics
18 Trapshooter's shout
19 Hardly robust
20 Get the gold
21 Bowling team?
23 Drink in a bottle
25 Awaken
26 Give a deposition
27 Big Band saxophonist Al
28 Underhand throw
31 Eagle model
33 Pitcher's achievement
34 Kind of sandwich
35 Bowler's home?
38 ___ Piper
39 Passage for Paulus
40 "As You Like It" locale
41 For example
42 Lunkhead
43 Auto racer Granatelli

44 How-to
45 Swallows
48 Bowler's winnings?
52 Mauna ___
53 Singer ___ Minogue
54 River through Pisa
55 Let out one's emotions, maybe
56 Chain gang restriction
57 Salacious look
58 Wallet fillers
59 Calvin of the P.G.A.
60 Byron poem
61 Gymnastics coach Karolyi

DOWN

1 Broadway fare
2 Sound
3 Bowler's dead end?
4 Luau entertainer
5 Paris, to Helen
6 Seize
7 1953 Leslie Caron film
8 Discusses
9 Dracula's resting site
10 Ballfield bobble

11 "The Owl and the Pussy Cat" writer
12 Not clerical
13 "Monty Python" troupe member
21 Exhausted
22 Aunt of Caroline
24 Steer clear of
27 ___ in (yielded)
28 Bowler's battle site?
29 John Berger's "___ in Europa"
30 Rheinland road
31 Recipe amts.
32 Samoan capital
33 Pirates of the N.C.A.A.
34 Late: Sp.
36 Purple bloomer
37 Cattle drive locale
42 Partner of 13-Down
43 Sweater material
44 Not electronic
45 Type of tube
46 Hand-held dryer
47 Taco salad topping
48 Pass up
49 Fiery stack
50 Shampoo ingredient
51 Precinct

55 Move up and down

488 by Raymond Hamel

ACROSS

1 Turkish title
6 Not adventurous
11 Prayer site
14 Dairy section selection
15 "Filthy" money
16 Rope-a-dope exponent
17 Religious Bronco center?
19 Bonus
20 Whilom
21 Odysseus's advisor
22 Middle mark
23 Soaks a bag
25 Form of pachisi
27 Religious basketball star?
32 Ratify
35 Invoice stamp
36 With 30-Down, a night sight
38 "___ Got Tonight" (hit song)
39 Actor Most of "Happy Days"
40 Skinny
41 Wanton look
42 Half of sedecim

43 Philadelphia skater
44 Religious Dodger pitcher?
47 Year of Columbus's death
48 Toady
52 1773 jetsam
54 Where Mark Twain is buried
58 Singer Turner
59 Fitting
60 Religious Rams end?
62 Start of a winning line
63 Cleveland Secretary of State Richard ___
64 Eye twisters
65 German pronoun
66 Some United Nations vetoes
67 Emerson product

DOWN

1 Rib ticklers?
2 On the ball
3 Take, at law
4 Easily riled
5 Lenten symbol
6 Open, in a way
7 1975 ZZ Top hit

8 Have pains
9 Thatcher nickname
10 Home of the Blue Demons
11 Author of "The Great Santini"
12 Nobelist Wiesel
13 Dry dishes
18 The low notes
24 Kind of roast
26 Plays two notes simultaneously
28 Long time
29 "A votre ___"
30 See 36-Across
31 Peon of yore
32 Saddlemaker's tool
33 Philosophical
34 Surpass
37 Robert Burns's birthplace
39 Without a fight
43 Challenger
45 Last name in fashion photography
46 Meg of "Sleepless in Seattle"
49 Talkative birds: Var.
50 The end of ___

51 Disagreeable
52 "Mon Oncle" director
53 Of majestic proportion
55 Pride of lions

56 Rapper né Tracey Marrow
57 Orbison and Rogers
61 Coffee, in slang

489 by Rich Norris

ACROSS

1 Some cards
7 Bodybuilder's concern
13 Ricocheted
15 Central American capital
16 Fashionable
17 "___ Swings" (1965 Roger Miller hit)
18 Armchair necessities for 46-Across
20 Thomas Moore subject
21 Something to lend or bend
22 Imbues with gravity
26 Kind of sauce
31 Hermitage figures
32 "Platoon" actor
33 Bit
34 Solar warmers
35 Word with house or mouse
36 Like summer days, often
37 W.W. II locale, in brief
38 Novi Sad natives
39 ___ Gables
40 Burial places
42 Antibody producers
43 To a fault
44 Ho do
46 Armchair activity, colloquially
53 Add one's two cents' worth
54 Furniture worker
55 Anticipate
56 Astor Cup competition, e.g.
57 Gets wind of
58 Flip again

DOWN

1 Deface
2 Blanch
3 Composer Khachaturian
4 Major ending
5 Thespians, perhaps
6 Spring rituals
7 Joked
8 Lodge
9 Weight watcher's concern: Var.
10 On even terms, old-style
11 Puzzle clues, sometimes
12 Inferior, as an excuse
14 Numerical prefix
15 Lavatory sign
19 Alert
22 Curtain fabric
23 Boston Symphony maestro
24 Mississippi feature
25 Uncertain syllables
27 Moves via twists
28 ___ 2600 (old game-playing machine)
29 "East of Eden" director
30 Eclogues
32 Archaic form of address
35 Rap sheet list
36 Breakfast delicacy
38 Next available time
39 Mettle
41 Floral organ
42 Not as slack
45 Country in a 1969 Beatles song
46 Ice-cream flav.
47 Take on
48 Ship's heading
49 Edict
50 Wild about
51 New Jersey five
52 Mardi ___
53 Baseball position Abbr.

490 by Gregory E. Paul

ACROSS

1 Grizzlies
6 Tennyson, e.g.
10 Mrs. Chaplin
14 Dragon of puppetry
15 Up to the task
16 Caspian Sea feeder
17 Put all one's eggs in one basket
19 "Cheerio!"
20 A.P. rival
21 Cracker spread
22 Pan coating
24 Cassandra, e.g.
26 Crooner Perry
27 One: Fr.
28 Drench
32 Senator Lott
35 Nursery cry
36 Unspecified shape
37 50/50 share
38 Star in Orion
39 Moon goddess
40 Guthrie of folk
41 Mideast carrier
42 Part of NOW
43 Almost a pin, in wrestling
45 Box office window letters
46 Detective's job
47 Masters champion Craig
51 Silverware tray compartment
54 Ugandan tyrant
55 Comedian Philips
56 Sportscaster Albert
57 Available
60 Formerly
61 Safari sound
62 Flood control embankment
63 First or reverse, e.g.
64 To be, in Toulon
65 Tinker-Chance middleman

DOWN

1 Phony
2 Emulate Romeo and Juliet
3 1966 Michael Caine film
4 Orinoco, e.g.
5 Garden of Eden dweller
6 Labor's partner
7 Cousin of the bassoon
8 Antlered animal
9 Go on the wagon
10 Revengeful
11 Spoken
12 1949 alliance
13 Novelist Paton
18 Military HQ
23 Down Under bird
25 Seek safety
26 Bedouin's transport
28 Katey of "Married . . . With Children"
29 Grad
30 "At the sound of the ___ . . ."
31 Israel's Abba
32 Comparison word
33 Scarce
34 Music's Fitzgerald
35 Choreographer Agnes de ___
38 Give comforting words to
42 Argue
44 Ceiling fixture
45 Mix
47 Round-the-campfire treat
48 Skedaddle
49 Hot coal
50 Valentine's Day bouquet
51 Health hazard
52 Window section
53 "Jaws" boat
54 From a distance
58 Flower holder
59 Title for Jesse Jackson: Abbr.

ACROSS

1 Scarlett's place
5 Entrée to the Internet
10 Relinquish
14 "___ as we speak . . ."
15 Blazing
16 World War II foe
17 Turn down
18 Yankee great Roger
19 Coin
20 Dairy case item
23 Stockings
24 Polka ___
25 Nautical quarters
28 Consecrate
31 Pizzeria appliance
32 Traveling bag
34 Pollster Harris
37 Protest formally
40 Profound respect
41 747's route
42 Parasites
43 Archipelago components
44 Outfield hits
45 Wile E. Coyote's supplies
47 Cohorts
49 Expose
55 Touchdown

56 Swashbuckler Flynn
57 Tennis's Lendl
59 Novelist Bagnold
60 Paul Anka tune
61 Hacienda, e.g.
62 Horne or Olin
63 Fools
64 Panache

DOWN

1 Danson of "Cheers"
2 ___ plaisir
3 Janet of Justice
4 "___ you can do . . ."
5 Half of a 1960's pop group
6 Coming ___
7 Desperate
8 Newsman Sevareid
9 Dovetail
10 Walk-on parts
11 Be
12 Sups
13 Erhard's discipline
21 Won ___ soup
22 Classic Ford
25 Soft drink
26 Swear
27 Literary carpenter Adam

28 Huffs and puffs
29 Succotash bean
30 Spot
32 Colorado skiing haven
33 Farmer's measurement
34 Next-to-last year in Claudius's reign
35 In days of old
36 Colorado Indians
38 Slackened
39 Popular pie seasoning
43 Mrs. Marcos
44 24-hour ___
45 In unison
46 Kind of letter
47 Call
48 Greek strongman
50 Helen's mother
51 Spring flower
52 Mardi ___
53 Elliptical
54 Cape Canaveral org.
55 Set
58 Bert Bobbsey's twin

ACROSS

1 Actress Moore
5 Grade school grade
9 More peculiar
14 Attorney Dershowitz
15 Chill
16 "Superman" star
17 Élan
18 High schooler
19 Trembling tree
20 "South Pacific" co-star
22 NO₂
23 Bounced, as a baby on the knee
24 "I, Claudius" attire
26 Literary collection
27 Part of a bridge auction
31 "I ___ a clue"
35 Maidenform purchase
36 Hosiery shade
37 Tours school
38 Carrier from Stockholm
39 "Sweeney Todd" prop
40 Et ___

41 90's convenience, for short
42 Prove a failure
43 Lasting
45 Part of a shark sighting
46 Kind of nut
47 Luanda resident
52 Assail
55 "The Godfather" writer
57 "Mazeppa" composer
58 Singer Clapton
59 "The Figure of ___": Dickinson
60 "Let's Make ___"
61 File's partner
62 Exceptional
63 Shouldered
64 Do in
65 ___ bien

DOWN

1 In a fog
2 Professor Higgins's pupil
3 "The ___ the White Suit" (1951 film)
4 "___ We Trust"
5 Like Job

6 To-do list
7 ___ Canal
8 Capitol Hill gang
9 Lunchbox item
10 Bandleader/TV star of old
11 ___ of Educ.
12 At any time
13 America West destination
21 DC-10
25 Eggs
28 Fly low over
29 Golden calf
30 "___ Mable" (1918 bestseller)
31 Superintendent
32 Bill of Rights defender, for short
33 ___ dire (court procedure)
34 "Gentleman's Agreement" director
35 Ka-pow!
38 Clambake fare
39 Fab Four name
41 Part of A.P.B.
42 Hard to please
44 Perfume holder
45 Cooked cereal

48 Modern museum display
49 Kind of module
50 Sky blue
51 I.O.U.'s, e.g.

52 "Spare tire"
53 Resort near Venice
54 River to the North Sea
56 Sea east of the Caspian

493   by Cathy Millhauser

ACROSS
1 Old math aids
6 The color of honey
10 Leave off
14 Play salesman
15 "The Morning Watch" author
16 Polaris bear
17 Light-headed?
18 Patricia of "Hud"
19 Culture site
20 Opinions of Greg Louganis?
23 Skater's leap
24 Shadow
25 Barker of 40's films
28 "Cheerio, Luciano!"
30 Drug shipment
33 Cockpit reading: Abbr.
34 Speck
35 "Sweet Lavender" playwright
37 What a Beach Boy's firecracker might do?
40 Loot
41 Tiny ringing sound
42 Speck
43 Seat of Jackson County, Tex.
44 Soup bean
45 Colon's meaning, in analogies
46 Foreign friend
48 Birds in herds
50 Qualities of Bennett Cerf's food?
56 Dyeing plant
57 Spicy cuisine
58 Cream of the crop
60 Port, e.g.
61 Sports period
62 Own up (to)
63 Pentagram
64 Vogue competitor
65 Erstwhile catalogue

DOWN
1 Celebrant's robe
2 Forward
3 Marne mine
4 Sailcloth
5 End table?
6 Nerve center
7 Kind of arch
8 Hobo's shelter
9 It may be found around the mouth
10 Showing cowardice
11 Exhort
12 Second of an ancient trio
13 Gobs
21 Right-hand pages
22 Hägar of the comics, e.g.
25 Binges
26 Abscond
27 Bore
29 Violinist's heirloom
31 City on the Aire
32 "Ready ___, here I come!"
34 Blazing
35 Hat made from jipijapa
36 Conductor Klemperer
38 Crafty one
39 Source of many book series
44 Murderous
45 Wagnerian title woman
47 "___ Mood" (1940 hit)
49 The eyes have them
50 Kit's mitts
51 Part of B.T.U.
52 Perfumer ___ Ricci
53 Ebb
54 Abel's "Green Mansions" love
55 Arouse
59 U.F.O. pilots

494   by Rich Norris

ACROSS
1 Thicket
8 Most cool
15 Charges
16 Worship
17 Farm equipment
18 Turns in
19 Some diktats
20 Upset
22 Actor with a partly shaved head
23 See 1-Down
24 Pasture
25 Gamin
26 Cambodian money
28 Mudslinger's charge
30 Thomas with three Emmys
31 Unfriendliness
33 Person in a pet
34 Return
36 Pool competitor's request
39 Discuss in detail
43 Throws out
44 ___ five
45 Specify
46 Tar
47 Provost of TV's "Lassie"
48 Auto ad stat
49 Start of many an essay title
50 Enthusiastic
53 Evening abroad
54 Soup accompaniment
56 Like some breezes
58 Steams
59 "Odyssey" trees
60 Do doer
61 Sommelier's consideration

DOWN
1 With 23-Across, a 1966 hit song
2 Vast
3 Computer add-on
4 Golf targets
5 "Peer Gynt" character
6 Actor Frobe
7 It, in Italy
8 Critic
9 Children's writer Turin
10 Guitar relative
11 Year in Edward the Confessor's reign
12 Designate
13 Lacking originality
14 Try to find, in a doctor's office
21 Pawn
25 Cameo
27 Have a few
28 Canal device
29 Press coverage
30 Frequently
32 Apple products
33 French door component
35 Musical piece
36 Rests
37 Issuing forth
38 Yankees vs. Red Sox, e.g.
40 Scram
41 Domains
42 Withdrawal
44 Upright
47 Vacation times
50 Best Picture of 1958
51 Nelson, e.g.
52 ___ about
53 Avoid
55 Loser to Botvinnik in 1961
57 Pen

ACROSS

1 List ender
5 Intrinsically
10 N.Y.C. station
14 Coveted review
15 Love in Limoges
16 "___, Brute?"
17 Part of the eye
18 Rams and Jets, e.g.
19 Newspaperman Adolph
20 "No guarantees"
23 ___ Alte (Adenauer)
24 540–1600 on a radio
27 Calpurnia's husband
31 Oner
35 Fluorescent-lamp filler
36 Intoxicating drink of the gods
37 Follower's suffix
38 Unwelcome one
42 Shad delicacy
43 Tight positions?
44 Record
45 Second self
48 Declare
49 Thrall of yore
50 MS. perusers
51 Willy-nilly
59 Concerning
62 Related maternally
63 Assist a prankster
64 ___ bene
65 Adder or asp
66 Secure, in a way
67 Not up
68 That is
69 ___ Domini

DOWN

1 "The Red"
2 "G.W.T.W." locale
3 Tel ___
4 Majesty lead-in
5 Little feet do it
6 Title in Turkey
7 Indulge one's wanderlust
8 Waste reservoir
9 Once, once
10 Bradley University site
11 Another list ender
12 Highest degree
13 Mus' followers
21 Hersey novel town
22 Harem room
25 Control a 747
26 Antiseptic-surgery pioneer Joseph
27 "Lost Horizon" director
28 Tissue gap
29 They may be snowy
30 "Mayday!"
31 Musical form ending a sonata
32 Freeman Gosden radio role
33 Sought office
34 Embark
36 Squealed
39 Society-page word
40 Artist's paste
41 T.L.C. is their forte
46 Nonet, for one
47 Early auto
48 Commercial, in British slang
50 ___ Park, Colorado
52 Jeans maker Strauss
53 Write Bagnold
54 Neck part
55 Miss Cantrell
56 "Voice of Israel" author, 1957
57 Nürnberg no
58 Capital of Manche
59 ___ nutshell
60 San Francisco hill
61 I-95, e.g.: Abbr.

ACROSS

1 Dumbfounded
5 Acquire, as expenses
10 Singer Campbell
14 Colombian city
15 Hughes' plane, Spruce ___
16 1890's Vice President ___ P. Morton
17 1959 Rodgers and Hammerstein hit
20 "You can ___ horse to . . ."
21 Bridal path
22 Predicament
24 Obote's successor
26 1956 Comden-Green-Styne collaboration
33 On ___ (counting calories)
34 Man with a title
35 Russian space vehicle
36 Pride and envy, e.g.
37 Old hat
38 "Aurora" painter
39 Kind of cap or cream
40 Radio host of note
41 First U.S.-born saint
42 1930 Gershwin musical
46 Sigmatism
47 Achy
48 Whiz kid
51 Blotto
54 1983 Herman-Fierstein musical
60 "Metamorphoses" poet
61 Wish granters
62 TV's Oscar
63 Hitches
64 Mill material
65 Murder

DOWN

1 Part of a play
2 Star of TV's "Wiseguy"
3 "Waiting for the Robert ___"
4 Puts out of commission
5 Desert critter
6 Persona ___ grata
7 How some packages are sent: Abbr.
8 R. & R. org.
9 Ring leader?
10 Sticking together
11 Decreasingly
12 Demonic
13 Garibaldi's birthplace
18 Keats or Shelley
19 Popular street name
23 Invent
24 Snaps handcuffs on
25 Gentle, as breezes
26 Grounds
27 Kingly decree
28 Passenger ship
29 Gobble
30 "___ man with seven . . ."
31 Curtain material
32 Nine-to-five routine
37 Conks out
38 Mutinied
41 ___-comic (play type)
43 Long narratives
44 Alan, Larry or Stephen
45 Tap-dance
48 Crushing news
49 Four-star review
50 ___ rain
52 Admiral Zumwalt
53 Actress Moore
55 Chicken's counterpart
56 Atmosphere: Prefix
57 Prefix with lateral
58 Omicrons predecessors
59 Thesaurus listing: Abbr.

497 by Raymond Hamel

ACROSS

1 Room between rooms
5 Handouts
9 Farm building
13 Opera solos
15 West Virginia resource
16 Sack starter
17 1970 Tommy Roe hit
20 Spain's locale
21 Leslie Caron role
22 Hesitation sounds
23 Writer Bombeck
25 Swindle
26 Sweet treat
30 "Fiddler on the Roof" fellow
35 Literary collection
36 Weep loudly
37 Arctic, for one
38 Recurring theme
41 French denial
43 Lisboa's sister city
44 1985 Kate Nelligan title role
45 Big shot
47 Calendar ender: Abbr.
48 Anglo's partner
49 Tentacled sea creature
52 Ostrich's cousin
54 Author Bellow
55 Lemon drink
58 Meadow bird
60 Drinkers' toasts
64 "Black Bottom Stomp" performer
67 Came down
68 Christmas centerpiece
69 The elder Judd
70 Critic Rex
71 Cruising
72 Tiff

DOWN

1 Pilgrim to Mecca
2 Pilgrim to Mecca
3 Citrus flavor
4 Emblem of victory
5 Item up the sleeve
6 Take it easy
7 Slander
8 With cunning
9 Visit Vail, perhaps
10 "Come Back, Little Sheba" playwright
11 Cowardly Lion portrayer
12 Chooses
14 Helical
18 Doorway parts
19 Perfect
24 Long, long time
26 Caan or Cagney
27 ___ Gay
28 Type of rubber
29 Superior to
31 Author Umberto
32 "Rigoletto" composer
33 Film director Peter
34 Tennyson's "___ Arden"
39 Odysseus's rescuer, in myth
40 Exquisitely
42 Guitarist Lofgren
46 Ecto or proto ending
49 Panel of 12
50 Alaskan river
51 Groups of indigenous plants
53 "I Remember Mama" mama
55 Partly open
56 Take out of print
57 Nobelist Wiesel
59 "Red Balloon" painter
61 On
62 ___ Linda, Calif.
63 Fit of anger
65 Former Ford
66 ___ & Perrins

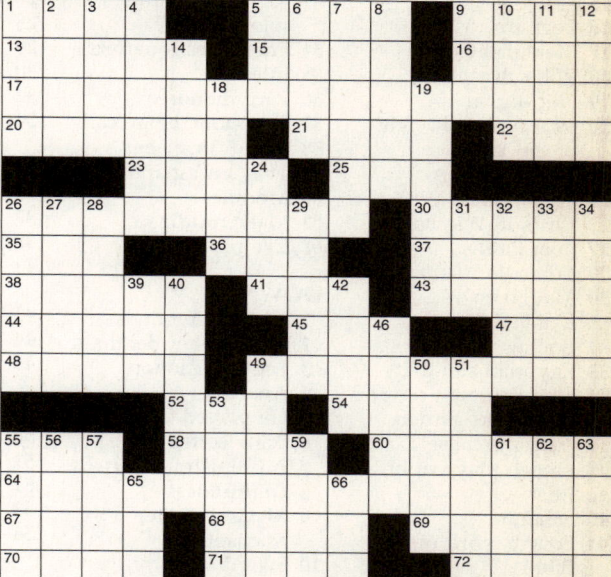

498 by Richard Thomas

ACROSS

1 By the side
6 In the back
10 Hoarded
14 1936 Leslie Howard role
15 Nose (out)
16 Actress Nazimova
17 Foes at Gaugamela
20 Mythological lineup
21 Whomps
22 ___ Claire
23 Loyal
24 Foes at the falls of Reichenbach
31 Topple
32 Leisure
33 Card
35 June honoree, for short
36 Taxable income
38 Philippine island
39 Plaintive
40 Out of business
41 Camera carriage
42 Foes at Troy
46 Fix, artwise
47 "Flying Down to ___"
48 Bundle barley
51 Cosmetic items
56 Foes at Tenochtitlán
58 Mayberry moppet
59 Simulacrum
60 Ferber title
61 Level
62 Not stifling
63 Levels off

DOWN

1 Not give ___
2 "Damn Yankees" role
3 Sign from on high
4 Barber's call
5 Green light
6 Pilot's vision problem
7 Nirvana
8 Cabinet dept.
9 Group based in Geneva
10 First name in the N.B.A.
11 Literary pseudonym
12 Jack Horner's surprise
13 Itar-___ (news agency)
18 Circa
19 As ___ (generally)
23 "Take ___!"
24 Tankard's kin
25 Rival of Sally
26 "The Cloister and the Hearth" author
27 N.Y.C. subway line
28 Busybody
29 Reb general Richard
30 Dear pelt
34 Fellows
36 Colonial African land
37 Prefix with Disney
38 Mil. rank
40 Caniff's "___ Canyon"
41 Bishop's bailiwick
43 Oregon's ___ Lake
44 Narrow opening
45 "Hey you!" sound
48 Dundee denizen
49 Original Arizonan
50 Gannon University home
51 Marston ___ (1644 battle site)
52 Don River's outlet
53 Hayseed
54 Ugandan exile
55 Needs a facelift
57 AT&T alternative

499 by Chuck Deodene

ACROSS
1 Nightwear, for short
4 Scruff
8 Kind of year
14 PAC donee: Abbr.
15 Holly shrub
16 Lock up
17 Mentalist Geller
18 Roll-call yell
19 Not digital
20 1991 N.B.A. Rookie of the Year
23 P.C. messages
24 "___ a Small World"
25 With, in Wiesbaden
27 Poet Plath
29 Wheedle
30 Maugham's "___ of Lambeth"
31 Boiling
33 Egyptian sun deity
34 Sinclair Lewis novel
37 Lawn-and-garden shop purchase
39 French playwright Jules
40 Saharan
41 Fourth word of the Bible
42 Zealous

46 Phyllis Diller accessory
47 Los Angeles D.A. Garcetti
48 Perfumery ingredient
49 Kelsey Grammer TV role
54 Phone headquarters
55 Inter ___
56 Party honoree
57 Drooping, botanically
58 Breath freshener
59 That, en español
60 Modifies
61 Make muffins
62 Eye problem

DOWN
1 Hardly libertines
2 Philosopher Bentham
3 Football motion
4 Anarchy
5 He played Obi-Wan
6 Brew coffee
7 Administrator, briefly
8 Faithfulness
9 Mystery writer Michael
10 Swindle
11 Disaster

12 Ponder painfully, with "over"
13 Pants part
21 Competed with
22 J. Paul Getty, for one
26 Bronzed
28 Noshed
29 Summoned
30 Ring of short stories
32 Flynn and others
34 Move to foreign shores
35 Pester
36 Cut short
37 Jurisprudence
38 Platinumlike metal
41 Candlestick Park team
43 K to 12
44 "That's the truth!"
45 Good ___ (Dixie chum)
47 Use a whetstone
50 Tartlike pastry
51 da-DUM
52 Director Kazan
53 Rangers locale
54 Genetic stuff

500 by Christopher Hurt

ACROSS
1 Spiral-horned sheep
7 Noël ___
13 Unnumbered spheres
16 First act
17 It can be a charm
18 Butterfly, e.g.
19 Crowlike bird
20 Caveat ___
22 Shriver of tennis
23 Mirror fogger
26 Sorority character
27 Volcanic island in the Aegean
29 Sanction
31 Alternative to Rep. or Dem.
33 Solicits
34 Noël's hit of 1941
37 10,000 square meters
38 Cole's hit of 1934
43 Mexican Indian
45 Alternative to Rep. or Dem.
46 Sagan's "pale blue dot"
47 Out of place
49 Opposite of fast
51 "The Merry Widow" composer

53 L.A. summer zone
54 Inn
57 Imitate
58 Religious works of art
60 Studies
63 Galápagos creature
64 Made a splash
65 Cole ___
66 Resells for a big profit

DOWN
1 Substances with low pH
2 Drink on credit
3 Hallmark sentiment
4 Court grp.
5 Slip behind
6 ___-et-Vilaine, France
7 TV host, 1948–63
8 Swirls and such
9 Made a commitment to
10 Short, short, long
11 Crack, so to speak
12 Tragedies, e.g.
14 Flaccid
15 Noël and Cole, e.g.
21 ___ Alley

24 Three-time champ
25 Infested, in a way
28 "Bali ___"
30 Uses a strop
32 Tennyson's "Break, Break, Break," e.g.
35 Bounces back
36 Stately
38 College athlete
39 Forty winks
40 Return on a deposit?
41 The kick in kirsch
42 Become orderly
43 "Cheerio!"
44 Musical mood?
48 Scottish title
50 Words
52 Breathers
55 Glacial ridges
56 Luang Prabang's land
59 Matter of retribution
61 Slipper, for short
62 Lupino of "High Sierra"

501   by Thomas W. Schier

ACROSS

1 Front line, maybe
7 Scoot along
10 Couple
14 Grammatical connector
15 Brian of British rock
16 ___ many words
17 Crows
19 Evening in Paris
20 Whitish
21 "___ won't!"
22 Boardwalk purchase
23 Schedule
25 Neck protector
27 Paycheck stub inits.
30 Of the universe in its present state
33 Enthuse
35 Harry James's "Don't ___ Go 'Way Mad"
37 Villain's laugh sound
38 Rattle
39 Publisher Ballantine
40 Chemical suffix
41 Celebrated jurist of the 10's–50's
43 Contributes to
45 Pond organism
46 Twenty: Prefix
47 Short snort
49 Cattle breed
51 Tankerful
53 Don't exist
57 Software buyer
58 Depreciate
60 Employment form category
61 ___ de dents (toothache): Fr.
62 Harvest fly
63 Falls for
64 Work at, as a trade
65 Tennis player's sock

DOWN

1 Part of a nuclear arsenal
2 Arias
3 Word after fire or harlequin
4 Two-handed carpenter's tool
5 Hydrocarbon group
6 Mortar beater
7 W.W. II Japanese plane
8 Not clear
9 Neg.'s counterpart
10 Render harmless
11 Not recognized
12 Like
13 Fishing boat
18 Cosmopolitan
22 Experienced
24 Solidarity
26 Meet
27 E trailer
28 Erin personified
29 In a unified manner
31 Extra printed sheets
32 Tennis star Michael
34 Mythical beast in Chinese art
36 "Shave ___ haircut . . ."
42 Foyer item
44 Tallies
48 Actress Linda
49 Speechless
50 Birthright barterer
52 Without effort
54 Mideast airline
55 Au naturel
56 Sow feature
58 Plate watcher
59 David Sarnoff's command, once

502   by Kenneth Witte

ACROSS

1 Word before "of health" or "of directors"
6 Adroit
10 Notion
14 See eye to eye
15 Lamb's nom de plume
16 Netting
17 Makes a good start
20 Understand
21 Mr. Onassis
22 Celebrity
23 Bearing
24 Common Market money
25 Isolated
32 Peter and Paul, e.g., but not Mary
33 Defeat decisively
34 Eggs
36 It marches on
37 Bar seat
39 Nasty, as a comment
40 ___ of a kind
41 Caesar and Vicious, e.g.
42 Radarange maker
43 Attempt to win approval
47 Enemy
48 Lasses' mates
49 Blueprint
53 Letter before omega
54 Jiang Qing's husband
57 Trying hard
60 Sicilian spouter
61 Intend
62 Architectural style
63 Light for serenaders
64 Terrier type
65 Parisian river

DOWN

1 Catches, as game
2 S-shaped curve
3 Jovial Johnson
4 Legal matter
5 Holds in custody
6 Emulate Webster
7 Inventor Whitney
8 Evergreens
9 Not gross
10 Stain
11 Conked out, as a battery
12 Conoco competitor
13 "Pardon me . . ."
18 Oka River city
19 Unspoken
23 Bog
25 "Beetle Bailey" pooch
26 Taking advantage of
27 Not as wild
28 "The Road Not Taken" poet
29 Besides
30 Like the 11:00 news, usually
31 Gulf of Riga tributary
35 Call it ___ (stop working)
37 Pistols, swords, etc.
38 N.F.L. scores
39 Sound equipment
41 Sleep loudly
42 More than devotees
44 Kabul native
45 Type of skiing
46 Boss Tweed nemesis
49 Carpe ___
50 Division word
51 ___ time (never)
52 Earth inheritors, with "the"
54 The south of France
55 Forthwith
56 Folklore villain
58 Remunerate
59 Cry's partner

503 · by Marie Heller

ACROSS

1 Year before jr.
5 Dhaka dress
9 Bacteria destroyer
14 Command to Dobbin
15 Desertlike
16 First duke of Normandy
17 Women's rights advocate Lucretia
18 Mathematician Descartes
19 Church instrument
20 Military bigwigs
23 Chemical relative
25 "A Lesson From ___"
26 Brig, for one
30 Like some tabloid headlines
31 To the point, as a remark
32 Evening hour
35 Rank between viscount and marquis
36 Fishing basket
37 Infested, in a way
38 Reagan mil. program
39 Bel ___ (cheese)
40 Relating to pitch
41 "Jules and Jim" situation
43 Relinquish, as a right
45 Skiing event
46 Post-Derby site
50 Writer of boys' tales
51 Mexican girl
52 Yen
55 Barnyard sound
56 Formerly
57 London restaurant district
58 Beforehand
59 Prosperity
60 Freshly

DOWN

1 Personal ad abbr.
2 Exclamation of surprise
3 Mishmash
4 Nasty letters
5 French existentialist
6 Neighborhood
7 Wagnerian cycle
8 Prefix with gram or logical
9 Bugbear
10 "Friday the 13th" genre
11 Pond cover
12 Word with drinking or looking
13 Ages and ages
21 Dork
22 Old movie star Conrad
23 Enchanted places, perhaps
24 Military unit
27 Street show
28 Words before a clarification
29 "The Female Eunuch" author
32 One heart in hand
33 Actor Calvino
34 Woody tissue
36 Spelunker
37 Big draw at the Louvre
39 Destitution
40 Soft mineral
41 Of direct descent
42 Tel Aviv's land
43 Author Cather
44 Fury
46 "Jabberwocky" word
47 Cable TV clears it up
48 Art film theater
49 One whom Pizarro encountered
53 ___ Guevara
54 "By what means?"

504 · by Gene Newman

ACROSS

1 Hollywood do
5 Coat, with "on"
9 By surprise
14 Favorite
15 ___ facto
16 Kind of pad
17 Heart of the matter
18 Jerk: Var.
19 Bogart in "High Sierra"
20 Barely
23 Linear
24 Toss (out)
25 Doyle's "___ in Scarlet"
28 Diner lunch order
29 "It's fun to stay at the ___" (1978 song lyric)
33 "Little Lulu" cartoonist
34 50's Yankees great Hank
36 Not in, in Innsbruck
37 Barely
40 PC key
41 Rummages (through)
42 Toot
43 Campus org.
45 Scheduled
46 Some 16th-century engravings
47 "Looks like trouble"
49 Japanese writing sticks
50 Barely
57 "Smoking gun"
58 Pitcher Wilhelm
59 "The Art of Love" author
60 Exploded
61 English composer
62 "So long"
63 Pants parts
64 Tournament ranking
65 Leave rolling in the aisles

DOWN

1 "Thank Heaven for Little Girls" musical
2 Tennis score
3 Without a clue
4 Notwithstanding that
5 ABC's owner
6 It eats its vegetables
7 "Semper fi" grp.
8 Literary circles
9 Hebrew A's
10 "Dick Tracy" star
11 Farm prefix
12 Not windy
13 "The Mocker Mocked" artist
21 Make beloved
22 Cowboy flick
25 Stoplight light
26 Express authority
27 Pamphlet
28 Thrash
30 Part of Felipe's family
31 Better-looking
32 Hardwoods
34 To-dos
35 Job hunter's need
38 Crystalline antiseptic
39 California crop
44 Regis or Kathie Lee
46 Prepared to lift prints
48 Tests the weight of
49 Composer Jule
50 P.D. alerts
51 Exact
52 Part of a Japanese pilot's war cry
53 Resentful
54 Planetary path
55 Actress Naldi
56 Normandy event

505 by Alfio Micci

ACROSS

1 Axis flier, in W.W. II headlines
4 Consommé
9 1936 Luce play, with "The"
14 "Honest" one
15 Disprove
16 Piano key wood
17 Start of a comment by G.K. Chesterton
19 Bar seat
20 Org.
21 A Gabor
22 A Guthrie
23 Oahu neckwear
24 Part 2 of the comment
28 Beethoven's "___ Solemnis"
30 Harrow's rival
31 God
33 Helps for Reps. and Dems.
34 Droop
37 Part 3 of the comment
41 Turquoise, e.g.
42 Electric unit
43 Bucolic
44 Regal term of address
45 It has a wheel on its heel
47 Part 4 of the comment
51 Autumn tool
54 Prefix with culture
55 Future fish
56 Traitor Aldrich
57 Mild cigar
59 End of the comment
61 More than miffed
62 Less cordial
63 Architectural prefix
64 Utopias
65 Heals
66 Swindle

DOWN

1 Jazz pianist Ahmad ___
2 Mistreat
3 Negative attitude
4 Origin of some PBS series
5 Takes another mate
6 "Twelfth Night" countess
7 Giant
8 Scornful cry
9 N.B.A.'s Unseld
10 Get
11 Othello's people
12 ___ Gay
13 Popular stocking
18 Positioned
25 Undiluted
26 Delineate
27 Pulpits
29 Poet Plath
31 "Understand?"
32 Suffix with ethyl
33 Poker win
34 In a steady flow
35 Palindromic exclamation
36 Set
38 Ripped
39 Wasn't colorfast
40 Beat in a relay
44 Slalom trail
45 Easy winner
46 Fell in a faint, with "over"
47 Store
48 Gave the eye
49 Speechify
50 Moment
52 Author Ken
53 Bar, at the bar
58 Photo ___ (campaign events)
59 Pep
60 April initials

506 by William S. Cotter

ACROSS

1 Soup order
4 Is afflicted with
7 Long-range weapons
12 Genetic letters
13 ___ National Accelerator Laboratory
15 Ultimate object
16 Cases for a zoo vet?
18 Popular Handel composition
19 Whence the phrase "God save the King"
20 Conductor Anderson et al.
22 Start of a Caesar quote
23 More: Prefix
24 Scottish headwarmer
27 Bosnian ___
28 Scottish explorer John
29 Pennsylvania's ___ Mountains
31 Dress
34 Ultraviolet ray absorber
35 Lamenting one
37 Corn oil brand
39 Man of La Mancha
40 Beer mug with a hinged lid
42 Mitigate
44 Soph., jr. and sr.
45 Back talk
49 Chatter
50 Parts of a Road & Track course
52 Dead duck
53 Poison remedy
55 Without much trouble
56 A Curie
58 Phone a rock group?
60 "Island of the Blue Dolphins" author Scott
61 La Scala production
62 Literary compilation
63 Portends
64 Proteus' domain
65 Prefix with fuel

DOWN

1 N.A.A.C.P. magazine, with "The"
2 Loosen, as a corset
3 Of the center of the hand
4 Recover
5 Tentacle
6 Punier
7 Summer problem for Eskimos?
8 Bluesman Robert
9 Pub seat
10 Cold war plane
11 Highway caution
13 Run
14 "That explains it"
17 Rheumatisms
21 Castigate
23 Poker holdings
25 Sigmund's daughter
26 Skiing gold medalist Tommy
28 Itinerary abbr.
30 McKinley's assassin
32 Fisherman's catch?
33 Arabian noblemen
35 "___ pin . . ."
36 Brilliant
38 Show stoppers?
39 Foxy
41 Ophthalmologists' equipment
43 Pres. advisory group
46 Old Colt Johnny
47 Grand theft, for example
48 Spider
51 Former Cincinnati Red Chris
52 Area under Arafat's control
54 Stack
55 Biblical scribe
56 Kind of rule
57 Stir
59 The end

507   by Rand H. Burns

ACROSS
1 Person in a cast
8 Salts
15 Product of the mountains of Italy
16 One who can't get a seat
17 Obsolescent symbol
19 Head lock
20 Press
21 Embattled funding org.
22 Caesar's sidekick
24 Kin of "-kin"
25 Fax button
26 High-tensile steel product
29 Tikal dwellers
30 Show fallibility
31 Inability to smell
33 Colorful pottery
36 It's usually inadmissible
40 Arctic sheet
42 Indiana humorist
43 Byrd book
46 Entry mode for full gainers
49 Yap
50 Overseas relative
51 Chronicle
52 "Take On Me" pop trio
53 Prefix with surgery or transmitter
55 Blown-up area
58 Snug joint
61 Like some alkaloids
62 Subject of Newton's first law
63 Lot
64 Catholicon

DOWN
1 Zwei cubed
2 Burn
3 It gets punched
4 Garlic variety
5 Menuhin's mentor
6 Gibr., for one
7 Famous twins' birthplace
8 Two-tone oxford
9 Dinsmore of children's literature
10 One of seven big things
11 One of seven small things
12 ___ Islands (Scapa Flow locale)
13 PbS
14 Slammin' Sammy's family
18 Prefix with surgery or transmitter
23 Informed
25 Mosel tributary
26 A head
27 Dudgeon
28 Futility
29 War stat
32 Fulfills
34 Subtle signal
35 Crack
37 Site of Florida's first golf course
38 Deuce followers
39 Nonetheless
41 Absorb
43 Died down
44 City in Kipling's "Kim"
45 Arboreal apes
47 Like Snow White, vis-à-vis the Queen
48 Bypass
50 Link
53 Ormandy's successor in Philadelphia
54 Lyrical
56 Base
57 Shade of blue
59 Fetched
60 Brindled beast

508   by Randolph Ross

ACROSS
1 Like Job
8 Bob or beehive
14 Leisurely musical pieces
15 Decrees
17 Pentagon advocate?
19 Parlor piece
20 Ex-Knick coach Jackson
21 Author of "Life in London"
22 Heart of France
24 Part
25 Visit Robert Reich?
31 Medical apprentice
32 Ease
37 Blue "Yellow Submarine" characters
38 Revised
40 Ancient beginning
41 Off course
42 Foggy Bottom boat?
46 Narc's collar
50 "Since ___ Have You"
51 Not for
52 Juan's uncle
53 Pescadores neighbor
59 Reno's piano practice?
62 Tympanic membrane
63 Guides, in a way
64 Brews tea
65 Menu listings

DOWN
1 Falsifies accounts
2 Chick ender
3 White House heavyweight
4 Beach Boys' "___ Around"
5 "___ kleine Nachtmusik"
6 Titan tip
7 Poetic monogram
8 Spa installation
9 Maestro Toscanini
10 Words often exchanged
11 Twice as unlikely
12 Down Under dog
13 "Love Story" star
16 January 1 song ending
18 Riding the waves
23 Bullfight cries
25 Walk with difficulty
26 Unwanted classification, once
27 Printing style: Abbr.
28 Hawaiian state bird
29 Kingston and others
30 Fee schedule
33 Friend of Ernie
34 Sills solo
35 Caterpillar construction
36 Advantage
38 Calling company
39 Intersection maneuver
43 Asks for a loan
44 They trip up foreigners
45 Magician's sound effect
46 First or home, e.g.
47 Last of the Mohicans
48 Genesis
49 Spanish squiggle
54 ___ were (so to speak)
55 Ovid's way
56 Oenologist's interest
57 Entr'___
58 Costner character
60 Prior, to Prior
61 G.I. ___

ACROSS
1 Actress Winger
6 Park, in Monopoly
11 "Honest" fellow
14 Where Gauguin visited van Gogh
15 Funnyman O'Brien
16 Bloodshot
17 "Cheers!" in Cherbourg?
19 Chang's Siamese twin
20 Brand of lemon-flavored drink
21 Daydream
23 Koch and Wynn
24 Pampering, for short
26 It's heard in a herd
27 Garibaldi in Genoa?
33 Pickle
36 Paparazzi prey
37 Avaricious one
38 October gem
40 Beam fastener
42 1963 Oscar winner
43 Arose
45 Danger
47 Hang in the breeze
48 Madrid's equivalent of a Texas university?
50 Performance
51 Had lunch
52 Montana and Moon, in brief
55 Gladstone rival
60 Real
62 "Poppycock!"
63 Pre-photo pronouncement in Geneva?
65 Some
66 Skirmish
67 "Dallas" Miss
68 Simonize
69 Classic theater name
70 4-Down again

DOWN
1 Peri opera
2 Made a boner
3 Post-sneeze word
4 Take money for a spare room
5 Loner
6 Agt.'s share
7 Creator of Lorelei Lee
8 Med. subj.
9 Winter melon
10 Competitor
11 Vicinity
12 Early German carmaker
13 Barely beat, with "out"
18 Woman's top
22 Cartoonist Wilson
25 Islamic leader
28 Crowbar
29 Portugal and its neighbor
30 Barely managed, with "out"
31 Raise
32 Alternative to Charles de Gaulle
33 Clinton's runs
34 Each
35 First name in spying
39 Moon-based
41 Alternative to Certs
44 "Desmoiselles d'Avignon" artist
46 Bloodletting practitioner
49 Potted
52 Put down
53 Count in music
54 Winter weather
55 Extract
56 New Rochelle college
57 Charon's domain
58 Kind of beer
59 Relationship words
61 Prefix with play or scope
64 Favorite relative in politics?

ACROSS
1 Rustic lodging, informally
6 The Fighting Tigers: Abbr.
9 Bust
14 Make ___ out of (contradict)
15 Rustic lodging
16 ". . . partridge in ___ tree"
17 "Alone" composer Brown
18 To catch a thief
19 Yo-Yo string?
20 With 53-Across, 1940 Reagan film
23 Reagan TV series
27 Singer Tucker and others
28 Language suffix
29 On the Baltic
30 Opposite of nord
31 Courage
33 Ultrasound is one
34 Part of NASA: Abbr.
35 ___ homo
38 Part of The Shadow's attire
41 Yellowish red
43 Old hand
46 Colorado Indians
47 TV frequency
48 Used a blender
50 Much-maligned Reagan flick
53 See 20-Across
54 Contradict
56 Certain savings, for short
57 Oil-well capper Red ___
60 With no letup
61 French seasoning
62 One of the Fab Four
63 Piece of pie
64 N.F.L. scores
65 ___ Hall (South Orange school)

DOWN
1 Prohibit
2 ___ carte
3 ___ Nora Charles ("Thin Man" pair)
4 Delicate
5 Uproar
6 Start of a tax form
7 Angry dog
8 Dim the spirits of
9 Exuding kitsch
10 Scheduling break
11 Dismissal
12 "My gal"
13 Spanish gold
21 Family room piece
22 Middling mark
23 Drunk's affliction
24 ___ Claire, Wis.
25 Affirmation
26 Took a load off
32 Scientific charlatan
34 A little bird
36 Isle of song
37 Pullman units
38 ___ games (Reagan announcing job)
39 Lunched
40 Biked
42 Put up for sale
43 Kind of race
44 ___-de-chaussée
45 Prefix with meter
47 Thurman of "Johnny Be Good"
49 Tour assistant
51 ___ France
52 Some exams
54 Arc
55 Opposite of WSW
58 Goodman's "When ___ A-Dreamin' "
59 Diminutive Reagan

511 by Bryant White

ACROSS

1 Beelike
6 Longtime record label
9 Funny Anne
14 Popovich or Gagarin, e.g.
16 Michaelmas daisy
17 Sandwich devotees?
19 Greek vowels
20 Expressed wonder
21 Singapore's Kuan Yew ___
22 Cube with 21 spots
23 Passeport info
25 Du Maurier's "Jamaica ___"
26 Year in the reign of Pius I
28 Perfect
31 Sum of one's virtues, to the Greeks
33 Palmer of "Twin Peaks"
35 Stravinsky and others
36 Sandwich fit for royalty?
38 British P.M., 1970–74
39 "Aminta" poet
40 Is left undecided
41 Hemingway moniker
42 In ___ (following)
45 Shaver
46 One vote
48 Grosbeak's beak
50 Fred Astaire's daughter
51 Laundromat appliance
55 To ___
56 Chicken sandwich?
60 Mounted lancer
61 Synthetic rubber
62 Hypothesize
63 Lion's ___
64 They're more than rare

DOWN

1 Hurt
2 Graceful, in a way
3 Acre's acres?
4 Freeman Gosden radio role
5 "Move it!"
6 ___ avis
7 Astrological point
8 Villa Albani statue in Rome
9 Plan
10 It's psychic
11 Painting locales
12 Sublets
13 Lupin of detective fiction
15 Eggy quaff
18 Familiar vow
24 Balthazar, e.g.
27 Work translated by Chapman
28 The "H" of W. H. Auden
29 Spanish Main cargo
30 Issue of 1993
32 Obedient helper
34 Nervous
35 Ingrid in "Casablanca"
36 Actresses Kay and Suzy
37 Shako, for one
38 Final throw
40 Emphasize
41 Diagrammed
43 Punctual
44 Freud, e.g.
47 Relative of Geo. or Chas.
49 Parts of boilermakers
52 Kind of tide
53 Statesman of 3-Down
54 Want ad abbr.
55 Elvis ___ Presley
57 My ___
58 Minn. neighbor
59 From ___ izzard

512 by Harvey Estes

ACROSS

1 Friendly spirit
7 Promising places
13 Panicky
15 China cabinet display
17 Montmartre painter
18 Dunderhead
19 Not crisp
20 Game without losers
22 Greene of "Bonanza"
23 On one's ___
24 Chesterfields
26 Latvia's capital
27 Traveler's rest
28 Headed a committee
30 Turner of channels
31 Single-masted vessel
33 Window ornamentation
35 Northern seabird
36 Actress Farrow
37 Fracases
41 Fort Knox holding
45 Not just any
46 Ear pleaser
48 One abroad
49 Hip-hop songs
51 Basketball defense
52 Taunts
53 Acrylic fiber
55 W.W. II battle site, for short
56 Unwelcome reflection
57 Kudos
59 Handout
61 Feeling
62 Danced last in Paris?
63 Dracula killers
64 Council chiefs

DOWN

1 That's a lye!
2 Pennsylvania city
3 "Madame X" painter
4 Bluenoses
5 Dickens's Little ___
6 Electrical unit
7 Fundamentally
8 Actress Thompson
9 Dark and handsome companion
10 Regarding
11 New draft
12 Shoulder-launched missile
14 Perform punctiliously
16 High school sweetheart
21 The Beatles' "___ Fell"
24 Radical reorganization
25 Parental talks
28 Two-door
29 Many a newspaper
32 Call for a shepherd
34 Blackguard
37 Barbers' needs
38 "Georgia on My Mind" singer
39 Change the flora
40 Lemon-lime drinks
41 Become lax
42 Bête noire
43 More sore
44 Sows anew
47 Go chop-chop?
50 Master of marches
52 Nostalgic poem
54 Sask. neighbor
56 Actress Rowlands
58 Follower's tail
60 Butt

513 by Manny Nosowsky

ACROSS

1 One often called on for answers
12 One for the road
15 Pointedly punctuated
16 Atty.'s assn.
17 Monitor for 12-Across
18 Throw
19 Reddish-brown horses
20 Ship's peril
22 Malta or Martinique: Abbr.
23 Food cooker
24 Part of the plot?
25 Current status
28 Magnetic attraction
30 Get ___ of (see)
31 Fourth Spanish letter
32 Jalopy
33 Graceful and slim
34 Ministry, perhaps
36 Androgen, e.g.
37 Sign up
38 Jamie of "M*A*S*H"
39 Holiday serving
40 Union targets
41 Long dress
42 End of a 1/1 song
43 All dried up
44 Forest god
45 Jazz grp.
47 1980's United Nations name
49 Roman statesman Marcus Vipsanius ___
53 Uncover, poetically
54 Persian
56 Some advice
57 Certain brother
58 Vane direction
59 Agree

DOWN

1 ___ Millay of "Red River"
2 Big showcase
3 Maple genus
4 Priest
5 Charon's destination
6 Skin softener
7 ___ horn (shofar)
8 Fr. holy one
9 Sleeping ___
10 At attention
11 Phoenician city
12 The British seized it in 1795
13 Oddity
14 The brink
21 Cotton machine
23 Detonate
25 9 on a hotel phone, e.g.
26 Run into
27 "Don't You Know" singer
29 Unprestigious publication
30 Say it's so
32 Leak indicator
33 Western attire
35 Subject of media law
36 Presidential instrument
38 Geisha's accessory
41 Thalassic
42 Reach by ship
44 Gay ___
46 Leaflike part
48 Easy questions
49 One of the Gibb brothers
50 ___-dieu
51 Brawnless
52 Palindromist Jon
55 Shoe width

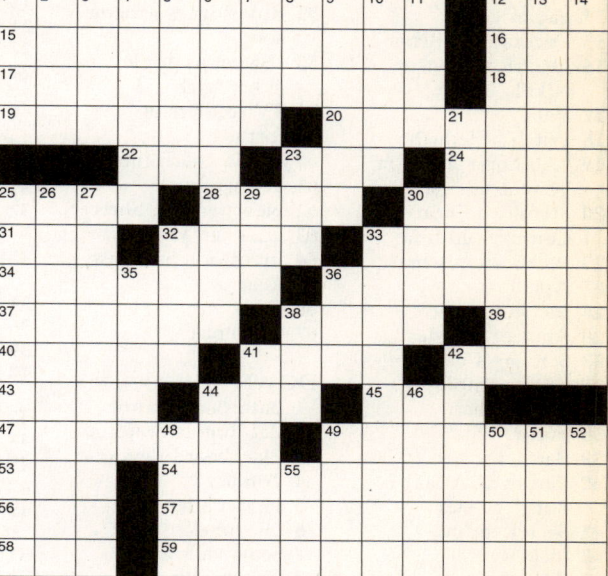

514 by Sidney L. Robbins

ACROSS

1 I.B.M. rival
6 How a deer might attend a party?
10 Info
14 Unobstructed
15 Peru's capital
16 Historic periods
17 Seaside aerialist
19 Give orders
20 Pass receivers
21 Repair
22 Movie pooch
23 Mata Hari, e.g.
24 Hold in high regard
26 Morality
30 Judge Ito
32 Miss Morgenstern of 70's TV
33 "If You Knew ___, Like . . ." (1925 hit)
34 Ft. Worth campus
37 Unburden oneself
40 German spa
41 "Yours ___" (letter closing)
42 Two under par
43 Smiles broadly
44 Lovers' meetings
45 B flat equivalent
48 Wall Street order
49 Booty
50 Starman
53 Birthday party necessity
57 Not keep a secret
58 Loiter
60 Architect Saarinen
61 Without repetition
62 Mr. Burr
63 Water whirl
64 Card game for three
65 Rio de la ___

DOWN

1 Yearn
2 Blueprint
3 Remain unsettled
4 Stays behind
5 Energy unit
6 Like algae
7 Ebb, e.g.
8 "You said it, brother!"
9 Corsage flower
10 Pre-election event
11 Came up
12 Discernment
13 Silkmaking region
18 Baby holders
23 Strew about
25 Stage background
26 Gardner of mysteries
27 Those characters
28 Romantic attraction, slangily
29 Uganda's Amin
30 Soothes
31 Wan
33 Rundown area
34 Clothes
35 Close-knit religious group
36 Salt Lake City athletes
38 Algonquian group
39 Jovial
43 Diamond helper
44 ___ fish sandwich
45 "Virginia Woolf" playwright
46 Like shoes
47 Squirrel away
48 Sire, biblically
51 Tall and thin
52 Early Peruvian
53 Newcastle's pride
54 Atmosphere
55 Shoelace problem
56 Author Ferber
59 Some MTV music

515 by Gregory E. Paul

ACROSS

1 Tijuana's locale, informally
5 Pro ___ (proportionately)
9 Amount bet
14 Pagan god
15 Decorative pitcher
16 Electrical pioneer Nikola
17 Valley
18 Witch's blemish
19 "All hope abandon, ye who ___ here!"
20 Home addition
21 Century-old time
23 Polk's successor
25 Auction
26 McGuffey book
29 Kind of measles
33 Scrooge's visitor
35 Circus employee
37 Sooner than
38 Furor
39 Bates, for one
40 Barbra's "A Star Is Born" co-star
41 Secret ending
42 Jockey rival
43 Buenos ___
44 Fright
46 Exquisite
48 Ancient land east of the Tigris
50 Prepared, as tomatoes
53 Roy Rogers's theme song
58 "Sweet as apple cider" girl
59 TV soldiers of fortune
60 N.F.L. coach Jim
61 Tennis score
62 Newswoman Shriver
63 ___ even keel
64 Investor's purchase
65 Rear
66 Darn
67 Influence

DOWN

1 Bathroom fixture
2 ___ Rogers St. Johns
3 Blackbeard flew one
4 Totality
5 Finder's fee
6 "Begone!"
7 Sea swallow
8 Cager Gilmore
9 Three Rivers Stadium player
10 Campground denizen
11 ___ spumante
12 Swiss painter
13 Roasting items
21 One with kids
22 Conrad of "The Kiss"
24 ___ majesté
27 Thames town
28 Appraised
30 Lehár operetta, with "The"
31 Indy 500's Luyendyk
32 Eliot of "The Untouchables"
33 It's stuck in beach sandals
34 Contain
36 Miniplateau
39 Corday's victim
40 Pass, as a forged check
42 Francis of Assisi, e.g.
43 Aardvark's meal
45 Fix
47 Hispaniola, e.g.
49 1983 Michael Keaton film
51 Minneapolis suburb
52 Beaut
53 Easter dinners
54 Rat-___
55 Balzac's "Le ___ Goriot"
56 Tiptop
57 Kurdish home
61 Stomach muscles, for short

516 by David J. Kahn

ACROSS

1 Former Toyota model
6 Grenades, e.g.
10 This may be tiled
14 Church recesses
15 Roaster's place?
16 Humorist Bombeck
17 "Romeo and Juliet" event
18 Slight trace
20 Gaping, as the mouth
22 Dizziness
23 Bat wood
24 Indulge, in a way
26 Type of servitude
29 1 + 1 = 3, for example
33 Noted name in puppetry
35 Buzzer
36 Theme of this puzzle
43 Birds ___ feather
44 Woody vine
45 Trial conference
50 Whole lot of apples
54 Marilyn role
56 Transfer ___
57 Actress De Mornay
59 Most lucid
62 Unfavorably known
64 Eastern princess
65 Swear
66 Spider nests
67 Trimming tools
68 Cross products
69 Narrow valley
70 Is not allowed to, for short

DOWN

1 Minor despot
2 Revolt
3 Analysis start
4 Breathing spell
5 Fictional wirehair
6 Source of TV revenue
7 Purple color
8 Chintzy ones
9 Fish-eating hawk
10 Enumerate
11 Not a copy: Abbr.
12 Melville classic
13 Cooler
19 "I'd consider ___ honor"
21 Subject for Aristotle
25 ___ Beach, Fla.
27 Brokaw's network
28 "Wonderful!"
30 Quick score in baseball
31 "I didn't know that!"
32 Approval
34 M—CCCL
36 Santa's laughs
37 "___ Loved You" ("Carousel" hit)
38 Bit
39 Bad check
40 1960's single-season home-run king
41 United
42 Churchill symbol
46 Jostles
47 Literally, farmer
48 Following a curve
49 Flinch
51 Violent agitation
52 Hidden
53 Fashion maven's quest
55 Honors word
57 Meander
58 ___ collar
60 Composer Khachaturian
61 Zilch
62 Be off guard
63 Break a Commandment

517 by A.J. Santora

ACROSS

1 Relay stick
6 Like bad news
10 Working hard
14 Like a lot
15 Sub ___
16 Writer Jaffe
17 Five-and-ten-cent store chain
19 Golf club
20 Dined
21 Chop ___
22 "The Thrill Is Gone" bluesman
24 "Amazing Grace," e.g.
25 Queen of the heavens
26 Jerk: Var.
29 Boyfriend
31 ___ Israel (Hebrew homeland)
35 Taken care of
37 All the way
39 Kilmer of "Batman Forever"
40 "Now We Are Six" author
42 F.D.R.'s successor
43 Edmonton resident
45 Physicist Fermi
47 Large African lake
48 Front's opposite
50 Set ___ on (limit)
51 Ridicule
53 Track tipster
55 Popular catalog company
58 Has ___ good authority
59 Worthless amount
62 Gentleman's title
63 "1 × 1" poet
66 "Hear no ___ . . ."
67 ___ College, N.C.
68 Start of a Dickens title
69 Appraise
70 See 26-Down
71 Slangy refusals

DOWN

1 Mexicali area
2 Kind of gen.
3 Richness
4 Tram cargo
5 Informative
6 Novelist Graham
7 Actor Calhoun
8 Medit. land
9 God willing
10 Dakota Indian
11 Singer Amos
12 Apprised of
13 Distinctive taste
18 Provisions provider, around a harbor
23 German port
24 Sweetie
25 Throw
26 With 70-Across, a whodunit writer
27 Mary of TV's "Peter Loves Mary"
28 Peach ___
30 "That's ___ how-do-you-do!"
32 Body of values
33 Puccini opera
34 Rock group that sang "Tush"
36 1943 U.S. victory site
38 Like early schoolhouses
41 Wal-___
44 Actress Getty
46 Squealer
49 Adjust, as in harmony
52 The Temptations' "All ___"
54 Frighten
55 Lecher's look
56 Kilauea flow
57 Fergie, for one
58 Symbol
59 Easy task
60 Stare
61 Applies
64 Yale student
65 "Was ___ blame?"

518 by Cathy Millhauser

ACROSS

1 Went with the flow
6 Chicken pox symptom
10 Nellie Melba, e.g.
14 Harmony
15 Rightful
16 Left agape
17 Old wheels of Wisconsin?
20 Head out of port
21 Royal Scots
22 Synthesizer inventor
24 "Hail to the Chief" chief
25 Mescal and others
29 Prefix with polar
32 Throwing out a moldy vegetable, e.g.?
38 Room at the Alhambra
39 Curtain sheer
40 Caliph who founded Cairo
42 Campaign slogan of 1856?
45 Loafing
46 "Midnight Cowboy" role
47 1982 Disney film
50 As soon as
53 Poulard
56 Sudden swell
61 Why the hot dog vendor made the grade?
63 Commercial endorsement person, maybe
64 "Lou Grant" paper, with "The"
65 Like some kitchens
66 Biblical miracles site
67 Lummox's cry
68 Alexander, once of "60 Minutes"

DOWN

1 Makes it
2 Hungarian patriot ___ Nagy
3 Reduced fare
4 Tour de France times
5 Vigorous
6 Fascist aviator Balbo
7 Sample
8 Quart quartet
9 Race part
10 Senegal's capital
11 Au courant
12 "I Love Lucy" name
13 TV's Byrnes and Hall
18 Book jacket item
19 Noted matchmaker
23 1989 NASA launch
25 "All in the Family" network
26 Kyrgyzstan's ___ Mountains
27 Branch Davidians, e.g.
28 Society affairs
30 ___ fides (bad faith)
31 Uncle Remus term of address
33 "Heroides" writer
34 Laze
35 Spanish castanet dance
36 Bleep
37 Sounds of impact
41 Model T contemporary
43 Some stoles
44 Shifts
47 Bara, the Vamp
48 Wisconsin college
49 City SSE of Gainesville
51 Anesthetizes
52 Computer center, for short
53 Smart
54 "___ perpetua" (Idaho's motto)
55 "Camelot" Lancelot Franco ___
57 Dixie National Forest site
58 Pro ___
59 Beam
60 Actress Best
62 Brief swim

519 by Manny Nosowsky

ACROSS

1 Taking care of business
16 Ones with lots of inventory
17 Fitting companions
18 ___-cone
19 Open-ended cigar
20 O.T. book
21 Insulting remark
22 Camera diaphragm
24 Lovelace's "To ___, From Prison"
27 Chekhov and Bruckner
31 "___ Theme" (1965 tune)
32 Brought to the surface
35 Like-not link
36 Seeing: Prefix
37 Tabouli holder
38 Mark's cry
40 Martini go-with
41 Nomads' pads
42 Early German
43 Okinawan port
45 "Quiet," to Shakespeare
46 Office equipment, for short
49 One in a hundred
51 One way to go
54 50's–60's ABC series
57 "Seeds in a dry pod, tick, tick, tick" writer
58 Goes on and on, in a way

DOWN

1 Vase occupants
2 80's hit "The Heat ___"
3 Concern for Claudius
4 Bug killer
5 Christmas tree trimming
6 Daniel Webster College site
7 "The Female Eunuch" author
8 Autocrat
9 Capital on the Red River
10 "The Gilded One" of myth
11 Word with trend or table
12 Philosopher Lao-___
13 Hawks' home court, with "The"
14 Old cars
15 Italian resort city
21 Give an edge
23 Leave for just a while
24 Leaning
25 Coffee-and-milk order
26 Go as a throng
28 Keats was one
29 Loony
30 Cape Trafalgar site
32 Seventh-century year
33 Have some remorse
34 Magic forest inhabitant
36 1985 #1 song
39 Promos
40 Invigorate
42 "Alas!"
44 Put in a chip, perhaps
45 Leaf opening
46 Roman commoner
47 Transfer, as property
48 It's a long story
50 Suit to ___
51 Maintain
52 Kind of pronoun: Abbr.
53 Talk of the Gaelic
55 Wine storer
56 ___ zed

520 by Rich Norris

ACROSS

1 Like some mountain condos
10 Feline, often
15 Children's collectible
16 Acid type
17 Kind of gland
18 Gift giver
19 Shirt size: Abbr.
20 Imperfection
21 Soundly defeated
22 Ampule
24 Imbeciles
26 Brahms's "___ Rhapsody"
27 Tedium
29 Actor Robert
30 Suture material
31 Cream ___
33 Empowerment term
35 Notice
36 Clothing store employee
38 Puts up
40 Part of the Trinity, with "the"
41 Foreman foe
42 Rocket
43 Sister of Ares
45 Bring in
47 Leaves unceremoniously
51 Beatrice d'___ (fabled beauty)
52 Ruhr city
54 Phone lead-in
55 By and large
57 Seeks favor with
59 Regal : Buick :: Wolverine : ___
60 Shirk duties, slangily
61 Treacherous
63 "Grand" sight
64 Nervous
65 Upright
66 Drink made with crème de cacao

DOWN

1 High time
2 Announce with ceremony
3 Incan, e.g.
4 Promising words
5 Game factor
6 Shoot
7 Plans of a kind
8 Political symbol
9 Survey
10 El ___
11 Some kitchen appliances
12 Captain's offering
13 Qualifies
14 Albemarle Sound island
21 "Cape Fear" star
23 Driving desire
25 They're often in the field
28 Bit
32 Sci-fi writer Lester ___
34 Trading unit, once
36 Derelict
37 Fraternity man
39 Heart
40 "It ___ me . . ."
44 Forwarded
46 In addition
48 Host
49 Request starter
50 Jayhawk rival
53 Benefit of some mail-order shopping
56 Provide
58 ___ spell (relax)
61 Small inlet
62 Football Hall-of-Famer Ford

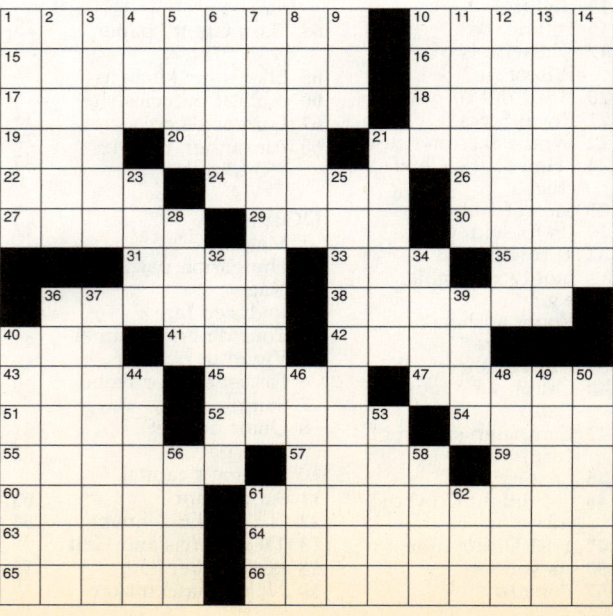

by A.J. Santora

ACROSS
1 Ace depository
7 Peter Lorre typecast
13 In no hurry to buy
15 Inexpensive
16 Table spread
17 Humiliate
18 Twice-told
19 Fairy tale kid
22 Hoodwink
26 Mosaic piece
28 ___-per-view
29 University of Maine town
31 Jazz star, with 36-Down
34 Dialing for dollars?
37 Slums Mother
38 Heavy bundles
39 Einstein's birthplace
40 Indy 500 occurrence
44 Humdrum
46 Vodka cocktail
49 Coach Holtz of Notre Dame
50 "All systems ___"
52 Survey
53 Spying on who's buying?
59 Alternatives to malls
60 "Marriage is ___": Cervantes
61 Saint-Tropez is one

DOWN
1 Makes confetti
2 Company trademark
3 Clean water agcy.
4 Prefix with glottis or gram
5 Pinot ou Chardonnay
6 Downstairs: Fr.
7 For beginners
8 Armored god
9 Like many football stadiums
10 Scheduled
11 Reception site
12 N.Y. summer time
13 Chambre
14 Kotter of 70's TV
15 Start, as a computer
19 Start of a toast
20 Spray, perhaps
21 Grandma
23 Knowing about
24 Bit of distress
25 Goggle
27 Fish entree
30 Sun or moon
31 Bear riot
32 "This is only ___"
33 Not discounted
34 ___ off (scold)
35 Anecdotal Bombeck
36 See 31-Across
37 Butter container
41 Writer at Orchard House
42 Guffaws
43 ___ out (ignore)
45 "It ___ Be You" (Kahn-Jones hit)
46 Romance or sci-fi, e.g.
47 Pop music's ___ Pop
48 Drive
51 Bravo and Grande
52 Ending with spin or speed
53 Art deg.
54 Golfer Woosnam
55 Sgt., for one
56 Color
57 U.F.O. occupants
58 ___-mo (replay technique)

by Harvey Estes

ACROSS
1 Zubin with a baton
6 Old streetlight
13 Daley and others
14 Gravel-voiced actress
15 Iron shortage
16 Commit
17 Just the highlights
18 Slammin' Sam
19 Trendy
20 Getting better, as wine: Var.
22 Up to now
24 Size up
26 Paints amateurishly
28 Almost shut
32 Kind of symbol: Abbr.
33 One whom Jesus healed
34 Rodeo rope
35 Dashboard reading, for short
36 Leave the pier
38 Acquire
39 Ask on one's knees
41 Had
42 Short lunch order
43 Belgrade dweller
44 In abeyance
45 Sciences' partner
46 Tooth
48 Comfort
50 Probe
53 Some pads
55 Accident mementos
58 Serves a sentence
60 Byrnes of "77 Sunset Strip"
61 Brown paint, e.g.
62 Six-footer?
63 Resort locale
64 Newspaper section

DOWN
1 Lion's pride?
2 It's hard to miss
3 Respect
4 Nonsense
5 Simile center
6 Comic Kaplan
7 Assuages
8 Picture with its own frame
9 Wheel bolt holder
10 King of comedy
11 Part of a pair
12 Sound of relief
13 Scuff up
14 It's hard to say
18 Fastens with a pop
21 "I have no ___!"
23 ___ chi ch'uan
24 Tail ends
25 Temptation for Atalanta
27 1991 American Conference champs
29 It's hard
30 Listing
31 Sounds off
33 Digital-watch readout: Abbr.
34 Postal letters
37 Have a hunch
40 1970 Jackson 5 hit
44 Looking while lusting
45 Waylay
47 Time and again
49 In unison
50 Tots up
51 Afternoon TV fare
52 Lifetime achievement Oscar winner Deborah
54 Mingo portrayer
56 Puerto ___
57 Play place
59 Take part in a biathlon
60 Kipling novel

523 by Fred Piscop

ACROSS

1 ___ and hounds (outdoor game)
5 Section of the brain
9 Palindromic name in pop music
13 Mideast carrier
14 Flower part
15 Regrets
16 MANTLE
19 Bars
20 Kind of bed
21 Hubbub
22 Olympus queen
23 RUTH
30 Indian princess
31 Offended
32 Street sign abbr.
33 "Ars Amatoria" author
34 Manages, as for oneself
35 Signaled
36 Command to Rover
37 Absorbed by
38 Prefix with dollars
39 AARON
43 With eyes and ears open
44 Antipollution grp.
45 St. Francis's home
48 Confirming
53 JACKSON
55 British P.M. ___ Douglas-Home
56 Jerks' works
57 Westernmost Aleutian
58 Ritzy
59 Word repeated before "1, 2, 3"
60 Nikita's no

DOWN

1 Fab Four flick
2 Controversial orchard spray
3 Zany Martha
4 Dignified
5 Hightailed it
6 ___ out (withdraws)
7 Cry from Scrooge
8 Euclid's grand work
9 Ark's terminus
10 Pat baby on the back
11 One of Alcott's little women
12 Sickly, as a complexion
14 "___ a gun!"
17 Color anew
18 Prefix with dollars
22 ___ hearing
23 One of a road crew
24 Architect Jones
25 Pioneer of the twist
26 Reach in total
27 ___ couture
28 Tinker-Chance link
29 Second draft, informally
30 L.B.J. son-in-law
34 Most passionate
35 ___ section
38 Easy catch
40 Jerk
41 Greasy-spoon fare
42 Southwestern formations
45 P.D.Q.
46 One-man band
47 Courts
48 No ifs, ___ or buts
49 Command to Tabby
50 ___-bitty
51 N.B.A.'s Thurmond
52 Flood
54 Ebbets Field's Preacher

524 by Daniel R. Stark

ACROSS

1 It's no loss
10 Grouch
14 Where Croesus's kingdom was
15 Cellular ___
16 Rabelais's amiable giant
17 Monks' hour when psalms are recited
18 One skilled in match play
19 Kind of jumper
20 "Brooklyn Bridge" actress Aquino
21 Hint
22 Calls upon
26 One of the Dionnes
27 Skirt style
28 Bossed
32 Rembrandt's "The Noble ___"
33 Bridge marker
34 Thin necktie
35 Quasimodo's love
37 Answer a charge
38 "I, Claudius" attire
39 Cal State branch site
40 Alley Oop and Fred Flintstone
43 Hefner's color?
44 "O tempora! ___!": Cicero
45 Inclined
50 Port near Hong Kong
51 Plantation crop
52 1985 film "___ Dancing!"
53 Assume
54 Popular fashion magazine
55 Dostoyevsky novel, with "The"

DOWN

1 Hero's tale
2 Peter or Nicholas
3 Melodies
4 Titicaca, por ejemplo
5 Flow (from)
6 Pharmacists' measures
7 Overeager
8 Race track figure
9 Baseball stat
10 Fickle
11 It makes you blush
12 Inca empire locale
13 Assail
15 Connect
19 Marble worker's tool
21 Site of a Margaret Mead study
22 Flower holder
23 Troubles
24 "Anna and the King of ___"
25 Dyed-in-the-wool
26 Cheese coatings
28 "Blowin' in the Wind" singer
29 Digits
30 Dash
31 Extinct bird
33 Leafs
36 Lover boys
37 Take steps
39 Railroad flares
40 Monte Cristo title
41 Menotti's "___ and the Night Visitors"
42 Outspoken
43 Does
45 Producer De Laurentiis
46 Picks, with "for"
47 Hot springs
48 Actress Sommer
49 Act
51 Kind of tent

ACROSS

1 Nimble
7 Warbler James
11 Ammo
14 Shed
15 Glad rags
16 A month of Sundays
17 Start of a question
19 Murmur
20 Sprinkle
21 Stood by, as an alibi
23 Sleeve
26 It's a long story
28 Returned
29 Meter ___
31 Part 2 of the question
33 39th Veep
35 Bottle size
36 Effectiveness
37 Part 3 of the question
38 An Allen
42 Stringency
44 Amusement park feature
45 Part 4 of the question
50 Constantly
51 Takes advantage (of)
52 1937 Tommy Dorsey hit
54 Purpose

55 Choral piece
57 "Otello" baritone
59 Upset
60 End of the question
65 You can spend it in Romania
66 Solar deity
67 Uneasy
68 W.W. II craft
69 Voters' choices
70 ___ d'état (for the good of the country): Fr.

DOWN

1 TV's Bundy and others
2 ___ gratias
3 Encouraging word
4 ___ about (legalistic phrase)
5 "___ a dark and stormy . . ."
6 Biblical adversary of Nehemiah
7 Bloke
8 Little ones
9 Used the most
10 Humans on flying saucers, e.g.

11 Crook a finger at
12 It covers little piggies
13 Head wraps
18 Actress Swenson
22 Victor's laugh
23 Latin I word
24 Fad
25 First word of "The Battle Hymn of the Republic"
27 Wing feature
30 Lion locale
32 On
34 Triple Crown winner in '41
37 Meshech prince, in the Bible
39 Swarm
40 Yemen port
41 One who's not in
43 Develop slowly
45 Betty Joan Perske, familiarly
46 Weasels out of
47 Disperse, as a search party
48 Kind of cloth
49 Orange or lemon, e.g.
53 Rocket stage
56 Cruising

58 "You're the ___ Care For"
61 ___ and outs
62 Sports scores, for short

63 Kind of mania
64 Cave

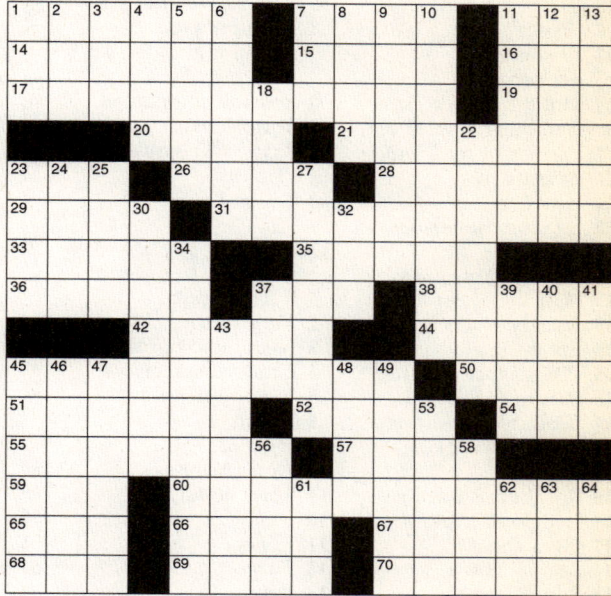

ACROSS

1 Pizarro victim
5 ___ and dangerous
10 Rights org. estab. 1960
14 One who's socially challenged
15 With 4-Down, M.L.K. declaration of 8/28/63
16 Pentateuch: Var.
17 Gen. Bradley
18 Invoice word
19 "Love ___ leave it"
20 M.L.K. honor, 1964
23 In the past
24 Blaster's need
25 Passing mark
26 Cabinet department
31 Tosspot's spot
33 Chinese tea
34 Saint of Avila
36 Rights org. estab. 1942
38 Mr. Onassis
39 Rights org. led by M.L.K.
43 M.L.K. and others
47 Writer Rosten
48 ___ rasa

51 Inferential
54 Pizarro's theft from 1-Across
55 Up to, briefly
57 Luau dish
58 Song sung by M.L.K. and others
65 See 71-Across
66 Nonswimmer, maybe
67 Drawn tight
68 Hanging loosely
69 Surrounded by
70 Lawyer: Abbr.
71 With 65-Across, former French president
72 Play areas
73 Sci. class

DOWN

1 Aware of
2 Verne's captain
3 Cancer, zodiacally
4 See 15-Across
5 Heathrow, e.g.
6 Onetime Korean president
7 Doll's cry
8 Force out
9 Peace policy

10 Swizzle
11 Handbill heading
12 M.L.K.'s alma mater, 1951
13 Drive recklessly
21 T-shirt size: Abbr.
22 Sch. orgs.
26 New Deal grp.
27 Cry of surprise
28 Bang up
29 Tête-à-tête
30 Ghostlike
32 ___ deferens
35 Marmalade ingredient
37 Outback bird
40 XV × X + I
41 Potok's "My Name is Asher ___"
42 Miler Sebastian
44 Lady Bird's middle name
45 One that keeps track?
46 Certain skiing events, slangily
48 Wrecker
49 Interstice
50 ___ University (where M.L.K. earned his doctorate)

52 Intersection: Abbr.
53 Candy mint
56 Andean animal
59 Ballyhoo
60 Scent

61 Sell
62 "Drat!" is a mild one
63 Silent
64 Word origin: Abbr.

527 by Gregory E. Paul

1 Jobs to do
6 "Excuse me . . ."
10 Sentry's command
14 Mr. North, informally
15 ___ contendere
16 "Tosca" tune
17 Absolutely dependable
19 Monthly check
20 Gambling site: Abbr.
21 Partner of read 'em
22 Latest news
24 Have on
25 London Magazine essayist
26 One of Santa's team
29 Half volley, in tennis
33 Speedy
34 Enfant terrible
35 PBS science program
36 Part of Q.E.D.
37 Beethoven dedicatee
38 Rat ___ (knocking)
39 Achy
40 Rosalind Russell role
41 Religious work of art
42 Gym shoes
44 See 47-Down
45 Filly's father

46 Droops
47 Celebration
50 Farming unit
51 Lawn square
54 Mideast's Gulf of ___
55 Almost weightless
58 Matador's foe
59 Pulled a gun, as in a shootout
60 Bedside companion
61 Tortoiselike
62 Actress Thompson of "Family"
63 ___ and true

DOWN
1 One way to order at a restaurant
2 Very much
3 Neatnik's counterpart
4 Grade-schooler
5 Natural fish food
6 Wrath
7 Hula-___
8 Angled annex
9 Tone down
10 Steely
11 Zone
12 Fuzz
13 London's ___ Gallery

18 Char
23 "Great Expectations" boy
24 Completely pale
25 Wipe out
26 Gown
27 Alphabetically advanced boy
28 Bowling score
29 Prunes
30 Arthur Hailey novel
31 Egg-shaped
32 Golden Horde member
34 Trumpet
37 May birthstones
41 Miss America, e.g.
43 First-aid box
44 Witch's blemish
46 Unstressed vowel
47 With 44-Across, "Ain't Misbehavin" songwriter
48 Teen's fave
49 Mr. Saarinen
50 Elderly
51 Rani's garb
52 Seine feeder
53 Slave Scott

56 Savings for the elderly: Abbr.
57 California's Big ___

528 by Gregory E. Paul

ACROSS
1 Ms. Midler
6 Cotton pod
10 Oasis tree
14 Senator Hatch
15 Felipe of the Expos
16 Actress McClurg
17 Colorado River site
19 Not reticent
20 Dallas-to-Houston dir.
21 Chow
22 Talk incoherently
24 Baby woe
25 Where streams flow
26 Acapulco, e.g.
29 Menu
30 French for 52-Across
31 "Holy cow!"
33 Portly plus
37 Cat's saucerful
38 Allegro
40 Adam's arboretum
41 Do more than trim
43 ___-majesté
44 School data
45 Frigid
47 Withdraw
49 Actor Grodin
52 Accompanying

53 Start of a ringmaster's announcement
54 Jeanne ___
55 Source of Clampett wealth, on TV
58 Stravinsky ballet
59 Neolithic mystery
62 Marionette man Tony
63 Seine feeder
64 "Daniel" singer John
65 J.F.K., for one
66 Urgent want
67 70's TV drama

DOWN
1 Short haircuts
2 Valentine's Day figure
3 Quiz choice
4 ___ Tuesday (pop group)
5 Make well-liked
6 "The Sot-Weed Factor" author
7 Cutlass Supreme, e.g.
8 Mauna ___
9 Type of vertebra
10 P.G.A. stop
11 Sun-dried brick

12 Pharmaceutical giant
13 Ancient people
18 Lent ender
23 Kind of sax
24 Wyoming's fourth-largest city
25 "Quo ___?"
26 Butts
27 Good's opponent
28 Actress Ward
29 Prank
32 Festive parties
34 Hem
35 Farmer's purchase
36 Massachusetts's motto start
39 Yen
42 Mender's target
46 Assignment
48 Albrecht Dürer, e.g.
49 Fastener
50 Cartoon Viking
51 Idolize
52 Approached extinction
54 Two pills, maybe
55 Savvy about
56 "___ You Babe" (1965 song)
57 Brownie point?

60 Railroad track part
61 "Xanadu" group

529 by Frank A. Longo

ACROSS

1 Stuff of which heros are made?
7 Add to the pot
11 April 15 org.
14 Novelist Lurie
15 Tide controller
16 Card game
17 Inkling
18 One-story cottage
20 1984 Dillon coming-of-age film
22 Paddle
23 Corroded
24 Confederate soldier
25 1978 Burton adventure
31 Razor brand
34 Savage Island, now
35 Civil rights leader Wilkins
36 1969 Eastwood action film
41 Lode load
42 Blue dye
43 ___ du Salut
44 1989 Duvall miniseries
49 J.F.K.'s predecessor
50 Pollution control grp.
51 Links letters
54 1975 Wayne western
59 Confused states
60 Undid
61 Informercials
62 Ending with slug or song
63 Ride a seesaw
64 Stinger
65 Mainz Mrs.
66 Highly decorated

DOWN

1 ___ Domingo
2 Hilo hello
3 Bottle capacity
4 "___ I cared!"
5 Dough
6 Natural
7 Two-way prefix
8 It may be proper
9 Chinese secret society
10 Gluts
11 Narrow-minded
12 Crucifix
13 Barnyard female
19 Tropical tree
21 Kitten's cry
25 Lime-juicer, in English slang
26 Fireplace
27 ___ Bad Wolf, of the comics
28 Payable
29 Irked
30 They may get 40 lashes
31 Military no-show
32 Poet's preposition
33 Sign again
37 Abates
38 Electronic music pioneer
39 Archer's skill
40 Run out of steam
45 Biblical kingdom
46 Yr.'s end
47 Portuguese city
48 Less clear
51 ___ Arenas (Chile's southernmost city)
52 Welcome
53 Wrestling's ___ the Giant
54 Uncivil
55 Deck
56 Actress Lanchester
57 Queue after Q
58 Artesian "well"
59 Bill

530 by Frank A. Longo

ACROSS

1 St. Louis hrs.
4 Daughter of Zeus
9 Essential
13 Suffix in taxonomy
14 Straw-colored
15 Informed about
16 Head, in slang
17 Basketry twigs
18 God's ___ (churchyard)
19 See 54-Across
22 River in Hesse
23 Clockmaker ___ Terry
24 Snack
26 See 54-Across
32 Records that may be broken?
33 Class head
34 ___ Minor
35 Train by oneself
39 Cuatro doubled
42 "Maude" producer Norman
43 Editorial reading: Abbr.
46 See 54-Across
51 Canvasses
52 Popular card game
53 Car part
54 Theme of this puzzle
60 Kin of "wham!"
61 Opera set in Cyprus
62 Debussy's "La ___"
63 Gambol
64 Put on again
65 "We ___ Not Alone"
66 Change, often
67 Burning desire?
68 Barrett of rock's Pink Floyd

DOWN

1 Solidify
2 Didn't meet
3 School supplies
4 Old radio host Maxwell
5 Form of transportation
6 Skating maneuver
7 Toyota model
8 Discounted
9 Fortress surrounder
10 Fuzzy
11 Window washer's leavings
12 Sock part
14 Palm (off)
20 Curly coif, for short
21 "Deck the Halls" contraction
25 It may be in the bag
27 Speed letters
28 ". . . man ___ mouse?"
29 Physique, slangily
30 Poker player's comment
31 Often-rented item
35 Another name for Phoebus
36 Entanglement
37 Cotswold's call
38 1949 Peace Nobelist John Boyd ___
39 ___ slow boat to China
40 It comes from a drawer
41 Be personally meaningful
43 Some Nissans
44 Lustrous, in a way
45 Turned up one's nose (at)
47 Ancient Mongol
48 Goat type
49 Mustered roll?
50 Needlefish
55 Troublemakers
56 Woods used in cabinetmaking
57 Ersatz butter
58 ___ Bator, Mongolia
59 Golden: Fr.
60 Good buddy

531 by Gerald R. Ferguson

ACROSS
1 Miffed
10 "___ as that goes . . ."
15 Trail guides
16 1953 Oscar nominee
17 More than a third of the residents of Canada
18 ___ de ville (city hall)
19 Golfer's launches
20 Eccentric
21 Pay back
22 Now, on "E.R."
23 Smooches
27 Law force since 1873
31 Mining tunnels
32 Opposes, as the wind
33 Hand, to Herrera
34 Hiker's woes
35 Grumble
36 Place in space
38 Annuity in France
39 Bygone political slogan
40 Coercion
41 Walkers, for short
42 Base V.I.P.'s
43 Blueprint
46 Saddam Hussein, e.g.
51 Papal cape
52 Like basset hounds
53 None the ___
54 Murmur
55 Bushels
56 Savvy

DOWN
1 Air particulates
2 Air
3 Suffix with Rock
4 Show horse
5 French fighter-bombers
6 Officials of ancient Rome
7 Passed out
8 Amphorae
9 Letter addenda
10 Waste receptacles
11 Soldier near the end of a tour of duty
12 Kismet
13 From square one
14 Bank
20 Flabbergasts
22 English architect Sir John
23 Phylline's mate, in a 1942 film
24 J.F.K.'s Interior Secretary
25 Exodus mountain
26 Put away for a rainy day
27 First name in country music
28 Words with all or hole
29 The "E" in E.-U.
30 Loudness measures
32 Appearance
34 Say "tut-tut"
37 Big ones, to an angler
38 Some linemen
40 Persevering
42 Seabee's motto
43 Dust-ups
44 Folk singer ___ Anderson
45 Bambino's home
46 Sonny of Sonny and Cher
47 Pudding flavor
48 "East of Eden" character
49 Cubs' hangouts
50 New pensée
52 Oaf

532 by Sidney L. Robbins

ACROSS
1 Preferred group of invitees
6 Normandy campaign town, 1944
10 Speaker's platform
14 New Zealand native
15 Watered down
16 Teen woe
17 Start of an old romantic song lyric
20 Take up again, as a claim
21 First month of the año
22 Vase
23 Midwest clock setting: Abbr.
25 Narrow waterway: Abbr.
26 Cosmetician Lauder
30 "I smell ___!"
31 Capitol topper
32 Explain once more
34 Deposited
37 Part 2 of the lyric
40 Light brown
41 93, e.g., at the pump
42 Curved molding
43 Wine sediment
44 Dictatorial
45 One ___ time
48 Netanyahu's land: Abbr.
49 Before: Prefix
51 Diamond measure
53 Fish that swims upright
58 End of the lyric
61 One of the O'Neills
62 Canal to Buffalo
63 Meal from the garden
64 Study, as text
65 "Lights out" music
66 Arduous journeys

DOWN
1 Mideast leader
2 Not on time
3 Where Ames is
4 Spanish ladies: Abbr.
5 Kleenex
6 Stem's opposite
7 "Anything but ___!"
8 Actress Ullmann
9 Quarter of four
10 Start of a new day
11 Pains
12 Motionless
13 "Si, si!" man
18 Any ship
19 Tiny sting
23 Uncle of Antigone
24 Unguentine, e.g.
26 Cut and paste
27 Divan
28 Fed. tax agents
29 Wriggly fish
30 Book of maps
32 Reduces to tiny bits
33 "Come in!"
34 Sty inhabitants
35 Colorado Indians
36 Unnamed ones
38 Underage heartbreaker
39 Go a-courting
44 Directive
45 Hollywood type
46 Nevada resort
47 Sports spot
49 "Oh, for ___ sake!"
50 Gridiron cheer
52 "Diary of ___ Housewife"
53 Barber's motion
54 Bridge expert Sharif
55 Part to play
56 Clean, as dentures
57 Pass receivers
59 Tennis judge's position
60 Lyricist Gershwin

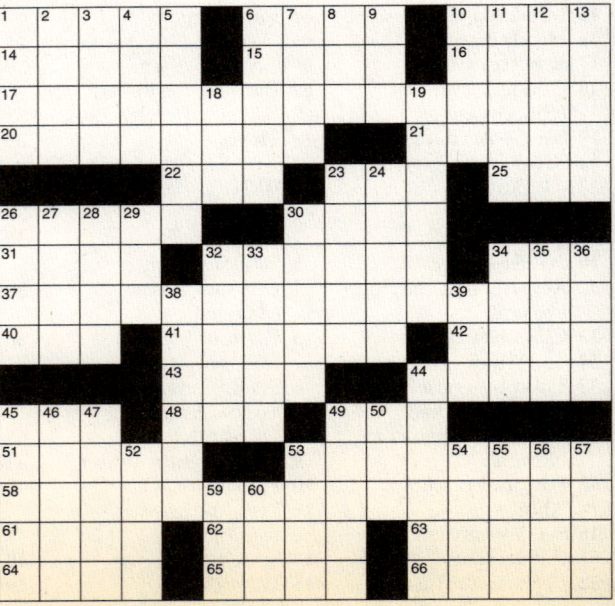

533 by Rich Norris

ACROSS
1 Kind of mass
9 Dull
15 Tangolike dance
16 Pleistocene epoch
17 Breakfast order
18 Printing, carpentry, etc.
19 Geom. figure
20 Allay
22 Alphabet string
23 "Nothing ___"
25 Messenger
26 Mechanical, after "by"
27 Consternation
29 Make a foozle
30 Humdinger
31 Prevail
33 Unpaved surfaces
35 Fed. watchdog
37 "Peter Pan" character
38 Episodes
42 Stung
46 Italian artist Guido
47 Corker
48 1940s Chief Justice
49 Elvis's middle name
50 Remove via percolation
53 Recorded proceedings
54 Year in a Roman sci-fi film?
55 Danish
56 Relief
57 Starting time?
59 Certain vaudeville act
62 Villa
63 1953 Emmy-winning actress
64 One of a team of eight
65 Organization founded by Jean Henri Dunant

DOWN
1 Mississippi native
2 Ristorante offering
3 Basque, e.g.
4 Stain
5 Chemical suffix
6 Wrap up
7 Unlawful firing
8 Airport event
9 Short, impassioned poem
10 It may be a lot
11 "Give ___ break!"
12 Boss
13 Cast out
14 Family types
21 Plaza de ___
24 Enter marching
26 "Smoke Gets in Your Eyes" musical
28 Nonnegotiable item
32 1992 Robert Altman film
34 Jupiter or Apollo, e.g.
36 Early sign of spring
38 Studied
39 Shade of pink
40 Oils
41 Go all over
43 "Sorry, that's impossible!"
44 Allures
45 Anesthetizes
51 Desire
52 Promoted to excess
55 Cracker topper
58 T, to Morse
60 ___ Lac (Vietnamese province)
61 J.F.K. event: Abbr.

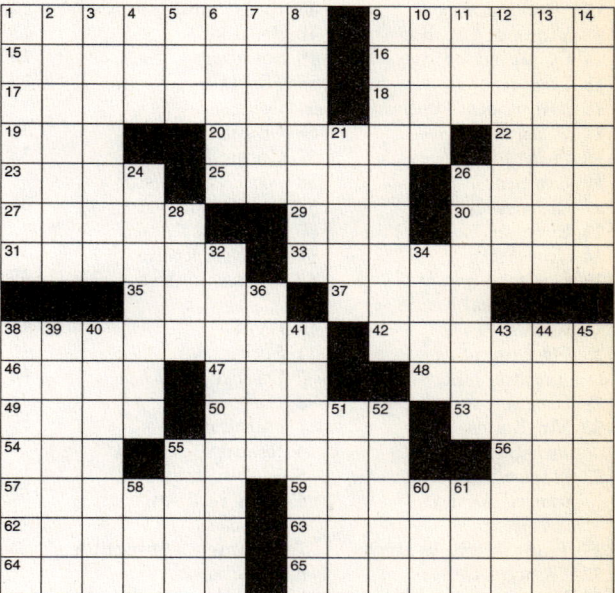

534 by Joel Davajan

ACROSS
1 Atop
5 Clubbed
10 Motes
14 New York Cosmos star
15 Chou ___
16 Oklahoma tribesman
17 Lord Nelson site
20 Part of an electrical switch
21 Zeroes
22 Hectored
23 Sans verve
24 Medicament
27 Winter woe
28 Ottoman official
31 The Donald's ex
32 Fly like Lindbergh
33 Aits in Arles
34 Prepare for an Indian attack
37 Raison d'___
38 30's actress Grey and others
39 Nighttime noise
40 Beam
41 Sponsorship
42 Feeds a furnace
43 Belgian river
44 Baseball union boss Donald
45 Like llamas
48 Sends quickly
52 Ships' drop-off location?
54 Sea flyer
55 Gnawed away
56 Composition closure
57 Crazy bird?
58 Monopoly payments
59 Formerly

DOWN
1 Goes (for)
2 ___ Beach, Fla.
3 Airline to Jerusalem
4 Testimonial
5 It's hummed
6 1973 hit by the Rolling Stones
7 Covered
8 The "E" in E.N.T.
9 Prohibit
10 Wampum
11 I-70's western terminus
12 Ilk
13 Golf course 18
18 Of some electrodes
19 Printer's spacer
23 Tree trunks
24 Potato preparer
25 "Requiem for ___"
26 Take the plunge
27 Lawyer Roy M. and others
28 "Take ___ at this!"
29 Type
30 Bridge of ___ (Euclid proposition)
32 Way up?
33 Blissful state?
35 Produce
36 Wheezing cause
41 Birthright seller
42 TV listing
43 Modern-day Sheba
44 Tops
45 Ex-steelworkers chief
46 Fiery fiddler
47 1962 Bond villain
48 Solar disk
49 Mr. Stravinsky
50 Lawyers' degrees
51 Install in office
53 "___ you sure?"

535 by A.J. Santora

ACROSS

1 Bit of lowlife?
6 Unyielding
10 Spacewalk, e.g.: Abbr.
13 "Reflections on Violence" author
14 Occupied with
15 Lose it
16 Brit's potato chip
17 Headliner
18 Hunt hint
19 Example
21 Riddler of old
23 Burnish
24 Careening
25 Use face cream
27 "Perpetual Peace" writer
28 First name in daytime talk
29 Brit. ref. work
30 Mr. Bones, in a minstrel show
33 Hard-rock band named for an inventor
35 Train schedule abbr.
37 French pupil
38 Nahuatl speakers
40 Cable TV inits.
42 Oklahoma city
43 Writer Hubbard
44 Guides
46 Refute
47 By ___ and bounds
48 Bearlike
49 Set apart
53 Flip talk
54 Spice
56 Missile depots
57 Comic Kamen
58 Art Deco master
59 Bar, legally
60 "___ luck?"
61 Env. enclosure
62 Expressionless

DOWN

1 Spore sacs
2 Daybreak
3 Discordia's counterpart
4 Readers' perusal
5 Woolly fabric
6 They're thrown at meets
7 Became a competitor
8 ___ glance
9 Abandon
10 Hitch
11 Boast of
12 High point
15 Spielberg film
20 Don't do it
22 Smooth
25 At the home of
26 Sans esprit
28 Concerned citizens' org.
31 Alamo competitor
32 Hammett detective Beaumont
34 Flip ___ (decide randomly)
36 Kind of ballot
39 Signs of a cold
41 Wood sorrels
45 Literary works
46 Einstein
48 U.S. Grant's school: Abbr.
50 Countertenor
51 Saturday TV fare, slangily
52 Glimpse
55 Paleozic, e.g.

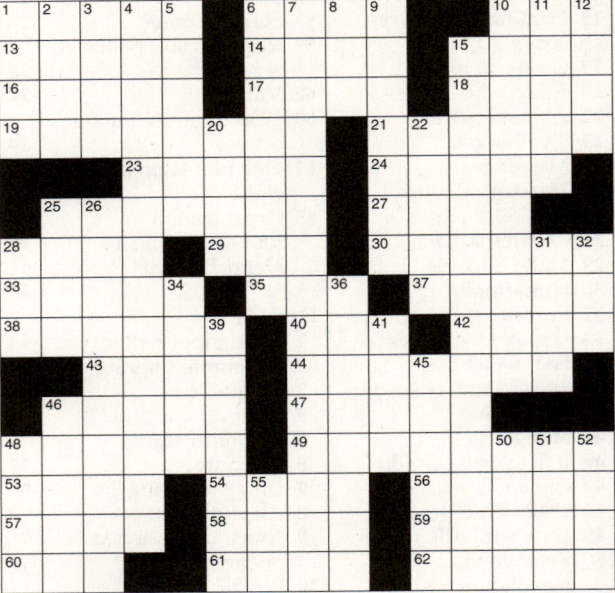

536 by Mel Taub

ACROSS

1 He wrote "The Bronx? No, thonx!"
5 Cramped Mother Goose dwelling
9 Renaissance beauty Isabella ___
14 Anent
15 Follow the game
16 Send packing
17 "Dark Lady" singer
18 Tallinn native
19 Actor Keach
20 Hollywood palmist?
23 Make cherished
24 Ump's purview
25 Roget's entry: Abbr.
27 Percussion at a powwow
31 Actor Davis
35 Well-oiled grp.
38 New Rochelle college
39 Hollywood quack?
42 For takeout
43 Ex of 17-Across
44 He wrote "The Proper Bostonians"
45 Available for
47 West Point subject
49 Yield slightly
52 Sports jacket
57 Hollywood's leading undertaker?
60 Originated
61 The last Mrs. Chaplin
62 Member of 35-Across
63 In accord (with)
64 Skidded
65 Scottish tongue
66 Heavy of old comedies
67 Location
68 M-G-M co-founder Marcus

DOWN

1 Mother-of-pearl
2 Pale-faced
3 Bed frame
4 Genghis Khan's mass
5 Jerez product
6 Silence
7 Ready if needed
8 Word on old gas pumps
9 Mississippi discoverer
10 Ultra credo
11 Minor dispute
12 Georgia ___
13 TV Tarzan Ron
21 Canvas prop
22 Do guard duty
26 Say ___ (refuse)
28 Kansas pooch
29 "___ about . . ."
30 Lots and lots
31 Tetra × 2
32 The Old Curiosity, e.g.
33 Nestor
34 Unyielding
36 Review a flop
37 Adequate, way back
40 Domicile
41 Confederate general Jubal
46 Dempsey's nemesis
48 Scrape
50 Luster
51 Carlo Levi's "Christ Stopped at ___"
53 Swiss diarist Henri Frédéric ___
54 Man in a mask
55 Get rid of
56 Freshen
57 "___ smile be . . ."
58 Borodin's prince
59 Singleton
60 "Phooey!"

ACROSS

1 Macintosh predecessor
5 Fish feature
10 Crumples
14 Joie de vivre
15 Less racy
16 Unbalanced
17 Start of an excerpt from an Edna St. Vincent Millay poem
19 Elvis, for one
20 "Read this"
21 Chaser, perhaps
22 Norm's wife, on "Cheers"
23 Physicist Joliet-Curie
25 Excerpt, part 2
29 A, to Mozart
30 Not sanguine
31 Ball perch
32 Having a ranking
34 Chateau-dotted valley
36 Wind up
37 Excerpt, part 3
40 Pendant
43 Zigzags
44 Oscitates
48 Antecedent period
49 Year of Trajan's victory over Dacia
50 Ruined
51 Excerpt, part 4
55 Comical Anne
56 Province
57 Young men's club
59 Moore's "___ the Last Rose of Summer"
60 Kind of stew
61 Excerpt, part 5
64 Icicle holder
65 What a skimmer skims
66 Box
67 Half-note feature
68 It's a crying need
69 Baseball Hall-of-Famer Coveleski

DOWN

1 More verdant
2 "Twelfth Night" setting
3 Conspicuous
4 What's more
5 Eye problem
6 Old Testament scout
7 Dean Martin subject
8 Deighton or Dawson
9 Dyne-centimeter
10 Give up
11 Not too soft
12 Openers
13 Like a newborn's legs
18 Tad's dad
24 1970 Nobel physicist Louis
26 Most bears, biologically
27 One of TV's Cleavers
28 Them, with "the"
33 Quit flying
34 Massenet opera
35 Black or red tree
38 ___ bean
39 Pave the way
40 Is mannerly
41 Pig out
42 Leave desolate
45 This and that
46 Onetime dictator
47 Eisenhower confidant
52 1692 trial site
53 Commonly
54 Inflict
55 V.J. employer
58 Land force
61 "___ liebe dich"
62 Powerful D.C. lobby
63 Superways

ACROSS

1 Came up
6 Good farm soil
10 Son of Seth
14 1981 John Lennon hit
15 Formerly
16 Songbird
17 "Blithe Spirit" playwright
19 Wearing-out point for pants
20 Creek
21 Tidy
23 Vintage
24 Fr. ladies
26 Toboggans
28 Fondle
31 "Not guilty," e.g.
33 Stow in a ship's hold
36 ___ bomb
38 Miss Cinders of early comics
40 Spy work, for short
41 Songs sung from house to house
44 Succinct
45 Looped handle
46 Within: Prefix
47 Kind of hammer
49 Texas pioneer Houston et al.
51 ___ es Salaam
52 Midnights' counterparts
54 "Alice" diner
56 Pussy
58 Tie fabric
60 Lariats
64 Sills solo
66 Seasonal worker
68 Bridge feat
69 Heinz number, to Ovid?
70 Happening
71 "O ___ Night"
72 Town near Padua
73 Schmoes

DOWN

1 Bristles
2 Cheer (for)
3 Hebrew dry measure
4 City of witch hunts
5 Pitch tents
6 Temperature extreme
7 ___ even keel
8 Lots of lots
9 Military awards
10 Antlered animal
11 Not much time
12 Pitcher Hershiser
13 Calendar à la Variety
18 Eggs-and-cheese dish
22 Aquarium fish
25 1965 march site
27 Lawn mower brand
28 Agreements
29 Miss Barrymore
30 Like a downpour
32 Astronaut Shepard et al.
34 Upper ___ (now Burkina Faso)
35 TV newsman David
37 Err
39 State of India
42 Lilies
43 Minolta, e.g.
48 Isolate
50 Cut
53 Serbs and Croats
55 Round of cheers
56 Neither check nor charge
57 Singer Guthrie
59 Make stockings
61 Far East weight
62 Polly, to Tom
63 Fast planes
65 1948 song "Once in Love With ___"
67 Come out even

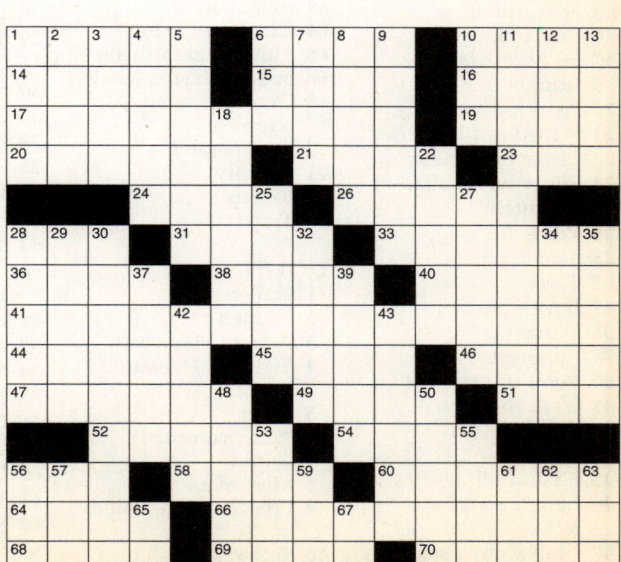

539 by Gregory E. Paul

ACROSS

1 Witches
5 "The Metamorphosis" author
10 Office honcho
14 Skin soother
15 Violas' neighbors in an orchestra
16 It's west of Ark.
17 "Love ___ leave it"
18 "Hungry Like the Wolf" singers
20 Vegetarian's no-no
22 'Twixt 12 and 20
23 Actor Dick of "Bewitched"
24 Defense acronym
25 ___ cum laude
27 Freight weight
28 Poet laureate Cecil Day ___
32 Juárez ones
33 Remove vital parts from
34 Scold
35 6 on a phone
36 Bullfighter
38 Actor Cariou
39 San Diego nine

41 Panhandle
42 Fakir's income
43 More cagey
44 "Kidnapped" monogram
45 Eliminate
46 See eye to eye
48 Defect
49 They're far out
52 Candy from a machine
55 1969 hit by the Archies
57 Mr. Nastase
58 Counterfeiters' foes
59 Muslim prince
60 Hawkeye Pierce's portrayer
61 Dian Fossey subjects
62 British tube
63 "A bit of talcum / Is always walcum" writer

DOWN

1 Tresses
2 Der ___ (Adenauer)
3 Self-righteous
4 O'Hara's "___ and Soda Water"

5 Minolta rival
6 Adjoin
7 Part of F.Y.I.
8 1977 Oscar actress
9 Seven-time Emmy winner Ed
10 Rascal
11 Green pods
12 Dross
13 Mentally sound
19 Casino employee
21 Victorian, for one
24 Distinguished
25 Parotitis
26 Historical record
27 Howard Carter's 1922 discovery
29 Whitman College site
30 Paraphernalia
31 Taste or touch
33 Oil alternative
34 Swamp
36 Wall Street news
37 TV host O'Connor
40 Former White House family
42 Kind of coffee
44 Job hunter's need
45 Slippery ___
47 Calibrate anew

48 Like winter animals
49 Hammett hound
50 Low-cut shoe
51 Double curve
52 Food critic Greene

53 Pots' tops
54 Wife of Jacob
56 Toothpaste type

---

540 by Sidney L. Robbins

ACROSS

1 Victim of Corday
6 Reminder
10 Kind of tongue
14 Wonderland lass
15 Graceful horse
16 Buy U.S. bonds
17 66-Across laurels
19 Bridge
20 Asserted
21 Wiped out in battle
23 Lover of sweets
24 Suffix with ballad or mountain
26 Wan
28 Taxi
31 Taste
33 Burlesque
36 Wings
38 Puppeteer Tony
40 Point of view
41 66-Across cry
44 Revolutionary War spy Major ___
45 First of all
46 Letters on a love letter
47 Peep show customers
49 Historic period
50 Napoleonic general

51 ___ Unis (United States, to Pierre)
53 Time Inc. workers
55 A Gershwin
57 Puppy bites
59 Acid salt
64 Cincinnati team
66 This puzzle's theme
68 Spoon-playing locale
69 One turn of an odometer
70 ___ operandi
71 Classify
72 Ripens
73 Trap

DOWN

1 Gullets
2 Landed
3 Actress Hayworth
4 Eight, to Hans und Franz
5 Titter
6 "___ overboard!"
7 Cupid
8 Miss Maples
9 Preoccupy the mind of
10 Silly one
11 66-Across garb
12 Ill-tempered czar

13 Car insurance case
18 Black Sea port
22 Plains harvest
25 Cowboy's rope
27 City south of Dallas
28 Chocolate source
29 Tag ___ with (accompany)
30 66-Across V.I.P.
32 Hardly a libertine
34 Arm bones
35 Vexatious
37 White heron
39 Hostile look
42 Broadcast again
43 Substance used to ignite firework fuses
48 Reputation harmer
52 Offshoot
54 Shuts with a bang
55 Irritates
56 City near Tahoe
58 Store event
60 Uniform collar
61 Verdi opera
62 Visitor's trip
63 Start of Massachusetts's motto

65 Collection
67 ___ Moines

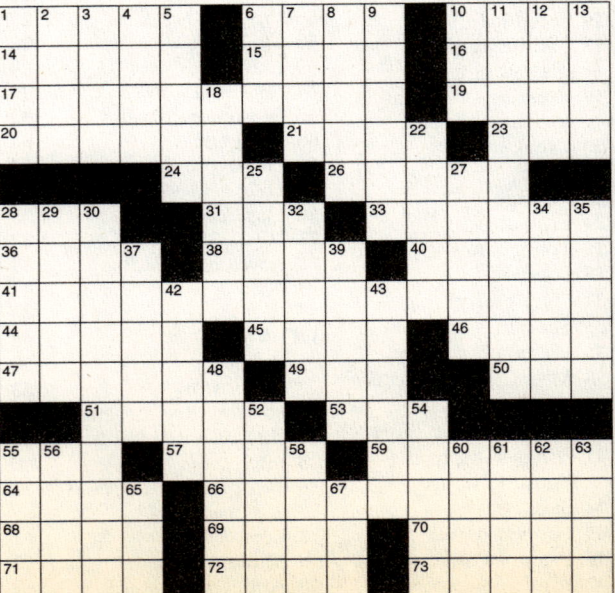

541   by Richard Hughes

ACROSS

1 Open a bit
5 Attach
10 "Four Weddings ___ Funeral"
14 Ecce ___
15 Ball in the game of pétanque
16 Like some college volleyball
17 Start of a quip
20 Switch positions
21 Fred's familial partner
22 Pry
23 Justice Fortas
24 Garment with laces
25 Part 2 of the quip
31 "Wanted" poster name
32 100 paise
33 Microscopic
34 Ulan ___
35 Inventory system, for short
39 Three-time British Open golf champ
40 Reflected on, with "over"
41 Part 3 of the quip

45 Musician's equipment handler
46 Singer, in a way
47 Change
48 Mark
51 ___ Tunas, Cuba
54 End of the quip
57 Modern sci. course
58 Stop work, slangily
59 ___ a soul
60 Stet's opposite
61 Construction equipment
62 Logic diagram

DOWN

1 Mr. Moto comment
2 Most common papal name
3 Book after Joel
4 Scuffle
5 Job, for one
6 Nap
7 Word with citizen or purpose
8 Ye ___ Shoppe
9 Ariz. neighbor
10 Yield
11 What a monkey senses, in a saying

12 Catch sight of
13 More than like
18 ___ breath
19 Words starting many bumper stickers
23 Call it ___
24 Kind of blast
25 Make lace
26 Hebrew judge
27 Racket
28 Some finals
29 Surpass
30 Parody
34 Use a kiln
35 Four-time Indy winner
36 Item listed on an I.R.S. form
37 Marsh
38 Out of the ordinary
39 Wand wielder
40 "The Bell Jar" author
41 Comfort
42 Beat work
43 Channel swimmer Gertrude
44 Sibelius's "Valse ___"
45 Hied
48 Skiers' aid
49 Gulf of ___ (Baltic arm)

50 Opposed to, in dialect
51 Polygraph failer
52 Caldwell's "God's Little ___"
53 Inner Hebrides island
55 Broadcast channel
56 Cable channel

542   by Lois Sidway

ACROSS

1 Anderson of rock's Jethro Tull
4 Gruesome
9 Rose's fella
13 It's full of ginger
15 Keen
16 Bears' adversaries
17 Clear finish?
18 Reform
20 "Good job!"
22 Sam Spade portrayer
23 Oz traveler
24 Great-grandma's picture, maybe
26 "Dallas" star
29 First-class
30 Architect Saarinen
31 Like some old fashion
36 Mobster's lady
37 "Murphy Brown" housekeeper
38 Verge
39 Withdrawn
41 Efforts
42 Land of the Midnight Sun dweller
43 Plains Indians
44 Reckon

48 Ireland's ___ Islands
49 Fix, as golf greens
50 Former Pirate slugger Willie
54 Square-shooting
57 I-79 terminus
58 Bingo call
59 Roger of NBC News
60 Goes pfft
61 Slip (into)
62 Minimum payment
63 Appeal

DOWN

1 What "vidi" means
2 Green Gables girl
3 Salt
4 Snorkeling site
5 Huskies of coll. basketball
6 Subterfuge
7 Conglomerate founded in 1920
8 ___ Spiegel (German magazine)
9 Running amok
10 Like some trousers
11 1965 Frishberg-Dorough tune

12 Lauder lady
14 Confusedly
19 A Yokum
21 Lever 2000 competitor
24 Viz.
25 ___ instant
26 Fiber source
27 Felipe of the Expos
28 Breathing organ
29 Seem reasonable
31 Split to get spliced
32 Psycho
33 "Gotcha"
34 Baseball's Tommie
35 Nitti's nemesis
37 Imported cheese
40 Shake off
41 Red foe
43 One way to take medicine
44 Investigation
45 Oscar de la ___
46 Sen. Kefauver
47 Frau's boys
48 Had a traditional dinner
50 Cinematographer Nykvist

51 Sister of Ares
52 Place
53 ___-majesté
55 Cut (off)
56 Storm heading

DIAGONAL

1 Eminently persuadable

543 by Fred Piscop

ACROSS

1 ___ d'oeuvres
5 "Without delay"
9 Gardener's tool
14 Came to ground
15 Boxer's wear
16 Sheik's bevy
17 "___ Zapata!"
18 Hint
19 Man and Wight, e.g.
20 Unsolicited, as manuscripts
23 Prefix with meter
24 "Watch your ___!"
25 Informal language
29 Loves to death
33 Who's Who entry
36 Fencing blades
38 Enthusiastic review
39 Ill
43 Map rds.
44 Newton of gravity fame
45 Spanish Mrs.
46 Cosa ___
49 Come in
51 Gossipy Barrett
53 Goes hither and thither
57 Stroll path, perhaps

62 Aristophanes comedy, with "The"
63 Savings' partner
64 1953 Leslie Caron film
65 Corner map
66 "Leave ___ Beaver"
67 Vigor
68 Petty officers
69 Hive denizens
70 "Peanuts" expletive

DOWN

1 Utter devastation
2 Popeye's gal
3 Torn apart
4 Begins
5 Curved gateway
6 ___ proprietorship
7 Border on
8 Jury members
9 Spruced up, as shoes
10 Globetrotter's need
11 Singer Guthrie
12 Consider
13 Printer's widths
21 Mosaic maker
22 ___ loss for words
26 Fitting

27 Royal Crown Cola brand
28 Silly birds
30 Stadium cheers
31 "Did you ___!"
32 Blood fluids
33 Beachgoer's worry
34 Look ___ (probe)
35 Pindaric verses
37 Ugly duckling, ultimately
40 Female hormone
41 Chow down
42 Bitter
47 Drags out of bed
48 ___ Arbor, Mich.
50 Word with high or holy
52 Ignore the script
54 "There!"
55 Acclaim
56 Injures slightly
57 Florence's river
58 Seamstress Betsy
59 Shopper's bag
60 Detest
61 Baseball's Slaughter
62 Stretch the truth

544 by Stephanie Spadaccini

ACROSS

1 Fixed up again
6 Highest point
10 Off-base, unofficially
14 Solo
15 Cajole
16 Venus de ___
17 Worthless types
20 "Your excellency"
21 Tell a whopper
22 Bob Marley's music
23 Fed lines to
25 Late-night schmoozer Jay
26 Recovered consciousness
29 Total
30 Dateless
34 "___ you ready yet?"
35 Straitlaced
37 Zeta's follower
38 Classic invention
41 Singleton
42 Horse holders
43 Walkway
44 Protective covering
46 Gobbled up
47 Comedian Marty
48 Eyebrow shape
50 The "C" of C.O.D.
51 Magic charm
54 Droop
55 Arboretum item

59 Part of making a favorable impression?
62 Funeral stand
63 Debaucher
64 "Alfie" star Michael
65 Artist Warhol
66 D.H. Lawrence's "___ and Lovers"
67 Append

DOWN

1 Tatters
2 "The Time Machine" people
3 Entranceway
4 Vulgarly dressed
5 Rock group ___ Leppard
6 Bitter
7 Dairy Queen order
8 Long March leader
9 In ___ (near death)
10 Buddies, in Baja
11 Museum extension
12 Gymnast Korbut
13 Mislay
18 Bogus butter
19 Barnyard clucker
24 Say

25 Hawaiian cookouts
26 Explorer Sebastian
27 Meadowlands ___
28 It may have quarters downtown
29 Item slung in a sling
31 Brief and to the point
32 Whatsoever
33 Stares open-mouthed
35 Blues singer Bessie
36 University bosses
39 Nuclear plant apparatuses
40 Skinflint
45 Piddling
47 "Othello" villain
49 Ump
50 Parisian snack sites
51 "Dancing Queen" pop group
52 Chow ___
53 Previously owned
54 Stupefy
56 Surprise attack
57 "Cubist" Rubik
58 Paradise
60 Tic-tac-toe win
61 Early broadcasting inits.

545 by Janet Bender

ACROSS

1 Ornamental stone
5 Beige
9 Play part
14 Yoke wearers
15 Diving bird
16 Cinematography units
17 Pupils
20 Versatile blackjack holdings
21 Mideast export
22 Changes actors in a play
26 Narrow waterways
30 Warns
31 Butter servings
32 "Mamma ___!"
33 Brawl
34 Lima's land
35 Serenade
36 Whites
39 1910's–20's art style
40 Prefix with series
41 "Cool!"
43 From ___ Z
44 Agile
45 Blockhead
46 Cincinnati footballers
48 "Sh" or "th," linguistically
49 Grow old
50 Trompe l'___ (optical illusion)
51 Irises
59 Sounds from a sty
60 Et ___
61 Aeronautical maneuver
62 Shivaree
63 Loretta who sang "You Ain't Woman Enough"
64 Hunter's quarry

DOWN

1 Tiny amount
2 Lumberjack's tool
3 Narcs' org.
4 S.A.S.E., e.g.
5 Votes into office
6 Apple remains
7 Betsy or Diana
8 Chapel Hill campus, for short
9 Elevator alternative
10 Rhea's role on "Cheers"
11 Cardiac readout, briefly
12 Born
13 Snaky curve
18 Hightail it
19 Whirlpool site
22 Dodge truck
23 Raise
24 Gray-green
25 Boxing venue
26 Famed New York restaurateur
27 Do an impression of
28 "God bless us every one" speaker
29 Droop
31 Something "for your thoughts"
34 Skating event
35 Dutch painter Jan
37 More capacious
38 Join the class
39 Small bit, as of cream
42 Long distance call start
44 Most wise
45 Contribute, as to a poker pot
47 Stares stupidly
48 A square ___ a round hole
50 No more than
51 Watch pocket
52 Capp's ___ Abner
53 Out ___ limb
54 Suffix with different
55 Swiss peak
56 Neither's companion
57 Boot's end
58 Snoop (on)

546 by Dean Niles

ACROSS

1 & 8 Former world leader and his successor
15 Pastoral piece
16 One who might deck you
17 Aristotle tome
18 Stocking warmer?
19 Blvd.
20 Jewish village
22 Having a bouquet, maybe
23 Roughly forever
24 Boners
26 ___ Verde (Texas county)
27 Prowler
30 Kind of cream
31 Writer Hite
33 Gametes
35 Lightheaded ones?
36 Cars once built in Lansing
37 Will of "The Waltons"
38 1864 Mississippi battle site
41 Drinks since 1929
45 Evening soap actress Christine ___
46 Cries at fireworks
47 Castigatory
48 Spoil
49 Reader's Digest co-founder Wallace
52 One of the Khans
53 Surveyor's work
55 Cincinnati university
57 Cyst
58 Acting as guardian
60 Tailed
62 Beryl variety
63 Distributes by plan
64 Autocrats
65 Rent payers

DOWN

1 Push, as a button
2 Transition zone between plant communities
3 Cold comfort
4 Auction parcel
5 Auspices
6 Collar lace
7 Small falcons
8 Jenn-Air maker
9 Full-size
10 Cambodia's Lon ___
11 Selected
12 Rejuvenate
13 "Fifty-two Pickup" crime novelist
14 Some socks
21 One foot-pound = 13,560,000 ___
25 Out
28 Landed property
29 Capsized, with "over"
32 Marilyn of the Met
34 Game with forfeits
35 Part of a restaurant bill: Abbr.
37 Of bodily motion
38 Attracted
39 Poe poem
40 "Peter Pan" extras
41 Switchblade
42 Ignorant
43 Range of colors
44 Wile
46 Stars and bars
50 Acclaim
51 Razz
54 Maryland player, for short
56 Director Meyer
59 Doctor of film
61 Windows platform

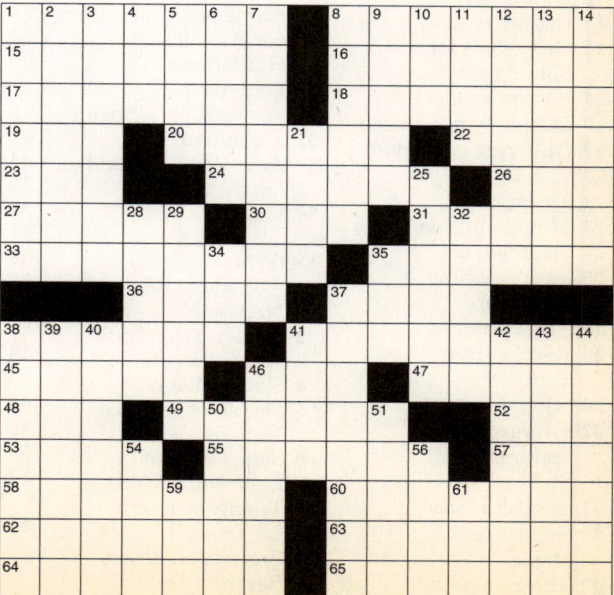

547 by Kenneth Haxton

ACROSS

1 Swiss river
4 New Orleans's Vieux ___
9 Child shot
12 Pique
14 Mix 'n match collections
15 Fisher's boat
16 Rhapsodic
17 Opening of 4/11/91
19 "My Cup Runneth Over" singer
21 Church teachings
22 Pitch
24 Opening of 3/13/47
26 Dialect
28 Beatles's "___ Mine"
29 Responsibility
30 Pope of 1775
34 Kitchen item
37 Song from "Mondo Cane"
38 Beauty parlor service
39 Nutmeg spice
40 Kind of money
41 Soda fountain indulgence
42 Back up, in a way
43 Actor McKellen
44 Singer Don
46 Opening of 3/26/64
52 Be a breadwinner
53 Flu variety
54 Memorial Coliseum player
56 Opening of 4/23/63
58 Smack
62 Schiller drama subject
63 Composer Bruckner
64 Gab
65 Name suffixes
66 Not in the ___
67 "Rosemary" of film

DOWN

1 Timber tree
2 Cuckoo
3 Oil drilling equipment
4 Robin Cook best seller
5 Out on ___
6 Stage stand
7 Martini's partner
8 Snake
9 In concealment
10 Advertising ploy
11 Theater critic Kenneth
13 1979 Midler film
15 Electron tube
18 "Turandot" librettist
20 Sixth-century date
22 Eastern capital
23 Often illegal auto maneuver
25 "___ Hell Harry"
26 Magnificence
27 Out of jail
31 ". . . kerchief and ___ my cap"
32 Berlin connector
33 Retirees' agcy.
34 Flutter
35 Vast expanse
36 "Roberta" composer
39 Bunkum
41 "Just ___"
43 Together
45 Medium grade
46 Crash diets
47 Poe family
48 Nobel physicist Bohr
49 Soames Forsyte wife
50 Certain Jamaican
51 Broadway cars
55 Parking mishap
57 Comics prince
59 "___ Woman" ('72 hit)
60 Astr. or biol.
61 Some popular music

DIAGONAL

1 Opening of 5/4/93

548 by Brett Blaylock

ACROSS

1 Game with numbers 1 to 20
6 Crosby to Hope, often
12 Adulterate
13 Deceptive alloys
15 One who's left holding the bag?
16 Pontiac model
17 Definitely not ascetic
19 Gulf War combatant
20 ___ ski
21 Thrombus
23 Mini-peninsula
24 Hautboy, e.g.
25 Capital east of Jerusalem
27 Exact point
28 Roy Orbison's "___ Baby"
30 Silo fan
32 George C. Scott feature
35 Fox
37 English martyr
41 French cooking staple
42 Those opposed
44 Wagner's earth goddess
45 Opportunist
47 Chinese: Prefix
48 Spirit
49 Postulate
51 Flagging conversation?
53 Headstrong
55 Pedigreed
56 Personal personnel
57 ___ in (curbed)
58 American saint and family
59 Sniggler

DOWN

1 A financée of Napolean
2 Kindergarten book
3 Nerve branch
4 Slavic sovereign
5 People of the Five Nations
6 Something you go by
7 Eight-time Norris Trophy winner
8 ___ to say
9 Brown and others
10 Reach in amount
11 More fit
12 Smart
14 Clobber
15 Boy Scouts of America founder
18 January birthstone
22 Tahitian dish
26 Shuttle group
29 Former U.S. poet laureate ___ Van Duyn
31 Bell's ringer?
33 ___ best friend
34 Master hands
35 Lives
36 Ennoble
38 Hatchery
39 Put on a pedestal
40 Like a newborn
41 Sweetie
43 Funereal, in Folkestone
46 Word on a bill
48 Baby
50 Second leader
52 Away from harm's way
54 Wimple wearer

549 by Wayne Robert Williams

ACROSS

1 Helen Gahagan film role of 1935
4 Mirthful
10 Guzzle
14 Electioneerer, for short
15 One-two bet
16 Perpetually
17 Start of a letter arrangement
19 Broadway's Kirk
20 Blowout
21 They can't be beat
23 Mother's charge
25 Show eagerness
26 More of the arrangement
30 Laminated rocks
31 Fade in the stretch
32 Motorists' org.
33 Film maker Craven
34 End of the arrangement
37 Start of the explanation of the arrangement
41 Wide width
42 Laurel and Hardy
43 Alfonso XIII's queen
44 Actress Anne
47 More of the explanation
50 Pyrenees resident
52 Stowe girl
53 Wider in scope
54 Get out of the way
58 Venetian honcho
59 End of the explanation
63 Men's names meaning "lion"
64 Receive as a member
65 Former
66 ___ gin
67 Perks
68 The end (appropriately)

DOWN

1 Initials in ancient Rome
2 Six-time N.H.L. M.V.P.
3 Mountain road abbr.
4 Flying woe
5 Acetylene starter
6 ___-de-Vire (historic French valley)
7 Here, in Tours
8 Lacking a key
9 Collar extension
10 Air
11 Egg receptacle
12 100 centimos
13 Gets the lead out
18 Sailing hazard
22 Copied
24 "Macbeth" title
25 Jamaican beat
26 Finishing tool
27 Early evening hour
28 Winter mo.
29 Tight spot
33 Drafted
35 Like Shakespeare's Valentine and Proteus
36 Goat feature
37 At lunch, maybe
38 Scale notes
39 Pioneer performance artist
40 Stir the air
42 ___ mother
44 A Gabor et al.
45 Join the party
46 Slowly
47 Speech source
48 Turns outward
49 Mr. Shankar
51 Get back to even
55 The gamut
56 Excise
57 Mahler's "Das Lied von der ___"
60 Statistical abbr.
61 Suffix with command
62 New Deal prog.

550 by Gregory E. Paul

ACROSS

1 Handle the situation
5 Harbinger
9 Pancake topper
14 Drifters' "___ the Roof"
15 Application form information
16 Monopoly purchase
17 Alex Raymond comic strip
19 Peter of Peter and Gordon
20 C.I.A. forerunner
21 Tokyo, once
22 Coin side
24 Feature of five U.S. Presidents
26 Apollo vehicle
27 Manager Anderson
30 Following orders
35 Corporate emblems
36 Clumsy dancer's problems
37 The Magi, e.g.
38 Christie or Quindlen
39 Things to crack
40 Part of E.M.T.: Abbr.
41 Kind of tea
42 Pearl Buck heroine
43 Sacred song
44 Western Hemisphere
46 Sliding dance step
47 The Red Baron, for one
48 Curtain fabric
50 Musicians
54 Electric swimmer
55 Telephonic 3
58 Kind of board
59 Legendary cowboy
62 Attach to a lapel
63 Wicked
64 Come in last
65 Adlai's 1956 running mate
66 Broad valley
67 Sloth's home

DOWN

1 Stephen King novel
2 Musical composition
3 Operatic Lily
4 H.S. course
5 "Sometime . . ."
6 Captain's superior
7 Record label with Capitol
8 Commander of the Nautilus
9 Attacked the whiskers
10 Ornery Warner Bros. cartoon character
11 Essen's river
12 Manipulates
13 Father, in France
18 Vichyssoise ingredients
23 Give a benediction
24 Namath's nickname
25 Gadgets
27 Done in
28 Puerto Rican port city
29 1973 resigner
31 Existed
32 Humorist Bombeck et al.
33 Physicist Bohr
34 The Velvet Fog
36 Bridge fee
39 Kitchen utensil
43 Collins and Donahue
45 Seas
46 Louisiana lingo
49 Heavy-hitting Fielder
50 "Essay on Man" author
51 San ___ Obispo, Calif.
52 "You ___ seen nothin' yet!"
53 Raced
55 New Look designer
56 If not
57 Head for the hills
60 Stowe girl
61 Lunch order, briefly

551 by Joy L. Wouk

ACROSS

1 Sobbed
5 Dangerous March date
9 First-class, in slang
14 Lotion ingredient
15 Kind of tide
16 Boisterous festivity
17 Bottle tops
18 ___ Rivera, Calif.
19 Warner ___ (Charlie Chan of film)
20 1943 musical composed by 37-Across
23 Poker opener
24 "High" time
25 Parts of table settings
28 Source of some PBS programs
29 Six-foot two, for example
33 Prying tool
34 Mother of Hermes
35 "Get outta here!"
36 Numero ___
37 Composer Kurt
38 Popular oil additive
39 Gabby bird
41 ___ of Fame

42 Grudge
44 Bridge option
45 Light switch positions
46 Loewe's partner on Broadway
47 Trudge
49 Othello's ancient
50 1928 work composed by 37-Across, with "The"
57 Ache (for)
58 Moses' attire
59 One corner in Monopoly
60 Coke rival
61 Hardly ___ (rarely)
62 Sicilian spewer
63 Vaudeville's Ole
64 June honorees
65 Sounds of reproof

DOWN

1 Texas city
2 Dash
3 John Paul, e.g.
4 Having a valid will
5 Feeds the computer
6 Clear the winter windshield

7 Apiece
8 One may be roseate
9 Utah city
10 Caves in
11 ___ the Terrible
12 Diner's card
13 Early auto maker
21 It's unique
22 Kind of point
25 Well-padded
26 See 31-Down
27 Three English rivers
28 Fights to save a sinking boat
30 Bret Harte character
31 With 26-Down, wife of 37-Across
32 Gentle runner
34 Rambled
37 Rodeo yell
40 Slander
42 Utah lily
43 Turbo engine plane
46 Cake features
48 Red Square figure
49 Not yet risen
50 Printer's goof
51 Dog command
52 Hip songs
53 Exploding star

54 Gobbles
55 Where to do figure eights
56 "Oh, woe!"

552 by Frances Hansen

ACROSS

1 Singer Ed
5 Songbird McEntire
9 Shortstop Ernie
14 Historic Adriatic port
15 Skip over
16 Tatum or Ryan
17 Cobb's "___ Laughing"
18 Novel set in Tahiti
19 Kind of blonde, once
20 Speed demon's way to go
23 "The works"
24 Chan portrayer
27 1930's power prog.
30 Navy waiter
34 Sandy's woof
36 Bunny's way to go
38 Crazy ___ ("O Pioneers!" hermit)
39 Dogie catcher
40 Outlawry
41 Adult insect
42 Mr. Cassini
43 Pig buyer's way to go
45 "___ doll . . ." (start of a request)
46 Bleach ingredient

47 Cricket sides
48 Wedding dress feature
50 Dock org.
52 Tumbler's way to go
59 Taper off
62 Buck extension
63 Satiate
64 Bakery order
65 Course offerer
66 Emilia's husband
67 Cancel
68 Wrangle
69 Physician's photo

DOWN

1 First shepherd
2 Ankle-length
3 Guitarist Clapton
4 Alaskan city
5 Ivy offshoot
6 Award since 1949
7 Short lives?
8 Over
9 In the flesh
10 "La Navarraise" heroine
11 Pince-___
12 1970's TV law drama
13 Wily

21 Gantry or Fudd
22 Chicago area, with "the"
25 Prized rug
26 Bring home by the ears
27 Pulsate
28 It may be ultra
29 Show up
31 Dame Thorndike of the English stage
32 Chases flies
33 One of a pair of drums
35 Aristophanes comedy, with "The"
37 Identify, in a way
38 "Am ___ brother's keeper?"
41 Shelley's "Paradise of exiles"
43 Dec. 31 follower
44 Delete text
46 Still
49 Chasing
51 Attach
53 Actress Dawber et al.
54 Kind of school
55 Island west of Scotland

56 Ananias
57 Gymnast Korbut
58 Stratagem
59 Org. founded by H.H.H.

60 Duck for apples
61 Kind of dye

553   by Wayne Robert Williams

ACROSS
1 Musical postscripts
6 No longer in vogue
11 Chum
14 Flooded
15 Computer correspondence
16 Infamous Amin
17 Misdirections
19 Crux
20 Rhea's cousins
21 Jeer from the stands
23 Missile trajectories
26 Egotist's claim
29 Fiery gemstone
30 Big ___
31 Hard one to convince
32 Sudden flood
33 Shot (at) from the sidelines
35 Left high and dry
37 Measured stretches
39 It may get dunked
40 Western outlaws
43 With the result
46 Low-budget prefix
47 One with sticky fingers
49 Biblical priest
50 Spots for teens?
51 Old-fashioned contraction
52 Idle of "Monty Python"
53 Input anew
55 Cartoonist Drake
57 Half of MMCII
58 Monte Carlo game
64 Days of yore
65 Baseball strike figure
66 Best
67 Mother deer
68 Selling feature
69 Mountain climber's spike

DOWN
1 Auto
2 Be in the red
3 "Dear old" fellow
4 England-Australia cricket prize, with "The"
5 One of Noah's sons
6 Individual
7 French friend
8 ___ Joaquin Valley
9 Spectacle
10 Otherwise
11 Peter Sellers movie, with "The"
12 Hero-worship
13 Maligned
18 "A Raisin in the Sun" actress
22 Lame excuse
23 Bonehead
24 Printing
25 Alabama
27 Purpose
28 Great number
31 Yo-Yo Ma's instrument
32 Start of a sequel title
34 60's singer Gene
36 Floral ornament
38 Mlle., in Spain
40 Activated again, as a missile
41 Italian artist Paolo
42 Less than forward
44 Scheherazade hero
45 Muscle spasm
48 Filler
51 Feline inquiries
52 Boredom
54 Swift Malay boat
56 Surmounting
59 Young ___
60 "Gosh!"
61 Legendary Giant
62 Bachelor's last words
63 Wood of the Rolling Stones

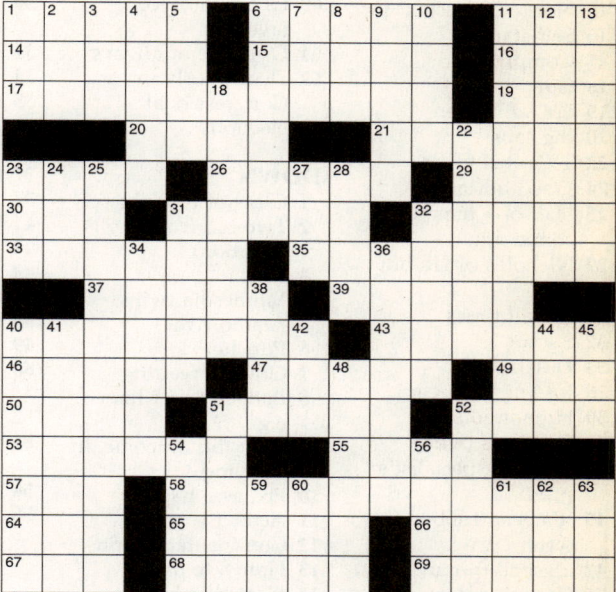

554   by David J. Kahn

ACROSS
1 Winter workers
10 Woodsy area
15 Place for the self-serving
16 Alternative to a Movado
17 Projects, in a way
18 Gulf of ___
19 Tint again
20 Group
22 ___ de plume
23 Hot time in Paris
24 What a commuter mustn't miss
27 Cuckoo
28 Underworld figures
30 Take a risk
31 Caramel-topped dessert
32 Disney pooch
34 Sad Sack's girlfriend, in the comics
35 Direct
40 ". . . ___ from our sponsor"
41 Wore
42 Miss out on a prize
43 Schiller's "___ Joy"
45 Fast fliers
49 Wolfed down
50 Some soon-to-be marrieds
52 Designate
53 ___ good turn
54 Samoan port, if repeated
55 Heavy clay
57 One-time Reagan co-star
59 Woman's magazine founded in 1989
62 Wing
63 "Sugar Babies" star
64 Frail
65 Like some tableware

DOWN
1 Went home
2 Must
3 "East ___"
4 To a high degree
5 Mertz or Merman
6 Grazing area
7 Directional suffix
8 Direct
9 Southwest Japanese port
10 Last year's srs.
11 He speaks: Lat. abbr.
12 "The Four Seasons" director
13 Cary Grant-like
14 Grilled
21 Part of a dog pound
25 Put ___ in one's ear
26 Dickens's Pecksniff
29 Replacement item
31 Babes in the woods
33 Pot top
34 Sign of success
35 Restaurant feature
36 Fairly solid, as odds
37 Emmy-winning comedienne
38 Lot
39 Repute
43 Spanish wave
44 Beliefs
46 Aussie tennis champ Fred
47 Turn the ___
48 Tridents
50 Sticky stuff
51 Vaccine developer
56 Secluded spot
58 British finale
60 Ribosomal ___
61 "___ Blue?" (1929 hit)

555　by Randolph Ross

ACROSS

1 Subject of "The Bridges of Madison County"
11 Tree house
15 Not to be wished for
16 Self-starter
17 Comprises
18 Gin
19 Pol. affiliation
20 Big tops
22 TV's Ricky
24 Freed hostage
25 Half of a famous comic duo
29 Nicholas of "Room 222"
30 For all times
32 Succor
33 Desert dare
38 José or Juan, e.g.
39 Humongous
40 Connects (with)
44 Medical specialist's prefix
45 It's been rubbed the wrong way
47 ___ ball (popular toy)
51 Count's place
55 One of the 13 colonies: Abbr.
56 Head of the class
57 New York eatery
59 Wise about
60 Of an embryonic layer
61 Opposite of always
62 Does poorly in Congressional elections

DOWN

1 Clear of thought
2 Two-___ (court situation)
3 Sells
4 Minnesota twins
5 Alamo rival
6 Puncher
7 Oracle's reading
8 Pollock and Kline, e.g.
9 Coin flip outcome, in a saying
10 Fix, as a napkin
11 Actor Lane
12 Continental hybrids
13 Home, to Yanks
14 #1 at Wimbledon
21 Social register word
23 "___ Old Cowhand"
26 Linguistic suffix
27 "___ said . . ."
28 Oysters ___ season
30 Brussels-born fashion designer
31 Record writing
34 Pinafore, e.g.
35 Ambulance driver: Abbr.
36 Date
37 Quotation notation
38 Affix, as a date
41 Tolerated
42 Real London ending
43 Place for Jefferson
46 Maine town
48 Tomato blight
49 Kindled anew
50 Police officers, in slang
52 Last wrapper
53 Guitarist Nugent et al.
54 Railway car cargoes
58 Dr. of rap

556　by Sidney L. Robbins

ACROSS

1 Island south of Sicily
6 One of the three B's
10 Church nook
14 Once more
15 Melville novel
16 Brag
17 Decide against, from fear
19 Present
20 Topeka native
21 On ___ (for later approval)
23 She, objectively
24 Coolio's music
26 Quench
28 Conducted
31 Iowa college town
33 Dish cleaner
36 "Take ___ from me"
38 Grand saga
40 Comforted
41 Hans Christian Andersen story
44 Foreword
45 Wall Street order
46 Toward shelter
47 Clink, clank, and clunk
49 Smack
51 Curved letter
52 Contractual matters
54 Big ___, Calif.
55 Inventor Whitney
57 Locale
59 Barely conceal one's anger
64 Cargo
66 Ballroom dance to ragtime music
68 Florence's river
69 Jane Austen novel
70 Wipe out
71 Bird pad
72 Quarrel
73 Store sects.

DOWN

1 Built like a ___ truck
2 Turkish bigwig
3 Reclined
4 Spasms
5 Turkish capital
6 ___ mot (witticism)
7 Famous cookie man
8 Ends of juntas
9 Monopoly purchases
10 "___ du lieber!"
11 Like a monkey's tail
12 Kind of loser
13 Pitcher
18 Tooth layer
22 "R.U.R." dramatist
25 Diarist Samuel
27 Australian "bear"
28 Language of Lucretius
29 Prefix with centric
30 Food gurus
32 Borders
34 Heredity determinants
35 Borders
37 Prize money
39 Selects
42 Traveling types
43 Word with escalator or subordinate
48 Deals a heavy blow to
50 Victimized, with "upon"
53 Nonplus
55 Dash
56 Folk wisdom
58 Witty Bombeck
60 To be, in Paris
61 Snare
62 Party thrower
63 French seasons
65 Speck
67 Cartoondom's Krazy ___

557 by Jonathan Schmalzbach

ACROSS
1 Put on the burner
5 Post-larval
10 Bullfight cries
14 Willa Cather's "One of ___"
15 Wipe out
16 Org. with a mission
17 Dr. Seuss's diner order?
20 Skipper's plea
21 "___ a Grecian Urn"
22 Like TV's "Tales From the Crypt"
23 "Roses ___ red . . ."
24 Certain computer, informally
25 "Here come de judge!" comic
33 Reindeer driver
34 Bounds
35 Coach Parseghian
36 Partner of kisses
37 Categorizes
38 Fortitude
39 Bedbound
40 Champagne buckets
41 Diminishes
42 Popular hors d'oeuvres
45 Play part
46 Carrier letters
47 Island off Venezuela
50 Road hazard warning
53 Moo goo gai pan pan
56 1676 Virginia uprising
59 Tulip's base
60 Jury
61 Cartoonist Peter
62 Woeful cry
63 Impatient
64 Pooped

DOWN
1 Monopolizes
2 Prefix with dollar or trash
3 Father of Deimos and Phobos
4 Mao ___-tung
5 Carolina river
6 Compulsion
7 When repeated, a Samoan port
8 Professional grp.
9 Grazing area
10 Up next
11 "The Wizard of Oz" actor
12 Actor Morales
13 Unvarying
18 Bellini opera
19 Gets close
23 C.I.A. types
24 Hammond products
25 Pope of A.D. 757
26 Fireside
27 Fragrant East Indian wood
28 ___ cotta
29 Taiwan-controlled island
30 "The Outcasts of Poker Flat" writer
31 Strong and fierce-tempered one, supposedly
32 Wrestling areas
33 Switchblade
37 "Away with you!"
38 Pranks
40 Early Peruvian
41 Swiss city
43 Powerful persons
44 "Of course!"
47 Father, in the Bible
48 Actor Julia
49 Abdul-Jabbar's alma mater
50 Humorist Lebowitz
51 Advanced
52 Lincoln and Burrows
53 Fence material
54 One of the O'Neills
55 Half hitch, e.g.
57 Health restorer
58 Rat-racing room, for short

558 by Randall J. Hartman

ACROSS
1 Jacuzzis
5 Box office hit
10 Man in a garden
14 Boston's Faneuil ___
15 Busch Gardens site
16 Singer Horne
17 One of the Guthries
18 Swiss mountains, to the French
19 City blight
20 What the photographer-turned-policeman said
23 Indian carving
24 Model Macpherson
25 Compadre of Fidel
27 Years at the Sorbonne
28 Cool ___ cucumber
31 Main course
33 Kind of shelter
36 P.B.A. Hall-of-Famer Anthony
37 What the sculptor-turned-policeman said
40 Man-eating giant
42 Bloodhounds' trails
43 Kind of scream
46 Weep
47 Berne's river
50 Notebook divider
51 Santa ___, Calif.
54 Way to the altar
56 What the manicurist-turned-policeman said
60 "___ Karenina"
61 Tricks
62 Tibetan priest
63 Compote fruit
64 Awaken, as feelings
65 Drei minus zwei
66 Actress Raines
67 Prevent
68 Skirt feature

DOWN
1 California peak
2 "9 to 5" actress
3 Metes out
4 Schussing site
5 Twinkler
6 Its capital is Bamako
7 Plentiful
8 Be in a bee
9 Harass
10 Too
11 Bill Clinton, e.g.
12 Second helping
13 Oui or Us, e.g.
21 Muscat resident
22 Biddy
26 Conger
29 Start of a cheer
30 "Lucky Jim" author
32 Miss Trueheart
33 "Excuse me"
34 Nile viper
35 Neighbor of Cambodia
37 Court of justice
38 Halloween cry
39 Population classification
40 Choose
41 Small anchor
44 Suffix with honor
45 Came into view
47 Lace into
48 Diploma holders
49 Banquet
52 Debonair
53 Underworld talk
55 Waits at the stoplight
57 Scarlett's home
58 Quarterback's command
59 Pete Sampras, in a way
60 Huxley's "___ and Essence"

559 by Christopher Page

ACROSS
1 Peck's Oscar role
6 Where Epsom is
12 Rapids transit
13 Snares
15 Mojo
16 Site of 25,000 workers
17 They provide zest
18 1902 erupter
19 Wee, in Wick
20 Like some antique shops
21 Decorticates
22 Good long bath
23 Sara of "Timecop"
24 Inclines
25 Billy's mate
26 Rest time
28 Rackets
29 Abrogate
30 Lackland trainees
33 & 34 Treatment for the faint
36 Embattled
39 First Oscar winner for a foreign-language performance
40 Reverse image, for short
41 Immersed
42 Fire fighter
43 German admiral
44 Stavros's archrival
45 PBS pledge premiums
46 Antennae
47 Decoration for a parade
49 One way to take café
50 Intensifies
51 Roofing material
52 Sci-fi group
53 Matzoh meal

DOWN
1 Attendant spirit
2 Swamp
3 German Expressionist Emil
4 Copyright symbols
5 33d Prez
6 Relieves
7 French ballot boxes
8 Practice
9 Genetic messenger
10 Needles
11 Savoyard guard
12 Glances
13 Alka-Seltzer mascot, in bygone ads
14 Winding
18 Kind of offense
21 Piano mute
22 Clog
24 Doctor
25 First name in strikeouts
27 Ruffled
28 Bannister, e.g.
30 Alveolae
31 Do a whitesmith's job
32 Less bustling
34 See 42-Down
35 Gets rid of
36 Top dogs at 16-Across
37 Kittenish Kitt
38 Screwy?
39 Nears a deadline
42 With 34-Down, some league members
43 Rabbit food
45 Measuring aid
46 Whimper
48 Verdi aria "___ tu"
49 Palm Sunday mount

560 by Richard Silvestri

ACROSS
1 Obsolete
6 Serpent song
10 Up to snuff
14 Type type
15 Put a stake on the table
16 Mr. Kadiddlehopper
17 Campaign-poster word
18 Night light
19 Litter littlest
20 Marquis de Sade's favorite side dish?
23 Before, to bards
24 Grandiose poetry
25 Wound reminder
28 Lingerie buy
31 Undiminished
35 Start of M-G-M's motto
36 Pop singer Abdul
38 Seven-time N.L. homer champ
39 Marquis de Sade's favorite entree?
42 Start of the año
43 Begin, as winds
44 Morn's opposite
45 Wanted-poster word
47 Snitch
48 Shelley output
49 Lab bottle
51 Former Mideast monogram
53 Marquis de Sade's favorite vegetable?
60 Ambition
61 At the summit of
62 More than manly
63 Move like the Blob
64 A little
65 Cultural characteristics
66 Ran in the laundry
67 Had no doubt
68 Ocean areas

DOWN
1 Regard
2 ___ breve (2/2 time)
3 Dad's Day gifts
4 Whistler was one
5 Dissuade
6 Fastening device
7 '85 film, "___ the Night"
8 Washington, e.g.
9 Ranchero's wrap
10 Verse with a message?
11 In a funk
12 Brownie's eye?
13 CPR specialist
21 Interdict
22 Hanoi's region
25 Fencing weapon
26 Brom Bones's prey
27 In ___ (agitated)
29 Has misgivings about
30 Birch kin
32 Readied the press
33 Christopher of the screen
34 Crossword birds
36 "Will it play in ___?"
37 Official records
40 Made a basketball boo-boo
41 Ask for a loan
46 Upholstery fabric
48 Baroque
50 Admit
52 Aligned the crosshairs
53 Air-conditioned
54 Bulldoze
55 Igloo shape
56 Gush forth
57 Need a backrub
58 Karate motion
59 Ponderosa name
60 Lump

561 by Eileen Lexau

ACROSS

1 Hazard
9 Rumor
14 Took to mean
15 Prevention dose?
16 Lousy tips
17 Be maître d'
18 "A Chorus Line" song
19 Electrical unit
20 Couple's org.
21 High-pitched
24 Moon valleys
27 One of the Chaplins
28 Fineness
29 Crash sound
31 Dire
34 St. Paul's top
35 See 42-Across
36 1964 Berne best seller (and a hint to seven other answers in this puzzle)
39 Falls off
40 D. J. Jazzy Jeff songs
41 Orders of the court
42 With 35-Across, a cleanser
43 Lean
44 So-so grade
45 Hears tell of
47 Least prevalent
50 Comedian's date
51 Wallops
52 Writer Buruma
54 Went chop-chop?
57 After-dinner drink
60 Breezing through
61 Lifeless
62 Italian summit
63 Matter for the Federal Trade Commission

DOWN

1 Butcher's cut of meat
2 Reply to a knock
3 East, in Berlin
4 School org.
5 Country music's Tennessee Plowboy
6 Lacy dress trimming
7 Judge
8 Track-meet measure: Abbr.
9 Amaze
10 From the sticks
11 Nice article
12 Diamonds
13 Asian holiday
14 U.S.N. rank
20 Computer dot
22 One of Adlai's running mates
23 Toodle-oos
24 Beef roasts
25 Princess ___ ("Don Carlos" figure)
26 Anwar of Egypt
28 Nuts
30 N.L. M.V.P., 1954 and 1965
31 Becomes gray
32 Intriguing group
33 Like Uriah Heep
34 ___ list
35 Tear
37 Tine
38 Jug
43 George Washington, e.g.
44 Harrah's, e.g.
46 Representative
47 Style of type
48 Twine fiber
49 Flavorsome
51 Relative of lotto
53 Born
54 Son of Noah
55 Umberto of Italy
56 Be lucky in the lottery
57 Turn down
58 Bit of advice
59 Latin I verb

562 by Joel Davajan

ACROSS

1 Unhappy
5 Man with the world on his shoulders
10 Israeli carrier
14 "Mona ___"
15 Scarlett's love
16 Comic Rudner
17 What we celebrate on July 4
20 Honor, with "to"
21 Form 1040 amount
22 Buntline and Rorem
23 Sean Connery, e.g.
24 Duke's home
27 Fifth Avenue name
28 Catch in the act
31 Gaucho's rope
32 Golfer Ballesteros
33 Old Russian assembly
34 What we celebrate on July 4
37 Bronze and Iron
38 Some intersections
39 Think
40 Stag party attendees
41 Scorch
42 Ranch
43 Tools locale
44 ___ de foie gras
45 Book after Nehemiah
48 Fortification
52 What we watch on July 4
54 A lulu
55 Miss Brooks portrayer
56 Muck
57 Witnessed
58 Stocking material
59 Some whiskies

DOWN

1 Happy
2 Green shade
3 Employed
4 Seasons, as meat
5 Teen hangout
6 Dean Martin's "___ Amore"
7 ___-majesté
8 Arm of the Treasury Dept.
9 Ill
10 Construct
11 Island near Venice
12 Mighty mite
13 Costly cloth
18 Hangover soother?
19 Son of Seth
23 Baseball and hockey stats
24 Father of Hector and Paris
25 Danny of the N.B.A.
26 Weighed down
27 Passover feast
28 Blue entertainment
29 Hotpoint rival
30 Sang to the moon
32 Golf legend Sam
33 Doctor's instrument
35 Intangible
36 Egypt's ___ Church
41 "Good night, ___" (old TV phrase)
42 Briny
43 Like Samson, once
44 Kind of truck
45 Heroic poetry
46 "Auld Lang ___"
47 It's better known for its bark than its bite
48 Third degrees, usually
49 Seaman's shout
50 Nod off
51 Rams' dams
53 Dernier ___

563 by Raymond Hamel

ACROSS
1 "St. John Passion" composer
5 In vogue
9 Carpet variety
13 Nepal's location
14 Leftovers dish
15 Prowess
16 "Lost Horizon" paradise
18 Public sentiment
19 "Message received"
20 Songwriter John
21 Long, deep bow
25 More than a snack
27 First look
30 1901 Churchill novel, with "The"
34 With masts fully extended
35 Imprint on glass
37 Posted
38 Puny pup
39 Dweller in Gulliver's Houyhnhnmland
40 Wash
41 Deuce topper
42 Skater Heiden
43 Idolater
44 Snow remover?

46 Seven Cities of Cibola seeker
48 George Takei TV/ movie role
50 Confuses
51 Shore bird
54 Soprano Nixon
57 Dik Browne Viking
58 Town visited by Tommy Albright
63 Subtle twist
64 Like elbowing, e.g.
65 Paris landing site
66 Aromatic herb
67 Prepared brandy
68 Start for "of honor" or "of silence"

DOWN
1 ___-relief
2 Ski wood
3 "The Company"
4 Solo of "Star Wars"
5 Plating material
6 Nixon chief of staff
7 Sunny vacation spot
8 Mojo
9 King Kong's home
10 Saber handle
11 To boot

12 ___ Burnie, Md.
15 Aborigine's weapon
17 Woodworker's concern
21 City attacked by Cleon
22 Fabric with a raised pattern
23 Near ringer
24 "Jaws" locale
26 Canyon sound
28 Bring up
29 Work ___
31 Action star Steven
32 Blitz
33 Typing pool members
36 Designer Chanel
39 Make oneself heard in the din
43 Lecterns
45 "Tumbling Tumbleweeds" singer, 1935
47 Traveled far and wide
49 Eclipse shadow
51 Kind of splints
52 Butler's quarters?
53 Operatic prince

55 "... as a bug in ___"
56 Sally of NASA
59 Medic
60 Spanish gold
61 Timeworn
62 TV comic Louis

564 by Harvey Estes

ACROSS
1 "All done"
8 Nina of jazz
14 "Strangers in the Night" singer
15 Actor Jack of "City Slickers"
16 "Wait a minute!"
18 Member of Cong.
19 A dot in the ocean
20 The Rail Splitter
23 Declaration of interdependence
25 Bridge feat
29 Bergen of "Murphy Brown"
32 Wall St. regulator
35 Tyrant Amin
36 The British Museum's ___ marbles
37 Sales spiel
39 RCA products
40 "Rough ride ahead!"
43 ___ jiffy
44 Old Testament prophet
45 ___ cum laude
46 R.E. Lee, e.g.
47 Printers' widths

48 Now available
50 Jekyll's counterpart
52 Ocean
53 Tiny
54 Tutor
58 ___ man (unanimously)
61 "Get ready for hard times!"
68 Having a liking for
69 Give-away: Var.
70 Allergy sufferer's bane
71 Nuclear treaty

DOWN
1 Reproof sound
2 Hurry
3 Suffix with meth- or hex-
4 Bugle solo
5 Eye problem
6 Satirical, maybe
7 T in Sparta
8 Comedian Mort
9 Nasty racket operator?
10 Stores
11 Que. neighbor
12 Sgt., e.g.

13 Nighttime, in poetry
15 Letter endings: Abbr.
17 "Flying Down to ___"
20 Like certain poker hands
21 Poppycock
22 "Oh, to be in ___ ...": Browning
24 Bottommost area
26 Actor John
27 Make progress
28 Boner
30 Performed
31 "Two mints ___"
32 Block
33 Logical beginning
34 Pals
38 Debtor's letters
41 Site of 60's service
42 Inform (on)
49 Word with mother or human
51 Lucy's landlady
52 Bashful
55 Little: Suffix
56 Time spent in line, seemingly
57 Atlanta-based network

59 Bauxite and others
60 Aid and ___
61 Kitchen meas.
62 ___ Jima
63 Toothpaste, perhaps

64 Frequently
65 Tide's retreat
66 Actress Thompson
67 Perfect rating

ACROSS

1 More pronounced
7 Ladies
13 Law of the land
14 Run
16 Proceeds as in a car chase
17 They can't be beat
18 Bird: Prefix
19 Pre-Bond Moore role, with "The"
21 "On Boxing" author
22 Zodiac animal
24 Wooden Mortimer
26 Like autumn leaves
27 Adam's-apple warmer
29 Succession of wins
31 90's cartoon character
32 Yankee #9
34 Governess of Thornfield
36 New Hampshire's "Live Free or Die"?
38 Bessemer product
41 Jalapeño hot stuff
44 San Antone sobriquet
45 Director Lubitsch
47 Ugly looks
49 Iron pumper's routine
51 Golden ___ (retirees)
53 Turkey meat request
54 Varsity
56 Giving the once-over
58 Year in Canute's life
59 Dodgson's illustrator
61 Utah emblem
63 Hall of broadcasting
64 Was useful
65 Canary's cousins
66 Greased the roast

DOWN

1 Throwback
2 Dance with dips and leaps
3 New Mexico's ___ Lake
4 Amer. election day
5 Lab heaters
6 Oozings
7 Habitants' home
8 Compliment, in a way
9 Deejay's disk
10 Precincts
11 Total control
12 Three-card monte shill
13 La ___, Milan
15 Palestinian sectarian
20 Just-born cow?
23 Ibsen, for one
25 Hockey great Potvin
28 Champion's claim
30 Kind of farm
33 Prickly pear
35 Sniggled
37 Peelable fruit
38 Class levels
39 Prepares for a fall
40 Tax form deduction
42 About 6,080 feet
43 Hit town
46 Like certain customs
48 Went downhill
50 Better balanced
52 1983 Indy 500 champ
55 Small model
57 Duds
60 Strauss's "___ Heldenleben"
62 Holed up

ACROSS

1 Cavort
5 Half an old radio team
9 Fall preceder
13 ___ Ben Adhem
14 Indian boy of film
15 Electron tube
16 X
19 Art lover
20 Riverbed item
21 Vane dir.
22 Stash
23 Act peevishly toward
27 Kind of stock
28 Fixes, illegally
32 Found a vein
33 Washington help
35 Tennis call
36 X
39 Bro., e.g.
40 Disgusted
41 Actor Jack of the 30's and 40's
42 Stew
44 Kickoff aid
45 Candy
46 Legislation
48 Bank convenience, for short
49 Error
52 Lineate
57 X
59 Start for a weaver
60 Urchin
61 Legal preceder
62 Salad cheese
63 Depend add-on
64 Pretentious one

DOWN

1 Pro ___
2 Theater award
3 Footwear, for short
4 Short shot
5 Rise
6 Fotomat choice
7 O, once, to hams
8 Litigate
9 Logs
10 60's Presidential in-law
11 Sacred statue
12 Soccer great
15 Did a hairdresser's job
17 Leading
18 Easter bloom
22 Invited to one's apartment
23 Blue cartoon critter
24 Montana, once
25 Tibia neighbor
26 Write
27 Dudgeon
29 Start of a 50's political slogan
30 "Understand?"
31 Eye problems
33 Lake Titicaca locale
34 Winter creations
37 Rainier
38 ___ kwon do
43 City on Commencement Bay
45 Pepper
47 Parish V.I.P.
48 Popular storage spot
49 Offend
50 About, in legalspeak
51 Fitzgerald forte
52 Browse
53 Cobras
54 Actress Nancy from Hong Kong
55 Architect Saarinen
56 Lackluster
58 Ram's mate

567 by Wayne Robert Williams

ACROSS
1 Classifieds
4 Light, old-style
10 Overlook
14 S. Amer. country
15 Hit dead-center
16 ___ mapping (modern science effort)
17 Monterey product
19 Actress Turner
20 Sign of controversy
21 It goes with the flow
23 Sounds like
24 Federalist paper
26 Ask a lot of questions
27 Beam
29 ___ dare
31 Lhasa ___
34 Baked dessert
39 Award of honor
40 One of Stalin's cronies
41 First-century Roman emperor
42 Sunday brunch fare
44 Runner Wyomia ___
45 Thickness
46 Versified romance
48 Ceiling
50 Fully sink (in)
53 Use a soapbox
57 Of the deep-sea floor
59 Uncivilized one
60 Pacific nation
61 Corn bread on the griddle
64 Old Testament kingdom
65 Journalist Fallaci
66 Wine classification
67 Dates
68 Trial separation?
69 Mach topper

DOWN
1 Menu phrase
2 Arrange artistically
3 Bolivian capital
4 Liquid, in a way
5 Oz lion
6 Golf-ball position
7 Diminutive suffix
8 Arizona features
9 Swelling
10 Eyeball
11 Burger
12 Spiritual
13 Melodramatic
18 Soviet youth group
22 Advice-column abbr.
24 Zimbalist, Sr. or Jr.
25 Computer capacity
28 Dear one
30 Recent
31 Manhunt letters
32 Chum
33 Ground beef sandwich
35 Belushi bio
36 Votes against
37 Calendar-watch abbr.
38 Attention-getting calls
43 Color changers
47 Harding and others
48 Smokey Joe's and others
49 Tolerate
51 Base V.I.P.
52 Actor Eric
54 Build up
55 Accepts uncomplainingly
56 First-rate
58 Beautician Naomi
59 Novelist Radcliffe et al.
62 ___ jacet (epitaph start)
63 Stirling denial

568 by Elizabeth C. Gorski

ACROSS
1 Corporate head, for short
4 Scotch or masking, e.g.
8 Disco light
14 Patient care grp.
15 Food gelling agent
16 Home on the reservation
17 "Apollo 13" actor
19 Tough time
20 Come back into, as the atmosphere
21 Livesaving skill, for short
22 14-Across employees
23 Sumatra's land
25 Alley ___
27 ___ Moines
28 Crier of "Wolf!"
32 Yields
35 "When ___ Loves a Woman"
36 Gymnastics coach Karolyi
37 Follower of Mar.
38 Meetings of presidents
41 Pussy
42 Bridle part
44 Noël Coward and others
45 Pet ___
47 Borrowing as a financial tool
49 It's south of Ga.
50 Greek letter
51 Mail recipient
56 All-out fight
58 Hypodermic amts.
60 Magazine deal
61 Attack
63 Modern college lodging
64 "Burnt" Crayola color
65 Auto maker Ferrari
66 Bullfight cry
67 Like football clothes
68 ___-do-well
69 Part of m.p.h.

DOWN
1 "Mon ___"
2 German city
3 Expressed wonderment
4 Feature of Granny Smiths
5 Concurs (with)
6 Skating couples
7 Uhs' kin
8 Halt
9 Fright
10 Crimson
11 Newspaper essay, maybe
12 Chicago footballer
13 Wrigglers
18 Battery part
21 French port city
24 60's TV sign-off, straight from the horse's mouth
26 Fed. money overseer
29 Picnic ruiner
30 Czech or Pole
31 London's ___ Gallery
32 Runner Lewis
33 Fencing rapier
34 Where to learn parallel parking
35 Some computers
39 "Surfin' ___" (1963 hit)
40 Magnificence
43 Center court sight
46 Facilitated
48 Molière contemporary
49 Police yell
52 Talk on and on
53 In one fell ___
54 Baseball Hall-of-Famer Combs
55 Mr. Fudd
56 Hornet
57 Pacific rim region
59 Bedecked
62 Plus
63 100 yrs.

569 by Norma Steinberg

ACROSS

1 Namath et al.
5 Famous cookie maker
9 Where to hang a hat
12 It's west of Ark.
13 Nominates
15 Wahine's dance
16 Financial district
18 Award for a sitcom
19 Old cleaning substance
20 In tatters
21 Slip by
23 Overly thin
24 Impish kid
25 Yellow bird
28 Snubbed
32 By oneself
33 Announcer's cry at a soccer match
34 Burn
35 Item on a to-do list
36 Kind of juice
37 Minstrel's accompaniment
38 Give off
39 Split
40 Mosaic components
41 Grudge carrier
43 Errand runners
44 Enumeration, as of errands
45 Explore, as the Internet
46 Cell centers
49 Lhasa ___ (dog)
50 Actress Dawber
53 Plowing unit
54 She said "Mmmmmwah" at the end of her shows
57 Smear
58 Comic Kovacs
59 Fitzgerald who sang "A-Tisket, A-Tasket"
60 Wailing horn
61 Castle material
62 Irrelevant

DOWN

1 Cheek neighbor
2 "You bet!"
3 Model Macpherson
4 Actor Mineo
5 Cleopatra's love
6 Get hitched
7 Augury
8 "___ you later!"
9 Ship's engine part
10 Street shaders
11 Singer Marvin
14 Free of germs
15 Brontë hero
17 Warehouse
22 Fall behind
23 One with many bills
24 Insipid
25 Actress Phoebe
26 Crockett's last stand, with "the"
27 Plebe's answer
28 In good condition
29 Greenland military base
30 Restaurant patron
31 Gown
33 Like some grandparents
36 Have the chair
40 Bullring bulls
42 Go in a hurry
43 Spoke effusively
45 Toledo's location
46 Catches red-handed
47 Bruins of the N.C.A.A.
48 Pivotal point
49 "___ Karenina"
50 Informal shirt
51 Guthrie the younger
52 Butcher's stock
55 Tax people, for short
56 Haw's partner

570 by Francis Heaney

ACROSS

1 Piano part
6 Trot and canter
11 Jamaica-based music
14 Integra maker
15 ___ Joe's (classic sign)
16 Tennis's Shriver
17 Camel rival
19 "___ we having fun yet?"
20 Linked, in a way
21 Persia, today
22 Hot mo.
25 Weekday: Abbr.
26 Gem sides
28 Daze
30 Small piano
32 Reveal
33 Whirling ones
36 Johnson of "Laugh-In"
37 Golfer with an army
38 Six: Prefix
39 Banal bit of versification
41 Mushroom
42 Gully
43 Do over
44 Gave the wrong impression
46 Shepherd's beckoning
47 Sot's woe
48 Novelist Tyler
49 Leaves the office early?
53 Schuss
54 Dairy Queen offering
58 Cool, old-style
59 Mountain chain
60 Steaming
61 Summer quencher
62 Commencement
63 Mike with a punch

DOWN

1 Buddy
2 Common Market money
3 Vietnam's Le ___ Tho
4 Synagogue cabinets
5 Tell frankly, in slang
6 "___ to the Church on Time"
7 Switzerland's Gorge of the ___
8 Medical suffix
9 Go on break
10 Marie, e.g.: Abbr.
11 Be lenient
12 Gold standard
13 Hymn finales
18 Ancient reptile's suffix
21 Rink event
22 Be ___ in the face
23 In ___ (unborn)
24 Bit of riffraff
27 Black cuckoo
29 "The Pit and the Pendulum," e.g.
30 Pick up on
31 Stiffly neat
33 Albanian river
34 Use, as influence
35 Physician Jonas and kin
37 Environmental problem
40 "___ had it!"
41 Is serious
43 Indian music
44 One of Chekhov's "Three Sisters"
45 Smeared indelibly
46 I.Q. test name
50 Goals
51 Pundit
52 Nimble
54 Sis's sib
55 ___ Vegas
56 Lance of L.A. law
57 Perfection in gymnastics

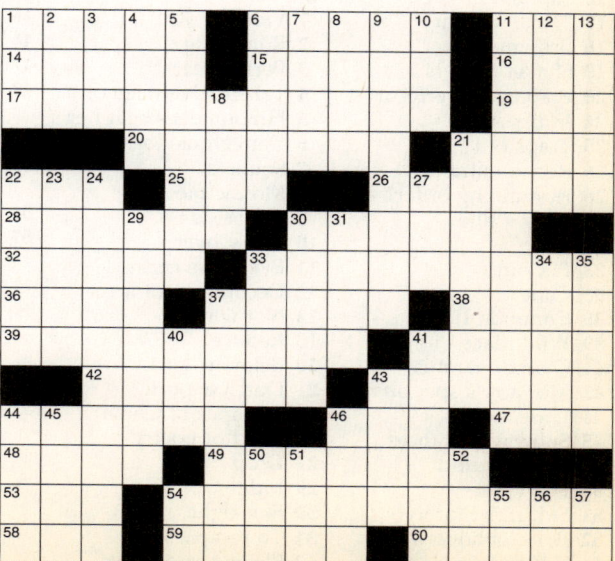

571   by Richard Hughes

ACROSS

1 In effect
6 Fast one
10 Hindu deity
14 Persian Gulf tongue
15 Clothing
16 Oscar winner Jannings
17 Fightin' words
20 Bat wood
21 Calhoun of "How to Marry a Millionaire"
22 Like some columns
23 Auto servicing
24 "See you later"
26 Fightin' words
32 Lifeless
33 Signals approval
34 E.P.A. rating
36 Clock
37 Reimbursable amounts
39 Have a look-see
40 Popular Formula One formula
41 Round-the-campfire stories
42 Rhône feeder
43 Fightin' words
47 Enfant, across the Pyrenees

48 Formerly, formerly
49 Polio vaccine developer
52 Face-to-face test
53 Pop
56 Fightin' words
60 Aviation-related
61 Scold, with "off"
62 Flavius's master, in Shakespeare
63 Govt. agents
64 Hopalong Cassidy portrayer William
65 Where Jimmy Carter teaches

DOWN

1 TV handyman Bob
2 Warlike Olympian
3 Lattice strip
4 Test figs.
5 Throw a monkey wrench into
6 Prefix with phonic
7 Clone
8 Gone by
9 East Lansing sch.
10 Drench again
11 African despot
12 Calf-length dress

13 "Tess of the d'Urbervilles" cad
18 Illustrated mug
19 Emperor after Vespasian
23 Entice
24 Horse race
25 Foots (up)
26 Worst possible situation, with "the"
27 Common design goal
28 Beat
29 Remove stitching
30 Arab chieftain
31 Kind of whale
35 "Riders of the Purple Sage" author
37 R.I. neighbor
38 Church calendar
39 Exam for H.S. juniors
41 "The Divided Self" author
42 1959 Ricky Nelson hit
44 Harmony
45 Boston paper
46 Ancient Syria
49 Hit a homer, e.g.
50 Polite interruption
51 Drill
52 Just
53 Try this!

54 Boy with a bow
55 Gainsay
57 Kind of parlor, for short
58 Classical beginning
59 British defector Philby

572   by Richard Silvestri

ACROSS

1 Kind of soup
9 Alley "oops"
14 Not absolute
15 Cream
16 Sap and sweat
17 "Taxi" co-star
18 Brownie's eye?
19 Shaker leaders
20 Prepare to perform
24 Indisposed
25 Traps out
26 Rodeo entrant
28 Restraining order?
29 Lady's title
30 Butt
33 Put out
35 Cant
38 Common ID
39 Wild place
41 Gym apparatus
42 Moriarty's specialty
44 Limelike
45 Subway entrances
48 Grace period
50 Flat taker
51 Sidi ___, Morocco
52 Refer obliquely
53 Self-satisfied
58 Let

59 Do over
60 Humble
61 Heston film, with "The"

DOWN

1 Verb for you
2 Roman law
3 Perfect start?
4 Taken advantage of
5 Hippomenes beat her
6 Dangerous dogs
7 Squares
8 Mosaic piece
9 Put aside
10 Chew over
11 Eye enhancer
12 Decorators, of a sort
13 Not windy
15 Reduce
20 Belmont card
21 Dutch exports
22 Province of China
23 Land of poetry
27 Drop
29 Judge
30 Sky sight
31 To recap
32 Skein components
34 Sick

36 Frank plus
37 Mississippi Senator
40 Part-time player
42 Grandfather ___
43 Make available
44 Eyetooth
45 Play for time
46 Prefix with logical
47 Wedding acquisition
49 Stu of "77 Sunset Strip"
54 Spacewalk, to NASA
55 Genealogical study: Abbr.
56 Hagen of the stage
57 60's singer Barry

573 by Joel Davajan

ACROSS

1 Christiania today
5 Noggin tops
10 Hind's mate
14 Hullabaloo
15 Open-eyed
16 "Damn Yankees" vamp
17 Ike was one
20 Track officials
21 Testify
22 "Rule, Britannia" composer
23 Early Briton
24 Social groups
27 Garlic relative
28 Asian holiday
31 Culture mores
32 Coxswain's crew
33 ___ Marquette
34 G.I. newspaper
37 Cures leather
38 "That's interesting"
39 Opt
40 Two-by-two vessel
41 Reared
42 Worth
43 Shed
44 Escape
45 Roman villa locale
48 Apollyon adherent
52 Biblical beacon
54 Seller's caveat
55 Backcomb hair
56 Mechanical memorization
57 Smoker's sound
58 Mead research site
59 Animal team

DOWN

1 Switch settings
2 Eye opening
3 Kind of flow
4 Bell workers
5 Thin metal disks
6 Cognizant
7 Salts
8 Dr.'s graph
9 Most rundown
10 Nodded
11 Pamplona runner
12 Hale of "Gilligan's Island"
13 10 on the Beaufort scale
18 Pressure
19 Spoon
23 Intrinsically
24 Jai alai basket
25 It makes scents
26 Part of the evening
27 Put on cargo
28 Dakota digs
29 Upright
30 Blood and acid, e.g.
32 Beginning
33 Bohemian beers
35 Berlin events of 1948
36 Recap
41 Machetelike knife
42 Wimbledon champ Gibson
43 Code name
44 1980 DeLuise flick
45 Royal Russian
46 "___ girl!"
47 Ski spot
48 Coal stratum
49 Hotcakes acronym
50 Bristle
51 Revenuers, for short
53 "___ sport"

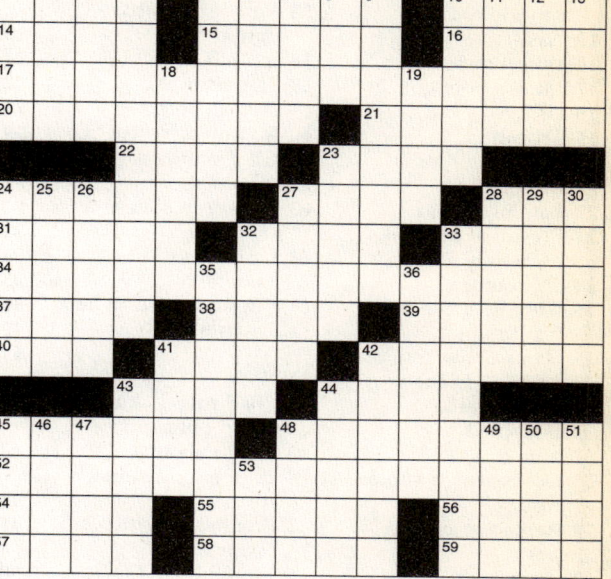

574 by Sidney L. Robbins

ACROSS

1 Wealthy person
5 Takes advantage of
9 "The Forsyte ___"
13 Likeness
15 Kind of stick
16 Sheriff Tupper of "Murder, She Wrote"
17 Social hangout
19 Sea swallow
20 Home turnover
21 Knock out of kilter
23 Illuminated
24 Terminator
25 Bear up there
29 Steep slope
33 Crier of Greek myth
35 Wakens
39 Bettor's challenge
43 Show fright
44 Weird
45 Followed orders
48 N.Y. Police ___
49 Exodus priest
53 Mauna ___
55 Responded unintelligibly
58 "Last stop! ___!"
62 Abner's pal and namesakes
63 Diamond coup
66 Relative of the clarinet
67 Auction actions
68 Indian boat
69 Part of Halloween makeup
70 Church nook
71 Endure

DOWN

1 Informal greetings
2 Eastern V.I.P.
3 Wind instrument?
4 They'll be hunted in April
5 Big sports news
6 Loudly weep
7 "Holy moly!"
8 Kind of loser
9 Beelzebub
10 Change
11 Watkins Glen, e.g.
12 "Lou Grant" star
14 Lod airport airline
18 Nobelist Wiesel
22 Esteem
25 German link
26 Kind of squad
27 Lemonlike
28 Singer Lane
30 Cuomo's predecessor
31 Son of Prince Valiant
32 Australian hopper
34 Long Island town
36 Tool storage area
37 Limerick site
38 Barber's cut
40 Wane
41 Bullring shout
42 Receive
46 Pass
47 Cabbage patch item
49 Visibly happy
50 Caribbean getaway
51 "___ has it . . ."
52 Start
54 Actor Guinness
56 Old lab burner
57 Trapdoor
59 Milky gem
60 Arm bone
61 Pueblo town
64 Employee card and others
65 Still and all

ACROSS

1 Razor sharpener
6 Health resort
9 More than a mere success
14 Mussolini's notorious son-in-law
15 Assist
16 With uneven gait
17 Mink's poor cousin
18 Ushered
19 Truism
20 Item to cut for dessert
23 Late-night star
24 President Manuel, ousted by Franco
25 TV rooms
26 New Rochelle institution
28 Game show sound
30 Princess Diana's family name
33 Bedecked
37 Mea ___
38 Get repeated value from
39 Replaceable shoe parts
42 Agrees
44 Carry on
45 30's and 40's actress Anna
46 Porcine cry
49 Kind of system
51 Weakens
55 Popular poultry entree
58 ___ hilt (fully)
59 "Le veau ___" ("Faust" aria)
60 Roomy dress cut
61 Chef's attire
62 Consume
63 American statesman Cyrus
64 Oceans, to Longfellow
65 Season on the Riviera
66 Lawn tool

DOWN

1 "Bad mood" look
2 Small obligation
3 Snitch about
4 Entree for a solitary diner
5 Scrutinize, with "over"
6 Marathoner Alberto
7 Michelangelo work
8 Afterthoughts
9 Bridge desideratum
10 Dieter's dish
11 A miss's equivalent
12 Dish's companion in flight
13 Songs of glory
21 Diminish
22 Foray
27 Florida city
29 Like Eric the Red
30 H.S. subject
31 So-called "lowest form of wit"
32 Bygone trains
34 Sally Field TV role
35 Erhard's training
36 ___ Plaines, Ill.
40 Prefer follower
41 Latecomer to a theater, maybe
42 Ancient fertility goddess
43 Suffix with young or old
46 Santa's reindeer, e.g.
47 "___ you're happy!"
48 Potassium salt
50 Summer ermine
52 Geriatric process
53 ___ de León
54 Lip curl
56 Understands
57 Pan's opposite

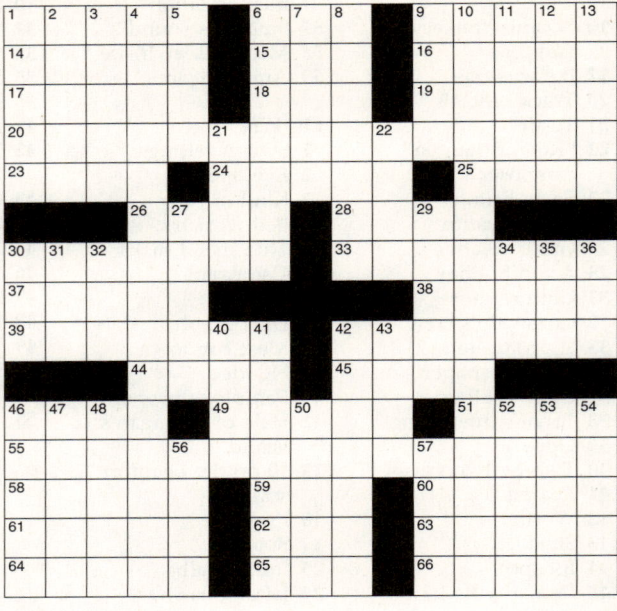

---

576 by Harvey Estes

ACROSS

1 Hunter's prey
5 Batter's woe
10 They're big for conceited folks
14 General under Dwight
15 Resort lake
16 Author Émile
17 Cabdrivers do this
20 Start for step or stop
21 Fix, as in gambling
22 Wild talk
23 Uganda's Amin
24 Show biz routine
28 Rummy cry
30 Repetitive goodbye
32 Simile center
33 "What Kind of Fool ___"
34 Its symbol is five rings
39 Write
40 Optometrists do this
44 Silent communication
45 Tributes
46 Expert
47 Kind of room
48 Animal stomach
52 Stole
53 Battery's partner
57 Show to a seat, informally
58 What you pay at sales
60 Way of Lao-tzu
61 World traveler of note
62 Lip readers do this
67 Conductor Klemperer
68 Friend of Mercutio
69 Cabin wood
70 Unmixed, at a mixer
71 Hanker
72 Busy bodies

DOWN

1 "Get cracking!"
2 Blake of "Gunsmoke"
3 Succeed
4 Before
5 Having a stiff upper lip
6 Har-de-har-har
7 TV band
8 Stock response
9 Each
10 Metrical Pound
11 Flipping
12 Nostalgic
13 Enclosed with an MS.
18 '93, '94, etc.
19 Aquatic zoo
25 Pudding ingredient
26 "Of Thee ___"
27 Big stickers
29 Diamond digit
31 Fine, to a pilot
35 Caustic agent
36 Letter sign-off
37 Slippers for the stubborn?
38 1989 comedy "___ Devil"
40 Page (through)
41 Kiss
42 Victor Herbert work
43 Computer key abbr.
49 Emphasizes, as an embarrassing error
50 Obliquely
51 "Certainly!"
53 Lenten symbol
54 Absolute
55 Imperative to Macduff
56 Overly
59 Dundee dweller
62 Persuaded to marry
63 Not straight
64 Millet's "Man With the ___"
65 Doctors' org.
66 Put ___ fight

577   by Harvey Estes

ACROSS

1 Composer Henry
8 Used an aerosol
15 Fellow who was called on the carpet?
16 Turn in the wash
17 Scot's squeeze
18 Footrest
19 Pop band ___ Lobos
20 Actor Linden
21 "Hit the road!"
24 Bamako's country
27 Treehouse underpinning
31 High-seas greeting
32 Watches, e.g.
34 Guy's date
35 "There Is Nothin' Like a ___"
36 Annul
37 Shooters' org.
38 Jams
40 Hug
42 "___ Lay Dying"
43 Reign of glaciers
47 Nonsense comedy of 60's TV
48 One in the cooler
49 Chico's boss
50 Russo of "In the Line of Fire"
51 Wounded ___, S.D.
53 Whitney and Wallach
54 Nonswimmer, perhaps
55 Mayberry address
57 "Just a ___"
58 Leave
62 "Woman With the Hat" painter
66 Batman?
67 Adequate
68 Colonist
69 Phone playback

DOWN

1 Fairy queen
2 ___ carte
3 Bug, in a way
4 Music maker
5 Dialect
6 Pinches
7 Glass ending
8 ___ Tomé
9 Cinema warning
10 Beatles' meter maid
11 Bikini, for one
12 Orange vegetable
13 Hellenic H
14 Cubs' home
21 Cartoon private
22 "___ de Roland" (medieval romance)
23 Iceberg alternative
24 Actress Farrow
25 Co. that made Ramblers
26 Meadow
28 Experienced bliss?
29 Lola portrayer, in 1930 film
30 Football lining
32 Newspaper listings
33 Rep.'s counterpart
39 English ___
41 Some wave catchers
44 Skinny swimmer
45 Bon ___ cleanser
46 Tankful
52 Upright
54 Electrical units
56 Referee's call
57 Masking, e.g.
58 A.M.A. members
59 Wash. neighbor
60 Chemical container
61 Salt
62 Mother's flower?
63 Nautilus locale
64 Droop
65 Before, in verse

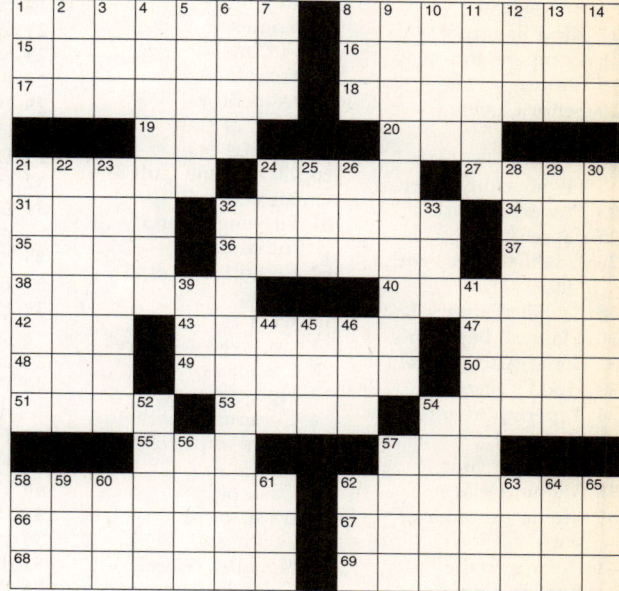

578   by Richard Thomas

ACROSS

1 Sloughs
5 1978 Bujold film
9 Tousle
13 Deseret, now
14 Shows skittishness
15 Within: Prefix
16 Get one's goat
17 Ivory tusk thief?
19 Zitherlike instrument
21 Give up
22 Noted Norman
23 Go without air conditioning
25 Animal to hop into bed with?
29 Girder
30 Was a mentor to
35 Put down
36 Museum near Malibu
38 Brazilian booter
39 Dramatic musical work
41 Poplar
42 Very large apparitions?
45 De Staël and others
49 Redolence
50 Tea-party crasher
51 1968 Winter Olympics site
55 Zookeeper?
58 Florida ___
59 Pass over
60 Kid's name
61 Fonda in "My Darling Clementine"
62 Unthinking response
63 Deal preceder
64 Layover

DOWN

1 Pat on the back
2 Football's Armstrong
3 Wingding
4 Swindle
5 Mexican horseman
6 Pinguid
7 Debussy's "La ___"
8 Tempe sch.
9 Palladium, e.g.
10 Awaiting ignition
11 Cooperstown's Carlton
12 More vexed
14 ___ off (renounce)
18 Treacly
20 Pair off
23 Peep shows and the like
24 Lean and strong
25 Rodin work with "The"
26 Up to the job
27 At hand
28 In reserve
31 Some brushwork
32 "___ Man" (1984 flick)
33 I, O or U: Abbr.
34 Cubs' hangouts
36 Flag waver
37 Vacation times abroad
40 Peloponnesian valley
41 Quotation notation
43 Roman odist
44 Gland prefix
45 College declaration
46 Budget rival
47 Pinkie, e.g.
48 Critical
51 Essence
52 Pooped
53 Vega's constellation
54 Lay eyes on
56 TV mfr.
57 Cacophony

579 By Rich Norris

ACROSS
1 Agape
11 French cleric
15 Toddler's vehicle
16 Austin ___ (Tenn. university)
17 Kind of carpet
18 Compete, in a way
19 Grouse
20 Señor Guevara
21 Ascetics
22 "Travels in Hyperreality" writer
23 Powerful shark
25 Close
26 Establishment, with "the"
28 "X-Files" topics
30 Classical beginning
31 Some road workers
33 Hood's piece
34 Tapering toward each end
36 Monet or Manet
38 Majolica glaze
39 Movie preceder of yore
41 River into the English Channel
42 Anemometer's measurement
43 Impression
47 Eloper's need, maybe
49 Toasted ___
51 Key letter
52 Comes to
53 Put on
54 Fell off
55 Josip Broz
56 Kind of state
59 St. crossers
60 City on the Gulf of Mexico
61 Fire-engine and Indian, e.g.
62 Robin Hood et al.

DOWN
1 Crossword squares
2 Craziness
3 Houston nine
4 Computer marvel
5 There are 1.609 in a mi.
6 Dash off
7 By surprise
8 Lacking
9 Nobelist Wiesel
10 Calendar abbr.
11 Fringe, on a golf course
12 Starts of bench-clearing brawls
13 Kind of driver
14 Sight
21 Causes of some falls
23 Mixtures
24 Beginner
25 1994 Oscar role
27 Cable network
29 Dread
32 Puts on buttons
34 Denture wearer's purchase
35 Like a first draft
37 Harmful
38 Early communications satellite
40 Played the straight man
44 Fine-grained granite
45 Flu symptom
46 Whom seekers seek
48 Refinery residue
50 Lend ___ (listen to)
53 Take out
54 Penn., et al.
56 Household entertainment abbr.
57 Trio in Torino
58 Cries of disappointment

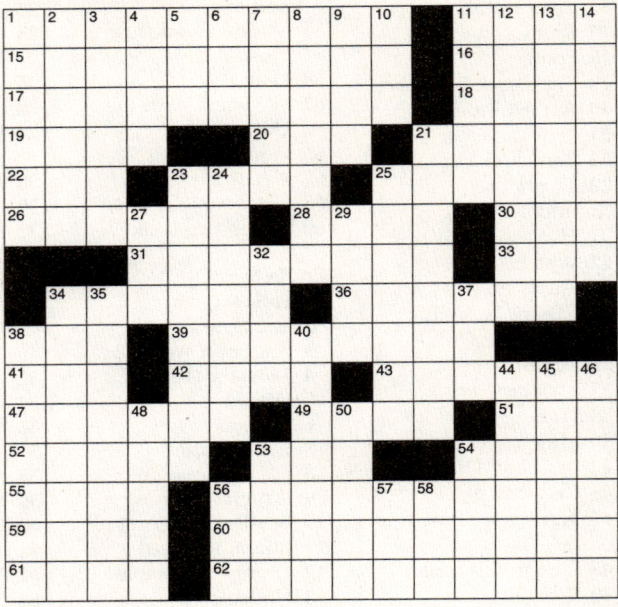

580 by Sidney L. Robbins

ACROSS
1 Large bodies of water
6 ___ mater
10 Stint
14 Separated
15 Friend of Androcles
16 Actor Jannings
17 Imprecise measurement
19 Competent
20 Last
21 Part of CNN
23 Arthur Godfrey instrument
24 Sample tape
26 Calyx part
28 Drink cat-style
31 Socialist Eugene
33 Describe
36 Israeli port
38 Sandy tract
40 Well-known
41 Imprecise age
44 "Quick, ___, the Flit!"
45 Columnist Bombeck
46 The "A" in A.M.
47 Halts legally
49 Life is a long one
51 Three-time George Burns film role
52 Snoozed
54 Jacob or Esau
56 Short cheer
58 Dear follower
60 Out of bed
64 De-wrinkle
66 Imprecise reply
68 Tobacco holder
69 Miss Cinders of old comics
70 Cacklers
71 Sunup site
72 Kind of car or machine
73 Sea eagles

DOWN
1 Animals, to hunters
2 On top of
3 Tub of ___
4 Wizard of id
5 Packed away
6 The whole shebang
7 Property claim
8 City planner Robert
9 Reply
10 4:00 social
11 Walking
12 Tie material
13 Swiss artist Paul
18 It's good for what ails you
22 Exhausted
25 On the heavy side
27 Shalom, in Honolulu
28 Metal shaper
29 Yearns
30 Letterhead suppliers
32 Jiggerful
34 50 minutes past
35 Won by a nose, with "out"
37 Actor Flynn
39 Irish patriot Robert
42 Does steno work
43 Cause of hearing loss?
48 Backbones
50 Illusion
53 Cave dweller
55 More friendly
56 Ready to pick
57 Domingo forte
59 Manche capital
61 British gun
62 Otherwise
63 Humorist Bill et al.
65 After expenses
67 Dine

581 by Stanley B. Whitten

ACROSS

1 Skiing or skin diving, e.g.
6 Gossip bit
10 Molecule component
14 More aged
15 Golfer's cry
16 Conserve
17 One of the Judds
18 Doesn't draw, in draw
20 Try hard
22 Italian wine region
23 Summer, in St.-Denis
24 Done by oneself
27 Traditional Christmas drink
30 "___ scale of 1 to 10 . . ."
31 Mrs. Perón
32 Block traffic, in a way
38 Intravenous fluids
40 Ocean off N.C.'s coast
41 Guy with an Irish Rose
42 Large marine fish
46 Ron of "Tarzan"
47 Charged particle
48 Separable components
51 Dim-witted cartoon dad
56 Son ___ gun
57 Verdi opera
58 Upstate New York City
62 Aliens
65 "Amo, amas, amat," e.g.
66 Disclose
67 Catch
68 Decree
69 It can close clothes
70 Murder
71 Classroom furnishings

DOWN

1 TV's "My Three ___"
2 Bit of real estate
3 What the nose knows
4 Negligent
5 "Jeopardy!" info
6 Suppositions
7 Sum
8 Clear the board
9 Smoker's choice
10 Nincompoop
11 Recorded
12 Egg-shaped
13 Allotted
19 Newswoman Sawyer
21 Oklahoma city
25 Be a bad winner
26 California's ___ Valley
27 Sunset direction
28 Allege
29 Mrs. Gandhi's garb
33 Actress Hagen
34 Goodyear flier
35 Brother in "Am I my brother's keeper?"
36 Irk
37 Low islands
39 ". . . baked in ___"
43 Ship's guidance system
44 Naval banners
45 Be beaten
49 Fancily dressed, with "up"
50 Like beds before a maid
51 Emcees
52 Frequently
53 Actress Gibbs
54 Perfect
55 "Ava ___"
59 "Tell it like ___!"
60 Barry of basketball
61 Formicary residents
63 Swiss peak
64 Foxlike

582 by Gregory E. Paul

ACROSS

1 Jacob's first wife
5 Senator from Kansas
9 Rock's ___ and the Dominos
14 Life of Riley
15 Perfect place
16 Chopin work
17 Greek peak
18 Hero's hidden flaw
20 Speedometer part
22 Neapolitan evening
23 Ambulance letters
24 Pennsylvania coal city
26 Rolling in dough
28 Havana man
30 Coot
34 Pile up
37 California's ___ Valley
39 Prefix with -naut
40 Vacuum's target
41 Kind of candle
42 Bumps, as in bumper cars
43 Locale
44 "Paradise Lost," e.g.
45 Rand McNally work
46 Zero of "The Producers"
48 Allegro, e.g.
50 Camelot lady
52 49ers coach George
56 "Caught ya!"
59 Judge
61 Fictional Simon
62 1957 Andy Williams song
65 Washington's bills
66 Hoopster Hal
67 ___-Lackawanna Railway
68 Register
69 Sailing
70 Hankers
71 Low marks

DOWN

1 Hotelier Helmsley
2 Studio stand
3 Balance sheet item
4 President or monarch, e.g.
5 Stick up for
6 Keats work
7 Sediment
8 Computer command
9 Mar
10 And so forth
11 "___ Britannia"
12 Round cheese
13 Ivories
19 Fountainhead
21 Teri Hatcher TV role
25 Greek fabulist
27 Generous nature
29 Confine
31 Enthusiasm
32 First name in humor
33 The New Yorker founder Harold
34 Eliot's Bede
35 Dali contemporary
36 Father of Eros
38 Medieval weapons
41 Welfare
45 Cap-___ (from head to toe)
47 "Bewitched" witch
49 Free-for-alls
51 Manila Bay hero
53 Kovacs of 50's TV
54 40's–50's Dodger star
55 Exams
56 Pond organism
57 Trumpeter Al
58 Chimps and such
60 Deep mud
63 Envision
64 Diarist Anaïs

583 by Francis Heaney

ACROSS

1 Not roundabout
7 Let in on
11 Stomach muscles, for short
14 Red pencil wielder
15 Devoted
16 Champagne-opening sound
17 Best Picture of 1950
19 Air pressure abbr.
20 Start of a giant's chant
21 Reporter's credit
22 Swing around
23 Mr. Kadiddlehopper
24 Mean
26 Whacks hard
29 Former French province near Flanders
31 Word with city or circle
32 180 degrees
35 Approval
36 Approval
37 Calm
38 Nickname for Michigan
40 "Excalibur" actor Williamson
41 Keep secret, in a way
42 No-no at cards
43 Rutabaga
45 Hi and Lois's pet
46 Mayberry denizen
47 Loses it
50 Fertility lab supply
53 ___ Jesse Jackson
54 Classic palindrome
56 Rachmaninoff's Symphony No. 2 ___ minor
57 Jejune
58 Port in Italia
59 Mil. chief
60 Author Ferber
61 Main course

DOWN

1 Unpersuadable
2 Twiddling one's thumbs
3 Heat up
4 H, to a Greek
5 Saver of soles?
6 French poet Chrétien de ___
7 "Jour de Fête" director and star
8 Kiln
9 Have fun
10 H.S.T.'s successor
11 Nonsense
12 Petty officer
13 Did "Mission: Impossible" work
18 Port on the Danube
22 Oppressive
23 Foes of Custer
25 "Wayne's World" word
26 Branch of 39-Down
27 Singer Paul
28 Site of a Knievel jump
29 Let up
30 Road nexus, proverbially
32 Not much
33 Folk dancer's shoe
34 Popular fashion magazine
36 "Arcadia" playwright
39 Sch. subject
40 Sam Donaldson, e.g.
42 Playwright Jean
43 Doughnut-shaped
44 Flip
45 Not too smart
48 Tennis score
49 Zip, to Zapata
50 Stench
51 ___ of tears
52 Friend of the famille
54 West of "I'm No Angel"
55 Quick to learn

584 by David J. Kahn

ACROSS

1 Tobacco pipe
6 Emulate Lorelei
11 Platters, now
14 "Help!" co-star
15 Keep ___ to the ground
16 Circus exclamation
17 "Where's my watch?" asked Captain Hook ___
19 Nautical chain
20 Burning
21 Buffalo area
23 Actor Gulager
24 1955 Kentucky Derby winner
27 Wyoming peak
28 Prefix with -gram
30 Penpoint style
32 Emaciated
33 Toast
35 Old toothpaste brand
37 "Get lost, Toto!" shouted the Tin Man ___
39 Stop by unexpectedly
40 1961 Heston role
41 TV detective Houston
42 Start of a fast break, often
44 "Like ___ not . . ."
48 Circular
50 "It's ___ in the face"
52 Soul, in St.-Lô
53 Summons, e.g.
55 Straightened (out)
57 Snaps
58 "I'm a beauty," said Venus de Milo ___
61 Like big shoes to fill?
62 Designer Simpson
63 Donnybrook
64 Giants make them, briefly
65 "Chill"
66 Inge contemporary

DOWN

1 Open up, in a way
2 Turn hastily
3 Continuous arrival
4 Foreign title of honor
5 Goes without purpose
6 Bit
7 Dir. heading
8 One beheaded by Perseus
9 Insect's sense organ
10 "Romeo and Juliet" event
11 Trancelike state
12 500
13 Lustrous
18 Nursery arrivals
22 "Tosca" soprano
25 Smell ___
26 Roper subjects
29 Germfree
31 Deny
34 Trombonist Winding
36 ___ phenomena
37 Steam rooms
38 Mideast flier
39 Deflected, as a question
41 Child
43 Cordlike ornament
45 Hair problem
46 Diner order
47 Goes back to brunette, e.g.
49 Durable wood
51 Ensemble's leading part
54 Team
56 Like a line
59 In the manner of
60 Popular name for a dog

ACROSS

1 Sports legend with a 20-1 record
8 Tops
14 Hardin-Simmons University site
15 Ethylene, e.g.
16 Summer time
17 Entertainer
18 Old-style driving iron
19 Tone poem by Liszt
21 Singer's syllable
22 Life support?
23 Actor Neill et al.
24 Act
25 Pressure meas.
26 Kind of infection
27 Worry
28 Is generous
31 Eastern title
32 Cabinet Dept.
33 Avoided attention
42 They're virtually pointless
43 Disengages
44 Half of a popular cuisine's name
45 Litter cries
46 Chaps
47 Drivel
48 Outer, at the outset
49 TV pioneer John
51 Lowlife
53 Bridge operators?
55 Ushers
57 Open
58 Boxed
59 Tea choices
60 Furnace devices

DOWN

1 Reckless ones
2 End
3 Neighbor of Cameroon
4 From times past
5 Implausible
6 Even a little
7 Computer instruction
8 Knights
9 Ready for
10 Kennedy Library architect
11 Strengthen
12 Meditation location
13 Scope
15 Rural fight
20 Oriental housemaid
23 Binding material
24 Tower over
26 1970's–80's Robert Urich series
27 Some lilies
29 Shipper's posting
30 Gives safety information
33 Excited
34 Androgynous
35 Half-time event, maybe
36 Smart looking
37 Use
38 Fraternity house decorations
39 Negotiators' problem
40 Less secure
41 Lays out
49 Jean Renoir film "La ___ Humaine"
50 Bows
51 White Mountains river
52 State since 1889: Abbr.
54 Doctor in a 1964 movie
56 Suffix with respond

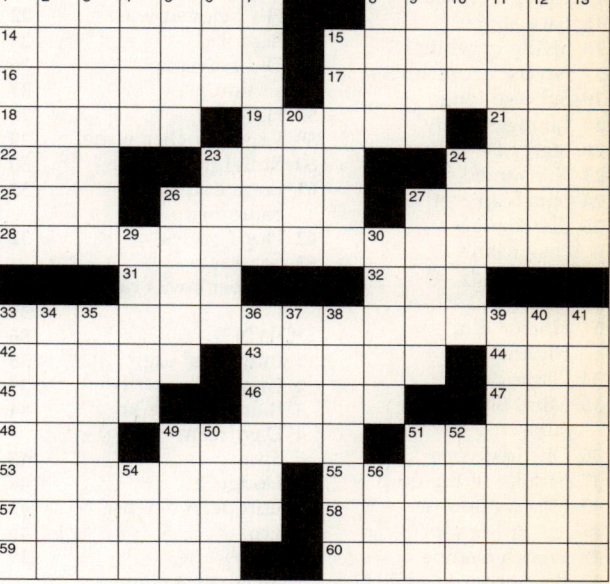

ACROSS

1 Hearth debris
6 Atmosphere
10 Columnist Bombeck
14 Room to ___
15 Skater Heiden
16 High time?
17 Critical juncture
20 Parade
21 Some oranges
22 Roasting items
25 Sometimes they get the hang of it
26 Woolly one
30 Carnegie Hall event
32 Where Marco Polo traveled
33 Tomb tenant
34 All fired up?
37 Future brass
41 Modeled, maybe
42 Mountain ridge
43 Peruvian of yore
44 Neptune's fork
46 Physicist Niels
47 Work, work, work
49 Its password was "Mickey Mouse"
51 Trotsky rival
52 Straight shooters?
57 Stops rambling
61 Algerian seaport
62 Broadway groom of 1922
63 Sister of Thalia
64 Bridge seat
65 Bank holding
66 Prepare to shave

DOWN

1 Cleo's snakes
2 Flyspeck
3 "Let the Sun Shine In" musical
4 Sea bird
5 Bristles
6 W.W. I grp.
7 Mausoleum item
8 "Road to ___"
9 Beginnings of poetry?
10 Involve
11 Beauty aid
12 Folkways
13 Writer Beattie and others
18 Poet translated by FitzGerald
19 Toledo locale
23 Depended
24 Perfumed
26 Senate output
27 On the briny
28 "Gorillas in the ___"
29 Hit a fly, perhaps
31 Mean
34 Host Jay
35 Yen
36 Ivan, for one
38 Church front area
39 Expensive rug
40 Fish in a way
44 Aptitude
45 Weight allowance
47 Pack away
48 "Falcon Crest" star
50 "Egad!"
51 Barge
53 McHenry, e.g.
54 Münchhausen, for one
55 Within: Prefix
56 Common sign
58 Sash
59 Cause for overtime
60 Clucker

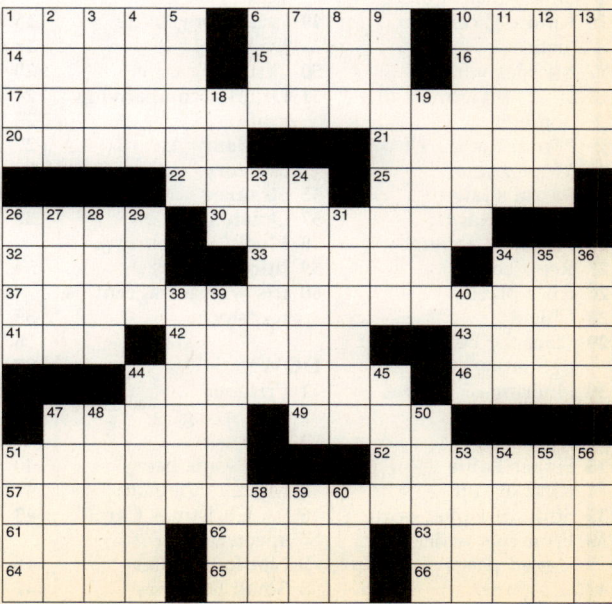

587 by Betty Jorgensen

ACROSS

1 One who reunes
5 Bic or Parker products
9 Lox's partner
14 Computer offering
15 Face shape
16 Shade of white
17 No ifs, ___ or buts
18 Soho so-long
19 Lounges lazily
20 Start of a quip
23 Consumed
24 Israeli airport
25 ___ chango (magician's command)
29 "That was close!"
31 Horror film frightener
34 Oscar de la ___
35 Mimi Sheraton subject
36 Obstinate one
37 Middle of the quip
40 Hor.'s opposite
41 ___ of March
42 French avenue
43 It's north of Calif.
44 Chance ___ (meet accidentally)
45 Not present
46 Columbus univ.
47 One, in Orléans
48 End of the quip
55 His beloved was Beatrice
56 Old newspaper section
57 Hide
59 Rags-to-riches writer
60 Roughneck
61 Bombeck, the columnist
62 Hops brews
63 Sea eagle
64 Cooper's was high

DOWN

1 Internists' org.
2 Give temporarily
3 Remove, as a knot
4 Daydream
5 Spud
6 Dodge
7 European defense grp.
8 Dross
9 Swell, as a cloud
10 Have nothing to do with
11 Course game
12 A Gardner
13 Fleur-de-___
21 Old Nick
22 Coasters
25 Utah city
26 Allude (to)
27 ___ nous
28 Editor's mark
29 Part of NOW
30 Breaks up clods
31 Company B awakener
32 ". . . in tears amid the ___ corn": Keats
33 Ism
35 Rover's playmate
36 Tormé and Gibson
38 Raise the end of
39 Cacophonous tower
44 Does a groomsman's job
45 Whosoever
46 Bewhiskered animal
47 Author Sinclair
48 Fabric texture
49 "Come Back, Little Sheba" playwright
50 Prod
51 Rating a D
52 Aboveboard
53 Florida's ___ Beach
54 Pollster Roper
55 A tiny bit
58 Ecru

588 by Arthur S. Verdesca

ACROSS

1 Entertain from house to house
6 Sirs' counterparts
12 Horse show locales
14 Slow musical pieces
16 Kind of license or justice
17 Measles variety
18 W.W. II German bomber
19 "From the ___ of Montezuma"
21 Pascal's law
22 Part of H.R.H.
23 Fixed, as a gauge
25 Reposed
26 Iris's place
28 Chichi
29 Place for belt-tightening
30 Flooring of marble chips
32 Ibsen play
33 Singer Laine
34 Kind of suit
35 Strait of Dover port
38 Women's wide-legged pants
42 ___-garde
43 District
44 Orient
45 Shower attention (on)
46 Jeans
48 Third-millennium year
49 "___ Along Little Dogies"
50 Gist
51 Drum accompanying a fife
53 Academy Award category
55 Strainers
57 Quietus
58 Pluck, as eyebrows
59 Juicer
60 Iris with a fragrant rootstock

DOWN

1 Prisoner
2 Alarm, e.g.
3 Stink
4 Like some beer
5 My ___, Vietnam
6 "A Christmas Carol" specter
7 Not for kiddies
8 Small flatfishes
9 Questionnaire info
10 "Pizarro Seizing the Inca of Peru" artist
11 Recital singer
13 Sonata's third movement, often
15 Louisiana 11
18 Folded up
20 Respecting
24 Demolishes
25 Founder of Taoism
27 Esoteric
29 Avast, on land
31 Got off
32 Robot, in Jewish legend
34 Most like the Marx Brothers
35 Sponged
36 Dodger
37 Trellis
38 Singer Lily
39 Africa's fourth-longest river
40 Seeps
41 Pen
43 Early American publisher Peter
46 Stupid
47 Beef cattle
50 Where Anna Leonowens taught
52 Affirm
54 Japanese drink
56 W.W. II battle site, for short

ACROSS

1 Enjoys at leisure
5 Lucifer
10 Likely
13 "Flower Song," e.g.
14 Harden
15 A Guthrie
16 Start of a quip
19 Part of a flick?
20 French holy women: Abbr.
21 First
22 Egg : oval :: ___ : pyriform
23 Supports
25 1973 Elton John hit
28 Burnt, in cooking
29 Environmentalism: Abbr.
30 Large: Prefix
31 "The Conqueror Worm" writer
34 Middle of the quip
38 Foreign exchange listing
39 Come to ___
40 O.K. Corral figure
41 Unstable
42 Elegant
44 Know-it-alls
47 Highlander
48 Treasured violin
49 Repugnance
50 "Whiffenpoof" syllable
53 End of the quip
57 Rotunda resting place
58 Prospero's sprite
59 Kind of ox
60 TV "clutter"
61 Curt
62 Arguments for

DOWN

1 "Völsunga ___"
2 Infuriates
3 Material for a topi
4 Had a session
5 Kind of anguish
6 Choler
7 Wash sites
8 Dernier ___
9 That girl
10 Spinning
11 Argue
12 Lincoln's in-laws
15 "For want of ___ the horse was lost"
17 Understanding words
18 Black ___ (sensational 1947 murder case)
22 Tiresome one
23 Coaxes
24 Boxlike sleigh
25 Slightly wet
26 Be heartsick
27 Time for mad dogs and Englishmen
28 Nuts
30 Grades
31 Vegetables
32 Not just mine
33 Glimpse
35 Kind of food
36 Capital
37 Kind of cutlet
41 Lecher
42 Kine
43 Lascivious look
44 Brazilian dance
45 "The way of a man with ___": Proverbs
46 Windmill arms
47 Rubbernecks
49 He's got it coming
50 Smudge
51 To boot
52 Bids
54 Topper
55 Long start
56 Little dickens

ACROSS

1 Rational belief in God
6 Tee off
11 Terrorist's weapon
14 Addled
15 Scout master?
16 Brief time
17 Forgiving country singer?
19 B.O. announcement
20 Ruler measure
21 Ruth topper, 1974
23 Smith or Jones
27 Sick country singer?
33 Radii neighbors
34 Dueling method
35 Energy source
37 Doubles team member
39 Fix the shower wall
41 Attention
42 Flintstones pet
46 Seiko competitor
47 Tired country singer?
50 Likes immediately
51 Put down
54 Modern site of ancient Illyria
60 Coffee server
61 Comical country singer?
65 In the past
66 Ham it up
67 Bare
68 Gaining currency?
69 80's TV sleuths Jonathan and Jennifer
70 Accouterment

DOWN

1 Pedestal part
2 007's alma mater
3 Spot in the ocean
4 Auto-
5 Cinco de ___ (Mexican holiday)
6 Height
7 Scenic-view spot
8 Purpose
9 From ___ Z
10 Address for a French friend
11 SALT participant
12 Close (in on)
13 Symbol
18 Nosegay
22 Bubble machine
24 Dr. Dre's specialty
25 Laugh maker Louis
26 Declare
27 Ewe said it!
28 Mural starter
29 Bemoans
30 Grazing site
31 Practical
32 Cobbled
33 Mom's bro
36 Tex-___ (cooking style)
38 Minn. neighbor
40 Palindromic preposition
43 Mineral suffix
44 Fraternity characters
45 Pump numbers
48 God, in Judaism
49 Rheinland city
51 Wharf
52 Press
53 In the near future
55 Combo
56 Way off
57 Microwave, in slang
58 Fateful day
59 Tags on
62 Singer Sumac
63 Negative correlative
64 Giant star

591   by Wayne Robert Williams

ACROSS

1 Camera settings
7 Reprobate
15 1970's Best Picture
16 "Shogun" rite
17 Secluded spot
18 Like Toons
19 Cedar Rapids college
20 Verdugo and others
22 Not share
23 Partake of
24 Work long and hard
25 Store, in a way
28 Air bubble
30 African sorceress of fiction
32 At the age of: Lat., abbr.
33 Agamemnon's father
36 Rocky ridge
38 1940 Hope film
43 Lissome
44 Stealth craft
45 Scratchy shrub
48 Chopper
50 ___ bene
51 Camels' kin
53 Furthermore
56 Prefix meaning failure
57 Roy Orbison's "___ Over"
58 Playwright Norman
60 Queen before Sophia
61 Refute
64 Personal spa
66 Dubai and others
67 Disentwine
68 Security
69 Hitchcock book "A ___ of a Different Color"

DOWN

1 Longest key
2 City north of Sunnyvale
3 And like that
4 Ike's arena
5 Peaceable types
6 New Zealand runner Peter
7 1932 Dietrich film
8 Miracle site
9 Greet the day
10 Flight
11 Police-blotter letters
12 Hip
13 Interstice on an insect's wing
14 Role for seven actresses
21 Sister of Selene
26 Durban's province
27 Enter gradually
29 Chaos
31 Directional suffix
34 City on the Mohawk
35 Soak
37 Fellow, in slang
39 ___ Na Na
40 Part of a dash
41 Hangers-on
42 Penciled-in
45 Vacation mementos
46 Last syllable of a word
47 Backbone of a mountain range
49 1994 U.S. Open golf champ Ernie
52 Walloped
54 "Yup"
55 Rhone tributary
59 Ancient greetings
62 Before indicator
63 Tore
65 Singer's syllable

592   by Deborah Trombley

ACROSS

1 Fold of cloth
6 Puts a lid on
10 Oats for horses
14 Main artery
15 Came to earth
16 "___ silly question..."
17 Unravel
19 Brings up the rear
20 Come into view
21 O'Hare abbr.
22 Luxuriant, as vegetation
23 Secreted
25 Amo, ___, amat
27 "A Hard Day's Night" group
31 Fits and ___
35 Natural inclination
36 Pouches
38 "Carmen," e.g.
39 5½-point type
41 Distance from the equator: Abbr.
42 Hysteria
43 Café order
44 Ensnare
46 Smell to high heaven
47 Say under oath, with "to"
49 Was coquettish
51 Fawn's father
53 Reverse of WSW
54 Saunter, with "along"
57 Pistol-packing org.
59 One who calls balls
64 Neighborhood
65 Unravel
67 Coconut's source
68 Come to earth
69 Eyeglasses
70 Mont Blanc site
71 Nephew of Abel
72 Brawl

DOWN

1 It may be picked up or set
2 Weaving machine
3 Épée ou pistolet
4 Anatomical passage
5 Schooled
6 Ne'er-do-well
7 Healing plant
8 One of a Columbus trio
9 Prepares, as rice
10 With 29-Down, unravels
11 Jacob's twin
12 Ticker tapes?
13 Hyphen's cousin
18 Sedaka and Armstrong
24 Handed out
26 Over
27 Fathered
28 Pass, as legislation
29 See 10-Down
30 Babushka
32 "Walk Away ___" (1966 hit)
33 Endeavored
34 Fire
35 Tuscaloosa university, informally
37 Like old potato chips
40 Steinbeck's "___ of Eden"
45 Calendar girl
48 Snarl
50 Derelict
52 Response to a pun
54 Hemingway nickname
55 Face-to-face exam
56 Health food from the sea
58 ___ time (never)
60 ___ Le Pew
61 "Body Count" rap star
62 Quadrilateral fig.
63 Bygone gas brand
66 "___ bodkins!"

593   by Sidney L. Robbins

ACROSS

1 Companies
6 Concerning
10 Priests' robes
14 Dickens's ___ Heep
15 Blood carrier
16 "Road" picture destination
17 With 55-Across, a handyman's description
20 "Now it's clear"
21 Elevator, in Exeter
22 Wight and Capri, e.g.
23 Greek weights
25 Like Irving's "Hollow"
26 Sneak showing: Var.
29 Two-wheeler
31 Buenos ___
32 Hose down
33 Taxi
36 Agitate
37 Brand of wrap
38 Go it alone
39 Golfer's ___ time
40 Pythias's pal
41 Serious offender
42 Israeli desert
43 Installed in office

44 41-Across's wish
47 Mr. Kefauver
49 Water jet
50 Actor Jannings
51 Milky white gem
55 See 17-Across
58 Whom Zeus visited as a swan
59 A Brontë
60 Malt kilns
61 Baseball's Say Hey Kid
62 Frisks
63 Grace word

DOWN

1 Japanese volcano
2 Savings for the elderly
3 "Minute" dish
4 Thorough beauty treatment
5 "___ nuff!"
6 Benefit
7 17-Across's ongoing program?
8 Pinball no-no
9 Toronto's prov.
10 Demeaned
11 Soup scoop

12 Censor, as a tape
13 Not a manly man
18 Ice sheet
19 "When the Frost is on the Punkin" poet
24 Greyhound vehicle
25 Bridge
26 History
27 Baptism, e.g.
28 Toledo's lake
30 Algerian seaport
32 Ditto
33 Pistol company
34 Burn soother
35 007
37 Wise guy
38 Like the Christmas card business
40 "D" in radio talk
41 Agent's 15%, e.g.
42 Actress Shearer et al.
43 French city in W.W. II fighting
44 The 23rd, for one
45 Sleeping problem
46 Reddish
48 Fathers
50 Sicilian spouter
52 Model

53 Exterminator's targets
54 Minus
56 Schmo
57 Watch chain

594   by Matt Gaffney

ACROSS

1 Stir-fry need
4 Angelic headwear
10 Saudi Arabia neighbor
14 Nigerian language
15 Country on Lake Victoria
16 Baseball squad
17 Tales of woe
19 Delivery vehicles
20 Command to Spot
21 Noble name part
22 Cap
23 Ottoman dynasty founder
26 Organizations
27 In
30 Moolah
31 Bowed tree
35 Polar worker
36 Purchasing option
37 Holed up
40 Best Picture nominee of 1992
43 "Gotcha"
44 Opera set around Seville
45 Lite-rock radio fare
48 1941 Leningrad event

50 X-rated
51 Autograph seeker's accessory
52 O.K. Corral fighter
56 Linda Ellerbee's "And ___ Goes"
57 "Terms of Endearment," e.g.
60 Therefore
61 What bargain hunters look for
62 Altar words
63 Impertinent one
64 Harrelson and Woodpecker
65 Doze (off)

DOWN

1 What precedes a blowout?
2 Melancholy instrument
3 1995 earthquake site
4 Pizza ___
5 In the past
6 Baby bug
7 Garden item appropriate for this puzzle
8 Jeannie portrayer

9 KLM rival
10 Taped, in a way
11 Dolphin home
12 Andrea McArdle Broadway role
13 Branch headquarters?
18 Single-masted vessel
22 Goof off
24 Is friendly to
25 Terrorized
26 Checkbook column
27 Wow
28 ___ Aviv
29 Weight
30 New Zealander
32 Circular motion
33 Give ___ (yield)
34 Kapow!
38 "___ Mine" (Beatles song)
39 Reading room
41 Castle site, often
42 "Mrs. Miniver" star Garson
45 Diamond corners
46 Festoon
47 One of the Mario Brothers
48 Bygone pact

49 1935 hit "The Lady ___"
51 South-of-the-border money
53 Related

54 Make over
55 Encourage
57 Playing marble
58 Rival of Dave
59 Chicago trains

595   by Fred Piscop

ACROSS
1 Easing of tension
5 They go down when it's sunny
11 Va. clock setting
14 Quattro maker
15 Menu pick
16 Big initials in old films
17 Man with a 36-Across
19 Prefix with conservative
20 Crop-___ (having short hair)
21 Connecticut town
23 Thwarted
26 Return to class
27 Gofer's task
28 Brand of vacuums
29 Pours none too neatly
30 Ancient Iranians
32 Dictionary abbr.
35 Under: Fr.
36 Theme of this puzzle
37 Bayh of Indiana
38 S.A.S.E., e.g.
39 Body of law
40 Egg-shaped

41 Learned via the grapevine
43 Army helicopter
44 Drink with Scotch
45 Blubber stripper
46 Big bang maker
47 Ali/Foreman battle site
48 Nutritional abbr.
49 Man with a 36-Across
54 ___ Lingus
55 Set apart
56 Home of 49-Across
57 "Anonymous"
58 They slide down chimneys
59 Kind of poll

DOWN
1 Make "it"
2 Shade
3 Uproar
4 Watergate-type crimes
5 Turned aside
6 Sacked out
7 Collar fastener
8 Rink great
9 Giver

10 Cracker seeds
11 Man with a 36-Across
12 Shooter's game
13 Bugs Bunny, e.g.
18 Capital ___
22 VCR button: Abbr.
23 "Siddhartha" author
24 Wrinkle-resistant fabric
25 Man with a 36-Across
26 Tokyo destroyer, in film
30 Dawber TV role
31 It's sometimes bruised
33 Wash
34 Scornful utterance
36 English colony until 1729
37 Fade away
39 Vessels outside port?
40 La Scala performance
42 Flow's partner
43 "___ Restaurant"
44 Golf cup name
45 Spanish composer Manuel de ___
46 Stuff (in)

47 Joie de vivre
50 Racket
51 Prom attire
52 Diamond stat
53 Dobbin's nibble

596   by David J. Kahn

ACROSS
1 Polling unit
7 "Pathétique," e.g.
13 Teacher of the deaf
15 Reporter, at times
16 Sway
17 Lennon classic
18 Dvořák's Symphony No. 9 ___ minor
19 Kind
21 Med. service providers
22 Sudden acceleration
27 ___ Jima
28 Colorful flowers
29 Unpretentious food
32 Swelling reducer
36 Cosmetician Lauder
37 Roping target
38 Climbed, as a pole
41 Spring time
43 Brilliantly colored bird
45 Lacrosse team
46 Crazed
51 Final say?
52 Wholly
53 Corrode
54 18th-century hairpiece

57 Hebrew prophet
61 Exalt
62 N.B.A. Raptors' city
63 Lease again
64 1964 Roger Miller hit

DOWN
1 Disperse
2 "Exodus" hero
3 Tubular pasta shells
4 Drop suddenly: Var.
5 Meat dish
6 Journal ending
7 Ampersand, e.g.: Abbr.
8 Spanish swell
9 Cabaret
10 Jung's inner self
11 Jan Peerce was one
12 "Give it ___!"
14 Twelvesome of Israel
15 Beach attraction
20 80's merger inits.
22 Kids
23 "A Dream Is ___ Your Heart Makes"
24 Copy
25 Behavioral trait
26 Rundown
30 Uncertain

31 Actress Olin et al.
33 Rabble-rousing
34 Something hard to drink?
35 New Hampshire city
39 Former Spanish queen
40 1992 Louis Malle film
41 Dry red wine
42 Compass line
44 "My ___ Sal"
46 Sulking sort
47 White poplar
48 More extreme
49 "Do I ___ Waltz?"
50 Wore
55 Lacking color
56 Sheraton's parent
58 Hunk's pride
59 Cash dispenser, for short
60 Weed remover

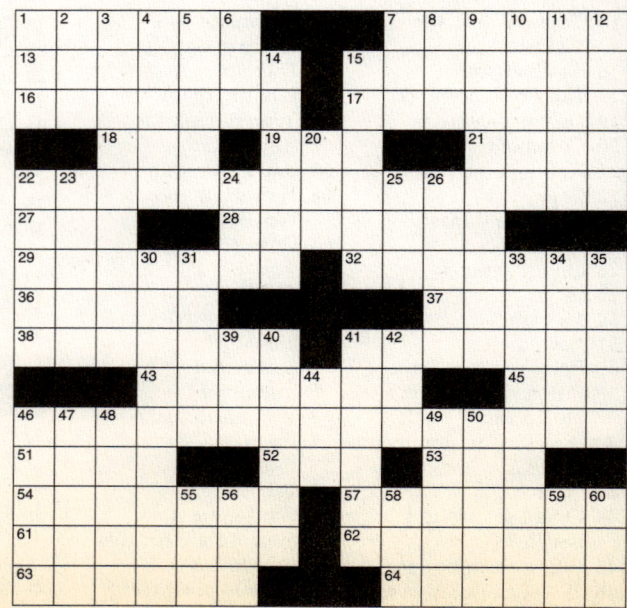

597 by Bob Sefick

ACROSS
1 "Schindler's List" symbols
10 70's vogue
15 Section of the globe
16 What a marriage may produce?
17 Ready to run at Pimlico
18 Author Hite
19 It's full of traps
20 Betting aids
22 Commercial symbol
24 Athletic wear
25 Sock necessity
28 Fats Domino's real first name
30 History, basically
32 One of the Brontës
33 Break beverage
36 Popular 70's talk show
37 Initials at sea
38 Passes up
40 She has one
41 Breakfast restaurant, for short
43 Two-sided
44 Pineapple, to a G.I.
46 First appearance, as of dawn
47 Turn ___ (upset)
49 It's right on your map
51 "Here Is Your War" author
53 60's TV host Robert
57 Raised strip
58 National personae non gratae
60 Unrelenting
61 Nights of old
62 Garr and Hatcher
63 Port authority headquarters?

DOWN
1 Univ. subjects
2 Quite the bookworm
3 Penny, maybe
4 Exile site
5 Connect with
6 Suffix in many sports names
7 Famous deadpan comic
8 Con
9 They've joined the family
10 Not on the level
11 Naturally belong
12 Hard fall
13 Links transportation
14 Isn't free and clear
21 Climb
23 Blather
25 Assyrian's foe
26 National competitor
27 Sawbucks
29 Buccaneer's base
31 Undesirable blackjack hands
33 Flag
34 Sport played to three points
35 Drippy
37 Breakfast fruit
39 Persisted
42 PC key
43 Marine
44 African amulet
45 Become more serious
47 Worn-out
48 Kind of secretary
50 Some Spanish paintings
51 Once, once
52 1890's Vice President ___ P. Morton
54 Give a face lift
55 Creepy look
56 Being, to Brutus
59 Of the same mind

598 by Wayne Robert Williams

ACROSS
1 Varnishes
7 Mormon councilmen
15 Hatred
16 Squash
17 Having belts
18 Merchant
19 Utopias
20 Part of a locomotive
21 Unprocessed grain
22 Atahualpa, for one
23 Former Cleveland Symphony conductor
25 Prefix with liter
26 Numerical suffix
27 Fervent
29 "Help!"
30 Popular mixer
32 Kind of alert
34 Candies
35 Proceed easily
39 Lounger's perch
41 Flower with colorful leaves
42 Avant-garde sculptor
45 Executioner of 22-Across
47 Family docs
48 Uris's "___ 18"
50 Guardian of Crete, in myth
51 Sensitivity
52 Hackers and others
54 Frequent tabloid subject
55 Actor Max von ___
56 Contemporary panhandler's prop
58 Mock or knock
59 Like Istanbul
60 Does community service, e.g.
61 Give more thought to
62 Most sound

DOWN
1 Flashy in the extreme
2 Consecration performer
3 Jack of diamonds and queen of spades
4 KitchenAid competitor
5 Excessive buffs
6 Pilot's dir.
7 Angel of death, in Judaism
8 Brick homes
9 Calendar abbr.
10 Heroin, to addicts
11 It precedes home
12 Easter décor
13 "Romanian Rhapsodies" composer
14 Marina of "Star Trek: The Next Generation"
20 Drug ___
23 Considers proper
24 Walks clumsily
27 Texas-based rock trio
28 Forage grass
31 Future profs
33 Storm maker
36 Swiss valley known for its resorts
37 Delivery aids
38 Kind of relations
40 Blooming shrubs
41 Last name in Communism
42 Entertainer
43 Blue
44 Chest cavity membrane
46 1986 James Cameron thriller
49 Sectors
51 Innsbruck is its capital
53 Shrink time: Abbr.
55 Bristle
57 Hand over, to Angus
58 Morse bit

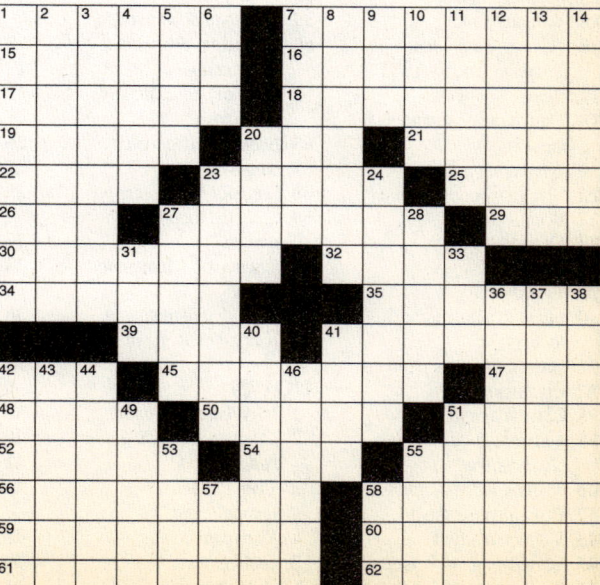

599   by Lois Sidway

ACROSS

1 Mississippi Senator Cochran
5 Nutty
9 Gangbusters at the box office
14 River to the Rhine
15 Lena of recent films
16 Like the skies in "Ulalume"
17 Sorts
18 Carty of baseball
19 Oh, so many moons
20 Go astray
23 Stack-blowing feeling
24 Countdown start
25 Tak's opposite
26 Alphabetical run
27 As a whole
31 Bit
33 Mezzo-soprano Marilyn
34 Santa Fe Trail town
35 Pickle
38 Red of firefighting fame
39 Words of wonderment
40 With respect to
41 "Whip It" rock group

42 Drawing card
43 The Divine Miss M
44 Play the siren
46 Smelt, e.g.
47 Aquarium oddity
49 Cry of delight
50 It has its point
51 Harvest goddess
52 Not yet in full bloom
58 Tubby the Tuba creator Paul
60 Reed of note
61 Light-footed
62 Hint
63 An order of the court
64 W.W. I German admiral
65 Pond covering
66 Silent O.K.'s
67 With defects and all

DOWN

1 Shadow
2 Christmas play prop
3 Synagogue cabinets
4 Not dose
5 World's third-largest island
6 '79 sci-fi thriller
7 Muscle spasms

8 Bird that summers in the Arctic
9 Agree
10 Sugary suffix
11 Many skiers use these when they (see diagonal)
12 Writers Jean and Walter
13 Assault
21 Mink's relative
22 Pretension
27 '64 musical "___ a Ball"
28 Leaf's starting point
29 Getting across
30 Stew ingredient
31 Skier Phil
32 Original Jed Clampett
34 Score for Barry Sanders
36 Observe
37 Great Scott of 1857
40 Sound as ___
42 Animal that sleeps with its eyes open
45 Noodle topper
46 Candy
47 Must, slangily

48 Part of an Argentine autumn
50 Steer clear of
53 River of Spain
54 Greek peak

55 Third addendum to a letter
56 "... ___ saw Elba"
57 Shoemakers' bottles
59 Trevino's org.

600   by Jonathan Schmalzbach

ACROSS

1 Granitelike
5 Paris' ___ Monceau
9 Paradigm of happiness
13 Melville book
14 Toledo ta-ta
16 "Guys and Dolls" Tony winner, 1951
17 Lose freshness
18 The Rock Island Line?
20 Argus-eyed
22 Pin down, in a way
23 Born
24 Othello, e.g.
25 Police BBQ?
27 Triathlete
30 Next-to-last Greek letter
31 Non compos mentis
32 Fit together
35 Chloroform kin
39 "The ___ of Innocence"
40 Men's accessories
42 Parisian season
43 Vitamin start
45 Sandberg of baseball
46 Give ___ whirl

47 Showstoppers
49 Propriety
52 Markdown at the marina?
57 Type of luck
58 In the past
59 ___ many words
60 Popular women's magazine
62 Mirror, brushes, perfume?
65 Storytelling dance
67 Regular
68 Drinks with straws
69 "... unto us ___ is given"
70 Laura of "Jurassic Park"
71 Bread grains
72 Jerry-built structure

DOWN

1 In what manner
2 "What ___ mind reader?"
3 The Pillsbury Doughboy?
4 Pamper
5 Deli meat
6 Punch's cousin

7 Public uprisings
8 Woo
9 Wheels, so to speak
10 Southwest plain
11 Tours ta-ta
12 "Spanish Guitar Player" artist
15 Meet Morpheus
19 Joshes
21 CD-___ (modern "book")
26 Pioneer Carson
27 Muslim priest
28 Francesco Rinaldi competitor
29 Not e'en once
33 Nathan Hale, e.g.
34 Kind of legs
36 Removal of Junior from a will?
37 Part of Caesar's reproach
38 Enlarge, as a hole
40 Morsel
41 Unnecessary
44 Menlo Park monogram
48 Some TV's
50 Hint
51 Nebraska Indians

52 Economized
53 Tequila plant
54 Asocial person
55 With respect to
56 Truckler

61 ___ gin
63 Publican's place
64 Actress ___ Dawn Chong
66 As well as

ACROSS

1 Gather
6 Radar gun reading: Abbr.
9 Bend
14 Collector's items
15 France's ___ d'Yeu
16 Throng
17 Lewis's Gantry
18 "The Beggar's Opera" author
19 Yeats's ___ Theatre
20 Singing sister of old Hollywood
23 American skiing medalist at Lillehammer
27 Cry of disgust
30 Twerp
31 Gross-weight deduction
32 "A miss is as good as ___"
34 Toddler
35 Where Zeno taught
36 Filmdom's Sam Spade
38 What's-his-name
40 Annealing oven
41 High school problem
45 In abeyance
46 Over, in Essen
47 ___ et quarante (betting game)
49 Posthumous duettist of 1991
50 "The Big Chill" actress
53 "Cheers" star
57 Shortcoming
60 Telephone button
61 Actor Reeves
62 Spy
63 "Gimme ___!" (end of a Yale cheer)
64 Patti LuPone role
65 Kind of bag
66 Writer Deighton
67 Attack

DOWN

1 Maintain
2 Venus's home
3 Weaponry
4 Expensive
5 Thinker
6 ___ worker
7 Magazine since 1953
8 "Lo!" modern-style
9 Music of the Benedictine monks
10 Noted televangelist
11 Sun, e.g.
12 Hafiz work
13 Pivotal
21 Alas, to Helmut
22 Sideways
24 Sups at home
25 Beethoven's Third
26 Reception china
27 Trite ideas
28 Microscopy subject
29 More costly
33 CNN personality
37 Mongol
39 Cornmeal concoctions
42 Stemware
43 Voyager II subject
44 Animate
48 ___ kwon do (Korean karate)
51 Pot
52 Student abroad
54 Café au ___
55 Within: Prefix
56 China's dollar
57 Parent
58 Personal pride
59 Importune

ACROSS

1 Chew the fat
4 Feature of Doyle's "The Adventure of the Dancing Men"
8 Faceup card in faro
12 Fraternal one
13 Region in NW Greece
15 Don Juan's mother
16 Mr. Potato Head accessory
17 Poser
19 Lab tube
21 Busy
22 Lobster claw
24 Kind of acid
25 Poser
30 Golden statuette
31 Jejune
32 Humbug?
35 Drink of old
36 Incite a hen?
38 Farm baby
39 Prince Valiant's son
40 Approach
41 Physics particle
42 Poser
45 Wooden shoe
48 Louis XVI's wife
49 Air-raid warnings
51 Angry
55 Poser
58 ___ Ben Canaan of "Exodus"
59 Soprano Moffo
60 Reduces
61 Slate-cutting tool
62 Spotted
63 Boris Godunov, e.g.
64 TV Tarzan

DOWN

1 Vehicle since 1940
2 Jai ___
3 Cincinnati letters
4 Tyson of "Sounder"
5 Two-time Smythe Trophy winner
6 Couple in Rome
7 This: Sp.
8 Use a heliograph
9 Best Supporting Actress, 1973
10 Tooth: Prefix
11 Montezuma, e.g.
13 Old Testament book
14 Gunn with a gun
18 Partner of dangerous
20 Outward
23 Coasters for Socrates, e.g.
25 Site for a Cézanne: Abbr.
26 W.W. I battle site
27 Scrutinize
28 El Dorado loot
29 Sauterne, e.g.
32 Ruth's husband
33 Manor head, maybe
34 Actress Sommer
36 Some doctor's reading: Abbr.
37 Empty talk
38 Large-headed match
40 Capone's chief enforcer
41 Counterpanes
42 River in an old spiritual
43 Football's pop
44 Poet Matthew
45 "Heimskringla" et al.
46 Solo
47 European capital
50 Save, with "away"
52 Stupefy
53 Caspian feeder
54 Folklore figure
56 Vetoes
57 ___ Zulu (South African region)

603　by Randolph Ross

ACROSS

1 Branch of algebra
11 Literary garlands
15 Chekhov relative
16 Fair
17 Cockpit dials
18 List extender
19 1936 Tommy Dorsey hit
20 T. ___
21 Nissan model
23 Clayey soil
25 Is forthright
27 Rival of Helena and Max
29 Weaken
30 Go ballistic
32 Hide-hair connector
33 Many M.I.T. grads
34 Roll
38 Like some welfare hotels: Abbr.
41 Item of dancer's attire
42 Winter vehicle
46 Former Scandinavian monarch
49 Time to remember
50 More than bushed
52 Years ago
53 Making the most sense
54 Going concern?
56 Painter ___ Borch
57 Nerve network
58 Suited to a tee
62 Toward the mouth
63 Agents of change
64 Colloquial "not"
65 Old street cry

DOWN

1 Former Washington family
2 Free
3 Impel
4 Sixth-century date
5 "Losing My Religion" rock band
6 State
7 "Soap" family
8 Small token of appreciation
9 St. ___-l'École, France
10 Root beer root
11 In ___ (somewhat)
12 One of Hamlet's choices
13 Generally
14 Liquefies a gel
22 ___ out a living
24 One of the exchanges, for short
26 Country Slaughter
28 Auction ending
31 W.W. II general Jimmy
35 Steel support
36 Conn.-to-Me. direction
37 ___ Gigio (old TV mouse)
38 Baseball great with the nickname "Moose"
39 San Remo locale
40 Bad movie rating
43 Reach
44 Wish granter
45 Actress Russell
47 Possessive
48 Sudden-death periods: Abbr.
51 Old Swedish money
55 Parlor piece
59 City north of Marseilles
60 Caviar
61 Game show mystery guest

604　by Sidney L. Robbins

ACROSS

1 Mosquito marks
6 It might be arched
10 Talks gangsta-style
14 "The Tempest" spirit
15 Country path
16 Dutch cheese
17 Pirates' flag
19 Medical researcher's goal
20 Aardvark snacks
21 More than big
22 Onetime hostess Maxwell
23 ___ Alamos
24 Spendthrift
26 Goods cast overboard
30 Halts
32 Kind of label
33 Con artist's aide
34 Baden-Baden, e.g.
37 Popular sort
40 Take advantage of
41 Unaccompanied
42 Clamor
43 Babble
44 In the open, as beliefs
45 High-spirited horses
48 Etch A Sketch, e.g.
49 Mil. defense systems
50 Escargot
53 Book after John
57 Swag
58 All-for-one feeling
60 It's just for openers
61 Russia's ___ Mountains
62 Make amends
63 Antler wearer
64 Red-ink amount
65 Stared open-mouthed

DOWN

1 ___ California
2 Collar straightener
3 Pinball no-no
4 Slippery fish
5 On the ___ (furtively)
6 Lumps
7 Fury
8 Change for a five
9 "___ of London" (1935 film)
10 Playtime
11 Grown-up
12 Analyze grammatically
13 Libel
18 Kitchen, e.g.
23 Rigging rope
25 In generous amounts
26 Amulet
27 Son of Seth
28 Bathroom feature
29 The sun
30 Glowed
31 Cause of beach erosion
33 Lampblack
34 Use a letter opener
35 Sit
36 Overwhelmed
38 Generous drink serving
39 Mauna ___
43 Ask, ask, ask
44 Like Lindbergh's flight
45 Meal starter
46 Hearty steak
47 Overact
48 Money drawers
51 Roman "fiddler"
52 "Oh, woe!"
53 Movie pooch
54 Mince
55 Fork prong
56 Hightailed it
59 Joker

605 by Gregory E. Paul

ACROSS

1 Impressionist Edgar
6 Phrase of understanding
10 Dan Blocker TV role
14 It may be blessed
15 Make airtight
16 Ready for business
17 "American Graffiti" actress
19 Alliance since 1949
20 Myrmecologist's subject
21 Ring of water
22 Bray
24 Thailand, once
25 "Richard ___" (E.A. Robinson poem)
26 Embroidery yarn
29 Top-notch, in ratings
33 Hounds' prey
34 Unexpected advantage
35 Coax
36 Rose's lover, on Broadway
37 Might
38 Intl. relief org.
39 Warsaw ___
40 Back muscles, for short
41 Irving Berlin's "Blue ___"
42 Linksman Craig et al.
44 Singer Rudy
45 Used the library
46 Time starter
47 Rock dove
50 Eagerly expecting
51 Cultural Revolution leader
54 Battle song
55 1963 chart topper
58 0 on the Beaufort scale
59 Geraint's wife
60 1935 Triple Crown winner
61 Means justifier
62 Parsnip, e.g.
63 Meddlesome

DOWN

1 Prefix with -hedron
2 Novelist Hunter
3 Urbane fellow
4 Common conjunction
5 Blocks
6 Malcolm X's faith
7 Pants part
8 Musical skill
9 Norwegian dog
10 Fragrant flower
11 Brightly colored fish
12 Bristle
13 Bamboozle
18 Fossil fuel
23 Flub
24 1985 Jessica Lange film
25 Chills
26 Wrangler's wear
27 Morocco's capital
28 Susan Lucci soap role
29 Hall of Fame QB Dan
30 Follow
31 See eye to eye
32 Pee Wee ___
34 Partner of room
37 Comet, e.g.
41 Ralph of the N.B.A.
43 Sign after Cancer
44 ___ dire (jurors' examination)
46 München, e.g.
47 Tempo
48 OPEC member
49 Aurify
50 Exchange premium
51 "Serpico" author Peter
52 Persistent pain
53 Approve
56 Popular card game
57 Med. insurance plan

606 by John R. Conrad

ACROSS

1 False arguments
9 Most washed out
15 Esthetically pleasing
16 1963 Broadway hit
17 Beethoven opus in C-sharp minor
19 "___ Rosenkavalier"
20 Served at a restaurant
21 Forest fledgling
24 Shopping place
25 Computer key abbr.
26 Rumor
28 Midafternoon
30 Mai ___
31 Throw, as a buckaroo
35 Infrequently
41 Squalid environment
42 Quadri- minus one
43 Couldn't hit the broadside of ___
46 Not given to schmoozing
49 Dismiss abruptly
50 Smallmouth fish
53 Pedal
54 Intestinal parasite
57 Bank adjunct, for short
58 Brecht-Weill chorus line
63 Wandered
64 Like some city railways
65 Tears along
66 Pittsburgh team

DOWN

1 Uncle ___
2 Cortez's gold
3 School grp.
4 Impede
5 Specks of land in the water
6 Budge
7 Russian-built fighter
8 Unstressed vowel
9 Set down as fact
10 Oodles
11 Motor vehicle bureau feature
12 Dodger
13 Bristly
14 Hypnotic spell
18 Cigarette stat
21 "___ be in England": Browning
22 Withdraw from a habit
23 Of churchgoers
24 One with nothing original to say?
27 Polly, to Tom Sawyer
28 Mao ___-tung
29 It may be taken up in sewing class
32 Cable TV option
33 Southwestern stews
34 Regrets
36 Be mistaken
37 Author Fleming
38 Pertaining to the ear
39 Exam type
40 "Cleopatra" setting
43 Thespians
44 Paint the town red?
45 Souls: Lat.
47 Musical range
48 Crash maker
50 Ties up
51 Enero a diciembre
52 Bank repositories
55 Arrive
56 Gardened, in a way
57 Sheltered, nautically
59 Elev.
60 Snacked
61 ___ Mediterranée
62 Madison Avenue offerings

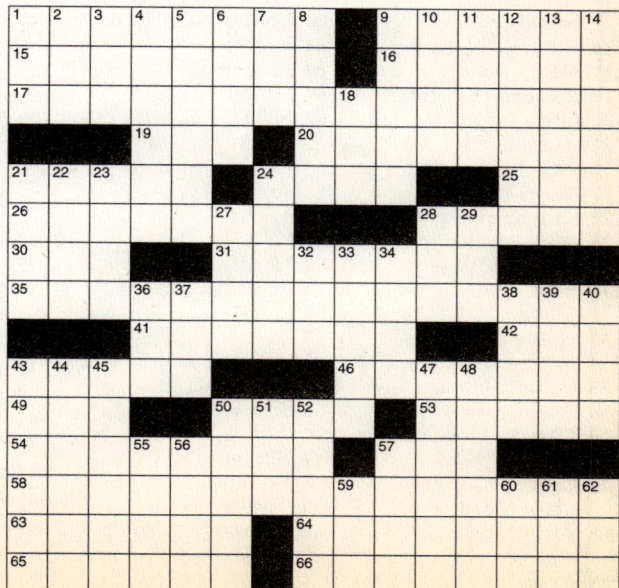

ACROSS

1 Shakespearean prince
4 Harridans
8 Chopped
13 Modern musician Brian
14 Iroquoian language
15 At whom Peeping Tom peeped
16 Freudian topic
17 Actress Swenson
18 Let up
19 Food meant for Lent
22 Geometry subject
23 Torments
27 Sub's activity
32 Ordinary writing
33 Part of P.R.
34 Gardner of "Mogambo"
37 French feminist's goal
41 Baseballer Williams
42 Irritate
44 Start of a famous boast
46 Imperturbable
53 Like most record albums
54 Southeastern Kansas town
55 Snub
60 Orchid organ
63 Keeps an account of
64 Elvis's "___ Lost You"
65 Clios and Obies
66 Au fait
67 Not-so-impressive grade
68 Via Sacra attire
69 Piggies
70 Cincinnati has three

DOWN

1 Bray
2 Goat breed
3 Pirate at work
4 Next in line
5 Cartoonist Peter
6 Musicians' engagements
7 Half ___ over (drunk)
8 Rub elbows (with)
9 "The Gathering" star
10 Sparkling gift?
11 Impending time
12 "Dear old" one
15 Test
20 Some skit humor
21 "A Christmas Carol" cry
24 "What's ___ for me?"
25 ___ homo
26 Like workhorses
28 High dudgeon
29 Eggy drink
30 Youth grp. founded in 1912
31 Having a purpose
34 Bridges of electricity
35 Bass ___
36 Sunburn soother
38 Hosp. section
39 Tic-___ (candy)
40 Zoo bird
43 Sophocles tragedy
45 Jannings of "The Blue Angel"
47 Steers clear of
48 They may be hard or soft
49 Put in
50 Dress part
51 Cricket squad
52 Street shows
56 Chair part
57 Bindlestiff
58 Make goo-goo eyes at
59 Exploits
60 Bit of encouragement
61 ___ Jima
62 Slump

ACROSS

1 Prospector's aid
4 Crawl, e.g.
8 Suddenly regain attention
14 ". . . ___ quit!"
15 Soap bar
16 Kind of collision
17 Sleuth out
19 Relative of euchre
20 One's all
21 Automaton
23 1958 Edgar winner Rex
24 Ship, in poesy
25 Some Duchamp art
29 Chinese dynasty
30 Book and TV crime solver
32 Utility customers
34 Northern native
35 Historic launch
38 Suitcases
40 Like dogwood leaves
41 Stendhal hero
42 Crime solver from St. Mary Mead
45 Part of the U.S. arsenal
49 Linear
50 Twosome
51 Prefix with logical
52 Incorporate
54 Kind of note
55 Labiate
58 Tie
60 Beethoven's Third
61 Exhort
62 ___-Cone
63 Lizards
64 N.F.L., e.g., with "the"
65 Fabric measures: Abbr.

DOWN

1 Hardly given to exhibitionism
2 Awn
3 Detroit cager
4 Apollo 9 and 15 astronaut
5 Silent goodbye
6 Alibi ___
7 Big business doings
8 Reeking
9 "Well done!"
10 P.D. James's crime solver from Scotland Yard
11 Figure to shoot for
12 Small songbird
13 Bauxite, e.g.
18 Poe's pioneering crime solver
22 ___ hill 'n' dale
24 "The King and I" actress
26 Cruising
27 McClure of "The Virginian"
28 A chip, maybe
30 Stew morsel
31 Old sorcerer
33 Florist's cutting
35 W.W. II leader
36 1985 Edgar winner Hunter
37 Wagon path
38 Lightning zigzag
39 Live
41 Step on the gas
43 Some gym gear
44 Groove
46 Coyly mannered
47 Name in a 1928 pact
48 Common inscriptions
51 Knots
53 Make out
54 When repeated, a Samoan port
55 French article
56 Exasperate
57 Luau fare
59 Fumble

609 by Rich Norris

ACROSS
1 Tie
9 Whispered words
15 Entertain
16 Follow
17 Turnpike feature
18 Like almost immediately
19 Film box letters
20 Sea eagle
21 Copy
22 Comics expletive
24 Slangy assent
25 Experienced (in)
26 Get an out-of-state license?
28 Crowbar, e.g.
30 Five-foot runner
31 Mock
33 Skedaddled
34 Measure
35 Complicated affair
38 Shopaholic's hangout
41 Banking trans.
42 Case determinants
46 Collection
47 Fertilized, in a way
49 Squawbush, e.g.
50 City south of Ft. Myers Beach
52 Limit
54 "Down at ___ Joe's" (1963 hit)
55 When some local news is on
56 Red-bearded god
58 Card table call
59 Very large number
61 Fancy
63 Domain
64 What "R" might indicate
65 Complex
66 Beach book, e.g.

DOWN
1 Without a coat
2 Default consequence, sometimes
3 Pilot
4 Bottom line
5 Relief
6 Pistil part
7 Aromatic herb
8 Stage designer's technique
9 Govt. employee
10 Eagle, at times
11 Press mechanism
12 Far back
13 Limit
14 Resisted, with "to"
23 High-chair hazard
25 Ill will
27 Tokyo, once
29 Vineyard need
32 "The ___ in sight"
34 Dessert sweetener
36 Treasure
37 ___ alienae (legal term)
38 Gets by
39 Makeup class?
40 Some notebooks
43 Fancy
44 Dessert made from a Brazilian export
45 Input, in a way
47 Poe poem
48 Cactus ___
51 On the up and up
53 Some shirts
57 Like good behavior, jocularly
60 Space program acronym
62 Sun. talk

610 by Fred Piscop

ACROSS
1 Arrives
6 "Dancing Queen" pop group
10 He loved Lucy
14 Stick out like ___ thumb
15 Late newscaster Sevareid
16 "Did you ___?"
17 Pen, but not for credit
19 Kind of cabinet
20 American, in W.W. II
21 Extra-ample shoe width
22 Contribute
23 Bar mitzvah, e.g.
27 Paris's river
29 Spooky
30 Jeans line
32 Beavers' project
33 An NCO
37 Pseudonymous surname
38 Famous oversleeper
40 Beer barrel
42 "What ___ the odds?"
43 Old gas name
45 Marked wrong
47 Farm horse
49 Dictation taker
51 Advertising lights
52 "Bonanza" boss
57 Love affair
58 Ireland's ___ Lingus
59 Two-syllable foot
62 Hammer or sickle
63 Square feature
66 Sicilian mount
67 Brainstorm
68 ___ Rogers St. Johns
69 Moose, for one
70 End of a fishhook
71 Desirable trait

DOWN
1 Shrewd
2 Worker protection gp.
3 Night sights on the eastern horizon
4 Writer Caldwell
5 "Game, ___, match"
6 Stamp on mail from Mexico
7 Informed
8 Took the bait
9 King topper
10 Does bomb squad work
11 Mrs. Perón
12 Baseball bigwig Bud
13 "Goodnight, ___" (1950 hit)
18 Itsy-bitsy
22 Tire abbr.
24 Salty drop
25 Mountain
26 Partner of dangerous
27 One of six on a cube
28 Son of Seth
31 Kitchen appliance
34 Incapacitates, illegally
35 Sheepish look
36 Scores for Comaneci
39 Shut (up)
41 Alarm sounder
44 Pertaining to kissing
46 King's widow, e.g.
48 Rumps
50 Cigarette stat
52 Like some breath
53 Ham it up
54 Nary a soul
55 Drug-kicking program
56 N.Y.C. subway line
60 Fr. miss
61 Cop's route
63 Tease
64 Sweet-as-apple-cider girl
65 Motorists' org.

611 by Gerald R. Ferguson

ACROSS
1 Bygone policy
10 "This can't be!"
14 Taunt in early motoring
15 Porch
16 "Come to think of it"
17 "___ woods these are I think I know": Frost
18 Kind of mile
19 Excavate
20 Popular tour sponsor: Abbr.
21 Antelope's playmate
22 Sour
26 Booby trap feature
30 Brown shade
31 Bridge
32 With it
33 Ceiling support
34 Europe's Gulf of ___
35 Lie
37 Petitions
38 Fluctuated
39 Flummox
40 Old World game animals
41 German title start
43 Bereft

46 Poisonous plant with milky juice
50 Listens to
51 City west of Madras
53 Standing
54 Lay open
55 Miffed
56 Distaff diviners

DOWN
1 Ottoman officer
2 Church hassock, in England
3 Persevering
4 Unusual, in Caesar's day
5 Tubby, in a Paul Tripp book
6 Start of a conjurer's phrase
7 One of nine sisters
8 Key
9 "Runaway" singer Shannon
10 Heaven or hell
11 Wicket
12 It may be stuffy
13 Unguarded
15 Important TV period

19 Benjamin Franklin was one
21 Chaff
22 NOW and others: Abbr.
23 Aborigine's call
24 Paris's ___ Polytechnique
25 Silver Spirit maker
26 Took a bite, maybe
27 Like Brown's walls
28 Splendid
29 Obliterate
31 Father-and-daughter singers
33 Gossiped
36 Lao-tzu, e.g.
37 Cook partly in an oven
41 Gifted one
42 Actress Samantha
43 Manages
44 Catalonian river
45 Change course
46 Truth alternative
47 Baba and others
48 French denials
49 Late fashion illustrator

51 Air-gun load
52 Sister of Selene

612 by Tap Osborn

ACROSS
1 "Spare tire"
5 Ferris wheel, e.g.
9 Shares quarters (with)
14 Furor
15 Airline to Haifa
16 Point with intent to shoot
17 General Bradley
18 Yarn irregularity
19 Roman goddess of flowers
20 Notorious 30's criminal
23 Smoker's intake
24 Subterfuge
25 German physicist Georg
28 Skin problem
31 Chinese veggie
35 F. ___ Bailey
36 Shankar's strings
38 Unaccompanied
39 Notorious 30's criminal
43 Killer whale
44 Massenet opera
45 Links position
46 Some flights

49 Janet of Justice
50 Mark's competitor
51 Quite ready
53 Road warning
55 Notorious 30's criminal
62 By radio, e.g.
63 New York Public Library figure
64 Cheater's aid
66 Rubbish
67 War god
68 He wrote "My Way" for Sinatra
69 Misogynist
70 Communications leader?
71 Walter ___ Hospital

DOWN
1 To's opposite
2 Reader's aid
3 Seaweed derivative
4 Special Forces cap
5 Put in a straitjacket
6 Not wisely
7 Smear
8 Pipe joint
9 Church drawing

10 Subject of the Teapot Dome scandal
11 Melville novel
12 ___ Tyler Moore
13 Native African village
21 Ankle bones
22 Pup's sound
25 Actor Edward James ___
26 Love, on bumper stickers
27 Muslim's holy place
29 Watch part
30 "Horrible" comic character
32 Parrot's moniker
33 North, of Irangate
34 Senior leader
37 Ancient letter
40 O'Neill play, with "The"
41 Balderdash
42 Hillock
47 Ransacker
48 Baden-Baden, e.g.
52 Razzle-dazzle
54 Filmdom honor
55 City near Bristol

56 Atmosphere
57 Englishman, in slang
58 Cork's locale
59 "The First ___"
60 Normandy river

61 Winged Victory
65 Spoiled

613 by Ed Stein

ACROSS

1 Sibelius's "___ Triste"
6 Where pins are made
10 Masochist's start
14 "Tempest" spirit
15 Late king of Norway
16 Popular rapper
17 Impractical idealist
19 Venus's home
20 Legal add-on
21 "___ goes" ("Slaughterhouse-Five" refrain)
22 Casserole tidbit
24 Port, e.g.
26 Son of ___
27 Gardner of "Mogambo"
28 Hollywood comer
31 Butler portrayer
34 First king of Israel
35 Leprechaun's land
37 French state
38 Father: Prefix
39 Oscar-winning song of 1958
40 "The Wind in the Willows" character
41 Deadlocked
42 Peacocks do it
43 Hook and crew
45 Kind of ball or card
46 He talked horse sense
47 Super-remedy
51 Hamlet's weapon
54 Jolts
55 Copacabana locale
56 Send forth
57 Performer of prodigious feats
60 Set of type
61 Sea into which the Amu Darya flows
62 Persian
63 Deuce topper
64 Caravel of 1492
65 Strong tastes

DOWN

1 "Star Wars" villain
2 Went up
3 Like some pads
4 Et ___ (footnote abbr.)
5 Slippery
6 Spirit
7 Scads
8 Make antimacassars
9 Bad influence
10 Cruel employer
11 Folic, e.g.
12 "Heigho! the derry oh" setting
13 Tribe in the Winnebago nation
18 Early center of Celtic learning
23 Sharing adjective
25 Daydreamer
26 Take ___ for the worse
28 Makes replete
29 Navy battle site of 1813
30 Comics bulldog
31 Masterpiece
32 Superior to
33 Site of a "Road" film
34 Redeemed
36 "Delta of Venus" author
38 Immature adult male
42 Livelihood
44 Art today
45 Bridle
47 Arum lily
48 Nordic
49 Chinese weight
50 Actress Anderson, et al.
51 Deprived, poetically
52 Subject in Virgil's "Eclogues"
53 Furniture wood
54 Don ___
58 "Exodus" role
59 Blue Eagle agcy. of the 30's

614 by Richard Silvestri

ACROSS

1 Symbol of stiffness
7 Brewing ingredient
11 Leave it to beavers
14 Julia, on "Seinfeld"
15 Mayberry moppet
16 Mistress Braun
17 "Wait 'Til My Bobby Gets Home" singer
19 Marshy area
20 Dockworkers' org.
21 Four laps, sometimes
22 A Sesame Streeter
23 X rating?
25 Sticker
27 Come to a halt
28 Patron saint of Norway
30 Co-star of "The Producers"
32 Government health program
34 "Hail, Caesar!"
35 Forge materials
36 Where Naxos is
39 Hard water?
40 Contest entry, perhaps
42 The Babe Ruth of Japan
46 Science writer Gernsback
47 Ease up
48 Hymn accompaniment
50 Record
51 Site of the 1960 Olympics
52 Ad writer's honor
53 Lend a hand
55 Cousin of Fortran
56 Former E Street Band member
60 Baseball throw
61 Working away
62 Bar perches
63 Journal addendum
64 Coolers
65 Lake Huron port

DOWN

1 It's seen in anger
2 According to
3 Tenderizing sauce
4 Brook
5 Hoopster Shaquille
6 Place to relax
7 "The Misanthrope" author
8 Harlem theater
9 As it occurs
10 Driving need
11 Trounce
12 Disinclined
13 Place for trophies
18 Barbecue leftovers
22 Implore
23 Tabby's mate
24 Kind of sch.
26 Rhododendron relative
27 Break the 10th Commandment
29 Impair
31 Warfield of "Night Court"
33 Secret supply
36 10^{100}
37 Witch's vessel
38 Therefore
40 They go by the book
41 Cerberus or Argus, e.g.
42 Ranchero's wrap
43 Homes
44 Vandalize
45 Arrive at last
49 1993 treaty
52 Give as a reference
54 Dr. Frankenstein's assistant
56 Shut-eye
57 C.I.A. forerunner
58 "Boola Boola" singer
59 Hush-hush D.C. grp.

615 by Martin Ashwood-Smith

ACROSS
1 Come clean, with "up"
5 Attitudinize
9 Matthew, originally
13 Lung opening?
14 "___ Speaks!" (1961 autobiography)
15 Well briefed about
16 Disarmament treaty concerns
19 Douglas, e.g.
20 Coeur d'___, Idaho
21 Draw out
22 The difference between Jan and Joan?
23 Kingdom east of Fiji
24 Air freshener option
25 Edwin Drood's betrothed
27 1991 flick "Bill & ___ Bogus Journey"
29 Suffix with exist or insist
30 High muck-a-mucks
32 Frequent figure in Renaissance paintings
35 Shoreline drive
37 Wipeout
39 Turning points
43 "Welcome" item
44 Apple-pie pros
45 Hard to believe
46 Chipped in
49 Mogul mogul
52 Swell place?
53 Shooter's request
54 Connacht county
55 Certainly may
56 Curaçao, e.g.
59 Classical theaters
60 Stop-___
61 Shaving cream additive
62 Joanne Dru's "Red River" role
63 Hwys.
64 Mystery writer John Dickson ___

DOWN
1 Hoopla
2 September event
3 Sweetener
4 1905 song girl
5 Minor need, at times?
6 Toast topping
7 Leave the nest
8 Sister of Selene
9 Montreal Monday
10 Shoulder piece
11 Spitfire, so to speak
12 Creepy-crawly
14 Overhead projection?
17 Dig in
18 It's shocking!
26 Experts
28 Mrs., abroad
31 Serpent's sound
33 Author LeShan
34 Copy
36 Robin's co-star in 70's TV
37 Artificial
38 Get-ups
40 Where "Turandot" premiered
41 Wife of England's Henry II
42 Calumny
43 Billiken
47 Literature Nobelist Canetti
48 Party girl
50 Exchange premium
51 Derek and others
57 Except for
58 Varnish ingredient

616 by Jonathan Schmalzbach

ACROSS
1 Iraq's second-largest city
6 Drain problem
10 Actress Garr
14 Dominant
15 Hockey's Gordie
16 Flair
17 Poker loser's retort
20 Hindquarters
21 Western Indian
22 French fighter jet
23 Amo, ___, amat
24 Transfusion liquids
25 Ambiguity
30 Kind of loser
31 Publicizes
32 "How dry ___"
34 Plenty
35 Plaintiff or defendant
37 Cruel one
38 Midmorning
39 Slug
40 Twisted
41 Some baseball games
46 Bargain hunter's delight
47 Dental photo
48 Mummify
51 "King ___"
52 Apply with a light touch
55 Insurance provision
58 "___ just take a minute"
59 In ___ of
60 Golfer with an army
61 Prefix with gram or graph
62 Prevaricates
63 Gift ideas for prisoners?

DOWN
1 Foretoken
2 Ever and ___
3 Collar fastener
4 Morrow of "Quiz Show"
5 Savoir-faire
6 Pick
7 Knowledge
8 Have
9 "There is no royal road to ___": Euclid
10 Ayatollah's capital
11 "On the Waterfront" director Kazan
12 Summoned, as a servant
13 "Picnic" playwright
18 Kin of etc.
19 Radials, e.g.
23 Fritzi Ritz, to Nancy
24 Show of anger
25 Distributed charity
26 Home of Maine's Black Bears
27 ___ Day (April 22)
28 Tony of cereal fame
29 Works hard for
30 Horror-film prop
33 Happened upon
35 Headlong
36 Toward shelter
37 Old-fashioned wedding word
39 "Hoops"
42 Of service
43 Uris best seller
44 English composer Thomas
45 "Broadway Open House" regular, in 50's TV
48 Fix text
49 Speck of dust
50 Positive Wall Street figure
51 Banjo site, in song
52 Rackets
53 Eagerly expecting
54 Ciao, adiós, etc.
56 Three, on a sundial
57 F.D.R.'s Blue Eagle grp.

ACROSS

1 "Lights out" tune
5 U.S. terr. until 1912
9 Dieter's lunch
14 Opposite of sans
15 ___ Raton
16 Noted violinmaker
17 Chaucer's Wife of ___
18 Radar screen image
19 Kayak
20 Pre-Utah team
23 Breakfast-in-bed item
24 Comic Johnson
25 Put on years
26 Hushed
28 Priest's robe
30 Clairvoyance
33 Alcohol awareness org.
35 Writer Fleming
37 Slender
39 Pre–Los Angeles team
42 Elicited
43 Anglo-Saxon letter
44 "Typee" sequel
45 Like Gen. Powell
46 Dadaist Hans
48 Ukr. or Russ., once

50 Some dash widths
51 Eurasia's ___ Mountains
53 King ___
55 Pre-Indianapolis team
61 Furnish
62 Artful
63 Manhandle
65 American Kennel Club rejects
66 Sister and wife of Osiris
67 New York canal
68 Mississippi tributary
69 Mammilla
70 Cell: Prefix

DOWN

1 Bill
2 Trend-setting, perhaps
3 Waned
4 Vowel sound
5 This ans., e.g.
6 Kind of bed
7 Colder
8 Revolutionary Emiliano
9 Pouches

10 Key of Mozart's Symph. No. 29
11 Actress Turner
12 The gamut
13 Number after nueve
21 Olive that's very thin
22 TV family, 1952–66
25 Jurassic Park compound
27 Crude container
29 Brief letters?
30 Basic
31 Forte
32 Mexican moola
34 Happy associate
36 Opposite SSE
38 I, to Claudius
40 Mauna ___
41 Reading problem?
47 Loss's partner
49 Orson Welles studio
52 Stood up
54 Early Mexican
55 The Ronettes' "___ Baby"
56 Shade of blue
57 Jump for Oksana Baiul
58 One of the Jackson 5
59 ___ facto

60 Skin abnormality
64 Pope who excommunicated Martin Luther

ACROSS

1 Temporary protector
5 Baker's wares
9 Bassoon relatives
14 New Rochelle college
15 Part of a platform dive
16 Dakar's cape
17 Hopper
20 Field hospital routine
21 Effluvia
22 Pool employees
23 Printers' measures
24 Health care lobby grp.
27 Nolan Ryan, once
30 "___ 17"
32 Oriental tea
35 Criticizes
37 El primer mes
38 Skipper
42 Fling
43 Mouse catcher
44 Very important
45 Like some 20th-century compositions
47 Generous
50 Plant
51 Apprehend the perpetrator

53 Matador's whirling maneuver
57 Caught 40 winks
59 Congenital
60 Jumper
64 Passage
65 Game played with a knife
66 Name on many locks
67 Colony resident of yore
68 Worker
69 Spoken

DOWN

1 Winnows
2 Pursue, in a way
3 Pulitzer-winning author E. ___ Proulx
4 Kind of split
5 Ancient gymnasium
6 Fed. collection agency
7 Mimic
8 Protection of a kind
9 Exceed improperly
10 Four-posters
11 Mars, for one
12 Former name for Tokyo

13 Safe follower
18 Selves
19 Diva Lily
24 Dripping
25 Donny's singing sister
26 Suffering
28 Carry on
29 Dvorak's "Russia," e.g.
31 Pismire
32 Barcelona abodes
33 Informed about
34 Tell projectile
36 Hoax
39 Write
40 One might do this backward
41 Notified
46 Use a hammock
48 Advance
49 Future fetus
52 Sir Toby of "Twelfth Night"
54 Aft
55 Inventor Nikola
56 One of the Fords
57 Take out
58 Oscar ___ Renta
60 "My Gal ___"

61 Golfer's concern
62 Sixth sense, for short
63 Tan

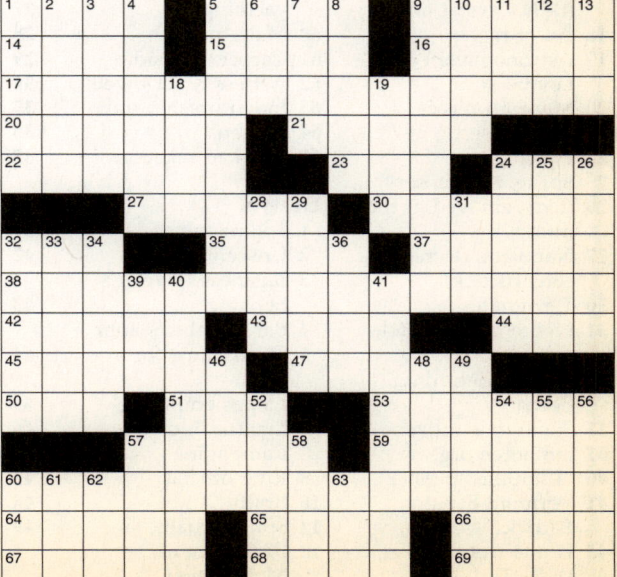

619 by Peter Gordon

ACROSS
1 Methuselah-like
4 ___ Mama (rum drink)
10 Louisville Sluggers
14 Trouble
15 Dream interrupters
16 Buffalo's county
17 French director Jean ___ Godard
18 Game show regular Charles Nelson ___
19 One 'twixt 12 and 20
20 Honor for 35-Down in 1991 and 1992
23 Ending for switch or smack
24 Half of sei
25 35-Down's position
30 Breakfast's partner
32 Genuine
33 Sigher's words
34 In reserve
37 Fleur-de-___
38 Into separate pieces
40 Gullible person
41 Stared lustfully
43 Actresses Farrow and Sara
44 Guernsey, e.g.

45 Thanksgiving tuber
46 35-Down's team
48 Flange
50 Figueras, Spain, museum subject
51 Honor for 35-Down in 1991
58 Piglet's friend
59 Equivalent of 21 shillings
60 D-Day figure, familiarly
62 Aware of
63 Insane, slangily
64 Teacher's org.
65 Nudnik
66 Prospectus listings
67 Bearded antelope

DOWN
1 Strigiform bird
2 Yankee who played a record 2,130 consecutive games
3 In a proper manner
4 ". . . And God Created Woman" star
5 Shake ___ (hurry up)
6 Storm pellets

7 Woody's son
8 2055, to Terence
9 Until now
10 'Twixt
11 Section
12 Stadium section
13 Delight
21 Oral history
22 Shady place
25 Capital of Manche
26 Airline to Malmö
27 Hitchhiker's need
28 ___ vincit amor
29 Step on it
31 Breaking up
35 Player with a record 2,131st consecutive game on 9/6/95
36 Pentathlon equipment
38 Own up to
39 Guinness suffix
42 Hearing range
44 Mosque priest
47 Goals
49 Igneous rock's source
51 Each
52 Solitary

53 Many
54 Has second thoughts about
55 Wins in a card game
56 Chip in a chip

57 Spam, ham or lamb
61 Perrier, par exemple

620 by Chuck Deodene

ACROSS
1 Conventions
6 Take, as testimony
10 Doctrines
14 Phrase of clarification
15 "Memories ___" (Billy Crystal film)
16 Set of races
17 Astronomical Willy Ley book
20 Museum pieces
21 Drive insert
22 Flinch
23 Sprite, to Spenser
26 Item removed at the pump
27 Napoleon decreed its construction
30 Terminate
31 Lieutenant of Fidel, once
32 Painter Gerard ___ Borch
33 Some moisturizers
37 Jamboree org.
40 "Ulalume" penner
41 Vermont Senator Patrick
43 Home-front plot of W.W. II

48 Some microwaves
50 Sock style
51 Blanches
52 "Even ___ speak . . ."
54 Satyajit Ray hero
56 Considerations in yachting
60 Malta moolah
61 Carpenter's aid
62 Actress MacDowell
63 Indentureship unit
64 Hubbub
65 Shocked reactions

DOWN
1 Foliate mineral
2 Unscented
3 Business traveler's booking
4 Bar member's abbr.
5 Good name for a cook?
6 L'eggs employee
7 Lizards, old-style
8 Rampaging
9 Ring official
10 Bratty
11 Spirited gathering
12 Birthplace of Mohammed

13 Precipitous
18 Touch up
19 Give and take
24 Bradley and O'Neill
25 Film amount
26 Feds
27 Shtick
28 Less demonstrative
29 Exultant cry
34 ___ out (withdraws)
35 Overly
36 Molten waste
37 1978 Springsteen song
38 Pre-shearing bath
39 Author Rand
42 Suffix with eat or boot
43 Irish statesman Eamon De ___
44 "Well, ___!" (huffy phrase)
45 Durango abode
46 Tedious affair, slangily
47 Baseball's Luzinski
48 Administer
49 1842 story "The Mystery of ___ Rogêt"

52 Stepped down
53 "Yes, indeed," in Madrid
55 Benefits
57 E.R. hookups

58 Jokester
59 ___ nutshell

621 by Cathy Millhauser

ACROSS

1 Shadow
6 Kind of bar
10 Choler
14 Actor Lloyd of "Peyton Place"
15 Opposite of windward
16 Chancel sight
17 Cut short, NASA-style
18 Eft-wing politician?
19 Yemeni port
20 Home of Briar Cliff College
23 In motion
24 Lo mein base
25 Johnny Cash hit of 1969
28 Suffix with king
29 Kind of short, for short
30 Enter the realm of Morpheus
34 Over
36 Jack of "Barney Miller"
38 Start to kick?
39 M*A*S*H worker
41 Sans mixers
44 "Winter of Artifice" writer
45 Valueless
49 Result of a head injury, maybe
52 Some sale settings
53 Place for locks
56 "Kon-___"
57 Ward of TV's "Sisters"
58 60's boxing champ Griffith
61 Kind of column
62 "Trinity" author
63 Less bats
64 Digs of twigs
65 What rakes make
66 Elmer the Bull's mate

DOWN

1 Women's rights periodical of 1853
2 Throng
3 Thrived
4 Curio
5 Fats Domino's real first name
6 Tailless cat
7 Actor Baldwin
8 Cassette button
9 Donnybrooks
10 Cornrow creators
11 Antiseptic compound
12 "Camelot" composer
13 Fashion editor Chase et al.
21 Caspian Sea feeder
22 "___ Be So Nice to Come Home To"
23 Have ___ to pick
25 Man in a garden
26 Enero or febrero, e.g.
27 ___ Lodge (motel chain)
31 Brains
32 Chihuahua "ciao"
33 Restaurant reading
35 Restaurant reading
37 National anthem contraction
40 Penalty
42 Girl starter
43 Saint called "The Little Flower"
46 Sneeze stopper
47 Thin, in a way
48 Barbarian
49 ___ Martin (classic car)
50 Election bellwether
51 SALT subject
54 Writer Wiesel
55 Service at St. Peter's
59 Hibiscus wreath
60 Before

622 by Sidney L. Robbins

ACROSS

1 Hubert's comic strip wife
6 Segment
10 Title for Nemo or Queeg: Abbr.
14 Eagle's nest
15 Was in debt
16 Slick
17 July–August period
20 On an ocean liner
21 Slippery ones
22 "... ___ evil..."
23 Neighbor of Libya
25 Euripides productions
26 Less hard
29 TV's "The ___ Bunch"
31 Run, as a meeting
32 Not a copy: Abbr.
33 Mobil product
36 Auto option
40 One of the Stooges
41 Rim
42 One who obeys all orders
43 Intimidates
45 Actress Black and others
46 Erie and Suez
49 Engulf
51 "There Is Nothin' Like ___"
52 Zoom
53 Clerical title
57 What a cold remedy gives
60 Gen. Robt. ___
61 Otherwise
62 Sheep's plaint
63 Foxx of "Sanford and Son"
64 Wagers
65 "Mr. Tambourine Man" band, with "The"

DOWN

1 Cry of success
2 Classic cars
3 Coax
4 Instructive
5 Pro vote
6 Sat
7 Dissatisfied soldier
8 Umps
9 Six-pointers, for short
10 "A Midsummer Night's Dream," e.g.
11 Girl's name meaning "loved"
12 Full assemblies
13 Rookies
18 1492 or 2001
19 Took unfair advantage of
24 Two-handed sandwich
25 Trio visiting Jesus
26 Con man's con
27 Akron's home
28 Transit token
29 Ship's prison
30 Baptism, for one
32 Probability
33 Mock
34 Shortly
35 Noncoms: Abbr.
37 Part of CNN
38 Intense exam
39 As a rule
43 Pitched tents
44 Margarine
45 Actress Deborah
46 Try to please, with "to"
47 "The Story of ___ H"
48 No longer anonymous
49 Defeat
50 Garfield's predecessor
52 Store event
54 Coffin stand
55 Item of wampum
56 Newts
58 Soldier under 60-Across
59 Dwindle

623 · by Stephanie Spadaccini

ACROSS
1 "Our Gang" producer Hal
6 Kind of nerve
11 Married
14 Get used (to)
15 Madrid museum
16 "Are you a man ___ mouse?"
17 Forestry worker?
19 Stoolie
20 Queen of Eng.
21 Mine material
22 "___ Fideles"
24 Tennessee Williams's "The Night of the ___"
27 Old Pontiacs
28 Clear as ___
30 Money held by a third party
33 Stage
34 French farewell
35 Actress Thurman
38 Actor Yves
40 Newswoman Norville
42 Dict. entry
43 Ruckus
45 Sculptures on pedestals
46 Day to wear a bonnet
48 The Divine Miss M
49 Take apart
51 Rodeo entrants
53 Aspirin, e.g.
56 Former Rep. Rostenkowski
57 Word between Friends
61 "___ monkey's uncle!"
62 Ocean liners' employees?
65 100 yrs.
66 Lacks, in brief
67 Some change
68 Make sense, with "up"
69 The end
70 Vice President Agnew

DOWN
1 "Interview with the Vampire" author Anne
2 Scott Turow book
3 German car maker
4 Most zany
5 That girl
6 "Pagliacci," for one
7 Dressed fussily
8 Little bit
9 Brainstorm
10 Big stack of firewood
11 Least appetizing sausage?
12 Muse of poetry
13 Palm tree fruits
18 Aretha Franklin's singing style
23 Freudian component
25 Twinkles
26 Out of the way
28 "Hey!" on the Hesperus
29 Outcast orchestra?
31 Bee follower
32 Kind of match
33 Brit. leaders
34 Chicago's ___ Planetarium
36 Spouse
37 Sounds of satisfaction
39 Trawler's equipment
41 Get the better of
44 Wearing away
47 U.S. modem-driven company
48 Giovanni's "good"
49 New York city
50 Christened
52 Macaroni, e.g.
54 Reverberate
55 21-Across carrier
58 Prefix with sphere
59 Pitcher
60 Bygone oil company
63 Exploit
64 Some I.R.A. investments

624 · by Bob Klahn

ACROSS
1 Kind of course
9 The terrible twos, for one
14 Poison pen letters
15 "Dover Beach" poet
17 Dents-ly populated?
18 Take baby steps
19 Shakespearean eulogist
20 Kids
22 Aspire
23 Approximate
24 Failings
25 "The Simpsons" storekeeper
26 Low notes
27 German spa city
28 Bear country?
29 "___ Girls"
30 President who was a Princeton graduate
32 Antiquated
33 Attempts
36 Letters from mom?
39 Wang Lung's patient wife
40 Laurey's aunt
41 Carson's Carnac, e.g.
42 Pabst brew, familiarly
43 "Inside the Third Reich" author
44 "Beetle Bailey" character
45 Seat on the aisle
46 One of the Sinatras
47 Tees, e.g.
48 Shalamar Gardens locale
50 Spiteful
52 Like 5's and 10's, e.g.
53 Slowly disappear
54 R.E.M. vocalist Michael
55 Canola oil source

DOWN
1 1959 Neil Sedaka hit
2 With no exceptions
3 Two of the Seven Wonders of the World
4 Jackson Hole backdrop
5 Rephrase
6 Ingrid's "Notorious" co-star
7 Little white thing
8 Noted 60's activist
9 "Love is a Battlefield" singer, 1983
10 ___ Perot
11 Further
12 Na_2CO_3
13 Orbital track
16 Reserved
21 Modern cubist?
24 Platinum-selling debut rock album of 1978
27 How some fast-food chicken is sold
28 Large server
30 Foment
31 Fisherman's profit?
32 Answer to the riddle of the Sphinx
33 Ballyhoo
34 Very attentive
35 "Eh?"
36 Chinese restaurant flower
37 Leaves for lunch?
38 Two-timed
41 Smothers with muck
43 Peel
44 End of the line?
47 Cinch
49 It's a cinch, in Japan
51 "Die Meistersinger" heroine

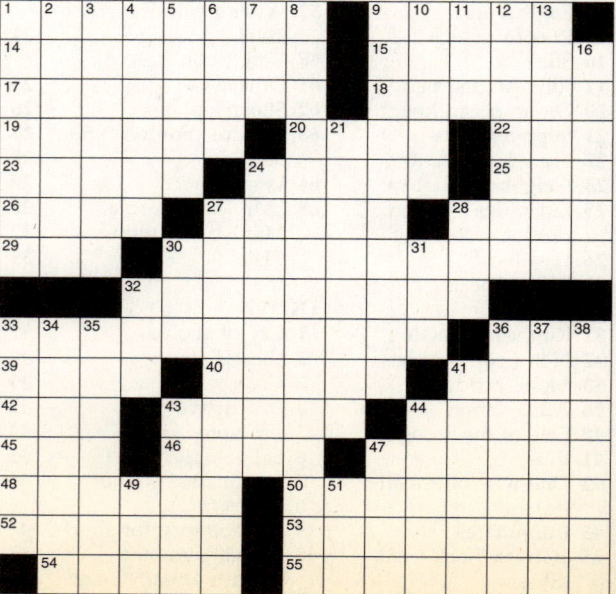

625   by Albert J. Klaus

ACROSS

1 John Denver's "Christmas in ___"
6 "Tuna-Fishing" painter
10 Among
14 "___ Eyes" (1969 song)
15 Actor Richard
16 Bounty rival
17 Refinement
18 Witticisms
19 Vigor
20 1950 Sinatra hit
23 West Bank org.
24 "Just a ___"
25 Three strokes, perhaps
28 Actress Sommer
31 Shares
36 Feared test
38 Troubles
40 Weaken
41 1955 Sinatra hit
44 Improve
45 Rig
46 Shut off
47 Beachwear
49 Relax
51 Audit conductor, for short
52 Guy's date
54 Eternity
56 1961 Sinatra hit
64 "Warm"
65 Minnow eater
66 Driving hazard
68 Petruchio's mate
69 Shillelagh land
70 10th-day-of-Christmas gift
71 Swerve
72 Henna and others
73 Follow

DOWN

1 Blue-chip symbol
2 Lively dance
3 Chihuahua change
4 Bar, in law
5 Compass part
6 Half begun?
7 Excited
8 Stucco backing
9 Foot part
10 Swear
11 Ryun's run
12 Basil's successor
13 Niels Bohr, e.g.
21 The Man Without a Country
22 More aloof
25 Propels a gondola
26 Bouquet
27 Bird "perched upon a bust of Pallas"
29 Toddlers
30 Dramatist Rice
32 Goddess of discord
33 Raccoon kin
34 Lawn tool
35 Is apparent
37 Impart
39 Ditto
42 Saw
43 Elevated
48 Stood up
50 Kind of switch
53 Distrustful
55 Run site
56 Prepares the presses
57 Plumber's concern
58 Behind
59 Ale
60 Pennsylvania port
61 Roadhouses
62 They go into locks
63 Relative of Hindustani
67 Volte-face WNW

626   by Fred Piscop

ACROSS

1 G.E. subsidiary
4 Mob member
8 Robotic rock group of the 80's
12 Emphasized, in a way
15 Gov. Bayh of Indiana
16 Mercury
18 "Ich bin ___ Berliner"
19 Uses a scope
20 Lipton competitor
21 Snap request?
22 Spread
23 Mars
30 "Pardon me"
31 Successes
32 Hubbub
33 Strings of yore
34 Prevailing mood
36 Stash the bags
37 Jersey call
38 Sea east of the Caspian
39 Down to the ___
40 Saturn
45 Stack part
46 "Now ___ me down . . ."
47 Knowing
50 Fair-to-middling
51 Ashen
54 Pluto
57 Woody's kid
58 Hidalgo highway
59 Ancient Mexican
60 Parcel (out)
61 Guinness Book suffix

DOWN

1 Nostalgic soft-drink brand
2 "Très ___!"
3 Gridiron pos.
4 Three-horse sleigh
5 "U Can't Touch This" rap singer
6 Western Indians
7 "___ a life!"
8 With dexterity
9 Kind of eye
10 Singer Jerry
11 One and ___
12 Numbered rd.
13 High-tech memos
14 Diplomats' quest
17 Interprets
21 TV correspondent Brit
22 Wound
23 Majorca seaport
24 "___ Beautiful Doll"
25 Nafta opposer
26 Kind of dog
27 Hand-dyed fabric
28 Love to death
29 Galley drudge
34 Double ___ (puzzle type)
35 Etna locations
36 Influence
38 Change
41 "___ customer"
42 "I ___ Like That" (60's hit)
43 Comic Bossler
44 Hot cereal name
47 Did the crawl
48 Irene of "Fame"
49 Unfavorably
50 "Don't tread ___"
51 Trials
52 One ___ (ball game)
53 Flyer's org.
55 Actor Waterston
56 Tram contents

627 by Kiran S. Kedlaya

ACROSS
1 Radio station supply
6 Dismay
10 Louis who was guillotined
13 Flu ward sound
14 "You said it!"
15 Regular Cosmo feature
16 Betraying, briefly
18 Lhasa ___ (dog)
19 Colony member
20 Strove (for)
21 Told (on)
23 Advance
24 Antigun lobbyist Brady
25 Congresswoman Waters
28 Respectful
31 Commencement
32 Wizards
33 Prevent
34 Four on a four, e.g.
35 Tint
36 Coffee
37 Nationality suffix
38 Flapjack places, for short
39 Punished, perhaps
40 Like some pizzas
42 Punish, perhaps
43 Speak monotonously
44 Soothing instrument
45 Knee/ankle connector
47 Glow
48 "Look here!"
51 Eager
52 It indicates what's happening, briefly
55 Womanizer
56 Raison d'___
57 Bud Grace comic strip
58 Unified
59 Antique store tag
60 Kind of statement

DOWN
1 Arp art
2 What a model might become
3 Barricade, with "in"
4 Inner ear
5 In the black, like a dry cleaner?
6 Sent, in a way
7 Within
8 Form of Buddhism
9 Currier or Ives
10 Start playing, briefly
11 Tight gripper
12 ___ Lacoste
15 Mideast nation
17 "___ Kleine Nachtmusik"
22 God shown with a burning torch
23 "Fairy tales"
24 Utah lilies
25 Two-wheeler
26 Liqueur flavor
27 Two-wheeler, briefly
28 "Lord of the Flies" leader
29 Object of contemplation?
30 Business
32 Bullwinkle, for one
35 Waters off Hong Kong
36 Green shade
38 Pop star, say
39 Wine orders
41 Bluenose
42 Lighting specialist, informally?
44 Crescents
45 Betting game
46 Tolstoy hero
47 Prefix with culture
48 "Yikes!"
49 Son, usually
50 Farm team
53 "___ a Joke, Son" (1947 flick)
54 Big inits. in credit reporting

628 by Albert J. Klaus

ACROSS
1 "Woe is me!"
5 Inn, informally
10 Dollop
14 Frolic
15 Title holder
16 Burt's ex
17 Jai ___
18 Former auto executive
20 Two-pointers
22 Differs
23 Saucer occupants, for short
24 Mozart's "___ fan tutte"
25 Ball girl
28 Vacation spot
30 "Jerusalem Delivered" poet
34 Border lake
35 Car in a procession
37 Spring mo.
38 West Point salutatorian, 1829
41 Language ending
42 Off course
43 City two hours south of Lillehammer
44 Spreads the word
46 Bit of voodoo
47 Grueling tests
48 Sword with a guard
50 Louis Freeh's org.
51 Rubbed
54 Ascendant
58 Two-time U.S. Open golf champion
61 Kind of shark
62 Suffix with buck
63 Pentax rival
64 Sicilian rumbler
65 Poet Robert ___ Warren
66 Exhausted
67 Sunup direction

DOWN
1 Bedouin
2 She gets what she wants
3 Amo, ___, amat
4 Modern film maker
5 Leaves in a hurry
6 Wows
7 Jet's heading
8 Mercury and Jupiter, e.g.
9 "Well done!"
10 Actress DeHaven
11 Places
12 ___ over lightly
13 Kind of crime
19 Mobile unit?
21 Season of l'année
24 Polish producer
25 Cap
26 Having an irregular edge
27 Defame
28 Boil
29 Military chaplain
31 Hot sauce
32 Word with cold or breathing
33 Chocolate snacks
35 Elevations: Abbr.
36 Remark
39 Hardly one with a lilting voice
40 Neoprimitive American artist
45 Unextinguished
47 Kimono sash
49 Paradises
50 Weather line
51 Keep time manually
52 "You are ___"
53 Ages and ages
54 Soon
55 Ninth Greek letter
56 Actress Woods and others
57 Pest
59 One who gets special treatment
60 W.W. II hero

629 by Norman S. Wizer

ACROSS
1 ___ Hatteras, N.C.
5 Clearheaded
10 Egyptian cobras
14 Mimics
15 Video arcade name
16 Turn obliquely
17 SCRAM
19 Antitoxins
20 Football's ___ Bowl
21 Safety org.
22 Current, as accounts
24 Russian grassland
26 Black Sea resort
28 Actors Silver and Howard
30 Illegal trader
33 Words preceding war or God
36 Young 'uns
38 Half of MCII
39 SPLIT
43 Indiana Jones's quest
44 Franchise
45 Vertical
46 Made tea
49 Crimson and carmine
51 Adulates
53 Standards of perfection
57 Plant pests
59 Italian wine district
61 Hawaiian garland
62 Cut in a skirt
63 BEAT IT
66 The Mikado's Lord High Executioner
67 Papal vestment
68 One of the Brontës
69 Suffix with road or hip
70 Opera voice
71 Miss Trueheart of the comics

DOWN
1 Summer getaways
2 "You'll always be ___ of me"
3 Tea type
4 Language ending
5 Yankee pitcher Don
6 Great Salt Lake state
7 Chocolate bean
8 Get on one's nerves
9 Allocate
10 St. Francis's home
11 VAMOOSE
12 Llama land
13 Barter
18 Finish
23 Dolt
25 Egg on
27 Mental confusion
29 Took deliberate steps
31 Grammy-winning Fitzgerald
32 Peril
33 Discoverers' cries
34 "Dead ___" (Dick Francis novel)
35 SKIDDOO
37 Hall-of-Famer Mel
40 Went too far
41 Finnan ___ (fish dish)
42 ___ dixit
47 Film cutter
48 Pea holder
50 One of two
52 Guy with a tail
54 "Home ___"
55 Shows partiality
56 Allies (with)
57 Proposes
58 Scheme
60 Normandy invasion town, 1944
64 Dander
65 Tell (on)

630 by Gregory E. Paul

ACROSS
1 Snitch
6 1986 World Series champs
10 "You said it!"
14 More washed out
15 Over
16 Pop singer Laura
17 Senator Specter
18 Pro ___
19 Bushy hairstyle
20 1970 George Harrison hit
23 Astronaut's "fine"
24 Catch sight of
25 Tropical animals
27 Bill Haley's band
30 Tackle box gizmo
32 Jazz's Kid
33 Stendhal hero Julien
35 Wedding guest
38 Take à la magicians
40 Sinatra standard
42 Wise
43 February forecast
45 Katmandu's land
47 Narcs' grp.
48 "So Big" author
50 Robert Shapiro, e.g.
52 Singer West
54 Pocket bread
55 Shoemaker's helper, in story
56 60's sitcom
62 Composer Janacek
64 Nabisco brand
65 Walkie-talkie
66 Landlocked Asian country
67 Void's partner
68 In ___ (stuck)
69 Scurriers
70 Strike out, as copy
71 Post offices have them

DOWN
1 W.W. II meat
2 On one's guard
3 Woes
4 Shortstop Reese
5 Hemingway and others
6 "Back to the Future" role
7 List shortener
8 Baum dog
9 "In the Heat of the Night" locale
10 Literary olio
11 Lerner-Loewe musical
12 Inaccuracy
13 Crannies
21 British college
22 "Tuna-Fishing" painter
26 Bic products
27 Flatfoots
28 Ph.D. exam
29 1989 Daniel Day-Lewis film
30 Underground way
31 Applaud
34 Sandberg of the Cubs
36 "The African Queen" screenwriter
37 Abrade
39 Track contest
41 Ivy Leaguer
44 Barbershop request
46 Football fling
49 ___ question (certainly)
51 Japanese mustard
52 Perry's secretary
53 City SSE of Buffalo
54 Capitalist tool
57 Quiz choice
58 Terrible rigor
59 Norse chief
60 Supreme Court complement
61 Lays down the lawn
63 Draft letters

631 by Chuck Deodene

ACROSS
1 Explorer Vasco ___
7 Exchange
11 Brewery item
14 Support group for drinkers' families
15 Mafia chief
16 "___ American Cousin"
17 Riches, derogatorily
19 Charlemagne's domain: Abbr.
20 Eyeballs
21 Woodwind
22 Potter's material
23 Storm heading
24 Pitcher's stat
25 Surgery reminders
27 Deprive of sustenance
30 To no ___ (fruitlessly)
32 Mints
34 Tiny organisms
35 Shady financial activity
39 Hall-of-Fame QB Johnny
40 Make an offer for
41 Sticker
42 Kleenex
45 "___ Luck" (1973–74 sitcom)
47 German "bugs"
48 Needlefish
50 Where it's happening
51 "Star Trek" counselor
53 Entrap
55 Prefix with cycle
56 Tidy sum, slangily
58 Gamepieces
59 Deputy
60 " 'Crocodile' ___"
61 Smelter input
62 Southwestern art colony
63 Golfers Sam and J.C.

DOWN
1 "Platoon" Oscar nominee Willem
2 Straightens
3 Stone chip
4 Poker chip, maybe
5 ___ scale (hardness measure)
6 Whichever
7 Treasure hunter's gear
8 Baylor University site
9 Post, in Paris
10 "The Tell-Tale Heart" writer
11 Cabbage kin
12 Like the Urals
13 "Riders of the Purple Sage" novelist
18 Brazilian city west of Rio
22 Grottoes
24 Satan's doings
26 Special appearances
28 Transparent sheet
29 1985 World Series champs
31 Support
33 Undersea prowler
34 ___ Ababa, Ethiopia
35 Woodstock '94 feature
36 Witticism
37 Smoker's fix
38 Dunce
43 "Raid on Entebbe" setting
44 Netted
46 Heart chambers
47 Yea and nay
49 Spanish kings
50 Kind of wrestler
52 Give a new look
53 Rotated
54 Endangered goose
56 Butter serving
57 Ground gained in the N.F.L.

632 by David J. Kahn

ACROSS
1 Recently
7 A Caesar partner
11 Pizazz
14 "The Vicar of Wakefield" daughter
15 "Boyz N the ___" (1991 film)
16 Promising words
17 Organically foolish?
19 Classical beginning
20 Lean
21 Kind of hunt
23 Sports page figure
25 Excitement
26 Organically loud?
32 Actor Mantegna
34 Western justice, once
35 Roost
36 Hardy boy
38 Quiets
40 Tijuana treat
41 ___ lodge
43 Source of family traits
45 Just opened
46 Organically sad?
49 Hockey's Tikkanen
50 Common fertilizer
51 Lively dance
56 Where Pocatello is
60 Rock's Rose
61 Organically afraid?
63 Isr. neighbor
64 Marble marking
65 Ridicule
66 Saatchi products
67 Late fashion illustrator
68 Test formats

DOWN
1 Sounds of pleasure
2 Tizzy
3 San Remo currency
4 Disinclined
5 Dalai Lama, e.g.
6 Audience
7 Stylish
8 A Chaplin
9 Of the same age
10 Made sense
11 Criticize cleverly
12 ___ fixe
13 Needy
18 Like
22 Trio trebled
24 First half of the alphabet
26 Resulted in
27 First name in beauty
28 Give a new gloss to
29 MGM ___
30 ___ homo
31 Lateen-rigged boat
32 Sidepiece
33 ___ about (lawyer's phrase)
37 Rube
39 Antitoxins
42 Settle a dispute
44 Contends
47 "Cats" designer John
48 Church officials
51 Celebration
52 Let go
53 Law degrees
54 Came down
55 Unit of force
57 Jessye Norman speciality
58 Miss Lamarr
59 Browning works
62 Chemical suffix

633 by A.J. Santora

ACROSS

1 Mean
5 Brisk, in mus.
9 Heartthrobs
14 One suited to go for a walk?
16 Sky-colored blossom
17 Dog with an upturned tail
18 Serious
19 Slick
20 Capital
22 Stage of development
23 This one, to Ovid
25 Blossomed again
27 Name in spydom
29 Because of
30 Kind of grant
31 City on the Golden Horn
33 Bartender's accessory
35 Seek a handout from
36 Favor
37 Roman laws
38 Italian love songs
41 Assn.
42 Vaquero's rope
44 Brought back
45 X'es
48 Painter thinner, for short
49 Start another hitch
50 Botanical apertures
52 White House nickname
53 The river, in Juárez
55 Hardly humble
57 Bremen's river
58 Coming back strong
59 Render
60 Travelers' timesavers
61 Civil endings, in London

DOWN

1 "South Pacific" song
2 Dumps
3 Persevered
4 R.N.'s stations
5 Have ___ about oneself (seem distinctive)
6 Took in eagerly
7 Lecherous
8 King Henry II portrayer
9 Some shot
10 Secretly leave
11 Bo Jackson and others
12 Camp shelters
13 Fellini film, with "La"
15 Kind of cakes
21 Peter Rabbit's creator
24 Stevens of "Peter Gunn"
26 Loudspeaker
28 Puts in
32 Keeps occupied
34 Small choir
36 SE Texas city
37 Siren
38 Underlings
39 Rotary engine
40 Guesses, informally
41 Bats
43 Late bloomers
46 Pitch
47 Goodbyes
51 Family girl
54 California's historic Fort ___
56 Part of a coll. curriculum

634 by Stanley B. Whitten

ACROSS

1 Surviving
6 Police radio messages, for short
10 Come clean, with "up"
14 Rich veins
15 Word to a fly
16 "Step ___!"
17 1995 Kline-Ryan comedy
19 Monster
20 Look up to
21 One who works at a stable
23 Free, as a subscription
25 Think out loud
26 Make misty
29 Naval fleets
33 Buckeyes' school: Abbr.
34 Exertion
36 Slender
39 Dobbin's dinner
41 Redhead's dye
42 Hawaiian seaport
43 Filth
44 Bars at Fort Knox
46 Chablis or Beaujolais
47 He's cool
49 Check recipient
51 Quarrel
53 Walk heavily
55 Celebrates
58 Make possible
62 Words of understanding
63 Beef entrée
66 Close
67 Riot spray
68 Chicago's ___ Field
69 Concordes
70 "Iliad," e.g.
71 Area of corporate expenditure, in brief

DOWN

1 Italian auto ___ Romeo
2 McGarrett portrayer
3 The same as before
4 City of canals
5 Home seller deposits
6 Inquire
7 ___ Beta Kappa
8 "Poppycock!"
9 Middling
10 Walker's lane
11 Ornamental vine
12 Ambulance's warning
13 Cubic meter
18 Dress's bottom
22 Square of lawn
24 Ma or pa
26 Cannon's sound
27 Jacob's twin
28 Separate-checks occasion
30 Distance
31 Class AAA baseball
32 Med. sch. course
35 "___ Magic Moment" (60's hit)
37 Nastase of tennis
38 "And Then There Were ___"
40 Runs lightly and rapidly
45 Advertiser
48 Luau dish
50 Christie who wrote 38-Down
51 Rotates
52 Facilitates
54 "___ Misérables"
56 Salinger girl
57 Trade
59 Lima, for one
60 Cooking fat
61 ___ out (barely got)
64 Here, in Nice
65 Jiffy

635 by Ed Early

ACROSS

1 Having more gains than losses
6 Rock's Jagger
10 1910 boxing champ Willard
14 ___ Gras
15 To me, in Marseilles
16 Nanjing nurse
17 Flack
19 Bamako is its capital
20 Word with run or jump
21 Help for the stumped
22 Photoelectric cell component
24 Pop
25 Military guards
26 Native of northern Spain
29 Valleys
30 Circa
31 Counterpart to paper
32 Long, drawn-out story
36 Riviera resort
37 Dungeon items
38 Perfect representative
39 Deceive, on the ice
40 Torpedoed
41 Popular game of deduction
42 Goes in a hurry
44 Bob Dole, e.g.
45 Says yes
48 Medics
49 Adagio non ___
50 Down with the flu
51 Down
54 Rossini subject
55 Miser
58 Brainstorm
59 Canal of song
60 Sheeplike
61 Teapot covering
62 Exhausts
63 Spud

DOWN

1 Rock band equipment
2 Return to, with "back"
3 ". . . ___ saw Elba"
4 Classifieds
5 Dispense, as advice
6 Diploma word
7 "___ Him in Paris" (1937 film)
8 Kind of artist
9 Rooms adjoining sculleries
10 Jazz performances
11 Internet missive
12 Granada toast
13 Adjusts with a wedge
18 White House operative
23 German one
24 Call from the third base coach
25 Proceed embarrassedly
26 Troop
27 Rose lover
28 Slug
29 Thugs
31 Does last-minute studying
33 Doesn't wait
34 "___ match?"
35 In a while
37 Atoms with the same number of protons
41 Gambler's goal
43 Across the way: Abbr.
44 Ed who asked "How'm I doin'?"
45 Storage area
46 Belief
47 Composer Porter and others
48 Cuts into cubes
50 Impertinent one
51 Peevishness
52 Henry VIII's second wife
53 Textile worker
56 Lyricist Gershwin
57 Spacewalk, for short

636 by David J. Kahn

ACROSS

1 Kind of team
5 Irving Berlin's "___ to Be Home"
9 Country lad
14 Parkay, e.g.
15 Learning method
16 1953 John Wayne role
17 Barnum & Bailey circus fake
20 Nursery outfit
21 Sunfish with colorful gill covers
22 Tout's place
23 Sneaker brand
24 Mideast sultanate
27 Modern locale of ancient Palmyra
29 "Usher" man
32 "The Shadow" medium
34 Like some fiction
37 Elroy of football fame
40 California dessert wine
41 Cato, e.g.
42 Spot
43 Haul: Var.
46 Pamplona attraction
47 ___ speak
49 Fodder figure
51 Pluck, in a way
54 Opening night opiners
58 Old Steve Martin phrase, with "a"
61 Early three-handed card game
62 Fire
63 Smut
64 Flash
65 Actor Rob
66 Illustrious illustrator

DOWN

1 Turkeys and such
2 Et ___ (and others)
3 Bank (on)
4 Update
5 For nothing
6 Without company
7 Z preceder
8 3, on a telephone
9 Did stable work
10 Have ___ (argue)
11 Actress Archer
12 "Good ___!"
13 Hussein's queen
18 1959 Kingston Trio hit
19 Hiatus
23 Rodin sculpture, with "The"
24 Killer whales
25 W.W. I battle site
26 Saw
28 Kingly
29 ___ Beach, Calif.
30 Code word for "O"
31 Prefix with history
33 Olive ___
35 Gas station offering
36 Patent office submission, maybe
38 Pay attention
39 Send back
44 Kind of account
45 Willie Stargell, e.g.
47 Exodus commemoration
48 Bygone airline
50 Columnist Smith
51 Uncommon bills
52 Chicken, so to speak
53 Noted exile place
55 Composer Stravinsky
56 Brusque
57 "Auld Lang ___"
59 Two-bagger: Abbr.
60 Bill's partner

by Rand H. Burns

637

ACROSS

1 Bridge column leaders
6 Battle site soon after D-Day
10 Abrade
14 1935 Triple Crown winner
15 Hearty greeting
16 Barbra's 1968 co-star
17 Sealskin mukluk
18 Marine fossil
20 Criticizes severely
22 Ersatz
23 Connections, of a sort
24 Artois article
25 Lens settings
26 Cane material
28 Tunnelers
30 "I Love Lucy" name
31 Dinners outdoors
32 Saturday-night special
35 Al Capp detective
38 Tom Hayden was its first pres.
39 Overcharges but good
40 Monteverdi opera
41 Outpouring
42 Actor Jeremy and others
43 Milk solid
46 Creosote source
48 Retiring
49 Clawlike
50 Carreras performance
53 Like the Manhattan Project
55 Broadcaster
56 Indigene of the Great Lakes area
57 Address fit for a king
58 Intermediate, in law
59 Hand's handful
60 Lob
61 Shellshocked

DOWN

1 Yan's pans
2 Underfed
3 TV witch and namesakes
4 One with a hankering, as for knowledge
5 "Reginald" writer
6 Victoria's Secret fabric
7 Ritz Brothers portrayal of 1939
8 Hi's helpmate
9 "Thimble Theater" surname
10 Some factory workers
11 Compadre
12 Took notice, in a way
13 Court defense?
19 One with a one-track mind
21 Lots of laughs
25 Chemical prefix
26 They're paid to make calls
27 Jamaican export
29 Clods
31 Hurdle for an aspiring atty.
32 The Trojans' undoing?
33 Torch fuel
34 Bout enders
36 Of the dawn
37 More formal
41 Felt
42 Buddy
43 "What's the ___?"
44 Really fancy
45 Maintenance maintainer
47 Up-front money
50 Rock music's Police, e.g.
51 Name of nine Thai kings
52 Turgenev's birthplace
54 It's observed in Pensacola, Fla.

---

by Morton B. Braun

638

ACROSS

1 Eve's second-born
5 Selves
9 Recipe direction
14 Venetian traveler
15 Baby's cry
16 Nuts-and-honey snack
17 Syllabus
18 Scottish group
19 Bean or Welles
20 Kind of joint between boards
23 Angers
24 British statesman Sir Robert
25 Pursued
28 It can provide a moving experience
29 "___ La Douce"
33 Pregame rah-rah meeting
34 1948 Hitchcock nail-biter
35 Close
36 Island prison of history
37 Days of celebration
38 Roof projection
39 Hammer head
40 CompuServe patron
41 Joseph of the Senate
42 Viewed
43 "All Things Considered" network
44 Be annoyed
45 Utah's state flower
47 Knot in wood
48 The Iron Chancellor
55 Pre-Columbian Mexican
56 Father of Enos
57 Tennis champ Yannick
58 African antelope
59 Suffix with kitchen or usher
60 Old Russian assembly
61 Race to a base, perhaps
62 Bird feeder fill
63 Observed

DOWN

1 Date with an M.D.
2 Heavy Army knife
3 Verve
4 View from Port Jefferson
5 Hosted a roast
6 Big parties
7 Mideast gulf
8 Alternative to a plane?
9 Kind of leave or dinner
10 Group containing Truk, Belau and Yap
11 Too
12 City in Ukraine
13 Hans Christian Andersen, e.g.
21 1934 chemistry Nobelist
22 Heredity units
25 Holiday paper
26 The Tin Man portrayer
27 "Seascape" playwright
28 Person in a booth?
30 Author of "The Cloister and the Hearth"
31 Expert
32 "You ___ kidding!"
34 Survey data
37 Baseball practice
41 Road shoulder
44 Hurried
46 Avoid
47 Please, to 48-Across
48 Singles
49 Fanciful, as a story
50 Popular cuisine
51 ___ noire
52 Rake
53 Arrived
54 Tatar chief

639   by Norma Steinberg

ACROSS
1 "Major Barbara" playwright
5 Sierra Club founder John
9 Phrygian king
14 Per capita
15 ___ facto
16 "Have ___ day!"
17 Proctor's cry at the end of a test
18 Pierce
19 Coast
20 Imprisoned feline's call?
23 Cornucopia
24 "Star-Spangled Banner" contraction
25 Avaricious
28 Nostalgic song for cows?
33 Greenstreet's frequent co-star
34 Monk's hood
35 Flag
36 Neighbor of Afr.
37 Bluish-gray cat
40 Famous diarist
41 Beginning (then)
43 Harness part
44 Desert plant
46 Rex Stout's canine sleuth?
48 Disclaimer
49 Kind of shot
50 Temperament
51 Kind of relationship for crows?
57 Isaac's mother
58 Pierre's breakfast choice
59 Cheer (for)
61 Blazing
62 In addition
63 Author Vidal
64 Sales prospects
65 More than misled
66 Tom Joad, e.g.

DOWN
1 Get ___ (ready)
2 Reagan Secretary of State
3 Wile E. Coyote's supply company
4 If
5 1990 Kathy Bates film
6 Author Sinclair
7 "... ere ___ Elba"
8 Kind of cop
9 Old word for a harasser
10 Get by will
11 Parisian house of design
12 Plat portion
13 Comment before "I told you so"
21 Computer add-on
22 Cons
25 Learn through research
26 Awaken
27 Goof
28 Pattern
29 TV lawyer ___ Marshall
30 Leonardo's hometown
31 Author Jong
32 Of the kidneys
34 Singer Laine
38 Whiff
39 "___ newt..."
42 Word before march
45 Experience
47 Fancies
48 Tipped, in a way
50 Verdun's river
51 Eatery
52 Kathleen Battle offering
53 Holiday season
54 Takeout shop
55 Kitchener
56 Actress Spelling
57 Former baseball All-Star Bando
60 Driver's aid

640   by Bernice Gordon

ACROSS
1 Like some eagles or tires
5 Poker Flat chronicler
10 Price
14 "Now ___ me down..."
15 Dillies
16 Patron saint of physicians
17 In need
19 "Miss ___ Regrets"
20 Former Washington nine
21 Journalists Joseph and Stewart
23 Bog
24 Dutch painter Jan
25 Actor Peter
28 Fleet cats
31 Comic Costello
32 ___ incognita
34 Psalms word
35 "Bon" words
37 Appears
39 Flintstones pet
40 Bit of clowning
42 Soup ingredients
44 Cattle call
45 Newborns
47 Shortly
49 End of a tunnel, proverbially
50 Came in horizontally
51 Manhandler
53 Fellow crew member
57 Have an itch for
58 "Fantastic!"
60 1949 hit "___ in Love With Amy"
61 Sky-hued flower
62 Shoe support
63 Glassmaker's oven
64 Broadcasts
65 Asserts

DOWN
1 Invitations
2 A lily
3 Mowing site
4 Ball of fire
5 Feted ones
6 Tennis's Agassi
7 Collectors' cars
8 Robert Morse stage role
9 Subject of a will
10 Shut up
11 In a tenuous position
12 Leave hastily
13 1994 film "Guarding ___"
18 Like Pisa's tower
22 Sediment
24 Humiliate
25 Broadway tune "___ River"
26 Ten-___ odds
27 Not with it
28 Northern Indians
29 Vietnam's capital
30 "Darn it!"
33 Rent out again
36 Presaging trouble
38 One-way transporters
41 Zoo fixture
43 Cuts
46 Pulses
48 Owns up to
50 Protected, as the feet
51 Subject to court-martial, maybe
52 Curse
53 Bedaze
54 Taj Mahal site
55 "___ also serve who..."
56 Hot times on the Riviera
59 Little: Suffix

641　by Charles Arnold

ACROSS

1 Guzzles
7 Bebop
11 Certain muscles, informally
14 Dislocate
15 Woodwind
16 Varnish resin
17 Ancient ascetic
18 Letter writing: Abbr.
19 Japanese admiral Yuko
20 Battleship
23 Mesmerized
27 "Or ___!" (veiled threat)
28 "Torero Saluting" painter
29 Rioting
31 Despicable
32 Greek market
33 Mitigates
35 Actor Matheson or Allen
38 Dictionary
40 Rogers's partner
42 Wily
43 Topple
45 Fudd of cartoondom

46 Director's cry
47 Bee activity
49 ___ Downs (English racetrack)
52 Contented sound
53 ___ fixe
54 Bluff, with a gun
57 Nuclear defense grp.
58 Russia's ___ Mountains
59 Slanted
64 Petition
65 Scoop (out)
66 To wit
67 "___! We Have No Bananas"
68 Whirlpool
69 Like Parmesan

DOWN

1 Neighbor of Ont.
2 Raises
3 "___ Gratia Artis" (M-G-M motto)
4 Enemy
5 Dear, as memories
6 Two-track
7 Oedipus's mother
8 Lodging

9 Swedish painter of "At the Granary Door"
10 "Fiddler on the Roof" star
11 Straighten
12 Wash up
13 "Waverley" novelist
21 Burstyn and Barkin
22 Labor org.
23 Iranian dollars
24 Theater backer
25 Stand-in
26 Actress Garr
30 Transistor predecessor
31 "___ Misérables"
34 Cronus, to Romans
35 Meek
36 "The woman" for Sherlock
37 Traffic sign
39 Choose
41 Prefix with meter
44 Just as much
46 Bill's partner
48 Vexing
49 Emerson piece
50 Aspect

51 Noted White House resident
52 Multicolored pattern
55 Slender nail
56 Sirius, e.g.

60 Drs.' org.
61 Tennis call
62 ___ de France
63 Dancer Charisse

642　by Gerald R. Ferguson

ACROSS

1 "X" denotes it
8 Swiss abodes
15 Continental, e.g.
16 Regular
17 No-___ (easy decision)
18 Radius, e.g.
19 Defeats
20 Brit. legislators
22 Posts
23 Debtors' notes
24 Runs amok
26 Bit of Livorno lucre
27 It's north of Afr.
28 Petrarch products
30 Crow's cry
31 Move back (from)
33 Make ___ at (try to pick up)
35 Felt the heat
37 Soviet cooperative
39 Demonstrated via charades
43 Baden-Powell offshoot org.
44 Besmirched
46 Computer's heart: Abbr.

47 Off-road conveyances, for short
49 Handed (out)
50 Suffix with slug or song
51 Old hat
53 Trojans' sch.
54 ___ the good (beneficial)
55 Tiniest
57 Arranged in rows and columns
59 "The flower of my heart" in song
60 Office of a Muslim leader
61 Fit in perfectly
62 Emergency indicator

DOWN

1 Female felines
2 Take on a freelance job
3 Deletion
4 Narrow openings
5 Bowling targets
6 Washington bill
7 Bus depot

8 Squeaky clean
9 Start of a Ralph Kramden laugh
10 Airborne defenses, for short
11 Smear
12 Alternative to Nikes
13 Frozen expanses
14 Playground apparatus
21 Easy-maintenance hairstyles
24 Urged on with spurs
25 Began
28 Cut (off)
29 Something to get up to
32 "Hey, you!"
34 Annex
36 Wide-ranging, as tastes
37 In the saddle
38 Gulches
40 Having eyelike spots
41 Like Albany vis-à-vis New York City
42 Coached
43 Top film of 1989
45 Bumped illegally
48 Clown's prop

50 Water channel
52 Actor Jannings
54 Have ___ hair day
56 Dijon donkey
58 Te ___ (cigar brand)

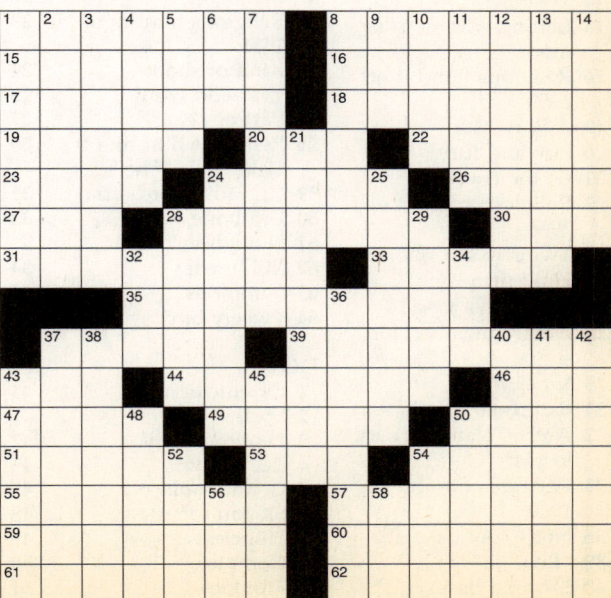

643   by Wayne Robert Williams

ACROSS

1 Disfigure
5 Shopaholic's activity
10 Grouch
14 Nick and Nora's pooch
15 ___ Selassie
16 Sharpen
17 1954 Laurence Harvey movie
20 University sessions
21 Blunt-edged swords
22 Summer on the Somme
23 "Chicks"
25 Mystery stories?
29 Junket
30 Vacation spot
33 Surrendered
34 Like workhorses
35 W.W. II gun
36 1976 Walter Matthau movie
39 Name of three English rivers
40 Campbell of the N.F.L.
41 Two under par
42 Squealer
43 Line of cars
44 Rescuee, in fairy tales
45 Take the bus
46 Humorist
47 Ruhr valley city
50 Media attention
55 1963 Marlon Brando movie
58 Mediocre grades
59 Yearning
60 Dull sound
61 Fabled loser
62 Exhausted
63 Jellied delicacies

DOWN

1 Wilander of Wimbledon
2 Arthur of Wimbledon
3 News bit
4 Epiphany honorees
5 Piglets
6 Missionary's title, maybe
7 Eliminates
8 Actor Wallach
9 Ample shoe width
10 Axes
11 Lecher
12 Helen Keller's teacher ___ Sullivan
13 Petitions
18 Iroquois League tribe
19 Cry of pain
23 Stomach sound
24 Contributes
25 Player
26 Tree with red flowers
27 That is to say
28 Daniels of the silents
29 Jerzy Kosinski's "Being ___"
30 Lone men
31 Hostess Mesta
32 Photographer Adams
34 Low character
35 Ore locale
37 Unusable
38 Word with egg or rug
43 Flash Gordon villain
44 Shunt
45 Practice conservation
46 Part of NOW
47 Make a lasting impression?
48 N.L. stadium
49 Clairvoyant
50 Confine
51 Communion, e.g.
52 Hypochondriac's complaint
53 France, once
54 Boundaries
56 Guitarist Paul
57 One of the Caroline Islands

644   by A.J. Santora

ACROSS

1 Kind of weight
5 Go one over
10 Expert in Exeter
13 Sparks's sister city
14 Together
15 Ending with nod- or mod-
16 Religious film hit of 1959
19 A.P. rival
20 Fire and fury
21 Of the cheeks
22 Religious film hit of 1966
25 Twins in the sky
26 Hold firm
27 Decorative vase
28 Family member, for short
29 Vinegar
31 Bathroom installation
32 Arches National Park locale
33 Religious film hit of 1960
36 Not 47-Across
39 "Rob ___"
40 Set up a base
44 Word with cheese or skinny
45 Set the dog (on)
46 Northern hemisphere?
47 In
49 Religious film hit of 1951
52 Kind of shoot
53 Year-end word
54 Part of i.e.
55 Religious film hit of 1956, with "The"
59 "___ tu" (Verdi aria)
60 Leg bone
61 "Laugh-in" comic
62 Mil. medal
63 Summons
64 Tweety bird

DOWN

1 Of nutrition
2 Spell
3 Lennon's lady
4 ___ Kippur
5 Commonplace
6 Siouan tongue
7 Hopeless
8 Complete
9 Flunkies
10 Aaron Burr, e.g.
11 Where Tirana is
12 Pessimistic
16 Buddha sermon
17 Planet
18 Prosciutto
23 Harold Robbins novel, with "The"
24 Live ___
25 Adorn
27 Work ___ sweat
30 Old-time actress Dressler
31 Pig's retreat
32 Sch. at New London, Conn.
34 Fox sitcom
35 Rice, e.g.: Abbr.
36 Reworked
37 Shrivels
38 Silent
41 One way to cook pasta
42 Wet
43 Puts up
45 Urbane
48 Whence Its. graduate
49 Shrink with fear
50 Armbones
51 Anomalistic
53 Prefix for both
56 "Mamma ___!"
57 Gullet
58 Foul up

645 · by Rich Norris

ACROSS
1 In addition to that
5 Thoroughly scold
10 Czar of 1800
14 Hide
15 Actor Werner
16 "You Are My Destiny" singer
17 Soil: Prefix
18 Practical
19 Tpks.
20 90's TV spinoff series
22 Squeeze (out)
23 Diamond group, e.g.
24 Mashes
27 Periodontist's deg.
28 Square dance call
30 Cause for rescheduling
31 Factor in military planning
33 Depleted
34 Plant called lady's-finger in England
37 Wire measure
38 Certain explorers
39 Tiptop
40 Some closets
43 Salad bar ingredients
45 Vane dir.
46 ___ Paulo
49 Original
50 Plays the guitar, in a way
52 Fed. employee
53 Orbital station
56 Words to a traitor
58 "There is no Frigate like ___": Dickinson
59 Popular snack
60 Stage bit
61 Motorless craft
62 New Mexico natives
63 It's guarded by military planes
64 Hikes
65 Instrument with a crossbar

DOWN
1 Got away
2 Account
3 Warnings
4 Leave via ladder?
5 Cad
6 Italian wine region
7 Cheat, slangily
8 Whopper
9 Prior to
10 Metropolitan rarities
11 Foyer
12 Maui music maker
13 ___ Palmas
21 1957 onward
22 Yale Bowl player
24 Summer cooler
25 Strain
26 Actress Anna
29 Bombeck et al.
30 "Die Sonette an Orpheus" poet
31 Serving no purpose
32 Suffer
34 Org. since 1960
35 Five-in-a-row game
36 Hisser, at times
40 Couple
41 Certain valves
42 Critic of Bill
44 Check for accuracy
46 Indignant
47 Amicable one
48 Dialyze
51 Tangled
53 Typewriter feature
54 Cornmeal cake
55 Collier's rival
56 Emissions watchdog: Abbr.
57 Pod starter
58 Pretense

646 · by Sidney L. Robbins

ACROSS
1 Tempest
6 Ace of spades, e.g.
10 Potatoes' partner
14 Prophet after Daniel
15 Region
16 "___ la Douce"
17 Heroine's cry in silent movies
20 Plow animals
21 "Absolutely!"
22 Grand pursuits
23 Dover's state: Abbr.
24 Actress Hepburn
25 Inebriated
29 Author Wiesel
30 Painter's stand
31 ___ out? (pet's choice)
32 Baden-Baden and Ems
36 Frequent subtitle in silent movies
39 Feeling insulted
40 Prefix with legal or medic
41 Laughing
42 Christmas
43 Flings
44 Punctual
47 Saying
48 House's counterpart
49 Sum total
50 "___ it the truth?"
54 They killed silent movies
57 Words of comprehension
58 Group with roles to play
59 Bakery by-product
60 Soaks, as flax
61 Ogles
62 Wayne ___ (Batman's home)

DOWN
1 Close
2 Color quality
3 Job hazard regulator: Abbr.
4 500 sheets
5 "___ overboard!"
6 R.J. Reynolds brand
7 War deity
8 Gun, as an engine
9 Blender-mixed cocktail
10 Distance runner
11 Wipe out
12 Friendship
13 Makes leather
18 Artificially blonde, say
19 Illicit drug, in slang
23 Wooded valley
24 Shalom in Honolulu
25 Genesis son
26 Honolulu's site
27 Employer
28 Aug.-Oct. divider
29 ___ nous
31 Country on a continental tour
32 Takes to the slopes
33 Stew vegetables
34 Prince Charles's sister
35 Fast planes
37 Conspicuous wealth
38 Brag
42 Abominable Snowman
43 Baby powder
44 Taunt
45 Shore recess
46 Auto brands
47 Small cuts
48 Agitate
49 Church nook
50 Surrounding glow
51 De-wrinkle
52 Verne captain
53 Nicholas, e.g.
55 Like old Paree
56 Highlands hat

647 by Gregory E. Paul

ACROSS
1 Show fright
5 Big rig
9 "The Two Gentlemen of Verona" character
14 Smelter refuse
15 Old Testament book
16 Tom Sawyer's aunt
17 To boot
18 Highway sign
19 Holmes's "___ Venner"
20 Court call
21 Degas painting, with "The"
23 Agatha Christie genre
25 Noshed
26 ___ Major
27 Radio receivers
32 Redcap's domain
34 Look of contempt
35 ___ de la Cité
36 Like a good listener
37 Basketballer
38 Jim Croce's "___ a Name"
39 Mad. ___
40 Consumer protector Ralph

41 Inferior grade of tea
42 Computer adjunct
44 Wimp's word
45 LAX letters
46 Seasoning seed
49 Monet painting
54 Old TV's "You ___ There"
55 Actress Alexander of "The Cosby Show"
56 "The Highwayman" heroine
57 Wineglass feature
58 February forecast
59 Machu Picchu builder
60 Clearasil target
61 Yankee manager Joe
62 It gets into a jamb
63 More ___ meets the eye

DOWN
1 Sacred song
2 Kind of cat
3 Leonardo da Vinci fresco, with "The"
4 Super ending
5 Mali's desert
6 One of the Brontës

7 Gangster's gal
8 Elba, e.g.
9 Ghost
10 Sneeze cause
11 Socialite Maxwell
12 New Haven collegians
13 Uses henna
21 Defeat
22 Spud
24 Jog
27 Harp player
28 Poetic contraction
29 Rembrandt painting, with "The"
30 Skin softener
31 ___ bad example
32 "Shucks!"
33 Roof edge
34 Actress Thompson of "Family"
37 Florida's Saint Lucie, e.g.
38 New Rochelle college
40 Fertilizer
41 Universal Product Code elements
43 More submissive
44 "All hail ___!"
46 Name for a Kid

47 Gladiator's spot
48 Sheba, today
49 Toward sunset
50 "Alice's Restaurant" singer
51 Row
52 Footnote abbr.
53 Late-night host
57 Coll. entrance exam

648 by Richard Hughes

ACROSS
1 ___ O'Rourke of "F Troop"
4 Incarcerates
9 Vexes
14 Tiny
15 Miss Dinsmore of children's books
16 Husband of Bathsheba
17 Give ___ whirl
18 Slanted
19 Home in a dome
20 B-less figure on a coin
23 Volcano, at times
24 Defeat soundly
28 "___ the house"
31 French sailing vessel
32 Play at full volume
35 Picture, in commercial names
37 Powerful D.C. lobby
38 B-less U.S. leader
42 Santa ___
43 Sch. founded in 1845
44 ". . . ___ which will live in infamy"
45 Pass play
48 Bad news for Exxon

50 Shivaree
52 Purse parts
56 B-less film legend
59 Animal track
62 Myanmar, formerly
63 Kind of cake
64 Shade of gray
65 Make dim
66 Actor Erwin
67 Concur
68 Walk furtively
69 Mount, with "on"

DOWN
1 Like many watches
2 Costume
3 Rag
4 MacDonald of old films
5 Where sacrifices are made
6 "The doctor ___"
7 Cheerful tune
8 Biblical brother and namesakes
9 21 shillings
10 Scottish pattern: Var.
11 Like Abner
12 Southeast Asian
13 "___ 'nuff!"

21 Make-___ Foundation
22 1977 George Burns film
25 Tony-winning singer Lotte
26 Stop, in France
27 Stop
29 Rubs out
30 Middays
32 Audacity
33 Meal in a box
34 Arcade name
36 Door on the floor
39 Like some ancient inscriptions
40 Crayola's parent company
41 Dwight's opponent in 1952
46 Repeat performance
47 Channel swimmer Gertrude
49 Cool guy?
51 Former Redskins coach Joe
53 Not stay still in a container
54 "Republic" author
55 Arrange
57 Pause

58 Eins + zwei
59 Workout site
60 Little Margaret
61 Row

649 by Karen Hodge

ACROSS

1 Zeus's wife
5 "Nearer, My God, to Thee" writer ___ Adams
10 See 59-Across
14 Tiptop
15 Critical
16 10 C-notes
17 Person next door in Honolulu?
19 Aretha Franklin's "___ No Way"
20 Tough nut
21 Clothes hamper in Gary?
23 Lace with liquor
26 Word on a French valentine
27 Musical sets
31 Dapper one
33 Tea holder in Pittsburgh?
35 Make new furrows
40 They can take a yoke
41 Wyeth's "___ Pictures"
43 Fictional slave girl of Egypt
44 Fidget
46 Circus employee in Cambridge?

48 Tide alternative
50 Tex and John
51 Tend to the turkey
55 200 milligrams
57 Pen in Tulsa?
59 Weapons limited by 10-Across
64 It means nothing to Nanette
65 Jewelry in Pocatello?
68 Belly-button type
69 Family relation
70 Grammy
71 Certain NCO's
72 Author Richard Henry and others
73 Goon

DOWN

1 A light laughter
2 Kind of proportions
3 Cabinet member Janet
4 Canner?
5 Droop
6 "Oh my," to Ohm
7 Cube creator
8 Made up (for)
9 Sage or thyme, e.g.
10 Secret supply
11 "Take ___!" ("Scram!")

12 Recluse
13 ___-frutti
18 Little map on a big page
22 Dermatologist's case
24 Commotion
25 Land in the ocean
27 Difficult situation
28 Danza/DeVito sitcom
29 Scraped (out)
30 Rip
32 Yemen's peninsula
34 Blight victim
36 Take different paths
37 Go for
38 Baltic feeder
39 Treaties end them
42 1974 N.L. batting champ Ralph
45 Once-over, maybe
47 Hideout for Anne Frank
49 Evangeline's home
51 First name in the Kremlin
52 Fit for ___
53 Chanel product
54 Awards for Neil Simon
56 Veep Barkley
58 Orange exterior

60 Penny
61 Hardly exciting
62 Diner's card
63 Dateless
66 Nipper's co.

67 D.D.E.'s 1952 and 1956 rival

650 by Jim Page

ACROSS

1 Oil-fire fighter
6 Sarcophagus decorations
10 Certain protest
14 Threefold
15 Fly ash
16 Contemporary of Agatha
17 Left Bank's thanks
18 Bleacher feature
20 Noted virologist
21 Sticky matter
22 Soft
24 Ease
25 French author ___ Prévost
26 Cowboy
30 Holds up
31 "If ___ make it there . . ."
32 Growing out
36 Political commentator ___ Thomas
37 More scintillating
39 Wouk topic
40 Head of a ranch
42 Scout's dinner
43 Fund-raiser, often
44 Renoir and others

46 Torah holders
47 Cuts out
50 Chisel, e.g.
52 Curbside sights
56 Containers in Castile
58 Dude
59 Paris's ___ Rivoli
60 Pulitzer-winning biographer Leon
61 Draft designation
62 Beast of Borden
63 "Le Néophyte" artist
64 Splices
65 Fix a course

DOWN

1 People withdraw from these
2 Hunk
3 Champagne feature
4 Sparks
5 Dauphin's mother
6 Author of biblical novels
7 Noted gallery locale
8 Pound, e.g.
9 Basic commodity
10 Swag
11 Precincts

12 Bluish gray
13 Jackson Hole's county
19 Word before "in sickness and in health"
23 Year in St. Symmachus's papacy
25 Bows
27 Booth, e.g.
28 Its capital is Doha
29 Rally
33 Perception
34 Alternative to Top 40
35 Chapters in history
37 Squirm
38 Start of North Carolina's motto
41 Missive
43 Debate restriction
45 Something money is put in
47 Silver, e.g.
48 Home of Bosch's "Garden of Earthly Delights"
49 Holographer's tool
51 German artist of the Renaissance

53 Last Stuart ruler
54 Call for
55 Relatives of Mmes.
57 Tournament V.I.P.

651   by Norma Steinberg

ACROSS
1 Outlet center?
5 Wheat ___ (crackers)
10 Stick around
14 The last Mrs. Chaplin
15 Storyteller of old Greece
16 Opening for a sweat bead
17 Ballerina's skirt
18 Strainer
19 Novelist Murdoch
20 Colonist's command
23 "Piggies"
24 Have a hunch
25 Like crazy
28 Waikiki dances
31 Dungeons & Dragons beast
32 Row, e.g.
34 School grp.
37 Judy Garland's command
40 Embroider
41 Bowling lanes
42 The hunted
43 Feeds the flame
44 ___ Haute, Ind.
45 Thursday's eponym
47 In a mo

49 February command
55 Invitation word
56 Heretofore mentioned
57 House nickname
59 ___ even keel
60 Basic belief
61 Ballooned
62 Took off
63 Shorthand, for short
64 Fair to middlin'

DOWN
1 Kitty
2 Musical forte?
3 Golden Rule word
4 Knight's glove
5 Discrimination
6 Will-reading attendees
7 "Um-hmm"
8 Award-winning science show
9 Expedited
10 Places for titles
11 "The Velvet Fog"
12 "The Little Mermaid"
13 Sandburg's "The People, ___"

21 1982 Pryor film, with "The"
22 Best ___
25 May honorees
26 "Let Us Now Praise Famous Men" author
27 Columnist Pearson
28 Sharpens
29 ___ daisy
30 O.K.'s
32 Athlete from Tres Coracoes, Brazil
33 Brooklet
34 Good engine sound
35 Level
36 "___ sow . . ."
38 TV host Povich
39 Job vacancies
43 Incite
44 Candidate for day care
45 Butcher's cut
46 Rambo, e.g.
47 Early evening
48 ___ a customer
50 Winery fixtures
51 Drive the get-away car, maybe
52 Sole

53 Claudius's adopted son
54 Sheepcote matriarchs
55 Intimidate
58 Brace

652   by Martin Schneider

ACROSS
1 Expire, as a membership
6 Show hosts, for short
9 Fill
13 Secretary of State Root
14 Dadaist Hans
15 Like Old King Cole
16 Baseball bigwig Bud
17 Assurance
19 Not brand-name
21 Spring blooms
22 Wildebeest
23 Entomological stage
25 Less original
28 Monks and nuns
32 Apartment sign
33 Lebanese symbol
34 Soup container
35 Immense, poetically
36 Mine find
37 Lift the spirits of
39 From ___ Z
40 Most Egyptians
42 Meet official
43 Louvre highlight
45 Insult
46 1983 Streisand role
47 Scottish denial

48 Value
51 Lethargy
55 Prohibition establishment
57 Chain of hills
59 Country music's Tucker
60 Drunk's problem, with "the"
61 Near Eastern chieftain
62 Bettor's starter
63 Opposite of WNW
64 Pores over

DOWN
1 Broadway's "___ Miz"
2 Words after shake or break
3 Mass
4 Roof worker
5 Noted name in puzzling
6 Biblical trio
7 Fancy term for 5-Down and 15-Down
8 Vacation destination
9 Grad-to-be
10 Liberal ___

11 Corner
12 Potato features
15 Noted name in puzzling
18 Lasso
20 Capek play
24 Styles
25 It may come in a head
26 Kemo Sabe's companion
27 Crazy as ___
29 "___, I saw . . ."
30 Eroded
31 Dummy Mortimer
33 Slide
38 Cable choice
41 Washer cycle
44 "Roger," at sea
45 ___ for the books
48 Film dog
49 Breadth
50 Faxed
52 Wall Street abbr.
53 Brainstorm
54 Like some cheeses
56 Suffix added to fruit names
58 Speech stumbles

653   by Cathy Millhauser

ACROSS
1 Use a letter opener
5 Dadaist poet Tristan
10 Bus. bigwigs
14 Bear of "very little brain"
15 Grant portrayer
16 Emerald City princess
17 Cogwheel comparison?
20 Skewers
21 Nuke
22 Tool for Bo-Peep
23 Focuses
25 Emmy winner Arthur
26 Totaled car, perhaps?
33 Made a touchdown
34 Got ruined in the wash
35 Manche capital
36 Sci-fi regulars
37 Quieted with Quaalude
40 "Do ___ say!"
41 Brews
43 Palm (off)
44 Financial success
46 Inflamed toe cause?
49 Big Ben?
50 Mayberry boy
51 Math discovery
54 Nameless one
56 Nolan Ryan was one
60 Mega-marathon?
63 Arabic name starter
64 Christmas Eve flier
65 Eye at the beach
66 Botch
67 Into pieces
68 Source of abundance

DOWN
1 Spring spots
2 Dropped, maybe
3 Isle near Mull
4 Bob Dylan back-up group
5 Make lace
6 Famed cop slapper
7 Anatomical loop
8 Glean
9 Dadaist painter Hans
10 Aiken and Hilton
11 Basso Pinza
12 "Typee" sequel
13 Dropped, maybe
18 Stage remarks
19 Bakery worker
24 Words before "TV" or "each other"
25 Crams
26 Hat-tipping cartoonist
27 Start
28 Curmudgeons
29 Eliot's "Jennyanydots," e.g.
30 Author Calvino
31 The Folger Lady, Mrs. ___
32 Jet, at Orly?
33 Levi's mother
38 Bashes
39 Defense mechanism
42 Swimming classes?
45 Hides
47 Dennis the Menace's dog
48 Word with baby or schuss
51 Surrey carriage
52 "Mike and Ike" creator Goldberg
53 Heavy load
54 It's most useful when it's cracked
55 Prefix re honeycombs
57 Buster Brown's bulldog
58 Kaiser, e.g.
59 Like Nash's lama
61 Public works inits.
62 S. & L. accrual

654   by Manny Nosowsky

ACROSS
1 "Alas"
6 "Chariots of the Gods" author Erich Von ___
13 John Denver's "___ Song"
15 Iridescent
16 Jordan River's outlet
18 Extirpates
19 Yodeler's perch
20 Apt to fall apart
22 Astuteness
23 Start of a classic question
25 Twinkle-toed
26 Size up
27 Abram's wife
29 Ship's heading
30 Husky-voiced singer from Vienna
31 Post-kickoff game status
34 Rudolph Valentino, e.g.
36 Kind of suit
38 Israel's Arens
41 "My mamma done ___ me"
42 Welles of the Mercury Theater
44 Play money?
45 Fire fighter
47 God of destruction
48 Reagan program: Abbr.
49 1966 musical featuring 30-Across
51 Calif. neighbor
52 Food preservative
54 Get cozy
56 Mark a marker?
57 House Speaker, 1977–86
58 Some car deals
59 Singer James and others

DOWN
1 Former Al-Qubbah Palace residents
2 15 slices, maybe
3 Visored hat style
4 Go to bat for
5 Family tree abbr.
6 Traitorous ones
7 Beatles record label
8 ___ a one
9 1969 Nobel Peace Prize winner: Abbr.
10 Of a Plains people
11 Something or someone
12 Lipton competitor
14 Word repeated in a Doris Day song
17 Site of one of Hercules's labors
21 F. Scott Fitzgerald's birthplace
24 Otologist's case
26 Impressionist collection
28 Carpet fiber
30 Resulted in
32 Argentine aunt
33 Mannerism
35 Blowing one's cool
37 "Billy Budd," e.g.
38 Chess or bridge ranking
39 Sir Frederick Ashton ballet
40 Smarts
43 Adam and Eve lacked them
45 Give up
46 Where exes are made
49 Scuttle load
50 Adjust
53 Brother
55 Pick up

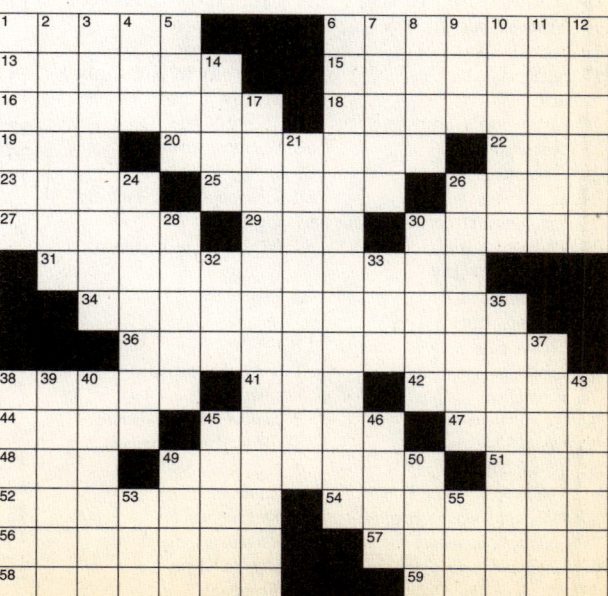

655 by Sidney L. Robbins

ACROSS
1 Winter precipitation
6 Pay, with "up"
10 Ivan the Terrible, e.g.
14 Proportion
15 "___ Smile" (1976 Hall & Oates hit)
16 Regulation
17 Bad loser's reaction
19 More than eager
20 Prolonged attack
21 Pacific Rim locale
23 "Eureka!"
24 ___ Vegas
26 A few
28 Scrutinizes
33 Watermelon's coat
34 "Tamerlane" playwright Nicholas
35 Frequent reduction targets
37 Delay
40 Outlawed explosion
42 Kind of service
43 Do-___ (all-out)
44 Take care of
45 Golf pegs
47 Author Ferber
48 Guided excursion
50 Innocent
52 Guy with a racket
55 Unknown John
56 Pleasant tune
57 Litigates
59 Train tracks
63 Ballet movement
65 Montana's state flower
68 Having little fat
69 Genesis son
70 ___ Rae (Sally Field role)
71 Flubs
72 Kind of tide
73 High-hat's look

DOWN
1 12th graders: Abbr.
2 Vientiane's land
3 Sewing case
4 It's west of England
5 Transverse pin
6 "___ matter of fact . . ."
7 California valley
8 Lock
9 Less difficult
10 ___-la-la
11 Gold digger's "mine"
12 Shalom in Hawaii
13 Like royalty
18 It's within grasp
22 Dispatch boat
25 Long-legged bird
27 Main dish
28 Nest eggs: Abbr.
29 Memo
30 Virginia women's college
31 Spaghetti sauces
32 Snooped
36 Race
38 Queue
39 Starring role
41 Race track tipsters
46 Gave an oath
49 Corned beef sandwich
51 Pines
52 Joplin's "___ Leaf Rag"
53 Ship from Kuwait
54 Marie Antoinette, e.g.
58 Greek portico
60 Remove the wrinkles from
61 Tradition
62 Not too many
64 Printers' measures
66 Recipe amt.
67 Old salt

656 by Matt Gaffney

ACROSS
1 Kind of acid
6 ___ de Triomphe
9 Doesn't read carefully
14 Another kind of acid
15 Mousse alternative
16 Apportion
17 Santa Clara Co. address
19 Lose one's amateur status
20 Affront
21 ___ Speedwagon
23 Finsteraarhorn is one
24 Property restriction
25 Bowling alley buttons
28 Bobby, here
29 Draft org.
30 Obsess
31 Filmflam
32 Carnation spot
33 Less 32-Down
34 Baseball slugger, 1988 A.L. M.V.P.
37 Political pamphlet
39 Skylark maker
40 City near Sparks
41 Tutu event
43 Summit
46 Summer drink
47 "Rabbit, Run" and "Rabbit Redux," e.g.
48 "___ Lisa"
49 Colorado Indian
50 Be in the red
51 Bullet type
53 "A Year in Provence" author Peter
55 "Forget it!"
58 Shower time
59 In high spirits
60 Cicero's was Tullius
61 Oozes
62 Make a palindromic living?
63 Upright

DOWN
1 Two Byzantine emperors
2 Some Mideasterners
3 Gets the soap out
4 ___ Joe, of "Tom Sawyer"
5 Refrigerate
6 Census info
7 Room type
8 Bordeaux, e.g.
9 Nigeria's former capital
10 Jeff Lynne rock band
11 "The Godfather" actor
12 "A Chorus Line" song "What I Did ___"
13 Cork in a bottle
18 Zebra feature
22 Summer on the Seine
26 Bigwig
27 Having a market, as goods
30 Speedy
31 Part of a royal flush
32 Batty
33 Splinter group
34 Brontë heroine
35 Void's partner
36 Bedtime for Alonzo
37 Psychological injuries
38 Bureaucracy
41 Theatrical finale
42 Settle a score
43 Still ahead
44 "Hold on"
45 Company with a subsidiary
47 Christmas songs
48 Word before league or domo
52 Sandberg of baseball
54 Back talk
56 Maryland's state tree
57 Three-way circuit

ACROSS

1 Ruined, slangily
5 Transparent
10 "O, ___ fortune's fool!": Romeo
13 Excellent
14 Siva follower
15 Year in the reign of Philip I
16 Impending disaster
19 Hydra's slayer
20 Armstrong et al.
21 Building extension
22 Imago, for one
24 Olds model
30 Object of a misanthrope's malice
31 Word with parking or breathing
32 Freudian stage
33 Current units, for short
35 Colorado Indian
36 Runs off at the mouth
37 Rockefeller Center muralist
38 Economic news
40 Titleist's support
41 Dealing in espionage
45 Swings for Tarzan
46 Cycle of verse prefix
47 Iowa community
49 Fixing the driveway
54 Fred Flintstone's cat, for one
57 Out of control
58 Rafsanjani, e.g.
59 Iditarod destination
60 Mariner's dir.
61 "Attention must be paid" to him
62 Corsair's quaff

DOWN

1 Obi
2 Julia Ward ___
3 ___ about (approximately)
4 Three lines of verse
5 Mojave plants
6 Chaim, to Potok
7 Goals
8 Critic ___ Louise Huxtable
9 The punch in planter's punch
10 Untaught
11 Skating maneuver
12 Strindberg's "___ Julie"
15 Secretary of Defense, 1957–59
17 Tedious
18 "Get ___" (1967 Esquires hit)
22 Climb
23 Fitting
24 Advertising figure Joe ___
25 Like certain math propositions
26 Rejects
27 Gratified
28 Creator
29 Differently
30 Virile: Abbr.
34 Like chapel glass
38 Menlo Park monogram
39 Eldest son of a French king
42 Wood knot
43 Biting insect
44 Generous
47 ". . . ___ forgive our debtors"
48 Conduit
49 Meander
50 View from Catania
51 Inventor Sikorsky
52 Verne captain
53 Diver Louganis
55 Before, briefly
56 Pizarro's plunder

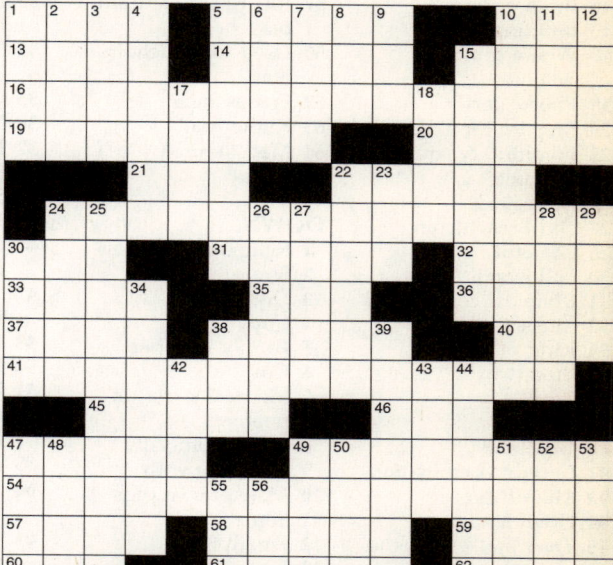

ACROSS

1 City west of Montgomery
6 Machine-repair pros
11 Any ship
14 One way to read
15 Provide with gear
16 Frisbee, e.g.
17 1960's movie or song
20 Dark side
21 Word of lament
22 Wassailers' song
23 Like Gen. Schwarzkopf
24 Russian river
25 Bring up to code, electrically
26 Hang-ups
28 Greenspan's domain, with "the"
29 ___ offensive
30 "Brand New Key" singer, 1971
34 Stick in the rec room
35 Excessive idolatry
37 Darlin'
38 Vegetarian's bane
39 Scooby-___
40 Tooth puller's deg.
41 Fit for a king
45 Talk-show fodder
47 Three-card monte, e.g.
50 Was a consumer
51 First-stringers
52 Alda colleague
53 Olympic skating gold medalist Gustafson
54 Office napper of note
57 Self-importance
58 Bronze finish
59 It comes with a pad
60 Kitty comment
61 Alex Trebek, e.g.
62 Amphetamine

DOWN

1 Mystery writer Dorothy
2 Cricket squad
3 Nabokov creation
4 Think
5 Shakespearean fuss
6 U.S.-Croatian inventor
7 Jury member
8 1907-08 World Series champs
9 "That guy?"
10 Out of touch with reality
11 Classic 1973 Bob Marley song
12 One who's toasted or roasted
13 Small hole
18 Card game for two
19 Eddie Murphy movie
24 Computer owner
25 "Don't You Know" singer
27 J. Edgar Hoover underlings
28 Grisham thriller, with "The"
31 Some nobility
32 Knocks the socks off
33 Land of ___
34 Recognize
35 Poky
36 Detriment
37 Terrorist's insurance
39 Crown
40 Knock down a peg
42 Threw in the towel
43 1967 Eisenhower book
44 Bank, often
46 Detroit grp.
47 Buffalo skater
48 Oil-field oil
49 Branch
52 Bank letters
53 Point on a bus map
55 Some resistance
56 Dallas sch.

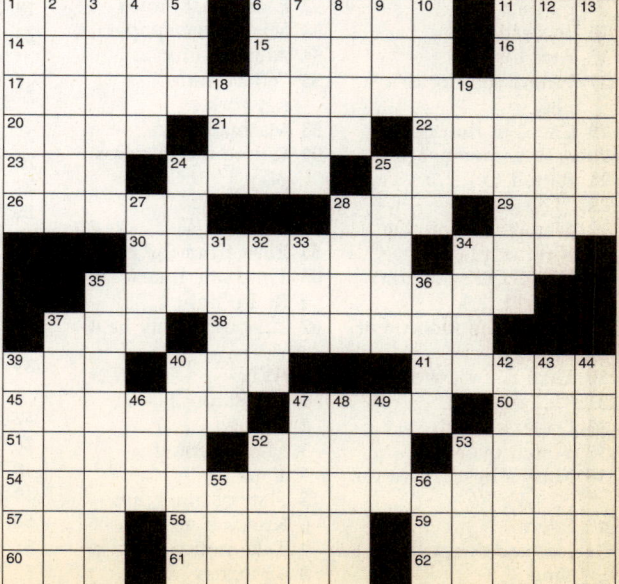

659 by Rich Norris

ACROSS
1 Pre-Cretaceous, in geologic history
9 Roughen
15 By emergency
16 Brain cover
17 Building lot
18 Where to find a donjon
19 Police alert
20 Prepare for 21-Down
22 Involuntary sound
23 Triangle
26 Disregards
27 Old French coin
28 Guileful
30 Follower
31 Charcoal component
32 Links
34 Kind of bean
35 Broadway's "___ of Love"
38 Drift
40 Goldbrick
41 Certain combination
43 Mil. officers
44 Govt. lender
45 They make forays for morays
49 Literary monogram
50 Grant
52 Storage area
53 Jr.'s junior
54 Disallowed
56 Latin I word
57 Riverfront Stadium player
59 Used too much, in a way
62 Possessions
63 Know-it-all
64 Mall fixtures
65 Soppy

DOWN
1 Religious conflicts
2 Shut
3 Digress
4 Copy
5 Family member
6 Cut
7 Metrical stress, in poetry
8 Arrive, officially
9 Go along with
10 Male guinea pigs
11 Some utils.
12 Finally
13 Fine
14 Heir raiser?
21 Lover's request
24 Idahos
25 Get ___ out of
29 As previously
31 Corn flour
33 Meteorological indicator
34 Showed impatience, as a horse
35 Credits
36 Most striking
37 Enter en masse
39 Saison d'___
42 Strait
44 Land depressions
46 Greek provincial governor
47 "Night of the Living Dead" director
48 Put away
50 Fall off
51 Troublemaker
55 60's group Dino, ___ & Billy
58 Needlefish
60 Handle the orders (for)
61 Court figures, for short

660 by Gregory E. Paul

ACROSS
1 ___ metabolism
6 The Beatles' "___ a Woman"
10 Western lily
14 Kukla and Fran's partner
15 Soccer legend
16 Auditorium
17 Where the Rockies play
19 Canal to Buffalo
20 A.B.A. member
21 Ratted (on)
22 "The Glass Menagerie" mother
24 Kind of phone
25 Old G.O.P. politico Harold
26 Poster announcement
29 Candy
30 Take ___ view of
31 "___ homo!"
33 Dieter's lunch
37 Watch over
38 Mary's best friend on 70's TV
40 Spent
41 Haggadah-reading time
43 T.V.A. product: Abbr.
44 Scintilla
45 Defense acronym
47 Discernment
49 Skit
52 Economist Smith
53 Miami newspaper
54 A-apple link
55 "60 Minutes" network
58 Maintain
59 Where the Red Sox play
62 Thrill
63 Scottish isle
64 Blast from the past
65 Time-line times
66 Rialto light
67 ___ out (barely beat)

DOWN
1 ___ Raton, Fla.
2 Oodles
3 Mail opening
4 Tune
5 Flatt of bluegrass
6 Knock over
7 Take notice
8 45 inches
9 Calm
10 Where the Mets play
11 Pockets
12 Dance movement
13 Upstate New York city
18 Dossier
23 Fannie ___ (securities)
24 Where the Orioles play
25 Alfred Nobel, e.g.
26 Fordham team
27 Singer Brickell
28 "Inherit the ___"
29 Chew out
32 Defraud
34 Weaving machine
35 Chip in a chip
36 College official
39 Maine's ___ National Park
42 Attendance list
46 Minnow
48 Echo site
49 Stage
50 Prying tool
51 Coliseum
52 City on the Nile
54 Part of A.D.
55 Rogues
56 Soft cheese
57 TV Guide chart, for short
60 Help wanted ad abbr.
61 West Bank org.

661 by Elizabeth C. Gorski

ACROSS

1 Applaud
5 Sweetheart
10 Nuclear weapon, for short
14 As well
15 Derbies
16 Fly high
17 Go pfft!
18 Kilns
19 Wraps up
20 Notes in cyberspace
23 Sidewalk ___
24 Sailor's assent
25 Sailor
28 Singer James et al.
32 Roomy
34 Mediator: Abbr.
37 "Nixon" character
40 Where to get a hoagy
42 Cleaver's "Soul ___"
43 Scorer on serve
44 Part of Chopin's Opus 10
47 Doubles team
48 Imps
49 Fly-fishing, for one
51 "For shame!"
52 "Well, ___-di-dah . . ."
55 In the lead
59 Dangerous strain
64 "The Second of May" artist
66 Start of a Dickens title
67 "Cheers" patron
68 Attend Choate, e.g.
69 No-Tell, for one
70 Paradise
71 Just okay
72 Beginning
73 Hardy heroine

DOWN

1 Sights along the Champs Élysées
2 Large, furry pet
3 Chinese, e.g.
4 Like Miss Manners
5 Word on a gift tag
6 Wash
7 They're good with tricks
8 The brainy bunch
9 E.B. White piece
10 "Peekaboo, ___ . . ."
11 Build
12 Rotten
13 ___ Malaprop
21 Running behind
22 Neuter
26 "Nixon" character
27 Small rocket engine
29 Thunder god
30 Tops
31 Actress Loretta and others
33 "There you are!"
34 Masterful
35 Twin brother of legend
36 Shiners
38 "We'll tak ___ o' kindness yet": Burns
39 Make over
41 Alphabet trio
45 Scandinavian port
46 Q.E.D. midsection
50 1995 Sandra Bullock film
53 1836 battle site, with "the"
54 Try to pick up
56 Wear away
57 Buenos ___
58 Denounces
60 Mafia chief
61 Fruity
62 Toward shelter
63 Scot or Breton, e.g.
64 Family docs
65 Conquistador's cache

662 by Gregory E. Paul

ACROSS

1 ___ au rhum (cake with a punch)
5 Mrs. Copperfield
9 Action-film highlight
14 Friend in battle
15 Dutch export
16 Actress Berry
17 Claim on property
18 Variable star
19 To no ___ (useless)
20 Halibut's home
21 "Sultans of Swing" Top 40 group
23 Turkey capital
25 Billboard
26 Semi
29 Snoopy, for one
33 Assail, as the ramparts
35 Taxi's ticker
37 Like steak tartare
38 It may be bloodless
39 Restrict
40 Refer to
41 Neighbor of Hung.
42 Three-dimensional figure
43 Mayberry gas station attendant
44 Compact
46 Intense fear
48 Waikiki Beach bash
50 Former Gretzky team
53 Large marsh near Virginia Beach
58 Prepare to fire
59 Blood of the gods
60 Israeli dance
61 Lhasa ___
62 Perch
63 Moran of "Happy Days"
64 Calendar unit
65 Speed units at sea
66 Riverfront Stadium players
67 Fish-eating eagle

DOWN

1 Model airplane wood
2 Mork, e.g.
3 Charles Dickens novel
4 Author Rand
5 Disbelief
6 Scent
7 Five-star review
8 Accumulate
9 Steed
10 Chief port of the West Indies
11 Jai ___
12 Buttonhole, essentially
13 Lampreys
21 Tap rhythmically
22 Home of the 61-Across
24 Seniors' PAC
27 Olympic runner Zatopek
28 Send in payment
30 Scythe carrier
31 Past due
32 Water pitcher
33 Sing like Ella
34 Sightseeing trip
36 Bay of Fundy feature
39 True
40 Groovy, updated
42 British royal family
43 Clutch
45 Nearly
47 Caesar's subjects
49 Wedding attendant
51 Gotten up
52 Cure, in a way
53 Actor Bogarde
54 Computer screen image
55 "Beat it!"
56 Had on
57 Parched
61 Reverence

663   by Frank Longo

ACROSS
1 Vinegar, essentially
11 Physics units
15 Noted 15th-century reformer
16 Source of interest
17 Before birth
18 Prefix with bond
19 Unaccented
20 Emulate a rodent
21 Sound stage
22 Gnatlike insect
23 Put on sale
26 In a stew
29 Bore
30 Masters
32 ___ soda
33 Fireballs
34 Reddish-brown
36 It often features articles about dating
38 Mound
39 Noted American ornithologist
40 Schumann's "___ From Childhood"
42 Jazz's ___ Shapiro
43 Instance, to Ingres
44 Somali-born supermodel
45 Double-dealing
52 Foreign princess
53 Traits that rate 10's
54 Usher tack-on
55 Timely
56 Whitetails
57 Supercharger

DOWN
1 Old World snakes
2 Help for airport baggage
3 "Did I ___?"
4 Exercises
5 Momentarily, slangily
6 Singer now known as Yusef Islam
7 Sea near Novokazalinsk
8 First black to host a TV series
9 Misfortunes
10 Dog ___
11 Matthew Arnold's "Thyrsis" and others
12 Like some tournaments
13 Pack rat's paradise, perhaps
14 Overwhelmed with flattery
22 Conductance units
23 Address abbrs.
24 Puzzler's pen, possibly
25 Amateur
26 Take pride in (oneself)
27 Chief Big Kansas, for one
28 Blushes
31 Give ___ (curse)
33 Bare
35 Absolutely
37 Having more lines, as a leaf
38 Málaga moolah
39 Bigeminal
41 Like a boxer
45 Kind of brake
46 Prefix with logical
47 Suture
48 Lid fastener
49 Family members
50 End: Prefix
51 W.W. I battle river

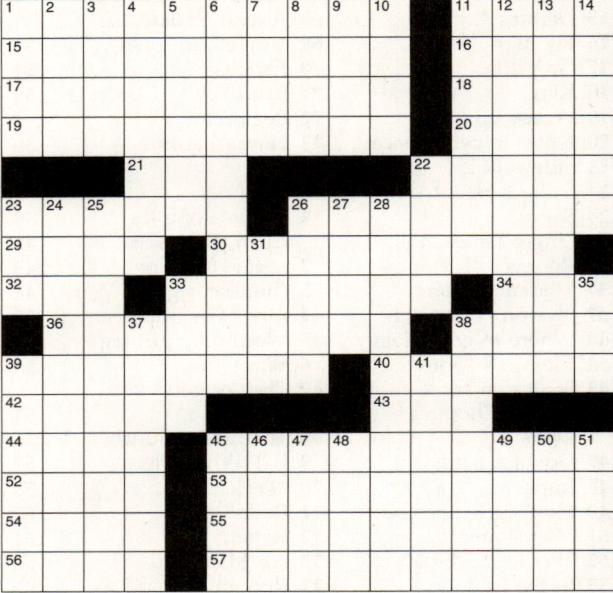

664   by David A. Rosen

ACROSS
1 Rumble
6 Not fancy?
10 Difficult obligation
14 "___ of do or die"
15 Bing Crosby best seller
16 Guthrie the younger
17 Hearty entree
20 Kibbutzniks' dance
21 Reverse
22 Must
23 Place to crash
25 Kipling novel
26 Tasty side dish
35 Mortgage matter
36 Words before "in the arm" or "in the dark"
37 Detective's cry
38 Them in "Them!"
39 Common key signature
40 Composer ___ Carlo Menotti
41 Cpl., for one
42 Feed a fete
43 Stood for
44 Yummy dessert
47 Cherbourg chum
48 Latin I?
49 Lamb Chop's "spokesperson"
52 Oceania republic
55 Windmill segment
59 Eventual bonus?
62 Cream-filled sandwich
63 Debouchment
64 Internet patrons
65 Blubber
66 Yeltsin veto
67 Koch's predecessor

DOWN
1 Calculator work
2 Radar blip
3 Thieves' hideout
4 They're loose
5 "Yikes!"
6 "The Afternoon of a ___"
7 In the thick of
8 First name in perfumery
9 Venture
10 Japanese mat
11 Olympic hawk
12 Bed-frame crosspiece
13 "Mikado" executioner
18 Sport whose name means "soft way"
19 Polo, e.g.
24 Circulars
25 Carpenter's woe
26 French bread?
27 High-priced spread?
28 "... and eat ___"
29 Subj. of a Clinton victory, 11/17/93
30 Key
31 Midway alternative
32 River nymph
33 The Gold Coast, today
34 "À votre ___!"
39 Java neighbor
40 Columbus, by birth
42 "Nancy" or "Cathy"
43 Puss
45 Server on skates
46 Dos + cuatro
49 Take third
50 Take on
51 "___ on Film" (1983 book set)
52 Conniving
53 Coach Nastase
54 Rock's Joan
56 Sphere
57 "Cheers" habitué
58 Alternatively
60 Lady lobster
61 Ungainly craft

665 by Randolph Ross

ACROSS
1 Funny pages favorite
11 Composer Satie
15 Exciting adventure
16 "I came," to Caesar
17 Recruiter's objective
18 Professional suffixes
19 Three after B
20 Cousin of "Eureka!"
21 Shows how
23 Stout
24 Hawaii's state bird
26 Screen's partner
27 Post
29 Show anger, in a way
32 According to
33 They make a bloom blossom
35 Satisfied subscribers
37 Profligate
40 Tubular pasta
43 Victoria's Secret selections
47 Blown-up photo: Abbr.
48 Discovery of 1781
51 Stevedore's, e.g.
52 Philatelist's item
54 Little pest
56 One over due
57 Shade maker
60 Twosome
61 Season in St.-Lô
62 Turner and Pappas
63 Way back
66 Furniture wood
67 Crudity
68 Guinness Book suffixes
69 Creator of 1-Across

DOWN
1 Start of a Gardner title
2 C.B.ers' names
3 Brennan and Ford
4 Calendar abbr.
5 Match play?
6 Chung's former partner
7 Singer Nina
8 Real ending in London
9 1978 Yankee hero
10 Renowned costume designer
11 Bounce
12 Amend
13 Whole amount
14 "Pow!" places
22 Quakers
25 Loop for a lobe
28 Oscar ___ Renta
30 Like Gen. Schwarzkopf
31 Prefix with cycle or sex
34 Gym exercises
36 TV host, 1955–82
38 N.Y.C. div.
39 Bambi's aunt
40 Break
41 Pipe openings
42 Show anger, in a way
44 Hospital personnel
45 Feature of many court buildings
46 Increase the angle of elevation
49 Without cause
50 Long, bony fish
53 Mardi Gras sights
55 Friendly Islands
58 First ed.
59 Actress Olin
64 Dutch painter Gerard ___ Borch
65 Thrash

666 by James L. Beatty

ACROSS
1 Outbuildings
6 Hobgoblin
10 "___ sesame"
14 Mischievous sprite
15 Selves
16 Nuclear reactor
17 Ahead of the times
19 Prefix with marketing
20 Sleep stage
21 Accurate
22 Made an incursion
24 Medicine that's not all it's promised to be
26 Bewails
27 Fictitious
30 Trigonometric function
32 Sashes
33 Oil city of Iran
34 Memorable period
37 Melts
40 It may be penciled in
42 Ott or Gibson
43 Appraised
45 Inland sea east of the Caspian
46 Rephrased
48 Lord Peter Wimsey's creator
50 Caper
52 Uproar
54 Evades
56 ___ of arms
57 Small amount
60 Woodwind instrument
61 Restaurant special
64 Add-on
65 Swearword
66 Valletta is its capital
67 Not the pictures
68 Nautical chains
69 Stocking material

DOWN
1 Box
2 Busy place
3 Word with eye or final
4 Gunga ___
5 Resolve
6 ___ Arts
7 Monstrously cruel
8 The Almighty
9 River to the North Sea
10 Right to purchase
11 Secondary residence
12 Actress Burstyn
13 Desiderata
18 Electric power network
23 Astound
24 Noted lioness
25 Take new vows
27 Froth
28 French ecclesiastic
29 Love letter
31 Low island
33 Fall bloomer
35 Bellow
36 Piercing tools
38 Instant
39 ___ one's words
41 Reddish-brown horses
44 Give a little learning
47 Reader's ___
48 Miner's nail
49 Cooling-off time
50 Take as one's own
51 Aristocratic
53 Closet pests
55 Espy
57 Kewpie, e.g.
58 Prefix with graph or crat
59 Breakfast fiber source
62 Ballad
63 Blue bird

667 by Wayne Robert Williams

ACROSS
1 Impudent youngster
6 Salesmen, briefly
10 Impudent talk
14 Cheapskate
15 Beasts of burden
16 Baseball's ___ brothers
17 1994 film role for Jim Carrey
19 Movers' trucks
20 More like winter sidewalks
21 Singer Estefan
23 Inge play
26 Closet spook
28 Nabokov novel
29 Clique
31 Norse deity
32 Film maker Wertmuller
34 Window surrounding
36 Fiery gems
41 Photographer's instruction
44 Rob
45 Neophyte
46 Paradise
47 Wedding vow
49 Soak (up)
51 Actor Tognazzi
52 By airmail from France
57 Dealer in cloth
59 "___ Twist"
60 England's Scilly ___
62 Call to the phone
63 Happy camper?
68 Kuwaiti honcho
69 Nile queen, for short
70 Neutral shade
71 Does lawnwork
72 Bakery bite
73 Of the eyes

DOWN
1 New Deal grp.
2 Sot's interjection
3 Just manage, with "out"
4 Writer Ira of "Sliver"
5 Concise summary
6 Old-fashioned learning method
7 Long-distance commuter's home
8 For each
9 Full of obstacles
10 "Stompin' at the ___"
11 Wake-up noise
12 Actress Braga
13 "Black-eyed" girl
18 Most hospitable
22 "Vive ___!" (old Parisian cry)
23 Becomes tiresome
24 Ninny
25 Tippy transportation
27 Those not mentioned
30 Arm art
33 Letters before an alias
35 Not outgoing
37 Leading prefix
38 Make sense
39 Feudal lord
40 Man of the casa
42 ___ and kicking
43 Bribe money
48 Straightforward
50 Magician's word
52 Vatican leaders
53 Texas shrine
54 Strict
55 Declares
56 Neighbor of Chad
58 Songwriters' grp.
61 Tab's target
64 Pie ___ mode
65 No longer chic
66 Wire service
67 Old-time gumshoe

668 by Lois Sidway

ACROSS
1 They rank above Pfc.'s
5 Address for a lady
9 Lamb servings
14 "Whoops"
15 "___ You" (Platters hit)
16 Protection
17 Metric prefix
18 Tetley products
19 Stag-party attendees
20 Many a Fifth Avenue habitué
23 Yevtushenko's "Babi ___"
24 ___ of March
25 Young faddist
30 Toy gun ammo
33 Overhead lighting?
34 Salt Lake City player
35 Lacking, with "of"
37 Hecklers' missiles
38 "Get lost!"
41 Drama award
42 Tsetses
44 Rhoda's mom, in 70's TV
45 Part of a paper roll
46 Countdown start
47 Nightclub gadabout
51 Role for Leontyne
52 Sloppy ___
53 Stovetop appliance
59 Life-jacket innards
60 Noodle
61 Commercial endorsement
63 Harsh
64 "Mystery" host Diana
65 Adm. Zumwalt
66 Snappish
67 Give ___ up (assist)
68 Engrossed

DOWN
1 Cow's chew
2 "That was close!"
3 Mathematical sets of points
4 Rudolph has one
5 Tourist transport
6 Once more
7 Voiced sigh
8 Gershwin-Weill ballad
9 Park patrons
10 Piles
11 Girl-watch
12 Fishing site
13 Draft org.
21 24 hours
22 Poem of praise
25 It's a steal
26 Two under par
27 Illinois city
28 How some stocks are sold: Abbr.
29 Jeopardy
30 Appear suddenly
31 Payola
32 Have the helm
36 It makes salsa picante
39 "Fables in Slang" author
40 Bridge alternative
43 Remain loyal to
48 Hubbub
49 Ms. Streisand
50 "Alley ___"
51 To the left, to Bligh
53 Stride
54 Unlocks, to Milton
55 Diamond of fame
56 Summon
57 Fitzgerald of scat
58 Roast cut
59 "Krazy ___"
62 Understood

669 by Norma Steinberg

ACROSS

1 Bridge option
5 Reunion group
9 Sound before "Gesundheit!"
14 Computer text function
15 One of two teams
16 The good dishes
17 Badgered
18 Sherbets' cousins
19 Apple drink
20 Shipboard regulations?
23 Steppenwolf's creator
24 Flashiest
28 Actress Stapleton
32 Pooh's middle name?
33 Words of self-control?
37 California-Nevada lake
39 Serpentine greeting
40 Parking
43 "Show Boat" composer
44 Early Peruvians
46 "Charlotte's Web" and "Animal Farm"?
48 D.C. vitamin monitors
49 Bulletin
52 Warm wrap
54 Colorado resort
59 Marriage?
63 Sentry
66 Hitchcock nail-biter
67 German valley
68 Cry of surrender
69 Epitome of thinness
70 Hgt.
71 Go by car
72 1978 Village People hit
73 Cautious

DOWN

1 Bird cage swing
2 Cherish
3 Walls
4 Fricassees
5 With it, sartorially
6 In ___ parentis
7 Revival meeting shout
8 Snuggle
9 Version
10 The French Chef
11 Put out of sight
12 Word before person and vote
13 Sculler's need
21 Convoy component
22 Caviar
25 Singer Waters
26 Coast
27 Adolescents
29 Dolt
30 Diamond arbiter
31 Harvests
33 Hint of fragrance
34 Indian believer
35 Levant of "Information Please"
36 Simile's center
38 Police blotter abbr.
41 Bush's old command
42 Scrambled item
45 Do a slow burn
47 Oolong and green
50 Nosh
51 Like clear night skies
53 Sophia's spouse
55 Scatter
56 Singer Abdul
57 Clear sky
58 Chutzpah-driven
60 Meander
61 DeMille genre
62 Crème ___ crème
63 Moscow department store
64 Numero ___
65 Behave

670 by Manny Nosowsky

ACROSS

1 Vaulted
7 "You're welcome," south of the border
13 Elegant
14 Thick soups
15 Without an angle
16 "Joueurs de Cartes" and "Les Baigneurs," e.g.
17 Apr. collectors
18 Small portable cabinet
20 Reading matter on an urn
21 Defeat soundly
23 Unsettled
24 Leader in the dunes
25 Any chapter of the Koran
26 M-G-M motto start
27 "___ we all?"
28 Asset for Jack Benny
32 Where the Althing sits
33 Lion of Judah
37 Make merry
38 "Enterprise" leaders
39 No more than
41 The "Odyssey," e.g.
42 Silly trick
44 Word with pen or pet
45 Nuclear defense acronym
46 Passes
48 Fashionable wrap
49 Delphic
51 Spring farm work
53 Bo with guitar
54 Quinze doubled
55 Kept someone awake, perhaps
56 Sidewalk ___

DOWN

1 Oil-rig firefighter Red et al.
2 Post-setback order
3 Ending
4 Horde member
5 Theater sign
6 Coffee order
7 Nodded off
8 "L'___ c'est moi"
9 Masefield's "The Tragedy of ___"
10 Moniker
11 Transferring property
12 Claim
14 Process accompanying digestion
16 Yorick was one
19 Super Bowl terror movie
22 Hangs around
24 "Childhood and Society" author
27 "Lucky Jim" author
29 Cut down
30 Peek at
31 ___ Toguri (Tokyo Rose)
33 Anticoagulant
34 Guacamole need
35 Strapped
36 Southern California city
37 Fixes bare spots
40 "The Right Stuff" role
42 Felt lousy
43 William Paley's realm
46 Principle
47 Knight time
50 Rank below capt.
52 Sebaceous cyst

671   by Manny Nosowsky

ACROSS
1 "Actually . . ."
16 Persisted
17 1980 Seymour-Reeve love story
18 No for Burns
19 Shapes again
20 Aquamarine, e.g.
21 Arthurian knight who sought the Holy Grail
22 Move about
24 Composed
27 Gladdens
31 Poker Flat chronicler
32 Shoot-out danger
35 "L' ___ c'est moi": Louis XIV
36 Rushmore is one
37 Blue hue
38 Sports doctors' supplies
40 Hardly windy
41 U.S. Gold Bullion Depository site
42 Analyzes sentences
43 Quick with a reply
45 Goes for the bronze
46 School figure, for short

49 Emotionally cold person, informally
51 ___ tai
54 Cold-war collections
57 Law chief
58 Puts in more chips, e.g.

DOWN
1 Part of P.T.A.: Abbr.
2 Columned walkway
3 "I would give all my ___ for a pot of ale": "Henry V"
4 Parliamentary stand
5 Did major editing
6 Stick
7 Arises (from)
8 "Comin' ___ the Rye"
9 Ends of a loaf
10 Defining challenge
11 Adenoids' neighbors
12 Kind of reaction
13 Not a copy: Abbr.
14 Seal in Disney's "20,000 Leagues Under the Sea"
15 Give the impression
21 Kind of average
23 Whitewater sight

24 Storage spot
25 Enjoy something enormously, with "up"
26 Drained
28 Ranks
29 Clear the boards
30 1991–92 U.S. Open tennis champ
32 Jailer's charge
33 Daily grind
34 Switch positions
36 Rivera and Orozco, e.g.
39 "The Miser" playwright
40 It doesn't go in circles
42 Coin holders
44 Picasso topper
45 Twill
46 Growl like a dog
47 "___ lid on it!"
48 Pre-intermission period
50 Evan from Indiana
51 Squiggle, e.g.
52 Aves have them
53 Cuba and Aruba: Abbr.

55 ___ Altos
56 King Features competitor

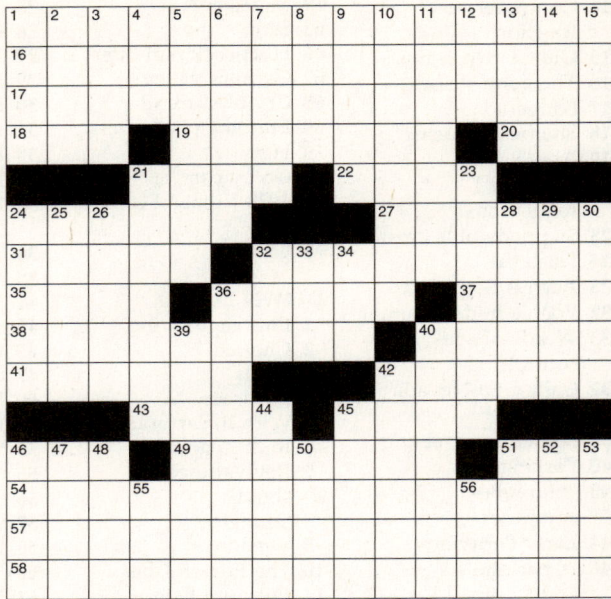

672   by Randall J. Hartman

ACROSS
1 Start of an auctioneer's windup
6 "Fairy tales"
10 Grump
14 Moving about
15 ___ Stanley Gardner
16 Bobcats of college football
17 1983 De Niro film
20 Musical ability
21 Lament
22 Methamphetamine
23 Toward sunup
24 Scintilla
26 1981 Sidney Lumet drama
33 Petite's opposite
34 "Losing My Religion" rock group
35 Birch or larch
36 Bambi's aunt
37 Bridge feats
39 Fed. air quality org.
40 Book after John
42 Charged particle
43 More sensible
45 1951 Hepburn-Bogart adventure
49 Mortgage

50 Magician Henning
51 Like a $3 bill
54 Arias
55 Soupy Sales faceful
58 1995 kids' film
62 Shoebox datum
63 Green land
64 Charlie Chaplin persona
65 Rime
66 ___ and crafts
67 Wimp

DOWN
1 Field entrance
2 Govt. watchdog grp.
3 Road to ancient Rome
4 Suffix with beat or peace
5 Pained look
6 Smooth, musically
7 Fe, in chemistry
8 One with a Claus in his contract?
9 "Wait a ___!"
10 Purse item
11 Korea's Syngman ___
12 Gofer

13 Hopalong Cassidy portrayer William
18 Rocket's front
19 Bone: Prefix
23 Our lang.
24 Detail
25 ___ law (electricity principle)
26 Skirt fold
27 Ponderosa, e.g.
28 More than peeved
29 Coin in Cannes
30 Dancer Castle
31 "Dances With Wolves" home
32 Pine (for)
37 Equine parent
38 Cut of beef
41 Private, often
43 Looks into the sun, e.g.
44 Sept. predecessor
46 Boxer's weapon
47 Embellishes
48 ___ me tangere
51 Gala
52 Mishmash
53 Sphinx site
54 Barbecue bar
55 Like ___ in a pod

56 Tenets
57 Spot
59 Grassland
60 Slip up
61 Dernier ___

ACROSS

1 Triviality
6 Deli order
10 Kan. neighbor
14 English truck
15 Towel word
16 Wet forecast
17 Mr. T series, with "The"
18 Sci. course
19 Analogy words
20 Unhelpful spelling tip #1
22 Surround
23 Escapade
24 Play during the day
26 Sound of a sock
29 In __ land (spacy)
31 Tall and slender
32 Russian river
34 Fluid parts of blood
36 Barge's path
39 Unhelpful spelling tip #2
42 It might let a person off
43 Glut
44 Kind of lord
45 Capone foe
47 River through Khartoum
49 Novelist Harper
50 Collaborate on a screenplay
53 Barber's cry
55 Il cambio currency
56 Unhelpful spelling tip #3
61 Tons
62 Walked all over
63 St. __ (West Indies spot)
64 Quebec's Lévesque
65 Vogue competitor
66 It may be perfect
67 Physics units
68 Does batik
69 Secretaries: Abbr.

DOWN

1 Indy 500 prop
2 Roster
3 Some search for these in vein
4 Be behind
5 Sunday songbook
6 Unappreciated
7 Wine: Prefix
8 Senator Phil
9 Bone-related
10 First generations
11 Unhelpful spelling tip #4
12 Austin Rover gas unit
13 Battery side
21 Understand
25 Lunch with a crunch
26 Cocoon's contents
27 Unwritten
28 Unhelpful spelling tip #5
30 Indo-European
33 Frees
35 Radioactive elements
37 Malaria symptom
38 Old __, Conn.
40 Unless, to Cato
41 Paris abductee
46 Explicit
48 Betting combo
50 Journalist __ Boothe Luce
51 Houston athlete
52 Betimes
54 Auto foursome
57 Part of a pump
58 Pearl S. Buck novel
59 Tilt to one side
60 Past spouses

ACROSS

1 Read carefully (over)
5 Elephant of children's books
10 Nourish
14 Soon, in verse
15 Flavorful seed
16 Aware of
17 Swing standard
20 Gains altitude
21 Indy 500 time
22 Matter in court
23 Searcher for the Northwest Passage
24 Mad, Elle and Mademoiselle, briefly
27 "__ went thataway"
29 "I could __ horse!"
33 Pal, in Arles
34 Carson's predecessor
35 Individual beings
37 Rock standard
40 "Puppy Love" singer, 1972
41 Diamond star Willie
42 Suffix with project
43 Projection room item
44 Window part
45 Kennedy, for one
46 Sachet scent
49 Suffix with cash
51 Miracle-working
54 Turned out, so to speak
58 Folk standard
60 Compact, e.g.
61 Put into law
62 Lady of La Mancha
63 Unwelcome cloud
64 Clockmaker Thomas et al.
65 Judge's order

DOWN

1 Mama's mate
2 Burden
3 Some college training
4 Walks in
5 Longtime Dick Clark show, for short
6 Years in Spain
7 Storage unit
8 Off the right path
9 Betty Ford Center activity
10 Prognosticate
11 Oklahoma city
12 Singer James
13 Ready to conk out
18 Like Bach's Violin Sonata No. 3
19 Environmental prefix
23 Earthenware
24 College choice
25 Entertain
26 "__ Shelter" (1970 movie)
28 Leon Uris novel, with "The"
30 Use
31 Inventor Nikola
32 Wan
34 Access to an A.T.M.
35 Attic windows
36 Awful grades
38 Tadpole
39 Baseball's Ripken
44 Kind of solution
45 Throngs
47 Here, to Henri
48 Olympic pool divisions
50 Toronto-to-Montreal dir.
51 Wharton grads
52 Grad
53 "__ Jail" (Monopoly directive)
54 Problem for a person in handcuffs?
55 Really funny person
56 Sicilian resort
57 June 6, 1944
59 __ King Cole

675 by Rich Norris

ACROSS

1 Go for game
5 Put up with
10 Pinochle holding
14 Onetime B.&O. rival
15 "The Prisoner of ___"
16 Mimicked
17 One eager for dinner
19 She played Ginger on "Gilligan's Island"
20 Rallying words
21 Real one
22 Devious
23 Collectible car
24 Dash gauge
26 Big hit on the diamond
31 Overly emotional
34 Terrific, slangily
35 Ethereal
36 Bread spread
37 "Pal Joey" writer
39 Hoods in hoods
40 Change, sometimes
41 60's battleground, briefly
42 Former Attorney General Edwin
43 Unwelcome guest
47 Seven days in May, e.g.
48 Wine cask
49 Tooth doctor's org.
52 Not together
55 Makeshift desk area
57 Highway hauler
58 Child of the 50's, e.g.
60 Many
61 PC communications
62 Small winning margin
63 Short dog, for short
64 Greene of "Bonanza"
65 J.F.K. arrivals

DOWN

1 Succors
2 Archangel of the Apocrypha
3 Rather cool
4 Boards, e.g.
5 Flowering shrub
6 Call
7 Seals, as deals
8 Running mate for R.M.N.
9 Musical talent
10 Yente, in "Fiddler on the Roof"
11 Miniseries, maybe
12 Letterman rival
13 Make-or-break time
18 Hook up with
21 Big inits. in records
24 Winter Palace resident
25 Capt. Pierce portrayer
26 Work behind the scenes, in a way
27 "Chicago Hope," e.g.
28 What a marker may mark
29 Important periods
30 Baseball's Sandberg
31 Sticky stuff
32 Part of the arm
33 Oracle
37 Less than rarely
38 "Listen!"
42 ___ Park, N.J.
44 At this time
45 Not leave home
46 Big name in big telescopes
49 Vapor, in Greece
50 Accomplish, as thou might
51 ___-ski
52 "Make it snappy!"
53 Brazilian soccer star
54 Frenziedly
55 Skier's aid
56 Ages and ages
58 ___ canto
59 Latin 101 word

676 by Rich Norris

ACROSS

1 Sailor's garb
8 Braces
15 Stretch
16 "L.A. Law" role
17 Swindles
18 Emote
19 Editor's mark
20 Bar supplies
22 Mastered perfectly
23 Vote (for)
24 Beldams
25 First word in a Mozart title
26 Buzzing
28 Prefix with revisionist
29 "The Devil and Daniel Webster" writer
30 Modifies
32 Natal natives
34 In a protective wrapper
36 Tub floater
40 Embroidery loop
42 Jo portrayer in 1994's "Little Women"
43 Thomas Cromwell, Earl of ___
46 Alternative to "smoking"
48 Spruce
49 Manufactured baloney?
50 Vestiges
52 Director Wenders
53 Withdrawal aid: Abbr.
54 Rose of a Stephen King best seller
55 Lucille Ball title role
56 Opposite of below
58 Sierra Nevada peak, with "El"
60 It spans 12 time zones
61 "Medical Center" co-star of 70's TV
62 Reproduction method
63 Málaga misters

DOWN

1 Roles
2 Biennial news tool
3 Stomach
4 Set group
5 "___! it is an ever-fixed mark": Shak.
6 Concerning
7 Polytetrafluoro-ethylene, familiarly
8 Satisfy expectations
9 Gads
10 Clumsy, stupid fellows
11 Average
12 Attach quickly
13 Open to view
14 Former cager Bob
21 "Mockingbird" singer Foxx
24 Neck, anatomically
25 Aeronautics pioneer Clyde
27 Exuded
29 Some stock acquisitions
31 Watchdog grp. for 29-Down
33 Depleted
35 Negotiations outcome
37 Trouble
38 Friend
39 Accounting department
41 Related
43 Gives a lift
44 Skip
45 Always, musically
47 Reunion attendees
50 Pie cuts, essentially
51 Desire
54 Etc. category
55 Harvard muralist
57 Japanese honorific
59 It comes to a point

677 — ACROSS

1 Irrational art
5 One of the Huxtables
10 Summer getaway
14 Not on the level
15 Radio-related
16 ___-Altaic (language group)
17 Start of a quote by Will Durant
20 Isaac or Howard
21 Put into difficulties
22 Old spy grp.
24 "On Golden Pond" playwright Thompson
25 Quote continued
31 Prefix with valence
32 Jabir al-Sabah, e.g.
33 Take forcibly
38 Local life
40 Storm heading
41 Pang
42 Mount
43 Pedal pushers?
45 Greek peak
46 Quote continued
49 Shaver
53 Pricing word
54 Touch a chord
57 Racket
61 End of the quote
64 Crosses
65 In heraldry, having small projections in the upper corners
66 Distribute
67 Glamour rival
68 Assemblies
69 Kind of money

DOWN

1 Judo levels
2 Much
3 Fawn
4 Choice of Paris
5 Preserve
6 Blockhead
7 The blue of baby blues
8 Opposite of gormandize
9 Small posy
10 Show rudeness in traffic
11 Glacial formation
12 Shocks of a sort
13 Spy of a sort
18 Split sec.
19 "Groovy"
23 1967 Monkees song
25 Yaks
26 Drop
27 Reed
28 John Ciardi's "___ Man"
29 Curtain fabric
30 Esurience
34 Places for displaying wares
35 Constellation name
36 Optimistic
37 They're sometimes split
39 Arithmetic figure
44 Easy mark
47 Stumped
48 Advanced
49 Babble
50 Kind of eagle
51 Nary ___
52 Constrictor
55 Language akin to Shan
56 Site of Galway Bay
58 Noncommittal response
59 Give a bellyful
60 Surveyed
62 Bottom line
63 Mdse.

678 — ACROSS

1 Bakery byproduct
6 Went by plane
10 Copied
14 Arizona features
15 Scottish isle
16 Lemon's partner
17 With 36-Across and 55-Across, a sales pitch disclaimer
20 Baden-Baden and others
21 Shea team
22 Eastern V.I.P.
23 Mr. Caesar
24 Ship to ___
25 "Swan Lake," e.g.
29 Tiny bit
31 Not native
32 Printer's employee
33 Printer's measures
36 See 17-Across
39 His wife took a turn for the worse
40 Obsolescent piano key material
41 Bellini opera
42 Hoarder's cry
43 Telescopist's sighting
44 Strength
47 Opponent
48 Xerox competitor
49 "When I was ___ . . ."
51 In ___ of (instead)
55 See 17-Across
58 Person 'twixt 12 and 20
59 "The King and I" setting
60 Singer Cara
61 Misses the mark
62 Paddles
63 Waco locale

DOWN

1 Concert hall equipment
2 Harvest
3 Greek mountain
4 Wrestlers' needs
5 Type of cobra
6 Shot
7 Artist's pad?
8 Son of Seth
9 Revolutionary, e.g.
10 "Remember the ___"
11 Heartbroken swain
12 Leno, for one
13 Bucks and does
18 Give forth
19 Indian noblewoman
23 Feeling
24 Suffix with tip or dump
25 Get-out-of-jail money
26 In addition
27 Bit of fluff
28 Mr. Durocher
29 Harden
30 "Sure, why not?"
32 Borodin's "Prince ___"
33 To be, in Paree
34 Secretarial work
35 Burn
37 Confess
38 "___ on your life!"
43 Fashion
44 "60 Minutes" regular
45 Reason out
46 Sentence subjects
47 Country homes
48 Pigeon coop
49 ___ da capo
50 Noted James Earl Jones stage role
51 Entice
52 The holm oak
53 Erupter of 1669
54 Applications
56 G.I. entertainers
57 Command to Fido

679 by Harvey Estes

ACROSS

1 On the ___ (very angry)
8 For the well-to-do
15 November winner
16 Savannah's place
17 "Evil Ways" band
18 Bar members
19 Dynamite's kin
20 Christian Science founder
22 Pope's "An ___ on Man"
23 ___ way (incidentally)
25 Murals and the like
26 Free-for-all
29 Play callers
31 Ill-fated sibling rival
35 Put on a pedestal
36 Ark builder
37 Singer Falana
38 String player
40 "Hop to it!"
42 Cancer's symbol
43 Reds' Rose
45 2:1, e.g.
46 "A-one and ___"
47 "I smell ___"
48 TV pitchman Merlin
49 "A Christmas Carol" boy
51 Study of optometry?
53 Edinburgh dwellers
56 Aloe ___ (lotion ingredient)
57 Retirement kitty, for short
60 Evangeline, e.g.
62 Last-place finisher, so it's said
65 Unyielding
66 Fence in
67 Reneges
68 Quotes poetry

DOWN

1 Frontierward
2 Chester Arthur's middle name
3 Monthly due
4 %: Abbr.
5 ___ loss for words
6 Belief
7 Edith + Holly
8 Hideous
9 Black-eyed one, perhaps
10 Farmer, in the spring
11 Billy + Lucille
12 "Rock of ___"
13 Italian bread
14 Word before come and go
21 Car for test-driving
23 Alexander + Timothy
24 Abominable Snowman
25 Tennis's Arthur
26 Islamic center
27 Bring to bear
28 Steven Bochco TV drama
30 Patti + Lana
32 Boxing matches
33 Borden bovine
34 Instructions to Macduff
39 Lunch meat
41 "Star Trek" counselor
44 Record
50 Basketball's Thomas
52 "Common Sense" author
53 "Saint Joan" playwright
54 Sign over
55 Reverend Roberts
56 Animal docs
57 "___ You Babe"
58 Misleading move
59 Senate votes
61 SSW's reverse
63 New Deal grp.
64 Yale player

680 by Robert Herrig

ACROSS

1 Speleology topic
5 Plane egresses
10 Pedestal topper
14 C.I.A. profiler Philip
15 Paradigm
16 Savvy about
17 Canine laryngitis?
19 Mutant heroes of modern comics
20 Not gross
21 Gain
22 Fanciful
24 Doubtful story
25 Fancies up
26 Record lists
29 Uses a cheat-sheet
30 "The Many ___ of Dobie Gillis"
31 Watkins ___, N.Y.
32 Gridiron period
36 Candid
37 First-aid contrivance
38 Stage curtain
39 Encircle
40 Way with words
41 Sneak preview
42 Posh
44 Like some hair
45 Words preceding film credits
47 Kingsley et al.
48 Warned with a horn
49 South of France
50 Shocking word
53 The least concern
54 Experimental canine?
57 Adjective for an antique store
58 TV exec Spelling
59 Hors d'oeuvre spread
60 Former empire
61 Acknowledge
62 Like certain trays

DOWN

1 "Three Coins in the Fountain" lyricist
2 Chills
3 Third piece of three
4 "A mouse!"
5 Richard Sheridan play, with "The"
6 Be gaga over
7 Chow ___
8 Lobbying acronym
9 Winter sport
10 Canine underwear?
11 Frighten to the core
12 Cut flowers
13 "West Side Story" beau
18 Lady Gregory cohort
23 Deprive (of)
24 Stylish canine?
25 "___ You Glad You're You?" (1946 hit)
26 Stop (up)
27 Snake dancers
28 Maintain
29 Succeed, informally
31 Endocrine, e.g.
33 Loads
34 Juice flavor
35 Rations
37 Not get hit?
41 Dither
43 Miniature
44 Failing business's woe
45 Trunk items
46 Gangsters
47 Plains critter
48 Commandment word
49 Vidal's Breckinridge
50 "Gil ___"
51 Courtroom ritual
52 Comply with
55 Contemptuous cry
56 Bath, for one

681 by Susan Smith

ACROSS

1 Big party
5 Enclose
9 Back-of-paper news item
13 Wrinkly fruit
14 Kind of eye
16 It's in a jamb
17 Projecting rock
18 ___ at all costs
19 Site in Sicily
20 Trail-blazing black modern dancer
23 A bean
24 Cloth measures: Abbr.
25 Architectural projection
28 Cookbook abbr.
31 One of the three D's
35 Director Fritz
36 Stored fodder
38 ___ v. Wade
39 First black poet to win a Pulitzer Prize
42 Santa ___
43 Some singing groups
44 Utilities
45 Gravelly glacial ridge
47 H.S. big shots
48 Songwriter Jule
49 Former President of Pakistan
51 "Mayday!"
52 Legendary black folk singer and composer
61 Costa ___
62 Remove
63 Mr. Guthrie
64 ___ about (time phrase)
65 Political party offering
66 Sound of waves
67 Novelist George
68 Court hero
69 O'Brien or Ferber

DOWN

1 Resist obstinately
2 Taj Mahal city
3 Blind part
4 Discreet warning
5 Bone-tired
6 Sitarist Shankar
7 Stravinsky ballet
8 Ballet movement
9 Danish city
10 One and the other
11 Scottish abbey site
12 Streetcar
15 Christian Science founder
21 Dawn goddess
22 Milk container
25 Pond film
26 Future queens?
27 Weasel
28 Jousts
29 More cunning
30 Dog breaths
32 Dull
33 Memento
34 "Magister Ludi" novelist
36 Leftist political label: Abbr.
37 Literary monogram
40 Andrea ___ (ill-fated liner)
41 Win a "no blinking" contest
46 Boxer Charles
48 ___ Canals
50 Fundamentals
51 Rock debris
52 Libido
53 Film director Wertmuller
54 Sacred image
55 Raines of 40's films
56 Afternoon gatherings
57 Biblical verb
58 Trampled
59 Dash
60 ___ Barnacle (Mrs. James Joyce)

682 by Alex Vaughn

ACROSS

1 Declined
5 Trapdoor
10 Lose pep
14 Whopper
15 Creighton University site
16 Smooth the flower bed
17 Certain Ivy Leaguers
18 Not as common
19 Miami of ___
20 Veer 120°
23 Veer
24 Mouth part
25 Without causing much excitement
28 Correspond
32 Male delivery?
35 Greek "H"
36 Name in small railroads
37 Don't do anything suspicious
41 Voice a conviction
42 Foreman stat
43 ___ out (add to)
44 Very much
45 ___ fugit
48 "You talkin' to me?"
50 Three-fifths of the world's people
54 Be evenhanded to clients
58 "Farmer," in Dutch
59 Fahd's faith
60 Rio nitery, for short
61 Ensured
62 Popular camera
63 Not injected
64 Bypasses, as commercials
65 ___ Park, Colo.
66 "Alice" diner

DOWN

1 Slows, as the flow
2 Steven Bochco TV series
3 "___ your style"
4 Saguaro locale
5 Ingredient of some pet foods
6 Eastern nurse
7 Georgia plantation
8 Sundae topper
9 "___ Speaks" (1962 autobiography)
10 Overadornment
11 Actor Bert
12 Comparable
13 Chevrolet division
21 Gardner of "The Naked Maja"
22 Namely
26 Time-saving abbr.
27 Potato pancake
29 As to
30 Furniture wood
31 Fashion magazine
32 Cartoonist Drake
33 Approximately
34 Wall St. workplace
36 Canary Islands port
38 First-down requisite
39 Gavel pounder's demand
40 Charlemagne, e.g.
45 Propositions
46 Cable network
47 It's just for laughs
49 Nimble
51 Ere
52 Katmandu's kingdom
53 Navy unit
54 Comic Imogene
55 Dickens villain
56 Touched down
57 Stand before
58 Industry, informally

683   by Rand H. Burns

ACROSS

1 Freshly
5 "Tony n' ___ Wedding" (off-Broadway hit)
10 Cheek's neighbor
14 Actress Copley
15 Père's frère
16 Mayberry lad
17 Efficient
18 Give a wide berth to
19 One End of London
20 Fainéance
22 Effervesces
24 Mordant
26 Varsity regulars
29 Snail or slug, e.g.
33 In an obvious way
35 Horizontal timber on an open boat
36 Simpson case judge
37 Arctic explorer John
38 Bygone bird
39 Ancient highway
40 Place-setting item
42 Brit's midday snack
44 Large dog
46 Crinkly gauze
47 Clad
49 Court

52 Benne seeds
56 Vast
57 Ex-President of Uganda
59 Salon product
60 Letter after aleph
61 Sturdy, as a beam
62 Dye-yielding plant
63 Contrarian
64 Lachrymal
65 Clamor

DOWN

1 King in the "Volsunga Saga"
2 Essential
3 Of an age
4 Jonathan's cousin
5 Brown
6 Ensnare
7 U.S.O. user, perhaps
8 Outs
9 Don Juan activity
10 Average guy
11 Shade of blue
12 Smart-alecky
13 Net calls
21 Roadside assister
23 Hull huggers
25 Sunbeam

26 Mocker's ploy
27 Russia's ___ Autonomous Republic
28 Run for one's wife?
30 Asphalts
31 Unmatched sets
32 Colonial figure Silas
34 Ratlike marsupial
38 Pale cheese
41 Arabian Sea port
42 It's collinear with SSW
43 Cached
45 Unicellular life
48 Fibber McGee's little friend
49 Singer McEntire
50 Dentist's request
51 Hand holder
53 Rider's grip, perhaps
54 Diabolic
55 Bears do it
58 Volga tributary at Gorki

684   by Amy Goldstein and Julian Ochrymowych

ACROSS

1 Claudia ___ Taylor (Lady Bird Johnson)
5 Write with acid
9 ___ and ruin
14 Cooking fat
15 Eight on a sundial
16 Capital of Vietnam
17 Reason for not attending
20 German port
21 "Holy moly!"
22 Average grade
23 Dodos
24 Weight, as on the mind
26 "___ bodkins!"
27 Gym moisture
29 Word after waste and want
30 Chicago suburb
34 16-Across's Le Duc ___
36 Upon
38 1955 Frank Sinatra hit
41 ___ dokey
42 Ballet dancer's digit
43 Sack cloth
44 Mine metal

45 Rouse
47 Regular: Abbr.
48 This ___ of tears
49 Milan opera house, with "La"
54 German first person
55 "You're it" game
56 Tommy gun noise
58 Classic Jackie Gleason series
61 Ohio rubber plant site
62 Silver wear?
63 Exhaust
64 Composer Camille Saint ___
65 Fill
66 Author Seton

DOWN

1 Omega's opposite
2 "___ Theme" ("Doctor Zhivago" tune)
3 Decorates the tree
4 Pueblo home
5 Always
6 Feel pins and needles
7 Short smoke
8 Longfellow chief

9 Exclamation of relief
10 Computer space, for short
11 Nonscientific, as evidence
12 Prairie wagon
13 Toy with strings attached
18 Bear country
19 The Almighty
25 Breakfast mush
26 Being broadcast, as a radio show
28 Departed
30 Traffic caution
31 Expressionist artist Oskar
32 George M. Cohan W.W. I song
33 Typed (in)
35 Kill ___ killed (law of the jungle)
37 Vim
39 Older society women
40 Totals
46 "Sesame Street" frog
48 Moving vehicle
50 "Why ___ woman be more like a man?"

51 Stayed home for dinner
52 Boxer Holmes
53 Confused
54 "Play ___ it lays"
55 Lots and lots
57 First-class
59 Dearie
60 Voter registration?

685 by Gregory E. Paul

ACROSS

1 N.Y.C. gallery
5 Personnel
10 ___ Nostra
14 Diabolic
15 Blender setting
16 Pink-slipped
17 Cozy place
18 Official publication
19 Pore over
20 Little Bear
22 Chic
23 Brown brew
24 Health enthusiast's dish
26 Entreat
30 Lodge resident
32 Technique
34 Jack Horner's last words
35 ___ facto
39 Chorister
40 Following
42 Egg on
43 Squad
44 Sturgeon delicacy
45 Plotter's plot
47 Mistreat
50 "The Wind in the Willows" character
51 Deere product
54 Swiss peak
56 Senator Charles and family
57 Little Flower, in old New York
63 Part of A.D.
64 Faneuil and Tammany, e.g.
65 Stable particles
66 Appear
67 Marina's place
68 Theaters
69 Oregano, e.g.
70 Unkempt
71 Republican V.I.P. Jack

DOWN

1 Waiter's offering
2 Walkie-talkie word
3 Strindberg's "___ Julie"
4 Province east of B.C.
5 Go bad
6 Cable TV man
7 Cornstarch brand
8 Intimidating
9 Swamp
10 Little Joe, e.g.
11 Kind of daisy
12 60's radical Bobby
13 Totaled
21 Composed, as a bed
22 Manuscript encl.
25 Mideast rulers
26 H.S. jr.'s exam
27 Singer Lovett
28 Word following dónde
29 Little Boy, e.g.
31 "You Must Remember This" author
33 Thomas of "That Girl"
36 Lyricist
37 Ditto
38 Frankfurt on the ___
41 Like many interstates
46 Noted nightclub
48 Sgt.'s superiors
49 "Best of My Love" rock group
51 Rubbish
52 Actress Blakley
53 Lum's partner
55 Hot-blooded
58 Shakespeare title start
59 Corner piece
60 Miami's county
61 News bit
62 Pronto
64 Unnamed fellow

686 by Rich Norris

ACROSS

1 Biblical verb ending
4 Dress
10 Logician's abbr.
13 Biblical pronoun
15 Confiscates
16 "What's the ___?"
17 Really solid
19 Boor
20 "Love Story" co-star
21 Change colors
22 Phys ed
23 Tar
25 Put in an all-nighter
27 Operating at capacity
33 Singer McEntire
37 Bud Grace comic strip
38 ___ da capo
39 Goofs
40 Handicapper's hangout: Abbr.
41 Retained
42 Broadcast
43 Hog hangouts
45 Former name at the pumps
46 Acknowledged responsibility
49 Zone
50 Big name in typewriters
55 Position
57 Military muckamucks
61 Fleet
62 Scull
63 Similar but unspecified things
65 Depot: Abbr.
66 Cash in, as chips
67 Not a weather
68 PC panic button
69 Visit
70 Grads-to-be: Abbr.

DOWN

1 System of beliefs
2 Title for Macbeth
3 "___ cow, there a cow . . ."
4 Beast of burden
5 Rip
6 Kind of pump
7 ___ Lacoste
8 Environmental buzzword
9 Geological ridges
10 Swamps
11 Wordsmith Willard
12 Reckon
14 Mild cheese
18 Jai ___
24 Wind dir.
26 With eyes open
28 Suds
29 Let loose
30 Legal record book
31 Bites
32 Cat, in Castile
33 Cause of grounding
34 Writer Bombeck
35 Curios
36 Fall bloomer
43 Budding actress
44 Pouch
47 Excludes
48 Dessert wine
51 Hindu nobility
52 October birthstones
53 "My Life in Court" author
54 Cutting tools
55 Canseco of baseball
56 Feedbox filler
58 Actor Ray
59 Measure
60 "The Purple People Eater" singer Wooley
64 Irving of "Micki & Maude"

687 by Brendan Emmett Quigley

ACROSS

1 Oreo's center
6 Dotty
10 Karate school
14 Boring tool
15 Share a side with
16 Israeli airline
17 "The Cloister and the Hearth" author
18 Kind of stockings
19 Auto brand
20 1986 Robert Palmer hit
23 Midpoint: Abbr.
24 Filth
25 Definitely, south of the border
28 "Ich bin ___ Berliner"
31 Asylum seeker
35 "Moneyline" channel
36 Blaupunkt product
38 Yard pests
39 Popular education aid
42 Cellular phones lack them
43 Kind of gloves
44 ___ good deed
45 Heads-up notices
47 Agcy. for retirees

48 Last word of "For He's a Jolly Good Fellow"
49 Bombard
51 Caviar
53 End of a classic Eubie Blake title
60 Hump-shouldered bovine
61 Bamboozles
62 Parting word
63 ___-contra
64 Pants part
65 Kidney-related
66 Become attentive, with "up"
67 Scorch
68 It's just over a foot

DOWN

1 Irene of "Fame"
2 Felt sorry about
3 "Holy moly!"
4 Italian dynasty name
5 Upright
6 Willing
7 Not up
8 Storm winds
9 Not out

10 Military punishment
11 Norwegian king until 1991
12 Senator in space ___ Garn
13 Matador's cheer
21 Word with "water" or "the boards"
22 Oaf
25 Pronunciation symbol
26 How sardines are packed
27 Saw wood
29 Screen favorite
30 Hirschfeld's hidings
32 Move effortlessly
33 Scouting mission
34 Susan Sontag piece
36 Refreshed
37 Decides
40 Dropping sound
41 Courage
46 Casual pants
48 Anesthetize
50 Steak type
52 Mitchell belle
53 "___ Off to See the Wizard"

54 Bridge support
55 Readily draftable
56 Ultimate buyer
57 Winter Olympics venue
58 Bona fide
59 Gift-giving time
60 Fast speed

688 by Matt Gaffney

ACROSS

1 Goofs
5 Carefully engineer
10 Unhitched
14 Sweetie
15 Site of Hercules' first labor
16 Like garage floors
17 Shelley poem
19 "A Death in the Family" author
20 Roller coaster features
21 W.W. II camps
23 Novelist Beattie
24 Caged pet
28 Skater Babilonia
29 Lawyer's abbr.
31 Indian exports
32 Hardly modest swimwear
34 One of eight popes
36 Satisfy
37 Happy 50's couple
41 Lustrous
42 Site for a Christie mystery
43 Model/actress Eleniak
44 Ring

45 Mexico City newspaper, with "El"
48 San Francisco's ___ Hill
49 Onetime alternative to a Camaro
52 Kit ___
54 Words of reproof before "you"
56 Gladden
58 Table d' ___
59 Purportedly weakening shield
63 Boot
64 Hungarian airline
65 Health food
66 Align
67 Cassette half
68 Rival of Ben & Jerry's

DOWN

1 Zaire menace
2 Draw new lines
3 Synthetic fabrics
4 Cesspool
5 Channel since 1980
6 Upper, maybe
7 "___ wrong?"
8 Bountiful occasions

9 Esthetic preference
10 One with a stable family
11 Pasta choice
12 Class
13 It needs some perspective
18 Hardwood
22 Maestro Toscanini
25 Cornered
26 Important statistic
27 Mister in a 1954 #1 song
30 Oddity
33 Misters, abroad
35 Tell
36 Kind of session
37 Easy 2-pointer, maybe
38 Time to attack
39 Japanese industrial combination
40 First name in Danish literature
44 War cry
46 Gave the go-ahead
47 These days
50 Hotel capacity
51 Sportscaster Allen
53 Maryland players

55 Dole (out)
57 Superior designation
60 On in years
61 Born
62 Stowe girl

689 by Gerald R. Ferguson

ACROSS
1 Impala, e.g.
8 ___ Palace
15 One way to stop
16 Back of the head
17 Football fling
18 "Good going!"
19 R.R. stop
20 Virginia Woolf novel
22 "___ gather"
23 Small fry
25 Two-time U.S. Open tennis champ
26 Phaser setting
27 Impala's relative
29 Part of a winning combination
30 Sheds
31 Delay
33 Makes an effort
35 ___ colada
37 Conductor's intro
38 Shows up
41 Like a patchwork quilt
45 Noted coloratura
46 Bashful colleague
48 Outlet, e.g.
49 Rock's Mötley ___
50 "Lost in Yonkers" character
52 Tommy's gun
53 Coat part
54 Instrument panel
56 Cable TV giant
57 Spoof
59 Schedule again
61 Colorless solvent
62 Whole number
63 Movie do-overs
64 Neptune's gardens

DOWN
1 Colt's home
2 Director Litvak
3 Rapper's sound
4 E.T.O. commander
5 Novice
6 Baseball's Vizquel et al.
7 Ball
8 Bonds
9 Litmus reddeners
10 Behold, to Bellini
11 Prussian pronoun
12 Mark, for one
13 Expirations
14 Bud holders
21 "I am miserable"
24 Popular quencher
26 Reds
28 Towels off
30 Rogers and others
32 Some trial evidence
34 Account exec
36 Battle of the Bulge locale
38 High-drama competition?
39 Fall
40 Musical notes
42 Kind of industry
43 Put up
44 "Nay" sayers
45 Graduated
47 She played Phyllis on TV
50 Kentucky county
51 Coeur d'___, Idaho
54 Doctor, in a way
55 This, to Pedro
58 Open-house org.
60 Kahlil Gibran's homeland: Abbr.

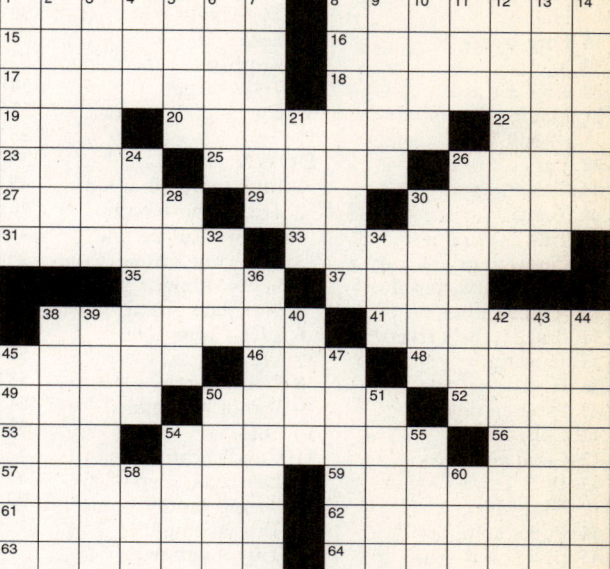

690 by Ronald C. Hirschfeld

ACROSS
1 They're plucked
6 Busy as ___
10 Lake formed by Hoover Dam
14 Bye
15 Druid, e.g.
16 Presque ___, Me.
17 Close behind
20 Chair plan
21 Setter or retriever
22 "Fables in Slang" author
24 Part of a bridal bio
25 Words after "The last time I saw Paris"
34 Buck follower
35 Muddies the water
36 "The Company"
37 Bara and Negri
39 Years in Paris
40 Mole
42 Native: Suffix
43 Comedienne Fields
45 Hebrides language
46 Completely unperturbed
50 Olympian: Abbr.
51 Knock-knock joke, e.g.
52 Sounds the hour
56 1967-70 war site
61 Discourage
63 Japanese aboriginal
64 Assassinate
65 Put up
66 Cuff
67 Cod relative
68 Drinks with straws

DOWN
1 It's a laugh
2 1985 film "My Life as ___"
3 ___ of passage
4 Drudge
5 Dairy bar order
6 Otto's "oh!"
7 English channel, with "the"
8 Like many textbook publishers
9 Adjective for Rome
10 Cellar growth
11 Old gas brand
12 Sleep like ___
13 Excellent, in slang
18 Cry of achievement
19 Ancient capital of Macedonian kings
23 Corrigenda
25 June in Hollywood
26 Sister of Thalia
27 Alfa ___
28 Sock ___
29 Quinine water
30 Smarten
31 Lip-puckering
32 Hair-coloring solution
33 ___ et Magistra (1961 encyclical)
38 It causes sparks
41 Lapidarist's object of study
44 City on Lake Winnebago
47 Tar
48 Actor Gooding
49 Glues
52 Earth
53 Bluefin
54 Scat cat
55 It's north of Neb.
57 Flying: Prefix
58 TV exec Friendly
59 Cape ___ (westernmost point in continental Europe)
60 Colonists
61 ___ de deux
62 Fork

691   by Robert Zimmerman

ACROSS

1 Rig
5 Big dos
10 At a distance
14 Ur locale
15 New York's ___ Tully Hall
16 Berg opera
17 M
20 Kicker's aid
21 Names in a Saudi phone book
22 Bury
23 Cut and run
24 Yearn
26 Talk radio guest
29 Playwright O'Casey
30 Army rank, for short
33 African lily
34 Brazzaville's river
35 Through
36 H
40 Fabergé objet
41 Collection
42 Candied items
43 1969 Three Dog Night hit
44 Pup's complaints
45 Lively wit
47 Some heirs

48 Time founder
49 "Orlando" author
52 Forum fashion
53 Quarry
56 Y
60 Organ setting
61 Type style
62 Eros
63 Ruptured
64 Tell's target
65 Currycomb target

DOWN

1 Investigate, in a way
2 Tribe whose name means "cat people"
3 Old gray animal?
4 Some ratings
5 Newgate guard
6 1966 Caine role
7 Wagons ___
8 German cry
9 Bishop's domain
10 Solo
11 Candid cameraman
12 Der ___ (Adenauer)
13 Krupp family home
18 Tall writing?
19 Tiny swimmer
23 Took off

24 Director Marshall
25 "Othello" plotter
26 Literary sketch
27 Collimate
28 Moose, e.g.
29 Divans
30 Opera prop
31 Pioneer atom splitter
32 Kingfisher's coif
34 ___ de ballet
37 Opposite of hire
38 St. Patrick's home
39 Publicity
45 Conductor Ormandy
46 Analyze verse
47 Skier's site
48 Dietary
49 ___ Point
50 "___ victory!"
51 Stink
52 Substitute
53 Cougar
54 Caddie's offering
55 Home of Jezebel
57 ___-la-la
58 School dance
59 Scottish cap

692   by David Ellis Dickerson

ACROSS

1 Masquerades
6 "Fe, fi, fo, ___!"
9 Batman foe, with "The"
14 Native Alaskan
15 Prince Hirobumi
16 Sheeplike
17 Irving's "A Prayer for Owen ___"
18 The lambada, once
19 Grand mountain
20 Dr. Seuss title
23 Actress Skye
24 Ho Chi ___
25 Car job
28 ___ Bingle (Crosby)
30 God Almighty
34 A year in Mexico
35 Put to the grindstone
37 Studio prop
38 Dr. Seuss title
41 Plant seeds again
42 ___-scarum
43 Coach Parseghian
44 Shakespearean oath
46 Smidgen
47 Love of Greece?
48 Dance or hairstyle
50 Calf's meat

52 Dr. Seuss title
59 One-___ (short play)
60 Crystal ball, e.g.
61 Keep busy
62 Violinist Isaac
63 Part of R.S.V.P.
64 Wrestling's ___ the Giant
65 Western film title of '75 and '93
66 Golf peg
67 Relaxes

DOWN

1 Like venison
2 Out of the wind
3 Carroll contemporary
4 Em, e.g.
5 Pen, for Pierre
6 About mid-month, with "the"
7 Brigham Young's home
8 Computer-phone link
9 Norse land of giants
10 Make out at a party?
11 Songstress Eartha
12 Organic compound
13 Philosopher Descartes

21 Conclude with
22 Small bird
25 Dens
26 Hungry
27 Idaho city
29 Betty Ford program
31 1991 Stallone comedy
32 Brain surgeon's prefix
33 Columnist Maxwell et al.
35 Author from Salem, Mass.
36 Inferable
39 Dinner chickens
40 More like Shirley Temple
45 ___ Solo of "Star Wars"
47 Sir Galahad's mother
49 Popular word game
51 "___ Is Born"
52 Fastener
53 VIII, to Virgil
54 Blvds. and rds.
55 Toledo's vista
56 Hitches
57 William of "The Doctor"
58 Unlocks, in a sonnet

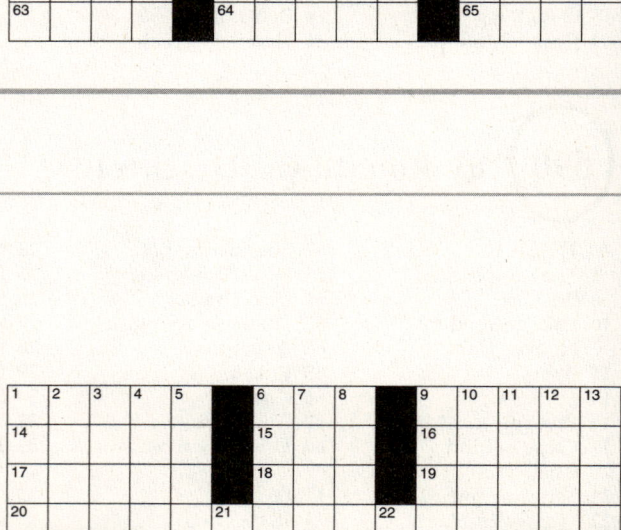

693   by Alfio Micci

ACROSS

1 Be a party to
5 Breakfast strip
10 "___ corny as Kansas..."
14 Judd Hirsch sitcom
15 Jagged
16 ___ me tangere
17 First place
18 Spry
19 Future flower
20 Start of an old proverb
23 Gran Paradiso, e.g.
25 Mideast export
26 Russian co-op
27 Part 2 of the proverb
32 Ancient city on the Gulf of Aqaba
33 Reduce
34 Muralist José
35 Irritable
37 Give the eye
41 Don Corleone
42 Circa
43 Part 3 of the proverb
47 Birchbark
49 One may be high at 5:00
50 ___ Plaines, Ill.
51 End of the proverb
56 ___ supra (see above)
57 Understand
58 Mr. Saarinen
61 Graph start
62 École attender
63 Leave shore
64 Apollo craft
65 Playwright Rice
66 Stepped

DOWN

1 Downed
2 Michael Jackson album
3 Archetype
4 A Turner
5 Grin's partner
6 Historic county in Scotland
7 Hairdo
8 Frogner Park locale
9 At no time, to poets
10 Natural
11 Nelson Eddy in "Rose Marie"
12 French avenue
13 Fortune-teller
21 "Goodbye, Columbus" author
22 Lion's pride
23 Iowa university town
24 Singer Lovett
28 Communications conglomerate
29 ___ Downs
30 Took a chair
31 Rossini's "Count ___"
35 Spasm
36 Ordinal ender
37 Gram. case
38 Firestone rival
39 Darth Vader's son
40 Vacation times abroad
41 Opinion
42 Wise ___ owl
43 Garland
44 Loggers' tourneys
45 When some local news is "live"
46 Render impotent
47 Kind of service
48 Stage comment
52 Business exec William
53 Cheerleader's routine
54 Watch part
55 Hatching post?
59 John Wayne's "___ Lobo"
60 Used

694   by Bryant White

ACROSS

1 Whom Simple Simon met
7 Worn out
11 Marciano stats
14 Ancient mystic
15 Alternative to Charles de Gaulle
16 A Mrs. Mickey Rooney
17 Lunch item
19 Pro ___
20 Make even
21 Stringed grp.
22 Ahab's father
23 D.C. summer hrs.
24 Lith., formerly
26 Of the first category
28 Fishing equipment
30 Curling inning
32 Francophone's income
33 Cosmetician Lauder
35 Like Pinocchio
36 Lunch item
39 "As You Like It" character
40 Physicist Bruno
41 Disgruntled employee's words
42 Pub serving
43 Thin wood strip
47 Fertilizers
49 Nettle
51 Fourth letter of the Arabic alphabet
52 Hairdresser's preparations
53 Pound for one
56 Cigar tips
58 "___ tu" (Verdi aria)
59 Lunch item
61 New Yorker cartoonist Chast
62 ___ out (scrapes by)
63 Greek markets
64 Mariner's dir.
65 Foreign start
66 Attacks on all sides

DOWN

1 Effervescent "Dr."
2 Tristram's beloved
3 Possessions left behind
4 Intend
5 Starts a pool
6 Art movement prefix
7 Planck contemporary
8 Red navigator
9 Capital of Attica?
10 Cobb and others
11 Capital of Nepal
12 Exceed, in a way
13 Japanese guitar
18 Ophthalmologist's study
22 Margarine ingredient
25 Paving stones
27 Greek or Maltese, e.g.
29 Author Ursula et al.
31 Actress Winger
34 Take care of
35 North Sea feeder
36 Southwestern cowboys
37 Make uniform
38 Light of Humbert Humbert's life
39 Tots of liquor
44 Clothes
45 Start of a Seuss title
46 Talks (over)
48 Nietzsche's "Thus ___ Zarathustra"
50 Small anchor
54 Presage
55 Conoco rival
57 Deux, dos, due et al.
59 Do voodoo
60 Collar

695 by Christopher Hurt

ACROSS

1 BBC competitor
4 Spoils
8 Furry swimmers
14 Curtain
16 Business group
17 Depressions
18 Emergency processing
19 Antiperspirant's target
20 Best of all possible worlds
21 This may have come first
22 K.G.B. predecessor
24 L.I. clock setting
25 Like some juices
29 ___, Bravo, Charlie, . . .
31 Like a bump on ___
32 Boss's last words
37 Gull-like birds
39 Italian artist ___ Bartolommeo
40 Notched
41 Humankind
44 Frame part
45 Brian Boru's land
46 Makes hard to read
48 Noun after a verb: Abbr.
51 Without a clue
53 Factory second: Abbr.
54 Crotchety folk
56 Took up residence
60 Mardi Gras mask
61 Hunter
63 Badge
64 Religious title
65 Improvise, in music
66 Educational org.
67 Ran into

DOWN

1 You can believe it
2 Warm up
3 Field mouse
4 "Sophie's Choice" role
5 Flippant fellow
6 Iowa State's home
7 Surface for painting
8 Eightfold
9 Molière hypocrite
10 Fates, e.g.
11 Troop encampment
12 First name in TV talk
13 Sound between Skye and Scotland
15 1973 news topic
23 Breezeway terminus
25 File object
26 She was Sylvia in Broadway's "The Women"
27 The rounds
28 1959 Fiestas hit
30 Popular sneaker
33 Coffee container
34 It may have broad shoulders
35 Salinger girl
36 Five-time Presidential candidate
38 Dangerous debris
42 Supple
43 Mewls
47 Acknowledge
48 Chicago's first mayor William
49 Fizzy remedy
50 Family-size
52 On both sides: Prefix
55 Easy to take
57 "Straight ___ the rocks?"
58 Detail
59 Airplane part
62 Alphabet snippet

696 by Gregory E. Paul

ACROSS

1 Be an omen of
5 Sen. Henry ___ Lodge
10 Discharge
14 Confess
15 "Let sleeping dogs lie," e.g.
16 Bestow
17 Wise
18 Skin holes
19 Quiet valley
20 Where ___ at (the scene)
21 Pack of trouble
23 Conceal
25 Corporate V.I.P.
26 Employ
27 Cowboy
32 Dodge
34 "The Road Not Taken" poet
35 Investment inits.
36 Compos mentis
37 Crop up
38 "Daily Planet" reporter
39 ___-tac-toe
40 Kind of clown
41 Cowboy's home
42 Circus heavyweight
44 Puts on TV
45 Org. overseeing the Atlanta games
46 Where visas are made
49 Living end
54 Clear weeds
55 Fever
56 Nero, e.g.
57 Grand old party
58 Sacramento arena
59 Lily-livered
60 "Antony and Cleopatra" character
61 Screwdriver, e.g.
62 ___ Gay
63 Mardi Gras follower

DOWN

1 Foundation
2 Egg-shaped
3 Little likelihood
4 Lamb's mother
5 "Breakfast at Tiffany's" writer
6 Hold dear
7 Farm building
8 Double-curved molding
9 Legal precedent
10 Yuletide drink
11 Ryun's run
12 "As I was going to St. ___ . . ."
13 Camp shelter
21 In this spot
22 Faxed
24 Roller coaster, for one
27 Place for a bracelet
28 Mr. Perot
29 Largest part
30 Guitarist Clapton
31 Baby's diaper problem
32 Villa d'___
33 Colorado resort
34 Football's Tarkenton
37 One way to order on a menu
38 "Doctor Zhivago" heroine
40 Hew
41 Barbecue entree
43 Firing range weapon
44 "The Glass Menagerie" role
46 Computer messages
47 Athenian lawgiver
48 Bakers get a rise out of it
49 Heart-to-heart
50 Prefix with nautical
51 Cantina snack
52 Amalgamate
53 Bullets
57 Hair fixative

697 by Diane C. Baldwin

ACROSS
1 Panama, e.g.
6 Touch
10 Speck
14 Zipping along
15 Ballet attire
16 City southeast of Milan
17 Hook
20 Corset feature
21 Pledge
22 Computer adjunct
23 Kin's partner
24 Parishioner's seat
25 "Messiah" composer
29 Verve
31 Bygone gas station freebie
34 Actor Delon
35 Water container
36 Diva's piece
37 Line
40 Song for the Everly Brothers
41 Harrow's rival
42 Hippy dances?
43 Gridiron gains: Abbr.
44 Fall in a faint, with "over"
45 Excessively sweet
46 Seal group
47 "Tarzan" actress Markey
49 Unresponding
52 Appearance
53 Wide-eyed
57 Sinker
60 Kind of sax
61 Extorted from
62 North from Virginia
63 Sequence position
64 Leaning
65 Airfield tower

DOWN
1 Stand vehicles
2 Give ___ on the back
3 Zilch
4 Having pains
5 Hilo neckwear
6 Up
7 Fall for hook, line and sinker
8 1941 Pearl Harbor ship
9 Harbor boat
10 Tolerate
11 Health food item
12 Laudatory works
13 Swampy area
18 Hard labor
19 Oracle's utterance
23 Lottery game
24 Young salmon
25 "Jude the Obscure" author
26 Vocally
27 Scruffs
28 Japanese parliament
30 Writer Uris
31 Scratch
32 Bride's destination
33 Erato's realm
35 90 degrees from norte
36 Tightfitting
38 Clarinet part
39 Falling sound
44 Big Apple ex-mayor
45 Chinese: Prefix
46 Lace loop
48 They're not hip
49 Vichy and Ems
50 Cash holder
51 Sgt. Snorkel's dog
52 1551, on monuments
53 Skillfully
54 Temerity
55 Gallimaufry
56 Dell
58 Fall back
59 Champagne-opening sound

698 by Wayne Robert Williams

ACROSS
1 Corridors
6 1968 U.S. Open winner
10 "Count ___!"
14 Author of "Daniel Deronda"
15 Secure, in a way
16 Sharpness
17 Thrifty maxim
20 Take a load off
21 Denials
22 Graduating classes
23 Sign of healing
24 Singer Guthrie
26 Irwin Shaw novel
32 Cold-cuts section
33 Z-zebra link
34 Snacked
35 One Italian
36 Saddle parts
39 Kind of kite
40 R&B's Boyz II ___
41 Mayberry lad
42 Whip mark
43 Ultimate thing
48 Model Macpherson
49 Accomplishes
50 Stag
53 Frigid suffix
54 Alphabet trio
57 Joke category
61 Level
62 Seed bed
63 Spine-tingling
64 U.S.
65 Stance
66 Former "London Times" editor Harold

DOWN
1 Fells
2 Jai ___
3 Schindler's aid
4 Building site
5 Cause for nose-holding
6 One-celled organism
7 Drunkards
8 Know-___
9 Memorable time
10 Kind of shower
11 Author O'Brien
12 Borodin's prince
13 Meadowlands Arena team
18 Linguist Chomsky
19 Hose
23 Sch. class
24 Church recess
25 Muddy waters
26 "Walk Away ___" (60's hit)
27 Massey of "Love Happy"
28 Dubbed
29 Actress Normand
30 Trans-Pacific refueling spot
31 Waiting room word
32 Speechless
36 Allergy stimulant
37 Fire
38 Miser's pronoun
42 Used to be
44 Bank, at times
45 Like some mushrooms
46 Mrs. Charles
47 Myers, formerly of the White House
50 Indian tourist mecca
51 Clayey soil
52 Seep
53 Sale tag phrase
54 Hospital supplies
55 Identical match
56 Functions
58 Psychic power
59 Court
60 Ore. neighbor

699 by Mark Diehl

ACROSS
1 Pickled utterances
5 Attack
10 Red-coated food item
14 Tract
15 Setting for a 1968 Neil Simon play, with "the"
16 Cockeyed
17 What a busboy clears
20 Chicken's complaint?
21 Pricey
22 TV host Rick
24 San Francisco's ___ Tower
25 Butter units
28 Lummox
30 Glacial masses
34 Wood used for tool handles
35 Dictator before Caesar
37 Curriculum follower
38 What a criminal lawyer clears
41 A.A. Milne character
42 Peace Nobelist of 1987
43 Slowpoke at the track
44 Startles
46 Word in the MGM motto
47 Ballet leap
48 Veterans Day honorees
50 Back talk?
52 Annual vaccine target
56 In flames
60 What a pickpocket clears
62 Prefix with sphere
63 Sewing kit portion
64 "The jig ___!"
65 Isle of exile
66 On edge
67 Given to eavesdropping

DOWN
1 Items in the ring
2 Where dinars buy dinner
3 Oldest Spanish city in the Philippines
4 Side orders, at times
5 Was forthright
6 Polar toiler
7 Dashboard dial, for short
8 ___ dye
9 Lively dances
10 Full of juice
11 ___ harm to (leave be)
12 Romans predecessor
13 Guinness superlative
18 Flock member
19 Den denizens
23 Nacho topping
25 Subsidizes
26 Like ___ in the face
27 Zoo beast
29 Vegetation
31 United (with)
32 Diamond figure
33 Papyrus plant
35 Weaving in and out
36 In flames
39 I problem?
40 Like Bugs Bunny
45 Least perilous
47 Adjective for Joe DiMaggio
49 Ski area
51 Showtime rival
52 Liniment target
53 Satirist Silverstein
54 Part of a meter, maybe
55 Tabloid topics
57 Chan comment
58 Olympian leader
59 Catch sight of
61 Army sleeper

700 by Rich Norris

ACROSS
1 Made ___ of things
6 Business abbr.
10 Victuals
14 Feathery
15 Jon Arbuckle's dog
16 Will Rogers line
17 Tee off
18 Humphrey's "Casablanca" role
19 Radius neighbor
20 Everything, with "the"
23 Saga
24 Zip
25 Everything
32 Passionate
33 Weather
34 Teachers' org.
35 Troubles
36 Put an end to
38 Crux
39 Unagi, at a Japanese restaurant
40 Composer Khachaturian
41 Kind of bird
42 Everything
46 ___ Z
47 Sea divers
48 Everything
55 Luxury car name
56 Servant of Antony in "Antony and Cleopatra"
57 Not rosy
58 Part of A.D.
59 Entice, with "in"
60 Permission
61 Bite
62 Raced
63 Like some seals

DOWN
1 There ought to be one
2 Ho Chi ___
3 Breakfast brand name
4 Gazebos, e.g.
5 Not monochromatic
6 Trumpet relative
7 Like some Keats works
8 Lucky in the lottery, maybe
9 Lap dog
10 Is
11 Anne Lindsay's "___ Robin Gray"
12 Actress Louise
13 Place for a masseuse
21 "Boola Boola" singer
22 Dryer detritus
25 Home contractor's hiree
26 Opening word
27 Surgery aid
28 Bamboozles
29 Powerless to move
30 Actress Patricia et al.
31 Girl of a 1918 song
32 Feudal estate
36 Crosby and Como, e.g.
37 Agua, in Arles
38 Some shrines
40 Cinematic canine
41 Elevate
43 Seder staple
44 Like big hair, e.g.
45 Telescopic sighting
48 Lotto-like game
49 Keepers keep them
50 Small amount
51 Handle, with "with"
52 Prized
53 Wash
54 Squeezed (out)
55 Interdiction

701 by A.J. Santora

ACROSS

1 Rush Limbaugh medium
10 Kind of artery
15 Everybody
16 Headword
17 Riding, in a way
18 Flavor
19 Doll's cry
20 Mai ___
21 1882 Sardou drama
22 Live
23 Assertive ones
25 Certain Hill
26 1976 Olympics star
28 Spanish ayes
29 Yeats's "The Lake ___ of Innisfree"
30 Flowery ornamentation
32 Foundation timber
33 Disturbances
35 Comic Bill and others
37 Asia's Trans ___ Mountains
38 Straightforward
42 Nash fellow
43 Perfect
44 "___ cold . . ."
47 Burt's "The Killers" co-star, 1946
48 Measles symptom
50 Nickname
51 Miner
53 N.T. book
54 Treat with milk
55 Florida's ___ National Forest
56 Decide in advance
58 Long narrative
59 Leave oneself at risk on Wall Street
60 Imparts
61 Care centers

DOWN

1 Without exception
2 Cochise player of 50's TV
3 Song standard from 1875
4 Ted Kennedy's eldest
5 Code material
6 Supplement
7 Arp was one
8 Backdoor
9 Spectator's cry
10 Pianist Von Alpenheim et al.
11 Kind of story
12 Song standard from 1996, with "The"
13 Without principles
14 Chewy candy
21 1969 Economics Nobelist Ragnar ___
23 Boughpot
24 Slangy ending
27 Area colonized by ancient Greeks
29 Printing
31 Biblical queen celebrated at Purim
33 Lettuce spray?
34 Collarbone
36 Liquidates, so to speak
39 Heater
40 Demoralize
41 Places to raise a flap?
45 Charisma, from the Spanish
46 Habitations
48 Auditions
49 Top
52 Like some bags or rags
54 Other: Sp.
56 ___ favor
57 Utmost

702 by Mike Shenk

ACROSS

1 Was a dud
9 Sect's manuals?
15 Out early
16 "Wayne's World" town
17 Like Henry Sweet's alphabet
18 "Cabaret" setting
19 Electronic drug in Shatner books
20 Church events
22 Getting on
23 Like most testimony
25 Fingerprint part
26 Eye of the wolf?
27 Needle holders
29 Concert souvenirs
30 Humdinger
31 Dump outputs
33 Packing
35 Gaggle : goose :: knot : ___
36 Turn on the lights, in a way
37 Move with stealth
39 Jitterbugs
43 Gallant
44 Scandal
46 Singles player
47 Wax bananas?
48 Kernite component
50 Sir Charles and chums, in basketball
51 "___ in hoary winter's night": Southwell
52 Balloon
54 Draw upon
55 Year, symbolically
57 Never
59 Admission
60 Orlando paper
61 Psyched up
62 Slickers' counterparts

DOWN

1 Fab Four features
2 Come into
3 Inland Empire capital
4 Summer cooler
5 Ticks off
6 Wankel engine part
7 Brought out
8 Gets off the fence
9 Cellar contents
10 Plan de Paris lines
11 Dep.'s opposite
12 Christmas gift for a man
13 Sang like a bird
14 Plane's kin
21 Minor drinking problem?
24 Not in the stacks
26 Brass band sounds
28 Refuse transport
32 1973 hit for Cher
34 Its teeth are conical
36 Forte
37 Robert Burns, the ___ Bard
38 Met
39 Compact cleaner
40 Everyday
41 Left to the imagination
42 Father's reading
43 Readies for impact
45 Forfeit-paying game
49 Billy's partner
52 18th-century part song
53 Wee bits o' whisky
56 Dwight Gooden moniker
58 Deuce, for example

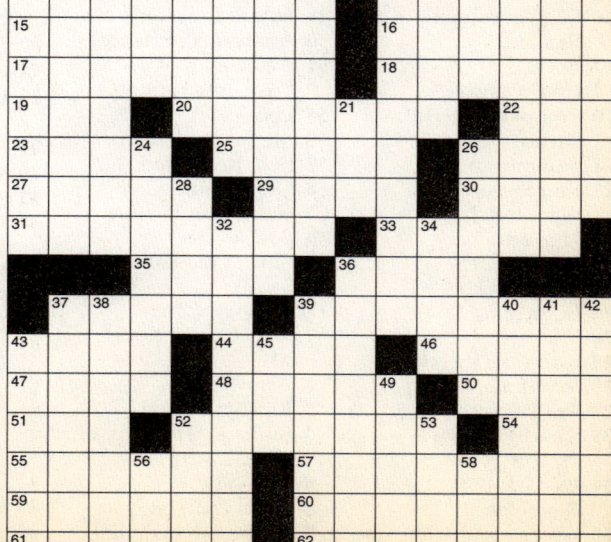

703 by Janie Lyons

ACROSS
1 Child's getaway
5 Nurse's stick
9 Malpractice target
14 Margarine
15 Part of a cash register
16 Sam or Tom, e.g.
17 Businessperson's oxymoron
20 Crowbar
21 Runner Devers
22 Sums
23 "Get ___!"
25 Cut up
27 Vipers
30 Indignant person's oxymoron
35 Actor Erwin
36 Breezy
37 Refer (to)
38 Dinner bird
40 Command to Fido
42 Jewish dinner
43 Mideast language
45 Flood survivor
47 W.W. II grp.
48 Oxymoron for a homely person
50 Cheek

51 Riches' opposite
52 Took a powder
54 Jacob's brother
57 Bare
59 Speechify
63 Coffee drinker's oxymoron
66 Passé
67 Within: Prefix
68 Model married to David Bowie
69 Steeple
70 Slumber
71 Library item

DOWN
1 Monk's hood
2 Lotion ingredient
3 Former talk-show host
4 Fireplace equipment
5 Penn, e.g.: Abbr.
6 Belly dancers
7 Edison's middle name
8 Mathematician Pascal
9 Sine ___ non
10 Straighten out
11 Sarcasm

12 Dolt
13 Barbies' mates
18 Enrage
19 Bow of silents
24 Black bird
26 Three-time Super Bowl–winning coach
27 Tin Pan Alley org.
28 One of the Beatles
29 Chrysalises
31 In competition
32 Lindley of "The Ropers"
33 Creativity
34 Indoor balls
36 Writer Loos
39 Busybody
41 Stashes
44 Caesar's swans
46 Certain vote
49 Shylock
50 Magellan, e.g.
53 Lee to Grant
54 Concludes
55 It's seen in bars
56 Against
58 Unit of force
60 BB's
61 Word after "go!"

62 Sea eagle
64 Humorist George
65 "Oh, darn!"

704 by William P. Baxley

ACROSS
1 Artistic skill
6 Card game also called sevens
12 Holed out in two under par
14 Warned
16 English essayist Richard
17 Burglar
18 Cools, as coffee
19 Pumpkin eater of rhyme
21 Summer drink
22 Employee health plan, for short
23 Horse trainer's equipment
25 Black cuckoos
26 Long, long time
28 Like some schools
29 Sweetens the kitty
30 Smart alecks
32 Traffic circle
33 Charlie Brown's "Darn!"
34 Ex-Mrs. Burt Reynolds
35 Charge with gas
38 Adorned

42 Vineyard fruit
43 Kismet
44 Snick's partner
45 Detest
46 Alternative to eggdrop
48 A Gershwin
49 Drunk ___ skunk
50 Analyze a sentence
51 Actor John of TV's "Addams Family"
53 Locale
55 Money-back deal
57 Boot camp denizen
58 Noted family in china manufacture
59 Arabs
60 Cancel the launch

DOWN
1 "L'état ___": Louis XIV
2 Army grub
3 Ripening agent
4 Butler's "The Way of All ___"
5 ___ Aviv
6 Observed Lent
7 Change the hemline
8 ___ -do-well

9 "La-la" leader
10 Home of the '96 Olympics
11 Poorer
13 Arranges strategically
15 Smart
18 Sullivan's "really big" one
20 Summers, in Haiti
24 Sharp
25 Clowning achievements?
27 Mexican shawl
29 Top-flight
31 Arena receipts
32 Drive in Beverly Hills
34 Epistles
35 Shocked
36 Pencil ends
37 Knocking sound
38 Forbids
39 Bootee maker
40 Most Halloweenlike
41 Doyen
43 Smithies
46 Dwindled
47 High-muck-a-muck
50 Fir

52 Prefix with masochism
54 Item of office attire
56 Fuel efficiency rater: Abbr.

705 by Jim Page

ACROSS
1 Hang up one's jersey
7 Roll of bills
10 Chi. time zone
13 It ties the score
14 Palatine Hill site
15 Pi follower
16 Less messy
17 Actor Estrada
18 ___-hoo
19 Old bandleader Edmundo
20 Keeled over
22 Library censures
24 Eats at the beach
26 They follow morns
27 Common suntanning locale
29 Eager to leave the picnic?
30 Atlanta Hawks arena, with "The"
31 Bites ineffectually
33 "Blech!"
34 Olympics skiing champion Alberto
36 "Car 54, Where Are You?" creator Hiken
37 Tiny mark
40 Nope's opposite
41 Was friends with
43 "My People" author
44 Xerox copy, for short
46 Equestrian competition
48 Director Kazan
49 Plains Indian
51 Woman's bio word
52 Jackie's hats
54 Turndowns
56 Prince Edward, e.g.: Abbr.
57 Sailor's direction
58 Rambo types
61 Classical start
62 Iodine source
63 To whom the Parthenon was dedicated
64 Vane direction
65 Speech pauses
66 Prepare fruit for eating

DOWN
1 Stimpy's pal
2 Adam's apple?
3 Little Anthony and the Imperials hit
4 "___ the Night," 1985 film
5 ___ Peanut Butter Cups
6 Drop the ball
7 Not so good
8 Wrong
9 Hockey fake
10 1970 Vincent Price film
11 Huzzahs
12 Foot, in slang
14 Poker-table phrase
20 Nowheresville
21 Hangs like an earring
22 It can be soft or blind
23 ___ sapiens
25 18-wheeler
28 Rush Limbaugh target
29 "___ Wiedersehen"
32 Backs
35 G.I.'s address
38 Tweety's home
39 Bender, of a sort
42 Very early
44 Fixes diapers
45 Molière miss and namesakes
47 Group of 100
49 Gondola guide
50 Nancy Kerrigan jumps
53 Shirr
55 Publishing notable Adolph
58 Like the woman of Chaillot
59 "A Chorus Line" showstopper
60 Rueful

706 by Manny Nosowsky

ACROSS
1 Bombay V.I.P.
6 Hacienda part
10 Money grp.
13 With 16-Across, financially O.K.
14 By its very nature
16 See 13-Across
17 Lab containers
18 Hemmed
20 James Murray work: Abbr.
21 Air hero
24 Pro ___
25 Kind of violet
29 Hawaiian verandas
31 Cousin of a mlle.
32 Inseparable
33 Lake ___ (Mississippi's source)
34 German "I"
35 Musical ending
36 Composer with a clavier
37 Mississippi waterway
39 Gland finale?
40 Der ___ (Adenauer)
41 Coll. srs. exam
42 Sophisticated
44 Scare word
45 Jungle squeezers
46 California team
47 Approve
49 The nth degree?
50 Festival time
51 Postal abbr.
52 Soviet workers' cooperative
54 Robin's transport
58 See 63-Across
62 Cost containment measure
63 With 58-Across, blockaded
64 Firecracker's path
65 Fun-house cries
66 Pretender

DOWN
1 Green
2 "The ___ Daba Honeymoon"
3 Write a bit
4 Former ova
5 Abélard, e.g.
6 Rushed
7 Balaam's beast
8 See 9-Down
9 With 8-Down, a reply's start
10 Banned chemical compound
11 Had a little lamb
12 Lettuce variety
14 Agenda listing
15 German import
19 See 45-Down
21 Legendary Arabian hero
22 Make a list
23 Doer
25 With a bow, musically
26 Radiator fluid
27 Faster than adagio
28 Least remote
30 Late apartheid opponent
31 Appraises, with "up"
35 Sierra Maestra country
38 Flaherty's "Man of ___"
43 Takes the elevator, perhaps
45 With 19-Down, predeparture words
48 Author Bombeck
49 Make ready, informally
52 "Poor pitiful me!"
53 Prefix with type
54 Merit badge grp.
55 Swiss river
56 Hosp. attention
57 Word of disgust
59 Both Begleys
60 "Huh!"
61 Sin

707 by Bob Klahn

ACROSS
1 Surely he jests
5 Comme ci, comme ça
9 Produce
14 Turning point
15 Bundle
16 Brooks of baseball
17 Piquancy
18 Homeowner's hangover?
19 Circus Maximus, e.g.
20 Startling revelation
22 Eland land
23 Keystone Kops creator
24 Kind of rock
26 "Clinton's Ditch"
27 Freight weight
31 Midlothian misses
34 Attracts and holds
35 Right from the beginning?
36 Multimedia format
37 Vitamin prescription
40 Boutonniere's counterpart
42 Not quite major-league
43 It's often thrust upon someone

44 Throwaway part
45 Most trim
49 Nomadic Mongol tribe
52 Fifty-fifty
54 Kind of committee
55 Deprivation
56 Burg
57 "Camelot" composer
58 March 15 question
59 Parmenides's birthplace
60 Dutch artist Hals
61 Lop the crop
62 Senator in space, 1985

DOWN
1 Rattles
2 Small round window
3 Novelist Tillie
4 Relax, literally
5 Snookums
6 '75 U.S. Open winner Manuel
7 Computer command
8 Do business
9 Hair-raiser?
10 Become angry, literally

11 Mr. Magwitch of "Great Expectations"
12 Crank (up)
13 Spruce
21 They're historically evocative
25 Hornswoggle
28 Mogul capital until 1658
29 Rand McNally subj.
30 Salinger's "For ___ —With Love and Squalor"
31 "The Talmadge Girls" author
32 "Tom Thumb" composer
33 Stanch
38 Son of Val and Aleta
39 Peak performer?
40 Relative of the organ
41 Begins firing
46 First name in aviation
47 "Les Miz" setting
48 Theater critic Kenneth
49 Moiety
50 Effluvium

51 Poseidon's mother
53 Have one's say, in a way

708 by Sidney L. Robbins

ACROSS
1 "You can say that again"
6 Papa's partner
10 Plays on stage
14 Perfection
15 Son of Adam
16 Tropical root
17 Tuxedo, slangily
19 Collar type
20 Otherwise
21 Starry
23 Computer headache
24 Nursery rhyme Jack
26 Counters by argument
28 Jam bottle
31 Push
32 Prophet
33 "___ Yankee Doodle dandy"
34 Like most colleges today
35 Taj Mahal site
38 Book before James
40 Inventory
43 "I Do, I Do, I Do, I Do, I Do" singers
44 With 22-Down, a cake brand

45 Imitate
46 Bumstead dog and namesakes
49 Cut, as nails
50 Visibly embarrassed
51 This and ___
52 Horseshoers' tools
54 "The Raven" poet
56 "Not a ___ too soon"
58 Pete Sampras org.
62 Novelist Paton
64 Locomotive's front
66 Become fatigued
67 Leg's middle
68 Don't exist
69 Jay Leno, e.g.
70 Three feet
71 Absorbs books

DOWN
1 Two nickels
2 Object of adoration
3 7 + 3, 5 + 5, 1 + 9, etc.
4 Instances of filming
5 Bullring shout
6 Rubdowns
7 Adjoined
8 Israel's Golda

9 Priests' places
10 Feasted
11 Second-story man
12 Rainbow fish
13 Hymnal contents
18 Peter of Peter, Paul & Mary
22 See 44-Across
25 Purplish brown
27 Schnozzola
28 Holy war
29 One-celled animal
30 V on a TV?
36 Lariat
37 Matured
39 Impetuous
40 On an even keel
41 Beard of grain
42 Li'l Abner's creator
44 Carpenter, often
47 Sweet potato
48 Solid and sturdy
53 Capital of Bolivia
54 Lane
55 Mixture
57 ___ Lisa
59 Mets milieu
60 Take care of
61 Partner of crafts

63 Basketball champion's "trophy"
65 Old salt

709   by Robert Zimmerman

ACROSS

1 "The Inferno" poet
6 Number after sieben
10 Highest point
14 Bay window
15 Scottish hillside
16 Fillmore, politically
17 Noted Swiss peak
19 1880 Zola novel
20 Grp. that dispatches ambulances
21 ___ Prism
22 Deserved
24 Rows
26 After-dinner candies
27 Potato order
30 Get retribution for
32 Ancient Andeans
33 Informal words
34 Letter after pi
37 Baseball's ___ the Man
38 Singer Bonnie
39 Israel's Abba ___
40 Be in season
41 Dads, in Dijon
42 Stand of trees
43 Boring tool
45 Piltdown Man and others
46 Make fun of
47 Political pamphlet
49 Weekly Wall Street paper
51 Novelist Levin
52 Sorbet
55 Winter Olympics event
56 Pattern on old horse blankets
59 Composer's work
60 Author Wiesel
61 Forum attire
62 Traveled
63 Beavers' constructions
64 Etched in ___ (permanent)

DOWN

1 Rotunda's crown
2 Saroyan character
3 Tiny criticisms
4 Hanoi holiday
5 Laments
6 Detest
7 ___-Magnon (early human)
8 Damage
9 Slumlord property
10 Sunshade
11 Motormouth
12 "King Solomon's ___"
13 "Zounds!"
18 Marsh plant
23 Wagner cycle
24 "More ___ You Know" (1929 song)
25 Prominent, as a feature
27 Hit or ___
28 The "A" in ABM
29 Firearm with an unfocused shot
31 Tubs
33 Poet Teasdale
35 Own
36 Change for a five
38 Felt regret
39 The "E" in Q.E.D.
41 Small change in Chihuahua
42 Racing vehicles
44 Most unusual
45 Animal with big ears
46 Brownish gray
48 Ceremonies
49 Sudden shock
50 Parlor, in La Paz
52 Shakespearean villain
53 MacGregor, e.g.
54 Otherwise
57 Conway or Curry
58 Barfly

710   by Jonathan Schmalzbach

ACROSS

1 Potassium ___ (astringent)
5 Ruse
9 Revue segment
13 Period of penitence
14 1992 Literature Nobelist ___ Walcott
16 Anent
17 New Year's figure
19 Capital of Togo
20 Sinatra's "I'm ___ to Want You"
21 "Israel in the World" author
23 Evict
26 Merit
27 Guardian of the comics
32 #4 of the Bruins
33 Baseball's Slaughter
34 River ducks
36 Ogler
38 Curvy letters
41 Bad mood
42 Vegas casino
44 Jai ___
46 Baseball club V.I.P.s: Abbr.
47 Literary sobriquet
51 Important periods
52 Room, to Ricardo
53 Max Ernst, Man Ray, Hans Arp et al.
57 Advanced exams
61 Licorice or sassafras
62 Balzac character
65 Cash for cards
66 Argument
67 Sandusky's lake
68 ___ off (miffed)
69 Sail support
70 Machine-gun bunker

DOWN

1 "A" in radio lingo
2 Page (through)
3 "Do ___ others . . ."
4 Volcanic peak in Ore.
5 T.E.D. opponent
6 Lease
7 Met solo
8 "The ___ of the Wedding" (McCullers novel)
9 Muzzles
10 Door handle
11 "The Joy of Cooking" author Rombauer
12 High schooler
15 Skewered meal
18 Escape capture by
22 In ___ (stagnant)
24 Since, New Year's Eve-style
25 Couples
27 Evaporate
28 Boxing locale
29 Silk-making region
30 Jumpy Milne character
31 Offensively vile
32 Brit. lexicon
35 Avenues: Abbr.
37 Echoed
39 Yale Bowl hosts
40 Capital of Yemen
43 Indian wear
45 Nome home
48 Hinged fasteners
49 Regard highly
50 Chief Justice Earl
53 "Fudge!"
54 Top-drawer
55 Show fondness
56 Mlle.'s neighbor
58 Suffix with billion
59 Maxwell of 007 films
60 Undo a dele
63 French connections?
64 Received

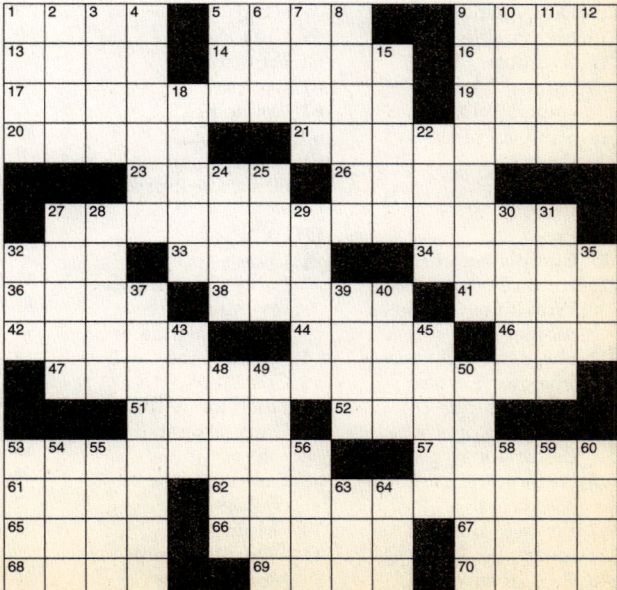

711   by Cliff Lundberg

ACROSS

1 Practical joke
5 Malice
10 Opera house box
14 Kind of history
15 Southwest home
16 During
17 Cluckers
18 More than angry
19 Rankle
20 What the N.B.A.'s Thurmond did in Lhasa, palindromically?
23 Gum unit
24 England's F.B.I.
25 Bank statement entry
28 Pen name
31 Wackos
35 Big birds
36 Threaten
38 Logical prefix
39 Like Napoleon, palindromically?
42 Itinerary section
43 Idolized
44 Spring
45 Rendezvous
47 Di-Gel target
48 80's top-rated TV star
49 Winter woe, in Wittenberg
51 Ages and ages
52 Wallop Nebraska tycoons, palindromically?
61 Soup ingredient
62 Buzzer
63 Land east of the Urals
64 Succulent plant
65 Spread out
66 Seven-foot, e.g.
67 McCartney's instrument
68 Scornful cries
69 Small amphibians

DOWN

1 One of 23 popes
2 Zone
3 Puff
4 Differently
5 Legal
6 Revise
7 Bygone Chevy
8 Notice of departure
9 Front-line physician
10 Texas city on the Rio Grande
11 Elide
12 Arizona river
13 Sir Anthony
21 Be up
22 Cycle enthusiast
25 Distributed
26 Fire remnant
27 Not flat
28 Obscure
29 Prefix with red
30 Sidewalk umbrella sites
32 Eyes
33 Shish ___
34 Needing a rinse
36 60's fashion plate
37 Oil source
40 2:1, e.g.
41 Stretch
46 Transitions
48 Lover's sound
50 Big hit
51 September TV special, with "the"
52 Pierce
53 Gwen Verdon role
54 Subjects of 58-Down investigations
55 Rival rival
56 Light ring
57 Smell ___
58 Fliers' mil. branch
59 Sing with grace
60 Mineo and others

712   by A.J. Santora

ACROSS

1 "This ___ test"
4 Sandwich topping
8 British ailment
14 "Under a Glass Bell" writer
15 Delinquent, of a sort
16 Memorable soirees
17 It's south of Scot.
18 "Mercy Mercy Me" singer, 1971
19 Stow, as cargo
20 Pantry
23 Only
24 Briny
25 Pro
27 Byron's before
29 Kind of change
30 Worshiper of Jesus's mother
33 She played 38-Across
35 Inventor Elisha
38 1985 film title role
39 Vincent Lopez's theme song
40 Author and son of 38-Across
43 Begin to burgle
44 Swears
48 Evergreen
49 H.S. dept.
50 Good name
51 It's a long story
53 Identify (with)
56 Science class
58 "Je Vous ___" (1947 song)
59 Crewman
60 Protozoans
61 Explorer
62 Coffee holder
63 Mother ___
64 China neighbor
65 60's protest grp.

DOWN

1 Living, to Livy
2 Politically attractive revenue source
3 Where Luanda is
4 Purplish red
5 Conscious
6 Fluctuate wildly
7 Dairy aisle item
8 Literary initials
9 Base for some cookies
10 "Mmmm"
11 1940 #1 Vaughn Monroe song
12 Setback
13 Journal's end
21 Nanjing buggy: Var.
22 Way to prepare chicken
26 Lashes
28 Sicilian mount
30 Griffith of Hollywood
31 "___ of robins in her hair"
32 Ancient city on the Tigris
34 Purposeful
35 Dionne Warwick's "Walk ___"
36 Fatiguing
37 Summer cooler
41 Skater Baiul et al.
42 Sock holders
45 Distasteful
46 Magician
47 Rear sections
50 Onyx decoration
52 Actor Kaplan
54 Rough up
55 Tower site
56 Halloween decoration
57 One for passage

ACROSS

1 Cowcatchers
8 ___ rule
11 Disney frame
14 Convertible
15 W.H.A. absorber
16 Pig & Whistle order
17 "Wake up!" in Teheran
18 Slow boat
19 Tippler
20 John Hancock rival
21 Mars sightings
23 Japanese "yes"
25 "Step on it!" in Jerusalem
27 "___ well!"
29 Exhausted
30 ___ buco
31 Home of the brave
33 Deep-blue mineral
36 "Candidly, Scarlett," in Paris
40 Gear computation
41 Sports stats
43 Fourth-century date
46 Tropical fruit
48 Nicholas I or II
49 "Put money on it?" in Beijing
52 Watering place near Koblenz
53 Solidify
54 Mt. Narodnaya locale
58 Alphabet chain
59 Scrape (out)
60 "Sorry to cut you off," in D.C.
63 Classified abbr.
64 Parasite's egg
65 Undistinguished follower
66 Snake sound
67 U.S.N. petty officer
68 Mantilla wearers

DOWN

1 Diary
2 Copy
3 Storekeeper
4 As to
5 Busy
6 Means ___ end
7 Small serving of coffee
8 Site of a Gen. McClellan victory
9 Open, as oysters
10 "Three Tall Women" writer
11 Cello maestro
12 Proceeds sans parental consent
13 Releases
22 Most nigh
23 Panama, e.g.
24 Letter before beth
26 Connecticut River city
28 Economical
29 Faction
32 Bambi's aunt
34 TV marine
35 Words with a ring to them?
37 So inclined
38 Local government position
39 Stationery purchase
42 Grads-to-be
43 Dishwasher listings
44 Former Albany first family
45 Where the Palme d'Or is awarded
47 Parlor pieces
50 Small
51 Old-time actor Jack
55 Ready to eat
56 Ugandan exile
57 Brand name that happens to be Latin for "I read"
61 Actress Merkel
62 Latin foot

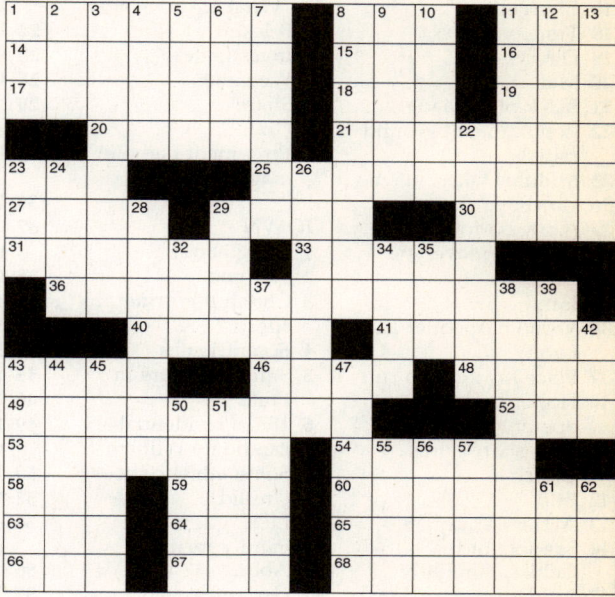

ACROSS

1 Queen Latifah songs
5 Less than 90 degrees
10 Mouth-to-mouth
14 Director Kazan
15 Andrews and Carvey
16 Appoint
17 "Right on, brother!"
18 Sheepish?
19 Use a Smith-Corona
20 1972 U.S. Olympic hero
22 "Get ___ of yourself!"
23 Dimwit's brain size
24 Francis and Dahl
26 Falsely incriminate
30 Part two of an election
32 Ebb
34 Diaper holder
35 Some VCR's
39 Parroted
40 In front
42 Breakfast restaurant chain, for short
43 Actress Spelling
44 Catch some rays
45 Gas rating
47 Changes
50 Nahuatl language
51 Hitting with short punches
54 Right off the stove
56 Grown-up
57 Plum brandy
63 "The ___ Never Sleeps" (bank slogan)
64 Business exec T. ___ Pickens
65 Farm: Prefix
66 Etta of the funnies
67 "The Age of Anxiety" poet
68 Tavern light
69 Mideast canal
70 Uses a spoon, maybe
71 Eye problem

DOWN

1 500 sheets
2 ___ mater
3 Ship's landing
4 Went under
5 Ali's "rope-___"
6 Champagne go-with
7 Part of B.T.U.
8 Neighbor of Kenya
9 Suffix with Japan or Sudan
10 Broken
11 Skirt material
12 Copious
13 Yorkshire's largest city
21 Went 80 m.p.h.
22 80's TV alien
25 Sonata movement
26 Toga party venue
27 "___ Man" (1984 film)
28 Excellent server
29 Publicist's coup
31 Turn over
33 Consumed
36 Chew the fat
37 Super-duper
38 On ___ (like some writers' assignments)
41 Loiters with friends
46 Ancient Roman censor
48 Cambridge sch.
49 Black eye
51 Raises, with "up"
52 Goodbye
53 Montana city
55 Hot spots
58 New Jersey city
59 U-Haul rentals
60 "___ a Kick Out of You"
61 Where Helen was abducted to
62 Amateur publication, informally
64 Undergrad degrees

715 by Rich Norris

ACROSS

1 Falls, e.g.
11 Short coats?
15 Fall back
16 Rodin sculpture
17 Charged
18 Time past
19 Directs
20 Mai ___
21 Black nightshade
22 Popular campground initials
23 Minutes taker, maybe
26 Cowboys' org.
27 [How boring!]
31 It might move you
32 Dander
33 Limit
36 Verne harpooner ___ Land
37 Place for bulls to run
40 Honor society opening
41 Tool sharpening device
42 Butt
43 Actress Thurman
44 Sanders of the Celtics, familiarly
47 Wild
48 Kind of swing
51 Gym unit
53 Protests of a kind
55 "How soothing!"
57 Flirt
58 "What I Am" singer Brickell
59 Investigates
62 Wee one
63 Share
64 Graf ___
65 Prominent name in magic

DOWN

1 Bring about
2 Sun god
3 Clutch performer, in sports
4 Eccentricities
5 Summer hours in Phila.
6 1832 Presidential candidate William
7 Some athletic shoes
8 Unsaid
9 J.F.K. guess
10 Family member: Abbr.
11 Certain spread
12 Trimming
13 Blithe
14 Was obviously not legit
21 Where the Tongue River flows
24 Run out
25 Crispy snacks
28 Plata's partner
29 Makes up
30 ___ Pie
34 Pertaining to anatomical tissue
35 Dr.'s orders
37 Got one's act together, so to speak
38 Geological comparison
39 Realize
40 Requests
45 Head start?
46 Moses portrayer
49 Flower with a pure white spathe
50 Ruin
52 Call
54 A Rose by another name
56 "Darn!"
57 It may be catching
59 Spot
60 Wing
61 Airline out of Stockholm

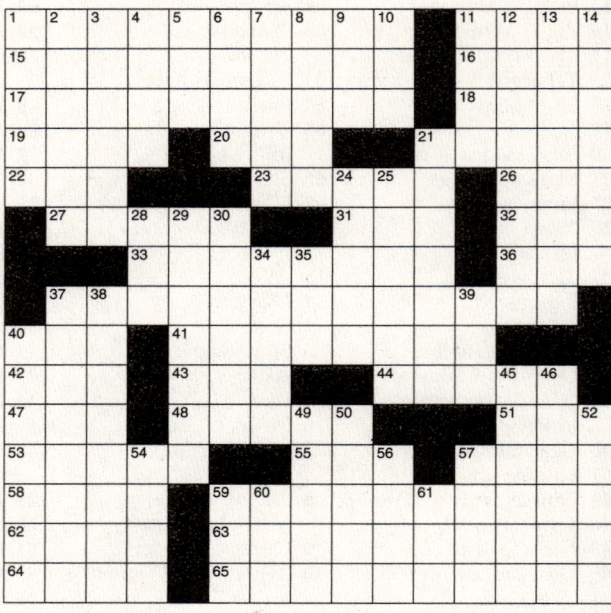

716 by Harvey Estes

ACROSS

1 They have pins at one end
6 Military bigwigs
11 Put in chips
13 Pan-fried
15 Mary Tyler Moore's old boss
16 Queen Victoria's family
17 Strikes out, perhaps
18 Nautilus habitat
20 Unflattering
21 Cub groups
22 Rock music's Tears for ___
24 London essayist
25 Calendar periods: Abbr.
26 Posthumous Forster novel
28 Persuaded
29 San Francisco pants-maker
31 Ancient fly prison
33 Troubles
34 The hunted
35 Offer an apple in Eden
37 Threadbare
40 Spending limit
41 Taunted
43 Quangtri locale
45 Last words
47 Bearded
48 "The ___ Report" (1976 best-seller)
49 Buddy of Irene Ryan?
51 Record number?
52 Hay holders
53 Carbon attachment
55 They're sometimes tickled
57 Put under
58 Bond, once
59 Smarts
60 Lacks

DOWN

1 Painters' equipment
2 Con
3 Egg containers
4 Some eagles
5 Use the peepers
6 Ewe said it!
7 Scores of diamonds
8 Make up
9 Barber's town
10 Less upscale
11 Like abandoned gardens
12 "Hunches in Bunches" author
13 Lamb Chop's voice
14 More than misgivings
19 Shoots an average score
22 Deducted style points from
23 Like Capone's face
26 Ralph of "Happy Days"
27 Touch up
30 Canyon edge
32 Party letters
34 Political tract
35 Purr-fect pets?
36 Show piece
37 Station that went on the air in 1978
38 Like one 1992 Olympics team
39 Ragamuffin's attire
40 Sorority possibles
42 Gave a rap
44 Topsy-turvy
46 L.B.J., e.g.
48 Lena of "Stormy Weather"
50 Picky people pick them
52 Like a star for a 46-Down
54 River to the Irish Sea
56 Bismarck's predecessor

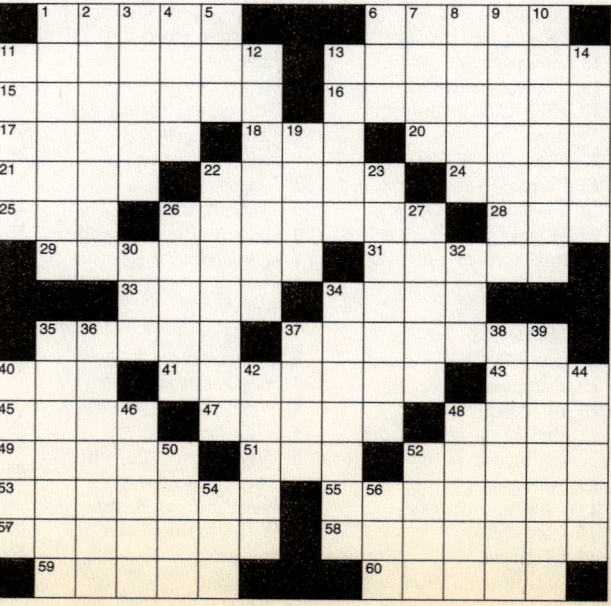

by Peter (Lefty) Gordon

ACROSS

1 Spirogyra or frog spit
5 Impression
9 Diamond protector
13 Burpee bit
14 Conclude, as negotiations
16 See 31-Across
17 Lefty celebrity relative
20 Turkish title
21 Customary practice
22 Strengthens, with "up"
23 Tugs
25 "Babes in Toyland" star, 1960
28 Head of the costume department?
30 Leonard and Charles
31 With 16-Across, former Phillies manager
34 "Queen ___ Day" (old game show)
35 Corporate abbr.
36 Have a hunch
37 Lefty artist
41 Shows one's humanity?

42 Bud
43 ___ Fein
44 Voted
45 Great
46 Overwhelms with humor
48 Catch in a net
50 Pipe type
52 Highest point in Sicily
55 Course for a newcomer to the U.S.: Abbr.
57 Lament
58 Lefty actor
62 French 101 word
63 Copy of a sort
64 Noted rap artist
65 Gloomy
66 Overdecorated
67 Danson, et al.

DOWN

1 Composers' org.
2 Three miles, roughly
3 Lefty President
4 Foofaraw
5 Horus's mother
6 Star in Cygnus

7 Baa maid?
8 Razor-billed bird
9 Kind of sax
10 Publican's offerings
11 Ridicule persistently
12 Is worthwhile
15 Lefty actress
18 Five-year periods
19 Refusals
24 Pontiac Silverdome team
26 Camden Yards team
27 Polaroid inventor
29 Lefty comedian
31 Lefty comedian
32 Continental trading grp.
33 Lawyer in both "Civil Wars" and "L.A. Law"
36 Student's worry
37 Roman law
38 Before, to Byron
39 Jutlander, e.g.
40 In a despicable way
45 Writer Quindlen
47 Blotto
48 Old-time knockout
49 Subs
51 Bridge seats

52 Horse that made sense?
53 One of the Jackson 5
54 Tannish color
56 Hot

59 Chaperoned girl
60 Actress Joanne
61 Paroxysm

---

by Manny Nosowsky

ACROSS

1 Dries (off)
7 The color of honey
12 Wining and dining place
13 Bob of reggae
15 The "thee" of "Of Thee I Sing"
16 Teases
18 ___ soda
19 Napoli night
21 Least big
22 Football no-no
24 Prefix equivalent to -ish
26 Way on or off
27 He told a hare racing story
29 Outlets
31 Hemingway novel setting
32 Furniture trim
34 Property restriction
36 Site of a Lewis and Clark stop, 1804
38 Inevitable
41 Up, in a way
44 Glaciate
45 Arises (from)
47 "It's ___ never"

49 "Stuffed Shirts" author
51 Blithe
53 Find, with "out"
54 Wassail flavor enhancer
56 Penicillin target, for short
58 Sermon subject
59 Semisoft Danish cheese
61 Approved
63 Modern phone option
64 Dürer and others
65 Oboelike in sound
66 Rest-less, perhaps

DOWN

1 Wrapped food
2 Giant stele
3 Disturber of the peace
4 Hibernia
5 Rimsky-Korsakov opera opener
6 Park art
7 Definitely not a know-it-all
8 Fannie ___

9 Steep
10 Venerable one
11 Legal O.K.
12 Abettor of Brutus
14 Rubber stamps
17 March honoree (with an aptly numbered clue)
20 Free of duties
23 Balance
25 "___ the bag!"
28 Fussbudgets
30 "Dragonwyck" author
33 Nail's companion
35 "Discus Thrower" sculptor of ancient Greece
37 With worry
38 Rip off
39 Eyepiece, in jargon
40 Bounce back
42 Ballroom dance
43 Nylons
46 Toots
48 Pulls apart
50 Get around
52 Streisand title role
55 Detroit River's destination

57 Runners try to pick it up
60 Just a bit
62 Amigo of Fidel

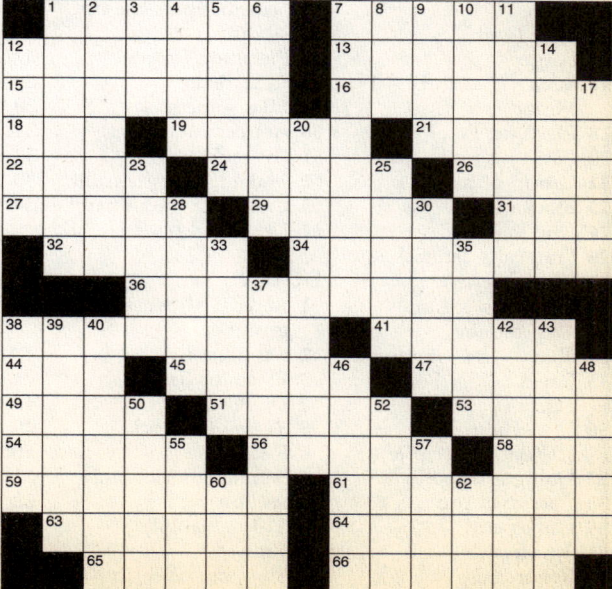

719 by Bob Klahn

ACROSS
1 Apple competitor
4 Gambler Holliday
7 Fifth-century pope
12 Green
14 The "S" in T. S. Eliot
16 Men of La Mancha
17 Farmer's tipcart
18 Cartridge type
19 Aviatrix, for short
20 Point of no return?
21 Hidden theme of this puzzle
24 Last word of "Finnegans Wake"
25 Make an appeal
26 White House monogram
27 Outfit
29 Make an appeal
30 Miners' sch.
32 Out of sorts
33 Friend of 21-Across
35 Affected by pollen
38 "Clan of the Cave Bear" heroine
39 Chosen number?
42 Anwar's successor
43 Pickpocket
44 Slangy hello
45 New York eng. sch.
46 Like 33-Across's apple
50 Suffix meaning "small one"
51 Pack animal?
52 Laid-back
53 Quick to blush
56 London barrister
58 Game officials
59 Making out
60 Hot time in Chile
61 Umpteen's ordinal?
62 Green lights

DOWN
1 Hosp. hookups
2 Doctors often carry them
3 Franciscus TV drama of the 60's
4 "Dream Lover" singer
5 With no letup
6 Price abbr.
7 Material
8 Pro follower
9 Dog, for short
10 Proof goof
11 Minimal ante
13 A bit obtuse
14 Maze word
15 Droopy-eyed
19 Corset result, perhaps
21 Where fat cats get thin
22 "I'm glad that's over!"
23 Sealy rival
28 N.H.-Vt. neighbor
30 Open
31 Whirligig
32 Actor Gerard
33 Boxer's title, briefly
34 Short shot?
35 Daphne and hazel
36 It's like home?
37 Bomber Boomer
39 Beethoven's only opera
40 Sight saver?
41 Peaked
43 Cockpit display
44 Mrs. Rockefeller
47 Former capital of Bolivia
48 Underground event
49 __ gland
54 It ended in 1806: Abbr.
55 Two or go follower
56 X
57 Football linemen: Abbr.

720 by Bernice Gordon

ACROSS
1 Record player
5 Retrieve, as fly balls
9 Conclude successfully
14 The King's middle name
15 Deal (with)
16 Forgo
17 Bach's "__ in B Minor"
18 Place for Pete?
20 Part of a radio wave
22 Group of nine
23 Blockaded
24 One-liner
25 Fraternity letter
26 Kind of cue
28 Con artist's game
32 Thai money
34 "Easy Aces" medium
35 Rap's Salt-N-Pepa, e.g.
36 __ Annie ("Oklahoma!" role)
37 Doing a takeoff
38 Canadian prov.
39 Upper cut?
41 Spirited
42 Regarding
43 "Dallas" actor Howard
44 Diner sign
45 "__ Doubtfire"
46 Ousted Ugandan
48 Argentine grasslands
51 Seasonal pick-me-up
54 90° arc
56 Place for Tyrone?
58 "__, Brute?"
59 Like some gases
60 Actress Merrill
61 A whole lot
62 Make the air fragrant
63 Call from the minaret
64 Unnamed ones

DOWN
1 Radical Mideast group
2 Shiraz native
3 Place for Jodie?
4 Discernment
5 Young haddock
6 Ruffian
7 Semicircular church section
8 $1000, slangily
9 Ritzy
10 Showing sincerity
11 Not on target
12 Part of the eye
13 Hang in the balance
19 Science course
21 Prefix with liberal
24 Nightclubs
26 Port Moresby resident
27 Pindar, e.g.
29 Place for Ben?
30 "__ We Got Fun?"
31 Marquand sleuth
32 Trunk cover
33 Direction for Solti
34 Andrew Johnson's birthplace
40 Carpentry machines
42 Antimacassar locale
45 Epithet for Anthony Wayne
47 Malory's "Le __ d'Arthur"
48 Hymn of praise
49 Architectural piers
50 Book-lined room
51 Like Homer's "Iliad"
52 Missing
53 Verdon of "Red Head"
54 "Jeopardy!" is one
55 Annapolis inits.
57 Ladies' room, of a sort

ACROSS

1 Vacuum tube filler
6 Wanders
11 Underwear initials
14 March composer
15 Key above G
16 Majors or Myles
17 Happenchance
19 Once ___ while
20 Barber of baseball
21 Sprite
22 Made
24 City near Utah Lake
26 "Desire Under the ___"
29 Head of a familia
30 Peeved
33 When Operation Overlord took place
34 Bygone coif
36 Mmes., across the Pyrenees
38 Dined
39 Jodie Foster's directorial debut, 1991
43 Douglas or alpine, e.g.
44 Choir members
45 Pub quaffs
46 Seventh day activity
48 Improves
51 Monkeyshine
53 Carriage, in the country
54 Cousin of the English horn
58 Bushy-tailed animal
60 Princess's sleep disturber
62 Dishcloth
63 Greek vowel
64 Child's means of propulsion
68 Soak flax
69 More cheerful
70 Takes to the trails
71 Opposite NNW
72 Brainstorms
73 Apply

DOWN

1 Houston player
2 Oarsman
3 Tour leader
4 W.W. II intelligence org.
5 N.B.A.'s Archibald
6 Club fund-raiser
7 Light switch position
8 Miss. neighbor
9 Chess finale
10 Robert Fulton's power
11 Notoriously risky social event
12 Respects
13 Sharpshooter
18 Fashion's Cassini
23 "Far out"
25 Shopping place
27 1939 James Stewart title role
28 Que follower, in song
31 ___ bene
32 Mr. Quayle
34 Drives away
35 A number 1
37 Christmas tree topper
40 Atty.'s degree
41 Parisian summers
42 What's more
43 Constitution creators
47 Actor Matheson
49 Narrows
50 Watchful one
52 Welsh dog
55 Accelerator's counterpart
56 Western
57 Cast out
59 Little hopper
61 North Carolina county
65 Drain cleaner
66 Pasture
67 General Mills cereal

ACROSS

1 Called, as a crow
6 English actor McCowen
10 Presage
14 Licorice flavor
15 Lake in northern Italy
16 Aloe
17 & 19 The Orient
20 Dad
21 Driver's lic. and others
22 Actress Matlin
24 Small boy
26 Verdi opera
27 Author of "The Meaning of Treason"
35 Wish undone
36 Misleading appearance
37 Fistfight
38 Culture base
40 Individual performances
42 "Beat it!"
43 Studio models
45 Neutral shade
47 Grab some grub
48 Canada
51 Rings of blooms
52 Tram
53 Mean-spirited
56 Prefix with glottis
58 Harbor pole
62 & 63 "Zip-A-Dee-Doo-Dah" movie
66 Moran of "Happy Days"
67 Finish line
68 Kazakhstan's ___ Mountains
69 800 exams
70 Boiled repast
71 Charged leptons

DOWN

1 Rustic stopover
2 Author Seton
3 Stray strand
4 What you will
5 One of the Tweedles
6 LSD
7 Writer Anita
8 Cassowary look-alike
9 Grand
10 Subdues by intimidation
11 More than a snack
12 Highland Gaelic
13 Thurmond of the N.B.A.
18 Bill attachments
23 Stage actress Rehan et al.
25 Comic strip bark
26 Pantomime
27 Sturm und ___
28 Soothsayer
29 Winner at Gettysburg
30 Carnival setups
31 Chou ___
32 Flammable anesthetic
33 Brown ermine
34 Gear element
39 Gets back to true
41 Coined money
44 Old-time actress Anna
46 Alfonso's queen
49 ___ peak (forehead point)
50 Imitation gold
53 Functions
54 Asta's mistress
55 Intertwine
56 Tours to be
57 "That was close!"
59 Mobile starter
60 Mikita of hockey
61 "___ Is Spinal Tap" (1984 movie)
64 Fill the bill
65 "Cheers" bartender

723 by James Nesi

ACROSS

1 Exclamation point
5 Nonvarsity player
10 Stinger
14 Bit of fishing gear
15 Produce a copy of
16 Opposite of aweather
17 Young Guthrie
18 Networks
19 Peruvian or Ohioan city
20 Homemade bomb
23 Pout
24 "Smoking or ___?" (waiter's query)
25 Photographic image, for short
28 Japanese lacquer box
30 Bird in the spring
35 Needle case
37 Joint Chiefs member: Abbr.
38 Blackmore's "___ Doone"
39 Pennsylvania insurrection, 1794
43 Inventor Nikola
44 ___ king
45 Spanish painter
46 Accommodates, as a Pullman
48 Escapade
50 Martial arts degree
51 Louvre pyramid architect
53 TV ad award
55 Lots of fun
63 With the bow, to a cellist
64 Cream
65 Like some food orders
66 Self-important people, colloquially
67 Mont ___, Alpine invasion route to Italy
68 Literary pen name
69 "Nana" writer
70 Financial plus
71 Woodworking tool

DOWN

1 Author Stoker
2 Dynamic start
3 ___ Gwyn, sweetheart of Charles II
4 ___ and doom
5 Disheveled
6 Wittier
7 Campus military org.
8 Kind of label
9 Naval guide
10 Poet Whitman
11 Inter ___
12 Trailer
13 Sound, as a bell
21 French pronoun
22 Sound, as a bell
25 Salamanders
26 Singer Merman
27 Semblance
29 Ryan or Tatum
31 Auctioneer's cry
32 Three-toned musical chord
33 ___ Gay
34 Arrested
36 ___ of Man
40 Honor society letter
41 Formal, but not too
42 Most prompt
47 One of the Iroquois
49 Frontiersman Carson
52 Wastes time
54 Weasellike mammal
55 Folk singer Joan
56 Therefore
57 School subj. for environmentalists
58 Diva Ponselle
59 Seven are deadly
60 She gets what she wants
61 Athena's shield
62 Daytime show

724 by Chuck Deodene

ACROSS

1 Bootlegging or extortion, e.g.
7 Enamored (of)
11 Gullet
14 Tropical lizard
15 Surmounted
17 Actress d'Abo
18 Like a desert water, usually
19 Missile's heading
21 Subject of many an ode
22 Develops slowly, as an idea
24 ___ mecum (handbook)
25 Insurgent, briefly
26 Eyewear for Col. Klink
29 Not a science, but ___
32 Trolley
36 Involving dispute
38 Smug
39 Nobel-winning poet Quasimodo
41 Tooth, in Torino
42 Drink recipe words
44 "___ the season . . ."
45 The "first martyr"
48 Retired
51 Erratic driver
54 Bonsai gardener
55 Medicinal herb
57 In a reverie
60 1994 Olympic rink star
61 Covered with soft hair
62 Somme season
63 1972 pact
64 Posture

DOWN

1 Lip
2 Muslim official
3 Unexpected pitch
4 Sammy and Danny
5 Make into law
6 Gong
7 Landlord's sign
8 Eggs
9 Trawlers' gear
10 Radiator drainpipe
11 Craze
12 Modify
13 Doorstop, maybe
16 Sporty Chevy
20 Ear doctor's device
22 ___ salami
23 Wizard
25 Hip-hop hits
27 Capt. of industry
28 Advance
30 Russian roulette need
31 Fed
33 Roman army commander
34 Those opposed
35 66 and others: Abbr.
37 Adherent: Suffix
40 Widespread
43 One-ups
45 Attentive
46 "Western Star" poet
47 Tidal bore
49 Greenland native
50 Magnetic induction unit
52 Some Ivy Leaguers
53 Baltic capital
56 Ripken, Jr. or Sr.
58 Pres. advisory grp.
59 "Well, I'll be!"

by David J. Kahn

ACROSS

1 1935 Triple Crown winner
6 Like some basements
10 Rely (on)
14 Horses, so to speak
15 "Essays of ___," 1823
16 Ball game finale?
17 Roof worker
18 Housing, as soldiers
20 Grenade with a wooden handle
22 Geometric curve
25 Tolstoy subject
26 Complain
27 Nebraska footballer
31 Urban map abbrs.
32 Meander
33 Actress Charlotte et al.
35 Tight-fisted exec, slangily
40 "A Teenager in Love" singer
41 Weekend wear
44 ___ Dhabi
47 Toy blowgun
50 Settle, in a way
53 Math ratios
54 ___ dye
55 1964 Anne Bancroft film, with "The"
59 Behind
60 See 25-Across
64 Teen worry
65 Ersatz
66 Cast a spell on
67 Costner role
68 Source for Pravda
69 Kind of shooter

DOWN

1 Go (for)
2 Longtime Kenyan president
3 Upholsterer's tool
4 Dickens villain
5 Kansas City stadium
6 Precludes
7 Descended
8 Actor O'Shea
9 Finnish composer Selim ___
10 "Midnight Cowboy" character
11 Root and Yale
12 Most reasonable
13 Paris zoo animals
19 Audience
21 Fraternity letter
22 Feign
23 Quarrel
24 Cheat
28 Compass heading
29 100 öre, in Sweden
30 ___ Claire, Wis.
34 Philadelphia university
36 Most chilly
37 70's-80's British track star
38 Workplace initials
39 Pro ___
42 Pince-___
43 Sign of a full house
44 ___ Way
45 Send packing
46 Deprives of strength
48 Myotonic reactions
49 Reason for a full house
51 W.W. I battleground
52 Where Kiev is: Abbr.
56 Okinawa's capital
57 Chronological periods
58 Stink
61 Chopper
62 Honor student's blemish
63 Summer Mass. hours

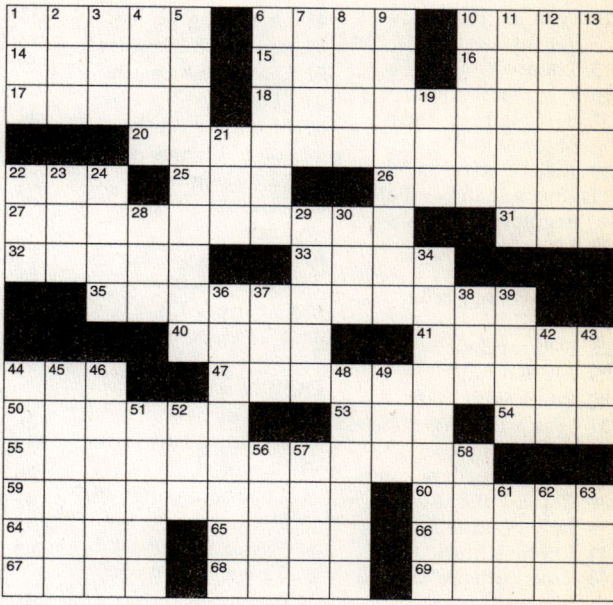

by Stephanie Spadaccini

ACROSS

1 Voting group
5 And so on . . .
8 Connection
13 The Hawkeye State
14 Money to tide one over
16 Cat-___-tails
17 Gambling game
19 Feeling of anxiety
20 Metric fractions
21 Is sick
23 Santa's laughs
24 12-mo. periods
25 It's frozen in Frankfurt
27 "What are you trying to ___?"
29 Wyoming Indian
31 Fleur-de-___
33 Began to melt
36 Rope fiber
38 Leopard features
39 Marx's "___ Kapital"
41 Stay
42 Open-air rooms
43 First Lady, 1969–74
45 Bering, for one: Abbr.
46 Procedures
48 Streisand title role
50 Abner's partner on old radio
51 Resort
54 Brit. fliers
56 Platoon, e.g.
58 Parish leader
60 First people to get invited
62 Booth Tarkington book
64 Turn
65 Cleveland's lake
66 Opposing
67 Down-at-the-heels
68 Bell and Kettle, e.g.
69 Pinocchio's give-away

DOWN

1 Itty-___
2 Take down, as a flag
3 1936 Olympian Jesse
4 Quitter's word
5 ___ fields (mythical paradise)
6 Overly
7 Site of Jesus's first miracle
8 Wedding reception speech
9 Hostel
10 Chuck out
11 ___ many words
12 New Jersey five
15 Corral sound
18 "Black Widow" actress Russell
22 Author Buscaglia
26 Hightailed it
28 Excuses
29 Duds
30 Get used (to)
32 Prefix with masochism
33 Agcy. that's got your #
34 Makes a choice
35 Old record
36 Sleepy-time guy
37 "The Ipcress File" author Deighton
40 Comedian Mort
44 "Rugs"
46 Shasta, e.g.: Abbr.
47 Beethoven dedication "Für ___"
49 Harebrained
51 Office worker
52 Rhymesters
53 Golf's Palmer, informally
54 Knocks
55 "I cannot tell ___"
57 Semester
59 Getz or Kenton
61 Turf
63 By way of

727 by Rose White

ACROSS

1 Close of a musical composition
5 Cancer
9 Bit of dust
14 Wall ___ (furniture item)
15 Tramp
16 Vietnam's capital
17 Bart Simpson catch phrase
20 Artist's stand
21 One side in baseball negotiations
22 Manet or Monet
25 Part of m.p.h.
26 NNW's opposite
27 Avoid
28 Deli sandwich
29 "Watch out!"
30 Prefix with byte
31 "Saturday Night Fever" locales
33 Classic cowboy song
38 Capital of Taiwan
39 Jolly good fellow
41 Coolio's music
44 Cole Porter's "___ Do It"
45 Aspiring actor's major
46 Inventor Whitney
47 Suffix with child or fiend
48 One going 75, e.g.
50 Approach intrusively
52 Diamond measure
53 "Ha!"
58 Musical with the song "Buenos Aires"
59 "___ delighted!"
60 "The ___ of the Lock"
61 Scout's work, for short
62 Faculty V.I.P.
63 1775 or 2001

DOWN

1 Cow's chew
2 Lennon's lady
3 Racket
4 Coatroom employee
5 Fox hunt, e.g.
6 Friend for Fido
7 Cain's victim
8 Jungle snake
9 Part of an auto dealership
10 Chess sacrifice, often
11 Tangle up
12 Unrefined
13 40's sex researcher
18 Loathe
19 Engage in arm-twisting
22 Coatroom hook
23 Keen
24 "Othello" villain
25 "GoodFellas" Oscar winner Joe
28 Dancer Gregory
31 The third dimension
32 Last-week-in-April honoree
34 Lucky charm
35 Party, south of the border
36 "If ___ a Hammer"
37 Reputation
40 Score to beat, in golf
41 Library patron
42 Nook
43 Ant-attracting activity
45 Start of a card game
48 Brazilian dance
49 Groom
51 "Beetle Bailey" dog
52 Surrender
54 Baby goat
55 Abu Dhabi's country: Abbr.
56 Student's 4.0, e.g.
57 Him's partner

728 by Bryant White

ACROSS

1 Upper Great Lakes Indian
7 Cheat
14 "Mme. Charpentier and Her Children" artist
15 Flirt
16 Chemical warfare gas
17 Weathercock's roost
18 Chisels, e.g.
19 Famously touchy one?
20 Address abbr.
21 Apple alternatives
22 Kind of colony
23 Tommy Atkins, e.g.
24 United Nations vote
25 Went off course
26 Homes abroad
27 Merrymaking
29 Car engine part
30 Object of a hunt in a 1929 mystery
34 Intl. org. based in D.C.
35 Forty-niners' equipment
37 Brews
40 Naval personnel
41 Evil spirit
42 Color in a Spanish sunset
43 Leftover
44 Wife of Lamech, in the Bible
45 War hero
46 Bake, in a way
47 Photographic surface
48 Gold coin of old
50 Beau
51 Modern time-waster
52 Consent
53 Pre-Life picture magazine
54 Removed, with "out"

DOWN

1 Panegyrics
2 Three-liter bottle
3 Sometime woe for Thurber
4 Is angry
5 Sports page stats
6 "You ___" (1983 Lionel Richie hit)
7 Thingamajig
8 Uniform
9 Stew
10 Female sandpiper
11 Scents
12 No man's land?
13 Stopping points
15 Subject of a 1926 Charlie Chan mystery
19 Famille members
22 Crowbars
23 ___ de Roma (Italian financial giant)
25 Sundance Kid's girlfriend and others
26 Repairs, in a way: Var.
28 Gold-mining province of Ecuador
29 Dared
31 Fin
32 Became rusty
33 Roundworm
36 Made round
37 1985 Jonathan Pryce film
38 Epoch in which mammals arose
39 Boots
40 Complains feebly
43 Fancy
44 "Falstaff" soprano
46 Mister, in Madras: Var.
47 Purplish brown
49 Animation frame
50 Crosscut

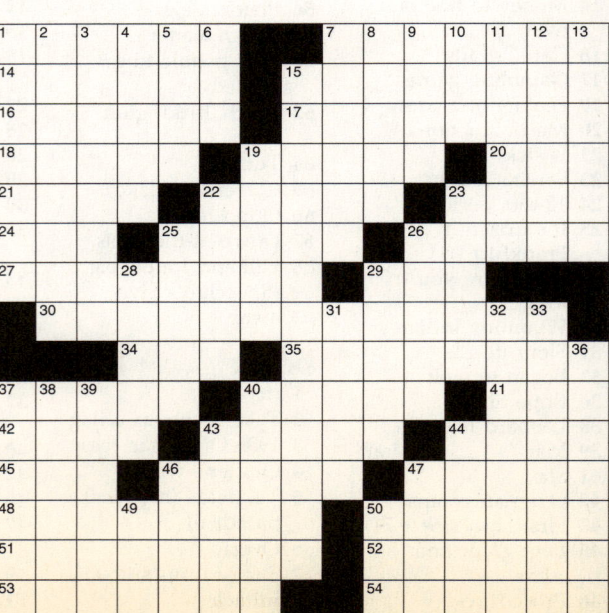

729

ACROSS

1 Tiller's place
4 Flop's opposite
9 Merchant R.H. ___
13 Money maker
14 Dessert bean
15 Newton knighted in 1705
17 Keg contents
18 "Help!" star
19 1959 Ritchie Valens hit
20 Behave
23 Multicolored
24 ___ Palmas, Spain
25 On an errand, maybe
26 Mortgage interest
27 Purple Heart, e.g.
30 "Low bridge! Everyone down!" canal
31 Officeholders
32 Circle of angels
33 Belief system
35 Is meticulous, with 53-Across
41 Abbr. in car ads
42 Many millennia
43 Word in an obit
44 Garroway of 50's TV
47 Itty-bitty map
49 "Interview with the Vampire" author
50 E.T.'s ship
51 "Life ___ beach"
52 Alta. neighbor
53 See 35-Across
59 Kind of wave
60 Scrub a tub, maybe
61 Bolivian export
62 Triangular treat
63 Be a ham
64 It's in the bag
65 NASA green lights
66 Make current
67 Catching of thought waves

DOWN

1 First bone donor
2 Tagalog speaker
3 Most microscopic
4 Seafood dish
5 Water artery
6 An embarrassing problem to face?
7 Is in a slump
8 Celebration
9 The original Goldfinger?
10 "Unto us ___ is given"
11 Openness
12 American in Habana
16 Brahman, for one
21 Study
22 Pronounced
26 Topper
27 Lack of oomph
28 Edifice extension
29 Spoils, with "on"
30 Trio of mommies?
32 Chance
34 Family nickname
36 Equal a bet
37 Ground-breaker
38 Sweet liqueur
39 Striped apparel, often
40 Heart of Billy Williams
44 Heating pipes
45 "Out of ___"
46 Spelling exercise?
48 Gamal of Egypt
49 Fan noise
51 Sailors' keys
52 Litter
54 Went to the bottom
55 Ne plus ultra
56 Diving bird
57 Guitar's ancestor
58 Piece of cake

730

ACROSS

1 Garden chemical brand
6 Good times
9 Bub
12 Pumice features
13 Gp. that sticks to its guns
14 Firefighter Red
16 It may be found on a lid
18 1920 Douglas Fairbanks role
19 Ethiopian prince
20 Slip ___ (blunder)
21 Dancers' railings
22 10-Down's food, perhaps
24 Post production
26 S.S.N.'s, e.g.
27 Repellent one
28 Fly in the tropics
29 Thun's river
30 ___ dixit (dogmatic statement)
31 Rove
33 Hotbed
34 Discombobulated
36 Shorten, as a sail
37 Greener
39 Der ___ (Adenauer monicker)
40 It's game
41 80's Nicaraguan president
44 Fan belt?
45 Solver's shout
46 Doctor's accessory
47 Field unit
48 À l'anglaise
50 ___ errand
52 It follows directions
53 Moony?
54 Kind of Majesty
56 Tricky curves
57 When Nancy bakes
58 ___-um (gnat)
59 Permanent job
60 Jenny, e.g.
61 Says it's so

DOWN

1 Centers of some theaters
2 Covent Garden feature
3 Violate
4 Guys
5 Worker's watchdog gp.
6 Annuls
7 Interim papers
8 Saying
9 Essential in knot-tying
10 Yorkshire dog
11 Encyclopedia features
14 Flowering shrub
15 Dali's "L'âge ___"
17 Svgs. ___
21 Iraqi city
23 "The Silent Partner" playwright
25 Suffix with ranch
32 Persona ___ (welcome guest)
34 Shown
35 Head of Haiti
38 Dries out, with "up"
42 Lamp spirits
43 Smell ___
49 New Guinea city from which Earhart made her last flight
51 Darling dog
54 "___ dear . . ."
55 Armistice mo.

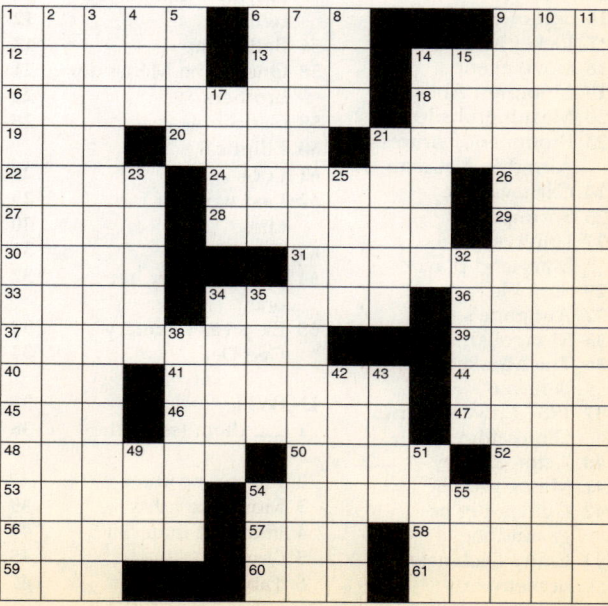

731 by Cathy Millhauser

ACROSS
1 "Alice in Wonderland" figure
6 Disney classic
11 Overcrowding antidote, initially
14 In ___ (prenatal)
15 Film director Resnais
16 Different ending
17 God
18 Minolta rival
19 Carrie married to Cavett
20 Modern choice #1
23 Former Swedish P.M. Ullsten
26 Ventnor or Vermont, e.g.: Abbr.
27 Sassoon creations
28 Modern choice #2
33 Theda "The Vamp"
34 Example, for example
35 Modern choice #3
42 Triple-layer treat
43 Cocoon-stage insect
45 Modern choice #4
51 Leading
52 She sang "At Seventeen"
53 Give a wave
54 Modern choice #5
59 That, in Spain
60 Suitor
61 Hoople or Houlihan
65 P.R. concern
66 "Unsafe at Any Speed" author
67 Logical starting point
68 First degs.
69 Plumbing tool
70 Gait problems

DOWN
1 Holy city of Iran
2 Tony winner Hagen
3 Comic book squeal
4 "___ Tu" ('74 hit)
5 Illinois State University site
6 Angel
7 Jai ___
8 Jazz flutist Herbie
9 Life story: Abbr.
10 Greenhorn
11 Showy flower
12 Welcome culmination
13 Valleys
21 Caesar's salad ingredients?
22 "Arabian Nights" flyer
23 Globe
24 Riffle
25 Earthy prefix
29 Egypt and Syr., once
30 ___ the other
31 Milne marsupial
32 It's "hard" for the French
36 "Do-si-do" dos
37 Muff
38 Car monogram of yore
39 Jupiter's mother
40 Courage
41 Bee's charge, in Mayberry
44 Shtick
45 Cycle parts
46 Word in a children's title
47 Contemptuous utterance
48 Coyote State capital
49 Shaver
50 Varmint
51 Bitter
55 Like Robinson Jeffers's stallion
56 End notes?
57 Need a bath
58 Approach the terminal
62 Lord of fiction
63 Alley from Moo
64 Apt. ad info

732 by Julian Ochrymowych & Amy Goldstein

ACROSS
1 ___ Rica
6 Job for Perry Mason
10 Career summary
14 Top grade
15 "___ We Got Fun?"
16 Son of Seth
17 Jockey's handful
18 Govt. agent
19 Mounties: Abbr.
20 Meaningful silence
23 Prominent features of Alfred E. Neuman
24 Carnaval site
25 Shrimpish
27 University of Maryland player
29 Stumble
32 Antigone's sister
35 Mongolian desert
36 The Monkees' "___ Believer"
37 1987 Edward James Olmos film
40 Actor Chaney
41 Minor profits?
42 Guinea pig or groundhog
43 Emily Dickinson's hometown
45 Air freshener scent
46 Nixon and Schroeder
47 Black-eyed item
48 Shows approval
52 Film in which Hayley Mills played twins
56 Ballet leap
58 One of the Menendez brothers
59 Gaucho gear
60 Elliptical
61 Look
62 Last word of fairy tales
63 Cravings
64 Flexible Flyer, for one
65 Ex-press secretary Dee Dee

DOWN
1 ___ diem (seize the day)
2 Puccini product
3 More like a fox
4 Filament material
5 Org.
6 Tabby treat
7 "We ___ please"
8 Breeze
9 Mediterranean spouter
10 Against
11 Stimulus
12 Mix of westerns
13 Venomous viper
21 Debts
22 Greek vowel
26 It's south of Saudi Arabia
28 Sign a check
29 Stylish, in the 60's
30 Basque, e.g.
31 Hair splitter
32 Mallorca, por ejemplo
33 Lively dance
34 Whisky-vermouth cocktail
35 Mdse.
38 Place to meet following a tennis match
39 Pick out of a lineup
44 Mertz and Merman
45 Looked too soon
47 Cracker Jack bonus
49 Speechify
50 Library gadget
51 Trains, in a way
53 Cribbage counters
54 Asia's ___ Sea
55 Streetcar
56 "The ___ Luck Club"
57 Night before

ACROSS

1 Punchline reaction
5 Detective with a number one son
9 Dramatist Chekhov
14 Algerian seaport
15 Novelist Jaffe
16 "The Cloister and the Hearth" author
17 He's timely and reliable
20 Admits
21 Stream animals
22 "The shakes"
23 Troubles
24 Writer W. E. B.
28 Gielgud and Olivier, e.g.
29 Command to Fido
32 Woodwinds
33 Sicilian smoker
34 Bullring figure
35 He's friendly and party-loving
38 "... ___ best friend"
39 Prong
40 Sam's sweetheart on "Cheers"
41 Gobbled
42 Regarding
43 Secured
44 ___ bien
45 Spoil
46 Go at
49 Window type
54 He's versatile and adept
56 "A Message From ___"
57 November word
58 Actress Lollobrigida
59 Paris subway
60 Pulitzer-winning author Herbert
61 Road for Caesar

DOWN

1 Popular roadside chain, for short
2 "Pretty Maids All in ___"
3 Nuclear fission discoverer
4 Novelist Radcliffe and others
5 Horror movie locales
6 Says "to-whoo"
7 ___ Domini
8 Turner or Cole
9 Mountain ridges
10 Tree houses
11 Record
12 Bouquet
13 New Jersey five
18 Not the modest sort
19 Cheer
23 Recoil
24 Belief
25 Ship sinker
26 Singer in white buck shoes
27 Multivolume dicts.
28 Shorthand user
29 Energy type
30 "Goodnight" girl of song
31 Trifled
33 Gives out
34 50-Down, e.g.
36 An end in ___
37 One of 50-Down
42 Light musical piece
43 Maven
44 Selfish one
45 Island near Sicily
46 In ___ (stuck)
47 Garage event
48 Burns, e.g.
49 Block
50 Christmas travelers?
51 Delete, with "out"
52 Hawaiian goose
53 Winter Palace resident
55 Actress Gardner

ACROSS

1 Wasn't colorfast
4 "Le ___ de Monte Cristo"
9 Napoleon's force
14 Gardner of "Mogambo"
15 1935 Triple Crown winner
16 Closes in on
17 Coastal area
19 Birdlike
20 Unyielding
21 Driver's need
23 Old town official
25 Gets the soap out
26 Investigated, with "about"
29 No-caffeine drink
31 Drives
33 Freight weight
34 Part of Q.E.D.
37 ___ capita
38 Had a hankering
41 Anger
42 Barber's action
44 Stars and Bars inits.
45 Commandment breaker
47 Batman, to the Joker
50 Astronomer Carl
51 "___ and rejoice": Psalms
53 Under, in verse
55 Largest newspaper in Calif.
57 Became less clear
61 Chilean port
62 Major pipe
64 Family car
65 "Hard ___!" (nautical command)
66 Mr. Gershwin
67 Idyllic spots
68 Legal wrongs
69 "___ Miz"

DOWN

1 Pro ___
2 Eager
3 Zilch, to Zapata
4 Like Lahr's lion
5 Mideasterner
6 Dull finishes
7 Word before more and merrier
8 Jazzman Hines
9 Tylenol alternative
10 Income
11 Watch's center
12 Clear the slate
13 Workers of puzzledom
18 Host
22 Worth and Castle
24 Give new job skills
26 Small drinks
27 Augury
28 Full moon occurrence
30 "___ Ryan's Express"
32 Leave the union
35 Space
36 Slender-billed sea bird
39 Palm Sunday mount
40 Warps
43 Big-billed sea bird
46 Biblical prophet
48 Marseille moms
49 Pie slice, in geometry
51 World-weary
52 Like many seals
54 On the qui vive
56 The Sultan of ___
58 Dublin legislature
59 Dublin's country
60 Genetic materials
63 G.I.'s address

735 by Wayne Robert Williams

ACROSS

1 Huck Finn's craft
5 Lacking
8 Propped-up shelter
14 Composer Satie
15 Tripmeter setting
16 Make well-liked
17 Site of Iolani Palace
19 No big thing
20 Docs united
21 Monkeylike
23 Baseball's Tommie et al.
24 Counterpoise
26 Itchin' (to)
28 "The Age of Innocence" director
30 Asian holiday
33 Wet
36 Sort
37 Faction
38 Zodiac sign
39 Hosp. employees
40 Commended for merit
41 Russian's neighbor
42 Large expanse
43 Peaceful demonstrations
44 Author Amy
45 Highest large lake in the world
47 Author Jong
49 Cupidity
53 Bo-o-oring
55 Become spoiled
57 Lon ___ of Cambodia
58 Muse of astronomy
60 Violin virtuoso
62 Not making one's quota
63 Request of Vanna
64 "Yikes!"
65 Jargons
66 Article in a periódico
67 Rib or jaw

DOWN

1 Treatment center
2 Appetite stimulant
3 Ultimate
4 Ref's decision
5 Just a bit
6 ___-than-thou attitude
7 Certain pronouns
8 Allowed to
9 Infuriate
10 River into the Gulf of Venice
11 Ikhnaton's wife
12 Whopper
13 Magnetite and malachite
18 Pricks
22 Cads
25 Resort in the Rockies
27 Put to
29 Site of 1956 warfare
31 Paradise
32 Turner and Williams
33 Crackers
34 "Elsa's Dream," e.g.
35 Longfellow maiden
37 Raga instrument
39 Mark sale prices
40 Bug with a loud love call
42 [as printed]
43 Cannibals and headhunters
45 The when of an event
46 Changing booth
48 Small to-do
50 Architect Jones
51 Schwarzenegger title role
52 Slur over
53 Primary intersections
54 Hurler Hershiser
56 Fiery gemstone
59 Classifieds
61 Woodpecker's tool

736 by A.J. Santora

ACROSS

1 Former Fox sitcom
4 Eat, with "down"
8 Sir Henry ___ (Hotspur)
13 Physical, e.g.
15 Hot-rod engine, for short
16 Loren's love
17 "99 Luftballons" singer
18 Door
19 Ring attire
20 Perplexity
22 TV premiere of 1/23/83
24 Suddenly goes crazy
26 Opposite
27 Enjoy, as gossip
29 Newswoman Wertheimer
31 Maximum rating, often
32 Unnamed others
33 Curvaceous leg
34 Actress ___ B. David
36 TV premiere of 1/16/81
42 Phon. alphabet
43 Cowboy's sweetie
44 Front end
45 ABC countries and more
48 Boston and Kenilworth, e.g.
50 Rubik's Cube company
51 Decent
53 Vegetarian purchase
55 TV premiere of 11/4/53
57 Strike out
60 Clear
61 Scoreboard number
63 Wall ___ (furniture purchase)
64 "___ Mio"
65 Leading surrealist
66 Erupter of 1832
67 Checks out
68 Daze
69 Bando of the A's

DOWN

1 Chateaubriand hero
2 They have pull
3 Kitchen container
4 Miserly
5 Machinist's ___ nut
6 Drop
7 Not outside
8 Mine-sweeping apparatus
9 Overdramatize
10 Bob, at times
11 Goalie's turf
12 Toadies
14 TV premiere of 12/11/80
21 Plan, with "out"
23 Ultimate object
25 Serb or Czech
27 Biblical verb finale
28 "So that's what you mean!"
30 Show on a screen
33 More serious
35 TV premiere of 9/21/93
37 Incidents
38 Eye shade?
39 Shows
40 ___ T
41 Pointed tool
45 Wall Street sale
46 Waken
47 Some murals
49 Distinct styles
50 Dander
52 Wading bird
54 Pelé's first name
56 Stop
58 Rock's Turner
59 Bibliography abbr.
62 1990 Robert Morse Broadway role

ACROSS

1 Place for a bucket
11 After-afterthought
14 Driver's rest
15 Sole protector
16 Kind of boat
17 Marble tower site
18 Low-voiced ladies
19 Limb extenders
21 Threatening words
25 Originate
26 Creek constrictors
29 Cries of pain
30 The Beatles' "I'm a ___"
31 G.E. bought it in 1986
32 Peppard TV role
35 On ___ (from the barrel)
36 Paul's singing partner
37 Incline
38 British verb ending
39 Me, to a griever?
40 Walked heavily
41 "Smoking or ___?"
42 Jack of rhyme
44 Haw alternative

45 Flying eagle of the 1850's
46 Dark meat option
47 "Potemkin" locale
50 Responded like Simba
52 Worked in whiteface
55 Practiced
56 1963 Chiffons hit
61 Trick
62 Too-willing witness
63 For example
64 Ride and others

DOWN

1 World banking org.
2 Brown beverage
3 Card catalogue abbr.
4 "Be prepared" and "Semper fi"
5 Branch shelter
6 Decided on
7 On a roll
8 Addams Family cousin
9 New beginning
10 Shady ones
11 Goliath, e.g.
12 Like most bowl games

13 Cecil of cartoons
15 Dick's running mate
20 Spilled the beans
22 In the distant past
23 Overran
24 Search dogs' target
26 Decide by chance
27 Window washer's problem?
28 Much
32 "Nothing ___ truth . . ."
33 Calendar abbr.
34 Dutch city
43 Have the same tense, e.g.
45 Recovered
48 Look favorably (upon)
49 Tendon
51 The i's have them
53 Red rind contents
54 Chip's chipmunk chum
57 Be off guard
58 Hellenic H
59 Commerce regulator: Abbr.
60 Foreign money

ACROSS

1 Dwellers on the Upper Oder
10 Coasts
15 Attaching
16 "The Forsyte Saga" novel
17 It's been said
18 ___ bug in one's ear (gives ideas)
19 Praise
20 Perrault's "La ___ au bois dormant"
22 Popular toy company
23 Pompous fellow
24 Boston literary family
26 Denials
27 Fido's offering
28 Été month
29 Skippy rival
30 Perniciousness
32 More than unpleasant
33 "Double Fantasy" singer
34 Quincy specialty
37 John Scopes, for one
39 $C_7H_5N_3O_6$, familiarly
40 Enwreathe
42 Eschews robots

43 Résumé info
44 Actress Swenson
45 Oomph
46 Musical notes
47 Not completely clean
49 New Deal grp.
52 Cultural matters, with "the"
54 Many a Lett
55 Hard up
56 Second-generation Japanese-American
58 Northern California city
60 "Murphy"
61 Dial number
62 It's currently positive
63 1983 Jackson-McCartney hit

DOWN

1 Five-time Super Bowl coach
2 Nitpicking amounts
3 Kind of position
4 Squeezed (out)
5 Gawain's title
6 One way to tie a knot

7 Only Veep from Maryland
8 Word with family or winter
9 Make crystal-clear
10 Gas station display
11 Galoot
12 Singer whose middle name is Hercules
13 City on the Raccoon
14 Remains to see
21 Remain free
24 Like the streets of Holmesian London
25 Like an angry lobster?
27 Ex-con, maybe
30 Language of 14 million
31 Certifies
34 Swift runner of myth
35 U-boat gear
36 "A nickel ain't worth a dime anymore" et al.
38 Salary limit
41 Hypothetical supercontinent
45 Some hotels

48 Flavorful
49 Brewer Adolph
50 Met soprano Mary
51 Perot theme song
53 Pit

55 Weaker ones
57 Displeasure
59 "Now I get it!"

ACROSS

1 Wise man in a turban
6 Cleopatra's snakes
10 Furniture buildup
14 Belly button
15 Blood obstruction
16 Disappear ___ thin air
17 Perfect
18 Sailor's tail one
19 Protected, as the feet
20 Vacation memento
23 Foam
24 ___ Park, Colo.
25 Sign up with again
29 Tina Turner's ex
31 Texas shrine
32 Better half
34 Knife
38 Start of a message on a 20-Across
41 Narrow wood piece
42 Termites' kin
43 Frozen
44 Mata Hari, e.g.
45 Cider ingredients
46 Perspire
50 Agitate
52 End of a message on a 20-Across
59 "Besides that . . ."
60 Baseball's Musial
61 Passover feast
62 Orange waste
63 Cooking fat
64 More logical
65 "Auld Lang ___"
66 ___ law (principle of electricity)
67 Gems

DOWN

1 Barber's motion
2 Desert stream
3 With: Fr.
4 Companion of potatoes
5 Magic trick
6 Performed
7 Smacks
8 Visitor to Kublai Khan
9 Marie and others: Abbr.
10 Records
11 Take off the topper
12 Five-and-ten, e.g.
13 Lincoln's in-laws
21 Hasten
22 Caddie's offering
25 Stadium cheers
26 Carrier to Tel Aviv
27 Coffee, in slang
28 Leave out
29 "How sweet ___!"
30 Barbie's beau
32 Lots
33 Where the rudder is
34 Red's signification
35 Money drawer
36 Gallic girlfriend
37 Infirmary capacity
39 Clothing chain since 1969, with "The"
40 After-dinner order
44 Hogs' home
45 Tire filler
46 Exchanges
47 Aviator Post
48 City on the Ruhr
49 ". . . like ___ in the head"
50 Group of bees
51 Watches over
53 Norway's capital
54 Salt Lake's home
55 Pile
56 Author Ferber
57 Movie unit
58 Misses the mark

ACROSS

1 Discontinue the countdown
6 Sweet raisin cake
11 Black bird
14 The Pineapple Island
15 An archangel
16 Salt Lake City athlete
17 One way to make a million
19 Madrid Mrs.
20 Takes too much, in a way
21 Tree trimming
22 Fuss
23 Not "for here"
24 Eventually
26 Israelites' home, in Genesis
29 Continental line
31 Made a parabola
32 Feline property
35 Slobodan Milosevic, e.g.
36 Party handout
37 It freezes your flippers
38 Gives maximum effort
40 Eyelashes
41 Long-eared hound
42 Particular photo
43 Frasier's ex
45 ___ of faculty
46 1979 revolution site
47 Stun guns
50 "___ Lay Dying"
53 "Smoking or ___?"
54 Tightly sealed containers
56 Remnant
57 Caper
58 China's Zhou ___
59 Prefix with functional
60 Play for the Red Wings, e.g.
61 Decisive wins

DOWN

1 Besides which
2 Madam
3 Half the binary system
4 Charlotte of "The Facts of Life"
5 Went quietly
6 Belushi catchphrase
7 Mr. Parseghian and others
8 Kind of messenger
9 Collapse
10 Gore and Capp
11 Small whirlwinds
12 Open-air rooms
13 Pooped
18 Converse with the deaf
22 Treasonous talk
23 Damon Runyon's name for gangster Arnold Rothstein
25 Zip
26 Short-of-breath breath
27 Hydrox rival
28 Wild expanse
29 Fairway damage
30 Not excluded from
32 Archibald of basketball
33 Yalies
34 Canine command
36 Home made of glass
39 Transportation that's booming?
40 Gripper
42 Start, as of an idea
43 Like notebook paper
44 Literary device
45 Trey preceder
48 Ancient Roman decrees
49 Business attire
50 Human rights org.
51 Three-handed card game
52 Sister of Nephthys
54 Anatomical duct
55 Enero-to-enero period

741 by Glenton Petgrave

ACROSS
1 Prologue
8 Beats
14 Cracks
15 Greet, in a way
16 Courting chair
17 Slow-witted
18 Easily seen
19 Soaked
21 Wore away
22 Major, for example
23 Game from the French for "five winning numbers"
24 "The Bronx Zoo" star of 80's TV
26 "A Song of Old Hawaii" accompaniment
27 Masking
29 Chaps
30 Beachhouse, often
32 Home on a height
34 Whirling
36 Ornamental badge
40 The Mets, but not the Yankees, for short
42 Zero
43 Crown
46 They may be wild
48 Reproductive necessity
49 Singes
51 Winter comment
52 Payments
53 Blackguard
54 Crinkled fabric
56 Sweetheart
57 Uncut
59 Outfit
61 Porter
62 Takes up
63 Diner table staples
64 Part

DOWN
1 Angry, and not by accident
2 King's title
3 1922 Ted Lewis hit "___ Day"
4 Show of anger
5 Close friend, in slang
6 Broke off
7 Land on Lake Peipus
8 Kind of kick
9 Where dinars buy dinners
10 Army member
11 Baja creature
12 On the Big Board
13 Says with scorn
14 Parliamentary procedure
20 One done for
23 Baked in an oven
25 To Milton it was "dewy-feathered"
27 Huzzah
28 Certain store owner
31 Jazz pianist McCoy ___
33 Veil of ___ (mystery)
35 Cousin of the loon
37 Menace
38 Ghetto sight
39 Stationer's supplies
41 Outdo
43 Get to
44 Thickset
45 Saint, maybe
47 Nativity representation
50 Free-for-all
52 Tall, slender wineglass
55 Capitol Hill workers, for short
56 Word with tax or free
58 Hospital sect.
60 Sprocket

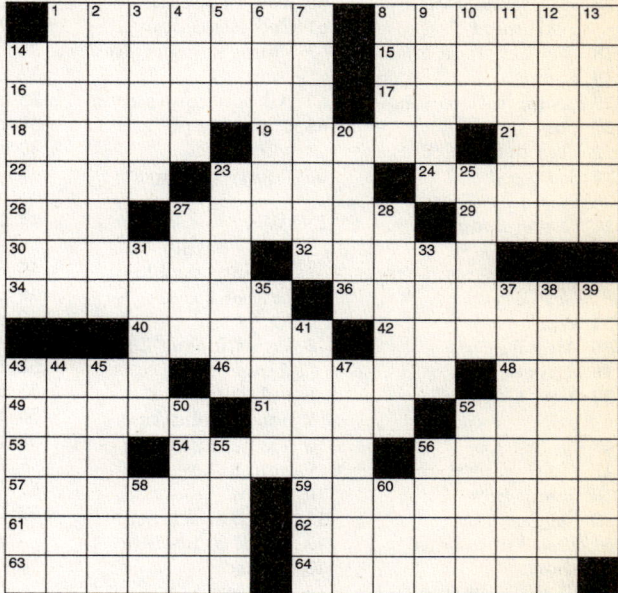

742 by Edward Early

ACROSS
1 Gutter site
5 Insomnia cause?
9 Marmon ___ (first auto to win the Indy 500)
13 Sick as ___
14 Onetime Aegean land
16 Actress Chase
17 Start of a quotation by 9-Down
20 Neighbor of Braz.
21 Popular machine
22 Detroit products
23 Kind of code
25 25, e.g.
28 Runway
30 ___-daisy
31 Signal since 1912
34 Indulgent
35 Sister of Selene
36 Straddling
37 Middle of quote
41 All ___ (attentive)
42 Zinger
43 Acht, ___, zehn
44 1994 U.S. Open golf champion
45 Star of "Mon Oncle"
46 Tidy up
48 Poznan's location
50 Seats, slangily
52 Peacock "eyes"
55 Addition
57 Suffix with insist
58 End of quote
62 "___ boy!"
63 Ruth's mother-in-law
64 Western star Richard
65 Admit, with "up"
66 Girlie show props
67 Certain investor's agreement, for short

DOWN
1 Gobble
2 More than appreciates
3 1985 Tom Hanks comedy
4 Kind of maniac
5 Losing proposition
6 Offspring of 7-Down
7 Rest stop
8 Noisy bird
9 See 17-Across
10 ___ Romeo
11 Potato part
12 Mountain route
15 1991 Sondheim show
18 Bag
19 Like a haunted house
24 Hamas adherents
26 San ___
27 Savvy about
29 Galatea's sculptor, in myth
31 Salisbury Plain attraction
32 Comic strip reaction
33 Aix-les-Bains, e.g.
36 Chills
37 One of 18
38 Movie computer
39 Bit
40 ___, Minn. (1862 Sioux uprising site)
45 Highway robbery?
47 Ballpoint part
48 Guilty and others
49 Stuffed deli delicacy
51 Dictator's aide
52 One of five Norse kings
53 Île de la ___
54 Salamanders
56 Ad exec George ___
59 Capture
60 Gunk
61 ___ Lingus

743   by Rich Norris

ACROSS
1 Wackos
10 Certain deodorant
15 Exotic
16 Uplift
17 Servopneumatic instrument
18 Diet beverage brand
19 Blemish
20 Bears, in Barcelona
21 Too
22 Plan detail
24 Scattered
26 Fortune 500 orgs.
27 Descendants
29 Signs
30 Big-house connector
31 Get cozy
33 Work
35 Alphabet trio
36 Exceeder
39 New Deal org.
42 Idle
43 Pianist José
47 Help wanted abbr.
48 Seine sights
50 Demanding
51 1960 Pirate hero, for short
52 Fictional beamer
54 Barbecue accessory
55 Betting window option
57 Gather
59 Long ___
60 Montana, once
61 Red chalcedony
63 Plume's owner, in song
64 Albuquerque's river
65 The arms of Morpheus
66 Poorly equipped

DOWN
1 Stuffs hastily
2 Patient's problem
3 One in a cast
4 X
5 Word for the Lone Ranger
6 Publicity
7 Some mollusks
8 Vachel Lindsay poem
9 Sun. talk
10 Brains
11 Truck attachment
12 Track competitor
13 Baffled
14 Reprimands
21 Saint's home
23 Shares
25 Theaters of old
28 Month after Av
32 Symphony originally dedicated to Napoleon
34 "I'm game!"
37 ___ Alto
38 Sticking places
39 Binds
40 Kind of cable
41 "The Card Players" artist
44 Prepare the house for sale, e.g.
45 Bucket passers
46 Sang
49 Solid, polycyclic alcohol
52 Throat trouble
53 Honks, as a goose
56 Badger group
58 Where the Ucayali flows
61 Dernier ___
62 Old French love poem

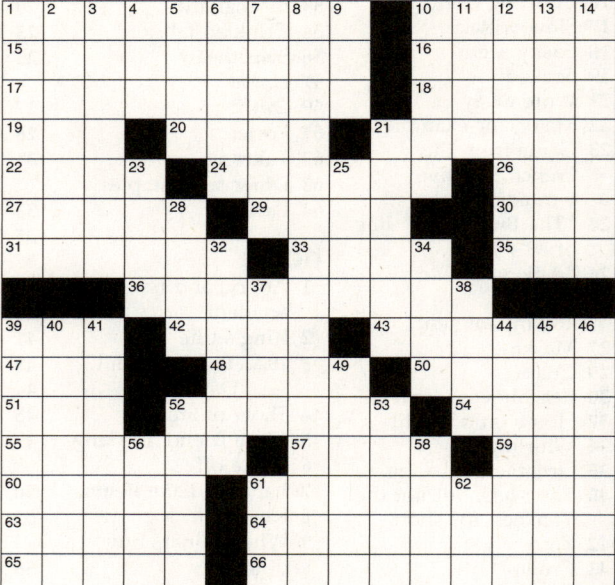

744   by David Ellis Dickerson

ACROSS
1 Kindergarten instruction
5 Onetime La Scala tenor
11 Shake up
14 Brook
15 Unlocked
16 Hollywood's Thurman
17 Star of "The Invisible Man"
19 Hoover, for one
20 Zeus or Jupiter, e.g.
21 School grp.
22 Wood-shaping tool
23 Fleur-de-___
25 Mr. Sondheim
27 Not left in the lurch
32 "The Time Machine" people
33 Speckled horse
34 Poet Wilfred
36 Meanies
39 Religious offshoot
40 Pay by mail
42 Onetime Texaco rival
43 Not on the level
45 Talkative Barrett
46 Prefix with plasm
47 Not cleric
49 Two-pointer, the hard way
51 Comes out
54 Kin of calypso music
55 Beats it
56 Piggie
58 Orientals, e.g.
63 Belief
64 Star of "The Vanishing" (1993 version)
66 Bedlam site
67 Spoke from the soapbox
68 Pull off a coup
69 Author Beattie
70 Choir voices
71 Minus

DOWN
1 Electrical paths
2 Gyp
3 Ali, once
4 Coin that's not a coin
5 One who shares a masthead billing
6 ___ financing (car ad phrase)
7 Sow's opposite
8 Rightmost column
9 A century in Washington
10 ___ bodkins
11 Star of "Without a Trace"
12 Flabbergast
13 Japanese noodle soup
18 Kewpie
22 Orbiting points
24 Betsy Ross, e.g.
26 "Don't Bring Me Down" rock band
27 Nocturnal bear?
28 They might be heard a thousand times
29 Star of "Missing"
30 All broken up
31 Disband, postwar
35 Hirschfeld hides them
37 This, in Madrid
38 Chimney grit
41 Ale mugs
44 Barrister's headgear
48 The "c" in etc.
50 Actress Lemmons
51 "My Fair Lady" lady
52 Stoneworker
53 Divans
57 Newts
59 False god
60 Dickensian chill
61 Eerie loch
62 Concorde et al.
64 Book after Esther
65 A stingy fellow?

ACROSS

1 Buddy
5 Balance sheet listing
10 Helper: Abbr.
14 New Rochelle college
15 They fly in formation
16 Wife of ___ (Chaucer pilgrim)
17 Ordnance
18 Fill with glee
19 Out of the weather
20 Battle in which Lee defeated Pope
23 Sunday talk: Abbr.
24 Activity
25 Fountain treat, for short
26 Battle in which Bragg defeated Rosecrans
31 Singer Coolidge et al.
32 Corner
33 11th-century date
36 Heaven on earth
37 Change
39 Earth sci.
40 Marry
41 Fine poker holdings
42 Hawks
43 Battle in which Grant defeated Bragg

46 John Wilkes Booth, e.g.
50 Tempe sch.
51 Items on a "must" list
52 Battle in which Lee defeated Burnside
57 Retread, e.g.
58 Go along (with)
59 Wrangler's pal
61 Overlook
62 Some are heroic
63 Mideast land
64 Promontory
65 Kilmer opus
66 Niño's nothing

DOWN

1 Spy grp.
2 Baseball, informally
3 Not deserved
4 Not fem.
5 Work to do
6 Infrequently
7 Petticoat junction
8 "Cómo ___ usted?"
9 Chelsea Clinton, e.g.
10 Embarrass
11 Nacho topping

12 Rib-eye
13 Ones nearby
21 Dumbarton ___ (1944 meeting site)
22 P.D.Q.
23 Item in a hardware bin
27 Fire
28 Nuclear experiment
29 Coffee server
30 Start for fly or about
33 Three-hanky film
34 City once named for Stalin
35 Rick's beloved et al.
37 Herr's "Oh!"
38 "Cry ___ River"
39 General Motors make
41 Parcel of land
42 High-hat
44 Words before "I'm yours"
45 Tax
46 "Sweet" river of song
47 Record blot
48 Actress Garr et al.
49 Playwright Clifford
53 Engrossed
54 Mr. Stravinsky

55 Saskatchewan tribe
56 Atop
60 Kind of testing

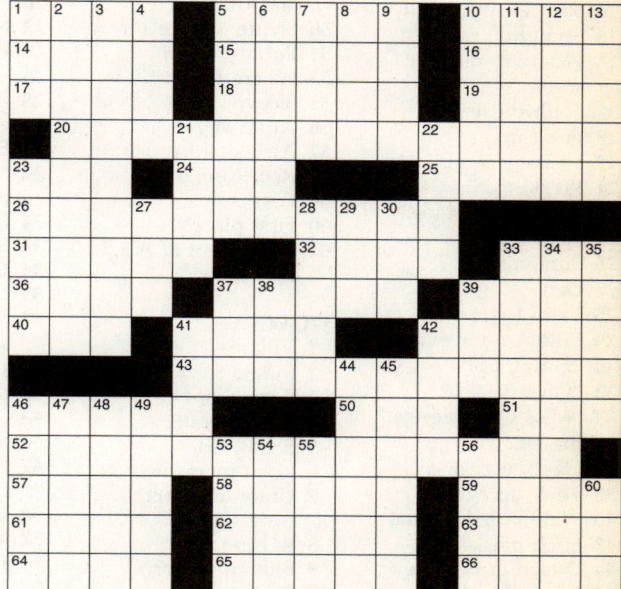

ACROSS

1 Shakespearean title start
5 Rock's UB40, e.g.
10 Sailor, informally
14 Marciano match
15 Doorbell
16 Shooter of thunderbolts
17 Alexander the Great's horse
19 Strauss's "___ Nacht in Venedig"
20 Studio
21 Not a member of the reserves
23 "The Wizard of Oz" producer Mervyn
25 Indy champ Luyendyk
26 Mr. Levant
29 Henpeck, in a way
31 1966 Michael Caine role
34 Cicadas' sounds
36 L-P connection
38 "Lohengrin" heroine
39 A dog's age
40 Winter wear
43 Blue chip initials

44 Sacramento arena
46 Trivial Pursuit piece
47 Skirmish
49 Sedaka and Simon
51 Mouths
53 Dentist's gas
54 Peace Garden State: Abbr.
56 Luigi's ladder
58 1957 Henry Fonda film, with "The"
61 Surfaces
65 Latin 101 word
66 Dale Evans's horse
68 Past due
69 City SSE of Buffalo
70 ___ breve
71 Kuwaiti leader
72 Quasimodo's charges
73 Harper's Weekly cartoonist

DOWN

1 Palindromic pop group
2 Oaf
3 Time founder
4 Brilliant
5 Fall color
6 Styx ferryman

7 Up to
8 Big birds
9 Seed cover
10 Hospital-clean
11 Tex Ritter's horse
12 Top of the line
13 ___ Rabbit
18 General Beauregard
22 Southern constellation
24 Bellyaches
26 Indian, for one
27 "Encino Man" star Pauly ___
28 Ulysses S. Grant's horse
30 Wildebeest
32 Cordage fiber
33 Glutton
35 Spring riser
37 Frequently, in poetry
41 Cruise port
42 Gas station attendant
45 Graybeard
48 1984 sci-fi film
50 Plopped down
52 Solvent
55 Barbecue entree
57 Solemn assents
58 Yarn

59 Teheran V.I.P.
60 "I before e, except after c," e.g.
62 Desert monster
63 Plumbing joints
64 Three-handed card game
67 ___ Aviv

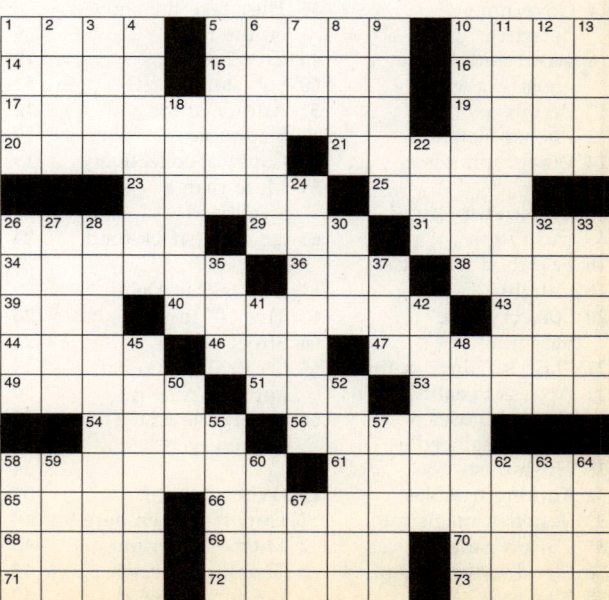

747 by A.J. Santora

ACROSS

1 C.D. follower
4 Goodbye, to Gaius
8 Release
13 Ex of Mickey
14 Secures, informally
15 Straight
16 Where to make a scene
17 Sophisticated
18 Fired up
19 Holiday exhibit
21 Working
23 French seasoning
24 Finery
25 Sundials?
27 Den
28 Latin I word
29 Like Amundsen
30 "Hurry up!"
32 "Give it ___"
33 "Miss Otis Regrets," maybe?
37 Hanoi occasion
38 Took up again
40 Web-footed animal
43 High pair
44 Queen of heaven
45 Kind of crab
47 Bel ___ (operatic style)
48 "What a good boy ___"
49 Home of the 40-Down
50 Shade of blue
51 Pottery luster
53 Where Bountiful is
55 Sleeve
56 At an angle
57 An old story
58 Red Rose, e.g.
59 Fusses
60 First place
61 Equivalent of A.S.T., for clocks

DOWN

1 Villains
2 Inflate
3 Equipment
4 French water
5 Starve (for)
6 Luau memento
7 Union contract provision
8 Raising
9 Blowup: Abbr.
10 Brief promo
11 Dungeons & Dragons devotees
12 To avoid the alternative
15 Café additive
20 Like some staircases
22 N.F.L. scores
25 Forbear
26 Saskatchewan city
28 Part of an M.D.'s educ.
31 Exceeds
32 "Famous" cookie name
34 Be giddy
35 Swamp
36 Emotionally secure
39 "Welcome" site
40 Family in a 1936 best seller
41 Least wild
42 Bagatelle
43 ___ Lingus
46 Venom
47 "Over There" composer
50 Beep
52 Weather system
54 Little bit

748 by Lois Sidway

ACROSS

1 Stepquote [starting across and making four turns in the grid]
4 Government detective
8 Word with China or ghost
12 Permit
13 Pitcher Hershiser
14 What hiphuggers hug
15 Comic strip cry of frustration
16 Fast-food franchises
18 Caught
20 Subject of the Stepquote
21 "Jake's Thing" author
23 Actress Elizabeth
24 One who uses a threadless needle
28 Hush-hush
32 Tummy troubles
33 Venetian magistrate
35 Casino game
36 Stand in the way of
38 Flap
39 It often gets a lick
41 Roman bear
42 Was nourished by
44 Put in the microwave, maybe
46 They take the show on the road
48 Criticizes
50 Sub station?
51 Author of the Stepquote
55 Canines, collectively
59 More than a swellhead
61 ___ Lay (snack-food company)
62 City SSE of Delhi
63 The "T" in TV
64 Street urchin
65 "A Bridge Too Far" author Cornelius
66 Where the Kon-Tiki is preserved

DOWN

1 Farsi is spoken here
2 Mitchell mansion
3 Thankless wretch
4 Pessimist's word
5 ___ League (Mideast group)
6 Summarize
7 Not far apart, as the eyes
8 Curtain holder
9 Stewpot
10 Desire
11 Pelé's org.
12 Fill-up filler
17 Nota ___
19 God, to Giorgio
22 Commemorative feast
24 Fifer's drum
25 Without ___ in the world
26 Astonished
27 Swelter
29 English playwright
30 Kipling poem
31 Boo Boo and Bugs, for two
34 Poky person
37 Meet by chance
40 Ben-Hur was one
43 Bit of wit
45 Spectacular suffix
47 Respected ref. work
49 Pigs' digs
51 Back
52 Like zabaglione
53 "Dumb" girl
54 Dining area
56 Stop on a ___
57 Mayberry jail habitué
58 Dude, Jamaican-style
60 Bus. V.I.P.

749 · by Chuck Deodene

ACROSS

1 Marshal Tito
5 A Cartwright
9 Seek water, in a way
14 Burt's ex
15 "You've Made ___ Very Happy" (1969 hit)
16 Spa on Lake Geneva
17 Quattuor doubled
18 Drill sgts., e.g.
19 Irish
20 Cardiologist's drastic remedy?
23 Early photos
24 G.P.'s org.
25 Acupuncturist's fee?
32 All ears
35 "Over There" songwriter
36 Ganymede, e.g.
37 Freudian topic
38 Dallas cager, briefly
39 Listener's gesture
40 Greene's "Travels With My ___"
42 Trained with LeMond
44 Quizzes
45 Dermatologist's pronouncement?
48 Kernel's locale
49 Best Picture of 1982
53 Arthroscopic surgeries?
57 Stone marker
59 Jellystone bear
60 Vajrayana teacher
61 Awaiting tenants
62 Scheme
63 "What ___ mind reader?"
64 Mild
65 Start of a chooser's rhyme
66 Chessboard line

DOWN

1 Alliances
2 Novelist Mazo de la ___
3 Barroom sign
4 Champion of Israel
5 Forgetful
6 Erté's art
7 Beginning
8 Revel à la rock fans
9 Aide-___
10 Baseball pitcher's style
11 Droop
12 Used a sedan
13 U.S.N. officer
21 Heater
22 Merit
26 Performer at Caroline's
27 Military hue
28 Overhangs
29 Solar wind particles
30 Camp employee
31 Termini
32 Rise up
33 Juanita's water
34 Longtime Met soprano
41 Pythagorean nugget
42 Swiss capital
43 Sense of self-respect
44 Ring-shaped
46 Fine pastry, e.g.
47 Bit of granola
50 Acting major
51 Encircle
52 Singer-songwriter Chris
53 Eikenberry of "L.A. Law"
54 Pound the keyboard
55 Mouse-like rodent
56 Painter Schiele
57 Wrigley Field player
58 Literary olio

750 · by Gregory E. Paul

ACROSS

1 Type of novel
5 Knucklehead
9 Continuing thought
14 Greek Mars
15 "___ Rebel" (1962 song)
16 Vacillate
17 Harangue
18 MTV prizes
19 Old toy company
20 Wyoming's motto
23 Postal worker's path: Abbr.
24 Pick on
25 "___, Brute?"
27 Bank (on)
30 Skyline sight
33 Language suffix
34 Belief
37 More inexperienced
38 Mighty bit
40 Cut off
42 Mt. Etna flow
43 Mt. Everest locale
45 Stitched
47 Matter at court
48 Abandon one's principles for money
50 Hawk
52 One, to Hans
53 String quartet member
55 Drum site
57 Arizona's motto
62 Say abruptly, with "out"
64 Premed course: Abbr.
65 Hillbilly's belt
66 "The Hobbit" hero
67 Frank Herbert sci-fi novel
68 Mayberry boy
69 Ale vessel
70 Nostradamus, e.g.
71 Shirt measurement

DOWN

1 Bell the cat
2 Gulf war foe
3 Carte du jour
4 Probate concern
5 Party picker-upper, maybe
6 Some jeans
7 Plains Indian
8 Recipe amount
9 Chubby Checker, for one
10 "It ___ to Be You"
11 New York's motto
12 Entrée, often
13 ___ Stanley Gardner
21 Pre-Easter time
22 Hanoi holiday
26 Dabbling duck
27 ___ list
28 First name in cosmetics
29 Arkansas's motto, with "The"
30 Brunswick, e.g.
31 Carpenter's tool
32 Clear a cassette
35 Snuggery
36 Morn's opposite
39 French Sudan, today
41 Newsperson
44 2,240 pounds
46 Takeout shop
49 Grp. that puts the show on the road
51 Wrinkle-resistant fabric
53 Trial's locale
54 Ludicrous
55 Declines
56 Touched down
58 Root beer brand
59 Rhode Island's motto
60 Not just an ordinary novel
61 Dig for
63 Slugger's stat

751   by Timothy S. Lewis

ACROSS

1 ___ Marie Presley
5 Trusted
10 Quarters
14 Excited
15 Give off
16 St. Columbia's island
17 With 26-, 45- and 60-Across, a line by Edna St. Vincent Millay
20 Sphere
21 Dolphin hazard
22 "Lady Lazarus" poet
23 Semi radios
25 Court
26 See 17-Across
34 Animal squeezer
35 Dislocate
36 Ponte Vecchio site
37 Phrase-book entry
39 S.D.I. component
40 Alternative to high heels
41 Marvin or Bernard
42 Not tippy
44 U-2 overseers
45 See 17-Across
48 Admirer's sound
49 Real-life Fogg

50 Without empathy
53 He, e.g.
56 A safari quarry
60 See 17-Across
63 Perfect
64 Mountebanks
65 Fasten permanently
66 Not post
67 Overburden
68 Notice

DOWN

1 One-l Nash subject
2 Lab assistant, of film
3 Peeved
4 ___ France-Presse
5 That boat
6 Ex-bulls
7 Brownish purple
8 Rephrase
9 Gillespie standard "Tin Tin ___"
10 Ratlike
11 "The Bridges of Madison County" locale
12 No-see-um
13 ". . . and threw up the ___"

18 Mush
19 Directly over
24 Taste
25 Wisdom's partner
26 Yesterday, tomorrow
27 ___ Selassie
28 Persona non ___
29 "Riddley Walker" author Russell ___
30 Skiing champ Alberto
31 Goosefoot family herb
32 Disunite
33 Eco's "Il nome della ___"
34 Messenger's vehicle
38 Like slide rules
40 Chap
42 "Hush!"
43 Legal deg.
46 Slinky et al.
47 Power of films
50 "The Joy of Cooking" author Rombauer
51 Originate
52 Fails to be
53 Nibble
54 Aleutian island
55 Ark deckhand

57 Nest eggs
58 No big thing
59 Without urgency
61 Suppositions
62 Dubious "gift"

752   by Diane C. Baldwin

ACROSS

1 Quetzalcoatl worshiper
6 Poet Teasdale
10 Tie type
14 1912 political symbol
15 Medical care grps.
16 Author Hunter
17 Famous Fidos
20 Indulge to the limit
21 Attila's horde
22 Book list
23 Living quarters, informally
24 ___ alai
25 Boston ___
29 Prep school attire
33 "For want of ___ the shoe . . ."
34 Geological period
35 Golf's Woosnam
37 Famous Fidos
41 Court divider
42 Top 10 items
43 Hymn player
44 Annoys
47 Putt, e.g.
48 Roguish

49 Too amusing for words
51 Puccini soprano
54 Love of Radames
55 Moolah
59 Famous Fidos
62 Cupid
63 Lady Chaplin
64 Sheepish
65 Schism
66 Go-ahead cues
67 Beau ___

DOWN

1 Current matters
2 "Germinal" author
3 Ballyhoo
4 Punta del ___, Uruguay
5 Company honcho
6 Indifference indicator
7 Fido, proverbially
8 CD-___
9 Symbol on a sarcophagus
10 Brownie topper
11 Roman poet
12 Shoot a light gun
13 Shade of black

18 Dilute
19 Longtime Mexican dictator Porfirio ___
23 Cutie
24 Part of a jungle pair
25 Actor James
26 Beginning
27 Dull finish
28 Woody's love, once
30 Superman's sweetie
31 Fab Four name
32 Game show spinmeister
34 Just like
36 Inches in a span
38 Sailing hailing
39 Not just one
40 Lapse, perhaps
45 Small Ford
46 Affront
47 Jazz singing
50 Impressions
51 "Terrible" title
52 "Lean ___" (1989 movie)
53 Before you know it
54 Peek ending
55 Jupiter, in an interjection

56 Alamo rival
57 Lincoln head
58 Kind of jerk
60 Thither
61 Not share

753 by Karen Hodge

ACROSS

1 Barrelhead bills
5 Cartel
9 Prepares, with "up"
14 Leleiwi Point site
15 Abandoned
16 Astrodome athlete
17 Perfect place
18 "The __ lama, he's . . .": Nash
19 Stiff necks
20 Specs for Elmer Fudd's gardener?
23 Bore
24 Baby buggy?
25 Elmer Fudd's quiet frontier?
32 Use the ax
35 Stand in the Rockies
36 "Now __ me down . . ."
37 Adjust, as the wheels
39 Turncoat
40 Dinner partner of film
41 Avis lead-in
42 __ ladder
44 Raise, with "to"
45 Elmer Fudd's colonial cooking utensil?
47 Former queen of Spain
48 Unsavory
52 Elmer Fudd's borrowed troubles?
58 Kind of law
59 Punjabi princess
60 Ne plus ultra
61 Restaurateur of song
62 Fictional pooch
63 Where to meet the Mets
64 Gives orders, in a way
65 Something to say?
66 First name in fairy tales

DOWN

1 Wad
2 Staffers
3 February forecast
4 "S.W.A.T." lieutenant of 70's TV
5 Ones who are fair
6 Protracted
7 Rare blood type, for short
8 Pen chamber
9 Rumors
10 Brain
11 Skin cream ingredient
12 Yankees' counterparts
13 Alums-to-be: Abbr.
21 Herbert Hoover, e.g.
22 Author Beattie et al.
26 Nursery rhyme name
27 Emulate Mr. Chips
28 Under one's control
29 Pierce's portrayer
30 Check for ID
31 Gave the once-over
32 Beethoven's "__ Quartet"
33 Airline name that's derived from Hosea
34 Lean and flexible
38 Fighting bird
40 Put it to
42 A Perón
43 Citizen of Mostar
46 Words before "toes" or "best behavior"
49 Swamped
50 Starbucks order
51 Land on the Red Sea
52 Ward of "Sisters"
53 Gulf war figure
54 Pull a pistol
55 Jumble
56 Penny __
57 Geographical heptad
58 Science course requirement

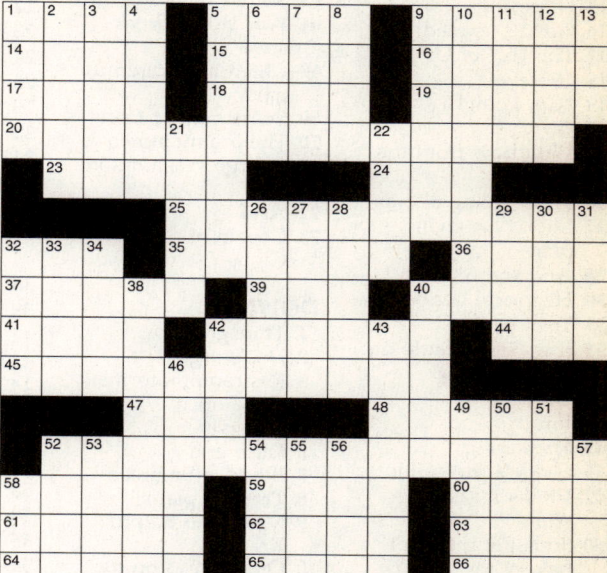

754 by Frank Longo

ACROSS

1 Flubs
6 Handles
11 Digital display
13 Caviar source
15 Ancient capital of Syria
16 What one may see on a Cree's knee
17 Fez's place
18 Jafar al-Sadiq's rule
19 "Whew!"
20 Added to the staff?
21 Bell __
22 Matches, in a way
24 Anatomical canals
25 Computer attachment?
26 Munich's river
27 Moves slightly
28 Kind of drill
30 It's often waxed
32 "What __!" ("Groovy!")
33 Forenoons
36 Declivity
37 Warm-up exam, for short
38 The conductor keeps it
39 It's hot stuff
41 Left-handed, in a way
43 About 26,000 square miles of Asia
44 Rehearse one's lines
45 "Star Trek II" ship
46 Animal, to granny
47 "Old Gringo" author Carlos
48 Like some golfers
49 Spending time?
50 Observers

DOWN

1 They're not available in Spain
2 Capitol architect Benjamin
3 Rocket scientists they're not
4 Kitty alternative
5 Hits
6 This may be A or B
7 Like benzene
8 Oft-relocated employee
9 Perfumery employees
10 Mounts
11 Maunder
12 Noted transcendentalist
13 Casino rounds
14 Shanter start
23 "Aunt __ Cope Book"
26 Numb
27 Redwood or magnolia
28 Fabric resembling broadcloth
29 Edible mushrooms
30 Sudden outburst
31 More patriotic
33 Wheat-preserving device
34 Postgraduate
35 Shepherds, in a way
36 Wolfs
37 Fuel sources
38 Wodehouse's Wooster
40 Gray-brown goose
42 Like an old hand

755 · by Stephanie Spadaccini

ACROSS
1 Pre-entree dish
6 Sit in the sun
10 Cozy home
14 Reflection
15 Opposing
16 Go ___ (exceed)
17 The "N" of U.S.N.A.
18 "Forever"
19 "Get going!"
20 Go
23 Withdraw from the Union
26 Those going 80, say
27 Med. cost-saving plan
28 And so on
30 Historical period
31 Teen woe
33 It makes an auto go
35 ___ latte
40 Go
44 Intuit
45 Hankering
46 Castle's protection
47 Chef's measure: Abbr.
50 Something to go to a bakery for
52 Wash. neighbor
53 Delivered a sermon
58 Comments to the audience
60 Go
62 Milky-white gem
63 Sacred Egyptian bird
64 War story, Greek-style
68 Chant at a fraternity party
69 Swiss painter Paul
70 The brainy bunch
71 George Washington bills
72 Arid
73 Cousin of a Golden Globe

DOWN
1 Transgression
2 Doc's org.
3 Restroom, informally
4 Wide-open
5 Deceive
6 False god
7 Black cattle breed
8 Treeless plain
9 Mouth, to Ralph Kramden
10 One always on the go
11 Call forth
12 Cut off
13 Lock of hair
21 "Take your hands off me!"
22 Instruct
23 Pre-Ayatollah rulers
24 Host
25 Sir Arthur ___ Doyle
29 Saturn, for one
32 Mag workers
34 Pigpen
36 Order between ready and fire
37 Result of a bank failure?
38 Distress signal
39 ___ Park, Colo.
41 "Go get it, Fido!"
42 Jitterbug's "cool"
43 First digital computer
48 Arab leaders
49 Little rock
51 Inuit
53 Kind of ID
54 Wisconsin college
55 Story, in France
56 Ayn Rand's "___ Shrugged"
57 Less moist
59 South Sea getaways
61 Words of comprehension
65 Business abbr.
66 Simile's middle
67 ___ es Salaam

756 · by Stephanie Spadaccini

ACROSS
1 Poet Sandburg
5 Sand bar
10 Jemima, e.g.
14 Guy with an Irish Rose
15 "College Bowl" host Robert
16 Chew (on)
17 Off-color
19 New York theater award
20 Escalator alternative
21 Boat propellers
23 "___ Maria"
24 Tear-jerker in the kitchen
26 "Bald" baby bird
28 Big toe woe
30 Patsy's pal on TV's "Absolutely Fabulous"
31 Dapper fellow
32 Foe
34 Numbskull
37 Catch sight of
39 Saccharine
41 Garbage boat
42 Chartres chapeau
44 "Deutschland über ___"
46 High season, on the Riviera
47 Before the due date
49 African antelopes
51 Actress Loren
53 Four-time Gold Glove winner Garvey
54 Chicken ___ king
55 ___ platter (Polynesian menu choice)
57 Bug's antenna
61 What not to yell in a crowded theater
63 Off-key
65 Tied, as a score
66 Revolutionary patriot Allen
67 Lo-cal
68 Funnyman Foxx
69 Horned zoo beast
70 Son of Seth

DOWN
1 Elliot of the Mamas and the Papas
2 Be next to
3 Latvia's capital
4 French Foreign ___
5 Rap or jam periods
6 Stetson, e.g.
7 Betelgeuse's constellation
8 Thomas Edison's middle name
9 Looked lecherously
10 In the past
11 Off-center
12 Innocent
13 Sound from an aviary
18 Sgt. Bilko
22 Stated
25 Street sign with an arrow
27 Wildebeests
28 Pedestal
29 Off-guard
30 Embroidered hole
31 Cotillion V.I.P.
33 Director Brooks
35 Bunkhouse beds
36 Female sheep
38 "You bet!"
40 It's used for a call in Madrid
43 Excursion
45 Lifeguard, sometimes
48 Giver of compliments
50 Thread's partner
51 Morley of "60 Minutes"
52 Martini garnish
53 Japanese dish
56 ___ helmet (safari wear)
58 Reclined
59 Inner: Prefix
60 1 and 66, e.g.: Abbr.
62 Finis
64 Campbell's container

757 by Betty Jorgensen

ACROSS
1 Incarcerate
5 Wife, in Madrid
11 U.S./U.K. divider
14 Wearer of an aiguillette
15 Warehouse charge
17 Start of a quip
19 Slippery swimmer
20 Axis end
21 Lift, as ice or oysters
22 Ilk
23 Enormous
26 Stress
29 "McSorley's Bar" painter John
30 Good earth
31 New Zealand native
32 Family V.I.P.'s
35 Middle of the quip
39 Pigpen
40 Brainy group
41 Something to cop
42 Mork's gal
43 Like schlock
45 Extra leaves
48 Ireland's ___ Islands
49 Spread for a spread
50 Manchurian border river

51 Sunny day production
54 End of the quip
59 Starlet's hope
60 Lackawanna's partner in railroads
61 Draft agcy.
62 Dallas's ___ Plaza
63 Become tiresome

DOWN
1 Rib
2 Yorkshire river
3 Worshiped one
4 Rock's ___ Zeppelin
5 Police accompaniment
6 Clown's prop
7 Corn bread
8 Assn.
9 Writer Rohmer
10 Farming: Abbr.
11 "Flow gently, sweet ___": Burns
12 Coming-of-age period
13 Shelf
16 Consumed
18 "___ the Roof" (1963 hit)

22 It's good for the long haul
23 Actress Massey
24 Filipino
25 Hotel housekeeper
26 Pauper's cry
27 Old feller
28 Guinea pig
29 Impertinent
31 Obeys
32 House slipper
33 Lincoln and Vigoda
34 Dog command
36 Head of Abu Dhabi
37 Shipped
38 Unguarded, as a receiver
42 Reagan Attorney General
43 Like a curmudgeon
44 Mata ___
45 Bridge declaration
46 D.E.A. workers
47 Swizzles
48 Provide divertissement
50 Soviet spy Rudolf
51 Now's partner
52 Siberia's site
53 River of Flanders

55 Proof's ending
56 Half of deux
57 Seventh Greek letter
58 Like a crescent moon

758 by Joan Yanofsky

ACROSS
1 Petite or jumbo
5 Gobs
9 Final Four rounds
14 Composer Satie
15 ___ avail
16 Gather into folds
17 Fashionable African land?
19 Chain of hills
20 Till compartment
21 Tartarus captive, in myth
22 Military encounter
25 ___ projection (map system)
27 Escargots
28 Embarrassment
30 Accede (to)
31 Places of refuge
32 Neither's partner
34 "The Twilight of the ___"
35 Unites
36 Deal (out)
37 ___ Lanka
38 Birdie beater
39 "Give My Regards to Broadway" composer

40 Meeting musts
42 "Canterbury Tales" inn
43 Gabriel, e.g.
44 Curmudgeon-like
45 Composer Duparc
47 Courts
48 "___ Cowboy"
49 Fashionable state?
54 Enact
55 Zone
56 Arched recess
57 "Flowers for Algernon" author Daniel
58 ". . . leave no ___ unstoned"
59 Haydn's "Nelson," for one

DOWN
1 Wine description
2 George's lyricist brother
3 Address part
4 ___ out a living
5 Some temps
6 "Two Women" Oscar winner

7 Remnants
8 Tale of ___
9 Naiads' homes
10 Donizetti's "The ___ of Love"
11 Fashionable Canadian city?
12 "Othello" villain
13 Actress Anna
18 Curtain fabric
22 Silky-haired cat
23 Fashionable Welsh body of water?
24 Bonds
25 Scold
26 Rest on one's ___
27 Is weary
28 Summons
29 Person with a seal
31 Kind of tender
33 Rip
35 1977 Wimbledon champ
36 Crowds around
38 Turbojet and others
39 Movement
41 Infuriate
42 Paris or Hector
44 Cringe

45 Corn covering
46 Russian-born designer
47 "___ off to see . . ."
49 King Cole

50 Computer capacity, for short
51 Site of rejuvenation
52 Double twist
53 "You bet!"

759   by Fran and Lou Sabin

ACROSS
1 Concede, with "up"
5 Star in Cygnus
10 Door-closing sound
14 Proceedings
15 The end for Socrates
16 Wonderland creature
17 Accomplice in 64-Across
20 Poker-faced TV sidekick
21 Workbench item
22 Pop
23 Restaurant freebie
26 Discus thrower Oerter et al.
28 Time of 64-Across
36 Tokyo of yore
37 Blacksmith
38 Now
39 See 3-Down
41 Inflexible
43 Enliven, with "up"
44 Finger, in a way
46 "___ the news today, oh boy" (Beatles lyric)
48 ___ Félicité, Que.
49 Places where 17-Across sat
52 Give the boot
53 Hamlet
54 Pumper's pride
57 Swimming champ Kristin
60 Drawn-out fight
64 Downfall of 17-Across
68 Egg on
69 Nail file
70 Guardianship
71 Will's wife
72 Took it from the top
73 Physics unit

DOWN
1 Actuality
2 She loved Narcissus
3 With 39-Across, "The Girl From Ipanema" saxophonist
4 Nobel Prize refuser, 1964
5 Everyman John
6 Fat letters
7 St. Petersburg's river
8 Major Hoople's exclamation, in the comics
9 Japanese battle cry
10 "Pinball Wizard" band, with "the"
11 Rocky
12 Acreage
13 Patch
18 Despoils
19 Blue-and-white pottery
24 Glassmaking oven
25 Pope of 795–816
27 "Cool it!"
28 Silent star
29 Concepts
30 "___ worry . . ."
31 Part of U.N.C.F.
32 Quaker
33 That is
34 Terra firma
35 Gettysburg general George
40 "Germinal" author
42 Actress Maryam
45 Island in Greek myth
47 Animals' backs
50 Grazer's limiter
51 Thought
54 Shade of blue
55 Overcook
56 Speak with the hands
58 Bibliophile's purchase
59 Was in arrears
61 Nervous
62 Football yardage
63 "What ___ is new?"
65 Dutch waterway
66 Indian title
67 Dancer Charisse

760   by Susan Smith

ACROSS
1 Mangle
5 Palindromic exclamation
8 The Mad ___
14 Magic phrase starter
15 Septuagenarian's kitty, for short
16 Shoe part
17 Leave in a hurry
19 Twisted
20 Say again
21 Actress North and others
22 Throbs
24 Where pins are made
27 Guarantee
28 Triple-A handout
31 Sharp as ___
33 1st Earl of Beaconsfield
36 Navajo "hello"
38 Nonstick coating
39 Popular citrus drink
42 Forepart
43 "Dear ___"
44 Greedy eater
47 Vietnam's ___ Dinh Diem
48 Cruel
50 Pampers
53 Error
58 Kind of punch
59 Slightly later than optimal
60 Fold of skin under the throat
61 Ruby, e.g.
62 Military subdivision
63 Liabilities' opposites
64 ___-la-la
65 Computer info quantity

DOWN
1 Half of a Hawaiian fish
2 "Isn't that ___ much?"
3 Spur
4 Cowardly Lion actor
5 Gap
6 Mountain gazelles
7 Shakespearean prince
8 Type of gas
9 A year in Provence
10 Ivan and Nicholas
11 Ripped or zipped
12 International fashion magazine
13 Actor Fernando et al.
18 Start the beer bust
21 Indian dress
23 South, in Soissons
24 Minnesota clinic founders
25 Computer-game maker
26 Mongol tribesman
28 Breakfast fruit
29 Onward
30 Spotted horse
32 100 yrs.
34 Invigorate
35 It's south of Eur.
37 Sneakers type
40 Entre ___
41 Provide with weapons
45 More like overripe meat
46 Puzzle
48 Carpet fiber
49 ___ the job (inexperienced)
50 Closing musical passage
51 Snake eyes
52 Stitches
54 Ticket part
55 Like Albee's Alice
56 Send forth
57 Much is done for his sake
59 Elev.

761 by Arthur S. Verdesca

ACROSS

1 Finance
6 Tore
10 Trick
14 "There!"
15 Drench, with "down"
16 Patron saint of Norway
17 Mississippi quartet
18 Plenty
19 ___ Bay, Hawaii
20 Like Chablis
21 Butcher?
24 Nell portrayer in a 1994 movie
26 With 46-Across, a successor to Buster Crabbe
27 Like Schoenberg's works
29 Anomalous
33 Daly role
34 Recoiled
35 Time-worn
37 Civic organization
38 Manilow's "___ It Be Magic"
39 Group of turtles
40 Receive
41 Cook squash, perhaps
42 Early tennis star ___ Hull Jacobs
43 Nerve impulse point
45 Aristocracy
46 See 26-Across
47 Afflict suddenly
48 Cattleman?
53 Magic org.
56 Trace
57 Superior
58 Tribal leader
60 Quechua
61 French chef's dish
62 Tuscan city
63 Marquess or viscount
64 Like ___ of bricks
65 Dangerously seductive

DOWN

1 Eventful times
2 Ship's prow
3 Orthopedist?
4 Violinist Bull
5 Toilsome part of the week
6 Ignominy
7 Kind of shirt
8 Workers' purchase arrangement, for short
9 Dissuaded
10 Herr Goethe
11 Got down
12 ___ Alto
13 ___ excellence
22 Trouble
23 Artery
25 A good deal of binary code
27 Tourist city near Nîmes
28 Lies
29 "On the Beach" author
30 Roofing item
31 Guidance counselor?
32 "Oklahoma!" aunt
34 Bygone coins
36 Gainsay
38 Largest living rodent
39 Auto pioneer
41 Polio pioneer
42 Doris Duke, e.g.
44 Sweet drink
45 Plow horse command
47 Flock of wild fowl
48 Send
49 Prong
50 If ever
51 Radix, botanically
52 Hip about
54 Nota ___
55 Flaherty's "Man of ___"
59 Weeks per annum

762 by Elizabeth Gorski

ACROSS

1 Muscle malady
5 Fitzgerald and others
10 Computer-drive capacity, in slang
14 Weaver's apparatus
15 Intimidate
16 With the stroke of ___
17 At times it's a stretch
18 Secretary's instrument
20 Opening for a coin
21 Tick off
22 New York's ___ Mansion
23 Evergreens
25 One more
26 Louts
28 Muscle malady
29 Parallel to
30 Evening's opposite
31 In the center of
35 Ashen
36 Discharge, as a liquid
39 Flightless bird
40 Gladly
42 Butter squares
43 Boston airport
45 Doesn't include
47 Turned into
48 Post office deliveries
51 Expletive replacement
52 Titillate
53 Miler Sebastian
54 Pequod's captain
57 Band member's instrument
59 It's off-limits
60 Carry
61 Like oxfords
62 "What's gotten ___ you?"
63 Ed of "Daniel Boone"
64 1923 Literature Nobelist
65 Average marks

DOWN

1 "___ Well That Ends Well"
2 Snake's shape
3 Punster's instrument
4 Feeling
5 Whirling currents
6 Dens
7 Gambler's need
8 Industrious worker
9 Not moving
10 Gandhi's title
11 Geologic time
12 Wish granter
13 Show of contempt
19 U.S. Open players, usually
24 Yuletide drinks
25 "___ moi le déluge"
26 Two-master
27 Jai ___
28 Does prelaundry work
30 Exams for future drs.
32 Cheerleader's instrument
33 Muslim leader
34 Sand formation
37 Neurontin treats it
38 Gen. Robt. ___
41 Zeroes in (on)
44 Relating to the sea
46 Natural table
47 Runs, as a color
48 Trattoria plateful
49 Woolf's "___ of One's Own"
50 Way to go
51 Lisa of "The Cosby Show"
53 Pepsi, e.g.
55 Sometimes it's upped
56 Opposite of huzzahs
58 Garden tool

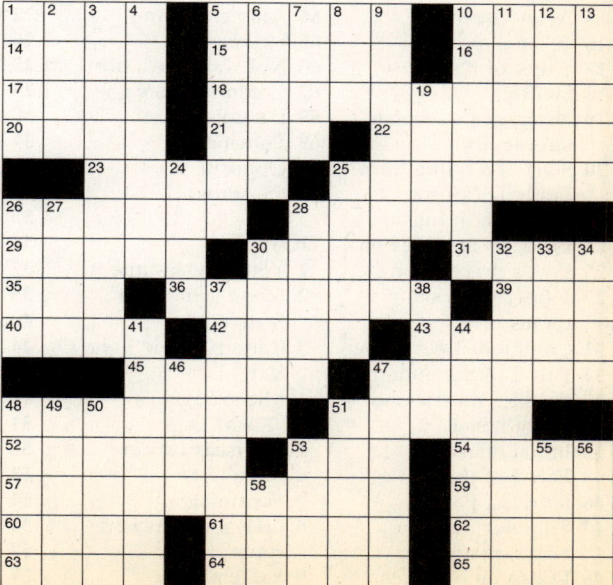

763 by Bernice Gordon

ACROSS
1 Timber-dressing tool
4 Spy secrets
9 Federal investigator
13 Maya Angelou, e.g.
15 Sky-colored
16 Conquering ___
17 Isle of exile
18 Washington Zoo animal
19 The "U" in B.T.U.
20 Obstinate
23 Nexus
24 Play ___ with (do mischief to)
25 Old joke
28 Restaurateur Toots
30 Second-century date
33 City in SE Kansas
34 To the left, to a sailor
35 Vandal
36 Conceited
40 Remote viewing
41 Improves, as text
42 Gallic girlfriend
43 Toast order
44 Mardi ___
45 Slept under the stars
47 "Bali ___"
48 [I am shocked!]

49 Nuts
57 Mesa's location: Abbr.
58 Holy scroll
59 Norwegian saint
60 Methodology
61 Crazy
62 Split
63 One the Army wants
64 Indianapolis team
65 Letters from Xanthippe

DOWN
1 King Kong's kin
2 Numbskull
3 Indian ox
4 1975 gangster movie
5 Onetime airline
6 Country music's Holly
7 Earth goddess
8 Locale for clam diggers
9 Browse (through)
10 Maître-d's offering
11 Seed covering
12 Paper money
14 Striking scene

21 Hollywood, with "the"
22 Arterial trunk
25 Rain clearer
26 Equine-related
27 Get hitched in a hurry
28 Gaiters
29 Brewer's need
30 Munch noisily
31 One of the Arnazes
32 Signed on the dotted line
34 The East
37 "La classe de danse" artist
38 Croatia's sea
39 Moth repellent
45 Stockpiles
46 Tree of the olive family
47 Nut tree
48 Research funds
49 Family V.I.P.
50 Lined up
51 Queen of Carthage, in myth
52 Pre-stereo sound
53 34-Down's ___ Sea

54 Trebek of "Jeopardy!"
55 Rajah's mate
56 Small amphibians

764 by Richard Hughes

ACROSS
1 Tries to take (out)
5 Mischievous
10 Novelist Mario Vargas Llosa's home
14 Carnival tune
15 Actor Greene
16 40's foe
17 Think of it!
18 Swiftly
19 Nicaragua's second-largest city
20 Start of a quote from Emily Dickinson
23 Direction in music
24 Picks up readings on
25 Poet's preposition
27 Indoor-outdoor rooms
31 Common street name
34 Part 2 of the quote
39 Feeding time sound
41 Set of beliefs
42 Initial offering?
43 Part 3 of the quote
46 John ___ Passos
47 Time for a coffee break, maybe
48 Lunch on

50 Rags
55 Esteem
59 End of the quote
62 Tel ___
63 Run with one's mouth open?
64 Arab chieftain
65 Strike out
66 Not wait one's turn
67 Communion, e.g.
68 It's unique
69 Transport
70 Opposite of 65-Across

DOWN
1 You may assume it
2 Move somewhat furtively
3 Certain movie light: Var.
4 Michelangelo's "Pieta," e.g.
5 Overseas carrier
6 Runs
7 Formulate
8 Like some ancient ruins
9 Exigencies

10 Athletic training site, in Greek antiquity
11 Divorcees
12 Portuguese rivers
13 American mil. wing
21 Actress Garr
22 Certain tide
26 Postal letters?
28 Peel
29 Division word
30 Seeming eternity
31 Spew
32 ___-majeste
33 Cut
35 Italian number
36 Stag goers
37 Old Tokyo
38 A little
40 "Anything you say"
44 Eclipse, maybe
45 Overhang
49 Selfish ones
51 "Is that ___?!"
52 Frere's sister
53 Verdi aria
54 Zeno follower
56 Restrict
57 Join
58 Plume's source

59 Flat
60 Revolting
61 "Baywatch" type
62 Foofaraw

ACROSS

1 Astrology concern
6 Gladiatorial combat site
11 Pileup
14 Young screecher
15 Approaches
16 Literary olio
17 Places where singer Joel sings?
19 Late-breaking story carrier
20 Play the ham
21 Novice
23 Issues a decree
26 Bubble gum collectibles
27 Snare loops
28 "Oh! Susanna" composer
29 Infamous 1972 hurricane
30 Swindles
31 Half of a 1955 merger: Abbr.
34 Cloister inhabitants
35 ___ hand (assist)
36 Qualified
37 Susan of "L.A. Law"
38 Longing looks
39 Monastery head
40 Valuable coins
42 Photoelectric cell element
43 Old English sheepdog feature
45 Lab liquid measurer
46 Culinary cover-ups
47 Hank the slugger
48 ___-tse, Chinese philosopher
49 Entrée for actor Norris?
54 Traffic caution
55 Borden bovine
56 Kukla's pal
57 Invite
58 Pairs
59 Prevarication

DOWN

1 Blubber
2 Light beginning
3 The whole enchilada
4 Press statements
5 Baffles
6 Citibank nos.
7 Stage part
8 Outback bird
9 Eight-time Orange Bowl champs
10 Classifies, in a way
11 Pet for a nursery rhyme boy?
12 Sandy's mistress
13 Artist Édouard
18 Shem and Ham, to Noah
22 Coleridge verse
23 ___ off (intermittently)
24 Scoundrel
25 Watering spot for one of the Osmonds?
26 Sniffles cases
28 More splendid
30 Ring holding a watch crystal
32 Treat with scorn
33 "___ Call You Sweetheart"
35 With extravagance
36 Without thinking
38 Ricocheted
39 Kind of spray
41 Simpson trial judge
42 Junkyard dogs
43 Raft material
44 Girasol and hyalite
45 Swelters
47 Sour
50 Dos Passos trilogy
51 Pharmaceutical giant ___ Lilly
52 Department in France
53 Powder holder

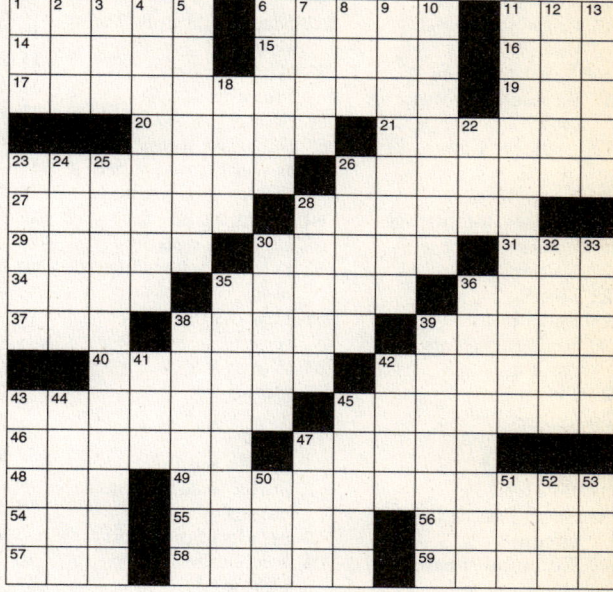

ACROSS

1 Hajj destination
6 Correct
11 RR stop
14 "___ With a View"
15 Baby doll
16 Toy with a string
17 1978 movie scripted by Oliver Stone
20 Got no return from
21 Baloney
22 Weird
23 Thor's lord
25 Comes in
26 1990's sitcom set in Arkansas
31 Preacher's admonition
32 Galley propellers
33 Mom's mate
36 Monopoly card
37 Experiment
38 Femur, e.g.
39 Aldous Huxley's "___ and Essence"
40 Jungle cry
42 German ballads
44 1967 Otto Preminger film
46 Las Vegas sight
49 Machu Picchu resident
50 "Pagliacci," e.g.
51 One of the Baldwins
53 Utah national park
57 Rod Serling TV show
60 "A Christmas Carol" boy
61 Greet the morn
62 Choir members
63 Coupon sites
64 "The Wild Swans at Coole" poet
65 Chicago team, with "Da"

DOWN

1 Michelle Phillips, e.g., in 60's pop
2 Skater Heiden
3 Message concealer
4 Tacitly approved
5 Friend of Henri
6 Sore
7 Remote control button
8 French summers
9 Veto
10 "It all ___!"
11 Cubic meter
12 "___ With Love"
13 Church nooks
18 Sparkle
19 Nerve network
24 Cacophony
25 Beagle feature
26 "Das Rheingold" role
27 Number two
28 Dueler's weapon
29 "My mistake!"
30 Farm food
33 Dunderhead
34 Freshly
35 "Jurassic Park" actress Laura
37 Feather's companion
38 Blind
40 1961 Del Shannon hit
41 El Dorado treasure
42 Midday break
43 Corp. abbr.
44 Trumpeter Al
45 Fort-capturing operations
46 Terra ___
47 Rose pest
48 Appears
51 Inter ___
52 Telephone book, essentially
54 Smidgen
55 ___ about (approximately)
56 "The Untouchables" protagonist
58 Wrath
59 Bill

767 by Matt Gaffney

ACROSS
1 Farmer's field: Abbr.
4 90's singer Mary ___ Carpenter
10 Caesar and others
14 Actress Joanne
15 Conference USA powerhouse
16 Turn ___ profit
17 Best-selling author of 1978
19 Explorer Cabeza de ___
20 ___ reflection
21 One for the history books
22 Rather
23 Sleep
25 Focal point
26 Innsbruck is its capital
27 Photo ___
30 Winter holiday
31 Site of a 1967 civil war
34 Boy lead-in
35 Short-lived 1986 TV sitcom
40 Common theater name
41 Art songs
42 Penny, sometimes
43 Quietus
44 TV cartoon dog
49 Top dogs
50 Cuts, in a way
52 MacLachlan of "Twin Peaks"
53 Author Zora ___ Hurston
56 Scope
57 Suffix with flex
58 It went down when the Valdez crashed
60 Grant basis
61 Miss the deadline
62 Word teachers like to hear
63 H.S. dropouts' redemptions
64 Worth a look
65 Ocean

DOWN
1 Fiddle with
2 Suffix in many class names
3 London Sun tidbit
4 Price abbr.
5 Offended
6 1966 Michael Caine film
7 Au ___
8 "Suicide Blonde" rock group
9 Following
10 Much of Cuba
11 Not at the counter
12 Say one will
13 Requirement to wear seat belts, e.g.
18 Not exo-
24 Hamburg's river
27 Rubbed out
28 Give a pointer to?
29 Old duchy in royal family names
32 Not going anywhere
33 It's not the breaking point
35 Spy satellite activity
36 One with a comb
37 Glorified
38 Some crop starts
39 Inside look
45 Piece of info
46 Frog's place
47 Deep canyon feature
48 Certain Japanese
50 New York's ___-Kettering hospital
51 Metric prefix
53 Bills
54 Company hotshot
55 Car bar
59 Instant

768 by David J. Kahn

ACROSS
1 African scourge
7 Stepping
15 Ultimatum word
16 Orderly place
17 Takes in, for example
18 Trenchant
19 Light on the set: Var.
20 "It's no ___!"
21 Volcanic elements
22 These might cover fires
25 Amigos
26 Verdi masterpiece, with "La"
29 Concert prop
31 "___ Said" (Neil Diamond hit)
32 Agcy. issuance
33 October handout
36 Quick hands artist
40 "Have ___ day"
41 ___-Magnon
42 Tooth part
43 Integration symbol
44 Lower jaw
46 Black shade
49 1951 Giant hero
51 "___ moi . . ."
53 Some clock-radios, or their settings
54 Quick
58 Food poisoning
60 You can count on it
61 Jerry Seinfeld contemporary
62 Stomach corrosion
63 Least sufficient
64 Sofa type

DOWN
1 Shipbuilding wood
2 Shades' stopping point
3 Suffix with disk
4 H. G. Wells's mad scientist
5 Composer Rachmaninoff
6 Hesitant sounds
7 Favorite 60's song of 36-Across?
8 Actress Blakley
9 Computer key: Abbr.
10 Make ___ of oneself
11 Favorite feat of 4-Down?
12 "___ far, far better thing . . ."
13 This may be contemplated
14 Daly's TV co-star
20 You, in the Yucatan
23 Most cautious
24 Olympic roster
26 Longtime Capitol Hill nickname
27 ___ avis
28 Revival word
30 "D.C. Cab" actor
34 From ___ (opening bit)
35 Drive (along)
37 Fort Worth sch.
38 Lab units
39 Homophone of 42-Across: Abbr.
45 Within reach
46 Melville's Vere and others: Abbr.
47 Instrument's lens
48 Bakery attraction
50 Big name in briefs
52 1972 agreement, for short
55 "Rhyme Pays" rapper
56 Bait, sometimes
57 Actual being
59 View on the Seine
60 Out of: Ger.

ACROSS

1 "Stat!"
5 Grow dim
9 Stop ___
14 "___ Barry Turns 40" (1990 best-seller)
15 Oak variety
16 Begot
17 Mark left by Zorro?
18 Ring site
19 1954 Oscar-winning composer
20 "Anatomy of a Murder": Defense
23 Singer with the 1991 #1 hit "Rush, Rush"
26 Pupils' spots
27 "Anatomy of a Murder": Prosecution
32 Affectedly creative
33 Stadium since 1964
34 ___ Club (retail chain)
38 ___ du Diable
39 Because
41 Chance
42 Rebuilder of Rome
44 Plenty
45 Zhivago's love
46 "Inherit the Wind": Prosecution
50 Classic work by Montaigne
53 Extra
54 "Inherit the Wind": Defense
59 The Law of Moses
60 Ages
61 Unhinged
65 Missouri river
66 Players
67 "Whoops!"
68 Not as bright
69 MOMA artist
70 Risque

DOWN

1 Pitches
2 Animal pouch
3 A Gardner
4 Swearing falsely
5 Medium of this puzzle's theme
6 ___ vera
7 Presidential candidate who campaigned from prison
8 They've split
9 Maintain
10 Dolts
11 ___ dust
12 Category
13 "Golden Boy" playwright
21 High school subj.
22 Uncle Jose
23 Once more
24 Tuesday night fixture on early NBC
25 Adoring one
28 Double curve
29 Tot
30 Gent from Argentina
31 Chollas
35 "___ Day's Night"
36 ___ Island, Fla.
37 Hall-of-Fame pitcher Warren
40 Computer key
43 At the point in one's life
45 Word repeated in a children's rhyme
47 Higher in fuel-to-air ratio
48 Vane dir.
49 Big ___
50 Prevent legally
51 Bride, in Brescia
52 Pertaining to ecological stages
55 Torture device
56 Small duck
57 A Kennedy
58 Pot starter
62 "I see!"
63 Big gobbler
64 Short

ACROSS

1 Garden tool
6 "Gimme Shelter" band, with "the"
12 Explain visually
14 Brecht's "Mother ___"
15 With 16-Across, Canadian speech
16 Anagram of 15-Across
17 Kind of fingerprinting, nowadays
18 Pollen holder
20 By way of
21 Left-fielder Ron
23 "For" words
24 Screen ___
25 Dubai royalty
27 Lush
28 Suffix with kitchen
29 Reminisce
31 Siege site
34 Midafternoon on a sundial
35 Suffix with sonnet
36 Make no change
41 Iced dessert
45 Heavy reading?
46 One for the road
48 La Scala locale
49 Banned apple spray
50 Error's partner
52 Druggie's nemesis
53 Ukr. neighbor
54 Land of ancient Smyrna
55 Earl Grey, e.g.
56 With 58-Across, hires recording artists again
58 Anagram of 56-Across
61 ___ list
62 Enrage
63 Satrap
64 Ad signs

DOWN

1 Like Rushdie's verses
2 Tour org.
3 T.W.A. info
4 Kind of wheel
5 Hams it up
6 Boils
7 Malaysian gent's title
8 Table scrap
9 Ingénue's trait
10 Self-ish folks
11 Upper chambers
12 Ebbets Field player
13 ___ only
14 Regain consciousness
19 Beginning (then)
22 With 24-Down, instructor's turf
24 Anagram of 22-Down
26 Coasted
30 Back talk
32 Person in stripes
33 Four years, for a President
36 Headlined
37 The second T in TNT
38 Accumulates
39 Puzzle direction
40 Follow
42 Typewriter rollers
43 Price cutters, in a sense
44 Box up
47 ___ bran
50 Believe it
51 Singer Frankie
54 Currency premium
57 Rascal
59 Enlisted V.I.P.
60 A superior of 59-Down

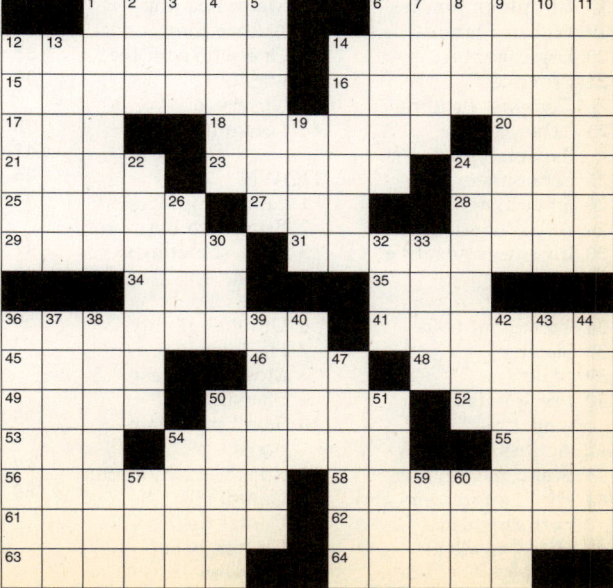

771 by Nancy Joline

ACROSS

1 Some swabs
6 Ski champ McKinney
12 1964 Hitchcock film
13 Renders drug-free
14 Logical thinker
15 Praises: Var.
16 Lovable
18 Assent
19 River inlet
20 Swiss river
22 Sequel to Buck's "The Good Earth"
23 Group of gangs
26 Bank claims
28 Geo. and Thos., e.g.
29 Adjusts
31 Belles-___
33 "Ars Amatoria" author
35 Word repeated in a Doris Day song
36 Brownies
39 Meal
43 Balkans map abbr.
44 Some boxing jabs
46 Pasta variety
47 Latin I word
49 Drying method

50 "___ the ramparts . . ."
51 Barbara follows it
53 Numbers in parentheses
57 Tough guy of filmdom
59 Break down
60 Oil and water, e.g.
61 Mend a coat
62 Emulated an oenophile
63 Boar or boor

DOWN

1 Libyan strongman
2 Word with blue or believer
3 Atahualpa, e.g.
4 Loading/unloading locale
5 "Flash Gordon," once
6 ___-Mex
7 "___ boy!"
8 Electronic synthesizers
9 Guns N' Roses leader
10 Softens
11 Evaluate
12 Not grandiose

13 Master's and others
14 Skin
17 One that gets hit on the head
21 Stage direction
24 Mr. Sikorsky
25 Smith's need
27 Kind of throat
30 Located
32 Shakespeare's "The ___ of Lucrece"
34 Pays part of
36 Mogadishu's locale
37 Manners
38 The slammer
40 Pain reliever
41 Dismiss lightly, with "at"
42 Blunt
43 Volcanic rock
45 Asparagus servings
48 Publican's offering
52 Indy champ Luyendyk
54 Once more
55 City southwest of Bogotá
56 Actor Ken or actress Lena
58 Append

772 by Rich Norris

ACROSS

1 Lotto lures
9 Warehouse: Abbr.
13 Djibouti neighbor
14 Took it easy
16 Cut-and-dried
17 Antiphon, for one
19 Walrus feature
20 Logical abbr.
21 Provoke
22 Compass heading
23 "The Age of Anxiety" poet
25 Economize
26 Smooth again, as soil
28 Abba hit song, 1975
30 Inverness negative
31 Lively
33 Bristle
34 Treatment plan
37 Sisterly
39 Make
40 Precipitated, in a way
42 Actress Joanne
43 Scandinavian flier
44 Hired supporters at a performance
48 Hired workers
51 Restless

53 Young ___ (tots, in dialect)
54 Tentacled mollusks
56 Informant
57 Switch's partner
58 Lawyerdom
59 Menu heading
61 Author Jong
62 One who's on the way out
63 Observed
64 Lookouts, e.g.

DOWN

1 Court employee
2 Bring into harmony
3 Beer, sometimes
4 Twist
5 Seed vessel
6 Unintelligibility
7 Hackneyed
8 Most downcast
9 Blackthorn
10 Small mountain pools
11 Rock's ___ Mountain Daredevils
12 Dental device
15 Church beliefs
18 Abrogate

23 Actor ___ Tamiroff
24 Clamor
27 Related
29 Office need
32 Chou
33 Word with cream or ice cream
34 Passionate
35 Otologist's case
36 Weight lifters, at times
38 Count (on)
41 TV actor Erik
45 Book size, in printing
46 Minister, at weddings
47 Lauder et al.
49 Maynard's "good buddy" of 60's TV
50 Room
52 Godwin's "The Adventures of ___ Williams"
55 Zagros Mountains site
57 One of the Simpsons
60 Hospital bed

773 — by Harvey Estes

ACROSS
1 Holiday companion
10 Hacks
14 Lucky charm
15 Sister ___ of "Guys and Dolls"
16 Plan of action
17 Painter Franz
18 Practitioners, for short
19 Puff
20 Enlarge
21 Catwoman of 60's TV
22 Dresses to the nines
23 Kind of skating
26 Syrup source
27 Callisto and Ganymede
28 Tireless tire maker
32 Walk wearily
33 Threescore
34 Pistol, in gang slang
35 Dramatist from Colonus
37 Neighbor of Tibet
38 Student stumpers
39 " 'Night, Mother" playwright Norman
40 Falls on
43 Brother of Poseidon
44 Stalwart
45 Roll at a hole
46 Go to pieces
49 Cheap jewelry
50 "My Land and My People" author
52 Prestigious schools
53 She played Jane to Weissmuller's Tarzan
54 Lack
55 Kaffeeklatsch activity

DOWN
1 Fancy
2 Over there, archaically
3 PBS topics
4 Philosopher Lao ___
5 Bowling
6 All you own
7 "I can take ___"
8 Fundamental
9 Cooler for cons
10 WKRP, e.g.
11 Libretto features
12 African tribesman
13 Followers
15 Gifts
20 Silent dwarf
21 Capable of compassion
22 Dodge cars
23 Misbehavers
24 Beginning of a plea
25 In the ___ (informed)
26 Bakers' shortcuts
28 Rolls the tape
29 Cousin of "uh-oh"
30 Nautical zookeeper
31 Actress Raines
33 Like serpent skin
36 Rust and others
37 Spiral shell dwellers
39 Silver and gold
40 Whirling
41 Song verse
42 "Wake Up Little ___" (1957 hit)
43 Z's, in code
45 El trailer
46 Sitarist Shankar
47 Muscat's country
48 Surprise for the taste buds
50 Follow around
51 Sass

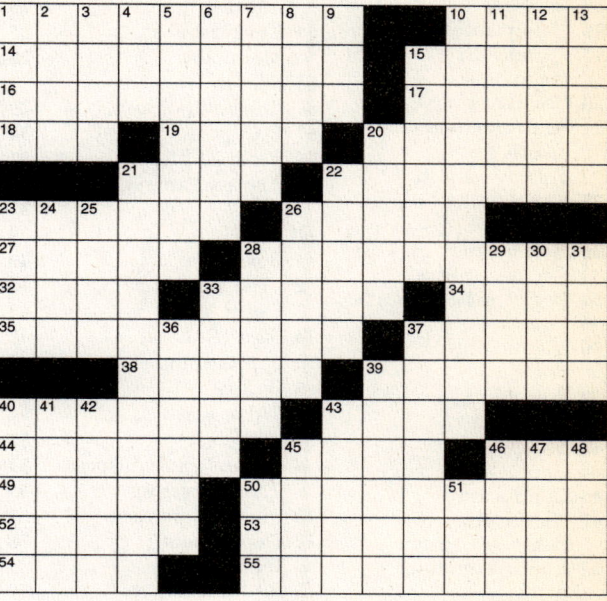

774 — by Randall J. Hartman

ACROSS
1 City near Kyoto
6 Saturate
10 Gallows reprieve
14 Threesome
15 "So long"
16 Cro-Magnon's home
17 Jungle dweller
20 Poet and tentmaker's son
21 It's unique
22 Buckeye State
25 Burn
27 Christopher of "Superman"
31 Campaigned
32 Sunday songs
34 Anticrime boss
35 Zest
38 Synthetic rubber
40 17 Across's formal title
43 Ailments
44 Skirt movement
46 Elderly
47 Descendant
50 Opposite of WNW
51 Bowling lane button
53 Playwright David
54 Like target pigeons
55 Pout
57 Mrs. Peel from "The Avengers"
59 Phrase from 17-Across
66 Declare
67 Legal memo starter
68 Kind of eclipse
69 Sneaky look
70 Constellation component
71 Stage direction

DOWN
1 Giant slugger
2 Mexican Mrs.
3 Inner-tube innards
4 Hummer's instrument
5 Edenite
6 Building floor, in London
7 Lummox
8 Johnnie Cochran, e.g.
9 Actress Madeline
10 Ray Bolger film role
11 Astaire specialty
12 "Hail, Caesar!"
13 "___, ma'am"
18 Partner of Crosby and Stills
19 Always, to a poet
22 Assn.
23 Trucker's business
24 Shoe pads
26 More than forgetfulness
28 Old Testament prophet
29 Singer Williams
30 Before
33 Message from the Titanic
36 NBC's peacock, e.g.
37 Uneven
39 Two of these make a qt.
41 Platoon members, for short
42 Coward
43 Deface
45 Relative of "pssst!"
48 Complier
49 Jules Verne captain
52 Craggy peak
54 Kind of cooking
56 Terrorists' weapons
58 Wagon train puller
59 Glove compartment item
60 Mate of 5-Down
61 Golf ball's perch
62 Gun lobby grp.
63 Colony pest
64 Scot's denial
65 Flub

775 by Jonathan Schmalzbach

ACROSS
1 Grocery holders
5 60's ___ sign
10 Gradient
14 Henry Gray's subj.
15 Inert gas
16 Slangy suffix
17 "Spoon River" anthologist
20 Cowboy's rope
21 Arab chieftain's jurisdiction
22 Tolstoy's Ilyich
25 Prefix with photo or type
26 "On Boxing" essayist
33 Cry of surprise
34 Peggy Ashcroft's title
35 Pit
36 Islamic prayer portion
38 French noggins
41 Not main
42 Miss Garbo
44 Choral voice range
46 Conducted
47 "Seven Keys to Baldpate" author
51 Edison's middle name
52 He sang about Alice
53 Shelley's elegy to Keats
56 Sea eagles
60 "Red Square" novelist
64 Kyrgyzstan's ___ Mountains
65 Reason why
66 Breakout, of a sort
67 D.C. pols
68 Violinist Mischa
69 Actress Patricia

DOWN
1 Boxer Max
2 "The King ___"
3 Dotty
4 Sign of an approaching storm
5 Buddy
6 "Able was I ___ . . ."
7 Add years
8 Regain consciousness
9 Tooth covering
10 Places of privacy
11 Department
12 Death: Fr.
13 Sit for a camera
18 Wrote a four-star review
19 Missile sites
23 ". . . way to skin ___"
24 Dub
26 Author Amado
27 Scarlett of Tara
28 One who teams up oxen
29 Apply more pitch to
30 Sheer cotton
31 Caboose, e.g.
32 Burpee products
37 Legendary island
39 Exile island
40 Start waking up
43 Statesman Stevenson
45 Eyes thighs, e.g.
48 Show clearly
49 Naughty one
50 First Miss America Margaret ___
53 Part of a Latin I trio
54 Broad valley
55 Algerian seaport
57 Not naughty
58 Europe's highest volcano
59 Writer Silverstein
61 Drink from Jamaica
62 ___ Today
63 ___ Buddhism

776 by Lois Sidway

ACROSS
1 Austrian peaks
5 "Get outta here!"
10 Drink of the ancients
14 Seldom seen
15 Eta-iota link
16 Oiler's target
17 Foreman?
19 Refs' decisions
20 Cackleberry
21 Ready for picking
22 Gauguin's last home
24 Pop music style
26 Thumb, e.g.
27 Kind of sch.
29 Words on a minimart front
32 Hayseed
35 Certain navel
37 Prefix with center
38 Amatory poet
39 This puzzle is missing some
40 Hardware item
41 D.D.E.'s rank
42 Glorify
43 Fresh
44 Operational
46 "Beverly Hills Cop" org.
48 1-2-3 software company
49 Breakfast beverage
53 They've been framed
55 Many a used car
57 Actor Wallach
58 Table salt
59 Like Santa Claus?
62 Miss Huber of tennis
63 TV, radio and such
64 Tantrum thrower
65 Go by
66 Studio prop
67 Bill and Carrie

DOWN
1 Like Lendl's lobs
2 Key ___
3 Spaghetti sauce brand
4 Stitch
5 Charity ___ (free-throw line)
6 Guacamole support
7 Debussy's dream
8 Had dinner
9 Refreshments for 007
10 "Chances Are" crooner
11 Cats?
12 Scads
13 Lucie's dad
18 Waggish
23 Baseball's Tommie
25 Dandelion, e.g.
26 "No kidding"
28 Part of a Perle Mesta epithet
30 Numbered work
31 Compassion
32 Boo Boo's buddy
33 Pizzeria need
34 Family reunion mementos?
36 G.I. hangout
39 "What say?"
40 Young 'uns
42 Art Deco name
43 Yarn holder
45 Scads
47 Take to a higher court
50 Lachrymose
51 Radii's partners
52 Paws
53 Breeze
54 Turner of "Peyton Place"
55 Some rtes.
56 Albany canal
60 Meadow
61 Son of, to Fahd

777 by Stephanie Spadaccini

ACROSS

1 Enter
5 Throaty utterance
9 Up, as the ante
14 Ancient alphabetic character
15 Singer Guthrie
16 Get straight A's, e.g.
17 Lot of land
18 "Greetings ___ . . ." (postcard opening)
19 Opinions
20 Lose some weight
23 Looks perfect on
24 Not pos.
25 Flier Earhart
29 Part of T.G.I.F.
30 Place to crash
33 Recluse
34 60's hairdo
36 ___ fide
37 Criticize formally
40 God of war
41 Where the Mets meet
42 Pulitzer winner Pyle
43 Actor Beatty
44 Señor Guevara
45 Certain marbles
46 "We ___ the

Champions" (Queen tune)
47 He loved Lucy
49 Nears, as a target
56 Hardly the brainy type
57 "Othello" villain
58 Golfer's cry
59 The Little Mermaid
60 Quite a rarity
61 Writer Lebowitz
62 Raison ___
63 Marquis de ___
64 Jodie Foster's alma mater

DOWN

1 Pate de foie ___
2 "That hurt!"
3 Concerning
4 Exigency
5 Basket material
6 Stop, in France
7 Puts on the brakes
8 Splendor
9 Variety shows
10 Getting rid of
11 Decorated, as a cake
12 Uses needle and thread

13 Overhead trains, for short
21 Blazing
22 "___ of Old Smoky"
25 Nebbishy comic Sherman
26 Sculptor Henry
27 Signed off
28 Diamond, of gangsterdom
29 "___ la Douce"
30 Gist
31 Vanity Fair photographer Leibovitz
32 Palm tree fruits
34 Word with head or heart
35 Enemy
36 Silent film star Theda
38 Hearth residue
39 On the up and up
44 New Orleans cuisine
45 On dry land
46 Yellowish-brown
47 Rigg or Ross
48 Pushed, with "on"
49 Take on, as an employee

50 Leave out
51 Grande and Bravo
52 Questionable
53 "A Doll's House" heroine

54 Like much testimony
55 Hawaii's state bird
56 Good, in street talk

778 by Joy L. Wouk

ACROSS

1 Fellow
5 Hardly a blabbermouth
9 "Saturday Night Live" bit
14 Priest of the East
15 "Ritorna vincitor" singer
16 Form of electric power
17 "I smell ___!"
18 Farm feed
19 On ___ (succeeding)
20 Swizzle stick
22 Like some vans
24 Longer-lived
25 Interweave
26 Expo '70 site
28 California event
32 Boccaccio's "Life of ___"
35 Sills offering
37 Confine
38 Liquid fat
39 Owned
40 Greenland base
41 Meeting of ministers association
42 Gump of the comics

43 Over
44 Tidbit
46 Nicholas Gage book
48 News media
50 Part of a 10-Down
54 Basketball strategy
57 Public face
58 Be in harmony
59 Astronaut Bean
61 "What ___ God wrought!"
62 Political alliances
63 Fictional detective
64 Toast topper
65 Vision
66 Fret
67 Pottery

DOWN

1 One may be easily dismissed
2 Author Bret
3 Vigorously
4 July Fourth celebration feature
5 Security equipment
6 Fabulist
7 Spots
8 Taj ___

9 Former Israeli Prime Minister
10 July Fourth celebration feature
11 Air freshener target
12 Shield border
13 Quit, in poker
21 Baseball great Al
23 Pro ___
25 July Fourth celebration features
27 Songwriter Gus
29 Tennyson poem
30 Leer
31 He wrote "Ten Days That Shook the World"
32 Awful end
33 Rival rival
34 "___ the twain shall meet"
36 Pastoral poem
40 Martinelli or Caruso
42 Silk-trading city of France
45 Conductor Ansermet
47 Heretofore
49 Fashion lines
51 Australian critter

52 Pierce
53 California resort
54 Taps or pats
55 He, to Enrico
56 Kermit, e.g.

57 Top of the head
60 Auction offering

779 by Jim Page

ACROSS
1 "How revolting!"
4 Roman road
10 Pugilists' org.
13 Purchasing agent's job
16 Gee's opposite
17 Flowerlike marine creatures
18 Where the C.S.A. was organized
19 Cherry
20 With greater rainfall
22 Has ___ (knows somebody)
23 Angel's dread
27 Like a highway
28 Settlings
29 Tear apart
30 1990 Best Actor
31 Lapse
32 Standout
33 Elects
34 Margays, e.g.
37 "... bring forth ___": Matt. 1:23
39 Woeful word
40 Year in Septimius Severus's reign
43 Muffler
44 Soft rock
45 King of clubs?
46 Up (to)
47 Flirtatious one
48 Singers Shannon and Reeves
49 Pen
51 Theorize
53 French biography
54 Champion
58 Afore
59 Bit of theatricality
60 Cherry
61 Prompt
62 Some A.L. batters

DOWN
1 Gentrified
2 Like some grass, in a phrase
3 Less fresh
4 Phoenix five
5 Amphibian with sticky feet
6 "Losing My Religion" band
7 Latin trio member
8 Retreat
9 De novo
10 Étagère
11 Whalebones
12 Grants
14 Doris Shannon novel "___ Daughters"
15 Old Possum, really
21 They're saved for a rainy day
24 Striped
25 Transparent sheet
26 Sheet fabric
34 It's read on Saturday
35 Some drafts
36 Attributed
37 Pick up
38 Browned, in a way
40 Spiked
41 Operator of the Palomar Observatory
42 Stays, e.g.
43 "Miracle Mets" pitcher
45 Turn ___ ear to
50 Stagnates
52 Brave
55 Hip-hop music
56 T-shirt size: Abbr.
57 Common middle name

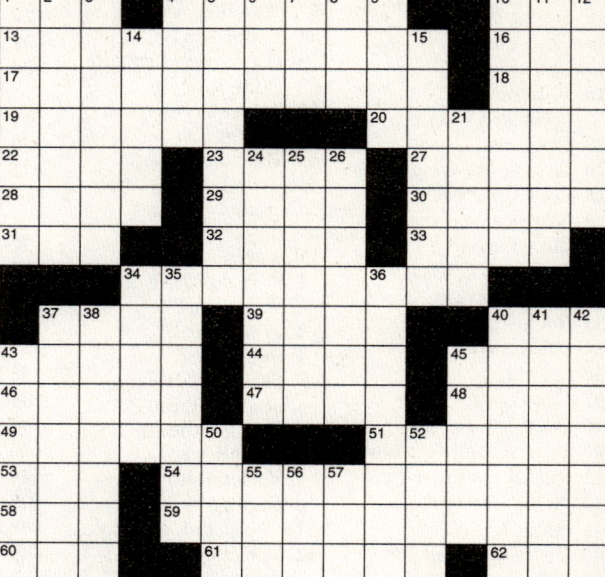

780 by Nancy Joline

ACROSS
1 Some vacation digs
11 Throws
15 Breeze on a hot day, e.g.
16 Auto part
17 Bandleader nicknamed El Rey
18 Scrap
19 ___ clip
20 Word with dish or piano
21 Blank
23 Plateaued, with "out"
26 Kind of check
28 Roman alternative
30 Furniture wood
31 It may be said for openers
32 Certain hotel, briefly
33 Mark Rudd's org.
34 Knit
36 Kind of history
39 What lats and pecs adorn
42 Thrice, in prescriptions
44 Released
48 Modest beachwear
51 Hard
52 Specialists' patients, usually
54 "It Ain't Me Babe" composer
55 Green
56 Fleur-de-___
58 Plus
59 Tray item
60 Batting position
64 Major addition
65 ABC-TV's first big hit, with "The"
66 Offspring
67 Somnolence

DOWN
1 Japanese mats
2 Copy
3 Greek brandies
4 "Hold On Tight" rock group
5 Taste
6 Time
7 Parts
8 Four-time Stanley Cup champs
9 Tolkien creature
10 Pier sights
11 Programming language
12 Increases
13 Ricocheted
14 Some volleyball players
22 Ancient Rome's ___ pacis
24 Actor Jack
25 Torch bearer
27 ___ Beach, Fla.
29 Model position?
35 Numerical prefix
37 Dismissed
38 Impose
39 Three kings of Bulgaria
40 Rodgers and Hart's "Johnny ___"
41 Puncture
43 Chili ___, Tex-Mex menu item
45 Mixture
46 Capers
47 Offers
49 Made the tiniest complaint
50 1994 cease-fire grp.
53 Resilience
57 Lat. and Lith., once
61 ___ favor
62 ___ chi
63 Actress Rutherford

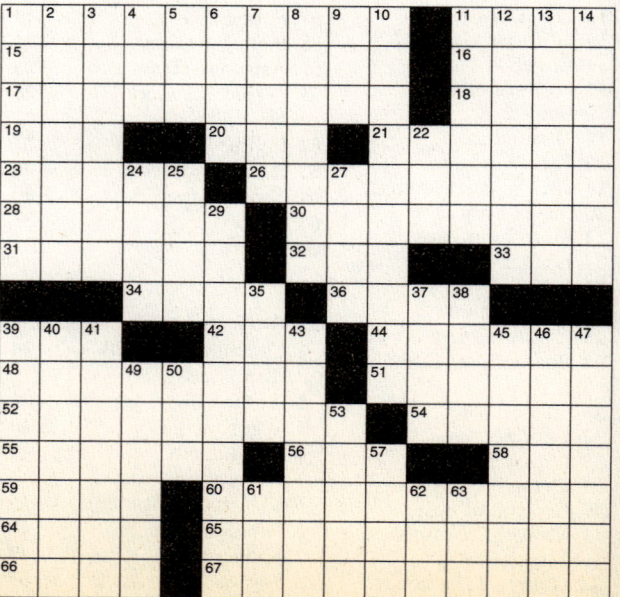

781   by Norman S. Wizer

ACROSS

1 Cheek
5 Runs in neutral
10 Latitude
14 Woody's son
15 State capital or its river
16 Artist Magritte
17 Ham operator's dog?
19 Prefix with -hedron
20 Napkin's place
21 Buffalo hunter
22 Feast of Lots honoree
24 Dam
25 Showing a fancy for
26 Cooked cereal
29 Kind of roll
33 Think a thought
34 Reading, for a famous example
35 Mishmash
36 Called the butler
37 Not set
38 Large green moth
39 Work units
40 They're kept under lids at night
41 ___ the hills
42 Drop in
44 Least laugh-out-loud, as humor
45 Parroted
46 Can't stand
47 Two-dimensional
50 Future jr.
51 Leg. title
54 Kharagpur queen
55 Hairdresser's dog?
58 30's migrant
59 Flip chart site
60 Woolen caps
61 Farmer's locale?
62 Metric unit
63 Boxer's stat

DOWN

1 Satirist Mort
2 Gazetteer info
3 Big shot in ice hockey
4 Lay turf
5 Locale of the Cantabrian Mountains
6 Mother hen, e.g.
7 Low-cal
8 Lubbock-to-Fort Worth dir.
9 In a calm manner
10 Diplomat's dog?
11 Poland's Walesa
12 Kitty feed
13 Junior, e.g.
18 Scape
23 Peter and Paul: Abbr.
24 Pilot's dog?
25 Best Actor of 1990
26 Shouts on the links
27 Disjointedly
28 Spoken-word #1 hit of 1964
29 One administering corporal punishment
30 Shake off
31 Hirschfeld hidings
32 Brown
34 Reinforced with a rope
37 Exhibits dyslexia
41 Lawn products brand
43 W.W. II agcy.
44 Parti-colored
46 Noted marine watercolorist
47 Egg on
48 Cottage site
49 Indigo dye
50 Enclosure with a MS.
51 Neighbor of Minn.
52 Pollster Roper
53 Hero of 60's TV and 80's film
56 Toque, for one
57 Six-time home run champ

782   by Elizabeth C. Gorski

ACROSS

1 "Let's go!"
5 Miss Cinders of old comics
9 Stravinsky's "Le ___ du printemps"
14 It's pulled on a pulley
15 Music for two
16 Farm units
17 Once more
18 Schooner part
19 Signified
20 Hit 1990's NBC comedy
23 Passing grade
24 Director Howard
25 X's in bowling
27 It's behind home plate
32 Sugar source
33 "___ American Cousin" (1859 comedy)
34 Results of big hits?
36 "Gandhi" setting
39 Shiite, e.g.
41 1997 has two
43 Brothers and sisters
44 Flattens
46 Plains home
48 Tam-o'-shanter
49 Yin's counterpart
51 Not the subs
53 Liberace wore them
56 A.F.L.'s partner
57 Tempe sch.
58 Novelty timepiece
64 Cinnamon unit
66 ___-Seltzer
67 First name in supermodeldom
68 Actress Berry
69 Alice doesn't work here anymore
70 Campus authority
71 Buzzing
72 Organic fuel
73 Klutz's utterance

DOWN

1 Pack in
2 "___ Lisa"
3 Like a William Safire piece
4 Alternative to J.F.K. and La Guardia
5 Oilers' home
6 Molokai meal
7 For fear that
8 Esqs.
9 Belushi character on "S.N.L."
10 Expert
11 Bartender's supply
12 "Walk Away ___" (1966 hit)
13 ___ Park, Colo.
21 Pear type
22 Like some stocks, for short
26 Lodges
27 Part of an old English Christmas feast
28 Atmosphere
29 Hodgepodge
30 Cross out
31 Glazier's items
35 Back-to-school time: Abbr.
37 Building support
38 Egyptian threats
40 Romeo
42 Maine's is rocky
45 Tee-hee
47 Psychiatrist Berne
50 Bearded creature
52 "Holy ___!"
53 Russian-born violinist Schneider, informally
54 These, in Madrid
55 Rascal
59 "Twittering Machine" artist
60 Neighbor of Kan.
61 Nondairy spread
62 Bit of thunder
63 Dolls since 1961
65 Cato's 151

783 by A.J. Santora

ACROSS

1 Hopeless
6 Where the tiller is
9 Zingers
13 Free
14 Colorado skiing mecca
16 Not right
17 How natives communicate
20 Type of mail
21 Mighty mite
22 ___ Rabbit
23 Rebuffs
25 Sort of
29 Droll 1993 best-seller
32 "The proof of the pudding ___ . . ."
34 Foofaraw
35 Seed
36 Dressing-down
41 Actor Holm
42 Old B'way sign
43 Latch ___
44 Not the secretive sort
49 Innumerable
50 Yearbook classmates: Abbr.
51 To live, to Livy

55 Richard Harris movie of 1977
57 Hornless
59 Communicating (with)
63 Mr. Hulot's creator
64 Cabal
65 "___ e Core" (1954 pop song)
66 On ___ (freelancer's terms)
67 Mamie Eisenhower, ___ Doud
68 Wanderer

DOWN

1 MacLaine's "Out on ___"
2 Individualist
3 Soprano Lehmann
4 Heralds
5 Look searchingly
6 Photographer Richard
7 Kind of cry
8 Actress Louise
9 Tribesmen in the film "Simba"
10 Wise one

11 Singing syllable
12 Neighbor of Leb.
15 Hispanic community
18 "I came," to Caesar
19 Reps. and Sens.
24 Lillehammer events
26 "Rome ___ built in a day"
27 Part of old discothèque names
28 Hedge shrub
30 H.S. course
31 Palindromic lady
32 Three-time World Cup winner
33 Sub detector
37 It's sold in lots
38 Bungle
39 On a roll
40 Native
41 Computer co.
45 Spike Lee's "Malcolm X," e.g.
46 Uncover
47 Old English royal house
48 New London grp.
52 More bruised
53 Diploma word

54 New Republic piece
56 Related
58 Greek letters
59 Military sch.
60 Rest

61 Geneviève, e.g.
62 Bach's "Partita ___ Minor"

784 by Daniel R. Stark

ACROSS

1 Snacks in Santa Rosalía
6 Upright
14 Aligned
16 Elephantine
17 Rainier locale
18 Globe flattener, in a way
19 Interest rate: Abbr.
20 Negotiates a puddle
22 ___ Khan
23 Superman's mother
25 Lake resort
26 Galway Bay isles
27 Accommodate
29 ___ openers
30 Positive, for a shutterbug
31 Mugged a snoozer
33 Husky runners
35 Gouda's cousin
37 Berlin one
38 One kind of clutch
41 Sarge, for one
45 Playwright-lyricist Comden
46 Buff
48 Reuniongoer

49 Harry Golden's "___ in America"
50 Watered silk
52 ___ rug
53 Altiplano tuber
54 Where Holstein cows originated
56 Catch some rays
57 Shaven, as a priest's head
59 Fix, as boundaries
61 Rooming-house convenience
62 Foul-ups
63 Quiet firework
64 "Hero and Leander" episode

DOWN

1 Charteris detective Simon ___
2 Alligator pear
3 Old telephone exchange
4 Stop ___ dime
5 Slangy instants
6 Private eye
7 Kind of town
8 Think alike
9 Resins

10 Actress Zadora
11 Least of the Great Lakes
12 Rallying cries
13 Not an easy boss
15 Blockhead
21 Clod
24 More than enough
26 It's south of the Caucasus
28 Lingerie item
30 Tree with edible seeds
32 Apply makeup
34 Aunts and others
36 Ill-fated bullfighter
38 Place for brooding
39 1996 Olympics site
40 Dutch coin
42 Notarize
43 The eldest Titan
44 Most Scroogelike
45 Fair constructions
47 ___-la-la
50 Fable's point
51 Tackles' neighbors
54 "The Incredible ___"
55 Hollow
58 Time of yr.
60 ___ and away

ACROSS

1 Erle Stanley Gardner pen name
7 Bo Derek's film debut
11 Jack or jenny
14 Kind of association
15 Preliminary race
16 Penn, for one: Abbr.
17 A, to Ludwig van Beethoven
20 Octogenarian's goal in life?
21 Thorns in one's side
22 Ask overpersonally
23 Framework
25 Flood residues
26 Presided over, as a case
29 Chevron wearers: Abbr.
31 ___ facto
32 Humble
34 Dog-tired
36 B, to Samuel Morse
40 Kind of kingdom
41 ___ Aires
43 Sharpen
46 Critic Pauline

48 Italian "please"
49 Playwright Connelly
50 Marched along
52 Fresh
53 Last words
56 Grammy song of '83
59 C, to Albert Einstein
62 The elected
63 Humorist Bombeck
64 Waterford worker
65 Middle grade
66 Monopoly piece
67 Platforms

DOWN

1 "Pooh" monogram
2 TV voice of Fred Flintstone
3 View from Tokyo
4 Egypt's ___-Ra
5 Legal memo starter
6 Laugh-a-minute comedies
7 Electrical unit
8 "Beverly Hills Cop" co-star
9 Beat, in a way
10 Building block of nature

11 Invites, as to an apartment
12 Lippizaners
13 Insists
18 Ford role in "Clear and Present Danger"
19 String on a finger, e.g.
22 Third degree?
24 Break up
27 Things to be paid
28 "Chitty Chitty Bang Bang" screenwriter
30 Oscar Madison, e.g.
33 Mont. neighbor
35 Live ___
37 Phrase after "Variations"
38 Type of stand
39 As a unit
42 Farm mother
43 Like ipecac
44 Strauss opera
45 Dolphin Hall-of-Famer Bob
47 Wolf, in Juárez
51 Put off
54 Mimed
55 One of the Dumas

57 Musical part
58 Spasms
60 Pop
61 Refrain intro

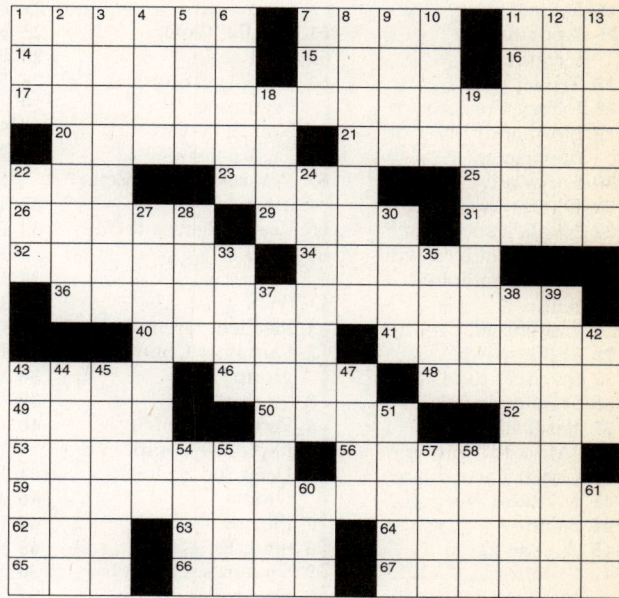

ACROSS

1 March instrument
5 Succeed in life
10 Brigham Young's home
14 Desertlike
15 Sky blue
16 Jesus's attire
17 Date tree
18 Sight at sunup
20 "___ Need Is the Girl" ("Gypsy" song)
21 Nav. rank
22 Hosts' counterparts
23 Nullify
25 Has ___ with
26 Undamaged
28 Hemmed
32 Move like a crab
33 Membership on Wall Street
34 Days of the dinosaurs
35 Card game
36 Salesmen sometimes leave them
39 Neighbor of Md.
40 Touch
42 N.B.A. star Thurmond

43 Escorted
45 Capital of Baja California Norte
47 Early invaders of England
48 Gallup product
49 Father, to Li'l Abner
50 International org.
53 Untold centuries
54 Butterfingers' cry
57 Stamp on some mail
59 Tallow source
60 Baldie's head
61 Individual items
62 Narrowly defeat
63 Jim-dandy
64 Discharge
65 Destine for trouble

DOWN

1 Tidbit in Toledo
2 Caspian feeder
3 Love letter
4 Halsey, for one
5 Most willing
6 Layer in the atmosphere
7 Minks and sables
8 Prince Valiant's firstborn

9 Flare up again
10 Imperativeness
11 Bushy clumps
12 Help in the holdup
13 Chops
19 Night, in Nîmes
24 Court coups
25 Start of a Dickens title
26 Farrakhan's belief
27 Weeper of myth
28 Seven: Prefix
29 "Hello"
30 Watergate Senator Sam
31 College heads
33 Minute
37 Similar item
38 Light punishment
41 Race track figure
44 Told all about
46 Caesar's partner in 50's TV
47 Most reasonable
49 Displays petulance
50 Sweeping hairstyle
51 Lunchtime
52 Salinger girl
53 Actress Adams

55 "___ My Heart" (1913 hit)
56 Stalk
58 Chang's Siamese twin

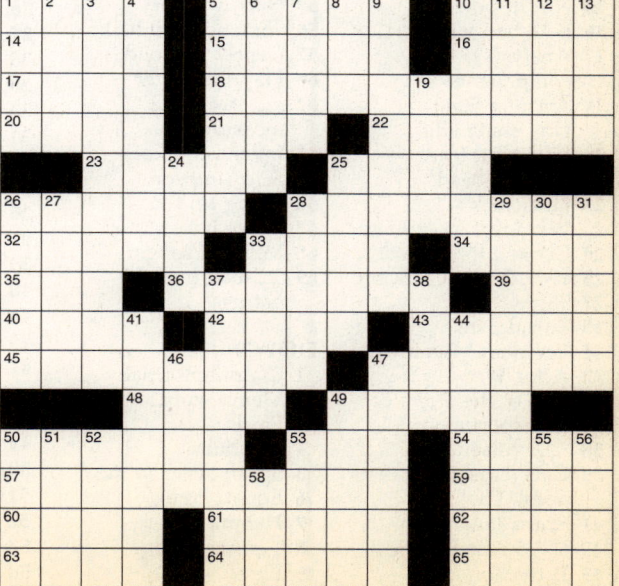

ACROSS

1 Overfill
5 Attorney ___
10 Gulf of Aden vessel
14 Don of talk radio
15 Dade County city
16 Appian Way terminus
17 Trivial pests?
18 Jockey Cordero
19 Normandy river or department
20 Superlative suffix
21 Diminutive suffix
22 Nikita's successor
24 Nocturnal bird with an onomatopoeic name
27 Cottonseed product
28 "Like wow!"
32 Swedish toast
35 State of India
37 Baseball's Brock
38 "Mikado" refrain
42 Coach Parseghian
43 Mythical weeper
44 Salary
45 Arcade game
47 "Tea for ___" (1925 hit)
49 Chimera
55 Visit to the Serengeti
58 Trim
59 ___ es Salaam
60 All-comers' tournament
61 Cordial flavor
63 Skirt style
64 Carpal or physical beginning
65 Skate's cousin
66 ___-Rooter
67 Returnees from Reno, maybe
68 Keanu Reeves thriller
69 Lead

DOWN

1 Resilient strength
2 Lancaster County group
3 ___-frutti
4 Road twist
5 Explosive compound
6 Deep red Spanish wine
7 Pilsner
8 Soul: Fr.
9 Violent squall in the near-polar regions
10 Slobbers
11 ___ of plenty
12 Atlanta arena, with "The"
13 Pull dandelions, e.g.
21 Prefix with center
23 Fragrant resin
25 Pre-election product
26 Fritter away
29 ___ podrida
30 Synthesizer
31 30's chess champ Max
32 Trade
33 Dame ___ Te Kanawa
34 Paton of "Cry, the Beloved Country" fame
35 Bikini, e.g.
36 Bro. or sis.
39 Walking ___ (elated)
40 John of the Boston Pops
41 Former Polish city
46 Masters, in Africa
47 Filament
48 Small
50 Suppose
51 Savor
52 ___ savant
53 Sleigh driver
54 Before, with "to"
55 A few
56 Top
57 Gala
62 Forty winks
63 ___ Butterworth

ACROSS

1 The "D" of C.D.
5 Fog
9 Heavenly instruments
14 Worldwide: Abbr.
15 Not in port
16 Be a bad winner
17 Analysis of components
19 Arizona State University site
20 Like pant legs
21 Swelled head
23 Hitchcock's "___ Window"
24 Cooked to perfection
25 1965 Petula Clark hit
27 Slight
30 Turndowns
31 Levin and Gershwin
32 Actor Warren
35 Part of the Dept. of Transportation
38 "___ Misérables"
39 Gary Larson cartoon, with "The"
41 Scuba tank supply
42 6-1, 5-7 or 6-4, e.g.
43 Perfection
44 Noncom: Abbr.
45 Bat wood
46 Pizza divisions
49 Row house
54 BBC nickname, with "the"
55 Harrow rival
56 Something to hail
57 Deprive of food
60 Play the guitar
62 ___ Act (1862 measure)
64 Inventor Nikola
65 Sen. Simpson
66 String up
67 "Give it ___!"
68 Minstrel songs
69 ___-Ball (arcade game)

DOWN

1 Claim, informally
2 Memo words
3 Firm
4 Hubbubs
5 Sportscaster John
6 Equal: Prefix
7 Hemmed
8 ___ Argentina
9 Elev.
10 Sirens
11 Juliet's beau.
12 Custard apple
13 Radio star Howard
18 Vegas game
22 Possessed
26 On the ___ (precisely)
27 Aches
28 Complimentary
29 Double-timed
33 Crazy ___ loon
34 Hacienda roofing material
35 Basketball offense
36 Temperature extreme
37 ___ and sciences
39 Bass, for one
40 Type of committee
44 Scabbards
45 Voids
47 "Ghosts" writer and kin
48 Understands
49 Seed cover
50 Valuable fur
51 For better or for ___
52 Taj ___
53 African virus
58 Barn topper
59 TV's "The ___ of Night"
61 Where pins are made
63 Flowering time

ACROSS

1 Great guy?
6 Boston bunch
10 Political suffix since the 70's
14 Comfortable
15 At capacity
16 Soprano Mills
17 None of the above
18 Jovial roly-poly of legend
20 Exhaust
22 Squirrel treats
23 Actress Reinking
24 Shin's neighbor
25 Debut auto of 1960
29 Catch, as a dogie
33 "That's clear"
34 Devilkin
35 Last-place spot
36 Turn on the waterworks, so to speak
37 Galilee, e.g.
38 Christmas need
39 Verse heading
40 Nuggets
42 He feeds 54-Down

43 Dole (out)
44 George of "Where's Poppa?"
45 "The Best Man" playwright
47 Crusoe's creator
49 Friday, for one
50 Bind one's boots
52 Alternative fuel
56 Pussyfoot
58 Decline
59 Insolent tad
60 An Autry
61 Entrance courts
62 Heave
63 Davis of TV's "Sinbad"
64 Like most movies

DOWN

1 Cargo vessel
2 Baby-faced
3 Labor Dept. arm
4 Very in
5 Guthrie of the theater
6 Fizzling sound
7 "___ Town"
8 Easily bent
9 Lax

10 "C'mon, quit kidding"
11 Give ___ for one's money
12 Muscle spasms
13 Cartoon cry
19 Kind of derby
21 These can be brief
24 Dadaist Hans
25 Harrow blades
26 "___ Mio"
27 Correct the defects in
28 Org. for Doogie Howser
30 Swung around
31 ___ Maria
32 Bay window
35 ___ vérité
37 Bad temper
38 In place of
41 Daredevils
42 Typical guy
43 Canon competitor
45 Its tunnel vision is poor
46 Alma mater of Meryl Streep
48 "Oh, darn!"
50 Jay of note
51 François's friends

52 Lola player in "Damn Yankees"
53 "Cotton Candy" trumpeter
54 Comic canine

55 Be the bellwether
56 F.D.R. follower
57 Cuckoo bird

ACROSS

1 Twain character
7 To the extent that
14 Lacking nothing
15 Closet
16 Blinker
17 Art of arguing
19 Traditional areas of knowledge
20 Defraud
21 High-paying easy job
22 Geraint's love
23 "___ Johnny!"
24 Part of an equine family tree
25 Room with an easy chair
26 Become entrenched
27 ___ Aviv
28 Football team
30 Part of elopement plans
32 Egg on
33 Fuzzy fruit
35 Holds back
38 Accolade
40 Conflict
41 Negotiations
42 D.C. summer time
45 Flag

47 Wall decoration
48 Blackthorn fruit
49 Derive (from)
50 Thin
51 Sign of life
52 Table
54 Rodeo rope
55 One on a walkout
56 Repay
57 Hobo's garb
58 Business news

DOWN

1 Prepared potatoes
2 "Who'll volunteer?"
3 Of the same mother
4 Stacked
5 Goddess of discord
6 Danger signal
7 Unlined tablet
8 Hot
9 Kith and kin
10 Live
11 On/off routes
12 Nimbleness
13 Ties down
18 Refine
20 Procreate
23 Busy place
26 Socialist Eugene

29 Amateur
30 Terrible ___
31 Fit out
33 Czar-era bourgeois
34 Sorts
35 Food that's hole-some?
36 Most acidic
37 Short melody
38 Breadwinners
39 Commotion
41 Merchant
43 Medicinal amount
44 Be indecisive
46 Brainy
47 Much the same
48 More confident
51 Blacktop
53 Be in session
54 Escape

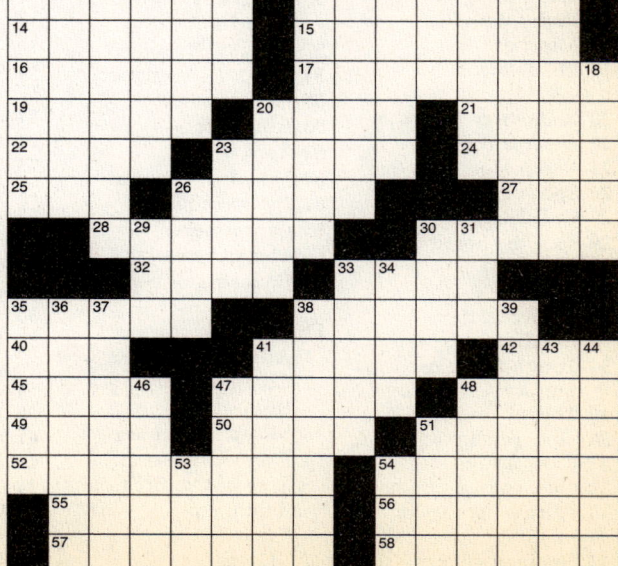

791 by David J. Kahn

ACROSS
1 "Rock of ___"
5 Press output
15 Brest bridge
16 Subject of a Longfellow poem
17 Raised nautically
18 Be mature
19 Short poem
21 Sounds of dismay
22 Rx giver
23 Ticks off
24 "What happened next?"
25 Give a price
27 Swear words
28 Negri of silents
30 Game divisions
31 Fall mo.
32 Moonfish
33 Towel word
34 50's TV game show
40 Norfolk inits.
41 Absolute worst
42 Cenozoic, e.g.
43 Is snoopy
45 Old-fashioned fuel
46 Patriotic soc.
47 Yale students beginning in 1969

48 Barrett of Pink Floyd
49 Heston film role
51 Relevant
52 "What's the ___?"
53 Fitting-room activities
54 1957 #1 song
58 Spanish linen fabric
59 Down-to-the-wire campaigns
60 Subject of peer pressure?
61 Words of despair
62 Or ___ (if not)

DOWN
1 Terse saying
2 "I like that!"
3 Surrounds
4 Inscribed slab
5 Give ___ on the back
6 F.E.C. file entry
7 "Bye Bye Birdie" song
8 Chaplin contemporary
9 Atlantic fliers
10 Passing grade
11 Hosp. hookups
12 Precisely correct

13 Cereal plant diseases
14 Volleyball's Gabrielle
20 Takes up, in a way
24 Orchard spray
25 Wit
26 ___ Major
29 Debuts
30 Eighth in a series
35 Chewable wad
36 Lost vitality
37 Marine life used for jewelry
38 Workout figures
39 Event in a classified
43 54-Across, e.g.
44 Puts new prices on
47 Western plants
48 Fiber named for a town in Mexico
50 Élève's place
52 Classic Latin work "___ Rustica"
53 1979 Polanski film
55 Madame ___ of 60's Vietnam
56 Pennies: Abbr.
57 ___ judicata

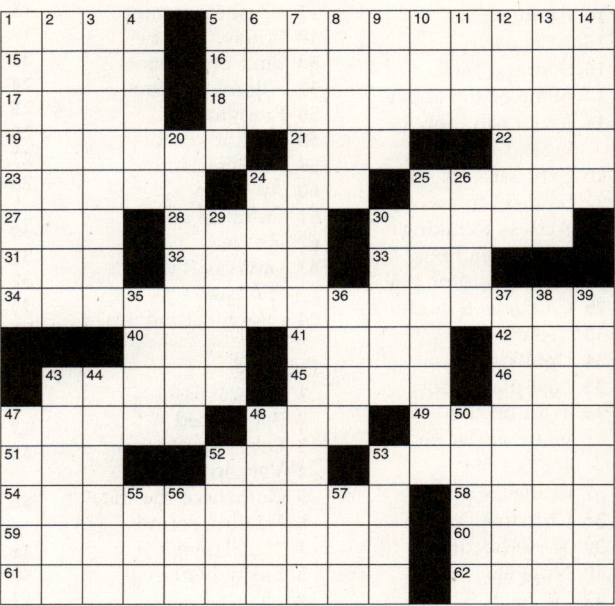

792 by Fred Piscop

ACROSS
1 Puccini opera
6 Very much
10 A.E.F. conflict
13 Bay window
14 Rain cats and dogs
15 "And ___ goes"
16 Bored with life
18 Miseries
19 Pb, elementally speaking
20 Relative of the wasp
22 Ice cream pattern
24 Robin Hood, for one
26 Sheep cries
27 Golf hazard
29 "___ the Sheriff" (1974 hit)
32 Landed
33 Jimmy Carter's middle name
34 Tough fabric used in uniforms
35 The "S" in R.S.V.P.
36 Slow-pitch pitch
37 Card up the sleeve
39 Oil treatment inits.
40 Patrick Ewing, for one
42 Game of chance

44 Resting on
45 ___ Wences (frequent Ed Sullivan guest)
46 Extremities
47 Asset
48 Poltergeists
50 Gradually decrease, with "off"
52 Lady of "Ivanhoe"
54 Der ___ (Adenauer)
55 Gen. Bradley
56 Irresolute
62 Yard digger
63 "Exodus" novelist
64 Propositioned
65 Office seeker
66 Mexican moolah
67 Equestrian's controls

DOWN
1 Auto club service
2 Conquistador's treasure
3 Ma'am's counterpart
4 Pablo Casals, e.g.
5 Tree of the birch family
6 Copied
7 Mauna ___

8 Dickens's "___ Mutual Friend"
9 Rendezvous
10 Would-be Romeo's call
11 "Where there's a ___ . . ."
12 ___-bitsy
15 Any provincial college
17 Army surgeon Reed
21 Carroll adventuress
22 Like seawater
23 Jerusalem prayer site
24 Galley propeller
25 High elevation area
26 Sunbathes
28 Bootlegging or extortion
30 Traveling, as a band
31 Big name in baseball cards
36 Tire-producing city
38 Expensive
41 Stick together
43 Nav. officer
44 Negotiate à la Chamberlain
49 Cut into logs
51 In armed conflict

52 Win easily, in the sports pages
53 Melville novel
54 Mr. Moto's reply
57 Dander
58 Family girl
59 Do slaloms
60 Farm cackler
61 Gridiron gains: Abbr.

793   by Gerald R. Ferguson

ACROSS

1 Husband one's resources
7 Take stock
13 1980's sitcom
14 Getting nowhere
15 Cruise ship sighting
16 Big name in desserts
18 Letters in an F.B.I. file
19 One of the orig. 13
20 Dispatched
21 Refusals in Rouen
23 Numb
26 The Lion of God
27 Because of
29 Chuck wagon fare
30 "___ it" (delayed reaction to a joke)
31 Pearl collection
33 Glistens
35 May Day pace
37 Sneeze cause
40 Click beetle
44 Hopper
45 Cannon sound
47 Group of three
48 No-good
49 Famed assassin
51 Clue finders
52 Glorified
54 Half of a 1955 merger
56 Something often sweetened
57 Encumbers
59 Wardrobe
61 The Spectator writer
62 Erudite
63 Top of a cornstalk
64 Kind of fracture

DOWN

1 Hit the hay
2 Janitor
3 Graycoat
4 Hot
5 Up to the hubs
6 Pirate's feature, sometimes
7 Sloths
8 Drink of half hard cider and half beer
9 Lethal gas
10 Of historic time
11 Waste matter
12 Terry Bradshaw, for one
13 Victuals
17 Cuts and splices
22 Not spontaneous
24 Place for powder
25 Morons' comments
28 ___ about (legal phrase)
30 Communicate
32 Just keep one's head above water
34 Dissolve
36 Person of the future
37 Practicing law
38 Most eye-catching
39 1980 De Niro role
41 Men's jewelry items
42 Showstoppers?
43 Not overworked
46 Tavern habitués
49 Astronomical discovery of 1801
50 River to the Danube
53 Explorer John et al.
55 Versifying astronomer
58 Bifteck seasoning
60 Nev. neighbor

794   by Fred Piscop

ACROSS

1 Singer-actress Lane
5 "___ Mia" (1965 hit)
9 Choreographer Agnes de ___
14 Watery
15 Stratford-Avon link
16 Firefighter Red
17 TV/film actor Jack
19 Comparatively modern
20 Scott's "___ Roy"
21 Got a move on
22 Honeybunch
23 Humdingers
25 Octave followers, in sonnets
28 It's hoisted in a pub
29 T'ai ___ ch'uan
30 Phillips University site
31 Writer Jack
34 Form 1040 completer
35 Scourge
38 Idolize
39 Escritoire
40 "Boola Boola" singer
41 Pugilist Jack
43 Savoir-faire
45 Skater Midori
46 Superaggressive one
50 Barrow residents
52 Licked boots?
54 Grasslands
55 Crash diet
56 Absorbed, as an expense
57 AOL memos
59 Movie actor Jack
61 Haggard
62 "Garfield" dog
63 Grid coach Alonzo Stagg
64 Loquacious, in slang
65 Kind of blocker
66 Sit in the sun

DOWN

1 Oscar and Obie
2 Wisconsin college
3 Psycho talk?
4 Manage to get, with "out"
5 Doll
6 Church recesses
7 Crucifix
8 Gloucester's cape
9 Currycombs comb them
10 Imagine
11 Lyricist Jack
12 "The check is in the mail," maybe
13 Blow it
18 Kind of wine
22 Clears for takeoff?
24 Word of Valleyspeak
25 High-pitched
26 Much of a waiter's income
27 Mount Rushmore's site: Abbr.
29 Former New York governor
32 Transmits
33 "Golden Boy" dramatist
35 ___ noire
36 Griever's exclamation
37 Golfer Jack
39 Twosome
42 Sister of Calliope
44 Some commercial promotions
47 Poisonous atmosphere
48 Caused to go
49 Danish city
51 Like beer
52 Unspoken
53 Actor Milo
55 Bona ___
57 "Rotten" missile
58 Ewe's sound
59 San Francisco's ___ Hill
60 Part of a science class

795 by Shannon Burns

ACROSS

1 Pickle
5 Klinger portrayer, in 70's–80's TV
9 Tubby
14 Chief Whitehorse, for one
15 Cousin of a clarinet
16 Winning
17 "Yeah, right!"
18 First name in country
19 Explorer Amundsen
20 High points
23 Places for aces?
24 Operculum
25 Opposite of post-
28 Stone smoother
29 Mr. Jaggers's ward, in Dickens
30 Brat's Christmas present
31 Largest moon of Neptune
33 Sounds of a leak
34 Burdensome possession
37 Pandemonium
38 Hologram producers
39 Cold war capital
40 Price word
41 Stand for a portrait
44 Down
45 Actress Tyler of 90's films
46 Small quantity symbol, in math
48 Extremely exasperated
51 Flabbergast
53 It's next to Mayfair, in London
54 Signs
55 Director known for spaghetti westerns
56 It's all the same to moi
57 Cut, maybe
58 Joined together
59 "It just isn't ___"
60 Employees' ID's: Abbr.

DOWN

1 Swine
2 The "se" in per se
3 "Beats me!"
4 Shield's purpose
5 Ontario city just west of Buffalo
6 Gives a yegg a hand
7 Biblical attire
8 Army's back section
9 Unit of capacitance
10 Sailor's salutation
11 Recipe measure
12 Baseball's Bando
13 Anomalous
21 Turns inside out
22 Dance maneuver
26 Enthralled
27 City rattlers
29 Like 19-Across's expeditions
30 Ranks
32 Broadcast
33 Musical passage
34 Horse's halter
35 Manual
36 Door feature
37 Safer workplace?
40 Pizzeria order
42 Twisty-horned animals
43 Ensure
45 Drew in
46 Actor Hawke
47 Branch headquarters?
49 Like Silver's rider
50 Inoperative
51 It's at the end of the line
52 King's name

796 by Louis Sabin

ACROSS

1 Spring runner
4 Pole at sea
9 Dieter's measure
13 Robust drink
14 Delete-key function
15 TV tease
16 Golf ball's position
17 Sedaka and Simon
18 Play the fink
19 "Falstaff"
22 Marked down
23 "The Woman in the Dunes" author
24 It's big in London
25 Hard or soft approach
27 Scout's group
30 Quatrain's pattern
33 Seville snack
35 Sister of Charlotte
37 "The Misfits"
40 Barkin of "Sea of Love"
41 Genealogist's work
42 It may be cured
43 Monaco cube
44 Speech site
46 Actress Carrie
48 Cobbler's tool
49 Imperfect bridge holding
53 Homer #521
59 Blotter entry
60 Waugh and others
61 Eunuch's unit
62 Disk-shaped marine fish
63 Challenger's quest
64 Political abbr.
65 Hound's quarry
66 Semicircular recesses
67 Wordsworth's "We ___ Seven"

DOWN

1 Military blast
2 Refuge seeker
3 Duke and earl
4 More than forgetful
5 Favors
6 Tout's post
7 ___ Mujeres, Mexico
8 Chester Gould femme
9 Smooth-skinned edible
10 Learning method
11 It makes the mundus go round
12 Actress Washbourne
15 Gordian knot, for one
20 Show amateurish interest (in)
21 Chess's Mikhail
25 Works with Riddick Bowe
26 Facility
27 Belly flop, e.g.
28 Lamb of yore
29 "No way Sergei!"
30 Elderly
31 Java neighbor
32 Up to snuff
34 Choral voices
36 Tick of time
38 On edge
39 Seaquarium arm
45 Like
47 Swains' requests
48 Like Pegasus
50 Now, in Nogales
51 Autumn beverage
52 Marchers' camp
53 Wear's partner
54 Chase of Tinseltown
55 Pre-rehab Pinocchio
56 ___ Hari
57 Underdress
58 "___ Do It" (Porter tune)

ACROSS

1 Author Bret
6 Oberon's imp
10 Not vivid
14 "Goodbye, mon ami"
15 King Harald's capital
16 Cameo stone
17 "___ to Belong to You" (1939 song)
18 McKern and Carroll
19 "Auld Lang ___"
20 Tough toy
21 Apollo, Aphrodite, etc.
23 Without exception
25 Scrap
26 Interstate haulers
27 What's sweet about parting
31 Discouraging word
34 Burden
35 "Behold!"
36 Massachusetts vacation spot
38 Brandy cocktail
40 Loose
41 Bruce or Laura
42 Elephant's org.
43 Offering vistas
45 Long tales

47 High note
48 Site of 36-Across and 22-Down
51 Accept, after negotiation
55 Like a mouse
57 Kind of arch
58 1986 #1 hit by Starship
59 "La Gioconda," e.g.
60 Taximeter reading
61 In ___ (stuck)
62 Alate
63 Tennis score
64 Seven Hills site
65 What roll calls count

DOWN

1 Reagan pal Al
2 Extemporize
3 Spanish wine
4 Domingo and others
5 1936 Literature Nobelist
6 Victim of Hamlet
7 Vain
8 Become tiresome
9 Greek universe
10 Physics particle
11 Author Seton

12 Actress Redgrave
13 Alimony getters
22 ___ Players (theater group)
24 Atlanta sports site, with "The"
28 Diana of "The Avengers"
29 Ersatz butter
30 Twist
31 So
32 Lip-___
33 Model Moss
37 Sophomore's age, maybe
38 Divide
39 Stumble
41 Propriety
44 Onetime chief of 64-Across
46 Opponent of Hannibal
49 Foreshadowings
50 Lament for the dead
51 It can hide a bed
52 "Oh, my!"
53 Garr of "Tootsie"
54 Casino game
56 Calendar pages

ACROSS

1 Arabian sultanate
5 Muddle
9 Insiders' talk
14 Take on
15 Word-of-mouth
16 Former Spanish P.M. ___ y Montaner
17 Semifictional movie
19 Circumvent
20 Alliances
21 One of the Huxtable kids
23 Increased, as inflation
27 ". . . on the Dead ___ Chest"
28 Like most music
29 Trounce
31 Photo repro
34 Plunders
36 The Emerald ___
38 Cider-sweet girl
39 "Metric" prefix
40 England-France connector
42 Witticism
43 Gender abbr.
44 Tedious undertaking
45 Much of Mali
47 Biblical beginning

49 Rounded ottoman
51 ___ Tots (grocery purchase)
52 Hold sway
54 Eulogists
56 Perry Como classic
59 B & B's
60 Hockey infraction
61 Mexican border language
66 Do detective work
67 Actress Garr
68 Lackawanna's railroad partner
69 Swiss mathematician
70 Good life
71 "Do Ya Think I'm ___?" (1979 hit)

DOWN

1 Unmatched
2 Chinese chairman
3 Trajectory
4 Sitting on the fence
5 Mushroom
6 Cleaned, as a disk
7 "Cheers" bartender
8 Eastern European
9 Frigidaire rival
10 Harsh-voiced birds

11 Number in the ballpark?
12 Hockey's Bobby et al.
13 "See ya"
18 Local lingo
22 Moseys
23 Discord
24 On one's mark
25 Paid-for TV program
26 Bar request
30 Adm. or capt.'s org.
32 Worshiper
33 13th-century invaders
35 Circle and octagon, e.g.
37 Raising spirits
41 Road show grp.
46 Tribulations
48 Shade of meaning
50 Some mendicants
53 German gun
55 Gal with a gun, on Broadway
56 Fisherman's hope
57 Beige shade
58 Italian art patron
62 Spherical food
63 Wrath
64 Evening hour
65 "You there!"

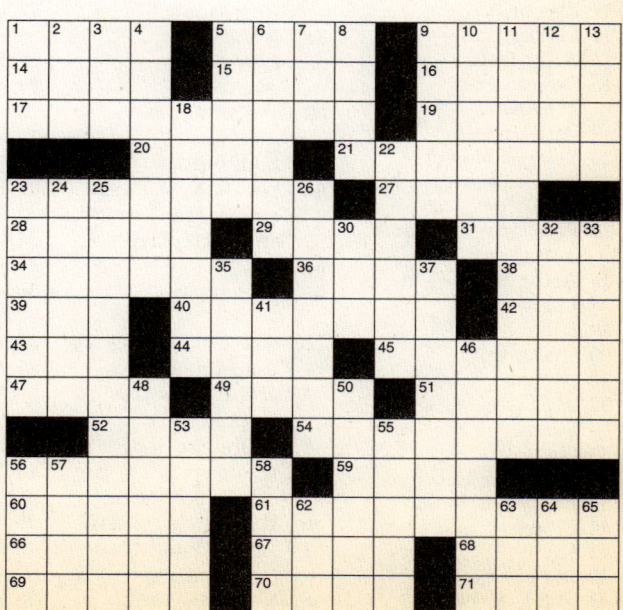

799 by Richard Hughes

ACROSS

1 Blvd. crossers
4 #2, informally
8 Defeater of Hannibal at Zama
14 Pasture
15 Shakespearean villain
16 Chaucer's ___ Inn
17 Civil war, e.g.
19 List ender
20 Mr. Rathbone
21 Dour
23 Chicago-to-Atlanta dir.
24 Slept "soundly"
26 "Hud" Oscar winner Patricia
28 Snap, crackle and pop, e.g.
34 Criminal charge
37 City on the Mosel
38 Razor sharpener
39 Help in the getaway
41 Architectural piers
43 Location
44 Catcalls
46 Moffo and Magnani
48 In low spirits
49 Fe, fi, fo, fum, e.g.
52 Willing
53 Swimwear manufacturer
57 Perform
60 Pole figure
63 Be unfaithful to
64 "Calm down!"
66 "Life is a bowl of cherries," e.g.
68 White winter coat
69 Primary
70 More than none
71 Clears of hidden problems
72 Rival rival
73 Born

DOWN

1 Neatniks' opposites
2 Ross Perot, e.g.
3 First authority
4 Cataclysmic
5 Attention
6 Sometimes they're super
7 ___ l'Évêque (French cheese)
8 Not monaural
9 Dozes
10 Olympic basketball coach Hank
11 Buddies
12 Rainbow goddess
13 Garfield's foil
18 Spanish Surrealist
22 One in the running
25 "Dumb ___" (old comic)
27 Plenty
29 Mosque feature
30 Big name in insurance
31 Goddess of discord
32 Least bit
33 Mimicked
34 Indian prince
35 Victim of sibling rivalry
36 Sir Robert of London's bobbies
40 Advanced math
42 "Je ne ___ quoi"
45 Averring
47 Elsa in "Lohrengrin"
50 Overacts
51 ___ tide
54 Wharton's Frome
55 Lorna of an 1869 romance
56 Deli phrase
57 Scored a hole-in-one
58 Inner workings
59 Grave
61 Poet Lazarus
62 More than a snack
65 N.Y. school
67 Waitress's bit

800 by Alfio Micci

ACROSS

1 Police action
5 Express displeasure at
8 Sandwich decoration
13 Part of A.D.
14 Plagiarize
15 Actor Delon
16 Composer of 24-Down
19 Parisian's soul
20 Ready follower
21 Not walk a straight line
22 Personnel director's duty
24 Artist Nicolaes ___
26 Literary olio
29 Spotted
30 Understand
32 Alphabet quartet
33 Says on a stack of Bibles
35 God
36 A pair of 24-Down
39 Lecherous looks
40 Protect
41 Kiln
42 Brand of brew
43 The least bit
47 Early Beatle Sutcliffe
48 Scout groups
49 Mortarboard adjunct
51 Sprinkle
53 First word of "Home, Sweet Home"
54 Moisten
55 Noted 24-Down of fiction
60 Companion of Artemis
61 Ladder unit
62 "Let Us Now Praise Famous Men" writer
63 San Diego player
64 Artful
65 Circle dance

DOWN

1 Eastern potentates
2 Lack of values, as in a people
3 Naturally belong
4 Put on
5 A fez lacks one
6 J.R. Ewing's concern
7 Cummerbund for a geisha
8 Detectives' work
9 ___ vera
10 "Lonely Boy" singer
11 Frozen Wasser
12 Genetic stuff
14 Redbug
17 Give a poor review
18 Kind of school
23 Book extra
24 Subject of this puzzle
25 Attack
27 Holiday song
28 Filing time: Abbr.
31 Former grape
32 Islamic prophets
34 Sentence parts: Abbr.
35 Caesar's 1550
36 Accomplishment
37 Rose anew
38 Avian activity
39 Pop music's ___ Lobos
42 Transportation Secretary Federico
44 Upstate New York city
45 Wobble
46 Gibson of tennis fame
48 Electron tube
50 Total
52 Not fully closed
53 "___ are called . . ."
55 Unruly locks
56 Historic time
57 "___ Miniver"
58 Actor Brynner
59 Humbug preceder

801 by Eileen Lexau

ACROSS
1 Real beauty, in old slang
5 Make sense
10 Crowds around
14 Hymn word
15 Seville tower
16 Bushy hairdo
17 Free
19 "Make the most ___"
20 Cobble
21 Tex-Mex treats
23 Has title to
25 Play in the water
26 Attempts to convey
30 Perfumer's compounds
33 Ancient letters
34 Stowe character
36 Court
37 Hill dwellers
38 Respighi's "___ of Rome"
39 Simon of song
40 Last degree
41 Prongs
42 Model wood
43 German poet
45 Tot's wheels
47 "Little Women" surname
49 Ilk
50 Debate curbs
53 Plies
57 Em or Polly
58 In a fix
60 Singer Jacques
61 "Cheers" perch
62 Comic "Dame"
63 Terrier type
64 Nixon's undoing
65 Has the nerve, in Dogpatch

DOWN
1 "New Look" designer
2 Gov. Carlson of Minnesota
3 Charlie Brown exclamation
4 Is incumbent on
5 Parthenon site
6 "Zip-a-Dee-___-Dah"
7 Defeat decisively
8 Bear, in old Rome
9 Incomparable
10 Chinese hard-liner
11 Pretty zany
12 Verve
13 Bar habitués
18 Cary of "Bram Stoker's Dracula"
22 Optimistic
24 Used, as a chair
26 Sturm und ___
27 Cost
28 Rich
29 Shades
31 Shake awake
32 Kind of energy
35 Irksome ones
38 It should be flaky
39 Equivocated
41 Fast-food drive-___
42 Kind of acid
44 Rat (on)
46 Spur attachments
48 Seven: Prefix
50 Crane operators' perches
51 Lie in wait
52 Huxley's "Time Must Have a ___"
54 Mother of Castor and Pollux
55 Couch potatoes' spots
56 Three-handed card game
59 Get at the weeds

802 by Matt Gaffney

ACROSS
1 Shoelace end
6 They have arches
10 Legal scholar Guinier
14 Follow back to the source
15 Nullify
16 It follows deuce in tennis
17 Reason to wear a hat?
19 Grandmother
20 Working
21 Replay feature
22 Midwest university town
23 Japanese cabbage
24 Ones with cases
25 Lover of Pyramus
27 Phrase of agreement
29 Côte de ___ (French entrée)
31 Tore
32 Lined up
34 Train company stocks
36 Leader of 1547
40 "Mother Goose Suite" composer
41 Focus (on)
42 "Aladdin" prince
43 Certain kitties, for short
45 Fistfight
48 Less of a mess
50 TD's are worth 6
51 Rap sheet abbr.
53 Having as a hobby
54 Jose Cruz, notably
57 Croat, e.g.
58 Having a pH value of less than 7
59 Bewitching stare
61 Spanish boy
62 Seemingly forever
63 Schlemiel
64 Can't stand the weight
65 Popular pencil-and-paper game
66 English music festival site

DOWN
1 Held off
2 Problems for high heels
3 Judeo-Spanish
4 Real: Ger.
5 British break
6 Rolls up
7 Opposite of exo-
8 Kind of cheese
9 Car since 1935
10 ___ City, Hawaii
11 Eve, biblically
12 Pool hall game
13 From one perspective
18 Whence the line "For unto us a child is born"
24 "Be honest!"
26 Goes chop-chop
28 Banquet
29 Democratic doings
30 Pitcher
33 ___ Pahlevi, former Shah
35 Four Tops hit "___ No Woman"
36 33-Down's subjects
37 Variety of orange
38 Flying
39 Russian city on the Don
44 Unfit for kids
46 "Honor Thy Father" author
47 Confirmed
49 Fusses
50 Weightroom choice
52 States
55 Word to a fly
56 Scout shelter
57 Liqueur flavor
60 Poorly

803 by Frank A. Longo

ACROSS

1 Calendar mo.
4 Up
9 Jerome Kern's "They ___ Believe Me"
14 Bikini part
16 Word with city or circle
17 Copy
18 It's often bid
19 Kenilworth and Boston, e.g.
20 Engenders
22 Abbreviated version
23 Blvds.
25 Ocular socket
26 Dicker
29 Takeout sign
30 Acerbity
32 Kvass ingredient
33 Three-person card game
34 Kansas City paper
36 Boat bigwig, briefly
39 Winter driving need
42 In ___ (stuck)
44 Cranesbills
46 Explain anew
48 Brain-wave record, familiarly
49 Louse eggs
51 Springer and Sussex, e.g.
53 Anglican headdress
54 "The Secret Garden" Tony winner Daisy
55 Rote procedure
58 "___ We All?"
59 Clerics
60 Peevish
61 Au fait
62 Comment of surprise

DOWN

1 Filled to overflowing
2 Four-time Oscar-winning film scorer
3 Property seizures
4 Unfixed
5 Jerk
6 Benaderet of "Petticoat Junction"
7 Craftsman
8 High schooler
9 Logbook
10 "Without a doubt!"
11 Black Sea feeder
12 With open palms, maybe
13 Fiduciary
15 Cutters
21 Swelling cause
23 Bowstring
24 Walk stealthily
27 Twelve ___ ("G.W.T.W." locale)
28 Seed coverings
31 Pakistani garment
35 Make up
36 Toddler's safety item
37 Set the stage
38 Storm problems
40 Wrung
41 Hitting hard
43 Kind of farming
45 Took major steps
47 Full of fuzz
50 Discern
52 100 centesimi
53 Trading center
56 French writer Curie
57 Theater group, informally

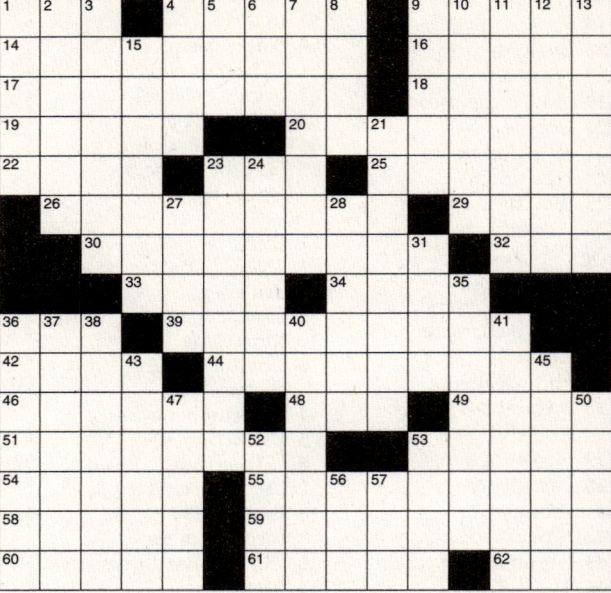

804 by Glenn E. Skyes

ACROSS

1 Graycoats
5 Whirlpool alternative
10 Copycats
14 Territory
15 La Scala's city
16 Fountain treat
17 Gangster's gal
18 On one's toes
19 Capri, for one
20 "Ninotchka" with music, 1955
23 Author Umberto
24 Circumference-figuring figures
25 Kunta Kinte's tale
28 Woodcutter
30 Part of una casa
33 "La ___ en Rose"
34 Rope step on a ship
37 Actor Wilder
38 "Romeo and Juliet" with music, 1957
41 Mandate
42 Confessors
43 Nav. rank
44 "Beau Geste" author P.C. ___
45 Out in front
49 Saying
51 "___ dreaming?"
53 Mao ___-tung
54 "My Sister Eileen" with music, 1953
59 On
61 Uproars
62 Demeanor
63 Fortune profilees
64 Queen ___ War (1702–13 conflict)
65 Jai ___
66 Whirlpool
67 Beat
68 Circus props

DOWN

1 One of 12 pharaohs
2 Beethoven's Third
3 Elephant's sound
4 Polio vaccine developer
5 Cremona craftsman
6 Director Forman
7 Smart ___
8 Stoolie
9 "No" voter
10 Friend of Francisco
11 Disregard
12 Building wing
13 Fr. holy woman
21 Lean eater
22 Second Amendment advocate: Abbr.
26 Wee
27 Call, in poker
29 Once, once
30 Ancient Phoenician city
31 Once more
32 ___-majesté
35 Romanov leader
36 Not taped
37 "You don't say!"
38 Skid row type
39 "The Bridges of Madison County" co-star
40 Not lead
41 Gender: Abbr.
44 Carried the day
46 Ballet headliner
47 Perspiring
48 Bulls' Rodman
50 Stowe character
51 "The Morning ___"
52 Untidy
55 Tie
56 Die Zeit article
57 Hollywood insider Barrett
58 Govt. agent
59 Hole in one
60 "Nightline" name

805 by Miriam D. Frankel

ACROSS

1 Red ink amount
5 Give as an example
9 Make ashamed
14 Inter ___
15 Alack's partner
16 Jouster's weapon
17 Fraternity letter
18 Light, happy tune
19 Flowery perfume
20 Choice at a singles bar
23 Bloodshot
24 Actress Thurman
25 Lost vitality
29 With 12-Down, a hospital procedure
31 Sobriquet
35 Hollywood's Flynn
36 Parade feature
37 Trendy
38 Choice at a casino
42 Church denom.
43 Kind of bag
44 "___ la vista!"
45 "The Lion King" lion
47 "Three ___ Match"
48 "...and soft the ___ blows": Thomas Gray
49 K-O connector
51 Barely lit
52 Choice at a faculty department
61 Deux's follower
62 Popular food chain, informally
63 Just
64 Useful quality
65 Glib comment
66 Abscond
67 Impudent
68 Word with pigeon or open
69 Salinger dedicatee

DOWN

1 Having no get-up-and-go
2 Stick in the fridge
3 In ___ (as originally positioned)
4 Coal-rich area in Europe
5 Telephoned
6 Trojan War epic
7 Fine-grained mineral
8 First Family of Ferrara
9 Modern car feature
10 Robin's mentor
11 One opposed
12 See 29-Across
13 Roll call word
21 Competitor of Pert
22 Surpass in performance
25 Four-door, maybe
26 Fragrance
27 Thin porridge
28 Tar
29 Magna ___
30 Shakespeare's Hathaway
32 Some Pennsylvania Dutch
33 ___ Python
34 Mystery writer's award
36 Blessing
39 Some jackets
40 Unifying idea
41 Start for hazard
46 Axis foes
48 Moved speedily
50 Having light fog
51 Remote-controlled plane
52 Span. coins
53 Heavenly bear
54 Office chief
55 Sword part
56 Glenn's state
57 Thorny flower
58 Prepares the printing press
59 Svelte
60 Public relations overkill

806 by Joe DiPietro

ACROSS

1 Ginger
10 Old coin of Italy
15 Evenhanded
16 Identified as
17 Produced
18 Place of worship
19 Barely beat
20 Detailed spirits of ancient Rome
21 Diamond preservers?
22 Ghost writer?
24 Mercedes-Benz model designation
25 Kind of support
27 Tennis shot
30 "___ me ae spark o' Nature's fire": Burns
31 Kicker's object
33 Hot
34 Floor
36 Some pollutants
39 Keen
43 Drop the ball
44 Fisherman's equipment
45 Drafted
46 Lets have it
48 It's made in balls
49 Cesar Romero role
50 Means of support
55 Before now
56 Tie the knot
57 Kind of treatment
59 French revenue
60 Planet's center
61 Crop fungus
62 Some John Constable paintings

DOWN

1 Honey, for one
2 September occurrence
3 Profess
4 A.T.M. entry
5 Twosome
6 Goose egg
7 Dark, to Donne
8 Pivot
9 Goes down
10 Weight lifter's move
11 Power-seeking clique
12 Offense
13 Throw away
14 Trip
23 Informants, in slang
24 Bar
26 System that connects computers: Abbr.
27 Black Sea resort
28 Basketball Hall-of-Famer George
29 Tennis's Agassi
32 They're sometimes struck
33 Noise that annoys
35 Captain's heading
36 Lie, with "oneself"
37 Balladeer
38 Downhill action
40 Sweet drink
41 Open-shelved piece
42 Lowers
44 Coarse, as language
47 Melee
50 Eye part
51 Italian well
52 Mystery writer Buchanan
53 First-rate
54 French brandy
58 Old Philco competitor

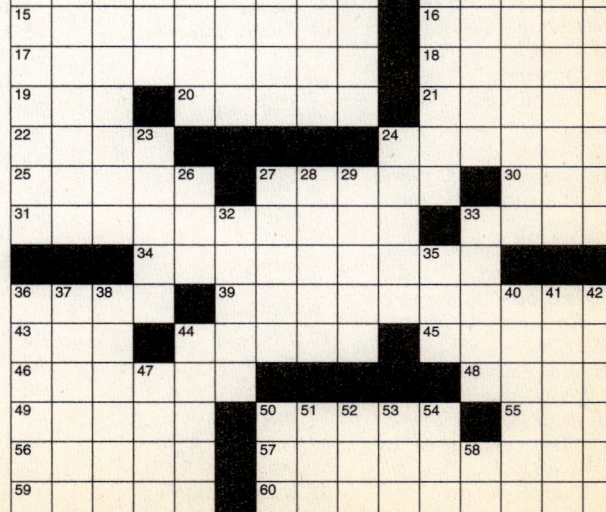

807 by Teresa M. Hackett

ACROSS
1 Hairdo
5 Inquired
10 Surrender
14 Stratagem
15 "Mars Attacks!" genre
16 They can take a yoke
17 Cake finisher
18 Guardian of Crete, in classical myth
19 Actor Arnaz
20 Agatha Christie title
23 "All ___ day's work"
24 Legal thing
25 Keats's work on melancholy
28 Biased
32 Grp. that oversees I.C.B.M.'s
35 Ironworker's workplace
37 Decree
38 Kent's state
39 Investigative tool
42 "EZ Streets" actor Ken
43 Mars: Prefix
44 Playful aquatic animal
45 Old TV comedian Louis
46 Hi-fis

48 Aegean, e.g.
49 Worker with a stethoscope
50 Ex-G.I.
52 Dismiss lightly
61 Work over Time
62 Profit
63 687 days on Mars
64 Bridge site
65 Jeune ___ (girl, in France)
66 Word repeated in "It's ___! All ___!"
67 Russian autocrat
68 Skedaddles
69 Word ending a threat

DOWN
1 Lit ___ (college course, informally)
2 "That hurts!"
3 Words of enlightenment
4 Physicist Enrico
5 Stellar
6 Old wound mark
7 Drug shipment, maybe
8 ___ effort
9 Separate
10 Musical finales

11 Prez
12 Where a student sits
13 Geraint's lady
21 Miniature map
22 Scarlet
25 Go ___ a tangent
26 Frilly place mat
27 Bert's "Sesame Street" buddy
29 Ere
30 Gunpowder ingredient
31 California-Nevada resort lake
32 Some immunizations
33 Evangelist McPherson
34 Army attack helicopter
36 Powell or Westmoreland, e.g.: Abbr.
38 Halloween mo.
40 Grain by-product
41 Units of medicine
46 Drunkard
47 Seeds-to-be
49 Restrain through intimidation
51 Mint family member
52 Lady's escort
53 Altar vows

54 MasterCard alternative
55 Wicked
56 Cotton quantity
57 Make angry

58 Trompe l'___
59 Pre-air conditioning coolers
60 Gratis

808 by Jeff Herrington

ACROSS
1 Japanese or Korean
10 Dutch Abstract Expressionist
15 ___ Springs, Fla.
16 Energy
17 Diviner, of sorts
18 Hardly sweet talk
19 Angler's needs
20 The Celtics' "Hondo"
22 Quarter of a calendrier
23 Kind of resort
24 Generous gifts
28 Game to 5,000 points
31 The Ayatollah, for one
35 They're called stations in Australia
36 Sardou play written for Sarah Bernhardt
39 Hike
40 What a juggler may practice with
41 Whence the phrase "Thou shalt love thy neighbor as thyself"
46 Loudly mourn
48 ___ Khan
51 Precedent setter

53 Fills the hold
55 Academy founder
56 Millionaire makers
58 Mickey Mantle, on the ball field
59 Hard white pottery
60 Classic advertising annual
61 Titled Italians

DOWN
1 Old coin
2 Rat island resident
3 Reserve
4 Mild
5 Latin 101 verb
6 Junior
7 Creep
8 Military command
9 Anxiousness
10 Counsel
11 Niceties
12 Yearned
13 Bring up
14 "Solaris" author Stanislaw
21 Musical notes
24 Flat
25 Rowan, e.g.

26 Interstate sign: Abbr.
27 Interstate sign
28 Device used in an A.T.M.
29 Swiss river
30 Austin-to-Dallas dir.
32 Cause of Chinese restaurant syndrome
33 Expert
34 Attachment to Christ?
36 Law, in Lyon
37 Circle section
38 Kind of cross
42 John and others
43 Hoover, e.g., informally
44 Slanted
45 Cache in the Sierra Madre
46 Newsman Garrick
47 Split
48 "So long"
49 Oscar winner Davis
50 Boobs
52 It's across the Thames from Windsor
53 ___ majesté

54 The Muses' domain
55 Free TV ad: Abbr.
57 Metal shell filling

809 by Norman S. Wizer

ACROSS

1 Spring weather forecast
5 Grey and others
10 Docs
13 Personal prefix
14 "Simon Boccanegra," e.g.
15 Defense mechanism
16 Tramp
17 Motherly type
18 Seep
19 Plant holder
21 Quickened pace
23 Coin on the Spanish Main
24 Can
25 1995, 2005 and 2003, in China
30 Vowel sounds in "melee"
31 Wheel part
32 Cry out
34 Released felon
35 Spoon
36 High-minded
37 Adolescent
38 Multitude
39 Dresden's location
40 1996, 2001 and 2002, in China
43 Road to Roma
44 Lee or Teasdale
45 Elastic cord
48 Used a pony
52 Parrier's equipment
53 Its capital is Kinshasa
56 Western necktie
57 Fighter of 1899–1902
58 Dreaded computer word
59 Nation on the Strait of Hormuz
60 Remnant
61 Slumgullion and pepper pot
62 Decimal system

DOWN

1 Spray
2 Lay off
3 Important person
4 1994, 2000 and 1998, in China
5 They have many signs
6 "Rocky" villain ___ Creed
7 Bottom line
8 Before, before
9 Unbecoming wit
10 Debatable
11 Stun
12 Road ending
15 2004, 1997 and 1999, in China
20 Encored, in a way
22 "___ du lieber!"
24 Blackout
25 Onetime Chinese rebel
26 ___ year (annually)
27 Haunted house sound
28 Saarinen namesakes
29 Nonelectric shaver
30 Court call
33 Layer
35 Seckel or Anjou
36 Austronesian language
38 Blessed events?
39 Philanthropists
41 Geneviève e.g.: Abbr.
42 Place in trust
45 Actress Daniels of the silents
46 Over
47 Shortfall
49 Endured
50 Panache
51 Grandees
54 High school class
55 Sharp feeling

810 by Jim Page

ACROSS

1 Cleo player
4 Nods
7 Healing waters
10 Bottom-of-letter abbr.
13 Greek nickname
14 "Barney Miller" regular Jack
15 1964 Murray Schisgal play
16 Vietnam's My ___
17 Place for coming to grips?
18 Prom flowers
20 Toast word
21 Oven for a singer?
23 Peking finale
24 Mr. Buchwald
25 Sign maker
27 "Damn Yankees" team
30 "___ well . . ."
32 Pope's "An ___ on Man"
33 Immensely
34 Man's name meaning "red"
35 "Le Coq ___"
36 Amenable
37 Big name in top 40
40 Backbiter?
43 Govt. help for mom-and-pop stores
45 "Alice" role
46 Radar reception
47 Come about
49 "Runaround Sue" singer
50 Get in return
51 Skipper's command
53 Jazz's ___ Winding
55 Oxlike critter
56 Sea for a singer?
61 First name in tyranny
62 More sluggish
63 By way of
64 Literary monogram
65 Long spell
66 Exactly right
67 Charley Weaver's Mt. ___
68 Author Harper
69 ___-Cat (arctic vehicle)
70 Kidnapping grp., 1974
71 Bandleader Brown

DOWN

1 Religious leader
2 It's south of Georgia
3 Tubular pasta
4 Award for "Wings"
5 Actress friend of Prince Andrew
6 Take up like a sponge
7 Quenches
8 Washington waterway
9 Staved off
10 Grain for a playwright?
11 Revulsion
12 Like apple juice
19 Forte for an actress?
22 Flavor sensor
26 Arcane
27 Annoyer
28 Menu phrase
29 Voyage for an actor?
31 Mauna ___
38 "Xanadu" rock grp.
39 Rare aquatic
41 Half a dance
42 Keystone figure
44 Plowed lands
47 #1 hit for the Chi-Lites, 1972
48 Wicked one
49 Family name of F.D.R.'s mother
52 Squash
54 It comes straight from the heart
57 Puppies' barks
58 Baudelaire's "The Flowers of ___"
59 Orderly
60 Senate votes

811 by Alex K. Justin

ACROSS

1 Catches in the act
5 Composer Franz
10 R.N.'s "touch"
13 Singer Guthrie
14 Kind of daisy
15 Where the Mets play
16 1934 Shirley Temple musical
19 Volcano spew
20 Protest that gets out of hand
21 Bizarre
22 Striped fish
23 Uses to achieve later success
25 Infuriate
28 Place to get all steamed up
29 Hideaway
30 Mode
31 President Lincoln
34 Take time out
38 Hearty mugful
39 Batter's position
40 Battering wind
41 Mailman's beat
42 Plant reproductive bodies
44 One just let out of jail
47 Couples
48 Perfect
49 Bushels
50 "So that's what you meant!"
53 Goldbrick
57 Not so much
58 Kareem ___-Jabbar
59 Back of the neck
60 Take to court
61 Social position
62 Mandated safety sign

DOWN

1 Mars Pathfinder launcher
2 Partner of crafts
3 Ho-hum
4 Prodigal ___
5 1991 buddy film "Thelma & ___"
6 Montréal team
7 Miami team
8 Writer Rand
9 Deeply blushing
10 Eta follower
11 Skeptical
12 Gives a hoot
15 Six-time Super Bowl coach Don
17 Downer
18 Safe place in the ring
22 Fishhook's end
23 "Band of Gold" singer Freda
24 "___ Lang Syne"
25 "Born Free" lioness
26 It gets hit on the head
27 ___ of passage
28 Condition
30 Rink need
31 Outlawed spray
32 Cotton bundle
33 "First Wives Club" members
35 Moon-landing program
36 Tip-off
37 Subjects of psychoanalysis
41 Highways and byways
42 Nonobvious
43 Deluxe
44 Multivitamins, e.g.
45 Goodbye
46 Shortstop Pee Wee
47 Glazed food item
49 Olympus dwellers
50 Rival of Bon Ami
51 Southwest Indian
52 Help in a heist
54 Servicewoman, briefly
55 Hawks' and Bucks' org.
56 Opposite WSW

812 by Cathy Millhauser

ACROSS

1 Italian sports car, informally
5 Prez's helper
9 Beat with feet
14 View from some dorms
15 Science magazine
16 Burned up
17 Perennial basketball powerhouse
18 Lo-fat
19 Checkers master
20 Elec. coolers
21 THEATRICAL
23 Nap in Nogales
25 Start of 36-Down's motto
26 Type of stripe
27 Type of chatter
29 Long March leader
32 COMICAL
36 Revealing dress
37 N.B.A. coach Unseld
38 Coal-dousing sound
39 UNETHICAL
44 Skiing champ Tommy
45 Enlightenment philosopher
46 Chablis, e.g.
47 Expose
48 Occupy
52 RHYTHMICAL
58 Have a bout with
59 Alimentary canal section
60 Slave of Amneris
61 Quale successor
62 Distress signal
63 Trudge
64 "Your turn," via radio
65 Worked with nails
66 Tunnel, e.g.
67 Propensity

DOWN

1 Sea shades
2 Soap star Susan
3 Bogus
4 Nabokov heroine
5 Stromboli, e.g.
6 Radiate
7 Within: Prefix
8 Boardwalk abutter
9 Mosque feature
10 Skater Heiden and others
11 Curbside cry
12 Beau Brummell's school
13 Escalator inventor Jesse
21 Persevering
22 Cronies
24 Parsley part
27 More than lethargic
28 Platter
29 Chief
30 Domed projection
31 Saturn's wife
32 Slangy goodbye
33 Writer Rice
34 TV lawyer Marshall
35 "Up in Smoke" co-star, 1978
36 "The Wizard of Oz" film company
40 Kind of milk
41 Estate near Atlanta
42 Middling
43 Quaff quantity
47 Skylike, maybe
49 Heavenward
50 Bridge king
51 Strain
52 Instant
53 1934 hit "___ Do Is Dream of You"
54 Ardor
55 De Soto contemporary
56 Hawaii County capital
57 Tiki, e.g.
61 Good & Plenty amount

813 by Martin Schneider

ACROSS

1 Polly, perhaps
7 Boy's partner, out West
10 Relative of a foot-pound: Abbr.
13 Book after Solomon
14 Iffy weather guide
16 Bar food
18 Game of numbers
19 Huck Finn's transport
20 Actor Beatty
21 Whichever
22 National Gallery of Art architect
23 Slack-jawed feeling
25 Lamprey
28 More bar food
31 Tyler or Taylor, e.g.
33 Kind of ear
34 Monopoly card
35 Bunk
39 Duck's habitat
40 Mexican Mrs.
41 Brewery fixture
42 Reaction to a ghost
46 Auto financing letters
47 A pocketful, in rhyme

48 Old Mideast alliance: Abbr.
49 Dance part?
52 Lout
54 British informer
56 Lute feature
57 False display of sympathy
60 Refine
61 Emu or ostrich
62 Approximately
63 Ghent river
64 Anthem part

DOWN

1 Words preceding number or card
2 Pallid
3 Like London
4 Con mucho dinero
5 Cork source
6 1994 Denis Leary movie
7 Fisherman's hook
8 Big name at Leonardo da Vinci
9 K-O bridge
10 Patch place
11 Contrary Mary and others

12 Hosts
15 Ford replaced him
17 Lacking savoir-faire
22 Boxers, informally
24 Custom
26 Discharge
27 $C_{20}H_{25}N_3O$
28 Aristophanes drama, with "The"
29 80's TV crime battlers, with "The"
30 Some of them are crazy
31 Joyful cry
32 Speakers' remuneration
36 Catch sight of
37 Kind
38 Cultivator
39 Nick Price's org.
43 At attention
44 Knitting stitch
45 California team
49 Noted business publisher
50 Budget alternative
51 Befuddled
53 Nosegay
55 Afflicts
56 Goat's milk product

57 Modern records
58 Source of Rockefeller wealth
59 Make lace

814 by Dorothea E. Shipp

ACROSS

1 Buccaneer's home
6 Waylay
12 Witches' brews
14 ___ Rico
15 *Patient's worry*
16 *Event for select customers*
18 ___ nutshell
19 To be: Sp.
20 Old spy org.
21 Novelist Josephine
22 Jazzman Herbie
24 Charlotte ___ (dessert)
26 Ancient, in bygone days
27 Necessity for Hillary
29 "Little old me?"
30 Huxtable boy and others
31 Linda of "Alice"
33 Not alfresco
35 Where Rome and Athens are
37 Fashion again
40 Bashkir's belief
44 1985 Michener best-seller
45 W.W. I body: Abbr.

47 Dutch export
49 Dutch export
50 Holmes novel "___ Venner"
52 Actress Lollobrigida
53 Word before and after "in"
54 Diminutive suffix
55 Haile Selassie, e.g.: Abbr.
57 Witticism
58 *Some laws*
60 *Ballerinas, in a way*
62 Polish, e.g.
63 Propriety
64 Unruffled
65 Oscar de la ___

DOWN

1 Pedicure's target
2 XXVI Olympiad site
3 "Mamma ___!"
4 Daddy-o
5 Goose genus
6 Next-door
7 A mummy may have one
8 So-so grades
9 Surgery sites, for short

10 Music's ___ Brothers
11 Steel-bladed swords
12 Get the hair just right
13 Blood ___
17 Hurricane centers
23 Ballot time: Abbr.
25 Elite parties
26 "What have we here?!"
28 Nears, old-style
30 Anniversary offering
32 Teachers' org. since 1857
34 Sixth-century date
36 Shimmer
37 Satisfaction
38 Instruction clarifier
39 Newsman Donaldson
41 Kind of sail
42 Food
43 Balearic island
44 It may be taped
46 Word with "of honor" or "of vision"
48 Pushover
50 Mystery writer Stanley
51 Qatar V.I.P.
54 Locale for Ali Baba

56 Tempo
59 Listener
61 Parker, e.g.

815   by Peter Gordon

ACROSS
1 Hikers' needs
5 Place for hydrotherapy
8 Marine deposits
14 One way to run
15 Trouble
16 Greets the day
17 Multishot firearm
19 With 61-Across, 1930's Cardinals All-Star (born 2/29/1904)
20 Funeral sound
21 Guiding maxims
23 It might have a black eye
24 Hair color
25 White's partner?
29 Like___ out of hell
31 Hägar the Horrible's dog
33 Send urgently
34 Hooky player
36 Role for Myrna
38 Curie's title: Abbr.
39 & 41 Director of "Wings" (born 2/29/1896)
43 Kimono sash
44 ___ Rabbit
46 Comic Boosler

47 Trompe l'___
49 Weathered
51 Frigg's husband
52 Helps with the dishes
54 Parapsychologist's study
55 L.A. law figure
56 Thin
58 About
61 See 19-Across
64 Generally available
66 Five spaces, perhaps
67 Name part
68 Depilatory brand
69 Bags
70 Provoke
71 New Year's song ending

DOWN
1 Take notice of
2 "It is so"
3 Excommunicator of Henry VIII (born 2/29/1468)
4 Kind of system
5 Posed
6 Certain baker
7 1953 A.L. M.V.P. (born 2/29/1924)
8 Hook or Cook: Abbr.

9 Double Stuf cookies
10 Woodshop tool
11 Egyptian cobra
12 See 62-Down
13 Old Communist state: Abbr.
18 ___ mode
22 Shawl
26 Noted bandleader (born 2/29/1904)
27 Italian designer
28 Actor ___ Ivory Wayans
29 "The Circle Game" poet
30 Party to payola
31 Big shots
32 Cornered
35 Quill point
37 Nothing but
40 Olympics length
42 Thai neighbors
45 "Semiramide" composer (born 2/29/1792)
48 Economist Thurow
50 Key
53 Hardcover part
55 Guarantee
57 Some queens
59 "Barton Fink" director Joel
60 Two chips, e.g.

61 Start to understand?
62 With 12-Down, founder of the American Shakers (born 2/29/1736)
63 Vitamin abbr.
65 Date

816   by Frank A. Longo

ACROSS
1 Gertrude Stein portraitist, 1906
8 Range
15 Comical
16 Like some charged atoms
17 Sun blocker
18 One way to row a boat
19 Qabus bin Said's domain
20 "And Still I ___" (Maya Angelou poem)
22 Kudos
23 Meal starter
24 Misters abroad
26 Fifth gear
27 Cousin of the spoonbill
29 One who helps tie a knot
31 Once called
32 More eldritch
34 Uncentered?
36 With vehemence
38 Majesty
41 Buckwheat plant
45 Coach Parseghian

46 Drain
48 Supermodel Campbell
49 Homebuilder's supply
51 Preoccupy
53 Asian holiday
54 Coins of minuscule value
56 Write back
57 Brusque
58 Colombia-Venezuela border river
60 Orchestrate
62 Line of drying hay
63 Snake
64 Playground fixtures
65 Stalin's economic plans, e.g.

DOWN
1 Babe in a bundle
2 Yemen, before 1962
3 Art professional
4 Strong ___ ox
5 One in the family
6 Insomnia cause
7 Flirting with, in a way
8 Yaoundé is its capital

9 "A Chorus Line" hit
10 Muck
11 Swing site
12 Kind of dye
13 Fermented fodders
14 Hilts : swords :: snaths : ___
21 Morgan le Fay, e.g.
24 Knitting bag items
25 Alphabetizes
28 Cleave
30 Products of vines
33 Buckjumper's event
35 Neighbor of Cygnus
37 Hardly museumgoers
38 Turns yellow
39 Kind of dog
40 Camp sight
42 Hotel lobby, sometimes
43 Surfaced
44 Ambulance equipment
47 Overhaul
50 Custody
52 River through Berlin
55 Marsh bird
57 Insincere talk
59 Bullyrag
61 Campaigned

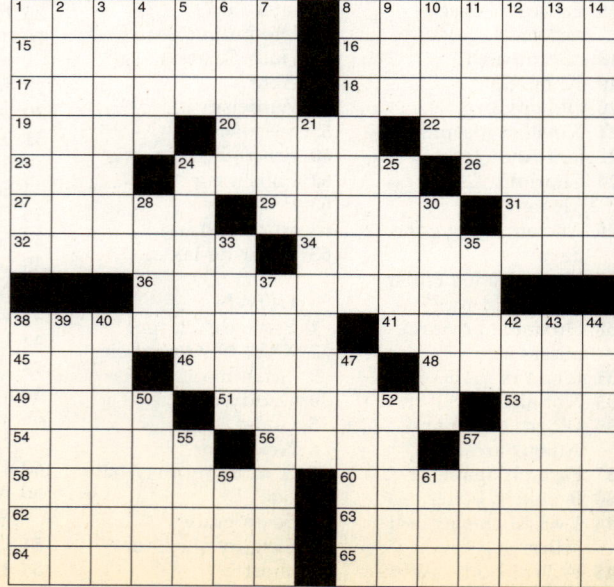

817 by John Scott Marrone

ACROSS

1 Edward Teach, familiarly
11 Watch chain
14 Art of bullfighting
15 Father
16 Article of "Ben-Hur" attire
17 Abbr. part, often
18 Mushroom stems
19 Forces
21 Boy starter
22 Latin 101 word
23 ___ case
24 Pizzeria ___ (restaurant chain)
25 Hosp. picture
26 Views
27 Gulf Coast city
30 ___ gone
31 Refuges
32 Ponder awhile
36 Robert Morse Tony-winning role
37 Stands
38 Count ___ Kansas City Seven (old jazz group)
41 Spanish queen until 1931
42 Kind of room
43 ___ lunch
44 Shadow, with "on"
45 Spanker, e.g.
47 Ribbons and ruffles
49 Kitchen gadget
51 Provisions
52 Say tongue twisters, maybe
54 Heraldic band
55 Unite with
56 Eur. airline
57 Sins

DOWN

1 A.C. capacity
2 Tropical shrubs
3 Acoustic
4 Stole
5 50's service site
6 Some N.Y.C. trains
7 ___ minérale
8 Leg muscle atrophy
9 Zoo creature
10 Scottish painter William
11 1968 Fred Astaire film title role
12 East
13 "___ Wedding" (1990 film)
15 Cohort for Paul Revere
20 Small brook
22 They may be fine
24 Olympic jacket letters
25 "La Bohème" cafe
26 Energetic dance
28 Something to gain from flying?
29 Certain about
32 Fisher rival
33 Roundheads
34 Breakfast at a brasserie
35 Hush-hush grp.
37 Fend off
38 Theatrical hits
39 Rosy-fingered goddess
40 Counter parts?
44 Kind of battery
45 Historic rival of Florence
46 "Hair" hair
48 Toast to the chef
49 Dance bit
50 Classic cars
53 "___ only money"

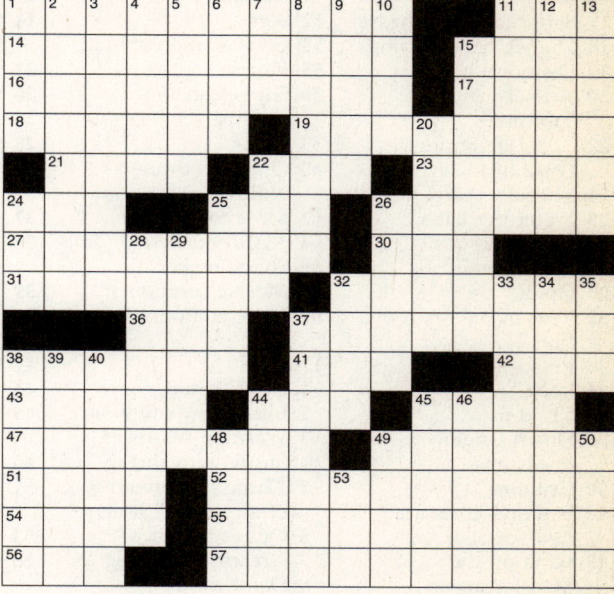

818 by Nancy S. Ross

ACROSS

1 Shaw title starter
5 Blue ribbon place
10 Build up interest?
14 Diamonds, e.g.
15 Isolated
16 "Time's Arrow" novelist
17 "Don Juan"
20 Protector of 56-Down
21 Plot
22 Onetime London transportation
25 Essence
26 Military inits., 1946–92
29 Glinka hero ___ Susanin
31 Confiscates
35 Put ___ fight
36 Rabin's successor
38 Landlord's due
39 "The New Moon"
43 At no charge
44 Related on the mother's side
45 Mr. Onassis
46 Rages
49 Try
50 Aleppo's land: Abbr.
51 Brewing grain
53 Last month of the Jewish calendar
55 Cords
59 Poke fun at
63 "Passion"
66 On the briny
67 Answers to charges
68 Kind of bag
69 Soldiers for old Dixie
70 Mushers' vehicles
71 Juno's Greek counterpart

DOWN

1 Abbr. in an office title
2 Legendary Yankee
3 Spanish Surrealist
4 Commencement
5 Musical syllables
6 Parisian pronoun
7 Campus org.
8 Pry
9 Chang's game
10 Deep blue
11 Mine, in Aix
12 Competitor
13 Salinger girl
18 Green
19 Villa-building family
23 Affirm confidently
24 One of the Simpsons
26 Roams, as the Net
27 Command to a helmsman
28 Small role, sometimes
30 Lights that glow
32 Greek characters
33 Way in
34 Flight segment
37 Inundation
40 Cut-off 55-Across?
41 Bibliographer's abbr.
42 Counters
47 Pulverize
48 Lies dormant
52 Sutherland specialty
54 Sometime Olivier co-star
55 Nicholas or Alexander
56 American Beauty, e.g.
57 Ground-floor apartment
58 "Peter Pan" pirate
60 Large lot
61 Moselle tributary
62 Where Portoferraio is
64 Deranged
65 Maritime letters

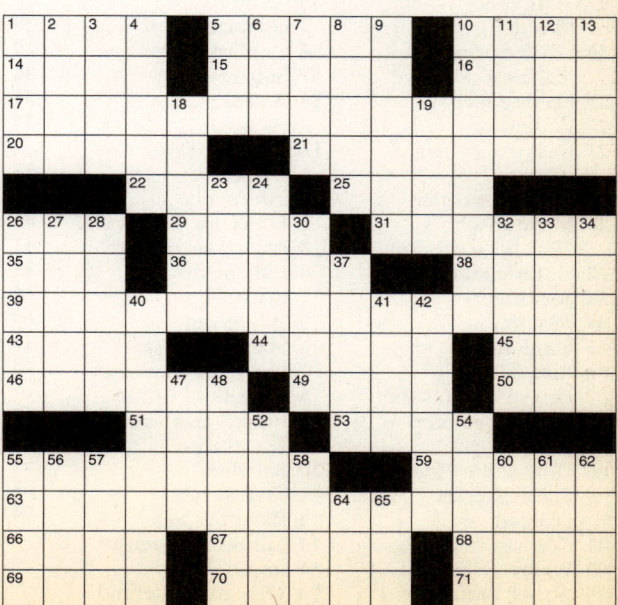

819 by Rich Norris

ACROSS

1 Leave
8 Shower purchase
15 Garment worker
16 Wall-to-wall alternative
17 Señorita's sweetheart
18 Highest violin string
19 Diamond head
20 Nursery rhyme surname
22 "___ Life Strange" (1972 hit)
23 Yucatán years
25 Fraternity letter
26 Act villainously
27 A multitude
29 Open
32 Year in the reign of Pius I
33 Puckish
34 Loop
35 Child meas.
36 Down Under opossums
39 Criticize
42 Ball and cross are two varieties
43 Land on the Mediterranean
47 Miss modifier
48 Upstart 90's politician
49 Mount
50 Shopper in a children's ditty
52 Sort
54 Constellation animal
55 Flurry
56 Soul-cleansing activity
59 Drink
60 Opposed to the N.R.A.
62 Most convenient
64 NASA concern
65 Shade maker
66 Mosaic component
67 More contoured

DOWN

1 Drafting aid
2 Like many reunions
3 Warning words
4 Suffix with slogan
5 "Time the devourer of all things" writer
6 Out of patience
7 Dreadful, in slang
8 Dairy prefix
9 Have ___ of hope
10 Itch
11 Skip dinner reservations
12 Apportion, in a way
13 Secret ways
14 Self-indulgence of a kind
21 Popular Burgundy
24 Fuss
26 Bouts
28 Short-tempered
30 Certain borders
31 "Do ___ say . . ."
37 Formerly
38 In ___ (naturally positioned)
39 Breakfast for the eat-and-run sort
40 Title recipient
41 Cancels
44 Mad
45 Words of understanding
46 Fitting device
51 Embarrassed expressions, at times
53 Toll
56 1973 Gore Vidal best-seller
57 "The Cherry Orchard" girl
58 Ready for action
61 Airfone company
63 AAA map abbr.

820 by Gerald R. Ferguson

ACROSS

1 Academic division
10 Chubby
15 Unruly
16 Harder to find
17 Temporary winter havens
18 Silver Springs neighbor
19 Having feelings
20 Rotten
21 Business owner's concern
24 Room freshener
28 Mendelssohn's "Elijah," e.g.
32 Guthrie and others
33 Backfire
34 "South Pacific" lass
35 Discloses
36 Rub out
37 Part of Pedro's diet
39 Martinique erupter of 1902
40 How some "Melrose Place" stories proceed
41 German sausages
42 Where to buy a suit
44 Writer Barthelme
47 Giant star in Scorpius
52 "There was ___ woman . . ."
53 Audience
55 "Argonautica" character
56 Cupbearer, for one
57 Squeeze
58 Booms

DOWN

1 Dispose of, informally
2 Letter for Cynewulf
3 Lay ___ (exaggerate)
4 Puts blades to blades?
5 Wipes out
6 Shelled
7 Butchers' measures
8 "The Lord of the Rings" creature
9 Postal rtes.
10 Ballyhoo
11 Twisthand
12 River at Orsk
13 Cartoonist Lazarus
14 Implore
20 They can be grand
22 Cheers
23 Cleaving tools
24 Shellbacks
25 Running wild
26 Ada of "Bleak House"
27 Bombshells
29 Certain stocks
30 Estuary feature
31 Gives the double O
33 One two of two-and-two
35 Duck ___
38 Mrs. Marcos et al.
39 Jamboree structure
41 Accustomed
43 Must
44 Extinguish
45 Pip
46 Central point
48 ". . . ___ can't get up!"
49 Stationery order
50 River to Donegal Bay
51 J.F.K. sights
53 Trail
54 1994–95 name in the news

821 by Gregory E. Paul

ACROSS
1 "Too bad!"
5 Sen. Lott
10 Hardly colorful
14 Parks who wouldn't take discrimination sitting down
15 12-inch stick
16 Superb
17 Water conduit
18 China's Zhou ___
19 Do, re or mi, e.g.
20 "Little Orphan Annie" character
23 "There ___ young . . ." (common limerick start)
24 WNW's reverse
25 Plant dripping
28 ___ Kippur
31 Newsman Pyle
35 Puts up
37 Spigot
39 Switch positions
40 Santa Claus
44 Noted business conglomerate
45 Great Lakes cargo
46 C_2H_6
47 Sweetie
50 1040 grp.

52 Last name in cosmetics
53 Photo ___ (media events)
55 Supreme Court Justice Black
57 Nobel author, informally
63 Pack (down)
64 To no ___ (worthless)
65 Snake eyes
67 Lemon go-with
68 Menu at Chez Jacques
69 One of the corners at Four Corners Monument
70 Blockhead
71 Gouged sneakily
72 Akron product

DOWN
1 It may be slung in a sling
2 Dumptruckful
3 Where China is
4 B.L.T., e.g.
5 Deuce toppers
6 Takeoff site
7 Actress Raines
8 Not distant

9 Cree or Crow
10 Martha Graham, e.g.
11 Castle, in chess
12 Orkin targets
13 Quilting party
21 "The Divine Comedy" poet
22 Take advantage of
25 Install to new specifications
26 Poet's Muse
27 Brawl
29 Partner for this and that, with "the"
30 Spoil
32 Wanderer
33 Absurd
34 Ruhr Valley city
36 Box-office letters
38 Bit of Trivial Pursuit equipment
41 Dernier ___
42 Coach Amos Alonzo ___
43 Discard
48 Went one better than
49 Place for a little R and R
51 Devout Iranian
54 Rough cabin
56 Proceeding independently

57 Item for Jack and Jill
58 Bullets and such
59 Writer Hunter
60 Stallion's mate
61 The "A" in ABM

62 Vintage
63 Special attention, for short
66 "___ Drives Me Crazy" (1989 #1 hit)

822 by Randolph Ross

ACROSS
1 ___ temple
8 Grippers
14 Like the White Rabbit
15 Unrefined metal
16 Hawk's home
17 Benedictine, e.g.
18 Bar servings
19 December 31 event
21 Biblical writing on the wall
22 Seasons
23 Diamond girl
24 Uru. neighbor
25 ___ Lama
26 Supports
28 Cable alternative
31 "Double Fantasy" singer
32 Bit of reproof
33 Tabloid topics
40 Throw for ___
41 1980 fadmaker
42 Cutup
44 Pop hit "Da ___ Ron Ron"
45 Nice nights
46 Crystalline rock
47 Diamond point

50 Coast
51 Version
52 Not a run-of-the-mill entertainer
54 Milk-curdling agents
55 Dock
56 Awards for P.D. James
57 Letterman lists

DOWN
1 Effluvium
2 Pollen bearers
3 The original Miss Saigon
4 Speak to the Senate
5 They have their orders
6 Practitioner's suffix
7 "12 Tribes" painter
8 TV transmitter in space
9 Cause of gray hair
10 Extension
11 Camden Yards ennead
12 Against.
13 Tackle box items
15 N.B.A. Hall of Famer Bob

20 Kyrgyz range
22 Permanent place?
25 Patron saint of France
26 "Wanna buy ___?" (old radio comedy line)
27 Snack
29 Robin Williams film
30 Notions holders
33 Overwhelmed
34 On the horizon
35 Sounds of strain
36 Prove acceptable to
37 Bow to bow, perhaps
38 Comeback
39 Polish, with "up"
40 Stick
43 Acts foppish
45 Vegas equipment
46 Top
48 Lab vessel
49 Landing
50 Red's signification
53 Sorority letter

823   by Manny Nosowsky

ACROSS
1 The Garden of Eden?
11 "I understand now"
15 Eloquent
16 Agent's income
17 Don's family
18 Unit of fat
19 Articles in Le Monde
20 Hospital employee
21 One asking for a handout
22 Things one sings?
24 Skywalker mentor
25 Beach playthings
26 Pitch, in a way
28 O.K. sign, maybe
29 When prompted
30 Camel country
32 Salad style
34 Slant
36 Unwelcome word at an antique shop
37 Words before "signed, sealed, delivered" in a Stevie Wonder hit
40 Find abhorrent
44 Nightclub charge
45 Med. country
47 Monkey or pony
48 Another name
49 "Yes, ___"
51 Ones ranked E-4 to E-9: Abbr.
52 Painter Anthony Van ___
53 Slightly black
55 ___ Lunas, N.M.
56 Where el sol rises
57 Tactless
59 Do-well intro
60 Fainted
61 Williams and Kennedy
62 Shoot-'em-up

DOWN
1 Intent
2 Taconite, e.g.
3 Grapples with, as a critter
4 Depot: Abbr.
5 Signal on the hour
6 Stockholder's prerogative
7 Loser to Ali
8 Followed, as advice
9 Benzi box
10 Enthusiasm
11 Flemish : Belgium :: Pashto : ___
12 Extravagant behavior
13 Aqua-colored
14 Filtrate
23 Party picker-uppers
25 Dog-tired
27 Judges and juries
31 Popular sushi fish
33 Icelander's catch
35 Oscar-nominated "Exodus" actor
37 Vatican City jurisdiction
38 Tossed out
39 Wander aimlessly
41 Surrounded territory
42 Kid's transport
43 Tile square
44 Rhythmic
46 Deli wares
50 Free-for-all
53 Punjabi believer
54 Lover of Aeneas
58 Bluecoat

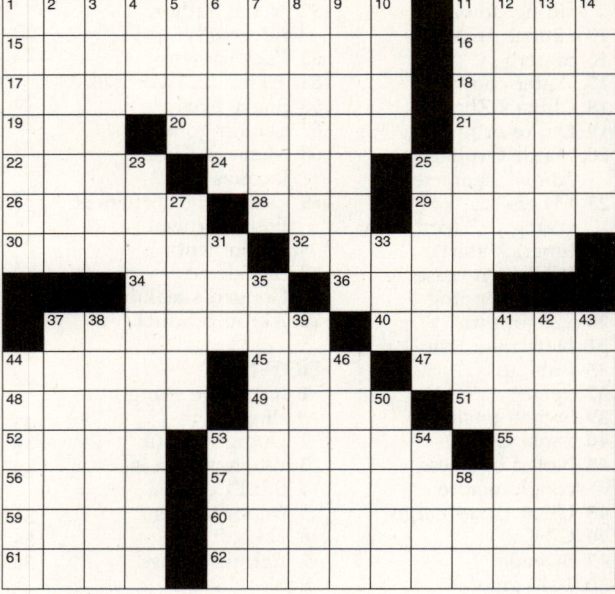

824   by A.J. Santora

ACROSS
1 Bleat
4 Abandon
9 Falsehood
13 Hosp. chart
14 Computer scooter
15 Iron Eagle of W.W. II
16 Sin
17 Built (on)
18 Dream girl of song
19 Start of a quip
22 Roger of the balcony
23 Get high marks
24 Failure
26 Novelist ___ Mae Brown
27 Despicable ones
30 Next in line
31 Reproducer
33 Inferior
35 More of the quip
37 Optimally
40 Mideast river to the Mediterranean
43 Rough finish
44 Passed
46 ___ College, N.C.
48 Pivot
49 Bind
50 Capri, to Loren
51 End of the quip
56 Superior to
57 Relish
58 Treasury dept.
59 Improve a rough draft
60 Bomb site of 1943–45
61 Peeples of "Fame"
62 H.S.T. or D.D.E.
63 "The Minister's Wooing" author
64 "Polly" playwright John

DOWN
1 Pager
2 Kind of dancing
3 Accept
4 Sting
5 Scout of renown
6 Designer Gernreich
7 Exploits
8 Madhouse
9 Actress Garr
10 Made alterations
11 Spiritless
12 Vision
15 Performing
20 In a corner
21 Skating extravaganza
25 Desiccate
27 Terrier
28 Pathet ___ (Communist group)
29 "I Can Get ___ You Wholesale" ('62 musical)
30 Most popular
32 '90 and '95, e.g.
34 Solo in space
36 Three, in Capri
37 Mountain tree
38 Walter Mitty's creator
39 "Road" star
41 Running for one's wife?
42 Sunrooms
45 Is noncommittal
47 Oppose
49 Some U.S. agents
50 ___ fell swoop
52 Designer St. Laurent
53 Supplant
54 Sinclair rival
55 Onetime flight attendant, slangily
56 3-D art pioneer

825 by Daniel R. Stark

ACROSS

1 Gardener's foe
6 Atkins or Huntley
10 Flat-bottomed boat
14 Do-re-mi
15 Sasquatch cousin
16 "No dice!"
17 "Caribbean Queen" singer
19 Suggestive
20 That one: Sp.
21 Kind of order
22 Liquor purchases
24 Patch up
26 Malt shop order
27 Young ___
28 Wine in a straw-covered bottle
31 Seventh sign
34 Writer Sheehy
35 Cold and wet
37 Novelist ___ S. Connell, Jr.
38 Pair of socks
39 Shade
40 Nob
41 Tavern fare
42 ___ Galore of "Goldfinger"
43 Intellectual

45 ___ Spiegel (German magazine)
46 Tackles' neighbors
47 Cap feature
51 Part of a Vandyke
54 Et ___ (and others): Lat.
55 Saccharin's discoverer ___ Remsen
56 Hawks' arena, with "The"
57 Disturbs the status quo
60 Catch
61 Hero's tale
62 Brainstorms
63 Off duty
64 "___-a-Cop" (Burt Reynolds flick)
65 Scrub

DOWN

1 Fossil resin
2 Composure
3 Pits
4 Under the weather
5 ___ 500
6 Bike
7 Command to Rover

8 Flight board info: Abbr.
9 Crinkly wrappings
10 Menu option
11 Exchange pleasantries
12 Cry of dismay
13 Kids' questions
18 Paddles
23 Mountain overlooking Troy
25 Make a comeback
26 Balks
28 Feed en masse
29 New Mexico art locale
30 Tourist establishments
31 Piece of dark meat
32 Composer Charles
33 Judge's bench
34 Festive occasions
36 Choirmaster's announcement
38 Landlubber's plaint
42 Male fashion of Washington's time
44 Series opener?
45 Platform
47 Pick
48 Iron-rich dish
49 Zones

50 Out-of-date
51 Game on the greens
52 Jerusalem's Mosque of ___
53 Mrs. Lindbergh

54 Similar
58 Make like
59 Foofaraw

826 by Christopher Page

ACROSS

1 ___ tunnel syndrome
7 Less lenient
14 Feudal tax
15 One "T" of TNT
16 Big wheel in Moscow?
18 Doctrine: Suffix
19 Striped
20 Marry
21 "Miss ___ Regrets"
23 Comedian Louis
24 Actress Anderson
25 Former capital of Alaska
27 Airline to Stockholm
30 Commedia dell'___
31 Canton cab?
35 "___ Te Ching" (classic work by Lao-Tzu)
36 "Ben ___"
37 A well-made fez, for example?
45 Fencing tool
46 ___ man (unanimously)
47 Scimitar
49 Put safely away
50 W.W. II fliers

53 Addict
54 Word of advice
55 Mohammed's daughter and namesakes
59 Mao ___-tung
60 Chattanooga choo-choo?
63 Apartment dwellers
64 1964 pop sensation
65 Ancient ascetics
66 Size up

DOWN

1 Severely critical
2 1928's Happy Warrior
3 Literary monogram
4 Bucket
5 Once more
6 Baseball's Dykstra
7 Greek portico
8 Recommend publicly
9 Pronoun for a Parisienne
10 Wish otherwise
11 ABC or UPN, e.g.
12 ___ cordiale
13 Less robust, as a musical sound

14 Certain chamber groups
17 Singer Della
22 Schuss
24 Fond du ___, Wis.
26 No voter
28 Reason for balm
29 Synagogue
32 Compass point
33 Palace Theatre locale
34 Discordant deity
37 Having a will
38 Periods when the computers work
39 Takes down the "Closed" sign
40 London's ___ Gardens
41 "Mack the Knife" singer
42 Sch. near the White House
43 Inns
44 Locks
48 Attire
51 Microscopic creature
52 Modern messages
55 Huckleberry ___
56 Entr'___
57 Source for Pravda

58 Bath and Baden-Baden
61 "Norma ___"
62 Hwy.

ACROSS

1 Capital east of Abidjan
6 Three-time Oscar director
11 ___-wolf
14 Sports show ending
15 Liquid fat
16 Boar's Head product
17 Power for an electric blanket?
19 Mill shipment
20 Rug exporter
21 Riding
23 Cooper Indian
27 Second-century astronomer
29 Philippine headhunter
30 46-Down character
31 Confine
32 1911 Nobel chemist
33 Jamaican music
36 Holiday beginnings
37 Pentateuch author, traditionally
38 Library index abbr.
39 Legal matter
40 Certified
41 Apollo attendant
42 Calamitous
44 W.W. II's Uncle Joe
45 Luther was one
47 Illegal, in a way
48 Varnish ingredient
49 Sentence subject
50 River sight
51 Urban rainwear?
58 Mythical bird
59 April Fools' sign
60 Stand up
61 Kind of degree
62 1986 Janet Jackson hit
63 A bit cool

DOWN

1 Lob's path
2 Corp. head
3 Roman 205
4 "Diff'rent Strokes" actress
5 Brandy source
6 "Give My Regards . . ." composer
7 Author Paton
8 ___ se
9 Fix
10 Buttercup family member
11 Bridal party postponement?
12 Sheik's ladies
13 Beauty parlor item
18 Pluto or bureau add-on
22 Pamplona cry
23 Certain track athlete
24 Pointed arch
25 Ell?
26 Eye part
27 Reduced
28 Baseball's Speaker
30 Swing, e.g.
32 Baby discomfort
34 Couric of "Today"
35 With
37 New Testament trio
38 Part of Q.E.D.
40 Sistine Chapel site, with "the"
41 Gladstone, e.g.
43 "Losing My Religion" group
44 Cleaver's "___ on Ice"
45 1995 Tony winner George
46 Literary pen name
47 Controlling
49 Raisa's refusal
52 Part of a tax plan: Abbr.
53 "___ the season . . ."
54 Dernier ___
55 Laotian dollar
56 Thought waves
57 Carlos, for one

ACROSS

1 Long-tailed parrot
6 Willy Wonka's creator
10 School orgs.
14 Fighting ___
15 Mine, in Menton
16 Isle of Mull neighbor
17 Spokes
18 "On Liberty" writer
19 Engaged in a particular activity
20 #23
23 #14
26 Actor Lloyd ___
27 Directional suffix
28 Mimic
29 Stretch, with "out"
31 "Mona ___" (art fakes)
33 God, in Gorizia
34 "Be ___" ("Help me out")
38 What each number in this puzzle refers to
42 Kind of flute
43 Conk out
44 Retract, as words
45 Coleridge work
46 Not be passive
48 Like some theater performances
49 Role in "Falstaff"
53 #21
56 #12
58 Bakery worker
59 Paper quantity
60 Emulate Cato
64 Ready to pick
65 Ratio words
66 Indemnity
67 Lunches
68 Tag warning
69 Weird

DOWN

1 Russian orbiter
2 Parrot genus
3 El ___
4 Flu variety
5 Rear-ender injury
6 Harm
7 Old-fashioned sort
8 Dairy cow
9 Leslie Caron role
10 Instrument for any 38-Across
11 Wreck
12 Bryant or Gillette
13 "Paradise Lost" figure
21 "Great Expectations" lad
22 ___ to grow on
23 Opera's Dame Nellie
24 Bay window
25 Start
30 Ring wins
32 From ___ Z
33 Just passing mark
34 Bay State cape
35 Out
36 Space Invaders game maker
37 Cry to Macduff
39 Singular
40 Like basement flats
41 Beat in competition
45 Poet's preposition
46 Los ___, N.M.
47 Rank below capt.
49 Burning
50 Donizetti heroine
51 Bungling
52 Demeter's Roman counterpart
54 Stradivari's teacher
55 Low dice roll
57 Sills solo
61 Spring mo.
62 ___ chi ch'uan
63 Iris locale

829   by Rand H. Burns

ACROSS

1 Aesop, e.g.
9 Rogues
15 Slowly fade
16 McKinley's first Vice President
17 Lute family member
18 A.A. affiliate
19 Diminutive suffix
20 Born
21 Comparison test item
22 Novelist Jaffe
24 Object of a literary hunt
26 Hoover and Roosevelt, e.g.
28 Breaks
30 ___-Magnon
31 Shakespeare edition
32 Familial marker
34 Tenfold
35 Shining example
38 Renounces
40 "You bet!"
41 Los ___
43 Cowboy's rope
45 Blue material
46 Corral
47 Agamemnon's home
51 Does lawnwork
52 Hitchcock nail-biter, with "The"
54 Physiognomy
55 Qualmishness
57 Yellow ___
59 View from the French Rivera
60 Woman pincher, maybe
61 Jawbone
63 60's weather satellites
64 Distaste
65 American Dadaist
66 Suffuse

DOWN

1 Thighbones
2 Land of Arthurian legend
3 Tropical flavor
4 Sturm ___ Drang (turmoil)
5 Mr. Trotsky
6 British ___
7 Ologies
8 Perfect rating
9 "Jaws" terror
10 Drink type
11 Strand
12 ". . . from Rangoon to ___": Kipling
13 Senator who gave Golden Fleece awards
14 A.M. or F.M. broadcaster
21 Sib
23 Quick to learn
25 Munitions maker
27 Fermented sauces
29 Site of iniquity in antiquity
31 Mediterranean holiday
33 "___ the season . . ."
34 Genetic strands
35 Flits (about)
36 Tragedienne ___ Duse, 1859–1924
37 Chinese
39 National park near Mount Rushmore
42 Warranty violator
44 Kennel sound
46 ___ mater (brain cover)
48 Its only neighbor is Senegal
49 Spotted cat
50 Unruffled
52 "Heavens to ___!"
53 More logical
56 Actress Ward
58 House ad abbr.
60 Overhead item, at Daytona
61 Triple-A handout
62 British verb ending

830   by Matt Jones

ACROSS

1 Sitcom star with a drawl
10 Tie ___ (carouse)
15 Handicaps
16 Infamous Ford
17 China's Father of the Revolution
18 Shoelace end
19 Sets (on)
20 When to spring forward: Abbr.
22 Mata ___
23 Biblical verb suffix
24 Merry, in a game name
27 Offensive football play
29 Conversion figure
32 Willow pattern locale
34 Unveils
38 Workers in masks
39 Columbia River port
41 Handles
42 Draining
44 She played "the movie star" in 60's TV
46 Style of disco music
49 Two fives for ___
50 Actor Gulager
53 Lotion ingredient
54 Causing tears, maybe
56 Shropshire sounds
57 Noggin
59 Like a human pregnancy
63 Amphetamine
64 Answer questions fully
65 In sorry shape
66 Kitten with a string, e.g.

DOWN

1 Frank's brother
2 "No more!"
3 Welcomers in Oz
4 Registrations of opposition
5 Resembling
6 While
7 Wts. at McDonald's
8 More like an oboe
9 Personnel data: Abbr.
10 ___-Locka, Fla.
11 Bistros
12 Zhou ___
13 New Mexico county
14 Away
21 Shoe part
24 Egyptian town of W.W. II fame
25 Kitty Litter inventor Edward
26 Blake of "Gunsmoke"
28 Kind of shampoo
30 Harvested
31 Article of 32-Across
32 Latin dance "step"
33 Early Eastern dynasty
35 Clinton accomplishment
36 "Henry & June" diarist
37 Slump
40 Pivot
43 Seventh heaven
45 Japanese drama
46 Lisbon's river
47 Run off
48 Two-door
51 Java concoction
52 Bring (in)
55 As soon as
56 1976–80 Wimbledon champ
58 Unbuttered
60 Often-contracted word
61 Emissions watchdog: Abbr.
62 Game pieces

831 by Stephanie Spadaccini

ACROSS
1 Wolf, in Juárez
5 Little bit
9 At the acme of
13 Desert caravan stops
14 Londoner, e.g.
15 1984 film "___ Man"
16 "Au revoir"
19 Hot, so to speak
20 Framework
21 Gypsy Rose's last name
22 "___ Plenty O' Nuttin' "
24 Close loudly
26 Jewel
29 Belonging to us
31 Ancient
35 Dangerous March date
37 Firearms
39 Mosaic, e.g.
40 "Au contraire"
43 Autumn color
44 Energetic one
45 Declare positively
46 Winnie-the-Pooh companion
48 Speaker's platform
50 ___ gratia artis

51 Prefix with cure
53 Harvest
55 Attack riotously
58 Warble
60 Yell
64 "Au courant"
67 Shipbuilder's wood
68 Word-of-mouth
69 Mideast leaders
70 Jekyll's alter ego
71 Nothing, south of the border
72 "See, I did it!"

DOWN
1 Café au ___
2 Sonja Henie's hometown
3 Attorney Melvin
4 Upstate New York city
5 Blue chip co.
6 Portland's state: Abbr.
7 Wedding cake layers
8 Well-known Hun
9 Evita's country: Abbr.
10 Greenish blue

11 Ronny Howard TV role
12 Corn bread
13 Extra playing periods, for short
17 "That will do!"
18 Slowly, in music
23 Lined up perfectly
25 High I.Q. society
26 W.W. II soldier
27 Draw out
28 Netted
30 Headband
32 Baseballer Tony
33 "See ya!"
34 Easter egg colorers
36 Barber's razor sharpener
38 Canapé picker-upper
41 Actress Wright or singer Brewer
42 Churchman
47 Phonograph's inventor
49 Little perfumed bag
52 The "I" in IV
54 ___ donna
55 Arith.
56 Do what you're told
57 Actor Pitt

59 Egg on
61 Sir Geraint's wife
62 Taj Mahal site
63 Ed.'s documents

65 ___ out a living (get by)
66 St. Augustine's state

832 by Rich Norris

ACROSS
1 Dish made with sour cream
11 Athens's ___ of Hadrian
15 Megadeth's music, e.g.
16 Name of six popes
17 Subject to omission
18 Stage beginning
19 Classic Maugham short story
20 Strip (of)
22 Some dashes
23 Big fans
27 Whole lot
28 Cause resentment
30 Base gesture
32 Appointed by an interested party, in Roman law
34 What Babe Ruth wore
35 Kind of end
37 Popular Christmas gifts
39 What's more
40 Signs of organization
42 Choice segments
44 Opposite of love

46 Brings up
50 Subject of a Keats poem
51 Fanatic
53 Back-road hazard
54 30's–40's force
56 Europe's Gulf of ___
57 Twist
58 Reeling
63 ___ de la Société
64 Colorful marine creature
65 Bite
66 Scenic walkways

DOWN
1 Actress North
2 Football's Chiefs, originally
3 Intolerant one
4 Thermometer site
5 Kind of joint
6 Invoice abbr.
7 King Features competitor
8 N.Y.C. parlor
9 1989–90 Masters champion
10 Companies' trucks
11 Boom

12 Tight-lipped
13 In the minority
14 Title recipient
21 Jr.'s exam
23 Delete, as a file
24 Tolkien creatures
25 Mentally quick
26 Landscaping machine
29 Man of many words
31 Buddhist sacred city
33 Ancient Roman official
35 1959 Bock-Harnick musical
36 "Laugh-In" sportscaster
38 Originate
40 Activates, in a way
41 Queens park
43 "___ of Destruction" (1965 hit)
45 Investigative report
47 Shooting aid
48 City on the Willamette
49 Stoppages
52 Sounds
55 "Entertainment Tonight" co-host
56 Piazza di Spagna site

59 Utilize
60 "2001" name
61 Alfonso's queen
62 Bacon's "Footloose" role

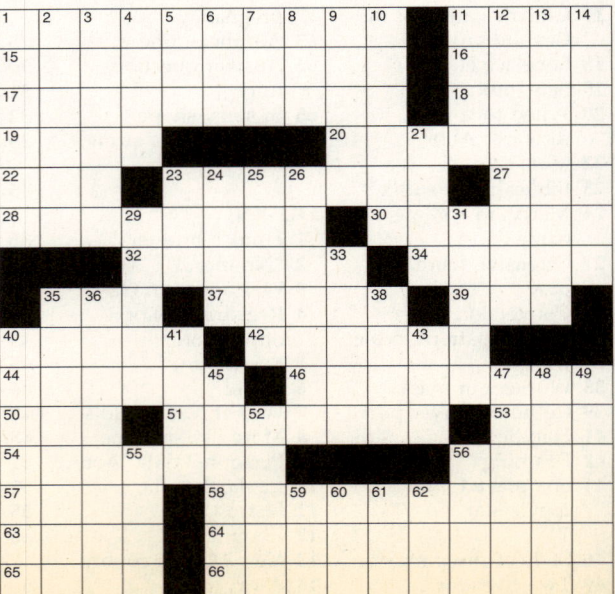

833 by Mark Elliot Skolsky

ACROSS

1 Abnormal vesicle
5 Longtime Boston Symphony conductor
10 D.E.A. officer
14 Miles per hour, e.g.
15 Suburban San Francisco county
16 Like an octopus's defense
17 Inter ___
18 Parenthetical comment
19 Saintly
20 The Flintstones' favorite track star?
23 "___ pray"
24 NASA launch concern
28 Carl Reiner's "Where's ___?"
32 Daunt
33 Drink from a dish
36 The Flintstones' favorite dancer?
39 Greek concert sites
41 Steal away
42 Cattle encourager
43 The Flintstones' favorite Congressman?
46 Calendar spans: Abbr.
47 Drain
48 Popular Deco lithographs
50 Covets
53 Organize, as an exhibit
57 The Flintstones' favorite baker?
61 Skater Starbuck
64 Bunk
65 Word in many Gardner titles
66 "The Art of Love" poet
67 Fish
68 "¿Como ___ usted?"
69 Pebbles, e.g., on "The Flintstones"
70 Actress Patricia et al.
71 Day of ___

DOWN

1 Swimming stroke
2 Bulldog
3 Circus prop
4 Join forces (with)
5 Bradley or Sharif
6 Pitts of "Life With Father"
7 Droughtlike
8 Golf ___
9 Give extreme unction to, old-style
10 Brandy, perhaps
11 Year in Spain
12 "Citizen Kane" studio
13 Dancer Charisse
21 Beginning
22 History
25 Dangerous, colloquially
26 Trial's partner
27 Oboes, e.g.
29 Quarry
30 Ill-gotten gains
31 Put on a pedestal
33 Like oak leaves
34 "There Is Nothin' Like ___"
35 Police blotter types
37 Be on ___ with (equal)
38 Posted
40 Immunity unit
44 Australia's largest lake
45 ___ Sabe
49 Football
51 Wharton's "___ Frome"
52 Best Director of 1986 and 1989
54 Imperial decree
55 Settles in
56 Doctor
58 Hatha-___
59 Word with T or dry
60 Whiskies
61 Psalms preceder
62 Fertility clinic needs
63 Foresail

834 by Alan Arbesfeld

ACROSS

1 Certain drapes
6 Atlantic food fish
10 Gator's kin
14 Cop ___ (confess for a lighter sentence)
15 White-tailed flier
16 Deli offering
17 Colt 45, e.g.
19 List member
20 "That's a lie!"
21 Household
23 70's–80's robotic rock group
25 The United States, metaphorically
27 Uris hero
28 Dance, in Dijon
29 Member of the 500 HR club
30 Rock impresario Brian
31 Surgical fabric
33 Ant, in dialect
35 "Texaco Star Theater" host
39 Cut down
40 Brilliance
43 High dudgeon
46 Mai ___
47 Go on to say
49 "Bravo!"
50 It once settled near Pompeii
53 Part of a whole
54 Kangaroo movements
55 Hayfield activity
57 Prefix with China
58 Kind of cereal
62 Shade of red
63 Conception
64 Bizarre
65 Bronte heroine
66 Pre-1821 Missouri, e.g.: Abbr.
67 He had Scarlett fever

DOWN

1 Uncle of note
2 New Deal prog.
3 Stream deposit
4 "I can't ___" (Stones refrain)
5 Morton product
6 "Rocky II," e.g.
7 Diabolical
8 Due halved
9 Words of assistance
10 "I ___" (ancient Chinese text)
11 Record again
12 Where to find Eugene
13 Awaken
18 Early Shirley role
22 Signed up for
23 U.N.'s Hammarskjold
24 Former polit. cause
26 ___ of the Unknowns
28 Like some greeting cards
32 Nine-digit number, maybe
33 Ultimate point
34 R.N.'s offering
36 Send
37 Trompe l'___
38 Stretch
41 He KO'd Quarry, 10/26/1970
42 Asian holiday
43 Tipple
44 "Didja ever wonder . . . ?" humorist
45 Successful escapee
47 Incarnation
48 Spanish Surrealist
51 Certain investment, informally
52 More competent
53 Jesse who lost to Ronald Reagan in 1970
56 Composer Stravinsky
59 Ending with quiet
60 N.Y.C. subway
61 Modern information source, with "the"

835 · by Jim Page

ACROSS

1 Swit co-star
5 Record label abbr.
8 ___ E. Coyote
12 Foreman
14 Superdome and Silverdome, e.g.
16 Nursery rhyme listeners
18 Dig it!
19 Puzzlement
20 Kind of badge
22 "The Counterfeiters" author
23 ___ hound
24 Mail client
27 Model Carol
28 Corn chip topping
30 Lacoste and others
32 Karl Malone's team
34 Pleases
36 Large number
37 Pave over
39 Heroic story
41 Actress Farrow
42 More retiring
44 Outshines
46 "... ___ saw Elba"
47 Eniwetok, e.g.
48 Brooklyn Bridge designer
52 Early TV's Denise
53 Pretty Maid's nursery rhyme declaration
58 Former Philly mayor Wilson et al.
59 Fiddle-faddle
60 Toshiba rival
61 Band's booking
62 Campaign

DOWN

1 Just dandy
2 Year in Nero's reign
3 Reading room
4 Zeals
5 Certain firearms
6 Actress Ryan
7 Modern site of ancient Kish
8 1962 Dion hit, with "The"
9 "The very ___!"
10 Line to the Hamptons, for short
11 "Don't overdo it"
13 Subway ___
14 Conservative
15 Like grade-A meat
17 Lively tots
20 Soda jerk's drink
21 Property
23 "Ironside" actress Elizabeth
24 Basketry twig
25 Kind of paint
26 Another round
29 Coasting at Lillehammer
31 Union and others: Abbr.
33 Opposite of 8-Down
35 Thievery
38 1970 Ossie Davis musical
40 Lauds
43 Holds one's horses?
45 First-rate joke
48 Fixes
49 Novel set on Tahiti
50 Designer von Furstenberg
51 The Daltons, e.g.
54 Miss Piggy word
55 ___ flash
56 Wash. advisory grp.
57 Command to a plow horse

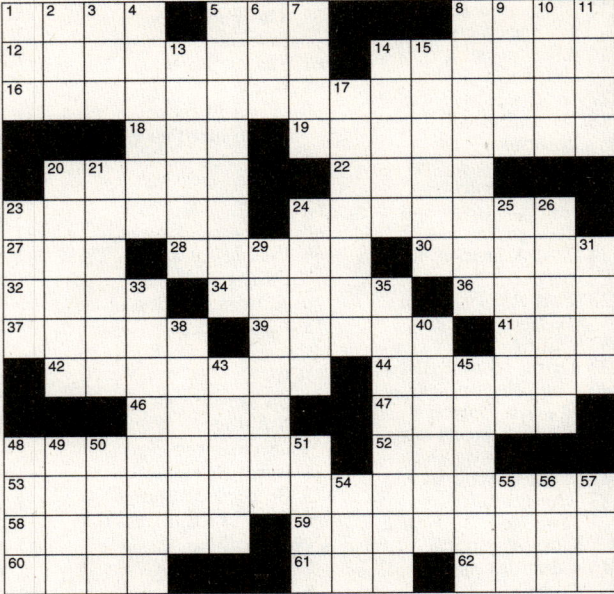

836 · by Richard Silvestri

ACROSS

1 Bar fare
6 "Merry old" king of rhyme
10 Drivel
13 Shiraz native
14 Moundsman Hershiser
15 Make a pitch
16 Trattoria staple
17 Noodges
18 Atahualpa was one
19 When an actress can see forever?
22 "Gunsmoke" appeared on it
25 Original sinner
26 Kickoff aid
27 Suffix with labyrinth
28 Black-and-white snack
30 Golden Fleece craft
32 Horse opera
34 Jamboree locale
36 Hwy.
37 Obese author's admission?
42 E.R. devices
43 More exquisite
44 Lawn game
47 Terrarium plant
48 China setting
49 A "Road" destination
50 Columbus initials
52 Candle count
54 Strive
55 Masochistic trumpeter's prediction?
59 Fine-edged
60 Peek-___
61 Disconcerted
65 Messes up
66 Oversupply
67 Hopping mad
68 Compass pt.
69 Antitoxins
70 Himalayan kingdom

DOWN

1 Sample, as wine
2 Coach Parseghian
3 Vegas opening
4 Opposed
5 "Cheers" character
6 Orchestral offering
7 Spoken
8 Smoothly, to Solti
9 Old comic actress ___ Janis
10 Learned one
11 Secret
12 Cast member
15 Get a move on
20 Profits
21 Go back into business
22 Caesar's sidekick
23 Source of fiber
24 Highway hauler
29 Kind of nerve
31 Crystal-lined rock
33 Dog from Japan
35 Delivery person?
36 Emotional pang
38 Circus Hall of Fame site
39 Main point
40 One who succeeds
41 Busboy's pickup
44 Part of a road test
45 Edmonton icemen
46 Stick together
47 Gridiron mishap
51 Bucks
53 Puckish
56 Election winners
57 Part of B.Y.O.B.
58 Make out
62 Skip, as commercials
63 Hellenic vowel
64 Singer Shannon

837   by Sidney L. Robbins

ACROSS

1 High rung on the evolutionary ladder
6 Alternative to a shower
10 Quatrain rhyme scheme
14 Like ___ from the blue
15 Environs
16 Wise guy
17 Popular chocolate snack
19 On the level
20 River through Florence
21 Mother ___
22 Help in crime
23 Quad number
24 Lock
25 Torah readers
29 Forgiving one
32 Oscar, e.g.
33 Prefix with cycle
34 Draft org.
37 March events?
40 Lolita
42 Phony prefix
43 Fond du ___, Wis.
44 New Zealand native
45 Where Spain and Portugal are
48 Seasoning
49 Afterward
51 Kind of show
53 Singer Minnelli
54 Kick locale
56 Dumb ___
60 Paid promotion: Abbr.
61 Give up hard drink?
63 Vegetarian's no-no
64 Sheltered
65 Similar
66 Wan
67 Lease
68 Little ones

DOWN

1 It's a laugh
2 "Deutschland ___ Alles"
3 Daybreak
4 What's more
5 To the ___ degree
6 Louisiana waterway
7 Bowers
8 Socials
9 Tortoise's competitor
10 Glaring
11 Place to have one's head examined
12 Bouts of chills
13 Borscht ingredients
18 Selves
23 Hoedown musician
24 Shortened
25 Criticizes
26 Not at home
27 Coming-of-age event
28 Cross-one's-heart garment
30 Play on words
31 Some
35 Dried
36 Agitate
38 Unit of corn
39 Phys. or chem.
41 Baby food
46 "Reds" star
47 Out of bed
48 Bygone
49 Andean animal
50 Gofers
52 Commencement
54 Box lightly
55 Patriot Nathan
56 It's full of baloney
57 Final notice
58 Roué
59 War deity
62 Hardly an underperformer

838   by Harvey Estes

ACROSS

1 Bon mot from Julia Child?
8 "Cotton Candy" trumpeter
14 Literary hero of 1605
15 Child's conveyance
16 Wild
17 George Eliot, e.g.
18 Not know from ___
19 The Third
21 Disputed heights
22 Reason for a patch
23 Smeary mark
26 The outside
27 Call ___ day
28 Exit
30 Want ___
31 Aft
33 Removes solids from
35 Shoemaker
37 Aforementioned
38 Writer from Hannibal, Mo.
41 Seers
45 ___-la-la
46 Porky Pig's sweetheart
48 It's measured in minutes
49 Possess, in the Bible
51 Like Tarzan's friends
52 Japanese dance-drama
53 Anesthetic
55 Ill. zone
56 Teen tormentor
57 Give a roar of approval?
59 Guglielmo, in America
62 Chilled desserts
63 Encroach
64 Started stud: Var.
65 More palatable

DOWN

1 Swimming sites
2 Opinion offerers
3 Sound of rain on a roof
4 Student stressor
5 Cruise in Hollywood
6 Follower: Suffix
7 Ennui
8 Topflight
9 Over the limit
10 Blackman of "Goldfinger"
11 Type of dressing
12 Sends back
13 Now people set them
15 Taps
20 Midmonth date
23 Husband one's resources
24 "Valleri" band, 1968
25 The Urals divide it
29 Republic of China
32 Wind heading
34 Wyo. neighbor
36 Attracts adroitly
38 It might be a mess
39 Respond angrily
40 Additional answers?
42 "Dear Heart" composer
43 Period starting about 1000 B.C.
44 Intriguing person
45 Actress Ritter
47 Pinhead
50 Present, e.g.
54 Hill
56 Landed
58 End of the British Empire?
60 Kaye's "___ Big Girl Now"
61 Bygone vinyl

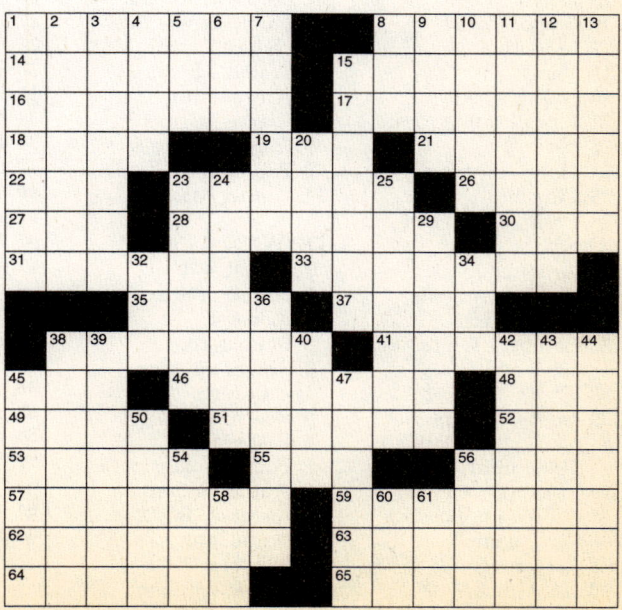

839 by Rich Norris

ACROSS
1 Scoundrels
10 Victoria et al.: Abbr.
14 Conciliatory fellow
15 Plug outlet
16 Nutmeg State resident, for one
17 Untidy, as the hair
18 Actress Gardner
19 Notes
20 Sacrificed, in a way
21 ___ avis
23 Flag feature
25 Lotto variant
26 Liszt symphonic poem
29 Indecent literature
31 Loud noise
32 Laotian dollars
34 Ordinarily
36 Busy
38 Remnants
39 De Klerk's successor
40 Serenaded
41 Naval letters
42 Garden sites
44 Sacred song
47 Urban problem
49 Realizes
51 Entre ___

53 Kind of scout
55 Kett of old comics
58 W.W. II vessel
59 About
60 Ogreish
62 Beethoven's "Choral Symphony," with "The"
63 Reunion locale
64 Way out
65 Scoundrel

DOWN
1 Campaign tactic
2 Neckwear
3 Michael of TV's "Broken Arrow"
4 Afire
5 King toppers
6 "If I ___ . . ."
7 One of the de Milles
8 Invitees
9 Turk. neighbor
10 Mettle
11 Sensory device
12 Storehouses
13 Blue Jays' home
15 1983 Cotton Bowl champs: Abbr.
20 Review

22 "Since you ___ . . ."
24 Gather
27 Cassette tape notation
28 Well-to-do
30 Mountain pools
33 Bogart role
35 Ronald's Donald
36 Home of the devil?
37 More than fresh
39 Famous Ford
43 "The Tattler" essayist
45 Humbert's obsession
46 Rifle forerunner
48 People, in Ponce
50 It goes in a corner
52 Metric measure
54 Ultimate
56 Former Russian ruler
57 Sphere starter
60 Soap unit
61 Etna locale

840 by Sidney L. Robbins

ACROSS
1 Belgian Congo, today
6 Midwest Indians
10 Choir member
14 Back-of-book feature
15 Narrow board
16 Brandy fruit
17 Individually
19 Wan
20 Approached
21 Pipes leading to the roof
23 Hoity-toity sort
25 Litigant
26 Positive pieces of advice
29 Arboreal locale
31 Remit in advance
35 Rink surface
36 Bombeck who's "at wit's end"
38 Trap
39 Bratty child phase
43 "A ___ the Dark" (1988 film)
44 "I cannot tell ___"
45 WNW's opposite
46 Card game
48 Advantage
50 ___ Moines

51 20th-century illustrator
53 Sea eagles
55 Stressful position
58 Devours
62 Suffix with buck
63 Homeowners in a children's story
66 Waiter's handout
67 Army outfit
68 Clark's partner
69 Chimney grime
70 Fountain treat
71 Painter Max

DOWN
1 Holy Land
2 House of Stuart monarch
3 Brainstorm
4 Brings up, as children
5 Reach
6 Fast plane
7 Poetic boxing champ
8 Author Albert
9 Increase, as production
10 Obvious
11 Secrecy problem

12 Paul Bunyan account
13 Silver containers
18 Worshiper
22 Succinct
24 Yogi ___
26 Jettison
27 Autumn color
28 Slangy goodbye
30 Rousseau work
32 Handled indelicately
33 Came up
34 Pro responses
37 Stay
40 Grows weary
41 ___ nous
42 Infamous Simon
47 Position
49 Give power to
52 Prefix with centric
54 It may be bum
55 Sandwich meats
56 Sandwich cookie
57 ___ avail
59 Cut, as logs
60 "QB VII" author
61 "Hey, you!"
64 Eliminate
65 Second letter after epsilon

841   by Matt Gaffney

ACROSS

1 Half of an old radio duo
5 German Expressionist Franz ___
9 Like many football stadiums
14 Queen's home
15 Where most people live
16 Out
17 Stock heading
18 Leg crosser
19 Computer accessory
20 1915 film epic, with "The"
23 Goddess, in ancient Rome
24 Leb. neighbor
25 Bradbury adjective
29 Not uncut, as a film
33 "___ little teapot . . ."
34 60's U.N. name
36 Met's home
37 1965 Beatles lyric
41 Picnic ruiners
42 Red as ___

43 Polite "du"
44 Odor eater?
47 Listen
49 Point of law
50 Rock's ___ Lobos
51 Classic Poirot case
59 New Age musician
60 Crèche figure
61 Pressed cheese
62 Coordinate
63 Shirt stitching
64 Big rig
65 Jason deserted her
66 Ajax rival
67 Erstwhile despot

DOWN

1 Husband of Jezebel
2 Actress Rogers
3 Banking blunders
4 The Brady kids, e.g.
5 Minnesota clinic
6 Since
7 Baltic capital
8 Dean of "Lois & Clark"
9 Finger or toe
10 Ancient Celtic tongue
11 Barcelona-born artist

12 Jet
13 Slow-witted
21 Columbus landfall, 1492
22 Snake charmer's snake
25 City of Lombardy
26 ___ acid
27 Relaxed sighs
28 Like some blockades
29 Throat problem
30 Didn't engage in fence-sitting
31 Chilling
32 Obsolete
35 Lincoln's home: Abbr.
38 Alienate
39 Verily
40 Do, as hair
45 Image receiver
46 Approximately, in times
48 "It's true!"
51 Valley
52 Oklahoma city
53 Drop
54 Hitlerite
55 Stepped (on)

56 Park visited by Sherlock Holmes
57 Buddhist priest
58 Mideast bigwig
59 Starchy dish

842   by Rich Norris

ACROSS

1 Knack
8 Pettifogger
15 Before
16 Bust used as an architectural adornment
17 Helping
18 Will subject
19 Fine service
20 Regular alternative
22 "F Troop" corporal
23 Inconsiderate
25 Last frame
27 Cut
28 Jagged
30 Emblem
32 Shoshonean
33 Stetted
35 Like an eagle, e.g.
37 Mild epithet
39 Abounding
40 Made roomier, as a sleeve
44 Paranormal TV fare, with "The"
48 Genetic material
49 Dig find
51 Mass vestment
52 Rich person's suffix

54 Asian capital
56 Stained
57 Approve, in a way
59 Eminent
61 Gregory's "On the Beach" co-star
62 Catania's island
64 Target, as with a ball
66 View from Darjeeling
67 Remind, in a way
68 Feeling
69 Smashed

DOWN

1 Wear
2 Come by
3 No longer interested in
4 Satiric riposte
5 Mother of battles, in myth
6 Brown fur
7 Shelley's "Ozymandias," for one
8 Deep-fryer's concern
9 Charlemagne's reign: Abbr.
10 Spiritual discipline
11 Forest males

12 Aggregate
13 Retired
14 Join anew
21 Door feature
24 Actor Rob of "Silk Stalkings"
26 Coil
29 Peak in a Trevanian title
31 Diva Anna
34 N.B.A.'s Archibald and Thurmond
36 Odd
38 Assign
40 Sorghum and others
41 Promoting togetherness
42 Crusades fighter
43 Big name in fashion
45 Kind of plan
46 Promote
47 Under medication
50 Chalk site
53 Arab chieftains
55 Actress Christine
58 Defense ___
60 Corner
63 Adherent
65 Tramful, maybe

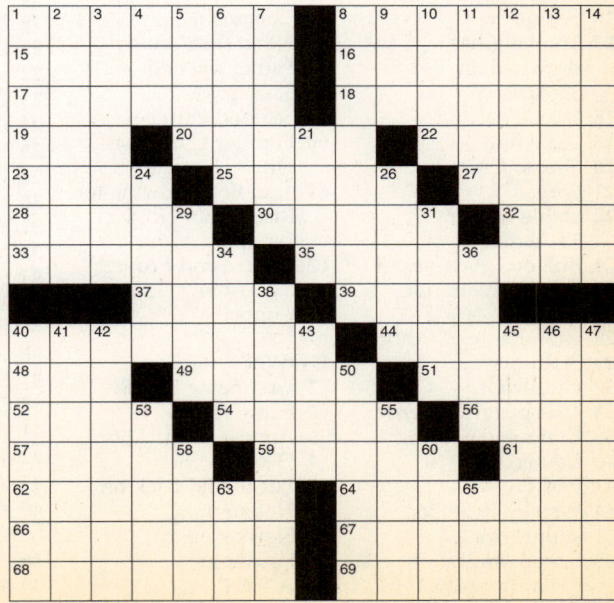

843 by Matt Gaffney

ACROSS
1 1984 sci-fi film
8 Snafu
15 Catherine the Great was one
16 Where Al Capone went to prison
17 Appellate court orders
18 Use as a base
19 Clique member
20 Covering ground
21 G.O.P. consultant Roger
22 Name in 1995 news
24 Word with time or life
25 Moon over München
26 It keeps Rover from roving
28 "Tootsie" co-star for Dustin
29 Sault ___ Marie
30 Neighborhood sign word
31 "Battleship Potemkin" locale
33 Gunk
34 Is afflicted by
35 Freshen
38 Desert Storm terror
40 To be, in Buenos Aires
43 Bring (out)
44 Kind of heat
46 Presage
47 1988 skating gold medalist Gustafson
49 Headline with an exclamation point
50 Spot
51 Befuddled
53 "West Side Story" song
55 Sea cow
56 Get set
57 Swellhead
58 Mickey Mouse Club name
59 Common speeding speed
60 Agrees

DOWN
1 Currents
2 "Murder in the Cathedral" writer
3 "Enchanted Places" memoir subject
4 Like "Pulp Fiction"
5 60's attire
6 No ifs, ___ or buts
7 Unpleasant folk
8 Choir section
9 "Tell ___ the judge"
10 Certain garden flowers, for short
11 Requires
12 Salad greens
13 Some assailants
14 Drink in a pitcher
23 Retribution object
26 Sacks
27 Causing ennui
30 Actor Jacobi
32 Lead-in for gum
33 Prepared for the prom
35 Now and then
36 Archaeologist's period
37 Bygone dynasty name
38 Overwhelming amount
39 Simón Bolívar's birthplace
40 Glitterati
41 School
42 Some transactions
45 Sylvester's would-be prey
46 Celebrated Argentine writer
48 Protested, 1960's-style
50 Comic Bruce
52 Animation
54 Novelist Simpson

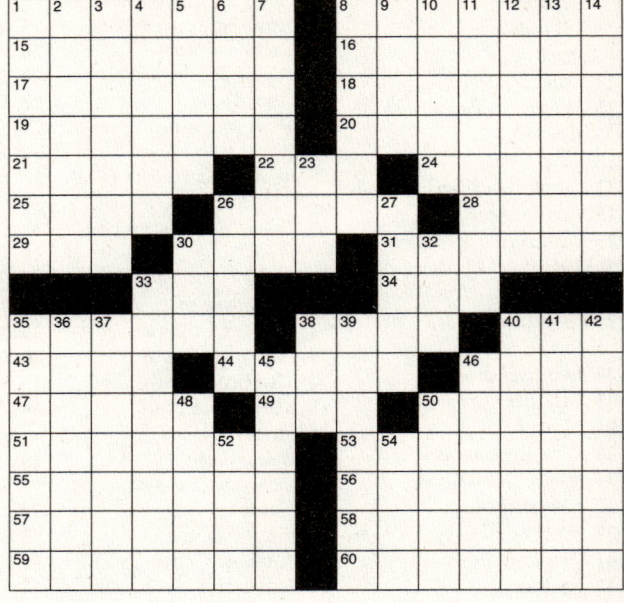

844 by James R. Leeds

ACROSS
1 Close in on, old-style
6 Pioneer Dadaist
9 Command in a western
13 Played
15 Sea duck
17 The king has drowned, in 33-Across?
18 Yarn
19 ___ whim
20 She, to Chanel
21 Spread
22 Stable fare, in 33-Across
24 Bulbous glass vessel
27 Sports finales, for short
28 Gibraltar, e.g.: Abbr.
29 Statutory ___
30 Paddled
33 This puzzle's theme
39 Con men, in slang
40 Cauterize
41 Baths
44 Whisky Rebellion suppressor
45 Noted family of philanthropists
47 Drag Miss DuBois to dinner, in 33-Across?
51 Her cow set Chicago ablaze, 1871
52 Buggy
53 Cousin of a Comanche
56 Naturalists' study
57 Father finch, in 33-Across?
59 Seafood entrée
60 Popular Christmas gift
61 "___ Bones Gwine ter Rise Again" (old song)
62 Psalms and Proverbs, e.g.: Abbr.
63 Copped

DOWN
1 First name in folk
2 Extra bright
3 Andean land: Abbr.
4 "Exodus" hero
5 Put the lid back on
6 Not straight
7 Newswoman Poussaint
8 A.S.A.P.
9 Hater
10 Confirmation and others
11 Aphrodite's amour
12 "You ___ kidding!"
14 "I haven't ___"
16 Mitch of 60's rock
21 No longer stocking
22 Inkling
23 Orch. leaders
24 Gov. Landon
25 Russian for "peace"
26 Princess's tormentor
30 Fishing basket
31 Atmospheric: Prefix
32 Villa ___
34 Stand
35 Words on a freshness label
36 Revivalist, for short
37 Skylark or Eagle, e.g.
38 Divs. of a day
41 Jeer
42 Wan
43 Anatomical ring
45 Ad salesmen have them: Abbr.
46 Eye-openers
48 Weight allowances
49 Smart one
50 Bouquets, to wine connoisseurs
53 Doing, so to speak
54 Asian unit of weight
55 In ___ (actually)
57 Writing tip
58 Bother, with "at"

845 by Fred Piscop

ACROSS
1 Title song of a 1973 Eagles album
10 Park feature
15 Prior to birth
16 Beat
17 Pearly gem
18 Pertaining to base 8
19 Al Fatah's org.
20 Element #50
21 Aperture for a lubricant
23 Turned blue
26 Van ___'s Land (Tasmania, once)
27 Head lines, for short?
28 Bug
30 Powerful D.C. lobby
31 "Concerto for the Left Hand" composer
34 Go-getter
35 Sylvester, to Tweety Pie
36 "Aladdin" prince and namesakes
37 Ran
38 Act grandmotherly
39 Wee
40 Brother of Cassandra
41 Grave matter
42 Hebrew letter
43 Quotable notable?: Abbr.
44 Light, in Lima
45 Fielding's last novel
47 Found after some effort
52 Boston's ___ Hall
54 Little time
55 LAX datum
56 Pitch ___ (prepare to camp)
57 Like much of the New Testament
60 Knot again
61 Strap for cash
62 Brand makers
63 Compounds of 20-Across

DOWN
1 Deadens
2 Name on a plane
3 Underwent
4 Big house
5 Strengthen
6 X, e.g.
7 Make up
8 Roseanne's man
9 Pat on the buns?
10 Encyclopedia name
11 Canadian novelist Mazo de la ___
12 Not the creative sort
13 No-win situation
14 Certain esters
22 Ran in neutral
24 School passes?
25 Some guests
29 "Concord" sonata composer
31 Selassie, to some
32 Beloved institution
33 Roman thoroughfare
34 Former Italian P.M. Aldo
37 Maui neighbor
38 Nod
40 Indians of the Great Basin
41 1974 Oscar winner
44 1956 World Series hero Don
46 Comintern's founder
48 Popular wedding gift
49 Struck out
50 Practical
51 Deals
53 Vehicles for Apollo
58 Ale holder
59 A geisha may tie one on

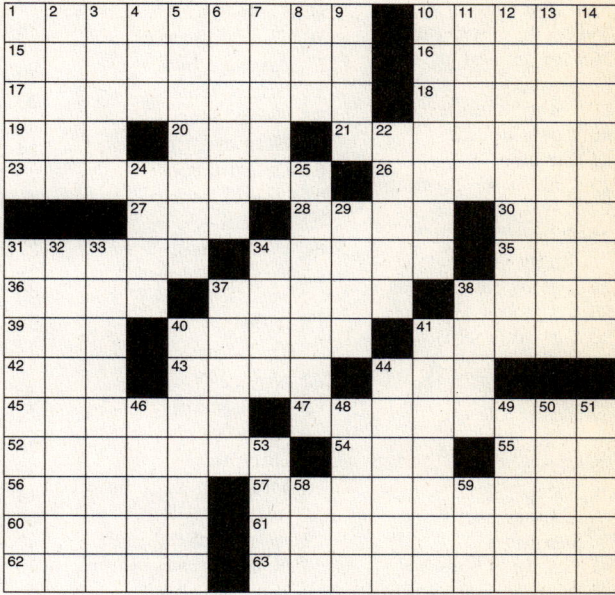

846 by Patrick Jordan

ACROSS
1 Greta who never actually said "I vant to be alone"
6 Howled like a hound
11 This instant
14 Extraterrestrial
15 Popeye's sweetie
16 Gardner of Tinseltown
17 Restaurant gadabout
19 Blend
20 Pesky insects
21 Christians' ___ Creed
23 Surfeit
26 Made fractions
27 Fold, as paper
28 One-dimensional
29 Forebodings
30 Zippy flavors
31 Uneaten morsel
34 Chaney Jr. and Sr.
35 Hats' stats
36 Fencing blade
37 Dehydrated
38 Star-to-be
39 Montreal baseballers
40 Held responsible (for)
42 "Accept the situation!"
43 Bing Crosby or Rudy Vallee, e.g.
45 Penny-pinching
46 Coarse-toothed tool
47 Stun gun
48 Egyptian snake
49 Dazzling performer
54 Victory sign
55 Cassettes
56 Speak
57 Be mistaken
58 Bewildered
59 Former Russian sovereigns

DOWN
1 Gangster's gun
2 Chicken ___ king
3 Barbecued treat
4 Antwerp residents
5 Unity
6 Pirates' plunder
7 Zurich's peaks
8 Sharp bark
9 Periods just past sunset
10 Infers
11 Egotistical conversationalist
12 Sheeplike
13 Like shiny floors
18 Despise
22 Spy org.
23 Chide, as a child
24 Knight's protection
25 Adolescent rock fan
26 Mel's on "Alice," for one
28 Lolled
30 Track official
32 Try to stop a squeak again
33 Snappish
35 To an extent
36 Quotes in book reviews
38 Rummy variation
39 Depose gradually and politely
41 ___ Angeles
42 Pugilist's weapon
43 Desire deeply
44 Part of a stairway
45 Term of address in "Roots"
47 Overly precious, to a Briton
50 Photo ___ (pol's news events)
51 Local educ. support group
52 Always, in verse
53 Southern Pacific and others: Abbr.

847 by Gerald R. Ferguson

ACROSS

1 Quark's place
5 Some are filled out
10 Org. for 7-Down
14 Command on a submarine
15 Beethoven dedicatee
16 Get ___ the ground floor
17 "Stop" sign
20 Costa del ___
21 Cleanse
22 One of the Brothers Karamazov
23 "Unforgettable" singer
24 Gas or elec., e.g.
25 To pieces
28 Lustrous fabric
30 Sailor
33 Assail
34 Ted's role on "Cheers"
35 "Dies ___"
36 "Stop" sign
40 Connecticut Ivy Leaguers
41 ___ de la Cite
42 Marconi's invention
43 Cub's home
44 To whom Tinker threw
46 Alamogordo event
47 Bouillabaisse, e.g.
48 Table d'___
50 Chairs on poles
53 Angler's luck
54 Guy's date
57 "Stop" sign
60 German article
61 Colorful rock
62 "Pistol Packin' ___"
63 Cherished
64 Wankel engine part
65 Procedure part

DOWN

1 Tacks on
2 Novice: Var.
3 Track shape
4 Kitten's cry
5 Untamed
6 Mount of ___ (site near Jerusalem)
7 Astronaut Sally
8 N.Y.C. sports venue
9 When to sow
10 This meant nothing to Nero
11 Operating without ___ (taking risks)
12 Skyrocket
13 "The King ___"
18 Three sheets to the wind
19 Ugandan dictator
23 Game featuring shooters
24 Where Provo is
25 Invited
26 English dramatist George
27 Supped at home
29 Starwort
30 School division
31 Watering hole
32 Infatuate
35 Furious
37 Exceptional, as a restaurant or hotel
38 Went by plane
39 Gadget for cheese
44 Sicilian volcano
45 Religion of Japan
47 Not a spendthrift
49 Aquatic mammal
50 Scurried
51 Buffalo's lake
52 Actress Merrill
53 Tuckered out
54 Midge
55 Crowning point
56 "Able to ___ tall buildings . . ."
58 Freudian factor
59 Early hrs.

848 by Cathy Millhauser

ACROSS

1 Jim at the bar
5 Long Island town
10 "Want to hear a secret?"
14 It's tender in Turin
15 Actress Gia
16 Bar assoc. member
17 Like a gemologist's drinks?
19 Kisser
20 Migrants' advocate Chavez
21 Sans mixers
22 Latest thing
23 Carafe quantity
25 Fictional hotel hellion
27 First-rate
30 Static ___
31 Film director Wertmuller
32 Adventure hero ___ Williams
35 Grateful?
38 Tailward, on jets
39 Sangria container
41 Gentle handling, initially
42 ___ dicit (legal refusal)
44 Ike's onetime singing partner
45 Luau entertainment
46 Skip over
48 Worker with a scythe
50 "The Song of the Earth" composer
52 Highly hackneyed
54 Baseball's Jesus
55 Actor Guinness
57 Gin flavorers
61 Asset
62 Like a platform diver's drinks?
64 Mislay
65 Fur source
66 Sparkling wine spot
67 Baa-maids?
68 In the poorhouse
69 Two semesters

DOWN

1 Voting group
2 Deutsche article
3 Song and dance, e.g.
4 Gospel's Jackson
5 Mt. Carmel site: Abbr.
6 Treat with tea
7 One who spikes the punch
8 Chase of "Now, Voyager"
9 Drawing that's easy on the eyes
10 Bar regulars, e.g.
11 Like an astronaut's drinks?
12 Deer sirs
13 Melville adventure
18 Lexicographer Partridge
24 TV's Hatcher
26 Detector target
27 Scotch family
28 LP player
29 Like a roofer's drinks?
30 Lawyer Roy
33 Diminutive suffix
34 Sprint rival
36 Word for a madame
37 Lasting impression
39 Barre room bend
40 Bring home
43 Mistreats
45 Vestibule
47 Tap
49 Part of SEATO
50 Fudge flavor
51 Let have
52 Davis of "Now, Voyager"
53 Hurt
56 Miller beer option
58 Seine feeder
59 "¿Como ___ usted?"
60 Do a bartending job
63 It may finish second

849 by David J. Kahn

ACROSS
1 Not occurring naturally
7 Beach resort near San Diego
13 Unfortunate landing spot for a parachutist
15 Fabric border
16 Workout expert
18 Bon ___
19 Not exactly PG-rated
20 Dos halved
21 Court wear
23 Incite
24 There was much of this in Shakespeare
25 Lilly of Lilly Pharmaceutical
26 N.B.A. venue, with "the"
28 Acclaim
30 H.M.O. employee
31 "Midnight Cowboy" role
33 "A bird," "a plane" or "Superman" preceder
34 Decorator, e.g.
38 Tic-tac-toe failure
39 Where the United Nations' setup was discussed
40 Pilot's announcement, for short
43 Insolent look
45 Bygone leader
46 Mo. to celebrate National Clown Week
47 Blacken
48 Actress MacDowell
51 Man with a mission
53 Abbr. after a comma
54 More urbane
56 "Tasty!"
57 Workout incentive
61 Most lenient
62 Rat
63 Ornate
64 It had many missions

DOWN
1 "The Racer's Edge"
2 Diva's device
3 Workout activity
4 "Beau ___"
5 W.W. II command
6 Family figures?
7 Skin: Prefix
8 Comedienne Boosler
9 Year in Nero's reign
10 Workout machine
11 Hidden items, sometimes
12 Transplant
14 How obvious? Very much so!
15 Solo, in a way
17 Kind of aide
21 Flushed
22 Gather on a surface, chemically
27 Fannie or Ginnie follower
29 Cannes co.
32 Sesames
35 Howard of comedy
36 D.C.'s Union ___
37 Irish national symbol
38 Rampaging
41 Hurly-burly
42 Sit in the cellar
43 Liquored up
44 Nonvolcanic eruptions
49 Cuckoo
50 Old Dodge model
52 Reply in a children's argument
55 Actress Lee of TV and film
58 Grunts, so to speak
59 "Bear"
60 Modernist, for short

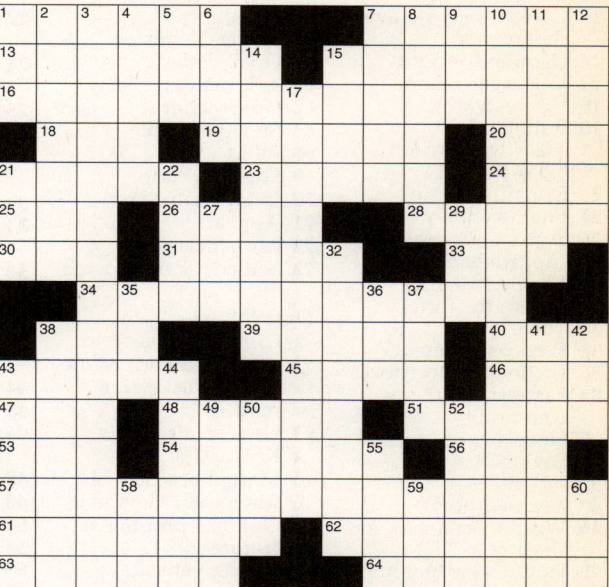

850 by Robert H. Wolfe

ACROSS
1 South of the border order
8 "I remember when . . ."
15 Cut off
16 Spark
17 Vandal
18 Had flashbacks about
19 Flaherty's "Man of ___"
20 Narrow inlets
22 Inscribed pillar
23 Makes tracks?
24 First name in gymnastics
26 Command to Rex
27 Conduit fitting
28 Karolyi who coached 24-Across
29 Perfectly
32 Hard to grasp
34 Fake
36 History chapters
38 Quod ___ faciendum
39 Suburb of Providence
42 Lacunae
45 Poseidon's domain
46 Neuwirth of "Chicago"
48 Third book of the Bible: Abbr.
50 Rubbish
51 Wage earner
53 ___ avis
54 Spring
57 "That's ___ blow!"
58 Emulate Ryan
59 Spice route procession
61 Thai towers
63 Nickel, e.g.
64 Like an encyclopedist
65 Minds
66 Governing bodies

DOWN
1 Philippic
2 Ordinarily
3 Not fixed
4 Actors Hale Sr. and Jr.
5 Retardation
6 Ageless, in poesy
7 Dickens, notably
8 Ankle bones
9 Sex-changing suffix
10 Wire measures
11 Give off
12 Greets from afar
13 Manet's workplace
14 Reserved
21 "Paradise Lost" character
25 Suffix with liquid
28 One of "The Usual Suspects" of film
30 Inedible orange
31 Heine poem "___ Troll"
33 Settings for idylls
35 Faithful wives
37 Posthaste
39 Lutheran hymn
40 Calls it a career
41 Ancient Greek coin
43 Expression of approval
44 Notched
45 Shipping inquiry
47 Meaning of "cave"
49 Ravel works
52 Carries on
53 70's TV spinoff
55 Indistinguishable
56 What one isn't
60 Tiny toiler
62 Report maker

851 by Peter Gordon

ACROSS

1 Comedian Mort
5 Small dent on a fender
9 Picket line crossers
14 Margarine
15 Cookie with a creme center
16 Diamond weight
17 Vegas card game
19 Dress style
20 Bullfight bull
21 Marx who wrote "Das Kapital"
23 Sault ___ Marie
24 Flue residue
26 Suffix meaning "approximately"
28 Lucille Ball, e.g.
30 Where the Eiffel Tower is
32 Feed bag contents
34 Distinctive doctrines
35 Fast-growing community
37 Housebroken animal
39 Savior
42 Till bill
43 Yearned (for)
46 Weapon in a silo, for short
49 Found's partner
51 Muse of love poetry
52 Organized absenteeism of police officers
54 Turf
56 "The ___ in the Hat" (rhyming Seuss book)
57 Writer Fleming
58 Greek letter
60 Ark builder
62 Greek letter
64 Stew vegetable
68 Build
69 Forearm bone
70 Indonesian island
71 Appears
72 Christmas carol
73 Settled, as on a perch

DOWN

1 Cry loudly
2 Start (and end) of the Three Musketeers' motto
3 London airport
4 Kooky
5 Martial arts schools
6 Rhymester Gershwin
7 Giraffe's prominent feature
8 Racing vehicle
9 Burn with hot water
10 Baseball's Ripken
11 Gets up
12 Small chicken
13 Spirited horses
18 Actress ___ Scott Thomas
22 Set a top in motion again
24 Police radio alert, briefly
25 ___ Paulo, Brazil
27 Inventor Elias
29 ___ and yon (in many places)
31 "Hi, honey!" follower
33 Egyptian symbols of life
36 Verdi opera based on a Shakespeare play
38 Incited
40 Kooky
41 Of the windpipe
44 Greek letter
45 "i" piece
46 Long-billed wading birds
47 Actress Bloom
48 Jumper's cord
50 Exceed in firepower
53 Decrees
55 Basketball's Shaquille
59 Woody Guthrie's son
61 Rhyme scheme for Mr. Eban?
63 1900, on a cornerstone
65 Opposite WSW
66 Rhyming boxing champ
67 Annual basketball event: Abbr.

852 by Martin Schneider

ACROSS

1 *"Toil and trouble" preceder
7 *Normal, in a way
13 The N. Platte, e.g.
15 Less sound
16 Increaser of one's growth potential?
17 Gifts
18 Pub supply
19 Garments for granny
21 Nintendo's Super ___
22 Tito's homeland
24 Slalom segment
27 Like some arches
28 Car part
29 Taxonomic div.
32 Willingly
33 Composer Mahler
35 "___ Male War Bride" (1949 movie)
37 Sound units: Abbr.
39 Fin de ___ (remainder): Fr.
40 Marinated beef strip
42 Official records
44 Cape ___
45 Some boxing wins
46 "The Thrill Is Gone" singer
48 "___ out!"
49 Adriatic port
50 Typewriter key
53 Pieces
54 "¿Que ___ es?" (Spanish 101 question)
55 Sneakers brand
58 Made of certain twigs
61 Many a Miamian
62 Corporate routine
63 *1990's sitcom
64 *Name in the news, 6/5/68

DOWN

1 *English pop group
2 "___ Mio"
3 Spurs
4 It's unfair
5 Year in Nero's reign
6 Poetic contraction
7 Out of the freezer
8 *Home of Whitman College
9 Squeezes (out)
10 Writer Anaïs
11 Hanoi festival
12 Age: Abbr.
14 Cobbled
15 What each star represents
20 Like the answers to this puzzle's 12 asterisked clues?
22 B
23 BBC's Italian counterpart
24 *Newsboy's cry
25 Assassinated
26 *Height of the N.B.A.'s Gheorghe Muresan
28 Peer Gynt's mother
29 *Evenly split
30 Open-eyed
31 *"Catch-22" character
34 Strunk & White subject
36 Family member
38 Clip
41 Rubber
43 Cable choice
47 Short hair, to Burns
49 *"It'll be O.K."
50 The Bible before Joshua
51 Asian palm
52 *European resort
53 Burlesque bit
54 Munster Mister
55 Duos: Abbr.
56 Defendants at law
57 Nail-biters: Abbr.
59 Eur. carrier
60 "Lord, is ___?"

853   by Matthew L. Jones

ACROSS
1 Letterman's last guest on NBC
9 Associates
14 Burn treatment
15 Springy?
16 "Little buddy" of 60's TV
17 Captivate
18 End of the year, e.g.
19 "Roll ___ bones!"
20 Base
21 Make out
23 Vice follower
25 Grandchild's seat
26 Catholic Bible version
28 First Nobelist in Physics
31 Woody
33 Woody pipe
34 Pop vocalist Annie
36 Magic act
39 "The door's open!"
41 Olympic statistic
43 Pacific island chain
46 Antisesquipedalian
47 1944 Bill of Rights subjects
48 Make confetti of
50 Friend en francais
51 Country with a blue, black and white flag
54 Def, to a slangster
56 Tilde carriers
57 Labor leader of note
58 Stimulus that causes strain
60 Literally, empty hand
61 Parting phrase
62 European cars
63 Probed

DOWN
1 Miscellanea
2 1980 Shelley Duvall role
3 Chemistry class model
4 Norse underworld queen
5 Passionate
6 Over half of Israel
7 "Seinfeld" character
8 ___ Ysidro, Calif.
9 Feller with Teller
10 Inferential word
11 Qualify
12 Eponymous Lord
13 It was azure-lidded, to Keats
15 Omission of all animal products from the diet
20 Rhône tributary
22 Julie ___, voice of Marge Simpson
24 Hold up
27 Single-named New Age musician
29 Be quiet, to a musician
30 Good egg's rank?
32 Certify, in a way
35 City near Dayton
37 Tortellini topping
38 Shakespearean locale
40 Bad-mouth
42 Fumes
43 Bit of bad luck
44 Gazing
45 Additional charge
47 Lizard with clingy toe pads
49 Arctic fur
52 Site for a race
53 Snags
55 Make judgments
58 Marie, e.g.: Abbr.
59 Phys., but not phys. ed.

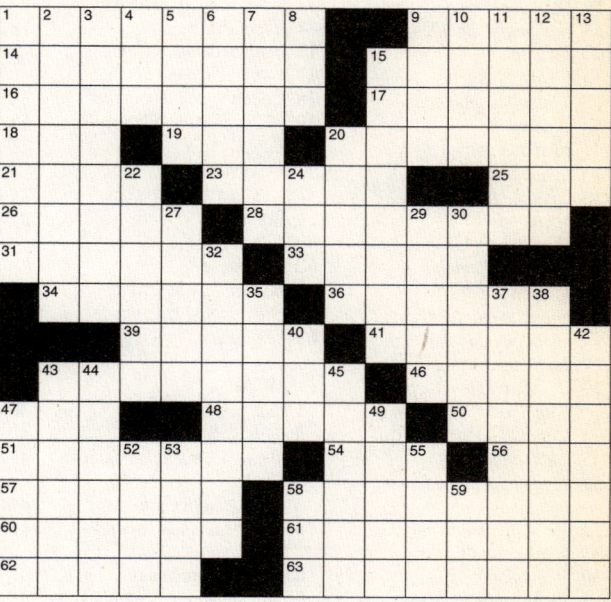

854   by Stephanie Spadaccini

ACROSS
1 The ex-Mrs. Bono
5 Money owed
9 Pharmacy items
14 Composer Schifrin
15 Anatomical passage
16 Like "The Twilight Zone" episodes
17 Actress Lena
18 This ___ of tears (life)
19 Do watercolors
20 Secondhand store
23 Showed respect for the national anthem
24 Sister of Osiris
25 Mr. O.
28 Cinematographer Nykvist
30 Arthurian sorcerer
32 Harvest goddess
35 Pass, as laws
38 Verdi heroine
39 John Glenn's Mercury spacecraft
43 Type assortment
44 Card catalogue entry after "Author"
45 Before, in verse
46 Overage
49 Boat propellers
51 Loaf with seeds
52 ___ to the throne (prince, e.g.)
55 Laid, as a bathroom floor
58 Member of the police
61 Without ___ in the world
64 Prefix with China
65 Nat King or Natalie
66 ___ says (tots' game)
67 ___-do-well
68 Popular fashion magazine
69 Israeli port
70 Microbe
71 Do one of the three R's

DOWN
1 Drain problem
2 Angels' headgear
3 Ness of "The Untouchables"
4 Musical movements
5 Stockholder's income
6 Catchall abbr.
7 Attorney Melvin
8 Lock of hair
9 Remove from office
10 Harvest
11 Spoon-bender Geller
12 Rummy game
13 Matched items
21 Made on a loom
22 That guy
25 Kicking's partner
26 Contract add-on
27 Nonsensical
29 Political cartoonist Thomas
31 "Norma ___"
32 Bidder's amount
33 Stockholder's vote
34 Subsequently
36 Letter before psi
37 Maverick Yugoslav leader
40 High season, on the Riviera
41 Railroad station area
42 Printing flourish
47 Singer Easton
48 Ocean
50 Deli machine
53 Cake decoration
54 "Walk Away ___" (1966 hit)
56 French school
57 Singer Reese
58 Univ. teacher
59 German border river
60 Marsh stalk
61 Cigarette waste
62 K.G.B.'s cold war foe
63 "___ the only one?"

855 by Brendan Emmett Quigley

ACROSS
1 Procter & Gamble bar
6 Native Alaskan
11 Spoil
14 Midwest airport hub
15 Sergeant at TV's Fort Baxter
16 Diamonds
17 Place to place a wallet or handkerchief
19 ___ Na Na
20 Thanksgiving meat request
21 "Entry of Christ Into Brussels" painter James
23 Scott Adams's put-upon comics hero
27 Nautical spar
29 Body parts shaped like punching bags
30 W.W. II Philippine battle site
31 Horse in a harness race
32 1924 Ferber novel
33 Little newt
36 It's NNW of Oklahoma City
37 Rounded lumps
38 Nicholas I or II, e.g.
39 Mule of song
40 Nash's two-l beast
41 Hardly elegant
42 Easy two-pointers
44 Concert halls
45 Starts of tourneys
47 Last course
48 Peres's predecessor
49 "___ That a Shame"
50 Eggs
51 "Come on!"
58 ___ canto (singing style)
59 Characteristic
60 Confuse
61 Right-angle joint
62 Steinbeck migrants
63 Dapper

DOWN
1 ___ a plea
2 "Now I see!"
3 Beatnik's exclamation
4 Skill
5 Sweetheart's assent
6 Cancel, as a launch
7 Drub
8 Lodge member
9 Luau instrument
10 Alternative to a purse
11 Err on stage
12 Cause for blessing?
13 Get ready for battle again
18 Average figures
22 Org. for Bulls and Bullets
23 Fools
24 Ex-Mrs. Trump
25 Four-time Emmy-winning comedienne
26 Ran, as colors
27 ___ the Hutt, of "Star Wars"
28 Medical suffix
30 Certain mikes
32 Knee hits
34 Mountebank
35 Lovers' engagement
37 Rather morose
38 Suns
40 Deceiving
41 Nuclear treaty subject
43 "The Greatest"
44 ___ cava (path to the heart)
45 Explore
46 "Bolero" composer
47 They're losing propositions
49 French friend
52 Bother
53 ___ tai (drink)
54 Nutritional abbr.
55 N.Y.C. summer clock setting
56 Model Carol
57 Lock opener

856 by Dean Niles

ACROSS
1 How the boss wants things done, briefly
5 Ditto
9 Devil dolls, e.g.
14 Kind of chop
15 "Family Ties" kid
16 Dander
17 "Oh, woe!"
18 Chimney covering
19 Nick name?
20 "Don't tell!"
23 "Losing My Religion" rock group
24 Scene of the William Tell legend
25 Norma Webster's middle name
26 Cash substitute
27 Certain corporate career path
33 Beam
34 Carthage founder
35 Julia, on "Seinfeld"
38 "___ Three Lives"
40 Reggae relative
42 Brit. decorations
43 New York county
46 Reaching as far as
49 Easter parade attraction
50 1948 Irene Dunne film
53 Foldaway, e.g.
55 Polit. designation
56 Maiden name preceder
57 ___ Arbor
58 Western mountain range
64 Shade tree
66 Equine shade
67 "Let's Make a Deal" choice
68 "Victory ___" (1954 film)
69 Secular
70 Designer Cassini
71 Forfeits
72 Swirl
73 "And away ___!"

DOWN
1 In ___ (having trouble)
2 George Takei TV/film role
3 Sixth-day creation
4 "Playing" critter
5 Japanese fish dish
6 Facial tissues additive
7 Doorsill cry
8 Obtain by force
9 Poker boo-boo
10 Mouths, anatomically
11 Eastern taxi: Var.
12 Prefix with arthritis
13 Sea World attraction
21 Walked (on)
22 Scarce
27 Chamber group, maybe
28 Dutch painter
29 See firsthand
30 Clinic workers, for short
31 Mammy ___
32 Lowlife
36 Linguist Chomsky
37 "¿Como ___ usted?"
39 German article
41 Police radio msg.
44 Japanese entertainers
45 Old Dodge
47 Period of a renter's agreement
48 Provo neighbor
51 Channel swimmer Gertrude
52 Grazing area
53 Plot
54 "You're ___ talk!"
59 Way to go
60 Bust, so to speak
61 Handout
62 Film director Nicolas
63 "Cogito ___ sum"
65 Middling mark

857 by Hugh Davis

ACROSS

1 Mad dog worry
5 Spy ___ Hari
9 Aware, with "in"
14 Water color
15 Valentine's Day matchmaker
16 Hawaiian veranda
17 "Brilliant idea!"
20 Ice Follies venue
21 Maid's cloth
22 Veteran
26 Pennilessness
30 ___ Strait (Russia-Alaska separator)
31 Confront
32 Wide shoe specification
33 Police operation
34 Knob
35 Nos. on a road map
36 Classic Bill Clinton phrase
39 Giant Mel et al.
40 Jazzy Fitzgerald
41 Remove, as a knot
43 Award for a knight: Abbr.
44 Neighbor of Vietnam
45 Like some kisses and bases
46 Novelist Hesse
48 Sentimentalists, maybe
49 Superlative ending
50 Subject of psychoanalysis
51 1962 Cary Grant/Doris Day movie
59 Actor Bruce of radio's "Sherlock Holmes"
60 Chess finale
61 "God's Little ___"
62 Lachrymose
63 Hardly any
64 Rural carriage

DOWN

1 Sheep's sound
2 Stats for eggheads
3 Egyptian boy king
4 Barber's obstruction
5 Cooking up
6 Change, as a motion
7 Swiped
8 Comic dog's bark
9 Split asunder
10 Jessica of 1976's "King Kong"
11 Prefix with cycle
12 ___ de vie
13 Insult, in slang
18 Pumpkin-colored
19 Food seller
22 Out-of-date: Abbr.
23 Last Beatles album
24 Gadabout
25 Jazzman "Fatha"
26 "The Taming of the Shrew" locale
27 Change names
28 Even smaller
29 "You bet!"
31 April ___ Day
34 Parachute material
35 Babbled
37 Shanty
38 Delay
39 Aah's partner
42 U.S.N. officer
44 Summing-up word
45 Flew alone
47 Olympic race unit
48 Conductor Zubin
50 "Get outta here!"
51 Explosive inits.
52 Hasten
53 ___ Khan
54 Thurman of "Pulp Fiction"
55 Mothers
56 "___ bin ein Berliner"
57 Gun enthusiast's grp.
58 Code breaker's discovery

858 by John D. Leavy

ACROSS

1 Bouquet holder
5 Bouquet makers
10 ___ Offensive
13 Deejay Don
14 Two-time Grand Slam winner
15 Missile housing
16 "Relax!"
19 ___ gratia artis
20 "I have half ___ to . . ."
21 Part of a bouquet
22 The Beatles' last movie
24 Brush, so to speak
25 Baseball's Charlie Hustle
26 Meager
28 Monopoly token
30 Mall component
31 Legal matter
34 "Relax!"
38 Be in hock
39 1977 U.S. Open champ
40 Likable
41 Manipulate
42 Predominant
44 Chiseler
46 James Bond backdrop
49 Not so bold
50 Former Soviet First Lady
52 Guinness specialty
53 "Relax!"
56 Cravings
57 "The Brady Bunch" housekeeper
58 Flying eagle, e.g.
59 Old polit. cause
60 Novelist Dostoyevsky: Var.
61 Trojan ally, in the "Iliad"

DOWN

1 "Myra Breckinridge" author
2 That's a subject for Dean Martin!
3 Summer ailment
4 Therapy fad
5 Like a plum pudding
6 "C'est ___"
7 Kenmore product
8 Crack the books
9 Semicircle
10 Indonesian island
11 Cousin of a gazelle
12 June award
15 Work like a slave
17 Items at a lost-and-found
18 First game
23 With 49-Down, "Say Anything" co-star
24 Cutting remark
26 Lieu
27 True-crime TV series
28 Simpson's criminal-case judge
29 Vulgar
30 Peddle
31 It's found in a runoff
32 And so on
33 1967 Monkees song
35 Zoo section
36 Dr. Atkins's plan
37 Oklahoma town
41 Blubbers
42 Participant at a 90's dance club
43 Jai ___
44 Root on
45 One raising a howl?
46 Pancho's amigo
47 Going stag
48 Signs a lease
49 See 23-Down
50 Preside over
51 Bone-dry
54 Clod
55 Admiral competitor, once

859   by Rose White

ACROSS
1 Unposed photo
7 Streisand, in fanzines
11 Cpl.'s superior
14 Tom, Dick or Harry
15 Year in Henry I's reign
16 Court
17 Military meal manager
19 Set off
20 Used a sauna
21 What "bathy-" means
23 Homeboys' "fraternity"
24 Consulate's kin
25 Somewhat firm
28 Track tournaments
29 Woolen cloth
30 Homes of the rich and famous
33 Beauty preceder?
34 Epoch
35 Hieroglyphic stone locale
40 Musical counterpoint
44 Prison guard, in slang
45 Air shafts for mines
46 Lewd
48 Sweep with binoculars
49 Decapitates
50 Hearty?
54 Clockmaker Terry
55 Embroidery style
57 Kind of camera: Abbr.
58 Margarita garnish
59 Author Welty
60 Grab a bite
61 "Waiting for the Robert ___"
62 Let live

DOWN
1 Rotating engine parts
2 Over
3 Amex alternative
4 Pharmacist's concerns
5 Coffee choice
6 Diplomat's quest
7 Mercedes competitor
8 University environment
9 Ancient galleys
10 Auxiliary wager
11 Diner entree
12 Al et al.
13 Hungarian wine
18 Nosed (out)
22 ___-cake (baby's game)
25 "Suppose they gave ___ . . ."
26 Sign of The Times?
27 Tuxedo accompaniment
31 River to Donegal Bay
32 Hurdles for srs.
36 Behold, to Pilate
37 Something cloying
38 Plant runner
39 Absolutely fabulous
40 Platters
41 Covers completely
42 Nascent company
43 Shaw play
46 Corpulent
47 Italian's word of approval
51 "Ripley's Believe ___ Not!"
52 4,047 square meters
53 Neighbor of Nigeria
56 Bishop's jurisdiction

860   by Martin Ashwood-Smith

ACROSS
1 Personal things?
4 It's full of roots
9 Rocky Mtn. highs?
13 Takes home
15 ___ Conferences of 1899 and 1907
16 ___ Maar (Picasso mistress and subject)
17 Some Havanans
19 Actor Morales
20 Round rolls
21 Sentimentality
23 Outer limit
24 Pizza topping
25 One that's over due?
27 1969 Hoffman role
29 Author ___ Yutang
30 "Independence Day" actor
32 Fleetwood Mac's "Walk ___ Line"
33 Mason attachment
34 Commercial prefix for many cold-weather products
35 Comic actor John
36 Like a shake roof
39 Mollycoddles
40 Military demolitions expert
41 Shoot the breeze
42 Take a bough
43 Nursery items
44 Monthly service
46 Trip
47 French story
48 Long ___
49 Millionths of a meter
51 Singer Ocasek of the Cars
52 Old-fashioned contraction
54 ___ one's welcome
56 Noted name in newspapering
58 Hospital helper
60 "___ Three Lives" (TV oldie)
61 "The Pirates of Penzance" heroine
62 Roulette bet
63 ___ Jr. (acting son, familiarly)
64 Beethoven dedicatee
65 Antis

DOWN
1 Body builder?
2 One usually precedes 15-Across
3 Infant's dessert, maybe
4 "Leaving Las Vegas" co-star
5 Hack's place
6 Palindromic title
7 Took a stab at?
8 Colombian coin
9 "The Sultan of Sulu" writer
10 Fall short in votes
11 50's innovation
12 Hoped for salvation
14 Whist variety
18 Roulette bet
22 They're all talk
26 Capital city till 1960
28 Chemical suffixes
31 Mouse manipulator
35 Hood
37 Take down ___
38 Right, in a way
39 Crews' quarters
41 Bender
44 Invitation notation
45 C.P.R. pros
50 "No man ___ . . ."
53 "Trust ___" (1937 hit)
55 Ubangi tributary
57 80's Pentagon letters
59 Diamond stat.

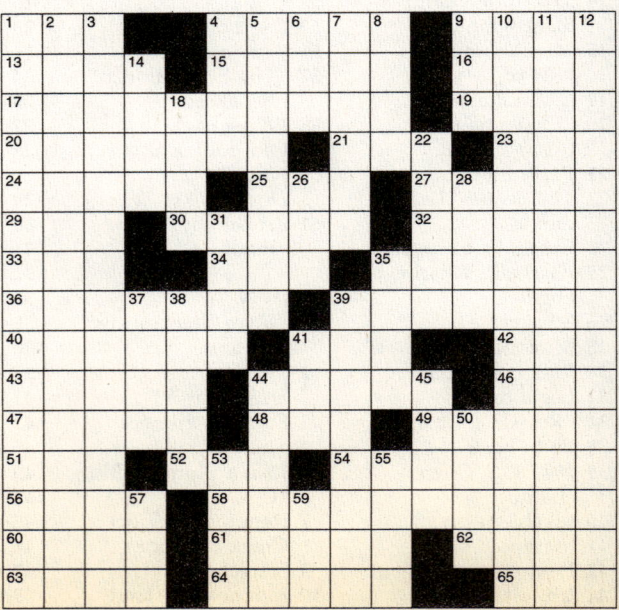

861 by Eileen Lexau

ACROSS

1 Prop up
6 Goddess pictured in Egyptian tombs
10 Fraud
14 Old autos
15 Short letter
16 Patriot Nathan
17 Feeling really good
20 Get-out-of-jail money
21 Hors d'oeuvre spread
22 Song for Aida
23 Chomped down
24 "___ cost to you!"
25 Novelist Waugh
27 Batter's goal
29 Frigid
30 "Turandot" slave girl
31 Moon-landing vehicle
32 ___ de Triomphe
33 "I ___ Grow Up" ("Peter Pan" song)
34 Heads of state get-together
38 "It can't be!"
39 Be in session
40 Nothing
41 Peas' holder
42 Pennies: Abbr.
43 Creeks
47 Storm warnings at sea
49 Clinton's #2
50 Wrestler's place
51 Site for a swing
52 Rikki-tikki-___ (Kipling mongoose)
53 Capable of
54 Little that's visible
57 Poker call
58 Mending site
59 Louis XIV, 1643–1715
60 Hawaii's state bird
61 Remove from office
62 Dunne of "I Remember Mama"

DOWN

1 Thick-trunked tropical tree
2 Italian soprano Scotto
3 Clarinetist Shaw and others
4 Refrigerate
5 One of Kreskin's claims
6 Wee one
7 ___ voce (almost in a whisper)
8 Spillane's "___ Jury"
9 Visualize
10 Beach
11 Set of bells
12 Relieving
13 Club ___
18 They expect the best
19 Undulating
24 "Um, excuse me"
25 Like a three-dollar bill
26 Cashew, e.g.
28 "Tickle me" doll
29 Anger
32 Quantity: Abbr.
33 Sly trick
34 Cable channel
35 Support
36 "___ the season . . ."
37 Radial, e.g.
38 Photo ___ (media events)
42 Musical sign
43 Bygone Russian group
44 Electrical unit
45 Female attendant
46 Cheap cigar
48 Sierra ___
49 Scottish Celts
52 10 C-notes
53 Opposite of unter, in German
54 Can's composition
55 Notwithstanding that, briefly
56 Biblical priest

---

862 by Ed Early

ACROSS

1 ___ World Service (radio provider)
4 ___ Pet (novelty item)
8 "My Life on Trial" author
13 Mine product
14 Dog : paw :: horse : ___
15 Lacking, with "of"
16 High-risk game
19 Plan
20 "___ to differ"
21 Coral ___
22 Gaze
23 Kind of acid
25 Dumb ___ ox
27 Republican V.I.P. Dick
31 Hemming and hawing
34 Charles Lamb, to readers
36 Exhibits scorn
37 Rot caused by bark beetles
40 Renaissance type
41 Course
42 ___ Alte (Adenauer)
43 Pulsate
44 Zorro's marks
46 Leg bones
50 Message on a Wonderland cake
54 Pac.'s counterpart
57 Beach, basically
58 Farmer's land
59 Montreal denizens
62 Distance on a radar screen
63 Peter Lorre role Mr. ___
64 Deception
65 Australian export
66 Effect of auto exhaust
67 Actor Mineo

DOWN

1 Tennis's Becker
2 Main thrust
3 Jai alai basket
4 Showy-flowered shrub
5 1956–57 Wimbledon champion Lew
6 Charged particle
7 Pertaining to the second-largest continent
8 Good herder
9 First lady
10 Plenty
11 Miller beer
12 Brainstorm
15 Piece for two
17 Word repeated after "Que"
18 Award bestowed by Queen Eliz.
23 Deep blue
24 Manitoba Indian
26 One of the Waughs
28 "Canterbury Tales" drink
29 Gaelic
30 North Sea feeder
31 Handle text
32 Dr. Westheimer
33 Hollywood Boulevard sight
35 Electric guitar hookup
36 Location
38 Congeal
39 Stupor
45 Hindu garment
47 Scornful cries
48 Co. name ending
49 Monroe's successor
51 Dabbling ducks
52 Craze
53 Collectible Ford
54 Opposite of a buzz cut
55 Pitfall
56 Moon of Jupiter
58 60's–70's Japanese P.M.
60 Zilch
61 Robespierre, e.g.

863 by Gilbert H. Ludwig

ACROSS

1 Thriving time
5 Seed covering
9 Make meek, in a way
14 Bring down
15 Kierkegaard, e.g.
16 Poolside turban
17 Scene of W.W. I fighting
18 "Black Beauty" author
20 Mourning
22 "Keep it up, fella!"
23 Don't believe it!
27 Pond dwellers
28 Ice ___
30 ___ populi
31 Sighting off the California coast
34 Spiffy
35 Noone
37 Newscaster Paula
39 Relents
40 Prefix with propyl
41 Screen
42 Can't take ___ an answer
46 Play by 21-Down
48 Film maker?
50 Knight
53 Slapstick, e.g.
56 Falkirk citizen
57 Harry Connick Jr.'s "___ and a Smile"
58 Lots of bucks
59 Some story
60 Brisk
61 Lith. and Azer., once
62 Suffix with huck

DOWN

1 Patronizes
2 At the scene
3 One-named folk singer
4 Subject for St. Thomas Aquinas
5 Hersey's bell town
6 Tall and wiry
7 Places to overnight
8 Rachel's sister
9 Singer Nicks
10 Author Barbara of "Laughing All the Way"
11 It's inspired
12 Football Hall-of-Famer Blount
13 Wing
19 Writer de Beauvoir et al.
21 See 46-Across
24 Maintain
25 Former part of Portuguese India
26 Inside no.
28 Blue-ribbon
29 Unhurried gait
32 Unfair employers
33 Word after over or clover
34 Family providers?
35 "Git!"
36 Piano pro
37 Move to the side
38 Soda ___
41 Hard to open
43 Contributor of big bucks
44 Mr. Chips portrayer, 1969
45 Flat dweller
47 Perform lousily
48 Freud contemporary
49 Many teamsters
51 Former Fords
52 They fit in sockets
53 Tube top
54 Take credit?
55 Earth orbiter

864 by Gregory E. Paul

ACROSS

1 Civil disorder
5 Urban haze
9 Diners
14 Workers' protection org.
15 Variety of fine cotton
16 Hold dear
17 Tizzy
18 The New Yorker cartoonist Peter
19 Chateau-Thierry's river
20 "Petticoat Junction" setting
23 Lyricist Rice
24 Granola grain
25 Copyists
27 Trim, as a tree
32 Arp's art
33 Military address: Abbr.
34 Fishing line
36 The "S" in WASP
39 State north of Ind.
41 Adventures
43 Battle of Normandy objective
44 Big news exclusive
46 Reading lights
48 Ames and Asner
49 Pub orders
51 Practice
53 Edmonton's province
56 Everything
57 Random number generator
58 "Father Knows Best" setting
64 Texas site to remember
66 Have ___ good authority
67 Sewing case
68 Georgia city, home of Mercer University
69 Color of linen
70 Final Four inits.
71 Pronunciation symbol
72 Make-believe
73 Eschew

DOWN

1 ___ ha-Shanah
2 "Money ___ object!"
3 Louisville's river
4 Dragon, perhaps
5 Big Ten team from East Lansing
6 Nuclear missile, briefly
7 Prefix meaning 56-Across
8 London lockups
9 Kodaks, e.g.
10 Nabokov novel
11 "The Phil Silvers Show" setting
12 Sgt. Bilko
13 Looks like
21 Prominent rabbit features
22 Digital readout, for short
26 Mrs. McKinley and others
27 Beavers' constructions
28 Kind of proportions
29 "I Dream of Jeannie" setting
30 Marsh duck
31 "Pomp and Circumstance" composer
35 Shiny fabric
37 Auto pioneer Ransom
38 Victory margin, at times
40 Tunnel
42 Moss for potting plants
45 ___ non grata
47 Prefix with starter
50 Nascar sponsor
52 Little green men
53 Revolutionary leader Samuel
54 Light purple
55 Pisces's follower
59 Scratch it!
60 Nick and ___ Charles
61 Make an aquatint
62 Hilo feast
63 Primatologist Fossey
65 Cut the grass

865   by Jonathan Schmalzbach

ACROSS

1 Support
5 Hindu gentleman
9 Indonesian island
14 Nautical direction
15 Part of the eye
16 Mirror ___
17 Charlemagne's legacy
20 Lepidopterist's equipment
21 Corrida cries
22 Condemned
23 Marking float
24 Tiny memory measures
25 "Nothing ___!"
27 James Buchanan, notably
31 Reign noted for magnificent porcelain
33 Actress Hagen
34 Commentators' page
35 Cricket sides
36 Play start
37 German direction
38 Virginia's nickname
42 Farewells
44 Chips in?
45 Rara ___
46 Semicircles

47 Gene Kelly's activity in the 30-Down
50 Hammett pooch
51 Stage of history
54 Disney realm
57 Draw a bead on
58 Subsequently
59 Venom
60 Cache
61 Stitches
62 Charon's river

DOWN

1 Where to take a Volkswagen for a spin
2 Shampoo ingredient
3 Breton, for one
4 Crucial
5 What John Scopes taught
6 Majority leader Dick
7 Partiality
8 Milit. branch
9 Coarse fodder grass
10 Levy
11 Impair
12 Bogeyman
13 Army surgeon Walter

18 Spherical
19 Pronouncement
23 Nickname for the Cowboys' hometown
24 One who sings the part of Boris Godunov
25 Boozehound
26 "And ___ grow on"
27 They were big in the 40's
28 "A Tale of Two Cities" heroine
29 Director Preminger et al.
30 See 47-Across
31 ___ synthesizer
32 Stem joints
36 Termites' kin
38 Render unnecessary
39 Fibbing
40 Forked-tail swallows
41 From early Peru
43 Buxom blonde of 50's TV
46 Crooked
47 B.&O. stops
48 "___ a New High" (1937 Lily Pons song)
49 Verne's captain

50 Lumbago, e.g.
51 Blue-pencil
52 ___-poly
53 Big Board's brother: Abbr.

55 "___ Not Unusual"
56 Literary monogram

866   by Nancy S. Ross

ACROSS

1 A single time
5 Stephen King's home state
10 Porgy's beloved
14 Gloucester's king
15 Jostle
16 Teatro ___ Scala
17 IRIS
20 Book addendum
21 Striped chalcedony
22 Guest room, frequently
23 Prosciutto
25 IRIS
33 Selfish sort
34 Ring shout
35 Chinese nurse
36 Bridge achievement
37 Snack items
39 In ___ (undisturbed)
40 Rival of Rival
41 Darling of the diamond
42 Boobs
43 IRIS
47 Wonder
48 Actor Beatty
49 Play for time
53 Academic term

58 IRIS
61 Shortly
62 Kind of flare or system
63 "___ Named Sue"
64 Well-bred chap
65 Porterhouse kin
66 Kesey and Follett

DOWN

1 One of Chekhov's Three Sisters
2 Tide type
3 Gefilte fish ingredient
4 Mahler's "Das Lied von der ___"
5 Tailor, at times
6 Describing some skiing
7 Old World goat
8 Neither's partner
9 One welcomed to the fold?
10 [Just like that!]
11 Lamb's pen name
12 Blind segment
13 Red-tag event
18 Where Saul consulted a witch
19 Identify

23 Servants
24 "The ___ have it"
25 Arum lily
26 Giraffe's relative
27 Fruit at the bar
28 Bringing off
29 Dated
30 Wrong
31 Hotel charges
32 Consequently
33 Nicholas or Alexander
37 Be exultant
38 Gordie of the N.H.L.
42 European viper
44 Debutante's affair
45 Kind of show or band
46 Shy and modest
49 Small setback
50 Sound quality
51 Bath's county
52 Mardi Gras follower
53 Manche capital
54 Mt. Rushmore's state: Abbr.
55 Start of a Hamlet soliloquy
56 Subj. for an M.B.A.

57 Actor John ___-Davies
59 Suffix with vocal
60 Sorrowful sound

867 by David J. Kahn

ACROSS
1 Bedim
6 Rude one
10 With 58-Down, a religious monogram
13 Contradict
14 "Same here!"
15 Hatcher
16 Graduation day V.I.P.'s
19 Newborn
20 Flunky
21 Nimbus
22 Short-legged hunter
24 Graduation day award
29 Biblical twin
30 1953 Leslie Caron role
31 Graduation day word
39 Dickerson of the N.F.L.
40 Captain, e.g.
41 Prize for 16-Across
48 Vaporize
49 The Supremes, e.g.
50 Bring (out)
51 Tree whose product is used in making soap
55 24-Across and others
60 "A Chorus Line" standard
61 ". . . woman who lived in ___"
62 Extremist
63 Old geographical inits.
64 100 sawbucks
65 Pried

DOWN
1 Overseas network
2 City NW of Madrid
3 Suffix with salmon
4 Troubles
5 Come back again
6 Words after 31-Across
7 Financial page heading: Abbr.
8 Sound at the circus
9 Aussie hopper
10 Suntanner's seat
11 Ranch worker
12 Some blowups
14 ___ Park, N.J.
17 Tackle
18 Cellar dweller's place
22 Composer Bartok
23 Very busy
24 Holiday mo.
25 Spanish bruin
26 Fire
27 Action on the shirt sleeves
28 "___ Liza Jane" (old glee club favorite)
32 Nautical danger
33 Dilettantish
34 Acapulco aunt
35 Subj. of a rollover
36 ___-leaf cluster
37 Compass heading
38 Jupiter's domain
41 Emotion of pity
42 Long-necked waders
43 Housekeeper, sometimes
44 ___-Honey (candy bar)
45 Take for ___
46 Fortune
47 Cork shooter
52 "Alice's Restaurant" name
53 "Why don't we?"
54 Nothing more than
56 Betray, with "on"
57 Object of E.P.A. monitoring
58 See 10-Across
59 Blue

868 by Gerald R. Ferguson

ACROSS
1 "Cheers!"
10 1995 Horse of the Year
15 Chesterfields
16 Julio's opposite
17 Opera cast members
18 Important boards, for short
19 Molecules that bind to receptors
20 If-looks-could-kill looks
21 Certain neckline
22 Humorist Lebowitz
23 Encrusted
26 Captain's log heading
30 Shows
31 Blisters, of a kind
32 Handicap
33 Force units
34 Still-life subjects
35 Foundry device
37 Kind of fair
38 Capable of being felt
39 ___ profundo
40 Chamber workers: Abbr.
41 Headlight setting
42 Lifter's asset
45 Singsong sounds
49 Press into service
50 Ships' sinkers?
52 Glorify
53 They get taken to dinner
54 Word with hard or hook
55 Duesenberg A's, e.g.

DOWN
1 Weave's partner
2 Geometry's ___ of Cassini
3 Actress Copley
4 Math class, informally
5 Parts of sonnets
6 Engaged in reverie
7 Horse racing Hall-of-Famer Earl
8 Western Athletic Conference team
9 They're not part of the body: Abbr.
10 Tornado refuge sites
11 Ropes, so to speak
12 Reverse, e.g.
13 Museo offering
14 "E.R." doctor
20 Homecoming V.I.P.'s
22 Town by Palisades State Pk.
23 Fighting force
24 Scientific discovery of 1894
25 Tallies
26 Airs
27 Rich tapestry
28 Fifty minutes past the hour
29 "___ quam videri" (North Carolina's motto)
30 Penitentiary count
31 Inventor McCormick
33 Blackmore heroine
36 Nourished: Var.
37 Young salmon
39 Not square
41 Words before hint or line
42 Ill-tempered
43 Ruin
44 B'way hits
45 "___ the mornin'!"
46 Settled
47 Low-cal
48 Impressionist
50 Ancient Roman spirit
51 Natl. registry org.

869 by Thomas W. Schier

ACROSS

1 Org. that safeguards pets
5 Prefix with port
9 Liability's opposite
14 Songwriter Gus
15 Plow animals
16 Marvy
17 "Yikes!"
18 Actress Hayworth
19 Mississippi ___
20 Lead singer with Dawn
23 Opposite of 42-Across
24 Alphabet trio
25 Reduced fare
26 ___ la Douce
28 What "hemi-" means
30 Odd
33 Popular record label
36 Cosmetician Elizabeth
37 Treaty
40 Seabees' motto
42 B or better
43 Impassive
45 Horses' home
47 Morning or afternoon travel
49 Vlad the Impaler, e.g.
53 Stallion's mate
54 Water, in Cadiz
56 "Do Ya" rock grp.
57 Kind of testing, in law enforcement
59 Los Angeles suburb
62 Sonata section
64 Mrs. Chaplin
65 Jazz performance
66 Dual conjunction
67 Men's business wear
68 Buster Brown's dog
69 Pirate's prize
70 Nobelist Wiesel
71 TV's "___ Three Lives"

DOWN

1 Artist's rendering
2 Chinese temple
3 Estee Lauder rival
4 Rooney of "60 Minutes"
5 Frightful
6 Banish
7 Free to attack
8 ___ instant (quickly)
9 Neighbor of Spain
10 Go out with
11 60's–70's A's third baseman
12 Ending with Henri
13 Wart-covered creature
21 Stench
22 Morse code click
27 Baseball owner Schott et al.
29 Bluebeard's last wife
30 Actress Thompson
31 Storm or Tracker, in the auto world
32 Finis
34 Postpaid encl.
35 It's a blast
37 Utilities watchdog grp.
38 From ___ Z
39 "Dirty Dozen" marauder
41 Inflexible
44 Superficial, as a look
46 Emulate Pisa's tower
48 Tetley product
50 Cosmetics applicator
51 Senior years
52 Blew a horn
54 Run ___ of (violate)
55 Bottled spirits
57 Cheerless
58 Banned act
60 Bloodhound's sensor
61 ___ spumante
63 Complete an "i"

870 by Gene Newman

ACROSS

1 Musicians' copyright grp.
6 King with a golden touch
11 Business fraud monitoring agcy.
14 TV exec Arledge
15 "Be ___..."
16 Spanish gold
17 Grant vs. Bragg, Nov. 1863
19 Tease
20 Sandwich choice
21 Parkers feed it downtown
23 ___-do-well
24 Black Sea port
25 Wakeful watches
28 Bush aide John
30 Neighborhood
31 Idiot
32 Chinese food additive
35 On, as a lamp
36 For fun
38 Place for a hole in a sock
39 Winter clock setting in Vt.
40 Union branch
41 Coal stratum
42 "Old ___" (1957 Disney film)
44 Lines of cliffs
46 Slugged
48 Salon job
49 Perth ___, N.J.
50 Unlike Mr. Spock of "Star Trek"
55 Brock or Costello
56 Rosecrans vs. Bragg, Sept. 1863
58 Continent north of Afr.
59 Eagle's nest
60 Listlessness
61 It follows a dot in many on-line addresses
62 Not our
63 Syria's Hafez al-___

DOWN

1 It may have fallen on a foot
2 Manhattan locale
3 Jacket
4 Cather novel "My ___"
5 Small sea bird
6 Millionaire's home
7 Elvis Presley, in the 50's and 60's
8 "I ___ it!" (cry of success)
9 H.S. math
10 Patrick Ewing specialty
11 Anderson vs. Beauregard, Apr. 1861
12 Attempts
13 Striking snake
18 Good blackjack holdings
22 Poet's dusk
24 ___ about (lawyer's phrase)
25 Caesar's farewell
26 Spring bloom
27 Meade vs. Lee, July 1863
28 Kind of energy or flare
29 ___ Mountains (edge of Asia)
31 Riot queller
33 Ivory, e.g.
34 Onyxes and opals
36 Night prowler
37 Auctioneer's last word
41 Pago Pago residents
43 D.D.E.'s command
44 ___ poor example
45 Sevastopol locale
46 Ancient: Prefix
47 Love affair
48 Fireplace rod
50 Dublin's land
51 1102, in dates
52 Women in habits
53 Tijuana water
54 Deposited
57 Sneaky laugh sound

871 by Robert Zimmerman

ACROSS
1 Bid
6 Mesa dweller
10 Nod off
14 Site of Cnossus
15 Big name in cosmetics
16 German biographer ___ Ludwig
17 "___ looking at you, kid"
18 Lady's man
19 Movers
20 Quirky
21 Impressive achievement
24 Sorbonne, e.g.
26 Tire channel
27 Peer, to his servant
29 Plant with a medicinal root
33 More than peeved
34 Charles's domain
35 Hemispheric assn.
37 Ready to come off the stove
38 Examined, as before a robbery
39 Skip
40 Business mag

41 Lawn
42 "The Taming of the Shrew" setting
43 Spy's byword
45 Police datum
46 Assistance
47 Like toast
48 Final stroke
53 Fate
56 The "A" in A.D.
57 Film ___
58 Pan-fry
60 Harness part
61 Gusto
62 Greek satirist
63 These may be fine
64 On the main
65 Driving hazard

DOWN
1 Cuatro y cuatro
2 N.F.L. receiver Biletnikoff
3 Tropical viper
4 Bastille Day season
5 Give back
6 World Court site, with "The"
7 Finished
8 Thoreau subject

9 Confined, as in wartime
10 Give, as time
11 Gen. Bradley
12 Over-the-counter cold remedy
13 Otherwise
22 Aged
23 Ado
25 ___ d'Azur (French Riviera)
27 Certain skirt
28 Actor Jeremy
29 Long-winded
30 Nouvelle Caledonie and others
31 Pseudonym
32 Julius Caesar's first name
34 W.W. II enlistee
36 Immediately, in the E.R.
38 Sideboard
39 Sculls
41 Part of a crossword
42 Clergymen
44 Poultry offerings
45 Compass tracing
47 Magna ___
48 Dear, as a signorina

49 Unique person
50 Military group
51 "Anything ___" (1934 or 1987 musical)
52 Levitate

54 Siouan tribe
55 Camp shelter
59 Be sick

872 by Stanley B. Whitten

ACROSS
1 Needy
5 Cautious advice
9 Rope fiber
14 Michigan town or its college
15 "___ be in England": Browning
16 Going too far
17 Act of faith
18 Ram
19 Like Dennis the Menace
20 Craze
22 Like some raises
24 Farm distance
25 Pie in the sky
28 Bro, e.g.
29 Not having a surrounding colonnade, in architecture
32 Sixth sense
35 Japanese wraps
38 Sierra ___
39 Guy in the sky
43 City on the Po
44 Function as a medical device
45 6 on the dial
46 Everlasting

48 Diamonds, to a gangster
51 Eye in the sky
57 Go for it
59 "Ben-Hur" garb
60 Bank patron
61 The "her" of "I've Grown Accustomed to Her Face"
63 Bo Derek's first major film
65 Inner tubes, geometrically
66 Musical composition
67 "There oughta be ___!"
68 First name in mystery
69 Shoe material
70 A or O, e.g.
71 Used henna

DOWN
1 Majorcan seaport
2 New York city on the Allegheny
3 Muscat native
4 Canoeist's danger
5 Kind of story
6 Hitting sound
7 Glossy brown fur

8 Some Sunday dinners
9 Foreign film feature
10 Sick
11 Pantry, e.g.
12 Cartoonist Peter
13 "This Gun for Hire" star
21 1996 Olympic torch lighter
23 Rascal
26 Inky
27 ". . . not always what they ___"
30 Shortly
31 Carson successor
32 Suffix with satin
33 Out of business
34 Swift falcon
36 Ornery farm animal
37 Put ___ good word for
40 Fantastical artist
41 Explain, in a way
42 Successor
47 Flurry
49 "I Love Lucy" appeared on it
50 Overjoyed
52 Premature
53 Abbr. on a C.D.

54 Banned article of trade
55 Actress Oberon
56 Snooped
57 Ballpoints

58 60's All-Star Felipe
62 From A to ___
64 Wonder

ACROSS

1 Deep-six
6 "I Ain't Marching Anymore" singer
10 Exult (over)
14 Puppeteer Lewis
15 Versifier
16 Hearty companion
17 Golden Horde member
18 It begins "In the first year of Cyrus king of Persia . . ."
19 "O patria mia" singer
20 General description of a 26-, 46- or 53-Across
23 "___! Come back!"(1953 movie line)
25 Diner
26 See 20-Across
30 Come apart
31 Promo pro
32 "Have a good time!"
36 Like good burgundy
38 Trig ratios
40 Gilbert of "Roseanne"
41 Catalogue illustration
43 Carries
45 Sidekick
46 See 20-Across
49 Pitch tents
52 Le Quai des Tuileries adjoins it
53 See 20-Across
57 Dark forces
58 Promise, e.g.
59 Extreme
63 It may be due on a duplex
64 Part of CPU
65 Some athletic shoes
66 It precedes quatro, in Rio
67 Raspberry ___
68 Certain retirement plan

DOWN

1 747 alternative
2 Part of a repeated dance movement
3 Deserter
4 1994 Peace Nobelist
5 It might bite the hand that feeds it
6 Trade grp. since 9/14/60
7 Homey
8 What a drover drives
9 Rude one
10 Jumps on
11 More chips for the pot
12 Born earlier (than)
13 Pooped
21 Base negotiating amounts
22 Slip (into)
23 Irish county
24 Crossed one's fingers
26 Stuff
27 Farrier, e.g.
28 Tonkin delta city
29 "You're ___ talk!"
33 40's foe
34 Spiel
35 Brown alternative
37 Bankers' woes
39 "Get"
42 Naive one
44 Explore caves
47 Little one
48 Actress Langtry
49 First president of the German republic, 1919
50 "When pigs fly!"
51 Queeg's minesweeper
54 Skeletal unit
55 Former Israeli P.M.
56 Street in New York's Chinatown
60 W.B.A. decision
61 Coffee order: Abbr.
62 Mountain ___

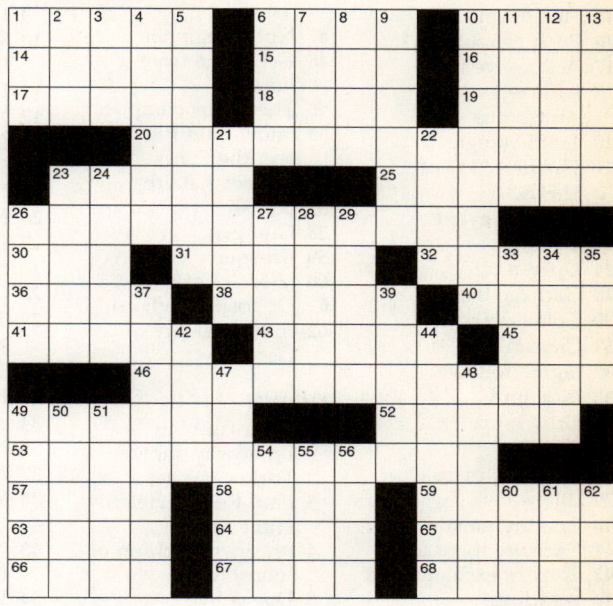

ACROSS

1 A flat's equivalent
7 Fortune-teller
13 Glacial matter
15 Violent struggles
16 Metalsmith's tool
18 Jazz lover's tag
19 Wrath
20 Herbal drink
22 Big heart?
23 Hawaiian goose
25 Enjoy
26 Distress signal
27 Perceive
29 Energetic, strong-willed type, supposedly
30 Introduction
31 Investigators sometimes follow them
34 Spawning ground of Atlantic eels
35 Challenges
36 Rental craft
37 Heavy-duty cleanser
38 Liszt piece
42 Elevation
43 Spanish playwright Calderon
45 Western Samoa's capital
46 Fiat model
47 Dreams of Daniel, e.g.
49 Third word in a limerick
50 Change the subject, perhaps
52 Kind of ears
54 Start of many Latin American place names
55 Glacier Garden city
56 Mason assistant
57 Cater basely

DOWN

1 Taunting
2 Bogeyman
3 Seat of Lewis and Clark County
4 Its first pres. was Samuel Gompers
5 Some corporal punishment
6 Court motions
7 Additional
8 Moon of Saturn
9 "Human Concretion" artist
10 Classic producer
11 Percolates, as water
12 Treasure
14 Leading court figures
17 Persevere
21 Snack item named after the inventor's 6-year-old daughter
24 Language of 350 million
26 Brief solo
28 Make sentence sense
30 Like yesterday's news
32 Golfing initials
33 California Rep. Dellums
34 Heliolater
35 Stadium disappointment
36 Hardly geniuses
39 Northbound, on most maps
40 One of the Lennon Sisters
41 A time to dye?
43 Wine grape
44 Early Ping-Pong score
47 Blackball, e.g.
48 Stray home
51 Before
53 Farm mother

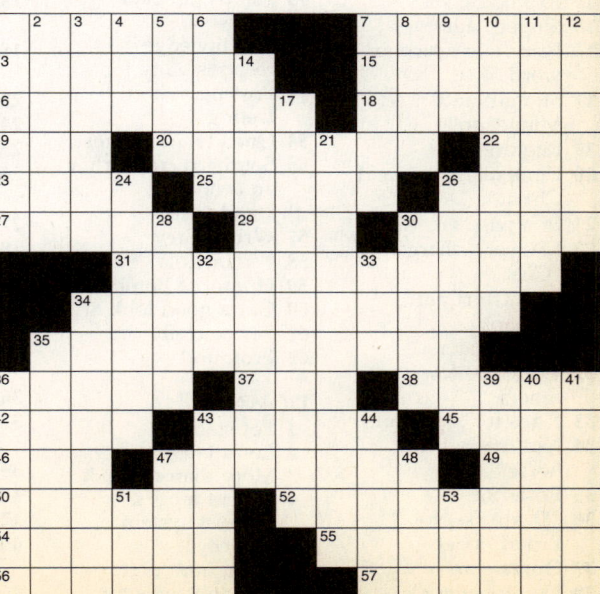

875 by Shannon Burns

ACROSS
1 Deep sleeps
6 Abbr. before an alias
9 Fragrant oil
14 ___-garde
15 Steal from
16 Push roughly
17 A Roosevelt
18 Afflicted with strabismus
20 Traffic tangle
21 The first "H" of H.H.S.
22 Quilting event
23 Cautious
24 Open a bit
28 Garbage barge
30 Come down
31 Clinton's #2
32 Sigma follower
33 Blue birds
34 Grown-ups
36 Snares
38 Shooting marble
39 Bill settlers
40 Coating metal
41 "Are we there ___?"
42 They're exchanged at weddings
43 Building block company
44 Goofs up
45 Of ships: Abbr.
46 Second-year student, for short
47 Not a beginner
48 Get down from a horse
50 Thesaurus compiler
53 Show with Richie and the Fonz
56 Dancer Astaire
57 Banish
58 Gun grp.
59 Brusque
60 "For ___ sake!"
61 Opposite NNE
62 Industrial city of Germany

DOWN
1 Long-running Broadway show
2 Turkey roaster
3 Paul Reiser/Helen Hunt series
4 President Jackson or Johnson
5 Do, as hair
6 Architectural frames
7 Ones with Seoul custody?
8 "All ___!" (conductor's cry)
9 Helper: Abbr.
10 Where Dutch royals live
11 Plaything
12 "___ Maria"
13 Like Time's border
19 Crafty
25 Pirate flags
26 More pretentious
27 Bowling alley buttons
28 Enter
29 The Great White North
30 Swimmer's regimen
33 Place for pickles
34 ___ time (never)
35 Nov. follower
37 Fasten papers again
38 Visited tourist places
40 Gentle breezes
43 "___ Run" (1976 sci-fi film)
44 Wears away
46 Rock singer Vicious
47 Chatter
49 Caustic solutions
51 Otherwise
52 Adolescent
53 Wise, man
54 Chop
55 Orchestra's location

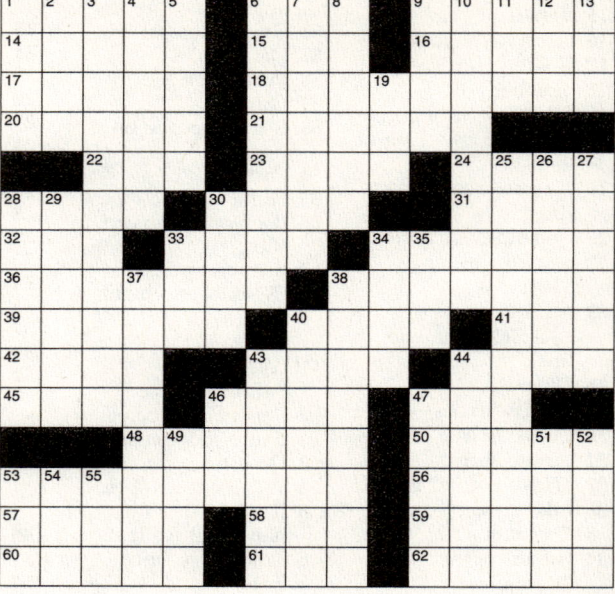

876 by Peter Gordon

ACROSS
1 Throat-clearing sound
5 Fencing weapon
10 Actress Rowlands
14 Exploding star
15 Singer Page
16 Fairy tale's second word
17 St. Paul and Minneapolis
19 Require
20 Comedians Bob and Chris
21 In a wise manner
23 Lawyer's charge
24 "Gee!"
25 Sweatshirt part, perhaps
27 Flush beater
32 Writer Bellow and others
33 Place for a pimento
34 Not the swiftest horse
35 Posterior
36 "Death Be Not Proud" poet
37 Opera star
38 Dog breeder's org.
39 Imply
40 Doled (out)
41 Leaders of hives
43 Like some tea
44 Praise
45 Santa ___, Calif.
46 Refuse to acknowledge responsibility for
49 Post-marathon feeling
54 Quickly, in memos
55 Southern crop, from an economic standpoint
57 Writer Grey
58 Writer Zola
59 Humorist Bombeck
60 Got a good look at
61 Saw socially
62 Profound

DOWN
1 Pot starter
2 Loud laugh
3 More than devilish
4 Part of a car's exhaust system
5 Malice
6 Light bulb unit
7 Elevator inventor
8 Road map abbr.
9 Liquefy
10 Very enthusiastic
11 Fencing weapon
12 Christmas song
13 Raggedy Ann's friend
18 Some college students
22 Tennis great Arthur
24 Quick flashes of light
25 17-syllable poem
26 Precious metal unit of weight
27 Paid, as a bill
28 Arm bones
29 Come together
30 Backed up on disk
31 "Holy cow!"
32 The N.B.A.'s O'Neal, familiarly
36 Exposed as false
37 Poured wine into another container
39 Chew
40 Actor Sal
42 Ran for one's wife?
45 Moved like a shooting star
46 Stun
47 British exclamation
48 Having all one's marbles
49 Tizzy
50 Leer at
51 To be, in Bordeaux
52 Not all
53 Jacket fastener
56 The Monkees' "___ Believer"

877   by Fred Piscop

ACROSS
1 The Hatfields or the McCoys
5 Trip to Mecca
9 Quench
14 Any one of three English rivers
15 "Summertime," e.g., in "Porgy and Bess"
16 Jazzman's cue
17 Woolen wear
20 Bizarre
21 Small ball
22 Makes certain
25 Long, long time
26 Toyota model
28 Govt. agent
32 Fortify, as a town
37 Brit's reply in agreement
38 Spot in a supermarket
41 Cowboys' entertainment
42 Said again
43 Not new
44 Scold
46 Court
47 Riddles
53 Names
58 A lot of Shakespeare's writing
59 Ambassador's stand-in
62 You can dig it
63 Island near Kauai
64 Touches lightly, as with a hanky
65 Soccer shoe
66 Ending with cable or candy
67 Command to Fido

DOWN
1 Drink served with marshmallows
2 Hawaiian feasts
3 Aides-de-camp: Abbr.
4 India's first P.M.
5 "Scots Wha ___" (Burns poem)
6 Sheet music abbr.
7 Goes kaput
8 Quartz variety
9 Oft-televised bishop
10 Polygraph flunker
11 Westernmost Aleutian
12 Canal to the Baltic
13 Raison d'___

18 Debussy's "La ___"
19 Rider's "Stop!"
23 "What's this, Pedro?"
24 "Star Trek" helmsman
27 Kind of lab dish
28 Melt ingredient
29 Catcher's catcher
30 Suit to ___
31 Taped eyeglasses wearer
32 Very light brown
33 Conductance units
34 "Venerable" English writer
35 Passed with flying colors
36 Bout outcome, in brief
37 "___ Sera, Sera"
39 Give up
40 Begin bidding
44 Baskin-Robbins purchase
45 Show off on the slopes
46 Isle of ___
48 Sweet-as-apple-cider girl
49 Diagrams
50 French Revolution figure Jean Paul

51 Microscopic creature
52 Giving a little lip
53 Electrical letters
54 Sen. Gramm
55 Noggin
56 Killer whale
57 Coal-rich European region
60 Home-financing org.
61 "Fe fi fo ___!"

878   by Richard Hughes

ACROSS
1 Sports Illustrated's 1974 Sportsman of the Year
4 Steep
9 English poet laureate Nahum ___
13 TV host who does "Headlines"
15 Vietnam's capital
16 Roman Eros
17 Like an inveterate procrastinator
18 Put together
19 Negri of the silent screen
20 Start of a Jonathan Swift quote
23 Col.'s boss
24 Sheriff Taylor's son, in 60's TV
25 Tit for tat?
26 "The Kiss" sculptor
28 Half of CXII
30 ___ Angeles
31 Political losers
32 Select
36 Part 2 of the quote
40 Mother-of-pearl source
41 In a bit
43 Mrs. Nixon
46 J.F.K. regular
47 Played out
48 Lyric poem
50 Largest of seven
53 Bird call
54 End of the quote
58 Surveyor's map
59 Do-___
60 ___-dieu
61 Konrad Adenauer, Der ___
62 Orchestra section
63 Architectural pier
64 "Gentlemen Prefer Blondes" author
65 "Haystacks" painter
66 Word part: Abbr.

DOWN
1 Lively bit of music
2 Omit
3 Plan on it
4 Early rocket traveler
5 Veranda
6 Mindless
7 Drop out, in poker
8 Put away, in a way

9 Tropical animal
10 Without scruples
11 Mid-American Conference team
12 Rubs out
14 Poet's contraction
21 Partner for hither
22 Iodine reaction
27 Mallorca, e.g.
28 Symbol of craziness
29 Hollywood cross street
32 Rock video prizes
33 Hide
34 Arafat's org.
35 Skier's aid
37 "Little Eyolf" playwright
38 Beasts on the royal arms of Scotland
39 Wholeness
42 F.D.R. accomplishment
43 One involved in foreign exchange?
44 Lover of Daphne
45 Campbell's choice
47 Bill
49 Times to remember?

50 "The Age of Anxiety" poet
51 Playground fixture
52 Phrase of explanation
55 Contemptible person
56 Chocolate snack
57 Govt. watchdog group

879 by Brendan Emmett Quigley

ACROSS
1 Behind
4 Group overseeing Fed. property
7 Playboy Hugh, familiarly
10 Rooked
13 Working together, with "in"
15 One reason to do something crazy
17 Sharp
18 Plain
19 Ask peremptorily
20 Night temps, usually
22 Nintendo's The Legend of __
23 "Are you game?"
25 Partner of Warner
26 Masters
28 "Dianetics" author __ Hubbard
30 Math finale
33 Hotelier Helmsley
34 Prior to, old-style
35 Altdorf is its capital
36 Some relics
37 1995 Robin Williams movie
38 Lightly cooked
39 Germanic negative

40 Bluegrass player
41 "L.A. Law" lawyer
42 "The Tonight Show" nickname
43 Former U.S. poet laureate __ Dove
44 European shipping units
45 First name in stunts
47 Shoddy
49 It shows the way
51 Similar
52 Katharine's role in "Adam's Rib"
55 Wild
57 Intelligent
59 Trapped
60 Poseidon's prop
61 Atlas abbr.
62 Passing need?
63 Start to collapse
64 Popular music variety

DOWN
1 Boarding sch.
2 Come to grips with
3 Classic 1956 spy film
4 Chunk
5 Artificial legs

6 It may be secured with a pin
7 Monopolizes
8 Compass reading
9 Amateur newsletter
10 Popular light reading
11 Parched
12 Numerical prefix
14 Predestines
16 Consider
21 Big name in radio, once
24 Spring playoffs org.
25 Geometrical solids
26 Hardly strutted
27 Eagle's home
29 Color of a Baja sunset
31 "Sesame Street" regular
32 Big blockers
34 West End classic "Charley's __"
37 Clink
38 Like magazine subscriptions
40 Buds are produced in this
41 "Now __ theater near you!"
44 Lady abroad
46 It's shocking!

48 Handles
49 Reuniongoer
50 Awestruck
51 Toward water
53 Cellarlike

54 Canadian prov.
56 Figure out
58 Musician's booking

880 by Manny Nosowsky

ACROSS
1 Word after a loss
5 It goes with being snowbound
15 Cost of occupation
16 "Forest primeval" figure
17 Marriage site in John 2:1
18 Nickname of Emperor Frederick I
19 Short summary
21 "Mission: Impossible" actress
22 Jerk
23 Abandon
24 Art follower
25 Make jerky?
26 Unaware
28 Second-century anatomist
29 Time of one's life
30 Abstract sculptor Sir Anthony
31 Table, so to speak
32 Cheapskate
34 Oahu outsiders
37 A hole in the wall?
38 Way to go: Abbr.
41 Park alcove
42 Ticket dispenser

44 Safari camp
45 Highly complimentary
46 Main line
47 Govt. org., 1887–1996
48 "Crucifixion of St. Peter" painter Guido __
49 Electrician's need
50 1961 Paul Newman film
53 Richard of "A Summer Place"
54 Maiden lover "in a kingdom by the sea"
55 Art philanthropist Sir Henry
56 Petite
57 River crossing France's Nord department

DOWN
1 Santa Anita race track site
2 Like some lizards
3 One of TV's Mouseketeers
4 Calorie category
5 Philippine island or its seaport

6 Actress Gardner
7 Opera with the aria "Largo al factotum," with "The"
8 Behind, with "of"
9 Marsh of mystery
10 Fossil impression
11 "Evil Woman" rock grp.
12 Warsaw's river
13 Guarantees
14 Chemistry lab selection
20 King, maybe
24 "Rats!"
25 Lt.-Maj. go-between
27 Roast site
28 Blanket
31 Loaded (with)
32 Wild plum
33 Better than never?
34 Home for ecologists
35 Weaver of myth
36 Bluer than blue
38 Krypton, e.g.
39 Perform a chemical test
40 "Roots" Emmy winner, 1977
42 Symbol of authority
43 Half
45 Adjust the tailoring

48 Lip shade
49 Hares, to hounds
51 Liu Pang's dynasty
52 Velvet finish

881 — by Gregory E. Paul

ACROSS
1 "Othello" villain
5 Flat-topped hills
10 Colonel Mustard's game
14 Eschew
15 Some of the Pennsylvania Dutch
16 Feed bag contents
17 Filly's mother
18 "Truly!"
19 Takes advantage of
20 Jalopy
23 Poker starter
24 "Roses ___ red . . ."
25 Like a lot
28 Fawn's mother
31 Necklace units
35 Come about
37 Department of Justice div.
39 Tiny
40 Autumn 1940 aerial war
44 Prior to, poetically
45 Mao ___-tung
46 Tenor Caruso
47 Council of Trent, e.g.
50 Flower holder
52 Spud
53 Lawyer's thing
55 Texas Western, today: Abbr.
57 Mule, e.g.
63 Kind of purse
64 Sidestep
65 Norse Zeus
67 Five-time Wimbledon champ, 1976–80
68 Vintner Ernest or Julio
69 Girl-watch or boy-watch
70 ___-Ball (arcade game)
71 Church officer
72 Marsh plant

DOWN
1 Doctrine: Suffix
2 Captain obsessed
3 Maven
4 Like some diamonds, sizewise
5 "Luncheon on the Grass" painter Edouard
6 Chewed the scenery
7 Fodder storage site
8 "___ I cared!"
9 Yemen, once
10 Grand ___ Dam
11 Word before laugh or straw
12 Salt Lake City students
13 Feminine suffix
21 Toll
22 Regalia item
25 French clerics
26 Hon
27 Time after time
29 Bid
30 Retrocede
32 Lie in store for
33 Winter windshield setting
34 Sir, in Seville
36 What may be followed by improved service?
38 Dander
41 Buckeyes' sch.
42 The "I" in ICBM
43 Cause of an unexpected fall
48 Jellybean flavor
49 ___ Plaines, Ill.
51 Marriageable
54 Old Wells Fargo transport
56 Elizabeth I was the last one
57 Library unit
58 Dublin's land
59 Elliptical
60 Quit, in poker
61 Winning margin
62 Longest river in the world
63 "60 Minutes" network
66 TV's "___ and Stacey"

882 — by Stephanie Spadaccini

ACROSS
1 "Woe is me!"
5 A wanted man, maybe
9 Miss in the comics
14 ___ Le Pew
15 Oldsmobile, e.g.
16 Sound during hay fever season
17 47-stringed instrument
18 Flair
19 "Jurassic Park" sound
20 Parental advice, part 1
23 ___ Moines
24 "O Sole ___"
25 Antislavery leader Turner
26 Call to Bo-peep
27 Once more, country-style
29 Name
32 See-through wrap
35 Scandinavian capital
36 "The Official Preppy Handbook" author Birnbach
37 Advice, part 2
40 ___ Major
41 Economist Smith
42 Listens to
43 "See ya!"
44 Utopia
45 Served with a meal
46 Choice of sizes: Abbr.
47 Not their
48 Twaddle
51 End of the advice
57 "Silas Marner" author
58 Derby distance, maybe
59 Small field
60 Training group
61 "Zip-___-Doo-Dah"
62 Wedding wear
63 Injured sneakily
64 Back talk
65 Mesozoic and others

DOWN
1 Garden pest
2 What all partygoers eventually take
3 After, in Avignon
4 Fall mo.
5 Flier Earhart
6 "Where's ___?"
7 "Sure, why not?"
8 Letterman rival
9 Hit game of 1980
10 Showy display
11 Call to a mate
12 Search, as a beach
13 Long (for)
21 Mideasterner
22 Merger
26 Where Bear Bryant coached, informally
27 Oriental
28 Grab (onto)
29 ___-a-minute (call rate)
30 Previously owned
31 Chorale part
32 The short end
33 Wrong
34 Floral gift
35 Ye ___ Tea Shoppe
36 Told a whopper
38 Soup scoop
39 "Ta-da!"
44 Hammed it up
45 90's group with the hit "Killing Me Softly," with "the"
46 Boutique
47 Looks at boldly
48 Track car
49 Open-air rooms
50 Skins
51 Isthmus
52 Pearl Buck heroine
53 Coastal flooding factor
54 Holiday season, for short
55 Verdi heroine
56 90's party

883 by Chuck Deodene

ACROSS
1 Monarch until 1979
5 Market amount
9 Texas A & M student
14 Attraction
15 "Button it!"
16 Hush money
17 Omnia vincit ___
18 1992 Edward James Olmos film
20 Travelers' needs
22 Not like a milquetoast
23 #1 hit for Helen Reddy
26 Actor Holbrook and others
30 Red-helmeted rock group
31 Precisely
33 Spheroid
36 Residents of Castel Gandolfo
39 Accommodate
40 Namibia, formerly
43 Paris plaza
44 Does go with them
45 Hipster
46 Making inquiries
48 Tony-winning actress Beryl
50 Parts of itineraries: Abbr.

51 Popular charity
56 Precept
58 ___ spout (water runoff site)
60 Quadrennial athletic event
65 Brooklet
66 Stradivari's teacher
67 Hardly racy
68 White House Scottie
69 Whence the Brahmaputra flows
70 Overpromotion
71 All-too-frequent Buffalo forecast

DOWN
1 Bulgar, e.g.
2 Like greenhouse air
3 Cropped up
4 Miami daily
5 1860's initials
6 Its symbol is an omega
7 Queen's land, once
8 Quarter's worth at a carnival, maybe
9 Fundamentals
10 Grecian Formula target
11 Mixologist's staple
12 PC maker

13 Specification at Thom McAn
19 George Harrison's "___ It a Pity"
21 "Portrait of the Artist" youth
24 Acknowledge
25 Numbskulls
27 Creepy household area
28 Nikon rival
29 French legislature
32 Ref's call
33 Grouchy Muppet
34 Hearty meal
35 Cleveland's ___ Lakefront Airport
37 Pa. hours
38 Sudden fright
41 Around a geographical meeting point
42 "Let Us Now Praise Famous Men" writer
47 Ho lead-in
49 Towers over
52 Below, in poesy
53 "Be that as ___ . . ."
54 Birdy
55 Mello ___ (Coca-Cola brand)
57 Discharge

59 It usually comes on the side
60 To the point
61 "___ Blue?"
62 Pick up
63 Nero, e.g.: Abbr.
64 "Didn't I tell you?"

884 by Matt Gaffney

ACROSS
1 Items often passed
6 41st in a series
10 Release
14 Ruin a bow
15 Conductor Klemperer
16 Dessert ___
17 Big name in zoos
18 M.V.P. of Super Bowls I and II
20 Controversial baseball owner
22 Place to unwind
23 Time of one's life
24 Possessive Latin pronoun
25 The buck stops here
26 Singer Zadora
27 Swallow flat
29 "Am ___ only one . . . ?"
31 Many an Olympic skiing gold medalist
32 Photo ___
34 Beats
37 Theme of this puzzle
39 Erstwhile warship
40 Part to grab hold of
41 Senator's claim
42 ___-a-porter (ready-to-wear)

44 1972 U.S. Open finalist
48 Football Hall-of-Famer Hendricks
49 Australian runner
51 The Fighting Tigers, for short
53 Life
54 Broke bread
55 Best Actress of 1969
58 Malcolm-Jamal Warner co-star
60 ___ Banks, N.C.
61 Afghan leader before the Soviet invasion
62 Russo of "Outbreak"
63 Sporty Pontiac
64 Chap
65 July 15, e.g.
66 Bad lighting?

DOWN
1 Underground Railroad leader
2 Tick off
3 Reserves
4 Bell sound
5 Sides in a classic battle
6 Rancher's threat
7 Canyonlands locale

8 Approached boldly, with "to"
9 Too ___ handle
10 Ambulance asst.
11 Empanadas
12 Devastated
13 Muslim wear
19 Part of many town names in Quebec
21 Geneve's country
28 In French it's frapper
30 Semilegendary Greek poet
31 Big name in workouts
33 A shot
35 Word from Tswana
36 Head of a syndicate
37 Gets rid of, as an old car
38 Questioned
39 When you can start to drive
41 Hogan's domain
43 Aristocracies
45 Treats maliciously
46 Straight
47 "Sleepless in Seattle" writer-director
49 Massachusetts Ave. bldg., in D.C.

50 Language of New Zealand
52 The States
56 Subject of passing concern?

57 Pioneering conservationist
59 Colony member

885 by Bob Klahn

ACROSS

1 Turpentine source
10 Splotches
15 Kept the lid on
16 Fashionably nostalgic
17 Popular comedienne
18 "Sweet" stream, to Burns
19 A White House scandal
21 Shepherd
22 Steno's need
23 It's a draw for astronauts
25 Pioneer bathyspherist
29 Natural
32 Psychiatrist who coined the term "inferiority complex"
33 Water tester
34 "Mail Order Bride" co-star, 1964
38 Hezbollah stronghold ___ Valley
39 Uncertainties
40 Mrs. Yeltsin
41 Quite a nose
42 Grass variety
43 A hundred smackers
44 Tees and ells
46 "Siddhartha" writer
47 Art and history, e.g.
50 Keebler character
52 Teen ___
53 Upbraided in no uncertain terms
60 Rudimentary thermos inventor
62 Renowned exile
63 Jane Curtin role
64 Small carriage
65 Final word
66 Hoax

DOWN

1 Go "shooby-doo" or just "shoo"
2 Unparalleled
3 "Finnegans Wake" wife
4 Put one's foot down
5 One playing on a band?
6 Michelangelo masterwork
7 Then
8 Octavia's husband
9 Cheesy town
10 Hidden means of support?
11 Unable to go home
12 Relative of a ferret
13 It may be broken on a ranch
14 High-altitude probe
20 Maniacal leader
24 Chips, to Mr. Chips
25 Another name for Barb
26 Fall setting
27 Pony express stop
28 Dry wine
30 Like some yogurt
31 It's #1
35 Tests the water?
36 Man's name meaning "mortal"
37 ___ the Great (juvenile detective)
45 Language suffix
47 Touchy fellow?
48 "A Passage to India" woman
49 Like a bloodhound
51 Letter paper?
54 Baseball's Blue Moon
55 She played "Diane," 1956
56 Oomph
57 Take out
58 City on the Skunk
59 Causing a pucker
61 Hudson contemporary

886 by Mark Elliot Skolsky

ACROSS

1 Tarzan's love
5 Bungle
10 Tickled
14 Johnny Cash's "___ Named Sue"
15 Before the due date
16 Singer McEntire
17 Formative Picasso phase
19 Terrible czar
20 It picks up readings
21 Hustler's tool, maybe
23 Religious council
25 Actor Davis
26 Assail
30 Football Hall-of-Famer Merlin
32 Newspaper publisher Adolph
33 Year, south of the border
34 Wouldn't proceed
39 Center of a 1994 chase
42 Apollo 13 commander
43 Holds
44 Tennis champ Bjorn
45 Cleaner/disinfectant brand
47 Connection
48 Octagon or oval
52 One of "The Honeymooners"
54 "Carnival of Venice" violinist
56 Tough
61 Jai ___
62 Sophie Tucker was the "last"
64 Opposite of ja
65 Writer Asimov
66 General's command
67 "Auld Lang ___"
68 Tailor
69 Bean counters, for short

DOWN

1 Quick punches
2 Up to the task
3 Verb preceder
4 Potato parts
5 Drunken
6 Paddle
7 July 14, in France
8 Sun blockers
9 F.D.R.'s ___ Park
10 Southern breakfast dish
11 Popular pants since 1850
12 Old-style calculators
13 "Thanks, Gerhard"
18 Hitching ___
22 Sub's "ears"
24 Taboo
26 New Year's Day game
27 22-Down reply
28 Hood's knife
29 Villa d'___
31 Trails off
33 Be ___ in the ointment
35 Earring locale
36 Fort ___ (gold depository site)
37 Stocking shade
38 Labradors and Yorkshires
40 Comedienne DeGeneres
41 Flamboyant Surrealist
46 Most mentally sound
47 Not masc. or fem.
48 Crosses over
49 Alex who wrote "Roots"
50 One more time
51 "Common Sense" pamphleteer
53 "Time in a Bottle" singer Jim
55 Pupil locale
57 Detroit financing co.
58 "The World According to ___"
59 Austen heroine
60 From nine to five, in the classifieds
63 Kubrick's "2001" mainframe

887 by Frank Longo

ACROSS
1 Top piece of a two-piece
4 Italian seaport
11 Timber wood
14 "Alley ___"
15 Zoom-in shot
16 Chinese principle
17 Sex determinant
19 ___ rampage
20 Ready to go
21 Taste test label
23 200 milligrams, to a jeweler
25 Funnyman Philips
28 Not have ___ in the world
29 Spinks defeater, 1978
30 Parallel bar exercises
32 Not nude
33 Complicated situations
37 Debussy contemporary
39 Treasure hunter's declaration
43 Pen
44 Parti-colored
46 Quite the expert
49 Having conflicting allegiances
51 ___ du Diable
52 Kind of fool
54 Wood splitter
55 Quite the expert
57 For adults only
59 Tickle one's fancy
61 Play (with)
62 Twenty-somethings
67 Jargon suffix
68 Earth, wind or fire
69 Squid secretion
70 Texas-Oklahoma boundary river
71 Tennis volleys
72 Gypsy Rose ___

DOWN
1 Word with band or sand
2 Dutton's sitcom role
3 "Art is long, life is short," e.g.
4 Astronaut Carpenter
5 Soprano Gluck
6 Blotto
7 Suffix with lion
8 Rock's ___ Speedwagon
9 Feeling the effects of Novocaine
10 "Don Giovanni," for one
11 Like Schoenberg's music
12 Bullock of "Speed"
13 Took in, in a way
18 Genetic stuff
22 Say "yes" to
23 Auto shaft, slangily
24 "Family Ties" boy
26 Anonymous man
27 Moonfish
31 Fruit/tree connector
34 Deemed appropriate
35 Miscalculate
36 "In Living Color" segment
38 Prefix with propyl
40 Greek portico
41 Salad dressing ingredient
42 Boob tube, in Britain: Var.
45 Hankering
46 Bandleader Les
47 Revolted
48 Not neat at the ends
50 More imminent
53 Pioneer in Cubism
55 Fido and friends
56 "___ recall . . ."
58 Take out
60 "Buddenbrooks" novelist Thomas
63 Surfing site
64 Big bird
65 Opposite SSW
66 Classic Jaguar

888 by Jonathan Schmalzbach

ACROSS
1 Solipsist's preoccupation
5 Harsh Athenian lawgiver
10 Employ a Singer
13 Anjou, e.g.
14 Casaba, e.g.
15 ___-Ball (arcade game)
16 Heroine of Tennessee Williams's "Summer and Smoke"
17 "___ Help Myself" (Four Tops hit)
18 Phoenician port
19 "Shut up!"
22 ___ broche (cooked on a spit)
24 Coach Parseghian
25 Iranian money
26 Lullaby start
31 Bandleader Shaw
32 They're in galley banks
33 Sow
34 "Flow gently, sweet ___": Burns
36 Yemen's capital
40 Game plan
41 Fancy watch
42 "Pipe down, Pierre!"
47 Hurler Reynolds of the 40's–50's Yankees
48 Go (for)
49 Assist
50 Director's directive
55 Amenhotep IV's god
56 Words repeated at the start of the "Sailor's Song"
57 Like ___ in a trap
60 Bookie's bookings
61 ___ around (near)
62 Rani's attire
63 Come-ons
64 Mystery writer Paretsky and others
65 Book after II Chronicles

DOWN
1 Health center
2 Electric ___
3 Berate
4 German wife
5 Composer Shostakovich
6 Supply with more varnish
7 Astronaut Shepard
8 Rabbit
9 Aware of
10 First U.S. space station
11 In a spooky way
12 Boohoos
15 Narrow furrow
20 Myth
21 City areas, informally
22 Triumphant cries
23 Tackle box item
27 Secreted
28 Smash to smithereens
29 Indochinese language
30 Directional suffix
34 Summer refresher
35 Shriner hat
36 Not worth a ___
37 Much-filmed prison
38 Radar's favorite drink on "M*A*S*H"
39 Fired
40 "___ a man . . ."
41 Popular fast-food chain, informally
42 Crimped, as a piecrust
43 T.S. and George
44 Trifles: Fr.
45 Goddess of wisdom
46 Covers with crumbs
47 Mideast's Gulf of ___
51 Revolutionary orator James
52 Soul singer Hendryx
53 Pre-Soviet royalty
54 Let up
58 Timetable abbr.
59 Aunt, in Madrid

889 by Wayne Robert Williams

ACROSS

1 Bryn ___ College
5 Quick drinks
10 Grouch
14 Prefix with -graph
15 It's the Law
16 ___ Bay, Hawaii
17 Back to the start
19 Porch raiders
20 Attacked
21 Breaking out, maybe
23 Group with the 1983 #1 hit "Africa"
25 Sharecrop
26 Sharpen
29 Abbr. in some military names
32 Highways
35 Aerial maneuver
38 Sucker
39 Grounded birds
40 Hebrew leader
41 Spaniard's other
42 Place to winter
43 Some chart analysts
45 Have one's back against the wall?
47 W.W. II arena: Abbr.
48 Indonesian island
49 Like vino tinto
51 Digestive juice
53 Heavy fabrics
57 Whip
61 1988 country album
62 Center of power
64 Military group
65 Take pleasure (in)
66 Muffs
67 Vocal inflection
68 Oodles
69 Keeps company with

DOWN

1 Tick off
2 Musical direction
3 Bucket locale
4 Some desks
5 Work period
6 Vert.'s opp.
7 1977 movie thriller with Bo Derek
8 Ready to be mowed, as grass
9 Storage space
10 Mexican cowboy
11 Circus figure
12 High: Prefix
13 Pear variety
18 Take over, in a way
22 The marshal in "Frontier Marshal"
24 "Otherwise . . ."
26 Popular Christmas gifts
27 "My Cousin Vinny" Oscar winner
28 Tournament type
30 Choice
31 C.E.O., e.g.
33 Asia's Amu ___ River
34 Tic
36 Osaka O.K.
37 "Ah, I see!"
41 Some colorful abstract paintings
43 ___ vu
44 Musical staff sign
46 Sniff out
50 They may be sniffed
52 The Fab Four, e.g.
53 Very dry
54 Vegas rival
55 Daredevil Knievel
56 Computer command
58 Republic since 1948
59 One to grow on?
60 "A Pure Woman" of an 1891 novel
63 Actor Ayres

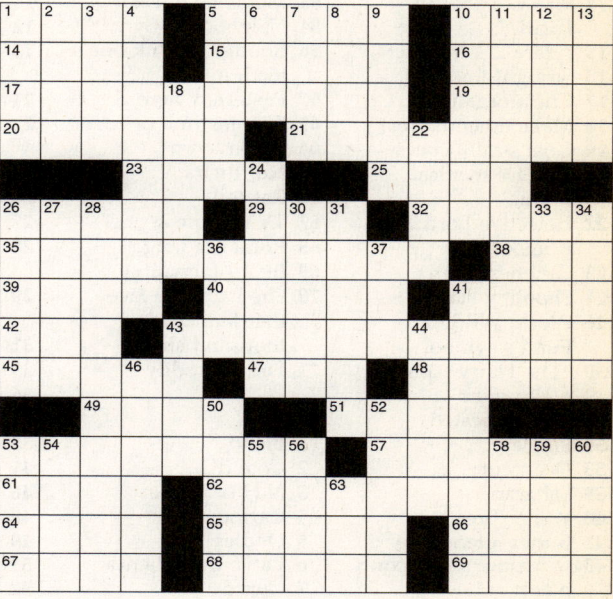

890 by Martin Ashwood-Smith

ACROSS

1 Hot stuff
8 U.S.N.A. rank
11 Ice, so to speak
14 Spark
15 Magazine
17 Visible
18 On the nasty side
19 Big brute
20 Soak
21 Discharged
22 Hogwash
24 Help wanted advertisement?
26 Fabled "Arabian Nights" creature
27 Rocket scientist Wernher ___ Braun
29 School tie?
31 Where the Storting meets
35 Descriptive words of honor
40 It can take your breath away
41 Screamers
42 "___-daisy!"
43 One billion years, in geology
44 H.S. class
45 "___ were you . . ."
47 Gained a lap
50 Taunt
53 Sty
57 Kind of part
59 Some fraternity men
60 Christmas crackler
61 Cliffside dwellers
63 Poker ploy
64 Italy's Gulf of ___
65 Hydrocarbon suffix
66 Grp. in old spy novels
67 90's catch phrase

DOWN

1 Flip side?
2 Cancel
3 Has trouble running
4 Brest friend
5 Brings up the rear
6 Moral element in literature
7 Words
8 Beat severely
9 Robotic: Var.
10 Medical prefix
11 "Get ___!"
12 Physiognomy
13 Skedaddled
16 Secreting securely
23 Chopin pieces
25 Ill humors
28 Local theater, slangily
30 Biological classes
32 Scrooge's attribute
33 ___-majesté
34 "___ of Solomon"
35 Popular cologne
36 Lot
37 Trunk items
38 Kind of chamber
39 Agatha contemporary
46 Big book
48 Looks out for, maybe
49 Part of the crown jewels
51 Isolated hill
52 Elizabeth's love
53 Brontë heroine
54 Beijing coin
55 Old news commentator ___ Abel
56 Things to sit on
58 Appropriate cry for Crusoe?
62 "School Daze" director

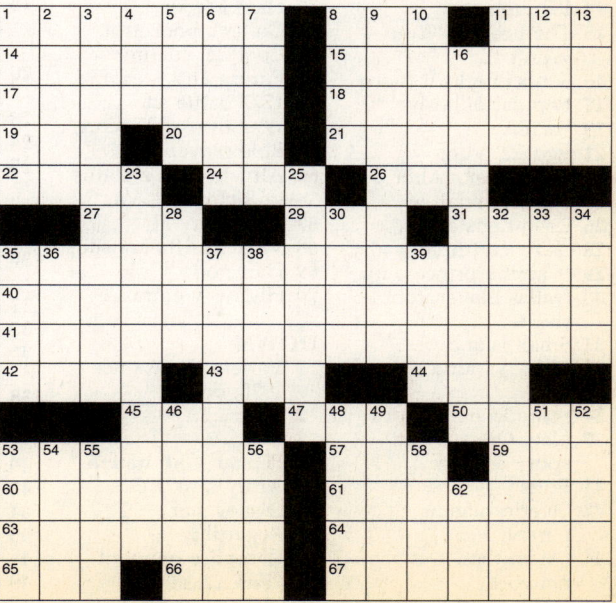

ACROSS

1 "Quite contrary" nursery rhyme girl
5 Sudden outpouring
10 June 6, 1944
14 Pinza of "South Pacific"
15 "Here ___ trouble!"
16 Straight line
17 Chest organ
18 Make amends (for)
19 Goat's-milk cheese
20 60's TV medical drama
22 Detective Lord ___ Wimsey
23 Guinness suffix
24 Shooting stars
26 World Wildlife Fund's symbol
30 "The Hairy Ape" playwright
32 Gets educated
34 Finale
35 Deep cut
39 Saharan
40 Writer Bret
42 Butter alternative
43 ___ contendere (court plea)
44 Kind of "vu" in a classified
45 Colossus of ___
47 Hardy's partner
50 Get used (to)
51 Medicine injector
54 Neighbor of Syr.
56 Enough to sink one's teeth into
57 Pasternak hero
63 "___ just me or . . .?"
64 Indian corn
65 Not theirs
66 Rat (on)
67 TV's "Kate & ___"
68 Romance lang.
69 In ___ (actually)
70 She had "the face that launched a thousand ships"
71 Fuddy-duddy

DOWN

1 Blend
2 Cote d'___
3 N.H.L. venue
4 Cartoon bear
5 Oodles
6 Latke ingredient
7 Cupid
8 Rent-controlled building, maybe
9 WNW's opposite
10 British rock group since the mid-70's
11 Because of
12 Take up, as a hem
13 Sophomore and junior, e.g.
21 Low-fat
22 ___ Club (onetime TV group)
25 Downy duck
26 Scheme
27 Prefix with dynamic
28 It gets hit on the head
29 1967 Rex Harrison film role
31 Moxie
33 Shoulder motion
36 Actor Alan
37 Trickle
38 Party thrower
41 Wiry dog
46 Spy Mata ___
48 Unspecified one
49 Tin ___
51 Wallop
52 O.K.'s
53 Train tracks
55 Luster
58 Streamlet
59 Empty
60 Garage occupant
61 Alum
62 Sonja Henie's birthplace
64 ___-jongg

ACROSS

1 N.B.A.'s O'Neal, familiarly
5 Nicklaus's org.
8 Orbital point
13 Cape Canaveral grp.
14 E.T. vehicles
15 The Beatles' "You Won't ___"
16 Santa checks it twice
17 Popular adhesive
19 Facility
21 Egg ___ yung
22 And others: Abbr.
23 Canasta relative
26 Cash register key
28 ___ trick (three goals)
29 It kept a princess up
30 Dallas player, for short
31 Small island
32 "Oh, ___ kind of guy . . ."
34 Score in horseshoes
37 New Orleans hot spot
41 Edits
42 Overindulgent parent, e.g.
44 "Meet the Press" network
47 Actress Sue ___ Langdon
48 Feather source
50 ___-Magnon
51 Conditioning, as leather
53 Ham holder
55 Golfer's pocketful
56 Cool ___ cucumber
58 Future atty.'s exam
59 1777 battle site
62 Worst possible score
65 Role player
66 Athlete with a statue in Richmond, Va.
67 Hydrox rival
68 Villa ___ (Italian site)
69 Hair goo
70 Highway entrance

DOWN

1 Variety show since 1975, briefly
2 "Bali ___"
3 O.K.
4 Persian Gulf nation
5 Army rank E-3
6 Disney star
7 Regarding
8 Campfire remnant
9 "For ___ sake!"
10 Washington State airport
11 Relative of a gazelle
12 Old vaudeville actress Blossom
14 1972 Bill Withers hit
18 Longtime Harvard president James Bryant ___
20 Second-biggest movie hit of 1978
23 Touch-tone 4
24 Poetic foot
25 "Cheers" bar owner Sam
27 Recording studio add-ins
30 Raymond of "East of Eden"
33 Shade
35 Tackle's neighbor
36 Custom Royale of old autodom
38 Popular pain relief cream
39 And so on
40 Trillion: Prefix
43 Engine part
44 So-so
45 Writer Ambrose
46 Footballer's footwear
49 Free-for-all
52 "Once ___ Enough"
53 Pay boost
54 Shadow eliminator?
57 Booty
60 Rap's Dr. ___
61 Devils' org.
63 Dream period, for short
64 Alley ___

893 by Brendan Emmett Quigley

ACROSS

1 "Battling Bella"
6 Booth in the theater
11 Part of what a biathlete does
14 "Crazy" singer Patsy
15 At any rate
17 1927 Virginia Woolf novel
19 Chem. or biol.
20 Where the wild things are
21 Baltic Sea feeder
22 Relish
23 Fall flat
26 "Java" man
29 Things to strive for
30 Very bright, as colors
31 Bouquet
32 Corp. money man or woman
35 Overly intelligent
39 Baseball's Fernandez
40 Kind of daisy
41 Patron saint of Norway
42 Truckers, perhaps
43 Trounces
45 Tell tale activity
48 Eccentric
49 1970 Kinks hit
50 Wrapped (up)
51 '45 battle site, for short
54 1962 Mitchum/MacLaine film
59 Kind of clause
60 Vampire hunter's weapon
61 Catcher locale?
62 Team for which Gretzky left the Oilers
63 Spoken for

DOWN

1 Groups on the program
2 Coalition
3 Penne alternative
4 Durham sch.
5 Coot
6 "Middlemarch" author
7 What grads earn: Abbr.
8 Crying sound
9 Partisan suffix
10 Utmost
11 Fahd or Faisal
12 Bandleader Kay
13 Rhone tributary
16 Marmaduke's comments
18 Confused
22 Element #30
23 One of the Bonds
24 Prosodic foot
25 Do in
26 Carpenters, e.g.
27 Pope who persuaded Attila not to attack Rome
28 Where the boyz are
29 Lady Jane and Zane
31 Cartoonist Tex
32 Storm preceder
33 Envelope part
34 Switch settings
36 Ear part
37 Phys. activity
38 Catchy part of a song
42 Rub the wrong way?
43 Really impresses
44 "I swear!"
45 Raised platform
46 Obstreperous
47 Part of a bulb
48 Ships' spines
50 Long nap?
51 Dinesen who wrote "Out of Africa"
52 Ship's trail
53 John Irving's "A Prayer for ___ Meany"
55 Fictional planet
56 Slugger's stat
57 Solder material
58 J.F.K. listing

894 by Randall J. Hartman

ACROSS

1 "Buffalo ___" (1844 song)
5 Speleologist
10 Guinea pigs, maybe
14 Tissue additive
15 Departure
16 Departure
17 Puccini soprano
18 Father of William the Conqueror
19 Anna Leonowens, e.g., in "The King and I"
20 They make wakeup calls
22 "Memphis ___" (1990 war film)
23 Drench, in a way
24 Hurt
26 Stocks and such
29 Tries
30 Whiskered animal
31 Stuck, after "in"
32 "The lie that enables us to realize the truth": Picasso
35 Shakespeare classic
39 Hurricane heading: Abbr.
40 Petrol unit
41 Kennedy's Secretary of State
42 Jibe
43 Calm
45 Severe critic
48 Star witnesses?
49 Actress Barkin
50 Parting word
54 Whim
55 Cast
57 Casa material
58 Mount whose name means "I burn"
59 Jackson and Jefferson, e.g.
60 "Mona ___"
61 Spots
62 ___ Rose
63 Pipe piece

DOWN

1 Gainesville athlete
2 "Not to mention . . ."
3 Wacky
4 Scallop, for one
5 Special touch
6 Cherish
7 They may be picked up
8 Poetic adverb
9 Sticking point
10 Hollywood producer Jon
11 Rejoice
12 King, for instance
13 Kept on the hard drive
21 Kindergartener
22 Genesis city
24 Wrap
25 Where Timbuktu is
26 Former Davis Cup captain
27 Writer O'Faolain
28 The very ___
29 Beach
31 It has many narrow rays
32 A pastel
33 Deteriorate
34 Kindergartener
36 Former Laker great Baylor
37 Cross-ply, e.g.
38 You can count on them
42 Circus sites
43 States as fact
44 I
45 Indicates
46 Blue bloods
47 Replicate
48 Best Picture of 1955
50 Chimney-top nester
51 Mine entrance
52 Rocketed
53 Nautical direction
55 Nautical direction
56 Bird sound

895 · by Harvey Estes

ACROSS
1 Part of Caesar's boast
5 Radio type
9 Art able to
14 Back
16 Duck
17 Resettle
18 Classic Vegas casino
19 Gets hot?
20 Really fancy
22 "Sometimes a Great Notion" author
24 Bugs
25 12-time baseball All-Star, 1976–88
27 It's parallel to the radius
29 Part of a long-distance company's 800 number
31 Nobility
32 Music genre
33 Unbuttered
34 Shooters
35 British servicewomen
36 10,080 minutes
37 "Chances ___"
38 Queensland native
39 Lowest par
40 Reagan prog.
41 Conclusion starter
42 Helmet plume
43 Fearsome fellows
45 Complain
47 Complains
49 2, to ½
53 Ouzo flavoring
54 Behind closed doors
56 Order members
57 Lubricating device
58 Midlife crisis symptom
59 Like a Friday crossword
60 Tiny type size

DOWN
1 Medical suffix
2 Certain
3 "Don't look ___!"
4 Narrow margins
5 Pick up
6 Gettysburg general
7 Skim milk extract
8 Vocal nag
9 Plants yielding senna
10 Profit
11 Bibliophobes
12 It's off the main drag
13 N.F.L. scores
15 Marsh birds
21 Sea birds
23 Christmas tradition
25 Strong-arm
26 Checking a fisherman's claim
28 50's–70's Soviet spacecraft series
30 Kid
31 They have open houses
32 Talk big
35 What things could always be
36 At a time of one's choosing
38 Most gung-ho
39 Commander of the Alamo
42 "Nostromo" author
44 Thieves may take these
46 More mellow
48 Suspire
50 Brand that offers "Chunky" style
51 Check mate
52 Start of a count
53 Professional org. since 1847
55 Grp. on the range?

896 · by Patrick Jordan

ACROSS
1 "If I ___ the World" (pop hit)
6 Boutique
10 Kind of carpet
14 Glue
15 Carbonated canful
16 Scarlett's plantation
17 Run to the altar
18 Brother of Cain
19 N.M. neighbor
20 Accounting principle, for short
21 Comic strip witch
23 ___ Steamer (early auto)
25 Land west of Britain
26 Brain wave reading: Abbr.
27 Track records?
29 Sine ___ non
32 Journalist Alexander
35 Isn't on the street?
36 Phoenix fivesome
37 Defeat decisively
40 "Ball!" callers
41 Scolds ceaselessly
42 Birchbark boat
43 Toothpaste type
44 Days of long ago
45 Inclined (to)
46 Feldman role in "Young Frankenstein"
48 Mill in 1848 news
52 Seal tightly, as a coffee can
56 Cleveland's lake
57 Memorable periods
58 Tiny bit
59 Area of corporate investment, briefly
60 1996 Broadway hit
61 Walked (on)
62 Popular watch brand
63 Plumb loco
64 Slangy assents
65 German industrial city

DOWN
1 Movie units
2 Illuminated from below
3 Bath sponge: Var.
4 Square numbers?
5 Hair coloring
6 Hair-raising
7 Traveling tramp
8 Bogus butter
9 Tree with fan-shaped leaves
10 Flight of steps
11 Clown
12 Dry, as a desert
13 Disputed Mideast strip
21 Entreat
22 Towel inscription
24 One of Jacob's wives
27 Unwelcome water on a ship
28 Seth's son
30 Next-to-last word of the golden rule
31 Tennis's Arthur
32 Self-satisfied
33 "Fourth base"
34 Resume submitter
35 From a distance
36 Specialized police units
38 Outrageousness
39 Sales slip: Abbr.
44 Last word of the golden rule
45 Northern diving bird
47 Bursts of wind
48 Gazillions
49 Sea eagles
50 Chain of hills
51 Alternative to a convertible
52 Sink or swim, e.g.
53 Vicinity
54 Skin opening
55 On the peak of
59 ___ v. Wade (landmark decision)

897 by Elizabeth C. Gorski

ACROSS

1 Free ticket
5 Watercress unit
10 Throw off
14 Neighborhood
15 Fraternity ___
16 Fast feline
17 Cheery tune
18 Bewildered
19 Kind of rain
20 1980 Neil Diamond hit
23 Yalie
24 Barker and Kettle, e.g.
25 "Siddhartha" author
27 ___-car
29 Injure
32 Nickname
33 Creature caught only by a virgin maiden
36 Prefix with -gramme
37 Secret competitor
40 Beam
41 Liqueur flavoring
42 Kind of stock: Abbr.
43 Sunrise direction, in Sonora
44 Pre-Revolution leaders
48 Solo in Berlioz's "Harold in Italy"
50 D'Amato or Dodd: Abbr.
52 Formerly
53 1978 Oscar-winning prison documentary
58 Pessimist's comments
59 Monastery figure
60 Rendezvous
61 Change for a ten
62 Argentine dance
63 Wings
64 About
65 Product of Bethlehem
66 Basketball's Archibald

DOWN

1 Telemarketer
2 Baltimore bird
3 Litigator Belli
4 Toast topping
5 Alexander, formerly of "60 Minutes"
6 "Designing Women" co-star
7 Hurry
8 Words of understanding
9 Trucker's choice
10 Part of NASA
11 Snake oil salesman
12 Go-between
13 June honoree
21 Saudi neighbor
22 Physicist Georg
26 Bruised item
28 Not go straight
29 Guts
30 Lincoln Center subject
31 Memo starter
34 Lupino and others
35 Copper
36 Tacks on
37 Masons, coopers and the like
38 Glance
39 Big insurance carrier
40 N.J.'s Whitman, e.g.
43 Pitcher part
45 Bassett of "Waiting to Exhale"
46 Warm up, as leftovers
47 Living room piece
49 Rancher's rope
50 Put on
51 Flynn of film
54 Newts
55 "Phooey!"
56 Kind of curve, in math
57 "___ old cowhand . . ."
58 Constrictor

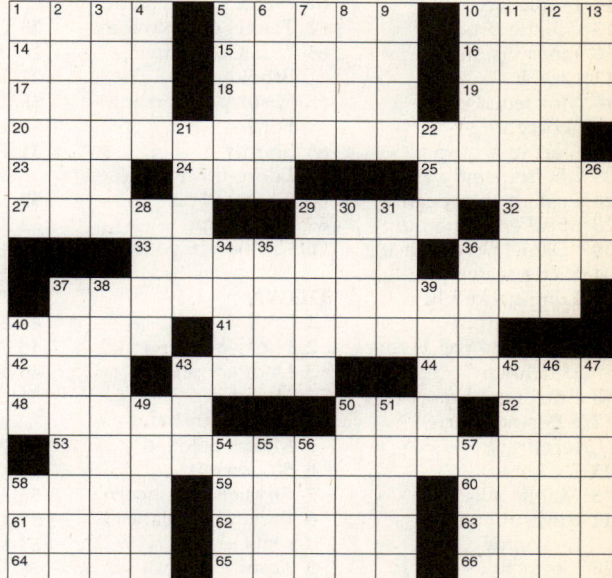

898 by John D. Leavy

ACROSS

1 You'd better believe it!
5 TV's Hawkeye
9 Bossy
12 "Dies ___"
13 Bloomsbury group writer
15 Showed up
16 Religious leader born in Wadowice, Poland
18 Stone with color flashes
19 Roadhouse
20 Formerly
21 Don sackcloth
23 Method
24 Nota ___
25 Sundae toppers
28 "Annie" showstopper
32 Controversial orchard spray
33 "King David" star, 1985
34 1922 Vincent Lopez hit
35 Actress Singer
36 Silo contents
37 Footnote abbr.
38 Fencer's weapon
39 Radiation units
40 Inlet
41 Minutemen's foe
43 Justice who replaced Brennan
45 Arm part
46 Bamboozles
47 Warehoused
50 Playwright Bogosian
51 Kind of chamber
54 New Zealander
55 Pianist born in Kurilovka, Poland
58 It popped into Descartes's head
59 Pool owner's headache
60 Novelist Paton
61 Cartridge holder
62 Young 'un
63 Motown's Marvin

DOWN

1 Big coconut exporter
2 The King's middle name
3 "Call Me Irresponsible" lyricist
4 Large shoe size
5 Plaques, maybe
6 No-goodnik
7 Nincompoop
8 Foreman's superior
9 Supergarb
10 Arab League member
11 Whipping memento
14 Relief pitchers, so to speak
15 Astronomer born in Torun, Poland
17 Working stiff
22 Roxy Music cofounder
23 Chemist born in Warsaw, Poland
24 Pushkin hero
25 Not so ruddy
26 Run to Reno?
27 Gave a fig
28 The yoke's on them
29 Kind of bomb
30 Ocher-green
31 Heron or egret
33 She vanted to be alone
36 White-bearded geezer, stereotypically
42 Grand ___ Opry
43 Formal bash
44 Exceptional occasion
46 Haunted house noise
47 Pass over
48 Beach sweeper
49 Novelist Wister
50 On pins and needles
51 Any of the Galapagos
52 "Why not?"
53 Common opening time
56 Supermodel Carol
57 Jokester

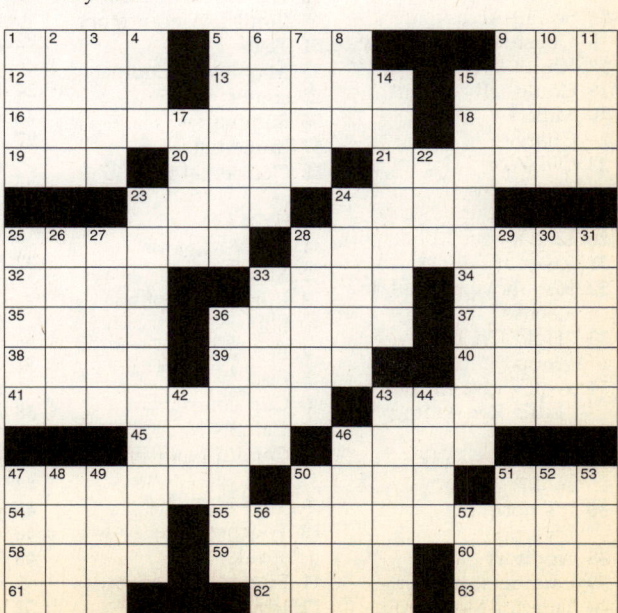

899 by Trip Payne

ACROSS
1 "Blue Sky" Oscar winner
6 Derbies
10 Washstand item
14 Emblazon
15 Gillette product
16 Inner vision
17 Lose it
18 Moistened clay
19 Worry
20 Start of a quip
23 It's frequently 72
24 Eastern European
25 Speaker of the quip
30 "Daniel Boone" actor
34 Vichy water
35 Long-necked lute
37 Play for time
38 Tenor in "The Flying Dutchman"
40 Brazilian seaport
42 I-79's northern terminus
43 Rx items
45 Manila's island
47 Revolutionary nickname
48 Go forth
50 Part 2 of the quip

52 "Camelot" actor Franco
54 Jack of "Barney Miller"
55 End of the quip
61 Prefix with distant
62 Tennis star Novotna
63 "___ Grows in Brooklyn"
65 History, according to Ford
66 Shortly
67 Loose-fitting dresses
68 Cornerstone
69 Cleo's lane
70 Car bomb?

DOWN
1 Trail
2 Hurly-burlies
3 Dodgers pitcher Hideo
4 Nana's husband
5 Makes beloved
6 50 percent
7 Physicist's concern
8 Parts of airplane seats
9 Taste
10 Mine

11 "King Kong" star
12 What otoscopes examine
13 Manhattan ingredient
21 Sen. Hatch
22 Fellas
25 Off-road vehicles
26 Actress Wilson
27 Put up
28 Underlining equiv.
29 Consume
31 First name in exploration
32 Donor Yale
33 Winter forecast
36 Flatten
39 Solitaire game
41 "___ luck!"
44 Petitions
46 Newborn
49 Hector was one
51 Searched for truffles, maybe
53 Muscat native
55 Greenish-blue
56 Cloistresses
57 Chemical compound
58 Glazier's item
59 Coffee brewers
60 French bean?

61 Abate
64 Immigrant's course: Abbr.

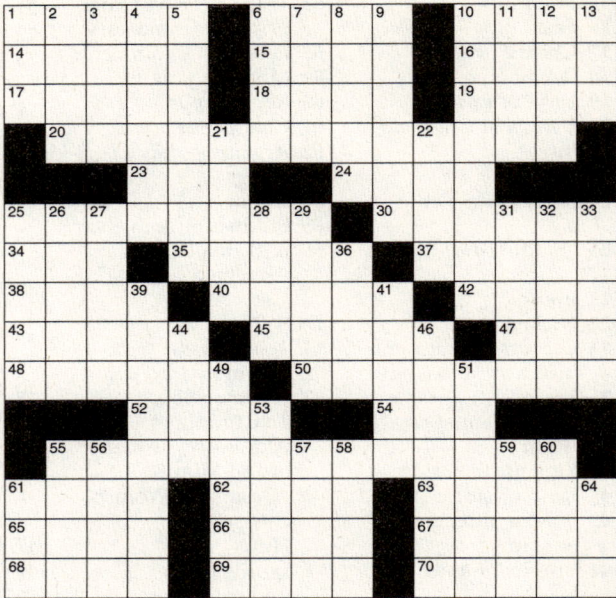

900 by Gerald R. Ferguson

ACROSS
1 Taps
10 With 15-Across, linguini topping
14 Connecting flight?
15 See 10-Across
16 Questioned, in a way
17 Kin of hyper-
18 Could tell
19 Milk
20 Charge
23 Old World evergreens
25 Bottom
26 Like loggers' boots
31 River at Rennes
32 Just above normal, in a sense
33 "Hold On Tight" group
34 Wolf's give-away in "Little Red Riding Hood"
35 Good name for a cook?
36 It's north of Liverpool
38 Auditory
39 Launders, in a way
40 Title for Marquette

41 Picnic hamperer
42 Tied up
44 Venomous snake
47 Compulsive
50 Western based on a Louis L'Amour story
51 Tears
55 Mayflower Compact signer
56 Summaries
57 Immediate
58 Occidental tourist?

DOWN
1 Trip instigator
2 Mineral suffix
3 Run up the phone bill
4 Bewhiskered
5 Essays
6 Clip component
7 Galoots
8 Certain plaintiff, at law
9 Toys since 1902
10 Touches base, so to speak
11 Fretted instrument
12 Israeli seaport

13 Drink for Robin Hood
15 Tubes
20 Off course
21 Place for an unwanted ring?
22 Artist's place, perhaps
24 Between: Fr.
26 Everywhere
27 This comes before a million
28 "Hey!"
29 Undivided
30 Mild expletive
32 Some Asian-Americans
34 Largest lake in central Europe
37 Much-covered R.&B. song
38 Kind of market
42 Turn outward
43 Dash
44 Tribal chief
45 Cameo, maybe
46 Lick ___ promise
48 Wild party
49 Clinches
52 Royal flush necessity

53 Kind of neck
54 Former Union member: Abbr.

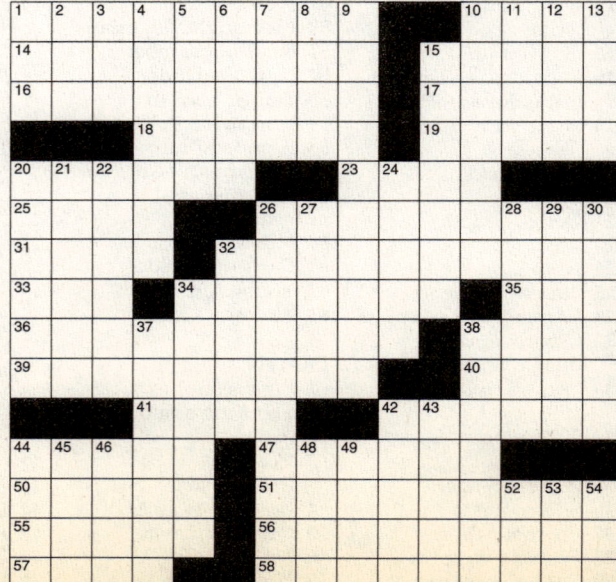

901 by Gregory E. Paul

ACROSS
1 Neanderthal's weapon
5 Basketballer
10 Tramp
14 Sharpen, as a razor
15 Dateless
16 Finished
17 Touch up, as text
18 Repeated Chris O'Donnell movie role
19 Org. expanding into Eastern Europe
20 Healthy
23 Toward the stern
24 September bloom
28 Mother that can't be fooled
32 Much of kindergarten
35 Sports venue
36 Woeful word
37 The first X of X-X-X
38 Spotless
42 No longer working: Abbr.
43 Parts of bytes
44 "Frasier" character
45 Weaken
48 Ulcer cause, in popular belief
49 Emergency room supply
50 Cosmonauts' space station
51 Taut
59 Certain boxing blow
62 Send, as payment
63 Seldom seen
64 Mitch Miller's instrument
65 "Goodnight" girl of song
66 The dark side
67 Still sleeping
68 Copier powder
69 A.F.C. division

DOWN
1 Worker with an apron
2 New Jersey city south of Paramus
3 Army outfit
4 VHS alternative
5 Chianti container
6 Skyward
7 Mongolian desert
8 Camelot lady
9 Split
10 "I'm telling you the truth!"
11 Lab eggs
12 Craps action
13 Treasure of the Sierra Madre
21 See-through wrap
22 Minstrel's song
25 Y.A. of the Giants
26 Novelist Zola and others
27 Alcove
28 Mother-of-pearls
29 Longtime "What's My Line" panelist
30 Wobble
31 Spanish article
32 Batter's position
33 Statutes
34 Baseball bat wood
36 "__ was in the beginning . . ."
39 Lawyers' org.
40 Prefix with venous
41 Madam's mate
46 Like a wagon trail
47 George Marshall's alma mater, briefly
48 Nun
50 Down East
52 Stick-to-itiveness
53 Submarine sandwich
54 Feds
55 Attracted
56 Strong thumbs-up review
57 "Mila 18" novelist
58 Liquefy, as ice cream
59 Mauna __
60 Decline
61 Antagonist

902 by Rich Norris

ACROSS
1 Understanding
6 Woodworking tool
9 Barks
13 A dime, dollarwise
14 Hideout
16 Calamitous
17 Filer's aid
18 "Rule, Britannia" composer
19 Rack site
20 Pink slip
23 Arafat's org.
24 Menu selection
25 Sebastiania seeds
31 First sign of spring
32 Takes it easy
33 Xmas gift recipient
36 Considerate
37 Grocery coupon value
38 Wharf
39 Mass. hours
40 "Piece of cake"
41 Bolivian capital
42 Plumbing convenience
44 Court stat
47 "Who, me?"
48 Means to an end
53 Jivers
54 Devoid of rocks?
55 Sen. Thurmond
58 "The Thin Man" dog
59 Semi support
60 Troy story
61 "Boy, that was close!"
62 Cap that may be partly plaid
63 Watchers

DOWN
1 Communications giant
2 Sleep state
3 Over
4 Short on cash
5 "The Mary Tyler Moore Show" spin-off
6 Jai __
7 "Nuts!"
8 Get in a good one on
9 Decides to use
10 Hudson, e.g.
11 Soeur's sibling
12 Brains
15 Undoes
21 __-Tiki
22 Reinking and Richards
25 Boxer LaMotta
26 "Battle Cry" author
27 Like new
28 Close in films
29 Actress Beulah
30 First name in rock
33 Passageway
34 River through Bern
35 One whose work is always changing
37 Southwestern saloon
38 With old-fashioned charm
40 Where Virgo meets Libra, e.g.
41 Actress Kurtz
42 Lumber mill fixture
43 All clocks are set by it: Abbr.
44 Musicians' org.
45 Thief's secret
46 Tre + quattro
49 Bakery call
50 Festive
51 Rose part
52 Northwest Pennsylvania city
56 Scull
57 Rx writers

903 by Mark Diehl

ACROSS
1 Memorable lines
5 ___ de mer
8 Whoop
13 Sports org. based in Boulder, Colo.
14 Rock singer Carmen
16 City on the Swan river
17 "Whoops!"
18 Succotash ingredient
19 Dentist's prefix
20 Org. with a secretary general
21 Jellystone Park denizen
23 Lively dances
25 Popular middle name
26 Econ. stat
27 Taps producer
29 Old-time actress ___ May Oliver
31 Fill
32 Brief outline
34 Nobleman
36 Quite limber
41 Wee hour
42 Best-selling picture book of the 70's

43 "Excuse me"
46 "Oh, bother!"
48 Cone-shaped heaters
49 Computer acronym
50 Cardinal insignia
51 Bar offering
53 Sign of affection
56 ___ Office
59 Long Island town, site of the Brookhaven Laboratory
60 Dickens's Mr. Pecksniff
61 Mrs. Charles Chaplin
62 Actress Verdugo
63 Return mailer: Abbr.
64 Yorick's skull, for one
65 Prank starter
66 ___ Royal Majesty
67 Thrill

DOWN
1 Physics particle
2 Dept. of Labor division
3 Aim, e.g.
4 Test site
5 Toast at mealtime

6 Melodic
7 It can move a star
8 It can create a stir
9 Rosemary, for one
10 Loser to Chamorro in 1990
11 World leader, 1961–71
12 Football Hall-of-Famer Jim
15 Poolside sights
22 Painting the town red
24 Scout's work
27 Pastoral sound
28 Periods of mania
30 Pulitzer category
31 Vie against Shaq
33 Familiar with
35 Infamous 1972 hurricane
37 Like some seals
38 Not a picky eater
39 ___ green
40 Twisted path
43 Contended
44 Big buildup
45 Ham
47 Pesky fly

50 Item on a sub
52 Program offerer
54 Last word before the gavel hits
55 "___, right"

57 Shortly
58 Columbo's employer, for short

904 by Martin Ashwood-Smith and Bob Klahn

ACROSS
1 Posts in the Hearst empire
16 Bailed out
17 Bark, generally
18 Gene Autry's "___ Faithful"
19 Wailuku welcome
20 Nobelist Morrison
21 "Woodstock" songwriter Mitchell
23 Voltmeter meas.
25 Mandela's land: Abbr.
26 Fighting bird
30 Memnon's mother, in Homer
32 Dispatch boat
33 One way to resign
38 Preseason staple
39 Animals: Suffix
40 Hamlet's relatives
41 A piece of one's mind?
43 More or less vertical
44 With 4-Down, perfectly
45 Digs
47 First name in horror

50 A.A.A. recommendation
52 Congregate
53 Compass
55 "Roustabout" star
57 "The Simpsons" storekeeper
60 They're debatable
64 International understanding
65 Snaps

DOWN
1 Prefix with -therm
2 "Kiss, Kiss" author
3 Hungarian poet Madach
4 See 44-Across
5 Suffix with Capri
6 Cheese made from ewe's milk
7 Underscore
8 "Now I see!"
9 Oblivion
10 Service piece
11 "___ make a lovely corpse": Dickens
12 Kind of D.A.
13 It ran in Ares's arteries

14 Wreckage
15 Print tint
21 Follower of Ignatius Loyola
22 Bunker player
24 "Live at Five" clip
26 Habit
27 Say for sure
28 Red giant in the constellation Cetus
29 Mound
31 "Enough!"
34 Trigger and others
35 Gershwin biographer David
36 Hitch or glitch
37 Priggish pronouncements
42 Pamper
46 Ditch
47 Record company
48 Maine college town
49 "Dagnabbit!"
51 Columnist Goodman
54 Chick's tail?
56 Number two
57 Chop-chop
58 1958 World Cup sensation
59 Mouse manipulator

61 No one has two of them
62 Do, re, mi
63 Object

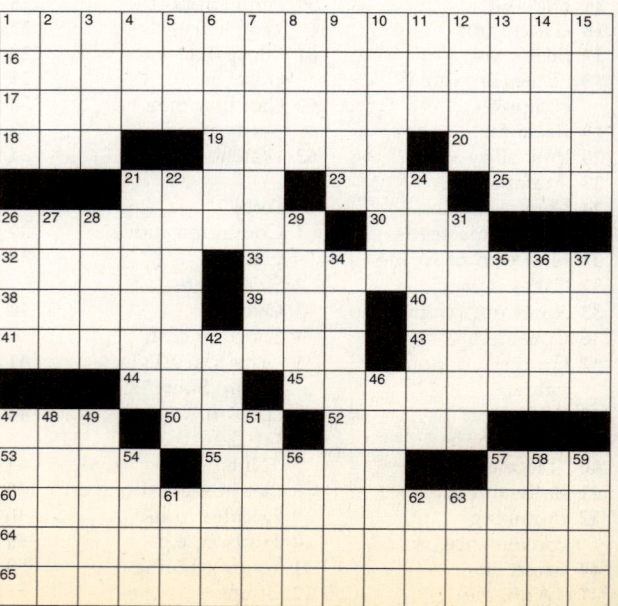

905 by Daniel Halfen

ACROSS
1 Webster's, e.g.: Abbr.
5 Ones easily fooled
9 Afflictions
14 Jacob's twin
15 "Not guilty," e.g.
16 Dwelling place
17 Green shot
18 Bibliography, basically
19 Cheek cosmetic
20 Parts of lbs.
21 Diagonally
23 Put safely to bed, as a child
25 Peewee
26 Steal cattle
29 Actor Nielsen of "Airplane!"
33 Practices in the ring
35 Be jubilant
37 Octopus's defense
38 Cheryl of "Charlie's Angels"
39 Louvers
40 Lavish affection (on)
41 Lubricate
42 Taxonomic divisions
43 Clerics' confab
44 2 or 3, maybe, on the Richter scale
46 Macbeth and others
48 ___ Normandes (Channel Islands)
50 Tidbit
53 Dry bouquet item
58 ___ and cry
59 Poppy product
60 Stead
61 1995 porcine Oscar nominee
62 Not so good
63 Muscat's land
64 Rainless
65 Lip-curling smile
66 Telegraphed
67 Caddie supplies

DOWN
1 Train stop
2 Trooper on the highway
3 Children's string game
4 Syllable of reproach
5 Aid for a fracture
6 Dismounted
7 Buzzy one
8 Mythical goat/man
9 British sir
10 Cuts short, as a space flight
11 Verb accompanier
12 Advantage
13 Prophet
21 Smooch
22 Picks out
24 Northern Iraqi
27 "The Windsor Beauties" painter
28 Praise
30 Biggest portion
31 Absorbed by
32 Scraped (out)
33 Coin hole
34 Twosome
36 Great Salt Lake site
39 Nagger
40 One turning color?
42 Nylon, for one
43 Skiers' wish
45 Treat badly
47 Quantity
49 Missile pits
51 Jazz pianist Blake
52 City north of Sheffield
53 Some camp denizens, for short
54 "Once ___ a time . . ."
55 Beget
56 Margarita fruit
57 Like Jack Sprat's diet
61 Dracula, at times

906 by Janet R. Bender

ACROSS
1 Poker holding
5 Study for finals
9 Shaping machine
14 "Crimes & Misdemeanors" actor
15 Wife of Zeus
16 Flynn of "Captain Blood"
17 Fast
20 Land, as a big one
21 Late Chairman
22 Blood supplies
23 Long, long time
25 Hall-of-Famer Drysdale
27 Swift
35 Didn't face the enemy
36 Chow down
37 Like a Jaguar or Miata
38 Was in a play
41 Ms. alternative
43 ___ raving mad
44 Deutsch, here
46 Swiss peak
48 Society page word
49 Fleet
53 Fat farm
54 Pouting face
55 "Dance On Little Girl" singer
59 Piercing tool
61 Opera house cries
65 Quick
68 Non-earthling
69 Otherwise
70 ___ Stanley Gardner
71 Old-fashioned
72 Fate
73 Aussie hoppers

DOWN
1 Henry VIII's sixth
2 Not into the wind
3 Not in use
4 Criticize harshly
5 Hong Kong residents, now
6 ___ Speedwagon
7 Calla lily family
8 Symbol of Jewish resistance
9 Hawaiian garland
10 Fine or liberal follower
11 "How ___!"
12 Frost
13 Singer Fitzgerald
18 Best Picture of 1958
19 They may need coloring at a salon
24 Deception
26 Small bites
27 Fort ___, N.C.
28 Indy entrant
29 Prelim
30 Horse stall covering
31 Go bad
32 Neighbor of an Afghani
33 Sore throat cause, briefly
34 Little squirts, so to speak
39 Big bird
40 Drops bait
42 Brickbat
45 Like some stocks
47 Bit of math homework
50 Acted servilely
51 Hang ten or shoot the curl
52 Medicine man
55 In the distance
56 Aswan's river
57 Make an afghan
58 "Hard Hearted Hannah" composer
60 Composer Schifrin
62 ___ Beach, Fla.
63 Norse capital
64 Tom Jones's "___ a Lady"
66 Brian of rock music
67 Prefix with metric

907 by Richard Silvestri

ACROSS
1 1958 Elvis song
5 & 10 1957 Elvis song
14 Personal prefix
15 "Dallas" matriarch
16 He sang about Alice
17 Somewhat, musically
18 Rey's mate
19 Part of N.B.
20 1962 Elvis song
23 Dedicatory phrase
24 Equals
25 "Little ___" (1961 Elvis song)
29 Man of La Mancha
32 Sleuthing dog
33 Room at the top
34 Health club
37 1956 Elvis song
41 Trouser half
42 Hotel posting
43 In apple-pie order
44 Attuned
45 1969 Elvis movie
47 Yellow-fever mosquito
50 Carpet cleaner, for short
51 1956 Elvis song
58 Mideast's Gulf of ___
59 Lightened one's billfold
60 Official proceedings
62 VHS alternative
63 Actor Williamson
64 Sting operation
65 Elvis's middle name
66 1964 Elvis song
67 1976 Elvis song

DOWN
1 Short swim
2 What the nose knows
3 "Treat Me ___" (1957 Elvis song)
4 Harbor alert
5 Brat
6 Actress Verdugo
7 Advanced Eng. degrees
8 Pebbles's pet
9 Pro votes
10 Full-width headline
11 Wear away
12 Take in or let out
13 Crowd noises
21 Shoshonean
22 Significant time
25 Satirical Mort
26 Words of understanding
27 Daddy deer
28 Pitch
29 Charger
30 Hellenic vowels
31 Beat ending
33 Commedia dell'___
34 Suffix with hip
35 Fruit baked in wine
36 Countertenor
38 Long lock
39 Airplane compartment
40 "Puppet ___ String" (1965 Elvis song)
44 Ed Wynn's son
45 Dungeons & Dragons locale
46 F.D.R.'s predecessor
47 Addis ___
48 Cain vis-a-vis Abel
49 Because of
50 Snake spit
52 Annapolis inits.
53 Prot. denomination
54 Flatten
55 Scout recitation
56 Stocking shade
57 "Flaming ___" (1960 Elvis movie)
61 Likely

908 by David J. Kahn

ACROSS
1 Whey-faced
4 Popular snack
10 Durable transports, for short
14 Proposal defeated in 1982
15 How some coffee is served
16 Administer
17 O.K.
19 ___ cava
20 Outcasts
21 Indiana : Hoosier :: Nevada : ___
23 Inca fortunes
24 Kyrgyz city
26 Most basic
27 61-Across, for example
28 They may be seeded
30 More than tubby
31 Automatic start
33 ___ East
35 1989 Jack Lemmon film
36 Epitome of sharpness
39 Prone
42 Swear by, with "on"
43 Dump
45 Monomaniac, informally
47 McCurry, to Clinton
49 5-Down, for example
52 Office staple
54 London theater Old ___
55 N.B.A.'s Nick Van ___
56 Put up
58 Shock
60 British title
61 O.K.
63 List ender
64 Take ___ of absence
65 Schoolboy
66 Forswear
67 Enthusiastic response
68 Mag. staff

DOWN
1 Club, say
2 Citation's jockey
3 Pearly: Var.
4 Sonoma neighbor
5 O.K.
6 Stylish
7 Book before Zephaniah: Abbr.
8 Works at the Met
9 Word with iron or bath
10 46-Down, for example
11 Tittered
12 Dustin's "Agatha" co-star
13 Like propaganda
18 Disney head
22 Soyuz 6 cosmonaut Shonin
25 Shakespearean play in two parts
29 "¿Comprende?"
32 Superstore
34 17-Across, for example
37 Suffix with pay
38 Little wrigglers
39 Assumed, with "to"
40 Apportion
41 Surveyor's assistant
44 Cotton or wool
46 O.K.
48 Unnerve
50 Fill up again, in a way
51 Merges
53 Indemnify
57 Red-pencil
59 "___ Death" (Grieg work)
62 Point, in law

ACROSS

1 Comes to pass
5 Sugar or starch, in slang
9 Present time
13 Tracy Marrow, familiarly
14 Apartment next to the super's, maybe
15 Sponge
16 Bumble Bee, e.g.
17 Whence the phrase "to give the devil his due"
19 Not moving
21 Sawer of logs
22 Author with a book subtitled "The Saga of an American Family"
23 Dinner wear
24 Imposes without invitation
28 ___ Z (everything)
29 "You can't mean me!?"
30 Word of the Prophet
32 Retreat
35 Preceding periods
37 W.W. II enlistee
39 Refrigerator bar?
41 Many A.B.A. members
43 His last work was "Pocketful of Miracles," 1961
45 Get up and it's gone
46 Kind of delivery
48 Token
50 Succeeded
53 Like Cheerios
54 "Yoo-hoo!"
55 Maternity surprise
58 Birds Eye offering
60 Plaster base
61 Stores
62 A person might earn one for a score
63 Christiania, today
64 Kind of dog
65 Fire
66 Break down

DOWN

1 Has real relevance
2 Slightly better than
3 Football coach's nightmare
4 Play maker
5 End piece
6 Betimes, updated
7 Torn
8 July 4th event, briefly
9 Letter sign-off
10 Sculptor Henry
11 Didn't wait
12 Former N.H.L. coach Fred
15 Advertising unit
18 Singles' grp.?
20 Curly cue?
25 Utter failure, in slang
26 Davis of baseball
27 Exerciser of spin control?
31 "Don't think so"
33 Uncomfortable
34 Whistler
36 Tight
38 Middle of a famous palindrome
40 Nonunion workplace
42 Churchill Downs features
44 Per
47 Submachine gun
49 Jaundiced
50 Winter wear
51 Four before a slash
52 Wild Asian dog
55 Bibliophile's purchase
56 Tevere's city
57 Romantic interlude
59 Cousin of a tarboosh

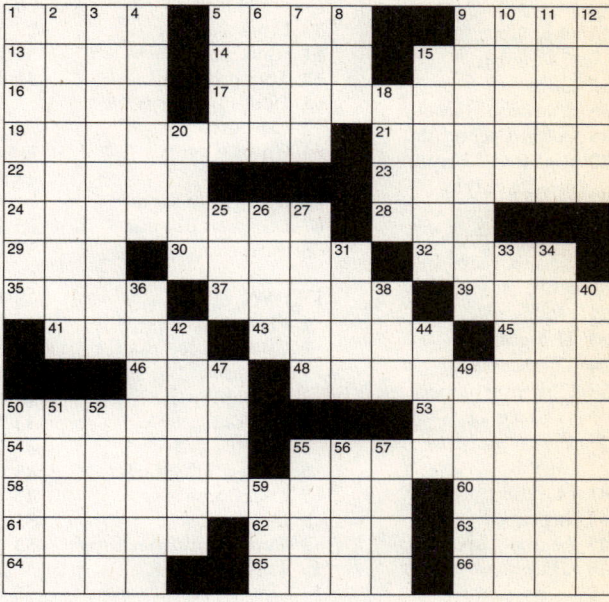

ACROSS

1 Cleopatra's love ___ Antony
5 Dressed like Dracula
10 Frozen waffle brand
14 Controversial orchard spray
15 Open-mouthed
16 ___ of Arc
17 Coffee, slangily
18 Half note
19 Roof's edge
20 Post-Derby interview spot
23 Camel rival
24 L-1011, e.g.
25 Sign after Aquarius
28 Land bordered by the Mekong
30 Beanie
33 With 54-Across, a Revolutionary hero
34 Algebra or trig
35 Scarlett's estate
36 1965 Gary Lewis and the Playboys hit
39 Four-star review
40 Andy of the comics
41 Otherworldly
42 Neighbor of Wyo.
43 Reps.' opponents
44 Parts of acts
45 The "L" of L.A.
46 Dullsville
47 Flabbergast
53 Freq. quotation attribution
54 See 33-Across
55 Mormon state
57 ___-deaf
58 For rent
59 Recipe directive
60 Washstand vessel
61 Mild oath
62 Many millennia

DOWN

1 Capt.'s better
2 "There oughta be ___!"
3 Sitarist Shankar
4 Engine housing
5 Relief carvings
6 "If I Had ___ Like You" (1925 hit)
7 Opposites of a 39-Across
8 Many a Cecil B. De Mille film
9 Large bottle
10 Tape deck button
11 Hockey score
12 Contributed
13 "My ___ and Only"
21 Immensely
22 Legal matter
25 ___ dish (lab item)
26 "___ to Be You"
27 Hindu Trinity member
28 Reading lights
29 Sitting on
30 Stone mound
31 70's sitcom
32 Capitol Hill gofers
34 Sir's partner
35 Branch office?
37 Emulate Oksana Baiul
38 Stick-on
43 Bespectacled dwarf
44 Viewpoints
45 Hardly a partygoer
46 Animal variety
47 Comprehend
48 ___ of the above
49 Whip
50 Stewpot
51 Director Preminger
52 Excedrin target
53 Had a hero?
56 Action film "48 ___"

ACROSS

1 "Shoo!"
5 Bishop of old TV
10 Like some furs
14 Forbidden: Var.
15 Ballroom dance
16 Novelist ___ S. Connell Jr.
17 Gobs
18 Sharon of Israel
19 Behind schedule
20 Righteous Brothers' musical style
23 Cool fabric
24 Crisp fabric
28 Coda's place in a score
29 House of ___
33 Thingamajig
34 Think about
36 Old-time actor Wallace ___
37 1967 Van Morrison hit
41 Handel oratorio
42 Say again
43 Teamed up (with)
46 CD player maker
47 Corp. giant
50 They practice girth control
52 Less convincing, as an excuse
54 Popular Southern vegetable
58 Lima's locale
61 Sao ___
62 Touch down
63 1934 Pulitzer writer Herbert
64 Church officer
65 "Or ___!"
66 Big Apple section
67 Logician in space
68 Sunbeams

DOWN

1 Place to start a ride
2 Check voice mail, perhaps
3 Be plentiful
4 Student
5 Judge's order
6 Fabled fast starter
7 Oklahoma city
8 Discharge
9 Type of mutual fund
10 Took the bait
11 One of Frank's exes
12 Krazy ___
13 Opposite WSW
21 Fund
22 Sky light?
25 German river
26 Peacock's pride
27 Supplement
30 Bed-and-breakfast
31 River through Frankfurt
32 Juan Carlos and others
34 Former Kremlin hotshots
35 Property taken back
37 Hope-Crosby's "Road to ___"
38 Govern
39 Hideout
40 Singer Crystal
41 Down
44 Sushi bar order
45 Window treatments
47 African antelope
48 Wee
49 Swaps
51 Resell at a profit
53 Philosopher Mortimer
55 Bit of praise
56 Util. bill
57 Duchess of ___
58 Dads
59 Kind of maniac
60 "Go, team!"

ACROSS

1 Dummy
5 More than unpopular
10 Sooty shaft
14 Kind of sch.
15 Dennis the Menace's mother
16 "___ That a Shame" (1955 hit)
17 Lamb's alias
18 Superior being
20 Compassion
22 Twofold
23 Ballantine brew
24 Annoying critic
26 Aswan Dam lake
28 Pizza
30 Foe of the Iroquois
31 Quick swim
32 The East
34 As well as
35 Kind of situation
39 Absolute flop
41 Deplete, perhaps
43 "___ your life!"
44 Poetic preposition
45 Had no doubts
46 ___ gestae
48 "Internal Affairs" star, 1990
50 "Der Ring ___ Nibelungen"
51 Yule garland
54 Talk turkey?
56 Mahler's homeland: Abbr.
57 Vow
59 "A Midsummer Night's Dream" king
62 Word to a cold sufferer
65 Permitted
66 "Paradise Lost" setting
67 Clear
68 Michener tale, e.g.
69 MGM Grand site
70 Africa's largest nation
71 Proof word

DOWN

1 Pager cue
2 Stew crock
3 Prevailing mood
4 College World Series site
5 Traditional wife
6 R.&B. singer ___ Sure
7 Like Grateful Dead attire
8 Beige
9 Insist on
10 Groupie
11 Loeb and Bonet of showbiz
12 Cry of defeat
13 Early anesthetic
19 Julia Louis-Dreyfus TV role
21 Flowery tribute
25 Fluff
27 Hybrid eating utensil
28 Hock
29 Golfer Aoki
33 Now, in Nogales
36 "Splendid!"
37 "Ah!"
38 Part of CNN
40 Gravel order, perhaps
41 Nabisco sweet
42 Prohibited
44 Brainiac
47 Secret Service eyewear
49 Recede
51 Vegas transaction
52 ___ Rivoli (arcaded Paris street)
53 Ruhr city
55 Pay for monthly
58 Like some traffic
60 Marathoner Markova
61 Tidy
63 Lively card game
64 "This ___ test . . ."

913 by Martin Ashwood-Smith

ACROSS

1 Road runners?
5 Make a move
8 Pastime
14 Plaudits, of a sort
15 "___ any drop to drink": Coleridge
16 Went easy on
17 Start of a quote
19 Snapper
20 Four, on the phone
21 Quote, part 2
23 ___ al-Khaimah (one of the United Arab Emirates)
24 Area of coll. study
25 Doo-wop part
26 Point on Magellan's compass
28 Summed up
30 Badgers
34 Not tacit
36 Toot
38 Aerialist's insurance
39 Money lender, for short
40 Quote, part 3
41 Terra ___
43 Familiar substitution
44 Holding steady
46 St. Francis's home
47 Exude
49 It may involve gas
51 Have words (with)
52 Russo of "Ransom"
54 Educ. group
56 Miltonian sea creature
57 End of the quote
61 Mauna ___
62 Nickels and dimes
63 Source of the quote
65 Warehouse worker, at times
66 Hotel sign
67 Bad spots?
68 Noted Titanic couple
69 Puncture sound
70 Strata

DOWN

1 Party places?
2 Hawaii
3 Freedom fighters
4 Its business is booming
5 Pepto-Bismol, e.g.
6 Term of familiarity
7 Leaves' home
8 English stage actress Winwood
9 Jet
10 Kind of copy
11 Uffizi display
12 Cosmos star
13 Carl Sagan's "The Dragons of ___"
18 4th of July cries
22 Person with the keys
27 Train sta. posting
29 Borders
31 Unable to stand the heat?
32 Circulates
33 Ways up
35 Little one
37 Mac rivals
40 Certain knife
42 C.I.A.'s forerunner
45 Bygone regiment
46 Seaport southwest of Nice
48 On the double
50 Branch of physics
53 Athirst
55 Valuable diamond?
57 Bruins' home
58 Greek characters
59 Hotel in "The Graduate"
60 Goddess of fertility
64 Test place

914 by William Bernhardt

ACROSS

1 One of 7-Down
6 Nicholas II, e.g.
10 Tattle
14 Kind of anesthetic
15 Roll call response
16 "I before E except after C," e.g.
17 Make amends
18 The witch's end in "Hansel and Gretel"
19 Where India is
20 Restorative
21 Attorney General Janet
22 Ollie's partner in slapstick
23 Popular oil additive
25 Tough as ___
27 One leads to Loch Lomond
31 Mounted again
35 Collection of anecdotes
36 One of 7-Down
38 Small drum
39 Signal for an act to end
41 Holy chalice of legend
43 Telephone sound
44 It increases by degrees
46 Make sense
48 The Red Baron was one
49 Curriculum vitae
51 Striped
53 Midsection, informally
55 It hangs next to 53-Across
56 "Hey, you!"
59 Growth on the north side of trees
61 Monastery staff
65 Reverberation
66 Satanic
67 1973 Broadway revival starring Debbie Reynolds
68 Pour
69 Singer Turner
70 Gypsy's deck
71 One of 7-Down
72 Midterm, e.g.
73 One of 7-Down

DOWN

1 Subdivision of land
2 ___-Rooter
3 It's clicked on a computer
4 Breakfast pastry for Hamlet?
5 Sophocles tragedy
6 God with a hammer
7 This puzzle's theme
8 "In the ___" (Nixon book)
9 Impressionist Pierre
10 High military muck-a-muck
11 One of 7-Down
12 Inter ___
13 Noggin
24 Ping-___
26 Serve to be reserved
27 Cartoon Viking
28 Hole-___
29 The Sharks and the Jets, e.g.
30 Taj Mahal site
32 German sub
33 Present
34 One of 7-Down
37 "___, Pagliaccio" (aria)
40 One of 7-Down
42 Moon goddess
45 Grounded bird
47 Drivers and hunters need them
50 Clown Kelly
52 Not concerned with right and wrong
54 Hollywood release
56 Dumas senior
57 Glance over
58 Thug's knife
60 Blinds piece
62 Peter or the Wolfe?
63 Half hitch, e.g.
64 Brother of Cain and Abel

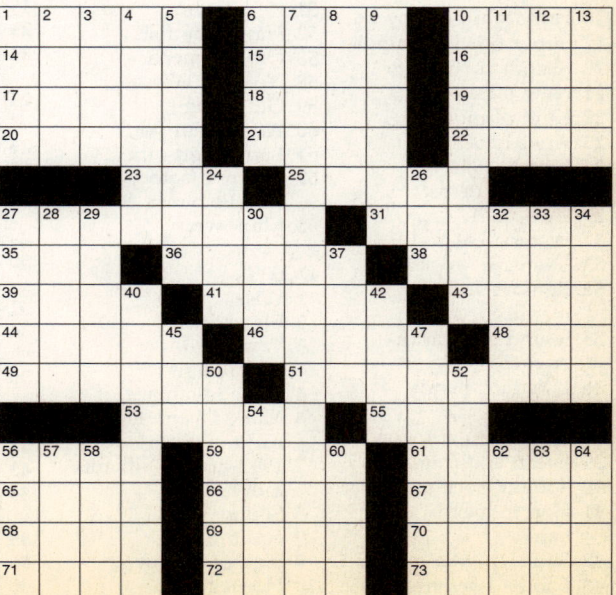

915 by Frank Longo

ACROSS

1 Telepathy and clairvoyance, e.g.
5 Diamond M.V.P., 1960–61
10 "Star Trek" regular Walter
12 Issuing, as from a source
14 Courtroom alibi, perhaps
16 "A Christmas Story" co-star Dillon
17 Sternly disciplined
18 Flustered
19 It's done in cages
21 Priest, at times
22 Some French wines, informally
23 Mythological trio
24 Spaces between lines, in printing
26 C.I.O.'s partner
27 Spanish missionary Bartolome de ___
32 "___ luego!"
37 Hershey bar
38 Bank figures
40 They help move calves

42 Massachusetts city, birthplace of N.C. Wyeth
43 Back up: Var.
44 Superlatively sarcastic
45 Beautifier
46 Classifies
47 Least vacillating
48 Not vacillating about
49 Barbed

DOWN

1 ___ Beach, Fla.
2 Potential White House hopeful
3 It'll keep you going
4 Rome's ___ Choir
5 Old Testament ender
6 "Friends" co-star
7 Being bombastic
8 Book lists
9 More than peeks
10 Algiers's old quarter
11 Megacorporation
12 Osman, for one
13 Texas county or its seat
15 1996–97 best-seller "___ Ashes"

20 Economical homes
25 Ancient land in eastern France
27 It may be poetic
28 Deity discreditor
29 Split
30 Actor Louis who starred in "Julius Caesar," 1953
31 After a lengthy delay
32 A sponge may get this
33 About 180 square miles of Europe
34 Pooh-pooher
35 Most wound up
36 Predicate
37 Part of the Louisiana Purchase
39 Imparts
41 "Chicago Hope" extras, familiarly

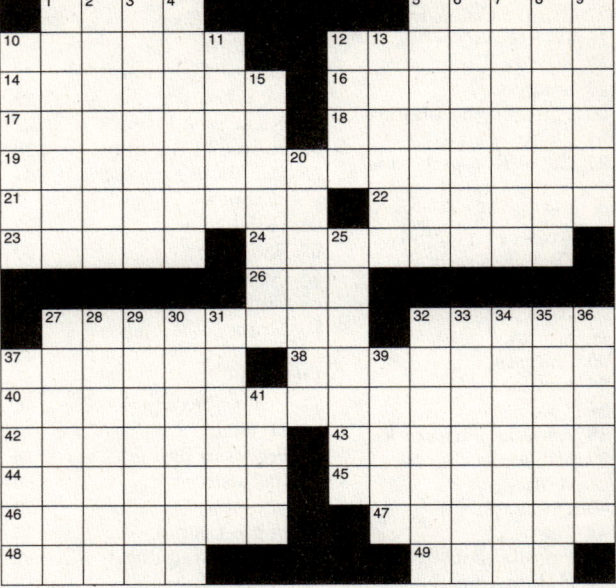

916 by Randall J. Hartman

ACROSS

1 Clinch, as a victory
6 R.B.I., e.g.
10 Keats, for one
14 Got out of bed
15 "Sock it ___!"
16 Fairy tale's first word
17 Super Bowl I champs
20 Slalom curve
21 New Jersey five
22 Kind of monkey
23 Anklebones
24 June 6, 1944
25 Yummy items
29 TV's "L.A. ___"
32 Waters: Lat.
33 "Xanadu" rock grp.
34 Remove from a manuscript
35 Sound of a cat or engine
36 Like Jack Benny, famously
38 More than a vogue
39 Pecan and pumpkin
40 Sought election
41 Had money in the bank
42 Sault ___ Marie
43 Football defensemen

46 It gets slapped around a lot
47 Skin cream ingredient
48 Book after Song of Solomon
51 Z ___ zebra
52 Hawaiian dish
55 On-line menaces
58 Nobelist Wiesel
59 Old Dodge
60 Artist's support
61 Bambi and others
62 When a factory whistle blows
63 Mink wrap

DOWN

1 Wise
2 Blows it
3 Trials and tribulations
4 Take advantage of
5 Mark Twain, for one
6 Kind of electricity
7 1992 Robin Williams movie
8 Soundstage equipment
9 Sign of sorrow
10 Hoosegow

11 Billfold bills
12 Light beige
13 "___ of the D'Urbervilles"
18 Dracula player Lugosi
19 Princely abbr.
23 Ivan and Nicholas
24 Boxer Oscar ___ Hoya
25 Northern Scandinavians
26 Phrase of resignation
27 Blender setting
28 Nancy Drew's creator
29 "Scram!"
30 Creator of the Ragged Dick books
31 Garden intruders
34 Circumnavigator Sir Francis
36 "Jurassic Park" novelist
37 Length of yarn
41 Candle brackets
43 Hawaiian do
44 Smash, as a windshield
45 Inter ___
46 Flutist
48 Clinched, as a victory

49 ___ survivor
50 Parisian lady friend
51 Florence's river
52 Baja buck
53 Pitcher Hershiser
54 Bermuda, e.g.
56 Comic Philips
57 Kit ___ Club

ACROSS

1 Dateless
5 Chitchat
9 Chorus voice
14 Pasty
15 Prince William's school
16 Cancel
17 "___ me."
20 Stop working
21 Pull a con
22 Clear tables and such
23 Where le nez is
25 Door opener
27 Do film work
30 Pillow cover
32 Coercion
36 Bikini tops
38 Provo neighbor
40 Medicine for what ails you
41 "___ me!"
44 Lethargy
45 Second of three virtues
46 Where to see a hula
47 Draw
49 Dick Francis book "Dead ___"
51 Make a mistake
52 Unopened
54 Porn
56 Nothing's alternative
59 "Phooey!"
61 Gets used (to)
65 "___ me?"
68 Eskimo boat
69 Christen
70 Suffix with billion
71 Stately place
72 Barks
73 Pig food

DOWN

1 Practice with Rocky
2 Saga
3 Got down
4 "Understand?"
5 TV money-raiser
6 Gobbled up
7 Passing shots
8 New York hoopster
9 Disparage
10 Hard-working insect
11 Snooty one
12 "Star Trek" character
13 Auto maker Ransom E. ___
18 Very, in Valence
19 Currency, in Capetown
24 "Planet of the Apes" planet
26 Range choice
27 Gaping pit
28 Bo-peep's staff
29 Brownish gray
31 French wine district
33 Follow
34 Sound of the 60's
35 Scrub
37 Glaswegians, e.g.
39 Is gloomy
42 Former Austrian prince
43 Home wreckers
48 Affronted
50 Star-Kist product
53 Lion-colored
55 Oompah instruments
56 Buzzing
57 Champagne Tony of golf
58 "___ Eyes" (Eagles hit)
60 Siamese, now
62 Stir up
63 Prefix with dollar or trash
64 Escalator part
66 ___-relief
67 Bit of electricity

ACROSS

1 Statesman Eban
5 Part of a wolf pack
10 Smidgen
14 Recline lazily
15 Kin of "shucks"
16 Billiard cushion
17 1934 Mae West song
19 Girl lead-in
20 Excitement
21 Need a doctor's care
22 Elite military unit
23 Account of a trip conducted by Virgil
28 Pretend
30 Sail spar
31 Abstract artist Milton ___
32 Hindu goddess of fortune
36 Romantic exploit
37 Repent
39 Regatta blades
41 Ingenue
43 Cooper hero
44 Show how
46 Weatherman Al
47 Cop's question to a speeder
52 Leporine creatures
53 Actress ___ Dawn Chong
54 Warriors' org.
57 Defenseman Bobby et al.
58 "Get lost!"
62 Siouan Indian
63 Verdi's "___ Chorus"
64 Leslie Caron role
65 Sprightly
66 60's catchword
67 Some are split

DOWN

1 Soprano Gluck
2 "Hopalong Cassidy" actor
3 Marriage prerequisite
4 The whole shootin' match
5 Ill-suited
6 Scarlett O'Hara and others
7 ___ e sempre (Italian motto)
8 It goes through withdrawals
9 Mao or Lao follower
10 Fuming
11 Western
12 Hyperion, for one
13 Col. Bowie's mission, with "the"
18 "___ Boy" (song of 1913)
22 P.M. times
24 Trunk line
25 Large stain
26 Country not in Rushdie's travel plans
27 Advertiser with a swoosh
28 Tarry
29 Sunset followers
33 It exists among thieves
34 The Yukon's ___ Mountains
35 "Dies ___"
37 Brews
38 Suckling spot
40 Communist land, once: Abbr.
42 U.S. 1 and others
43 Companion of Gabriel
45 Brave
47 Victory shout
48 Poker Flat's chronicler
49 Gaffe
50 Change, as a clock
51 Epigrammatic tale
55 Composer Bartok
56 How flawed goods are sold
58 Disparity
59 Singleton
60 Norris Dam's project: Abbr.
61 Mont Blanc, e.g.

919 · by Shannon Burns

ACROSS

1 Harper on the bookshelf
4 Procrastinator's time of action
14 Trouble
15 Some Pythagoreans
17 Certain ed. of the Bible
18 Festive
19 Midgard serpent's slayer
21 Cafeteria-goers
22 Salt
23 "If I ___ Rich Man"
25 It comes easily to hand
26 Abominable Snowman
27 Rigorous tests
28 Advantages
29 Gibbons on TV
30 Roscoe
31 Georgia ___
33 ___ de mer
34 Going on and on and . . .
36 Jack and Jill's burden
40 Annoy
41 Put out
42 Taking after
43 Candied
46 1969 Three Dog Night hit
47 Is not on the level
49 Genre of 46-Across
50 Slays, in slang
51 Beginning
52 "Lady ___ Train" (1945 film)
53 Cream puff
55 "Coming Home" co-star
56 Sneaky
59 Member of the familia
60 They may make you feel 18-Across
61 Mr. Cat
62 Desperate strategy
63 Stuff of mine

DOWN

1 Definitive statement
2 "Take your choice"
3 Pizarro's quest
4 Fond du ___, Wis.
5 Gentleman of the court
6 In need of repentance
7 Musical interval
8 Saunters
9 Prologue
10 Annuaire listings
11 Actress Thurman
12 Guinea pig, in a way
13 Synthetic
16 Site of ancient Palmyra
20 Luth. teaching, e.g.
24 Yearn
26 Cry out loud
29 Docked
32 Publicity
33 West of Hollywood
35 Shaving wound
36 1988 Connery film, with "The"
37 Unnatural high
38 Intentionally concealed
39 1-Across or 55-Across, e.g.
41 Babies
43 Get together
44 1970's Cambodian leader
45 ___ National Park, Maine
46 Recently
48 Perot follower: Abbr.
50 Yellowish
53 Formerly, formerly
54 Caboose, figuratively
57 Print measures
58 August hrs.

920 · by Mark Diehl

ACROSS

1 Pursuing
6 Part of a Mideast name
9 Bibliophile's suffix
12 Truman biographer ___ Miller
13 Atomic bits
16 Start of a quip
19 Blackmore heroine
20 Sticking spot?
21 Egoiste's concern
22 Event where one stands for a spell
24 Actress Dickinson
26 Suffix with scan
27 Quip, part 2
31 MASH procedure
32 Lend ___ (pay attention)
33 Liza's mentor, to Liza
34 Telecommunications letters
35 Obie-winning dramatist David
38 1982 Michener epic
40 Out of focus
42 Quip, part 3
46 Gives the heave-ho
47 Quilt stuffing
48 "Help!"
49 They make contact in "Contact"
50 Professional runner?
51 Foreign heads of state
54 End of the quip
59 Latin extension
60 Belittle
61 Brood
62 London-to-Lisbon dir.
63 Kind of star

DOWN

1 Grp. with a caduceus
2 Eliot Ness, e.g.
3 Swaps at a car lot
4 One who's tickled
5 Start again from scratch
6 Move over a bit
7 Big ___
8 Fuel for the body
9 Desert mount
10 Veterans Day mo.
11 Tiredness
14 Cop
15 Bird decoy
17 Without substance
18 It comes from a pen
22 Deli order
23 Where hurling originated
25 Like Mitch Miller, e.g.
26 Horror novelist Peter
28 St. Paul's birthplace
29 Memphis setting
30 British peers
34 Not so well-heeled person?
36 Pentagon big
37 Cubist Rubik
39 Patronized an inn
40 Part of W.W. II's Pacific theater
41 Broncos run for them: Abbr.
42 Super-duper
43 Clean up
44 Initiations
45 Bray
50 "Painter of the soul": D'Israeli
52 Nobelist Pavlov
53 Singer McEntire
55 Third-century date
56 1-Down members
57 ___ rule
58 State on the Atl.

921 by Gregory E. Paul

ACROSS

1 Destine to disaster
5 Pepper's partner
9 Fix (in)
14 ___ Major
15 Pop singer Brickell
16 TV's "Kate & ___"
17 Word with land or critical
18 Score before 15
19 One who raises a stink?
20 Famous Wall Street panic
23 Reverse of WNW
24 De-squeaked
25 Travel far and wide
27 Make war
30 Modern refrigerators do it automatically
33 Prefix with cycle
34 Actor Davis
37 Field enclosure
38 Marksman of Swiss legend
40 Exodus mountain
42 Mideast's Gulf of ___
43 Spud
45 Skin: Suffix
47 Yucatan year
48 Well-read
50 Kind of piano
52 Deftness
53 Faint, as through ecstasy
55 Sit-ups firm these
57 1971 Steve McQueen film
62 Officer-to-be
64 Fountain drink
65 Overhang
66 Mannerism
67 Lackawanna's partner in railroading
68 Pavarotti piece
69 Final approval
70 Poetic contraction
71 Old Fords

DOWN

1 Slow-witted
2 Like some vaccines
3 Bones
4 Army's mule, e.g.
5 Concerned only with others
6 Idolize
7 Enraged
8 Ready to be hit, as a golf ball
9 Popular oven cleaner
10 Jan. 15 initials
11 1957 Fats Domino hit
12 One, to Hans
13 Astronaut Slayton
21 Narc's unit
22 "All the Things You ___"
26 Side squared, for a square
27 Montana city
28 Lend ___ (listen)
29 "Voices Carry" pop group
30 Honeybunch
31 Happening place
32 Voice above baritone
35 Team
36 Suffix with elephant
39 Helen's mother, in Greek myth
41 Charlatan
44 Italian rice dish
46 Major League brothers' name
49 Half a score
51 Temper, as metal
53 Trap
54 Poet Elinor
55 ___ of the Apostles
56 Theda of Hollywood
58 "You said it, brother!"
59 Bull's-eye hitter
60 Ardent
61 Yes votes
63 Frozen Wasser

922 by Alan Arbesfeld

ACROSS

1 "Red" tree
6 Tues., for Tuesday
10 Poland's Walesa
14 24 sheets of paper
15 Peeved
16 First name in scat
17 Open, as a bottle
18 They produce a row on the farm
19 Swear
20 "Act your ___!"
21 Elated
24 Opera set in the time of the Pharaohs
25 Hershey brand
26 Elated
31 Handy
32 Large pitcher
33 Triangular sail
36 Fall cleanup need
37 Longed
39 Western writer Grey
40 P, in Greece
41 "Hi-___, Hi-Lo" (1953 film song)
42 Quarterback Brett
43 Elated
46 Countenance
49 Open
50 Elated
53 33 or 45, e.g.
56 It's taken out at the seams
57 Bucket
58 "Behold!"
60 Writer Lindbergh
61 Ever
62 Ballyhooed sitcom of 1997
63 Latvian
64 Lack
65 Chill, so to speak

DOWN

1 Shade of blue
2 It's breath-taking
3 Cut into cubes
4 Stat for Maddux
5 Dinosaur, e.g.
6 Depth charge, in slang
7 Engage, as an entertainer
8 Belgian songwriter Jacques
9 Not showing emotions
10 Ballet dancer, at times
11 Oft-cited sighting
12 Copy
13 Peddles
22 Uganda's Amin
23 Forest denizen
24 Competent
26 Extra-short haircut
27 Bryce Canyon locale
28 Anti-apartheid activist Steven
29 Magic wish granters
30 Be in debt
33 Cawfee
34 Letters for Jesus
35 Miller, for one
37 Join in a football heap
38 Kind
39 Wacky
41 Italy's ___ di Como
42 Eternally
43 Picture gallery site?
44 Threw out, as a runner
45 Word to end a card game
46 Song part
47 Hole-___
48 Meager
51 Scandinavian
52 Enjoyable
53 Brook
54 Emotional request
55 Domestic cat
59 Corrida cry

923 by Hugh Davis

ACROSS

1 They sweep at the regatta
5 Malay for "man"
10 Come to a ___
14 Unbending
15 Rhythmic pattern in poetry
16 Spindle
17 Leaf projection
18 City near Boys Town
19 Strike
20 Oscar winner for "Jerry Maguire"
23 Words to no one in particular
24 Star Wars program: Abbr.
25 Bluesman ___ Mahal
28 Born abroad
29 Certain tennis stroke
33 L.A. suburb near Sherman Oaks
35 Giraffe-like ruminants
37 Whet
38 Noted Italian religious philosopher
43 Advance
44 ___ Beach, Calif.
45 Former Big Apple mayor
48 Certain tide
49 Author LeShan
52 John ___
53 Help-wanted abbr.
55 Exclusive, as circles
57 Longtime welterweight boxing champ
62 Crossword maker's canvas
64 Honored the flag
65 France's 1947 Literature Nobelist
66 Church section
67 The Velvet Fog
68 Neck and neck
69 Hammer's end
70 Alaska's North ___
71 Let

DOWN

1 Garage squirter
2 Stir
3 Pop singer Dupree
4 Three-time Masters champ
5 Sequel to "Typee"
6 San ___, Italy
7 Not much
8 Certain grape sodas
9 Like some dames
10 Requirement of Islam
11 Sweat
12 Everyone
13 Scenic Scottish river
21 Small lizard
22 Ingredient in a boomerang
26 O'Neill's "___ Christie"
27 Smokey ___ (Broadway hit locale)
30 Show-off
31 Translucent gem
32 Galileo, e.g.
34 ___ Pet (novelty item)
35 "Horrors!"
36 Wise guy
38 Musher's need
39 Kind of list
40 Relax
41 Sine ___ non
42 Free, as clothing
46 Disney frame
47 Boosts
49 Salad ingredient
50 Muffle
51 Burning with desire
54 Laud
56 African river
58 Perfect place
59 Fighting bull
60 Gambol
61 Nice notion
62 Econ. statistic
63 TV actress Charlotte

924 by Richard Silvestri

ACROSS

1 Sitar music
5 Gyro bread
9 Weight of a stone
14 NATO member: Abbr.
15 Dark horse
16 Duck
17 Buy everyone beers?
19 Paint ingredient
20 "Go Tell It on the Mountain" family name
21 Japanese seaport
23 "Enough!"
25 Works on pumps, maybe
30 Historical trivia
32 Didn't shuffle
33 Like most houses
36 Change the fight card?
38 "___ takers?"
39 Cheerleader's act
40 Fi leader
41 Omit the lettuce?
44 Dutch genre painter
46 December ocean phenomenon
47 Colorado Governor Roy
49 Beneficiary
51 Meal
54 Off. helper
56 Walk quietly
58 "Sweeney Todd" prop
62 Join the cast?
64 Napoleon's punishment
65 Hydrox alternative
66 Humorist Bombeck
67 Things to worry over
68 Henry VIII's VIth
69 It holds the line

DOWN

1 Actress Diana
2 Sampras and others
3 "Savvy?"
4 Apple-pie order
5 Oktoberfest toast
6 Letters of credit
7 Kind of top
8 Legalese conjunction
9 Keyboard instrument
10 Prize televised on MTV
11 Cagney epithet
12 Suffix with some fruit names
13 Cowboy's moniker
18 Fix, as a sofa
22 Assail
24 Fiesta Bowl site
26 Symbol of sovereignty
27 Relaxed
28 Draw out
29 Take hold
31 Energy choice
33 Display stand
34 Spat spot
35 In competition
37 King of old movies
39 Al Bundy sells them
42 Daughter of Ingrid
43 Star in Scorpio
44 Photo tint
45 Hide seeker
48 Temporary skylight?
50 Bar, by law
52 Look and look and look
53 "Bewitched" singer, 1950
55 Mitchell mansion
57 And others, in brief
58 Yank's foe
59 Dismiss
60 70's–80's Pakistani president
61 Part of O.T.
63 Plop preceder

925 by Harvey Estes

ACROSS

1 Thoroughfares: Abbr.
4 1920's chess champion Capablanca
8 Nubian Desert site
13 Canvas coats?
16 Where to see Ben Franklin's portrait
17 Pump thump
18 Attorney modifier
19 Going around the world
20 Much of boot camp
21 Fax button
22 Give away
23 Projecting part
25 Cry of glee
26 A.C.L.U. concerns: Abbr.
28 Vogue
29 Cigs
30 One of Frank's exes
31 Bill and Bob's opponent
32 Sheds
33 Archly theatrical
34 Ab ___ (from the beginning)
35 Cornerstone of Cartesianism
36 Centers
37 Nonexistent
38 Air France terminal
39 Goggles
40 Threw over
42 !, to a printer
43 Particular
44 Greens, politically
48 Ardent
49 Quid pro quo
50 Sweetie pie
51 Monet subject
52 Physicist Mach
53 Raw material
54 Tarquin's title

DOWN

1 Area near TriBeCa
2 Class
3 Tabletop, perhaps
4 In agreement
5 Upright
6 Actaeon, ultimately, in Greek myth
7 Hrs. in Quebec
8 Hermes accessories
9 Free from restraint
10 Important monetary currency peg
11 Every minute
12 Intelligence
14 Cooler places?
15 Work on, with "to"
20 Hero's list
22 Butler of fiction
23 Support
24 Denouement
25 Young role on TV
27 Drains
28 Suffix in high-tech company names
29 ___-be
32 Prized mushroom
33 Rodeo rider
35 Most moronic
36 Psalms singer
39 Faux pas
41 Exchanges
42 She played Margo in "All About Eve"
43 See
44 Jim Carrey, in a 1997 movie
45 Sensation
46 Scheherazade specialty
47 An oath on it was once held to be inviolable
49 Company number

926 by Robert Goldberg

ACROSS

1 One of the Three B's of classical music
5 Milkshake conduit
10 Church recess
14 Field measure
15 Nile capital
16 Close, as an envelope
17 "Horse Feathers" stars
20 Put in stitches
21 Orders to plow horses
22 Eagle's nest
23 Pencil's innards
24 New York nine
26 Eastern philosophy
29 Scandalous gossip
30 Getty product
33 Broadcasts
34 Larger than quarto
35 9-to-5 grind
36 Genre of 17- and 56-Across
40 Vietnamese holiday
41 Picnic places
42 First murder victim
43 Gawk at
44 Prevaricates
45 Placid
47 Hairless
48 Stocking flaws
49 West Indies, e.g.
52 Connect, as girders
53 Where: Lat.
56 "The Outlaws Is Coming" stars
60 Jacket
61 Hot coal
62 Escape battle
63 "___ springs eternal"
64 Like many attics
65 Classify, as blood

DOWN

1 Cave dwellers
2 Feel sore
3 Rowing sport
4 Skirt's edge
5 Reaction on a roller coaster
6 Burdened
7 Barbecued dish slathered with sauce
8 Flightboard abbr.
9 Court
10 Cigar residue
11 Equal
12 Indian dress
13 "What ___ is new?"
18 Long, long time
19 Skin art
23 Speech problem
24 Dairy products
25 Newsman Sevareid
26 Flavor
27 Choreographer Alvin
28 Declaim
29 Links with a space station
30 Diving bird
31 Poet W.H. ___
32 Flair
34 Out of a job
37 Quite a display
38 Mermaid feature
39 Pathfinder's locale
45 Torrid
46 Inner: Prefix
47 Divine Miss M
48 Stopwatch button
49 Compulsive desire
50 "Begone!"
51 Quantum ___
52 Insect snares
53 Hideous
54 Pager sound
55 Expression of understanding
57 Claret color
58 Ostrich kin
59 Frequently

927 · by Elizabeth C. Gorski

ACROSS

1 Fruit of the Loom rival
6 Where boys will be boys
10 Frost
14 Word with time or rights
15 Indian music
16 Some mutual fund accts.
17 Ingratiate oneself, e.g.
19 Dust busters, for short
20 Film critic Pauline
21 Cuckoo bird
22 Style
23 Original state
27 "Virginia Woolf" dramatist
29 1955 children's heroine
30 Ogle
32 Charged particle
33 Mail carriers have them: Abbr.
37 With 6-Down, operator of a 63-Down
38 Auction offering
40 Butterfly catcher
42 Pitcherful, maybe
43 Droops
45 Post–W.W. II grp.
47 "Shucks!"
49 La Scala productions
52 Shark watchers' protectors
53 Sherlock Holmes player
57 Way in
58 Sale item marking: Abbr.
59 Big exam
62 Pulitzer writer James
63 Words of wisdom
66 "Twittering Machine" artist
67 Gulf war missile
68 Al ___ (firm)
69 Does lawn work
70 Summer shirts
71 Lock of hair

DOWN

1 "Shucks!"
2 Water color
3 Famed trial venue
4 Before now
5 Like Wile E. Coyote
6 See 37-Across
7 Italian cheese or meat dish
8 Give it ___ (try)
9 Roof top
10 Rosie the ___
11 Khomeini, for one
12 Computer shortcut
13 German Pittsburgh
18 The 2% of 2%
22 Dogfaces, today
24 Patricia of "Hud"
25 Twelve ___
26 Ate fancily
27 Word of resignation
28 "Star Wars" princess
31 Radio station need
34 Cousin of an orange
35 Peace Nobelist Wiesel
36 Places for props
39 "Gone With the Wind" setting
41 Guacamole's place
44 Evening get-togethers
46 Rundown feeling
48 Hurried next door, e.g.
50 Thickness
51 Tears up
53 Prominent toucan features
54 The "A" of WASP
55 Riding horse
56 Stagewear for Madonna
60 Plays the part
61 Some popular jeans
63 See 37-Across
64 Serve like Sampras, e.g.
65 Banned pesticide

928 · by Randall J. Hartman

ACROSS

1 They're hailed in cities everywhere
5 Ancient Roman senate house
10 Miles of Hollywood
14 Downwind
15 Mimicking
16 Helicopter builder Sikorsky
17 Compatriot, redundantly
20 Glorify
21 Miss ___ USA
22 Youth org.
23 9C, say
26 Clay pigeons, e.g.
28 St. Louis pro
31 Posted
33 Star in Cetus
34 Guitarist Clapton
36 Diminutive DC Comics superhero, with "The"
38 Quotes
41 Perceptible, redundantly
44 British cavalry weapon
45 Rant's companion
46 Off the hook
47 Paleozoic and Mesozoic
49 All hogwash
51 Tom Hayden's 60's org.
52 Aboveboard
55 Shoot off
57 Mauna ___
58 Long-distance starts
60 Fliers in V's
64 Strategizing, redundantly
68 Tenpenny ___
69 March
70 Crosby, Stills and Nash, e.g.
71 Unit of force
72 Mary of "The Maltese Falcon"
73 Match parts

DOWN

1 Site for a bite
2 " 'World Capitals' for 200, ___"
3 Gymnastics coach Karolyi
4 Moves, as cars
5 Crow's cry
6 It's shown in bars: Abbr.
7 Hit at Catch a Rising Star
8 Estuary
9 Shining brightly
10 Itinerary word
11 They might whip something up in the kitchen
12 Get out of bed
13 Fields
18 Mayberry sot
19 Improve
24 Fervor
25 PC key
27 "Good ___!"
28 Guns, in a way
29 Stage solo
30 Acting up, to Fats Waller
32 Add up
35 Wispy clouds
37 Three-reeler, e.g.
39 Regarded
40 Regards
42 Mariner's aid
43 Swarm
48 Holy places
50 Leo, for one
52 African antelope
53 TV staple since 1/14/52
54 Lustful looks
56 Safari lodgings
59 Fido's cousin
61 Leprechauns' home
62 Huffy state
63 Freudian subjects
65 Pub pint
66 Elton's john
67 Spring mo.

929 by Matt Gaffney

ACROSS

1 Grade school door sign
5 Chesapeake catch
10 Son of Judah
14 Indian tribe
15 Magnificent
16 Scent detection device
17 What's the point of annoying Leno's sheep?
20 60-Across, in other words
21 Served
22 Beverage cart locale
25 Intention
26 Planetary paths
28 "___ will throw thee from my care...": Shak.
30 "Endymion" poet
34 Happy post-accident statement
35 U.S. ally in the American Revolution
37 Best Actor nominee of 1992
38 Singers Starr and Kiki look at each other
41 Author LeShan
42 Lowest A, usually
43 London's ___ of Court
44 Kind of disk
46 Is for two
47 Nutritionist's amts.
48 Rough position?
50 U.S. foe of 1898
52 38-Across, in other words
56 17-Across, in other words
60 Fashion magazine is indebted to a pop group
63 Hammer part
64 Bury
65 Suffix with disk
66 Williams and Knight
67 Duma votes
68 Hardy soul?

DOWN

1 New Year's event
2 Emperor after Galba
3 Fad item of '61
4 Blows
5 Cliff sights
6 Musical notes
7 Information ___
8 Tijuana locale
9 Toil (away)
10 Like some kicks
11 Coward of note
12 "___ forgive those who trespass..."
13 Sine qua non
18 Protection: Var.
19 Pinstriper
23 One of the Bobbitts
24 Sites of some chalk deposits
26 Brazilian writer Jorge
27 Flush variety
29 Shoe section
31 Indianapolis's Market Square ___
32 Oft-rebellious group
33 Act saucy
34 Alibi ___ (excuse makers)
35 Memo letters
36 Baseball's Ron
39 Physicist Fermi
40 Failed to comprehend
45 1986 sci-fi hit
47 Confirmation, e.g.
49 Buzz Aldrin's real first name
51 Australia's ___ Rock
52 Preserved
53 Bauhaus artist
54 ___ 'Oléron (island off 35-Across)
55 Disallow
57 Ballet jump
58 Super Bowl III champs
59 Applications
61 Part of many Québec names
62 "Wanna ___?"

---

930 by Chuck Deodene

ACROSS

1 Honey badger
6 Drivel
14 École attendee
15 Vacation footage, e.g.
17 Microscopist's reagent
18 Smithsonian specialty
19 Dixie desserts
21 Cinnabar et al.
22 Shiraz resident
23 Like some paint
25 Armenian President Levon ___-Petrosyan
26 First name in humor
28 L.A.-based petroleum giant
29 D.C. summer hrs.
30 Freshman language course
32 Stutters
33 Cafeteria wear
34 Texas A & M rival
37 Register
38 Spotted amphibian
41 Egypt's ___ Church
43 Quarries
45 Windswept spot
46 Not aching
47 Marine phosphorescence
49 ___ Grande, Fla.
50 Tropospheric current
52 San Antonio arena
55 1964 #1 hit
56 Energy-saving cooker
57 Grant portrayer
58 Most clement
59 Jurors

DOWN

1 Time-out
2 Not in its original form
3 Server's trolley
4 Lake Geneva spa
5 "Of Mice and Men" character
6 Flexible armor
7 Togo's capital
8 Home of the N.C.A.A.'s Cyclones
9 According to
10 Pa. nuke plant
11 Post-Baroque
12 Profiteer's vice
13 It helps you get a grip
16 Canvas supports
20 Lingo
23 Crescent-shaped windows
24 Module
27 No longer anchored
31 Hard to brush off
33 Scion
34 Takes a dive
35 "Hamlet" highlight
36 Swank
38 French philosopher Gilson
39 One rummaging about
40 Aftershocks
42 Unanimously
44 Despotic governor
48 Thick upholstery fabric
50 Roman Zeus
51 Scottish uncles
53 Scrap
54 It makes a lot of cents: Abbr.

931 by Stephanie Spadaccini

ACROSS
1 Amo, ___, amat (Latin practice)
5 College prep exam
9 Thin and bony
14 Singer-actress Lorna
15 "Picnic" playwright
16 Daddy Warbucks's little girl
17 Prefix with phobia
18 Years and years
19 Get together
20 Demonstrate affection like a plumber?
23 Saharalike
24 ___ Khan (ex of Rita Hayworth)
25 Place to park a car
29 French cheese
31 Krazy ___ of the comics
34 "Tiny" Albee character
35 Tugboat sound
36 Prefix with dynamic
37 What a plumber says to noisy kids?
40 Days before big events
41 Bands' bookings
42 Preferred invitees
43 TV room
44 Therefore
45 Vertebral columns
46 Exploit
47 Gloomy guy
48 Declines, as a plumber?
56 Where Leonardo was born
57 Oklahoma city
58 Atmosphere
59 Part of the pelvis
60 Sicilian blower
61 Ribald
62 "E pluribus unum," e.g.
63 Like a busybody
64 Dummies' replies

DOWN
1 "Woe is me!"
2 Lots of
3 60's hairdo
4 Put away
5 South Dakota's capital
6 Very white
7 Lambs: Lat.
8 Experiment
9 Charles de ___
10 Bother
11 Purdue, e.g.: Abbr.
12 Evening, informally
13 Golfer's gadget
21 Made a border
22 Port-au-Prince's land
25 Stared openly
26 Breathing
27 Get ready to be picked
28 One-spots
29 Beatnik's drum
30 Paddles
31 Enter, as computer data
32 Got up
33 Praises loudly
35 Branch offshoot
36 "___ Wanna Do" (Sheryl Crow hit)
38 Monsters
39 Run out, as a subscription
44 Igloo dweller
45 Half a weekend
46 Not abridged
47 Procures
48 Where fodder is stored
49 Monogram unit: Abbr.
50 High schooler
51 "I'm ___ you!"
52 Voting district
53 Meal on Maui
54 Mezz. alternative
55 Paths
56 Energy

932 by Christopher Page

ACROSS
1 "Holy mackerel!"
5 Shady lady
9 Landscaper's tool
14 California wine valley
15 1847 South Seas adventure
16 Running bowline, e.g.
17 Desert mount
19 7-11 game
20 Full up
21 Aria, usually
23 "j" topper
24 "Yuck!"
25 Place for marbles
29 Baby blues
31 Hillbilly TV fare
35 Strait of Dover port
37 Got some shuteye
38 Hightail it
40 New Zealand native
43 Executive: Abbr.
44 Bit of parsley
46 "You've got my support"
48 Settles bills
50 How many bouquets are made
53 Desperation football pass
56 Native: Suffix
57 Bad Ems, e.g.
60 School sports org.
61 Gave a ticket
63 Caterpillar, for one
65 Irish locale of song
68 Caper
69 Go ___ detail
70 "The Masque of Alfred" composer
71 Kind of answer
72 Kind of tide
73 Humorist Bill and others

DOWN
1 Finishes
2 Home annex
3 Rx purveyor
4 Woman of distinction
5 Physique, slangily
6 Physicians' grp.
7 "What's the ___ that could happen?"
8 "___ mind?"
9 They follow standing ovations
10 Golden, in France
11 Spur
12 Hockey great Phil, familiarly
13 Take five
18 1957 Ford debut
22 ___-di-dah
26 Bygone London transport
27 Part of SEATO
28 Barker
30 Reverend's responsibility
32 Like many titles
33 "Tarzan" extra
34 Lb. and kg.
36 ___-disant (self-styled): Fr.
38 Recipe amt.
39 Emissions tester: Abbr.
41 Pro ___
42 Operatic prince
45 Camel's cousin
47 Rolls's partner
49 Paparazzo's prize
51 Ev'rlasting
52 Goes brunette this time
54 "E pluribus unum," e.g.
55 Bath's state
57 Leave laughing
58 Glazier's unit
59 Theater, opera, etc.
62 Tabriz's land
64 Bordeaux, e.g.
66 Educ. group
67 Top 40 music

933 by Karen Hodge

ACROSS

1 Grist for processors
5 Quizzes
9 Hurt
14 "L'___ c'est moi": Louis XIV
15 Train transportation
16 Word in a Yale song
17 Religious monster?
19 Sound louder than kerplop
20 Swimming pool problem
21 Athos, Porthos and Aramis, e.g.
23 1944 Pulitzer journalist
24 It's rolled out at parties
26 Wooden shoe
28 1940's Big-Band leader
30 Solidarnosc leader
33 Chattering birds
36 Not stiff
38 Frothy
39 Serpent's mark?
40 Popular men's magazine
42 Parisian way
43 "Mefistofele" composer
45 Biology subj.
46 Gets choked up
47 Charles's "Gaslight" co-star, 1944
49 "___ to bed"
51 Solicit cash from
53 Formation of bone
57 Spoils
59 Cream of the crop
61 Junta's act
62 Tigger's adopted mom
64 Macho dance?
66 Signed
67 Sound
68 December air
69 Compote fruit
70 Q-Tip
71 In ___ (existing)

DOWN

1 Make lean?
2 "I could ___ unfold . . .": "Hamlet"
3 Northern evergreen forests
4 Jumps on
5 S.A. republic
6 Patron of bread?
7 Narc's catch, maybe
8 Putdowns
9 Tummy muscles
10 "Apocalypse Now" director
11 Jerusalem?
12 One way to get to Jerusalem
13 Anniversary, e.g.
18 Take, as oral arguments
22 Cut
25 Wear the crown
27 Barbara, to friends
29 Popular appliance maker
31 Overproud
32 Words said in passing?
33 Skater Thomas
34 Shakespeare, the Bard of ___
35 Measure a pop singer?
37 Musical fish?
40 "Go ahead!"
41 Some old Fords
44 Set off
46 "Nice going!"
48 Name
50 Kind of aerobics
52 Pains in the neck
54 Farm towers
55 F.D.R.'s Interior Secretary
56 Several-days-old
57 Pass over
58 Diminish
60 Pack away
63 TV breaks
65 Miss out?

934 by Cathy Millhauser

ACROSS

1 Breeze
5 Appetizer for Juan
9 Cornrows alternative
13 Summer cabin site
14 Curaçao neighbor
16 Cherokee, for one
17 Suffix with sinus
18 Two of a 60's quartet
19 Loads
20 Hacked it, as a farmer?
23 Script scraper
24 Cling to
25 Bill Nye's subj. on TV
28 Forum matter
29 Médoc, merlot, etc.
32 Surpassed
34 Hacked it, as a highway engineer?
36 1986 World Series stadium
39 Long March leader
40 Smeltery input
41 Hacked it, as a candlemaker?
46 Informal hatrack
47 Medal recipient
48 Prefix with pressure
51 Literary inits.
52 Dawn deity
54 Lily-livered
56 Hacked it, as a pelican?
60 Salalah's land
62 "Vive ___!"
63 Restrain
64 [Get the joke?]
65 Microscopy supply
66 Inventor Elisha
67 "Don't be startled"
68 Some are horned
69 Lt. Columbo et al.

DOWN

1 Deli need
2 John Muir's interest
3 Muscular dogs
4 Rats, gnats, etc.
5 Like some jeans legs
6 80's–90's writer Saroyan
7 Kind of platter
8 Discompose
9 Open, but just
10 Crystalline mineral
11 Monogrammatic car of old
12 Choose
15 Perspicacious
21 Sister of Zeus
22 Eagerly excited
26 Grant
27 Middle of a mensis
30 Sample
31 Secret supply
33 Academic handle
34 Handle without care
35 Sharpen
36 Try for a fly
37 Geiger of Geiger counter fame
38 Pop music's Gloria and Emilio
42 Flake (off)
43 Longhaired fad dolls
44 Scamps
45 "Watch out!"
48 Do the Wright thing
49 Larry Bird was one
50 But
53 Handle
55 Prior's superior
57 Black and wet
58 Tie
59 Labor
60 Have a tab
61 Veterans' concern, briefly

935 · by Rich Norris

ACROSS

1 Gravely ill, once
6 Big name in auto supplies
10 Alphabet trio
13 Damfool thing
14 Machetes
15 Appear indecisive
16 Comics hero since 1947
18 Porter
19 Beers, maybe
20 Request of Rhonda, in a 1965 Beach Boys hit
22 Heavenly route
23 Consider appropriate
26 Have another picture taken
27 Helm of fiction
29 Stop using
31 Left
32 Invoice fig.
34 Unfair
36 Beverly Sills contemporary
39 Tom or Daisy of "The Great Gatsby"
40 1981 Tony winner McKellen
41 North Carolina county on the Blue Ridge Parkway
42 __-Roman
44 Trudge
48 More remote
50 Tanker's cargo
52 Provoke
53 Old nursery song word
55 V.I.P.
57 Wing
58 Subject of a 1930's mystery
61 "Norma __"
62 Anonym
63 Thunderstorm product
64 A.A.R.P. members
65 Cord fiber
66 Fast times

DOWN

1 F.B.I. sting of the late 70's
2 1962 monster film
3 Like "The Zoo Story," e.g.
4 Guns
5 Stuck
6 Prefix with dairy
7 One of the Khans
8 "Fiddlesticks!"
9 Seven-time Emmy winner
10 Liszt piece
11 Gene Krupa portrayer, 1959
12 Chirped
14 Computer language
17 Ready to break, as a wave
21 Multitudes
24 Certain witticism
25 1880 literary heroine
28 Wolfpack opponent
30 Kind of table
33 Hit song of 1959
35 Overseas Mrs.
36 Powerful
37 Victim of Paris
38 One whose work's a bust
39 Emergency boat workers
43 Salad ingredients, briefly
45 Maker of Wish-Bone salad dressing
46 Break in, so to speak
47 Categories
49 Indian chief
51 Register
54 Winter time
56 Goggle
59 Lower, in a way
60 Break

936 · by Gregory E. Paul

ACROSS

1 Separate, as flour or ashes
5 Forum language
10 Paul Bunyan's ox
14 Doughnut's middle
15 Primitive calculators
16 Military no-show
17 Bit of physics
18 "Dear friend!"
19 Door sound
20 Overjoyed
23 April 15 initials
24 Paper purchases
28 Egg-rolling time
32 Reddish-brown horse
35 Copper, e.g.
36 Greeting at sea
37 Hush-hush govt. group
38 Highly pleased with oneself
42 Afternoon hour on a sundial
43 Info
44 Country singer Crystal
45 Garbage-marauding critters
48 Present and future, e.g.
49 Borden's cow
50 Forbid
51 Bonkers
59 Opposite of all
62 Perch
63 "__ to leap tall buildings . . ."
64 Skunk's defense
65 TV duo Kate and __
66 Carbonated drink
67 Overhaul
68 Bread maker
69 Trial balloon

DOWN

1 Mideast ruler of years past
2 Small amount
3 Dud
4 Office fill-in
5 Actress Hedy
6 Vast chasm
7 Novelist Janowitz
8 Suffix with poet
9 One of Columbus's ships
10 Two-pointer
11 Cobbler's tool
12 Feathered stole
13 Shade tree
21 Submit
22 Four Monopoly properties: Abbr.
25 Pesters
26 Biceps, e.g.
27 Belmont __
28 Sovereign's domain
29 Antenna
30 Zeno and others
31 Fraternity "T"
32 Cowboy's wear
33 Aspiration
34 Hurricane's center
36 "Unto us __ is given"
39 Fuss
40 60's rocket stage
41 Soup container
46 Roman orator
47 Poet's preposition
48 Sampler
50 Count of jazz
52 Lebanese, e.g.
53 Defender of Dreyfus
54 Egg part
55 Wear well
56 Mitch Miller's instrument
57 The "O" in R.E.O.
58 Peachy-keen
59 Neither's partner
60 "__ to a Nightingale"
61 Doze (off)

937 by Nancy Salomon

ACROSS

1 Catherine who survived Henry VIII
5 Eden dweller
9 ___-ski
14 Theater award
15 Timber wolf
16 Fit to be tied
17 Dieter's credo?
19 One of Lear's daughters
20 French farewell
21 Program airing
23 State of high alarm
26 Praiseful poem
27 Dieter's credo?
32 Pitcher's pride
35 First name in scat
36 Flood embankment
37 Hijinks in a stolen car
40 Determines limits in advance
42 Had title to
43 Regarding
45 Realize
46 Dieter's credo?
50 Calamity
51 Comic musical work
55 Mt. Rainier's site, with "the"
59 "___ Pretty" (song for Maria)
60 Anticipate
61 Dieter's credo?
64 It results from work well done
65 Gamblers' mecca
66 This, in Mexico
67 Polk's predecessor
68 Dutch cheese
69 Bygone Tunisian V.I.P.'s

DOWN

1 Kind of bear
2 Stand for
3 Unbending
4 Fix, as leftovers
5 Draught, maybe
6 Mafia boss
7 Act of touching
8 Wear a long face
9 Terrier type
10 Comes before
11 Indian music style
12 Greek H's
13 On its way, as a message
18 Noted site of ancient Mexican ruins
22 British john
24 Managed, with "out"
25 Take the reins again
28 Portable PC
29 Place to broil
30 Lavish party
31 Suffix with gab or slug
32 "Get ___" (1958 hit)
33 English poet laureate Nicholas
34 Popular pet bird
38 Killing of a king
39 Blind worshiper
41 Banned Pete
44 Stinko
47 Like the gray mare
48 Actor Estrada
49 Officiated a game
52 Rib
53 Irascible
54 Choir voices
55 Nemo, e.g.: Abbr.
56 Not straight
57 Leave dock
58 To be, in France
62 One-million link
63 ___ de guerre

938 by Wayne Robert Williams

ACROSS

1 Flaccid
5 Writer Ferber
9 Port of Iraq
14 Neighborhood
15 Picture of a physician
16 Old-time strongman
17 Alternative to a tuning fork
19 New York city or its college
20 Mil. entertainers
21 "Sorry 'bout that!"
22 Some binary compounds
23 Apollo as god of the sun
25 Preserved for later
26 Wasn't fast . . . or was fast?
27 Joke's target
28 Darling of baseball
31 Car crime
35 Practice piece
37 Folk singer Phil
38 "___ I Don't Have You" (1959 hit)
40 Holm oak
41 Makes holes
43 Practical experiment
45 Lennon's widow
46 Potter's need
48 Guy's date
49 "Missing You" singer John
51 Stanches
55 Some T-shirts
57 Piano-violin piece
58 Stage signal
59 Masseur's offering
60 Get sick in the winter
62 Lacking sense
63 Melville novel
64 Church area
65 Shot out beams
66 Actress Armstrong
67 Symbol on California's flag

DOWN

1 Drink like a cat
2 ___ Sweeps Derby
3 "I want to, as well"
4 It washes Wash.
5 Explains in detail
6 Nerds
7 Siestas
8 Nautical assent
9 Principal ore of aluminum
10 Room at the top
11 Obsolete math aid
12 Family of man
13 Gray and others
18 White House architect James
22 Neighbor of Man.
24 Expunge
25 Light weight
27 Russian novelist Ivan
29 Some old poetry
30 Waiting room call
31 Wandering soul
32 Computer image
33 Dispose of
34 Search messily
36 Library catalogue heading
39 "View of Toledo" and "Adoration"
42 Adept
44 Vader of "Star Wars"
47 "___ a Living"
50 Coeur d'___, Idaho
51 Cars
52 Purview
53 Oklahoma city
54 Passover meal
55 Be up and about
56 Actress Washbourne
57 Lady's title
60 Male swan
61 Semi part

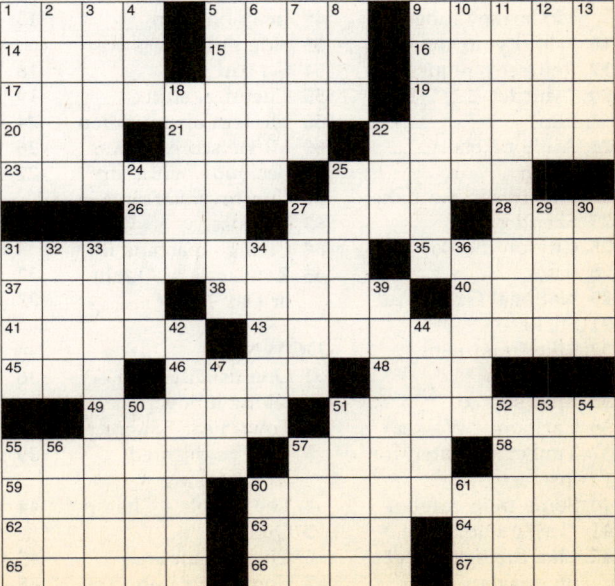

939 · by Mark Diehl

ACROSS
1 Checked for prints
7 "What fools these mortals be" writer
13 Under close scrutiny
15 Apple variety
16 Hopper
18 Wee
19 Lesley of "60 Minutes"
20 Fire ___
21 Sweeping
23 Put the pedal to the metal
24 Release forcibly
26 Birthplace of Columbus
28 Quarterback play
31 Sidewalk stand offering
32 Cold war grp.?
34 1963 Shirley MacLaine role
35 Russian river in a Sholokhov title
36 Skipper
41 Bother
42 Duds
43 Scratch the surface
44 Member of 32-Across
45 Master's degree requirement
47 Plows
51 Snaillike
53 Pastoral sounds
55 What chimney sweeps sweep
56 No-show
58 Kipling story setting
60 "___ Vadis?"
61 Jumper
64 "Driving Miss Daisy" co-star
65 Like TV's Ninja Turtles
66 So-called "Gateway to Australia"
67 Like Felix vis-à-vis Oscar

DOWN
1 Golf course feature
2 Green
3 Leader born in Georgia
4 Lead-in with angle
5 One overseas
6 Pub diversion
7 Taste
8 Within: Prefix
9 Tidal points
10 Lark
11 Came to visit
12 King Kong, e.g.
14 Track and field attempts
15 Skyscraper workers
17 The house white, perhaps
22 Kind of tar
25 Proceed
27 Southwest friend
29 ___ radio
30 Measure of purity
33 Gelatin substitute
36 Roams
37 Blind devotion
38 Cattle drive hazard
39 Like Scheherazade
40 Tennessee's state flower
46 1978 co-Nobelist
48 Plumlike fruit
49 Airport V.I.P. section
50 He brought Dracula to life
52 Common door sign
54 Police car device
57 Citrus fruit
59 To ___ (perfectly)
61 Qualifiers
62 Thumbs down
63 Genetic stuff

940 · by Chuck Deodene

ACROSS
1 Andean shrub
5 ___ Sanctorum
9 Crayola color
14 Caspian Sea feeder
15 1966 Lennon-McCartney tune
16 "Hold your tongue!"
17 Refugee's request
20 "Murder, ___" (1960 film)
21 Author Robert ___ Butler
22 Jazz trumpeter Baker
23 Skeptics
25 City on the Po
28 Fate
29 National Gallery ___
31 Slicker
32 Like fraudulent accidents
35 Milk source
36 Cartoonist Walker
37 Timber or water, for instance
40 Some train cargoes
41 "Undoubtedly"
42 Like the risk to bet on, maybe
43 "What a ___!" (beach comment)
44 Reno game
46 "Chuang Tzu" principle
47 Prefix with sphere
49 Infamous pen
53 Side in a 1980's war
54 Go bad
55 Chemical suffix
56 Modern air munition
60 Movie scorer Straus
61 Beclouds, with "up"
62 Controversial ripener
63 Verbose
64 Change machine fill
65 Rowlands of "Light of Day"

DOWN
1 One usually seen taking a bow
2 Town near Bangor
3 They're deemed worth taking
4 The People's Champ
5 Quick
6 Chicago suburb
7 Commuter hub
8 Completely
9 Gist
10 Industrialist Guggenheim
11 Babe Ruth, in 1914
12 French crown
13 "The One I Love" group
18 Barely walk
19 Taylor or Hayes, e.g.
24 Counterfeit
26 Busters
27 Chamber group, perhaps
30 Knock out, so to speak
32 Brahmins
33 Place to see a hanged man, e.g.
34 Dawn-till-dusk
36 Marshal under Napoleon
38 Roarer
39 ___ about (publicly visible)
44 Without a cover at night
45 Gunk
48 Expanses
50 Garnish leaf
51 Pitcher, of a sort
52 Kind of crossing
56 Part of a trunk
57 ___ precaution
58 Subject of a grainy picture?
59 Nab

941 by Randy Sowell

ACROSS

1 Response to an insult
5 Tibetan monk
9 Snack chip
14 Prefix with dynamic
15 Pastoral poem
16 "Not you ___!"
17 Expressway access
18 Big bag
19 Saltine brand
20 Attractions near the Nile
23 Doorway
24 Elderly
25 Orthodontist's org.
28 Sights around road repairs
33 "Quiet!"
36 Fishing equipment
37 ___ Ababa
38 Rural outing
41 Fine gold and enamelware
43 Viper
44 Swiss peak
45 Question's opposite: Abbr.
46 1, 8, 27, 64, etc.
51 That: Sp.
52 It's 21% oxygen
53 Stallone title role

57 Components of some auto engines
62 Screen symbols
64 Grand Dragon's group
65 Barely passing grades
66 "___ and Punishment"
67 Table of contents, e.g.
68 ___ spumante (wine)
69 18 on a golf course
70 Canyon effect
71 Distribute, with "out"

DOWN

1 "Beetle Bailey" character
2 Gain knowledge
3 Medieval helmet
4 Warhol's genre
5 Have trouble with esses
6 "An apple ___ . . ."
7 Sherlock Holmes's brother
8 Acid neutralizer
9 "Schindler's List" villain
10 Elderly

11 Prophetess of Greek myth
12 Strike
13 "Put ___ Happy Face"
21 Scandinavian war god
22 1600, to Cato
26 Condescend
27 Biblical beasts of burden
29 Common conjunction
30 Finder's ___
31 Taxi
32 "___ to the West Wind"
33 Mold
34 Devil's domain
35 Swift watercraft
39 Third man in the ring
40 Anger
41 Winter bug
42 Police alert, for short
44 Kind of paint
47 Convertible or coupe, e.g.
48 Amuse
49 White-tailed eagle
50 Iraq's Hussein
54 Reagan Attorney General Edwin

55 Royals great George
56 Actor Davis
58 "This one's ___"
59 Applies
60 Whip

61 "What's gotten ___ you?"
62 German "I"
63 ___-Magnon

942 by Patrick Jordan

ACROSS

1 Start to form, as a storm
5 "___-Dick"
9 Christie's Miss Marple
13 Exude
14 Village Voice award
15 Miser Marner
16 Where this answer goes
19 Singing syllable
20 Mysterious loch
21 Utah mountains
22 Villa d'___
23 Up to the task
24 Goodyear fleet
27 Train storage area
31 W.W. II hero Murphy
32 Seas, to Cousteau
33 Go a-courtin'
34 What this answer does
38 Suffix with ranch
39 ". . . unto us ___ is given"
40 Contemptible one
41 Narrow-necked bottle
44 Cried like a baby

45 Word with slicker or hall
46 Guns, as an engine
47 "Lucky" dice rolls
50 ___ over (carry through)
51 Point of decline
54 What this answer seems to have
57 Book with legends
58 The triple in a triple play
59 Author Bagnold
60 Exude
61 Phoenix neighbor
62 Thanksgiving dishes

DOWN

1 Ring engagement
2 First sound in an M-G-M film
3 Poet Pound
4 Little piggy's cry
5 Some MOMA paintings
6 More than plump
7 Strained pea catchers
8 Biblical affirmative
9 Small bus
10 Heaps
11 Cape Canaveral org.

12 Gentlemen: Abbr.
15 Expertise
17 Without obligation
18 Picasso-Braque movement
22 Bahrain bigwig
23 Hammerin' Hank
24 Bundled, as straw
25 Riches
26 Manner of speaking
27 Scouting mission
28 Horrendous
29 Stir from slumber
30 Parceled (out)
32 Like fine netting
35 Chinese philosopher
36 Football team quorum
37 Starts a crop
42 Polar feature
43 Pixie and Dixie's nemesis, in the cartoons
44 Mythological woman with unruly hair
46 Laughfests
47 Mineral springs
48 Suffix with cigar
49 Reprehensible
50 Veracious
51 Sicilian peak
52 Cup lip

53 Political campaigns
55 Mr. Turkey
56 Susan of "Looker"

943 by Janet R. Bender

ACROSS

1 Employee's reward
6 Person from Muscat
11 Civil War alliance: Abbr.
14 ___-garde
15 Repairman
16 Cause friction
17 Nervousness
19 Slippery fish
20 Lover of Sir Lancelot
21 Dawn goddess
22 Take it easy
23 Chooses
25 Computer-telephone link
27 Some New Year's resolutions
29 Gallows loops
32 Muppeteer Henson
35 Former pro footballer, briefly
37 Like mountains in winter
38 Very dry
40 Batman's sidekick
42 Yemeni port
43 Hotel employee
45 Words mouthed at a TV camera
47 "We ___ Not Alone" (1939 film)
48 Short sock
50 "Frasier" character
52 Red wine
54 Outline
58 Part of Q.E.D.
60 Prof's deg.
62 Jelly used for fuel
63 Coffeemaker
64 Numbskulls
66 Ripen
67 Out-of-date
68 Stan's partner, for short
69 Actress Susan
70 Place for grandma's trunk
71 Yorkshire city

DOWN

1 "___ in Toyland"
2 Small egg
3 Birth-related
4 Loose, as shoelaces
5 Sign painter's aid
6 Not at work
7 Miss's equivalent, in a saying
8 Adage
9 Actor Liam
10 April check payee: Abbr.
11 Certain soft drink
12 Mideast canal
13 Skillful
18 Open up a rip again
22 Hotelier Helmsley
24 ___ Brewery Co., of Detroit
26 Opposite of no-nos
28 Polio vaccine developer
30 Pitcher
31 Auld lang ___
32 Jakarta's island
33 Ayatollah's land
34 Small allowance for a schoolchild
36 Copycat
39 Took out
41 Like a win-win situation
44 "Nightline" host Koppel
46 Cough drop ingredient
49 Formal headgear
51 "The Spectator" essayist
53 Treasure container
55 Papal vestment
56 Ruined
57 What everything's coming up, in song
58 College area
59 Encourage
61 Lucy's husband
64 Bean counter, for short
65 Dry, as wine

944 by Jim Page

ACROSS

1 At first
7 Nudists
15 Sarge's superiors
16 Not to mention
17 Practice pieces
18 I.B.M. laptop
19 "___ dieu!"
20 Pet-carrier feature
22 Wee, to Burns
23 Bygone empire
25 Critic Roger
26 Lampblack
27 Trail
29 "At Seventeen" singer
30 Hobbits' home, with "The"
31 Late pop singer Franchi et al.
33 Whirlpools
35 Bar degree
36 "Unaccustomed ___ . . ."
37 Knight mares?
40 Scale
44 Family of Danish physicists
45 Certain suckler
47 Lake Tanganyika discoverer John
48 Cries for Joselito
49 Skating event
51 Lith. and Lat., once
52 Battle of Britain grp.
53 Compared
55 Daisy ___
56 Like Oedipus's curse in "Oedipus Rex"
58 Flip out
60 Nonuple
61 "FoxTrot" pet, in the funnies
62 Masthead names
63 Types

DOWN

1 The Rebels
2 Never
3 Disco feature
4 Auxiliary
5 "Did You Ever ___ Lassie?"
6 "Ah, Wilderness!" mother
7 Gibson of tennis
8 Renders harmless, in a way
9 Listing
10 Long hair
11 Nature
12 Bulb cover
13 Bewitches
14 Put under
21 Results of cleanup work?
24 Bass players?
26 Cocktail contents
28 Game pieces
30 O.K.s, in Toledo
32 "Hmm . . . !?"
34 ___-Mart
37 Glassed-in porches
38 Winkler role
39 Potted maritime plant
40 Geneva research ctr.
41 Tarnish
42 Chernobyl setting
43 Spanish cabbage
44 Ho-hum
46 Handles
49 Ornamental loop
50 Baseball exec Bud
53 Ride
54 Venetian V.I.P.
57 Name-dropper's word
59 It rises at dawn

945 by Alex Vaughn

ACROSS

1 Make silly
6 Undergoes
9 Out of cards in a suit
13 Peter ___ Tchaikovsky
14 Common-sense
15 River through Aragon
16 Ballgoer
17 Puling
19 Happy spymaster?
21 Heartfelt
22 Record-owning
25 Poolroom aid
26 "And thereby hangs ___"
28 A party to
29 Kind of beer
30 Interpretation
31 Summoned
32 Happy Wagner hero?
35 Trekkie idol
38 Province
39 Subject of academic study
42 Viking deity
43 Hodgepodge
45 ___ spumante
46 Certain riding horses
48 Like many gardens
50 Happy ex-Mayor of New York?
52 Play backup for
54 Make fit
56 "Damn Yankees" vamp
57 Plunked items
58 Eugene who wrote "Wynken, Blynken and Nod"
59 58-Across, e.g.
60 Minster seat
61 Business concern

DOWN

1 Dribble guard
2 Like a Thomas Gray work
3 Schoolmaster's order
4 Word of the hour?
5 Yonder
6 Doubter's outbursts
7 Member of a very old kingdom
8 Dotty, perhaps
9 Antonio or Bassanio, e.g.
10 Compliant
11 Investigator's employer: Abbr.
12 Hairstyles
14 Hon
18 Inadequately
20 Boardroom easel display
21 ___ Lanka
23 Miney follower
24 Omega
27 Year's record
30 Modern ink source
31 Singer Zadora
32 Item aboard a merchant ship
33 Awards for Sheryl Crow
34 Overhaul a soundtrack
35 Jean, for one
36 Witness's reply
37 Wonderwork
39 Pequod hand
40 Bell site
41 Prefix with life or wife
43 Grab
44 Tremulous
45 Park in Maine
47 Issue materiel
49 Toronto Maple ___
51 Resurgently
52 Swiss eminence
53 Pigeon sound
55 Kingdome scores, for short

946 by Brendan Emmett Quigley

ACROSS

1 It's hailed by city dwellers
5 "The final frontier"
10 Philosopher David
14 Plow pullers
15 Director Welles
16 Ukraine's Sea of ___
17 One socially challenged
18 Scottish estate owner
19 "Oh, my!"
20 Bad news
23 Philosopher John
24 It comes from the heart
28 Tampa neighbor, informally
31 Maladroit
33 "Common Sense" pamphleteer
34 Equestrian's handful
36 Smidgen
37 Lots of activity
41 Baseball stat
42 Like Superman's vision
43 Less tanned
44 Kickoff response
47 TV journalist Poussaint et al.
48 Highway curves
49 Window cover
51 Like some chicken
57 Talk
60 Alternatives to suspenders
61 Keen
62 One for the road
63 $100 bill
64 Reply to the Little Red Hen
65 "That was a close one!"
66 Planted
67 Word with high or hole

DOWN

1 Chinese dynasty
2 Skater's move
3 Dry: Prefix
4 Slothful
5 Comfort giver
6 Short-sheeting a bed, e.g.
7 Stage remark
8 Part of a parachute
9 Prefix with -morph
10 Upper part of a barn
11 Terrorist's weapon
12 Swab
13 "The Three Faces of ___"
21 "Psycho" setting
22 Sturdy furniture material
25 Tot's noisemaker
26 Rose's home, in song
27 Common vipers
28 Globe
29 Ford model
30 Galileo's kinsmen
31 Amos's partner
32 Part of "www"
34 Luke preceder
35 Santa ___, Calif.
38 First-rate: Abbr.
39 Flip over
40 Shoal
45 Confer (upon)
46 Volcano detritus
47 Got the suds out
49 "Look out ___!"
50 Starbucks serving
52 Kindergarten instruction
53 Gambling game
54 The Bard's river
55 Toy with a tail
56 Singer Brickell
57 Beret
58 "Come again?"
59 Noshed

947 by Thomas W. Schier

ACROSS

1 Title car in a 1964 song
4 Month after marzo, in Mexico
9 Indian prince
14 Urban music
15 Tired
16 Uneven, as the border of a leaf
17 Oscar director for "Gentleman's Agreement"
19 ___ Moore stew
20 N.Y. neighbor
21 Oscar actress for "The Accidental Tourist"
23 Dramatist Eugene
25 Taboo
26 Oscar actress for "Shampoo"
30 Doctrine: Suffix
33 Easy golf putt
36 In ___ land (spacy)
37 Make eyes at
38 Pleasingly mirthful
39 Rocker Brian
40 ___ water (facing trouble)

41 In unison, musically
42 Johann Sebastian ___
43 Stop holding
44 ___ de mer
45 Oscar actor for "Forrest Gump"
47 Bank job?
49 Shoot-'em-ups
53 Oscar actor for "The Color of Money"
58 Region
59 Beckon to enter
60 Oscar actor for "Harry and Tonto"
62 Depart
63 Fiend
64 "___ Got Sixpence"
65 Concentrated beam
66 Plant disease
67 Always, to a poet

DOWN

1 Artist El ___
2 Eagle's claw
3 Think out loud
4 Parrot's cry
5 Snoopy, for one
6 Bring down the house
7 Hymn "Dies ___"

8 City northeast of Boston
9 Measles symptom
10 Suffix with sect
11 Oscar actor for "Coming Home"
12 Italian wine center
13 Cries of surprise
18 Dye ingredient
22 "___ Karenina"
24 Pre-Easter season
27 Flash of light
28 Cowhand's home
29 Hilo hello
31 Work long and hard
32 "Take ___ your leader"
33 Monorail unit
34 Verdi opera
35 Oscar actor for "Watch on the Rhine"
37 Poor movie rating
40 Actress Chase
42 Snack for a dog
45 Leather worker
46 Sarge, for one
48 Martini garnish
50 "Sesame Street" regular

51 Christopher of "Superman"
52 Pop singer Leo
53 Cast a ___ over
54 On the briny
55 Walk in the surf
56 60's TV horse
57 "Look ___!"
61 Literary olio

948 by Shannon Burns

ACROSS

1 Game for the Joy Luck Club
9 Eyepiece, in jargon
15 Ornamental shrub
16 Sport from 4-Down
17 Spitfire, e.g.
18 Alonso or Markova of ballet
19 Slangy approval
20 Sound system staple
22 "I ___ idea!"
25 Lucky people?
26 Schedule abbr.
27 Like Herriman's Kat
30 Vietnamese coin
33 Cagey one?
35 1990–91 World Grand Prix champion
37 Montezuma, e.g.
38 With greater frequency
40 Retreats
41 Dodge cars
43 ___-Cat
44 French equivalent of the Oscar
45 It may be easily bruised

46 Max von ___
49 "The Wild Duck" playwright
51 Cinematic techniques
54 Nouvelle Caledonie, e.g.
55 Herschel discovered it
56 Orange-flowered plant
61 Frost in New England
62 Vast river basin
63 Team stat
64 Start of years past?

DOWN

1 Level the playing field?
2 Like
3 "And I Love ___"
4 "Walk, Don't Run" setting, 1966
5 Spectators
6 Site of Theo. Roosevelt Natl. Park
7 O.T. book
8 Adopt Hellenism
9 Relative of a giraffe
10 Demands, with "for"

11 'Umble Dickens character
12 Filigreed
13 What some games end in
14 Stern
21 Timber diseases
22 Old TV series based on a cartoon
23 Bouquets
24 Visitor
28 Vintage auto
29 Preserves flavor
31 "___ Song" (John Denver hit)
32 Anxious
34 Oils obtained from petroleum, coal or wood
35 Boil, perhaps
36 "Backdraft" crime
39 Monk's title
42 Rather, for one
47 Cahn-Styne's "___ My Girl"
48 Checks for prints
50 Fathered
51 Roll up
52 Ending with buck or stink

53 Pats
54 Neighbor of Turkmenistan
57 Start of Cain's query
58 Bit of binary code

59 Hammarskjold's predecessor
60 Rather, for one

949 by A.J. Santora

ACROSS

1 Santa ___
5 School subj.
9 McEntire and others
14 He follows the news
15 Perry creator
16 La Scala cheer
17 Jewish month
18 Kind of companion
19 Minipicture, maybe
20 Gawks
23 Six-foot Australian
24 Brilliance
25 Double curve
26 Uphill conveyance
27 Get it
28 Jumping-off place?
31 Squire
32 Sylvester's co-star in "Rocky"
33 Per ___
38 Expense
39 About-face
40 Luxurious
43 A long way to go?
46 "Give ___ break!"
49 Manual offerings
50 Hurler Hershiser
51 Clemson athlete

53 Indian whose tribe's name means "lovers of sexual pleasure"
54 Fastening device
56 Thoughtful sort
58 Slammer
59 First word in Massachusetts's motto
60 Utopias
61 ". . . ___ saw Elba"
62 Gulf capital
63 Back to zero, perhaps
64 Reddish-brown gem
65 Whipping site at sea

DOWN

1 Luce and others
2 Truncate
3 Impotent
4 Anthony Quinn title role
5 Semitic lang.
6 Magnetite, e.g.
7 Fruity liqueur
8 Like an old pay telephone call
9 Stat for which Cecil Fielder once led the A.L.

10 West end?
11 Summer game
12 Church recitation
13 Start of TV Guide listings
21 Bug-eyed monsters
22 Stag party staple
26 In every respect
29 Couples grp.
30 A.C. measure
33 Account, in a way
34 Disposition
35 They may be cross
36 Angers
37 Demolitionist's supply
38 Its symbol is an omega
40 Expresses
41 Pseudo fat
42 Less clear, as river water
44 Milit. rank
45 Milit. school
46 Where Kampala is
47 Physiological pentad
48 Eager
52 Skyscraper construction unit

54 Start for while
55 Crocus or freesia, e.g.
57 Wind dir.

950 by Trip Payne

ACROSS

1 ___ center
4 Protection against chills
9 Biting
14 Listening device
15 Shire of "For Richer, For Poorer"
16 Paint ingredient
17 Saddam Hussein's title
20 Playful water animal
21 "Speed" name
22 Popular N.B.A. nickname
23 They avail themselves of Vail
26 ___ Canals
29 "The Joy Luck Club" author
30 A & W rival
31 Con job
32 This is one for the books
33 Dwellers along the Volga
35 Informative dialogues
38 Not moving
39 Resell at inflated prices
40 Run amok
41 Marquee names

42 %: Abbr.
45 Computer's "guts," for short
46 Bomb tryouts
48 Prefix with space or stat
49 Title for Cervantes
51 Persian Gulf nation
52 Most typewriters have them
57 Spine-tingling
58 Freeze
59 "Hold On Tight" rock group
60 Office furniture
61 Part of a spool
62 "___ Miserables"

DOWN

1 Send another E-mail message
2 Actress Kitt
3 Canea resident
4 Move a muscle
5 "It ___ to Be You"
6 Pintful, perhaps
7 Take the gold
8 Potato pancakes
9 Code words for "A"
10 He went east of Eden
11 Ancient Italian

12 Stephen of "The Crying Game"
13 Diagonal chess capture
18 Et ___ (and the following)
19 "The Star-Spangled Banner" preposition
23 1978 Peace Prize winner
24 Actor Kristofferson
25 Mensa hurdles
27 Galley items
28 Meditation syllables
30 Signs of winter's end
31 Word in an octagon
32 Work without ___ (risk injury)
33 Some Romanovs
34 Suffers
35 Common swab
36 Firebrands
37 Imitate Mel Torme
38 Pinball path
41 Pianist Rudolf
42 "Stormy" sea bird
43 Hold protectively
44 Some sculptures
46 Poker payments
47 Slinky or yo-yo
48 Motel approver, briefly

50 Estrada of "CHiPs"
51 Hebrew letter before resh
52 Proof finale
53 Minuscule

54 "The Island of the Day Before" author
55 To date
56 Tampa Bay player, for short

951 by John R. Conrad

ACROSS
1 Smart
5 Diminished by
10 E, in Morse code
13 Nimbus
14 Makes amends (for)
16 Morn's opposite
17 Part of B.P.O.E.
18 Like some regions
19 Levy
20 No middle ground, successwise
23 Corn serving
24 Mornings, for short
25 Like some history
28 "Beau ___"
31 Not guzzle
32 ___ firma
33 Sounds from the stands
34 Approximately
36 Trial judge Lance
37 Dad's mate
38 Bit of hope
39 Turndowns
40 Words before taking the plunge
43 Certain breakout
44 Channels
45 Married
46 Newspapers
47 At bats, e.g.
48 Eternal queen, of book and film
49 Former Mideast merger: Abbr.
50 Eventually
56 Hawaiian necklace
58 ___ to go (eager)
59 The Clintons' alma mater
60 Possess
61 Pindar's country
62 Class with a Paul Samuelson text
63 Entreat
64 Pothook shapes
65 1958 Presley #1 hit

DOWN
1 One whose work causes a stir?
2 Robust
3 Actress Chase
4 Pampers
5 Estate home
6 Anatomical passage
7 Foul
8 Free
9 Appears
10 Hoped-for effect of having a big military
11 Eggs
12 Cowhand's nickname
15 ___ Lanka
21 ___ kwon do
22 Christmas carol
26 Cases for insurance detectives
27 Maidens
28 Operates, as a hand organ
29 Patronize restaurants
30 Highlighting
31 In an undetermined place, in dialect
32 Attempt
34 Back-to-work time: Abbr.
35 Paddle
37 ___ Olson (ad character)
41 Director Preminger
42 Eastern thrushes
43 In formation
46 Buddy
48 Trap
49 Prods
51 Assoc.
52 A long time ago
53 Sandwich with fixin's
54 Carolina college
55 1996 Tony musical
56 High return
57 Farm mother

952 by Manny Nosowsky

ACROSS
1 With 58-Across, 35-Across
9 Kind of cage
15 "Messiah," e.g.
16 Chicago Mrs.
17 Getting to the bottom of things?
18 Like a paramecium
19 ___ pooped to pop
20 The Force was with him
21 Problem-laden chores
22 Have trust
23 Stop making a scene?
24 Far from sharp
27 Good Citizens contest sponsor: Abbr.
28 They're filled with tracks
31 A raft, in diner slang
32 Where Edna Ferber was born
35 See 1-Across
37 Lingua franca, for some
38 Hub
39 A.A.A. suggestion
40 Itty-bitty
41 Didn't dawdle
42 Barbed comments
44 Cooped (up)
45 Duke's deputy in "Measure for Measure"
48 Twist in a drink
49 Bit of work
52 Writer aboard the Beagle
53 Jump past
55 Not in quantity
56 Proteus and Valentine, for two noted examples
57 Whence much color of fall
58 See 1-Across

DOWN
1 Between half and all
2 Snack since 1912
3 Kind of forces
4 Baseball All-Star, 1934–44
5 You needn't press it
6 Firebird
7 Popular 30's dance
8 Kind of master
9 City in Genesis
10 Massey of "Balalaika"
11 Stop working so hard
12 Roasting platform
13 Lawyer/writer Gardner
14 Chrome yellow and others
22 Charlotte ___
23 Face lost in the crowd
24 Besides what's here
25 Leg up
26 Mole-colored
27 He went through Hell
28 Like Milos Forman
29 Like life in Italy, maybe
30 "Alas"
32 "___ War" (Nick Stone book series)
33 The folks
34 Controversial event
36 Doc
41 Bickle's portrayer, in "Taxi Driver"
42 Watch bearing
43 Girl who meets the Duchess
44 Skinflint
45 Dweller in Paradise
46 Wine area
47 Traveling bag
48 Common request
49 "If you ___ . . . !" (threat)
50 Crash, so to speak
51 Certain horse
54 It's for the money

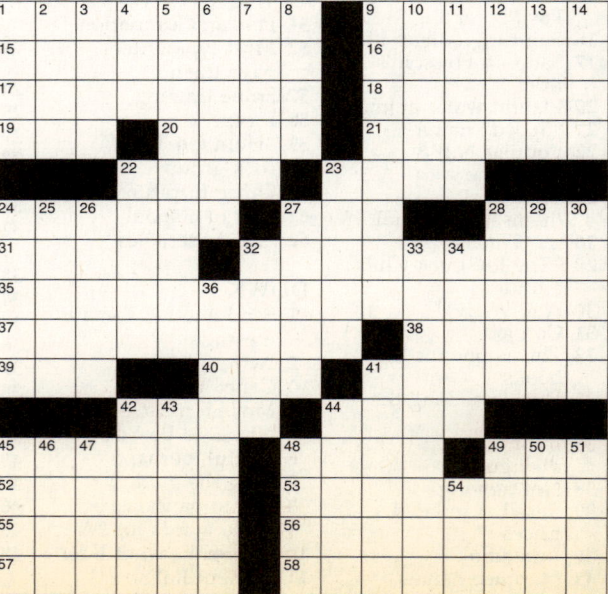

ACROSS

1 1979 exile
5 Double or triple, possibly
9 "Cantar de Rodrigo" hero
14 Actress Hatcher
15 Plod (through)
16 Nero's instrument
17 Neighbor of Albion
18 Kazakh-Uzbek sea
19 "Ghosts" writer
20 1983 Eddie Murphy movie
23 Like some letters
24 Opposite of idles
27 Run into
30 Kitchen needs
31 "Would ___?" (sleazeball's question)
32 Procter & Gamble brand
33 Penultimate fairy-tale word
34 Where 61-Across was "drawn"
35 Clock settings
36 Thing, in law
37 F.D.R. program
39 "How dry ___"
40 "Ah, But Your Land is Beautiful" novelist
42 Wax
43 Flamenco cheer
44 Foreign Secretary under Churchill
45 Transport to Sugar Hill
47 Mary's "Ink" co-star
48 Brave
49 Funnyman David
51 Stock market activity
56 "Chill"
58 Not very bright
59 Hirt hit
60 Sultan Qabus bin Said, e.g.
61 The ___-Neisse Line
62 Holly genus
63 Vegas casino, with "The"
64 June honorees
65 Kudzu, for one

DOWN

1 Let it stand
2 Title for Mozart
3 Horne solo
4 Caste member
5 Graceful descent
6 Chess and Risk
7 Electrical device
8 Manhattan Project physicist
9 "Beowulf," for one
10 Oldest republic in Africa
11 Big Mama
12 Bruckner's Symphony No. 7 ___
13 Mafia boss
21 Detain during wartime
22 Clio winners
25 Sports commentator Dick
26 Like old nylons
27 Cut the mustard?
28 Loser of 1588
29 Overall guide
34 What a bore!
37 Had a dispute
38 Expert advice
41 Kind of road
42 Island discovered by Columbus
45 Disney acquisition of 1995
46 This will help you shoot straight
50 Indira's son
52 W.W. II side
53 Buñuel collaborator
54 Neck and neck
55 Old German duchy name
56 Bacillus shape
57 Big bird

ACROSS

1 Follower of Mary
5 Return to base before proceeding
10 Hot springs
13 Resort town near Santa Barbara
14 "You ___ Beautiful" (1975 Joe Cocker hit)
15 Hard to comprehend
16 Sneaky thief
18 Flying-related
19 Mined metal
20 Real howler
21 In shreds
23 Dagger handle
24 Close
25 In ___ (intrinsically)
28 Comedy brothers of 60's–70's TV
32 Satirist Mort
33 Set in "Die Fledermaus"
34 Prez's stand-in
35 Skater's maneuver
36 ___ Carlo
37 Spanish general Duke of ___
38 A very good pair
39 Egyptian cross
40 Cherished
41 Bargain with the prosecutor
43 Jumpy
45 Signals at Sotheby's
46 Item on a cowboy boot
47 Slightly bounce
50 "Pardon me"
51 Draft org.
54 Double-reed instrument
55 Theme of this puzzle
58 Ship's spine
59 Chrissie of tennis
60 Jai ___
61 U.F.O. crew
62 Old yet new again
63 Toasty

DOWN

1 Nuts or crackers
2 Slightly open
3 Aussie buddy
4 It's usually served with lobster
5 Import duty
6 Shoptalk
7 Moolah
8 It's a free country
9 Window onto the ocean
10 Caught sight of
11 Lima's land
12 Each
15 Luke Skywalker's father
17 Russia's ___ Mountains
22 Not at home
23 Member of a notorious biker gang
24 Will of 55-Across
25 Writer Asimov
26 Tourist mecca near Mexico City
27 Blind followers
28 The daddy of decafs
29 Went congering
30 Pack again, as groceries
31 Fifth wheel
33 Tommy Lee of 55-Across
36 Seagoer's woe
42 Campaigner, for short
43 Not rejecting out of hand
44 Not feeling
46 Bake, as eggs
47 Speechmaker's opening
48 "Yeah, sure!"
49 Proceeds
50 Work without ___ (be daring)
51 Hacienda room
52 Wound reminder
53 Dairy-case choice
56 Adam's mate
57 Jurisprudence

 by Elizabeth C. Gorski

ACROSS

1 Zoning unit, maybe
5 Comic Bill, familiarly
8 Reception improver
13 Cartoonist Addams
14 "Critique of Practical Reason" writer
15 Heavenly hunter
16 Work between jobs
17 Brainstorm
18 Communion offering
19 1929 Hemingway book, with "A"
22 Sign by a door
23 Serpentlike
24 Toots one's horn
27 K-O bridge
28 Car launched by an aeronautics company
32 Come up
33 Vegans avoid these
35 Constructor of many dams: Abbr.
36 1950 Jean Simmons film
39 São Paulo-to-Rio dir.
40 "Go and catch a falling star" poet
41 Checked, as a computer program
42 ___ bird
44 God, in Roma
45 Tubs
46 50%
48 Accounting, e.g.: Abbr.
49 1934 James Hilton novella
55 Cruising
56 Good, long bath
57 Colorado resort
59 Philanthropist Wallace and others
60 Spinners
61 ___ time (never)
62 Accompanying music
63 Auden's "To My Pupils," e.g.
64 Ponce's birthplace

DOWN

1 Play the part
2 Child, for one
3 Avatar of Vishnu
4 Coffee bar order
5 Citadel student
6 First-year Harvard law student
7 Draw
8 Some computer programs are written in it
9 Groupings
10 Oktoberfest draft
11 Rich soil
12 Wraps up
14 Fuzzy fruit
20 Lengthen
21 Final Commandment
24 Stationed
25 Maine college town
26 Had the bug
27 ". . . ___ man put asunder"
29 Arcade name
30 Birdy
31 Old dance sites
33 Declaration
34 Angel
37 Pious
38 Mostly Mozart, for one
43 "My!"
45 Pub order
47 Put down
48 Hang
49 Guys' dates
50 Ear-related
51 European port
52 "___ Indigo"
53 Fancy chopped liver
54 Chinese: Prefix
58 First name in horror films

 by Christopher Hurt

ACROSS

1 Petit chapeau
6 Crosswordy ratite
9 Theater box
13 Its capital is Oranjestad
14 "___ Life of Johnson" (classic biography)
16 ___ Caesar (Caligula)
17 Genius
18 Teetotalers
20 Torso's washboard
21 British baby bearer
23 ___ Domini
25 French number with three 0's
27 Ones, when marching
28 Mrs. John Quincy Adams and others
30 Wraps
32 Actress Penelope ___ Miller
33 Use clippers
35 Turtle dove
36 Genius
42 "___ questions?"
43 Bartoli performance
44 ___ Berg, the intellectual of Baseball
45 Convertibles
49 Collected works
51 Substance from which the universe was created
52 Like a hermit
54 Robin's residence
55 It towers over Taormina
56 0
57 Univ. recruiter
59 Genius
62 Kind of board
65 Hotel chain
66 Like a carpet
67 Associate with riffraff
68 Lao-___
69 Hot pot and others

DOWN

1 It plays it
2 Mouths, to 16-Across
3 One who'd like to know more
4 Classic 1896 Alfred Jarry play
5 "No sweat!"
6 Tidal movement
7 Upright
8 In working order
9 Writer Deighton
10 Op-ed artist Pat
11 Expresses anger, in a way
12 Pleasant distraction
15 Know-it-all
19 Know-it-all
22 Submissions to S. & S.
23 Brand of daminozide
24 It's outlawed
26 Horned goddess
29 Shorthander, for short
31 First name in late-night TV
34 1990 Matsushita acquisition
37 Nepalese capital
38 Press
39 One who doesn't know much
40 ___-chef
41 Toe in the water
45 Manhattan ingredient
46 Changes a suit
47 Agreeable
48 Most artful
50 Just know
53 Medleys
58 Butterfingers' remark
60 Actor Alastair
61 22.5 degrees
63 Maimonides, for one
64 Spots

957 by Martin Ashwood-Smith

ACROSS

1 It works like a charm
9 Undertone
15 Former Big Apple mayor
16 Drill bit?
17 Saskatchewan city
18 Item of biblical attire
19 Touchdown point?: Abbr.
20 Porgy and bass
22 Foreign V.I.P.
23 Recreation center staple
26 Loudness unit
27 Ariz. neighbor
28 Music sheet abbr.
29 Seal
30 Comedian Howard
31 Tercel
37 An angry speaker might make it
38 Two-time Masters champ
39 Palindromist's preposition
40 Old Dodge
41 Bank accrual: Abbr.
42 More than a miss
44 Marshlands
45 Baltimore team, in sportspeak
47 Large copier
48 Hirsch of "Taxi"
49 Actress Meyers
50 Polar wear
52 Christopher Marlowe drama
57 Game keeper?
58 Western Sahara, once
59 They're great on Triple Letter Scores
60 Drummer

DOWN

1 Skye cap
2 Blood letters
3 Constellation near Hydra
4 "Ghosts" writer
5 Mind
6 Goya depiction
7 Health-care lobby grp.
8 St. John's people
9 Billiard stroke
10 1945 Roy Rogers–Dale Evans western
11 Half a cartoon duo
12 1943 Greer Garson title role
13 Lexicographer's concert
14 "Chill!"
21 Calculator display
23 See 24-Down
24 With 23-Down, "Zorba the Greek" actress
25 "See ya!" overseas
26 Out of harm's way
27 "Q & A" star
29 Sp. title
30 Trestletree site
32 Filer
33 Kotter of "Welcome Back, Kotter"
34 Ending with song
35 Town NE of Bangor
36 Coveys
42 Two-mile-high capital
43 Not counting, with "from"
44 They may be blown in boxes
45 Calling
46 Dad's rival
48 Nephrite
49 In trouble, in the Army
51 ___ Kan
53 Cinco de Mayo, e.g.
54 Monk's title
55 "Ça ___" (French revolutionary song)
56 Charged bit

958 by Rich Norris

ACROSS

1 Righteousness to a fault
9 Market grp.
15 Schubert song
16 City near Syracuse
17 Judged, in a way
18 Denver athlete
19 Storage areas
20 Ref. book
22 70's extremist grp.
23 "___ Three Lives"
24 Former TV co-host
25 Funeral stand
26 Cyberspace abbr.
27 Fakes
30 Ship's heading
31 ___ Hill (James Monroe's home)
32 Ashby of the 80's Astros
33 Fat, in France
35 North Dakota native or city
38 Mother of Levi and Judah
39 Bank acct. entry
40 Not classical
42 Comfort, in a way
45 Cinch
46 Not
47 Hungarian patriot Nagy
48 Bangkok money
49 Germany's Dortmund-___ Canal
50 Quite a while
51 Actress North
53 Fortune
55 Less relaxed
57 Japanese floor covering
58 Olympics sport discontinued after 1908
59 Hit song of 1968
60 Swore

DOWN

1 Sci-fi enemy
2 Like some speeches
3 Airport employee, at times
4 Fix
5 Caper
6 More than upsets
7 German pronoun
8 More angry
9 Cool
10 ". . . some kind of ___?"
11 Line part: Abbr.
12 Eats with enthusiasm
13 Astaire and others
14 Its capital is Doha
21 Iraqi, most likely
24 Net
25 Join
27 Trig function
28 Is smart
29 So much, musically
34 Oil of ___
36 Beekeeper
37 Fast food request
41 Faded (out)
42 "Hippolyte et Aricie" composer
43 Sham
44 Phoebe's sister on "Friends"
46 Salamanders
48 Castilian kisses
50 "Look ___ . . ."
51 Faction
52 Wonderland character
54 Chou En-___
56 A Turner

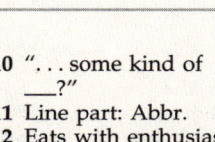

959   by Barbara Campitelli

ACROSS

1 The Bee Gees brothers
6 Subside
9 Big hit, in Variety slang
14 Journalist ___ Rogers St. Johns
15 Inlet
16 Zhou ___
17 Classic film duo
20 Andean animals
21 Entrance
22 Villa d'___
23 Old card game
26 Film ___
27 Sirs' counterparts
32 "Catcher in the Rye" author
37 "My Three Sons" son
38 Classic film duo
40 The "A" in RAM
41 Vanquished
42 Nearby things
43 Go over 212 degrees
44 Bird on a U.S. coin
45 Weaving machine
49 Actor Emilio
54 Old-time actress Ina
56 Classic film duo
59 Stradivari's mentor
60 Help
61 Itsy-bitsy
62 Without face value, as stock
63 Numbered hwy.
64 Swashbuckling Flynn

DOWN

1 Bit of Gothic architecture
2 False gods
3 Fathered, biblical-style
4 Hold responsible
5 F.D.R.'s mother
6 Cenozoic, e.g.
7 Coal container
8 Nag, nag, nag
9 Vanquished
10 A single time
11 Imperfection
12 F.D.R.'s pooch
13 Unctuous
18 Former Presidential aspirant Paul
19 Tollbooth part
24 Popular brand of faucet
25 Spaniel, for one
27 Look dejected
28 With 49-Down, former Israeli statesman
29 Border
30 Bog
31 FedEx, e.g.
32 Suffix with thermo-
33 Part of the foot
34 Shoestring
35 Boardwalk coolers
36 Where bulls and bears run: Abbr.
37 Mirror
39 Greeting to Hitler
43 Charity event
44 Poet's period after dusk
45 Cake part
46 Long-spouted can
47 University of Maine town
48 Streep of "Out of Africa"
49 See 28-Down
50 Japanese wrestling
51 Golf hazard
52 Jazz singer ___ James
53 To see, in Marseille
55 Overdue
57 Small point to criticize
58 J.F.K.'s predecessor

960   by Richard Hughes

ACROSS

1 Kind of layer
6 Applaud
10 Locking device
14 Of neap and ebb
15 Overconfident racer of fable
16 Charles Lamb pseudonym
17 Raise
18 Quickly, quickly
19 Charitable donation
20 Start of a Daniel Webster quote
22 "Act now!"
23 New England's Cape ___
24 Generally
26 Turn to cinders
29 Sentry's cry
32 Prevent from acting
33 Chicken
34 Syrup brand
35 Radical college org.
36 Middle of the quote
42 California's Fort ___
43 Cover for a diamond
44 Theater sign
45 Élève's place
48 Janet of Justice
49 Latin love
50 Whom Reagan beat in 1984
52 Tanner's tub
54 Tweed, for one
55 End of the quote
61 Related
62 Andes land
63 Sporty Toyota
64 Rudner of comedy
65 Protection: Var.
66 Diet guru Jenny
67 Hang onto
68 Gusto
69 Refuges, old-style

DOWN

1 Roman emperor after Galba
2 Utah national park
3 Garfield's foil
4 Racing org.
5 Singer John
6 Honolulu-based detective
7 Survive
8 Noah's landfall
9 English diarist Samuel
10 Whiplash preventer
11 Total
12 Cousin of a metaphor
13 Scrapbook user
21 "___ me, villain!"
25 Total
26 Navy noncom
27 Sweetie
28 It's swung in forests
30 "___ longa, vita brevis"
31 Singer Lenya
34 "M*A*S*H" setting
35 Endeavored
37 Sudden arrival of fall weather
38 Author Fleming
39 Belief
40 Spanish gold
41 Negative joiner
45 Set sail
46 Gingersnap, e.g.
47 Kind of inspection
48 Go back on a promise
49 Rose oils
51 "If I Had a Hammer" singer
53 Pet protection org.
56 Goddess of discord
57 Problem for Sneezy?
58 "Do as ___, . . ."
59 Buzz's moonmate
60 Eastern discipline

961 by Gilbert H. Ludwig

ACROSS

1 Where St. Pete is
4 Transmitter starter
9 Musical syllable
12 Create friction
14 Start
15 Pasty
16 Shared dwelling
18 Mary Steenburgen sitcom
19 Live
20 Big name in flying
22 With "of," in total agreement
24 Purple shade
25 Continental Div., e.g.
26 Early course
28 Serve a sentence
31 Yield
33 Collar type
34 "Sweet" stream of poetry
37 Further matter?
38 Answer to "You wouldn't believe it"
39 Croquet field
40 Stiff and formal
42 Raid site
44 San Marino money
45 Racket

48 Hokey
50 Tune-up, oil change, etc.
52 Smooth worker
55 Sulky person
56 Legal thing
57 Kind of experiment
59 Bridge between two vowels
60 Blake of jazz fame
61 "The King"
62 Vaudevillian Eddie
63 Alamogordo event
64 Short time

DOWN

1 Linguistically knowledgeable
2 Falls into disuse
3 "There's ___ chance of that"
4 Japanese drama
5 Sufficient, once
6 Diner order, with "the"
7 Decline again
8 Verdi opera
9 St. Paul, for one
10 Dancer with a few fans

11 "My Way" songwriter
12 Modern infokeeper
13 "The Fly" star, 1958
17 Element 54
21 Diner
23 Old gold coin
27 Step on it
29 Small business co-owner
30 Chemical suffix
31 Big bird
32 Like some columns
34 1936 campaigner Landon
35 Much
36 Bitten before?
38 First CinemaScope movie
40 Dispatched
41 Mourning band
43 First-class
45 Latin case
46 Peaceful
47 Social misfits
49 "Could ___ more specific?"
51 Selects
52 "Carmina Burana" composer

53 "___ My Heart"
54 Grand slam foursome
58 Court decision

962 by Cathy Millhauser

ACROSS

1 A pin may go through it
5 Cirrus cloud formation
9 Ankylosaur feature
14 Base
15 Angelic symbol
16 Sabbatical, e.g.
17 One of TV's Simpsons
18 One-named supermodel
19 It's spoken in Kuala Lumpur
20 Improvise, as a historian?
23 Deli buy
24 Impatient
27 Pane frame
29 Rat
31 Can. heads
34 Ramsey Lewis Trio song about Taoists?
36 Witness stand statement
38 Bear lair
39 Cinders in old strips
40 Film about burgling partners?

45 Count finish
46 What "nobody doesn't like"
47 Hankers
49 Old Renault
50 One-person boats
54 Baker's quote from "Romeo and Juliet"?
58 Nicholas Gage best-seller
61 Gardener's role
62 In ___ (as found)
63 Kind of machine
64 Late Norwegian king
65 Set foot (on)
66 Braves Hall-of-Famer Warren
67 Townshend of the Who
68 Horned vipers

DOWN

1 Benefits
2 Spain's Saint Teresa of ___
3 Rope fiber
4 Spanish beaches
5 Milky
6 A foot in a line
7 Do in

8 Small liqueur glass
9 Fact-filled reference
10 One of a bicycle pair
11 Bad start?
12 They're fertilized
13 Juan Carlos, e.g.
21 "___ the end of my rope!"
22 Merit
25 Clerical scarf
26 Caterwauls
28 Waffle
29 Cheap-seeming
30 Vitamin bottle info
31 Florists' needs
32 Taj ___
33 Cubic meter
35 Verily
37 Fragrant lily
41 Jubilance
42 Jewell of "The Facts of Life"
43 Merit
44 Black
48 Rest after almuerzo
51 Expositions
52 Camera setting
53 Supports for laths
55 Kind of talk
56 Lacquered metalware

57 Olympics preliminary
58 Staff of Life: Abbr.
59 Impudence
60 Greek letter

963   by Shannon Burns

ACROSS

1 Scrap
7 Makes merry
14 Output
15 Old-time buffalo hunter
16 Pump worker, perhaps
17 Magic, once
18 R.O.T.C. relative
19 Home built in a day?
21 Hit the road
22 "Yeah, right!"
24 Source of relief
25 Self-questioning reply
26 Rage
28 "Yes, ___"
30 Current line
31 Blot
33 Industrial fuels
35 Horseplay
37 Some parasites
40 Shocked
44 Hazzard County lawman
45 Mischievous
47 Overly sentimental
48 Small, for short
49 Scratches (out)
51 Esoteric
52 Melville work
54 Lorraine's partner
56 Bloomers worn around the neck
57 Rock's Milli ___
59 Tums alternative
61 Annual, as Mediterranean winds
62 Tchotchke
63 Striking out
64 Roscoe

DOWN

1 Is worried about
2 "Moses in Egypt" composer
3 Flap
4 "PT 109" actor
5 Biting
6 Flow
7 Zuppa di pesce ingredient
8 League member
9 Batman before George
10 Hyalite, e.g.
11 Collected abundantly
12 Position of prominence
13 Forays
14 Some tournaments
20 Diner stack
23 Doesn't give up
27 Paris pal
29 "Who's the Boss?" role
30 Succumbed to a swindle
32 Uttar Pradesh city
34 Xmas armfuls: Abbr.
36 Flunky
37 Dear
38 Fire
39 Silver eagle wearer
41 Simian
42 One over the limit
43 Keyboard whiz
46 Home
50 Noted script?
53 Seine feeder
54 Economist Greenspan
55 Three-time director for Marlon
58 Number of weeks per annum
60 Army member

964   by Fred Piscop

ACROSS

1 For a song
10 Not listed above
15 In need of bleeping
16 TV exec Arledge
17 Hole-positioning device
18 Supply with fresh troops
19 Many lounge combos
20 Cain raiser
21 San ___
22 Directional suffix
23 A.A.A. recommendation
24 Bum
26 Lose acuity
28 Midwest Indians
30 Tea server
31 Patek Philippe competitor
33 Puts in order
35 Like a victim of calumny
37 Jack Kerouac, e.g.
39 "I ___ it"
42 Shipping abbr.
43 Amplified
45 Scares
47 "Entertaining Mr. ___" (Orton play)
49 Dietary oil source
50 Book before Esth.
51 Whisper
52 Barely get, with "out"
53 Daytime Emmy actress Rena
55 Province west of Madrid
57 Make straight
59 Puerto ___
60 Responded disrespectfully
61 Out
62 Kitchen gadgets

DOWN

1 Channeled
2 By mistake
3 Met
4 Former leader of the nonaligned movement
5 Street: Abbr.
6 Laugh syllable
7 Campy's field
8 Spirited
9 "Our Gang" pooch
10 Three-time Hart Trophy winner
11 It's human
12 Great success, so to speak
13 Makes spoony
14 Celebrity
23 1987 Steve Martin film
24 Like a mountain goat
25 Medical prefix
27 Opera heroine who sings "Einsam in trüben Tagen"
29 "I hadn't thought of that"
32 First name in rock
34 Cabinet dept.
36 Game with matchsticks
37 Coffee producer
38 Much-debated school subject
40 It may be lit on the Fourth
41 Plucker's need
42 Tough key for pianists
44 Original "Star Trek" actor
46 Confetti
48 50's ICBM
52 Choice word
53 "The Chronicles of Clovis" writer
54 Utah city
56 Hydrocarbon suffix
58 Outer: Prefix

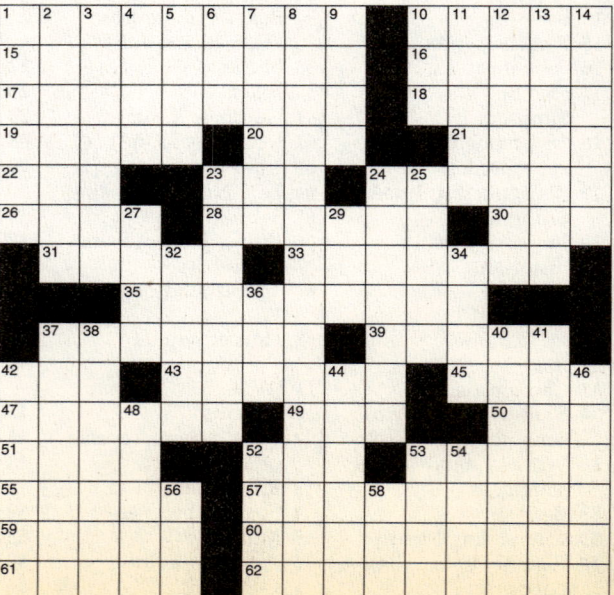

965   by Gregory E. Paul

ACROSS

1 "___ Network" (1980's comedy series)
5 False god
9 Phillips head item
14 ___ vera
15 Austen's Woodhouse
16 Mild cigar
17 Unload, as stock
18 Ruler's length
19 Hammerin' Hank
20 "Just one gosh-darn minute!"
23 Rebel (against)
24 Vim
25 Part of the Dept. of Trans.
28 Like a taxi
31 Scrooge's cry
34 The "A" in James A. Garfield
36 Tire fill
37 Inter ___
38 "Be polite!"
42 Actress McClurg
43 Handyman's vehicle
44 Detail map
45 Poor grade
46 Preschooler's auto accessory
49 Opposite NNW
50 Hockey's Bobby
51 Farm unit
53 "Hush!"
60 Stocking stuffer
61 Singer Guthrie
62 Russia's Itar-___ news agency
63 Musical eightsome
64 Peter the Great, e.g.
65 Nights before
66 Beach spot
67 Chumps
68 Start all over

DOWN

1 Window frame
2 Nile queen, informally
3 Tunnel fee
4 South African expanse
5 "Age ___ beauty"
6 Add up (to)
7 Love, to Livy
8 Builder's backing
9 With knees knocking
10 Purse part
11 Scarce
12 February 14 figure
13 Triumphed
21 Scrumptious
22 "La Bohème," e.g.
25 Widely known
26 Put up with
27 Golfer with an "army"
29 Takes home, as salary
30 Basketball blackboard attachment
31 Hallow
32 Buenos ___
33 Waste maker
35 Fruit drink
37 Landers with advice
39 Egg maker
40 Former Mideast inits.
41 Explosive, informally
46 Devise
47 Part of a cold-weather cap
48 The "A" in S.A.G.
50 Playful water animal
52 "Come in!"
53 "Brandenburg Concertos" composer
54 "___ each life some . . ."
55 Horse's mouthful
56 Celestial bear
57 Donated
58 Not new
59 Sinclair rival
60 "Send help!"

966   by Robert Malinow

ACROSS

1 Struck, old-style
5 Uneven hairdo
9 Winery in Modesto, Calif.
14 Yesterday's dinner today
15 Smog
16 To no ___ (futilely)
17 Actor John, once married to Shirley Temple
18 Appliance on a board
19 Greene of "Bonanza"
20 "The Lone Ranger" catchphrase
23 Carryall
24 "Eureka!"
25 "The Honeymooners" catchphrase
32 Monte ___
33 Filleted fish
34 One with filling work?: Abbr.
35 Woodwind
36 Ground grain
38 Big elephant features
39 Announcer Pardo
40 Chimney duct
41 "God bless" preceder
42 "The Goldbergs" catchphrase
46 Spanish gold
47 Rebellious one, maybe
48 "Star Trek" catchphrase
55 In concealment
56 Report cards' stats
57 Pained look
58 Writer Nin
59 Needle case
60 College in New Rochelle
61 Whom Jason jilted
62 Part to play
63 Hatfields or McCoys, e.g.

DOWN

1 ___ of Iran
2 Travelers to Bethlehem
3 "___, old chap!"
4 Choke
5 Many an Iranian
6 Home of poet Langston Hughes
7 Europe's Sea of ___
8 Trait carrier
9 Lancelot's son
10 Promise
11 Zhivago's love
12 Streaked
13 Matador's cheer
21 It borders Regent Street
22 Charged
25 Pork, to a Jew, e.g.
26 Maine campus town
27 Willow
28 Circus cries
29 Popular potato
30 Modern "book"
31 Where an Edsel filled up, maybe
32 Wild West Show star
36 Despondency
37 ___ and Coke
38 Business-related
40 Where Taipei is
41 One of the Baldwins
43 Grinder
44 State capital on the Mississippi
45 Singer Smith
48 Rib, for one
49 "Heavens to Betsy!"
50 Elbe tributary
51 ___ no good
52 Cat's-paw
53 Cape Cod catch
54 Bear young, as sheep
55 Beaver's work

967 — by Randall J. Hartman

ACROSS

1 South Seas paradise
5 Put in the cup
10 Attempt
14 "___ a Teen-Age Werewolf"
15 Taste stimulus
16 1970 Kinks hit
17 Sci-fi weapon, formally?
19 "A Prayer for ___ Meany"
20 Holy wars
21 Had title to
22 With it, once
23 Neptune's domain
24 Growing locale
26 Highway sight, formally?
31 Elaborate tapestry
34 G.I. with chevrons
35 Crosby, Stills and Nash, e.g.
36 Café au ___
37 Two-time U.S. Open tennis champ
39 Bedevilers
40 Ferrara family name
41 Dream Team's team
42 Armed band
43 Western chow dispenser, formally?
47 Rats run it
48 Ad word
49 Unexplained
52 Man of many words
55 Sensational headline
57 One gone but not forgotten
58 1930's design style, formally?
60 No-show's score
61 Vidal Sassoon's workplace
62 Turkish bigwigs
63 Genesis setting
64 Dubbing need
65 Giant great

DOWN

1 Hazel's cousin
2 In the know
3 Michael Jordan shot
4 Doctrines
5 "Water Music" composer
6 Tough going
7 Captain Kirk's records
8 Feathered six-footer
9 Fancy one
10 Replay feature
11 Atlas dot
12 Sheltered, nautically
13 Boston or Chicago, e.g.
18 Kalahari stopover
21 Celestial sphere
24 Mug
25 Book after Joel
26 Summer snack
27 Archie or Edith, to Mike
28 Weaponry
29 Tears
30 10 cc, perhaps
31 He played Obi-Wan
32 Baby's problem
33 The Beatles' meter maid
37 Red Sea access
38 Being, to Caesar
42 Authority
44 Back muscle, for short
45 Rather, e.g.
46 Verb-turned-noun
49 The end, in Athens
50 Rot
51 Smelting refuse
52 Bring down the house
53 Had markers out
54 Reason for an R rating
55 Historic Normandy city
56 Resident of 63-Across
58 Balaam's mount
59 Cold and wet

968 — by Brendan Emmett Quigley

ACROSS

1 Starts
6 Emily of "Our Town"
10 It takes a bow at a recital
14 Render harmless, in a way
15 Part
16 They, in Trieste
17 Tongue twister #1
20 Varsity starters
21 Comic strip tiger
22 It may have 6 rms, riv vu
24 Moore of "G.I. Jane"
27 River through the Lake of the Ozarks
28 Addict's need?
31 Time off
33 Kind of deer
34 Treasured spots?
36 [Oh no!]
38 Tongue twister #2
42 Jacket material
43 Foul up, as plans
45 Old what's-___-name
48 Rewrites
50 The Post or News, e.g.
51 Protozoan
53 Biblical brother
55 Rejections
56 You may have to send for it
58 Runabout?
61 Tongue twister #3
66 Stare at
67 "Clear as day"
68 Like Mork's spaceship
69 Loch ___
70 Difficulty, so to speak
71 Famous test participant

DOWN

1 Stick (out)
2 New England state sch.
3 Part of an ironman competition
4 Ready: Fr.
5 Hook's mate
6 "Getting close"
7 Before, to Byron
8 Old-fashioned party
9 Shellacking
10 Hit and run, e.g.
11 Map line
12 New York river to Lake Ontario
13 Tenant
18 The macarena, once
19 Cheered
22 Word with form or film
23 Where El Misti volcano is
25 Refrigerator decorations
26 About
29 Dollar rival
30 Hand down
32 "Harvey" character Elwood P. ___
35 Took to court
37 Half of a 1934 M-G-M couple
39 Newswoman Magnus
40 Kerplop maker
41 Part of kg-m
44 French-Belgian boundary river
45 Talk about endlessly
46 Reveal oneself
47 Civil War side
49 Pink-slipped
52 Diamond corners
54 Speech stumbles
57 Ireland
59 Breakfast chain, informally
60 CNN word
62 Consume
63 Originally named
64 Old-fashioned contraction
65 Star Wars: Abbr.

969 · by Alan Jay Weiss

ACROSS

1 Lacking significance
7 Deep Blue specialty
12 Laments loudly
15 Successor of Nikita
16 Ice cream flavor
17 It may have a berth to Perth
18 Pump
19 Brighten
21 Returns letters
22 Cutlet?
24 Danielle's darling
25 ___ B'rith
26 The Fair Maid of Kent and namesakes
28 Robert Morse tour de force
29 Dirt-court game
30 Raid
32 Art lovers
34 Garbed
36 Increase dramatically
37 Wolverines' rivals
41 Ahead
45 ___-midi
46 A.M.A. members
48 Burt Reynolds film
49 Somewhat
50 Coventry coolers
52 Losers at Vicksburg
53 Prog. Cons. opponent, in Canada
54 Turn bad
56 Diminutive suffix
57 Exclamation of exhaustion
59 Fussy dress
61 Handles
62 U.S. air-to-air missiles
63 User interface
64 Actress Madeleine et al.

DOWN

1 Robin Williams film
2 A going-over
3 Jalopy
4 Final: Abbr.
5 Chemist's condiment
6 Body of values
7 Thank the singer
8 Party member?
9 Gone
10 Yachting event
11 Mama's boys
13 Good Olympics score
14 Field
15 Here, in Honduras
20 Builder's framework
23 Found fault with
25 1899–1902 event
27 Company division
29 Hemp
31 It breaks in the morning
33 Unduly
35 "Women Ironing" artist
37 Belief in false gods
38 Operating periods
39 Found fault with
40 Lampoons
42 Was humiliated
43 "Class" star
44 Lorax creator
47 Impolite sound
50 Sunday-meeting link
51 Classical walks
54 Saturday night specials
55 Offended
58 "___ Beso" (Paul Anka song)
60 Back

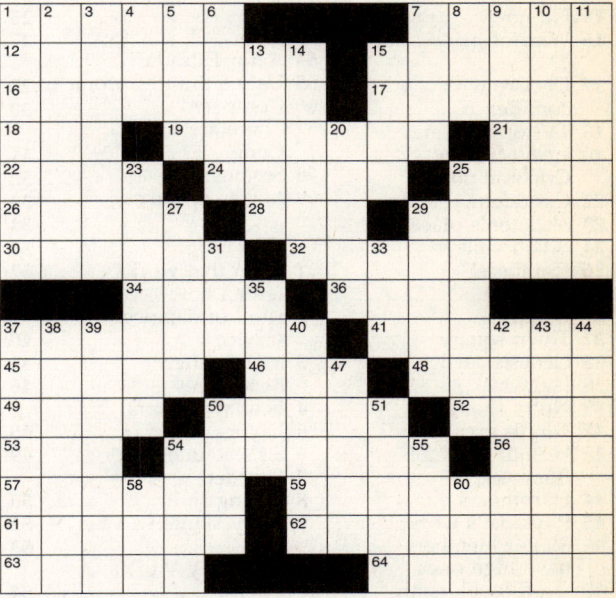

970 · by Rich Norris

ACROSS

1 Wins the draw, probably
11 Grouch
15 Pool feat
16 Pulitzer-winning microbiologist Dubos
17 1963 Chiffons hit
18 Plains Indian
19 Nutritional abbr.
20 Actress Felicia
21 Crack
22 Care for
24 Old "Supper Club" radio host
27 Old-fashioned ballot boxes
28 "Leave It to Beaver" pal
30 Like modern technology
32 Base appropriations?
34 Pass
35 Windswept point
36 Farmer's place, in song
38 Singer Dana
41 Relative of a bandicoot
42 "I Could Fall in Love" singer
44 Sticking together
47 Unprecedented
48 Low card
49 Shakespearean character who "had a tongue with a tang"
50 Neurotransmitter amino acid
51 Make sound
52 100 cents abroad
55 Void, in Vichy
56 Harassed
57 Gift shop item
60 Leading ammunition maker
61 Many Nobel Prize winners
62 German auto pioneer
63 Church clothes

DOWN

1 Losing straw in drawing straws
2 Personally left with
3 Ornamental dogbane
4 Not working
5 Expression of relief
6 Mideast capital
7 Passionate
8 Michael Crichton best-seller, with "The"
9 Overwhelming number
10 Go
11 Players may place stakes on this
12 Yield
13 Consecrate
14 Medical alerts?
23 Day, in Durango
25 Bit of biblical writing
26 Seniors' hurdles, maybe
29 John of song
31 Staff leader?
33 Meat cut
37 Noted English letter writer
38 Like Proteus
39 Sporadically
40 Spark
41 "Falling From Grace" actress, 1992
43 Restraint
44 Cuisine style
45 Opening
46 Vehement
48 Beat
53 Mexican child
54 Cartoonist Roy
57 Sound of a lit fuse
58 The Horned Frogs, for short
59 Point

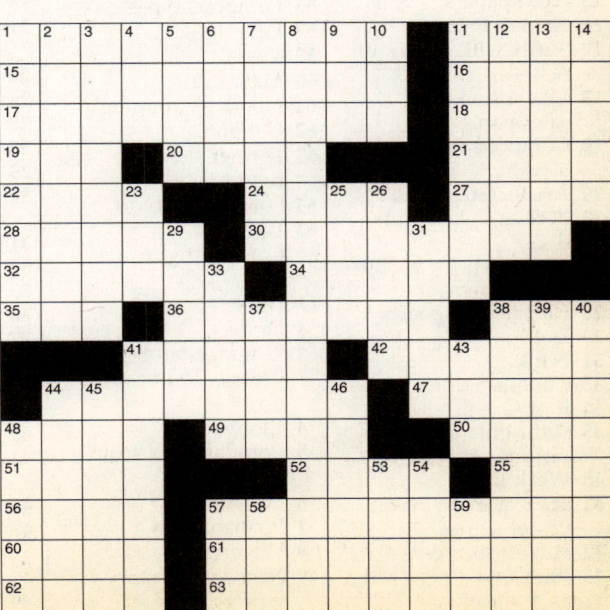

971 by Peter Gordon

ACROSS
1 Frosts, as a cake
5 Give off an odor
10 "Iliad" or "Aeneid," e.g.
14 Trig ratio
15 No-no
16 Warrior princess of TV
17 Declare with confidence
18 TV-top antenna
20 1996 Michael Crichton novel
22 Confidential matter
23 Skeleton's place?
24 Broad valleys
26 "So there!"
28 Sprinted
29 Dripping
32 Town square
36 Genesis garden
38 Jazzy talk
39 Nutty thought
42 Tennis great Lendl
43 Humor columnist Bombeck
44 Harbingers
45 Physicist's workplace
46 Mensa members have high ones
47 ___-fi (book genre)

49 Rockne of Notre Dame
51 Once a year
56 Set of advantages
59 Generosity
61 Beginners' skiing area
63 Price
64 Actor Estrada
65 Uses a Smith-Corona
66 Competed
67 There are 435 in Cong.
68 Sesames, e.g.
69 Makes mistakes

DOWN
1 Stern that works with a bow
2 Kind of engineer or service
3 Month after diciembre
4 Feudal workers
5 Layers
6 Sir's counterpart
7 Receded
8 Arcing shot
9 Perry White was her boss
10 Company V.I.P.'s
11 Prickly ___

12 Legal memo starter
13 It's made of plaster of paris
19 Selective Service registrant, agewise
21 Post-op period
25 Sports venues
27 Cosmopolitan publisher
29 Broad
30 Like left-hand page numbers
31 Lipton products
32 Comedian Hartman
33 Volcano output
34 United ___ Emirates
35 Kind of Buddhist
37 Not too intelligent
38 "Huckleberry Finn" character
40 Bands take them
41 Performing
46 Annual Memorial Day event
48 Gentle stroke
49 Difficulties to be worked out
50 Run off to the chapel
52 Chutzpah
53 Pan Am rival, formerly
54 Daisylike bloom

55 Yorkshire city
56 "Deutschland ___ Alles"
57 Undiluted
58 Scissors cut
60 Mimicked
62 Soapmaker's solution

972 by Elizabeth C. Gorski

ACROSS
1 Like fine wine
5 Revival shouts
10 Impertinent one
14 Where the Vatican is
15 Newspapers, TV, etc.
16 Actress Petty
17 Suffix with psych- or neur-
18 Like a snake-oil salesman
19 Components of elevens
20 Aristocratic types
23 Berlioz's "Les nuits d'___"
24 Contained, with "up"
25 Packs down
28 Isn't feeling good
29 Dolt
31 Brink
33 Conquistador's haul
34 E or G, e.g.
35 Self-righteously virtuous types
40 Work unit
41 Start of many naval vessel names
42 Subject to breezes
43 Phrase in a new way, as a question

46 Throw hard
48 Farm mudholes
49 Salespeople, informally
50 Sheepish reply
53 Pompous types
57 Deep laugh
59 Vassal
60 Mata ___
61 Nondairy topping
62 Get-go
63 Former sneaker brand
64 Something to do
65 Uproots?
66 Campus figure

DOWN
1 Stood
2 "I understand!"
3 Classic Rousseau novel
4 Clobber
5 Popular brew from Holland
6 Cantaloupes
7 Proclamation
8 Shaving cut
9 Noted short-story writer

10 "Just say no," for instance
11 Favorable life insurance category
12 Miff
13 Detectives, for short
21 Used binoculars, maybe
22 To the ___ degree
26 Where "e'en" is seen
27 Heaven
28 Long ___
29 Full house sign
30 Beloved comic's nickname
31 White heron
32 Small sharks
33 Cries of pain
36 "Tasty!"
37 Mao ___-tung
38 Draconian
39 Van Gogh's "Irises," e.g.
40 Hesitant sounds
44 Shot again, as a photo
45 Tempe sch.
46 Didn't give a definite answer
47 Unexpected wins
49 Singer Della

50 Intrepid
51 Courtyards
52 Kind of flu
54 Move like lava
55 Better than good

56 "___ the Craziest Dream" (1942 song)
57 Steamy
58 Ending with schnozz

973 by John D. Leavy

ACROSS

1 On the double
5 Peace Nobelist of 1984
9 Classic drinks
14 Jazz home
15 Letters of urgency
16 Impossible to miss
17 Tick off
18 Columbus : ___ :: . . .
20 Brunch staple
22 Much of Mongolia
23 Bird's bill
24 Distant
26 St. Louis attraction
28 Like the flu
30 "Hey Girl" singer, 1971
34 Bygone Ford
37 1970's Tony Musante series
39 Command to Rover
40 Sourpuss
41 Halfhearted
42 Kind of bread
43 Prop at a Christmas musical
44 Serpent's home
45 Plains roamers
46 Chrétien's capital
48 Essayist Sontag
50 Tex-Mex snack
52 Got (by)
56 Kramden vehicle
59 College basketball coach Adolph
61 Amend one's return
62 Kirk : ___ :: . . .
65 "Havana" actress
66 Astaire had it
67 The East
68 Outback critters
69 Antidote target
70 Injury
71 Feminine suffix

DOWN

1 Hue and cry
2 "___ to Kill" (Grisham novel)
3 City on the Willamette
4 Stubing : ___ :: . . .
5 One who sips
6 "Home of the brave"
7 Flavor to remember
8 ___ point (only so far)
9 Daily page
10 Reproductive cells
11 "Show Boat" composer
12 Native New Yorker
13 Wild guess
19 Overseas
21 What lurks in the hearts of men
25 Went with
27 Corcoran : ___
29 Runs
31 "Miss ___ Regrets"
32 Warsaw Pact counterforce
33 Cannon in Hollywood
34 Audio problem
35 Fieldsian expletive
36 Popeye, e.g.
38 Drawback
41 Service component
45 In the buff
47 Briar patch, maybe
49 Riot
51 Geraldo competitor
53 Series sample
54 "Cats" lyricist
55 None too bright
56 A+
57 "Do ___ others . . ."
58 Charon's crossing
60 Tower site
63 George Bush was one
64 Sidney Poitier title role

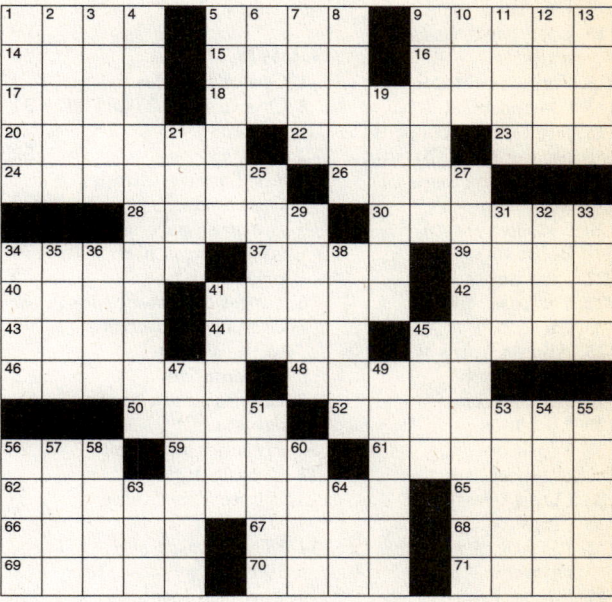

974 by Frances Hansen

ACROSS

1 Victor of piano antics
6 Doll's cry
10 Lawn ___
14 March sign
15 Muezzin's call to prayer
16 "O" in old radio lingo
17 Disneyland site
19 Superbright
20 Wistful word
21 Court call
22 Pretentious
23 Virginia tourist attraction
26 From the beginning
28 Some Mozart art
32 Bird with a cup-shaped nest
33 Razzing victim
36 Bother, with "at"
37 Complicated love relationship
41 Half a cartoon duo
42 Lampoon
43 Hotel booking
44 Too much, musically
47 Result of a burning desire
48 Primitive hearing aid
53 Cornered
56 Litter critter
57 Oscar ___ Renta
60 Lowdown
61 Pooh-bah
63 Colorless liqueur
64 Nick and Nora's pet
65 The taking of Troy, e.g.
66 Goad
67 "To ___ it may concern"
68 Much of Chile

DOWN

1 Eight-time Sugar Bowl champs, familiarly
2 Viva-voce
3 Oscar, Grammy, Tony and Emmy winner
4 Recovers from
5 Suffix with Peking
6 Muslim messiah
7 Kind of dye
8 Château-Thierry's river
9 Raggedy ___
10 Doctrine maker
11 "Not on ___!" ("No way!")
12 Where gnus snooze
13 Counting-out start
18 Informer
22 17-Across, e.g.
24 "High" time
25 French novelist Pierre
26 Ward off
27 Bad dog
29 On the rolls
30 Noted Finnish architect
31 "Skittle Players" artist
33 Day-___
34 Financial page heading
35 Vessel in a storm
38 "Orfeo ed Euridice" god
39 P.D.Q., updated
40 "The Barber of Baghdad" tenor
45 Vegetable container
46 Settle up
49 Refuse
50 Total
51 Fix a blockage
52 Urban transit org.
53 Per item purchased
54 Kind of bus
55 TV clown
58 Winter sport
59 Cathy of "East of Eden"
61 Handle clumsily
62 Hush-hush org.

975 by Frank Longo

ACROSS

1 Woodworking tool
7 Come to an end
12 Shortens a sentence, perhaps
14 Dreadful
15 Lose control at a buffet
16 Forbes alternative
17 Clarion blast
18 She helped Theseus escape the Labyrinth
19 One in the arms of Morpheus
20 Monster slain by Beowulf
21 Like italics
22 Teriyaki spices
23 Close call
25 Andy Capp's wife, often
26 Acquiescence
35 Like fans
37 Work on text together
38 Piano relative
39 First, e.g.
41 It's full of rye, in rhyme
42 Silver: Prefix
43 Tooth tissue
44 Cry of achievement
45 Put right?
46 Father of Fauvism
47 They follow Shebats
48 Convictions

DOWN

1 Ocelot features
2 One of over 2,000,000 Cubans
3 Gritty
4 San Diego's founder Gaspar de ___
5 Aaron's son and successor as high priest
6 Target of a swift kick
7 China and environs, to the French
8 Systematize
9 Cowboy on a cattle drive, e.g.
10 Preacher's pursuit
11 Detroit duds
13 Where Whirlaway waited
14 "The Abyss" star, 1989
16 Carousel locale
24 Japanese surname suffix
26 Rival of Montel
27 Raiser
28 Birds related to the goldfinch
29 Focused
30 Habitually humiliated one
31 Notorious London prison
32 Added just before time ran out
33 Like Simone Martini's art
34 Oligarchy proponent
35 "Evangeline" setting
36 Bank
40 Matrimony, bar mitzvah, etc.

976 by John Scott Marrone

ACROSS

1 1985 western starring two Kevins
10 Noted Boston conductor
15 Manuscripts at academic journals
16 French author Bazin and others
17 Museumgoers
18 Some sopranos
19 Adjust, in a way
20 Ardent
22 Thousand dollars, in slang
23 Folder filer's aid
26 Ornamental tag
27 It may be vaulted
28 Three in one
30 Michigan college or its town
32 Determined policy
33 Social reformer Wells and others
37 Word for a lady
38 "Tyranny, like hell, is not easily conquered" writer
39 Bank deposit?
40 River to Donegal Bay
41 Originates
42 It's hard to believe
43 Marie Antoinette and others
45 Yipper
46 Back up
49 Govt. org. since 1946
51 Horatio Alger sort
52 King, for one
54 Swindle
57 Minute hands, essentially
58 Exactly
61 Intestinal division
62 Inner city sights
63 Prefix with -plasty
64 Request help

DOWN

1 Lead
2 Sale item, maybe
3 Admired athlete
4 Care for
5 Kind of collar
6 Fasten firmly
7 Enzyme suffix
8 German article
9 Bones
10 Decree
11 Spirit of the time
12 Smith's station
13 Bob's companion
14 Plus
21 More than 120 1970's sitcom episodes
24 Hit
25 Cooks, in a way
27 "The shadow of Virtue": Seneca
29 "Rainbow After a Storm" artist
31 Element used in radiation research
32 "Obey your thirst" sloganeer
34 Pipe organ stops
35 Hints at
36 Recipe part
44 Parka wearer
46 Sharp
47 Kind of oil
48 Annual feast
50 Hurt
51 It's kept in the closet
53 Falls apart
55 Blood: Prefix
56 Reduced by
59 Name word
60 Grand Ole Opry broadcaster

977 by Mark Gottlieb

ACROSS

1 "Gee whillikers!"
5 Like a good lounge chair
10 Go steady with
14 Follow, as orders
15 ". . . like a big pizza pie, that's ___" (old song lyric)
16 Russian river or mountain
17 "St. Elmo's Fire" actor Rob
18 Sinks one's teeth into
19 Is sick
20 60's sitcom/90's movie
23 Aardvark's tidbit
24 Lumberjack's tool
25 Possesses
28 Shirt or dress
32 Monet supply?
35 What to make a dep. into
37 Dweeb
38 Allude (to)
40 60's sitcom/90's movie
43 Individually owned apartment
44 Opposite of a thinker
45 Airport conveyance
46 Sweltering
47 Invisible troublemaker
50 Where the iris is
51 Knot
52 "Hold on a ___!"
54 60's sitcom/90's movie
63 Artist's work
64 Flip out
65 Jazz lingo
66 Location
67 ___ Dame
68 Preowned
69 Kilt wearer
70 Kills, as a dragon
71 Emperor with a burning ambition?

DOWN

1 Credit card color
2 Clarinet cousin
3 Stitched
4 Laughing ___
5 Where to get a taxi
6 Exclude
7 Butterfly's cousin
8 Liberate
9 Flunky
10 One of the Allman Brothers
11 Operatic solo
12 Baby powder ingredient
13 Otherwise
21 Gerund's end
22 Bonus
25 "Down the ___!" (drinker's toast)
26 Sound before "Gesundheit!"
27 Bloodhound's trail
29 English author Charles
30 1983 Michael Keaton comedy
31 Ford flop
32 Flaming
33 Pass-the-baton race
34 Product sample's invitation
36 Little bit
39 CPR practitioner
41 Calf, to a cowboy
42 Flying toys
48 Acts as king
49 Born as
51 Den appliance
53 New Orleans cooking style
54 Any Buffalo Bills Super Bowl result
55 Grand, as an adventure
56 Car
57 Hammer or sickle, e.g.
58 "Toodle-oo"
59 Grand Ole ___
60 Workbench clamp
61 At any time
62 Start over

978 by Bernice Gordon

ACROSS

1 Lots
5 Desert streambed
9 Tennis great Rod
14 "Are you some kind of ___?"
15 Black
16 "___ at the office"
17 Vidal's Breckinridge
18 Roar at the shore
19 Count with an orchestra
20 1989 Madonna hit
23 Churchill's sign
24 Basic college degrees
25 Summit
29 ___-Jo (1988 Olympics name)
31 Mosque V.I.P.
35 Live, in a TV studio
36 Like Britain
38 Poetic palindrome
39 It may be used in minor surgery
42 Quattro minus uno
43 Freshman, sophomore, etc.
44 Revolving machine part
45 Reply to "Are not!"
47 I-80, e.g.: Abbr.
48 Item in a Mexican fiesta
49 Luau dish
51 Sound from Sandy
52 Bibliophile's treasures
61 Belief in sorcery and magic
62 Pre-tractor farmer's need
63 Plummet
64 "À votre ___!"
65 Grp. affecting gas prices
66 Go gently (into)
67 More correct
68 Brood
69 "Jeopardy!" host Trebek

DOWN

1 Charades, e.g.
2 Cameo stone
3 Pat on the back, as a baby
4 Asterisk
5 Setting for Thomas Hardy novels
6 Maltreatment
7 Boat with oars
8 Data
9 Astrologically, the thoughtful, diplomatic type
10 Tennis great Andre
11 Bouquet site
12 Satanicalness
13 Sailor's peril
21 Don or Phil of 50's–60's pop
22 W.W. II menace
25 Physicist Alessandro
26 Vast, old-style
27 Regattas
28 Spanish aunt
29 French brother
30 Minus
32 Acclaimed "Hostess with the Mostes' "
33 Unrestrained
34 Stiller's comedy partner
36 Buzzing pest
37 Savings and loan
40 Condor's home
41 Long time
46 Narcotic
48 William or Harry, e.g.
50 Word with woman or worldly
51 Take ___ breath
52 Bewildered
53 Construction support
54 Maitre d's offering
55 Condemn
56 Montreal player
57 Bright thought
58 Spoken
59 Winning margin, maybe
60 Glasses, in ads

979   by Kelly Clark

ACROSS
1 Trawler's haul
5 Man-___
9 Like 30% of the world's landmass
14 Color deficient
15 Typewriter type
16 Round Tabler's weapon
17 Later
18 Cross letters
19 Host
20 With 40- and 60-Across, a cautionary message
22 Dove call
23 Children's song refrain
24 Romantic interlude
26 "Right on, brother!"
29 Jim-dandy
31 Simpleton's utterance
33 Gaza force, for short
34 Isn't bold
37 Quite a tale
38 Lease
39 Jackie's "O"
40 See 20-Across
42 Planning time

43 Indy stop
44 Creative
45 On the docket
47 "Isn't that beautiful?"
48 What Dick, Jane and Spot did
49 Literary ___
50 Kind of job
52 Repeated role for Lorre
54 "All That Jazz" director
58 Old Mideast inits.
60 See 20-Across
62 Bubble-headed
64 Wild romp
65 Denials
66 One of the Horae
67 Dance instruction
68 Charlie, for one
69 Square dance partners
70 Green one
71 Blackjack option

DOWN
1 One in a black suit
2 Saigon's foe
3 Garbo-like

4 Most of a tooth
5 Mayberry boy of TV
6 Improvise
7 Caustic
8 Saver's eventuality
9 Actor Baldwin
10 Navigators' Islands, today
11 Like 60-Across
12 Air hero
13 Word before Bouvier
21 Turn-of-century British conflict
25 Actor who put teeth into his work?
27 Parisian pupil
28 Prominent
30 Hindu retreat
32 Cart away
34 Crime bosses
35 Whom Artemis loved
36 Like 60-Across
37 Pig's digs
41 Free
46 Applies holy oil to
49 Like Pinocchio's nose after a lie
51 "That ___ so bad . . ."
53 Somewhat sour

55 Schnoz
56 Saint Catherine's home
57 Opinionated work
59 Deli loaves

61 It may be found in a proof
62 Archeological site
63 It's west of G.B.

980   by Cathy Millhauser

ACROSS
1 Literary olios
5 Some nerve
10 They go over your part
14 Sweater eater
15 "___ Knows" (Dion & the Belmonts hit)
16 Chase in the movies
17 Group endured chickenhouse disaster?
20 Enduring
21 Mistreat
22 Relatives of Rafael
23 Oversupply
24 Spirit of an evil evil spirit?
29 Overturn
30 Billy goat's bleat
31 Sch. liaisons
33 Fury
34 Texas's Houston
35 Prefix with system
36 Rudely terse
38 Bristle on barley
39 Inviolate
42 Lass specified madras?

45 With 49-Down, "The Firm" actor
46 Smelter's stuff
47 ___ rasa (clean slate)
50 Periodic payments
54 Significant danger to beef?
56 Noted actress-model
57 Creepy
58 Lug
59 F.D.R.'s Scottie
60 Towels
61 Over

DOWN
1 Prefix with polar
2 Group standard
3 Bit
4 Grow rapidly
5 Treading the boards
6 K compound
7 Die, e.g.
8 Daughter of Cadmus, in myth
9 Every garçon has one
10 Sledder's starting point
11 Big surname in baseball

12 W.B.A. stats
13 "Smooth Operator" singer
18 Kind of press
19 Nasty bugs
23 Island discovered by Magellan
24 Discussion opportunity
25 Field of buffos
26 Yemeni's neighbor
27 Starter homes?
28 Spiked
29 Quirk
32 Turf
34 Pen that swims
37 Baja California city
38 Chagrined
39 Pixies
40 Beth's preceder
41 City NNE of Naples
43 Airhead
44 Country singer West
47 Weekly "Whew!"
48 First word of the "Aeneid"
49 See 45-Across
50 Indira's dress
51 Gas in Vegas

52 Number in a letter
53 Worry
55 Aye

ACROSS

1 Son of Noah
8 Book sizes
15 Con artist
16 Upstart
17 Electric horns
18 Camper
19 Actor Priestley et al.
20 Frosted
21 "Rin Tin Tin" shower
22 Bread and drink
23 Kings and queens, e.g.
25 Pulitzer dramatist Akins
26 Enduring
28 ___ pura
29 Kenyan president beginning 1978
32 Cut loose
33 Overwhelms
34 Confessed
36 Prince Philip's birthplace
37 Patron saint of France
38 TV's George Jefferson, e.g.
41 O.E.D. ender
42 Thomas Moore's homeland
43 How some are left
45 Menu words
46 Rough ___
47 City NW of Mascara
51 Kicks
52 Census data
53 Elegant garden feature
55 To such an extent
57 Circus follower
58 Sovereignty, in Sussex
59 Struggle
60 "No problem"
61 Chang, alternatively

DOWN

1 Celeb often seen in supermarket tabs
2 Put to rest
3 Porridge ingredient
4 Simple sugar
5 Budget subj.
6 Kid's present, perhaps
7 "48 ___"
8 Re sight
9 California artist's colony
10 Drive-in diner supplies
11 Bird: Prefix
12 "Las Meninas" painter
13 Tennis maximum
14 Discontinued
20 Tennis's Lacoste
24 Sportscaster Cross
27 Spanish crowd?
28 Picnicked
29 Prepared the punch?
30 How some business deals are made
31 View from Syracuse
33 Mlle. across the Pyrenees
35 Game aim
36 Loses it
38 "Tommy Boy" co-star
39 Ticked states
40 Warsaw Pact member, initially
43 Mozart subject
44 Out
46 A lot
48 Pardon
49 Full of lively gossip
50 Long time follower
54 Neuron part
56 Go one way or the other
57 Has a green light

ACROSS

1 "Silence of the Lambs" role
9 Prettifies
15 Traveler's need, perhaps
16 Dance
17 Rural science
18 Land design?
19 Hardly a site of decorum
20 1986–87 Emmy winner for drama
22 1944 N.L. M.V.P. ___ Marion
23 Actress Claire et al.
25 60's western co-star
27 One side in a battle of the sexes
28 Certain down
30 Mooring sites
31 Great Trek participant
32 Haile Selassie follower, for short
33 Paella cooker
34 "Need You Tonight" rock group
35 Breeze
37 Craving
39 Rock's Bon ___
42 Taxpayer reps, at times
44 Hinder
48 Dutch ___
49 Certain exchange, for short, with "the"
50 Casco Bay locale
51 Boxer's title: Abbr.
52 Lieutenant in "The Fugitive"
54 Site for an alligator bonnet
55 Instant
57 Wintry forecast
59 Society column word
60 Sailor's punishment
62 Aging problem
64 Altruist's opposite
65 Theater space?
66 Harder to follow, as prose
67 Weighed

DOWN

1 1964 Olympic boxing gold medalist
2 Garden perennial
3 Forays
4 ___ Z
5 The Jets, for one
6 Brussels's Royal Militaire, e.g.
7 Some status seekers
8 Aid for upwind maneuvers
9 Mil. classification
10 Acts restless
11 First name in humor
12 "Society and Solitude" author
13 Enclosed passage in a church
14 David and others
21 Televisions
24 Arrives
26 Son of Rebekah
29 Competed, in a way
31 PC image type
36 Cap
38 D.D.'s inst.
39 Pushed
40 Ineligible, in a way
41 Dish for Robin Hood
43 About 25,000 square miles of Asia
45 Cyborg science
46 One of the original Mouseketeers
47 Visibly grieving
52 Ninnies
53 Makes an impression
56 X's
58 Kind of iron or chain
61 Orch. section
63 Some mindless singing

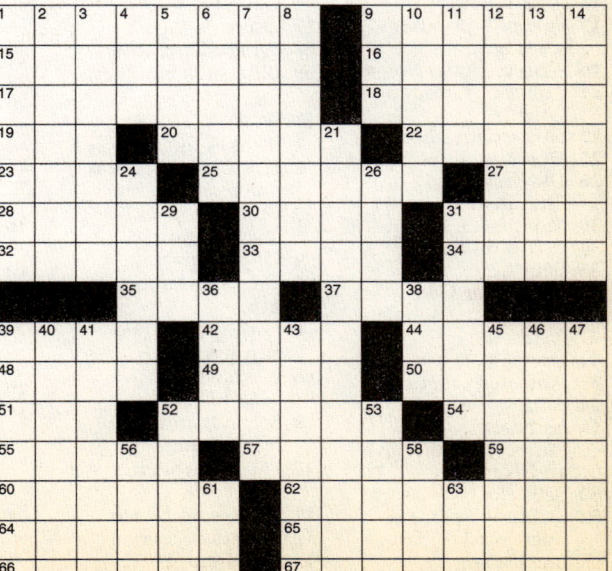

ACROSS

1 Freight
6 Watering holes
10 "Puttin' on the ___" (Berlin classic)
14 Completely foreign
15 Early part of the day
16 "Toreador Song," e.g., in "Carmen"
17 River to the Rhône
18 Italian man
19 Rope material
20 Parlors
23 Metal refuse
24 Hwy.
25 Stovetop item
28 Mailing ctrs.
31 "Damn Yankees" temptress
33 Predicament
35 Official proceedings
37 Cartoonist Gross
39 ___ diem (seize the day)
40 Applause, plus
43 Chili con ___
44 Vasco da ___
45 Back talk
46 Where some shoes are made
48 Bring home the bacon
50 "Yo!"
51 Martial arts expert Bruce
52 ___ Cruces, N.M.
54 Spanish rivers
56 Cane
61 Graduation month
64 Poi ingredient
65 Artist Matisse
66 Marco Polo crossed it
67 Catchall abbr.
68 Like certain seals
69 An American, to a Brit
70 Ownership document
71 Gobs

DOWN

1 Elliot, of the Mamas and the Papas
2 Jai ___
3 Uproar
4 Men's room sign
5 "Mourning Becomes Electra" playwright
6 Customs officer's concern
7 Opposite of rich
8 Knight's protection
9 High-hats
10 Cheerleaders' cheers
11 Anger
12 Director Burton or Robbins
13 Knock out, as with a remote
21 Supermodel Campbell
22 Muslim's destination
25 Outcast
26 Go up against
27 Wee
28 French mathematician Blaise
29 87 or 93 at the pump
30 Go on a hunger strike
32 Pond covering
34 "Fudge!"
36 Years, in old Rome
38 Roseanne's ex
41 Singer Reese
42 Brazilian airline
47 Stored, with "away"
49 Snacks
53 Use Rollerblades
55 Pilfer
56 Lacking strength
57 "Dies ___" (hymn)
58 Concerning
59 Ship's staff
60 Joshes
61 First Chief Justice John
62 Red, white and blue team
63 Writer Anaïs

ACROSS

1 Shopaholic's hangout
5 Out-and-out
10 Way to go
14 Pacific Rim locale
15 Shoe material
16 As a result
17 Part of a popular song lyric
20 Actress-skater Sonja
21 Chinese restaurant flowers
22 Suffix with idiom
25 Open, as an envelope
26 Old-fashioned illumination
30 Monticello, for one
34 1970's discipline
35 Bête ___
37 Book after Gen.
38 More of the song's lyric
42 Do-well starter
43 Anteater's feature
44 Actress Peeples
45 Not asea
48 Supporters of Ivan and Nicholas
50 Sells (for)
52 Onetime Spanish queen and namesakes
53 Draws
57 Midafternoon
61 Statement describing the subject of the song
64 Nectar flavor
65 Microwave brand
66 Gave the boot
67 Censor's target
68 Where Durban is
69 Baseball's Sandberg

DOWN

1 It takes figuring
2 U.S. Open stadium name
3 Property encumbrance
4 Of the lips
5 G.I. entertainment grp.
6 Large cask
7 Sermon basis
8 Newswoman Magnus et al.
9 Secondhand transaction
10 Did a horticulturist's job
11 Planets and such
12 Malarial fever
13 Children's connectibles
18 Eye layer
19 "Trinity" author
23 "___ a Name" (Jim Croce hit)
24 Debt markers
26 "I can't ___ satisfaction" (1965 lyric)
27 Visibly frightened
28 Shipment to Detroit
29 E.C. Bentley detective
31 Impulse transmitters
32 Namely
33 Author Ferber and others
36 Jagged
39 Exaggerator
40 Chinese dollar
41 Geologic layers
46 One noted for bringing couples together
47 Abase
49 Babylonian love goddess
51 1965 march site
53 Rewards for waiting
54 News bit
55 Son of Rebekah
56 Mattress support
58 Classic theater name
59 Gershwin biographer David
60 "Momo" author Michael
62 Actress Merkel
63 Actor Kilmer

985 by A.J. Santora

ACROSS

1 "Dragnet" force, for short
5 H & R Block workers
9 King ___
14 Bridge toll unit
15 Glen Gray's "Casa ___ Stomp"
16 Upright
17 Diana, with "the"
20 Overhang
21 Early Peruvian
22 Signal light
25 Famed Helen
29 Painfully sensitive
30 It may get higher with age
32 Take apart
33 50's–60's actress Debra
34 Club ___
35 Diana
39 One of Tom's rivals
41 Oscar de la ___
42 Own
45 Make enemies of
47 Field
49 It's full of slots
50 South African leader
51 Brain membrane
53 Socony rival
54 Diana tribute
61 Florida city
62 Superfine
63 Royal's school
64 One of Tom's rivals
65 Like show horses
66 Spanish lady

DOWN

1 Full circle
2 Pink-slip
3 U.N.-recognized grp. since 1974
4 Swear by
5 Witty
6 Brainteaser
7 Sound enhancer
8 Ranee's wrap
9 Symphonic composition
10 Available
11 Stinger
12 Ones providing IV's, maybe
13 Commercials
18 Area behind a dam
19 More black
22 A.C. unit
23 Sportscaster Berman
24 Paragraph starts
26 Citrus drink
27 WSW's opposite
28 Communist
30 Swiftness
31 Turkish title
33 Engine knock
36 Like table sugar
37 "The Raven" maiden
38 Tailed
39 Last mo.
40 ". . . lovely ___ tree"
43 Tennessee athlete
44 Actress Aulin
46 Sphinx's offering
47 Potato choice
48 Word in Massachusetts's motto
50 Subway
52 Snooty put-on
54 Swipe
55 One-spot
56 Slave leader Turner
57 Slangy refusal
58 "Who am ___ say?"
59 Sine qua ___
60 Genetic initials

986 by Nancy Salomon

ACROSS

1 Author Rona
6 Hits with a stun gun
10 Saudi or Iraqi
14 Sleep spoiler
15 Its motto is "Industry"
16 "___ Smile" (1976 hit)
17 Postgame activity
18 Off one's rocker
19 Porn
20 Loss of footing for a jockey?
23 Trophy locale
24 Spasms
25 What a champion jockey holds?
31 Montreal club
32 Indiana's state flower
33 Col. Sanders's place
36 Top of the heap
37 Gives notice
38 Lively dance
39 Put one past
40 Spirit
41 Sermon subjects
42 Nighttime jockey's gear?
44 Shook hands (on)
47 Suffix with boy or girl
48 Prizes for a winning jockey?
54 "Constant Craving" singer, 1992
55 Bedevils, in a way
56 Its symbol is two horns
58 Nose (out)
59 Wind, so to speak
60 Kind of eclipse
61 Vintage cars
62 José's hurrays
63 Tiffs

DOWN

1 Crock
2 Pub potables
3 It's true
4 Polite refusal, slangily
5 Catherine, for one
6 Bantu tribesman
7 Riding
8 Corcordat
9 Turns a maxi into a midi
10 Underwrite
11 Ex-Green Beret of film
12 As ___ (usually)
13 College in Lewiston, Me.
21 Red Cross workers, briefly
22 "Whatever will I do?"
25 C&W's McEntire
26 Board member, for short
27 ___ dixit
28 Words before "about" and "at 'em"
29 Rocks ahead
30 Actress Blakley
33 "The People's Court" judge, once
34 Stew
35 He ran against Taylor, 1848
37 Completely sold on
38 Bigwig
40 Highlander
41 Speech enliveners
42 Rushlike plants
43 Rye, e.g.: Abbr.
44 More adept
45 A, B or C
46 Fab Four name
49 Be hopping mad
50 Nasty sort
51 Manipulates
52 Ike's ex
53 Spot in the Senate
57 Promgoers: Abbr.

987 by Brendan Emmett Quigley

ACROSS
1 Partner of burn
6 "Enough already!"
12 Garden tool
14 Family need
15 1959 hit TV theme song
16 Connections
17 Semicircular recesses
18 Some trumpeters
20 No-goodnik
21 Last Pope to be sainted
22 Task
23 Objectionable
24 Switzerland's Bay of ___
25 Vocal effect
26 Lost cause
27 Dig discovery: Var.
29 As much
30 NBC slogan
32 "On the Sunny Side of the Street" songwriter
35 Charger
39 Heritage
40 Range rovers
41 Age
42 Accepts defeat
43 By accident, old-style
44 Formal accessory
45 ___ Miss
46 Kind of pool
47 "Michel Strogoff" author
48 Basque's kingdom
50 Blue Jay's song?
52 Opposing forces
53 Harder on the ears
54 "Archie" and "Cathy"
55 Go well together

DOWN
1 1945 Pulitzer poet
2 Case
3 Molar maladies
4 Is on the run
5 Common contraction
6 Essential beginning?
7 Coffeehouse equipment
8 It looks good on paper
9 Bullish
10 Gets rid of Dracula
11 Product checkers
12 Put the finishing touches on
13 Turn over a new leaf
14 Loose talk?
19 Blown about
22 Swagger
23 850 Turbo, e.g.
25 Gorillas
26 Third-century invaders
28 1940's South African P.M.
29 Like Dilbert
31 Near the beginning
32 Minstrel troupe member
33 Core fluid
34 Still
36 Prepare to change careers
37 Came across as
38 Win over
40 Pikas' kin
43 Signs up
44 Smarts
46 Boring one
47 Aspen alternative
49 Horner's last words
51 Part of the ear

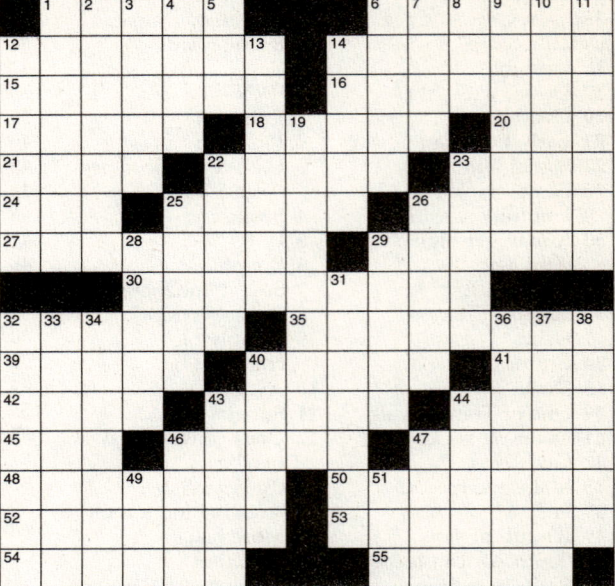

988 by Jim Page

ACROSS
1 Environmentalist's concern
10 Rudiments
14 Kind of zone
15 Stunts
17 Labor convenience
18 "In the name of ___"
19 "That's ___!"
20 Hilltop
21 Warhol's "___ Boxes"
22 Invoice word
23 Forget again
25 Anatomical tissue
26 Some assets, briefly
27 Verdi's "___ tu"
28 Reins
30 Barbell abbr.
31 Wool fats
32 Even, after "in"
34 ___ Lingus
35 Assyrian foe
36 Pizza order
38 Scepter
39 Implies
40 Member of the E.U.
41 Kind of catcher
44 African fox
45 ___ de Sévigné, French belletrist
47 Shoe box letters
48 Copies
50 First of a Latin trio
51 Chaps
52 Had food brought to the room
53 Stuffs
55 Bygone aide
56 Chart song
57 Hesse river
58 Passenger ships' sections

DOWN
1 Sitting, as a court
2 Provided fuel for an engine
3 Some footnotes
4 Account
5 '97 and '98, e.g.
6 Some Winter Olympians
7 Copenhagen park
8 When it's least chilly in Chile
9 Ball club V.I.P.: Abbr.
10 Way off
11 Depreciated
12 Bell Atlantic service
13 "Lock Up" star
16 Lighthouse site, maybe
21 "___ the alert!"
23 University of Nevada at Las Vegas team
24 Lasting effect
29 "Stop!"
30 Popular Warner-Lambert product
31 "The Magnificent Seven" gunslinger
32 After-dinner drink
33 Racing vehicle
34 Proceedings
36 Family in a 1936 novel
37 Big pet food brand
38 Sackcloth and ashes
40 Reproductive cell
41 Smooth-shelled ocean creature
42 Hawk
43 Toady's words
46 Longshoreman's device
49 ___ about
51 Actress Olin
53 Funhouse cries
54 Object of decoration

989   by Grace Fabbroni

ACROSS

1 Milky-white gem
5 Turned white
10 Inclusion with a MS.
14 Trucking rig
15 French love
16 Drug ___ (Washington pooh-bah)
17 Patronizing person
18 Sparkling headwear
19 Ladder step
20 Start of a quip
23 Son of Aphrodite
24 Fencing blade
25 Harmony
28 On the up-and-up
31 Rioter's take
32 Joins
34 Hen's pride
37 Middle of the quip
40 Adriatic, e.g.
41 Ryan and Tatum of filmdom
42 Verdi's slave girl
43 Tête-à-têtes
44 Awry
45 Feedback of a sort
47 Like auto shop floors
49 End of the quip

55 ___ and tell
56 Scarlett, for one
57 Snug
59 Sped
60 Heavy volumes
61 Lamb's sobriquet
62 Took advantage of
63 Kasparov's game
64 Red light directive

DOWN

1 C.I.A. predecessor
2 Await judgment
3 To me, in Paris
4 It kept Bizet busy
5 Outdoor lounging area
6 Faulty
7 Temporary use
8 Currency replacing the mark, franc, lira, etc.
9 "Phooey!"
10 Actor's "homework"
11 Sky-blue
12 "À votre ___!"
13 Work unit
21 Word repeated before "again," in a saying

22 Jefferson, religiously
25 Priests' garments
26 Grimace
27 Smidgen
28 Beans in a stew
29 List-ending abbr.
30 Catches on
32 Forearm bone
33 Boris's refusal
34 Actor Estrada
35 1947 Literature Nobelist André
36 Eat beaver-style
38 Not at all
39 Classic 30's–40's radio comedy
43 Reprimanded, with "out"
44 100%
45 Group character
46 Taking out the garbage, e.g.
47 Fairy tale villains
48 Bridge declaration
50 University mil. group
51 "Oops!"
52 Reputation
53 Revolver inventor
54 Pinza of the Met
55 Trio after R

58 Prattle

990   by Brendan Emmett Quigley

ACROSS

1 ___ de Boulogne (Paris park)
5 Constant complainer
9 Excite, as interest
14 Ancient inscription
15 Daughter of Cronus
16 Pluck
17 Start with boy or girl
18 "The jig ___!"
19 Much-played part of a 45
20 Led Zeppelin hit, 1969
23 English ___
24 Rocker Garcia, informally
25 Big Blue
26 "___ Yes!" (old political placard)
28 Jewel
30 Classic clown
32 It comes after Mardi
33 Gagging cry
35 Actor Beatty
36 Make out
37 Midgame broadcasts
42 Inch, e.g.
43 "Pish posh!"
44 Part of an academic yr.

45 Sicilian spouter
46 McDonald's founder Ray
48 Dance version of a pop song, e.g.
52 "Comprende?"
53 Clump
54 Make sense, with "up"
56 British verb ending
57 Alternative to a Whopper
61 Deceit
62 Engagement gift
63 Waters: Fr.
64 Part of a furniture joint
65 Pins and needles holder
66 Fair distance
67 Works with words
68 Do carbon-testing on
69 Table scraps

DOWN

1 Barroom fights
2 Do better than at bat
3 Altogether
4 Whiskered circus animal

5 Its capital is Santiago
6 Soak up again
7 In ___ (stuck)
8 Saint John, for one
9 Sacred song
10 ___ facto
11 Shaker
12 Just walk through a role, say
13 Stretch, with "out"
21 Cassette deck button
22 Homes
27 Questions
29 First-term Clinton victory
31 ". . . and ___ grow on"
32 Treasure-hoarding dwarf
34 Popular candy bar
37 Tinted
38 Artificially made to look old
39 Pasta favorite
40 Trounced, in sports
41 Hidden
47 Screw backer
49 Any point in a trapeze artist's routine
50 Tristram's love

51 Persian king who destroyed Athens
53 Brown songbirds
55 Cowboy's stray
58 Tons

59 Meter maid of song
60 Verne captain
61 AT&T competitor

991 by Randall J. Hartman

ACROSS

1 Doberman doc
4 Antony of antiquity
8 Match play?
13 Touch
15 Director Kazan
16 Tragic Montague
17 Asta's mistress
18 Afternoon affairs
19 In pieces
20 Joe DiMaggio's nickname
23 Completely lost
24 Teachers' grp.
25 Mai ___
28 "Edward ___"
33 Dawber who played Mindy
36 Hounds' quarry
37 Basketballer Shaquille
38 2001, for one
40 Cousin of a minibike
43 Salinger heroine
44 Miser's motivation
46 Go like lightning
48 J.F.K. sight
49 Member of the P.G.A. Seniors Tour
53 Exclamation of affirmation
54 Buddy Holly's "Peggy ___"
55 Coffee preference
59 Somerset Maugham novel
64 Panel member
66 Winners break it
67 Select at random
68 Under way
69 Home of Phillips University
70 Unit of loudness
71 Wins going away
72 Requirement
73 Damage

DOWN

1 Chekhov's "Uncle ___"
2 W.W. II menace
3 Changes colors
4 Dole
5 One of the Baldwins
6 Qum coin
7 1995 De Niro film
8 Oklahoma Indian
9 Skip it
10 Savvy
11 "___ the ramparts . . ."
12 "___ to worry"
14 Movie shots
21 Apiece
22 Apiece
26 President from Braintree
27 Cay
29 Beatles' "___ the Walrus"
30 Sign at the Bijou
31 Dividing membranes
32 Chemical suffix
33 African tribesman
34 Hawk's home
35 Powerful whirlpool
39 Fam. member
41 Always, to Keats
42 Smidgen
45 Gobi and Kalahari
47 1990 World Series champs
50 Capek classic
51 Whipped
52 Bassoon and oboe
56 PC feature
57 Capital of Guam
58 Not as many
60 Showy earring
61 "Riders of the Purple Sage" author Grey
62 Ron Howard role
63 Comedian Foxx
64 Jelly holder
65 ET's ride

992 by Manny Nosowsky

ACROSS

1 Scratch the surface of
4 "No bid"
9 People person
14 Old Foghorn, e.g.
15 "I Fall to Pieces" singer
16 Twinkle-toed
17 Nonsense
18 Pugilistic sweethearts?
20 Irons on stage
22 April honoree
23 Hurricane heading: Abbr.
24 Kind of cleaner
25 Curly do
26 Sweater
27 Girls who love books?
31 Hang it all!
32 Casanova
33 Waiting period, seemingly
34 It runs in the rain
36 Midwest city where Orson Welles was born
40 Non-earthlings, briefly
41 Prefix with dose
42 Four times a day, in prescriptions
43 Dog show event?
46 Seles foe
48 The bulk
49 "Veni, ___, vici"
50 "Frasier" role
51 "Minimum" amount
52 Japanese leader of old
54 The first four-minute mile, e.g.?
57 Band's booking
58 Wedding reception, say
59 "Pomp and Circumstance" composer
60 Baton Rouge sch.
61 Opening books
62 Color changers
63 Incas' realm, e.g.: Abbr.

DOWN

1 Oregano shelfmate
2 Plant used for skin lotions
3 Getaways
4 Part of a nuclear arsenal, for short
5 Ruse
6 ___-en-Provence
7 Cold sufferer's sound
8 Lady of la casa
9 Telephone
10 Cause of conflict, maybe
11 Adds zest to
12 1985 Nelligan film
13 Under siege
19 Zip
21 Terminal
25 Oaxaca water
26 Lotto variant
28 Breathing fire
29 Viking shipmate
30 Destroyer detector
35 Old "What's My Line" panelist
36 Ohio college town
37 Tilde, e.g.
38 Brahman's belief
39 Making sense
41 Cheap
43 Marketplace
44 Tenacious
45 Ab ___ (from day one)
46 White collar crime
47 "Arise, fair sun, and kill the envious moon" speaker
51 In the company of
52 Slash mark?
53 That lady's
55 When doubled, a Gabor
56 Wine improver

by Martin Ashwood-Smith

ACROSS
1 They help in the classroom
16 Étoile's medium
17 John Hancock's place
18 Take orders, in a way
19 Random one
20 Jimmy
21 Certain league: Abbr.
23 Alarmist?
26 Bara contemporary
28 N. Car. neighbor
29 What a patrol car might get, for short
30 Bad looks
34 Suffix with corrupt
38 Shakes hands
41 Saab model
42 Fly over the Equator
43 Casting requirement?
44 Pasternak lady
46 1974 Hoffman movie
48 Japanese mat
50 "___ It Romantic?"
51 Praying figure
53 Lot
55 Old fool
58 Three of a kind?
62 Bushel or inch, e.g.
63 Splurged

DOWN
1 Have ___ (freak out)
2 It parallels the radius
3 Singles spot
4 1987 Beatty flop
5 Monosaccharide
6 "Myra Breckinridge" author
7 Screen symbol
8 Letch
9 Final: Abbr.
10 One of the brothers of Warner Bros.
11 Soup server
12 Kind of reaction
13 "As ___ and breathe!"
14 Sandy tract
15 Trick ending
22 Mrs. Addams, to Gomez
24 Milestone
25 Travel needs
26 Japan's first capital
27 Sport played to three points
31 Aquarium acquisition
32 Tea-growing state
33 Canadian pol Bob ___
35 Springsteen's first hit
36 Author ___ Hubbard
37 Turning point?
39 Strainer
40 "Fantasia" frames
45 Getup
47 House
48 Home of the N.H.L.'s Lightning
49 Ethnic prefix
50 The Dow, e.g.
51 Mayberry sot
52 Cakewalk
54 Treater's words
56 Bobby and others
57 Prized Pacific salmon
59 El ___
60 State that borders Colo.
61 One's lot

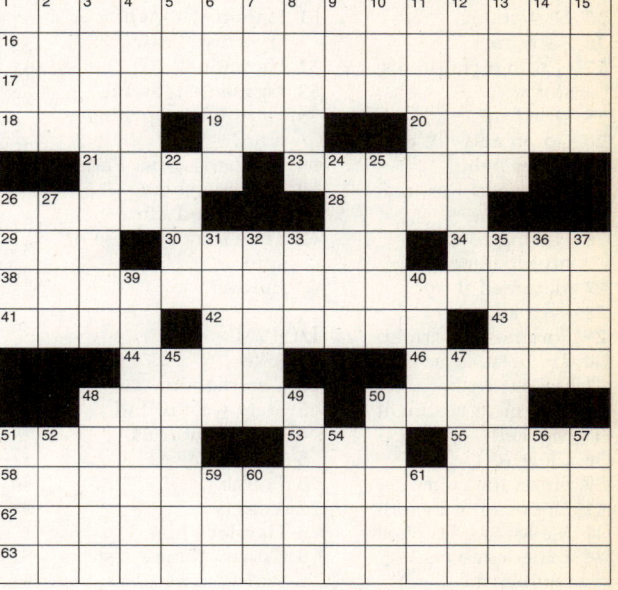

by Fred Piscop

ACROSS
1 Tapioca source
8 High-elevation areas
15 Most desirable
16 Horseshoe locale
17 Blue prints?
18 Of the blood
19 Strictness
20 The Mustangs, for short
22 Narc's find
23 Conflict resolver, at times
24 Of ___ (alike)
26 City near Padua
27 Poetic preposition
28 Part of a nuclear research facility
30 It may be curried
31 Kind of broker
33 Worshipers at the church of Santa Maria della Spina
35 Beat around the bush
37 Examine closely
40 Like some winds
44 Old greeting
45 Diamond displayers
47 Some M.I.T. grads
48 Jambalaya need
50 Looks
51 Word before 1 or 2
52 Girl's name in a 1990 Billy Joel title
54 When doubled, a David Merrick musical
55 Della ___ (St. Peter's architect)
56 "Ulysses" hero Stephen
58 Depleting
60 Narrowest of victory margins
61 You can feel it
62 Verse form used by Dante
63 Hick

DOWN
1 Involuntary
2 Based on hypothesis
3 Smelly smokes
4 Suppress
5 Mideast ruler
6 Hoover, informally
7 Tlingits and others
8 Slangy answer
9 Amount to be divided
10 Whales the tar out of
11 Steelie alternative
12 Bullwinkle archenemy
13 Popular cold remedy
14 Indian chiefs
21 Ready to cry
24 They make you laugh
25 Kicks out
28 March man
29 Rebels
32 I.B.M. "brain"
34 Abbr. in many Paris street names
36 Cape Cod town
37 Mardi Gras highlights
38 Curse, of sorts
39 Moves back
41 Debate anew
42 Stern reprimand
43 Like a slingshot
46 Professional companion
49 Praise
51 Alpes, e.g.
53 Part of a court game name
55 Fairy
57 Swabs' grp.
59 One of seven

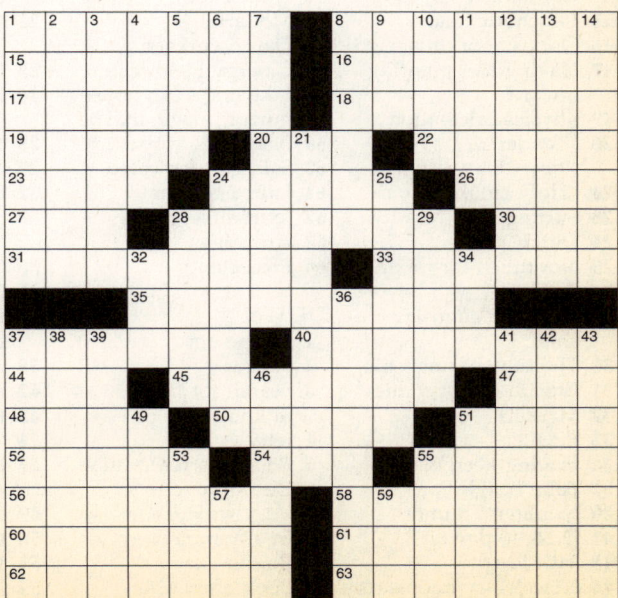

995   by Holden Baker

ACROSS

1 Walk, trot or canter
5 Cheese served with crackers
9 Cavort
13 Speak without notes
15 Loaf about
16 Race track
17 Girl in a children's story
19 Dried up
20 Go on and off, as a traffic light
21 Spain and Portugal
23 Polluted
26 Having round protuberances
27 Hammed it up
28 Irish accent
29 Foremost's partner
30 Try, as a case
31 Go out with
34 Liturgical vestment
35 Mocked
38 Clear (of)
39 Shirts for golfers?
41 Opposite of include
42 Mellowing, as cheese
44 Long-legged shorebird
46 90's music or fashion
47 These can be winning or losing
49 Scarlet bird
50 Readies, as a pool cue
51 Harold who wrote "Stormy Weather"
52 Harangue
53 Worse than awful
58 Fairy tale's opening word
59 They crisscross Paris
60 Grafting shoot
61 Bambi and kin
62 They may be loose or split
63 Burden

DOWN

1 Joke
2 Commotion
3 State west of Ind.
4 Choice morsels
5 Flaxen-haired
6 Boulder
7 Variety
8 Hamlet's home
9 Citizen Kane's last word
10 Domineering
11 Nobelist Curie
12 Beg
14 Military lodgings
18 Stretched the truth, so to speak
22 Peat locale
23 Trim, as a roast
24 Author Zola
25 Restraint
26 Velveeta maker
28 Comport with
30 Development developments
32 Touch of color
33 Landscaping tool
36 Overconfident
37 Sock menders
40 More slender and graceful
43 Wild llama
45 Acorn tree
46 Joyous celebration
47 Seafood order
48 Macbeth, for one
49 Lady's keepsake to a soldier, once
51 Not up yet
54 Convent dweller
55 Storage container
56 Costello or Grant
57 Printer's widths

996   by Peter Gordon

ACROSS

1 Golf hazard
5 Abound
9 A few
13 ___ law (old Germanic legal code)
15 Lunchbox treat
16 Opposite of unter
17 Having feet pointing inward
19 Physics calculation
20 "Tender ___" (1983 Robert Duvall film)
21 "Holy smokes!"
23 Surfing site
24 Dutch airline
25 Not much for mixing
27 Attire
29 Onetime Yugoslav chief
30 The time of one's life
31 Brenda of the comics
32 Markets
33 Bewitch
34 Having keen vision
37 Baby beagle
40 Nonliteral humor
41 Dusk to dawn
45 34th Prez
46 New Jersey hoopsters
47 Indian homes
48 Soup dishes
50 PC alternative
51 Home planet in a 1978-82 sitcom
52 One of the McCartneys
53 Dairy workers
55 Cinergy Field team
56 Like one's fun house mirror image, maybe
59 Baseball's Moises
60 Salinger dedicatee
61 Lace place mat
62 Journalist Hamill
63 Arousing
64 Protected

DOWN

1 Recipe amt.
2 Attire
3 Search for the unknown?
4 Jetty
5 Pole on a reservation
6 God of love
7 Very wide, shoewise
8 In a humble way
9 Poison ___
10 Book after Amos
11 Bit of E-mail
12 Hosp. areas
14 Foolish
18 Cairo's river
22 Flexible, like some lamp shafts
23 "Scream" director Craven
25 Choreographer Alvin
26 Big Apple subway stop, for short
28 Mine metal
29 Rebellious time
32 Casino machines
35 Soldiers' "pineapples"
36 Quick swim
37 Raucous card game
38 Tiny Tim's instrument
39 August birthstone
42 Where Athens is
43 Feminine pronoun
44 "Naughty, naughty!"
47 Like most N.B.A. players
49 Follow
50 Boy in Life cereal ads
53 1910, on cornerstones
54 Stars have big ones
55 Hip-hop
57 Put to work
58 Hair coloring

997   by Elizabeth C. Gorski

ACROSS

1 & 6 Attacked verbally
10 Key
14 Circumvent
15 Twelve, half of the time
16 Cast off
17 Ear-related
18 Zilch, so to speak
19 White-water carrier
20 Like some Halloween costumes
23 Erhard's claim to fame
24 "___ Tu" (70's hit)
25 Knot again
27 Charlotte russe, for one
30 More slick
31 Kind of support
34 Big section in a dictionary
35 "The Fabulous Baker Boys" actor
38 Journal publisher
40 Starts to cry
41 Venue
44 One of the Apostles
48 Where a bangle may dangle
49 Hunt and peck
51 Have a go at
52 Golden parachute, e.g.
56 Fly high
57 Onetime airline
58 ___ lunch
59 Drink with Stilton
60 Michelangelo's work
61 Part of a wood joint
62 Common links
63 The supreme Supreme
64 Observatory observations

DOWN

1 Paged
2 Tear apart
3 Gemologist's concern
4 Round cheese
5 Take out
6 Flotation device
7 Looped rope
8 Morrison and Braxton
9 Small bills
10 Handel's "___ in Egypt"
11 Hovels
12 Southpaws
13 Summer hrs. in D.C.
21 Send another way
22 Prefix with state
26 Sounds of fluster
28 Quito-to-La Paz dir.
29 Govt. watchdog
30 Senior citizen
32 Sp. lady
33 Places for flight patterns
35 Unenlightened
36 Gloomy guy
37 Center starter
38 Pie-mode connection
39 Wet time
42 Signals
43 Jackie's sister
45 Site of the forges of Hephaestus, in myth
46 Daniel Webster, e.g.
47 Hose
49 Complete, informally
50 "The Wild Swans at Coole" poet
53 It can give you a lift
54 Kindergarteners
55 Puccini's "Flower ___"
56 Place to unwind

998   by Raymond Hamel

ACROSS

1 Construct
5 Meadow sounds
9 Barbra's "A Star Is Born" co-star
13 "The Good Earth" heroine
14 Runs while sitting
16 Cassio's rival
17 Benchmark
18 Hotel employee
19 False locks
20 Cheesy TV comedy?
23 Witch's potential meal
24 A mean Amin
25 Cheesy TV cop show?
32 Doo-wop syllable
35 Floor model
36 Change
37 Chirac's state
39 Country singer Tillis
41 Sunni, e.g.
42 1970 Tony winner for "Applause"
45 Harsh words
48 Locomobile contemporary
49 Cheesy TV comedy?
52 Back, in a way
53 Muss up
57 Cheesy TV detective show, with "The"?
62 Clue
63 South African province
64 TV knob
65 Toiletries case
66 One of the Titans
67 Jim Davis canine
68 Member of a traditional establishment
69 First name in TV comedy
70 Russo of "Outbreak"

DOWN

1 Calendar page
2 Sandwich Islands greeting
3 Silkwood of "Silkwood"
4 Tangle up
5 Oyster, e.g.
6 Classic Rodin sculpture
7 Start of a Shakespearean title
8 Deem appropriate
9 Bird whose males incubate the eggs
10 Epitome of thinness
11 Rock singer ___ Pop
12 Urgent call
15 Sports facilities
21 Pooped
22 Peeve
26 Signal booster
27 Circus noises
28 Speculations
29 Tack, in a way
30 "___ homo"
31 "How to Make an American Quilt" author Whitney ___
32 Corporate concern
33 Bryce Canyon locale
34 Defensive spray
38 Flat hat
40 Welcome site
43 Outdoor party
44 Scale holder
46 Alit
47 One who leads class struggle?
50 "Foul!"
51 Swain
54 Water park sight
55 Order of ___ (bygone award)
56 Lauder of cosmetics
57 Romance writer's award
58 Load to bear
59 Bathroom cabinet item
60 Oklahoma native
61 Big name in mapmaking
62 Cabinet acronym, once

999 by Chuck Deodene

ACROSS

1 Israel, to some
9 Closet odorizer
15 Source of cubes
16 Individually
17 Jazzy rhythm technique
18 Four-wheeler
19 Promulgate
20 Hybrid
22 Ziegfeld offering
23 ___ Na Na
24 Like sex symbols
26 Hit bottom?
29 Italian monk
30 Gulf war ally
33 "L.A. Law" lawyer
34 Average guys
35 Plane capt.'s announcement
36 "Just simmer down!"
40 Kind of beetle
41 Aerosol
42 African antelope
43 A four-star meal it's not
45 Med. center ward
46 Leaks
47 Indian of southern Mexico
49 Prefix with handle
50 Tuscany town
52 Blow the joint
54 Frat letter
57 Bait
59 Symptoms of otitis
61 Operatives
62 Battle of Britain fighter
63 Dumas's "La Reine ___"
64 Work boot feature

DOWN

1 Heckle, in a way
2 VIII
3 Plaintive cry
4 Akihito, e.g.: Abbr.
5 Kind of kid
6 Director Kurosawa
7 Early comics name
8 Executive's fashion credo
9 Wilt
10 To the left
11 "O tempora, O mores!" speaker
12 It's just a racket to some
13 Decorator's shade
14 Where les yeux are
21 Optimal, as a bet
23 Salon sound
25 Truss
26 "Land ___!"
27 Alberto VO5 rival
28 Wind instrument
31 A-test site, perhaps
32 Some baby holders
34 Saliva
37 Drop
38 Soul mate
39 Bar selections
44 Heartsick (for)
48 Kind of knife
49 English novelist Corelli
50 Vein
51 Swenson of "Benson"
53 Absorbed
54 Voucher
55 Parade honoree
56 "Uh-huh"
58 Inflationary suffix
60 Toronto Argonauts' org.

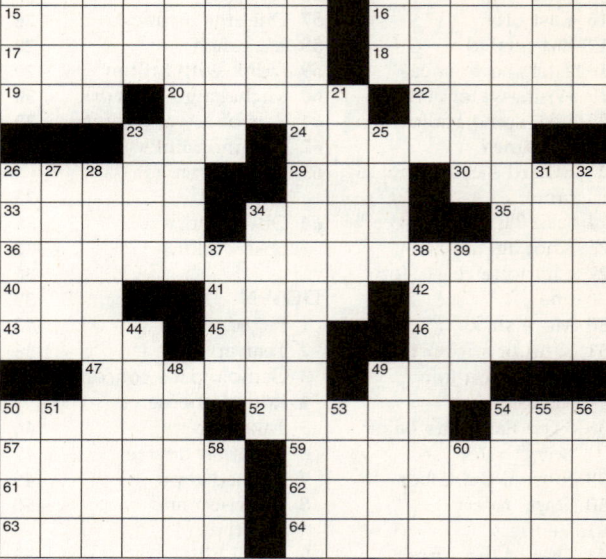

1000 by Nancy Schuster

ACROSS

1 Junk E-mail
5 Good engine sounds
10 Police cry
14 Tramp
15 Cause of an 1839–42 war
16 Giggler of Sesame Street
17 Telephone button
18 "Pagliacci" baritone
19 Carson's predecessor at NBC
20 Pleasantly drunk, so to speak
23 "Winnie-the-Pooh" baby
24 ___ chi ch'uan
25 Extra added detraction?
32 H.S. math
33 Hot
34 Vice ___
36 Bacteria-inhibiting drug
39 French nobleman
40 "Waiting for Lefty" playwright
41 Run ___ of (violate)
42 Name on over 75 whodunits
44 Comic screech
45 Paris attraction
49 Alphabetic sequence
50 Veto
51 Make a mistake
58 Japanese soup
59 Iranian V.I.P.'s
60 Hairdo
62 Art patron ___ Kahn
63 Hawley's tariff act co-sponsor
64 58-Across ingredient
65 Call from the minaret
66 Poet dramatized by Goethe
67 Shortly

DOWN

1 Sound at the movies
2 "Now you see it, now you don't!"
3 Skilled
4 Big Apple museum, for short, with "the"
5 Witches' brews
6 Well-informed about
7 Prize of the Nibelung
8 Bankrupt
9 Peanut butter choice
10 Working again
11 Jai ___
12 Single-named supermodel
13 Like first-place medals in Grenoble
21 Mauna ___
22 Nurmi, the Flying Finn
25 Cotton down
26 Yukon home
27 Gives over
28 Demographer's region
29 Sunrise to sunset to sunrise, e.g.
30 Feminist Germaine
31 First name in skin care
32 Simile's center
35 Quiz
37 Time for the werewolf alert
38 Out on ___
43 Che, formally
46 Collect, as volunteers
47 Tomcat
48 Combo bet at Belmont
51 Irish name part
52 Logo at Arthur Ashe Stadium
53 Austen heroine
54 Santa Fe Trail stop
55 Certain insurers
56 Nutcase
57 Acctg. principle
58 Kiwi's extinct cousin
61 Jollity

AVAILABLE NOW

Shortz says: The puzzle's clever theme is signaled by the circled letters in the middle of the grid. For the constuctor to get all these multi-checked letters to work could not have been easy.

 **1001** by Bill Zais

ACROSS

1 Passport feature
6 Role for Ingrid
10 Bridge toll unit
14 Overthrowing a base, e.g.
15 Select
16 Prehistoric terror, informally
17 Superhero's home
19 Go on and on
20 "Look, up in the ___!"
21 Playboy centerfold
22 Authority
23 32 pieces and a board
25 Speed: Abbr.
26 Certain teas
29 They go well with plaids
31 Diamond unit
32 Asian plains
35 River to Hades
36 Stayed at home
37 Best Picture of 1958
40 Dress store section
42 Feeling puffed up
43 Players in a dome, once

45 Taken care of
46 "___ Te Ching"
47 More skittish
51 Like much notebook paper
53 "The Unity of India" writer
54 Symbol on a cape
57 Et ___
58 Superhero's nickname
60 Drunks
61 Smooth (out)
62 Baseball Hall-of-Famer Combs
63 Deuce taker
64 "Pretty Woman" co-star
65 Berate

DOWN

1 Grad sch. classes
2 Trudge
3 Pretentious
4 Commercial suffix with "Sav-"
5 Prognosticator
6 Computer programs have them
7 Whoppers
8 Mooring spots

9 Gore and Bundy
10 Gillette brand
11 Superhero's skill
12 Filmed, in Hollywood slang
13 Praises lavishly
18 Slapstick comedy items
22 Clog (up)
23 Encourager
24 "SportsZone" airer
26 I.B.M. products
27 Partake of
28 Superhero's undoing
30 Fictional Simon
32 Used a bench
33 Mao ___-tung
34 Wasser in the winter
36 Smart-alecky
38 Belt tightener?
39 Altar reply
41 Snitched
42 Scans
43 Finally
44 Expert on spars and stars
45 Catch a wave
48 Catch
49 Mister, in Mendoza
50 Radiated
52 "___ does it"
54 Architect Saarinen

55 Talk up
56 Huskies' load
58 Russian plane
59 Middle of XXX

Solution for Bonus Puzzle 1001

S	T	A	M	P	█	I	L	S	A	█	A	X	L	E
E	R	R	O	R	█	C	U	L	L	█	T	R	E	X
M	E	T	R	O	P	O	L	I	S	█	R	A	N	T
S	K	Y	█	P	I	N	U	P	█	S	A	Y	S	O
█	█	C	H	E	S	S	S	E	T	█	V	E	L	█
P	E	K	O	E	S	█	█	S	O	L	I	D	S	█
C	A	R	A	T	█	S	T	E	P	P	E	S	█	█
S	T	Y	X	█	W	A	S	I	N	█	G	I	G	I
█	█	P	E	T	I	T	E	S	█	P	R	O	U	D
A	S	T	R	O	S	█	█	S	E	E	N	T	O	█
T	A	O	█	L	E	S	S	U	R	E	█	█	█	█
L	I	N	E	D	█	N	E	H	R	U	█	E	S	S
A	L	I	A	█	M	A	N	O	F	S	T	E	E	L
S	O	T	S	█	I	R	O	N	█	E	A	R	L	E
T	R	E	Y	█	G	E	R	E	█	S	C	O	L	D

1

```
LADD  OPENS  ABBE
OLEO  FRATS  SEAL
AVERYFISHERHALL
MARMOSET    EERIE
     YES   DABS
TEAPOT  AURA  OPT
ARLO  ERECT   PAW
NATIONALTHEATRE
GSA  LOVES   NIKE
OER  IDES  CANCAN
    IVES   BAD
BERNE   PANDEMIC
TEATROALLASCALA
URGE  ICIER  HILT
SOAR  LEERY  ODES
```

6

```
ATIT  MELS   SPAIN
TONE  ARUT   PASTE
STEN  RICE   ERASE
EARTHSCIENCE
ALTHEA  DREI   MAA
    SAL    AARONS
ASH  DAILYPLANET
SMEE   RIO    GERE
WORLDRECORD   TAR
ATTLEE    IAN
NEZ  APED   CRESTS
   GLOBETHEATRE
WHALE  SLUE   TAIL
OILER  ETES   ELEE
OPENS  NAST   NESS
```

11

```
SLAB  ABAFT   ADAM
PAPA  MELEE   GIBE
AVES  BABAR   ONUS
MAXIMUMSTRENGTH
    LESS    AMY
SLEIGH  OOZE   ALA
TALC   BLAZE   BUD
ADVANCEDFORMULA
LEI   ALLIS   ISUP
ENS  CUTE  ABLEST
    ARB   ONME
WHITERTHANWHITE
HURL  OHARA   IDES
EMMA  ORIEL   GELS
TEAS  MOLDS   HALO
```

16

```
KHAKI  HADJ   ASHE
NOCAN  ACRE   SLAV
OBEYS  SHAW   TORE
TODAYSNEWSPAPER
   KNIT   HERESY
ABJECT    SMART
BOOR   BOARD    CAB
CROSSWORDPUZZLE
SON   HOLED   OATS
HYMAN    THERES
ANGOLA    DOIT
FORTYNINEACROSS
LIAR  IDOL  COCOA
ASTO  SLOT  UPTON
TEED  HERA  PEONS
```

2

```
ARENA  AABB   SCAT
GOBEL  BURR   UHUH
AURAL  AREA   BIDE
STOLENCARS    PLEA
AOK    SWAIN
ALHIRT    ABHORS
LAIRS  SNEAK   AEC
ONTV  CUGAT   SULU
TAR  BARED   WICKS
ERASER   BOPEEP
SCENE    SEZ
BLOC  MOLTENLAVA
LIRA  ELIE  IOWAN
ADDS  NINA  AVANT
BEST  TODD  KEYES
```

7

```
MOSHE  CRIB   CAPE
ATEAM  HOAR   OXEN
THEHONEYMOONERS
TOMATO    BARR
    ETCH  DEARIE
AUDREYMEADOWS
HANG  EDMOND   LIS
ALTO   INS    ELLA
DEI  ANNALS   LILY
JACKIEGLEASON
INSETS    SMUT
ACTA    LEGATE
JOETHEBARTENDER
UNTO   GENE   LAIRS
GOON   GLAD   ERNIE
```

12

```
WARM  FORMA   ODDS
ALOE  ONEAL   RIOT
STATUEOFLIBERTY
HONOR    CLOTHE
OGRE    CIA
ESC  EMMALAZARUS
SHAM  SOME   ERASE
SIREN  TEA   DOZER
ENERO  INNS   NERF
NEWCOLOSSUS   SSS
DEN   EMIT
OTOOLE    ZOWIE
GROVERCLEVELAND
LAZE  EPOXY   LAKE
EYER  DANTE   SCAN
```

17

```
REBEL  EGBDF   WAG
AROMA  BROAD   EEL
MAXIMBOXCAMERA
OTIS   VEE    ODIN
ALF  ACHED   RAYED
DUFF   HELICES
MAILBOX  NAB   SHE
ENCOIL    JOSHUA
NNE  TAJ  BOXCARS
PERUSAL   IDLE
OPALS  KHMER   OYL
RICE   OER    SHAW
SQUAWKBOX   EMBER
OUT   ILOVE  ABOVE
NEE   TAXES  SIXED
```

3

```
HUTS   LISA   RICH
OLEO  MUSHY   EVIE
PURL  OILER   MANX
ELM  JOSE   FONDA
FAIRASASTARWHEN
OTTER   HRE    ORE
REED  ATRAIN   ESS
ONLYONEIS
BMT  ALICES   AMAS
OAR   ZEN   AMISH
SHININGINTHESKY
WALES  LIRA    LAS
ELLE  QUITO   PANT
LIED  USURY   RICE
LADY  ACME   ODER
```

8

```
SPACE  SAME   MASC
COLON  TRAY   INTO
ARCED  OOZEANDOZ
RCA  WILD   STOWE
FIZZEDCLASS   VAN
SNAILS    UNPEGS
ERTE   APSE    URE
HELLRAZOR
TRE  ALEX   LIST
LOIRET   DENIRO
ARP  SEIZERSALAD
SNOOP  DIVE    VIE
HAPPYDAZE   AMENS
EDER   THIN   CORES
SONY   SOTS   HOSEA
```

13

```
HECTARE    ERIN
EXHIBITS   ADENO
ACEPHATE  REBABS
DISPOSAL  INAROW
ESTER    FASTLANE
RESTSTOPS   ALBEE
INOSITOLS
CHINESEDATE
POORTASTE
GALLO  RESETTLES
ALLONYMS   ROAST
GAUCHE  SALINITY
ANDEAN  EROTICAL
CENTS   DETONATE
EDES    SINGLES
```

18

```
MACE  EMBARK   VON
ALAN  MAIDEN   IRA
RIDDICKBOWE   OAR
IVE  DEES  REALLY
SETTLER    MILLI
OED    LATEENS
FABER  FOYER   BIN
AMOS  IOTAS   BOZO
BED  ECRUS   BOWER
SIGNETS    BLY
DITCH   HEADSET
DODGER  YEAR    AXE
AXL  BEAUXGESTES
TEE  BARREL   HIRT
ANY  EMPIRE   ANTS
```

4

```
CARLO   SRI   FATAL
OPIUM   TEN   ANOUT
NISAN  RECORDERS
TEQUILASUNRISE
ECUS  APERS    HAW
SEE   TSP    BIOTA
BOHEA   VENEER
MIXEDDRINKS
OMANIS   MERES
LOREN   VIS    SAW
ENT  LABEL   ALDA
SINGAPORESLING
STAIRCASE   OCEAN
PENNI   RUN   BASTE
ARSON   TNT   ENTER
```

9

```
TAMP  ETAL   BRAVA
UTAH  LOCI   OILER
NORA  ALEG   OPERA
APUNSTERASKSCAN
TEED    MESA
STEAL  OPEN   WELT
CEASES  SNOB   SIR
APSYCHIATRISTBE
LEE  TILT   ASTERN
DESI  ELSA   TREED
SELF    BARI
CALLEDANIDOCTOR
AMEER  TODO   TILE
AMATI  EVER   EDGE
NORSE  DADE   READ
```

14

```
ATRIA  COUP   ARCH
NOONS  EASE   COLO
KNOCKEDFORALOOP
ASTAIRES    RUSSO
NED   FAG    TEN
GULAG    ALLY
ARAB  SAMUEL   APE
DISCOMBOBULATED
SST  ROBUST   TORI
IGOR    KAPUT
WAS  EST    IRA
AGAIN    STARTREK
FRUSTRATEDNOEND
TENN  ATOM   ATACK
SEAT  PEWS   KOREA
```

5

```
ELIZA  BEL    BOMB
MYGAL  ACE   LUNAR
MOONLIGHTSONATA
ANTE  REO   AUDITS
AIL    AMPERES
ACROSS    RISE
TAINT  GOSH   ACHE
ONCEINABLUEMOON
PEER  ELIE   LOVED
STAN    ASSESS
MOSLEMS    ORE
OCTANE  ETC    INCA
THEMANINTHEMOON
TENET  DOE   GAMIN
EROS   ISR   OMENS
```

10

```
PALMA  DODDERING
ONAIR  ENERGIZER
STINT  NEVERMORE
SIDNEY  ODE    DOW
ECTO    ORANGS
SLOWEDUP   ESCROW
SIR  RAPPED   RAPE
IMETA   EEL   MODES
VASE  SENSOR   INT
EXTANT   DISCLOSE
ERASES    OPER
AND   WIG   ORPHAN
PERCAPITA   APOSE
EVANGELIC   TENOR
DAMNEDEST   EDENS
```

15

```
MIMI  FIRST   OHMS
ERIN  ARENA   LEIS
LIST  RANON   ELSE
THEBOSTONPOPS
IAGO    PEI    MIR
SPROUTS   REPAVE
ATREAR    ETES
FATHERFIGURES
MIRE    PEDANT
ERODED  SISTINE
GEM  NAP    INON
DADDYLONGLEGS
LOTI  TAHOE   NOUN
EGIS  OTTER   CORA
ASCH  NOOSE   EDEN
```

19

```
CDE   SAMAR    EDA
WROTE  CREPE   PAC
PUTONTHEDOG    ILA
ASHINE   ILLICIT
HELENS    COES
LEADADOGSLIFE
DOI  DEKE   ANAT
EDNA  REPOT   MDSE
NODS   OTRA    ITS
TRYITONTHEDOG
DIRE   ENDUES
STDENIS   CLINIC
AHA  GOTOTHEDOGS
BOZ  ELLER   SAUNA
ERE  DEERE    SSE
```

20

```
DUAL  PACERS   BEG
OGLE  IMARET   UAR
CHICAGOHOPE   FRA
TIL   NOR    AFLY
DUNE    ESSAYS
INARUT    CASUAL
SOLE  SCHISM   ODD
MOLDS  OAR   SOBER
ERA  ARROYO   VILE
SEVENS    THELAW
FOGGED    HURL
AFRO   DOE    EMU
UTE  SEATTLESLEW
NEE  REFUEL   ESTO
ANN  ORSINO   DUCK
```

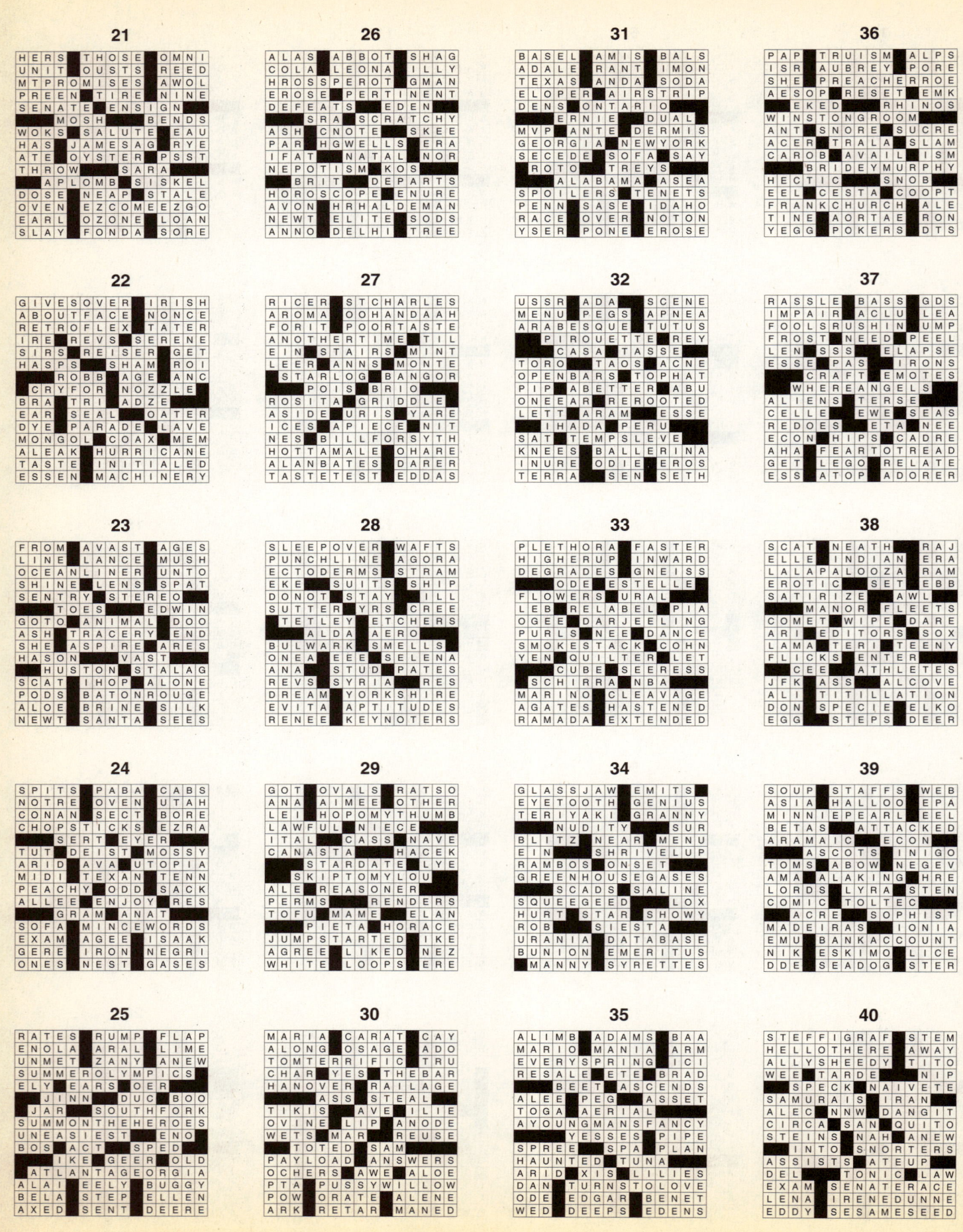

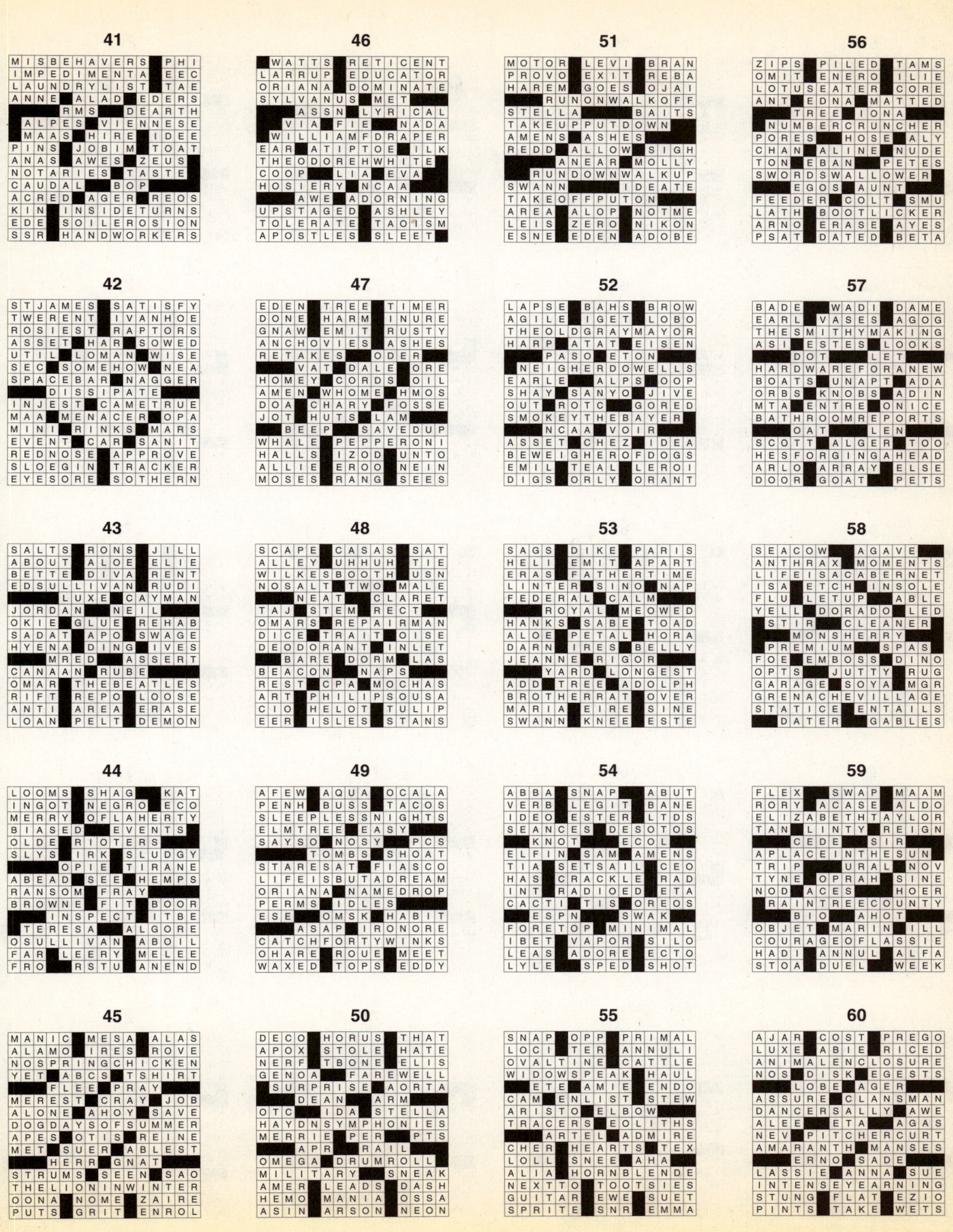

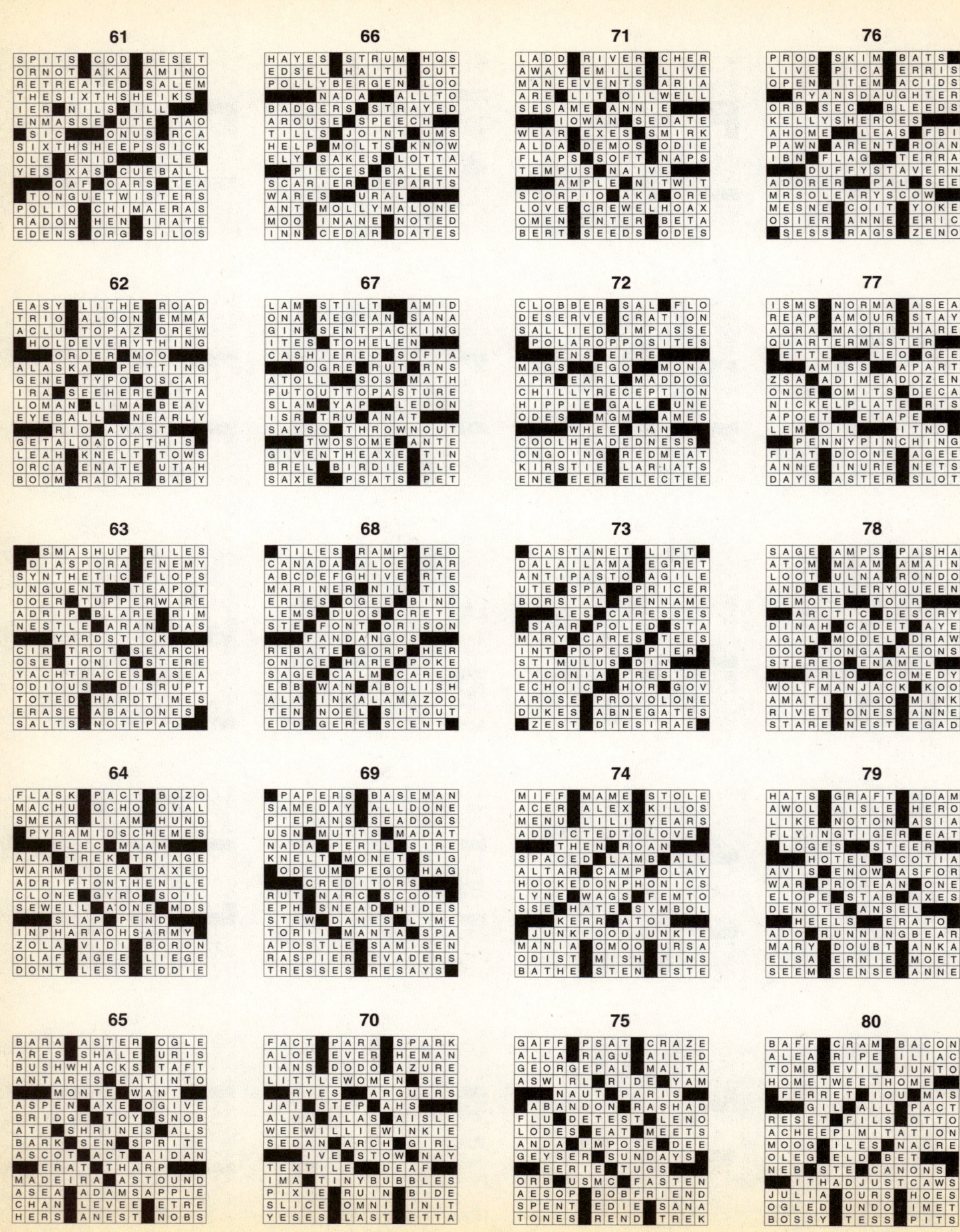

81

```
STEWS  THAI  IMAN
COXIE  HENS  COMO
AFAST  RAGE  EDEN
NFLCHEERLEADER
TET  REDO  LURID
YESMAAM  ALPACA
  INSIDER   TAB
NBCTELEVISION
FOR  REBOZOS
AMATIS  LOOTERS
TIMER  FAUN  NET
NBAALLSTARGAME
HALS  YETI  HUMOR
ATEE  EERO  EMOTE
MESS  STAN  APRES
```

82

```
CIGAR  EMBOSSING
OZONE  ROADTORIO
SEVENTYTHOUSAND
ATH  HARD   TOO
VCR  EREI  NEST
VIE  CBER  CSA
ASQUIETASAMOUSE
MOUNTAINCLIMBER
PRICEREDUCTIONS
USS  FLUE  ADE
SOFT  BALL  ETS
CRO  APET  USA
ACROSSTHESTREET
LAMBASTED  ELATE
ASSENTERS  PYREX
```

83

```
TREE  IGET  ATOM
WELL  RETRO  REDO
IWAS  ONAIR  CLOP
NATIONALANTHEM
GREENS   DORIC
EDS  THAT  TATARS
SHOER   DESKS
TICKETCOLLECTOR
ALBIN   YEAST
DESPOT  SWIM  OPT
EASES   CASTRO
EXTEMPORANEOUS
STER  PENAL  GODS
ATCO  SWIRL  ALEE
NASL  STAY  LESS
```

84

```
AFRO  STARR  ABBA
SLED  LEVEE  LAIR
HEADTOHEAD  MCLI
EEL  APER  EVOKED
EPEE   BEAST
ALFRED  SEMITONE
MEANS  HOVEL  BIN
INCA  SANER  TACT
STE  RIVAL  CACHE
HOTCIDER  HANKER
OATES   BARK
RIFLES  GALL  TAE
SLAM  HANDTOHAND
VICE  OSAGE  OBOE
PEER  WATER  GUNN
```

85

```
CORM  INCA  SCRAP
OLIO  MELD  AHOME
MENU  PAIL  SIMON
MISSMARMELSTEIN
ACETIC   BRAE
ATTU   TREBLE
EVICT  NAPE  TROY
WISHYOUWEREHERE
ELIE  LMNO  LOWER
SENSED   NOEL
LISP   SNORES
WHENWEMETAGAIN
ROMEO  ETTE  INDO
AMINO  WARN  STER
POLED  SLED  TORT
```

86

```
POTATO  DIAPERS
ERASED  CAPTIVES
ROCKED  OBSOLETE
ONE  STU  OPER
TOTAL  ENT  GPA
SINATRA  ERRS
TASSO  IOS  REAP
BREADANDHONEY
PART  ERG  EDENS
ERAS  SPHERES
PSI  SOS  STRAP
GAME  UPA  INA
PENNAMES  BESOTS
EVENTIDE  CREDIT
REDEALS  SENECA
```

87

```
CRAFTS  EDRED
THOREAU  READER
HANDSUP  MERINOS
UPDOS  PRIMETIME
DEER  ALAN  DOZEN
SAL  SCENE  REOS
USELESS  RINSE
NOSTALGIA
STARE  COUPLED
PUMA  SKIMS  VEG
INEPT  PETS  METE
CENTIPEDE  FARES
AUDUBON  RAIMENT
PERIOD  ENLISTS
DEALS  DELETE
```

88

```
MEN  EBOAT  SRI
ARAB  TAURI  SPAR
ERMA  TRIOSONATA
RWANDA  REWET
CEOS  SARABANDE
YANQUI   DID
ETTU  MINUET  LSD
ATEE  PLOTS  GATE
SYR  BALLET  ATOM
PAL  ELVERS
GAILLARDE  YORK
LEVEE  ARMLET
ARIADACAPO  TRUE
DOES  PEPTO  EURO
ESS  TREYS  BEN
```

89

```
MARACAIBO
JACKOLANTERNS
BALLROOMDANCING
OCA  OFFER  CEE
AARON  TOOT  AHEM
SMUG   EELERS
TAMOSHANTERS
SRS  TALENTS  MOS
WILLOTHEWISP
ATTIRE   ESTA
LAIN  RAMA  SETON
ERA  RANEE  ESK
CORONAAUSTRALIS
CATONINETAILS
SANDARACS
```

90

```
ACRE  MODEL  ELF
EARED  AROMA  VIE
GREENSTREET  EVE
GOTFAT  SNEERED
SNEE  ROB  DRAG
RAIDERS  GRAB
PEG  OPERA  DEERE
SIREN  SAD  ERECT
IRENE  STILE  NSA
SEED  CAESARS
NASA  SHY  ARFS
WALTERS  EATERY
IRA  WINTERGREEN
TIN  ONION  HASTE
HAD  NAPES  APES
```

91

```
CABOB  STABS  INC
ARENA  PANIC  NEO
LEWALCINDOR  LIZ
LOA  LANKY  EMILY
ALIMONY   DANE
SALUT  DORMOUSE
ISRAELIS   OER
MAWR  OLLIE  AFAR
IMA  INTENDED
ROTUNDAS  NOIRE
ERGO  MOISTEN
CURIE  CLANG  ADS
AXL  SKIPTOMYLOU
MOO  TINGE  AMICE
PRO  SNEAD  SACKS
```

92

```
CRAPE  DAMP  NOMS
OILED  OMAR  ORAL
SCOLD  MOLE  VALE
THELIBERTYBELLE
MEAD   ERNEST
ATTEST   MEDIA
COAL  AARON  TAU
HAULSOFCONGRESS
EDT  PRIES  ELIS
DIETS  OHDEAR
ACTORS   MOOR
THEMETALOFHONOR
RENI  EWER  OVINE
IRON  INON  HELEN
AERO  ASIS  OREAD
```

93

```
PITA  SOBIG  AFAR
IRAN  OUIDA  ULNA
POCAHONTAS  SYNE
ENTRANCE  PATIOS
CREE   SETIN
SACHER  STRANGLE
ENRY  SAKES  SCUD
AGA  MIL  RIG
LIZA  CEDES  ROSE
SOYBEANS  CREWED
HORUS   IRIS
AMORAL  INACTIVE
BART  KINGPHILIP
ELSE  ECOLE  VENI
DEED  DUNES  EXEC
```

94

```
ATLARGE  ABRAHAM
SHARERS  CLAMORS
TRIEDIT  TOTEBAG
RONALD   TOWER
OBESE  EUR  DINAH
TEXT   CODA
SPARTACUS  JAMAL
MACHETE  IRONAGE
ABHOR  LONCHANEY
SLED   DEAN
HOSES  SEW  DACHA
STATS  FELLIN
RAVIOLI  DUELING
INFAVOR  INRANGE
PAWNEES  STENGEL
```

95

```
MARGARET  PUSH
OVERSEER  INDUCE
SAYONARA  QUINOL
UAR  CHUM  TRE
GNP  TOE  HERA
MUD  IRON  CARON
DOASTHEROMANSDO
RADIOASTRONOMER
INALLDIRECTIONS
VALLE  DARK  HOT
ABCS  SUI  GIN
BOA  HEEL  SEL
LUNGED  ETCETERA
ETALIA  REASONED
LORN  SERENADE
```

96

```
ICALL  LOSTASTEP
MEDEA  ATLIBERTY
PROGNOSTICATION
AIL  AKSOP  STONE
ISPY  DOM  BEE
REHAB  SAFE  RAZZ
RIB  NORM  POE
CBLOBNDTOOLNE  ELECTED
AUR  SARA  ERR
TIAS  SASH  VALOR
AIT  PAS  BARA
AWARD  EERIE  MAP
MISTERPRESIDENT
OSTRACISM  RINGO
SHOELACES  ENTER
```

97

```
STOPSUP  PIERCED
TAXRATE  INFORCE
INFESTS  NETBALL
GTO  SETTERS  TIE
MARV  REACT  SEPT
ARDEN  RKO  PURSE
SASHAY  ENDORSED
INESSENCE
STACCATO  AUTHOR
TABLE  AVA  STOVE
ELSE  FRETS  ETES
ACE  TOWROPE  SRI
MONTOYA  NOTEPAD
ESCAPER  CONNOTE
DEEMERS  ENACTED
```

98

```
SNAG  DEFT  LEMAT
COVE  ELLA  IRANI
AMIN  DUET  LAINE
ROSEBUDWASASLED
ACE   ICE
SPARSE  BIG  SPIC
TAROS  EARN  ENO
APEWORLDISEARTH
REN  OILS  ALIEN
TRAP  GAY  FRILLS
LEE   AIL
SHEISREALLYAMAN
TONGS  PILL  RARE
ALOHA  IDEE  CREW
TESTY  CENT  HEAT
```

99

```
CUBE  SLASH  PIPE
APEX  MAINE  OVID
PORTLANDOR  CANI
ENG  URGE  ORANGE
ARTE   ICET
SMILEY  PROCESS
WILLS  GOOP  LEMA
ALOE  NOONS  LOAN
TENN  ONLY  COULD
RATINGS  REILLY
ONUS   WARD
AVOWER  AARE  WOE
NEON  BETHESDAMD
CAPP  ALTOS  ORIG
ELSA  NONOT  ANTE
```

100

```
PAPYRI  JIMI  ERA
ATRAIN  ANALYSES
THUMBNAILSKETCH
REDS  EMMAS  SHOO
INE  TRAINER  EAR
CENSE  ZED  EARLE
EUCLASE  SKIT
SMEARS  UNTRUE
KITH  PHALANX
LADEN  ELAN  EMIT
ARA  GETIT  HEAVE
URNS  NASHUA  DEN
PICTUREPOSTCARD
EVERMORE  FLENSE
RES  ALAR  LOOSED
```

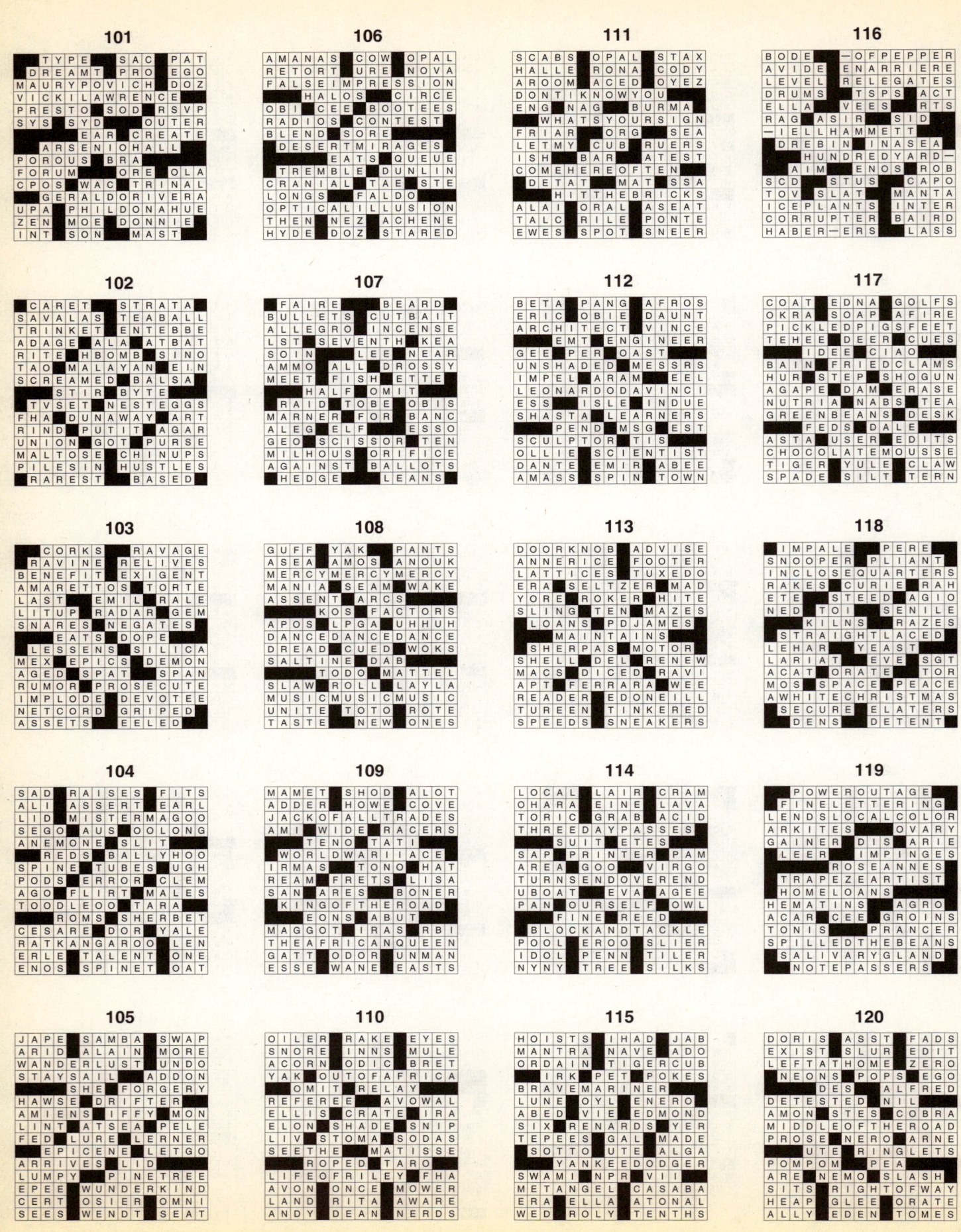

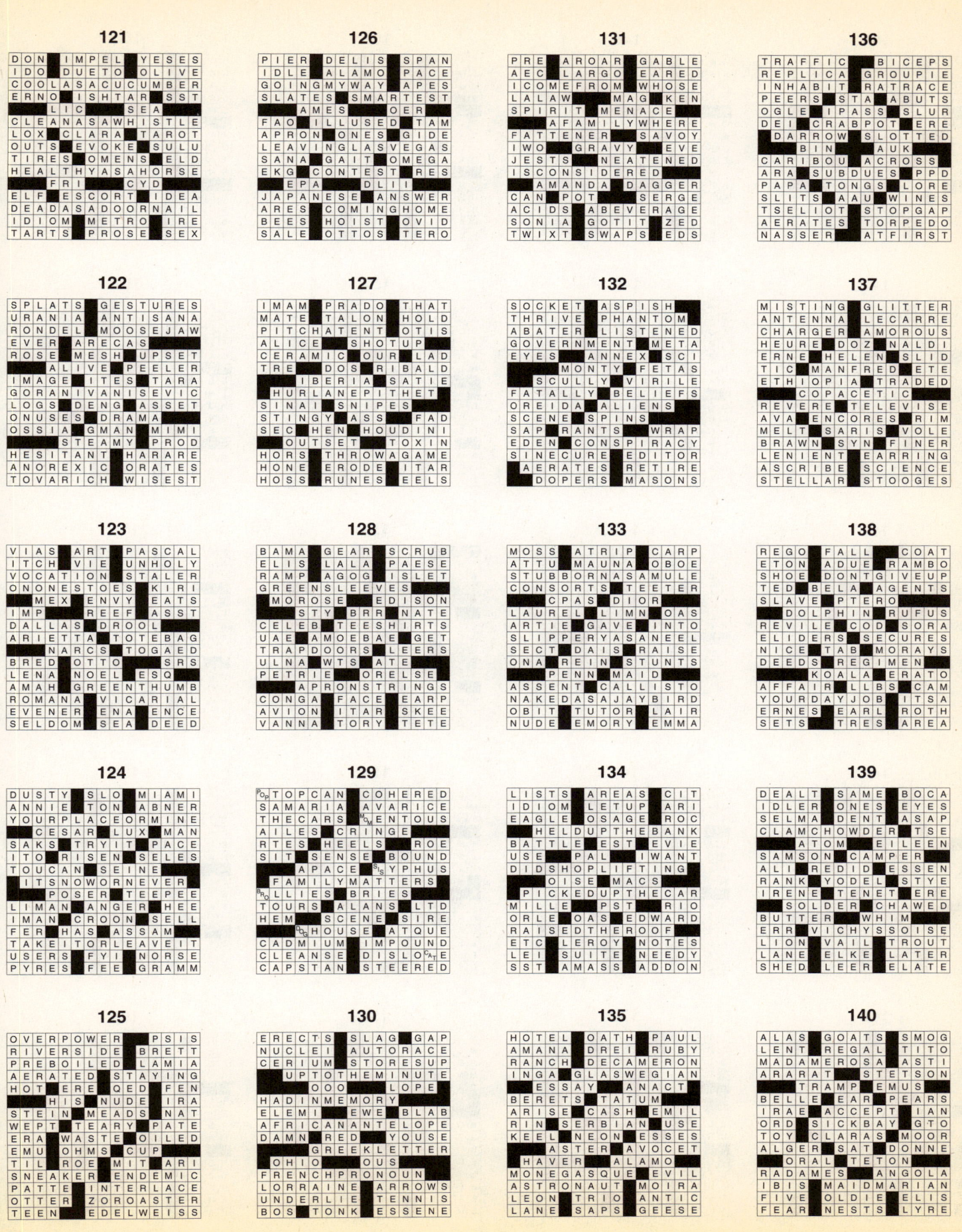

121
```
DON   IMPEL    YESES
IDO   DUETO    OLIVE
COOLASACUCUMBER
ERNO  ISHTAR   SST
      LIC   SEA
CLEANASAWHISTLE
LOX   CLARA    TAROT
OUTS  EVOKE    SULU
TIRES OMENS    ELD
HEALTHYASAHORSE
      FRI   CYD
ELF   ESCORT   IDEA
DEADASADOORNAIL
IDIOM METRO    IRE
TARTS PROSE    SEX
```

126
```
PIER  DELIS    SPAN
IDLE  ALAMO    PACE
GOINGMYWAY     APES
SLATES   SMARTEST
      AMES   OER
FAO   ILLUSED  TAM
APRON ONES     GIDE
LEAVINGLASVEGAS
SANA  GAIT     OMEGA
EKG   CONTEST  RES
      EPA   DLII
JAPANESE    ANSWER
ARES  COMINGHOME
BEES  HOIST    OVID
SALE  OTTOS    TERO
```

131
```
PRE   AROAR    GABLE
AEC   LARGO    EARED
ICOMEFROM      WHOSE
LALAW    MAG   KEN
SPIRIT    MENACE
AFAMILYWHERE
FATTENER    SAVOY
IWO   GRAVY    EVE
JESTS    NEATENED
ISCONSIDERED
AMANDA    DAGGER
CAN   POT      SERGE
ACIDS  ABEVERAGE
SONIA GOTIT    ZED
TWIXT SWAPS    EDS
```

136
```
TRAFFIC    BICEPS
REPLICA    GROUPIE
INHABIT    RATRACE
PEERS STA  ABUTS
OGLE  IPASS    SLUR
DEI   CRABPOT  ERE
DARROW     SLOTTED
      BIN  AUK
CARIBOU    ACROSS
ARA   SUBDUES  PPD
PAPA  TONGS    LORE
SLITS AAU      WINES
TSELIOT    STOPGAP
AERATES    TORPEDO
NASSER     ATFIRST
```

122
```
SPLATS    GESTURES
URANIA    ANTISANA
RONDEL    MOOSEJAW
EVER  ARECAS
ROSE  MESH     UPSET
      ALIVE   PEELER
IMAGE ITES     TARA
GORANIVANISEVIC
LOGS  DENG     ASSET
ONUSES    DRAMA
OSSIA GMAN     MIMI
      STEAMY  PROD
HESITANT    HARARE
ANOREXIC    ORATES
TOVARICH    WISEST
```

127
```
IMAM  PRADO    THAT
MATE  TALON    HOLD
PITCHATENT     OTIS
ALICE    SHOTUP
CERAMIC  OUR   LAD
TRE   DOS      RIBALD
IBERIA    SATIE
HURLANEPITHET
SINAI    SNIPES
STINGY  ASS    FAD
SEC   HEN      HOUDINI
OUTSET    TOXIN
HORS  THROWAGAME
HONE  ERODE    ITAR
HOSS  RUNES    EELS
```

132
```
SOCKET    ASPISH
THRIVE    PHANTOM
ABATER    LISTENED
GOVERNMENT     META
EYES  ANNEX    SCI
      MONTY   FETAS
SCULLY    VIRILE
FATALLY    BELIEFS
OREIDA    ALIENS
SCENE    SPINS
SAP   RANTS    WRAP
EDEN  CONSPIRACY
SINECURE    EDITOR
AERATES    RETIRE
DOPERS    MASONS
```

137
```
MISTING    GLITTER
ANTENNA    LECARRE
CHARGER    AMOROUS
HEURE DOZ  NALDI
ERNE  HELEN    SLID
TIC   MANFRED  ETE
ETHIOPIA    TRADED
COPACETIC
REVERE    TELEVISE
AVA   ENCORES  RIM
MELT  SARIS    VOLE
BRAWN SYN      FINER
LENIENT    EARRING
ASCRIBE    SCIENCE
STELLAR    STOOGES
```

123
```
VIAS  ART   PASCAL
ITCH  VIE   UNHOLY
VOCATION    STALER
ONONESTOES  KIRI
MEX   ENVY     EATS
IMP   REEF     ASST
DALLAS    DROOL
ARIETTA    TOTEBAG
NARCS    TOGAED
BRED  OTTO     SRS
LENA  NOEL     ESQ
AMAH  GREENTHUMB
ROMANA    VICARIAL
EVENER ENA  ENCE
SELDOM SEA  DEED
```

128
```
BAMA  GEAR     SCRUB
ELIS  LALA     PAESE
RAMP  AGOG     ISLET
GREENSLEEVES
MOROSE    EDISON
STY   BRR      NATE
CELEB    TEESHIRTS
UAE   AMOEBAE  GET
TRAPDOORS    LEERS
ULNA  WTS      ATE
PETRIE    ORELSE
APRONSTRINGS
CONGA FACE     EARP
AVION ITAR     SKEE
VANNA TORY     TETE
```

133
```
MOSS  ATRIP    CARP
ATTU  MAUNA    OBOE
STUBBORNASAMULE
CONSORTS    TEETER
CPAS     DIOR
LAUREL LIMN    OAS
ARTIE GAVE     INTO
SLIPPERYASANEEL
SECT  DAIS     RAISE
ONA   REIN     STUNTS
PENN     MAID
ASSENT    CALLISTO
NAKEDASAJAYBIRD
OBIT  TUTOR    LAIR
NUDE  EMORY    EMMA
```

138
```
REGO  FALL     COAT
ETON  ADUE     RAMBO
SHOE  DONTGIVEUP
TED   BELA     AGENTS
SLAVE    PTERO
DOLPHIN    RUFUS
REVILE COD     SORA
ELIDERS    SECURES
NICE  TAB      MORAYS
DEEDS    REGIMEN
KOALA    ERATO
AFFAIR LLBS    CAM
YOURDAYJOB     ITSA
ERNES EARL     ROTH
SETS  TRES     AREA
```

124
```
DUSTY SLO   MIAMI
ANNIE TON   ABNER
YOURPLACEORMINE
CESAR LUX   MAN
SAKS  TRYIT    PACE
ITO   RISEN    SELES
TOUCAN    SEINE
ITSNOWORNEVER
POSER    TEEPEE
LIMAN ANGER    HEE
IMAN  CROON    SELL
FER   HAS      ASSAM
TAKEITORLEAVEIT
USERS FYI   NORSE
PYRES FEE   GRAMM
```

129
```
POPTOPCAN   COHERED
SAMARIA    AVARICE
THECARS    MOMENTOUS
AILES    CRINGE
RTES  HEELS    ROE
SIT   SENSE    BOUND
APACE    SISYPHUS
FAMILYMATTERS
BROLLIES    BRIES
TOURS ALANS    LTD
HEM   SCENE    SIRE
DOGHOUSE    ATQUE
CADMIUM    IMPOUND
CLEANSE    DISLOCATE
CAPSTAN    STEERED
```

134
```
LISTS AREAS    CIT
IDIOM LETUP    ARI
EAGLE OSAGE    ROC
HELDUPTHEBANK
BATTLE EST  EVIE
USE   PAL      IWANT
DIDSHOPLIFTING
OISE     MACS
PICKEDUPTHECAR
MILLE PST      RIO
ORLE  OAS      EDWARD
RAISEDTHEROOF
ETC   LEROY    NOTES
LEI   SUITE    NEEDY
SST   AMASS    ADDON
```

139
```
DEALT SAME     BOCA
IDLER ONES     EYES
SELMA DENT     ASAP
CLAMCHOWDER    TSE
      ATOM   EILEEN
SAMSON    CAMPER
ALI   REDID    ESSEN
RANK  YODEL    STYE
IRENE TENET    ERE
SOLDER    CHAWED
BUTTER    WHIM
ERR   VICHYSSOISE
LION  VAIL     TROUT
LANE  ELKE     LATER
SHED  LEER     ELATE
```

125
```
OVERPOWER    PSIS
RIVERSIDE    BRETT
PREBOILED    LAMIA
AERATED    STAYING
HOT   ERE   QED  FEN
HIS   NUDE     IRA
STEIN MEADS    NAT
WEPT  TEARY    PATE
ERA   WASTE    OILED
EMU   OHMS     CUP
TIL   ROE   MIT  ARI
SNEAKER    ENDEMIC
PATTE    INTERLACE
OTTER    ZOROASTER
TEEN     EDELWEISS
```

130
```
ERECTS SLAG    GAP
NUCLEI    AUTORACE
CERIUM    STORESUP
UPTOTHEMINUTE
OOO      LOPE
HADINMEMORY
ELEMI EWE      BLAB
AFRICANANTELOPE
DAMN  RED      YOUSE
GREEKLETTER
OHIO     OUS
FRENCHPRONOUN
LORRAINE    ARROWS
UNDERLIE    TENNIS
BOS   TONK     ESSENE
```

135
```
HOTEL OATH     PAUL
AMANA DREI     RUBY
RANCH DECAMERON
INGA  GLASWEGIAN
ESSAY    ANACT
BERETS    TATUM
ARISE CASH     EMIL
RIN   SERBIAN  USE
KEEL  NEON     ESSES
ASTER    AVOCET
HAVER    ALAMO
MONEGASQUE    EVIL
ASTRONAUT    MOIRA
LEON  TRIO     ANTIC
LANE  SAPS     GEESE
```

140
```
ALAS  GOATS    SMOG
LENT  REGAL    TITO
MADAMEROSA    ASTI
ARARAT    STETSON
TRAMP    EMUS
BELLE EAR      PEARS
IRAE  ACCEPT   IAN
ORD   SICKBAY  GTO
TOY   CLARAS   MOOR
ALGER SAT      DONNE
ORAL     TETON
RADAMES    ANGOLA
IBIS  MAIDMARIAN
FIVE  OLDIE    ELIS
FEAR  NESTS    LYRE
```

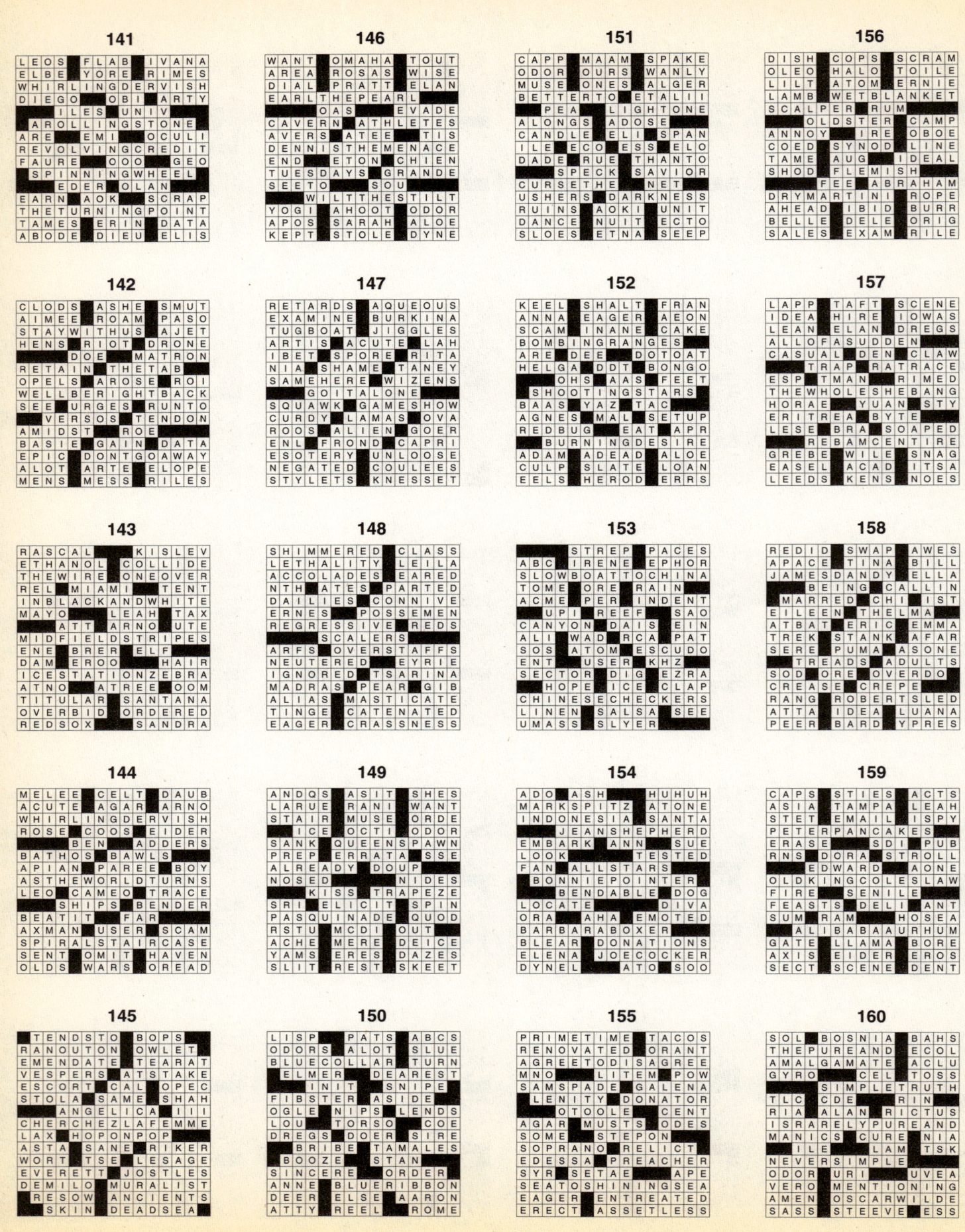

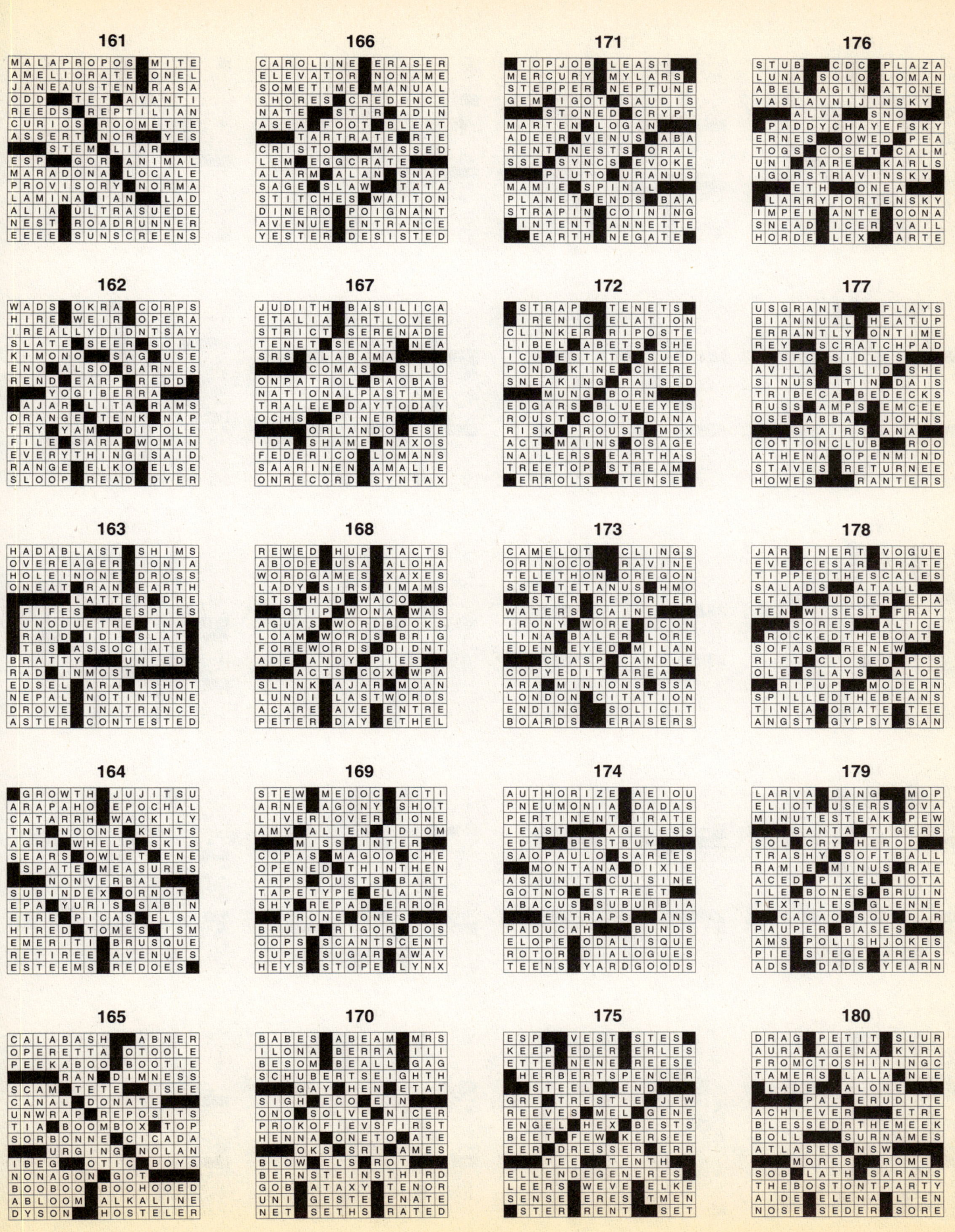

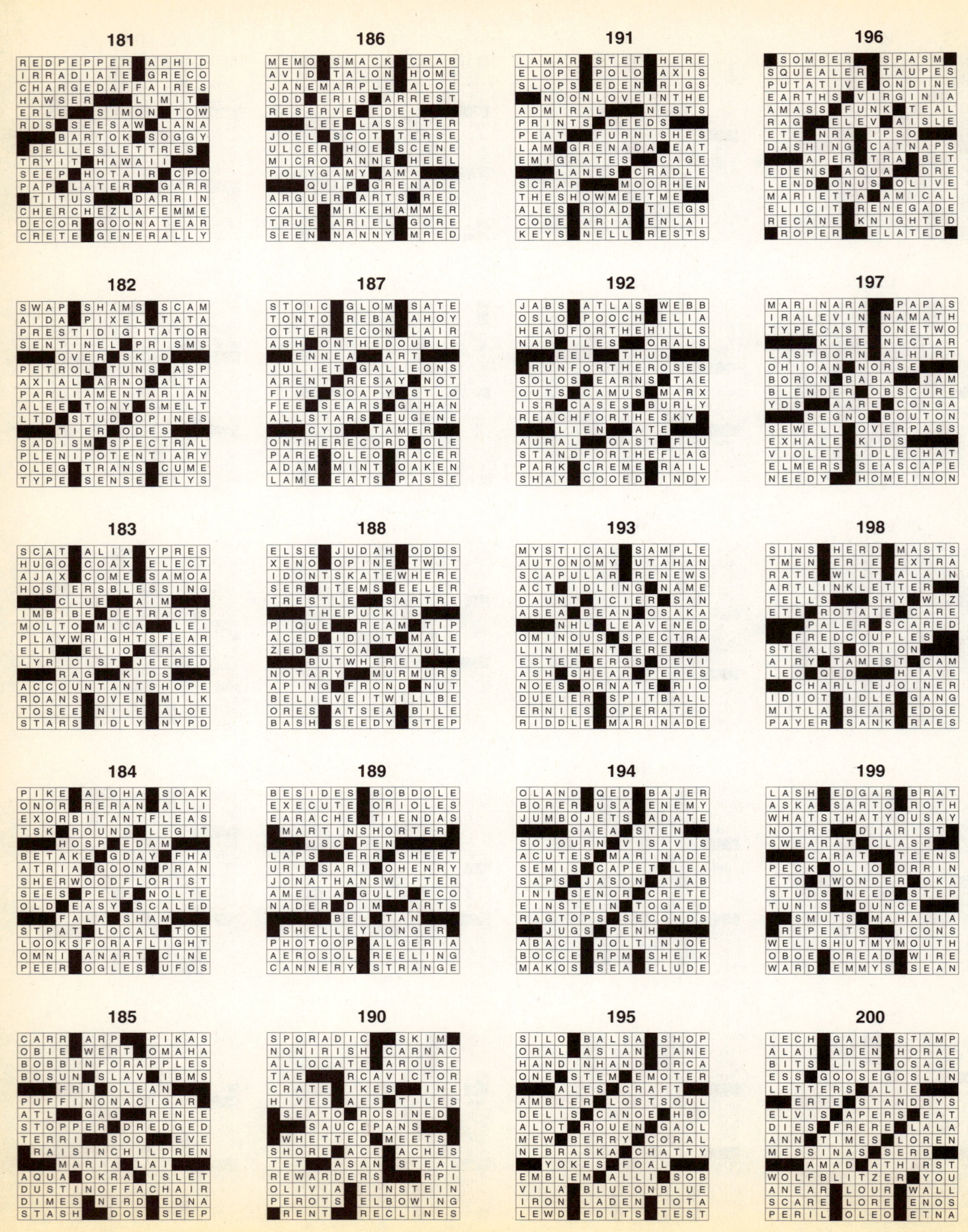

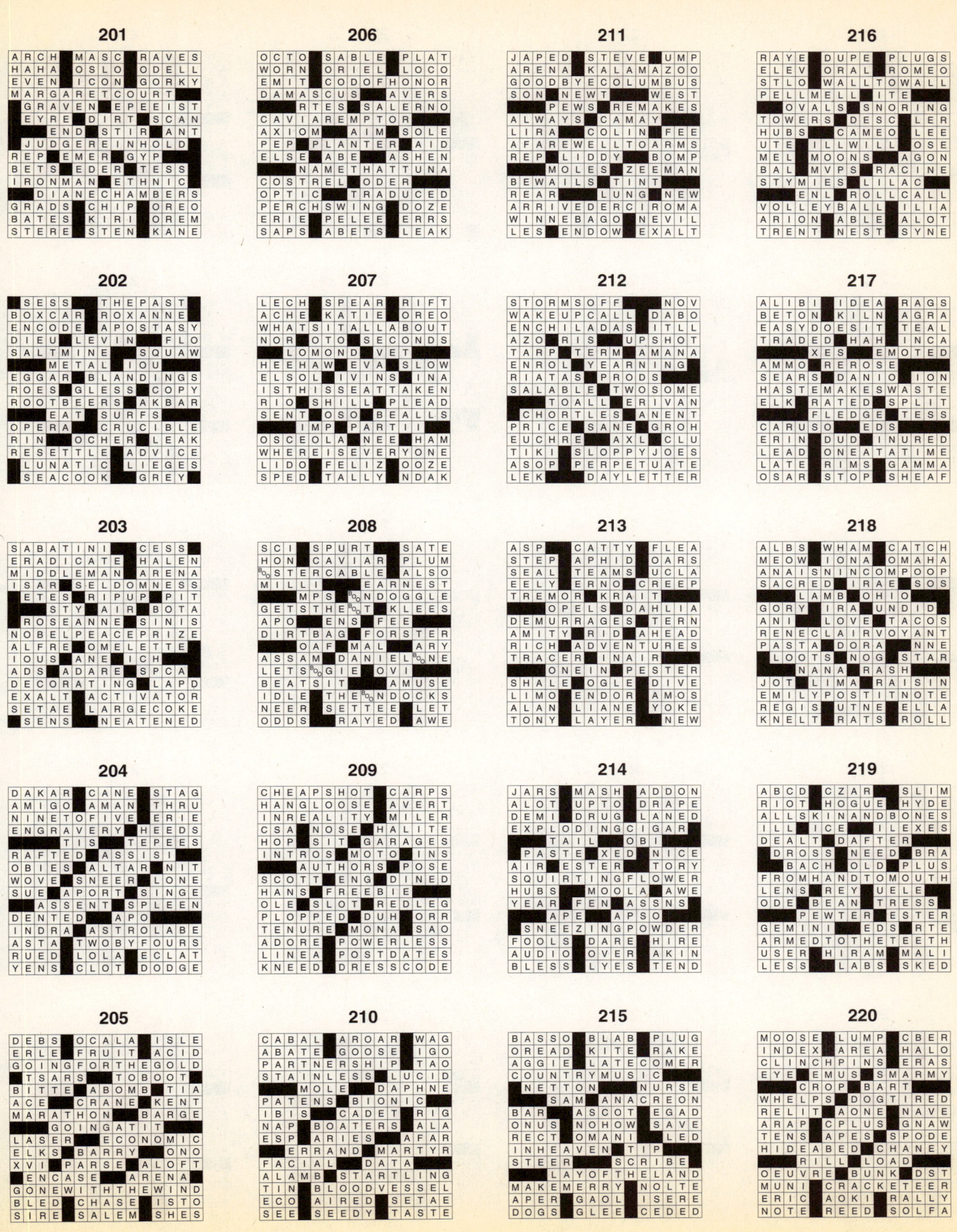

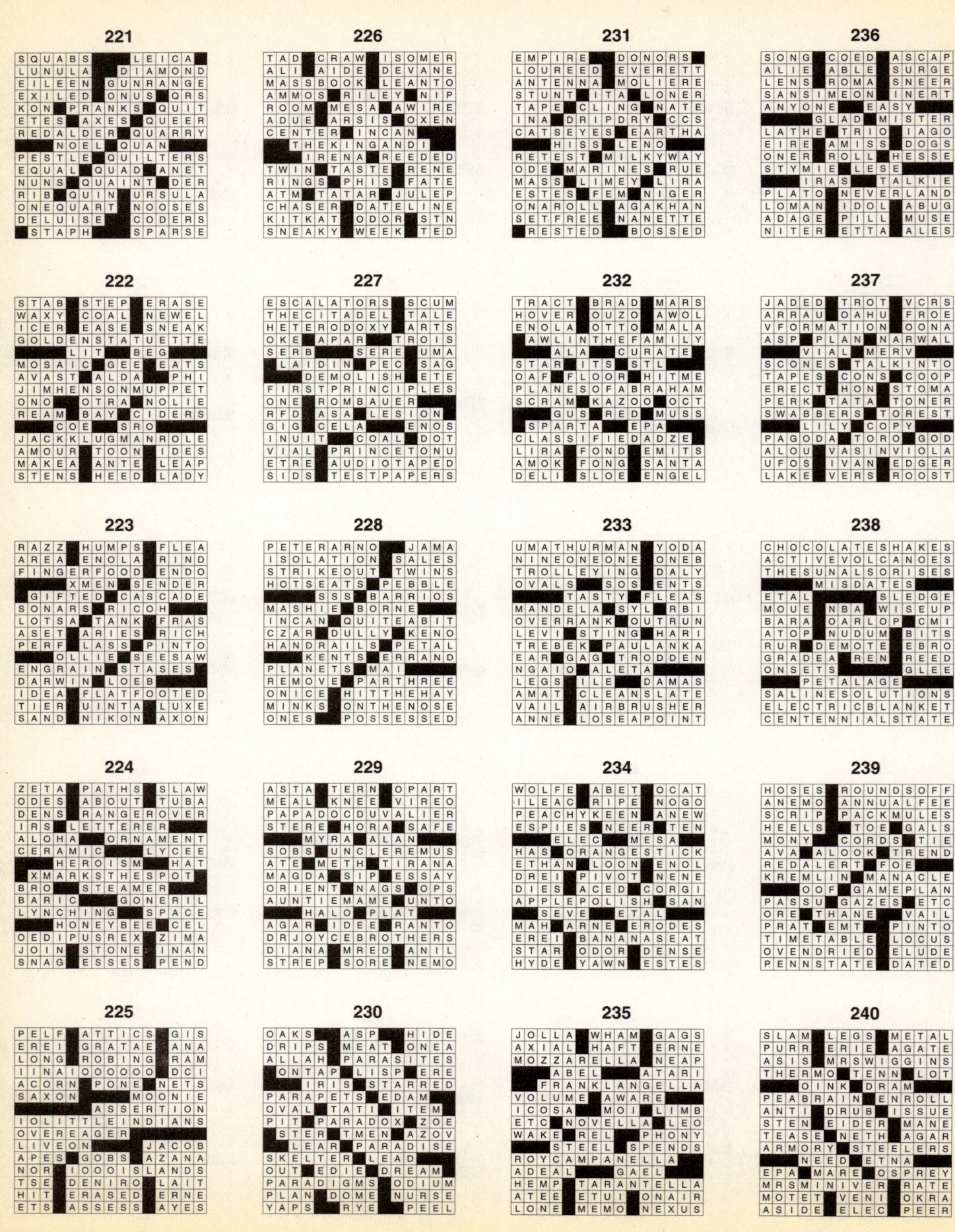

221
```
SQUABS   LEICA
LUNULA  DIAMOND
EILEEN GUNRANGE
EXILED ONUS  QRS
KON  PRANKS QUIT
ETES  AXES  QUEER
REDALDER  QUARRY
  NOEL QUAN
PESTLE QUILTERS
EQUAL QUAD  ANET
NUNS QUAINT  DER
RIB  QUIN URSULA
ONEQUART NOOSES
DELUISE  CODERS
 STAPH   SPARSE
```

226
```
TAD  CRAW ISOMER
ALI  AIDE DEVANE
MASSBOOK  LEANTO
AMMOS RILEY   NIP
ROOM MESA   AWIRE
ADUE ARSIS   OXEN
CENTER    INCAN
   THEKINGANDI
   IRENA REEDED
TWIN TASTE   RENE
RINGS PHIS   FATE
ATM TATAR  JULEP
CHASER  DATELINE
KITKAT ODOR  STN
SNEAKY WEEK  TED
```

231
```
EMPIRE    DONORS
LOUREED  EVERETT
ANTENNA  MOLIERE
STUNT ITA  LONER
TAPE CLING   NATE
INA DRIPDRY  CCS
CATSEYES EARTHA
  HISS   LENO
RETEST  MILKYWAY
ODE MARINES  RUE
MASS LIMEY   LIRA
ESTES FEM   NIGER
ONAROLL AGAKHAN
SETFREE NANETTE
 RESTED  BOSSED
```

236
```
SONG COED  ASCAP
ALIE ABLE  SURGE
SANSIMEON  INERT
ANYONE    EASY
   GLAD MISTER
LATHE TRIO   IAGO
EIRE AMISS   DOGS
ONER ROLL  HESSE
STYMIE   LESE
   IRAS TALKIE
PLATO NEVERLAND
LOMAN IDOL  ABUG
ADAGE PILL  MUSE
NITER ETTA  ALES
```

222
```
STAB STEP  ERASE
WAXY COAL  NEWEL
ICER EASE  SNEAK
GOLDENSTATUETTE
 LIT     BEG
MOSAIC GEE   EATS
AVAST ALDA    PHI
JIMHENSONMUPPET
ONO OTRA   NOLIE
REAM BAY  CIDERS
 COE     SRO
JACKKLUGMANROLE
AMOUR TOON   IDES
MAKEA ANTE   LEAP
STENS HEED   LADY
```

227
```
ESCALATORS  SCUM
THECITADEL  TALE
HETERODOXY  ARTS
OKE APAR   TROIS
SERB  SERE   UMA
LAIDIN PEC    SAG
DEMOLISH     ETE
FIRSTPRINCIPLES
ONE  ROMBAUER
RFD ASA   LESION
GIG CELA   ENOS
INUIT COAL   DOT
VIAL PRINCETONU
ETRE AUDIOTAPED
SIDS  TESTPAPERS
```

232
```
TRACT BRAD   MARS
HOVER OUZO   AWOL
ENOLA OTTO   MALA
AWLINTHEFAMILY
 ALA    CURATE
STAR  ITS    STL
OAF FLOOR  HITME
PLANESOFABRAHAM
SCRAM KAZOO   OCT
GUS RED    MUSS
SPARTA     EPA
CLASSIFIEDADZE
LIRA FOND   EMITS
AMOK FONG   SANTA
DELI SLOE   ENGEL
```

237
```
JADED TROT   VCRS
ARRAU OAHU   FROE
VFORMATION   OONA
ASP PLAN   NARWAL
 VIAL    MERV
SCONES  TALKINTO
TAPES CONS   COOP
ERECT HON   STOMA
PERK TATA   TONER
SWABBERS   TOREST
 LILY    COPY
PAGODA TORO   GOD
ALOU VASINVIOLA
UFOS IVAN   EDGER
LAKE VERS   ROOST
```

223
```
RAZZ HUMPS   FLEA
AREA ENOLA   RIND
FINGERFOOD   ENDO
 XMEN    SENDER
GIFTED  CASCADE
SONARS  RICOH
LOTSA TANK   FRAS
ASET ARIES   RICH
PERF LASS   PINTO
OLLIE    SEESAW
ENGRAIN  STASES
DARWIN   LOEB
IDEA FLATFOOTED
TIER UINTA   LUXE
SAND NIKON   AXON
```

228
```
PETERARNO   JAMA
ISOLATION  SALES
STRIKEOUT  TWINS
HOTSEATS  PEBBLE
 SSS    BARRIOS
MASHIE   BORNE
INCAN  QUITEABIT
CZAR DULLY   KENO
HANDRAILS  PETAL
 KENTS   ERRAND
PLANETS    MAI
REMOVE  PARTHREE
ONICE  HITTHEHAY
MINKS  ONTHENOSE
ONES   POSSESSED
```

233
```
UMATHURMAN   YODA
NINEONEONE   ONEB
TROLLEYING   DALY
OVALS SOS    ENTS
 TASTY   FLEAS
MANDELA SYL   RBI
OVERRANK  OUTRUN
LEVI STING   HARI
TREBEK  PAULANKA
EAR GAG   TRODDEN
NGAIO    ALETA
LEGS ILE   DAMAS
AMAT  CLEANSLATE
VAIL  AIRBRUSHER
ANNE  LOSEAPOINT
```

238
```
CHOCOLATESHAKES
ACTIVEVOLCANOES
THESUNALSORISES
       MISDATES
ETAL    SLEDGE
MOUE NBA   WISEUP
BARA OARLOP   CMI
ATOP NUDUM   BITS
RUR DEMOTE   EBRO
GRADEA REN   REED
ONSETS     GLEE
  PETALAGE
SALINESOLUTIONS
ELECTRICBLANKET
CENTENNIALSTATE
```

224
```
ZETA PATHS   SLAW
ODES ABOUT   TUBA
DENS RANGEROVER
IRS  LETTERER
ALOHA  ORNAMENT
CERAMIC    LYCEE
 HEROISM    HAT
XMARKSTHESPOT
BRO   STEAMER
BARIC    GONERIL
LYNCHING   SPACE
 HONEYBEE   CEL
OEDIPUSREX  ZIMA
JOIN STONE   INAN
SNAG ESSES   PEND
```

229
```
ASTA TERN   OPART
MEAL KNEE   VIREO
PAPADOCDUVALIER
STERE HORA   SAFE
 MYRA    ALAN
SOBS  UNCLEREMUS
ATE METH   TIRANA
MAGDA SIP   ESSAY
ORIENT NAGS   OPS
AUNTIEMAME   UNTO
 HALO    PLAT
AGAR IDEE   RANTO
DRJOYCEBROTHERS
DIANA MRED   ANIL
STREP SORE   NEMO
```

234
```
WOLFE ABET   OCAT
ILEAC RIPE   NOGO
PEACHYKEEN   ANEW
ESPIES NEER   TEN
 ELEC    MESA
HAS  ORANGESTICK
ETHAN LOON   ENOL
DREI PIVOT   NENE
DIES ACED   CORGI
APPLEPOLISH  SAN
SEVE    ETAL
MAH ARNE   ERODES
EREI  BANANASEAT
STAR ODOR   DENSE
HYDE YAWN   ESTES
```

239
```
HOSES  ROUNDSOFF
ANEMO  ANNUALFEE
SCRIP  PACKMULES
HEELS TOE    GALS
MONY CORDS    TIE
AVA ALOOK   TREND
REDALERT     FOE
KREMLIN  MANACLE
 OOF    GAMEPLAN
PASSU GAZES   ETC
ORE THANE   VAIL
PRAT EMT   PINTO
TIMETABLE  LOCUS
OVENDRIED  ELUDE
PENNSTATE  DATED
```

225
```
PELF ATTICS   GIS
EREI GRATAE   ANA
LONG ROBING   RAM
IINAIOOOOO   DCI
ACORN PONE   NETS
SAXON    MOONIE
  ASSERTION
IOLITTLEINDIANS
 OVEREAGER
LIVEON    JACOB
APES GOBS   AZANA
NOR  IOOOISLANDS
TSE DENIRO   LAIT
HIT ERASED   ERNE
ETS  ASSESS  AYES
```

230
```
OAKS ASP    HIDE
DRIPS MEAT   ONEA
ALLAH  PARASITES
ONTAP LISP    ERE
 IRIS   STARRED
PARAPETS    EDAM
OVAL TATI   ITEM
PIT PARADOX   ZOE
STER TMEN   AZOV
LEAR   PARADISE
SKELTER    LEAD
OUT EDIE   DREAM
PARADIGMS  ODIUM
PLAN DOME   NURSE
YAPS RYE    PEEL
```

235
```
JOLLA WHAM   GAGS
AXIAL HAFT   ERNE
MOZZARELLA   NEAP
 ABEL    ATARI
 FRANKLANGELLA
VOLUME   AWARE
ICOSA MOI   LIMB
ETC NOVELLA   LEO
WAKE REL   PHONY
STEEL    SPENDS
ROYCAMPANELLA
ADEAL    GAEL
HEMP  TARANTELLA
ATEE ETUI   ONAIR
LONE MEMO   NEXUS
```

240
```
SLAM LEGS   METAL
PURR ERIE   AGATE
ASIS  MRSWIGGINS
THERMO TENN   LOT
 OINK    DRAM
PEABRAIN   ENROLL
ANTI DRUB   ISSUE
STEN EIDER   MANE
TEASE NETH   AGAR
ARMORY   STEELERS
 NEED    ETNA
EPA MARE   OSPREY
MRSMINIVER   RATE
MOTET VENI   OKRA
ASIDE ELEC   PEER
```

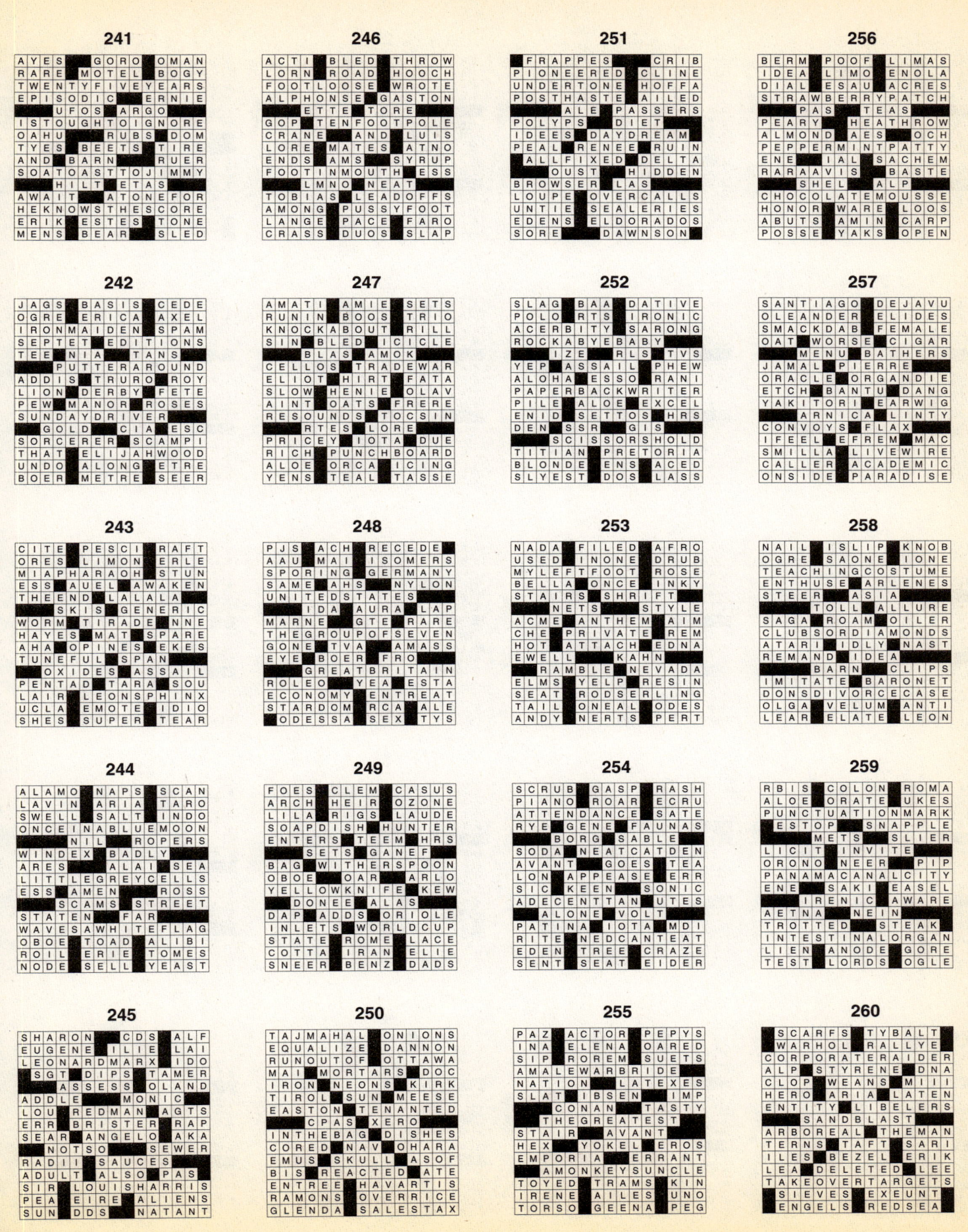

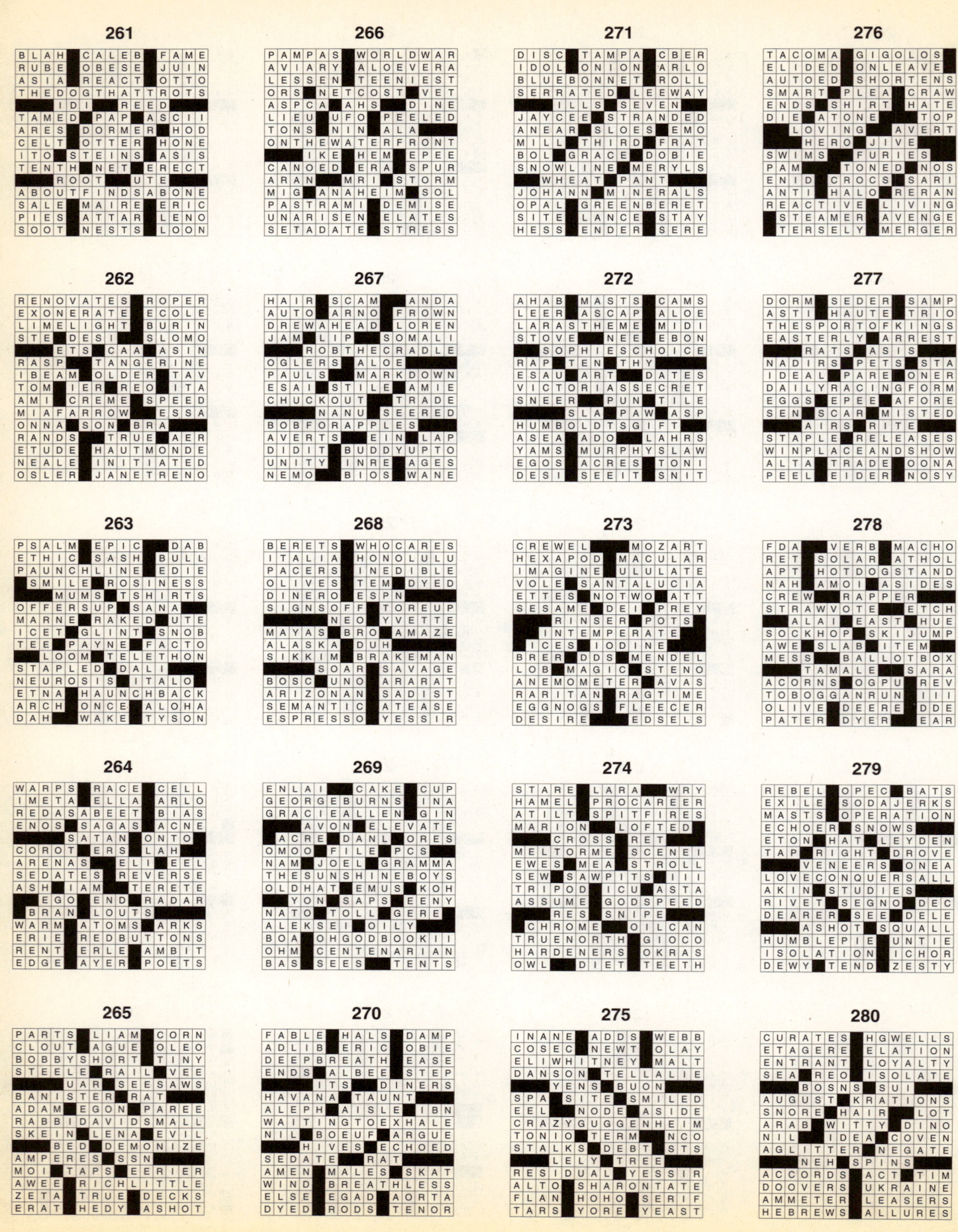

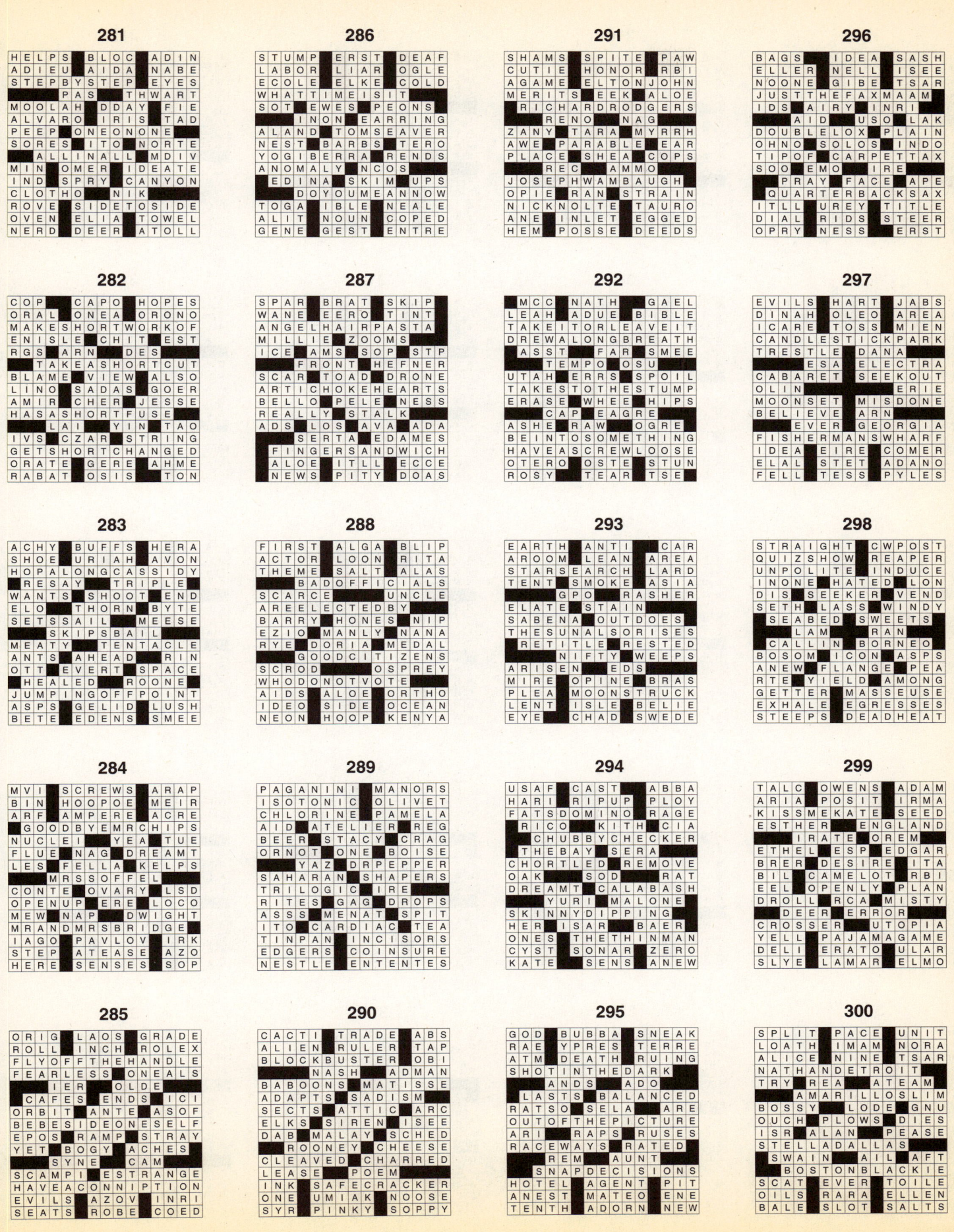

281

HELPS■BLOC■ADIN
ADIEU■AIDA■NABE
STEPBYSTEP■EYES
■■■■PAS■■THWART
MOOLAH■DDAY■FIE
ALVARO■IRIS■TAD
PEEP■ONEONONE■■
SORES■ITO■NORTE
■■ALLINALL■MDIV
MIN■OMER■IDEATE
IND■SPRY■CANYON
CLOTHO■■NIK■■■■
ROVE■SIDETOSIDE
OVEN■ELIA■TOWEL
NERD■DEER■ATOLL

282

COP■■CAPO■HOPES
ORAL■ONEA■ORONO
MAKESHORTWORKOF
ENISLE■CHIT■EST
RGS■ARN■■DES■■■
■■TAKEASHORTCUT
BLAME■VIEW■ALSO
LINO■SADAS■GOER
AMIR■CHER■JESSE
HASASHORTFUSE■■
■■■LAI■■YIN■TAO
IVS■CZAR■STRING
GETSHORTCHANGED
ORATE■GERE■AHME
RABAT■OSIS■■TON

283

ACHY■BUFFS■HERA
SHOE■URIAH■AVON
HOPALONGCASSIDY
■RESAY■■TRIPLE■
WANTS■SHOOT■END
ELO■■THORN■BYTE
SETSSAIL■■MEESE
■■■SKIPSBAIL■■■
MEATY■■TENTACLE
ANTS■AHEAD■■RIN
OTT■EVERT■SPACE
■HEALED■■ROONE■
JUMPINGOFFPOINT
ASPS■GELID■LUSH
BETE■EDENS■SMEE

284

MVI■SCREWS■ARAP
BIN■HOOPOE■MEIR
ARF■AMPERE■ACRE
■GOODBYEMRCHIPS
NUCLEI■■YEA■TUE
FLUE■NAG■DREAMT
LES■FELLA■KELPS
■■■MRSSOFFEL■■■
CONTE■OVARY■LSD
OPENUP■ERE■LOCO
MEW■NAP■■DWIGHT
MRANDMRSBRIDGE■
IAGO■PAVLOV■IRK
STEP■ATEASE■AZO
HERE■SENSES■SOP

285

ORIG■LAOS■GRADE
ROLL■INCH■ROLEX
FLYOFFTHEHANDLE
FEARLESS■ONEALS
■■■IER■■OLDE■■■
■CAFES■ENDS■ICI
ORBIT■ANTE■ASOF
BEBESIDEONESELF
EPOS■RAMP■STRAY
YET■BOGY■ACHES■
■■■SYNE■■CAM■■■
SCAMPI■ESTRANGE
HAVEACONNIPTION
EVILS■AZOV■INRI
SEATS■ROBE■COED

286

STUMP■ERST■DEAF
LABOR■LIAR■OGLE
ECOLE■ELKE■COLD
WHATTIMEISIT■■■
SOT■EWES■PEONS■
■■■INON■EARRING
ALAND■TOMSEAVER
NEST■BARBS■TERO
YOGIBERRA■RENDS
ANOMALY■NCOS■■■
■EDINA■SKIM■UPS
■■■DOYOUMEANNOW
TOGA■IBLE■NEALE
ALIT■NOUN■COPED
GENE■GEST■ENTRE

287

SPAR■BRAT■SKIP■
WANE■EERO■TINT■
ANGELHAIRPASTA■
MILLIE■ZOOMS■■■
ICE■AMS■SOP■STP
■■■FRONT■HEFNER
SCAR■TOAD■DRONE
ARTICHOKEHEARTS
BELLO■PELE■NESS
REALLY■STALK■■■
ADS■LOS■AVA■ADA
■■■SERTA■EDAMES
■FINGERSANDWICH
■ALOE■ITLL■ECCE
■NEWS■PITY■DOAS

288

FIRST■ALGA■BLIP
ACTOR■LOON■RITA
THEME■SALT■ALAS
■■■BADOFFICIALS
SCARCE■■■■UNCLE
AREELECTEDBY■■■
BARRY■HONES■NIP
EZIO■MANLY■NANA
RYE■DORIA■MEDAL
■■■GOODCITIZENS
SCROD■■■■OSPREY
WHODONOTVOTE■■■
AIDS■ALOE■ORTHO
IDEO■SIDE■OCEAN
NEON■HOOP■KENYA

289

PAGANINI■MANORS
ISOTONIC■OLIVET
CHLORINE■PAMELA
AID■ATELIER■REG
BEER■STACY■CRAG
ORNOT■ONE■BOISE
■■■YAZ■DRPEPPER
SAHARAN■SHAPERS
TRILOGIC■IRE■■■
RITES■GAG■DROPS
ASSS■MENAT■SPIT
ITO■CARDIAC■TEA
TINPAN■INCISORS
EDGERS■COINSURE
NESTLE■ENTENTES

290

CACTI■TRADE■ABS
ALIEN■RULER■TAP
BLOCKBUSTER■OBI
■■■■NASH■■ADMAN
BABOONS■MATISSE
ADAPTS■SADISM■■
SECTS■ATTIC■ARC
ELKS■SIREN■ISEE
DAB■MALAY■SCHED
■■ROONEY■CHEESE
CLEAVED■CHARRED
LEASE■■POEM■■■■
INK■SAFECRACKER
ONE■UMIAK■NOOSE
SYR■PINKY■SOPPY

291

SHAMS■SPITE■PAW
CUTIE■HONOR■RBI
AGAME■ELTONJOHN
MERITS■EEK■ALOE
■RICHARDRODGERS
■■■RENO■■NAG■■■
ZANY■TARA■MYRRH
AWE■PARABLE■EAR
PLACE■SHEA■COPS
■■■REC■■AMMO■■■
JOSEPHWAMBAUGH■
OPIE■RAN■STRAIN
NICKNOLTE■TAURO
ANE■INLET■EGGED
HEM■POSSE■DEEDS

292

■MCC■NATH■■GAEL
LEAH■ADUE■BIBLE
TAKEITORLEAVEIT
DREWALONGBREATH
■ASST■■FAR■SMEE
■■■TEMPO■OSU■■■
UTAH■ERRS■SPOIL
TAKESTOTHESTUMP
ERASE■WHEE■HIPS
■■■CAP■EAGRE■■■
ASHE■RAW■■OGRE■
BEINTOSOMETHING
HAVEASCREWLOOSE
OTERO■OSTE■STUN
ROSY■■TEAR■TSE■

293

EARTH■ANTI■■CAR
AROOM■LEAN■AREA
STARSEARCH■LARD
TENT■SMOKE■ASIA
■■■■GPO■■RASHER
ELATE■STAIN■■■■
SABENA■OUTDOES■
THESUNALSORISES
■RETITLE■RESTED
■■■■NIFTY■WEEPS
ARISEN■■EDS■■■■
MIRE■OPINE■BRAS
PLEA■MOONSTRUCK
LENT■ISLE■BELIE
EYE■■CHAD■SWEDE

294

USAF■CAST■■ABBA
HARI■RIPUP■PLOY
FATSDOMINO■RAGE
■RICO■■KITH■CIA
■■CHUBBYCHECKER
■THEBAY■SERA■■■
CHORTLED■REMOVE
OAK■■■SOD■■■RAT
DREAMT■CALABASH
■■■YURI■MALONE■
SKINNYDIPPING■■
HER■ISAR■■BAER■
ONES■THETHINMAN
CYST■SONAR■ZERO
KATE■■SENS■ANEW

295

GOD■BUBBA■SNEAK
RAE■YPRES■TERRE
ATM■DEATH■RUING
SHOTINTHEDARK■■
■■■ANDS■■ADO■■■
■LASTS■BALANCED
RATSO■SELA■■ARE
OUTOFTHEPICTURE
ARI■■RAPS■RUSES
RACEWAYS■RATED■
■■■REM■■AUNT■■■
■■SNAPDECISIONS
HOTEL■AGENT■PIT
ANEST■MATEO■ENE
TENTH■ADORN■NEW

296

BAGS■■IDEA■SASH
ELLER■NELL■ISEE
NOONE■GIBE■TSAR
JUSTTHEFAXMAAM■
IDS■AIRY■INRI■■
■■■AID■■USO■LAK
DOUBLELOX■PLAIN
OHNO■SOLOS■INDO
TIPOF■CARPETTAX
SOO■EMO■■IRE■■■
■■PRAY■FACE■APE
■QUARTERBACKSAX
ITLL■UREY■TITLE
DIAL■RIDS■STEER
OPRY■NESS■■ERST

297

EVILS■HART■JABS
DINAH■OLEO■AREA
ICARE■TOSS■MIEN
CANDLESTICKPARK
TRESTLE■DANA■■■
■■■■ESA■ELECTRA
CABARET■SEEKOUT
OLIN■■■■■■■ERIE
MOONSET■MISDONE
BELIEVE■ARN■■■■
■■■EVER■GEORGIA
FISHERMANSWHARF
IDEA■EIRE■COMER
ELAL■STET■ADANO
FELL■TESS■PYLES

298

STRAIGHT■CWPOST
QUIZSHOW■REAPER
UNPOLITE■INDUCE
INONE■HATED■LON
DIS■SEEKER■VEND
SETH■LASS■WINDY
■SEABED■SWEETS■
■■■LAM■■■RAN■■■
■CALLIN■BORNEO■
BOSOM■ICON■ASPS
ANEW■FLANGE■PEA
RTE■YIELD■AMONG
GETTER■MASSEUSE
EXHALE■EGRESSES
STEEPS■DEADHEAT

299

TALC■OWENS■ADAM
ARIA■POSIT■IRMA
KISSMEKATE■SEED
ESTHER■■ENGLAND
■■■IRATE■OREM■■
ETHEL■ESP■EDGAR
BRER■DESIRE■ITA
BIL■CAMELOT■RBI
EEL■OPENLY■PLAN
DROLL■RCA■MISTY
■■DEER■ERROR■■■
CROSSER■■UTOPIA
YELL■PAJAMAGAME
DELI■ERATO■ULAR
SLYE■LAMAR■ELMO

300

SPLIT■PACE■UNIT
LOATH■IMAM■NORA
ALICE■NINE■TSAR
NATHANDETROIT■■
TRY■REA■■ATEAM■
■■■AMARILLOSLIM
BOSSY■■LODE■GNU
OUCH■PLOWS■DIES
ISR■ALAN■■PEASE
STELLADALLAS■■■
■SWAIN■■AIL■AFT
■■BOSTONBLACKIE
SCAT■EVER■TOILE
OILS■RARA■ELLEN
BALE■SLOT■SALTS

301

```
GOTH  ANTIC  LSTS
ACHE  BIOTA  AHIT
PHANTOMJET  RAGU
ERR  OREO  ERODED
DEPARTS  AROSE
   BUS  OPERATED
APSES  BARRY  RYE
DEPT  DOTES  SEEK
ASI  NIXES  SUEDE
MOREOVER  SIE
   INNES  BENZINE
DOTTER  TATE  CIV
ERGO  GHOSTWRITE
SCUM  EERIE  OLAN
IAMB  DRONE  CYST
```

306

```
ADAM  CABAL  FEAT
MEGA  ELOPE  RENO
OPENINGPRESENTS
STRICT  SOREEYES
   CARP  NEAR
BAS  RIAS  DREWUP
USE  USLTA  IOTA
CHRISTMASDINNER
KEGS  SITES  TRI
ONEACT  DEVO  SOS
   BAIL  RIGA
INSERTED  LOCATE
TOALLAGOODNIGHT
EVIL  NUEVO  DEAN
MALA  SPRIG  SETA
```

311

```
DOMES  MASK  UMP
ALIVE  ALIE  APER
YINANDYANG  GALA
SOT  ADORES  ANEW
   TERM  WIDEN
LADLE  SESTINA
ALOE  DEER  BUN
DAWDLER  ANEMONE
SIN  OMAR  AUTO
ADAPTED  GETON
PINED  NUDE
RODE  STEREO  CPA
ATOM  NOWANDTHEN
TAUS  IRAN  EVICT
EST  PELT  SACKS
```

316

```
AFFRONT  RESIDES
TROOPER  EVIDENT
TEXTILE  TENAFLY
REG  ELMERS  SEAL
ABLE  YODA  ACE
COOPT  LACERATED
TOVAR  OMELET
STEREO  LATEST
   CARTED  MIXER
TIGHTROPE  SCENE
RNA  PELF  ACTS
ISTS  SHEILA  RIP
BOHEMIA  BANDANA
ELEMENT  ESTATES
SERINES  SHEKELS
```

302

```
ODES  LIZA  HASPS
LAVA  ARUN  ACCRA
IVAN  WALTERREED
VIDKUNQUISLING
IDEAL  PEDANT
ASS  TIC  ANY  RAH
   ARTHUR  FINE
JUDASISCARIOT
YUKS  CAESAR
EMU  IJK  DUD  POE
SPLICE  AKRON
BENEDICTARNOLD
CALAMITIES  AVIS
ELENA  EARP  VETO
OLSEN  MOMS  EDEN
```

307

```
ZAP  TUBA  ESKER
LOPE  ARAB  NOUSE
EDELWEISS  THROB
GIRLY  ROOT
SAC  ABT  CRO  SEW
CUTTER  RIP  ARI
STRATEGY  WIN
ESME  MUANG  HACK
CPA  DUMBNESS
HID  IDA  ARCTIC
OLE  VAS  SSE  SOL
LOVE  NAOMI
LAVER  STATESMAN
ANENT  LUCE  TETE
CERTS  OXEN  IRS
```

312

```
APSIS  NAZI  SLAW
GRANT  OMAN  PINA
TENCOMMANDMENTS
SPEAKEASY  ALDEN
ENDS  ATLAST
ABOARD  ORTS
SOON  EERIE  SST
HUNDREDYEARSWAR
ETA  ORIEL  AUTO
SCAT  ZOOMED
CAMPOS  STUN
OLEIC  SCHLEMIEL
CASTOFTHOUSANDS
ACHE  RAMS  EIGHT
SKYS  OBOE  CLASS
```

317

```
SLAM  RECAP  PASO
CAME  AMARE  IVAN
ALOT  DURER  ROIL
MAKEHASTESLOWLY
RUR  LIEU
DIM  EMIT  AVERSE
ANAS  ACES  ITEMS
WASTENOTWANTNOT
ENORM  NEAR  ETTE
SENECA  STOP  AES
EELS  UAW
HASTEMAKESWASTE
ERIC  OPERA  LOAN
ANNA  SPELL  TYRO
DOER  TYPES  ZAPS
```

303

```
SHAH  FOLIC  GMAT
POL&  IREL&  RAGE
EYES  NEELY  &REA
WASTRELS  SYSTEM
   &ERS  STAT
PIGSTY  TWOP&AS
ITO  HOAR  EL&S
SERB  BETTE  RIBS
ARM&  ONES  VAT
S&STORM  USHERS
TIKI  ONH&
VER&AS  ABLATIVE
ARAB  TEPEE  ODEA
REM&  &RESS  HERR
YIPS  SAXES  &EAN
```

308

```
VOICEOVER  ASSHE
INTHEHOLE  SQUID
STEELMILL  SUING
CORDS  LAYS  ESTA
EGAD  RES  QUASAR
RETAKES  JUNKETS
ANERVE  HAIRY
LYS  ENQUIRE  PAR
STAUB  RESAVE
MOROCCO  DELETES
ARIGHT  GEL  ARNO
DIAG  SHEP  ALIGN
RELIC  ANAALICIA
ENTER  SOREPOINT
STORY  PATRONAGE
```

313

```
JONAH  WACO  PAID
AMUSE  IRAN  ERMA
MEDIC  MIND  EGAN
SNEAKYPETE  PURE
   LAST  CRISIS
RAMJET  TOKEN
EZIO  ESAU  OGLER
FULLEST  RESTORE
TROLL  EAST  OBIE
YOUNG  ALMOND
BAIRNS  RATA
ARNO  EVENSTEVEN
DRUG  DIED  HUILE
GORE  UNTO  ERASE
EWER  POOR  SOLED
```

318

```
RATA  AMBI  LETUP
OGRE  CORN  IRANI
THERITEOFSPRING
SAXON  GAPS  PES
   ROMANA  SEAT
SUMMERINTHECITY
ASTI  ARSENIO
MANSE  STRAW
   SLIMIER  TIRO
AUTUMNINNEWYORK
OTIS  TRICIA
RAG  FRAT  DISCO
THELIONINWINTER
AARON  DANA  GONE
ENSUE  ALEX  EATS
```

304

```
PAPADOC  SERAPHS
OMIGOSH  ATECROW
REGATTA  YEARONE
TRITE  PCS  PETAL
EIRE  FELON  SELL
NCO  STROKES  SEE
TANGELOS  EMOTED
   OPENENDED
OFNOTE  COLLECTS
URB  ANNABEL  LAW
TEAS  JELLS  BENE
BEGAN  ALE  GRATE
AMATEUR  MINIVAN
CAMILLE  ETAGERE
KNEELER  NEWSDAY
```

309

```
AGES  STRIA  LOPS
GOTH  AWIDE  IMET
AUTO  VIPER  CORE
STEPBOXSMITHOUT
   TOUT  FOE
AFFAIR  AMORETTO
BILLS  AVER  AHA
BROKERCARMARKET
ESO  ERIE  MEESE
STREUSEL  KISSER
NAT  LISP
CHAIRORGANHOUSE
RANG  READD  NCAA
ATOM  EAGLE  SLAT
MESA  SPEER  EARS
```

314

```
ARISTOTLE  RIDER
MARIACHIS  URIAH
OVERREACT  BITSY
SID  BANK  SYSTEM
   HANK  AIRHOLE
BLOBS  PORES
HAIRY  DAREDEVIL
ERNS  DARTS  TERI
MACEDONIA  STRIP
TILTS  FLEAS
STARTLE  PEAR
TORAHS  CAMP  BAR
ELUDE  ELIASHOWE
WEBER  PURLOINED
STARS  ABSENTEES
```

319

```
TARP  THIEF  LOSS
ORAL  ROLLE  OPAH
LIZA  ORION  VETO
LAZYSUSAN  AERIE
   ETE  GARLAND
SHEBA  SHANTY
PEARLS  ETO  ROLL
ALSO  IDLED  IDEA
SLEW  NEO  ELTONS
NEGATE  EARTH
RAMBLED  VFW
ORIEL  PROUDMARY
MUST  BOILS  OVUM
ABET  SOLVE  DISC
NARY  ALLES  ESTA
```

305

```
GARAGE  SMALLOJ
ARETHA  SHINBONE
SMITES  TEXASTEA
CAVETT  ERIS  HAL
ADESTE  EEN  WACO
PASTORALE  TARTU
ELI  VARIES
TAKINGINVENTORY
INAFOG  DIN
TATAR  SUPERVENE
LIAT  EHS  ROOTER
ISR  OMIT  ALTHEA
SNIPPIER  BLINDS
TINSELLY  LEVINE
SNAILED  ERECTS
```

310

```
HOTWIRED  SHINER
AREACODE  PAVANE
CONTENDS  ALEUTS
KIN  TRIESTE  SEI
IDIS  EERIE  LEND
TESTCASES  DIODE
ARG  TACITURN
SURREAL  LOVESET
CLEMENTE  MER
ATLAS  CAMPDAVID
LION  MORAL  LORE
AMA  DOLLIES  LAT
WADSUP  ATTITUDE
ATEASE  PREVOTES
GEDDES  SESAMEST
```

315

```
SALSA  AKBAR  SKI
OLEAN  BELLE  POD
UPONTHEROOF  ASI
PONCHOS  CURACAO
TER  INERT
CHIMNEYSWEEP
YEATS  DOPED  RBI
ABLY  FAKES  TOUR
PUT  AIMEE  SABRE
EAVESDROPPER
GORSE  NED
ROTUNDA  NONAGON
AZO  GUTTERSNIPE
PEP  ENTER  ECLAT
EDS  RESOD  REALS
```

320

```
AVIS  SISAL  AMAN
CITY  TRALA  LUGE
EVEN  MONAD  TNUT
DAMONANDPYTHIAS
PALS  CIE
PASSGO  MARGARET
EPEE  DANAE  ATE
CAESARANDBRUTUS
ORT  DECOY  NEIL
STOPOVER  ODESSA
APE  IRAQ
FLATTANDSCRUGGS
LAIR  LEASH  ARIA
UNDO  ENNUI  LILY
BEAN  DELED  SPAS
```

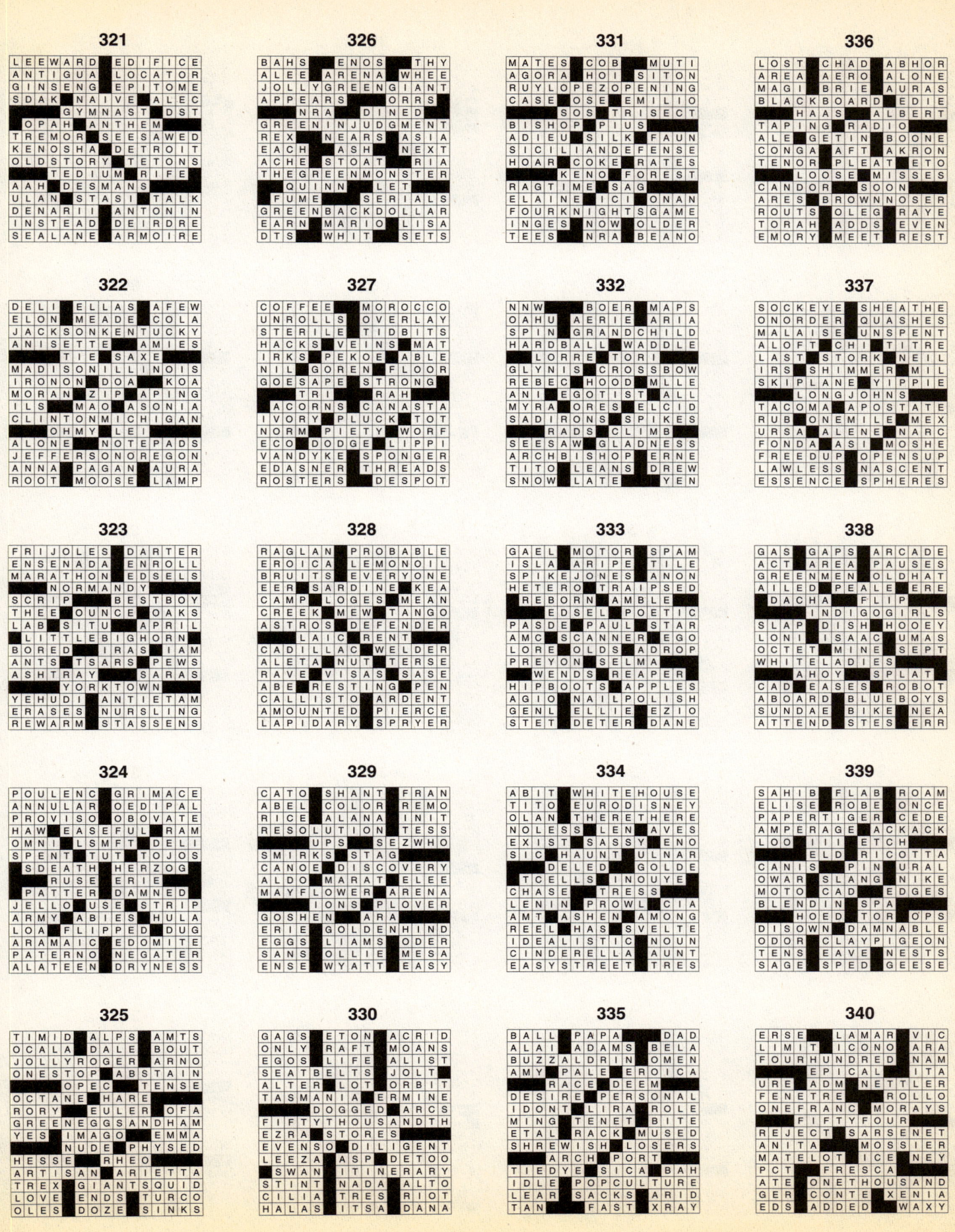

341

```
SELF GAGS  PELE
OVAL ACRES LAOS
FIREESCAPE URGE
ALDEN NICEST
   SIR DATE HOR
OAS  DESI  LIMBO
CLUB COLOR TOLD
ULNA ALONE EVAN
LUGS PIQUE METE
ARLES USSR  REY
REA  ASHE  EOS
  SATEEN OPERA
GASP WATERMELON
AGES SPLIT LIST
POSE SYNE  LESS
```

346

```
WARM CRAM  FACT
ASIA SHONE REAR
NECK PLUGS IDLE
TAKETOONESHEELS
  AIDED  KANSAS
AMEBAE THIRD
SOXER TROT SLOP
HOPEAGAINSTHOPE
ENOL HOPI  HIKES
IDEST  ARPINO
PLANET  IGLUS
ROBERTOCLEMENTE
IOOF OSKAR VAIL
DEVO ELECT ETTA
EYER DOTE  NOON
```

351

```
ORBS MESS  AROMA
POOH ALEC  LEDON
ESSE EAVE  LADEN
CASEYSTENGEL
SAPOTE  ALAMODE
MURDERERSROW
ROMERO FINS INE
ITON  FRO  SEER
NAG  SOLE  MACLES
GREATBAMBINO
SUNSUIT ASTROS
STEINBRENNER
GOMEZ RUBE ETRE
AROSE OKLA ROVE
GROSS NEED SPED
```

356

```
TOMATOPASTE OSS
ORIGINALSIN NOW
REGENERATED ERI
RATE  SRS  MOS
BRA  SONS  SIRS
LEMS ATTAR CLIC
OCEAN  EYETEETH
CORNEDBEEFONRYE
KNITWEAR  ETAPE
INCA ALECK SCIS
SOAS  DEER ENE
LIN  AMI  TIES
ATI SECRETSTORM
NEV CLEARHEADED
DRY HOTPASTRAMI
```

342

```
CASABA ADAM CAW
ELIDED BOUT ASH
LIBERALARTS SSE
ING  OLEO  SPAR
OWL ATOM  STAIR
REAP SINISTERLY
ONTIPTOE  PAN
DEALIN  BENGAL
SEM  PONDERED
LEFTBEHIND LANE
AGREE AVIS BOW
DOOR  TROT  ASI
LIS PORTOFSPAIN
EST  OBOE CHANCE
STY  LEWD CENSED
```

347

```
LACES SAGE HATS
ADULT OVUM ALAI
CELLO WISP NELL
STACKEDTHEDECK
  KIT  ALE
CALLEDONESBLUFF
OREAD OKIE SOL
WRAP SPIES SURE
LOS  ELIS  SERGE
SWEETENEDTHEPOT
  ANE  EAU
KEPTAPOKERFACE
EDIE SIAM FLOAT
PEER ISLE LARVA
INDY NEED ENDED
```

352

```
CAJOLES  COSMOS
MONOPOLY OCTOPI
INTHESUN LEADEN
SEENRED BLARING
  WARE  RUN
OSHA  SAD  ITSA
STATEOFTHEUNION
MISSOULAMONTANA
ANTONIOBANDERAS
NEON  MAS  LARS
  FAT  EMIL
TOWARDS RAREGAS
EMILIA COCACOLA
REDEEM IDENTIFY
INESSE DESISTS
```

357

```
IMAN ABBEY ASTA
NOGO WRITE ZAHN
GROW NONEWTAXES
ATNOTIME  ILENE
NONO  DATE
SEADOG NOTHANKS
ARRET CANOE ARY
BARR FOGUP ICON
ITO  TREAT ETHNO
NOWAYOUT LASTED
USER  BARN
OTERO  EATNOFAT
NONONSENSE URSA
EMIR ADOSE SAIL
SADA NOWINE ESTE
```

343

```
JILT CAIRD SOOT
ALOE OLDIE PENA
MEGA SAIDJULIET
TOROMEO  ETALII
ONO  ICES
IFYOU WONTSHAVE
DRUMS RATE LIL
LICS POKED DIAL
ETC  ONER  ARENA
ROADSIGNS LENDS
EENS  CSA
ALBERT  GOHOMEO
BURMASHAVE SAMS
ERIE TILES UTAH
TEED OPENS PANE
```

348

```
AMPAS ALEC AQUA
SARDI SOLO DUST
CREAM TIER ZOOM
OLYMPIASNOWE
TOSSES ALE JAM
  RAMS  LATELY
BALK NATHANHALE
ACING COO SANER
ROBERTHAYS WENS
BREWER  TAIL
SNL  EAU  LETTER
CRYSTALGAYLE
HAIR FAIL ELLEN
ALOU UGLY NIECE
MANX LETS DARTS
```

353

```
SPREADS LEADOFF
HEADSUP EMPEROR
INVITEE PIROGUE
SNEER CHER  ARA
HEN ACTOR MINSK
BLURB  SONICS
ATMO SUN  MATZOH
CHOW AMOCO AERO
EROTIC BOK CREW
REDINK  BLEST
BERET SEEDY HAM
ALI  SODS  LLAMA
TINFOIL LIVEDIN
ENGORGE ASININE
DESPOND WHATNOT
```

358

```
INDIAN SCAM SPA
NEEDLE PACE TAB
CHERIS ANTEDATE
IDOCTOR  ISIGHT
  PEST  AVER
CHOPS OMNI EMIL
LOPE  INS  ODE
OVER IEXAM IDEA
MER  NYE  WEAN
PRAM KERN GILLS
ORBS  CART
ILEVEL  IOPENER
FIREWOOD REELIN
FRO  ETRE ONSIDE
YES  DSCS NESSIE
```

344

```
CHART INCA CODE
AIDES NELL HAIL
THEHOUSEOFLARDS
SONE TADS OSSIE
ALAN  ESOS
GETTHEBUTTEROF
PRIED APES ECU
LADD TWIST SETS
OPE  HARZ  ELVES
THREEPIECESUET
MIEN  EYER
SOLID GEAR OBIT
PAYLIPIDSERVICE
AHOY INGE AEDES
RUNS AGED WREST
```

349

```
SLAP SHEAR AWAY
PERI EARLE WARM
AVON ARGOT ERIC
TIMEISMONEY IDA
SNATCH  GLESS
AHEAD  LASHES
TBAR LIRA TWERP
ILL ALMONDS LIE
COLON SPAR BLED
SWINGS  STEVE
SASHA  SIEGES
SEW TALKISCHEAP
CLEW STILL INGA
OSLO TOTIE VEER
WALK ASTER ETRE
```

354

```
BETA HACK CACTI
AMAS OBIE OCHER
REBA LOSE STORE
CROPCIRCLES PIS
AGO ASTO  LAMS
RESORT ALCOHOL
NAILED  KRONE
PACT CUTIN APED
ELLAS  VENOMS
SLIPUPS BASTER
PEPE SPOT  RAE
ENC PRUNEDANISH
VALSE LANI ESTE
INOUR NINE SHEA
LOPES ALES TART
```

359

```
ACAT CATER ASS
RAGES ORATE MIT
CRUNCHBERRY ONE
OPENAIR PENANCE
LEA  ANGEL
HARPERSFERRY
ALIAS IRED POM
REND PALED JAVA
PEG  TINT SORER
MATTHEWPERRY
IBEAM  CHE
NIAGARA HENREID
LOS LONDONDERRY
ATE ESTEE SAGAN
WAD SEEMS LONE
```

345

```
ORC COTTA RAISA
BAA AWARD ALDEN
VIS DEVIL ITALY
INCORRIGIBLE
ABATE  BURRITO
TODO TWA NOEVIL
EWE BOILS AGENA
PUNSTERDO
HUMAN HALAS TOW
EMERGE RFD TORI
MARSHAL  TAPIR
NOTINCORRIGE
BASIL MEADE CAT
ELOPE BASIN AMA
ABYSS OPTED LIP
```

350

```
SOAR PENAL APED
ETRE ENOLA FARE
NOTS EDGARALLAN
SOHO  TUG  CRO
ELUL ERICHMARIA
SERVE ENE  TODD
CEDED EBB  BOD
WOODEN  EASELS
IBN  NAP  ADLER
SOAK EAR  MATTS
HENRYDAVID SLUE
UAE ZAXES CORN
RALPHWALDO AURA
ATOP AVONS PIET
MEWS RENES ESTE
```

355

```
SHAPED  PRIDE
HOLEDUP SHOVING
ONORDER COMESTO
TOMMY IPANA PIE
ARAS HORDE TARA
TER GORES KATES
FOOTE  MUSCLY
JEFFFOXWORTHY
BELLES  PARTY
AREAR NODOZ PMS
SECT RISEN KEEP
EMT ZAXES NOTRE
SISTINE IWOJIMA
TATAMIS NEGATER
HOGAN  TOKENS
```

360

```
AWED  MAO  OSIP
LOVELY ASP DEMI
BROCAS THEBEARS
SNEAKER ERITREA
PERIL  AGTS
BOSOM GIG SATIE
ACADIA NOAH OLD
RAU CHICAGO WIN
ELL HALO EUREKA
RABBI KLM LURES
EEGS  NEEDS
VULGATE DRESSER
ILLINOIS GRIEVE
ANON ORA OSAGES
LAWS LEX  NAST
```

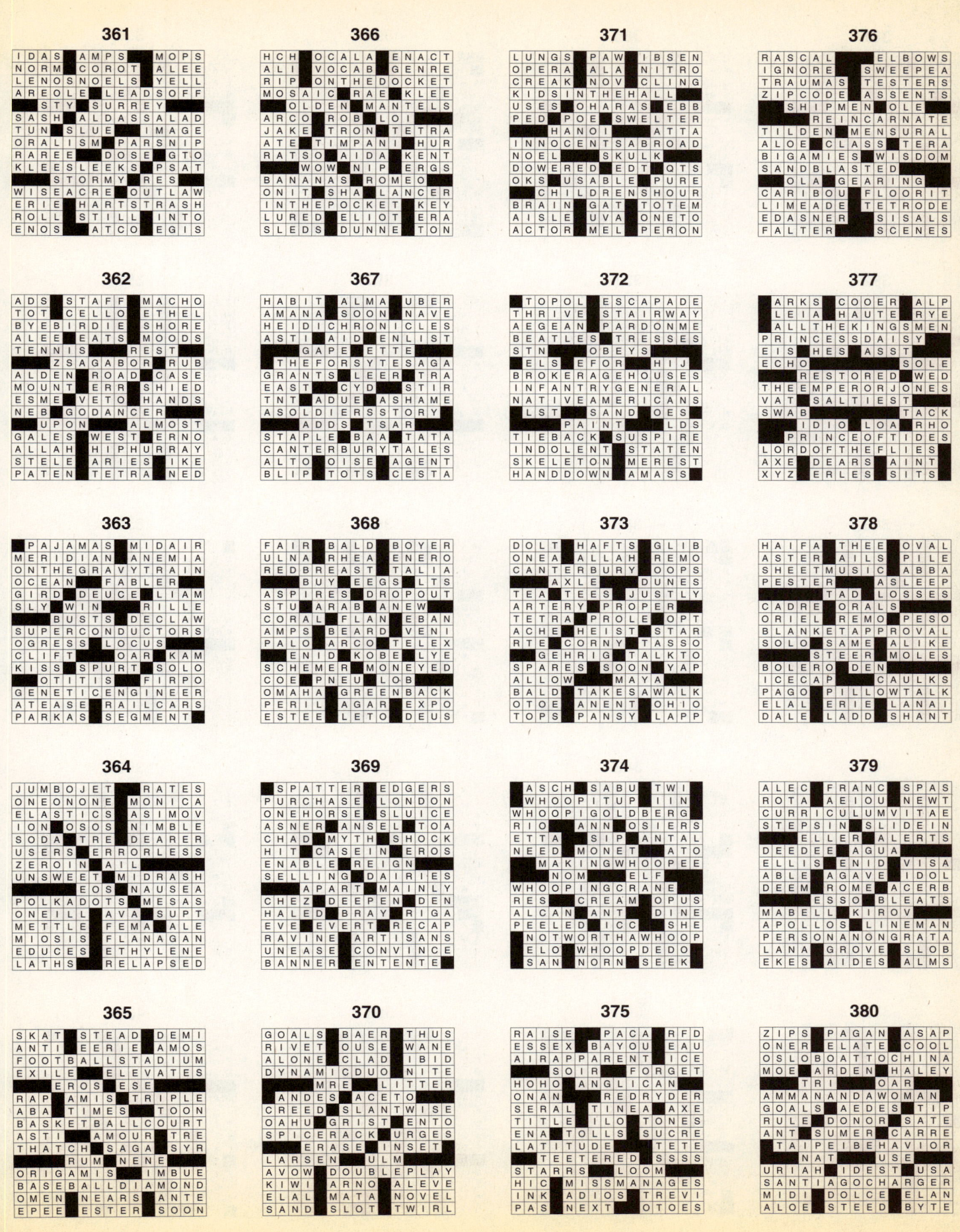

381

```
TRIBE DALI  CLAM
OOZED EBAN  RACE
GOODINVESTMENTS
ODD  FOIL  RADISH
     PITT  TORI
MALICIOUSINTENT
ANISE NATE  QUI
DIVA  HAIRS BURN
ATE   MEMO  SOUSE
MARKEDINCREASES
EDGE  AUNT
SORTIE ERIE  RAJ
WRETCHEDINGRATE
ANIL  OVEN  ADMIT
GENE  GANG  LASTS
```

386

```
CAPE  BOMBE SPEC
ARLO  ELIOT LEVI
GOOSEFLESH  ETAT
END   LOINS SWEDE
      SAGE  IGNORE
MACON SHERIFF
AVOIDS ISIT  IER
MILL  PARTS ONCE
ADD   BALE  TOUCHE
TOOTERS ATHOS
MUSTER PCTS
PERCH TAHOE THO
ILKA  PIGEONTOED
UBER  INERT ELLA
SAYS  AGREE ALLY
```

391

```
SPASM JOHAN
GLANCE ONAPAR
ARISTAS YEWTREE
DEP  ALSORAN RAT
DAPS DEVIL ROPE
USEIT DAD  SOWER
PERSIA LEFTTURN
YEGGS SARAN
TOWNHALL OUTDID
ASHOT EIS  MEESE
STER  MEMOS DRAB
KEN  LAPORTE PAU
SAWYERS REENACT
LEANTO ORLESS
TWAIN WESTS
```

396

```
ZELDA RACE  RAVE
ABOIL ELAN  AGED
LABOURCANDIDATE
ENORMOUS  EDISON
NOR  GALA
GREATSLAVELAKE
SUAVE IZOD  GAB
HAZE  MILER WEBB
ONE   NANA  GENUS
WORKINGCAPITAL
NONE  ION
STROBE SMUGNESS
TOILERSOFTHESEA
IDOL  LIDO  ABACK
ROTS  YEAR  MOUSE
```

382

```
SHEBA DUG  ABASE
AURUM ISO  SADAS
GRASPEDATSTRAWS
POSHEST SNO SEX
AAH  SLOYD
DRAPE CAMEOS
HELDONTIGHT
SLEETS YAHOO
SPOIL UNI
AIR  NRA  EVANGEL
CLINGINGVINE
CAMETOGRIPSWITH
ENERO LEA  OLLIE
LEDON OWN  NYLON
```

387

```
JOESIXPACK  LADY
IGNESFATUI  SNEE
BASELINERS  DIMS
EGO  ALE  VSO TIM
SERENE KEYS  AMA
ADSORB SOLOS
BEETS NIA  AFOOT
ALMS  ESL  FORE
MAFIA NHL  MISER
BLOND ONSPEC
OAR  ASTA  OLESON
OMS  MIR  DUO TRI
ZETA  DURANDURAN
LIEN  EMANCIPATE
ENRY  APPLECIDER
```

392

```
BIER  TAN  TAPS
UNLEAVENED  ERLE
FREDDIETHEGREAT
FEEDER  IRANIANS
YET  UNA
PAP  RUGS  SWAMPS
AGRA  ALOE  EXALT
SAINTLARRYRIVER
HINDU DESI  SINE
ANTICS STEM  NAP
STP  LEA
ATSTORES  DUNNER
QUEENANNIESTYLE
URGE  WAITRESSED
ANON  LPS  YEAS
```

397

```
SPASM PEZ  KNIFE
WALLA LAO  RURAL
ATLAS USO  AMARK
SHIVERMETIMBERS
HON  REEL  NEE
YAMS  BURROWS
STPAT DAS  MIA
WALKINGTHEPLANK
ATA  OAS  AYRES
BANDITS FORE
ANS  LEWD  SGT
DAVYJONESLOCKER
ELITE OAT  NOOSE
ADIOS UKE  MOATS
FAINT SYR  ELLES
```

383

```
PAPA  EDGAR CAFE
OLIN  VERNE USER
MICE  IREAD THEA
PICNIC  GREATEST
ADATE MYTH
AND  NITE  EARNA
LOIS  OATH  LOOSE
FILLINTHEBLANKS
ARLES SERA  TOMS
EYEOF LENO  NEE
PULP  ISLES
TELLTALE  HELENS
ERIE  MATTE INON
AGES  ENTRE ASTI
MOSS  STAYS SEAT
```

388

```
SPOCK SWIMS
CHACHI WARIEST
BRUSHED INASTIR
LETTERMAN  ESTA
OATER ALGEBRAIC
OMER  NASAL INK
MYRNA BECURLS
ARIMATHEA
ESKIMOS SCARF
SMU  SANTA  ELEA
EPICENTER SHEER
PITA  ARISTOTLE
TRISTAN STARTED
SENHORA TENSED
GAMIN ANGER
```

393

```
MACE  SOAP  SMA
IRON  PARSI LASS
FIRSTOFTHEMONTH
FAN  ALAS  DIETER
ICIER AMA  URE
SECONDINCOMMAND
AVERT OMNIA
MESS  BERET NMEX
ECLAT SCORE
BEETHOVENSTHIRD
ATE  OWE  ALIAS
SCLERO ASOF  TUN
THEFOURTHOFJULY
EERO  TIEUP ARNE
SYR  SANA  BEAT
```

398

```
SPONSOR  OFFISH
SEAHORSE LEANTO
PARADISE LEADEN
AWARE ILIAD IRE
CANE  MAIN  SAGES
ITO  SINNER MOOT
NEIGHS GRUMP
GRANOLA TSELIOT
ADEPT SIENNA
USSR  DARTER NET
REALM COAT  COST
GEL  OLEUM DEVIL
IGUANA PALISADE
NETHER ELEVATED
GREATS REVERED
```

384

```
GAB  CRAT  ACME
OURS  ROMEO NAIL
OREO  ATALL IMSO
DOWNINTHEDUMPS
IRE  NEE  GASPS
EARED RALPH IER
LES  GEE  ATNO
INEXPERIENCED
SMEE  ESE  NOR
APO  REPEL RYDER
LAPSE ELM  EVE
CHICKENHEARTED
ETYM  AROMA AARE
VETO  NOMAN WISE
ADEN  SENT  LOM
```

389

```
BALD  COED  PENN
ALIE  ORLE  LEVEE
ROBS  LAIT  INERT
BUREAU  HARVARD
DARTMOUTH  TABU
DEM  ITLL  IONIA
IVYLEAGUESCHOOL
VIRAL OVAL  SSE
ALASKA RIBS
PRINCETON
CORNELL KEEPUP
SAMOA ELLE  PEKE
BROWN SUER  PREP
ADOS  SSTS  EASE
```

394

```
BASK  DESI  MAVIS
LONI  AXON  ELEGY
ANUN  CIRC  SEXED
BEGGARSBANQUET
SLOT  ROUTS
JUSTIN  ANTIS
EZIO  BRACT MAC
DINNERATTHERITZ
ISE  VERSE ELEA
BONNY COCKER
OILED CHAR
AMOVEABLEFEAST
AMATI NEIL  ALLY
BENIN CANA  TEAR
USING EDGE  EXPO
```

399

```
DEAN  SCRUB PFCS
ETTA  HOFFA EROS
FUTURESCONTRACT
INTUIT  SIESTAS
ISLA  SRI
STOCKARBITRAGE
IOTAS RTES  ONT
ARAL  SPOOR SIDE
MIR  THIN  SINUS
CURRENCYHEDGES
AYE  AONE
ENSNARE HOARSE
LONGTERMOPTIONS
BRIE  STOOL TROP
EATS  TENSE EASY
```

385

```
ANALOGIST  TARP
RAREEARTH  BALER
DIMESTORE  AKITE
OVERTONES  LETAT
REDYE SEE  LATKE
SST  TVTABLES
TODOS SEEDIEST
IVEDONEIT
SANSERIF SCENE
PRETRIAL OAT
ACERB TAC  CARTA
RADII ORATORIES
EDICT MERRIMENT
SIETE IDEOLOGUE
TARS  COLDSNAPS
```

390

```
PARSE PEARS
CRANIUM AESOPS
RERATES CREMATE
ADELE REO  ARAP
SOSO  PLED  SIENA
GALEN RAN
IMA  VANE  ELEVEN
LAW  ANAGRAM IWO
KINDLE AERO  MEG
ROT  DAMNS
CHAIN DEMS  CROP
LOPE  SIS  PRADO
USEDCAR STRIPED
TRUDGE ISOMERS
SPEAR REAPS
```

395

```
BOTH  OFTHE HEN
ALOOF TAHOE APE
LEAVEITTOBEAVER
MODERN HUB  NEED
RANGE ION
SAD  LIAR  TREATS
ATE  NIK  TABOO
GILLIGANSISLAND
ALTAR OWN  TEA
STARES WAGS  ESS
IDI  STEPS
SOFA  EBB  SOLACE
THETHREESTOOGES
AIL  ERASE FERNS
GOT  MATTE SATE
```

400

```
AHSO  IMAM  CAR
BATMOBILE  REFER
ENLIVENED  ALTAR
ESOTERICA  BLESS
TRIM  LABORS
MANILA  MINISTER
AGONY DESKS ARE
ZING  FILTH ASTI
ETS  DOVES PUTON
LAKEERIE  CATERS
TILTED TOTO
TILDE ECONOMIST
DOLES NONVIABLE
SNERT DIGESTION
SDS  SLAY  EDEN
```

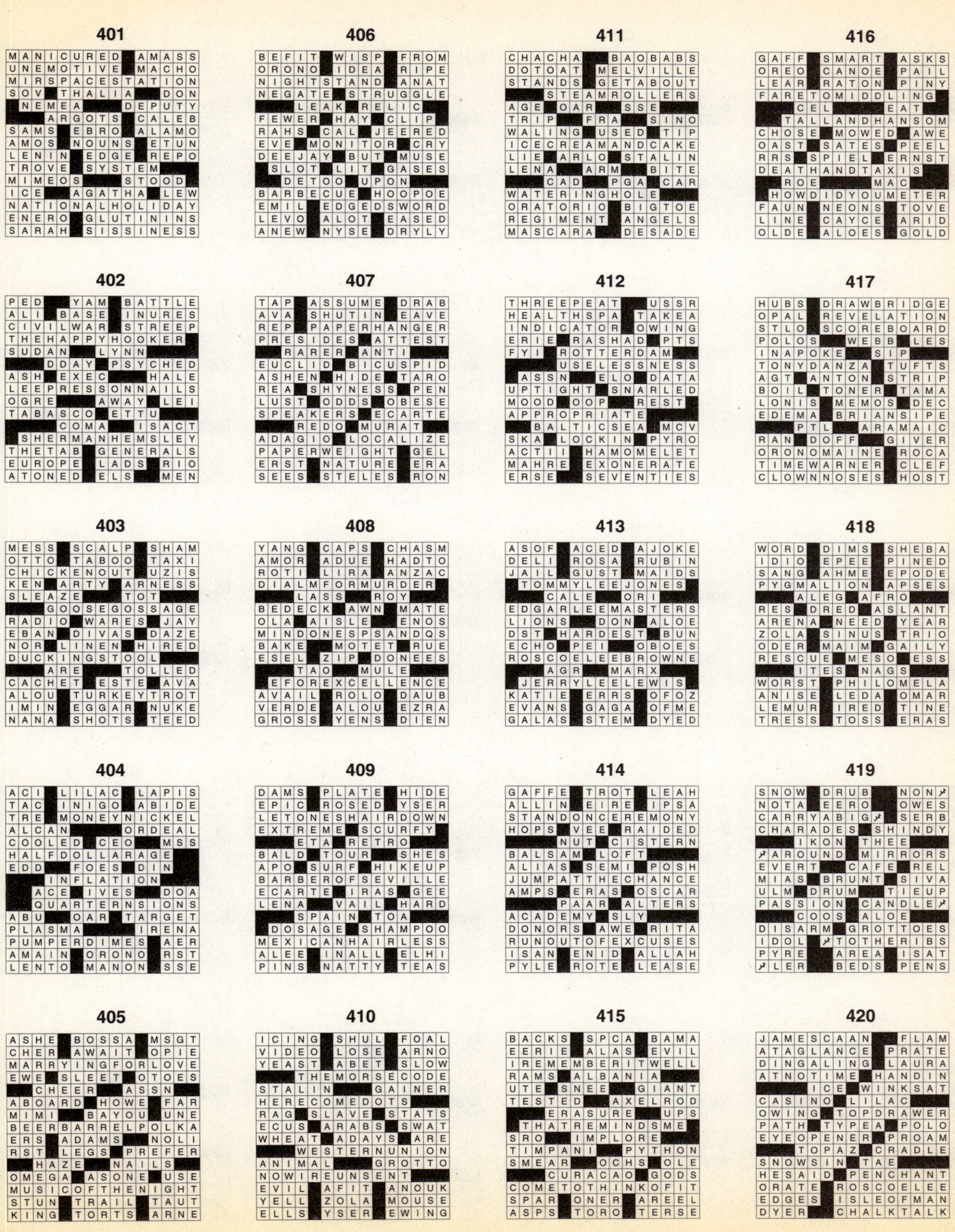

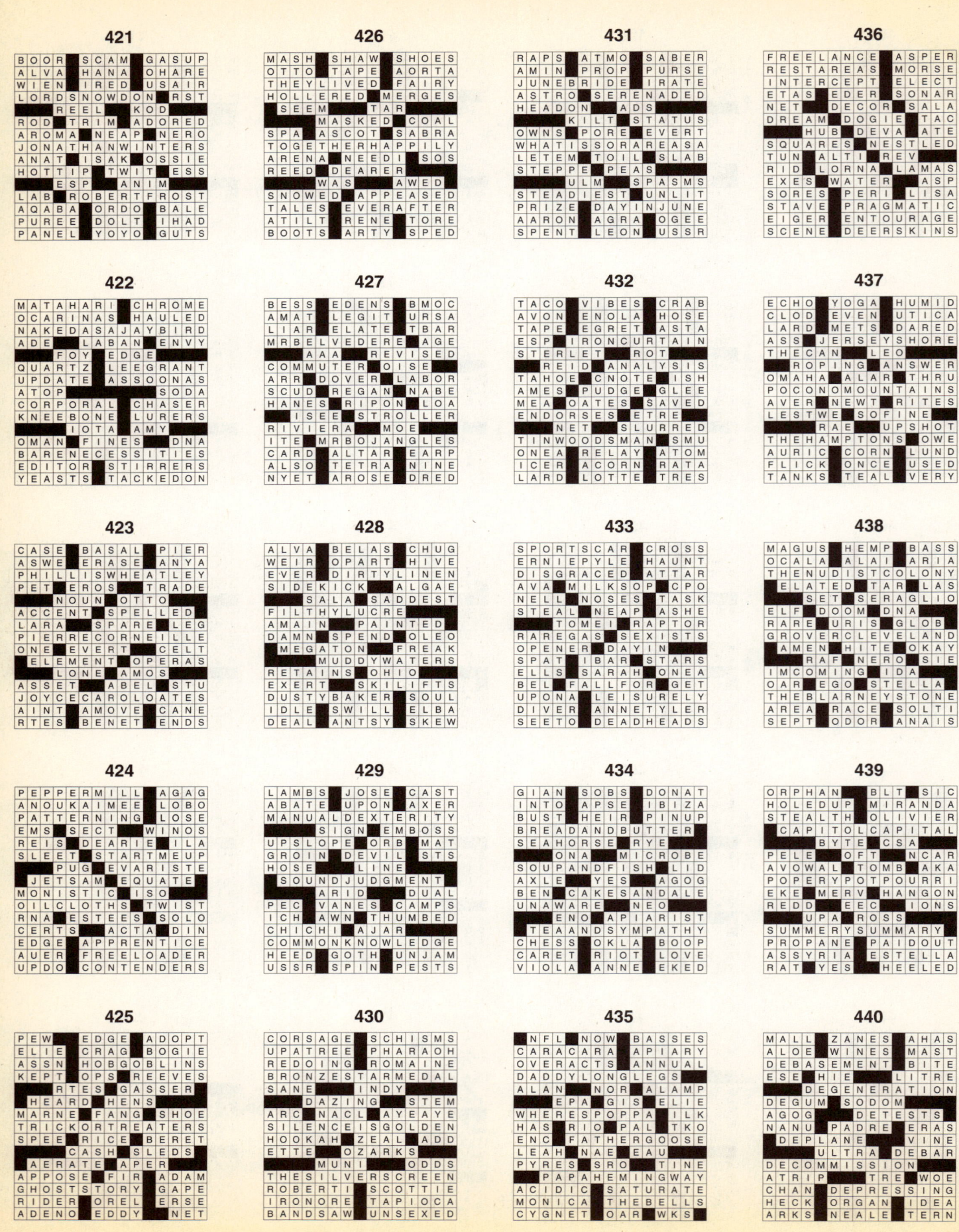

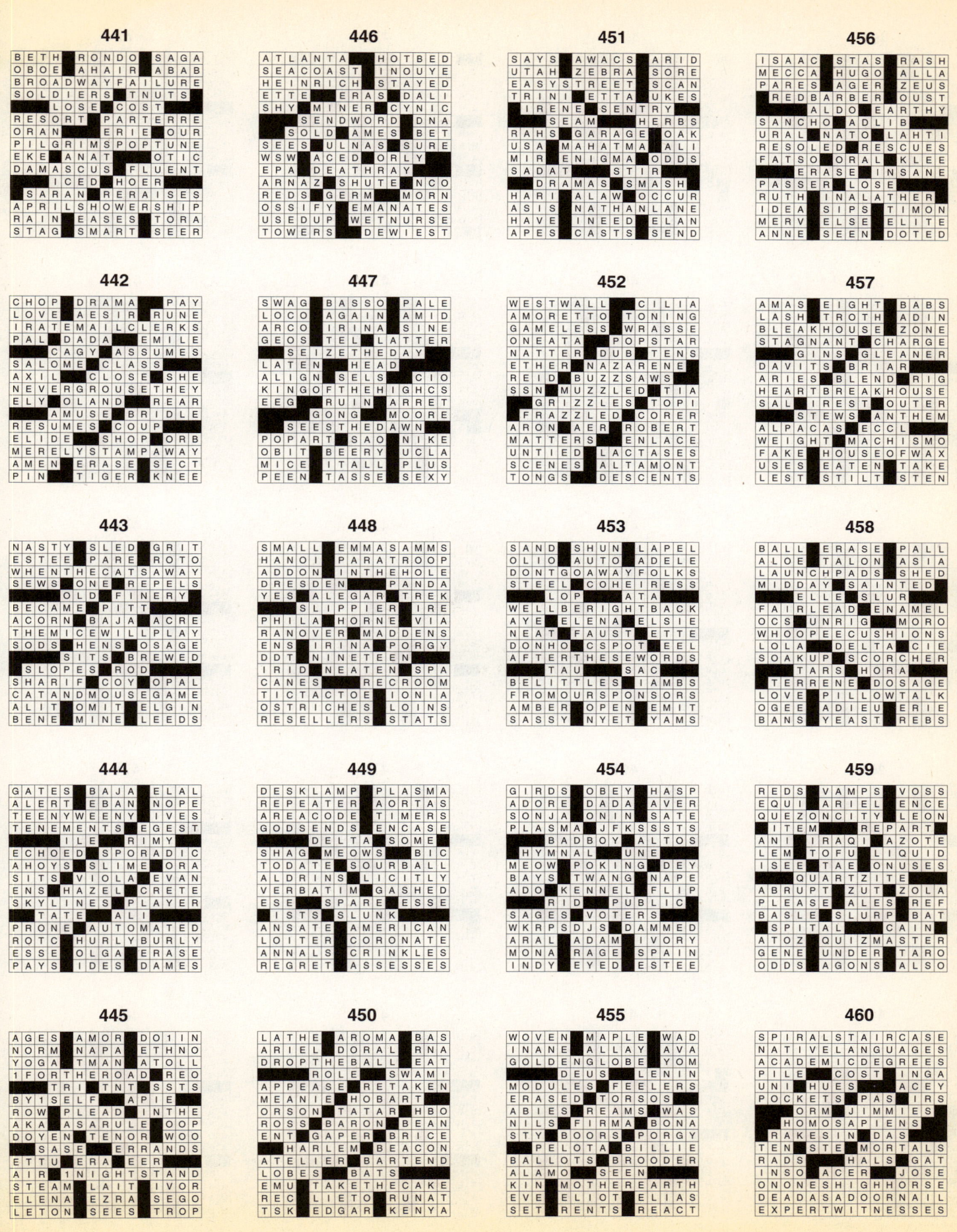

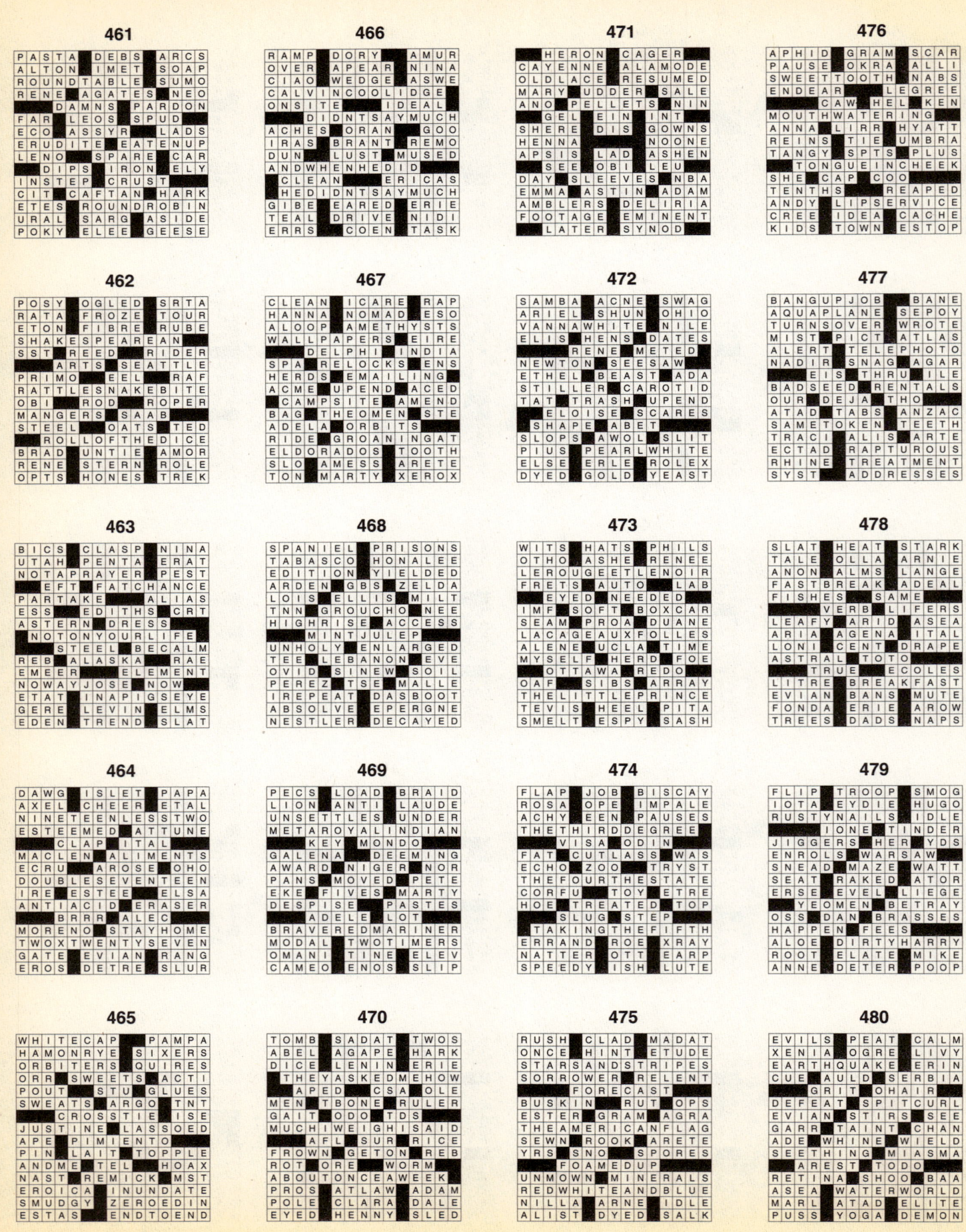

461

```
PASTA DEBS ARCS
ALTON IMET SOAP
ROUNDTABLE SUMO
RENE AGATES NEO
    DAMNS PARDON
FAR LEOS SPUD
ECO ASSYR LADS
ERUDITE EATENUP
LENO SPARE CAR
DIPS IRON ELY
INSTEP CRUST
CIT CAFTAN HARK
ETES ROUNDROBIN
URAL SARG ASIDE
POKY ELEE GEESE
```

466

```
RAMP DORY AMUR
OVER APEAR NINA
CIAO WEDGE ASWE
CALVINCOOLIDGE
ONSITE IDEAL
  DIDNTSAYMUCH
ACHES ORAN GOO
IRAS BRANT REMO
DUN LUST MUSED
ANDWHENHEDID
CLEAN ERICAS
HEDIDNTSAYMUCH
GIBE EARED ERIE
TEAL DRIVE NIDI
ERRS COEN TASK
```

471

```
HERON CAGER
CAYENNE ALAMODE
OLDLACE RESUMED
MARY UDDER SALE
ANO PELLETS NIN
GEL EIN INT
SHERE DIS GOWNS
HENNA NOONE
APSIS LAD ASHEN
SEE OBI LEU
DAY SLEEVES NBA
EMMA ASTIN ADAM
AMBLERS DELIRIA
FOOTAGE EMINENT
LATER SYNOD
```

476

```
APHID GRAM SCAR
PAUSE OKRA ALLI
SWEETTOOTH NABS
ENDEAR LEGREE
CAW HEL KEN
MOUTHWATERING
ANNA LIRR HYATT
REINS TIE UMBRA
TANGY SPTS PLUS
TONGUEINCHEEK
SHE CAP COO
TENTHS REAPED
ANDY LIPSERVICE
CREE IDEA CACHE
KIDS TOWN ESTOP
```

462

```
POSY OGLED SRTA
RATA FROZE TOUR
ETON FIBRE RUBE
SHAKESPEAREAN
SST REED RIDER
ARTS SEATTLE
PRIMO EEL RAF
RATTLESNAKEBITE
OBI ROD ROPER
MANGERS SAAB
STEEL OATS TED
ROLLOFTHEDICE
BRAD UNTIE AMOR
RENE STERN ROLE
OPTS HONES TREK
```

467

```
CLEAN ICARE RAP
HANNA NOMAD ESO
ALOOP AMETHYSTS
WALLPAPERS EIRE
DELPHI INDIA
SPA RELOCKS ENS
HERDS EMAILING
ACME UPEND ACED
CAMPSITE AMEND
BAG THEOMEN STE
ADELA ORBITS
RIDE GROANINGAT
ELDORADOS TOOTH
SLO AMESS ARETE
TON MARTY XEROX
```

472

```
SAMBA ACNE SWAG
ARIEL SHUN OHIO
VANNAWHITE NILE
ELIS HENS DATES
RENE METED
NEWTON SEESAW
ETHEL BEAST ADA
STILLER CAROTID
TAT TRASH UPEND
ELOISE SCARES
SHAPE ABET
SLOPS AWOL SLIT
PIUS PEARLWHITE
ELSE ERLE ROLEX
DYED GOLD YEAST
```

477

```
BANGUPJOB BANE
AQUAPLANE SEPOY
TURNSOVER WROTE
MIST PICT ATLAS
ALERT TELEPHOTO
NADIR SNAG AGAR
EIS THRU ILE
BADSEED RENTALS
OUR DEJA THO
ATAD TABS ANZAC
SAMETOKEN TEETH
TRACI ALIS ARTE
ECTAD RAPTUROUS
RHINE TREATMENT
SYST ADDRESSES
```

463

```
BICS CLASP NINA
UTAH PENTA ERAT
NOTAPRAYER PEST
EFT FATCHANCE
PARTAKE ALIAS
ESS EDITHS CRT
ASTERN DRESS
NOTONYOURLIFE
STEEL BECALM
REB ALASKA RAE
EMEER ELEMENT
NOWAYJOSE NOW
ETAT INAPIGSEYE
GERE LEVIN ELMS
EDEN TREND SLAT
```

468

```
SPANIEL PRISONS
TABASCO HONALEE
EDITION YIELDED
ARDEN GBS ZELDA
LOIS ELLIS MILT
TNN GROUCHO NEE
HIGHRISE ACCESS
MINTJULEP
UNHOLY ENLARGED
TEE LEBANON EVE
OVID SINEW SOIL
PEREZ TSE MALLE
IREPEAT DASBOOT
ABSOLVE EPERGNE
NESTLER DECAYED
```

473

```
WITS HATS PHILS
OTHO ASHE RENEE
LEROUGEETLENOIR
FRETS AUTO LAB
EYED NEEDED
IMF SOFT BOXCAR
SEAM PROA DUANE
LACAGEAUXFOLLES
ALENE UCLA TIME
MYSELF HERD FOE
OTTAWA REDO
OAF SIBS ARRAY
THELITTLEPRINCE
TEVIS HEEL PITA
SMELT ESPY SASH
```

478

```
SLAT HEAT STARK
TALE OLLA ARNIE
ANON ALMS LANGE
FASTBREAK ADEAL
FISHES SAME
VERB LIFERS
LEAFY ARID ASEA
ARIA AGENA ITAL
LONI CENT DRAPE
ASTRAL TOTO
TRUE ECOLES
LITRE BREAKFAST
EVIAN BANS MUTE
FONDA ERIE AROW
TREES DADS NAPS
```

464

```
DAWG ISLET PAPA
AXEL CHEER ETAL
NINETEENLESSTWO
ESTEEMED ATTUNE
CLAP ITAL
MACLEN AILMENTS
ECRU AROSE OHO
DOUBLESEVENTEEN
IRE ESTEE ELSA
ANTIACID ERASER
BRRR ALEC
MORENO STAYHOME
TWOXTWENTYSEVEN
GATE EVIAN RANG
EROS DETRE SLUR
```

469

```
PECS LOAD BRAID
LION ANTI LAUDE
UNSETTLES UNDER
METAROYALINDIAN
KEY MONDO
GALENA DEEMING
AWARD NIGER NOR
PANS MOVED PETE
EKE FIVES MARTY
DESPISE PASTES
ADELE LOT
BRAVEREDMARINER
MODAL TWOTIMERS
OMANI TINE ELEV
CAMEO ENOS SLIP
```

474

```
FLAP JOB BISCAY
ROSA OPE IMPALE
ACHY EEN PAUSES
THETHIRDDEGREE
VISA ODIN
FAT CUTLASS WAS
ECHO ZOO TRYST
THEFOURTHESTATE
CORFU TOY ETRE
HOE TREATED TOP
SLUG STEP
TAKINGTHEFIFTH
ERRAND ROE XRAY
NATTER OTT EARP
SPEEDY ISH LUTE
```

479

```
FLIP TROOP SMOG
IOTA EYDIE HUGO
RUSTYNAILS IDLE
IONE TINDER
JIGGERS HER YDS
ENROLS WARSAW
SNEAD MAZE WATT
SEAT RAKED ATOR
ERSE EVEL LIEGE
YEOMEN BETRAY
OSS DAN BRASSES
HAPPEN FEES
ALOE DIRTYHARRY
ROOT ELATE MIKE
ANNE DETER POOP
```

465

```
WHITECAP PAMPA
HAMONRYE SIXERS
ORBITERS QUIRES
ORR SWEETS ACTI
POUT STU GLUES
SWEATS ARGO TNT
CROSSTIE ISE
JUSTINE LASSOED
APE PIMIENTO
PIN LAIT TOPPLE
ANDME TEL HOAX
NAST REMICK MST
EROICA INUNDATE
SMUDGY ZEROEDIN
ESTAS ENDTOEND
```

470

```
TOMB SADAT TWOS
ABEL AGAPE HARK
DICE LENIN ERIE
THEYASKEDMEHOW
APED CSA OLE
MEN TBONE RULER
GAIT ODO TDS
MUCHIWEIGHISAID
AFL SUR RICE
FROWN GETON REB
ROT ORE WORM
ABOUTONCEAWEEK
PROS ATLAW ADAM
POLE CLARA DALE
EYED HENNY SLED
```

475

```
RUSH CLAD MADAT
ONCE HINT ETUDE
STARSANDSTRIPES
SORROWER RELENT
FORECAST
BUSKIN RUT OPS
ESTER GRAM AGRA
THEAMERICANFLAG
SEWN ROOK ARETE
YRS SNO SPORES
FOAMEDUP
UNMOWN MINERALS
REDWHITEANDBLUE
NILLA ARNE IDLE
ALIST DYED SALK
```

480

```
EVILS PEAT CALM
XENIA OGRE LIVY
EARTHQUAKE ERIN
CUE AULD SERBIA
GRIT OHAIR
DEFEAT SPITCURL
EVIAN STIRS SEE
GARR TAINT CHAN
ADE WHINE WIELD
SEETHING MIASMA
AREST TODO
RETINA SHOO BAA
ASEA WATERWORLD
MARL ATAD ELITE
PUSS YOGA DEMON
```

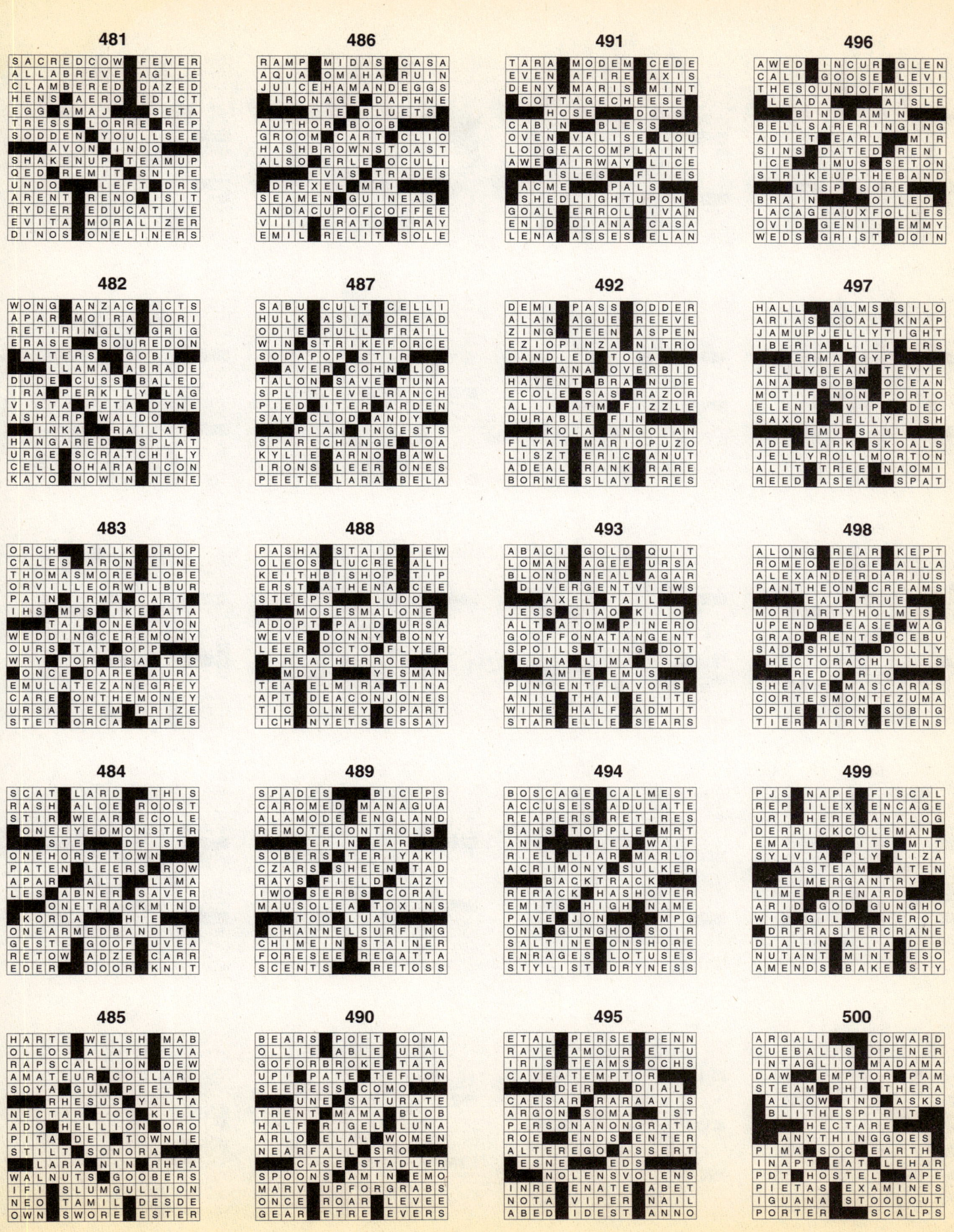

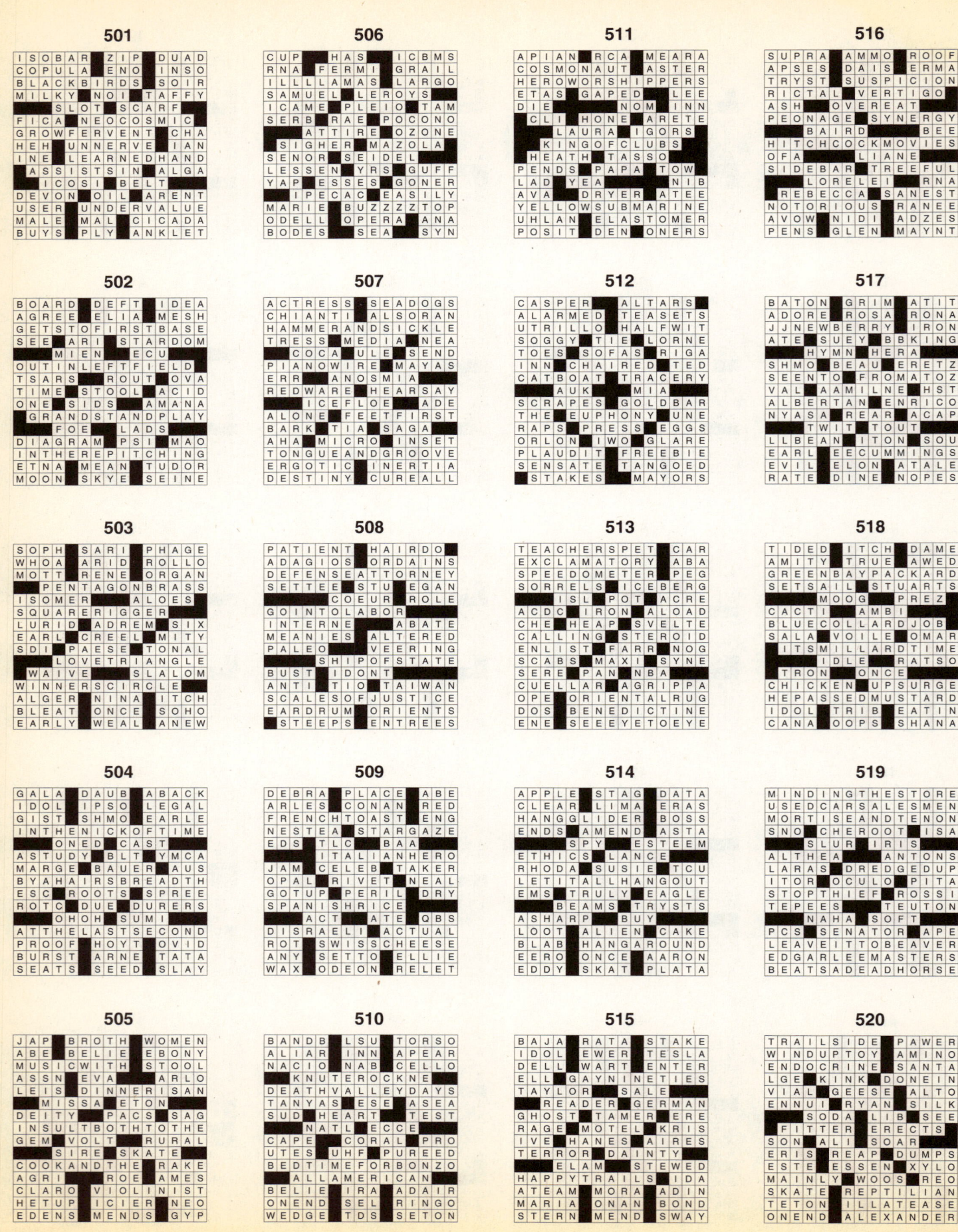

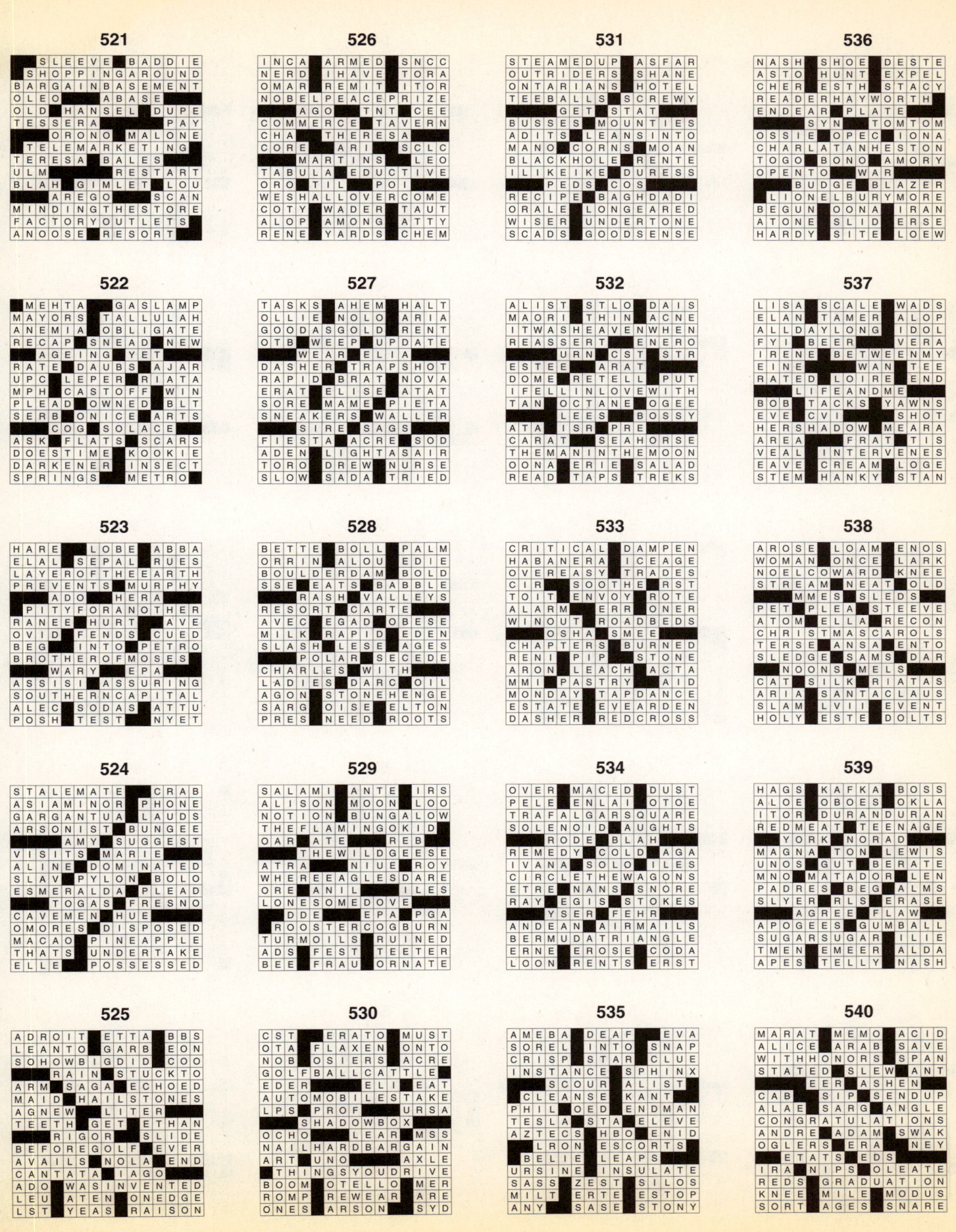

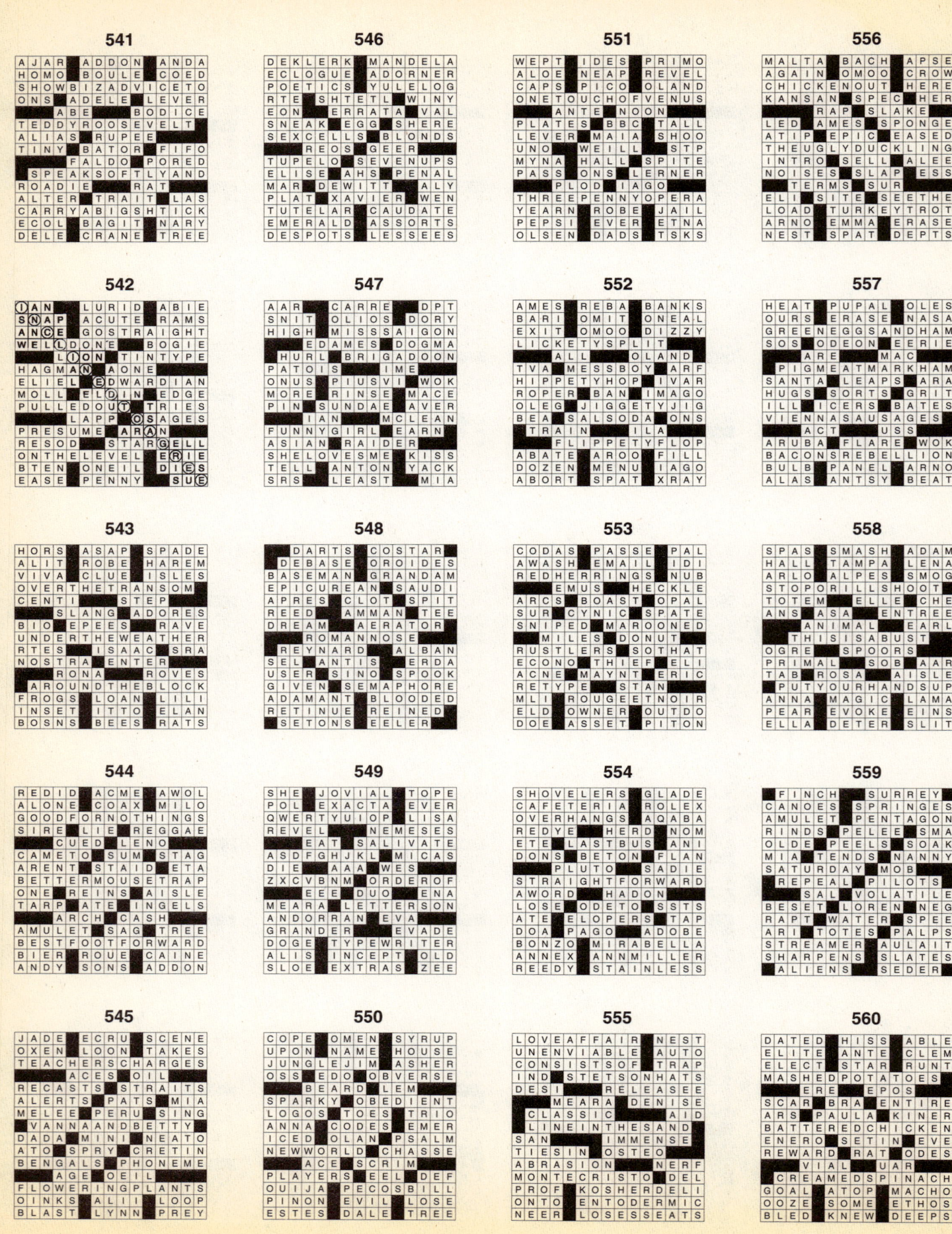

541
```
AJAR ADDON ANDA
HOMO BOULE COED
SHOWBIZADVICETO
ONS ADELE LEVER
    ABE BODICE
TEDDYROOSEVELT
ALIAS RUPEE
TINY BATOR FIFO
    FALDO PORED
SPEAKSOFTLYAND
ROADIE RAT
ALTER TRAIT LAS
CARRYABIGSHTICK
ECOL BAGIT NARY
DELE CRANE TREE
```

542
```
IAN LURID ABIE
SNAP ACUTE RAMS
ANCE GOSTRAIGHT
WELLDONE BOGIE
LION TINTYPE
HAGMAN AONE
ELIEL EDWARDIAN
MOLL ELDIN EDGE
PULLEDOUT TRIES
LAPP OSAGES
PRESUME ARAN
RESOD STAR GELL
ONTHELEVEL ERIE
BTEN ONEIL DIES
EASE PENNY SUE
```

543
```
HORS ASAP SPADE
ALIT ROBE HAREM
VIVA CLUE ISLES
OVERTHETRANSOM
CENTI STEP
SLANG ADORES
BIO EPEES RAVE
UNDERTHEWEATHER
RTES ISAAC SRA
NOSTRA ENTER
RONA ROVES
AROUNDTHEBLOCK
FROGS LOAN LILI
INSET ITTO ELAN
BOSNS BEES RATS
```

544
```
REDID ACME AWOL
ALONE COAX MILO
GOODFORNOTHINGS
SIRE LIE REGGAE
CUED LENO
CAMETO SUM STAG
ARENT STAID ETA
BETTERMOUSETRAP
ONE REINS AISLE
TARP ATE INGELS
ARCH CASH
AMULET SAG TREE
BESTFOOTFORWARD
BIER ROUE CAINE
ANDY SONS ADDON
```

545
```
JADE ECRU SCENE
OXEN LOON TAKES
TEACHERSCHARGES
ACES OIL
RECASTS STRAITS
ALERTS PATS MIA
MELEE PERU SING
VANNAANDBETTY
DADA MINI NEATO
ATO SPRY CRETIN
BENGALS PHONEME
AGE OEIL
FLOWERINGPLANTS
OINKS ALII LOOP
BLAST LYNN PREY
```

546
```
DEKLERK MANDELA
ECLOGUE ADORNER
POETICS YULELOG
RTE SHTETL WINY
EON ERRATA VAL
SNEAK EGG SHERE
SEXCELLS BLONDS
REOS GEER
TUPELO SEVENUPS
ELISE AHS PENAL
MAR DEWITT ALY
PLAT XAVIER WEN
TUTELAR CAUDATE
EMERALD ASSORTS
DESPOTS LESSEES
```

547
```
AAR CARRE DPT
SNIT OLIOS DORY
HIGH MISSSAIGON
EDAMES DOGMA
HURL BRIGADOON
PATOIS IME
ONUS PIUSVI WOK
MORE RINSE MACE
PIN SUNDAE AVER
IAN MCLEAN
FUNNYGIRL EARN
ASIAN RAIDER
SHELOVESME KISS
TELL ANTON YACK
SRS LEAST MIA
```

548
```
DARTS COSTAR
DEBASE OROIDES
BASEMAN GRANDAM
EPICUREAN SAUDI
APRES CLOT SPIT
REED AMMAN TEE
DREAM AERATOR
ROMANNOSE
REYNARD ALBAN
SEL ANTIS ERDA
USER SINO SPOOK
GIVEN SEMAPHORE
ADAMANT BLOODED
RETINUE REINED
SETONS EELER
```

549
```
SHE JOVIAL TOPE
POL EXACTA EVER
QWERTYUIOP LISA
REVEL NEMESES
EAT SALIVATE
ASDFGHJKL MICAS
DIE AAA WES
ZXCVBNM ORDEROF
EEE DUO ENA
MEARA LETTERSON
ANDORRAN EVA
GRANDER EVADE
DOGE TYPEWRITER
ALIS INCEPT OLD
SLOE EXTRAS ZEE
```

550
```
COPE OMEN SYRUP
UPON NAME HOUSE
JUNGLEJIM ASHER
OSS EDO OBVERSE
BEARD LEM
SPARKY OBEDIENT
LOGOS TOES TRIO
ANNA CODES EMER
ICED OLAN PSALM
NEWWORLD CHASSE
ACE SCRIM
PLAYERS EEL DEF
OUIJA PECOSBILL
PINON EVIL LOSE
ESTES DALE TREE
```

551
```
WEPT IDES PRIMO
ALOE NEAP REVEL
CAPS PICO OLAND
ONETOUCHOFVENUS
ANTE NOON
PLATES BBC TALL
LEVER MAIA SHOO
UNO WEILL STP
MYNA HALL SPITE
PASS ONS LERNER
PLOD IAGO
THREEPENNYOPERA
YEARN ROBE JAIL
PEPSI EVER ETNA
OLSEN DADS TSKS
```

552
```
AMES REBA BANKS
BARI OMIT ONEAL
EXIT OMOO DIZZY
LICKETYSPLIT
ALL OLAND
TVA MESSBOY ARF
HIPPETYHOP IVAR
ROPER BAN IMAGO
OLEG JIGGETYJIG
BEA SALSODA ONS
TRAIN ILA
FLIPPETYFLOP
ABATE AROO FILL
DOZEN MENU IAGO
ABORT SPAT XRAY
```

553
```
CODAS PASSE PAL
AWASH EMAIL IDI
REDHERRINGS NUB
EMUS HECKLE
ARCS BOAST OPAL
SUR CYNIC SPATE
SNIPED MAROONED
MILES DONUT
RUSTLERS SOTHAT
ECONO THIEF ELI
ACNE MAYNT ERIC
RETYPE STAN
MLI ROUGEETNOIR
ELD OWNER OUTDO
DOE ASSET PITON
```

554
```
SHOVELERS GLADE
CAFETERIA ROLEX
OVERHANGS AQABA
REDYE HERD NOM
ETE LASTBUS ANI
DONS BETON FLAN
PLUTO SADIE
STRAIGHTFORWARD
AWORD HADON
LOSE ODETO SSTS
ATE ELOPERS TAP
DOA PAGO ADOBE
BONZO MIRABELLA
ANNEX ANNMILLER
REEDY STAINLESS
```

555
```
LOVEAFFAIR NEST
UNENVIABLE AUTO
CONSISTSOF TRAP
IND STETSONHATS
DESI RELEASEE
MEARA DENISE
CLASSIC AID
LINEINTHESAND
SAN IMMENSE
TIESIN OSTEO
ABRASION NERF
MONTECRISTO DEL
PROF KOSHERDELI
ONTO ENTODERMIC
NEER LOSESSEATS
```

556
```
MALTA BACH APSE
AGAIN OMOO CROW
CHICKENOUT HERE
KANSAN SPEC HER
RAP SLAKE
LED AMES SPONGE
ATIP EPIC EASED
THEUGLYDUCKLING
INTRO SELL ALEE
NOISES SLAP ESS
TERMS SUR
ELI SITE SEETHE
LOAD TURKEYTROT
ARNO EMMA ERASE
NEST SPAT DEPTS
```

557
```
HEAT PUPAL OLES
OURS ERASE NASA
GREENEGGSANDHAM
SOS ODEON EERIE
ARE MAC
PIGMEATMARKHAM
SANTA LEAPS ARA
HUGS SORTS GRIT
ILL ICERS BATES
VIENNASAUSAGES
ACT USS
ARUBA FLARE WOK
BACONSREBELLION
BULB PANEL ARNO
ALAS ANTSY BEAT
```

558
```
SPAS SMASH ADAM
HALL TAMPA LENA
ARLO ALPES SMOG
STOPORILLSHOOT
TOTEM ELLE CHE
ANS ASA ENTREE
ANIMAL EARL
THISISABUST
OGRE SPOORS
PRIMAL SOB AAR
TAB ROSA AISLE
PUTYOURHANDSUP
ANNA MAGIC LAMA
PEAR EVOKE EINS
ELLA DETER SLIT
```

559
```
FINCH SURREY
CANOES SPRINGES
AMULET PENTAGON
RINDS PELEE SMA
OLDE PEELS SOAK
MIA TENDS NANNY
SATURDAY MOB
REPEAL PILOTS
SAL VOLATILE
BESET LOREN NEG
RAPT WATER SPEE
ARI TOTES PALPS
STREAMER AULAIT
SHARPENS SLATES
ALIENS SEDER
```

560
```
DATED HISS ABLE
ELITE ANTE CLEM
ELECT STAR RUNT
MASHEDPOTATOES
ERE EPOS
SCAR BRA ENTIRE
ARS PAULA KINER
BATTEREDCHICKEN
ENERO SETIN EVE
REWARD RAT ODES
VIAL UAR
CREAMEDSPINACH
GOAL ATOP MACHO
OOZE SOME ETHOS
BLED KNEW DEEPS
```

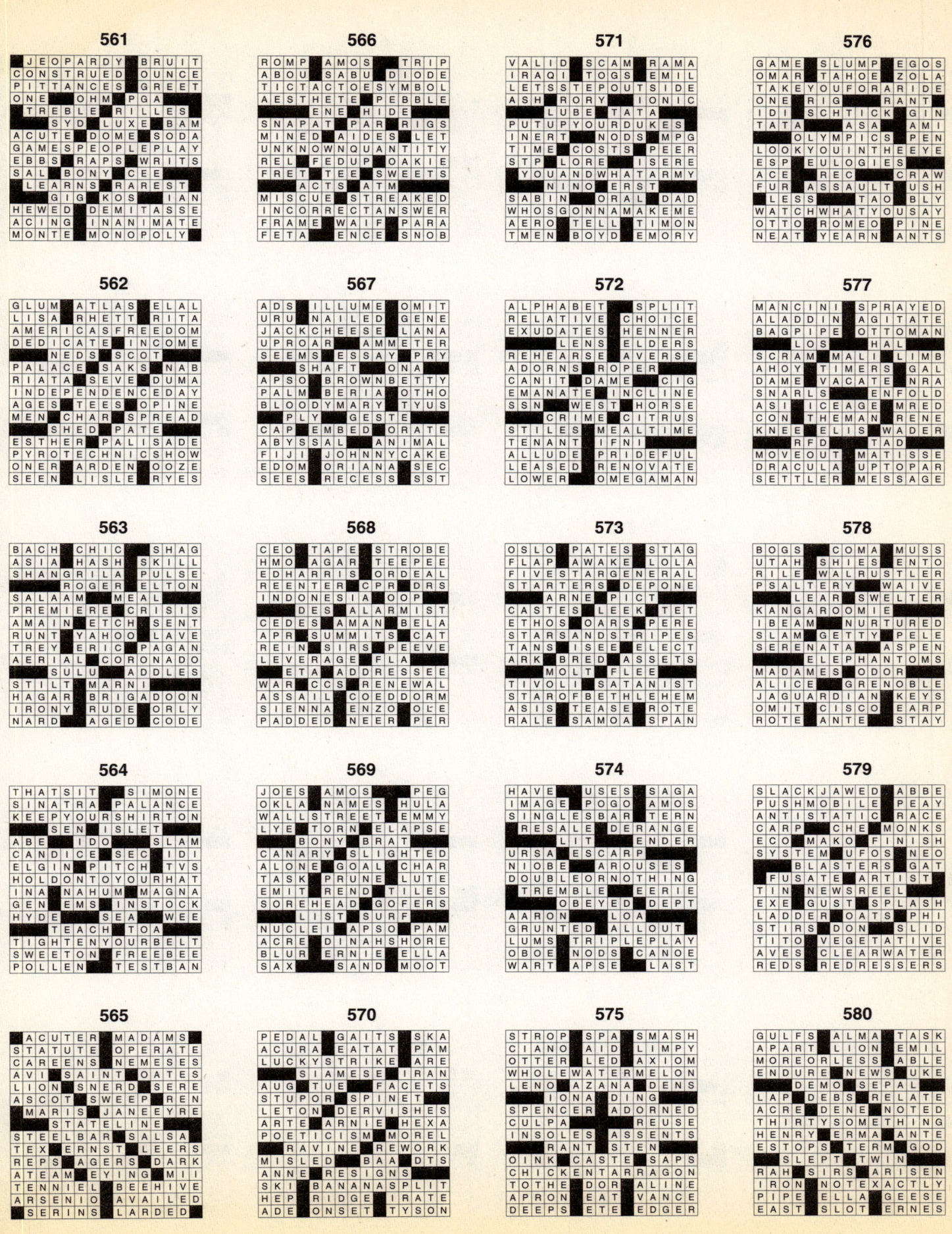

581
```
SPORT ITEM ATOM
OLDER FORE SAVE
NAOMI STANDSPAT
STRIVE ASTI ETE
  SINGLEHANDED
WASSAIL  ONA
EVA DOUBLEPARK
SERA ATL ABIE
TRIPLETAIL ELY
ION MODULES
HOMERSIMPSON
OFA AIDA ELMIRA
STRANGERS LATIN
TELL NAIL EDICT
SNAP SLAY DESKS
```

586
```
ASHES AURA ERMA
SPARE ERIC NOON
POINTOFNORETURN
STREAM OSAGES
  EARS SPIES
LAMB RECITAL
ASIA LENIN LIT
SAT ARETE INCA
TRIDENT BOHR
SLAVE DDAY
STALIN RIFLES
COMESTOTHEPOINT
ORAN ABIE ERATO
WEST LIEN STROP
```

591
```
SPEEDS SCALAWAG
PATTON HARAKIRI
ALCOVE ANIMATED
COE ELENAS HOG
EAT SLOG ENSILE
BLEB SHE AETAT
ATREUS ARETE
ROADTOSINGAPORE
LITHE GLIDER
SUMAC AXE NOTA
LLAMAS PLUS MIS
ITS MARSHA ENA
DISPROVE HOTTUB
EMIRATES UNREEL
SAFENESS HEARSE
```

596
```
SAMPLE  SONATA
ORALIST BYLINER
WINOVER IMAGINE
INE ILK HMOS
JACKRABBITSTART
IWO PEONIES
VITTLES ICEPACK
ESTEE DOGIE
SHINNED MAYTIDE
TANAGER TEN
MADASAMARCHHARE
OBIT ALL EAT
PERIWIG OBADIAH
ELEVATE TORONTO
RERENT  DANGME
```

582
```
LEAH DOLE DEREK
EASE EDEN ETUDE
OSSA FEETOFCLAY
NEEDLE SERA EMS
ALTOONA RICH
FIDEL GEEZER
AMASS SIMI AERO
DIRT ROMAN RAMS
AREA EPIC ATLAS
MOSTEL TEMPO
ENID SEIFERT
AHA DEEM LEGREE
LIPSOFWINE ONES
GREER ERIE LIST
ATSEA YENS DEES
```

587
```
ALUM PENS BAGEL
MENU OVAL IVORY
ANDS TATA LOLLS
DOESADOGSLIFE
    ATE LOD
PRESTO WHEW BAT
RENTA FOOD MULE
OFTENTIMESBEGIN
VERT IDES ALLEE
ORE UPON ABSENT
OSU UNE
WITHPUPPYLOVE
DANTE ROTO PELT
ALGER GOON ERMA
BEERS ERNE NOON
```

592
```
PLAIT CAPS FEED
AORTA ALIT ASKA
COMEUNDONE LAGS
EMERGE ETA LUSH
    HID AMAS
BEATLES STARTS
BENT SACS OPERA
AGATE LAT PANIC
MOCHA TRAP REEK
ATTEST FLIRTED
   STAG ENE
POKE NRA UMPIRE
AREA GOTOPIECES
PALM LAND SPECS
ALPS ENOS SETTO
```

597
```
SWASTIKAS DISCO
CONTINENT INLAW
INTHEGATE SHERE
SKEET TIPSHEETS
   LOGO SHORTS
MATE ANTOINE
EVENTS ANNE TEA
DINAH HMS SKIPS
ESS IHOP STEREO
GRENADE PEEP
TURTLE EAST
ERNIEPYLE EARLE
RIDGE DEPORTEES
STERN EVENTIDES
TERIS WINESTORE
```

583
```
DIRECT TOLD ABS
EDITOR AVID POP
ALLABOUTEVE PSI
FEE BYLINE SLUE
CLEM INTEND
BASHES ARTOIS
INNER ABOUTFACE
OKAY STAMP LULL
LAKESTATE NICOL
ENCODE RENEGE
TURNIP DAWG
OPIE PANICS OVA
REV MADAMIMADAM
INE ARID NAPOLI
CDR EDNA ENTREE
```

588
```
CAROL  MADAMS
ARENAS ADAGIOS
POETIC RUBELLA
STUKA HALLS LOI
HIS PRESET LAIN
UVEA ARTY WAIST
TERRAZZO GHOSTS
CLEO ZOOT
CALAIS PALAZZOS
AVANT ZONE EAST
DOTE DENIMS MMI
GIT SENSE TABOR
EDITING SIEVES
DECEASE TWEEZE
REAMER  ORRIS
```

593
```
FIRMS ASTO ALBS
URIAH VEIN BALI
JACKOFALLTRADES
ISEE LIFT ISLES
OBOLI SLEEPY
PREVUE MOPED
AIRES SPRAY CAB
STIR SARAN SOLO
TEE DAMON FELON
NEGEV SEATED
PAROLE ESTES
SPURT EMIL OPAL
ANDMASTEROFNONE
LEDA ANNE OASTS
MAYS PATS BLESS
```

598
```
JAPANS APOSTLES
ANIMUS ZUCCHINI
ZONATE RETAILER
ZIONS CAB GRIST
INCA SZELL DECI
ETH ZEALOUS SOS
SELTZER SMOG
TREATS BREEZE
SOFA BEGONIA
ARP PIZARRO GPS
MILA TALOS TACT
USERS LIZ SYDOW
SQUEEGEE DERIDE
EURASIAN ATONES
REASSESS HALEST
```

584
```
BRIAR TEMPT CDS
RINGO ANEAR AAH
OFFHANDEDLY TYE
AFLAME UPSTATE
CLU SWAPS TETON
HEXA BROAD BONY
SKOAL IPANA
HEARTLESSLY
POPIN ELCID
MATT STEAL ITOR
ORBIC ASLAP AME
PROCESS IRONED
PIX DISARMINGLY
EEE ADELE MELEE
TDS RELAX ODETS
```

589
```
SIPS MATCH APT
ARIA ENURE ARLO
GETTINGBIRDSEED
ASH STES AHEAD
PEAR UPHOLDS
DANIEL BRULE
ECOL MAGNI POE
WHOLESALEGAVEUS
YEN TERMS EARP
SHAKY CLASSY
SAVANTS GAEL
AMATI HATE BAA
MANYCHEEPTRILLS
BIER ARIEL MUSK
ADS TERSE PROS
```

594
```
WOK HALOES OMAN
IBO UGANDA NINE
SOBSTORIES VANS
HEEL VON LIMIT
OSMAN BODIES
ATHOME KALE
WEEPINGWILLOW
ELF LAYAWAY HID
THECRYINGGAME
ISEE CARMEN
BALLAD SIEGE
ADULT PEN EARP
SOIT TEARJERKER
ERGO ASTEAL IDO
SNIP WOODYS NOD
```

599
```
THAD BATS SOCKO
AARE OLIN ASHEN
ILKS RICO YEARS
LOSEONESWAY IRE
TEN GIE RST
INTOTO MORSEL
HORNE TAOS BIND
ADAIR OHS ASFOR
DEVO LURE BETTE
ENTICE SENSED
GAR OOH AWL
OPS UNDEVELOPED
TRIPP OBOE SPRY
TINGE WRIT SPEE
ALGAE NODS ASIS
```

585
```
MANOWAR SUPERB
ABILENE RIPENER
DOGDAYS ARTISTE
CLEEK TASSO TRA
AIR SAMS DEED
PSI VIRAL SWEAT
SHARESTHEWEALTH
AGA AGR
KEPTALOWPROFILE
EPEES WEANS MEX
YIPS LADS PAP
ECT BAIRD SNAKE
DEALERS LEADSIN
UNLATCH ENCASED
PEKOES STOKERS
```

590
```
DEISM STEAM UZI
ATSEA TONTO SEC
DOLLYPARDON SRO
ONEFOOT AARON
SURNAME
BILLYRAYVIRUS
ULNAE EPEE ATOM
NETMAN RETILE
CARE DINO ROLEX
TANYATUCKERED
TAKESTO
QUASH ALBANIA
URN WYNONNAFUDD
AGO EMOTE NAKED
YEN HARTS DRESS
```

595
```
THAW VISORS EST
AUDI ENTREE RKO
GEORGEBURNS NEO
EARED DARIEN
HOGTIED REMEET
ERRAND ORECK
SLOPS MEDES OBS
SOUS CIGAR EVAN
ENC CANON OVATE
HEARD APACHE
ROBROY FLENSER
CYMBAL ZAIRE
RDA FIDELCASTRO
AER ENISLE CUBA
MRX SANTAS EXIT
```

600
```
HARD PARC CLAM
OMOO ADIOS ALDA
WILT SEOULTRAIN
ALERT TREE NEE
MOOR STEAKOUT
IRONMAN PSI
MAD MESH ETHER
AGE TIEPINS ETE
MULTI RYNE ITA
ADS DECORUM
SALEBOAT DUMB
AGO INSO LEARS
VANITYFARE HULA
EVEN SODAS ASON
DERN RYES SHED
```

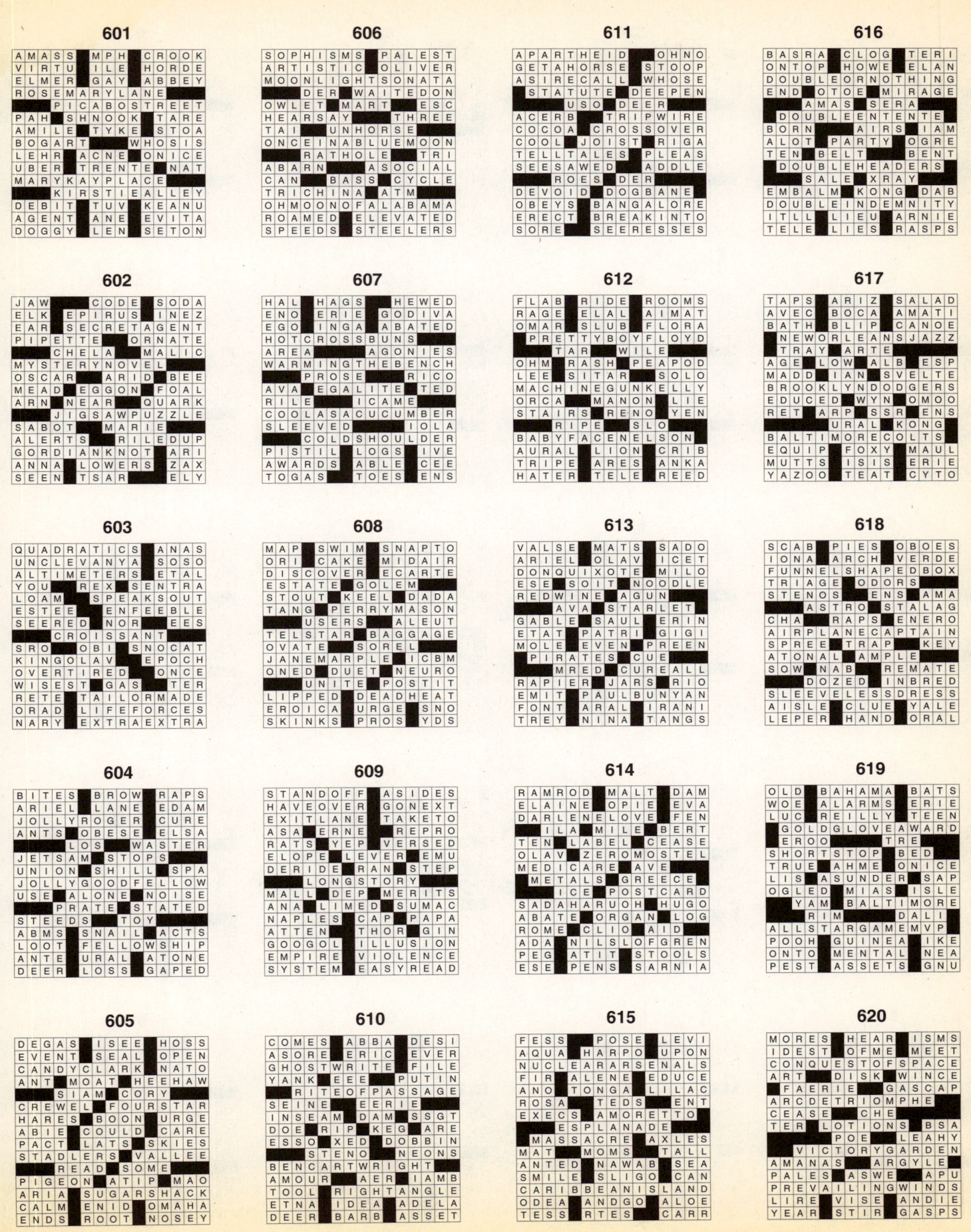

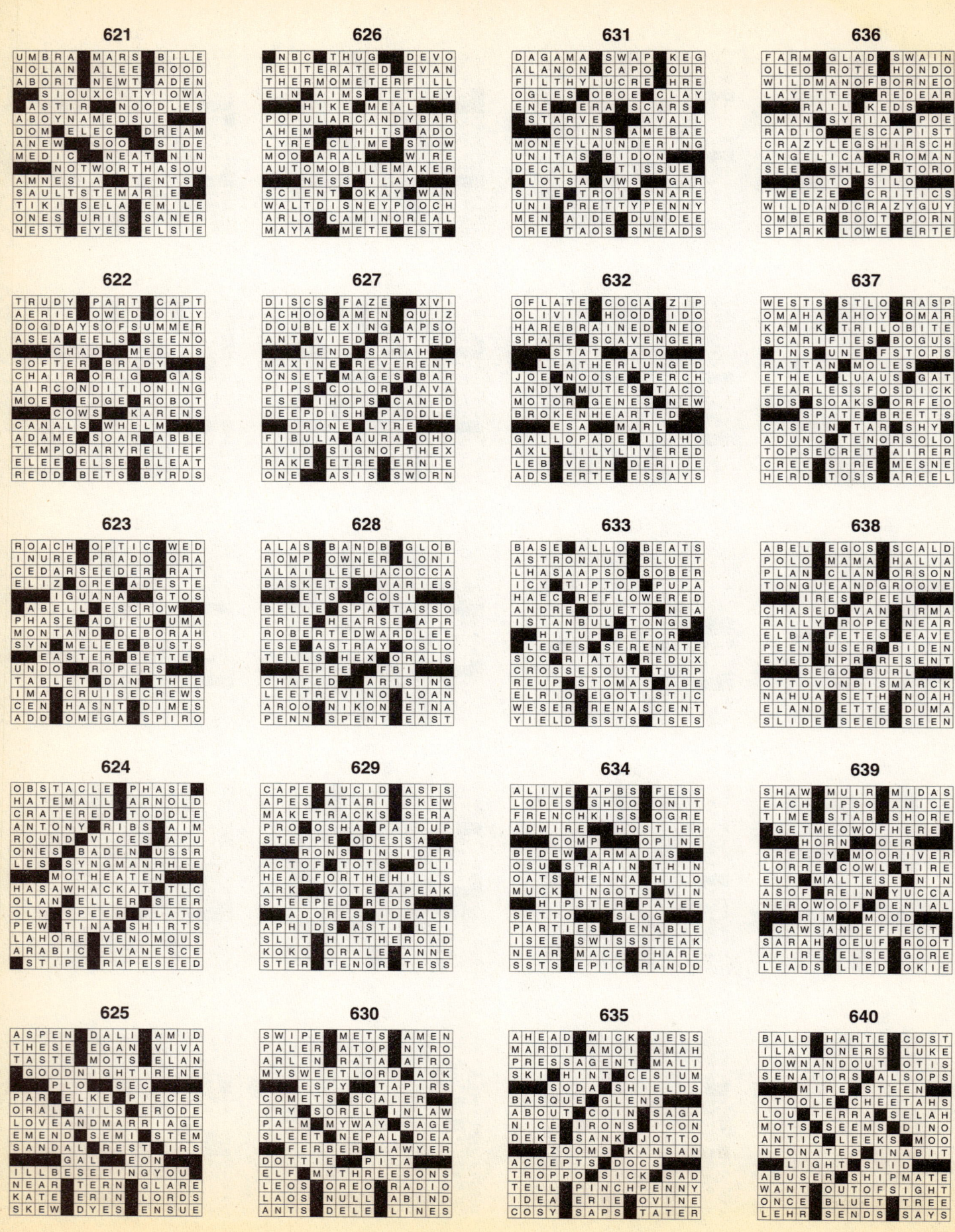

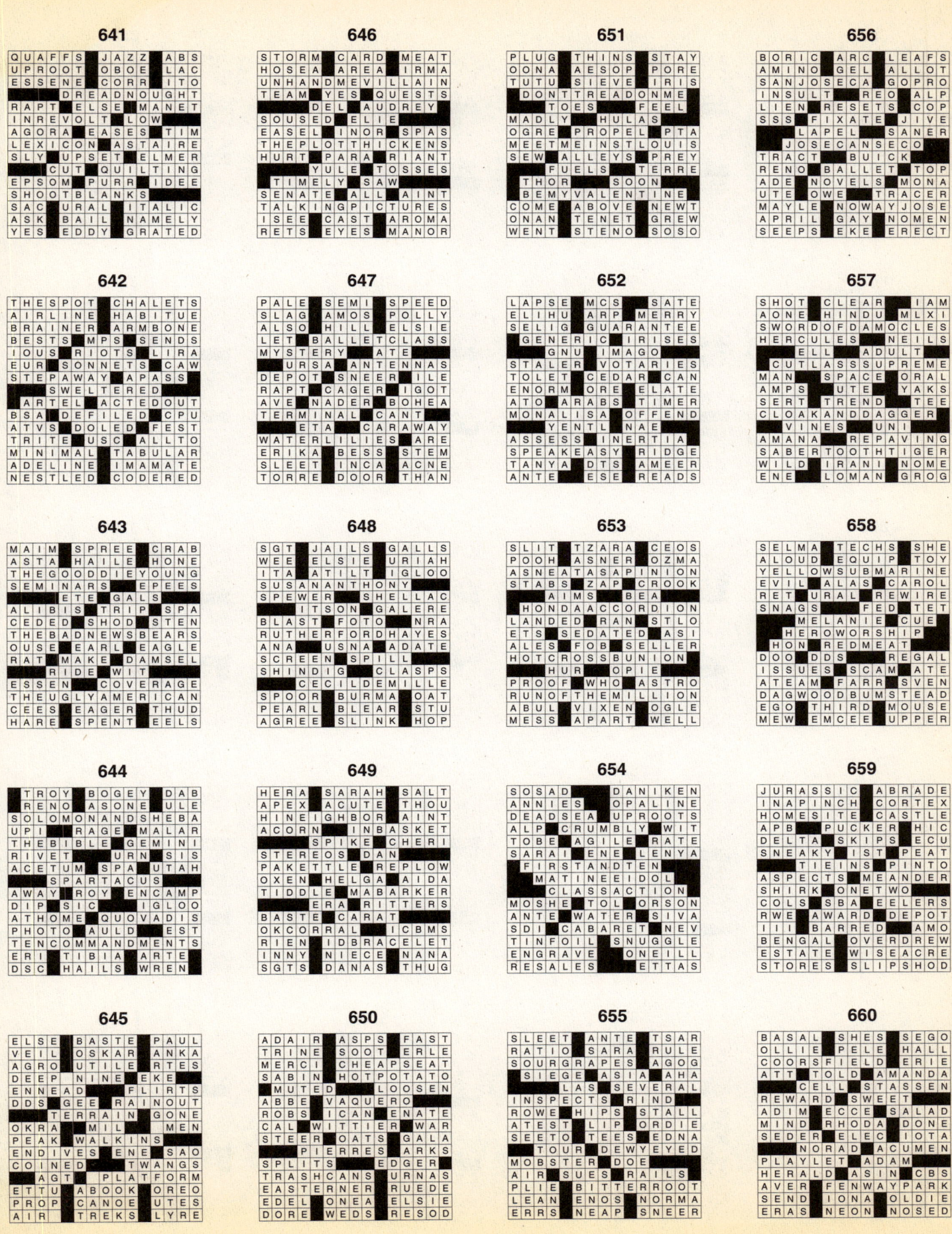

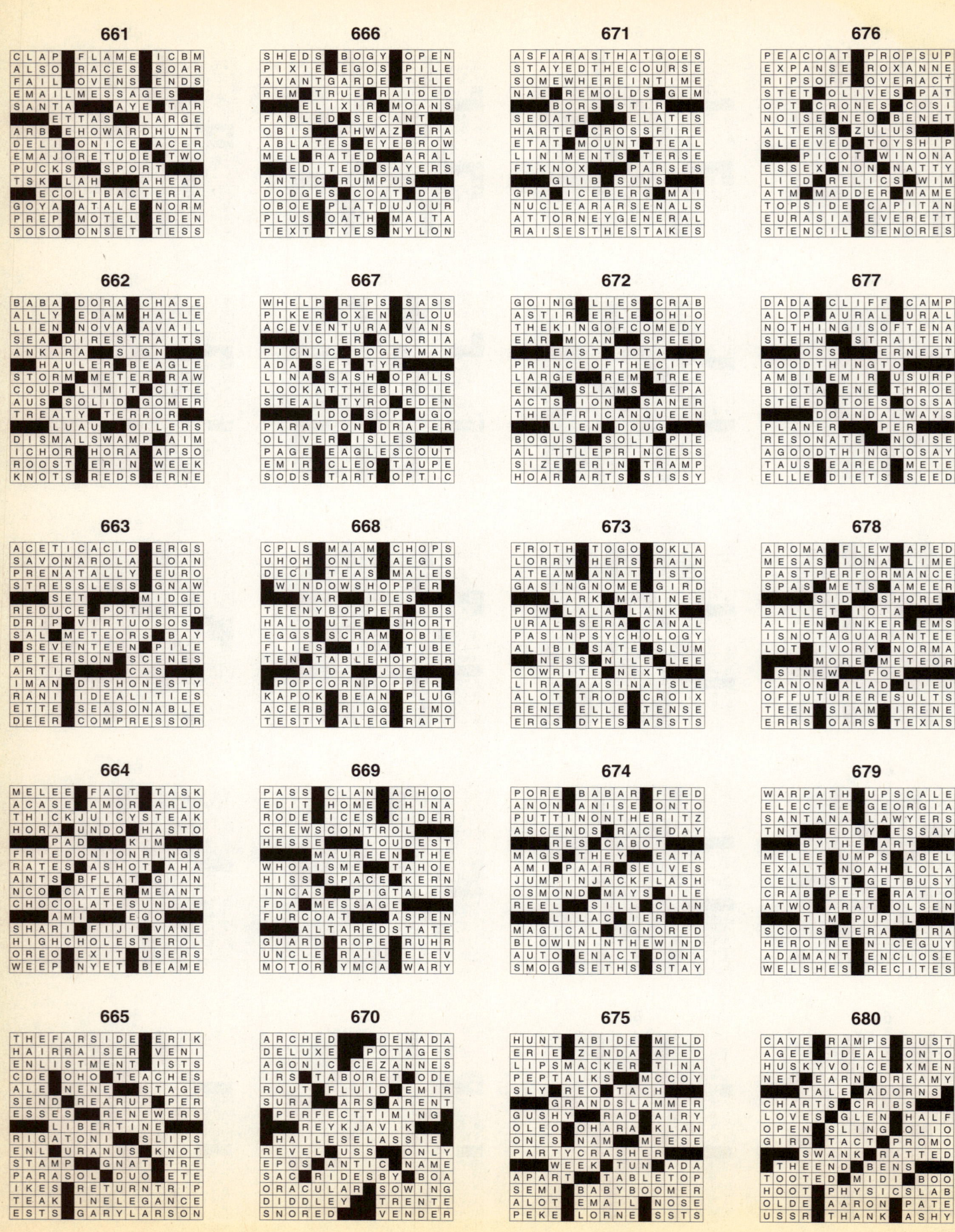

661

CLAP FLAME ICBM
ALSO RACES SOAR
FAIL OVENS ENDS
EMAILMESSAGES
SANTA AYE TAR
ETTAS LARGE
ARB EHOWARDHUNT
DELI ONICE ACER
EMAJORETUDE TWO
PUCKS SPORT
TSK LAH AHEAD
ECOLIBACTERIA
GOYA ATALE NORM
PREP MOTEL EDEN
SOSO ONSET TESS

666

SHEDS BOGY OPEN
PIXIE EGOS PILE
AVANTGARDE TELE
REM TRUE RAIDED
ELIXIR MOANS
FABLED SECANT
OBIS AHWAZ ERA
ABLATES EYEBROW
MEL RATED ARAL
EDITED SAYERS
ANTIC RUMPUS
DODGES COAT DAB
OBOE PLATDUJOUR
PLUS OATH MALTA
TEXT TYES NYLON

671

ASFARASTHATGOES
STAYEDTHECOURSE
SOMEWHEREINTIME
NAE REMOLDS GEM
BORS STIR
SEDATE ELATES
HARTE CROSSFIRE
ETAT MOUNT TEAL
LINIMENTS TERSE
FTKNOX PARSES
GLIB SUNS
GPA ICEBERG MAI
NUCLEARARSENALS
ATTORNEYGENERAL
RAISESTHESTAKES

676

PEACOAT PROPSUP
EXPANSE ROXANNE
RIPOFF OVERACT
STET OLIVES PAT
OPT CRONES COSI
NOISE NEO BENET
ALTERS ZULUS
SLEEVED TOYSHIP
PICOT WINONA
ESSEX NON NATTY
LIED RELICS WIM
ATM MADDER MAME
TOPSIDE CAPITAN
EURASIA EVERETT
STENCIL SENORES

662

BABA DORA CHASE
ALLY EDAM HALLE
LIEN NOVA AVAIL
SEA DIRESTRAITS
ANKARA SIGN
HAULER BEAGLE
STORM METER RAW
COUP LIMIT CITE
AUS SOLID GOMER
TREATY TERROR
LUAU OILERS AIM
DISMALSWAMP AIM
ICHOR HORA APSO
ROOST ERIN WEEK
KNOTS REDS ERNE

667

WHELP REPS SASS
PIKER OXEN ALOU
ACEVENTURA VANS
ICIER GLORIA
PICNIC BOGEYMAN
ADA SET TYR
LINA SASH OPALS
LOOKATTHEBIRDIE
STEAL TYRO EDEN
IDO SOP UGO
PARAVION DRAPER
OLIVER ISLES
PAGE EAGLESCOUT
EMIR CLEO TAUPE
SODS TART OPTIC

672

GOING LIES CRAB
ASTIR ERLE OHIO
THEKINGOFCOMEDY
EAR MOAN SPEED
EAST IOTA
PRINCEOFTHECITY
LARGE REM TREE
ENA SLAMS EPA
ACTS ION SANER
THEAFRICANQUEEN
LIEN DOUG
BOGUS SOLI PIE
ALITTLEPRINCESS
SIZE ERIN TRAMP
HOAR ARTS SISSY

677

DADA CLIFF CAMP
ALOP AURAL URAL
NOTHINGISOFTENA
STERN STRAITEN
OSS ERNEST
GOODTHINGTO
AMBI EMIR USURP
BIOTA ENE THROE
STEED TOES OSSA
DOANDALWAYS
PLANER PER
RESONATE NOISE
AGOODTHINGTOSAY
TAUS EARED METE
ELLE DIETS SEED

663

ACETICACID ERGS
SAVONAROLA LOAN
PRENATALLY EURO
STRESSLESS GNAW
SET MIDGE
REDUCE POTHERED
DRIP VIRTUOSOS
SAL METEORS BAY
SEVENTEEN PILE
PETERSON SCENES
ARTIE CAS
IMAN DISHONESTY
RANI IDEALITIES
ETTE SEASONABLE
DEER COMPRESSOR

668

CPLS MAAM CHOPS
UHOH ONLY AEGIS
DECI TEAS MALES
WINDOWSHOPPER
YAR IDES
TEENYBOPPER BBS
HALO UTE SHORT
EGGS SCRAM OBIE
FLIES IDA TUBE
TEN TABLEHOPPER
AIDA JOE
POPCORNPOPPER
KAPOK BEAN PLUG
ACERB RIGG ELMO
TESTY ALEG RAPT

673

FROTH TOGO OKLA
LORRY HERS RAIN
ATEAM ANAT ISTO
GASINGNOME GIRD
LARK MATINEE
POW LALA LANK
URAL SERA CANAL
PASINPSYCHOLOGY
ALIBI SATE SLUM
NESS NILE LEE
COWRITE NEXT
LIRA AASINAISLE
ALOT TROD CROIX
RENE ELLE TENSE
ERGS DYES ASSTS

678

AROMA FLEW APED
MESAS IONA LIME
PASTPERFORMANCE
SPAS METS AMEER
SID SHORE
BALLET IOTA
ALIEN INKER EMS
ISNOTAGUARANTEE
LOT IVORY NORMA
MORE METEOR
SINEW FOE
CANON ALAD LIEU
OFFUTURERESULTS
TEEN SIAM IRENE
ERRS OARS TEXAS

664

MELEE FACT TASK
ACASE AMOR ARLO
THICKJUICYSTEAK
HORA UNDO HASTO
PAD KIM
FRIEDONIONRINGS
RATES ASHOT AHA
ANTS BFLAT GIAN
NCO CATER MEANT
CHOCOLATESUNDAE
AMI EGO
SHARI FIJI VANE
HIGHCHOLESTEROL
OREO EXIT USERS
WEEP NYET BEAME

669

PASS CLAN ACHOO
EDIT HOME CHINA
RODE ICES CIDER
CREWSCONTROL
HESSE LOUDEST
MAUREEN THE
WHOAISME TAHOE
HISS SPACE KERN
INCAS PIGTALES
FDA MESSAGE
FURCOAT ASPEN
ALTAREDSTATE
GUARD ROPE RUHR
UNCLE RAIL ELEV
MOTOR YMCA WARY

674

PORE BABAR FEED
ANON ANISE ONTO
PUTTINONTHERITZ
ASCENDS RACEDAY
RES CABOT
MAGS THEY EATA
AMI PAAR SELVES
JUMPINJACKFLASH
OSMOND MAYS ILE
REEL SILL CLAN
LILAC IER
MAGICAL IGNORED
BLOWININTHEWIND
AUTO ENACT DONA
SMOG SETHS STAY

679

WARPATH UPSCALE
ELECTEE GEORGIA
SANTANA LAWYERS
TNT EDDY ESSAY
BYTHE ART
MELEE UMPS ABEL
EXALT NOAH LOLA
CELLIST GETBUSY
CRAB PETE RATIO
ATWO ARAT OLSEN
TIM PUPIL
SCOTS VERA IRA
HEROINE NICEGUY
ADAMANT ENCLOSE
WELSHES RECITES

665

THEFARSIDE ERIK
HAIRRAISER VENI
ENLISTMENT ISTS
CDE OHO TEACHES
ALE NENE STAGE
SEND REARUP PER
ESSES RENEWERS
LIBERTINE
RIGATONI SLIPS
ENL URANUS KNOT
STAMP GNAT TRE
PARASOL DUO ETE
IKES RETURNTRIP
TEAK INELEGANCE
ESTS GARYLARSON

670

ARCHED DENADA
DELUXE POTAGES
AGONIC CEZANNES
IRS TABORET ODE
ROUT FLUID EMIR
SURA ARS ARENT
PERFECTTIMING
REYKJAVIK
HAILESELASSIE
REVEL USS ONLY
EPOS ANTIC NAME
SAC RIDESBY BOA
ORACULAR SOWING
DIDDLEY TRENTE
SNORED VENDER

675

HUNT ABIDE MELD
ERIE ZENDA APED
LIPSMACKER TINA
PEPTALKS MCCOY
SLY REO TACH
GRANDSLAMMER
GUSHY RAD AIRY
OLEO OHARA KLAN
ONES NAM MEESE
PARTYCRASHER
WEEK TUN ADA
APART TABLETOP
SEMI BABYBOOMER
ALOT EMAIL NOSE
PEKE LORNE SSTS

680

CAVE RAMPS BUST
AGEE IDEAL ONTO
HUSKYVOICE XMEN
NET EARN DREAMY
TALE ADORNS
CHARTS CRIBS
LOVES GLEN HALF
OPEN SLING OLIO
GIRD TACT PROMO
SWANK RATTED
THEEND BENS
TOOTED MIDI BOO
HOOT PHYSICSLAB
OLDE AARON PATE
USSR THANK ASHY

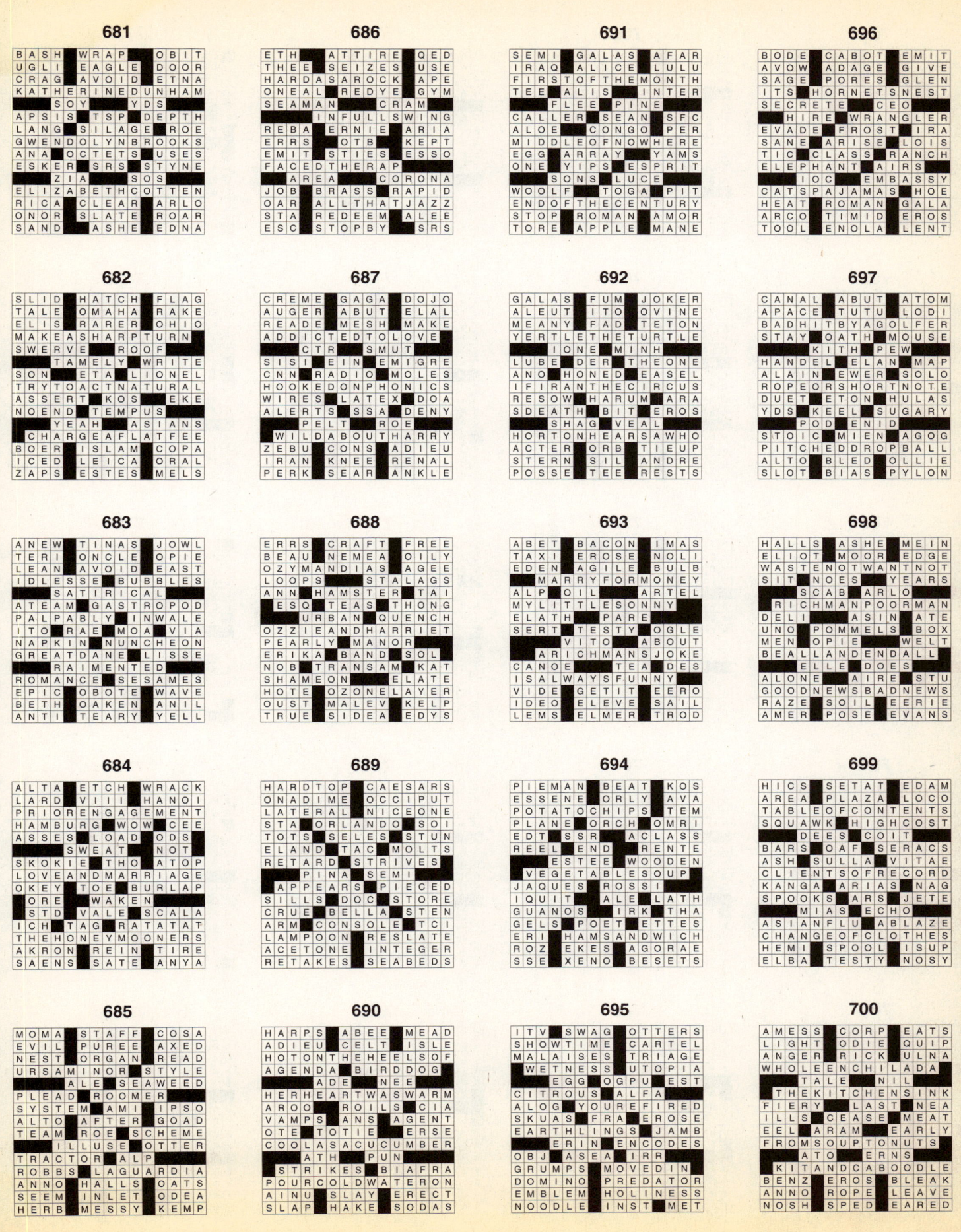

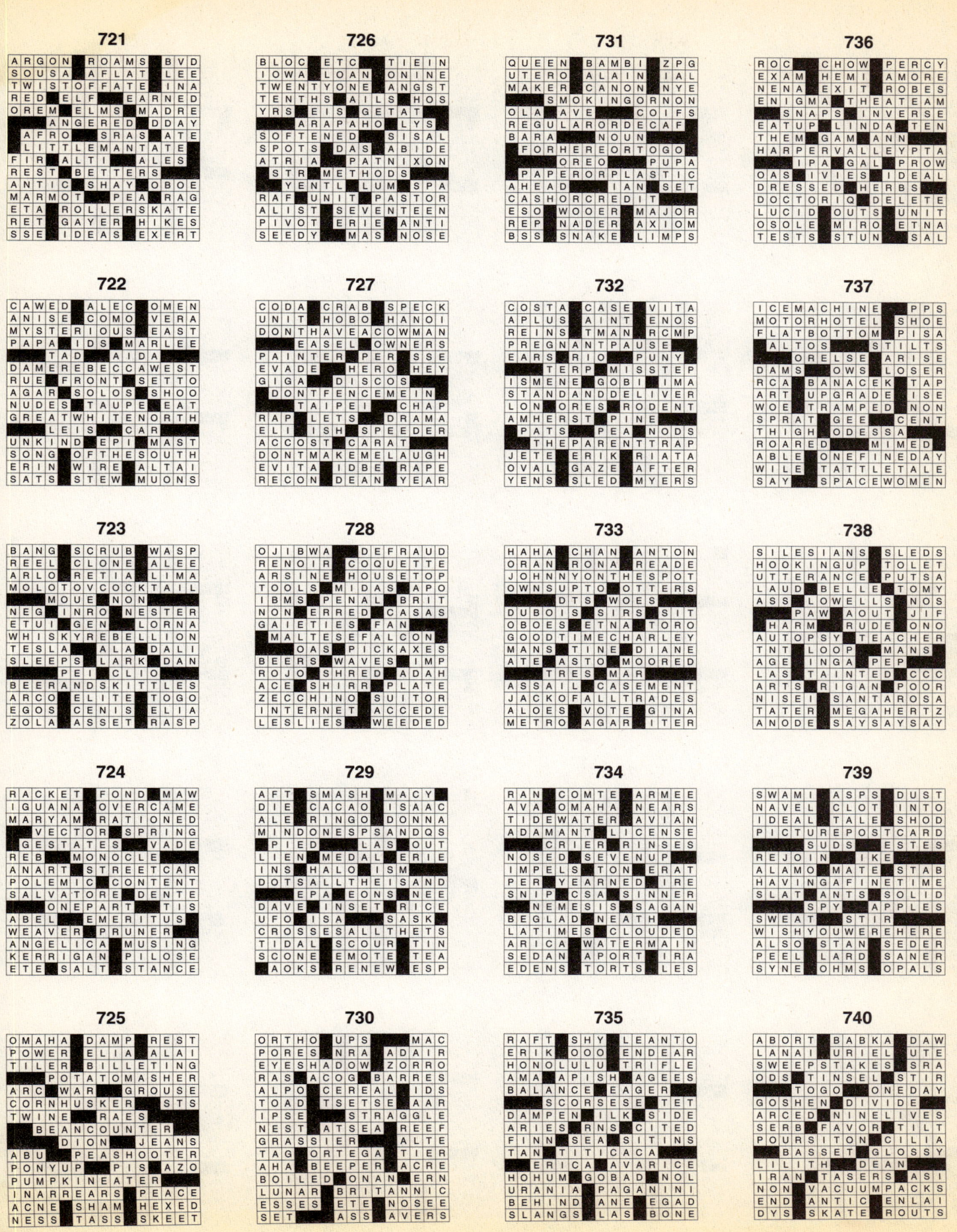

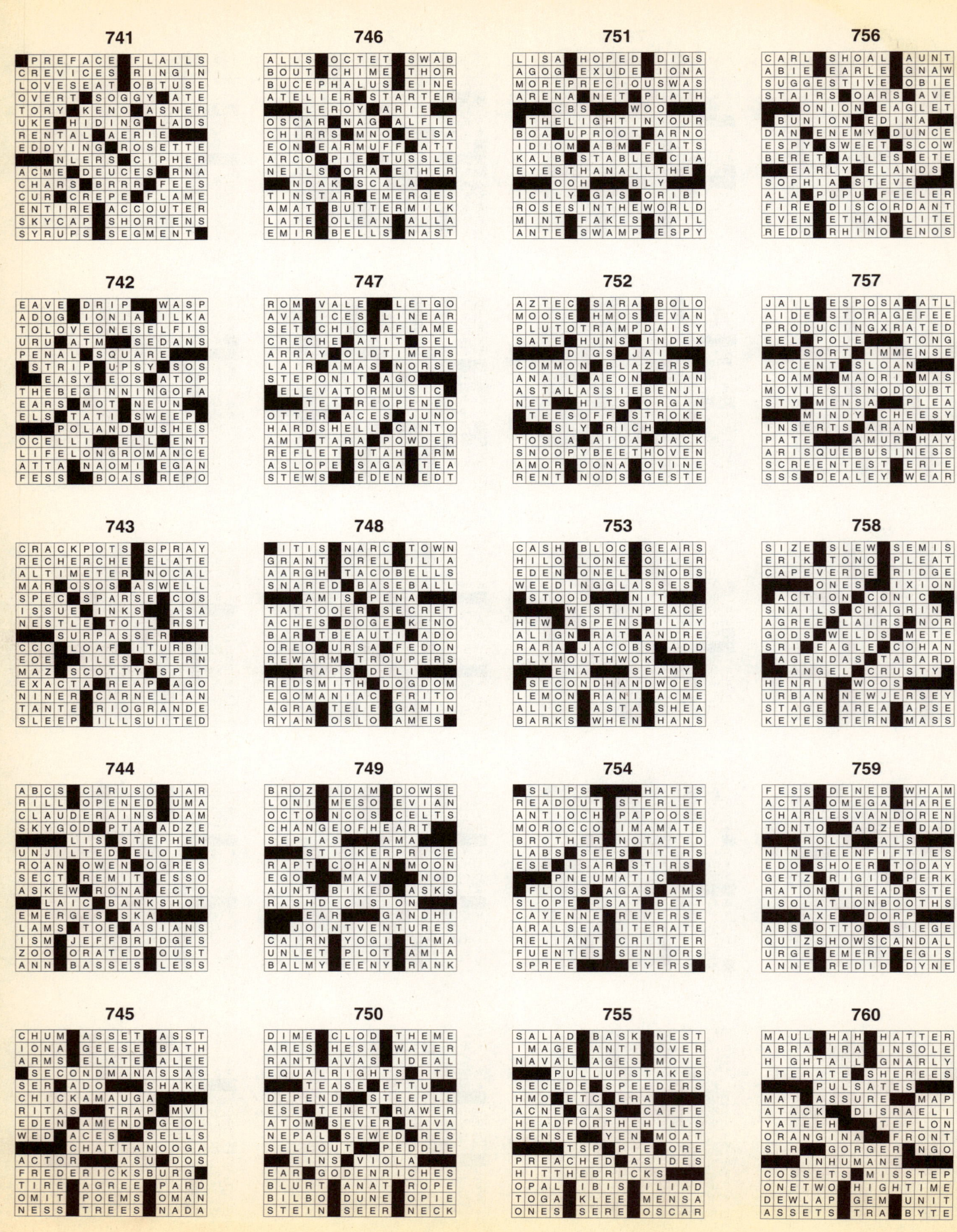

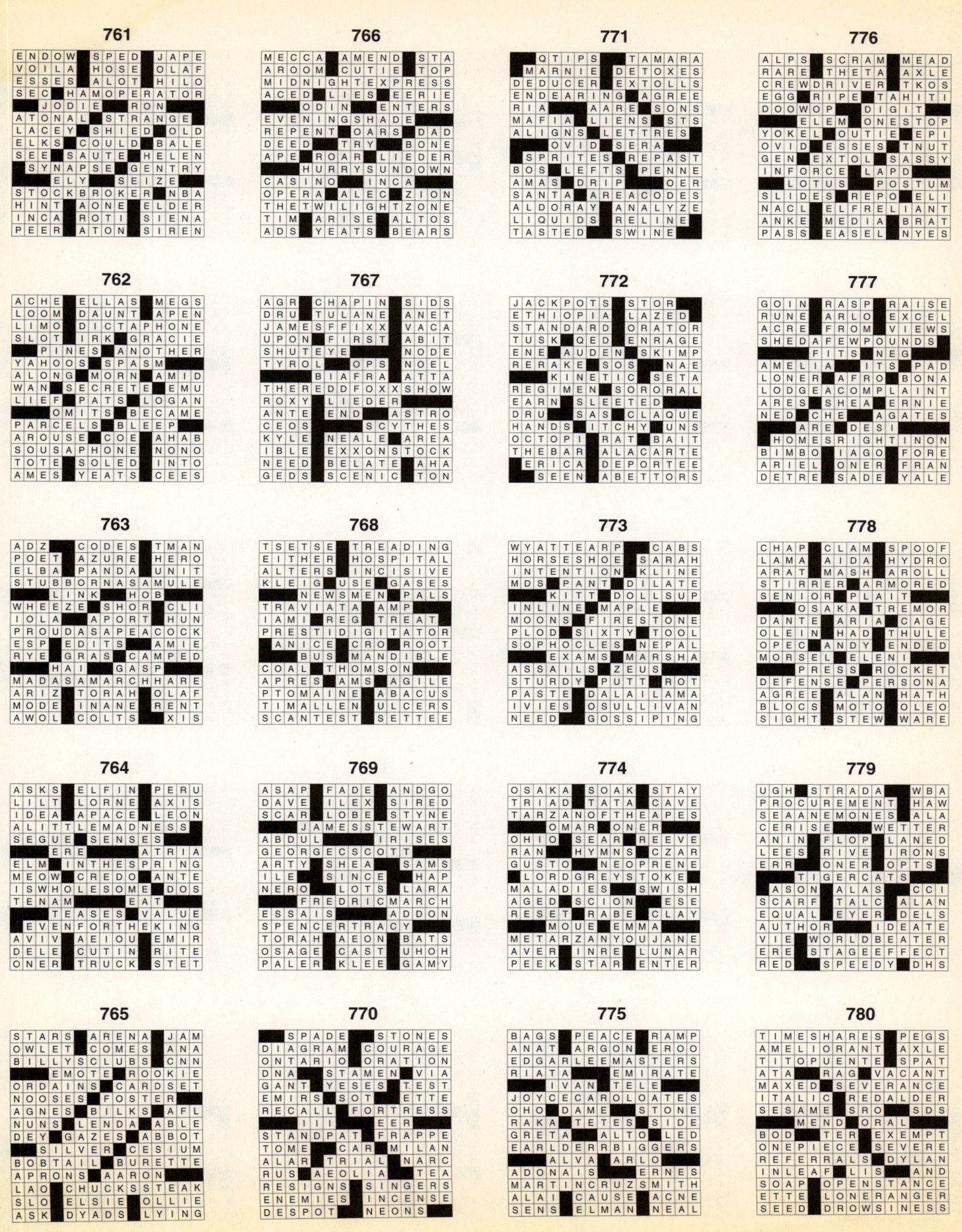

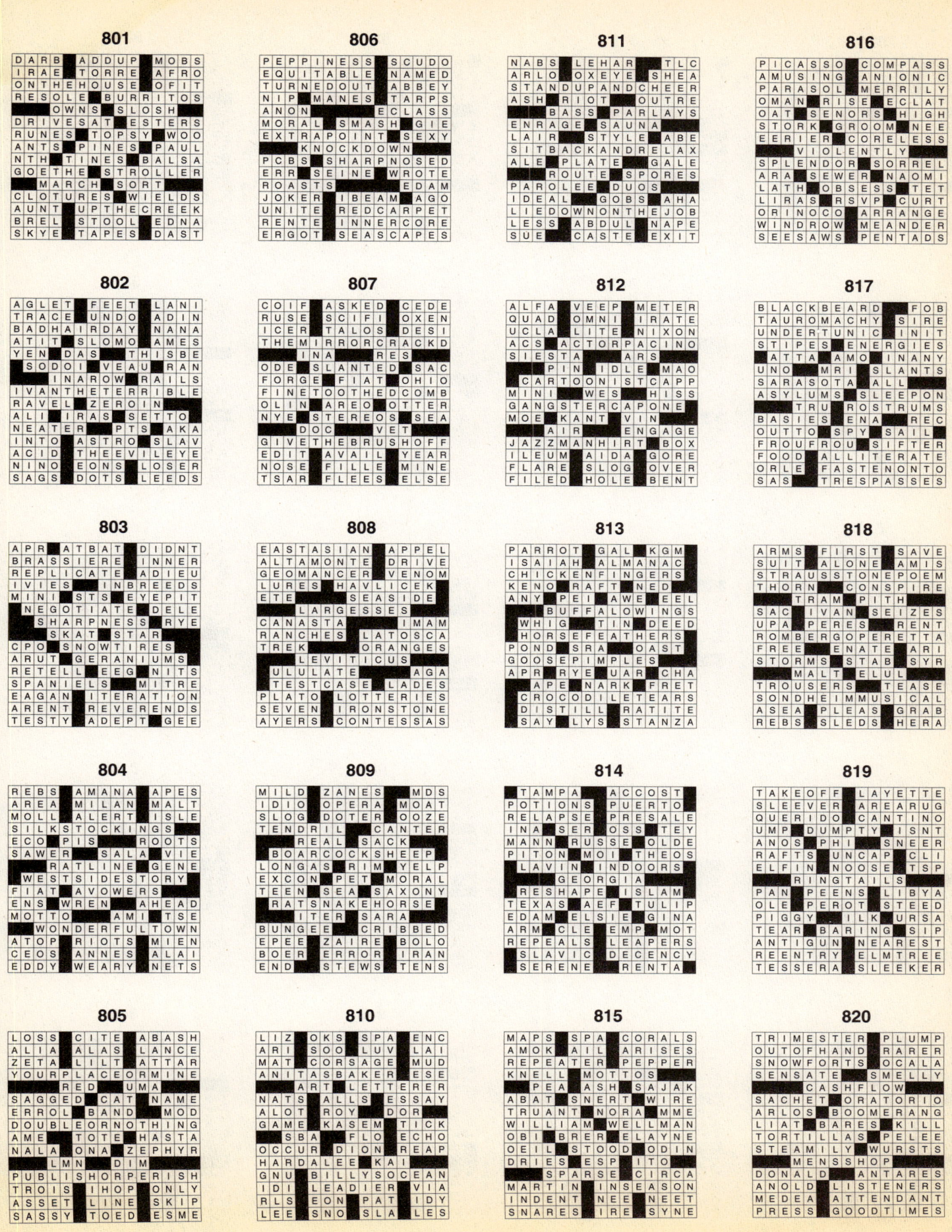

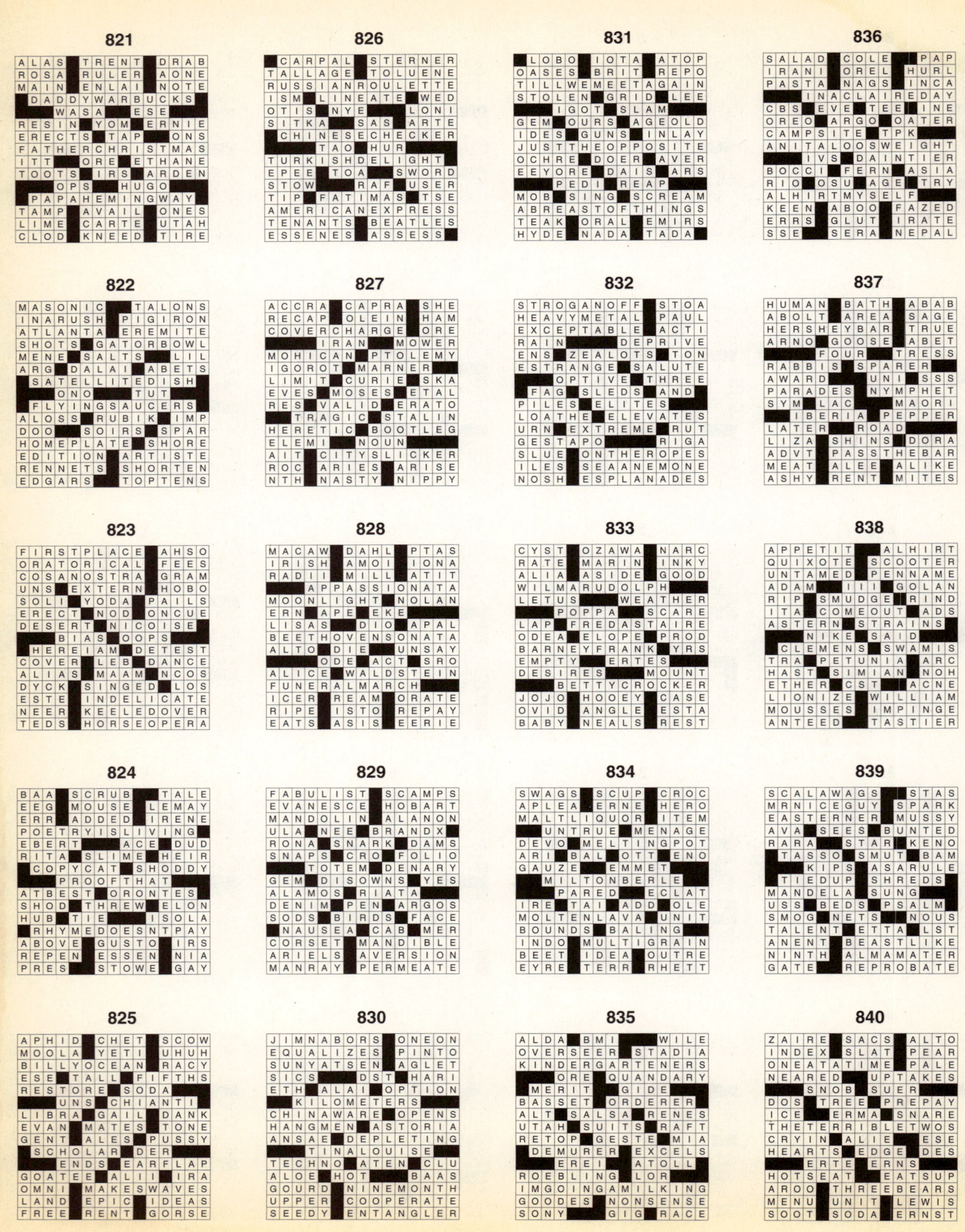

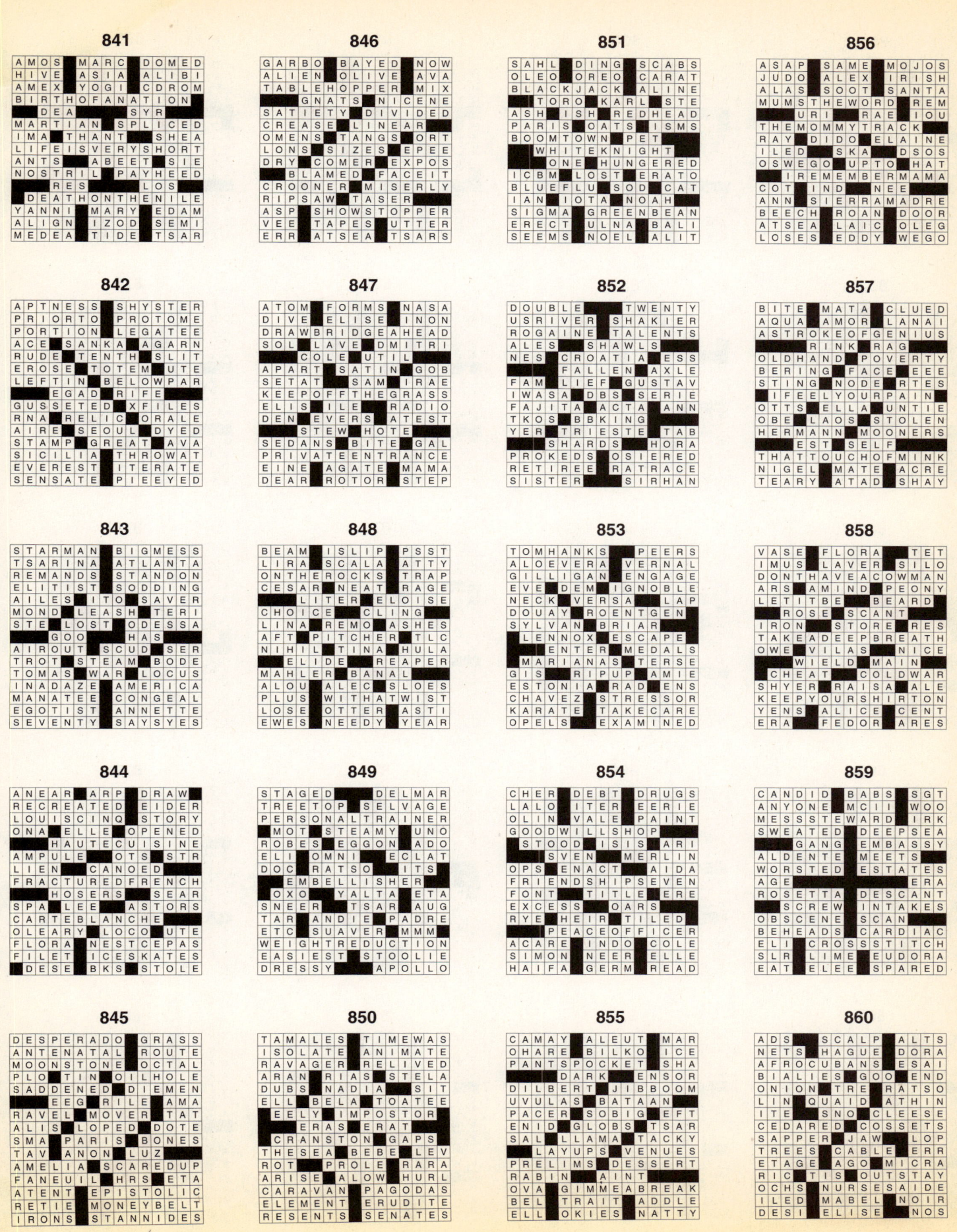

861

```
BRACE ISIS SCAM
AEROS NOTE HALE
ONTOPOFTHEWORLD
BAIL PATE ARIA
ATE ATNO EVELYN
BASEHIT ICY LIU
LEM ARC WONT
SUMMITMEETING
OHNO SIT NIL
POD CTS STREAMS
SWELLS GORE MAT
TREE TAVI UPTO
TIPOFTHEICEBERG
IMIN HOLE LEROI
NENE OUST IRENE
```

866

```
ONCE MAINE BESS
LEAR ELBOW ALLA
GARDENPERENNIAL
APPENDIX AGATE
DEN HAM
COLOREDEYEPART
TAKER OLE AMAH
SLAM CHIPS SITU
ALPO RON ASSES
RAINBOWGODDESS
AWE NED
STALL SEMESTER
NOVELISTMURDOCH
ANON SOLAR ABOY
GENT TBONE KENS
```

871

```
OFFER HOPI DOZE
CRETE AVON EMIL
HERES GENT VANS
ODD TOURDEFORCE
ECOLE RUT
MILORD GINSENG
IRATE WALES OAS
DONE CASED OMIT
INC GRASS PADUA
SECRECY ARREST
AID CRISP
COUPDEGRACE LOT
ANNO NOIR SAUTE
REIN ZEST TIMON
ARTS ASEA SLEET
```

876

```
AHEM SWORD GENA
NOVA PATTI UPON
TWINCITIES NEED
ELLIOTTS SAGELY
FEE GOSH
HOOD FULLHOUSE
SAULS OLIVE NAG
HIND DONNE DIVA
AKC GETAT METED
QUEENBEES ICED
LAUD ANA
DISOWN SORENESS
ASAP KINGCOTTON
ZANE EMILE ERMA
EYED DATED DEEP
```

862

```
BBC CHIA BELLI
ORE HOOF DEVOID
RUSSIANROULETTE
INTEND IBEG SEA
STARE ACETIC
ASAN ARMEY
ERS ELIA SNEERS
DUTCHELMDISEASE
ITALIC PATH DER
THROB ZEES
TIBIAE EATME
ATL SAND SPREAD
FRENCHCANADIANS
RADIUS MOTO LIE
OPALS SMOG SAL
```

867

```
BLEAR BOOR CHI
BELIE METOO HEN
COLLEGESCHOLARS
NASCENT AIDE
HALO BASSET
DOCTOROFLETTERS
ESAU LILI
CONGRATULATIONS
ERIC RANK
PHIBETAKAPPAKEY
AERIFY TRIO
TROT OILPALM
HONORARYDEGREES
ONE ASHOE ULTRA
SSR THOU NOSED
```

872

```
POOR STOP SISAL
ALMA OHTO ULTRA
LEAP BUTT BLOND
MANIA MERIT ROD
ANIDLEPROMISE
SIB APTERAL
ESP OBIS LEONE
THEMANINTHEMOON
TURIN LASE MNO
ETERNAL ICE
GOODYEARBLIMP
PAR TOGAS SAVER
ELIZA ORCA TORI
NONET ALAW ERLE
SUEDE TYPE DYED
```

877

```
CLAN HADJ SLAKE
OUSE ARIA HITIT
CASHMERESWEATER
OUTRE SPHERULE
ASSURES EON
SUPRA TMAN
EMBATTLE QUITE
CHECKOUTCOUNTER
RODEO REPEATED
USED CHIDE
WOO ENIGMAS
APPOINTS DRAMA
CHARGEDAFFAIRES
DITCH OAHU DABS
CLEAT GRAM STAY
```

863

```
BOOM ARIL SHAME
UNDO DANE TOWEL
YSER ANNASEWELL
SITTINGSHIVA
ATTABOY MIRAGE
TEALS FLOE VOX
SEALION NEAT
SINGERPETER
ZAHN EASESUP
ISO SIFT NOFOR
GHOSTS ACETATE
TITLEDBRITON
COMICSTYLE SCOT
AWINK DEER TALE
PERKY SSRS STER
```

868

```
BOTTOMSUP CIGAR
OVERCOATS ENERO
BARITONES LSATS
LIGANDS GLARES
VEE FRAN
CAKED STARDATE
BARES COLDSORES
EDGE DYNES URNS
DROPFORGE STATE
SENSUOUS BASSO
SENS DIM
MUSCLE TRALALA
ENROL LOOSELIPS
ADORE APPETITES
NOSED ROADSTERS
```

873

```
SCRAP OCHS CROW
SHARI POET HALE
TATAR EZRA AIDA
FANCYDRESSER
SHANE EATERY
CLOTHESHORSE
RIP ADMAN ENJOY
AGED SINES SARA
MODEL TOTES PAL
FASHIONPLATE
ENCAMP SEINE
BEAUBRUMMELL
EVIL OLEO ULTRA
RENT UNIT NIKES
TRES TART KEOGH
```

878

```
ALI CLIFF TATE
LENO HANOI AMOR
LATE INALL POLA
EVERYMANDESIRES
GEN OPIE TRADE
RODIN LVI LOS
OUTS APPOINT
TOLIVELONGBUT
ABALONE ANON
PAT SST TRITE
EPODE ASIA CAW
NOMANWOULDBEOLD
PLAT ORDIE PRIE
ALTE REEDS ANTA
LOOS MONET SYL
```

864

```
RIOT SMOG CAFES
OSHA PIMA ADORE
SNIT ARNO MARNE
HOOTERVILLE TIM
OAT SCRIBES
DECORATE DADA
APO SNELL SAXON
MICH SAGAS STLO
SCOOP LAMPS EDS
ALES REHEARSE
ALBERTA ALL
DIE SPRINGFIELD
ALAMO ITON ETUI
MACON ECRU NCAA
SCHWA SHAM SHUN
```

869

```
SPCA HELI ASSET
KAHN OXEN NEATO
EGAD RITA DELTA
TONYORLANDO BAD
CDE DIET IRMA
HALFOF STRANGE
ARISTA ARDEN
PACT CANDO GOOD
STOIC STABLE
COMMUTE DESPOT
MARE AGUA ELO
DNA SANFERNANDO
RONDO OONA SCAT
ANDOR SUIT TIGE
BOOTY ELIE ILED
```

874

```
GSHARP ORACLE
ICEFALL THROES
BALLPEEN HEPCAT
IRE SAGETEA ACE
NENE SAVOR ACHE
GRASP LEO PROEM
PAPERTRAILS
SARGASSOSEA
RUNSAGAINST
CANOE LYE ETUDE
HILL PEDRO APIA
UNO VISIONS WAS
MOVEON ELEPHANT
PUERTO LUCERNE
STREET PANDER
```

879

```
AFT GSA HEF HAD
CAHOOTS ONADARE
ACERBIC GENERIC
DE D LOWS ZELDA
WANTTO TIME
SAHIBS LRON QED
LEONA AFORE URI
URNS JU JI PINK
NIE BANJO ARNIE
KEV RITA STERES
EVEL CHEAPO
ARROW AKIN A DA
LAWLESS LOGICAL
UPATREE TRIDENT
MTS YEA SAG SKA
```

865

```
BACK BABU TIMOR
ALEE IRIS IMAGE
HOLYROMANEMPIRE
NET OLES DOOMED
BUOY BITS
DOING BACHELOR
MINGDYNASTY UTA
OPED ONS ACTI
OST OLDDOMINION
GOODBYES ANTES
AVIS ARCS
SINGIN ASTA ERA
THEMAGICKINGDOM
AIMAT THEN BILE
STORE SEWS STYX
```

870

```
ASCAP MIDAS FTC
ROONE ADOLL ORO
CHATTANOOGA RIB
HOTORCOLD METER
NEER ODESSA
VIGILS SUNUNU
AREA MORON MSG
LIT ASALARK TOE
EST LOCAL SEAM
YELLER SCARPS
PASTED PERM
AMBOY EMOTIONAL
LOU CHICKAMAUGA
EUR AERIE ENNUI
ORG THEIR ASSAD
```

875

```
COMAS AKA ATTAR
AVANT ROB SHOVE
TEDDY CROSSEYED
SNARL HEALTH
BEE WARY AJAR
SCOW LAND GORE
TAU JAYS ADULTS
ENTRAPS STEELIE
PAYERS ZINC YET
IDOS LEGO ERRS
NAUT SOPH PRO
ALIGHT ROGET
HAPPYDAYS ADELE
EXILE NRA TERSE
PETES SSW ESSEN
```

880

```
ALAS CABINFEVER
RENT EVANGELINE
CANA BARBAROSSA
APERCU BAIN TUG
DITCH DECO CURE
INTHEDARK GALEN
AGE CARO REPAST
SKINFLINT
HAOLES SAFE RTE
ARBOR METERMAID
BASE RAVE AORTA
ICC RENI PLIERS
THEHUSTLER EGAN
ANNABELLEE TATE
TEENYWEENY YSER
```

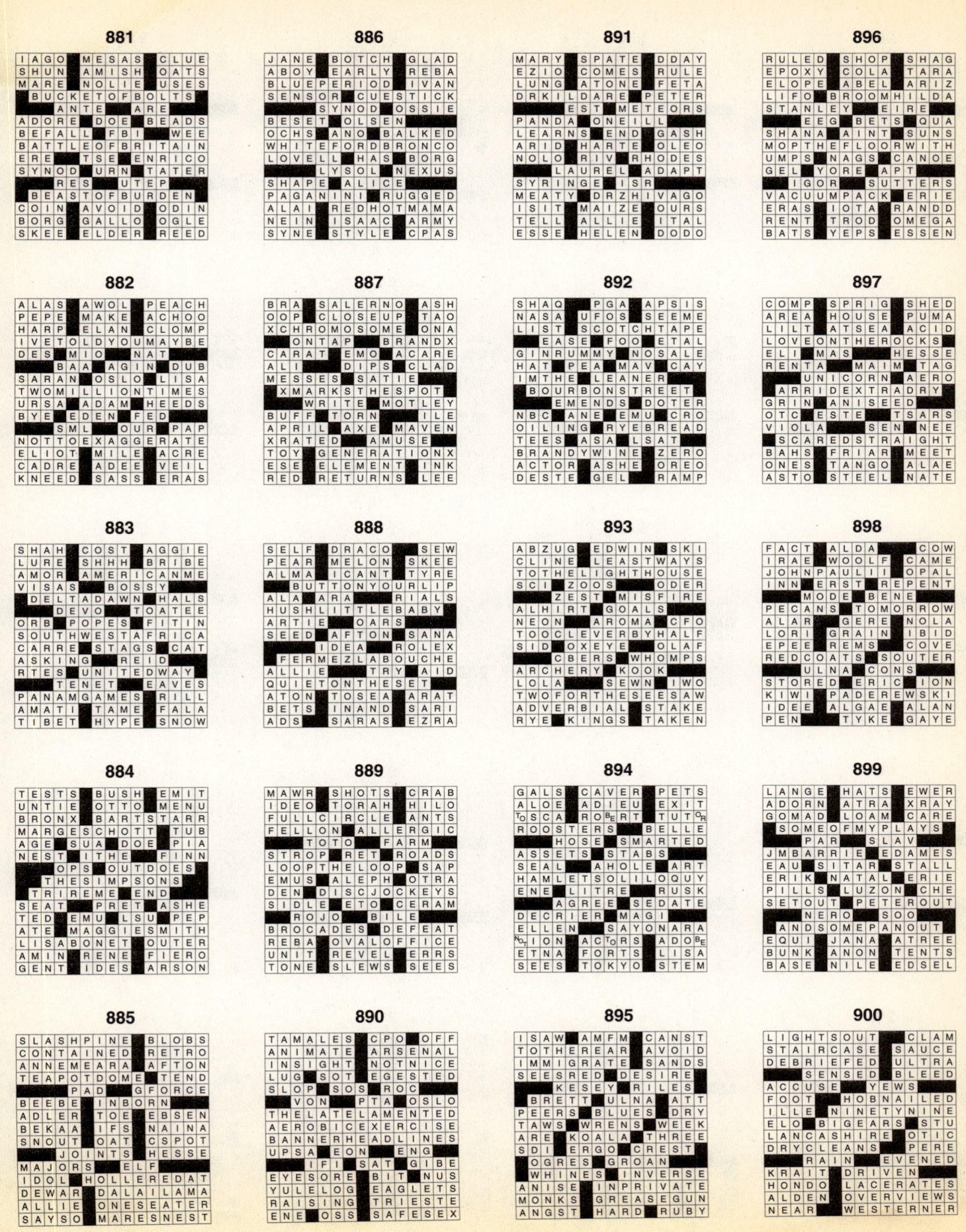

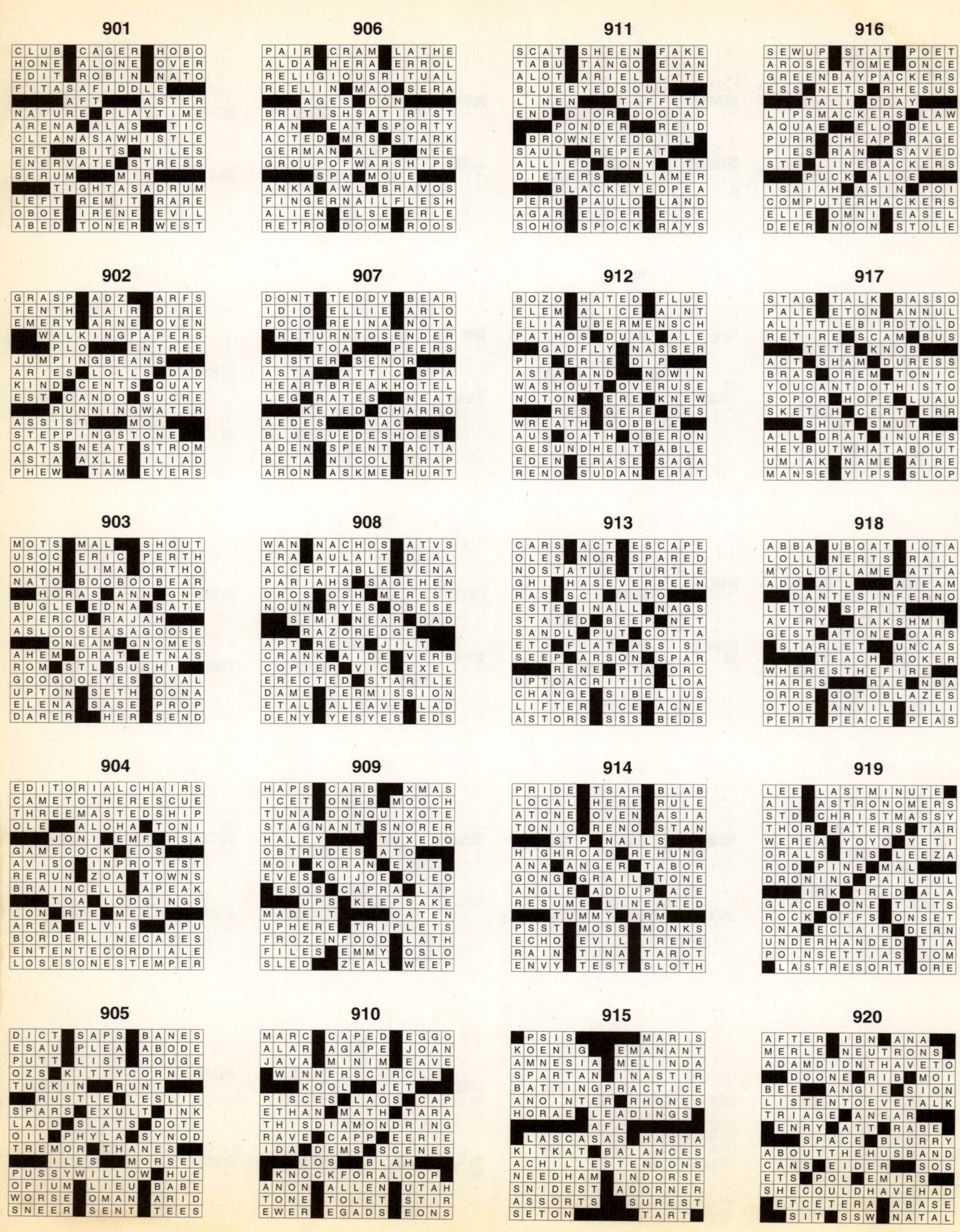

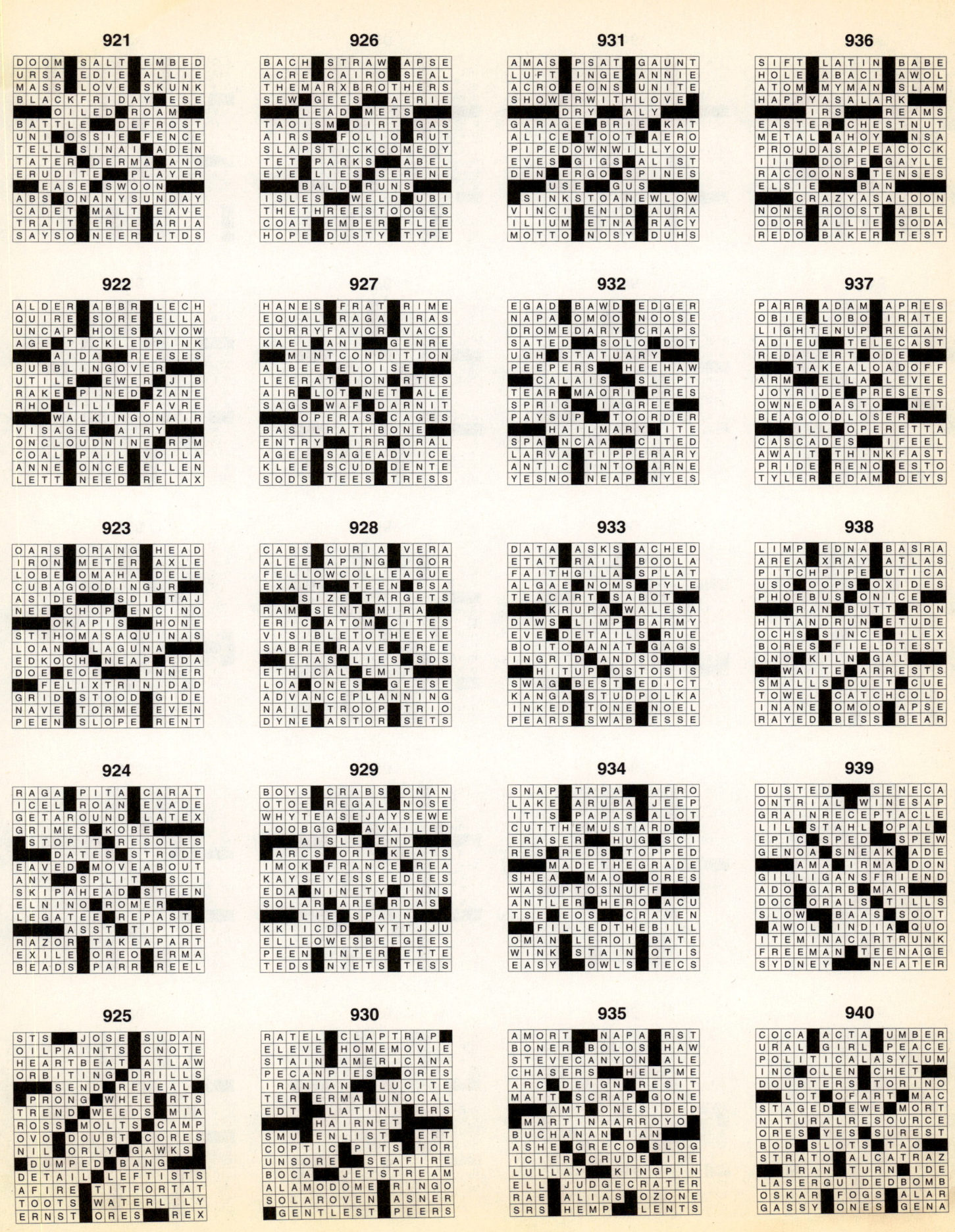

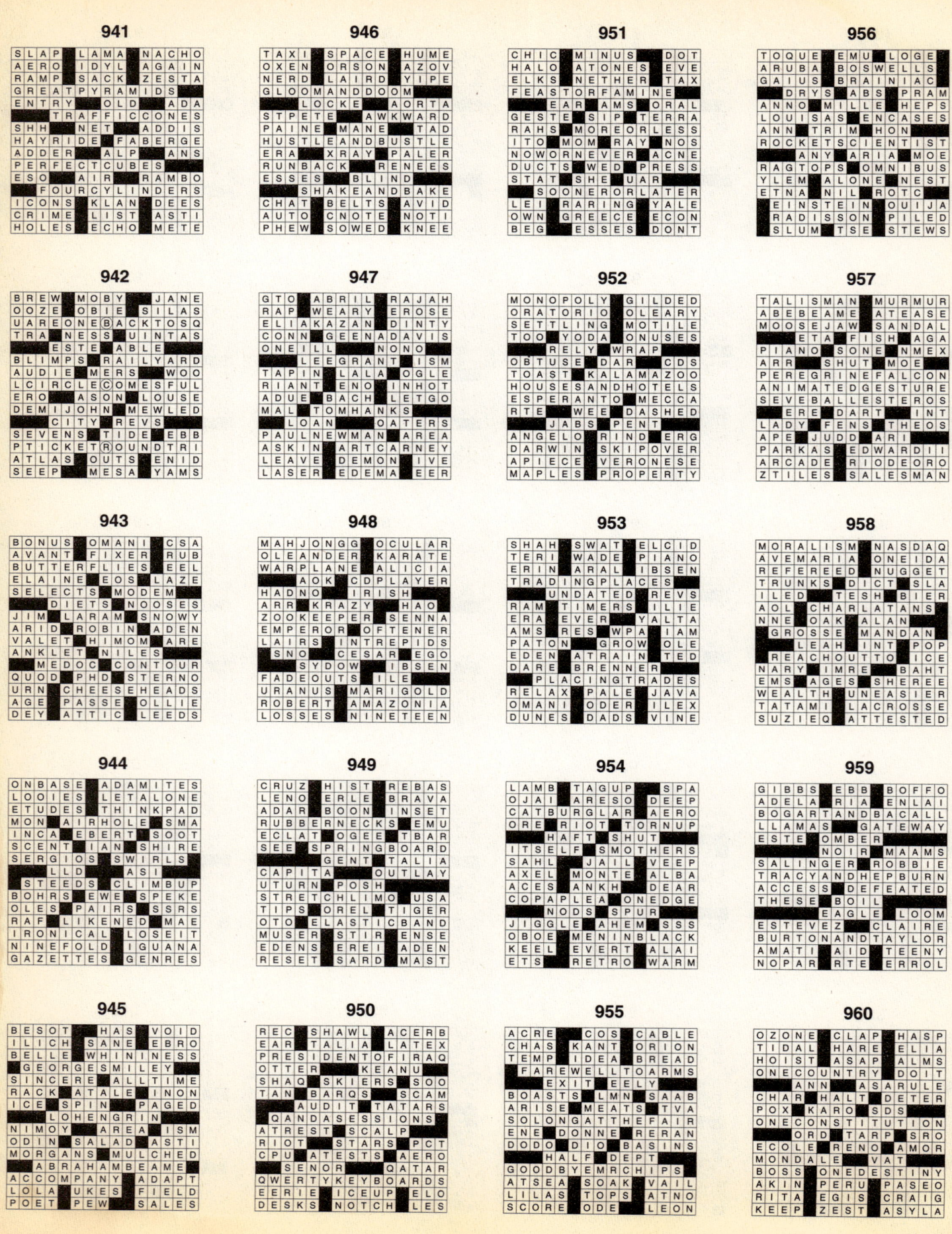

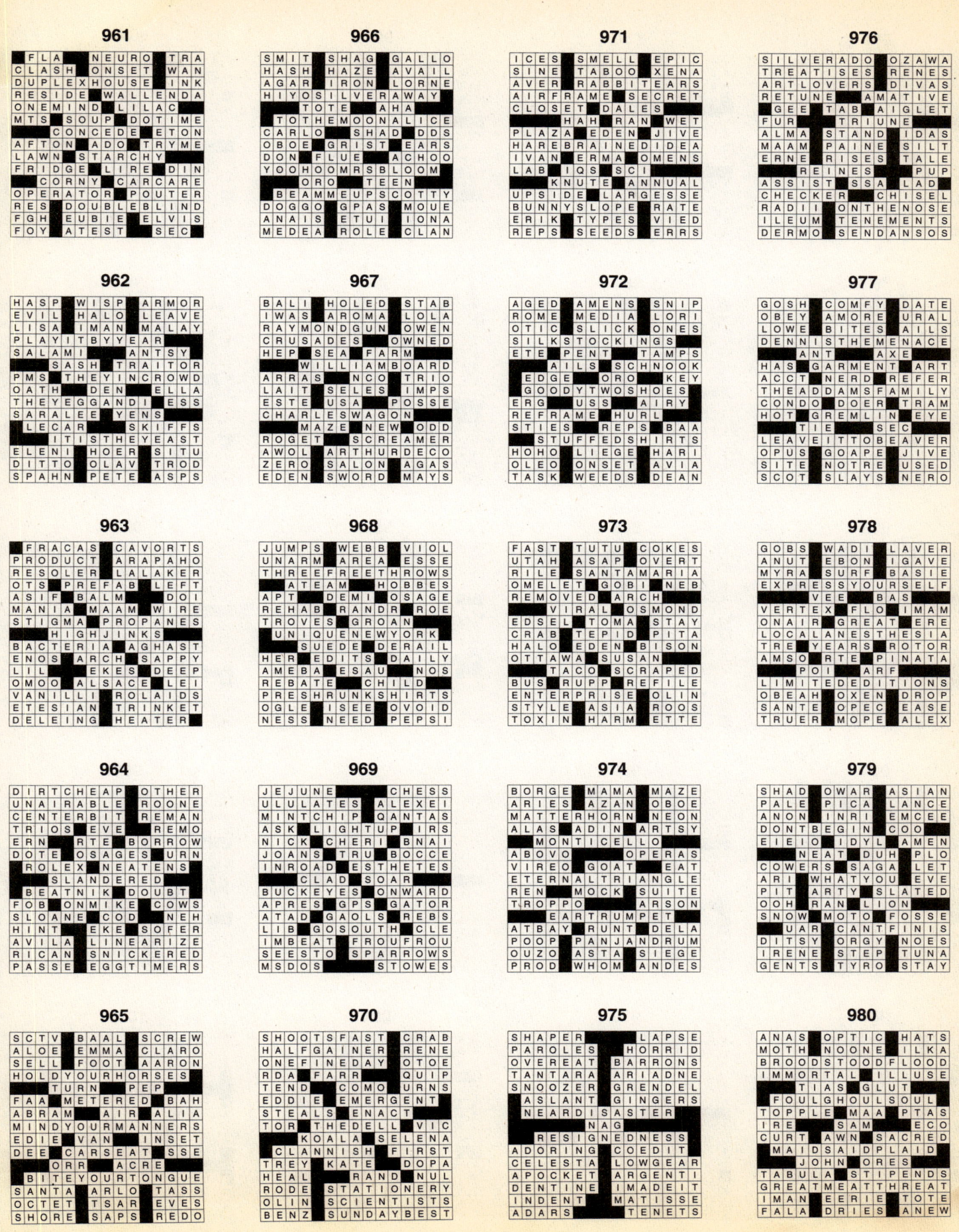

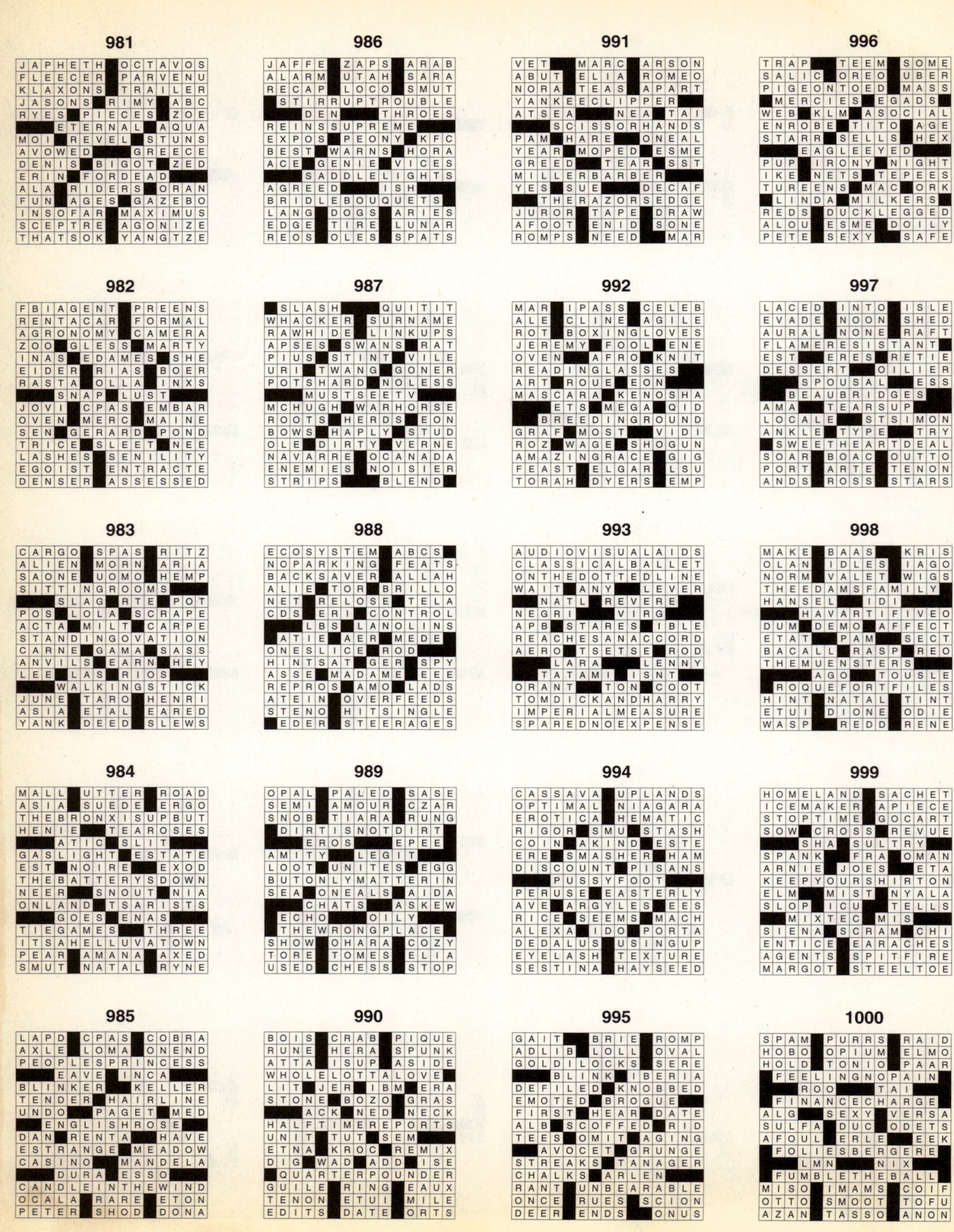

The New York Times
Crossword Puzzles

The #1 name in crosswords

Millions of fans know that *New York Times* crosswords are the pinnacle of puzzledom. Challenge your brain with these quality titles from St. Martin's Griffin.

Available at your local bookstore or online at **nytimes.com/nystore**